M000221210

SOME GEORGIA COUNTY RECORDS
VOL. 1

BEING SOME OF THE LEGAL RECORDS
OF
COLUMBIA, HANCOCK, JEFFERSON AND WARREN COUNTIES, GEORGIA

96 - 1214

COMPILED BY:
  THE REV. SILAS EMMETT LUCAS, JR.
PUBLISHED BY:
  SOUTHERN HISTORICAL PRESS

1st Printing: 1977
2nd Printing: 1994

Southern Historical Press, Inc.
P.O. Box 1267
Greenville, S.C. 29602

ISBN # 0-89308-044-6

Printed in the United States of America

INTRODUCTION

For the person interested in Georgia genealogical research, this book is the attempt to meet some of the growing need for new source material. Georgia is one of the few Southern states for which there has been a reasonably adequate amount of printed original source material. However, most of the original source material for Georgia county records was done from the period of about 1910 to about 1933 and little new material has been done in the past 40 years in book form.

The Publisher also being the Editor of the Georgia Genealogical Magazine, the oldest genealogical quarterly on Georgia source material, has found that there is a vast difference between persons who subscribe to a genealogical quarterly and those persons who purchase books containing source material,i.e., most of those persons who subscribe to the Georgia Genealogical Magazine do not buy books of source material, and those who buy books for some reason do not subscribe to quarterly genealogical magazines containing source material on Georgia.

Therefore, to try and meet the needs of both groups of people, I have taken source material that has run in the Georgia Genealogical Magazine in more or less continuous form and put it together as one block of material for a given county and likewise for other counties. The reader will notice that much of the material in this book has appeared in the "GGM" over the period from 1961 to 1976. HOWEVER, there has been a considerable amount of material added to that which has appeared in the "GGM" which has required new and additional research so as to try and make some of the county records appearing in this book more complete.

I have set out a plan for at least three books on Georgia County Records to appear in 1977. This Volume is the first in this series; the second will be a book containing records from *Clark, Greene, Morgan, Oglethorpe and Putnam Counties, Georgia*. The third volume will contain legals records from *Butts, Fayette, Henry, Jasper, Jones, Monroe and Newton Counties*. None of these books, including this volume one is an attempt to present all of the legal records for the counties under consideration but rather to try and present as many different legal records for as many counties as possible for the genealogist interested in these counties. It is hoped that in future years I can bring additional books dealing with other counties and their records to the reader.

Comments and contributions of original source material from readers will be appreciated for possible use in future books.

                  Good Luck In Your Research,

                  The Rev.Silas Emmett Lucas,Jr.,Publisher
                      Southern Historical Press
                  January 1977

TABLE OF CONTENTS

COLUMBIA COUNTY DEED BOOK A

NOTE: In transcribing these Deeds from the microfilm copy, the first
         two pages of Deed Book A are missing, so that the Deeds for
Book A begin on Page 3. At the top of Page 3 is found the completion of
a Deed that began on Page 2, but which has noted after the signature
and witnessing who this Deed was to, acres and county.

Page 3: ----- of the sd. ANDERSON CRAWFORD and RACHEL his wife have
         set hands and seals. Signed: A. CRAWFORD, RACHEL CRAWFORD.
Wit: PETER CRAWFORD, J.P. (Note: underneath this says "Conveyance
A. CRAWFORD to RICH'd REGAN, 300 acres in Columbia Co.)

Page 3: Recorded 8 April 1791, Power of Attorney dated 24 February
         1791 by MARY ELKINS, formerly MARY WHITNEY of Col. Co. --
to her son-in-law WILLIAM TAYLOR of same - to recover in Province of
Virginia --- but especially that part of my right to my uncle JEREMIAH
WHITNEY, dec'd, consisting of negroes and property. Signed: MARY (X)
ELKINS. Wit: JNO. TANKERSLEY, J.P., WILLIAM HUNT, JOHN LUCKEY.

Page 4: Recorded 8 April 1791, Deed of Gift dated 24 February 1791
         bet. MARY ELKINS of Col. Co. and WILLIAM TAYLOR of same..
for natural love & affection -- for her son-in-law property in Province
of Virginia, formerly property of her uncle JEREMIAH WHITNEY, dec'd
and also sum of 5 lbs. to her paid by WILLIAM TAYLOR. Signed: MARY
(X) ELKINS. Wit: JNO. TANKERSLEY, J.P., WILLIAM HUNT, JNO. LUCKEY.

Page 5: Recorded 19 May 1791 Deed dated 21 April 1791 bet. THOMAS
         CLASSCOCK of Richmond County, Esq. and MARY his wife to
WILLIAM REILY of Augusta ... consideration of 110 lbs. law money...
convey tract cont. 1800 acres in Richmond Co., now Columbia Co.
bounding: JAMES GRIERSON, JOSHUA SANDERS, ___ HERD, GERMANY, RICHARD
AUSTIN, EPHRAIM OWENS, DAVID BALDWIN and others. Signed: THOMAS
GLASCOCK, MARY GLASCOCK. Wit: RO. LEE. Richmond County, 21 April
1791, MARY, wife of THOMAS GLASCOCK rel. dower in the 1800 acres before
DALRIEL HUNTER, J.P.

Page 7: Recorded 26 May 1791, DEED dated 27 January 1789 bet. LEVI
         LANCASTER of Green Co., Ga., and HUGH BLAIR of Richmond Co.
consideration of 160 lbs. Ster... conveys tract in Richmond County
on Greenbrier prong of Great Kiokia Creek, containing 200 acres ...
part of 400 acre tract gtd. to ROBERT STORY on 7 July 1772. Signed:
LEVI LANCASTER. Wit: MICHAEL SMALLY, MOSES PARK.

Page 8: Recorded 30 May 1791, Deed dated 29 October 1790 bet. OWEN
         SULLIVAN and THOMAS SULLIVAN both of Rich. Co., and WILLIAM
KENNON of same... consid. 30 lbs law money... convey tract cont. 50
acres lying in same where THOMAS SULLIVAN now lives... bounding:
NORTH HOBSON, EDMOND SAMUELS, ABRAHAM BOOTHS, WILLIAM KENNON, L.
KENNON and SAMUEL ___. Signed: OWEN (OS) SULLIVAN, THOMAS (T)
SULLIVAN. Wit: JOHN WILLINGHAM, ADAM MANNON, _____ MCDOWEL, JOHN
TANKERSLEY, J.P.

Page 9: Recorded 30 May 1791, Deed dated 27 March 1790 bet. JONATHAN
         SELLS of County of Stokes in North Carolina and KINDRED
CARTER of Richmond Co.... consid. 50 lbs. Sterl.. conveys tract in
Richmond County... bounding SELLS land and vacant ... containing 100
acres... gtd. JONATHAN SELLS 2 November 1789. Signed JNO. SELLS. Wit:
JOHN (I) DAVIS, (T. H.? illegible) CARR, JP.

Page 10:   Recorded 27 June 1791, Deed dated 28 March 1791 bet. DAVID
           MILLER of Col. Co., and the heirs of REUBEN BLANCHARD,
dec'd of same ... consid. 100 lbs. law money pd by heirs of REUBEN
BLANCHARD ... convey tract of 200 acres in Col. Co. ... whereon widow
of R. BLANCHARD dec'd now lives ... on waters of Kegg Creek ...
counding: WILLIAM CANDLER, BLANCHARDS & SWINTS & vacant. Signed:
DAVID MILLER. Wit: JNO. TANKERSLEY, J.P.

1

Page 11:   Recorded 27 June 1791, Deed dated 14 November 1787 bet.
             FERDINAND O'NEAL of Liberty Co., Ga., and JOHN PEAK of
Richmond Co., ... consid. 50 lbs. law money ... conveys tract of 500
acres formerly property of CHARLES WILLIAM MCKINNON, one of persons
named in the persons named in Act. of Confiscation & Banishment ...
bounded by HUGH MIDDLETON, M. READ, JOHN GERMANY. Signed: F. O'NEAL.
Wit: JN. COBBS, J.P., TOM HAGAN.

Page 12:   Recorded 28 June 1791, Power of Attorney dated 10 April
             1789 by JOHN TARVIN a citizen of the Creek Nation who appt.'s
his brother GEROGE TARVIN of Richmond Co. to dispose of tract gtd him
by the State for 100 acres in Richmond Co.... on waters of Little
Kiokia Creek, part of which is sd. to be property of LEROY HAMM...
bounding: GEDEON BOOKER, ANDERSON CRAWFORD & WILLIAM TARVIN, dec'd.
Signed: JOHN TARVIN. Wit: W. (WM.) F. BOOKER, ROBT. DIXON, ISAAC
GARDNER, J. L. DIXON.

Page 13:   Recorded 28 June 1791, Deed dated 26 October 1789 bet.
             GEORGE TARVIN (lawful attorney of his brother JOHN TARVIN
on April 1789 in Richmond County) and WILLIAM F. BOOKER of same...
consid. 30 lbs. cur. money... convey tract cont. 37 acres in Richmond
Co. part of 100 acres gtd. to sd. JOHN TARVIN. Signed: GEORGE TARVIN.
Wit: GIDEON BOOKER, JOHN BOOKER, JACOB GORE.

Page 15:   Recorded 2 July 1791, Dated 6 July 1789. SARAH GERMANY
             (widow) and PAUL CALDWELL both of Richmond Co., bond by
STEPHEN HEARD of Wilkes Co., Esq.   full sum of 3000 lbs. Ster. to be
pd. to STEPHEN HEARD. Whereas a marriage shortly proposed to be
solemnized bet. sd. SARAH GERMAN, widow and sd. PAUL CALDWELL... and
sd. SARAH GERMANY being desirous to secure such part, both of land &
negroes as she may rec. of Estate of her late husband WILLIAM GERMANY
on a division being made acc. to law unto JAMES GERMANY, MARY GERMANY,
WILLIAM GERMANY, JOHN GERMANY, JEAN GERMANY & STEPHEN GERMANY, children
of sd. SARAH GERMANY & sd. WILLIAM GERMANY, dec'd... reserving same for
herself & PAUL CALDWELL for her natural life & at her decease to be the
only right property and Estate of above (children as named) share and
share alike... & JAMES GERMANY elder son. Signed: SARAH (X) GERMANY,
PAUL CALDWELL. Wit: JAS. STALLINGS, J.P., THOMAS DORSEY.

Page 16:   Recorded 2 June 1791, Deed dated 24 March 1791 bet. SOLOMON
             ELLIS & MARGRET his wife of Col. Co. and LEAKIN DORSEY of
same... consid. 50 lbs. Ster... convey tract in Col. Co. cont. 200
acres... bounding: BARNETTS, FULALRS, DAYS & vacant... which sd.
tract gtd. to WILLIAM MADDOX & conveyed to him to SOLOMON ELLIS.
Signed SOLOMON ELLIS, M. ELLIS. Wit: PETER CRAWFORD, J.P., CHARLES
ELLIS.

Page 18:   Recorded 30 July 1791, Deed dated 24 March 1791 bet. SOLOMON
             ELLIS & MARGRET his wife of Col. Co. and LEAKIN DORSEY of
same... consid. 100 lbs. Ster... convey tract of 92 acres in Col. Co...
bounding: STEPHEN DAYS, WILLIAM MADDOX, JOHN FULLARS & vacant... sd.
tract gtd. JOSHUA FULLAR & by him to SOLOMON ELLIS, the gt. cont. 100
acres, which since has been conveyed to JOSEPH DORSEY by SOLOMON ELLIS.
Signed: SOLOMON ELLIS, M. ELLIS. Wit: PETER CRAWFORD, J.P., CHARLES
ELLIS.

Page 19:   Recorded 1 August 1791, Deed dated 1 March 1790 bet. THOMAS
             COWAN of Richmond Co., Planter and HENRY CANDLER of same...
consid. 4 lbs. 6 shillings, 8 pence law money paid by THOMAS COWAN...
cont. tract of 26 acres in same county... being tract gtd. HENRY
CANDLER 1 February 1790... bounding STANDFORDS, DUNCANS & vacant.
Signed: H. CANDLER. Wit: ELDRIDGE HARGROVE, JNO. HARGROVE.

Page 21:   Recorded 2 August 1791, Deed dated 30 July 1785, bet. JAMES
             GROVES of Wilkes Co., Ga., Planter and MICHAEL GRIFFIN of
Richmond Co., Planter... consid. 40 lbs Ster... conveys tract 200
acres in Richmond Co... lying on South side of little River ... which
was gtd. JAMES GROVES 3 April 1770. Signed: JAMES GROVES, MARY (X)
GROVES. Wit: SAMUEL KEITS, EDM. CARTLIDGE, J.P.

Page 23:   Recorded 6 August 1791, Deed of Gift dated 4 August 1791
             by ROBERT BURTON of Col. Co., blacksmith... for consid. of
love & good will etc... I have towards my beloved son CALEB BURTON...
tract cont. 300 acres... in Col. Co., also cattle & their increase from
the year 1782, horse, feather bed, cloaths, pewter plates & dish etc.
Signed: ROB. BURTON. Wit: N. HARRIS, J.P., BLAKE (T) PURUY.

Page 24:   Recorded 6 August 1791, Deed dated 4 August 1791 bet. ROBERT
             BURTON of Col. Co. and CALEB BURTON of same... consid. 40
lbs. specie ... tract cont. 250 acres in Columbia & Richmond Counties,
on Rudy Creek, bounding TEMPLES, FRANKLINS & vacant. Signed: ROBT.
BURTON. Wit: JESSE HORN, N. HARRIS, J.P.

Page 25:   Recorded 22 October 1790, Deed dated 13 September 1789, bet.
             THOMAS SMYTH, Jr., now of Queen Ann County, Maryland and
RICHARD FOOTMAN of City of Philadelphia, merchant... consid. 500 lbs.
cur. money of Md... 2 tracts in Richmond Co., Ga., which sd. THOMAS
SMYTH purchased of a certain DANIEL STEARGISS. Signed: THO. SMYTH,
Jun. Wit: JA. O'BRYAN, ART. EMORY. Acknowledged: Queen Ann Co.,
Md. on 2 October 1790.

Page 27:   Recorded 23 August 1791, Deed of Gift in Trust from THOMAS
             HAMILTON of Col. Co. for consid. of love, good will, etc...
which I have unto my loving wife CONCORD HAMILTON... do freely grant
unto ISAIAH WRIGHT (in Trust) of Col. Co.... in behalf of my loving
wife CONCORD HAMILTON, all my goods, chattels, lands etc... together
with Doctor EDMOND DILLONS Bond and Mortgages dated 26 February 1789
and also ROBT. MONTGOMERYS dated 18 Jan. 1791... & negroes... 800
acres lying on both sides the trading road adj. each other... & 700
acres on waters of Little Kiokia each in Col. Co., horses, cows, hogs...
I have del. to ISAIAH WRIGHT in Trust on Inventory. Signed with my
own hand. THOS. HAMILTON. Wit: FREDRICK BROWN, PETER CRAWFORD, J.P.
Inv. made 17 August 1791.

Page 29:   Recorded 23 August 1791, Deed dated 15 January 1791 bet.
             JOHN WRIGHT and ALSEA his wife of Col. Co. and THOMAS COWAN
of same... consid. 15 lbs... convey tract in Col. Co. cont. 69 acres..
part of a 95 acre gtd. to JOHN WRIGHT 4 Dec. 1790. Signed: JOHN
WRIGHT, ALSSEA (X) WRIGHT. Wit: LEWIS (L) CRANE, JACOB LANGSTON.

Page 30:   Recorded 23 August 1791, Deed dated 28 July 1791, bet.
             JACOB GOARE & RACHEL GOARE his wife of Col. Co. and WILLIAM
F. BOOKER of same... consid. 70 lbs. cur.money... tract of 100 acres
in Col. Co. on waters of Little Kiokia Creek... bounding:JOHN YOUNG-
BLOOD, GIDEON BOOKER & WILLIAM ZACHRY... which sd. tract was conveyed
by JOHN YOUNGBLOOD & MARY YOUNGBLOOD his wife to sd. JACOB GOARE by
Deed. Signed: JACOB GOARE, RACHEL (X) GOARE. Wit: PETER CRAWFORD,
J.P., JOHN GOARE.

Page 32:   Recorded 24 August 1791, Deed dated 28 March 1791, bet.
             LEAKIN DORSEY & ANNA his wife of Col. Co. and RANDEL
RAMSEY of same... sum of 100 lbs. Ster... tract to RANDLE RAMSEY in
Col. Co., cont. 200 acres... bounding: BARNETTS, FULLARS, DAYS, &
vacant... tract gtd. to WILLIAM MADDOX & by MADDOX to SOLOMON ELLIS &
by ELLIS to LEAKIN DORSEY. Signed: LEAKIN DORSEY, ANNA DORSEY. Wit:
FRANCIS DORSEY, PETER CRAWFORD, J.P.

Page 33:   Recorded 24 August 1791, Deed dated 28 March 1791 bet. LEAKIN
             DORSEY and ANNA his wife of Col. Co. to RANDEL RAMSEY of
same... consid. 100 lbs. Sterl. tract in Col. Co. cont. 92 acres...
bounded by: STEPHEN DAYS, WILLIAM MADDOX, JOHN FULLARS & vacant...
sd. tract gtd. JOSHUA FULLAR & by him to SOLOMON ELLIS, orig. gt.
cont. 100 acres, 8 acres of which was conveyed by ELLIS to JOSEPH
DORSEY & by sd. ELLIS to LEAKIN DORSEY. Signed LEAKIN DORSEY, ANNA
DORSEY. Wit: PETER CRAWFORD, J.P., FRANCIS DORSEY.

Page 34:   Recorded 7 Sept. 1791, Deed dated 6 Sept. 1791 bet.
            ANDERSON CRAWFORD of Col. Co. and JOHN MCMUNN of same...
ANDERSON CRAWFORD & RACHEL his wife for sum of 50 lbs. convey tract in
Richmond Co., now Col. Co... cont. 195 acres... bounded by WILLIAM
MELESS & MOORES land, ISAAC JACKSON, THOMAS WATSON, CHARLES BURKES &
PETER PERKINS land on waters of Upton Creek... formerly gtd. HENRY
WRIGHT & sold by Sheriff of Richmond Co. to ANDERSON CRAWFORD 8 Sept.
1788. Signed: A. CRAWFORD, RACHEL CRAWFORD. Wit: PETER CRAWFORD,
J.P., MARY SINQUEFIELD.

Page 36:   Recorded 6 October 1791, Power of Attorney dated 29 July
            1791 by WILLIAM F. BOOKER of Col. Co. who appoints his
brother GEDEON BOOKER his lawful Att. to dispose of lands in sd. state.
Signed: W. F. BOOKER. Wit: JACOB GOARE, JOHN WALHON, JOHN BOOKER.

Page 37:   Recorded 6 Oct. 1791, Deed dated 22 November 1783 bet.
            ABRAHAM RAVOT, HUGH LAWSON & HEPWORTH CARTER, Esqs. Com-
missioners of Confiscated Lands... and ROBERT FLOURNOY of Rich. Co.,
consid. 204 lbs. Sterl. tract in Rich. Co., township of Wrightsborough,
formerly property of Sir JAMES WRIGHT and known as Quaker Meeting House
tract... bounded by: JOSEPH MADDOX, THOMAS JACKSON, JOHN DAVIS,
        PAGES, JOHN WATSON, JOB SMITH, SAMUEL OLIVERS, JONATHAN SALES,
JOHN SIDWELLS, ___ MCCLUNG, JOSEPH MADDOX, ISAAC VERNON... cont.
1579 acres. Signed: H. LAWSON, ABM. RAVOT. Wit: MAT. HUBERT,
WILLIAM HARTON, PHILLIP (P) SEFLEN.

Page 39:   Recorded 6 Oct. 1791, Deed dated 22 Nov. 1783, bet. ABRAHAM
            RAVOT, HUGH LAWSON, & HEPWORTH CARTER, Comm. of Confiscated
Lands... and ROBERT FLOURNOY of Rich. Co... tract of 1,000 acres in
Rich. Co., formerly property of JOHN GRAYHAM... bounded ___ by ___
HUNTERS, JOHN DOVERS, JAMES EMMIT... in Township of Wrightsborough on
sd. town creek & lying on both sides sd. creek. Signed: H. LAWSON,
ABN. RAVOTT. Wit: PHILLIP (p) SEFLEN, MAT. HUBIRT, WM. HARTON.

Page 41:   Recorded 14 Oct. 1791, Bill of Sale from SUSANNAH COLEMAN
            of Col. Co. to WILLIAM SHIELDS as Gdn. of ELIZABETH
ROSBOROUGH of same... following property to wit: (Negro slaves, cattle,
horses, beds & furn., tables, chairs etc.).. for the price or consid.
of 191 lbs., 10 shillings, 4 pence Sterl. Signed: SUSANNAH (A)
COLEMAN. Wit: JOS. SIMMS, J.P., PETER CRAWFORD, J.P.

Page 42:   Recorded 17 Oct. 1791, Deed of Lease dated 7 May 1774 bet.
            WILLIAM LYNN of Parish of St. Paul's, Planter and JOSHUA
PERKINS of District of Ninety-Six in Province of S.C., Carpenter...
consid. of 10 shillings cur. money of S.C.... tract containing 100
acres in St. Paul's Parish... Township of Wrightsborough, bounded by
vacant lands. Signed: WM. LYNN. Wit: WM. MATTHEWS, BENJAMIN ALLEN,
JAMES MCLEAN (MCCLEAN? as was difficult to read on microfilm).

Page 44:   Recorded 17 Oct. 1791, Deed of Release dated 8 May 1774,
            bet. WILLIAM LYNN of St. Paul's Parish, planter and JOSHUA
PERKINS of 96 Dist. S.C., carpenter, by grant dated 3 July 1770, Sir
James Wright did gt. sd. WM. LYNN, 100 acres... now WM. LYNN for sum
of 20 lbs. Sterl... conveys to JOSHUA PERKINS in his actual possession,
forever, all sd. tract in Wrightsborough. Signed: WM. LYNN (W).
Wit: WM. MATTHEWS, BENJAMIN ALLEN and JAMES MCCLEAN.

Page 47:   Recorded 19 Oct. 1791, Lease dated 22 Dec. 1774, bet. JOSHUA
            PERKINS of Prov. of Georgia, carpenter and WILLIAM WALKER of
96 Dist., Prov. of S.C., Planter... consid. of 5 shillings... doth
sell unto WILLIAM WALKER a cert. tract cont. 100 acres lying in
St. Paul's Parish in Township of Wrightsborough... for term of one
year. Signed: JOSHUA PERKINS. Wit: DAVID THWEATT, SAMUEL WALKER,
THOMAS GLASCOCK.

Page 48:   Recorded 19 Oct. 1791, Release, dated 23 Dec. 1784, bet.
            JOSHUA PERKINS of Pro. of Georgia, planter to WILLIAM WALKER

of 96 Dist. in S.C., planter... whereas in gt. dated 3 July 1770 to
WM. LYNN by Sir JAMES WRIGHT... tract cont. 100 acres... in St. Paul's
Parish... & conveyed to JOSHUA PERKINS... Wit. sd. JOSHUA PERKINS for
30 lbs. Sterl. doth sell & release... in fee simple sd. tract to
WILLIAM WALKER. Signed: JOSHUA PERKINS. Wit: DAVID THWEATT, SAMUEL
WALKER, THOMAS GLASCOCK.

Page 53: Recorded 20 Oct. 1791, Deed dated 20 Sept. 1784 bet. WILLIAM
WALKER and JOHN FLUKER of other... consid. 40 lbs. Sterl.
tract on Germany's Creek in Richmond Co., cont. 100 acres. Signed:
WILLIAM (X) WALKER. Wit: HENRY BELL, OWEN FLUKER.

Page 55: Recorded 20 Oct. 1791, Deed dated 4 Feb. 1790, bet. JOHN
FLUKER & his wife REBECCA & BENJAMIN FEW of other, all of
Richmond Co. ... consid. 300 labs. law. money convey tract in Rich.
Co., on German's Ck. cont. 100 acres... orig. gtd. WILLIAM LYNN dated
3 April 1770. Signed: JNO. FLUKER, REBECKAH FLUKER. Wit: P. BLEDSOE,
JNO. SMITH.

Page 57: Recorded 12 Nov. 1791, Deed dated 14 Feb. 1791, bet. ALEX-
ANDER SCOTT and his Minister of the Gospel wife, ELIZABETH
SCOTT of State of S.C. and County of Linkham... and ELI GARNETT of
Col. Co., Ga., consid. 100 lbs. Sterl. tract of 150 acres in Col. Co.,
bounded by vacant lands... orig. gtd. sd. SCOTT 2 Aug. 1774. Signed:
ALEX. SCOTT, ELIZ. SCOTT. Wit: JACOB HENRY, JOHN GERMANY, Sr.

Page 59: Recorded 12 Nov. 1791, Deed... whereas WALKER RICHARDSON on
10 Jan. 1787 did institute a case agst. EZEKIEL OFFUTT in
Sup. Ct. Rich. Co... and did on 26 March 1788 recover sum of 23 lbs.,
8 shillings & 2 pence... and did on 13 Aug. 1790 direct to all Sheriffs
of sd. state... commanding them that goods and chattels of EZEKIEL
OFFUTT of Rich. Co. and WILLIAM WALKER's of same, his Security... should
be levied the sum of 29 lbs, 2 shillings and a pence inc. entreat...
afterwards sd. tract sold at public auction... whereas GEORGE HANDLEY,
Sheriff of Rich. Co. for sum of 33 lbs. sold to ISAIAH WRIGHT of
Rich. Co., tract cont. 250 acres on waters of Kiokia Creek in Rich. Co.
bounded by: BLAIRS, SMITHS, GARDNERS & vacant, gtd. to WILLIAM WILKINS.
Signed: GEORGE HANDLEY, Sher. of Rich. Co. Wit: W. H. BOOKER, EDMD.
B. JENKINS.

Page 61: Recorded 15 Nov. 1791, Deed dated 6 Jan. 1791, bet. ISAIAH
WRIGHT of Col. Co., and JOHN BRISCOE of same... consid. 75
lbs. law. money ... tract cont. 250 acres (be the same 100 more or
less) in Col. Co., bounded by BLAIRS, SMITH, GARDNER... orig. gtd.
WILLIAM WILKINS in 1785. Signed: I. WRIGHT. Wit: N. DAUGHERTY,
CATY DUNN.

Page 63: Recorded 17 Nov. 1791, Deed dated 15 Sept. 1790, bet. ISAAC
LOWE of Rich. Co. and DAVID VINSON of same... consid. 25
labs. Sterl... tract of 50 acres in Rich. Co., orig. gtrd. to ISAAC
LOWE, Sr. on 31 Dec. 1787 & conveyed by ISAAC LOWE, Sr. to his son
ISAAC LOWE by a written will... bounded at time of survey by JOHN
MADDOX, DAVID VINSON, JAMES LACKEY. Signed: ISAAC LOWE. Wit: JOHN
RENNELS, ROBERT BELL.

Page 65: Recorded 23 Nov. 1791, Deed of Gift from Ann Lin of Col. Co.
for consid. of love, good will & maternal affection which I
have to my 3 youngest children, JANE LIN, ANN LIN & CHARLES LIN all of
same county... do voluntarily give unto sd. JANE, ANN & CHARLES LIN...
one negro girl in my house in Wrightsborough. Signed: ANN (H) LIN ,
Wit: THOS. WHITE, ALASANAH L ____ (illegible), RHISA HOWARD, J.P.

Page 66: Recorded 23 November 1791, Deed dated 23 October 1791, bet.
EDWARD BURKS of Col. Co. and ELIZABETH his wife and JOSEPH
DAVIS of same... consid. 10 lbs. convey tract cont. 86 acres in afsd.
Co... bounded by HAYES & DAYS land, LOWS and HIGGINBOTHAMS land.
Signed: EDWARD BURKS. Wit: HANNAH (X) BARNETT, PETER CRAWFORD, J.P.

Page 67:   Recorded 30 November 1791, Deed dated 13 May 1790, bet.
            WILLIAM TINDELL of Richmond County and BETSEY ANN his wife
and BIRD BOOKER TINDELL of same... consid. 75 lbs. law. money...
convey tract cont. 200 acres, orig. gtd. to JOHN TINDELL, also a parcel
lying on the Ucha Creek supposed to be 40 acres, part of old survey
gtd. to JOHN TINDELL. Signed: WILLIAM (X) TINDELL, BETSEY ANN TINDELL.
Wit: WILLIAM TINDELL, PLEASANT TINDELL.

Page 68:   Recorded 1 December 1791, Deed dated 13 Sept. 1791 bet.
            WILLIAM TINDELL, Sr., of Col. Co. and WILLIAM TINDELL, Jr.
of Col. Co... consid. 50 lbs. law. money convey tract supposed to be
160 acres, orig. gtd. WILLIAM TINDELL, Sr., lying on Ucha Creek in
Columbia County. Signed: WILLIAM (X) TINDELL. Wit: JOHN TINDELL,
JOSEPH BARROW.

Page 69:   Recorded 2 Dec. 1791... Power of Attorney by SAUL WARD of
            Col. Co. to his son THOMAS WARD, his lawful attorney to
dispose of all property real and personal which he has in State of
Maryland. Signed: SAUL WARD. Wit: A. CRAWFORD, PETER CRAWFORD, J.P.

Page 70:   Recorded 6 Dec. 1791, Deed dated 10 Jan 1777 bet. DAVID
            FLEMMING of Richmond County and WILLIAM CANDLER of same...
consid. 25 lbs. law. money... tract in County afsd. on Upton's Creek
cont. 100 acres... orig. gtd. DAVID FLEMMING 4 Feb. 1774. Signed;
DAVID FLEMMING. Wit: ABRAHAM SANDERS, JNO. OLIVER, J.P.

Page 71:   Recorded 6 Dec. 1791, Deed dated 26 Sept. 1778 bet. COLLO.
            WILLIAM CANDLER of Richmond County and COLLO. ANDREW BURNS
of same... consid. 75 lbs. Sterl. of Georgia... convey tract cont.
and laid out in Wrightsborough dist. on Waters of Upton's Creek, bounded
by vacant land... sd. tract orig. gtd. to certain DAVID FLEMMING on
4 Oct. 1774... & conveyed by sd. DAVID FLEMMING unto WILLIAM CANDLER
on 10 Jan. 1777. Signed: WILLIAM CANDLER. Wit: JAMES (X) LENNOX,
ELIZABETH (X) LENNOX.

Page 73:   Recorded 6 Dec. 1791, Deed dated 6 May 1791 bet. ANDREW
            BURNS of County of Wilkes and BENJAMIN FEW and RHESA HOWARD
of Col. Co., consid. 75 lbs. law. money... tract of 100 acres... orig.
gtd. DAVID FLEMMING dated 10 Jan. 1777 & gtd. ANDREW BURNS by WILLIAM
CANDLER 25 Sept. 1778. Signed: ANDW. BURNS. Wit: JAS. WILLIAMS,
R. ABERCROMBIE.

Page 74:   Recorded 6 Dec. 1791, Bill of Sale dated 25 June 1791 by
            WILLIAM ROSBOROUGH of Green Co., Ga. sells unto PAUL CLADWELL
of Col. Co., for 50 lbs. Sterl... 2 negro boys, Edmond and Will Edmond,
8 years old and 6 years old. Signed: WILLIAM ROSBOROUGH. Wit:
PETER CRAWFORD, J.P., SUSANNAH (A) COLEMAN.

Page 75:   Recorded 6 Dec. 1791, Deed dated 25 June 1791, bet. WILLIAM
            ROSBOROUGH of Green County, Georgia and PAUL CALDWELL of
Col. Co.... consid 50 lbs. Sterl.... convey 1/3 part of several tracts
in Col. Co., cont. in the whole 350 acres, orig. gtd. to GEORGE
ROSBOROUGH & bounded by: THOMAS MOORS, RANDEL RAMSEY, Sr., JOHN SMITH,
NATHANIEL BARNETTS... the 1/3 of afsd. tracts amounting to 116 1/2
acres, which sd. 1/3 part being the proportion of the real Estate of
GEORGE ROSBOROUGH, dec'd., due to the afsd. WILLIAM ROSBOROUGH as one
of the heirs of sd. GEORGE ROSBOROUGH. Signed: WILLIAM ROSBOROUGH.
Wit: PETER CRAWFORD, J.P., SUSANNAH (A) COLEMAN.

Page 76:   Recorded 10 Dec. 1791, Deed dated 17 Dec. 1787 bet. JOHN
            HODGINS of township of Wrightsborough, Co. of Richmond and
WILLIAM THOMAS & CAM THOMAS of county afsd., wheelrights... consid. of
55 lbs. Sterl... convey tract in Wrightsborough cont. 131 acres... on
waters of Upton's Creek, formerly gtd. to JOSEPH MADDOX and ISAAC
VERNON as sd. MADDOX and JAMES BROWN deed to sd. HODGINS will more
apply & fully appear, it dated 10 Dec. 1787... bounded by lands of:
heirs of sd. VERNON, dec'd. and heirs of GEORGE BECK, dec'd... by lands
surveyed for WILLIAM DANIEL & MERCER BROWN. Signed: JOHN HODGINS.

6

Wit: JOHN TORRENCE, THOS. WHITE, R. HOWARD, J.P. . . . 28 Oct. 1790
MARY HODGINS, relict of sd. JOHN HODGINS rel. dower bef. R. HOWARD,
J.P.

Page 79:   Recorded 17 Dec. 1791, Receipt dated 30 Aug. 1791 from Mr.
             SHERWOOD BUGG, Admnr. of Estate of PETER PARIS, dec'd. the
following negroes.. horses, furniture, being the unsold part of PETER
PARIS's Est. Signed: THOMAS WATKINS, J.P. Wit: ABRAHAM JONES.

Page 80:   Recorded 17 Dec. 1791, Deed dated 20 Dec. 1778 bet. WILLIAM
             SHEPPERD, planter of Richmond Co. and JACOB WEBSTER of
Wilkes County, Ga., sd. WILLIAM SHEPHERD and SARAH SHEPHERD his wife...
sell tract cont. 200 acres... in Parish to St. Paul, Co. of Richmond...
joining lands of JOHN (FINLETER? illegible)... gtd. to a certain
NATHAN SHEPHERD, dated at Savannah 19 Jan. 1773 & Rec. Book I, Folio
894, for sum of 350 lbs. Sterl. Signed: WM. (+) SHEPHERD, SARAH (X)
SHEPHERD. Wit: JAS. INGRAM, JNO. PALMER, ROBERT TONY.

Page 82:   Recorded 3 Jan. 1792, Deed dated 26 Jan. 1791 bet. LOVELESS
             SAVEDGE & ELIZABETH SAVEDGE his wife of Col. Co. & JOHN
FOSTER of same... consid. 5 lbs. law. money, convey tract cont. 200
acres on Germany's Creek... & being when surveyed in Richmond Co.,
now Col. Co., bounding lands of DAVID BOYD, WM. GERMANY, JOHN BOYD &
vacant... gtd. to SARAH RICHARDSON by Gov. JOHN HOUSTON 13 Sept. 1784.
Signed: LOVELESS SAVEDGE, ELIZABETH (X) SAVIDGE. Wit: JOHN (+) RUH,
MOLLY RUH. (Note: these later names were quite difficult to read and
could have been RICH, instead of RUH).

Page 84:   Recorded 9 Jan. 1792, Mortgage dated 9 Jan. 1792, bet JOEL
             CRAWFORD of Col. Co. and WILLIAM BARNETT, Esq. of Elbert
County... for consid. 30 lbs. Sterl. Mortgage unto WILLIAM BARNETT his
heirs etc... tract cont. 287 1/2 acres in Elbert Co. on Waters of
Broad River, joining lands of GARDNER & others... orig. gtd. JOHN
TISDALE... with privilege of redemption within term of 2 years. Signed
JOEL CRAWFORD. Wit: J. BARNETT, PETER CRAWFORD, J.P.

Page 85:   Recorded 11 Jan. 1792, Deed dated 26 Jan. 1791 bet. JOHN
             FOSTER & ELIZABETH FOSTER his wife of Col. Co. and LOVELESS
SAVEDGE of same... sum of 5 lbs. law. money, conveys tract cont. 200
acres... on Germany's Creek, being when surveyed in Rich. now Col. Co.
bounding lands of LOVELESS SAVEDGE, (HISCOKS?, illegible) or COURSONS
land, REES MORRIS, JOHN GARRETT, WILLIAM CANES, RICKITSONS... orig. gtd
ANN WOOD by Gov. SAML. ELBERT 4 Feb. 1785. Signed; J. FOSTER, ELIZA-
BETH FOSTER. Wit: JOHN RUH, MOLLY RUH.

Page 87:   Recorded 2 Feb. 1792, Deed dated 13 Jan. 1792, bet NATHANIEL
             PERREA of Augusta in Ga., Esq. and ANNA his wife and NOTLY
WHITCOMB of Col. Co., Planter...consid. of 100 lbs. law. money...
convey tract of 50 acres in Richmond, now Col. Co. being at time of
survey in 1774 on lands of THOMAS GREER, CRAWFORD, BACON, ANTHONY
DICKEY and vacant. Signed: NATE PERREA, ANNA PERREA. Wit: MERRYMAN
THORN, JP.
             In 1774, I made a survey of 500 on both sides of Uchee
Creek, adj. THOMAS GREERS land and others at the Instance of JAMES
MCFARLAND, Esq. for a cert. JOSEPH FARLEY... I also certify that on
request of Capt. NATHANIEL PERREA who saith he purchased sd. land.
Cert. 23 April 1789, WILLIAM SIMS, D.S.

Page 89:   Recorded 3 Feb. 1792, Deed dated 27 Aug. 1791, bet. WILLIAM
             REILY late of Baltimore County in Maryland, but now of
Augusta, Merchant... & by one Ind. of writing dated 21 April 1791 made
bet. THOMAS GLASCOCK of Richmond Co., Esq. & MARY his wife and afsd.
REILY of other... was conveyed tract cont. 1800 acres in Richmond Co.,
now Col. Co., bounding: JAMES GREVISON, JOSHUA SANDERS, HERD GERMANY,
RICHARD AUSTIN, EPHRIAM OWENS, DAVID BALDWIN & others... Recorded in
Clerks Office of Col. Co., Book A, Folio 5 & 6... Now this Ind.

witnesseth sd. WILLIAM REILY for consid. of 500 lbs. cur. money of Md.
doth convey to sd. WILLIAM SMITH the above tract of land... Signed:
WILLIAM REILY. Wit: EDW. D. BUPY, GEORGE P. KUPORTS (N.P. Baltimore
Co., Md.) Deed Ack. in Baltimore Co., 27 Aug. 1791 bef. GEO. GOULD, JAS.
CATHORN on appearance of WM. REILY.

Page 92: Recorded 8 Feb. 1792, Deed dated 1 April 1791 bet. JOHN
MCDONALD & NANCEY his wife of Col. Co. and ANTHONY HAYNES of
same... consid. of 30 lbs. law. money tract cont. 100 acres in Col.
Co. on waters of Uchee Creek, joining CHARLES CRAWFORD, SAMUEL HANSON,
WILLIAM SIMMS & sd. ANTHONY HAYNES line. Signed: JOHN MCDONALD,
NANCEY (X) MCDONALD. Wit: ALEXANDER THOMSON, WILLIAM (X) MCGEE.

Page 94: Recorded 8 Feb. 1792, Deed dated 1 April 1791 bet. JOHN
MCDONALD & NANCEY MCDONALD his wife of Col. Co. and ANTHONY
HAYNES of same... consid. 30 lbs. law. money... convey tract of 100
acres in Col. Co. on branch of Uchee Creek called back Creek and
bounding: SIMS, HAYNES, ROSS, ALDREDGE, CRAWFORD, SIMS, which was tract
gtd. sd. JOHN MCDONALD 18 July 1787. Signed: JOHN MCDONALD, NANCY (X)
MCDONALD. Wit: ALEXANDER THOMPSON, WILLIAM (X) MCGEE.

Page 95: Recorded 20 Feb. 1792, Power of Attorney dated 14 Feb. 1792,
from TURNER THOMASON of Col. Co. who appoints PUIHY BLEDSON
of Greene County, Ga., to rec. all money that may be due him in State
of Va., as a soldier in the late Wars with Great Brittain. Signed:
TURNER (I) THOMASON. Wit: PETER CRAWFORD, J.P., CHARLES CRAWFORD.

Page 96: Recorded 26 Feb. 1792, Deed dated 25 Feb. 1792, bet. WILLIAM
APPLING of Col. Co. for consid. of 5 shillings law. money
pd. by sd. Commissioners... do confirm unto sd. Com.'s to and for use
of a Court House & Goal in Co. afsd. all that tract of land which was
laid out of my premises by WM. WALTON, Esq., the 21 day this Instant...
cont. 5 acres, accepting a graveyard not exceeding 1/4 part of an acre
& shall be laid square-part of 2 surveys... one gtd. to EBENEZER SMITH
7 July 1772 cont. 200 acres... & the other gtd. JOSEPH WOOD 2 Aug.
1774, cont. 100 acres. Signed: WM. APPLING. Wit: J. M. NEIL.

Page 97: Recorded 26 Feb. 1792, Deed dated 25 Feb. 1792, bet
WILLIAM APPLING of Col. Co. & Trustees of the Anabaptist
Church on the Kiokias... consid. 5 shillings convey tract cont. 4 acres
being part of tract gtd. JOSEPH WOOD 2 Aug. 1774, cont. 100 acres,
bounded by lands of EBENEZER SMITH. Signed: WM. APPLING. Wit:
J. M. NEIL, J.P.

Page 98: Recorded 26 Feb. 1792, Deed dated 11 Feb. 1792, bet MARY
MUNCRIEF (widow) of Col. Co. and MICHAEL and JAMES MCNEIL
of same... consid. 25 lbs. law.money convey tract of 100 acres gtd.
to her 23 July 1784 in Col. Co.... bounding: JEREMIAH DUCKWORTH,
RANDAL RAMSEY. Signed: MARY (+) MONCRIEF. Wit: JAS. SIMMS, J.P.

Page 100: Recorded 26 Feb. 1792, Deed of Gift dated 7 Feb. 1792 from
THOMAS NAPIER of Col. Co... for consid. of love, good will
& affection, which I have to my son in law ROBERT RANDOLPH of same...
convey tract on East side of Germany's Creek below Malony branch,
included in a 300 acre tract orig. gtd. to JOHN SALE... also all that
parcel on north side of Maliony branch conveyed by ROBT. MCGINTY to sd.
THOMAS NAPIER adj. afsd. SELLS, cont. 320 acres (adjoins BENJ. FEWS,
WM. BATTOM, RICHARD RANDOLPH) Signed: TH. NAPIER. Wit: PETER
CRAWFORD, J.P.

Page 101: Recorded 26 Feb. 1792, Deed of Gift dated 7 Feb. 1792 from
THOMAS NAPIER of Col. Co... for consid. of love, good
will & affection towards my loving son in law RICHARD RANDOLPH... parcel
land in sd. Co. on west side Germany's Creek, being part of 300 acre
tract orig. gtd. JOHN SELL... also 30 acres orig. gtd. sd. THOMAS NAP-
IER and all that part of 200 acre tract orig. gtd. JOHN JONES on west
side Germany's Creek, adj. sd. 30 acres tract. Signed: TH. NAPIER.
Wit: PETER CRAWFORD, J.P.

Page 102:   Recorded 29 Feb. 1792, Deed dated 4 April 1791, bet.
              WILLIAM MILBANK at present of State of Ga. & Col. Co. and
JESSE SANDERS, Esq. of same... consid. 200 lbs. specie... convey tract
in Col. Co. formerly St. Paul's Parish, cont. 200 acres, lying on
both sides of Little Kiokia Creek, adj. BENJAMIN BEAVENS & EDWARD
CARTLEDGE... gtd. sd. WILLIAM MILBANK 3 Jan. 1775. Signed: WM.
MILBANK. Wit: HORATIO MARBURY, JOSEPH B. SPENCER, YANCEY SANDERS.

Page 103:   Recorded 5 March 1792 the marks (for cattle) of CHARLEY
              ATKINSON of Col. Co., CHARLEY ATKINSON appeared bef.
PETER CRAWFORD, J.P. & saith his mark is a smooth crop in the right
ear and slit in the left. Dated 1 March 1792.

Page 104:   Recorded 2 March 1792, Deed dated 27 Jan. 1791 bet. JESSE
              SANDERS of Col. Co. and JOHN DAUGED of same... consid. 310
lbs... convey tract 414 acres lying on bigg Kiokia Creek in Col. Co.
bounded by lands of: J. SANDERS, JEREMIAH LAMKIN, Mrs. RAYE & the
bigg Kiokia Creek, 300 of which known by name of CARTLEDGE tract which
was confiscated GREIRSONS property & sold by law... to J. SANDERS.
Signed: JESSE SANDERS. Wit: ANDW. FRAZER, WILLIAM JENNINGS, THOS.
LAWTON, PETER CRAWFORD, J.P.

Page 105:   Recorded 8 March 1792, Deed dated 26 April 1791, bet.
              RICHARD MOORE of Col. Co. Mason of the one part and PHILLIP
BRANTLY of same... consid. 300 lbs. Sterl. convey tract cont. 100
acres in Col. Co. on waters of Hearts Creek on all sides vacant...
transferred unto sd. RICHARD MOORE by SAMUEL TEMPLE SANSOME. Signed:
RICHD. MOORE. Wit: THOS. WHITE, R. HOWARD, J.P.

Page 107:   Recorded 9 March 1792, Deed dated 15 Feb. 1790, bet. HENRY
              CANDLER of one part and JOHN JONES of other, both of
Richmond Co. consid. 30 lbs. Sterl... tract in Richmond Co. on waters
of Sullivan's Creek, orig. gtd. HENRY CANDLER by grant dated 9 Feb.
1790... cont. 142 acres... bounding: SHILMANS, SIMS, WOODS & STUBBS.
Signed: H. CANDLER. Wit: JOHN DAUGHERTY, ALEXANDER (X) DAUGHERTY.

Page 108:   Recorded 9 March 1792, Deed dated 12 March 1790, bet.
              BURRUS HIGGINBOTHAM of Richmond Co., Planter and JONATHAN
PAIN of same... consid. 10 lbs. law. money convey tract in Richmond
Co. orig. gtd. to BURRUS HIGGINBOTHAM L 1787, cont. 100 acres...
bounded by ISAAC LOWE & DAVID WALKER. Signed: BURRHUS (X)
HUKINGBOTHAM. Wit: DAVID WALKER, PARKER RUNNELS, WILLIAM MCDOWELL.

Page 110:   Recorded 9 March 1792, Deed dated 21 Dec. 1791 bet. WILLIAM
              COUSINS of Col. Co. and NATHAN HARRIS of same... consid.
75 lbs... convey tract cont. 200 acres in Col. Co. on north side of
Greenbrier Creek, orig. gtd. to PETER LAURENCE 7 March 1775 & bounded
at time of survey by lands of: JAMES BROWN, WILLIAM FELPS... &
transferred by a Deed and Sale by PETER LAURENCE & ELIZABETH his wife
to REUBEN DYER on 13 Jan. 1776 & by sd. REUBEN DYER to WILLIAM COUSINS
5 Jan. 1779. Signed: WILLIAM COUSINS. Wit: JAMES COUSINS, WILLIAM
(W) COUSINS.

Page 111:   Recorded 9 March 1792, Deed dated 23 Nov. 1790, bet. JOHN
              MADDOX and MARY his wife and HUGH GOLIGHTLY of other...
consid. of 100 law. money... convey tract in Richmond Co. cont. 200
acres... bounded by: JACKSONS, BRYANTS, LACKEYS & LOWS... gtd. to
WILLIAM BARNETT 24 Feb. 1785, which tract was part of real Est. of sd.
WILLIAM BARNETT since dec'd... and left to JOHN MADDOX as one of
legatees of sd. Dec'd. Signed: JOHN MADDOX, SARAH (X) MADDOX. Wit;
DAVID VINSON, JOHN RENNOLS.

Page 112:   Recorded 9 March 1792 (CATTLE) MARK dated 1 March 1792,
              when JOHN TUDER appeared and said his mark was a slit in
each ear. Signed: PETER CRAWFORD, J.P.

Page 113:   Recorded 22 March 1792, Mortage of ROBERT WATKINS of
              Richmond County who sold to NEHEMIAH DUNN of same... tract

cont. 200 acres... bounding WILLIAM JACKSON... gtd. to WILLIAM BURGAMY..
in Book M. Folio 165,7 Sept. 1774 and by him conveyed to JOHN WALTON,
Esq. 21 Feb. 1775, Rec. In Book CC... NEHEMIAH DUNN gives bond to
ROBERT WATKINS under penalty of 200 lbs. Sterl. in gold and silver coin.
bef. 1 Jan. 1792. Signed: NEH. DUNN. Wit: J. C. WALTON (shown as
JOHN CARTER WALTON in the Wit. to Signature) GEORGE WATKINS.

Page 114:   Recorded 11 April 1792, MARKS & BONDS dated 11 April 1792
             bef. PETER CRAWFORD, J.P. of JAMES ALRIDGS in Col. Co. who
says his brand is (totiet), a swallow fork and under bit in right and
swallow fork in the left, brands thus I A. Signed: JAMES (A) ALRIDGE.

Page 114:   Recorded 15 April 1792, Deed, dated 1 Dec. 1789 bet.
             DREDZIL PACE of Richmond County and JAMES MCMILLAN of same.
consid. 150 lbs. law.money... conveys tract 200 acres in Rich. Co...
bounding Savannah River, JOHN GERMANY, Sr... orig. gtd. JOHN GERMANY
in two separate grants of 100 acres each, bearing date 3 Feb.1767.
Signed: DREADSIL PACE. Wit: JAS. GERMANY, JOHN MORRIS.
             Note: Richmond Co., we JOHN SHACKLEFORD & CATHERINE SHACK-
LEFORD of Rich. Co. do relinquish our right title, claim or demand of
above land... as dower... 1 Dec. 1789. Signed: JNO. SHACKLEFORD,
CATHERINE (C) SHACKLEFORD. Wit: JAS GERMANY.

Page 116:   Recorded 15 April 1792, Deed dated 4 Nov. 1791 bet. JOSEPH
             BATSON of Dol. Co. and JAMES READ of Rich. Co... sd. JOSEPH
BATSON & LUCY his wife for sum of 55 lbs. law. money... convey tract
100 acres in County afsd... bounded by SAMUEL SCOTT, Scotts Spring
Branch, Greenbryer Creek & JOHN MARSHALL... part of 550 acre tract
gtd. to THOMAS FORD. Signed: JOSEPH BATSON, LUCY (+) BATSON. Wit:
JAMES (R) REID, GEORGE LOFLIN.
             Note: Columbia Co.... personally app. JAMES READ, Sr.
who saith he see the with in deed signed & sealed & del. from JOSEPH
BATSON & his wife unto JAMES REED, Junior, 26 March 1792. JAMES SIMMS,
J.P.

Page 118:   Recorded 21 April 1792, Power of Attorney dated 18 April
             1792 of CHARLES TAYLOR of Elbert Co., Ga. who appt's JOHN
WALTON of Col. Co. his law. attorney. Signed: CHARLES TAYLOR. Wit:
JAS. TAIT, J.P., R. WATKINS, J.P.

Page 119:   Recorded 23 April 1792, Power of Attorney dated 23 April
             1792 from JOHN BEALLE of Col. Co. to JOHN WALTON, Esq. of
same, as his true & law. attorney. Signed: JOHN BEALLE. Wit: PETER
CRAWFORD, J.P.

Page 120:   Recorded 27 April 1792, Deed dated 12 Oct. 1789 bet. JOHN
             BECK of Richmond Co. and AMOS GREEN of same... consid. 30
lbs. Sterl... tract in Rich. Co. on Maddocks Creek cont. 150 acres...
bounded by: WILLIAM & CAMM THOMAS, WILLIAM DANIEL & Sawmill Tract
formerly gtd. to MADDOCK and VERNON. Signed: JOHN BECK. Wit: WM.
THOMAS, CAM THOMAS.

Page 121:   ... orig. gtd. by Gov. WRIGHT to GEORGE BECK of above land
             and one lot in Wrightsborough No. 59 and dated 3 July 1770.

Page 121:   ... we JOSEPH & PHEBE MIDDLETON of State of North Carolina
             do release & aquit our claims in above tract of land to
AMOS GREEN... dated 28 Oct. 1789. Signed: JOSEPH MIDDLETON, PHEBE
MIDDLETON. Test: SML. JONES, FRANCIS JONES.

Page 122:   Recorded 30 April 1792, Deed dated 1 Dec. 1791, bet
             WILLIAM BROWN, planter of Col. Co. and SARAH his wife and
WILLIAM EVANS of same, planter... consid 70lbs. Sterl. tract on waters
of Keo Creek in Col. Co... bounded by SAMUEL SCOTT, WILLIAM PAYNE &
land gtd. to BARBARA CLARK, GEORGE GOLPHEN, EDWARD CARTLEDGE & ANDREW
MCLANE, SAMUEL PAYNE... 100 acres being grant to WM. BROWN (see Bk.
GGG, Fol. 47), the remainder being part of 100 acres gtd. THOMAS

ADCOCK & by him to WM. BROWN. Plat dated 5 April 1785... remainder cont. 130 a. Signed: WILLIAM BROWN, SARAH (X) BROWN. Wit: JOHN TANKERSLEY, J.P.

Page 123:   Recorded 1 May 1792, Deed dated 5 Dec. 1789 bet. BENJAMIN JACKSON & SUSANNAH his wife of the State of Ga., and JAMES DOSIER of sd. state... consid.of 150 lbs. lawful mo.... convey tract of 150 acres in Rich. Co. bounding south side of Little River. Signed: BENJAMIN JACKSON, SUSANNAH (+) JACKSON. Wit: WILLIAM DOZER, JOHN DOZER.

Page 125:   Recorded 1 May 1792... Deed dated 18 March 1791, bet. JOHN MARSHALL of Wilkes Co., Ga., and ABRAHAM YOUNGBLOOD of Col. Co.... consid. of 30 lbs. cur. mo. convey tract of 100 acres in Col. Co... bounding: Upton's land... sd. tract was sold by JESSE MCNEIL to ANDREW WHITFIELD and by ANDREW WHITFIELD to JOHN MARSHALL. Signed: JOHN MARSHALL. Wit: JACOB GOARE, WM. BOOKER, J.P.

Page 126:   Recorded 3 May 1792... Deed dated 31 March 1791, bet BENJAMIN REES of Col. Co. and WILLIAM SMITH of Rich. Co... consid. 50 lbs. Sterl... tract in town of Wrightsboro, No. 67, which was gtd. unto a cert. JOHN SLATER, son and heir at law to 1st. ment. JOHN SLATER, dec'd... by Deed of Conveyance 19 Nov. 1789. Signed BENJAMIN REES. Wit: JAMES LAMAR, Jr., R. HOWARD, J.P.

Page 127:   Recorded 9 May 1792... Dated 24 Jan. 1789, bet. CALEB MONCREEF and MARY MONCREEF his wife and WILLIAM EVANS, all of Co. of Rich... consid. 500 lbs. law.mo... convey tract in Co. afsd. cont. 190 acres, bounded by RICHARD MIDDOWS, STURGES & MADDOX's Branch, THOMAS HOGAN... signed: CALEB MONCREEF, (-) his mark, MARY (-) MONCREEF. Wit: TOM. HOGAN, THOMAS THOMPSON, JNO. SHACKLEFORD, J.P.

Page 129:   Rec. 10 May 1792... Deed dated 19 Nov. 1789, bet JOHN SLATER of Rich. Co. & BENJAMIN REES of same... consid. 50 lbs. specie... convey tract in town of Wrightsboro cont. 1 acre, Lot 67... gtd. to a cert. JOHN SLATER, Dec'd. Signed: JOHN SLATER. Wit: CHARLES LIN, R. HOWARD, J.P.

Page 130:   Rec. 11 May 1792, Deed dated 24 Dec. 1790, bet. FRANCIS GRUBBS of one part, Planter and JOHN MONK of other part, planter, both of Col. Co... consid. of 50 lbs. Sterl. tract in Rich. Co. (now Col.) cont. 100 acres on both sides of Boggy Gut Creek and is part of tract orig. gtd. to EDWARD PRATER on 3 July 1787 cont. 150 acres... also all that tract cont. 200 acres orig. gtd. JOHN NORTH dated 4 Dec. 1790, bounding EDWARD PRATORS and GARDNERS land & other sides by JOHN GARDNERS land. Signed: FRANCIS GRUBBS. Wit: THOS. HAMILTON, J.P., GEORGE FOULES.

Page 132:   Rec. 12 May 1792, Deed dated 3 Oct. 1789, bet. EDWARD PREATER & SARAH PREATER his wife of Rich. Co. and FRANCIS GRUBBS of same, consid. 40 lbs. law.mo. convey tract cont. 100 acres in Rich. Co. on both sides Boggy Gut Creek & part of a tract cont. 150 acres gtd. EDWARD PREATER on 3 July 1787. Signed: EDWARD (X) PREATOR, SARAH (X) PREATOR. Wit: E. OFFUTT, D. HUNTER, J.P.

Page 133:   Rec. 22 June 1792, Deed dated _____ 1791, bet. BENJAMIN PORTER of Wilkes Co. and PATSEY CLAIBORNS his wife and CHARLES CROOKSHANKS of the State of Maryland, consid. of 1,000 lbs. law.mo., convey tract of 350 acres, as appears by grant to WILLIAM FEW, also 200 acres as gtd. to ANDERSON CRAWFORD, also part of tract cont. 200 acres gtd. to ALEXANDER DOUGLASS & conveyed to sd. PORTER by JOHN CARMICHAL & by DOUGLASS to CARMICHAL, sd. tracts in Col. Co. on waters of Greenbrier Creek. Signed: B. PORTER, PATSY C. PORTER. Wit: none shown. 15 May 1791, PATSEY CLABOURN relinquished her dower, bef. R. WORSHAM, J.P.

Page 135:   Rec. 2 July 1792, Power of Attorney made 18 April 1792 from
             JAMES HESTER of Wilkes Co. to JOSHUA GRINAGE of Col. Co.
Sgd. JAMES HESTER. Wit: JAS. TAIT, J.P., R. WATKINS, J.P.

Page 135:   Rec. 2 July 1792, Dated 18 April 1792, Power of Attorney
             from CHARLES TAYLOR of Elbert Co., Ga. to JOSHUA GRINAGE
of Col. Co. Signed: CHARLES TAYLOR. Wit: JAS. TAIT, J.P., R.
WATKINS, J.P.

Page 136:   Rec. 2 July 1792, Power of Att. dated 28 April 1792 from
             ROBERT DIXON of Col. Co. to JOSHUA GRINAGE. Signed:
ROBERT (X) DIXON. Wit: THOMAS MOORE, J.P.

Page 136:   Rec. 2 July 1792, Power of Att. dated 31 May 1792 from
             ROBERT NIXON of Col. Co. to JOSHUA GRINAGE, Esq. of Col.
Co. Signed: ROBERT NIXON. Wit: JNO. FOSTER, J.P.

Page 136:   Rec. 2 July 1792, Power of Att. dated 16 June 1792 from
             RICHARD BULLOCH of Col. Co. to JOSHUA GRINAGE of Col. Co.
Signed: RICHARD BULLOCH. Wit: JAS SIMMS, J.P.

Page 137:   Rec. 2 July 1792, Power of Att. dated 16 June 1792 from
             SAMUEL POOL of Col. Co. to JOSHUA GRINAGE of Col. Co.
Signed: SAMUEL POOL. Wit: JAS. SIMMS, J.P.

Page 137:   Rec. 2 July 1792, Power to Att. from WILLIAM DENNIS of
             Col. Co. to JOSHUA GRINAGE, dated 21 June 1792. Signed.
WM. (X) DINNIS. Wit: JNO. TANKERSLEY, J.P.

Page 137:   Rec. 2 July 1792, Power of Att. dated 28 June 1792 from
             ISAAC RAZOR of Col. Co. to JOSHUA GRINAGE. Signed:
ISAAC RAZOR. Wit: JNO. FOSTER, J.P.

Page 138:   Rec. 2 July 1792, Power to Att. Dated 29 June 1792, from
             LITTLETON YARBOROUGH of Col. Co. to JOSHUA GRINAGE.
Signed: LETTN. YARBOROUGH. Wit: PETER CRAWFORD, J.P.

Page 139:   Rec. 12 July 1792, Deed dated 8 Oct. 1791, bet. NICHOLAS
             H. BUGG and CHARLOTTE his wife and JAMES ALLEN both of
Rich. Co., consid. 125 lbs. law.mo. tract in Col. Co., part of tract
gtd. to ALEXANDER INGLIS by Comm. of Confiscated Lands, also 50 acres
by name of STORY's tract, joining lands of MICHAEL SMALLY, NICHOLAS
BUGG, SHERWOOD BUGG, cont. 100 acres. Signed: N. H. BUGG, CHARLOTTE
BUGG. Wit: P. CLAYTON, J.P. 21 April 1792 CHARLOTTE BUGG rel. dower
bef. P. CLAYTON, J.P.

Page 140:   Rec. 13 July 1792, Deed dated 26 April 1776, bet. JESSE
             REEVES of Barkley Co. & Pro. of S.C. and JOSEPH MOTT of
St. Paul's Parish, consid. 30 lbs. Sterl. Great Britain, conveys
tract of 100 acres in St. Paul's Parish gtd. to JESSE REEVES 2 August
1774... bounded by ROGERS, REDMARKS, THEOPHILUS DAVIS. Signed: JESSE
(X) REEVES. Wit: URIAH (+) MOTT, JNO. OLIVER, J.P.

Page 142:   Rec. 13 July 1792, Deed dated 31 March 1792, bet. ELIZABETH
             BOYD, widow of EDWARD BOYD, dec'd of Col. Co. and MARY
BOYD, dau. of sd. EDWARD & ELIZABETH BOYD, now about to be married,
for good will and affection she had for her former husband and to that
and that her only dau. shall have the property that was her fathers,
the sd. ELIZABETH BOYD doth this day move over all her right title,
dower etc., cows, calves etc. Signed: ELIZABETH (C) BOYD. Wit:
ELIZABETH FOSTER, JNO. FOSTER, J.P.

Page 143:   Rec. 19 July 1792, Deed dated 20 Jan. 1791, bet. JAMES
             INGRAM of town of Augusta, Esq. and NICHOLAS HOPSON BUGG,
of Col. Co., consid. of 1,000 lbs. Sterl. convey tract or several tracts
(to wit), one tract of 100 acres surveyed for NATHAN HARRIS 12 Feb.
1769, gtd. on 7 July 1772 bounded by vacant lands adj. following
tracts called Oak Hill which is also one other tract conveyed of 400

12

acres, surveyed for DANIEL COLEMAN on 19 May 1772 and gtd 7 June 1774, also one other tract adj. above 200 acres, formerly property of JAMES STORY, one other tract of 150 acres formerly property of THOMAS JONES, one other tract of 800 acres surveyed by ALEXANDER FRAZER. (Note total of 1700 acres) Signed: JAS. INGRAM. Wit: SHERWD. BUGG, J.P. WAGNON.

Page 145:   Rec. 21 July 1792, Deed dated 21 July 1792, bet. MANN SIMS and MARGARET SIMS his wife of Col. Co. and CHARLES COMER of Rich. Co., consid. 40 lbs. cur.mo, conveys tract of 500 acres in Col. Co. on both sides bigg Kiokia Creek, which land was gtd. MANN SIMS 14 Sept. 1789. Signed: MANN SIMS, MARGRET SIMS. Wit: PETER CRAWFORD, J.P.

Page 147:   Rec. 28 July 1792, Deed dated 10 June 1790, bet. WILLIAM STITH of Rich. Co. and JOHN COBBS, Jr., WILLIAM STITH, Jr. & JOHN STITH of sd. Co., consid. of 1,000 lbs. cur.mo., convey tract on waters of Sherils Creek near river Ogeeche in Co. of Wilkes, being the land sd. WILLIAM purchased of GEORGE REID cont. 250 acres, one other tract on waters of Greenbrier Creek in Rich. Co. purchased by sd. WILLIAM of ALEXANDER JOHNSON, cont. 300 acres, one other tract on Germany's Creek in Rich. Co. purchased by sd. WILLIAM of GILES CARTER cont. 600 acres, also slaves, cattle, furniture. Signed: W. STITH. Wit: RICHD. CALL, THOS. DAWSON, PAYTON R. STITH, PETER CRAWFORD, J.P.

Page 148:   Rec. 28, July 1792, Whereas WILLIAM STITH of Rich. Co. on 10 June 1790 did sell for 1000 lbs. cur. mo., sell unto JOHN COBBS, Jr., WM. STITH, Jr., & JOHN STITH, Esqs, the following lands, slaves etc., now wit. that JOHN COBBS, Jr. & WM. STITH, Jr. for divers consid. & 5 lbs. cur.mo. pd. by JOHN STITH do grant and quit claim the same unto JOHN STITH. Signed: JNO. COBBS, W. STITH, Jr. Wit: GEO. WALKER, N. HARRIS, J.P.

Page 150:   Rec. 30 July 1792, Deed dated 21 Feb. 1789, bet. ISHAM BYLIS of Rich. Co. and JAMES CARTLEDGE of same, ISHAM BAYLIS and wife ELIZABETH, for consid. of 200 lbs. Sterl. convey tract of land in Rich. Co. being one equal half of a tract of 250 acres conveyed from ROBERT GRAVES to ISHAM BAYLIS being 125 acres, bounded by DAYS GILE, JOSEPH HUTCHENSON, including old fields known by name of Johnsons field. Signed: ISHAM BAYLIS, ELIZABETH (X) BAYLIS. Wit: LUKE SANDERS, JESSE SANDERS, I. FEW, J.P.

Page 151:   Rec. 6, Sept. 1792, Deed dated 9 Oct. 1783, bet. JAMES MCFARLAND, Esq. of Rich. Co. and SAMUEL MADDOX of same, consid. of 30 lbs. Sterl., convey tract cont. 200 acres in Wrightsboro Dist. on Waters of Hearts Creek in Co. of Rich., bounded by JOHN JONES, JOHN STUBBS, JOSEPH BROWN, sd. tract gtd. to JAMES MCFARLAND 3 Dec. 1771. Signed: JAS. MCFARLAND. Wit: RHESA HOWARD, J.P., CHARLES LIN.

Page 153:   Rec. 12 Feb. 1793, Deed dated 21 Jan. 1791, bet. JOHN TOWNS & MARGARET his wife of Col. Co. and JAMES WILLIS, Sr. of same, consid. of 200 lbs, tract of 400 acres, 300 in one tract gtd. to MORDICAI MOORE, bounding JOHN KINGS, NAPIERS, SANDERS & GRAYHAM and JAMES MOORS, land late property of above JOHN & MARGRET TOWNS, also 100 acres just above described gtd. JAMES MOORE in 1784 and bounding GRAYHAMS, MORDICAI MOORS. Signed: JOHN TOWNS, MARGRET (X) TOWNS. Wit: THOMAS PORTER, WILLIAM SEAY, JOHN BINION.

Page 155:   Rec. 11 Sept. 1793, Deed dated 11 June 1793, bet JAMES MCDONALD of Col. Co. and JOHN TINDILL of same, consid. of 5 shillings, sd. JOHN TINDILL and MARY his wife have given to JAMES MCDONALD tract in Col. Co., bounding both sides of Ogchee Creek, cont. 100 acres, bounding WILLIAM TINDILL, JOHN MCDONALDS, tract orig. gtd. 17 Aug. 1705 (way deed reads, must be 1785) unto sd. JOHN TINDILL. Signed: JOHN TINDILL, MARY TINDILL. Wit: ANDREW MCDONALD, PLEASANT TINDILL.

Page 156:   Rec. 31 Jan. 1794, Bill of Sale dated 18 Oct. 1791 from
             PETER CULBREATH of Col. Co. to JAMES CULBREATH, one negro
woman for 50 lbs. specie. Signed: PETER (+) CULBREATH. Wit: BEVERLY
LOWE, PETER CRAWFORD, J.P.

Page 156:   Rec. 31, Jan. 1794, Bill of Sale dated 5 Aug. 1793 from
             PETER CULBREATH of Col. Co. to JAMES CULBREATH of Rich. Co.
4 negroes for 180 lbs. Signed: PETER (+) CULBREATH. Wit: DAVID
WALL, WILLIAM SILLIVENT (Note: Sullivan in affidavit).

Page 157:   Rec. 10 Feb. 1795, Power of Att. dated _____ from JOAB
             WATSON of PITTSYLVANIA Co., Va. to DAVID HARRIS of Col. Co.,
Ga., to recover from WATERS DUNN, Sr. of Col. Co., Ga., the amt. of a
judgment formerly obtained in Essex Co., Va., also the further sum of
14 lbs. Va. currency due from DUDLEY REYNOLDS of Wilkes Co., Ga., on a
bond given to a cert. JESSE CARTER indorsed to sd. JOAB WATSON. Signed
JOAB WATSON. Wit: A. CRAWFORD, J.P.

Page 158:   Rec. 17 Feb. 1795, Deed dated 30 May 1774, bet. JAMES HILL
             of St. Paul's Parish and JOHN KNOTT of Prov. of N.C. and
Co. of Granville, consid. of 20 lbs. Sterl., conveys tract in afsd.
Parish cont. 100 acres on west side of Germanys Creek bounded by the
Quaker Road and AMBROSE HOLADAYS, WM. LEAS, SAMUEL WILSON, gtd. to
JAMES HILL. Signed: JAMES HILL. Wit: SANDERS WALKER, JOHN HILL.

Page 160:   Rec. 17 Feb. 1795, Power of Att. dated _____ from JOHN
             KNOTT of Grandville Co., N.C. to WILLIAM WILLINGHAM of
Rich. Co., Ga. to recover lands in Rich. Co. Signed: JOHN KNOTT.
Wit: CALEB BRASFIELD, JAMES KNOTT, DAVID KNOTT, JUDAH (X) BRASFIELD,
WILLIS ROBERTS. Greene County, Georgia. Personally app. bef. me
CALEB BRASFIELD & JUDAH BOLIVER, who formerly was BRASFIELD and made
oath, that they saw JOHN KNOTT sign the above, dated 27 Dec. 1794.
WM. GREER, J.P.

Page 161:   Rec. 17 July 1795, Deed dated 6 Sept. 1788, bet. MAN SIMS
             and MARGRET his wife of Rich. Co. and FITZTS MORRIS HUNT
of same, consid. of 50 lbs. law. mo., convey tract of 200 acres in
Rich. Co. on Waters of Little River, bounding POALK and MIDDLETON
(Gtd. 17 Dec. 1784). Signed: MANN SIMS, MARGARET SIMS. Wit: JOHN
TINDILL, THOMAS CHAMBLERS.

Page 163:   Rec. 18 Feb. 1795, Deed dated 19 March 1794, bet. CHARLES
             GERGUSON and WINIFRED his wife of Col. Co. and NATHANIEL
PEARRE of same, consid. of 60 lbs. Sterl. convey tract cont. 300 acres,
orig. gtd. WILLIAM STANLEY and 180 acres of the afsd. 300 acres
descended to CHARLES FERGUSON & WINIFRED as sole heirs to afsd. WILLIAM
STANLEY, dec'd., 1/3 of the orig. survey or 90 acres being conveyed to
JOHN SURTHERLAND, the tract now conveyed in Col. Co. on White Oak Creek,
including 180 acres bounded by HICKS MELONES and SURTHERLAND. Signed:
CHARLES (X) FERGASON, WINYFRED FERGASON. Wit: JOSIAH HATCHER, MERRY-
MAN THORNE, J.P. On 19 March 1794 WINIFRED FERGUSON rel. dower bef.
JOSIAH HATCHER and MERRYMAN THORNE, J.P.

Page 165:   Rec. 18 Feb. 1795, Deed dated 3 Jan. 1793, bet. ROBERT
             BROWN and TEMPA his wife of Col. Co. and THOMAS BUTTRILE
of same, consid. of 3600 weight of tobacco, convey tract of 123 acres
in Col. Co., beginning at JAMES DOZER's corner. Signed: ROBERT
BROWN, TEMPERANCE BROWN. Wit: JAMES DOZER, THOMAS TRAVIS, WILLIAM
DOZER.

Page 166:   Rec. 18 Feb. 1795, Deed dated 21 Dec. 1793, bet. ALBERT
             WRIGHT of Col. Co. and ABEDNIGO WRIGHT of same, consid. of
150 lbs. law.mo., tract 300 acres, 150 acres orig. gtd. to WILLIAM HOL-
ADAY, Sen. and conveyed by sd. HOLADAY to DYONATIOUS WRIGHT and 150
acres gtd. to DYONATIOUS WRIGHT & beq. by him to me in Col. Co. on
Waters of big Kioka bounded by lands gtd. to: JOHN SMITH, BENJAMIN
HARRIS & WILLIAM HOLIDAY. Signed: ALBERT (+) WRIGHT. Wit: WALT.
DRANE, J.P., ALETHE DRANE, T. MCGRAW.

14

Page 167:   Rec. 19 Feb. 1795, Deed dated 8 March 1794, bet FITZ MORRIS
             HUNT and his wife SARAH of Col. Co. and LITTLEBERRY CREW
of Wilkes Co., Ga., consid. of 65 lbs, convey tract of 200 acres
formerly gtd. to MANN SIMS, in Col. Co. on a branch of Little River
and bounded by MIDDLETON, BOOTHE, gtd. to sd. MANN SIMS 17 Dec. 1784.
Signed: FITZ M. HUNT, SARAH HUNT. Wit: REBECKA THOMAS, WM. THOMAS,
J.P.

Page 169:   Rec. 19 Feb. 1795, Deed dated 15 Nov. 1792, bet THOMAS
             CLAYTON of Col. Co. and BENJAMIN WILLIAMS of same, consid.
of 30 lbs. law.mo. tract cont. 75 acres in sd. Co. in Parish of St.
Paul's bounding (from Plat look like RAYS lands, TELFAIRS, CRABBS),
part of tract gtd. 15 Nov. 1792, part of 1500 acres gtd. THOMAS CLAYTON.
Signed: THOMAS (T) CLAYTON, MILLEY (8) CLAYTON. Wit: JAS. FLEMING,
J.P.

Page 170:   Rec. 19 Feb. 1795, Deed dated 23 April 1793, bet ISAIAH
             WRIGHT of Col. Co. and ZACHARIAH SPIERS of other, consid.
of 74 lbs. 5 shillings pd to ISAIAH WRIGHT and REBECKAH his wife,
convey tract cont. 1650 acres in Co. afsd. on ____ branches of Great
Kioka Creek, orig. gtd. to DYONISIUS WRIGHT and beq. in Last Will and
Test. of sd. DYONISCUS WRIGHT to sd. ISAIAH WRIGHT the above 165
acres (plat shows it adj MAXWELL's land, WM. (SUTTON's?) land. Signed:
I. WRIGHT, REBECKAH (+) WRIGHT. Wit: STEPHIN COLLINS, A CRAWFORD,
J.P.

Page 171:   Rec. 12 March 1795, Received 2 March 1795 of JOHN BEALLE,
             Judgment in full proved agst. him by LACON DORSEY, I say
rec'd by me, the Judgment at Col. Court House. Signed: THOMAS WATSON.
Wit: J. GRINAGE.

Page 172:   Rec. 12 March 1795, Deed dated 24 Feb. 17__ ty4, bet. JOHN
             FOSTER and ELIZABETH FOSTER his wife of Col. Co. and JOHN
SHACKLEFORD of same, consid. of 75 lbs. law.mo., convey tract cont.
150 acres in 2 separate surveys, wit, the one in 100 acres and the
other in 50 acres, the 100 one gtd. to JESSE REEVES the 2nd. Aug. 1794
and the 50 acres in name of NATHAN MOATT on 21 March 1787, on road
leading from Augusta to Brownsborough in sd. Co., bounding: NICHOLSON,
REDMANS, THEOPHILUS DAVIS, DAWNS, MCNEAR's, JENKINSES. Signed: JNO.
FOSTER, ELIZABETH FOSTER. Wit: Z. LAMAR, Sr. (reads ZACHARIAH in
Affidavit), ISAAC (X) ROE. On 31 Jan. 1801 in Col. Co. ELIZABETH
FOSTER rel. Dower bef. JAS. GERMAN, J.P.

COLUMBIA COUNTY DEEDS & MORTGAGES - BOOK B

1792 - 1794

Page 1: Rec. 31 July 1792, Deed dated 6 August 1791, bet JOEL CRAWFORD of Col. Co. and JOHN PERREA of same, consid. of 1 lbs. 17 shillings of Ga., tract in Rich. Co. on Waters of Spirit Creek cont. 200 acres, bounded by RICHARD CALL. Signed: JOEL CRAWFORD. Wit: PETER BARRETT, JONATHAN PERREA, MERRYMAN THORNE, J.P. Received money on 6 Aug. 1791.

Page 3: Rec. 31 July 1792, Deed dated 21 Dec. 1791, bet. MORRIS KELLY, heir of SPENCER KELLY, dec'd. of Ga. and Co. of Col. and WILLIAM CONE, Jr. of same, consid. 80 lbs. law.m., tract cont. 100 acres in Parish of St. Paul bounded on all sides by vacant land when surveyed and gtd, to SPENCER KELLY 6 Sept. 1774 by JAS. WRIGHT, Gov., but now land of Col. Cocke. Signed: MORRIS KELLY. Wit: ELIZABETH FOSTER, JNO. FOSTER, J.P.

Page 5: Deed dated 10 Feb. 1790 bet. BENJAMIN MOSELY & wife of one part and JOSHUA GRINAGE, for consid. of 50 lbs. cur.mo., tract cont. 144 acres in Rich. Co. adj. CALWELLS, BEALES & HAYNES, GERMANY's land, MCNEILS land & GRIERS land, gtd. to us 31 March 1786. Signed: BENJAMIN (B) MOSELY, JANIE (+) MOSELY. Wit: MICHAEL MCNEIL, JOHN BEALLE. Rec. 1 Aug. 1792. Ack. 28 Oct. 1791, THOMAS MOORE, J.P.

Page 7: Rec. 16 Aug. 1792, Deed dated 2 Oct. 1784, bet. ABRAHAM DAVIS and ISAAC DAVIS of Co. of Rich. of one part and GEORGE CARTER of Virginia and Co. of Montgomery, consid of 20 lbs. Sterl., tract of 150 acres in Rich. Co. formerly St. Paul's Parish on Waters of Germanys Creek in Wrightsboro Dist. or Township, bounded by WATSON and vacant land, gtd. to JOHN DAVIS on 7 June 1774, and afsd. JOHN DAVIS left above tract to afsd. ABRAHAM and ISAAC DAVIS by his will, the afsd. tract cont. 150 acres. Signed: MARGARET (X) DAVIS, ABRAHAM DAVIS, ISAAC (X) DAVIS. Wit: JOHN (‡) DAVIS, PETER OVERBY, JOSEPH MENDENHALL. MARGARET DAVIS Rec. the consid., Wit: CHARLES SIN, J.P., WM. DEVOREAUX.

Page 10: Rec. 26 Aug. 1792, Deed dated 30 Dec. 1791, bet. JOHN BRYAN of Burk Co., Ga. and HENRY WAGGONER of Col. Co., consid. of 50 lbs specie, tract of 100 acres sit. in St. Paul's Parish, Wrightsboro Township, when gtd. vacant on every side, orig. gtd by His Majesty George 3rd on 4 Aug. 1772. I the afsd. JOHN BRYAN and my wife HELLEN do confirm the grant. Signed: JOHN BRYAN, HELLEN (X) BRYAN. Wit: BRITAIN DAWSON, WM. LITTLE, J.P.

Page 12: Rec. 5 Nov. 1792, Bill of Sale dated 3 Oct. 1792 from ROBERT DIXON of Col. Co., Planter, consid. of 50 lbs. law.mo. of Ga. pd. by JACOB DUCKWORTH in Col. Co., Planter, one soril mare valued at 10 lbs., one gray at 5 lbs., 1 bay at 5 lbs. one brind le Coco & calf at Ł 2 lbs., one brown cow and calf at 2 lbs., feather bed, furn., my household furn., one riding saddle, 200 bushels corn, 5 hogs, etc. Signed: ROBERT (6) DIXON. Wit: GEO. DOWNS, BENJAMIN REDMAN.

Page 14: Rec. 22 Oct. 1792, Deed dated 1 March 1785, bet. JONATHAN SELL of Rich. Co. and MATTHEW MOAT of same, consid. of 50 lbs. Sterl., tract of 100 acres in Rich. Co. on Waters of Germany Creek, bounded by SELL's land and vacant land, gtd. JONATHAN SELLS 3 July 1770. Signed: JON. SELLS. Wit: CHARLES LYN, J.P., SAMUEL JONES, PETER OVERBY.

Page 16: Rec. 2 Nov. 1792, Deed dated 25 July 1791, bet. ISAAC JUSTICE of Wilkes Co., Ga. and DAVID DOUGLASS of Col. Co., consid. of 80 lbs. Sterl., tract in Col. Co. on both sides of Sullivan's Creek, cont. 50 acres, whereon sd. DOUGLASS now lives, adj. LUKE LANDER, CLARKS, JAMES WRIGHT, JAMES LANDERS. Signed: ISAAC JUSTICE. Wit: LUKE LANDERS, JAMES LANDERS, TYRE LANDERS.

Page 18:   Rec. 4 Nov. 1792, ROBERT DIXON of Col. Co. but late a soldier
           in the N.C. State legion or State service, constitute and
app't. my trusty friend BRITAIN SANDERS, Esq. of N.C. and County of Wake
my lawful att., and received from the commissionery, to settle and
liquidate claims of the soldiers in State Troops of N.C. Signed:
ROBERT (X) DIXON. Wit: THOMAS MOORE, J.P., PETER CRAWFORD, J.P.

Page 19:   Rec. 8 Nov. 1792, Deed dated 9 July 1791, bet. JOHN KING of
           State of S.C. and JOHN ALLISON of State of Ga., consid.
100 lbs. Sterl., tract lying on both sides of Williams Creek, part in
Col. Co. & part in Wilkes Co., surveyed by LEROY HAMMOND, Nov. 27, 1766
& gtd. to him by sd. KING by JAMES WRIGHT, Gov. on April 7, 1767 &
Registered in Reg. Off. 8 May 1767, Folio 190, Cont. 250 acres. Signed:
JOHN KING. Wit: JONTHA. DOWNS, WILLIAM ALLISON, J.P. Cert. 1 Aug.
1792.

Page 20:   Rec. 8 Nov. 1792, Deed dated 7 Oct. 1791, bet. JAMES HICKEY
           of Rich. Co. and ISAAC BLUNT of same, consid. of 40 lbs.
law.money, convey tract lying in same state and county on Rocky Comfort
cont. 200 acres, gtd. to ROBERT WILKINS by gt. from his Honor GEORGE
HANDBY, Esq. dated 31 March 1788, bounded by THOMAS JOHNSON, WILLIAM
(BUSHAND?) and vacant land, GEORGE UPTON land. Signed: JAMES HICKEY.
Wit: MOSES GRANBERY, JESSE DYKES.

Page 23:   Rec. 8 Nov. 1792, Deed dated 8 Nov. 1791, bet. JOHN BENSON
           of Rich. Co. and MOSES GRANBERY of same, consid. of 50 lbs,
convey tract in afsd. county cont. 267 acres sit. on Rocky Comfort
Creek, which tract of land cont. 287 1/2 acres (bit supposing 20 & 1/2
to be taken off MCFARLINS line), which was gtd. to LEVI BUSHE by gt.
of GEO. HANDBY, Esq., dated 31 March 1788, bounded by MCFARLINS land,
LAWSONS & Rocky Comfort Creek. Signed: JOHN BENSON, NANCEY (X) BENSON.
Wit: ISAAC BLOUNT, JESSE DIKES.

Page 24:   Rec. 23 Nov. 1792, Richmond County, WILLIAM HOZICK of Green-
           brier County in State of Virginia, who saith a certain DAVID
COURSON made title to him, this deponent, for 200 acres in now Col. Co.
(formerly St. Paul's Parish), bearing date 9 Sept. 1774, deponent
verily believes from last information he is able to collect that he is
of full age or above the age of 21 years. Signed: WILLIAM HOZICK.
Sworn to in Augusta, 27 Oct. 1792 bef. THO. WATKINS, J.P.

Page 25:   Rec. 23 Nov. 1792, Deed dated 27 Oct. 1792, bet. WILLIAM
           HOZICK of state of Va. and county of Greenbrier to JOHN
FOSTER of Col. Co., consid. of 50 lbs. sterl., tract cont. 200 acres
orig. gtd. to DAVID COURSON by His Majesty, George 3rd., dated 6 April
1773, being the sd. tract that sd. DAVID COURSON deeded unto the sd.
FOSTER, which sd. WILLIAM HOZICK doth... quit claim to sd. FOSTER, on
waters of Savannah River, on Michaels or Germanys Creek. Signed:
WILLIAM HOZICK. Wit: ROBERT WATKINS, THO. WATKINS, J.P.

Page 27:   Rec. 24 Nov. 1792, Deed dated 23 Jan. 1787, bet. JOHN
           STANFORD of one part and MORDICA BENTON of other, consid of
50 lbs. Sterl., convey tract of 100 acres in Rich. Co. on waters of
bigg Kiokia, joining on NATHAN HARRIS, PERRIMANS, COBBS and COLLINS.
Signed: JOHN STANFORD, RACHEL (X) STANFORD. Wit: SAVIDGE LITTLETON,
JOHN WRIGHT. Ack. 20 Aug. 1792 bef. MERRYMAN THORN, J.P., NATH'L.
PERRIE.

Page 29:   Rec. 24 Nov. 1792, Deed of Gift from GEORGE WALTON of State
           of Georgia, Esq. for friendship and affection I bear to
JESSE WINFREE as also in consid. of 5 lbs. law.money, do convey in fee
simple all that plantation cont. 250 acres sit. near CLAIBORNS Mill
on the great Kiokia and adj. JOHN GLEN, Esq. & JOHN WALTON, dec'd.
Signed: GEO. WALTON. Wit: ROBT. WALTON, SEABORN JONES.

Page 30:   Rec. 26 Nov. 1792, Deed dated 2 Feb. 1790, bet. JOHN BEALLE
           and REBECCA his wife of Col. Co. and BENJAMIN FINNEY of same,

consid. of 100 lbs. law.money convey tract sd. JOHN & REBECCA live on sit. in Co. afsd. on the Uchee Creek, cont. 100 acres, being all that tract gtd. to RAWLS PERRY and at this time adj. land of WILLIAM BEALLE, WILKINS, JOHN RAMSEY and MOSSMANS. Signed: JOHN BEALLE, REBECCA (I) BEALLE, Wit: THOMAS HAYNES, J.P., JOHN HARGROVES, REBECCA BEALLE relinq. Dower 2 Feb. 1792.

Page 33:   Rec. 26 Nov. 1792, Deed dated 7 July 1791, bet. REUBEN DYER late of Ga. & Co. of Rich. but now of Tenesaw River and Mobile Dist. of one part and NATHAN HARRIS of Col. Co., consid. of 60 lbs., tract in Col. Co., bet. Kegg Creek and Little River orig. gtd to THOMAS CHADWICK, as a gt. for same cont. 100 acres, bounded by SAMUEL PAINES & vacant. Signed: REUBEN DYER. Wit: SAML. GERMANY, JOHN GERMANY.

Page 35:   Rec. 28 Nov. 1792, Deed dated 27 May 1791, bet. NATHANIEL BARNETT and SUSANNAH his wife of Col. Co., and FRANCES CRAWFORD, Extrx. of Estate of JOEL CRAWFORD of same, consid. of 100 lbs. Sterl. convey 1/2 tract land wherein NATHANIEL BARNETT lives, sit. in Col. Co. on waters of little Kiokia Creek, cont. orig. 400 acres & the 1/2 afsd. tract of land now to be gtd. to begin at ROSBOROUGHS Corner, bounded by JAMES MCFARLANDS, by HORNS & CRAWFORDS. Signed: NATHANIEL BARNETT, SUSANNAH (B) BARNETT. Wit: PETER BARNETT, PETER CRAWFORD, J.P.

Page 37:   Rec. 28 Nov. 1792, Deed dated 14 Dec. 1791, bet. JOSEPH THOMAS of Col. Co., Planter and RICHARD MERRIWETHER of County of Edgefield in S.C., consid. of 25 lbs. Sterl., convey all that tenement., on waters of Savannah River in Col. Co., bounded by Savannah River, JOHN LOTTS, THOMAS LAMARS, BOYDS, gtd. JOSEPH THOMAS, orig. Regis. in Secretary's Office, Book FFF, Fol. 709, cont. 100 acres. Signed: JOSEPH THOMAS, JOYCE THOMAS. Wit: JOHN TANKERSLEY, J.P.

Page 39:   Rec. (date not shown), Deed dated 14 Dec. 1791, bet. JOSEPH THOMAS of one part and THOMAS MERREWETHER, Jr., and NICHOLAS MERRIWETHER both of Col. Co., JOSEPH THOMAS and wife JOYCE for consid. of 150 lbs. Sterl., convey tract on Savannah River in Col. Co., bounded by Sav. River, THOMAS GRAY, BENJAMIN ARES, cont. 200 acres. Signed: JOSEPH THOMAS, JOYCE THOMAS. Wit: JOHN TANKERSLY, J.P.

Page 41:   Rec. 28 Nov. 1792, Deed dated 14 Nov. 1792, bet. JOHN SMITH of one part and JAMES MARTIN of other, both of Col. Co., sd. JOHN SMITH and wife REBECCA for consid. of 40 lbs. current money, convey tract cont. 97 acres gtd. to JOHN SMITH dated 17 Aug. 1785 (then of county of Richmond), lying on east side of Kiokia Creek, bounded by SAMUEL BLAIR, widow SMITH, SAMUEL MORTON. Signed: JOHN SMITH, REBECCA (X) SMITH. Wit: WALT. DRANE, J.P.

Page 43:   Rec. 29 Nov. 1792, Deed dated 12 Nov. 1792, bet. HUGH MCGEE of Col. Co. and ANNE BENNETT of same, consid. of 10 lbs. Sterl. conveys tract or part of tract of 400 acres orig. gtd. to ROBERT STORY, cont. 30 acres. Signed: HUGH MCGEE. Wit: MARTIN MILLOWA (MELONE shown later), JOHN BENNETT.

Page 44:   Rec. 29 Nov. 1792, Deed (month & day not shown), 1791, bet. JAMES SCRUGS of Col. Co. and WILLIAM WATKINS of same, consid. of (not given), tract in sd.Co. on waters of Green Brier cont. 30 acres, part of tract of 400 acres gtd. to ROBERT STORY (adj. MITCHELLS land, BUGGS, SMALLEYS & SCRUGGS, these names taken from the Plat). Signed: JAMES (X) SCRUGGS. Wit: MICHAEL SMALLY, HUGH BLAIR, JOHN LUCKEY.

Page 45:   Rec. 29 Nov. 1792, Deed dated 21 Sept. 1792, bet. WILLIAM WATKINS of Col. Co. and HUGH MCGEE of same, consid. of 60 lbs. Sterl., tract in Col. Co. on waters of Greenbrier Creek, part of a 400 acre tract gtd to ROBT. STORY. Signed: WILLIAM (X) WATKINS. Wit: MICHAEL SMALLY, HUGH BLAIR, JOHN LUCKEY.

Page 47:   Rec. 29 Nov. 1792, Deed dated 12 Oct. 1792, bet. GILBERT
             GREER of Greene Co., Ga., farmer, and LEVI MARSHALL of Col.
Co., farmer, consid. of 30 lbs. Sterl., conveys tract in Col. Co. on
waters of Greenbrier Creek, surveyed 11 Aug. 1784 and gtd by Hon.
SAMUEL ELBERT, bounded by SAMUEL CARTLEDGE and JOHN MARCUS, cont. 200
acres, GILBERT GREER and wife FRANCES renounce their claim. Signed:
GILBERT GREER, FRANCES (X) GREER. Wit: WM. GREER, PETER MALONE.

Page 48:   Rec. 29 Nov. 1792, Deed dated 12 Dec.1791, bet. MARGRET
             SHEILDS, Admnx. of WILLIAM MCFARLAND, dec'd of Col. Co. of
one part and ROBERT MCCORKLE of same, consid. of 47 lbs. 10 shillings
lawful money, conveys tract of 150 acres by gt. gtd. to WILLIAM MCFARLAND
bearing date 5 Dec. 1782 and Regist. in Book M., Folio 617, Aug. 2,
1774, in Col. Co. Letters of Admm. gtd. to MARGRET SHEILS dated 17
Jan. 1785 in Rich. Co., and by virtue of a Judgment of ELIZABETH DYSART
and HENRY CANDLER, Admr. fee of WILLIAM CANDLER an Exor., was levied on
sd. 150 acres by PETER CRAWFORD, Sheriff and sold at public auction to
sd. MARGRET SHEILDS for sum of 52 lbs. 2 shillings... and appeared in
deed from PETER CRAWFORD to MARGRET SHEILDS dated 18 May 1789. Signed
MARGARET SHEILDS. Wit: JOHN RUPAN (or ROUPAN or ROUSSAN), JAMES MC-
CORKEL.

Page 51:   Rec. 29 Nov. 1792, Deed dated 8 Nov. 1783, bet. SAMUEL MORTON
             and ANN his wife of No. Car. & Mulenburg Co., Planter and
EBENEZER SMITH, farmer of Rich. Co., Ga., consid. of 5 lbs. Sterl.,
convey tract in Rich. Co. on Great Keokia Creek, cont. 200 acres,
bounded by lands of EBENEZER SMITH, dec'd., of ABRAHAM AYERS, dec'd.,
of JOSHUA BRADLEY and BENJAMIN HARRIS and other sides vacant, gtd. sd.
MORTON by Warrant dated 6 Jan. 1773, and surveyed 28 June 1774 by
JEDEDIAH SMITH and conf. by patent dated 6 Dec. 1774, Rec. Book M.,
Folio 808 the 7 Jan. 1774 by WILLIAM HOUSTON, Regis. Signed: SAMUEL
MORTON. Wit: JOHN FINDLY, JAMES SMITH, JNO. TORRENCE.

Page 53:   Rec. 30 Nov. 1792, Deed dated 22 March 1791, bet. JAMES
             LOVELL and ANN his wife of Col. Co. and WILLIAM JENNINGS of
other, consid. of 25 lbs. Sterl. tract in Col. Co. cont. 50 acres,
bounded by LAWTONS land, branch on north, JOSEPH THOMAS and WILLIAM
JENNINGS. Signed: JAMES LOVELL, ANN (X) LOVELL. Wit: RICH'D. P.
WHITE, NATHAN WARD, NICK, MERRIWETHER.

Page 55:   Rec. 24 Dec. 1792, Deed dated 22 Oct. 1792, bet. RANDAL
             RAMSEY, Jr., and wife of one part and ISHAM BAYLIS of other
part (both of Col. Co.), consid. of 150 lbs. Cur.Money, convey tract
cont. 150 acres lying both sides of Little Kiokia Creek and in Col Co.,
gtd. to JOHN RAMSEY on 3 Jan. 1775, bounded by lands of JAMES GRAVES,
JAMES MCFARLAND & vacant. Signed: RANDOLPH RAMSEY, MARREY (X) RAMSEY.
Wit: JAS. FLEMING, J.P.

Page 57:   Rec. 6 Jan. 1793, Deed dated 25 Oct. 1792, bet. JAMES
             CARTLEDGE and JANE AYRES both of Col. Co. and NEAL DAUGERTY
of same, consid. of 60 lbs. law.mo., convey tract of 150 acres in Col
Co. bounded by lands vacant at time of orig. gt. lying bet. Greenbrier
Creek, and the Kiokia Creek, being tract gtd. to ABRAHAM AYRES, dec'd.
Signed: JAMES CARTLEDGE, JAIN (X) AIRES. Wit: MARTIN MELLOWN, JOHN
DAUGHERTY.

Page 59:   Rec. 6 Jan. 1793, Deed dated 27 Oct. 1792, bet. NEAL
             DAUGHERTY of Col. Co. and PATRICK DAUGHERTY of same of
other, consid of 60 lbs. law.money, convey tract of 150 acres in Col.
Co., orig. gtd. to ABRAHAM AYRES (same tract as above on Page 57).
Signed: N. DOUGHERTY. Wit: JOHN DOUGHERTY, J. EVANS.

Page 61:   Rec. 6 Jan. 1793, Deed dated 29 Oct. 1792, bet. NEAIL DOUGH-
             ERTY of Col. Co. and PATRICK DOUGHERTY of same, consid of
60 lbs, tract of 150 acres in Col. Co., bounded by lands of ROBERT COWINS
WILLIAM CANDLER, GEORGE UPTON & DANIEL MCCARTY formerly property of
JOHN LIGHINGSTON, same forfeited to state & gtd. to NEHEMEAH (WAD?)
by Co. of Conf. Est. of act of 1782. Signed: N. DOUGHERTY. Wit:
JOHN DOUGHERTY.

Page 63:   Rec. 6 Jan. 1793, Deed dated 19 Feb. 1791, bet. THOMAS
             LAWTON and ELIZABETH his wife of Col. Co. and WILLIAM JENNINGS
of the other part, consid. of 50 lbs. Sterl. tract in Col. Co., upon
Booths Branch Creek, about 1 mile from Savannah River, cont. 100 acres,
bounded by lands of SAMUEL PAYNES, Senr., JOSEPH THOMAS, part of tract
gtd. to THOMAS LAWTON on his own headright, (part of which THOMAS LAWTON
sold 100 acres to SAMUEL PAYNE) gtd. to THOMAS LAWTON 12 Aug. 1784.
Signed: THOS. LAWTON, ELIZABETH (X) LAWTON. Wit: HORATIO MARBURY,
JEREMIAH LAMKIN.

Page 65:   Rec. 10 Jan. 1793, Deed dated 13 July 1785, bet. Captain
             JAMES MCFARLAND of Rich. Co. and PETER OVERBY, Hatter of same,
consid. of 7 lbs. Sterl. tract of 1 acre lying in town of Wrightsboro,
known in plan of sd. town by #50, gtd. to sd. MCFARLAND ___ day
month ___ 17 & ___. Signed: JAS. MCFARLAND. Wit: R. HOWARD, J.P.,
other name illegible.

Page 67:   Rec. 10 Jan. 1793, Deed dated 2 July 1787, bet. PETER PERKINS
             of Wilks Co., Planter and SARAH his wife and PETER OVERBY of
Rich. Co., Hatter, consid. of 50 lbs. Sterl. specie, tract in town of
Wrightsboro in Rich. Co., cont. 1 acre, #48. Signed: PETER (X)
PERKINS. Wit: BENJ. REES, R. HOWARD, J.P.

Page 69*, 70:   Rec. 28 Jan. 1793, JOSEPH MORTON for consid. of sum of
             94 lbs. Sterl. of Ga. paid to (Capt.?) HENRY HAMPTON
sold to GERRARD BANKS of Wilkes Co., Ga., a good new well built wagon
with a team. Signed: J. MORTON. Wit: J. PANNILL. Ack. in Wilkes
Co., which says COLONEL JOSEPH PANNILL witnessed the above.
     *Note by Ed. In Deed Book Page 70 reads page 76.

THE ENTREES FOLLOWING SHOW A NEW CLERK BEGINNING MAKING ENTREES

Page 77*:   Rec. 12 Feb. 1793, Deed (no date given) from WILLIAM HUGHS
             and SARAH his wife of Col. Co., convey to JAMES MULLEN of
same, 300 acres, a survey of 14 May 1787 and gtd. to WILLIAM HUGHS 19
Aug. 1790, bounding lands of F. SANDERS, for consid. of 30 lbs. Sterl.
Signed: WILLIAM HUGHS, SARAH (X) HUGHS. Wit: FITS (FITZ) M. (MORRIS)
HUNT, JOHN DUNCAN, JOHN (X) HAM.
     * Note, this is actually Page 72.

Page 78:   Rec. 12 Feb. 1793, Deed dated 21 Jan. 1791, bet. JOHN TOWN
             and MARGARET his wife of Col. Co. and JAMES WILLIS of same,
consid. of 200 lbs. law.money tract of 50 acres in same, adj. MORDICA
MOORS, Upton's Creek, SANDERS Mill, Signed: JOHN TOWNS, MARGARET (X)
TOWNS. Wit: THOMAS PORTER, WILLIAM SEAY, JOHN BINION, B. CATCHING,
J.P. (Wilkes Co., Ga., within deed proved by oath of WILLIAM SEAY,
3 Dec. 1791.

Page 80:   Rec. 12 Feb. 1793, Deed dated 20 Jan. 1791, bet. JOHN KING,
             Esq. of Wilkes Co. and JANE his wife and CHARLES PORTER of
Rich. Co., consid. of 50 lbs. tract of 100 acres on both sides of
Upton's Creek bounded by lands of MORDICA MOORE, EUKLES on south and
west and confiscated as the property of WILLIAM MANSON inc. dwelling
house where CHARLES PORTER now lives. Signed: JOHN KING. Wit:
J. COSBY, J.P., WM. COATS.

Page 81:   Rec. 13 Feb. 1793, Deed dated 19 March 1789, bet. RHESA
             HOWARD and CHARLES LIN both of township of Wrightsboro, Co.
of Rich., Esq's and THOMAS MEREWETHER, Senr. of other, consid. 430 lbs.
Specie, convey tract in Col. Co. on Booths Branch Creek, ca. 1 mile
from Sav. River, cont. 450 acres, bounded by lands of THOMAS LOYD,
THOMAS LAWTON, MORDECA SHEFTELL, sd. tract gtd. to CHARLES PARKS 5
July 1779, in Book F, Folio 136. Signed: R. HOWARD, CHARLES LIN.
Wit: WILLIAM HUNT, THOS. WHITE, J.P.

Page 83:   Rec. 13 Feb. 1793, Deed dated 28 Dec. 1792, bet. JOHN MORRIS
             and ELIZABETH MORRIS his wife of Col. Co. and DREDZIL PACE

of same, consid. of 120 lbs. law.money, convey 2 tracts, one cont. 150
acres lying and being in sd. state and formerly St. Paul's Parish but
now Col. Co. on Michaels Creek or Germany Creek, orig. gtd. to THOMAS
MORRIS and beq. by him to sd. JOHN MORRIS his son and bearing date 7
April 1772, the other 45 acres adj. afsd. 150 acres formerly Rich. Co.
now Col. Co., bounding FOSTERS land and MORRIS land, DAVISES land and
orig. gtd. JOHN MORRIS 9 Feb. 1790, total of 195 acres. Signed: JOHN
MORRIS, ELIZABETH (X) MORRIS. Wit: JOSEPH GARNETT, STEPHEN JOHNSTON,
P. FOSTER, J.P., ELISABETH MORRIS Rel. Dower bef. P. FOSTER, J.P.

Page 85:   Rec. 14 Feb. 1793, Deed dated 10 Jan. 1789, bet. JOHN CAR-
            MICHALL of Rich. Co. and MARY his wife and BENJAMIN PORTER
of Col. Co., consid. 50 lbs. convey tract in Rich. Co. on waters of
Greenbrier Creek, cont. 150 acres, bounded by PORTER, BUGG and lands
belonging to sd. PORTER gtd. to ANDERSON CRAWFORD and on west by lands
now claimed by IGNATIUS FEW but 1st. survey by ALEXANDER DOUGLASS.
Signed: JNO. CARMICHALL. Wit: THO. NAPIER, J.P.

Page 87:   Rec. 28 Feb. 1793, Bill of Sale from James Hamilton,
            Sheriff of Col. Co. on 14 Dec. 1792, requiring that lands
etc. of LEW. JONES for debt of 4 lbs, 5 shillings with interest from
25 Dec. 1794, sale of cert. negroes (named), when Capt. THOMAS L. JONES
being highest bidder knocked off to him for sum of 72 lbs. Signed:
JAMES HAMILTON, Dated 5 Feb. 1793.

Page 88:   Rec. 28 Feb. 1793, Wilkes County, July 11, 1778, Receipt of
            JAMES HAWKINS for $1200, 300 lbs, clear of all demans for
tract of land lying on Kiokias joining JOHN COLEMANS land. Signed:
HOLL'D. MIDDLETON. Augusta 7 Dec. 1792, ROBERT MIDDLETON made oath
that the within hand writing signed HOLLY MIDDLETON is signed by him.
Signed: ROBERT MIDDLETON, 8 Dec. 1793, GEO. YOUNG, J.P.

Page 89:   Rec. 1 March 1793, State of Maryland, Prince George County,
            Deposition of MARGRET COBLEGE of same, saith in year 1785
she lent a negro boy named Providence to THOMAS P. CARNES, Esq. then an
Att. at Law in Co. and State afsd. and living at upper Marlborough
within a mile or two of the place of her residence and that the boy
remained with him until his departure for State of Georgia and sd.
THOMAS P. CARNES when about to leave State of Md. (she the Dep. has
been informed and believes) sent the afsd. negro boy to his the afore-
mentioned THOMAS P. CARNES fathers in St. Mary's County, for purpose of
carrying cloaths and that he left sd. boy then with directions to his
father to return him to his mistress (this deponent) and that THOMAS P.
CARNES has intention of taking residence in Ga., and she is desirous of
having the boy in her possession and service, sent to house of THOMAS
P. CARNES father and she believes the sd. THOMAS P. CARNES was not by
any dishonest or fradulent motives in sending sd. Providence to his
father. Taken Out 3 August 1792, bef. DAVID CRAWFORD, J. for P.G. Co.
Ct.

Page 91:   Rec. 21 March 1793, Relinquishment to Trustees of Quaker
            Meeting House for 43 acres. ROBERT FLOURNOY of Greene Co.
in Ga. for divers good consideration do relinquish claim to tract of
43 acres for use of Society of the People called Quakers, being part of
tract orig. gtd. to JAMES WRIGHT, known by name of Quaker Meeting House,
tract in Wrightsboro Dist. of Col. Co. gtd to DANIEL WILLIAMS and JOHN
STUBBS, Jr. as Trustees of Society by WILLIAM BROWNE, Deed bearing date
10 April 1787. Signed: R. FLOURNOY. Wit: CLEMENTIONS DAVIS, R.
HOWARD, J.P.

Page 92:   Rec. 26 March 1793, Deed dated 16 July 1790, bet. PHILIP
            MOSES of City of Savannah and SARAH his wife and ISAAC
BENEDIX of sd. city, merchant, consid. of 160 lbs. Sterl. convey to
ISAAC BENEDIX in his actual possession, tract in St. Paul's Parish,
Rich. Co., cont. 200 acres. Signed: PHILIP MOSES, SARAH MOSES. Wit:
CASHMAN PALOCK, LAM'L STIRKF (or SHARKF?) J.P. Wit. to Signature of
SARAH MOSES, ANPH'R PHILLIPS. SARAH MOSES Rel. Dower 9 Aug. 1790
bef. Justice Court of Common Pleas, County of Phila'd., WM. CRAIG.

Page 96:   Rec. 29 March 1793, Deed dated 12 Jan. 1792, bet. ISAAC
            VERNON of Col. Co. and JOEL SANDERS of same, consid. of 67
lbs. Sterl., convey tract sit. in Col. Co. on Upton's Creek or Moxdoc's
Creek, part of tract orig. gtd. JOSEPH MADDOK and ISAAC VERNON, dec'd.
cont. 150 acres, bounding lands, Mill Tract, formerly laid off for
JAMES BROWN and conveyed to MERCER BROWN, adj. MARION BROWNS line,
JOHN BUK and now property of AMOS GREEN. Signed: ISAAC VERNON. Wit:
CAMM THOMAS, ENOS BUTLIN, WM. THOMAS, J.P., MARGARET HODGEZ, MARY VERNON,
& REBECCA VERNON, mother, wife and sister to within named ISAAC VERNON
Relinq. & Quit Claim. Signed: MARY (X) HODGENS, MARY VERNON, REBECCA
(X) VERNON. Wit: WM. THOMAS, J.P., CAMM THOMAS.

Page 98:   Rec. 30 March 1793, Deed dated 17 March 1792, bet. BENJAMIN
            REES of Col. Co., Planter and ABRAHAM SANDERS of Wilkes Co.
in sd. state, consid. of 60 lbs. Sterl. convey tract in Col. Co. on
waters of Middle Creek, bounded by land sold by sd. REES to EDMOND HAYS,
north by land sold by sd. REES to JACOB SMITH and by land sold by
same to HUGH REES and south by Wilkes Co. line, near JANE GILMOUS line,
it being part of 1287 acres confiscated and sold as property of Sir
James Wrgiht, Esq. and it being then transferred to sd. BENJ. REES,
260 acres. Signed: BENJ. REES, SARAH REES. Wit: RICH'D. CARTER, JNO.
TORRENCE, J.P., Wilks Co.

Page 101:   Rec. 3 April 1793, Deed dated 10 July 1789, bet THOMAS
            GALPHIN of S.C. Esq. the only acting Qual. Exor. of L. W.
& T. of GEORGE GALPHIN late of the last ment. sd. state, Esq. dec'd.
who is qualified in State of Ga. of the one part and DANIEL MCMURPHY of
Rich. Co., Ga., Esq. consid. of 250 lbs. Sterl. conveys tract cont.
500 acres sit. on Keg Creek in Co. of Rich., formerly St. Paul's Parish,
butting and bounding vacant land, JOHN SCOTT, SWINTS land and LINSONS
land, sd. tract gtd. to GEORGE GALPHIN dec'd. 7 Feb. 1775. Signed:
THOMAS GALPHIN. Wit: ALEXANDER AVRIT, THOS. BROOKS. Sworn to 10
Aug. 1791.

Page 103:   Rec. 3 April 1793, Deed dated 4 Jan. 1791, bet. DANIEL
            MCMURPHY of Rich. Co. and EDMOND CARTLEDGE of Col. Co., sd.
DANIEL MCMURPHY and his wife SUSANNAH for consid. of 76 lbs. Sterl.
16 shillings, convey tract cont. 256 acres on Keg Creek in Col Co.,
formerly Rich. Co., butting SAMUEL PAYNE, part of a 500 acre tract gtd.
GEORGE GALPHIN, Esq., dec'd. Signed: DANIEL MCMURPHY, SUSANNAH MC-
MURPHY. Wit: JOHN GRAY, SAMUEL (SP) PAYNE, JOHN (X) CARTLEDGE, JAS.
TAYLOR. Sworn to 22 July 1793.

Page 105:   Rec. 3 April 1793, Deed dated 20 Feb. 1788, bet. THOMAS
            ADCOCK and JAMES ADCOCK and EDMOND CARTLEDGE, Jr., of other
part, consid. of 50 lbs. Sterl. convey tract cont. 50 acres on waters
of Keg Creek, being the land where JAMES ADCOCK now lives, half of 100
acres, orig. gtd. to sd. THOMAS ADCOCK. Reg. 5 April 1785, Book JJJ,
Signed: THOS. (X) ADCOCK, JAMES (Ȝ) ADCOCK. Wit: THOS. MERIWETHER,
Jr., HENRY (X) GOFF.

Page 107:   Rec. 4 April 1793, Deed dated 26 Jan. 1793, bet. THOMAS
            STAPLER and RUTH his wife, JOHN CURRIE and REBECCA his
wife, THOMAS JONES and SARAH his wife, which sd. RUTH, REBECCA & SARAH
are daughters and heirs of the sd. ROBERT STORY, dec'd of one part,
and PRUDENCE STORY, widow of ROBERT STORY dec'd, late of Chatham Co.
(PRUDENCE of Col. Co.) for consid. of 20 lbs. law.money pd. by PRUDENCE
STORY, grant to sd. PRUDENCE STORY her heirs and assigns their due
proportion & distributive shares as claimants under the sd. ROBERT STORY,
dec'd. of all that tract in Brier Creek and Col Co. cont. 17(5) acres,
adj. lands of HENSHAW, HUGH BLAIR, UPTONS Estate and lands of JAMES
ROSS, sd. tract orig. gtd. ROBERT STORY and at his death div. into
equal portions. Signed: THOMAS STAPLER, JOHN CURRIE, REBECCA (X)
CURRIE, THOMAS JONES, SARY (X) JONES. Wit: JOHN STAPLER, BENJAMIN (X)
MICHAL, JANE (X) CURRY. MICHAEL SMALLY swore to above on 20 Feb. 1793
bef. MOSES MARSHALL, J.P.

Page 109:   Rec. 4 April 1793, Deed dated 10 Feb. 1793, bet. PRUDENCE
              STORY of Col. Co. widow of ROBERT STORY, dec'd. late of
Chatham Co., of one part and SHERWOOD BUGG of Col. Co., consid of 34
lbs. law.money, tract cont. 58 acres on both sides of Green Brier Creek,
bounding BLAIRS line, part of tract of 400 acres gtd. to ROBERT STORY
and entered a Memorial in Auditors office Book B, Folio 3 (Note: plat
shows it adjoins RICH'D DUNNS land). Signed: PRUDENCE (P) STORY.
Wit: WATERS DUNN, Junr., ANDREW ALLEN, MICHAEL SMALLEY.

Page 111:   Rec. 4 April 1793, Deed dated 31 July 1792, bet. WILLIAM
              WALTON of Col. Co. and JOSEPH DARSEY of same, consid. of
5 shillings, convey tract in Co. afsd. cont. 179 acres on the big
Kiokia Creek. Wit: JOHN GLENN. Signed: WILLIAM WALTON. Other
Witnesses: GIEON BOOKER, BEN W. STUBBLEFIELD. (Plat shows this land
bounding: JAS. SMITH, JNO. LAZENBERRY, KENDRICKS land, W. LEIGH, ALLENS,
NELSONS land and NATH'L HICKS.

Page 113:   Rec. 2 May 1793, Deed dated 22 Oct. 1791, bet. THOMAS
              WILLINGHAM and OLLEY WILLINGHAM of Col. Co. and also
ALEXANDER JOHNSON, AYRES HOLLIDAY, JOHN WALKER, CORNELIUS JOHNSON,
JACOB JOHNSON, JOHN JOHNSON, SALLEY JOHNSON, MIJAY JOHNSON of Wilkes
County of one part and ROBERT ALLEN of Col. Co., consid. of 150 lbs.
Sterl. convey tract in Col. Co. on White Oak Creek, orig. gtd. to
RICHARD CASTLEBERRY by patent 29 July 1785 cont. 100 acres, being part
of 200 acre gtd. JACOB CASTLEBERRY. Signed: THOMAS (X)WILLINGHAM,
ALLY (X) WILLINGHAM, ALEXD. JOHNSTON, AYRES (X) HOLLIDAY, JOHN WALKER,
CORNELIUS JOHNSTON, JACOB JOHNSTON, JOHN JOHNSTON, SARAY (X) JOHNSTON,
MIJAY (X) JOHNSTON. Wit: MARY (X) GABY, MARGRET (X) GABY. On 5 Nov.
1791, OLLA HOLLIDAY, NELLY WALKER Relinq. Dower.

Page 115:   Rec. 8 May 1793, Deed dated 6 Oct. 1792, bet. JOHN BOYD of
              Col. Co. and NICODEMUS BOYD of same, consid. of 7 lbs.
Sterl. convey tract that was his fathers JOHN BOYD, dec'd. as his
proportion as legatee of sd. JOHN BOYD, dec'd, & in part 2 tracts gtd.
JOHN BOYD, dec'd. one of 400 acres now in Col. Co. orig. gtd. 7 Feb.
1775 and the other of 200 acres adj. to other, the former whereon
ELIZABETH BOYD, widow of sd. JOHN NOW lives. Signed: JOHN (X) BOYD.
Wit: JOHN BUGG, ELIZABETH FOSTER, JNO. FOSTER, J.P.

Page 117:   Rec. 8 May 1793, Deed dated 17 Nov. 1792, bet. DAVID BOYD
              and SARAH BOYD his wife of Washington Co., Ga. and NICO-
DEMUS BOYD of same place, Co. of Col., consid. 5 lbs. Sterl. convey 1/9
part of tract in formerly St. Paul's Parish, now Col. Co., cont. 600
acres, the one 400 acres and other 200 acres, and the 400 acre tract
the one whereon ELIZABETH BOYD, widow to JOHN BOYD, dec'd now lives,
the other near Savannah River orig. gtd. sd. JOHN BOYD, the 1/8 part
amounting to 75 acres, being his proportion of real estate of JOHN BOYD
due to DAVID BOYD as one of heirs. Signed: DAVID BOYD, SARAH (X) BOYD.
Wit: JOHN (I) BOYD, JNO. FOSTER, SARAH BOYD Relinq. Dower 17 Nov. 1792
bef. JNO. FOSTER, J.P.

Page 119:   Rec. 13 May 1793, Power of Attorney dated 2 May 1793 of
              PETER THOMAS late a Soldier in the 14th Va. Geg't. Commanded
by Col. ____ LEWIS, afterwards by ANTHONY WHITE, in the horse service,
do app't. JOSHUA GRINAGE of Col. Co., Ga. to ask, demand... all my
pay or arrearages of pay and bounty of land due me as a soldier.
Signed: PETER (X) THOMAS. Wit: MOSES MARSHALL, J.P., JAMES SIMMS, J.P.

Page 120:   Rec. 13 May 1793, Power of Attorney (no date shown) of
              CHARLES TAYLOR, late a Soldier in the 1st. Va. State Reg't.
commanded by Col. GEORGE GIBSON, do app't. JOSHUA GRINAGE of Col. Co.,
Ga. to ask, demand and rec. all my pay or arrearages of pay and bounty
lands due me as a soldier. Signed: CHARLES TAYLOR. Wit: JAMES MILLEN,
JAS. TAIT, J.P.

Page 121:   Rec. 14 May 1793, Deed dated 11 Feb. 1793, bet. THOMAS
              CRITTENDEN and ANN CRITTENDEN his wife of Washington Co.,
Ga. of the one part and MORRIS KELLY of Col. Co. of other, consid. of

60 lbs. Sterl., convey tract of 100 acres in Rich. Co. and Col. Co., bounding MCNEARS land, FOSTERS land and DAVIS land, orig. gtd. THOMAS CRITTENDEN 29 June 1792 by His Hon. EDWARD TELFAIR, Esq. Gov. Signed: THOMAS CRITTENDEN, ANN (X) CRITTENDEN. Wit: GEO. DOWNS, ARTHUR FORT, J.P. 20 Feb.1793, ANN CRITTENDEN Relinq. Dower bef. ARTHUR FORT, J.P.

Page 123:   Rec. 13 June 1793, Deed dated 10 April 1787, bet. WILLIAM BROWN (Major) of Rich. Co. and DANIEL WILLIAMS, Carpenter and JOHN STUBBS, Junr., both of Rich. Co., sd. WILLIAM BROWN and ANN his wife for consid. of 15 lbs. Sterl. pd. by DANIEL WILLIAMS and JOHN STUBBS, Junr. for themselves and the Society of People called Quakers convey tract in township of Wrightsboro in Rich. Co. cont. 43 acres on waters of Uptons Creek including a house called the Quaker Meeting House, a spring, part of a tract formerly gtd. Sir JAMES WRIGHT, sd. land sold to WILLIAM BROWN by Com. of Confiscated Est's. dated 22 Nov. 1783. Signed: W. BROWN, ANN BROWN. Wit: THOS WHITE, R. HOWARD, J.P., ANN BROWN, wife to Major WILLIAM BROWN Relinq. Dower 13 Nov. 1786 bef. THOS. WHITE & R. HOWARD.

Page 127:   Rec. 13 June 1793, Deed dated 21 Nov. 1791, bet. HENRY BOSSLER of City of Augusta and Rich. Co., Millright and THOMAS HAMILTON of Col. Co., consid. of 200 lbs. Sterl., convey tract of 500 acres in Parish of St. Paul, now Col. Co. bounded by land of DYONISIOUS WRIGHT, WILLIAM HOLLIDAY, JAMES PHILLIPS, bearing date 3 Jan. 1775. Signed: HENRY BOSSLER. Wit: JOHN MONK, BURRICK BULLOCK.

Page 129:   Deed dated 7 May 1793 bet. GEORGE HANDLEY Esq. Sheriff of the Co. of Richmond of one part and JOSHUA SANDERS of Col. Co Esq... for consid. of 6 lbs. Sterl. sold and by virtue of the powers in him as Sheriff and of a Writ of Fi__facias issued out of Sup. Ct. of Chatham Co. dated (blank) last part at the suit of GEORGE HOUSTON agst. ANN ROE (RAE) (now ANN COBBISON) which ANN is admnr. of Est. and effects of JAMES RAE dec'd which JAMES RAE was surviving copartner of JOHN RAE, ROBERT RAE, JAMES RA(LL or AE?), SAMUEL ELBERT, and THOMAS GRAHAM merchants and copartners all dec'd., doth bargain and sell unto sd. JOSHUA SANDERS, being knocked off to him at public out-cry as highest bidder on 5th day Feb. 1793, tract of land cont. 300 acres sit, on Little River in Col. Co. in 2 grants one of which of 200 acres gtd. to BARNERD HEARD on 2 Aug. 1768 bounded on all sides by vacant land and 100 acres gtd. to RICHARD AUSTIN on 3 July 1770 bounded by tract of BERNERD HEARD and other sides vacant. Signed: GEO HANDLEY. Wit: P. CLAYTON, J.P., B. CATCHING. Rec'd year and day above written.

Page 131:   Deed dated 29 Jan. 1791 bet. Captain ROBERT FLOURNOY of Wilkes Co. of one part and KINDRED CARTER of Col. Co., for consid. of 50 lbs. law.money a tract cont. (by survey) 200 acres in Co. of Col., bounding lands of sd. CARTER and others (in description mentions "corner to CARTER & STEEL), part of tract orig. gtd. to Sir. JAMES WRIGHT and sold by Com. of Conf. land to Captain ROBERT FLOURNOY, by deed bearing date 22 Nov. 1783, Signed: ROBT. FLOURNOY. Wit: GADWELL RAINS HARRISON, R. HOWARD, J.P.

Page 133:   Deed dated 16 April 1793, bet. PRUDENCE STORY widow of ROBERT STORY dec'd of Col. Co. and ELENDER SCRUGS wife of JAMES SCRUGS late ELENDER STORY dau. of sd. ROBERT STORY and sd. PRU-DENCE STORY of sd. Co. and State of the one part and HUGH BLAIR of Col. Co., consid. of 33 lbs. law.money, do convey cert. tract in Col. Co. of waters of Greenbrier Creek, bounding: corner of S. BUGG, BLAIRS line of his 200 acre tract, MITCHELS old line, to WATKINS tract of 30 acres, to large poplar by WATKINS & STORY's Spring branch, cont. 52 acres, it being part of tract of 400 gtd. to sd. ROBERT STORY as will appear in the ____ office in Book B, Folio 3, grant sgnd. by JAMES HABERSHAM, President. Signed: PRUDENCE (P) STORY, ELENDER (+) STORY. Wit: H. (HAMPTON?), JOHN ROUSSAU, SHERWD. BUGG, J.P., Rec'd 16 April 1793.

Page 135:   Deed dated 16 April 1793 bet. ANN BENNET of Col. Co. and
            JOHN SCRUGS, son of JAMES of same place of other part,
consid. of 30 lbs. law.money, convey tract in afds. Co. on Waters of
Greenbrier Creek cont. 30 acres, it being part of a tract of 400 acres
gtd. by grant to ROBERT STORY which sd. 30 acres was sold by JAMES
SCRUGS to WILLIAM WATKINS and sold by him to HUGH MAGEE and by him sold
to ANN BENNET bounding lands of SHERWOOD BUGG, MICHAEL SMALLY and the
tract formerly JOHN MITCHELL and remainder of the 400 acre tract.
Signed: ANN (A) BENNETT. Wit: H. HAMPTON, JOHN ROUSSAU, SHERWD.
BUGG, J.P.

Page 137:   Bill of Sale from WILLIAM WATKINS of Col. Co. unto SARAH
            UPTON the sundries to wit: sorril horse, bay horse, 2
bay mares, negro man AMOS, 5 head of cattle, 2 feather beds with furn.
together with all house and kitchen furn., 2 shot guns, thesd. named
articles the value of 150 lbs. Sterl. which sum I already have rec'd. in
hand. Signed: WILLIAM (+) WATKINS. Wit: WATERS DUNN, MARY BURGAMY.
Sworn to 18 July 1793.

Page 138:   Mortgage, Rec'd 10 July 1793. Indenture dated 26 Dec. 1792,
            bet. PELEG & TRUELOVE GREENE of Georgetowns in Wilkes Co.,
of one part and ROBERT BOLTON of Savannah, Co. of Chatham, Merchant of
other part, whereas sd. PELEG GREENE by a writing under his hand
commonly called a promissory note stands indebted to sd. ROBERT BOLTON
in sum of 88 lbs. 10 shillings & 7 pence, sd. note bears date 9 Jan.
1790. Wit: that sd. PELEG GREENE and TRUELOVE GREENE in consid. of sd.
debt, do sell unto ROBERT BOLTON a tract of land on Big Creek in Col.
Co., whereon MCKINDLY now lives cont. 300 acres bounding So. vacant,
MCKINLYS & WATKINS, CRAWFORDS and PEAVYS land (being part of 400 acres
gtd. by His Excellency EDWARD TELFAIR to JOSEPH MCKINLY 24 Jan. 1791.
Signed: PELEG GREENE, TRUELOVE GREENE. Wit: JOHN N. BRAILSFORD, JOHN
HOWELL, Not. Public.

Page 142:   Bill of Sale Recorded 23 July 1793. Whereas we Milly
            Farrier and ABSALOM FARRIER Admnx. and Admnr. of Est. of
GILBERT CLARK dec'd late of Co. of Richmond now Columbia, dec'd on
Feb. 19 did expose to sale the whole of afsd. GILBERT CLARK dec'd which
is cont. noticed or ment.'d in the Inventory, and ABSALOM FARRER being
the highest bidder, for the sum of 56 lbs. cur. money, do convey every
part and parcel to afsd. ABSALOM FARRER. Signed: MILLY (O) FARRAR,
ABSALOM FARRAR. Dated 20 July 1793 in presence of JAMES MCNEIL, J.P.

Page 143:   Deed dated 3 April 1792, bet. JAMES HAMILTON, Esq. Sheriff
            of Col. Co. and ROBERT MIDDLETON of Greene Co., whereas a
fire ficias was issued out of Sup.Ct. of Wilks Co. dated 24 Aug. 1791
under seal of HENRY MOUNGER clerk, requiring the Sheriffs of sd. state,
that goods, chattels, etc. of HORATIO MARBURY, SAMUEL JACK and ROBERT
MIDDLETON, you cause to be made as well a cert. debt of 523 lbs. which
RICHARD WYLY and LEONARD (CREEL)? recovered in sd. ct. held at Wilkes
Ct. House for Aug. term last, agst. them as also ____ which were adjudged
to the sd. WYLY and (CREEL?), where as sd. JAMES HAMILTON sheriff did
set up to sale for cash one tract of land cont. 100 acres, when ROBERT
MIDDLETON being highest bidder for sum of 51 lbs, the sd. 100 acres in
Col. Co. being part of tract of 200 acres gtd. to HENRY GOLDING on
2 Aug. 1774, bounding: GEORGE GALPHIN, GARNETTS land, which was conveyed
from sd. HENRY GOLDING to LEONARD MARBURY and from sd. MARBURY to
ELIZABETH FRAZIER and from her to HORATIO MARBURY. Signed: JAMES
HAMILTON. Wit: D. HUNTER, J.P., WM. GARDNER. Rec'd. 10 Aug. 1793.

Page 145:   Deed dated 3 April 1792, recorded 10 Aug. 1793, bet. JAMES
            HAMILTON, Sheriff of Col. Co. of one part and ROBERT
MIDDLETON of Greene Co. of other, a fire ficias issued from Wilks Co.
Sup. Ct. on 24 Aug. 1791 sells tract of 152 acres to ROBERT MIDDLETON
the highest bidder for sum of 70 lbs. in Col. Co. being a moiety of
Germany Island orig. gtd. to JOHN ROE (RAE). Signed: JAMES HAMILTON.
Wit: D. HUNTER, J. P., WM. GARDNER.

Page 147:   Deed recorded 13 Aug. 1793, whereas THOMAS GOLPHIN and
            WILLIAM DUNBAR the Exors. of GEORGE GOLPHIN on 6 Aug. 1791
did commence and institute action on the Coll.? and soforth agst.
EPHRIAM (L or S)ANDERS, Admnr. of Est. of WILLIAM GILPHIN, dec'd. in
Inf. Ct. of Col. Co. and on 12 Sept. 1791 received sum of 72 lbs., 10
shillings, Court ordered that goods chattels etc. of EPHRIAM LANDERS,
Admnr. of Est. of WILLIAM GILPHIN, they or either of them should cause
to be made and levied the sum of 72 lbs. 10 shil, which sh. writ the
tract wherein described was sold at auction for 52 lbs. by EDMOND
JENKINS, Esq. Sheriff of Col. Co. at which EPHRIAM LANDERS was highest
bidder, the tract cont. 100 acres sit. in Col. Co. on East side of
Little Kiokia Creek. Signed: EDMD. B. JENKINS. Wit: GIDEON BOOKER,
M. WALTON. Dated 20 Dec. 1791

Page 149:   Bond, rec'd. 14 Aug. 1793, bet. GEORGE JOHNSON of Burke
            Co., Ga. who is bound unto ISHAM BAYLIS of Rich. Co., in
the full sum of 500 lbs. Sterl. and dated 19 Nov. 1788, the consid. of
above obligation is such that whereas the sd. GEORGE JOHNSON hath
sold unto ISHAM BAYLIS a cert. tract cont. 250 acres in Richmond Co.,
which sd. land was orig. gtd. to ROBERT GRAVES on 4 Oct. 1774 and since
conveyed to "my father" GEORGE JOHNSON. Signed: GEORGE JOHNSON.
Wit: JOHN GRIFFIN, YANCEY (L or S)ANDERS.

Page 150:   Bill of Sale, rec'd 14 Aug. 1793 from JOHN RAMSEY the
            younger of Col. Co. who sold unto JOHN CULBREATH of same one
negro boy named JAMES about age of 10 years. Dated 8 Feb. 1793. Signed:
JOHN RAMSEY. Test. J. MCNEIL, J.P. (no price mentioned).

Page 151:   Deed dated 13 July 1793, rec'd 14 Aug. 1793, bet. THOMAS
            HENSON and ELIZABETH his wife of Col. Co., Shoemaker of
one part and JOHN FURY of town of Augusta of other, consid. of 50 lbs.
Sterl. convey tract cont. 100 acres in Col. Co. bounded by GERMANY's
land, MILLINS land and other sides by Savannah River. Signed: THOS.
HANSON, ELIZABETH HANSON. Wit: J. EVANS, J. FOSTER, J. P., ELIZABETH
HANSON Rel. Dower 13 July 1793.

Page 153:   Deed dated 16 Feb. 1778, recorded 15 Aug. 1793, bet. DANIEL
            WALKER of Richmond Co., Planter and WILLIAM STANFORD,
planter of other, consid. 500 lbs. Sterl. Money, doth convey tract in
Co. afsd. in Saint Paul's Parish, cont. 100 acres as more fully appears
by GEORGE C____ and by His Majestys Letter Pattant to sd. GEORGE
COU___ (ON), bearing date 5 July 1774. Signed: DANIEL (D) WALKER,
SUSANNAH (+) WALKER. Wit: NATHAN HARRIS, ROBT. (R) STORY.

Page 155:   Deed dated 13 Aug. 1793, Rec'd 15 Aug. 1793, bet. FREDRICK
            BROWN and PEACE BROWN his wife of Col. Co. of one part and
HEZEKIAH JONES of Richmond Co., consid. of 100 lbs. Sterl., convey
tract in Col. Co. bet. the Big and Little Kiokia Creeks cont. 200 acres,
bounded by LAMARS land, COLLINS land, WILLSONS land, VAUGHNS land,
N. W. by land orig. JESSE LOWES the sd. BROWN gtd. 200 acres 10 Aug.
1784. Signed: FREDRICK BROWN, PEACE BROWN. Wit: JAS. SIMMS, J.P.,
J. WRIGHT.

Page 157:   Deed dated 21 Jan. 1793, Rec'd 20 Aug. 1793, bet. SUSANNAH
            COLEMAN, DREDZIL PAU, and PAUL CALDWELL, legatees of Est.
of GEORGE ROSBOROUGH, dec'd Wit. that sd. Legatees do mutually agree
to devise the tract of land whereon sd. GEORGE ROSBOROUGH dec'd. lived
cont. 350 acres agreeable to the Plat in the Marhin, cont. each 116
and 2/3's acres. Signed: SUSANNAH (C) COLEMAN, PAUL CALDWELL,
DREDZIL PAU. Wit: JAS. SIMMS, J.P. (This name is PACE instead of
PAU in your editors opinion.)

Page 158:   Bill of Sale, Rec'd 20 Aug. 1793 from WILLIAM WILKINS of
            Col. Co. to WILLIAM LAUGHLIN of Col. Co., a certain negro
by name of Alse about age of 8 years which sd. girl I had of a certain
THOMAS LAUGHLIN, for and in consid. of sum of 30 lbs. to me paid.
Signed: WM. WILKINS. Wit: SAMUEL LAUGHLIN, WILLIAM LAUGHLIN, GEORGE
TARVIN. Dated 26 Feb. 1793.

Page 159:   Deed dated 25 Oct. 1792, Rec'd 20 Aug. 1793, bet. ABIGAL
             LOWTRIP of Col. Co. of one part and BENJAMIN RICKETSON of
same, consid. of 10 lbs. cur.money conveys tract of land cont. 50
acres in Col. Co. on a branch of Savannah River known by name of Dry
Branch, being part of a larger tract gtd. to sd. ABIGAL LOWTRIP by
grant dated 8 Feb. 1785. Signed: ABIGAL LOWTRIP. Wit: JOHN COTTIER,
JAS. JONES. (Later when payment received JOHN COTTIER is spelled
COLLIER.)

Page 161:   Bill of Sale dated 26 March 1793 in Augusta, recorded 20
             Aug. 1793, from THOMAS MOORE, planter of Col. Co. in consid.
of sum of 65 lbs. specie to sells to GODFREY ZIMMERMAN of Augusta a
negro woman named Lucy with her child Abia, Lucy about 26 years of
age, Abia her child about one year of age. Signed: THOMAS MOORE.
Wit; PETER CRAWFORD, J.P. Ack. 25 April 1793 in Open Court.

Page 162:   Bill of Sale dated 4 March 1793, Rec'd 20 Aug. 1793 from
             WILLIAM WILKIN of Co. of Burke state of Ga. unto WILLIAM
WILKINS of Col. Co., one negro man about age of 30 years named Dick,
for sum of 18 lbs. 2 shillings Sterl. Signed: WILLIAM (X) WILKINS.
Wit: THANKFULL WILKINS, MARTIN BEAVERS. Sworn to Aug. 5, 1793.

Page 163:   Deed dated 22 April 1793, Rec'd 21 Aug. 1793, bet. GEORGE
             TARVIN of Col. Co., planter and WILLIAM WILKINS of sd. Co.,
planter, consid. 150 lbs. Sterl. tract cont. 250 acres sit. in Parish
of St. Paul (now Col. Co.) and bounded by land sd. to be EDWARD BARNERD,
MICHAEL ILLY, WILLIAM CANDLER, orig. gtd. WILLIAM TARVIN on 3 Jan.
1775 JAMES WRIGHT, Baronet Governor of the then Province. Signed:
GEORGE TARVIN. Wit: THANKFULL WILKINS, A. CRAWFORD, J.P.

Page 165:   Deed dated 29 June 1786, Rec'd 22 Aug. 1793, bet. JOHN
             GARRETT of Augusta in Rich. Co. Gentleman and CATHERINE his
wife and BENJAMIN REES of Wrightsborough Rich. Co., Gentleman, consid.
of 250 lbs. law.money, convey tract cont. 1285 acres in township of
Wrightsborough, bounding lands of JOHN GRAYHAM, ____ HUNTER and SAMUEL
OLIVER, JOSEPH STUBBS, TRAVIS JONES, orig. Sir JAMES WRIGHT and sold as
his confiscated property to sd. JOHN GARRETT on 13 Sept. last past.
Signed: JOHN GARRETT, CATHERINE (+) GARRETT. Wit: LUCY FARISH, JOHN
SWEPSON, WM. HA_.

Page 167:   Deed dated 14 May 1793, Rec'd. 25 Aug. 1793, bet. MORRIS
             KELLEY of Col. Co. of one part and GEORGE NEWMAN of Co.
afsd. of others, consid. of 65 lbs. Sterl. grant tract in Col Co. cont.
100 acres and bounded by: WILKINS land, FOSTERS land, and all other
sides by DAVISES land, orig. gtd. to THOMAS CRITTENDEN on 29 June 1792
and conveyed by him to the sd. MORRIS KELLEY on 11 Feb. 1793. Signed:
MORRIS KELLEY. Wit: ELIZABETH FOSTER, J. FOSTER, J.P.

Page 168:   Power of Attorney, Recorded 10 Sept. 1793 from JOHN
             SUDTHARD, Late a soldier in Colo. ANTHONY W. WHITES Core
of horses, do app't. JOSHUA GRINAGE of Col. Co. to demand and receive
all my pay or arrearages of pay and bounty of land due to me as a
soldier from the United States or the State of Virginia. Signed:
JOHN SUDTHARD. Dated 3 May 1793. Wit: JONATHAN ARMSTRONG, WM. EVANS,
J.P.

Page 169:   Power of Attorney, Recorded 10 Sept. 1793, Dated _th. March
             1793 from CHARLES TAYLOR late a soldier in the first Vir-
ginia State Regiment commanded by Colonel GEORGE GIBSON, appt's.
JOSHUA GRINAGE of Col. Co. to demand and receive arrears of pay and
bounty of land due him as a soldier from the United States of State
of Virginia. Signed: CHARLES TAYLOR. Wit: JAMES M___. JAS. TAIT,
J.P. (In the microfilm, this Power of Att. has been crossed out with a
large "X".)

Page 169:   Power of Attorney Recorded 10 Sept. 1793, Dated 13 May 1793
             from JOHN BEALIE late a soldier in the Virginia line

27

commanded by Colonel E. BL___ appt's JOSHUA GRINAGE OF Col. Co. to demand and received arrears of pay and bounty of land due him as a soldier from the U.S. or State of Virginia. Signed: JOHN BEALLE. Wit: RICHD. KING, PETER CRAWFORD, J.P.

Page 170:   Power of Attorney dated 13 May 1793, Recorded 10 Sept. 1793 from ROBERT HASTINGS late a soldier in the Delaware regiment commanded by Col. VAUGHN and Capt.KIRKWOOD appt's JOSHUA GRINAGE of Col. Co. to demand and receive arrearages of pay and bounty of land due him as a soldier from the U.S. or State of Delaware. Signed: ROBERT (+) HASTINGS. Wit: MARMADUKE RICKETSON, ANDREW WHIT-FIELD, J.P.

Page 171:   Power of Attorney, Dated 7 Sept. 1793, Recorded 10 Sept. 1793 from GEORGE DOUGLASS late of South Carolina who appt's JOSHUA GRINAGE of Col. Co. to demand and receive certificates or due bills that may be due him for services, supplies or money funded in the state of S.C. from the U.S. or state of S.C. Signed: GEORGE DOUGLAS. Wit: P. CLAYTON, J.P.

Page 172:   Power of Attorney dated 11 May 1793, Recorded 10 Sept. 1793 from JULIUS HOLLAND late a soldier in the light Dragoons service commanded by Colo. WHITE appt's JOSHUA GRINAGE of Col. Co. to demand arrearages of pay and bounty of land due him as a soldier from the U.S. or State of Virginia. Signed: JULIUS HOLLAND. Wit: JS. HOLLAND, J.P., JOHN SUDTHARD. JULIUS HOLLAND appeared before JS. HOLLAND, Justice of Lincoln Co., N.C. and ack. his Power of Att.

Page 173:   Power of Attorney dated 7 Sept. 1793, Recorded 10 Sept. 1793 from WILLIAM BELLAMEY late of South Carolina appt's. JOSHUA GRINAGE to demand and receive all certificates, due bills that may be due him for supplies furnished to the Continental Army under the command of General Lincoln. Signed: WILLIAM BELLAMY. Wit: WILLIAM LONGSTREET, J.P.

Page 173:   Power of Attorney Dated 7 Sept. 1793, Recorded 10 Sept. 1793 from ALEXANDER JOHNSTON, late a soldier in the Inde-pendant Company commanded by Capt. JOHN MOORE, appt's JOSHUA GRINAGE of Col. Co. to demand and receive arrearages of pay and bounty of land due him as a soldier from U.S. or State of S.C. Signed: ALEXAR. JOHNSTON. Wit: SHERWD. BUGG, J.P., WM. GOB___.

Page 174:   Power of Attorney Dated 10 Aug. 1793, from WILLIAM CREEMOR late a soldier of the 15th Virginia Regt. commanded by Col. INNIS appt's JOSHUA GRINAGE of Col. Co. to demand and receive arrearages of pay and bounty of land due him as a soldier from the U.S. or State of Virginia. Signed: WILLIAM CREEMOR. Wit: JOHN SUDTHARD, WILLIAMS EVANS, J.P.

Page 175:   Power of Attorney Dated 29 Aug. 1793 from JOHANTHAN TAYLOR late a soldier in 3rd Regt. of L.D. Commanded by Colo. WILL. WASHINGTON appt's JOSHUA GRINAGE of Col. Co. to demand and receive arrearages of pay and bounty of land from the U.S. or State of (blank). Signed: JONATHAN TAYLOR. Wit: DANIEL PARKER, SAML. JACK, J.P.

Page 175:   Power of Attorney Dated 23 July 1793, Recorded 10 Sept. 1793, from WILLIAM HOLT, late soldier in the 6th. Pennsyl-vania Regt. commanded by Colo. THOMAS JOHNSON appt's JOSHUA GRINAGE to demand and receive arrearages of pay and bounty of land due him as a soldier from the U.S. or State of Pennsylvania. Signed: WILLIAM HOLT. Wit: RICHARD WORSHAM, J.P., RICHARD JOHNSON.

Page 176:   Power of Attorney Dated 6 Aug. 1793, Recorded 10 Sept. 1793, from JOHN MCCARTY late a soldier in the third Regt.

of S.C. Troop commanded by Colo. THOMASON appt's JOSHUA GRINAGE of Col. Co. to demand and received arrearages of pay and bounty of land due him as a soldier from the U.S. or State of S.C. Signed: JOHN MCCARTY. Wit: SAML. JONES, R. HOWARD, J.P.

Page 177: Power of Attorney, Dated 15 Aug. 1793, Recorded 10 Sept. 1793 from PATRICK MCMAHAN late a soldier 14th. Virginia Regt. commanded by Colo. LEWIS appt's JOSHUA GRINAGE to demand and receive arrearages of pay and bounty of land due him as a soldier from the U.S. or State of Virginia. Signed: PATRICK MCMAHAN. Wit: RICHARD WORSHAM, RICHARD JOHNSON.

Page 177: Power to Attorney, Dated 10 May 1793, Recorded 10 Sept. 1793, from HENRY MCCARDILE late a soldier in 6th Regt. or S.C. commanded by Colonel SUMPTER appt's JOSHUA GRINAGE of Col. Co. to demand and receive arrearages of pay and bounty of land due him as a soldier from the U.S. or State of S.C. Signed: HENRY (X) MCCARDILL. Wit: RICHD. KING, PETER CRAWFORD, J.P.

Page 178: Power of Attorney, Dated 1 Sept. 1793, Recorded 10 Sept. 1793, from ROBERT NIXON late a soldier in North Carolina line of Continental troops, appt's JOSHUA GRINAGE of Col. Co. to demand and receive arrearages of pay and bounty of land due him as a soldier from the U.S. or State of North Carolina. Signed: ROBT. NIXON. Wit: JNO. FOSTER, J.P.

Page 179: Deed dated 26 July 1792, Recorded 13 Sept. 1793, bet. JOHN MARSHALL of Col. Co., Planter of one part and ALEXANDER SCOTT of State of S.C. County of Lincoln, Doctor of Divinity of other, consid. of 150 lbs. paid to sd. ALEXANDER SCOTT and ELIZABETH his wife by JOHN MARSHALL, convey tract cont. 300 acres in Col. Co., bounded by Kiokia Creek below mouth of Greenbrier Creek and running up Creek being land gtd. DANIEL COLEMAN by JAMES WRIGHT, then Gov. and dated 2 Aug. 1774, having such shapes as on plat, thereof annexed to the grant cont. 100 acres, being the north part of a 200 acre tract, it being plantation whereon sd. COLEMAN formerly lived, the other tract bounded southwardly by Kiokia Creek and lands of sd. JOHN MARSHALL, and above ment. tract of land westwardly by lands of THOMAS FORD, land of RICHARD MEADOWS cont. 200 acres formerly gtd. to ALEXANDER SCOTT by Sir. JAMES WRIGHT in 1775. Signed: ALEXD. SCOTT. Wit: LEWIS HARRIS, LUD. HARRIS.

Page 181: Deed of Gift, Dated 27 March 1793, Recorded 13 Sept. 1793 from MOSES THOMSON of Col. Co. and in consid. of the love, good will and affection I have and do bear towards my loving and dutiful son JOHN THOMSON of the State and Co. afsd. do give and grant unto him 200 acres on south side of Brier Creek adj. JOHN POLKS land. Signed: MOSES (+) THOMSON. Wit: WM. WHITTINGTON, JAMES BOLAND. Sworn to bef. NATHAN HARRIS 28 March 1793.

Page 182: Deed of Gift, Dated 27 March 1793, Recorded 13 Sept. 1793 from MOSES THOMSON of Col. Co., for consid. of love, good will and affection which I have unto my loving and dutiful children JOSHUA THOMSON, REUBEN THOMSON, WILLIAM THOMSON and MARY THOMSON of the State and Co. afsd. do freely grant and give unto them to be equally divided among the four, one brown mare branded on the near shoulder (M) and one mare colt and 20 head of cattle, marked a half crop in the left ear and two slits in the right ear and my household furniture to have and to hold all the goods and creatures. Signed: MOSES (+) THOMSON. Wit: WM. WHITTINGTON, JOHN BOLAND, Sworn to bef. NATHAN HARRIS 28 March 1793.

Page 183: Deed dated 31 Dec. 1792, Recorded 14 Sept. 1793, bet. THOMAS HANSON and ELIZABETH HANDSON his wife of Col. Co. of one part and HENRY EVANS of the same consid. of 100 lbs. law.money, convey tract cont. 270 acres in Col Co. on waters of Red Creek but formerly in Co. of Richmond, bounding: SIMS, REDMANS, MORRIS and HANSONS. Signed: THOS. HANSON, ELIZABETH HANSON. Wit: J. EVANS, JNO. FOSTER, J.P., ELIZ. HANSON Rel. Dower bef. JOHN FOSTER 31 Dec. 1792.

Page 185:   Deed dated 4 Jan. 1793, Recorded 14 Sept. 1793, bet. JOHN
            RATTON and (LEYTHIA?) his wife of Franklin County and
State of Ga. of one part and HUGH BLAIR of Col. Co., consid. 100 lbs.
Sterl., convey tract in Col. Co. on waters of Greenbrier a prong of the
Great Kiokia Creek cont. 300 acres, bounding MIDDLETON and APPLINGS
land, the above ment. land being gtd. to (P or S diff. to read as blurred)
ROTTENS by virtur of a Plat and grant gtd. to him 17 years ago. Signed:
JOHN (R) RATTON, LEYTHIA (+) RATTON. Wit: ALEXR. JOHNSTON, WILLIAM
RATTON, ELIZABETH (+) SMITH. (Note: this name may be ROTTON instead
of RATTON, but was so blurred it was diff. to distinguish an O from an
A, Ed.) LETHANAH RATTON Rel. Dower 23 April 1793. (Also, JOHN RATTON's
wife's first name may have started with a "Z" instead of an "L".)

Page 187:   Deed dated 8 Nov. 1788, Recorded 16 Sept. 1793, bet.
            ANDERSON CRAWFORD of Richmond Co. of one part and BENJAMIN
PORTER of sd. Co. of other, consid. of 5 shillings, sd. ANDERSON
CRAWFORD and RACHEL his wife grant tract in Co. of Richmond on waters
of Greenbrier Creek cont. 200 acres. Signed: A. CRAWFORD, RACHEL
CRAWFORD. Wit: J. BARNETT, JOHN ZACHARY. Ack. 20 Aug. 1793. PETER
CRAWFORD, J.P. Col. Co.

Page 188:   Deed dated 15 March 1790, Recorded 16 Sept. 1793, bet. JAMES
            HUTCHINSON of state of Ga. and LUTHEA his wife of one part
and BENJAMIN PORTER of State afsd. of other, consid. of 5 shillings
tract in Rich. Co. on both sides of Germany's Creek, cont. 52½ acres,
bounded by JOSEPH BOGGS, on north by lands formerly owned by WILLIAM
OUSLEY and on south and S. W. by Colo. THOMAS NAPIER and Colo. BENJAMIN
FEW. Signed: J. HUTCHISON. Wit: FREDERICK SIMS, J.P.

Page 189:   Deed dated 8 Nov. 1789, Recorded 16 Sept. 1793, bet
            BENJAMIN PORTER of Wilks Co. of one part and ANDERSON
CRAWFORD of Richmond Co., consid. of 5 shillings. conveys in Richmond
Co. on Little River cont. 100 acres, adjoining lands of RAE (ROE?)
ELBERT & COMPANY, BENJAMIN PORTER and PATSEY his wife by these presents
do sell sd. tract. Signed: B. PORTER. Wit: J. BARNETT, JOHN ZACHRY.
Ack. 25 April 1793.

Page 190:   Deed of Gift, Dated 10 Dec. 1789, Recorded 16 Sept. 1793,
            from DAVID MAXWELL of Richmond Co. for love and good will
I have for JANE BULLOCK wife of DAN BULLOCK of State of S.C. do give
unto her one negro woman named Moll and her increase forever, also one
negro boy named Bobb, also one mare and colt, also one feather bed and
furn. Signed: DAVID MAXWELL. Wit: ROBERT CRAWFORD.

Page 191:   Deed dated 19 May 1788, Recorded 16 Sept. 1793, bet. CHARLES
            CRAWFORD Esq. of Richmond Co. of one part and TIMOTHY LEE
and RACHEL LEE his wife of Wilks Co., consid. of 10 lbs. law. money,
convey tract in Richmond Co. cont. 287 1/2 acres being part of a 937½
acres gtd. the above named DRAWFORD and LEE the 14 Nov. 1787.
Signed: TIMOTHY (+) LEE, RACHEL (R) LEE. Wit: A. CRAWFORD, BENJAMIN
NICHOLSON.

Page 192:   Deed dated 14 Nov. 1791, Recorded 17 Sept. 1793, bet. JOHN
            NORTH of Col. Co. of one part and FRACNIS GRUBBS of Richmond
Co. of other, consid. of 40 lbs. law.money, convey tract cont. 200 acres
in Xol. Co. and on south side of Boggy Gutt Creek gtd. to sd. JOHN
NORTH by grant dated 4 Dec. 1790, bounded by vacant, PRATERS & GARDNERS
land JOHN GARDNERS land. Signed: JOHN NORTH. Wit: JAMES BROOKS,
DANIEL (+) COBB.

Page 194:   Power of Attorney dated 20 Sept. 1793, Recorded 20 Sept.
            1793, from TURNER THOMASON late a soldier in the 2nd
Regt. commanded by Colonel WILLIAM STEWART, appt's P(UCH?)Y BLEDSOE
of Wilks Co. to demand and receive arrearages of pay due him as a soldier
from the U.S. or State of Virginia. Signed: TURNER (I) THOMSON. Wit:
R. HOWARD, J.P., THOS. WHITE, J.P.

Page 195:   Deed dated 22 Aug. 1792, Recorded 2 Oct. 1793, bet. NICHOLAS
             HOBSON BUGG of Richmond Co. and his wife CHARLOTTE of one
part and THOMAS GLASCOCK of Co. and State afsd., Merchant of other,
consid. 400 lbs. law.money, convey all those several tracts of land in
(formerly Richmond Co.) Col. Co., namely all that tract cont. 100
acres formerly Parish of St. Paul but now Col. Co. gtd. to NATHAN HARRIS
on 20 July 1772, also all that tract cont. 400 acres at time of grant
in Parish of St. Paul but now Col. bounding at time of survey lands
of B. WELLS, DANIEL COLEMAN and JAMES BROWN, MITCHELLS and ROBERT STORYS
which sd. tract was gtd. to DANIEL COLEMAN 7 June 1774, also all that
tract cont. 200 acres in Col. Co. on Greenbrier Creek bounding at time
of survey lands of LANCASTER, WELLS & MIDDLETON which sd. tract was
gtd. to ROBERT MIDDLETON on 16 Sept. 1785, cont. on whole 700 acres,
known and distinguished by name of Oak Hill, with all rights to sd.
several tracts cont. 700 acres. Signed: N. H. BUGG, CHARLOTTE BUGG.
Wit: ABRAM JONES, J.P., THO. WATKINS, J.P., CHARLOTTE BUGG Rel. Dower
in Rich. Co. 22 Aug. 1792.

Page 198:   Deed dated 28 March 1793, Recorded 4 Oct. 1793, bet. THOMAS
             GLASCOCK of Richmond Co., Merchant and MARY his wife of one
part and JOHN LIDDALE DIXON of Co. of Washington and State of Ga.,
Planter, consid. of 400 lbs. law.money all those tracts of land sit.
in Richmond Co. (formerly) in the Co. of Col., this grant is of the 3
tracts mentioned in Deed Page 195 preceeding. Signed: THOMAS GLASCOCK,
MARY GLASCOCK. Wit: D. HUNTER, J.P. Page 200, MARY GLASCOCK, Rel.
Dower on 28 March 1793, bef. D. HUNTER, J.P.

Page 201:   Bill of Sale dated 3 July 1792, Recorded 4 Oct. 1793 from
             JAMES HAMILTON, Sheriff of Col. Co. on writ of Sup. Ct. of
Richmond Co. dated 29 May 1790 and hand of THOMAS WATKINS Esq. Clerk
of sd., Ct. that good, chattles, etc. of LEWELLEN JONES be sold for a
debt of 363 lbs., interest which BENJAMIN FEW and JACOB DENNIS recovered in sd. Ct. held in Augusta, did set up to sell for cash the
following negroes, to wit: (18 are named) when Capt. THOMAS JONES
being the highest bidder they were knocked off to him for the price
and sum of 358 lbs. 15 shillings. Signed: JAMES HAMILTON. Wit: PETER
CRAWFORD, J.P.

Page 202:   Power of Attorney dated 9 Oct. 1793, Recorded 9 Oct. 1793,
             from LEWIS GARDNER of Col. Co. to trusty friend ALEXANDER
GARDNER of same, to sell all his rights and claim in cert. tract lying
in North Carolina in County of Bartee (Bertie, Ed.) the one parcel
lying joining on new lands belonging formerly to the Tuskarora Indians,
the other lying on the east side of Cashy Swamp. Signed: LEWIS GARDNER.
Wit: ASHEL GARDNER, JOHN GARDNER, A. CRAWFORD, J.P.

Page 203:   Deed dated 12 Feb. 1791, Recorded 28 Nov. 1793, bet. MARY
             MITCHELL and JOHN G(ALTNY?) of Col. Co. Exors to JOHN
MITCHELL Esq. dec'd of one part and N. H. BUGG of Col. Co., consid.
of 50 lbs. Sterl. law.money, convey tract surveyed for JOHN MITCHELL
of 150 acres surveyed 10 Aug. 1771 and gtd. 2 Dec. 1772, bounding lands
of ROBERT STORY and DANIEL COLEMAN. Signed: MARY (+) MITCHELL, JOHN
(I) GALTONY. Wit: WILLIAM   ? , SAMPSON LAMKIN.

Page 205:   Deed dated 12 July 1792, Recorded 28 Nov. 1793, bet. JOHN
             COBBS of Col. Co. and NICHOLAS H. BUGG of the other part,
consid. of 500 law.money, doth grant that tract in Col. Co. cont. 500
acres, called by name of Oak Hall, bearing date of grant 10 Feb. 1769,
gtd. to NATHAN HARRIS, also one other gtd. to DANIEL COLEMAN, bearing
date 7 June 1774. Signed: JNO. COBBS. Wit: RO. BURTON, JA. WILLIAMS,
ABRAM JONES, J.P.

Page 207:   Deed dated 27 July 1792, Recorded 30 Nov. 1793, bet. THOMAS
             CARR of Col. Co. and NICHOLAS BUGG of Co. of Richmond of
other, consid. of 500 lbs. law.money, doth grant tract in Col Co.,
formerly Richmond, bounded by lands of WILLIAM FEW and others known
by name of Oak Hill, cont. 436 acres. Signed: THO. CARR. Wit:
ABRAHAM JONES, J.P., NATHL. COCKE.

Page 209:   Deed dated 18 Oct. 1790, Recorded 30 Nov. 1793, bet.
             WILLIAM WALTON of Co. and State afsd. of one part and NICHO-
LAS H. BUGG of other, consid. of 5 shillings, convey tract in Richmond
Co., cont. 500 acres, bounded by lands of SHEREWOOD BUGG, JAMES STORY
and other sides vacant. Signed: WILLIAM WALTON. Wit: WM. GLASCOCK,
J.P., THO. WOOD (LIEF?).

Page 210:   Deed dated 3 Dec. 1793 and Recorded 5 Dec. 1793, bet. JOHN
             WILLINGHAM, Junr. and ANN WILLINGHAM his wife of Col. Co. of
one part and JOHN CHATTIN of Pitsilvania Co. and State of Virginia of
other, consid. of 70 lbs, convey tract in Col. Co. cont. 400 acres
gtd. orig. to MANN (SIMS) 17 Dec. 1784 and bounded by STURGESS line,
O'NEILS line, JORDANS line. Signed: JOHN (I) WILLINGHAM, ANN (A)
WILLINGHAM. Wit: WILLIAM WILLINGHAM, CLAYBORN (L or S)ANDERS, LUKE
LANDERS (or SANDERS).

Page 213-223:   Assignment dated 23 Aug. 1792, Recorded 9 Dec. 1793.
                This indenture of three parts bet. GEORGE HUNT, JAMES
STALLINGS and EZEKIEL STALLINGS of the State of Augusta in the Province
of Georgia in North America, Merchants and Copartners (and which sd.
GEORGE HUNT, and JAMES STALLINGS are at the time of the Execution of
these presents at the City of Londone of the first part the several
other persons Creditors of the sd. GEORGE HUNT, JAMES STALLINGS and
EZEKIEL STALLINGS who shall execute these presents within 12 calendar
months from the day of the date of the 2nd. part and CHAMBERLAIN BIRCH
and CHARLES OUVRY of Fleet Street in the City of London Paper Stainers
and Copartners the principle creditors of the (three before mentioned
men, Ed.) and trustees herein after named of the 3rd. part, the firm
of HUNT and STALLINGS are in debt to firm of CHAIMBERLANE BIRCH and
CHARLES OUVRY in the sum of 12,000 pounds, GEORGE HUNT, JAMES STALLINGS
and EZEKIEL STALLINGS assign over the above firm all their goods,
chattles, merchandize, wares, books, assets, debts, sums of money etc.
to the English firm, both in American and Great Brittain. Signed:
GEORGE HUNT, JAMES STALLINGS, CHAMBERLAIN BIRCH, CHAS. OUVRY. Wit:
CHAS. HARMAN, Att., No. 4 Wine Office Court, Fleet Street London;
ROBERT BROWN, At. Messers BIRCH & OUVRYS. Sworn to bef. DALZEIL HUNTER,
J.P. of Richmond Co., 2 Oct. 1793 by STRAFFORD BROWN.

Page 223:   Deed dated 25 Nov. 1793, Recorded 11 Dec. 1793, bet. WILLIAM
             FORD of State and Co. afsd. and JOHN DORSETT, Junior of Col.
Co., Planter, consid. of 50 lbs law. money, convey tract in Col. Co.
cont. 100 acres, bounded at the present survey by MARTAINS land,
ALLISON heirs land, vacant lands and LAZENBYS land, FLURRINCES land.
Singed: WM. FORD. Wit: RICHARD G. BOWDRE, MERRYMAN THORNE, J.P.
Ack. by WILLIAM FORD on 25 Nov. 1793 and CASIAH FORD wife of sd.
WILLIAM FORD Rel. Dower.

Page 225:   Deed dated 12 July 1791, Recorded 11 Dec. 1793, bet. WILLIAM
             WATKINS of Col. Co. and EZEKIEL SMITH of same Co., consid.
of 20 lbs. law.money, convey tract in Col. Co. on waters of Brier Creek
butting and bounding DAVID ROBIRTSONS, cont. 150 acres, the grant
dated 31 Dec. 1787. Signed: WM. WATKINS. Wit: LEWIS CRANE, WILLIAM
UPTON.

Page 227:   Deed dated 19 March 1793, Recorded 11 Dec. 1793, bet
             GEORGE TARVIN, Admnr. of Est. of WILLIAM TARVIN dec'd. of
Col. Co. and GEORGE TARVIN of State and Co. afsd. sd. GEORGE TARVIN
petitioned the Court for an order for the sale of 2 tracts of land.
Wit: 350 acres on Little Kiokia adj. land of THOMAS PACE at the time of
survey 250 acres on waters of Little River adj. lands of WILLIAM CANDLER
and others, both tracts orig. gtd. to sd. WILLIAM TARVEN dec'd., and
Court ordered by an Act for the sale after legal notice being given by
sd. Admnr, and GEORGE TARVEN being highest bidder, the same was knocked
off to him for sum of 48 lbs, Signed: GEORGE TARVEN. Wit: RICHARD
BULLOCK, A. CRAWFORD, J.P.

Page 229:   Deed dated 28 Aug. 1792, Recorded 12 Dec. 1793, bet. RHESA
             HOWARD and HANAH HOWARD both of Col. Co. and THOMAS SHORT
of same. sd. RHESA HOWARD and HANAH HOWARD his wife for consid. of 100
lbs. law.mo. do convey a parcel of land in the sd. county HENRY FLINT
now lives which shall contain 150 acres, being the one half of the 100
acres known by the name of JACOB WATSONS old place, bounded by land
claimed by EZEKIEL HADNALL and one other survey inc. the plantation
whereon HENRY FLINT now lives. Signed: R. HOWARD, HANAH HOWARD. Wit:
RICHD. JONES, MICAJAH LITTLE, EDWARD SHORT.

Page 230:   Deed dated 4 Dec. 1792, Recorded 12 Dec. 1793, bet. JOHN
             HARGROVE of Richmond Co., planter and JOSEPH BATSON and
LUCY his wife of the sd. Co. and state afsd. the sd. JOSEPH BATSON and
his wife LUCY for consid. of 90 lbs. law.mo. convey unto sd. JOSEPH
HARGROVE tract of land cont. 100 acres lying in county afsd., being a
tract orig. gtd. by Sir. JAMES PATE to Richmond as doth appear by grant
bearing date 1 Nov. 1774. Signed: JOSEPH BATTSON. Wit: ELDRIGE
HARGROVE, SOLOMON NEWSOM, JAS. SIMMS, J.P.

Page 232:   Deed dated 27 Nov. 1793, Recorded 12 Dec. 1793, bet.
             LITTLETON YARBOROUGH and ELIZABETH his wife of Col. Co., and
BENJAMIN FINNEY of Col. Co. of other, consid. 100 lbs. Sterl. do convey
tract cont. 300 acres in Col. Co., abounded S.W. WILLIAM TINDELLS land,
S.W. by lands of ANDERSON CRAWFORD and BOOKERS land, N.W. by vacant
land on the N. and N.E. by land of JAMES TINSLEY, sd. land orig. gtd.
to LITTLETON YARBOROUGH 29 April 1788. Signed: LITTLETON YARBOROUGH,
ELIZABETH (+) YARBOROUGH. Wit: THOMAS HAYNES, J.P., FRANCES HAYNES.
ELIZABETH relinquished Dower 27 Nov. 1793 bef THOS. HAYNES, J.P.

Page 234:   Deed dated 8 July 1793, Recorded 13 Dec. 1793, bet. PETER
             CULBREATH and wife of one part and CATHARINE CARR of other
part, consid. of 5 lbs. law.mo. convey tract in Col. Co. on waters of
Little Kiokia Creek, the same being part of a cert. tract cont. 200 acres
gtd. to WILLIAM MCINTOSH on 7 May 1771 and by him conveyed to DAVID
THWEATT on 1 July 1771 and by sd. DAVID THWEATT to us on 10 Sept. 1772,
together with a tract of land the same being gtd. to WILLIAM RAMSEY and
conveyed by him to JOHN RAMSEY and by JOHN RAMSEY to use exchange for
a part of the afsd. tract of land which was tgd. to WILLIAM MCINTOSH
which tract shall contain and include 100 acres, shall be laid off
beginning at N.W. corner of the bef. ment. tract of land gtd. to
WILLIAM MCINTOSH. Signed: PETER (X) CULBREATH, JANE (2) CULBREATH.
Wit: JAMES MCNEIL, J.P.

Page 236:   Deed dated 17 Jan. 1789, Recorded 14 Dec., bet. PHILIP
             UPTON and RACHEL UPTON his wife of one part and JOHN RIVES
of other, for consid. of 100 lbs. law.mo. pd. by sd. JOHN REAVES,
convey tract in Richmond Co. on waters of the great Kiokia cont. 200
acres pine land, bounding N.W. by WILLIAM DRANES, W. by WILLIAM WALTONS,
S. by JOSHUA FULLERS, gtd. to sd. UPTON by GEORGE HANDLEY Governor of
State. Signed: PHILIP (+) UPTON, RACHEL (X) UPTON. Wit: WALTR.
DRANE, WILLIAM DRANE, NANCY (X) UPTON.

Page 237:   Deed dated 17 August 1789, Rec. 14 Dec. 1793, bet. JOSEPH
             RICHARDSON and AMEY RICHARDSON his wife of Richmond Co. of
one part and JOHN TATER (TADER in body of deed, Ed.), convey tract
cont. 100 acres in Rich. Co. on waters of Uchee Creek which sd. 100
acres is part of tract gtd. JAMES ALDRIDGE 21 Feb. 1785, signed by
the Hon. SAMUEL ELBERT, Gov. of Ga. and since conveyed by sd. JAMES
ALDRIDGE, ROSA ALDRIDGE his wife to the above JOSEPH RICHARDSON by
deed dated 25 Nov. 1786, which sd. land bounded: ROSSES line etc.
Signed: JOSEPH (I) RICHARDSON, AMY (+) RICHARDSON. Wit: ANTHONY
HAYNES, JOHN SNOW.

Pages 240-241:   Deed dated May 13, 1789, RICHARD CALL of Richmond Co.
                 Gentleman, to DALZEEL HUNTER of Augusta, for 237
pounds, 10 shillings sterling, 950 acres on water of the Keikia and
Uche Creeks, bounding land sold by sd. RICHARD CALL to sd. DALZIEL
HUNTER, Dec. 9 last, also bounding NININ OFFAT MCGRUDEN, HUGH MILLIGAN,

33

ABEDNEGO WRIGHT, HENRY WRIGHT, ZACHERY, MARK ROBINSON, the heirs of
Miss WRIGHT, WILLIAM BENNET, Junr., WILLIA CARROL, RICHARD CALL (SEAL).
Wit: HORATIO MARBURY, JOSEPH SPENCER, JNO. SHACKEFORD J.P.   Rec. Aug.
29, 1794.

Pages 241-242:   RICHARD CALL and LAETHEA his wife to DALZIEL HUNTER
                 of Augusta for 100 pounds sterling, 400 acres, part of
a tract of 1300 acres granted to the sd. RICHARD CALL lying on the water
of the Keokia and Uche Creeks in Richmond County adj. JAMES WATERS
and EDWARD WALKER, RICHARD CALL (SEAL), ALETHA CALL (LS). Wit: C.
DYSART, PATK. JACK., JNO. SHACKLEFORD JP. Rec. Aug. 29, 1794, Dated
Dec. 9, 1788.

Page 243-244:   Jan. 5, 1789, JOYN COBBS of Richmond Co. to HENRY EVANS
                of same, for 30 pounds lawful money of sd. State of Ga.,
200 acres on a branch of Little River, adj. BUSH & SIMMS. JOHN COBBS
(SEAL). Wit: BA. JONES, THOS. HANCOCK NEVELL. Rec: Aug. 29, 1794.

Page 245:   Columbia Co., Ga., Dec. 28, 1793, ANDERSON CRAWFORD of
            State and County aforesaid to CHARLES PORTER, 200 acres in
Richmond County formerly, but now in Columbia. A. CRAWFORD (LS). Wit:
JOHN CRAWFORD, PETER CRAWFORD, J.P.

Pages 246-247:   May 17, 1790 MANN SIMS of Richmond County to JOHN
                 WILLINGHAM, Junr. of same for 60 pounds sterling, MANN
SIMS and MARGARET his wife, 500 acres originally granted to sd. SIMS
Dec. 17, 1784, MANN SIMS (SEAL), MARGARET SIMS. Wit: ABNER SIMS,
PURMELY DAVIS (X) (her mark). Rec: Jan. 30, 1794.

Pages 248-249:   May 2, 1790, MANN SIMS to JOHN WILLINGHAM for 20 pounds
                 sterling, 250 in Richmond County, adj. WILLINGHAM,
Miss FLEMING & others, part of an 800 grant to sd. SIMS, Dec. 17, 1784,
MANN SIMS (SEAL), MARGARET SIMS (SEAL). Wit: ABNER SIMS, PURMELY
DAVIS (X).

Page 249-251:   Dec. 26, 1793, RECE MORRIS and ELIZABETH his wife to
                THOMAS LAMAR DAVIS all of Columbia County, Ga., for
150 pounds sterling, 200 acres (formerly in St. Paul's Parish), granted
to sd. RECE MORRIS (?) MOVUS (?), Jan. 19, 1773 by JAMES HABERSHAM,
Esqr. RS. MORRIS (SEAL), ELIZABETH MORRIS (SEAL). Wit: DREADREL PACE,
BARNETT WHITTINGTON, JNO. FOSTER, JP. Rec.   31, 1794.

Pages 252-253:   June 22, 1793, WILLIAM JENNINGS of Columbia Co., Ga.,
                 and CATHERINE his wife to WILLIAM JONES of same, for
31 pounds sterling, land adj. SAMUEL PAYNE, SAMUEL SCOTT, JOHN SHACKE-
FORD & WILLIAM JENNINGS. WILLIAM JENNINGS (LS), CATY DYKE JENNINGS (LS),
Wit: JOHN TANKERSLEY J.P.

Pages 254-255:   Aug. 16, 1793, JOHN ZACHERY of Wilkes County to WILLIAM
                 TENDILL Junior of Columbia County, for 25 pounds law-
ful money of sd. state (Ga.), 100 acres in Columbia County, granted to
GARRET JORDAN, June 7, 1786, JOHN ZACKRY (SEAL), SARAH ZACKRY (X)
(SEAL). Wit: BENJAMIN FENNY (X). Rec. Aug. 16, 1793. JOHN ZACKRY
(SEAL), SARAH ZACKRY (X) (SEAL). Test: ABNER ZACKRY, BENJAMIN FENNY
(X). Rec. Jan. 31, 1794.

Page 256:   Columbia County, Ga., JULIUS SCRUGGS do make my friend
            JOSEPH BRADBERRY my lawful attorney to claim a judgment
against ENOCH GREGSBY in Henry County Court, Virginia, for sum of 200
pounds current money of Virginia. Jan. 2, 1793. JULIUS SCRUGGS (SEAL).
Wit: WILLIAM TAYLOR, MILLER BLEDSOE. Mr. GREGSBY pay the within amount
400 pounds Va. currency to Mr. GEORGE B. MOORE. JOSEPH BRADBERRY (X)
Jan. 31, 1794.

Pages 257-258:   Nov. 5, 1792, BENJAMIN WILLIAMS of Columbia County,
                 State of North Carolina, to JOHN WILLINGHAM, Junr. of
Richmond County, Ga., for 28 pounds, land in Richmond County, 100 acres
adj. STEPHEN ELLIS, BENJAMIN WILLIAMS ( ) (SEAL). Wit: THOMAS MOON,
JAMES KNOTT. Rec. Feb. 4, 1794.

Pages 259-261:   March 28, 1791, JAMES HABERSHAM of Chatham County and
                  HESTER his wife to DANIEL WILLIAMS of Columbia County,
Planter, for 4000 pounds weight of tobacco, 50 acres known as the mill
seat, a grist mill and saw mill, line of division run by mutual agreement of JAMES HABERSHAM and DANIEL WILLIAMS as Executor of L. W. & T.
of JAMES KENON (?) Dec'd, adj. heirs of JAMES VERSON, JAS. HABERSHAM
(SEAL). HESTER HABERSHAM (SEAL). Wit: JAS. HABERSHAM JP.

Pages 262-264:   Nov. 22, 1791, JAMES HABERSHAM of Chatham Co., Ga.,
                  planter to JACOB BULL of Wilkes County, for 553 pounds,
10 shillings and 8 pence, sterling, 300 acres in Columbia County, adj.
HENRY ASKFIELD, JOHN OLIVER and vacant on other sides at time of orig.
survey, and 200 acres known by the name of MADDOX, land originally
granted to JOSEPH MADDOX, adj. land of GEORGE BITCH, ISAAC VERNON, and
vacant land, and ROBERT MCCUNG (?), land has been resurveyed by JOHN
TORRENCE, Feb. 27, 1790. JAS. HABERSHAM (SEAL), HESTER HABERSHAM (SEAL).
Wit: JAMES COCHRAN J.P., JAS. HABERSHAM.

Pages 265-266:   January 13, 1794, JACOB BULL Senior, Planter to JAMES
                  HABERSHAM, Junior for 100 pounds sterling, 200 acres
by an original survey, in the parish of St. Paul's adj. land granted to
JOSEPH MADDOX adj. JOHN "EMPREE or EMERY", JACOB BULL (SEAL), RENNIS
BULL (SEAL). Wit: DANIEL WILLIAMS, JOHN TODD, WM. THOMAS J.P., Rec.
Feb. 6, 1794.

Pages 267-268:   JAMES BURROUGHS late of the state of Maryland and
                  county of St. Mary's, appoint my son BENNET BURROUGHS
of the county and state aforesaid, my lawful attorney to receive from
estate of BENJAMIN WOOD Senr. dec'd late of the state of Maryland,
county of Charles, my right and dower to all the negroes, JAS. BURROUGHS
(SEAL). Wit: ALEXR. GARDNER, JNO. LUTH, JNO. FOSTER, J.P. Dated:
Jan. 13, 1794.

Pages 268-269:   JAMES BURROUGHS late of St. Mary's County, Maryland,
                  but now of Columbia County, Ga., for 150 pounds sterling
to BENNETT BURROUGHS of the state and county aforesaid, deliver all my
interest in right and dower of at least five or more Negroes and their
increase, from estate of BENJAMIN WOOD, Senr. dec'd of Charles County,
Maryland. JAS BARROUGHS. Wit: ALEXR. GARDNER, JNO. FOSTER J.P.
Rec. Feb. 6, 1794.

Pages 269-271:   Jan. 13, 1794, JACOB BULL Senior to JAMES HABERSHAM,
                  Junior, for 75 pounds sterling, land known as the
horse pen tract in the vicinity of Wrightsborough and Columbia County,
300 acres granted to JOSEPH MADDOX, adj. HENRY ASHFIELD, JOHN OLIVER,
JACOB BULL (SEAL), RENNIS BULL (SEAL). Wit: DANIEL WILLIAMS, JOHN
TODD, WM. THOMAS J.P. Rec. Feb. 6, 1794.

Page 272-273:   March 22, 1793, LEWIS GARDNER of Columbia Co., to NINION
                 BEAL MAGROODER of same, for 30 pounds lawful money of
Ga., 50 acres, part of a tract of 160 acres granted to HUGH MILLICAN,
Sept. 16, 1785, adj. RICHD. CASTLEBERRY, and HOLTOR (?), (plat included
in deed), LEWIS GARDNER and MARY his wife, LEWIS GARDNER (LS), MARY
GARDNER (LS). Wit: WILLIAM MAGRUDER, JOHN OFFUTT (?). Acknowledged
before WALT. DRANE J.P., Oct. 22, 1793. Rec. Feb. 12, 1794.

Page 274:   RACHEL HOGG to her two children, JOHN HOGE and ELENOR HOGE,
             all my hosehold furniture, deed of gift. March 18, 1794,
RACHEL HOGG (X). Wit; PETER CRAWFORD J.P. Rec. March 18, 1794.

Pages 274-275:   FRANCIS GRIFFIN, late a soldier in the 3d. regiment of
                  South Carolina Troops comd. by Col. THOMSON do hereby
make JOSHUA GRIMAGE of Columbia Co., Ga., to demand and receive all my
pay or arreages of pay and bounty of land due to me as a soldier, Sept.
3, 1793. FRANCIS GRIFFIN ( ). Wit: JNO. FOSTER J.P.

Page 275:   I, JOSHUA GRIMAGE, late a soldier in the detachment command-
             ed by Col. WILLIAM HETH (?) at the siege of Charleston

belonging to the Virginia line do hereby make, appoint, the HO. ABRAHAM BALDWIN now in the City of Philadelphia my true & lawful attorney, to demand my payment from the state of Virginia. Feb. 1, 1794. J. GRIMAGE. Wit: WM. WALTON, PETER CRAWFORD J.P.

Pages 276-277:   Nov. 1, 1793, JOHN TINDALL of Columbia Co., to DANL.
                  MCNEAL of same, for 20 pounds sterling, 200 acres
adj. YOUNGS and vacant land, UPTONS land, originally granted to sd.
JOHN TINDALE Oct. 30, last, JOHN TINDALL (LS). Wit: SAMUEL ROBISON,
WM. HOGE. Proven: Feb. 22, 1794.

Pages 278-279:   Oct. 1, 1792, PHILIP UPTON of Columbia Co., to DANL.
                  MCNEAL for 100 pds. sterling, 100 acres on the great
Kiokee, granted to sd. PHILIP UPTON Aug. 17, 1785, PHILIP UPTON (X)
(LS), RACHEL UPTON (X) (LS). Wit: ABRAHAM YOUNGBLOOD, FERREL RILY,
WILLIAM UPTON. Rec. April 3, 1794.

Pages 280-281:   April 9, 1792, ROBERT MIDDLETON and ELIZABETH his wife
                  of Green County, Ga., to JOHN PARRUM of Columbia Co.
for 120 pounds lawful money of sd. state, 600 acres, adj. HOLLAND
MIDDLETON, formerly the property of JOHN JAMISON, sold to JOHN GARRET,
for confiscated estate, R. MIDDLETON (LS), E. MIDDLETON (LS). Wit:
R. FLOURNOY, JOHN PEAK (X). Sworn before THOMAS MOORE, J.P. Feb. 25,
1794.

Pages 282-283:   Nov. 16, 1793, JOHN MARSHALL and his wife MIRIUM of
                  Columbia County, to JAMES REED of same, for 200 pounds
lawful money of Ga., 79½ acres, part of a grant to ALEXANDER SCOTT,
200 acres, adj. RICHARD MALLOWS, dec'd and DANIEL LOFTIN, JOHN MARSHALL
(SEAL), MIRIUM MARSHALL (-) SEAL). Wit: EPHRAIM SANDER, MACHAEL SMALL,
KALEB MONCRIEF.

Page 284:   NATHL. COCKE of Columbia Co., Ga., for 80 pounds "spiece
             money" to AZCHARIAH SPIERS mortgage of Negroes. Aug. 18,
1791. NATHL. COCKE (SEAL). Wit: JAMES PEANE Senr., J. WRIGHT.

Page 285-286:   AMBROSE GORDON purchased from THOMAS JONES of Columbia
                 County, two negro slaves, April 24, 1793. AMBROSE
GORDON (LS). Wit: P. CLAYTON Clk.

Page 286-288:   Feb. 4, 1794, JOSEPH RAY and NANCY his wife of Columbia
                 County, to BASIL JONES of same, for 400 pounds sterling,
where WILLIAM JONES now lives, granted to PETER PARRIS Jan. 2, 1770,
sold to JOHN RAY Feb. 6, 1773. (plat in deed, says warrant Jan. 3,
1769, St. Paul's Parish), NANCY RAY (SEAL), JOHN RAY (SEAL). Wit:
WM. EVANS, J.P., JOSEPH SCOTT, POLLY PREAN(?).

Page 288-290:   Dec. 24, 1787, MORDECAI MOORE of Richmond Co., Ga., to
                 JAMES MOORE of same, for 50 pounds sterling, 33 2/3
acres of a mill included in said land in the county of Richmond, on
Upton's Creek, part of a tract of 300, MORDECAI MOORE (X) (LS). Wit:
R. MOORE, JESSE DOPSON, R. HARVARD, J.P.

Page 291:   THOMAS HAMILTON of Columbia County, in virtue of the power
             of attorney from NICHOLAS MILLER of Chatham County, to sell
two tracts of land in Washington County, 287½ acres each on Williamsons
Sway, for 100 pounds sterling for the use of Mrs. CONCORD HAMILTON
unto Mr. IASAIAH WRIGHT, her lawful trustee, THOS. HAMILTON (LS). Wit:
HENRY KINDALL, ELIZABETH KINDALL.

Page 292-293:   Dec. 28, 1793, JOHN SMITH and REBECKA his wife of
                 Columbia County, for 100 pounds current money to
WILLIAM FLOWRENCE, 200 acres on the Great Kiokee, adj. BRICOW's land,
MORTAINS land, JOHN SMITH (SEAL), REBECKA SMITH (SEAL). Wit: A.
WRIGHT JP.

Page 294-295:   Aug. 25, 1786, JOHN DANELLY, JOHN CURRY, JOHN STAPLAR
                 and WILLIAM SHEALDS of Richmond Co., to THOMAS STAPLAR

of same, for 50 pounds lawful money of Ga., land on Cane Creek, bound
by THOMAS STAPLAR and TELFAIR, (plat included in deed), JOHN DANELLY
( ) (SEAL), JOHN CURRY (SEAL), REBECCA CURRY (S) (SEAL), JOHN STAPLER
(SEAL), WM. SHIELDS (SEAL). Wit: JOHN CURRY, THOMAS CURRY, JOHN
SHEPPARD, J.P.

Pages 296-297:　　Feb. 24, 1793, WILLIAM F. BOOKER and ELIZABETH his wife
　　　　　　　　to JACOB GOAR of Columbia Co., for 70 pounds current
money, land on little Kioka Creek, bounded as follows: JOHN BOOKER,
GIDION BOOKER, JOHN YOUNGBLOOD, W. F. BOOKER (SEAL), ELIZA BOOKER (LS).
Wit: JOHN PETTIT, A. CRAWFORD, J.P.

Pages 298-299:　　Jan. 1, 1793, JAMES HAMILTON Sheriff of Columbia County
　　　　　　　　to Capt. NATHL. PEARCE, sold for debt of THOMAS CARR
and SHERWOOD BUGG (?), 2225 acres. JAMES HAMILTON (LS). Wit: PETER
CRAWFORD, Clk.

Pages 299-300:　　JOSEPH THOMAS of Richmond Co., do lease unto MARY
　　　　　　　　HENDERSON during her life, 10 acres, part of a tract
of 100, joining lands of JOHN READS, Sept. 30, 1793 (1783?), JOSEPH
THOMAS (SEAL). Test: JOHN BOYD. Sworn to Feb. 26, 1794.

Pages 300-301:　　CLEM K. HARRISON of Columbia Co., for 85 pounds and one
　　　　　　　　penny sterling, to RICHARD HARRISON of same, 10 negroes
CLEM K. HARRISON (LS). Wit: ABRM JOHNSON, J.P., JESSE WRIGHT.

Page 302:　　PATRICK DANNELLY, formerly an Indian trader, do give to my
　　　　　　　son JAMES DANNELLY, a minor of the aforesaid state & county,
born illegitimate of a white woman, my only son, PAT DANELLY (LS).
Wit: JOHN MCINTOSH, WILLIAM COBBS, July 1, 1794. Acknowledged July 2,
1794.

Pages 303-305:　　Jan. 29, 1777, JOHN BACON and OBEDIENCE his wife of
　　　　　　　　St. Paul's Parish, Prov. of Ga., to MARMADUKE RICKINSON,
70 pounds, 350 acres on branches of Germany's, adj. JOHN CRAWFORD and
ISAAC SKINNERS lines, granted to sd. JOHN BACON, JOHN BACON (SEAL),
OBEDIENCE BACON (SEAL). Wit: JOHN BEDINGFIELD, JORDAN RICKERSON,
WILLIAM SIMS. Sworn March 25, 1784 before WM. GLASCOCK A.J.

Page 305-306:　　May 21, 1794, MARMADUKE RICKETSON of the village of
　　　　　　　　Bedford, Shoemaker, to SEABORN JONES, for 100 pounds
sterling, 250 acres on branches of Germany's and Uche Creeks, MARADUKE
TECKETSON (LS). Wit: GILES GAYLORD, JNO. MILLES, WILLIAM POE.

Page 307:　　Received of ELIZABETH BOYD 50 pounds sterling for one
　　　　　　negro boy, WILLIAM KENNER (X) (SEAL), March 28, 1793. Wit:
JNO. FOSTER J.P. Rec. July 24, 1794. Test: ISAAC SKINNER (X).

Page 307-308:　　ELIZABETH BOYD widow and relict of JOHN BOYD, dec'd,
　　　　　　　　for 100 pounds sterling, to MANSEY BOYD, one negro and
furniture, ELIZABETH BOYD (X) (SEAL). Wit: ISAAC SKINNER (X), JNO.
FOSTER, J.P.

Pages 309-310:　　Feb. 14, 1794, ROBERT MIDDLETON and ELIZABETH his wife
　　　　　　　　to LEWIS GARDNER, for 150 pounds lawful money of Ga.,
land in Columbia County, originally granted to JOHN RAE Junior. R.
MIDDLETON (SEAL), E. MIDDLETON (SEAL). Wit: WM. GARDNER, WM. LONG-
STREET, J.P. Rec. July 24, 1794.

Page 311:　　MARY CARMICAL widow, of Columbia County, to her children,
　　　　　　　JOSEPH WADE CARMICAL, ELIZABETH GRAY CARMICAL, ELIZABETH
GRAY CARMICAL, PEGGY BYNUM CARMICAL, ABNER CARMICAL, when they arrive to
the age of twenty one years, land originally granted to BEVERLY LOW and
transferred to WILLIAM MADDOX, then to MARY CARMICAL, 150 acres, MARY
CARMICAL (SEAL). Wit: WILLIAM MADDOX, JOHN GARDNER, N. HARRIS, J.P.
Dated: June 7, 1792.

Pages 312-313: April 19, 1794, ANDERSON CRAWFORD and RACHEL his wife
to WILLIAM BINION, Senr. for 150 pounds, 600 acres on
Little River, originally granted to WILLIAM GOODGION March 7, 1775,
adj. land formerly called, THOMAS GILLANS, WILLIAM WHEAT, & DENNIS
DUGG, WILLIAM LYN, AMOS & THOMAS STAPLERS, JOHN HEARD, A. CRAWFORD
(SEAL), RACHEL CRAWFORD (SEAL). Wit: PETER CRAWFORD, J.P., JOHN BOOKER.

Pages 313-314: March 9, 1791, NATHANIEL VERNON and GRACE his wife to
AARON PARKER all of Columbia County, for 55 pounds,
100 acres on Upton's Creek, adj. JOHN MOORE, AARON PARKER, WILLIAM
MELONS (?), JOHN MCMINN, JOSEPH MONEY, NATHANIEL VERNON (LS), GRACE
VERNON (LS). Wit: DANIEL WILLIAMS, MERCER BROWN.

Pages 315-316: _____ 1793, EDWARD BURKS and ELIZABETH his wife to
ICHABUD PHILLIPS all of Columbia County, for 50 pounds
325 acres, EDWARD BURKS (SEAL), ELIZABETH BURKS (SEAL) ( ). Wit:
PETER CRAWFORD, J.P., SAMUEL POOL.

Pages 317-318: Sept. 13, 1792, BENJAMIN PORTER (as attorney in fact).
WILLIAM CALBON and PATSY his wife to MERRYMAN THORN
of Columbia County, for 75 pounds, 233 acres more or less in the lower
end of Franklin County, on both sides of Poter's Creek, granted to
WILLIAM CORBAN, Dec. 3, 1784, later listed as PATSY CLAIBORNE,
(evidently PATSY CLAIBORNE was the wife of BENJAMIN PORTER, and WILLIAM
CORBAN, another party to the deed), B. PORTER (SEAL), PATSY C. PORTER
(SEAL). Wit: ROBERT RANDOLPH, Justice of the Peace. Acknowledged
Sept. 13, 1792.

Page 319-320: May 6, 1790, NEHEMIAH DUNN, ROBERT WATKINS and ELIZABETH
MARTHA his wife to NEHEMIAH DUNN (this is how the deed
is worded) for 100 pounds, land adj. WILLIAM JACKSON, granted to WILLIAM
BURGAMY, Sept. 7, 1774, and conveyed to JOHN WALLON Feb. 21, 1775, 200
acres, ROBERT WATKINS (LS), E. M. WATKINS (LS). Wit: GEORGE WATKINS,
H. WALTON.

Pages 321-323: June 5, 1786, WILLIAM LOVE of Richmond County to
SAMUEL JOHNSON of same, for 50 pounds sterling, one
acre in town of Wrightsborough, #27, facing Habersham Street, originally
granted to JOSEPH MONEY, dec'd, with 500 acres, 1720, conveyed by
MARY MONEY, Extx. of JOSEPH MONEY May 17, 1784 to JOHN SMITH, then
to MATTHEW MILLER. Then to WILLIAM LOVE, on Nov. 9, 1785, WILLIAM LOVE
(SEAL). Wit: ALEXANDER JOHNSTON, DANL. JOHNSTON.

Pages 324-325: March 23, 1792, WILLIAM MADDOX of Columbia County,
Planter, to MARY CARMICHAEL, for 100 pounds, 150 acres
on Little Kiokee, formerly in Richmond County, now in Columbia County,
granted to BEVERLY LOWE, then to WILLIAM MADDOX & ANN his wife,
WILLIAM MADDOX (LS), ANN MADDOX (LS). Wit: LEWIS GARDNER, A. CRAWFORD,
J.P.

Pages 326-327: Richmond County, July 9, 1794, JAMES RICHARDS, Sheriff
of Richmond County to WILLIAM CHANLER NORMANT, for
75 pounds, 16 shillings, and eleven pence, sold by reason of a suit of
GREENHOW & HIGGISON, against ANDREW MCLEAN, 300 acres on Big Kiokee,
JAS. RICHARDS, S.R.C. (LS). Wit: ANDREW WHITEFIELD JP.

Pages 327-328: Aug. 13, 1790, JOHN TOWNS to NATHAN BENTON for 20 pounds
sterling, 100 acres in Richmond County, on Upton's
Creek, adj. MOONEY, FRANCIS JONES, PETER PERKINS, JOHN TOWNS (SEAL).
Wit: WALTN DRANE, J.P.

Pages 329-330: May 7, 1794, FRANCIS HORNSBY and NANCY his wife of
Richmond Co., to ABNER SIMS of Columbia County, for 30
pounds, 100 acres, on Ukee Creek, granted to GIBREAL EARHART, FRANCIS
HORNSBY (SEAL), NANCY HORNSBY (SEAL). Wit: THOMAS YOUNG, WILLIAM SIMS.

Pages 331-332: JOHN VANDERLINDER of Columbia County, cooper, appoint,
THOMAS HAYNES my attorney to recover from estate of

PETER CULBREATH late of Columbia County, dec'd, my legacy to me and
my wife MARY, JOHN VANDERLINDRE (LS). Wit: JOHN BEALLE, WILLIAM BEALLE.
Dated May 12, 1794.

Pages 333-334:   July 26, 1794, WILLIAM SMITH (son heir of CHARLES
                 SMITH, dec'd) of Warren Co., and TELITHA his wife to
JOHN L. DIXSON of Washington County for 300 pounds sterling, 200 acres
in Columbia County, originally granted to JAMES WRIGHT, Aug. 2, 1768,
WILLIAM SMITH (SEAL), TELITHA SMITH (X) (SEAL). Wit: HILLORY FOWLER,
SUSANNAH SMITH (X), ELISHABA FOWLER (X).

Page 335:   JANE CULBREATH, widow of PETER CULBREATH, appoint JOSHUA
            GRIMMAGE as my attorney, and impower Mr. JAMES CULBREATH
as my attorney. JANE CULBREATH (X) (LS). Dated Sept. 23, 1794.

Pages 336-337:   July 21, 1794, JAMES ROSS and ANN his wife to JOHN
                 HARGROVE all of Columbia County, for 30 pounds lawful
money, 104 on Greenbrier Creek, DOUGHERTY's line, granted to JOHN WALTON
and LUD WILLIAMS, then sold to sd. JAMES ROSS, JAMES ROSS (LS), ANN ROSS
(LS). Wit: WM. APPLING, THOS. DOSSETT, ANN ROSS relinquishes dower.

Page 338-339:   Sept. 26, 1794, JOHN BACON of Augusta to JOSIAH BOSWELL
                of Warren County, for 37 pounds, 10 shillings, lawful
money, land on both sides of Uchee Creek, and on both sides of the road
leading over Barnett's Bridge to the old Court House of Richmond County,
150 acres. JOHN BACON (LS). Wit: WM. F. TAYLOR, WILLIAM BEALE,
NATHL. COCKE.

Pages 339-341:   Jan. 11, 1792, JOHN ROBERTS of Wilkes Co., Ga., to
                 JOHN HUTCHINSON of Columbia County, for 100 pounds
sterling, 300 acres on Little River, GRIFFIN's corner, granted to sd.
JOHN ROBERTS June 1790, by EDWARD TELFAIR, JOHN ROBERTS ( ) (LS).
Wit: ROBERT WALTON, WILLIAM DOWSING, ROBERT ATKINSON.

Pages 342-344:   Jan. 9, 1794, JAMES SMITH and ELIZABETH his wife of
                 Columbia County, to NATHANIEL PEARCE of same, for 100
pounds specie, 200 acres on both sides of the Great Kioka Creek, adj.
JAMES SMITH, GRAVES & DORSEY, HICKS & MILLIGENS,, originally granted
to JOB SMITH, and conveyed to WILLIAM CANDLER, then to EBENEZER SMITH
and willed by him to his son JAMES SMITH, JAMES SMITH (SEAL), ELIZABETH
SMITH (SEAL). Wit: JAMES DAVIS, MERRYMAN THORN J.P., Jan. 9, 1793,
JANE SMITH, wife of EBENEZER SMITH, dec'd, relinquishes dower,
JANE SMITH (X) (SEAL).

Pages 344-346:   Sept. 4, 1794, JOHN L. DIXON of Washington County,
                 Planter, and MARY his wife, to NICHOLAS H. BUGG of
Richmond County, for 150 pounds sterling, several tracts containing
400 acres, granted to NATHAN HARRIS July 7, 1772, the other tract sur-
veyed for DANIEL COLEMAN on June 4, 1774. (Plats included in deed.)
J. L. DIXON (SEAL), POLLY DIXON (SEAL). Wit: LEVIN WAILS, ABRAM
JONES J.P.

Pages 347-348:   March 3, 1794, NATHANIEL JACKSON of Wilkes County
                 to WILLIAM SMITH of Columbia County for 30 pounds, land
on Upton's Creek, originally granted to sd. JACKSON, near Rightsborough
Feb. 7, 1775, adj. PETER PERKINS, 100 acres. NATHANIEL JACKSON (LS).
Wit: ABRAM JOHNSON JP.

Page 349:   WILLIAM BARNETT of Elbert Co., Ga., do relinquish a claim
            to 100 acres granted to NATHL. JACKSON, Feb. 7, 1775 in
Columbia County, WM. BARNETT. Wit: R. HOWARD J.P. Dated Nov. 7, 1793.

Pages 350-351:   Aug. 19, 1793, EDWARD UPTON and MARY his wife to
                 NATHANIEL WILLIAMS for 70 pounds lawful money, 50 acres
part of a tract of 250, on Great Kioka, surveyed by SANDERS WALKER,
Deputy Surveyor the 12th of May, 1773, bounded at time of survey by
vacant land, now by DANIEL MCKEE (?) (MCNEEL?), ABRAHAM YOUNGBLOOD and
JOSHUA FULLER, granted to sd. MARY UPTON in the time of her widowhood,
thru MARY EATON, EDWARD UPTON (LS) MARY UPTON (C) (LS). Wit: NATHR. DRANE,JP

Pages 352-353:   Sept. 5, 1793, WILLIAM TRIPLETT of Wilkes County,
                 Collector of Taxes to THOMAS STARK Senr. (STACK?),
taken from ABSALOM JACKSON for his taxes for the year 1792, containing,
100 acres originally granted to BENJAMIN JACKSON Senr., adj. Little
River, JAMES DOZAR, ROBERT BROWN, THOMAS TRAVIX, WM. TRIPLETT (SEAL).
Wit: WM. STARK, WM. G. GILBERT, JOHN SIMS.

Pages 354-355:   Oct. 23, 1794, NATHANIEL BARNETT and SUSANNAH his wife
                 of Elbert County, to CHARLES SEWALL of Columbia County,
for 80 pounds sterling money of Georgia, land at ROSBOROUGH Corner,
near Little Kioka Creek, formerly sold to JOEL CRAWFORD, two tracts of
200 acres each, NATHANIEL BARNETT (LS), SUSANNAH BARNETT (S) (LS).
Wit: WM. BARNETT, J. PEACE, NILSON BARNETT.

Page 355:   Rec. Feb. 10, 1795, received fo JOSHUA GRINAGE the Judgment
            in full the administrators of WILLIAM BARNETT against sd.
GRINAGE & JOHN GIBSON, Feb. 5, 1795. JAMES SMITH. Test: THOMAS
MOORE, J.P.

Pages 356-357:   Sept. 9, 1794, MOSES MARSHALL and MARY his wife and
                 BENJAMIN GARRISON and JOHN DOSS to WILLIAM BECKHAM of
Columbia Co., for 80 pounds, 160 acres on Green Brier Creek, part of
250 acres granted to WILLIAM CHANDLER, Aug. 1, 1769 and conveyed to
BENJAMIN BURNS (BEVINS?), then to his four children begotten on the
body of REBECKAH GARRISON, namely MARRY, BENJAMIN, SARAH and DANESLY (?),
by deed of gift, Sept. 10, 1777, land adj. MOSES MARSHALL, THOS. COBBS,
HUNTS, DENHAMS, (plat in deed) MOSES MARSHALL (LS), BENJAMIN GARRISON
(LS), JOHN DOSS (LS), MARY MARSHALL (LS). Wit: JOHN DOBBS, Junr.,
ALEXR. JOHNSTON, SHERW. BUGGS, J.P.

Pages 358-360:   June 9, 1794, JAMES SMITH and ELIZABETH his wife to
                 NATHANIEL PEARCE, for 25 pounds sterling, 47 acres on
Great Kioka, originally granted to sd. JAMES SMITH, adj. JAMES MORTON,
SAMUEL MORTON, JAMES SMITH (SEAL), ELIZABETH SMITH (LS). Wit: WM.
DEARMOND, MERRYMAN THORN, J.P.

Pages 360-361:   Oct. 17, 1792, WILLIAM WALTON to JAMES BAILEY all of
                 Columbia County, for 20 pounds, 100 acres, except that
a survey of ROGER QUARLES takes off a corner, on Big Kiokea Creek.
WILLIAM WALTON (LS). Wit: GARNER SMITH (V).

Pages 362-364:   Aug. 22, 1793, JAMES BAILEY of Columbia County, to
                 SARAH GLOVER, for 500 pounds, 100 acres on Kioka
Creek, adj. ROGER QUALLS, JAMES BAILEY (SEAL). Wit: WALTR. DRANE,
J.P., WM. HOGE, JOHN REEVE.

Pages 364-366:   THOMAS STARK Senr. of Wilkes Co. to JAMES DOZER of
                 Columbia County, Feb. 13, 1792, for land of ABSALOM
JACKSON sold for taxes, 100 acres granted to BENJAMIN JACKSON, THOMAS
STARK (LS). Wit: WM. STARK, R. SMITH, A. CUMMINS.

Pages 367-368:   Sept. 18, 1793, DALZIEL HUNTER to JOEL DEES for 10
                 pounds lawful money, DALZIEL HUNTER of town of Augusta,
50 acres in Columbia County, adj. CALLS, WATKINS, on head of Great
Kioka Creek, DALZIEL HUNTER (LS). Wit: AMBERS SEIGH, J.P.,
LITTLETON WYCHE.

Pages 369-370:   Oct. 23, 1793, RHESA HOWARD Esqr. of Columbia Co.,
                 to BENJAMIN PORTER of Wilkes Co., Ga., for 100 pounds,
200 acres in Kingores's Creek, waters of Little River, granted to sd.
HOWARD, Oct. 4, 1774, adj. WALTER JACKSON, RALPH KILGORE. R. HOWARD
(SEAL). Wit: THOS. NAPIER, ROBT. RANDOLPH, J.P.

Pages 370-372:   May 13, 1794, JESSE WINFREE of Columbia Co., to EDWARD
                 ONEAL of same, for 50 pounds sterling, 134 acres adj.
WILLIAM WALTON's land, JOHN PECKS land (plat included in deed), JESSE
WINFREE (LS). Wit: THOMAS MOORE, J.P., EDM. B. JENKINS.

Pages 373-374:   Oct. 1, 1787, JOHN MCMUNN and wife PRUDENCE to JOHN
                  TOWNS, Planter of Richmond Co., for 60 pounds lawful
money, 150 acres, originally granted to JOHN PURROLL, and part of 300
acres originally granted to MORDECAI MOORE, July 3, 1770 on Upton's
Creek, JNO MCMUNN, PRUDENCE MCMUNN. Wit: NATHANIEL VERNON, JOHN
MONEY (X).

Pages 374-375:   1792, JOHN FLEMING to RANDOLPH RAMSEY, Junior, JOHN
                  FLEMING of Lancaster Co., South Carolina, for 150 pounds
200 acres on Sullivans Creek, branch of Little River, granted to
NATHANIEL SHEPARD, Jan. 19, 1773, adj. JOHN TUNKLES (?), SARY WEBSTER
(SEAL), JOHN FLEMING (SEAL). Wit: JAS. FLEMING, J.P., Dec. 13, 1792,
received full amt. JOHN FLEMING.

Pages 376-377:   Dec. 9, 1794 (?) JACOB GOARE and RACHEL his wife to
                  WILLIAM F. BOOKER, for 65 pounds current money, land
on Little Kioka Creek, 100 acres, adj. JOHN BOOKER, GIDEON BOOKER, JOHN
YOUNGBLOOD, WILLIAM ZACHRY, purchased by sd. JACOB of JOHN YOUNGBLOOD,
JACOB BOARE (SEAL), RACHEL BOARE (X) (LS). Wit: SAM. C. LENEVE (?),
A. CRAWFORD.

Page 378:   STEPHEN COLLINS of Columbia County, for 5 shillings sterling,
             and natural love for my son in law RICHARD SHACKLEFORD, give
one negro woman, plantations, whereon I now live, etc. May 6, 1794.
STEPHEN COLLINS (SEAL). Wit: GIDEON BOOKER, WM. BOOKER, J.P.

(Next page not numbered):   Dec. 4, 1792, JOHN HARGROVE of Richmond Co.
                             and LUCY his wife from JOSEPH BATSON, for
90 pounds lawful money, 100 acres, originally granted Nov. 1, 1774 by
Sir JAMES RETE, JOSEPH BATTSONS (LS). Wit: EDLRIGE HARGROVE, SOLOMON
NEWSOME, JAS SIMMS, J.P.

Pages 1-2: July 20, 1793, WILLIAM WALLACE to DANIEL DANNELLY, for
40 pounds lawful money, land in the county of Richmond at
time of survey, adj. vacant land on all sides, 350 acres, headrights
from WM. GLASCOCK, presiding at a land court in Richmond County, June
11, 1785, WM. WALLACE (SEAL). Wit: GEO. BARNES. SARAH, wife of
WILLIAM WALLACE renounced dower on Aug. 26, 1793. Wit: WM. BARDEN,
Junr., GEO. BARNES. Recorded March 27, 1795.

Pages 3-4: Dec. 6, 1790 (in the 16th year of the sovereignty of the
USA), JAMES WILLIS & ANN his wife of Columbia Co., to
ROBERT JOHNS, of same, for 200 pounds sterling money, 200 acres granted
to MORDECAI MOORE, bound by JOHN KING, Upton's Creek, SANDER's land on
GRAHAM old survey & JAMES MOORE's land, and another tract 100 acres on
MORDECAI MOORE's old survey and a tract of 50 acres adj. MORDECAI
MOORE's line, on Upton's Creek, SANDERS' mill pond, total 400 acres,
JAMES WILLIS (SEAL), ANN WILLIS (SEAL). Wit: CHAS PORTER, SLARK
(STARK?) WRIGHT, MOSES WILLIS. Proven by CHARLES PORTER, Apr. 3, 1793.
Recorded April 5 (?), 1795 (1793?).

Pages 5-6: July 25, 1794, JOEL DEES of Columbia Co., planter to
DANIEL DANNELLY of same, planter, for 100 pounds sterling,
50 acres in Columbia Co., originally granted to Major CALL, adj. CALL's
land, WALKER's land, on head of Great Keokia Creek, JOEL DEES (SEAL)
( ). Wit: WALKR (?) DEANE, J.P., GEORGE MAGRUDER, JOHN OLIVE.
Recorded April 1, 1795.

Pages 6-8: Recorded April 2, 1795. Whereas GEORGE TARVIN, admr. of
est. of WILLIAM TARVIN, late of Columbia Co., deceased,
did on Oct. 26, 1791 on petition to Superior Court of Columbia Co.,
for an order to dispose of 2 tracts of land in sd. county, 350 acres
on Keokia adj. BEVERLY LOWE and another tract of 250 acres on Little
River, adj. lands of CANDLER, SOLOMON MARSHALL, Deputy Sheriff of sd.
Co., for 48 pounds do sell sd. 2 tracts to GEORGE TARVIN, S. MARSHALL
(SD) (LS). Wit: JOHN TUDER, PETER CRAWFORD, J.P. March 19, 1793.

Pages 8-9: Jan. 22, 1795, GEORGE TARVIN of Columbia Co. to THOMAS
FLINT, of same, for $1231.75, 379 acres originally granted
to WILLIAM TARVIN, deceased on Little Keokia Creek, adj. land originally
granted to THOMAS PACE (?), the SW corner of sd. survey before conveyed
to ANDERSON CRAWFORD, GEORGE TARVIN (LS). Wit: JOHN RINNELS, A.
CRAWFORD, J.P. Plat to sd. 379 acres on page 10, shows land adj. WM. F.
BOOKER & CULBREATH & BACON.

Pages 10-12: Nov. 29, 1794, NICHOLAS HOBSON BUGG of Town of Augusta,
Richmond Co., Ga., to SAMPSON LAMKINS of same, both
planters, for 75 pounds lawful money 150 acres on Green Brier Creek
formerly granted to JOHN MITCHELL, adj. lands of DANIEL COLEMON &
ROBERT STORY, N. H. BUGG (SEAL), CHARLOTTE BUGG (SEAL). Wit: ABRAM
JONES (?), J.P., CHAS GOODWIN, SOPHIA CHARLOTTE BUTT, wife of sd.
NICHOLAS H. BUGG relinquish dower ABRAM JOURS, J.P. (SEAL). Recorded
April 2, 1795.

Pages 12-13: March 21, 1795, JAMES DANNELLY of Columbia to ROBERT
FLOURNOY Esquire, for 10,000 pounds sterling lawful
money of Ga., 14,000 acres in 14 adjoining surveys of 1,000 acres each,
several grants bearing date March 20, 1795, adj. Richmond and Columbia
County lines, YOUNG, WHITICAN, COBB LANGSTON, GRAVES, OFFUTTS, JENKINS,
RICHARD CALL, WHITTINGTON, WHITE ROBERSON & CO., MCNEAR (?), JAS. DAN-
NELLY, MCNEIL, CALL, DANIEL DANNELLY, YOUNGBLOOD, POLLS, EDWARD BURK,
PRATERS, WILKINS, excluding 450 acres in the name of T. M. HUNT, 200
acres in the name of WILLIAM LEONARD, 200 in name of WILLIAM PACE, on
waters of Fork Creek and Boggy Gut. JAMES DANNELLY (SEAL). Wit:
EDM. B. JENKINS, R. MIDDLETON. Proven by EDWARD B. JENKINS April __,
1795. Rec. April 3, 1795.

Pages 14-15:   Oct. 16, 1787, JAMES MOORE of Richmond Co. to JOHN
                TOWNS of same, for 60 pounds sterling, land in Richmond
Co., adj. MORDECAI MOORE's land and land surveyed for JAMES GUIST, and
all other sides vacant land at time of survey, land granted to JAMES
MOORE, Aug. 2, 1786, JAMES MOORE (SEAL). Wit: WM. BROWN, R. HOWARD,
J.P. Rec. Apr. 8, 1795.

Pages 16-18:   Oct. 26, 1792, JOHN WILLINGHAM of Columbia Co., to
                BAZEL ONEAL of same, for 50 pounds lawful money, land in
Sullivan's Creek, adj. MOON's corner, granted to MANN (?) SIMS, Dec.
17, 1784, 100 acres (Plat in body of deed shows adj. BEN. WILLIAMS),
JOHN W. WILLINGHAM ( ) (SEAL). Wit: JOHN RUSSAU, JONATHAN SWAN (+),
JOHN W. WILLINGHAM rec'd. 50 pounds of BAZEL ONEAL, Oct. 26, 1792.
Wit: JOHN RUSSAU, RICHARD SIMS (?), JONATHAN SWAN (+). Rec. April 8,
1795. Proved by JOHN RUSSAU, March 2, 1793 before JAS FLEMING, J.P.
Before SHERWD. BUGG, EDW., a J.P. for Columbia, ANN WILLINGHAM, wife
of JOHN WILLINGHAM release dower. ANN WILLINGHAM (A). Jan. 20, 1794.

Pages 19-20:   Jan. 18, 1794, CALEB MONCREEF to JOHN GANLY, for 25
                pounds lawful money, 100 acres in Columbia Co., adj.
Col. ONEAL's line, on Great Keokia Creek, CALEB MONCREEF (+) (SEAL),
MARY MONCREEF (+) (SEAL). Wit: JAMES READ (R), STEPHEN COLLINS, JOHN
MARSHALL. Rec. April 9, 1795.

Page 21-22:   Feb. 7, 1791, FRANCIS WILLIS and ELIZABETH his wife of
                Wilkes Co., to JEREMIAH LAMKEN of Columbia Co., for 5
shillings current money of Ga., two tracts of land, one granted to
LEVI SHEFTAL (?), 300 acres on Savannah River and the Great Kiokea
Creek about 60 acres sold to Col. JESSE SANDERS, on the Sw side of
Kiokia Creek, adj. land of KILGORES, CHRISTEAU SUMBECKER, and 400 acres
adj. WM. KILGORE's, ELIAS X VOBRAVIRS, granted to GEORGE LEMBECKER (?),
FRANS WILLIS (SEAL). Wit: JOHN WALTON, GEO WALTON Judge. Rec. April
10, 1795.

Pages 23-24:   March 17, 1790, ALEXANDER STEEL and FANNY his wife of
                Wilkes Co., to CHARLES REYNOLDS of Richmond Co., for 50
pounds lawful money, land in Richmond Co., adj. DUNN's land, TIMOTHY
RICHETSONs, COOPER's land, ALEXANDER STEEL (A) (SEAL), FANNY STEEL (Q)
(SEAL). Wit: WILLIAM CARTER, BENJM. EVANS. Proven Dec. 8, 1794 by
WILLIAM CARTER. Rec. April 10, 1795.

Pages 24-26:   Oct. 22, 1792, ISHAM BALIS and wife to RANDOL RAMSEY,
                for 135 pounds current and lawful money, two tracts,
one of 125 and one of 135 acres, part of a grant to ROBERT GRAVES,
Oct. 1, 1774 for 250 acres in Columbia Co., on waters of Little River,
conveyance of ROBERT WHITTEN to us, Oct. 26, 1790. ISHAM BAYLIS (LS),
BETSEY BAYLIS (X) (LS). Wit: JAS FLEMING, J.P. Rec. April 14, 1795.

Pages 26-28:   Jan. 24, 1795, JOSEPH MONEY and HANNAH his wife and
                MARY MONEY from Newberry County, South Carolina, to AARON
PARKES of Columbia Co., for 50 pounds, 175 acres on Upton's Creek, adj.
SAMUEL BROWN, part of a 550 acres tract, granted to JOSEPH MONEY, July
3, 1770, MARY MONEY, mother of JOSEPH MONEY. JOSEPH MONEY (SEAL), MARY
MONEY (X) (SEAL), HANNAH MOONEY (SEAL). Wit: J. MOORE, RICHARD RYON.
Rec. April 14, 1795.

Pages 29-30:   Oct. 6, 1794, JOHN GANLY to JOHN LUKE both of Columbia
                Co., for 25 pounds lawful money, land on Great Kiokia
Creek, 100 acres, JOHN GANLEY (X) (LS), MARY GANLEY (LS). Wit: JAMES
MCNEEL, J.P. Rec. April 16, 1795.

Pages 30-33:   June 15, 1793, DAVID MURRAY Jur. of Wilkes Co., planter,
                & MARY his wife to AQUILA HOWARD of Columbia Co., planter,
for 275 pounds good and lawful money, 350 acres, granted by Sir JAMES
WRIGHT to ISAAC JACKSON, July 3, 1770 and conveyed to HENRY WRIGHT,
May 16, 1783, and conveyed to DAVID MURRAY, Dec. 11, 1790, DAVID MURRAY
(LS). Wit: ROBERT JOHNS, THOMAS WHITE, J.P.

Pages 33-36:   Dec. 25, 1787, WILLIAM HICKSON of Wrightsborough Township,
               Richmond County, to JONATHAN MOTE of same, WILLIAM HICK-
SON and ELIZABETH his wife, for 500 pounds sterling, 200 acres in
Wrightsborough Township, granted to WILLIAM HICKSON, by Sir. JAMES
WRIGHT, Gov. of Ga., July 4, 1769. WILLIAM HICKSON (W). Wit: DAVID
SMITH (D), ROBERT WALDEN (R). Proved by DAVID SMITH and ROBERT WALDEN,
July 20, 1789 before THOMAS WHITE, J.P. ELIZABETH HICKSON, release of
dower, July 20, 1789. WILLIAM HICKSON (W), ELIZABETH HICKSON (X). Rec.
April 16, 1795.

Pages 37-38:   April 5, 1791, ELI GARNETT of Richmond Co., to JOHN
               EUBANKS of same, for a free or figt donation, 95 acres
in County aforesaid, adj. WILLIAM WILLINGHAM's corner, GRIFFETH's line,
ELI GARNETT (SEAL). Wit: JOHN TANKESLEY, J.P. April 18, 1795, SARAH
GARNETT, wife of ELI, release of dower. Rec. April 16, 1795.

Pages 39-40:   Dec. 13, 1794, CHARLES REYNOLDS & MARY his wife of
               Columbia Co. to JOHN LANGSTON of same, for 40 pounds
sterling, 100 acres in Columbia County, on Jermaney's Creek, granted to
ALEXANDER STEEL, adj. where BENJAMIN ANDREW now lives, adj. land granted
to ISAAC COOPER & C., also one other parcel, 26 acres, adj. the aforesaid 100 acres, being part of a survey made for GETER CARTER, adj. to
the corner of land granted to ISAAC COOPER and ROBERT BAUR, CHARLES
REYNOLDS (LS), MARY REYNOLDS (X) (LS). Wit: DAVID LANGSTON, CHARLES
SPALDING (X). Proven Feb. 24, 1795. Rec. April 18, 1795.

Pages 41-42:   Oct. 16, 1787, MORDECAI MOORE of Richmond Co., to JOHN
               TOWNS, for (amt. not given), 200 acres, part of 300 acres
granted to MORDECAI MOORE, July 3, 1770, MORDECAI MOORE (M). Wit: WM.
BROWN, A. HOWARD, J.P. Rec. April 18, 1795.

Pages 43-44:   SARAH WEBSTER, of Lancaster County, South Carolina,
               Seastees do appoint my son in law JOHN FLEMING my lawful
attorney to make lawful title to my lands that is coming to me for any
parts of the United States and receive in my name any sums of money,
etc. April 24, 1792, SARAH WEBSTER ( ). Wit: BAILEY FLEMING, HANNAH
MCHUGH, JOHN BAKER. South Carolina, Keshaw (Kershaw) County, Appeared
BAILEY & JOHN BAKER before me THOS. BALLARD, J.P., on Nov. 24, 1792.
Rec. April 18, 1795.

Pages 44-45:   JEREMIAH LAMKIN of Columbia Co., have sold unto JOHN
               LAMKIN of same, six negroes for 250 pounds, March 2,
1794, JEREMIAH LAMKIM. Wit: BOSWELL SMITH, RICHD (?) WHITEHEAD.
Proven Feb. 19, 1795. Rec. April 20, 1795.

Pages 45-46:   THOS. MERIWETHER of Columbia Co., for 65 pounds do
               emancipate a certain MUSH COLEY, alias QUASH, later looks
like MICAH COLEY, Feb. 25, 1795, THOS MERIWETHER (SEAL). Wit: BOSWELL
SMITH, THOS. HOGAN, RICHD WHITE.

Pages 46-47:   WILLIAM SIMS for 5 pounds current money of Ga., for
               raising two negro girls I had of Col. LEONARD MARBURY,
sold to MANN SIMS, WILLIAM SIMS (LS). Wit: PETER CRAWFORD, J.P.,
March 17, 1795.

Pages 47-48:   THOMAS MERIWETHER for 90,000 weight of tobacco, to
               NICHOLAS MERIWETHER, 39 negroes, April 14, 1794, THOMAS
MERIWETHER (L). Wit: JOSEPH B. SPANCER, TOWD. STONE, LEONARD THOMPSON.
Proven Feb. 25, 1795. Rec. April 20, 1795.

Pages 49-50:   Aug. 3, 1793, LITTLETON YARBROUGH of Columbia Co., to
               THOMAS TARRY of same, for 10 pounds sterling, 150 acres
on waters of Spirits Creek, LITTLETON YARBROUGH (SEAL). Wit: MARY A.
CRAWFORD, PETER CRAWFORD, J.P.

Pages 50-52:   Feb. 25, 1794, HUGH MILLIGAN & MARTHA his wife to
               NATHANIEL PEARCE all of Columbia Co., for 20 pounds

sterling, 50 acres adj. MORTON's land, JOB SMITH, WILLIAM WALLACE, AB. AYRES, HUGH MILLIGAN (LS), MARTHA MILLIGAN (X) (LS). Wit: BUCKHAM, MERRYMAN THORN, J.P. Rec. May 28, 1795.

Pages 52-54:   Jan. 18, 1791, JOHN LANDERS of Columbia to HENRY SPALDING of same, for 74 pounds, 10 shillings, 200 acres on waters of Kegg Creek, adj. JOHN TANKERSLEY's line, GERMANY's line, JOHN LANDERS (SEAL). Wit: JNO. TANKERSLEY, J.P. Rec. May 28, 1795.

Pages 54-56:   April 11, 1795, JOHN YOUNGBLOOD and ANN his wife to WILLIAM Z(?) BOOKER, all of Columbia Co., for 500 pounds current money, 100 acres on Little Kiokia Creek, adj. GIDEON BOOKER, JACOB GOAR's old line, land originally granted to JOHN YOUNGBLOOD (I) SEAL), ANN YOUNGBLOOD (X) (SEAL). Wit: JOHN BOOKER, A. CRAWFORD, J.P. Rec. May 28, 1795.

Pages 57-58:   July 3, 1795, WILLIAM EVANS and EDITH his wife to DANIEL LOFTIN, for 200 pounds sterling, 190 acres adj. land granted to RICHARD MEADOWS, land formerly CALEB MONCREEF's, EDWARD ONEAL, WILLIAM EVANS (SEAL), EDITH EVANS (X) (SEAL). Wit: JAMES LANE, HUMPHREY EVANS, JAS BOYD, JAS. SIMMS, J.P. EDITH EVANS relinquished dower July 10, 1794. Rec. May 29, 1795.

Pages 59-60:   May 7, 1794, DREDZEL PACE to DANIEL LOFTIN, both of Columbia Co., for 50 pounds sterling, 116 2/3 acres adj. land formerly GEORGE ROBURG's, on Little Kokee Creek (plat included in deed, shows adj. R. RAMSEY Sr., DREDZIL PACE (LS), BETSEY PACE (LS). Wit: JAS SIMMS, J.P., Rec. June 9, 1795.

Pages 61-62:   ANTHONY HAYNES frees negro slaves June 10, 1795, ANTHONY HAYNES. Wit: JOHN TUDER, JOAB GRUBBS, PETER CRAWFORD, J.P. Rec. June 10, 1795.

Pages 62-64:   March 6, 1795, JOHN WILLIAMS and MARY his wife (heirs of THOMAS WILLIAMS, deceased) of Richmond County, to THOMAS HANSON of Columbia County, for 50 pounds sterling 200 acres on wouth branches of Uchee Creek, at time of original survey in St. Pauls Parish, now Columbia Co., at time of survey bounding on all sides by vacant land granted to CHARLES LUCAS Senior on July 5, 1774, JOHN WILLIAMS (SEAL), MARY WILLIAMS (SEAL). Wit: ELIZABETH FOSTER, JOHN (?) FOSTER, J.P., MARY WILLIAMS relinquish dower on March 6, 1795. Rec. June 15, 1795.

Pages 65-66:   June 4, 1794, JOHN LAMAR to JOEL JONES, JOHN LAMAR & LUCY his wife of Richmond Co., to JOEL JONES of Columbia Co., for 10 pounds sterling, 50 acres on Columbia Co., being the north corner of a tract granted to LEONARD MARBURY, bounding east on Kelly's Branch, south on JOHN LAMAR's land, west part of the survey laid off to ISAAC CLYATT (?), and north land granted to WELLS & WOOD (plat included in deed) JOHN LAMAR (SEAL), LUCY LAMAR (SEAL). Wit: D. QUIER, JOHN LAMAR Jurn. Rec. June 25, 1795.

Pages 67-68:   June 4, 1795, JOHN LAMAR & LUCY his wife to ISAAC CLYATT, for 10 pounds sterling, adj. to land laid off to JOEL JONES, Kellys Branch, land belonging to CRAWFORD, etc., JOHN LAMAR (SEAL) LUCY LAMAR (SEAL). Wit: JOHN LAMAR, Jur., (plat included in deed). Rec. June 26, 1795.

Pages 69-70:   May 21, 1795, FRANCIS HORNSBY and NANCY his wife of Richmond Co., to SAMUEL HANSON of Columbia Co., for 35 pounds, 200 acres on Uchee Creek, part of a tract granted to GABRIEL EREHART, FRANCIS HORNSBY (LS), NANCY HORSBY (LS). Wit: DAVID SWILIVAN, ABNER SIMS. Rec. June 26, 1795.

Pages 71-72:   April 7, 1795, JAMES HAMILTON Sheriff of Columbia Co., to JOHN L. DIXON of same, by order of the Inferior Court,

Dec. 1, 1794 under the hand of PETER CRAWFORD, Clerk of sd. Court, to
sell good & chattels land & tenement of MOSES (?) MARSHALL & JOHN DOSS,
for a debt of 59 pounds, 3 shillings, and 5 pence, which JOHN COBBESON
recovered in sd. court in April last term against them, tract of 119
acres on waters of Green Brier Creek, adj. BAZEL JONES, ELIAS JONES,
DENHAM, WILLIAM BUKUM & JOHN COBBS land, JAMES HAMILTON Sheriff (LS).
Wit: TH SHORT, A CRAWFORD, J.P.

Pages 71-73:   Feb. 6, 1789, JOHN MARSHALL of Richmond Co., to WILLIAM
               FEW of same for 10 pounds, 100 acres in Richmond Co.,
adj. to lands of WILLIAM FEW, DANIEL MARSHALL, JOHN MARSHALL. Heirs
of WILLIAM FELPS, part of a tract of 225 acres, granted to JOHN MARSHALL,
Jan. 7, 1786, (plat included in deed), JOHN MARSHALL (SEAL). Wit:
H. J. HUNT, J. FEW, J.P.

Pages 74-76:   ANTHONY HAYNES of Columbia Co., "in consideration of the
               confidence which I have and do repose in my friends
THOMAS HAYNES, Esquire & DAVID MAXWELL" property in my L. W. & T. in
trust for negroes, ANTHONY HAYNES (SEAL). Wit: JAMES ALDRIGE (A),
ABNER SIMS, GILES GAYLORD. Dated June 15, 1795. Proven: June 18, 1795.
Rec. July 2, 1795.

Pages 76-78:   Dec. 13, 1783, BENJAMIN WELLS and MARY his wife of
               Richmond Co., to WILLIAM FEW, Jr., for 80 pounds sterling
land originally granted to RICHARD WILLIAMSON, adj. to land belonging
to the estate of WILLIAM FELPS, dec'd, on both sides of Green Brier
Creek, on the north fork of the Great Kiokee, a tract granted to aforesaid BENJAMIN WILLS by George III, Feb. 10, 1770. BENJAMIN WELLS (LS),
MARY WELLS ( ) (LS). Wit: JOHN WELLS, JOHN COLEMAN, G. LEE, J.P.
Rec. July 2, 1795.

Pages 78-80:   Dec. 10, 1788, WILLIAM BARNET, Esquire, Sheriff of
               Richmond Co., to WILLIAM FEW Junior, Whereas WILLIAM FEW
Senior did lately in Superior Court of sd. Co. obtain a judgment
against the admr. of est. of JAMES BROWN, Dec'd, for 277 pounds, 17
shillings Specie, 700 acres in Richmond Co., granted to RICHARD WILLIAM-
SON, May 1, 1770, conveyed to JAMES BROWN, by deed June 1, 1770, WM.
BARNETT (LS). Wit: DANL. ELAM, WM. CARR, JR., Rec. July 3, 1795.

Pages 81-82:   March 22, 1786, JACOB CATLEBERRY, Blacksmith of Richmond
               Co., to SAMUEL JOHNSTON, TAYLOR, of same, for 50 pounds,
current money of Ga., 100 acres, part of a tract granted to JACOB
CASTLEBERRY, 200 acres, adj. WALTON's line, granted Oct. 5, 1784. JOEL
CASTLEBERRY (SEAL), MARY CASTLEBERRY (X) (SEAL). Wit: None. Rec.
July 9, 1795.

Pages 82-84:   Feb. 22, 1795, EDMOND B. JENKINS of Columbia Co., Planter,
               to THOMAS GLASCOCK of Richmond Co., Esquire, for 5
shillings lawful money, 4000 acres in Columbia Co., 4 separate grants
of 1000 acres each, three dated Oct. 2, 1794, the other Jan. 29 following
to sd. EDMOND B. JENKINS, also 2000 acres adj. JAMES DANNELLY's land,
RICHARD CALL's land and MESHACK MATHI's land, WILLIAM STITH's land,
REAVES & WILLIAM WALTON's land, SARAH PHILLIPS land, HEADSTALL Creek,
granted in 2 grants of 1000 acres each and 2000 acres adj. JOSEPH MAYS,
Wilkes Co. lines and EDMOND B. JENKINS, EDM. B. JENKINS (SEAL). Wit:
THOMAS MOORE, J.P., JNO. TODD. Rec. July 15, 1795.

Pages 84-86:   June 9, 1775, ROBERT DUNN and PRECILLA his wife of
               "Province of South Carolina, Granville County" to IGNATIUS
FEW of Parish of St. Paul, for 100 pounds sterling, land in Parish of
St. Paul, originally granted to ROBERT DUNN by his Magesty "sixth day
of ____", adj. ABENTON PHILLIPS corner, 350 acres, ROBERT DUNN (SEAL),
PRECILLA DUNN (SEAL). Wit: JOSIAH DUNN, JOHN CARPENTER. Rec. July
29, 1795.

Pages 87-88:   Sept. 27, 1794, NELSON CRAWFORD & SUSANNAH CRAWFORD of
               Columbia Co., to JOHN GARNETT of same, for 50 pounds

sterling land which we as heirs to Est. of JOHN CRAWFORD, Esq. dec'd., are by law entitled to in Columbia Co., adj. GREEN's land, granted to sd. JOHN CRAWFORD, Feb. 2, 1773, adj. JOHN GARNETT & THOMAS GREER (GREEN?), and a tract granted to JOHN CRAWFORD, Nov. 1, 1774, NELSON CRAWFORD (LS), SUSANNA CRAWFORD (LS). Wit: THOS. HAYNES, J.P., JAMES GARNETT. Rec. July 29, 1795.

Page 88:   RICHARD NAPIER to daughter MOLLY WELLS NAPIER, four negroes, deed of gift, RICHD NAPIER (LS). Wit: JOEL HANDLEY, H. MONTAGUE (?). Dated Aug. 1, 1793. Rec. July 31, 1795.

Pages 89-90:   March 20, 1795, WILLIAM GARNER of Effingham County, to THOMAS GLASCOCK of Richmond Co., for 2 shillings sterling land on waters of Briar Creek, 5000 acres, adj. POOL's land, YOUNG's and MCGARDER's land, WHITAKER's land, JONES' land, ROBERTSON's land, 5 tracts of 1000 acres each, grant Oct. 18, 1794, W. GARDNER (SEAL). Wit: JOHN WILSON, J.P., WURQUHART (?). Rec. July 31, 1795.

Pages 91-92:   July 16, 1795, RICHARD RANDOLPH of Columbia Co., to ROBERT RANDOLPH, Esquire of same, RICHARD and wife DOLLY for 1 pound lawful money, land on a branch of Germany's Creek, 400 acres, adj. land granted Sir. JAMES WRIGHT, SAMUEL WATSON, BENJAMIN FEW, part of 200 acres granted to JOHN SELL, RICHARD RANDOLPH (LS), DOLLY RANDOLPH (SEAL). Wit: J. A. CRAWFORD, J.P. Rec. Aug. 3, 1795.

Pages 92-93:   Oct. 14, 1790, JOHN STEWART of Richmond Co., to WILLIAM SEAY of same, for 60 pounds specie, 200 acres on Upton's Creek, granted Feb. 1, 1790, JNO. STEWART (LS). Wit: JOHN BIONION, ROBT STEWART. Sworn Dec. 3, 1795. Rec. Aug. 5, 1795.

Pages 94-95:   Nov. 2, 1790, JOHN STEWART & ROBERT STEWART of Richmond Co., to WILLIAM SEAY of same, for 73 pounds, 10 shillings 133 acres on both sides of Upton's Creek, on the Mountain Branch. JNO. STEWART (SEAL), ROBT. STEWART (SEAL). Wit: JOHN BINION, WILLIAM DUNN. Recpt. signed by JNO. STEWART, MARY STEWART, ROBT. STEWART. Rec. Dec. 10, 1791.

Pages 96-97:   Sept. 1, 1793, JOSEPH CLAY, of Chatham Co., Ga., Merchant, and ANN his wife to THOMAS CUMMING of Richmond Co., for 200 pounds specie, 500 acres, bounded at time of survey by lands of JOHN GERMANY, JOHN PITTMAN and vacant land, sold at public auction by the Sheriff to JOSEPH CLAY, May 12, 1775, JOSEPH CLAY (SEAL), ANN CLAY (SEAL). Wit: JOS. HABERSHAM, J.P., WM. WALLACE. Rec. Aug. 5, 1795.

Pages 98-99:   Sept. 23, 1794, JOHN LAMAR Senr. and LUCY his wife to ZEPHANIAH ATHEY of Columbia Co., for 20 pounds sterling, 100 acres near the Quaker Springs, on a branch of Savages Creek, WOODS line, JOHN LAMAR (SEAL), LUCY LAMAR (SEAL). Wit: JESSE GLOVER, JAS. JONES. Sworn to by JESSE GLOVER, Sept. 25, 1794. Rec. Aug. 6, 1795.

Pages 100-101:   March 3, 1795, ZEPHANIAH ATHEY of Columbia to MARMADUKE RICKSON of Richmond Co., for 20 pounds, 100 acres near the Quaker Springs (land described in above deed), ZEPHANIAH ATHA (X). Wit: BAXTER, JNO. LEITH, J.P., LUCY ATHA (X), relinquishes dower May 28, 1795.

Pages 102-103:   We, the heirs of the L. W. & T. of DANIEL MARSHALL, minister of the Gospel dec'd., late of Richmond County, L. W. & T. bearing date Nov. 28, 1783, sell of lot not exceeding 50 acres on Augusta Road on west adj. Kiokee Creek, we DANIEL MARSHALL, MOSES MARSHALL, SOLOMON MARSHALL, JOSEPH MARSHALL & ELIAS WILBURN for 30 pounds sterling, quit claim to ABRAHAM MARSHALL, Oct. 26, 1793, DANIEL MARSHALL (LS), JOHN MARSHALL (LS), LEVI MARSHALL (LS), S. MARSHALL (LS), JOSEPH MARSHALL (LS), MOSES MARSHALL (LS), ZACHARIAH MARSHALL (LS), ELIAS WILBURN (LS). Wit: JAS SIMMS, J.P. Rec. Aug. 14, 1795.

Pages 103-105:   July 8, 1795, JAMES RICHARDS Sheriff of Richmond Co.,
                 to LEWIS GARDNER of Columbia, for 82 pounds, 10
shillings, for an execution issued in Superior Court of Chatham County,
March 17, 1795. Wherein JOSEPH CLAY and JOSEPH HABERSHAM, Plaintiff
and JOHN COBBISON and ANN, his wife, SAMUEL HAMMOND and REBECKAH his
wife Defendants, doth bargain and sell to sd. LEWIS GARDNER, 116 3/4
acres, part of a tract of 220 acres originally granted to JOHN ROE (?),
1765 sold the 5th day of May last at public sale, JAS RICHARD S.R.C.
(SEAL). Wit: W. H. BACON, W. GARDNER, WILLIAM ROBERSON, J.P. Rec.
Aug. 14, 1795, (Plat included in deed.)

Pages 105-106: LEWIS GARDNER of Columbia Co., assign over to MARY
                CARMICHAEL all my interest in to property now in posses-
sion of sd. MARY CARMICHAEL, that I purchased at a Sheriff's sale on
Dec. 16, 1790, THOMAS NAPIER vs. JOHN CARMICHAEL at Richmond Court
house, negroes and furniture, May 13, 1792, LEWIS GARDNER (SEAL). Wit:
JOHN GARDNER, JASON GARDNER. Proven: July 2, 1794. Rec. Aug. 15, 1795.

Pages 106-107:   July 5, 1795, ASHEL GARDNER and his spows SARAH GARDNER
                 to JOHN ANDREWS, all of Columbia County, for 15 pounds
sterling land on Little Kiokia Creek, formerly belonging to MICAJAH
ANDREWS, ASHEL GARDNER (SEAL), SARAH GARDNER (X) (SEAL). Wit:
ALEXANDER GARDNER, J.P., JOHN PRATT. Rec. Aug. 15, 1795.

Pages 107-108:   Sept. 6, 1793, JOSEPH MCCORMACK & MARGRET his wife,
                 admrs, JOHN WATSON, THOMAS WATSON, BENJAMIN WATSON,
PETER WATSON, MARY WATSON now MADDOX, REBECAH WATSON now DURBIN, GEORGE
WATSON, HANNAH WATSON, WILLIAM WATSON, JAMES WATSON of Columbia Co.,
for 90 pounds paid by RICHARD HARRISON, 162½ acres where sd. HARRISON
now lives, part of 500 acres granted to THOMAS WATSON, surveyed by
IGNATUIS FEW, Esqr. JOSEPH MCCORMACK (LS), MARGARET MCCORMACK (M) (LS),
JOHN WATSON (SEAL), THOMAS WATSON (SEAL), BENJAMIN WATSON (SEAL),
HANNAN WATSON (X), PETER WATSON (SEAL). Wit: R. HOWARD, J.P. Rec.
Aug. 15, 1795.

Pages 109-112:   Aug. 1, 1795, GEORGE NAYLOR of Town of Augusta,
                 Richmond Co., to BENJAMIN SIMS of same, Esq., for
$40,105.72, tracts in Columbia County, 300 acres on Bigg Kioka, formerly
the property of the Rev. Mr. DANIEL STURGES, a half of all the property
the town and vicinity of Hardwick on the River Ogechee, purchased
jointly by sd. GEORGE NAYLOR & ISAAC POLOCK Vizt. one tract known as
JINCES (?) point, one island called Redbud Island, other property
including negroes, GEORGE NAYLOR (LS). Wit: L. SEWALL, J.P., LEVIN
WALLS. Rec. Aug. 22, 1795.

Pages 113-114:   May 7, 1795, JAMES RICHARDS, Sheriff of Richmond Co.,
                 to ROBERT WARE of Wilkes Co., for 80 pounds sterling,
400 acres in County of Columbia granted to CHARLES JORTLOR (?), Nov.
6, 1770, bounded by vacant land at time of survey, lately seized under
execution at the suit of JOSEPH CLAY & JOHN HABERSHAM against the admrs.
of ROSS, ELBERT & GRAHAM, late of Co. of Richmond, sold at public
auction. JAS RICHARDS (LS). Wit: WM. WALLACE, JOHN WILLSON, J.P.
Rec. Sept. 7, 1795.

Pages 114-116:   Feb. 2, 1793, JAMES BEALE of Augusta, Gentlemen and
                 his wife MARY, to DALZIEL HUNTER of Augusta, Esq., for
100 pounds sterling, 200 acres on Little River, adj. JACKSON's land,
granted Feb. 14, 1785 to JAMES MCDONALD Tavern-keeper, and conveyed to
JAMES BEALE, May 3, 1791, JAMES BEAL (LS), MARY BEAL (X) (LS). Wit:
JO RANDOLPH, ABRAM JONES, J.P., DALZIEL HUNTER (LS). A justice of
Richmond Co., JOSEPH STILES, also a justice swore to DALZIEL HUNTER's
handwriting June 26, 1795. Rec. Sept. 7, 1795.

Pages 117-118:   JOSEPH DAVIS of Columbia County, Planter, appoint "my
                 trusty friend" JESSE HAMLETT of State of Va., Prince
Edward County, Gentleman, to receive or recover from ROBERT HARDEN and

FRANCIS DEGRAFTENREID of State of Virginia and Lunenburg Co., a certain tract on both sides of Ledbetter Creek, originally the property of JONATHAN & WILLIAM DAVIS, part of 785 acres jointly claimed by the sd. JONATHAN & WILLIAM DAVIS, now deceased, the sd. JOSEPH DAVIS now claiming under the aforesaid WILLIAM deceased, as his legal representative, Sept. 8, 1795, JOSEPH DAVIS (+) (LS). Wit: A. CRAWFORD, J.P. Rec. Sept. 21, 1795.

Page 118:   THOMAS MERIWETHER of Columbia Co., for 45,000 pounds weight of inspected tobacco paid by ROBERT WARE in County of Wilkes, negro slaves, Dec. 7, 1791, THOMAS MERIWETHER (SEAL). Wit: RICHD. P. WHITE, JOHN WHITE. Sworn to Aug. ____, 1795. Rec. Sept. 30, 1795.

Pages 119-120:   May 18, 1795, PRUDENCE STORY of Columbia Co., to RICHARD SCRUGGS Junior and JAMES SCRUGGS Junior of same for 60 pounds sterling, land on Green Bryer prong of Kiokia Creek, 60 acres part of a 400 acre tract granted to ROBERT STORY, July 7, 1772, adj. WILLIAM WATKINS old tract, MEASE SMALLY, SHERWOOD BUGG, HUGH BLAIR, the land where PRUDENCE STORY now lives, PRUDENCE STORY ( ) (SEAL). Wit: SHERW. BUGG, J.P., HUGH BLAIR, HILLIARY PRATT. Rec. Sept. 28, 1795.

Page 120:   ELIJAH BRAGG of Columbia Co., for 30 pounds lawful money paid by BENJAMIN REES, two horses branded BR Jan. 7, 1793, ELIJAH BRAGG (LS). Wit: THOS WHITE J.P. Rec. Oct. 1, 1795.

Pages 121-122:   Jan. 15, 1795, NICHOLAS H. BUGG of Richmond Co., to ABRAM JONES, for __ pounds sterling money of Ga., land on waters of Green Brier Creek, in three surveys containing 1100 acres, a tract granted to THOMAS JONES, July 1, 1774, adj. lands of MICHEL & COLEMAN, the residue of a tract granted to NATHAN HARRIS & DANIEL COLEMAN, conveyed by JOHN L. DIXON to NICHOLAS H. BUGG, 400 acres known by the name of Oak Hall, and 50 acres adj. SHERWOOD BUGG. Originally granted to ALEXANDER INGLES & ANDREW FRAIZER, N. H. BUGG. Wit: JOHN COURSE, J.P., GEO. B. MOORE. Rec. Oct. 1, 1795.

Pages 122-123:   March 4, 1795, CHARLES FERGUSON and WINNEYFRED his wife of Columbia Co., to BENJAMIN KING of same, for 20 shillings, land on waters of White Oak Creek, part of WILLIAM STANLY's land, adj. JOHN SUTHERLAND, CHARLES FORGASON (LS), WINNYFRED FORGASON (LS). Rec. Oct. 1, 1795. Wit: MERRYMAN THORNE, J.P.

Pages 124-125:   Aug. 2, 1794, WILLIAM GRAVES of Wilkes Co., Merchant, to DALZIEL HUNTER, of Augusta by a certain bond dated Aug. 1, past, WILLIAM GRAVES is indebted to DALZIEL HUNTER for 77 pounds, 10 shillings, payable on the 1st day of Aug. 1795, for the purchase of land 620 acres on Little River in Columbia Co., adj. EDWARD TELLFAIR, WILLIAM LOCKER, REUBEN BLANCHARD, DAVID MILLER, EDWARD SPALDING, granted to DALZIEL HUNTER, April 26, 1787, then in Richmond Co., WM. GREAVES (LS). Wit: ALEX. MCMILLAN, NATHL. COCKE, Aldr. Rec. Oct. 2, 1795.

Pages 126-127:   Wilkes County, Jan. 29, 1789 DENNIS LINDSEY of Richmond Co., to JOSEPH LEWIS SHARPE of Wilkes Co., for 60 pounds sterling, 100 acres in Richmond Co., on the head of White Oak on the Quaker Road, joining the Widow JONES' land, originally grant made May 26, 1787, DENNIS LINDSEY & WILLIAM LINDSEY and their Mother MARTHA LINDSEY, MARTHA LINDSEY (+), WILLIAM LINDSEY (+), DENNIS LINDSEY (+). Wit: JOHN KELLY (+), JOHN LINDSEY (+). Proven before CHARLES LIN J.P. Sept. 12, 1789. Rec. Oct. 3, 1795.

Pages 128-129:   Feb. 6, 1789, JOSEPH LEWIS SHARPE of Wilkes Co., to RICHARD NAPIER of same, for 20 pounds sterling, 100 acres (land described in above deed). JOS LEWS SHARP (LS). Wit: JOEL HANDLEY, JOHN MCMINN (?), CHARLES LIN JP. Rec. Oct. 3, 1795.

Pages 129-131:   Aug. 16, 1794, BASIL JONES & JOHN COBBS of Ga., to
                   LEONARD MAGRUDER, THEODORE BEALL, and WM. D. BEALLE
of the State of Maryland, 200,000 acres in Montgomery County, for 46
pounds, 13 shillings, and 4 pence and 901 pounds in dry goods on return
of the warrant and surveys all duly executed into the surveyor Generals
Office with Mr. LEWIS SEWELLS certificate, to be made ready by Sept. 1,
Mr. THOMAS DAVIS or Col. MOORE of Hancock County, JN. COBBS (SEAL),
BASIL JONES (SEAL), LEOND MAGRUDER (SEAL), WM. D. BEALL (SEAL), WM. D.
BEALL (SEAL), THEO. BEALL (SEAL), Wit: LEVEN WALLES.

Page 131:   May 7, 1794, JOHN FULLAR delivered one colt to ELIZABETH
              MARTHIAS, JOHN FULLOR (LS). Wit: ELIZA. FULLER (EL).
Rec. Oct. 7, 1795.

Pages 132-133:   Nov. 30, 1793, ANDERSON CRAWFORD from GEORGE TARVIN
                   both of Columbia Co., for 3 pounds, 14 shillings, 8
acres on south side of Little Kioka Creek, in the south east corner of
a tract containing 350 acres granted to WILLIAM TARVIN (now deceased,
adj. CRAWFORD plantation, (plat included in deed), GEORGE TARVIN (SEAL).
Wit: BENJN. BLEDSOE, JOHN RENNALDS. Sworn to July 4, 1795. Rec.
Oct. 7, 1795.

Page 134:   Receipt from AMBROSE GORDON to THOMAS JONES, April 2, 1795
              for 52 pounds for a negro girl. THOS. JONES. Test:
ANANIAS COOPER. Rec. Oct. 7, 1795.

Pages 134-135:   July 15, 1795, WALTER LEIGH of Richmond Co., and
                   MARTHA his wife to BENJAMIN LEIGH of same, for 5
shillings, 250 acres in Columbia County on waters of Bigg Kioka Creek,
granted to WILLIAM CASTLEBERRY Oct. 3, 1769, adj. LEONARD CLAYBORN and
vacant land, WALTER LEIGH (SEAL), MARTHA LEIGH (SEAL). Wit: ABRAM
JONES, J.P., C. LINBURMAN (?), MARTHA LEIGH relinquishes dower July 15,
1795. Rec. Oct. 7, 1795.

Pages 136-137:   Oct. 12, 1784, THOS. JONES of Richmond Co., Planter, to
                   ROBERT MIDDLETON of same, for 5 shillings specie, 150
acres adj. DANIEL COLEMAN & JOHN MICHEL, originally granted to THOMAS
JONES July 3, 1774, THOMAS JONES. Wit: CHARLES FINCH, EDWD HAIL (+).
Proven by EDWD. HAIL in Washington Co., Ga., Aug. 10, 1795. Rec. Oct.
9, 1795.

Pages 138-139:   Oct. 13, 1784, THOMAS JONES and SARAH his wife of
                   Richmond Co., to ROBERT MIDDLETON of same, for 100
pounds specie, 150 acres originally granted to THOMAS JONES, July 3,
1774, THOMAS JONES (SEAL), SARAH JONES (X) (SEAL). Wit: CHARLES FINCH,
EDWARD HAIL (X). Rec. Oct. 13, 1795.

Page 140:   Columbia County, EZEKIEL HUDNALL, frees negroes, Sept. 3,
              1794. EZEKIEL HUDNALL (SEAL). Wit: MOSES MARSHALL, J.P.,
BENJN. FEW, JOHN BURDE, HADEN PRIOR.

Pages 141-142:   Columbia County, JOHN SHACKLEFORD to son MORDICAI
                   SHACKLEFORD, power of attorney to sell land in King
and Queen Co., Virginia, 200 acres or perhaps more, which said land was
given to my mother ISABELLA, by her father M (?) DAVIS WIDDENBURN and
reverted to the subscriber by being the only male heir, Oct. 16, 1795,
JNO. SHACKLEFORD (LS). Wit: T. W. MURRELL, JER DAY, MORRIS KELLY.
Rec. Oct. 16, 1795. Sworn to by THOMAS WILLIAMS MURRELL.

Pages 143:   RICHARD NAPIER to his son RICHARD CLAIBORNE NAPIER, deed
               of gift, negroes, Jan. 3, 1794, RICHARD NAPIER (LS). Wit:
H. MOUNGER, THOMAS TRAVIS. Sworn before MERRYMAN THORNE, J.P.
Oct. 16, 1795. Rec. Oct. 17, 1795.

Pages 144-148:   Columbia County: REUBEN BROWNSON became held and
                   firmly bound to AMBROSE HOLLIDAY, Planter, for 9900

pounds weight of inspected crop tobacco to be delivered in Augusta, in 3 annual payments, 1791, 1792 & 1793, at or upon Nov. 12, 1792, for 3 slaves, I have bargained to sell unto sd. AMBROSE HOLLIDAY the following tracts of land: All on GERMANY's Creek (1) 100 acres granted to KNOWLES PACE, Sept. 5, 1769 (2) a tract of 200 acres adjoining the first, bounded by HABERSHAMS, granted to AMBROSE HOLLIDAY, March 17, 1786 (30 287½ acres adj. CARMICHAEL's, granted to sd. HOLLIDAY, March 31, 1788 (4) 100 acres granted to sd. HOLLIDAY, the grant of which was consumed by accidental fire and (5) 70 acres adjoining the last grant adj. JOHN DAVIS' land granted to sd. HOLLIDAY, June 6, 1786, deed bearing date April 8, 1791, REUBEN BROWNSON (LS). Wit: JNO. TORRENCE, J.P., W. C., THOS. WHITE, J.P., R. HOWARD, J.P.

Pages 148-149:   June 10, 1795, PETER ZACHRY of Columbia Co., to WILLIAM BARNETT of same, for 22 pounds, 10 shillings lawful money, 150 acres adj. to lands of RICHARD HILL, PETER ZACHRY (LS). Wit: JOHN TINDELL, JOHN MARTIN STRAWZEN. Sworn to before PETER CRAWFORD, Nov. 24, 1795. Rec. Nov. 24, 1795.

Pages 150-151:   JAMES GRADY appoints JOSEPH RENNOLD of Spotsylvania Co., Va., attorney to demand all debts due him in state of Va., and to claim 150 acres 150 acres in Co. of Orrange, Dec. 4, 1795, JAMES GRASDY (X). Wit: RICHD. LONG, PETER CRAWFORD, J.P. Rec. Dec. 4, 1795.

Pages 151-152:   Aug. 20, 1795, WILLIAM FEW Junr., Esq. of Columbia Co., to WATERS DUNN, Junr. of same, for 60 pounds sterling 100 acres on waters of Green Brier Creek, adj. FORD, WELLS, DUNNS, FLEPS, LAWRONCE, granted to sd. WILLIAM FEW, Junr. Sept. 11, 1789, W. FEW (LS). Wit: MERRYMAN THORNE, J.P., R. HOWARD, J.P. Rec. Feb. 22, 1796.

Pages 153-154:   April 11, 1789, JAMES DANNELLY of Richmond Co., to FREDRICK COBBS of same, for 150 pounds sterling 150 acres on waters of Great Kioka, adj. DANNELLY, WARDEN, HOGER (?) land, JAMES DANELLY (LS). Wit: JAMES WATTERS, ANDREW DANELLY, NICHOLAS HARDON. Sworn to by ANDREW DANNELLY July 6, 1790 before WALTR DRANE, J.P. Rec. March 3, 1796.

Pages 154-155:   Sept. 29, 1795, FREDRICK COBBS of Columbia Co., to WILLIAM HOGE, for 100 pounds sterling, 100 acres on Great Kioka (land described in above deed), adj. WILLIAM HOGE, CLEMATUIS DAVIS, JAMES STEWART, JAMES OLIVE, FREDRICK COBB (LS), SARAH COBB (X) (LS). Wit: WR. DRANE, J.P., JAMES DANELLY. Rec. March 3, 1796.

Page 156:   Jan. 28, 1796, ROBERT WARE and JANE his wife of Wilkes Co., to THOMAS MOON of Columbia Co., for 200 pounds sterling, 400 acres in Columbia Co., known as Jordans Old-fields, bounding vacant land on all sides when surveyed ROBERT WARE (LS), JANEY WARE (LS). Wit: BENJAMIN FARMER, DAVID TOMLINSON (T). Rec. March 4, 1796.

Pages 157-158:   Feb. 19, 1793, JOHN SORRILS of Columbia Co. to THOMAS MOORE of same, for 14 pounds sterling, land on both sides of Sullivan's Creek, part of a grant to sd. JOHN SORRILS by a deed bearing date Sept. 20, 1787, adj. JORDAN's corner, 22 acres, JOHN SORRILS (LS). Wit: WILLIAM FARMER, Junr., BENJAMIN GARNER. Rec. March 4, 1796.

Pages 158-159:   MARTHA HOWARD of Columbia, widow and sole admx. of est. of LEMUEL HOWARD dec'd. appoint sons AQUILLA HOWARD & DEWEY HOWARD, attorney, to recover from Rev. JOHN COLEMAN, minister of the Protestant Episcopal Church in Harford County, Maryland, the full amt. of the bonds and interest due by the sd. COLEMAN to the est. of sd. A. LEMUEL HOWARD and in my name, Nov. 16, 1795, MARTHA HOWARD. Wit: R. HOWARD, J.P., THOS. WHITE, J.P. Rec. March 8, 1796.

Pages 160-161:   Dec. 3, 1793, JAMES ROSS of Columbia Co., to BENJAMIN BLEDSOE of same, for 100 pounds lawful money, 200 acres

on both sides of Little Kiokia Creek, originally granted to MARTIN
WEATHERFORD, March 15, 1771, JAMES ROSS (LS), ANN ROSS (LS). Wit:
THEODORE DORSETT, JOSHUA VAUGHN (+). Rec. March 14, 1796.

Pages 161-162:   DAVID HARRIS of Columbia Co., for 5 pounds paid by
                 BENJAMIN BLEDSOE, negroes Jan. 28, 1793, D. HARRIS
(LS). Wit: JNO. BURNETT, REUBEN REYNOLDS. Sworn before A. CRAWFORD,
J.P. Dec. 24, 1795. Rec. March 14, 1796.

Pages 162-164:   July 20, 1795, WILLIAM KENNON of Wilkes Co., to ROGER
                 KAGLE of Columbia Co., for 30 pounds sterling, land
on the Rockey in Columbia Co., JONES' line, 151 acres, WILLIAM KENNON
(LS). ELIZA. KENNON (LS). Wit: ISAAC KENT ( ), BEN WILLIAMS, J.P.
Rec. March 14, 1796.

Pages 164-166:   Dec. 10, 1795, ELIZABETH STORY, DINAH STORY, RACHEL
                 STORY of Washington Co., and THOMAS STORY, REBECCA
STORY & JOHN BROOKS of Warren County, to JAMES ALLEN of Columbia Co.,
for 25 pounds lawful money, 50 acres, adj. SHERWOOD BUGG, originally
granted to JAMES COBB, ELIZABETH STORY (X) (LS), DINAH STORY (LS),
RACHEL STORY (+) (LS), THOMAS STORY, REBECCA STORY (+) (LS), JOHN BROOKS
(+) (LS). Wit: WILLIAM WARE (+), JOHN WATTS, J.P., VINCENT THORP,
J.P. Rec. March 15, 1796.

Pages 166-167:   Nov. 18, 1795, ANNE FLOYD of State of South Carolina,
                 widow, to WINEFRED JOHNSTON, wife of THOMAS JOHNSTON
of Ga., for the natural love and affection, gift of negroes, ANNE FLOYD
( ) (LS). Wit: DANL ELAM, J.P. Rec. March 15, 1796.

Pages 167-168:   Feb. 14, 1794, DANIEL CONNELL & MARY his wife of
                 Richmond Co., to DREDZIL PACE of Columbia Co., for 80
pounds sterling, 100 acres, part of 200 acre tract, granted to JOHN
PARKER, July __, 1774, in St. Paul's Parish, on Mill Creek, adj. DANIEL
RICHARDSON, Mr. WOODS, LOVELACE DAVIS, DANIEL CONNEL (LS), MARY CONNEL
(+) (LS). Wit: JOHN STILES, WM. LONGSTREET, J.P. Rec. March 18, 1796.

Pages 169-170:   MARY MATHIS of Columbia to son WILLIAM MATHIS of
                 Warren Co., land on waters of Brier Creek, 100 acres
granted to MARY MATHIS, Sept. 21, 1785, adj. REEVES, the second tract,
150 acres granted to MARY MATHIS Oct. 14, 1788, MARY MATHIS (W) (LS).
Wit: JOHN WALTON, THOMAS JONES. Sworn to March 25, 1796. Rec. March
25, 1796.

On unnumbered pages following page 170: Plan for 21 tracts of land in
different waters of Kiokia joining unknown lands, surveyed in the same
of JOHN FEE, 18,000 acres dated Aug. 5, 1793.

Pages 171-174:   Sept. 12, 1794, JOHN FEE of town of Augusta, merchant
                 to Dr. THOMAS RESS of Philadelphia, Pennsylvania, for
5 shillings lawful money of Pennsylvania, 18,000 acres, JNO. FEE (LS).
Wit: CATHARINE BAKER, GEORGE A. BAKER, Receipt of payment witnessed by:
JOHN PHILLIPS, GEORGE A. BAKER. Certificate of credit signed by
THOMAS MIFFLIN, Gov. of Pa. Rec. April 3, 1796.

Page 175:   ALEXANDER E. BEALL of Columbia, to my father JAMES BEALL
            of Montgomery Co., Maryland, power of attorney, May 13, 1796.
Rec. May 14, 1796.

Pages 176-177:   Oct. 19, 1793, DALZIEL HUNTER of Augusta, to JAMES
                 WATERS of Columbia Co., for 50 pounds lawful money,
339 acres on Kiokia Creek and Uchee Creek, adj. MAGRUDER, CARROL, ALL,
DEES, DALZIEL HUNTER (LS). Wit: J. RANDOLPH, STEPHEN F. RANDOLPH.
Rec. June 14, 1796. (Plat included in deed.)

Pages 178-179:   Nov. 16, 1792, GEORGE HANDLEY, Sheriff of Richmond Co.,
                 to JOHN MILLIN of Savannah, Chatham Co., Bootmaker,

whereas FRANCIS CURVAISIE in Inferior Court of Chatham Co., did recover Judgment against est. of JOHN DOBBINS dec'd., for 25 pounds with 4 pounds, 6 shillings, and 10 pence, 200 acres granted March 3, 1777 to JOHN DOBBINS, GEO HANDLEY. Wit: SEABORN JONES, JOHN COURSE, J.P. Rec. July 27, 1796.

Pages 180-181:   Jan. 13, 1795, RICHARD NAPIER & MOLLY his wife of Columbia Co., to CHARLES FENNELL of same, for 5 shilling 100 acres on Upton's Creek, adj. PORTER, CHARLES FENNELL, PARKES, RICHD. NAPIER (LS). MOLLY NAPIER (LS). Wit: B. PORTER, ROBT. RANDOLPH, J.P. Rec. July 27, 1796.

Pages 181-182:   March 17, 1796, JAMES MOORE to ROBERT QUINN, both of Columbia Co., for 10 pounds, 100 acres, part of a 685 acre grant to JAMES MOORE, 1792, J. MOORE (LS). Wit: JOHN QUINN, JOHN MOORE (-). Rec. July 27, 1796.

Page 183:   JOSHUA MORGAN of Wilkes Co. to my Grand Children JOSHUA MORGAN, BETSEY MORGAN, BILLY MORGAN, JEREMY MORGAN & THOMAS MORGAN, all of Columbia County, cattle and furniture. Aug. 6, 1795. JOSHUA MORGAN (M) (LS). Wit: HADEN PRIOR, JANE REGERY (?). Rec. July 28, 1796.

(Two pages numbered 183.)

Pages 183-184:   March 12, 1788, JOSEPH MONEY of Newberry County, South Carolina, planter, to JOHN MONEY of Richmond Co., Ga., for 50 pounds sterling, 100 acres on Uptons Creek, part of a 550 acre grant to JOSEPH MONEY Senr. now deceased, July 5, 1769, adj. SAMUEL BROWN, JOS MONEY (LS). Wit: J. MOORE, REUBIN BAINE, DUNCAN, MCCOWEN. Rec. July 27, 1796.

Pages 185-186:   July 2, 1796, THOMAS CARR of Columbia Co., to RICHARD MATTHEWS, Jr., son of RICHARD MATHEWS begotten on CATHARINE his wife, for 20 pounds, land adj. WILLIAM LINDSEY, 100 acres, part of a grant of 830 acres granted to sd. CARR, Oct. 27, 1794, plat included in deed, THOS CARR (LS). Wit: NEIL DAUGHTERY, JNO. APPLING, J.P. Rec. July 29, 1796.

Pages 187-188:   Jan. 8, 1796, WILLIAM FARMER, Senr., planter of Columbia Co., to JOHN CONNERS of same, planter, for 12 pounds, 10 shillings, 200 acres granted to sd. WILLIAM FARMER, Sept. 20, 1787, adj. sd. W. FARMER & BROWN, RICHARDSON, WILLIAM FARMER (LS). Wit: ISAAC COOPER, SAMUEL OWEN, NATHAN JONES. Rec. July 30, 1796.

Pages 188-190:   June 3, 1796, ANN WALL to CHRISTOPHER MILLIRON, both of Ga., for 50 pounds sterling, 300 acres on waters of White Oak Creek, where I do now live, ANN WALL (X) (LS). Wit: MARTHA MELLOWN (?), BENJ. KING. Rec. July 30, 1796.

Pages 190-192:   July 11, 1792, DANIEL MCCARTY of Wilkes Co. to JOHN WRIGHT of Columbia Co., for 75 pounds sterling, 100 acres on Green Brier Creek, surveyed for DANIEL MCCARTY, Nov. 10, 1772, adj. R. UPTON, DANIEL MCCARTY (LS). Wit: RICHARD WRIGHT, GEORGE WRIGHT. Rec. June 30, 1796.

Pages 193-194:   JOHN WALTON of Columbia Co., make MATTHEW WALTON of State of Kentucky, attorney to make titles to land I hold in Kentucky, Aug. 18, 1796. JOHN WALTON (LS). Wit: MARY A. CRAWFORD, PETER CRAWFORD, J.P. Rec. Aug. 18, 1796.

Pages 194-195:   Sept. 15, 1776, IGNATUIS FEW of Parish of St. Paul, to WILLIAM FEW of same, for 100 pounds sterling, land beginning at ABBENTON FELPS corner, 350 acres granted to ROBERT DUN(?), Dec. 6, 1774, conveyed by DUNN to sd. FEW June 9, 1775, IGS FEW (LS). Wit: WM. FEW, BENJ. FEW. Proved by BENJAMIN FEW, June 15, 1796. Rec. Aug. 24, 1796.

Pages 196-197:   July 18, 1796, HUGH BLAIR of Columbia Co., to DAVID
                  PERRYMAN of same, for 70 pounds sterling, 275 acres,
HUGH BLAIR (LS).   Wit: JAMES PERRYMAN, ELISHA PERRYMAN. Proven by
ELISHA PERRYMAN, Aug. 2, 1796. Rec. Aug. 24, 1796.

Pages 197-198:   Aug. 3, 1796, SAMPSON LAMKIN to WILLIAM LAMKIN for 70
                  pounds lawful money, 150 acres on Green Brier Creek,
formerly granted to and known by the name of JOHN MITCHELLS tract, adj.
DANIEL COLEMAN & ROBERT STORY, and all other sides vacant at time of
survey, SAMPSON LAMKIN (LS). Wit: NATHAN CRAWFORD, PETER CRAWFORD, J.P.
Rec. Aug. 24, 1796.

Pages 199-200:   April 5, 1796, BENJAMIN HARRIS & JANE his wife, planter
                  of Columbia Co., to JAMES OLIVER of same, planter, for
100 pounds sterling, 173 acres registered in Secretary Office on Feb.
17, 1796, BENJAMIN HARRIS (LS), JANE HARRIS (LS). Wit: JOHN OLIVER,
JAMES OLIVER. Sworn to Aug. 2, 1796. Rec. Aug. 24, 1796.

Pages 200-201:   June 21, 1796, WALTER DRANE, Sheriff of Columbia Co.,
                  to THOMAS COBB the elder, of same, for $300, by two
writs of fiere facias of Superior Court of Columbia Co., April 6, 1796
at the suit of EDMUND BUGG, HENRY HAMPTON & HENRY HILL, Exrs. of L. W. &
T. of BENJAMIN ANDREW, dec'd. against JOHN COBB Junr. & PETER CRAWFORD
and another suit against CHESLEY BOSTWICK, Junr. & sd. JOHN COBB, land
where JOHN COBBS live on north fork of Kioka Creek, commonly called
Green Brier, 528 acres, near WALLIONS line, BEVINS old line, now
BUKHAMS, BAZIL JONES line, W. DRANE (LS), S.C.C.: Wit: J. L. DIXON, WM.
BUKHAM, J. FEW J.P. Rec. Aug. 24, 1796.

Pages 202-203:   June __, 1796, THOMAS COBB the elder to JOHN COBB of
                  same, for $300, 528 acres (land described in above
deed), THOS. COBB (LS). Wit: J. L. DIXON, WM. BUKHAM, J. FEW, J.P.
Rec. Aug. 24, 1796.

Pages 204-205:   Dec. 28, 1795, ISAAC PINSON of Columbia Co., Planter,
                  to EDMUND BUGG of same, for $300, 150 acres where sd.
PINSON now lives, granted to JOSEPH COBB, July 5, 1774, conveyed to sd.
PINSON by deed Dec. 14, 1782, also 100 acres joining the above tract
granted to WILLIAM PINSON, and conveyed to ISAAC PINSON, by deed Oct.
20, 1789, ISAAC PINSON (P). Wit: DANL. ELAM, J.P., NEHE: DUNN,
REBECCA, wife of ISAAC PINSON, relinquished dower Dec. 28, 1795, Rec.
Aug. 24, 1796.

Page 206:   Dec. 14, 1793, JAMES DANELLY to JAMES OLIVE, both of
             Columbia Co., for 100 pounds sterling, 150 acres on waters
of Great Kioka Creek, granted to MESHICK MATHIS, Aug. 7, 1774, adj.
MAGRUDER, JAMES STEWART, supposed to be BRYANTS land, JAMES DANELLY (LS).
Wit: WALTR. DRANE, J.P. Rec. Aug. 24, 1796.

Pages 207-208:   Sept. 20, 1794, THOMAS WATSON, Admr. & ELIZABETH WATSON,
                  EADY WATSON, MILLY WATSON, MARY COATS of Columbia Co.,
for 100 pounds, land on waters of GERMANY's Creek, 200 acres adj. JOHN
PERKINS, JOSEPH BOGGS lands formerly JACOB CASTLE, granted by GEORGE
III, June 7, 1774 to JAMES COATS, THOMAS WATSON (LS), ELIZABETH WATSON
( ) (LS), JOHN COATS, REBECKAH WATSON (X) (LS), EDEY WATSON (+) (LS),
MILLY WATSON (+), MARY COATS (+) (LS). Wit: JOHN WATSON, JOSEPH
WATSON. Rec. Aug. 25, 1796.

Pages 209-210:   Jan. 4, 1796, RICHARD MOORE of Columbia Co., to GEORGE
                  JONES, late of North Carolina, for 60 pounds, 100 acres
adj. CHARLES SIMS, JOHN STUBBS, FRANCIS JONES, SAMUEL JONES, land
granted to sd. RICHARD MOORE on bounty, 1770, RICHARD MOORE (LS). Wit:
J. MOORE, J.P., JAS MCFARLAND, J.P.

Pages 211-213:   June 21, 1796, JAMES RICHARDS Sheriff of Richmond Co.,
                  to WILLIAM JACKSON, of same, planter, by writ of

fiere facias March 17, 1794, Superior Court of Chatham Co., in the
name of JOSEPH CLAY & JOSEPH HABERSHAM against the goods & c. of JAMES
ROE, dec'd. in the hands of JOHN COBBISON & ANN his wife, of ROBERT
ROE in the hands of SAMUEL HAMMOND & REBECCA his wife to be admred. of
the goods and chattels of RAE, ELBERT & GRAYHAM, for the sum of 573
pounds, 1 shilling and 10 pence & 4 pounds, 5 shillings, cost of suit,
four tracts of lands in Columbia County, on Savannah River (1) 200 acres,
granted to ROGER QUARLES July 5, 1774 conveyed to ROBERT RAE, JAMES RAE,
JOHN RAE, SAMUEL ELBERT & THOMAS GRAYHAM, (2) 150 acres adj. Kioka
Creek and land of THOMY LLOYD, granted to THOMAS GILLELAND, Oct. 2,
1759, then conveyed to ANDREW MOORE and then to ROBERT RAY, JAMES RAE
& THOMAS GRAYHAM, (3) 250 acres, in district of Augusta, granted to
RALPH KILGORE Dec. 16, 1756, (4) 100 acres adj. CARTLEDGE, granted to
THOMAS HOGAN, Dec. 5, 1769, conveyed to ANDREW MOORE, JAS RICHARDS
S.R.C. (LS). Wit: GEO. WATKINS, ISAAC HERBERT, J.P. Rec. Aug. 25,
1796.

Pages 213-214:   Feb. 20, 1775, WILLIAM CASTLEBERRY Senr. & MARGARET his
                 wife of Parish of St. Paul, to GEORGE RAY of same, for
27 pounds sterling money, 100 acres granted July 4, 1769, WILLIAM
CASTLEBERRY (W) (LS), MARGRET CASTLEBERRY (N) (LS). Wit: JAMES YOUNG-
BLOOD (LS), LEWIS POWELL, RICHARD CASTLEBERRY. Proved in Wilkes Co.,
Oct. 17, 1793. Rec. Aug. 25, 1796.

Pages 215-216:   Aug. 10, 1775, RICHARD CASTLEBERRY & ANN his wife of
                 Parish of St. Paul, to GEORGE RAY of same, for 75
pounds, 150 adj. THOMAS AYRES, LEONARD CLAIBORNE, granted to RICHARD
CASTLEBERRY, Oct. 3, 1769, RICHARD CASTLEBERRY (LS), ANN CASTLEBERRY
(+) (LS). Wit: JOHN BRYAN, JONATHAN HUFF. Proven in Wilkes Co., Oct.
17, 1793. Rec. Aug. 25, 1796.

Pages 217-218:   Dec. 18, 1792, LEWIS BARNES, Esqr. & ELIZABETH his wife
                 of Columbia Co., to GEORGE RAY of same, for 40 pounds
sterling, 100 acres on waters of Big Kioka Creek, granted to JACOB
JONES, adj. when surveyed WILLIAM CASTLEBERRY, LEWIS BARNES (LS),
ELIZABETH BARNES (LS). Wit: OBEDIENCE SIMMS, LEWIS CRANE (L). Proven
by LEWIS CRANE, Aug. 2, 1796. Rec. Aug. 25, 1796.

Pages 218-219:   Aug. 28, 1792, WINNEFRED PINSON, widow of Columbia Co.,
                 to GEORGE RAY, for 30 pounds sterling, 100 acres,
granted to EZEKIEL OFFCETT (?), Sept. 17, 1787, adj. WINNEFRED PINSON,
WINN PINSON ( ) (LS). Wit: LEWIS BARNER, J.P., JNO. SMITH. Rec. Aug.
25, 1796.

Page 220:   Nov. 23, 1795, JOHN WOOD promises to pay Mr. SETH HOWARD,
            $15. Test WILLIAM ROSS, ENOS HOWARD, (signed on the back
"OLIVER BAXTER.") Rec. Sept. 13, 1796.
            Mr. JAMES BURROUGHS, J.P. swears that he mislaid a note of
hand given by JOHN WOOD to SETH HOWARD for $15, Sept. 12, 1796. JAS.
BURROUGHS.

Pages 221-222:   July 26, 1796, FERREL REILY of Columbia to DANIEL
                 MCNEIL Senr. of same, for 100 pounds lawful money,
200 acres on Great Kiokia Creek, granted to JESSE MCNEIL, Oct. 22, 1784,
FERRIL RILY (LS). Wit: SARAH JONES (+), MARY RAY (+). Rec. Sept. 13,
1796.

Pages 223-224:   Aug. 1, 1794, DALZIEL HUNTER of Augusta, to WILLIAM
                 GREAVES of Wilkes Co., merchant, for 77 pounds, 10
shillings, 620 acres, adj. EDWARD TELFAIR, WILLIAM LOCKLER, Little River,
DAVID MILLER, REUBEN BLANCHARD, HENRY SPALDING, DALZIEL HUNTER (LS).
Wit: NATHL. COCKE, ALEX MCMILLAN. Rec. Oct. 11, 1796.

Pages 225-226:   Oct. 4, 1796, JOSEPH WARE, EDW Sheriff of Richmond Co.,
                 to SEABORN JONES, for $41, 620 acres (land described

in above deed), suit of GEORGE HUNT against DALZIEL HUNTER, ABNMELECH HAWKINS & Exrs. of DANILE WALLION (?), JOSEPH WARE S.R.C. (LS). Wit: NICHOLAS WARE, THO. FLOURNOY, JOHN WILLSON,J.P.

Pages 226-228:   Sept. 9, 1783, JOHN RICHARDSON of Richmond Co., planter
                 to ENOCH RICHARDSON of same, planter, for 5 pounds
current money land on Savidges Creek, formerly called Red Mill Creek,
100 acres, ½ of a grant to DANIEL RICHARDSON, 1774, adj. JOHN RICHARDSONS
line, JOHN RICHARDSON (LS). Wit: MANN SIMS, WILLIAM SIMS. Sworn
July 6, 1788. Rec. Oct. 31, 1796.

Pages 229-230:   Jan. 3, 1793, MATTHEW DUNCAN to JOHN SOUTHERLAND, for
                 50 pounds sterling land granted to ABRAHAM HORN, 100
acres, YOUNGBLOODS line, JAMES WRIGHTS, Widow BENNETs line, MATTHEW
DUNCAN (LS). Wit: JNO. STITH, P. R. STITH, JOHN BENNETTV Proven
Aug. 2, 1796. Rec. Nov. 6, 1796.

Pages 231-232:   MARY CULBREATH wife of JOHN CULBREATH & MARY RAMSEY,
                 wife of JOHN RAMSEY, both of Columbia Co., cannot
without manifest inconvenience attent the Court of Mecklenburg Co.,
Virginia, to represent our third part in a 400 acre tract which was
granted to JOHN CULBREATH & MARY CULBREATH the heirs and minors of
EDWARD CULBREATH, late of Mecklenburg Co., Va., on southside of the
ROANOCK River, on waters of Grassy Creek, we authorize our respective
husbands to dispose of sd. land, Nov. 17, 1796. MARY CULBREATH (X)
(LS), MARY RAMSEY ( ). Wit: JAMES SIMMS, J.P.

Pages 232-234:   Jan. 5, 1797, JOHN CULBREATH & MARY his wife and JOHN
                 RAMSEY and MARY his wife all of Ga., to THOMAS GREEN-
WOOD of Mecklenburg Co., Va., for 250 pounds, land in Mecklenburg Co.,
MARY CULBREATH (+) (LS), JOHN CULBREATH (LS), JOHN RAMSEY (LS), MARY
RAMSEY (LS). Wit: JAMES SIMMS, THOMAS MOON J.P. Rec. Jan. 10, 1797.

Pages 235-236:   March 23, 1796, WILLIAM SHIELDS, Jnr. to ANDREW STUR-
                 GESS both of Columbia Co., for 15 pounds, 30 acres on
waters of Cane Creek, granted to JOHN SHIELDS Oct. 4, 1774, grant
containing 150 acres, WM. SHIELDS (LS). Wit: JOHN ROUSAU (?), JOHN
L. POGUE. Rec. Feb. 25, 1797.

Page 237:   Columbia Co., NANCY SANDERS, Admx. of Est. of EPHRAIM SANDERS
            dec'd. April 22, 1797, place under sale the est. of sd.
EPHRAIM SANDERS, NANCY SANDERS Admr. (LS). Wit: ROBT. TOOMBS, JAMES
MCNEIL. Rec. May 10, 1797.

Page 238:   Columbia Co., WILLIAM WALTON, appoints WILLIAM SHACKEFORD of
            Kentucky to sell his lands in Kentucky, Sept. 16, 1800.
WM. WALTON (LS). Wit: J. CRAWFORD, PETER CRAWFORD, J.P. Rec. Sept.
16, 1800.

Pages 239-240:   Oct. 18, 1796, JOHN KNIDAY (NIDY) of Columbia Co., to
                 THOMAS CARR of same, for $48, 15 acres on Green Brier
Creek, granted to MOSES LINDSAY, Dec. 13, 1785, conveyed to WILLIAM
JONES March 7, 1786 then to sd. NIDAY, JOHN NIDADY (LS). Wit: JOHN
FULLER, JOHN GRIMES (X). Rec. Oct. 14, 1800.

(Note, the page directly after page 239 is number 249.)

Pages 250-251:   Received of BENJAMIN REYNOLDS of Columbia Co., $100 for
                 slaves which we are entitled to from equity, est. of
the late BENJAMIN REYNOLDS, dec'd., of Orange County, Va., JAMES GRADY
& ELIZABETH his wife, formerly ELIZABETH REYNOLDS, JOSEPH REYNOLDS &
legally conveyed to BENJAMIN REYNOLDS, dec'd and now supposed to be in
possession of WILLIAM REYNOLDS, of Orange Co., Va., JAMES GRADY (X) (LS),
ELIZABETH GRADY (X) (LS). Wit: ELIZABETH BELGER (X) (?), JOHN FOSTER,
J.J.C. Rec. Nov. 27, 1800, Dated Nov. 24, 1800.

Pages 251-252:   Sept. 5, 1800, DAVID PERRYMAN to ELISHA PERRYMAN both
                 of Columbia Co., for $500, 116 acres on Green Brier
and Kioka Creek, granted to DAVID PERRYMAN by TELFAIR, adj. Widow
APPLING, RODDEY, WILLIAM FEW, DAVID PERRYMAN (LS). Wit: D. PERRYMAN,
WM. WILKINS, J.P. Rec. Dec. 1800.

Pages 252-253:   Aug. 12, 1800, JAMES ROSS to JOHN FULLER, Senr. both
                 of Columbia Co., for $10, granted to JAMES ROSS, July
4, 1800, adj. IGNATUIS FEW & MCDONALD, FULLER, 34 acres, (plat included
in deed), JAMES ROSS (LS). Wit: TERREL C. HARRISON, JAMES SHIELD,
JOHN FULLER. Rec. Dec. 9, 1800.

Pages 254-255:   Nov. 15, 1788, WILLIAM STURGES of Richmond Co., to
                 CHARLES KENNON of Halifax Co., Virginia for 100 pounds,
400 acres on Sullivans Creek, adj. RAY, SHEPHERD, WM. STURGES (LS). Wit:
JOHN FONTAIN, JNO. COBB, J.P. Rec. Dec. 9, 1800.

Page 256:   Columbia Co., JOSHUA WINN to my son JOSHUA WINN, 3 negroes,
            Oct. 5, 1800, JOSHUA WYNN (LS). Wit: JOHN TODD, JAMES
STEWART, J.P. Rec. Dec. 18, 1800.

Page 257:   Columbia Co., JOSHUA WINN to son JOHN WYNN, 3 negroes, Oct.
            25, 1800, JOSHUA WYNNE (LS). Wit: JNO. TODD, JAS. STUART
JP. Rec. no date.

Page 258:   JOSHUA WYNNE to son WILLIAMSON WYNNE, negroes, April 31,
            1800 JOSHUA WYNNE (LS). Wit: JAMES STUART JP. Rec. Dec.
29, 1800.

Pages 259-260:   Jan. 2, 1798, THOMAS JONES to ANTHONY COOPER of
                 Columbia Co., for two hundred lawful money, 150 acres
granted to EZEKIEL STALLINGS, on Red Bird (?) Creek, THOMAS JONES (LS).
Wit: JAS. STALLINGS, J.P., ELISHA WATKINS. Rec. Jan. 16, 1801.

Pages 260-261:   May 15, 1800, JACOB HIGGINBOTHOM & ANN his wife of
                 Elbert Co., to JACOB SHOVER of Columbia Co., for 88
pounds sterling 200 acres, formerly in Parish of St. Paul, now Columbia
Co., JACOB HIGGINBOTHAM Senr. (LS), ANN HIGGINBOTHAM (LS). Wit:
W. HIGGINBOTHAM, DUDDOIN CISTER (German Signature). Rec. Jan. 16, 1801.

Page 262:   RICHARD MERIWETHER of Columbia Co., frees slaves, Jan. 21,
            1800, RICHARD MEREWETHER (LS). Wit: J. WHITE, PETER CRAW-
FORD, JP. Rec. Jan. 21, 1801.

Pages 263:   Certificate that JAMES BELCHER sold about 1786 to THOMAS
             WASHINGTON, 380 acres in Richmond Co., on Little River,
believed originally granted to ROBERT HATCHER, purchased of IGNATIUS
FEW, Jan. 19, 1801, JAS BELCHER (LS). Wit: W. STITH, TH CARR. Rec.
Jan. 29, 1801.

Pages 263-265:   Chatham County: ARCHIBALD BULLOCK late, by his L. W.
                 & T. dated Feb. 11, 1775, did leave to JAMES BULLOCK,
ARCHIBALD S. BULLOCK & WILLIAM B. BULLOCK (each of said sons being
upwards of 21 years of age), division of land 400 acres adj. HUGH
MIDDLETON, ROBERT MIDDLETON, ROBERT MIDDLETON & GEORGE GALPHIUS,
ALEXANDER SCOTT, originally granted to sd. ARCHABALD BULLOCK, also 300
acres adj. SILLS, WILLIAM SHIELDS, JOHN SHIELDS, NATHANIEL COATS, ROSS,
and originally granted to sd. ARCH. BULLOCK, and 200 acres also granted
to sd. BULLOCK, BULLOCH (LS), A. S. BULLOCK (LS). Wit: SHEFTALL
SHEFTALL JP., S. FILE. Rec. Jan. 29, 1801.

Pages 266-267:   Feb. 4, 1800, JAMES PILKINGTON & PATSEY his wife of
                 Columbia Co., to HARRY MCCLENDON for $210, 60 acres on
both sides of MICHAELS or GERMANYS Creek, adj. PAINTER, FOSTER,
GRENAGY, originally granted to ANN WOOD, Feb. 4, 1785, JAMES PILKINTON
(LS), PATSEY PILKINTON (+) (LS). Wit: GEORGE DOWNS, JAMES FOSTER, JNO.
FOSTER, J.P. Rec. Feb. 7, 1801.

age 268:   THOMAS MOORE of Columbia Co., to daughter NANCY, one negroe
             girl, deed of gift, Feb. 23, 1801. THOMAS MOORE (LS).
Wit: MANN SIMS. Rec. Feb. 24, 1801.

Page 269:   SAMUEL BOWDRIE of Columbia Co., to JAMES STUART of same,
             planter, for $400, sale of negroe, signed at Augusta, May
3, 1800, SAML. BOWDRIE (LS). Wit: DAVID TAYLOR, JOHN WILLSON, JP.
Rec. Feb. 27, 1801.

Page 270:   FRANCIS SHACKLEFORD of Fayetteville, North Carolina,
             Sadler, to JOHN WILLSON & Co. of Augusta, Merchants, on
account of JAMES STUART of Columbia Co., planter, for $350, sale of
negroes, FRAS SHACKLEFORD (LS). Wit: GEO SCOTT, JOHN WILLSON, JP.
Rec. Feb. 27, 1801.

Page 271:   CHARLES DENHAM of Columbia Co., for paternam affection to
             JOHN HOLLINGSHEAD, JOHN's father being dead, JOHN now a
minor, gift of negroes Dec. 9, 1800, CHAR. DENHAM (LS). Wit: TRUMAN
BRISCOE, DANL. MCDUFFY. Rec. Feb. 27, 1801. SINAI DENHAM (+) relinquishes title.

Pages 272-273:   Oct. 13, 1800, THOMAS HANSON & ELIZABETH his wife to
                 THOMAS BEALL, all of Columbia Co., for $600, 138 acres,
part of a 200 acre grant to JOHN GARNETT, Feb. 21, 1785, adj. REESE
MORRIS, EVEHART, WILLIAMS, THOS. HANSON (LS), ELIZABETH HANSON (+)
(LS). Wit: JOHN BEALL, JNO FOSTER J.J.C. Rec. April 13, 1801.

Pages 274-275:   Sept. 24, 1798, NATHAN SIDWELL to JAMES GUIST (GIST)
                 both of Columbia Co., for $30, 10 acres on Germanys
Creek, granted to JOHN SIDWELL, then left to NATHAN SIDWELL by will,
beginning at SE corner of a tract formerly belonging to JONATHAN SELL,
NATHAN SIDWELL (LS). Wit: J. MOORE, SAMSON S. SLATE JP. Rec. April
14, 1801.

Pages 275-276:   April 19, 1800, MATTHEW BURNSIDES to JAS GUIST, for
                 $60, 7 acres on Germanys Creek, part of a grant to
SAMUEL WILLSON and sold to sd. MATTHEW BURNSIDES, MATTHEW BURNSIDES
(LS). Wit: MARK P. DAVIS, THOS WHITE JP.

Page 276:   WILLIAM THOMAS to JAMES GUIST, 17 acres adj. JOHN EWBRA,
             JAMES GUIST, MATTHEW BURNSIDES, adj. Augusta Great Road,
and late KINDRED CARTER's for $85, March 13, 1800, WM. THOMAS (LS).
Wit: ___ JONES, ___ THOMAS. Rec. April 14, 1801.

Pages 277-279:   Aug. 31, 1789, JOSEPH MENDINGALL of Surry County, North
                 Carolina & ELIZABETH his wife to JAMES GUIST of Rich-
mond Co., Ga., for 40 pounds sterling, 100 acres on Germanys Creek in
Wrightsborough Township, granted to JOHN HASTSHORN, Oct. 4, 1774, adj.
MATTHEW MOATS, NATHAN SIDWELL, JAMES WILLSON, JOSEPH MENDENHALL (LS),
ELIZABETH MENDENHALL (LS). Wit: DAVID MOTTS, SAMUEL JONES, ADAM GUEST.
Rec. April 24, 1801.

On unnumbered pages following 279: Sept. 20, 1794, THOMAS WATSON, Adr.
et. al to JNO. MOATS, (same deed as on Pages 207-208).

COLUMBIA COUNTY, GA. MARRIAGES

BOOK A

The dates given below are marriage dates unless marked "lic." for marriage license or "rec." for recorded date of marriage entry in the book. Names marked with a single asterisk are no longer in Book A but were recorded as being there in 1910 when they were published in HISTORICAL COLLECTIONS OF THE JOSEPH HABERSHAM CHAPTER, DAUGHTERS AMERICAN REVOLUTION, VOLUME III. Dates marked with a double asterisk have been taken from original marriage bonds which are on film at the Georgia Department of Archives and History.

	James Tinsley and Lucy Richards*	7 July 1806**
	Jonathan Gammon and Winifred Monk*	10 Aug. 1806**
Page 4	Henry Slaughter and Betsey T. Blackwell	18 Sept. 1806
	Jonathan Brooks and Nancey Monk	21 Sept. 1806
Page 5	Israel Blades and Elizabeth McDonald	11 Sept. 1806
	Nathaniel Cobbs and Flora Fee	6 Nov. 1806
Page 6	Joel Woolly and Patsey Leeth (? Luth)	21 Oct. 1806
	Solomon Ward and Jane Dannelly	18 Dec. 1806
Page 7	John Parks Bacon and Miss Mary Lamar	1 Jan. 1807
	John Hannon and Elizabeth Wright	8 Jan. 1807
Page 8	Joseph Cobb and Nancey Reynolds	11 Jan. 1807
	James McCord and Nancey Neal	12 Feb. 1807
Page 9	Juriah Harriss and Elizabeth Dantignac	12 Feb. 1807
	George W. Dent and Miss Nancey Hutcheson	21 Aug. 1806
Page 10	Gabriel Williams and Miss Sarah Williams	22 Feb. 1807
	Absolom Castles and Rebekah Jones	10 Jan. 1807
Page 11	James Williams and Nancey Hill	4 Jan. 1807
	Maurice Ronie and Nancey Flyn	28 Dec. 1806
Page 12	Daniel McDonald and Jane Fuller	8 May 1806
	Richard Jelks and Mrs. Hannah Germany	9 June 1807
Page 13	Willis Gammon and Rebekah Willis	14 May 1807
	John Sutherland and Hannah Martin	11 Aug. 1807
	Wm. Betts and Mary Cosby*	24 Aug. 1807**
	James Amos and Sarah Reese*	28 Aug. 1807**
	Edmund Cates and Nancy Cobb*	
	Willoby Slaton and Elizabeth Low*	16 Nov. 1807**
Page 16	John Smith and Levency (? Leveney) Payne	23 Jan. 1808
	David Willson and Anny Drane	21 Jan. 1808
	Robert Shaw, Jr. and Nancy McDonald*	9 Dec. 1807**
	Charles Lisles and Betsy Chisholm*	17 Dec. 1807**
	Wm. Griffin and Barbary Taylor*	
	Samuel Fuller and Eleanor Kendrick*	
	John Collins and Nancy Stuart*	
	John Farrer and Nancy Baker*	
	Samuel Linky and Philopena Jones*	
	Edmund Bowdre and Martha Hicks*	
	George Burbedge and Polly Sommers*	
	John Inglet and Winifred Moran*	21 Dec. 1808**
	Wm. A. Fuller and Polly Hoge*	31 Dec. 1808**
	Wm. Hansford and Peggy Rogers*	
	Robert Jones and Susanna Allen*	
	Solomon Simons and Sally Ware*	
	Jacob Miller, Jr., and Martha Newsom*	18 Feb. 1809**
	Wm. Adams and Delilah Lisles*	28 Jan. 1809**
	Jesse Albritton and Patsy Zachry*	23 Dec. 1808**
	David Thomas and Mary Sims*	
	Thomas Beall and Mary M. Maddox*	15 April 1809**
	Wm. Scott and Sarah Wilson*	
	Jesse Waller and Patience Collins*	15 May 1809**
	Daniel Killingsworth and Mary Greene*	8 May 1809**
	John Prescot and Margaret Millican*	17 June 1809**
	Wm. Bryan and Catherine Griffin*	23 May 1809**
	John Colvard and Sally Gibson*	8 July 1809**
	Thornton Gibson and Martha Jones*	

	Pleasant Benning and Milinda L. White*	23 May 1809**
	Thomas Yarborough and Polly Walton*	
	Robert Martin and Fanny Collins*	
	James Shaffer and Sarah Chambless*	2 Aug. 1809**
Page 33	Thomas Burton and Charity Wright	17 Sept. 1809
	John McDonald and Susan Jones	14 Sept. 1809
Page 34	Solomon Hoge and Nancey Southerland	8 Oct. 1809
	Thomas Yarbrough and Jane Warren	24 Dec. 1809
Page 35	Laurence Richardson and Nancey Glover	14 Jan. 1810
	Thomas Turner and Eliza Worshing	2 Mar. 1810
Page 36	George McKinze and Mary Lacey	22 Feb. 1810
	Burrell Richards and Ann Linn	9 May 1810
Page 37	Hendley Boswell and Polly Collins	31 May 1810
	William Lovlace and Jane Hunt	30 May 1810
Page 38	Walter Gray and Nancey Carr	6 Sept. 1810
	Booker Sutton and Nancey Stapler	6 Sept. 1810
Page 39	Isaac Russel and Ann Youngblood	29 April 1810
	John Watson Junr. and Casandra Hoge	12 Sept. 1810
Page 40	John Murray and Elizabeth Watson	19 Nov. 1807
	Taylor Wiley and Verlinder Finney	21 Oct. 1810
Page 41	Thomas Dooly and Palatur Jones	6 Dec. 1810
	Lewis Powell and Elizabeth Chenault	16 Dec. 1810
Page 42	Benjamin Johnson and Ann Allen	4 Jan. 1811
	John Dunn and Patsey Simms	6 Dec. 1810
Page 43	William Reynolds and Serena Fuller	23 Dec. 1810
	Peter H. Collins and Jane Stuart	3 Jan. 1811
Page 44	Thomas Johnson and Elizabeth Jones	9 Jan. 1811
	Greenberry Templeton and Betsey Mathews	17 Jan. 1811
Page 45	Zenue Parker and Elizabeth Burnsides	17 Dec. 1810
	Jesse Morris and Jane McCorkle	8 Sept. 1809 lic.
Page 46	George Roberts and Catharene Sheilds	5 Dec. 1808 lic.
	Reuben Eubanks and Polly Sturgess	24 Dec. 1810
Page 47	John Mitchell and Rebekah Crabb	28 Sept. 1809 lic.
	James Roussau and Levina Few	1 Feb.1810 lic.
Page 48	Amos Mitchell and Jane Taylor	19 April 1810
	William Sullivan and Betsey Burnsides	3 March 1811
Page 49	Herod Roberts and Linder Beall	7 March 1810
	Joseph Day Junr. and Lincey Dunn	17 March 1811
Page 50	David Walker Junr. and Polly Crawford	29 Aug. 1811
	Dawson Cash and Rebekah Miles	24 Dec. 1810
Page 51	James McCleary and Caty Edmondson	19 April 1811
	Thomas Culbreath and Catharene Heyans (?)	22 Sept. 1811
		22 Sept. 1809 lic.
Page 52	William Wiley and Pricey Youngblood	15 Sept. 1811
	Thomas Burnsides and Elizabeth Pierce	7 Nov. 1811
Page 53	James Wright and Casandra Drane	7 Nov. 1811
	Thomas Hunt and Sarah Miles	20 Nov. 1811
Page 54	David Banks and Camelly Wade	14 Nov. 1811
	Mordecai Johnson and Frances Cosby	15 July 1811
Page 55	Nehemiah Johnson and Elizabeth Wright	14 Nov. 1811
	Henry Wheat and Nancey Darsay	20 Nov. 1811
Page 56	Fredk. Robertson and Jane Crosby	5 Mar. 1812
	Thomas Willis and Jane Toms	10 Feb. 1812
Page 57	John Wooding and Elizabeth Drane	4 July 1811
	Benjamin Crabb and Rachel Wade	29 Apr. 1810
Page 58	Henry Copeland and Sarah McIntire	3 Dec. 1811
	William Day and Nancey McDonald	2 May 1812
Page 57	Peter Watson and Elizabeth McCormick	23 Oct. 1811
	Jeremiah Reese and Ann Hollyman	5 Mar. 1812
Page 58	Nimrod Jones and Eliza. Gray	22 Mar. 1812
	Cash Willingham and Martha Moon	3 Apr. 1812
Page 59	John McDonald and Finety Phelan	5 Mar. 1812
	John Walker and Lucinda Burnsides	4 May 1812 lic.
Page 60	Eldridge Revel and Francis Lacey	25 June 1812
	Elijah Lesley and Mary Wheeler	22 Oct. 1812
Page 61	James Young and Sophia Sommers	6 Oct. 1812
	James Washington and Nancey Revell	4 Feb. 1813

Page 62	Henry Youngblood and Alice Ray	20 Nov. 1812
	Clayborn Revell and Martha Bennefield	3 Feb. 1813
Page 63	William Binion and Peggy Harden	18 Aug. 1813
	James Ross and Sally Harden	5 Nov. 1813
Page 64	Samuel Shelly and Verlinder Gardner	11 Mar. 1813
	Isaac Evans and Nelly Rainey	27 May 1813
Page 65	Benjamin Maddox and Polly Franklin	11 Apr. 1813
	Berry Olive and Eliza Wilkins	18 May 1813
Page 66	George Roberts and Constantia Whie	11 Mar. 1813
	Willis Roberts and Mary Bolton	5 Aug. 1812
Page 67	Francis Jones and Nancey Maddox	4 Feb. 1813
	William Reese and Polly Walker	27 June 1813
Page 68	John Reeves and Alithea Drane	11 Jan. 1813
	Notley Whitcomb and Rebecca Lashley	7 Oct. 1813
Page 69	James Walker and Sarah Winfrey	11 Nov. 1813
	Peter B. Short and Margaret Short	1 Dec. 1813
Page 70	Nathl. Pearre and Rebekah Offutt	30 Sept. 1813
	Churchwell Tarvin and Elizabeth Philips	7 Oct. 1813
Page 71	John Ray and Mary Pate 4 Oct. 1813 lic.	30 Dec. 1813
	David Simpson and Burnette Porter	28 Jan. 1813
Page 72	Stephen Coleman and Winney Hunt	28 Mar. 1813
	Green Dozier and Constantia Hunt	29 Aug. 1813
Page 73	Benjamin Fuller and Rebekah Youngblood	11 Jan. 1814
	John Magee and Nancy Hood	20 Jan. 1814
Page 74	Collins H. Belcher and Rebecca Gilpin	10 Dec. 1813
	Henry Radford and Elizabeth Walker	17 Feb. 1814
Page 75	William Trudal and Rachel Grinage	3 Feb. 1814
	William White and Concord Brown	7 Sept. 1813
Page 76	Joseph Maddox and Mary Vaughan	12 Apr. 1814
	James Thompson and Amelia Gerrald	29 June 1814
Page 77	Philip Steed and Susan Ray	8 Feb. 1814
	Jefferson Pitman and Rachel Harden	7 July 1814
Page 78	John Ford and Syntha Cowan	14 July 1814
	Isaac McCoy and Jemima Nelson	28 Apr. 1814
Page 79	Jesse Jones and Polly Nelson	16 May 1814
	James Daniel and Eleanor Hunt	8 Aug. 1814
Page 80	Seymour Powell and Martha W. Cowling	4 Oct. 1814
	Edward Prather and Tabetha Smith	14 Oct. 1814
Page 81	Thomas Newman and Loisa Formby	18 Nov. 1814
	John Ford and Cassander Johnson	22 Jan. 1815
Page 82	John Lucky and Polly McNair	3 Jan. 1815
	Richard Cox and Lucey Johnson	15 Jan. 1815
Page 83	James McNair and Martha Fudge	25 Jan. 1815
	Hezekiah Lunday and Loisa Spivey	5 Mar. 1815
Page 84	Asa Marshall and Lucy McNeil	16 Sept. 1815
	Josiah Magee and Judah Stanford	16 Feb. 1815
Page 85	Hinchy Johnson and Miss Becca Cosby	7 Feb. 1815
	Sherwood Roberts and Lucey (Luke) Staples	16 May 1815
Page 86	William Pearre and Aggy Offutt	3 June 1815
	James Bohorn (? Cohom) and Nancey Ray	11 May 1815
Page 87	William Toller and Betsey Partker	4 July 1815 Warren Co.
	Ila Wheat and Miss Nancey Evans	10 Aug. 1815
Page 88	Blank	
Page 89	Thomas Dozier and Catharine White	3 Aug. 1814
	George Washington and Sophia Fitzgerald	9 July 1815
Page 90	Stephen Day Jr. and Mary Hobbs	8 June 1815
	Thomas Ronay and Polly Crosby	13 Nov. 1815
Page 91	William Page and Mary Landers	24 Dec. 1815
	Cary Johnson and Miss Rachel Young	1 Feb. 1816
Page 92	Washington Stone and Fetney Dorsay	30 Jan. 1816
	Isaac Powell and Sally Jones	4 Feb. 1816
Page 93	John McClain and Elizabeth Smith	14 Mar. 1816
	Mark A. Candler and Lucy White	5 May 1816
Page 94	John Hall and Elizabeth Barbaree	11 Dec. 1815
	William Young and Miss Rebecca Grinage	5 Sept. 1816
Page 95	John Cosby and Miss Nancey Barbaree	15 Sept. 1816
	Sherwood Roberts and Lucinda Staples	2 Jan. 1816

Page 96	Archibald McNeille and Miss Kitty Fears	4 Oct. 1816
	William Pace and Miss Patsey Hixon	23 June 1816
Page 97	Henry Hunt and Lucinda Sanders	10 Oct. 1816
	John Reed and Elizabeth Jones	22 Oct. 1816
Page 98	Horatio Sims and Elizabeth Flint	28 Nov. 1816
	Mitchell Wilkins and Nancey Gorley (?Gosley)	15 Dec. 1816
Page 99	Anselm Watkins and Casandra Youngblood	7 Nov. 1816
	Amen Newsom and Nancey Philips	15 Nov. 1816
Page 100	Stephen Hargraves and Nelly Barlow	1 Nov. 1816
	James G. Blunt and Miss Edna G. Roberts	15 Dec. 1816
Page 101	Hezekiah L. Embrey and Martha Low	4 June 1816
	John Bynam and Charity Wilkins	18 Mar. 1817
Page 102	John Buck and Mary Willis	29 May 1817
	James Rees and Matilda Bull	12 Mar. 1817
Page 103	James A. Cooper and Elizabeth White	11 June 1817
	Dreadsil Ayres and Mrs. Catharine Jones	28 Aug. 1817
Page 104	Thomas Pace and Miss C.E.M. Coleman	5 Apr. 1817 lic.
	"Ga. Hancock Co. Executed the within the	
	Thomas Lundy J.P."	
	Edward Bull and Sarah Warden	8 June 1817
Page 105	Philip Grant and Betsey Merriwether	4 Sept. 1817
	Thomas Seay and Miss Judey Winfrey	18 Dec. 1817
Page 106	John Tinsley and Miss Rebecca Yarbrough	25 Dec. 1817
	Charles Evans and Miss Margaret A. Reynolds	21 June 1817 lic.
		12 Jan. 1818 rec.
Page 107	Jonathan Jones and Penny Lashley	18 Dec. 1817
	John Ansley and Susan Shields	11 Sept. 1817
Page 108	Milton Gartrell and Lucey Culbreath	29 May 1817
	Merriday Edwards and Anny Lambert	3 Mar. 1817 lic.
	"married Sunday following"	
Page 109	Joseph Mooney and Caroline M. Mote	23 Dec. 1817
	Ambrose Brown and Miss Sabrey Lofton	11 Jan. 1818
Page 110	John Moon and Mary Hurst	3 Nov. 1812
	Robert Bolton and Lydia George	28 Dec. 1817
Page 111	Archibald Willingham and Ellener Belcher	12 Dec. 1809
	Timothy Hixon and Miss Ana Dickby	29 Dec. 1814
Page 112	James Smally and Rebecah Wright	20 May 1815 (? 13)
	William Norriss and Betsey Willingham	8 Aug. 1810
Page 113	Benjamin Bartlett and Thankfull Wilkins	2 Apr. 1818
	Thomas Kindrick and Miss Nancy Tindell	5 Dec. 1816
		4 Dec. 1818 lic.
		9 Dec. 1818 rec.
Page 114	Moses P. Willis and Miss Hester Ann Low	13 Nov. 1817
	James Barnes and Rebecah Turner	17 Feb. 1818
Page 115	James Harden and Polly Reeves	20 Jan. 1818
	David Roberts and Elizabeth Spalding	6 Feb. 1818
Page 116	Allen Jones and Miss Catharine Smith	5 Feb. 1818
	John Willingham and Rebecca Tylar	20 Dec. 1814
Page 117	Fayette Porter and Mrs. Jane G. Willis	19 Nov. 1817
	Elias Wilson and Miss Margarett Scott	1 Jan. 1818
Page 118	David L. Morris and Hannah Gardener	1 Jan. 1818
	John Older and Polly Hicks	20 May 1812
Page 119	John Cartledge and Miss Elizabeth Stuart	9 July 1818
	John Walker and Miss Charlotte McGaha	16 Apr. 1818
Page 120	James Quisenberry and Elizabeth Gibson	8 July 1818
	John Kindrick and Miss Nancy Locklin	4 Dec. 1816
Page 121	Joel Cooper and Miss Louisa White	27 Aug. 1818
	Obadiah Morris and Miss Rebecca Adams	24 Dec. 1816 lic.
Page 121	Bad Olive and Prudence Grinage	27 Jan. 1818
	William Atkinson and Susannah Dunham	8 Apr. 1808
Page 122	Jacob Paul and Miss Polly Going	9 Sept. 1818
	Leonard Mattox and Polly Wilkins	14 Jan. 1817
Page 123	Wiley Philips and Miss Veney Reeves	23 Dec. 1817
	John Avary and Mrs. Anna Marshall	1 Mar. 1818
Page 124	Randolph Jarrel and Nancy Poage	31 Dec. 1807
	John Tyler Allen and Frances A. Winfrey	20 Oct. 1818

Page 125	Thomas Newberry and Lydia Newberry	8 Oct. 1818
	Isaac Lucas and Miss Martha Pollard	17 Dec. 1818
Page 126	Benj. H. Berry and Elizabeth Bary	4 Jan. 1819
	Jesse Lolly and Miss Margaret Garner	8 Nov. 1818
Page 127	Simmons Crawford and Miss Pamela E. Moore	4 Feb. 1819
	David Fudge and Miss Jincey Dannelly	12 Jan. 1819
Page 128	John Pearre and Elizabeth Gibson	24 Nov. 1818
	Isham Phillips and Polly Youngblood	24 Dec. 1819
		18 May 1819 rec.
Page 129	Dancy Adams and Miss Polly Morriss	29 Dec. 1818
	Sterling Edwards and Henrietta Dorsett	12 Jan. 1819
Page 130	Stephen Drane and Miss Rebecca Wilson	7 Jan. 1819
	Sampson D. Jenskins and Jane Yow	23 Feb. 1819 lic.
Page 131	Hugh Patrick and Rachael Tipper	24 Feb. 1819 lic.
	William Wilder and Mary Drane	17 Apr. 1817
		22 Jan. 1820 lic.
		22 Jan. 1820 rec.
Page 132	John A. Fleming and Dicy (Uridice) Gardner	27 Aug. 1818
	license marked, "Warren Co."	
	John Cammack and Nancy Tankersley	28 Oct. 1818
Page 133	Eleazor Tracy and Sarah Gunby	14 Oct. 1819
	James Cain and Linday Lambert	25 Feb. 1819
Page 134	John Gray and Nancy Lovell	9 July 1819
	John Zillun (?Zilluer) and Martha Montcrief	7 Mar. 1819
Page 135	James Huies and Martha Gunby	25 Mar. 1819
	William C. Webb and Susan Colvard	24 Mar. 1819
Page 136	David Watson and Nancy Roland	30 Mar. 1819
	Augustus Wood and Sarah Watson	28 Oct. 1819
Page 137	E. Hinsdale Burrett and Ann Williams Watson	28 Oct. 1819
	James Waters and Miss Mary Reese	4 May 1820
Page 138	James Newberry and Miss Hannah Newberry	20 Feb. 1820
	Bowling W. Stark and Miss Nancy M. Johns	25 Nov. 1819
Page 139	George Gunby and Mrs. Mary Roberts	9 Dec. 1819
	Freeman Killingsworth and Cealia Parks	18 Nov. 1819
Page 140	James R. Ades and Elizabeth Prickett	30 Feb. 1820
	Thomas Dunn and Drucilla McNair	11 Nov. 1819
Page 141	Willis Magahee and Miss Peggy Magahee	6 Jan. 1820
	Henry Scott and Miss Mariah P. Rees	2 Mar. 1820
Page 142	Gideon Prickett and Mrs. Nancy Bell	4 June 1820
	Ebenezer T. Williams and Susan W. Jones	10 Feb. 1820
Page 143	Joseph Larken and Patsey Lazenby	30 Dec. 1820
	Hezekiah Young and Elizabeth Walls (Wall)	21 Dec. 1820
Page 144	Charles Bealle and Frances J. Walton	26 Aug. 1820
	John Walker and Miss Sarah Tindill	26 Dec. 1819
Page 145	George Wheeler and Miss Eliza Tindill	12 July 1819
	Felix Cochran and Miss Matilda Youngblood	16 Sept. 1819
Page 146	Henry Newberry and Mrs. Sarah Epps	15 Feb. 1820
	John Griffin Jr. and Rachael Moon	27 Jan. 1820
Page 147	William Bastion and Mary Smith	17 May 1820
	Seaborn P. Hutchinson and Martha S. Daugherty	23 Dec. 1819
Page 148	Robert Shanklin and Miss Martha Langston	15 Aug. 1820
	Thomas W. Battle and Francis F. Warrin	29 June 1820
Page 149	William Yarbrough and Miss Catharine Jones	21 Dec. 1819
	William Dozier and Pamelia Jones	20 Aug. 1820
Page 150	James Shipp and Rhoda Parker	9 Dec. 1819
	Jesse Moon and Miss Margaret Parker	3 Feb. 1819
Page 151	Daniel Freeman and Miss Elizabeth Youngblood	1 Jan. 1820
	John Moon and Miss Harriot Cole	2 Feb. 1820
Page 152	Thomas E. Burnsides and Miss Catharine Wood	23 Mar. 1820
	James Stallings and Nancy Winfrey	23 Apr. 1820
Page 153	James G. Powers and Miss Sarah Q. Short	6 Sept. 1820
	Samuel C. Rice and Miss Martha Martin	14 Sept. 1820
Page 154	James G. Huchinson and Martha Culbreath	14 Sept. 1820
	Elvey Langston and Miss Nancy Adams	12 Oct. 1820
Page 155	John Powers and Jamima Crosby	4 Nov. 1820
	Francis T. Allen and Jane Johns	18 Oct. 1820
Page 156	Sheldreck Brown and Nancy McKindrick	23 Nov. 1820
	Benjamin T. Rees and Miss Martha Mathews	20 Oct. 1820

Page 157	William Watson and Miss Nancy Lavender	23 Nov. 1820
	William W. Johnson and Elizabeth Reynolds	2 Mar. 1821
Page 158	W. Ganaway Martin and Miss Nancy Embree	21 Dec. 1820
	Samuel Jones and Eliza Johnson	24 Dec. 1820
Page 159	Daniel Carroll and Theodate Kindrick	12 Apr. 1821
	Samuel Moore and Betsey Gray	1 May 1821
Page 160	David A. Perryman and Effey Drane	22 Mar. 1821
	Nimrod Jones and Rebecca Gray	15 July 1821
Page 161	John Morriss and Nancey Gray	12 July 1821
	James Spragins and Nancey Powell	6 Aug. 1821
Page 162	Thomas J. (I?) Darby and India ONeal	10 Sept. 1821
	John McNeil and Nancey Moon	2 Sept. 1821
Page 163	John Spivey and Mrs. India McGee	11 July 1819
	Rowell Adams and Miss Lucy Ivy	21 Nov. 1820
Page 164	Henry Marks and Miss Margaret Daniel	25 May 1820
	Wilas Fitz Gerald and Miss Nelly (Milly) Palmore 15 Nov. 1821
Page 165	David Hodge and Elizabeth Bailey	25 Oct. 1819
	George G. Smith and Miss Mary Brooks	15 Feb. 1821
Page 166	Samuel Guy and Miss Rebecca Cobb	11 Apr. 1819
	John Parish and Miss Sally Phillips	4 Aug. 1819
Page 167	Hiram Jones and Miss Winny Radford	20 Apr. 1820
	Isaac Palmer and Miss Mary Revell	10 Feb. 1820
Page 168	Benjamin W. Few and Miss Sarah Shackleford	20 Dec. 1821
	Andrew Miller and Miss Caroline Sturges	10 Jan. 1822
Page 169	Isaac Palmer and Miss Mary Revall (Reval)	10 Feb. 1820
	marked "twice entered"	
	Hiram Jones and Miss Winney Radford	20 Apr. 1820
	marked "twice entered"	
Page 170	Thomas Martin and Mrs. Rebecca King	13 Jan. 1822
	James Newman and Alice Strother Blackstone	1 Nov. 1821
Page 171	James Finney and Martha Albritton	26 Dec. 1821
	Warrington (Warrenton) Hainey and	
	Miss Elizabeth Culbreath	27 Jan. 1822
Page 172	Robert Jones and Nancey Durden	27 Sept. 1821
	Thomas Tudor and (Miss) Martha Cliatt	21 Feb. 1822
Page 173	Phillip Steed and Miss Nancey Garnett	1 Mar. 1821
	Edward Wade and Luvenia Watson	20 Dec. 1821
Page 174	Seaborn Hixon and Mary Stallings	3 Jan. 1822
	John Orr and Miss Sarah Jones	17 Jan. 1822
Page 175	Samuel Paul and Mrs. Treacy Magruder	13 June 1822
	David Robinson and Ann Layden	20 Apr. 1822 lic.
Page 180	William H. McDonald and Margarett Phillips	5 (?8) Dec. 1822
	Jonathan S. (?L.) Rook and Miss Amy Holder	3 Apr. 1822
Page 181	John Roberts and Elizabeth Flinn (Flynn)	6 Mar. 1823
	Joseph Going and Miss Ide? (Jude?) Kindrick	1 Nov. 1822
Page 182	Caswell Wright and (Miss) Mary Neal	21 June 1821
	Rufus Ray and Mrs. Maryann Thompson	11 Feb. 1823
Page 183	Benjamin Bugg and Sarah D. Gibson	19 Dec. 1822
	Jeremiah Sampler and Miss Elizabeth Ann Jones	12 Jan. 1823
Page 184	Jeremiah W. Ray and Miss Nancy B. Ray	
	James Watson and Susanna P. Baggot	26 Nov. 1823
		26 Nov. 1822 lic.
		20 May 1823 rec.
Page 185	William Riley and Margarett Powell	21 July 1822
	Nathaniel Davis and Elizabeth Willingham	14 Aug. 1822
Page 186	Thomas Colvard and Ann L. Winfrey	25 June 1822
	Wike Ivey and Sarah Adams	14 Nov. 1822
Page 187	David Robertson and Ann Layden	16 May 1822
	marked "twice"	
	Abraham Prim and Miss Eliza Davis	20 Mar. 1822
Page 188	Peter Cody and Louisa Tucker	21 Mar. 1822
	Burrel Perry and Maria Sturgess	5 Nov. 1821
Page 189	Robert Flemming and Elizabeth Gunby	13 Jan. 1822
	Edward M. Crawford and Elizabeth Carolina Holton 6 Aug. 1822
Page 190	Richard Dozier and Rebecca Kendrick	28 Aug. 1823
	Samuel Millican and Miss Mary Wilson	11 Jan. 1824

Page 191	Henry G. Lamar and Miss Mary Ann Davis	28 Oct. 1823
	Mark Fleming and Miss Elanor (Eleanor) Jones	14 Dec. 1823
Page 192	Stephen Cole and Miss Martha Willingham	27 Jan. 1824
	William Palmer and Francis Revell (Revil)	8 Mar. 1822
Page 193	Joshua Hunter and Turecy Roberts	21 Nov. 1822
	Jacob Fudge and Matilda Carrol (Carroll)	24 Dec. 1822
Page 194	Samuel Turner and Mrs. Mary Maddox	9 Jan. 1823
	David Mims and Miss Mahala Kendrick	4 Feb. 1823
Page 195	Alexander Stephenson and Mrs. Sally Reynolds	27 Mar. 1823
	James Binion and Pamelia (Pamela) Davis	3 Apr. 1823
Page 196	William Lavendar and Miss Nancey Ray	1 Apr. 1823 lic.
	William Cunningham and Miss Sarah Cartledge	26 June 1823
Page 197	William Greenway and Miss Mary Sikes	7 June 1823
	Lovett Stallings and Alla Stanley	24 June 1821
Page 198	Thomas Caraway and Patience Ray	3 July 1823
	Silas Meacham and Miss Rebecca Watson	6 Aug. 1823
Page 199	Overton Reynolds and Miss Ann Fuller	2 Oct. 1823
	Jeremiah Bugg and Martha Hurst	29 Sept. 1823
Page 200	Sterling Jones and Miss Martha H. Winfrey	9 Nov. 1823
	John Barnes and Harriot B. Darsey	28 Dec. 1823
Page 201	Martin B. Reynolds and Miss Susan S. Culbreath	22 Jan. 1824
	Joel Darsey and Elizabeth Shields	22 Jan. 1824
Page 202	John Stapler and Polly V. Woolfolk	2 Dec. 1810
	Jesse McNeil and Nancy Kendrick	26 Oct. 1822
Page 203	Troy Griffin and Martha Willingham	19 Dec. 1823
	George A. Flinn and Patience Spivey	26 Oct. 1823
Page 204	Handy Alford and Dicey Fleming	13 Nov. 1823
	William Philips and Susan Megahee	22 Jan. 1824
Page 205	Dawson Satterwhite and Miss Martha Fuller	11 Mar. 1824
	Benjamin Hardin (Harden) and Sarah Corum?	1 Feb. 1821
Page 206	Thomas Culbreath and Miss Eunice Pullin	3 Apr. 1821
	Thomas Griffin and Miss Nancy Tindille	13 Dec. 1821
Page 206	James S. Jones and Miss Deborah Scott	21 Nov. 1822
	Nowell Kendrick and Miss Lucinda Going	29 Dec. 1826
Page 207	John F. Young and Miss M. Stanford	15 Jan. 1822
	Frederick Hill and Charlotte Fleetwood	3 Feb. 1822
Page 208	John C. Talbert and Cassandra Pearre	12 Mar. 1822
	Sterling Edward (s?) and Miss Susan Hicks	27 Mar. 1822
Page 209	Wm. B. Luke and Mrs. Martha Martin	7 May 1822
	Isaac Miles and Polly Pollard	26 Dec. 1822
Page 210	Wm. M. Williams and Miss Evalina Bealle	6 Feb. 1823
	Joel Culbreath and Mary Pullen	10 Mar. 1823
Page 211	Thomas (P.) Thompson and Miss Elizabeth Luke	Oct. 1823
	James Lamkin and Miss Elizabeth Fraser Luke	21 Dec. 1823
Page 212	Robert Atkinson and (Miss) Martha Wilkins	8 Jan. 1824
	Nelson M. Benton and Miss Maria Louisa Jones	5 Feb. 1824
Page 213	Ralph Briscoe and Miss Sarah Dougherty	12 Feb. 1824
	Wm. L. Crawford and Miss Artemissia Zachary	30 Mar. 1824
Page 214	James Young and Miss Aletha Tindille	8 Jan. 1824
	Clement Malone and Miss Margaret Foy	4 July 1824
Page 215	William F. Wilkins and Miss Mary H. Avary	10 Aug. 1824
	Samuel D. Bolton and Miss Jane Phelps	21 Sept. 1824
Page 216	Harriss P. Speir and Miss Ann M. Shaw	22 July 1824
	Joshua Stanford and Miss Louisa Johnson	19 Aug. 1824
Page 217	Thomas Cartlidge and Miss Susan S. Beard	7 Oct. 1824
	Allen Greene and Miss Pamela Tindall	14 Oct. 1824
Page 218	Burton Baggett and Miss Mary Moon	27 Nov. 1824
	James Cartlidge and Miss Frances G. Walton	5 Dec. 1824
Page 219	Robert H. Cleveland and Miss Mary Jones	8 Aug. 1824
	Larkin Reynolds and Miss Eliza Clayton	19 Dec. 1824
Page 220	Richard B. Huggins and Miss Mary Lambert	30 Nov. 1824
	Thomas Satterwhite and Miss Martha Matthews	23 Dec. 1824
Page 221	Josiah Hodgins and Serepta Lambert	23 Dec.1824
	Elisha Salton and Miss Mary Newman	20 Jan. 1824
Page 222	Ferdinand Luke and Miss Mary Bailey	15 Apr. 1824
	James Whitaker and Seanith Morriss	23 Dec. 1824

Page 223	Alfred Ansley and Miss Sarah Newsome	18 Nov. 1824
	John Wooding and Miss Betsy Drane	17 Mar. 1825
Page 224	Edward Wooding and Miss Rebecca Day	28 Apr. 1825
	Noel W. Binion and Miss Melissa Davis	4 Feb. 1825
Page 225	Henry Kendall and Miss Eliza A. Wright	9 Feb. 1825
	Leonard Weissinger and Miss Mildred Cobb	23 Dec. 1824
Page 226	Burton Hicks and Miss Ann (B.) Hattaway	27 Jan. 1825
	Stephen S. Phillips and Miss Mary Dozier	21 Apr. 1825
Page 227	Robert Allen and Mrs. Sarah Winfrey	1 Sept. 1825
	Peter W. Edward (s?) and Miss Sarah Whitaker	3 Sept. 1825
Page 228	Thomas Stewart and Miss Mary Ann Philips	20 Sept. 1825
	James H. Moore and Miss Nancy Hudgins	31 July 1825
Page 229	Alfred G. Barden and Miss Martha Harriss	29 Sept. 1825
	Lott Dodson and Miss Hebzibah (Hepzibah) Holmes 20 Oct. 1825
Page 230	Valentine Brewer and Miss Nancy Newman	21 Nov. 1825
	Berryman H. Embree and Mrs. Mary George	29 Sept. 1825
Page 231	Charles Wade and Miss Charlotte Short	25 Dec. 1825
	Abram A. Heard and Miss Harriett Magruder	5 Jan. 1826
Page 232	Sullivan Harrison and Miss Mary R. Baldwin	2 Feb. 1826
	William Lynn and Miss Sarah E. Price	1 Feb. 1826
Page 233	Harrison S. Patillo and Miss Elizabeth Dunn	2 Mar. 1826
	James Terry and Lucy Wilkins	27 Feb. 1826
Page 234	Wiley Roberts and Elizabeth Shipp	25 Dec. 1825
	Thomas Tudor and Miss Nazey Cliett	3 Jan. 1826
Page 235	Robert B. E. Burke and Elenor Tally	28 Dec. 1825
	Iverson R. Smith and Miss Rachel Philips	13 Apr. 1826
Page 236	William A. Baldwin and Miss Mary Ann Griffin 13 Apr. 1826
	Albert Collins and Miss Louisa E. Shaw	23 Mar. 1826
Page 237	Frederick B. Heath and Miss Elizabeth Clark	9 Feb. 1826
	Joseph Plunket and Susannah S. Ray	1 Apr. 1826
Page 238	John Moon and Miss Alea A. Cole	17 July 1826
	Richard Bennett and Polly Whitehead	15 Feb. 1824
Page 239	Henry W. Ray and Miss Sarah Gerald	18 May 1826
	Waters Briscoe and Miss Martha M. Wellborn	27 July 1826
Page 240	Lorenzo Willingham and Miss Mahala Jenkins	27 Aug. 1826
	Benjamin H. Gibson and Mrs. Mary M. Bealle	5 Sept. 1826
Page 241	Leroy Nance and Miss Frances Gibson	20 Aug. 1826
	Robert H. Woolfolk and Mrs. Ann Smith	8 Oct. 1826
Page 242	James Daniel Greene and Miss Sarah Harriss	20 Nov. 1826
	John C. Baldwin and Miss Mildred Winfrey	14 Nov. 1826
Page 243	Simeon Wimburn and Martha Wilkinson	18 June 1824
	Perryman H. Embre and Mrs. Mary George	29 Sept. 1825
Page 244	Solomon Ray Vickers and Miss Ann Cuttliff	5 Oct. 1826
	William L. Lochlin and Miss Nancy Messer	5 Oct. 1826
Page 245	William C. Avary and Mrs. Elizabeth Adams	21 Nov. 1826
	Gideon Lantern and Faithy Mims	31 Dec. 1826
Page 246	Robert Marks and Miss Nancy Bolton	3 Aug. 1826
	Thomas Crosby and Miss Vinah Megahee	7 Jan. 1827
Page 247	Edward Welch and Miss Cassandra Crosby	16 Jan. 1827
	John Milton and Miss Susan Amanda Cobb	9 Feb. 1826
Page 248	James D. Perryman and Cynthia Ray	21 Dec. 1826
	William Ray and Pamela Lavender	7 Dec. 1826
Page 249	Jacob Bailey and Jane Burnside	3 Dec. 1826
	Edward Miles and Miss Martha Malone	7 Feb. 1827
Page 250	James Holder and Miss Martha Willingham	2 Nov. 1826
	John P. Flake and Miss Mary Denson	12 Mar. 1827
Page 251	David Stanford, Jr. and Miss Sarah Faucette 20 Mar. 1827
	Hezekiah Boyd and Miss Constantia Scott	10 Apr. 1827
Page 252	Samuel P. (B?) Holliman (Holleman and	
	Miss Martha Harden	22 Mar. 1827
	Thomas M. Watson and Catherine Jones	8 June 1826
Page 253	Daniel Davis and Miss Nancy Going	22 Apr. 1827
	James McDonald and Miss Nancy Gray	7 Aug. 1827 lic.
	(Note: No date for marriage, page torn	
	off where record would be written.)	
Page 254	George W. Redman and Miss Elizabeth Sanders 12 Aug. 1827
	John Webster and Miss Jamima (Jemima) Folds 12 July 1827

Page 256	Jacob Paul and Elizabeth Melton	22 June 1827
		25 June 1827 lic.
	William Prescot and Elizabeth Guy	20 Sept. 1827
Page 257	Benjamin E. Alford and	
	Miss Ann Wilkerson (Wilkinson)	22 Nov. 1827
	Samuel Hicks and Miss Louisa Bowdre	25 Nov. 1827
Page 258	Hiram Drane and Miss Eleanor Magruder	20 Dec. 1827
	Thomas Burnside and Miss Nancy Davis	20 Jan. 1825
Page 260	Robert Pounds and Eliza Fuller	10 Jan. 1828
	Vincent Rees and Miss Susan Short	3 Feb. 1828
Page 261	William M. Dantignac and	
	Miss Mary Ann C. Harriss	7 Feb. 1828
	Dr. William A. L. Collins and	
	Mrs. Casandra Talbert	28 Feb. 1828
Page 262	John F. Jeffers and Miss Eliza W. Sutherland	10 Feb. 1828
	Luke Lively and Miss Louisa Lamkin	28 Mar. 1826
Page 263	Alexander Eady and Mrs. Rebecca B. Tinsley	27 Apr. 1828
	William Bastion and Miss Polly Jones	21 Feb. 1828
Page 264	William Drane and Mrs. Martha H. Jones	6 Dec. 1827
	Allen Green and Mrs. Ann Sikes	25 May 1828
Page 265	Daniel Stanford and Mary A. Morse	24 June 1828
	Bennett Crafton and Miss Mary H. Beale	15 July 1828
Page 266	Peyton Hawes (Haws) and	
	Miss?/Mrs? Arta Huchingson	26 Oct. 1828
	John E. Tindell and Prudence Olive	5 Aug. 1828
		21 Aug. 1828 lic.
Page 267	Ezekiel Reed and Miss Aletha Huchingson	Mar. 1828
	James Eshom and Matilda Beall	24 Mar. 1828 lic.
		4 Dec. 1828
Page 268	George Folds and Miss Jenny Combs	28 Sept. 1828
	James M. Darsey and Miss Mary Sutton	28 Dec. 1828
Page 269	Isaac Langston and Mary Daniel	25 Dec. 1825
	Josiah Spivey and Miss?/Mrs.? Olive Warren	11 Jan. 1829
Page 270	Samuel J. Lazenby and Mrs.? Frances A.M.L. Bacon	1 Jan. 1829
	Wade Prior and Miss Rebecca Poythess	4 Mar. 1829
Page 271	William Farr and Miss Mary A.M. Stanford	6 Nov. 1828
	George W. Persons and Alice S.N. Jones	27 Jan. 1829
Page 272	Micajah Thompson and Miss Mary Guy	29 Nov. 1827
	Augustus V. Denham and Harriot Bennefield	5 Feb. 1829
Page 273	Allen J. Fuller and	
	Sydaviar (Sydavier) Mary McDonald	1 Jan. 1829
	George S. Morriss and Mary Sharp	15 Jan. 1829
Page 274	George Gunby and Miss Obedience Johnston	21 May 1829
	Edmund Palmer and Fetina Taylor	25 Jan. 1829
Page 276	Sydney S. Holland and Miss Elizabeth Griffin	1 Sept. 1829
	Edmund Fuller and Rebecca Baggett	31 Aug. 1825
Page 278	Joel Whitaker and Vashte Philips	23 Dec. 1826
	Lewis Gardner and Keziah Youn	20 Apr. 1826
Page 280	James Yearby and Keziah Fuller	21 Jan. 1828 lic.
	Elias Barbaree and Mrs. Patsey Hamilton	31 Oct. 1825
Page 282	Leanus (?) (Lenus? Hill and Louisa Carroll	8 Jan. 1823
	William Guy and Sarah Whitaker	16 Dec. 1823 lic.
Page 284	Stephen Durden and Verlinda Powell	22 Sept. 1822
	Thomas Whitaker and Nancey Youn	16 Dec. 1824
Page 286	James Gray and Jamima Reynolds	4 Mar. 1827
		2 Mar. 1829 lic.
	Hiram Washington and Ellana Harriss	27 May 1828
Page 288	Nathan Mash and Miss Mary Evans	3 Jan. 1828
	William Thomas and Miss Mary Guy	2 Apr. 1825
Page 289	Thaddeus A. Jones and Miss Martha Wilkins	8 Oct. 1829
	Edward Wooding and	
	Miss Joicey (Joicy) Maddux (Maddox)	24 Sept. 1829
Page 290	Rhesa Hamilton and Miss Hetty Cole	28 Oct. 1829
	Robert Douglass and Miss Elizabeth Olive	24 June 1828
Page 291	Henry Adams and Miss Ann R. Gerald	26 Nov. 1829
	Nelson M. Benton and Miss Martha A. Wooding	26 Nov. 1829

Page 292   Joseph A. Marshall and Miss Naomi Doggett   10 Dec. 1829
      Ebenezer T. Williams and Miss Mary C. Martin 17 Dec.1829
Blank page with the following in the margin:
      James A. Cooper and Elizabeth White   7 June 1817
      Edward Bull and Sarah Warden   4?-6?th June 1817

COLUMBIA COUNTY, GA. MARRIAGES

BOOK B

Page 1	Nathaniel Scott and Mary K. Embre	5 Nov. 1829
	William Anderson and Miss Eliza Neal	31 Dec. 1829
Page 2	Ewell McCoy and Sarah W. Walker	24 Jan. 1830
	William White and Rebecca Mills	13 Dec. 1829
Page 3	Nicholas V. Prather and Miss Caroline Welch	8 Dec. 1829
	James Howard and Polly Edger	23 Dec. 1829
Page 4	Kennington B. Blackstone and	
	Cynthia M. Vaughn	10 Jan. 1830
	John Battimon Brown and Priscilla Smith	3 Jan. 1830
Page 5	Jesse Watson and Miss Vinah (Lavinah) Powell	31 Jan. 1830
	David Daniel and Miss Sarah Rowland	14 Feb. 1830
Page 6	Ayres Lynn and Miss Mary Moore	27 Jan. 1830
	James Drane and Miss Matilda B. Shaw	16 Dec. 1829
		16 Dec. 1830 lic.
Page 7	John Megahee Jr. and Miss Emily Carrell	7 Jan. 1830
	Reddick Tarver and Miss Mary Ross	3 Sept. 1829
Page 8	Benjamin Harden and Miss Elizabeth Davis	28 Jan. 1830
	Peter B. Short and Miss Elizabeth Watkins	10 Dec. 1829
Page 9	William Welch and Miss Keziah Lott	28 Feb. 1830
	Waters Dunn and Miss Nancy Doggett	23 Feb. 1830
Page 10	Richard Wiley Jones and	
	Miss Lovey Ann Durden	25 Mar. 1830
Page 11	John Reynolds and Ann Harden	11 Mar. 1830
	Joseph A. Collier and Miss Rebecca Blanchard	6 May 1830
Page 12	Robert McNair and Mary Adams	28 Feb. 1830
	William Odom and Miss Margarett Whitaker	6 Jan. 1830
Page 13	James W. Blackstone and Luquilla Carroll	13 May 1830
	William Anderson and Nancey Welsh (Welch)	16 Aug. 1830
Page 14	William C. Crisp and Cordelia Amanda Ivy	28 Sept. 1830
	Hugh Solly and Elizabeth Harrup	12 Sept. 1830
Page 15	Charles Evans and	
	Miss Mary W. Wiams (Williams)	21 Sept. 1830
	Alfred I. Dunn and	
	Miss Catharine Tankersley	21 Oct. 1830
Page 15	Jefferson B. Cochran and Miss Mary Barden	28 Oct. 1830
	William Crawford and Mary M. Allen	1 Sept. 1830
Page 16	Aron T. Kendrick and Eleanor L. Nesbit	23 Sept. 1830
	William B. Kendrick and Ann P. Shaw	23 Dec. 1830
Page 17	John Prather and Miss Catharine McNair	4 Jan. 1831
	George Augustus Tindall and	
	Miss Elizabeth Grimes	23 Jan. 1831
Page 19	James Saterwhite and Sarah Wright (White)	9 Dec. 1830
	Alfred Sturges and Miss Mary Darsey	19 Oct. 1830
Page 20	Ezekiel Smith and Susannah Powell	1 Feb. 1831
	Robert Harris and Miss Susan Gunby	1 Mar. 1831
Page 22	Joseph Barnes and Mrs. Louisa Matilda Rees	14 Oct. 1830
	John B. Harris and	
	Miss Harriett Matilda Stanford	29 July 1831
Page 23	Timothy T. Barham and Miss Adeline M. Barden	19 June 1831
	John Reynolds and Mahala Smith	3 June 1831
Page 24	William B. Tankersley Jr. and Mary H. Clay	7 July 1831
	James Whitaker and Miss Elizabeth Langston	3 July 1831
Page 25	Littleberry Lewis and Frances Blackstone	28 July 1831
	John B. Tindall and Martha Sarah Bugg	7 Aug. 1831

Page 26	Andrew Inglet (Inglit) and Mary Ann Smith	7 Aug. 1831
	David Welch and Miss Nancy Anderson	12 May 1831
Page 27	William Tankersley and Miss Mary Avary	22 Sept. 1831
	Thomas Reeves and Miss Gatey Elizabeth Watson	18 Oct.1831 lic.
	Compare Book B, p. 37	
Page 28	Nathan I. Day and Miss Martha E. B. Cole	1 Dec. 1831
	John Frasier and Mary Durden	15 Apr. 1830
Page 29	James Sutherland and Miss Jane Sutton	15 Dec. 1831
	John Augustus Stapler and	
	Miss Jane L. Collins	18 Jan. 1832
Page 30	William Powell and Elizabeth Prescott	14 Nov. 1831
		12 Dec. 1831 lic.
	Henry Radford and Polly Cosby	2 Dec. 1830
Page 33	George M. Magruder and	
	Miss Mary Emily Heggie	1 May 1832
	William Bell and Miss Hulda Marshall	3 May 1832
Page 35	Stephen G. Reeves and Patsey Washington	23 Aug. 1832
	Daniel Prather and Miss Lurana Newman	13 Sept. 1832
Page 36	James I. Morris and Miss Evalina Binion	13 Sept. 1832
	John B. Kennedy and Miss Eliza L. Cobb	25 Oct. 1832
Page 37	Thomas Reeves and	
	Miss Gatey Elizabeth Watson	20 Oct. 1831
	Alfred M. Landsdell and Miss Amelia Wilkins	5 July 1832
Page 38	John Brooks and Miss Ann Brown	19 July 1829
	Horatio Gartrell and Ann Cox	14 June 1832
Page 39	Mark Sullivan and Miss Lucy Baggett	15 July 1832
	William W. Hardwick and Frances J. Dozier	9 Aug. 1832
Page 40	James Burnside and	
	Miss Harriette Maria Pettit	14 Nov. 1832
	Robert W. Bell and Miss Mary Salina Marshall	15 Nov. 1832
Page 41	Thomas W. Burton and Miss Martha F. Boswell	17 Dec. 1832
	John A. Magruder and	
	Miss Rachel Evalina Shaw	20 Dec. 1832
Page 42	William B. Bealle and Miss Louisa Cochran	20 Dec. 1832
	William B. Hawes and	
	Miss Catharine Huchingson	30 Dec. 1832
		30 Dec. 1833 lic.
Page 43	William O. Rees and Prudence D. Rees	15 Mar. 1831
	Absolem (Absalem) Garrett and	
	Delany W. Lowe	15 Nov. 1832
Page 44	Lewis Linch and Emily Ann Moore	22 Jan. 1833
	Wyot Chamblin and Miss Prudence T.? Evans	12 Feb. 1833
Page 45	Thomas H. Dozier and Miss Martha L. Davie	25 Dec. 1832
	Gabriel Jones Esqr. and Miss Mary H.F. Allen	28 Mar. 1833
Page 46	Littleberry Mulkey and Miss Nancy Pearre	3 Feb. 1833
	George Davise and Mrs. Agness Moffett	18 Apr. 1833
Page 47	Bennington B. Blackstone and	
	Miss Sarah Ann Baston	30 May 1833
	Leonard B. Sims and	
	Mrs. Mary Cochran "morning of"	18 July 1833
Page 48	Henry Gray and Mrs. Frances Wells	13 Aug. 1833
	Thomas C. Cliett and Elizabeth Smith	2 Oct. 1833
Page 49	Richard E. Doggett and	
	Miss Mary Elizabeth T? Yarbrough	17 Oct. 1833
	Charles Y. Wilkerson and Miss Mary Ann Scott	27 June 1833
Page 50	Irby Roberts and Miss Mary Fuller	24 Oct. 1833
	Thomas I. Wright and Permelia Magruder	14 Nov. 1833
Page 51	Winsley Hobley and Martha Rowena Martin	1 Apr. 1834
	Edward Ballard and Elizabeth Pearre	6 Apr. 1834
Page 52	Mark J. Langston and	
	Miss Prisse (Priscilla) Lassiter	16 Dec. 1834
	Thomas Garnett and Miss Mary Toole	5 Mar. 1835
Page 53	John Lewis and Letticia Offutt	22 Dec. 1833
	Elisha P. Bolton and	
	Miss Eliza Burbidge (Burbudge)	17 Dec. 1833
Page 54	David P. Stanford and Miss Martha Steed	21 Jan. 1834
	Obediah Morris and Miss Sarah Binion	11 May 1834

Page 55	Bailey B. Wilkinson and	
	Miss Matilda A. G. Steed	10 Dec. 1833
	David Langston and Miss Mary Olive	18 Oct. 1834
		21 Oct. 1834 lic.
Page 56	Roderick W. Lassiter and Miss Vealy Perry	8 Feb. 1835
	William Bennett and Miss Margarett Bailey	1 Jan. 1835
Page 57	Benjamin E. Alford and Miss Phebe Burbidge	18 Jan. 1835
	William Newsom and Miss Ollief (Olief) Gray	10 Oct. 1833
Page 58	Robert Gray and Miss Lucy Richardson	28 Oct. 1834
	Henry W. Massengale and Rebecca Ann Lowe	12 Jan. 1832
Page 59	John H. Candler and Miss Permela Young	16 Oct. 1833
	William F. Strother and Miss Nancy Griffin	17 Apr. 1834
Page 60	Edmund Darsey and Miss Martha Stanford	2 Jan. 1834
	John W. Carlton and Sarah T. Barham	31 Mar. 1835
Page 61	Emberson Miller and Mrs. Margaret Binion	12 Feb. 1835
	James J. Dooly and Miss Julia Ann Scott	1 Mar. 1835
Page 62	Owen W. Baldwin and Miss Martha Magruder	30 Apr. 1835
	John C. Watson and Miss Patience Durden	3 May 1835
Page 63	Alexander Harrison and Miss Ellen Elkins	9 June 1835
	William B. Tindall and	
	Miss Martha E. Y. Russell	25 Dec. 1834
Page 64	James Fuller and Jane Jenkins	5 Mar. 1835
	Edward Wade and Miss Nancy Roberts	20 Aug. 1835
Page 65	Charles D. Stewart and	
	Miss Rebecca C. Appling	20 Sept. 1835
	Ambrose I. (J.) Avary and Miss Susan Pace	15 Oct. 1835
Page 66	John Miles and Miss Elmira Willingham	29 Oct. 1835
	Theodosius E. Massingale and	
	Miss Elizabeth Angelina Pettit	6 Oct. 1835
Page 67	John B. Cassells and Miss Lucy Magruder	23 Nov. 1835
	Revd Arthur L. Kennedy and Mrs. Arty Hawes	7 Jan. 1836
Page 68	Joseph Cotten and Miss Lucinda Pollard	7 Jan. 1836
	John McKorcle and Mary W. Reynolds	21 Jan. 1836
Page 69	James Yarbrough and Miss Mary E. Sturges	12 Feb. 1836
	Samuel McGuffin and Mrs. Mary E. Fleming	6 Apr. 1836
Page 70	Benjamin Moore and Miss Jane Ann Eliza Elkins	27 Jan. 1836
	Abijah Holliman and Mrs. Ann Carr	24 Mar. 1836
Page 71	Isaiah Ivey and Mary Holliman	14 Apr. 1836
	Joshua Stanford and Miss Louisa Johnson	19 Aug. 1824
Page 72	John Cartlidge Esqr. and	
	Mrs. Elcy (Eley?) Jones	1 May 1836
	(License 1 May 1836 marked over in	
	another hand 1 May 1834.)	
	Samuel Holliman and Miss Saloma McCarthur	24 Feb. 1836
	(License marked Columbia Co., marriage	
	marked Warren Co.)	
Page 73	William Colvard Jr. and Miss Martha A.M.Walker	12 June 1836
	Jeremiah Butt and Ann W. Thomas	4 May 1836
Page 74	James M. Pace and Miss Martha M. Cobb	15 Sept. 1836
	Gazaway W. Sims and Miss Ann B. Zachry	20 Sept. 1836
Page 75	Thomas Ross and Almedia M. Blackstone	6 June 1836
	Jeremiah Walker and Miss Martha Ann Davis	13 Oct. 1836
Page 76	John Lamar and Miss Mary Louisa Hill	23 Nov. 1836
	William Adams and Hetty Andrews	23 Nov. 1836
Page 77	Rezin Darsey and Miss Mary W. Bolton	18 Feb. 1836
	John Walker and Miss Eleanor Lambert	5 Apr. 1836
		26 Mar. 1835 lic.
Page 78	John C. Lambert and Miss Lavinia Gray	14 Jan. 1836
		20 Jan. 1836 lic.
	Archibald Dougherty and Miss Jane Ryan	22 Dec. 1836
Page 79	Sylvester F. Jordan and Rachel Gunby	1 Mar. 1836
	Charles T. Bealle Jr. and	
	Miss Eliza Ann Maddox	18 Oct. 1836
Page 80	Luna Payne and Miss Charity Culbreath	5 Jan. 1837
		26 Nov. 1837 lic.
	Napoleon B. Corbin and	
	Miss Emeline S. Steed	27 Feb. 1837

Page 81	Francis M. Darsey and Miss Jane F.M. Charlton 9 Nov. 1837
	William Jones and Nancy Watson	24 Apr. 1836
Page 82	John B. Moore Esqr. and Miss Mary O. Bacon	17 July 1836
	Isaiah W. Maddock and Miss Olivia Burnley	6 Oct. 1836
Page 83	Benjamin Leigh and Miss Emily C. Shaw	23 Feb. 1837
	Thomas Davenport and Miss Mary F. Dooly	25 Apr. 1837
Page 84	John Cliett and
	Miss Elvey Blackstone (Blackston)	4 May 1837
	William Hamner and Miss Malinda Mims	4 June 1836
Page 85	Almon Y. Day and Miss Sarah Ann Sykes	20 Aug. 1835
	Allen C. Young and Miss Elizabeth C. (A) Dye	6 July 1837
Page 86	Thomas Burns and Catharine Fuller	11 July 1837
	Marcus D. Benson and Mahala Simons	5 July 1837
Page 87	Thomas Bolin and Miss Salina L. Pearre	7 Aug. 1837
	Reuben Leatherwood and Sarah Spivey	29 Aug. 1837
Page 88	Washington Meese and Sarah Ann Spivey	27 Aug. 1837
	George A.P. Whitefield and Miss Sarah Stanford 31 Aug. 1837
Page 89	Benjamin Adams and Elizabeth Evans	25 Dec. 1836
	Frances T. Allen and Miss Rachel Langston	12 Nov. 1837
Page 90	Guilford A. Bunting and
	Miss Elizabeth Jenkins	14 Dec. 1837
	William Zachry Esqr. and
	Miss Lucy T. Lamkin	14 Dec. 1837
Page 91	Hosea Young and Mrs. Elizabeth Tindall	22 Dec. 1837
	James Quizenberry and Miss Nancy Sikes	21 Nov. 1836
Page 92	John P.J. Evans and Caroline R.A. Lamar	17 Mar. 1836
	Henry L. Corbin and Miss Adaline Steed	8 Nov. 1837
		1 Nov. 1836 lic.
Page 93	John Emerson and
	Mrs. Louisa Matilda Barnes
	(Louisa M. Emerson)	27 July 1836
	Benjamin Wiley and Miss Cassandra Pearre	26 Nov. 1835
Page 94	Jesse H. Chambers and
	Miss Catharine D. Steed	7 Jan. 1837
	Asa Paschal and Miss Louisa Walton	7 Feb. 1836
Page 95	Abel J. Huchingson and Miss Jane Taylor	11 Oct. 1837
	John Garnett and Miss Catharine Foster	10 Nov. 1837
Page 96	Isaac Newton Heggie and Miss Nancy Jane Evans 15 Dec.1836
	George Lewis and Miss Lucy H. Wellborn	18 Oct. 1837
Page 97	Daniel L. Marshall Esqr. and
	Miss Mary Smalley	10 Jan. 1838
	Griffin Tankersley and Miss Phebe L. Ray	21 Dec. 1837
Page 98	William Dozier and Mary Cash	1 Mar. 1838
	Roderick R. Moore and Lucinda W. Lambert	11 Mar. 1838
		3 Oct. 1836 lic.
Page 99	Freeman W. Holliman and
	Miss Loduska O. Wade	25 Mar. 1838
	Gamwell Flanagin and Matilda Somers	29 Apr. 1838
Page 100	Samuel Stanford and Miss Ellen P. Sanderlin 26 Apr. 1838
	Robert A. Gerald and Miss Mary E. Albea	4 Oct. 1839
		2 Oct. 1838 lic.
Page 101	Bashford Robbins and Mrs. Patsy Hood	17 June 1838
	Hensley Landers and Mahala Jordan	10 May 1838
Page 102	George J. McClesky (McCleskey) and
	Miss Naomi M. Lovelace	5 July 1838
	Peyton R. Sutherland and Miss Louisa E. Olive 13 Sept. 1838
Page 103	John Bynaum and
	Mrs. Mary A. Lansdell (Lansdale)	29 July 1838
	Obadiah P. Morriss and
	Miss Louisa M. Shields	18 Sept. 1838
Page 104	William L. Blount and Martha S. Bailey	25 Nov. 1838
	Richard Avary and Miss Mahala Reid (Reed)	23 Dec. 1838
Page 105	Eli J. Wheat and Miss Elizabeth A. Harden	20 Dec. 1838
	John C. Harrison and Miss Rebecca Stanford	6 Jan. 1839
Page 106	John W. Wood and Matilda Emma Hunt	17 Jan. 1839
	John Briscoe and Miss Elizabeth Dougherty	14 Feb. 1838

Page 107	Charles Fox and Miss Lucinda Toole	29 May 1839
		28 May 1838 lic.
	Madison Avary and Miss Phebe C. Avary	22 July 1838
Page 108	Daniel P. Marshall and	
	Miss Margaret A. Tankersley	22 Nov. 1838
	Thomas Blalock and Miss Virginia Benning	23 Dec. 1838
Page 109	Nathaniel Cooper and Martha M. Reynolds	12 July 1836
	Francis Maguire (McGuire) and Emily Gay	17 Mar. 1836
Page 110	Matthew Philips and Renza Sellers	1 Feb. 1838
	John Taylor and Eliza (Litha) Philips	1 Feb. 1838
Page 111	John Whitaker and Miss Elizabeth Rowland	11 Jan. 1837
	John Gay and Miss Louisa Fuller	27 Jan. 1839
Page 112	Dr. Moses Griffith and	
	Miss Elizabeth C. Lovelace	4 Apr. 1839
	Elijah Hughes and Miss Nancy Adams	29 Jan. 1839
Page 113	William Sills and Miss Mary Watson	1 Dec. 1838
	John C. Smith and Miss Martha S. Morriss	19 May 1839
Page 114	Wiley K. Jones and Sarah E.H. Tracy	30 May 1839
	Robert Jones and Nancy Ann Crawford	30 June 1836
Page 115	William A. Morriss and Mrs. Mary O. Graham	28 Feb. 1839
	William H. Dozier and Miss Martha S. Stapler	14 Aug. 1839
Page 116	Levi Fullbright and Zelpha (?) Roberts	8 June 1839
	Walter J. Jones and Mary C. Scott	30 July 1839
Page 117	Robert McDonald and Miss Lydia B. Bond	28 Aug. 1839
	Peter Branch Short and Miss Luraney Watkins	15 Sept. 1839
Page 118	John F. Young and Miss Mary Young	3 Oct. 1839
	William Raney (Rayney) and Miss A. E. Womble	31 July 1839
Page 119	John Addison Christian and	
	Miss Elizabeth Ann Harriss	1 Dec. 1839
	James Joiner and Elizabeth Sikes	
Page 120	William M. Carrell (Carrel) and	
	Miss Jincey Inglet	11 Jan. 1838
	Jacob Inglet and Catharine McDonald	20 Oct. 1839
Page 121	Asa G. Avary and	
	Miss Mary Ann Chapalier (Chappler)	blank Jan. 1840
		2 Jan. 1840 lic.
	David P. Downs and Mrs. Mary Howard	12 Dec. 1839
Page 122	Allanson (Alanson) A. Day and	
	Miss Permelia Tindall	23 Jan. 1840
	Michael Griffin and Miss Susan Harkins	24 Feb. 1840
Page 123	John W. Dougherty and	
	Mrs. Catharine J. Dougherty	5 Mar. 1840
	Floyd W. Finch and Miss Sarah H. Langston	8 Mar. 1840
Page 124	Joshua Eppes and Miss Leanner Burnside	8 Mar. 1840
	John Cartlidge and Miss Rebecca Willingham	10 Mar. 1840
Page 125	Curtis H. Shockley Esqr. and	
	Mrs. Martha R. Hobby	15 Mar. 1840
	Tilman F. Dozier and Catharine Patman	8 Feb. 1840 lic.
	"Ga. Oglethorpe Co. the above named parties	
	were joined together... 11 Feb. 1840."	
Page 126	Henry Harrison and Miss Zara Thigpen	16 Apr. 1840
	James T. McGee and Elizabeth Wilson	23 Jan. 1840
Page 127	Levi Marshall and Miss Eliza M. Pollard	7 May 1840
	Hezekiah Yown and Sarah Ann Richardson	28 June 1840
Page 128	Marshall Holesonbeck and Martha Wilkins	15 July 1840
	Dr. Horace Neeson and Elizabeth J. White	8 Nov. 1840
Page 129	Anderson Upton and Miss Eliza Ann Heath	17 Dec. 1840
	Wilkerson P. Finch and Miss Mary Langston	27 Dec. 1840
Page 130	Rowel Adams and Miss Nancy Phillips	2 Dec. 1840
	Washington W. Stone and	
	Mrs. Permelia Wright	14 Jan. 1841
Page 131	Thomas M. Bailey and Miss Laura Binion	3 Dec. 1840
	Townsend Watkins and Miss Sarah Ann Jones	14 Jan. 1841
Page 132	Henry P. Hampton and Miss Lavinia T. Pace	18 Feb. 1841
	Albert Holliman and Mrs. Louisa M. Emerson	22 Nov. 1840
Page 133	John W. Wade and Miss Malvina Lynn	17 Nov. 1840
	James Stanford and	
	Mrs. Elizabeth F. Thompson	25 Dec. 1839

Page 134	Gatwood S. Dunn and Miss Nancy Dunn	23 Jan. 1839
		23 Jan. 1840 lic.
	Benjamin Berry and	
	Miss Frances M. Alexander	13 Feb. 1841
		12 Feb. 1840 lic.
Page 135	Augustus Lamkin and	
	Miss Mary A. E. Alexander	27 June 1841
		25 June 1840 lic.
	James D. Heggie and Miss Jane Reid	29 Oct. 1841
		28 Oct. 1840 lic.
Page 136	Elisha Beall and Miss Martha Miles	11 June 1841
		11 June 1840 lic.
	Edmund Hardaway and Miss Mary J. Fleming	26 Feb. 1841
Page 137	George Roberts Esqr. and Loretta Ann Paul	14 Mar. 1841
	David Revil and Miss Nancy Fuller	9 May 1841
Page 138	William B. Cochran and Miss Mary B. Day	10 June 1841
	William Wall and Miss Cordelia S. Watson	9 Jan. 1840
Page 139	David W. Wilson and Miss Delilah E. Wall	19 Jan. 1840
	Robert Crag and Frances Ann Spivey	29 Dec. 1837
Page 140	Benjamin Clark and Elizabeth Simons	9 Jan. 1838
	David Daniel and Miss Mary Whitaker	28 Apr. 1838
Page 141	Joseph O. Hill and Rebecca Roland	26 May 1838
	Andrew Rogers and Jane Watson	17 Oct. 1838
Page 142	Thomas Watson and Miss Sarah Lewis	28 July 1839
	Felix Prior and Mrs. Martha A. Rees	3 Nov. 1840
Page 143	John Smith and Miss Eleanor Ann Lamkin	6 July 1841
	James Owens and Miss Sally Fuller	22 Aug. 1841
Page 144	William H. Johnson and Miss Dolly Lassiter	15 Apr. 1841
	James M. Johnson and Miss Elizabeth Stanford	6 May 1841
Page 145	Dr. Thomas E. Bowdre and	
	Miss Frances A. Wiley	2 Dec. 1841
	Thomas N. Hicks and Miss Eliza E. Magruder	5 Dec. 1841
Page 146	Edmund B. Bacon and	
	Miss Evaline (Eveline) M. Steed	28 Oct. 1841
	James Y. Carrell and Miss Catharine Revill	11 Nov. 1841
Page 147	Thomas Bussey (Bussy) and Frances Watson	22 Dec. 1841
	John F. Jackson and Mrs. Mary H. Bowdre	28 Dec. 1841
Page 148	Crosby S. Skidmore and	
	Miss Pamelia D. Sutherland	4 Jan. 1842
	James Anderson and Harriet E. Philips	6 Jan. 1842
Page 149	Robert Shields and Miss Eliza F. Morriss	6 Jan. 1842
	Henry O. Williams and Miss Nancy McKorcle	20 Feb. 1842
Page 150	Chapel (Chappel) Brooks and Elizabeth Mathis	29 Oct. 1840
	Jeremiah Wells and Miss Mary Elkins	15 July 1841
Page 151	William J. Evans and Miss Lucy M. Pearre	27 Feb. 1841
		24 Feb. 1842 lic.
	Frances A. Duffe and Annah Pearre	3 Mar. 1842
Page 152	Michael Megahee and Miss Jane Jenkins	28 Oct. 1841
	William Welch and Miss Mary Ann Lott	1 Dec. 1841
Page 153	William Grimsley and Miss Susan Pearre	20 Dec. 1841
	William Cliett and Miss Elizabeth Zachry	22 Feb. 1842
Page 154	Richard F. Harrison and Miss Louisa Doyle	20 Feb. 1842
	Thomas K. Collier and Miss Mary Ann Roberts	24 Apr. 1842
Page 155	William F. Johnston and	
	Mrs. Emily M. Stallings	2 Mar. 1842
	Levi Owen and Miss Frances E. Langston	23 July 1841
Page 156	Thomas Langford and Miss Martha Ann Langston	21 Apr. 1842
	William Flanagin and Miss Ann E.S. Collins	31 May 1842
Page 157	John F. Young and Miss Elizabeth Bosworth	19 June 1842
	Seaborn Anderson and Miss Adelia F. Sanders	19 Dec. 1841
Page 158	William J. Langston and Miss Martha A. Young	19 May 1842
	Dr. John A. (H.) Hanson and	
	Miss Rebecca Ann Cartlidge	3 May 1842
Page 159	Thomas (A) Carr (Car) and Elizabeth R. Prior	20 July 1842
	Marcus A. Huling and Miss Martha A. Clark	25 Aug. 1842
Page 160	Charles Ashley and Miss Ellen Gray	28 Aug. 1842
	Larkin B. Roberts and Miss Barbara Watkins	8 Sept. 1842

```
Page 161   William Watson and Pamela A. Fleming          3 Oct. 1842
                                                         19 Oct. 1842 lic.
           Job Dexter Gibson and Miss Martha Ann Martin 10 Nov. 1842
Page 162   Kitrel H. Morriss and Elizabeth Reynolds     24 Nov. 1842
           Capt. Hezekiah Grubbs and Malvina Pollard     1 Nov. 1842
Page 163   John Burnside and Miss Sarah A.E. Bartlett   27 Nov. 1842
           William J. Eubank and
             Miss Louisa J. Harden (Hardin)              8 Dec. 1842
Page 164   Robert Lott and Miss Mary Ann Hall            3 July 1842
           Patrick McGinnis and Miss Elizabeth Wade      6 Dec. 1842
Page 165   Edmund Palmer and Miss Martha Revill (Revel) 15 Dec. 1842
           Benjamin T. Rees and Blanche M. Wood          2 Feb. 1843
Page 166   Sydney Tillory and Miss Polly Gray            8 Jan. 1843
           Washington Edwards and Miss Nancy Roberts     7 Mar. 1843
Page 167   Littleton Barber and Miss Mary Johnson       28 Apr. 1843
           Jeremiah Paschal and Palatiah E. Dooly       22 Nov. 1843
                                                         21 Nov. 1842 lic.
Page 168   John Wilkins and Miss Alta Ann Henderson      9 Feb. 1843
           Thomas P. Wade and Eliza Story                1 Oct. 1840
Page 169   William Powell and Elizabeth Smith           22 Mar. 1843
           Dr. Thomas H. Dawson and
             Miss Martha A. Hardwich                    27 July 1843
Page 170   Albert Gallatin Ruffin and
             Miss Harriet C. Gilpin                     15 Aug. 1843
           James S. Kamilton and Rebecca A. Crawford    26 Sept. 1843
Page 171   James B. Knox Jr. and Miss Rebecca Adams     14 Sept. 1843
           Jefferson S. Briscoe and Louisa Stanford     28 Sept. 1843
Page 172   William H. Murray and Miss L. Eliza Barnett   5 Oct. 1843
           Anderson M. Crawford and
             Miss Lucy E. Williams                      24 Oct. 1843
Page 173   William Smith and Miss Elizabeth Winn        19 Nov. 1843
           John P. Ferdon and Miss Martha A. Lazenby    16 Nov. 1843
Page 174   Valentine A. Hatcher and
             Miss Sarah Jane Mercer                     30 Nov. 1843
           Isaac Thompson and Miss Catharine Adams      25 Oct. 1843
Page 175   James Dougherty and Miss Elizabeth Avary     16 Jan. 1844
           Isaiah Hancock and Miss Ann Tudor            17 Dec. 1843
Page 176   Marcus T.C. Dozier and Miss Sarah Hughes     22 Dec. 1842
           John Holliday and Miss Catharine Griffin     16 Mar. 1843
                                                         10 Mar. 1844 lic.
Page 177   Dr. William A. L. Collins and
             Miss Sarah L. Allen                        16 Apr. 1844
           Richard S. Neale and Miss Lucy Ann Dunn      30 May 1844
                                                         29 June 1844 lic.
Page 178   Absalom Phillips and Miss Isabel Rowland      7 Feb. 1844
           Benjamin Gainus and Miss Ellen Whitaker       4 Jan. 1844
Page 179   John Evans and Sophronia Jane Magruder       23 Nov. 1841
           Samuel M. Jackson and
             Miss Catharine Halsonback (Holsonback)     28 Feb. 1844
Page 180   Uriah L. Leonard and Cassandra M. Drane      11 Apr. 1844
           James McKannon (McKennon) and
             Miss Mary Culbreath                         1 Aug. 1844
Page 181   Mr. John Barnett and
             Miss Georgia Ann S. Harden                 20 July 1844
           Benjamin Watkins and Ann H. Yarborough        9 Oct. 1844
Page 182   Allanson A. Day and Sarah Ann Bosworth        8 Oct. 1844
           William Holliday and Miss Amanda Griffin      7 Nov. 1844
Page 183   James S. Walker and Miss Nancy Smith         27 Oct. 1844
           James Alfred Hall and Mary K. Paul            2 Jan. 1845
Page 184   James Carrell and Jane Chrosby               13 Nov. 1844
           Angus Weaver and Emily Chrosby               13 Nov. 1844
Page 185   Evander Rodgers and Miss Harriet Fuller      27 Oct. 1844
           William Winder Stanford and Mary Ann Offutt   5 Jan. 1845
Page 186   Wilson W. Johnson and Miss Mary C. Smith     19 Dec. 1844
           Randolph Newsom and Laney Philips            16 Jan. 1845
Page 187   Obediah P. Morriss and Sarah E. Smith         7 Dec. 1843
           William P. Beale Esqr. and Verlinda Magruder 27 Mar. 1845
```

Page 188	James M. Harriss and Miss Sarah C. Luke	18 Mar. 1845
	Jeremiah G. Rees and	
	Miss Frances W. Cartlidge	8 Apr. 1845
Page 189	Valentine Watson and Susan Cline Upton	17 Apr. 1845
	Jonathan Baker and Martha Jane Megahee	27 Apr. 1845
Page 190	Lindsey C. Pearre and Miss Emma Pearre	6 Feb. 1845
	William Megahee and Gracy Huff	6 Aug. 1844
Page 191	Arthur Street and Miss Eliza Ann Paul	3 Apr. 1845
	James B. Newman and Miss Frances E. Cosage	19 June 1845
Page 192	Claiborn Revill Jr. and Miss Mary L. Green	20 Mar. 1845
	Revd. John J. Triggs and Miss Nancy Allen	16 Sept. 1845
Page 193	Uriah D. Watson and Miss Arena N. May	16 Oct. 1845
	John Henry Holt (Hob?) and	
	Miss Maria Louisa Benton	20 Nov. 1845
Page 194	Robert M. Warren and Miss Ophelia B. Gibson	4 Nov. 1845
	Dr. William A. Martin and Ann T. Burch	16 Dec. 1845
Page 195	William Howard Morriss and	
	Miss Matilda Jane Watson	23 Dec. 1845
	Thomas Ingram and Miss Frances P.E. Baston	25 Dec. 1845
Page 196	Eaton Pugh Bonner and Martha Mills Hambrick	28 Nov. 1845
	John Harden Wiley and	
	Miss Eliza Matilda Massengale	21 Dec. 1845
Page 197	John W. Wiley and Miss Lucinda Jane Bell	1 Feb. 1846
	Francis M. Fuller and Sarah A.H.(A) Flint	17 Feb. 1846
Page 198	Richmond Harriss and Miss Mary F. Reynolds	6 Nov. 1845
	Thomas J. W. Newman and	
	Miss Sarah P. Killingsworth	15 Jan. 1846
Page 199	Mark M. Shipp and Ellen E. Griffin	8 May 1846
	(Note: bottom of page blank.)	
Page 200	Henry A. Ramsey and Isabella Jane Cartlidge	6 Jan. 1846
	Charles Baston and Miss Frances Kelly	15 Aug. 1846
Page 201	James Dougherty and Miss Ann Avary	23 Oct. 1845
	William F. Lazenby and Sarah E. Albea	28 Apr. 1846
Page 202	John M. Cutliff and Mary S. Jones	17 Dec. 1846
	Freeman Rees and Miss Susan Johnston	17 Dec. 1846
Page 203	Robert F. Watson and Elizabeth Hamilton	20 Dec. 1846
	Thomas Sills and Mrs. Jane Rogers	27 Dec. 1846
Page 204	Augustus M. Johnson and Savannah Whitaker	20 Dec. 1846
	James H. Alford and Miss Emily Prior	15 Jan. 1845
		25 Dec. 1847 lic.
Page 205	George Washington and Ann Z. Rowland	13 Mar. 1845
	Solomon R. Taylor and	
	Miss Elizabeth H. B. Elebee (Elabee)	22 Mar. 1846
Page 206	James Street and Miss Mary Ann Fuller	5 Apr. 1846
	Francis M. Johnson and	
	Miss Clarissa Phillips (Philips)	3 Jan. 1837
		2 Jan. 1847 lic.
Page 207	Raymond Sellers and Miss Mary Palmer	24 Jan. 1847
	Richard Parks and Miss Martha Pearre	22 Dec. 1846
Page 208	David Seay and Miss Eveline P. (R.) Pettit	16 Apr. 1847
	Erasamus John Dozier and Mary Ann Adkins	23 May 1847
Page 209	Henry T. Hammack and Sarah Jane Crawford	20 June 1847
	Thomas Wynne Jr. and Miss Celia Roberts	18 Mar. 1847
Page 210	Joel L. Sills and Miss Elizabeth Watson	3 Jan. 1847
	William Moughon and	
	Miss Parthenia Portia Ramsey	26 Oct. 1847
Page 211	William Baston and	
	Miss Martha Jalina (?) Downs	26 Aug. 1847
	Jesse S. Wood and Miss Emily Culbreath	4 Nov. 1847
Page 212	William Woodall and Alcena J. Griffin	2 Nov. 1847
	Augustus B. Jones and Mary A. Meriwether	2 Dec. 1847
Page 214	John M. Thomas and Miss Mary E. Torrence	11 Jan. 1848
	James Culbreath Esq. and Miss Penelope Steed	15 Feb. 1848
Page 215	George W. Newman and Mary Ann Prather	30 Jan. 1848
	Caleb R. E. Ramsey and	
	Miss Gracy Caroline Hardin	13 Jan. 1848

Page 216	Joseph D. Spears and	
	Mary Ann Harris alias Watson	2 Mar. 1848
	James Satterwhite and	
	Miss Elizabeth Ann Sears (Sayrs)	7 Oct. 1847
Page 217	William A. H. Marshall and Mary Hassel	4 Apr. 1848
	Thomas Howard White and	
	Miss Sarah Finley Johnson	15 June 1848
Page 218	Samuel L. Brinkley and	
	Emeline (Evaline) F. Darsey	29 July 1848
	Warren G. Bell and Miss Terua? McDonald	30 Jan. 1848
Page 219	Jesse C. Reed and	
	Miss Elizabeth Jane Adams	22 June 1848
	Robert L. Lamkin and	
	Miss Aurelia Amanda Berry	15 June 1848
Page 220	John S. Dunn and Matilda F. Martin	12 Oct. 1848
	Adam Jones Smith and	
	Miss Evalina Fletcher Young	14 Dec. 1848
Page 221	Ebenezer Welkins and	
	Miss Elizabeth O. Neal (O. Neael)	11 Mar. 1849
	Seaborn H. Roberts and Charlotte Dagnal	1 Apr. 1849
Page 222	John A. Faucett and Miss Martha R. Turner	28 Feb. 1849
	Barnabus C. Gay and Miss Margaret Beasley	20 Dec. 1848
Page 223	James A. Simons and Miss Susan R. Isdell	2 Sept. 1849
	Albert T. Candler and Susan E. Paschal	2 Oct. 1849
Page 224	Asa Paschal and Miss Vashti T. Collins	4 Oct. 1849
	John H. Wiley and Mrs. Eleanor N. Winfrey	11 Sept. 1849
Page 225	Thomas Smith and Miss Mary Ann Barber	26 Oct. 1849
	James Willingham and	
	Elizabeth (Elizabith) Ann Miles	17 Mar. 1850
Page 226	Charles Y. Wilkerson and Mrs. Mary A. Scott	19 Dec. 1849
		17 Dec. 1847 lic.
	Joseph H. Young and Miss Eliza Ann Simons	21 Dec. 1848
Page 227	Lindsey C. Pearre and	
	Sarah Ann Rebecca Flint	20 Dec. 1849
	Isaac Gibson and Louisa E. Martin	13 Dec. 1849
Page 228	Almon Y. Carrel and	
	Miss Barbary Ann Revel (Revil)	29 Nov. 1849
	James M. Hatcher and Sarah F. Lazenby	21 Dec. 1849
Page 229	Martin Ganard and Miss Barbary Street	2 June 1849
		30 June 1849 lic.
	Francis P. Powel and Isabella L. Spivey	2 Aug. 1849
Page 230	James L. Heggie and Miss Henrietta Heard	18 Dec. 1849
	William A. Dyer and Elizabeth S. Dozier	18 Dec. 1849
Page 231	Vergelius M. Barnes and Ann Eliza Darsey	12 Feb. 1850
	Louis Young and Frances Barber	18 Dec. 1849
Page 232	Middleton Parish and Mary Radford	20 Dec. 1849
	Philip Smith and	
	Mary Josephine Louisa Reynolds	6 Dec. 1849
Page 233	Edwin T. Jones and Miss Martha D. Wright	4 Apr. 1850
	Lycurgus P. Murray and Mary A. F. Sturgis	16 Apr. 1850
Page 234	Freeman W. Morris and Susan S. Reynolds	20 May 1850
	Gideon Young and Mary Francis Sills	31 Jan. 1850
Page 235	James W. Tucker and Miss Jane A. Knox	2 June 1850
	John M. Jennings and	
	Miss Frances B. (P.?) Dunn	12 Sept. 1850
Page 236	Revd. Wesley P. Arnold and Julia E. Candler	9 Jan. 1850
	Jeremah (Jeremiah) S. Griffin and	
	Miss Elizabeth Merceir	25 Sept. 1850
Page 237	Benjamin T. Rees and Mrs. Martha F. Embree	27 Oct. 1850
	William S. Smith and Caroline M. Young	8 Sept. 1850
Page 238	Walker Culpepper and Nancy Frasees (Frasier)	18 July 1850
	Gazaway D. Lamar and Susan B. Wright	6 Nov. 1850
Page 239	John A. Green and Mary A. A. Denham	27 Nov. 1850
	James A. Langston and Nancy E. Youn	26 Dec. 1850
Page 239	Robert Turner Washington and	
	Miss Martha Margery Young	28 Nov. 1850
	William A. Sturgis and	
	Parmelia (Permelia) O. Bugg	5 Dec. 1850

Page 240	James Dougherty and Mrs. Selina Bell	17 Dec. 1850
	Anderson Moon (Moore?) Crawford and	
	Miss Mary Casandra Collins	11 Feb. 1851
Page 241	Minor R. Jones and Frances Holleman	13 Mar. 1851
	George Lyon and Selina Ann Gray	28 Dec. 1850
Page 242	John Moore and Miss Frances M. Bartlett	29 Dec. 1850
	Furney (Funey) George and	
	Sarah Matilda Adams	27 Feb. 1851
Page 243	Jacob Anderson and Nancey A. Prather	26 Dec. 1850
	Walter D. Willson and	
	Miss Isabella C. Collins	20 May 1851
Page 244	Greene B. Alford and Martha Ann Arnett	14 Aug. 1851
	Isaac Harper and Savannah Ivey	7 Oct. 1851
Page 245	George W. Watson and	
	Miss Louisa M. Rice (Rece?)	6 Nov. 1851
	Robert Marten Jr. and	
	Arminia (Armema) J. Wilkenson	31 Oct. 1851
Page 247	Isaac Vaughn and Miss Patsey Blackstone	15 Aug. 1816
	Samuel Marshall and Miss Elizabeth Rawls	24 Dec. 1846?
Page 249	Benjamin Winfrey and	
	Sally (Miss Sarah) Tindill	15 Feb. 1816?
Page 251	Blank	
Page 252	Benjamin F. Bolton and Sarah F. Cartledge	4 Dec. 1851
	Memoy (Mernoy?) Cain and Elizabeth Hammock	9 Nov. 1851
Page 253	Green B. Alford and Miss Martha A. Amett	14 Nov. 1851
	(Note page 244)	
Page 254	Bradford Ivy and Anna Duffy (Duffie)	27 Mar. 1851
	Jonathan B. Huff and Miss Mary Revill	2 Nov. 1851
Page 255	Robert Sellers and Nancey E. Kindrick	25 Jan. 1852
	William F. Nance and Miss Sarah Ansley	18 Dec. 1851
Page 256	George L. Bosher and	
	Miss Eliza F. Hardwick (?)	27 Nov. 1851
	Octavius L. Barnes and	
	Miss Sarah Frances Boyd	4 Dec. 1852
		3 Dec. 1851 lic.
Page 257	Willis Howard and Maletda Odum	11 May 1851
	Felix Simons and Lennea D. Young	28 Aug. 1851
Page 258	Gilbert S. Mann and	
	Miss Martha Ann Eliz Jones	8 Jan. 1851
		7 Jan. 1852 lic.
	Isaac Harper and Miss Savannah Ivy	7 Oct. 1851
Page 259	Thomas Peter Wade and	
	Mrs. Narcissa E. Roney	9 Dec. 1851
	Freeman Walker and Elizabeth Pate	1 Feb. 1852
Page 261	Simeen (Simeon) F. Griffin and	
	Miss Elizabeth Sanders	8 Jan. 1852
	Robert Franks and	
	Caroline V. Powell (Franks)	21 Aug. 1845

HANCOCK COUNTY, GA. DEEDS
1793-1795

Pages 1-2:   State of Georgia, April 15, 1794, JOHN COBB (S?) and POLLEY his wife of Hancock Co., to DAVID ROSS or Richmond, Virginia, for 500 pounds. Five hundred and (torn) five acres run on the Bounty Warran (t) (torn) BROWN and ROBERT JONES situate by (torn) County of Hancock, (torn) which land was conveyed to the said (torn)chard CALL the third day of August (torn) one thousand seven hundred and (torn) JN. COBBS (SEAL), POLLY COBBS (SEAL). Wit: LEU JONES, MARY COBBS. LEW? JONES made oath fifteenth day of (torn) 1794.

Pages 2-3:   State of Georgia Hancock County, March 19, 1794, JOHN TENNYHILL of South Carolina to LITTLETON REESE of Hancock * (formerly Washington on Fort Creek, waters of Shoulder bone, adj. PACTONS & MARSHALLS land, granted to JOHN TENNY HILL, Jan. 24, 1791, JOHN TENNY-HILL (X) (LS). Wit: PEYTON SMITH JP.
        Green County, Ga., PEYTON SMITH, a Justice of the Peace for sd. Co. appear March 19, 1794. Note* (Should read as follows, "for 100 lbs. 287 1/2 acres in Co. of Hancock, formerly Washington on Fort Hill Creek...")

Pages 3-4:   Hancock Co., Ga., 1794, WILLIAM PAXTON of South Carolina to JAMES THWEATT of Hancock Co., Ga.; for 100 pounds, 287½ acres in Hancock formerly Washington, on Fort Creek, waters of Shoulder bond adj. COLEMAN's, HAMMOCK'S, MARSHALL'S at time of original survey, granted to WILLIAM PAXTON, Jan. 24, 1791, WILLIAM PAXTON (SEAL). Wit: G. W. FOSTER, J.P.

Page 5:   JOHN YARBOROUGH of Green County, Ga., to dau. REBEKAH MUSE (MURE?), one Negro woman, negro girl, negro boy, JOHN YARBOROUGH ( ) (SEAL). Wit: ELIJAH HERN, JOHN HEATH, HESTER HEATH (X), JOHN RAGAN, JP.
        LEONARD GORDY's mark is a smooth crop in the right ear and a Swallowford in the left ear recorded March 10, 1794.

Pages 5-6:   Feb. 9, 1793, JOHN MCLAIN (MCCLAIN?) of Pendleton County, South Carolina, and MARIENA his wife, to LEONARD GORDY of Green Co., Ga., for 25 pounds, land on Rocky Creek in Greene County (formerly Washington) granted to sd. JOHN MCCLAIN, Dec. 31, 1784, 287½ acres, JOHN MCLANE (SEAL), MARINA MCLANE (X) (SEAL). Wit: SIER STALLINGS, WILLIAM SHAKLEFORD, sworn to Jan. 7, 1794, SIER STALLINGS.

Pages 6-7:   Apr. 11, 1792, ROBERT MIDDLETON of Greene Co., Ga., to BENJAMIN THOMPSON of same, for 20 pounds, 185 acres in Greene Co. on Ogechee River, beginning at an old survey of sd. BENJAMIN THOMPSON... JAMES ORRICK's line... WILLIAM COLBERT's line... part of 1700 acres granted to ROBERT MIDDLETON Aug. 2, 1786, R. MIDDLETON (SEAL). Wit: SAML. LAWRENCE, JNO. HAMILL, Not. pub.

Pages 7-8:   June 20, 1793, BENJAMIN UPTON of Columbia Co., Ga., to JAMES THOMAS WILLIAMS of Wilkes Co. for 50 pounds, 200 acres, adj. a branch of Ogechee River, COL. BENJAMIN FEW, a plat in Washington Co. sold by COL. ANDREW BURNS, before Feb. 1, 1792, one lot sold to AYRES STEWART... BENJA. UPTON (SEAL). Wit: BENA.? EVANS, T. WELLS.
        Warren Co., Ga., on May 13, 1794, BENJAMIN UPTON ack. and relinquished claim of dower, his wife JUDITH UPTON. Above deed was for 119 acres, including the town of Lexington.

Pages 9-10:   May 2, 1794, JONES PERSONS of Hancock Co., to EDMUND DROWDER of same, for 12 Spanish milled dollars, 4 acres in the Co. of Hancock belonging to the Society of Powell's Creek meeting house, adj. JAMES HUTCHENSON, JONES PERSONS (SEAL). Wit: JAS. HARVEY, JP.

Page 10:   JOHN ADAMS & ELIZABETH DAY of Hancock Co., power of attorney to JOSEPH MCMEEN of Lancaster Co., South Carolina, June 16, 1794, JOHN ADAMS ( ) (SEAL), ELIZABETH DAY (X). Wit: HENRY MITCHELL JP., DAVID ADAMS.

Page 11:   SARAH SCURLOCK formerly the wife of ISAAC WILLIAMS, dec'd.,
acknowledge the will of my former husband unto the heirs therein
mentioned, dated Oct. 20, 1792, SARAH SCURLOCK (X) (SEAL). Wit: J.
HUTCHINSON, MOSES MILES. Ack. by J. HUTCHINSON June 10, 1794.

Page 11:   HENRY MCCOY of Hancock Co. appoint RICHARD RISPES of Beuford
(Beaufort?) Co., North Carolina as his attorney, to receive of THOMAS
SMITH of Craven Co., 25 pounds in my name, March 7, 1794, HENRY MCKOY
(SEAL). Wit: HEN. GRAYBILL, Ck. of Superior Court of Hancock Co.

Page 12:   May 1, 1794, BENJAMIN ANDERSON of Hancock to EDMUND WALSH in
trust for STEPHEN WALSH, for 60 pounds, 178 acres on Little Ogechee,
originally granted to sd. ANDERSON by EDWARD TELFAIR, his Excellency, adj.
CHRISTMAS, WHATLEY, LAMAR, BENJAMIN ANDERSON (SEAL). Wit: P. BOYLE,
THOMAS GORDON, Junr., MARY ANDERSON.

Page 13:   May 10, 1793, MICHAEL HARVEY & REBEKAH his wife of Greene Co.,
Ga., to BENJAMIN THOMPSON of same for 50 pounds, land on Powell's Creek,
3 acres including the mill, part of a tract originally granted to
MICHAEL HARVEY (SEAL). Wit: JAMES ORRICK, JOHN GREER, HEN. GRAYBILL
JP.

Page 14:   Feb. 6, 1794, WILLIAM MCCLELLAN of Hancock Co. to SEAVEN
ELLIS, for 85 pounds, 200 acres on Shoulder bone, adj. EDMUND KNOWLES,
ROBERT MIDDLETON, SILAS MERCER, granted to WILLIAM MCLELLAN, Feb. 2,
1786, WILLIAM MCCLELLAN (SEAL). Wit: HEN. GRAYBILL, RANDOLPH RUTLAND.

Pages 14-15:   March 10, 1790, DANIEL WHATLEY of Washington Co. to
JAMES HUDDLESTON of Greene Co. for 100 pounds, 400 acres, in Greene Co.
on Little Ogechee, adj. WEAZEY, HEARD's, granted May 24, 1787, DANIEL
WHATLEY (X) (SEAL). Wit: DAVID BARELY, JAMES JORDAN, SAMUEL EWING,
JOHN BARELAY JP.

Page 15:   HENRY TOWNSEND's mark is a slit in the left Ear and a swallow
fork and a half moon in the right, rec. June 10, 1794.
        JESSE SANFORD's brand is his mark a cropin the left ear and
a swallow fork in the right, rec. July 5, 1794.
        GABRIEL HUBERT's mark is a crop and slit in each ear, rec.
May 4, 179_ (6?).
        JONATHAN MILLER's brand is   his mark a swallow fork in each
ear and a half moon in the under side of each ear. Rec. June 2, 179_.

Page 16:   July 6, 1793, ABRAHAM REDDICK & HANNAH his wife of Greene
Co. to JOHN STROTHER of same for 50 pounds, land on Folsom's Creek,
waters of Ogechee, 50 acres, granted May 5, 1790, ABRAHAM REDDICK (X),
HANNAH REDDICK (X). Wit: SAAC EVANS, AGRIPPA ATKINSON. (Later above
was called ISAAC EVANS.)

Page 17:   JOSIAH BEAL, THOMAS DENT & THADEUS BEAL of Co. of Hancock,
bound to THOMAS LAMAR, for 1000 pounds, March 25, 1794, JOSIAH BEALE to
be Deputy Sheriff of Hancock Co., JOSIAH BEAL (SEAL), THOMAS DENT (SEAL),
THADEUS BEAL (SEAL). Wit: DAVID DICKSON, P. BOYLE, JOHN HAMILTON.

Pages 18:   Feb. 6, 1794, LEVIN ELLIS of Hancock Co. to JOSHUA CULVER,
for 3000 pounds of crop tobacco, 50 acres which LIVEN ELLIS bought of
WILLIAM MCCLELLAN. LEAVEN ELLIS (X). Wit: HEN. GRAYBILL JP, RANDOLPH
RUTLAND.

Pages 18-19:   May 16, 1786, JESSE STALLINS of Wilks Co. to JAMES YOUNG
of Richmond Co. 287½ acres on south prong of watery fork of Buffaloe
Creek, adj. JOHN WILLIAMS, WILLIAM AYRES, granted to JESSE STALLIONS
March 3, 1785. (Another place names purchaser as JAMES YOUNGBLOOD.)
JESSE STALLIONS (X) (SEAL), SARAH STALLIONS (SEAL). Wit: SANDERS
WALKER, SARAH WALKER (X), NANCY WALKER. Proved: April 11, 1793.

Page 20:   Feb. 14, 1789, MOSES MARSHALL of Richmond to HENRY PARRISH
of Washington Co. for 100 pounds, 287½ acres, on Derresoe's Creek,

granted to MOSES MARSHALL July 14, 1787. MOSES MARSHALL (SEAL), MARY MARSHALL (SEAL). Wit: SANDERS WALKER, JOSEPH MARSHALL, SAMUEL POOL. Proven: Wilkes Co., April 10, 1793.

Page 21:   State of Ga., Washington County, Dec. 27, 1791, JAMES YOUNG-BLOOD & JEMIMAH his wife to NATHAN YOUNGBLOOD for 50 pounds, 218 3/4 acres on Buffaloe Creek, adj. JOHN WILLIAMS, ARTHUR YOUNGBLOOD, WILLIS, BOLING... JAMES YOUNGBLOOD ( ) (SEAL), JEMIMAH YOUNGBLOOD (J) (SEAL). Wit: HUGH MONTGOMERY, HENRY ROGERS, (torn) MCKINNIE.

Page 22:   Feb. 17, 1794, HENRY PARRISH of Hancock Co. to ARTHUR DANILY for 50 pounds, 350 acres on Ocnie River & Town Creek, adj. WILLIAM SHUFFIELD, ROBERT SHUFFIELD, unknown and vacant land, granted Sept. 20, 1791, HENRY PARRISH (X). Wit: _____ BURNS, _____ (page torn at bottom).

(Next page is numbered 31.)

Page 31:   June 14, 1788, THOMAS JOHNSTON of Greene Co., to DANIEL SOW of same, for 50 pounds, 65 acres, bounded by twelve miles Beaverdam Creek, JACOB DANBY, SAMUEL HAWKINS, ABRAHAM RIDDLE?. Land granted to JACOB DANSBY, Nov. 30, 1784. THOMAS JOHNSTON (X) (S). Wit: HEN. GRAYBILL JP., EDMUND BUTLER.

Page 32:   Sept. 3, 1784, THOMAS LAMAR & wife ELIZABETH of Hancock Co., to SIMON DAY of same for five pounds, land on Shoulderbone Creek, 24½ acres, part of a grant to JOHN LAMAR March 15, 1785. THOS. LAMAR (SEAL), BETSEY LAMAR (SEAL). Wit: HEN. GRAYBILL JP., ALEXANDER MCDONALD.

Page 33:   June 10, 1794, WILLIAM MADDOX, Senr. of Hancock Co. to WM. MADDOX, Junr. of same for 100 pounds, land on Fulsom's Creek, adj. BAGBY, BRAN (BRAU?), MATHEW RAVEN, JOHN KILGORE, 1003 acres, 50 excepted. WILLIAM MADDUX (X) (SEAL). Wit: WM. OWNSLEY (OWNSBY?), ALEXANDER RICHESON (X). Proven: Oct. 10, 1794.

Page 34:   Hancock Co., Ga., Aug. 19, 1794, WILLIAM MADDUX to REUBEN JONES MARTIN ARMSTRONG for 100 pounds, land on Fulsom's Creek, adj. BAGBY, BRUSER, MATHEWS RABUNS, JOHN GILGOAR, 1093 acres. WILLIAM MADDUX. Wit: DONALD MCDOWELL (X), WM. OWSLEY, REBECHA OWSLEY ( ). Proven: Oct. 10, 1794.

Page 35:   Sept. 15, 1794, THOMAS KILLY of Hancock Co. to JONATHAN MILLER of same for 50 pounds, 287½ acres on Shoulderbone Creek, THOMAS KELLY (T) (SEAL). Wit: JAMES NICHOLSON, WILLIAM YARBROUGH, JOHN MCKENZIE JP.

Page 36:   May 31, 1792, JOSEPH RILEY of Washington Co. to JAMES BISHOP of Wilkes Co. for 8 pounds, 200 acres, adj. TRAWICKS, granted Dec. 20, 1786, JOSEPH RILEY (SEAL). Wit: JAMES RILEY, EDWARD LORD? Proven: May 31, 1794.

Pages 36-37:   Nov. 10, 1792, BRITAIN ROGERS of Green Co. to JAMES WILSON of same, for 25 shillings, 75 acres on Fort Creek, part of a grant to BRITTAIN ROGERS, 1784, adj. JOHN WHITE, BRITTAIN ROGERS (B) (SEAL). Wit: MARTHA DICKSON (X), DAVID DICKSON JP.

Pages 37-38:   Feb. 20, 1792, GEORGE IEA of Washington Co. to ASA ATKINS of Wilkes Co. for 125 pounds, land on Buck Creek, 550 acres, originally granted to SANDERS WALKER, March 3, 1785. GEORGE LEA (SEAL), LUCY LEA (SEAL). Wit: JOEL MCCLENDON, JOHN MILES, WILLIAM WILLIAMS.

Pages 38-39:   May 22, 1792, GEORGE LEA & LUCY his wife to WILLIAM MILES all of Washington Co., Ga., for 100 pounds, 87 acres on Buck Creek, originally granted to Reverend SANDERS WALKER, Dec. 31, 1784, conveyed to GEORGE LEA June 17, 1788. GEORGE LEA (SEAL), LUCY LEA (SEAL). Wit: JEREMIAH MILES, RANSOM LEA, SAML. BECKOM JP.

Pages 39-40:   July 31, 1793, WILLIAM ANDREWS of Greene Co. to SAMUEL BARRON for 60 pounds, 200 acres, part of 1700 granted to ROBERT

MIDDLETON Aug. 2, 1786, WILLIAM ANDREWS (X) (SEAL). Wit: (names very dim). Aug. 17, 1793, JOHN BARRON, one of wit. declared that he saw WM. ANDREWS ack. deed, and saw AZCHERIAH GLASS wit. also.

Pages 40-41:   Feb. 15, 1794, SAMUEL BARRON of Hancock Co. to JOHN BARRON, for 60 pounds (same land as above). SAMUEL BARRON (SEAL). Wit: ELIAS? WOODS, ZECHARIAH GLASS. Later mentions ETHELRED WOODS.

On Page 41:   This indenture made the 2nd day of October in the year of our Lord one thousand and seven hundred and inety four between MERREDITH PRICE of Hancock County and State of Georgia of the one part and (nothing else on page).

Page 42:   May 22, 1792, GEORGE LEA & LUCY his wife to RANSOM LEA for 100 pounds, 150 acres on Buck Creek, granted to REVD. SANDERS WALKER Dec. 31, 1794, GEORGE LEA (SEAL), LUCY LEA (SEAL). Wit: WM. MILES, JEREMIAH MILES, SAML. BECKIOM JP.

Pages 42-43:   June 5, 1794, ROBERT FLOURNOY to heirs of EPHRAIM VAUGHN, 30, 60, or 100 acres in Co. of Hancock on Waters of Little Ogeechee, adj. KELLEY, HUBBARD part of a grant to RICHARD CALL, R. FLOURNOY (SEAL). Wit: SARAH M. BOSTWICK, ISAAC BAUGHAN, JACOB WOOD JP.

Pages 43-44:   Oct. 2, 1794, GEORGE GRISLE of Pendleton County, South Carolina to RICHARD HEAD & WILLIAM HARGROVE for 50 pounds, 287½ acres on Shoulderbone Creek, granted to sd. GEORGE GRISLE on bounty, Sept. 10, 1784, GEORGE GRIZEL (SEAL). Wit: JESSE BROWN, ALEXR. MCMILLIAN, WILLIAM HERD (X), WM. HEARD made oath in Wilkes Co., Oct. 6, 1794.

Pages 44-45:   Nov. 1, 1794, STERLING CATO of Hancock Co. to CORNELIUS CLARK for 30 pounds 300 acres, granted to WILLIAM PHILLIPS, Nov. 25, 1788. STERLING CATO (SEAL), ABIGAIL CATO (SEAL). Wit: FRANCES BLACK-WOOD, JOSEPH CAHPPLE, JAS. AAMS JP. (ADAMS?)

Page 45:   JOHN PERMENTER of Washington Co. sold to AARON MCKINZIE 2 negroes, six head of cattle, for 60 pounds, July 1, 1793. Wit: RANDOLPH MCKINZIE, WM. MCKINZIE. Sworn to: Nov. 25, 1794.

Page 46:   Nov. 18, 1792, JOHN CAIN of Wilkes Co., Ga. to JOSEPH MCGLAUGHLIN of South Carolina, for 60 pounds, 287½ acres, granted to THOMAS GRAY Oct. 12, 1785. JOHN CAIN (SEAL), ELIZABETH CAIN (X) (SEAL). Wit: JOHN TOLBOT, ISAAC DAVIES MORGAN, ALEXANDER MURPHY.

Page 47:   March 4, 1793, NATHAN JONES & BETTY his wife of Greene Co., Ga. to PETER JACKSON of same, for 100 pounds, 200 acres on Powell's Creek, granted to sd. JONES April 7, 17__ (illegible), NATHAN JONES (SEAL), BETTY JONES ( ) (SEAL). Wit: HEN. GRAYBILL, WILLIAM JACKSON.

Page 48:   Dec. 24, 1792, REUBEN JONES of Greene Co. to DAVID STRICKLAND, for 100 pounds, 287½ acres, on Island Ck. and Rocky Crk., granted to ROBERT SMART, Oct. 13, 1785. REUBEN JONES (SEAL). Wit: WM. RABUN, JACOB STRICKLAND, NANCY JONES.

Page 49:   Dec. 2, 1794, CLEMENT MULLINS of Hancock Co. to JOHN BARRON of same, for 65 pounds, 115 acres, adj. CLEMONS, CLEMENT MULLINS (X) (SEAL). Wit: JOHN TAPLEY, SAMUEL BARRON, JOHN MCKINZIE.

Page 50:   Nov. 29, 1793, JOHN PURSE of Richmond Co. to THOMAS SHIP of Greene Co. for 65 Guineas, (later JOHN PIERCE)... JOHN PIERCE (SEAL). Wit: NOAH DADRIGE, WM. LONGSTREET JP.

Pages 50-51:   Jan. 30, 1784, (should be 1794), ROBERT FLOURNOY of Hancock Co. to WILLIAM BEVIN of same for 300 pounds, 138 3/4 acres, part of 933 of ROBERT FLOURNOY in Washington Co. on waters of Derisoes Creek, adj. MARSHALL, R. FLOURNOY. Wit: WILYE ABERCROMBIE, JNO. BAILEY JP.

Pages 51-52:   BENJAMIN BREAD, Nov. 21, 1794... THOMAS LAMAR... (later) BENJAMIN BREEDLOVE (this deed very dim), B. W. BREEDLOVE (LS). Wit: HEN. GRAYBILL JP.

31

Page 52:   March 14, 1793, LEVY LANCASTER of Greene Co. & BENJAMIN JONES. WILLIAM JONES of his own free will to the sd. LEVY LANCASTER & his mother... gives a certain negro girl... mother ANN LANCASTER... BENJAMIN JONES (SEAL), LEVI LANCASTER (SEAL). Wit: THADS. HOLT.

Page 53:   1792, LEONARD SWITZER of Wilks Co. to JEHEMIAH MOORE of Greene Co. for 100 pounds, 287½ acres, border at time of survey, vacant land... LEONARD SWITZER (SEAL). Wit: DANIEL PRICE, DAVID CRESWELL JP.

Page 54:   Jan. 9, 1792, JOSIAH DENNIS of Washington Co. to CHARLES STUART of same, for 45 pounds, land purchased of MATTHEW HUBARD on Little Ogeechee & Dry Creek, 100 acres, adj. KELLY, JOSIAH DENNIS (SEAL). Wit: JOHN CALLOWAY (X), IS. VAUGHAN, JNO. BAILEY JP.

Pages 54-55:   Aug. 24, 1792, JAMES MORGAN of Washington Co. to CHARLES STUART, for 30 pounds, 100 acres, granted to JAMES MORGAN 1784, JAMES MORGAN (SEAL). Wit: DEMPSEY STANDLEY (X), JOHN KELLY (X), HARMAN RUNNELS JP.

Pages 55-56:   July 27, 1794, JOHN BOOTH, Senr. of Hancock Co. to JOSEPH PARMOUR, for 20 pounds, 100 acres on Rocky Creek, adj. NOAH OWSLEY, JOHN BOOTH SEN. (SEAL). Wit: J. SANDORD JP.

Pages 56-57:   Nov. 22, 1792, WILLIAM BUCKHATTER of Wilkes Co. to LITTLETON BEAUCHAMP of Greene Co. for 50 pounds, 200 acres, adj. JNO. WARD, WILLIAM BURCHHALTER (SEAL). Wit: JOSEPH HOWARD (X), JESSEE HOWARD (X).

Pages 57-58:   Jan. 1, 1795, JOHN BARRON of Hancock Co. to SAMUEL BARRON of same, for 65 pounds, land on Rocky Creek, adj. CALMONS, TOLBORTS, JOHN BARRON (LS). Wit: JOHN BARRON, Junr., A. COMER, JP.

Pages 58-59:   March 3, 1791, ELIJAH CLARK of Wilkes Co. to ANDERSON COMER, for 100 pounds, 287½ acres, on Oconee River, adj. BUCKNER DUKES, in Greene Co. formerly Washington... ELIJAH CLARK (E) (SEAL). Wit: THOMAS BROWN, WM. OWSLEY.

Pages 59-60:   Nov. 2, 1787, WILLIAM HUNT of Richmond Co. to RHESE HOWARD, for 50 pounds, 230 acres, adj. CRESWELL, JOHN WARD, granted to WM. HUNT July 20, 1786. WILLIAM HUNT (LS). Wit: THOS. WHITE, WM. WATT. Proven: July 18, 1791.

Pages 61-62:   Apr. 28, 1791, RHESA HOWARD of Columbia Co. to ANDERSON COMBER of Greene Co. for 50 pounds, (same as above). R. HOWARD (LS). Wit: THOS. WHITE, ABRM JOHNSON.

Pages 62-63:   April 6, 1793, JAMES ADAMS & MARY his wife, for 35 pounds, to ANDERSON COMER, when original survey was made mistaken for Island Creek, but really Logdown Creek, granted to THOMAS HANNA Aug. 17, 1785, JAMES ADAMS (SEAL), MARY ADAMS (SEAL). Wit: DAVID DICKSON JP.

Pages 63-64:   Jan. 10, 1788, ?OHN PALMER of Edgefield Co., South Carolina, to JOHN LAMAR of Richmond Co., Ga., for 50 pounds, land on Buffaloe Creek, granted to JOHN PARLMER, Feb. 1785, JOHN PALMER (IP) (LS). Wit: H. ALLISON JP.

Page 65:   July 31, 1794, JOHN MCCARTIE of Columbia Co. to JOHN LAMAR of Hancock Co. for 200 pounds, 460 acres, granted to sd. MCCARLIE July 19, 1785, JOHN MCCARTLY. Wit: JONATHAN SMITH, THOS. WHITE JP.

Pages 66-67:   Jan. 17, 1792, JOHN LAMAR of Richmond Co. to JOHN LAMAR Junr. of Green Co. for 100 pounds, 287½ acres, on a fork of Buffaloe Creek, JOHN LAMAR (LS). Wit: ZACHARIAH LAMAR, Junr., B. W. BREEDLOVE.

Pages 67-68:   June 19, 1793, JOSEPH COOPER & SARAH his wife to JOHN LAMAR, for 270 pounds, 540 acres on Oconee River, including the mouth of Sandy Run, granted to STERN SIMMONS, May 24, 1786, JOSEPH COOPER (SEAL), SARAH COOPER (N) (SEAL). Wit: HEN. GRAYBILL JP, MARY GRAYBILL ( ).

Pages 69-70: April 2, 1791, HOLLAND MIDDLETON of Greene County to JOHN LAMAR, for 200 pounds, 250 acres, adj. THOMAS LAMAR, HOLLAND MIDDLETON (SEAL). Wit: HE. GRAYBILL JP, ZACHARIAH MADUX.

Page 70: June 1, 1794, ROBERT FLOURNOY of Hancock Co. to PERIMAN FLOYD of Washington, for 100 pounds, 287½ acres in Washington Co., R. FLOURNOY (SEAL). Wit: R. THOMAS JP, FRANCIS LAWSON JP.

Pages 71-72: Dec. 17, 1794, WILLIAM LANIER of Anson County, North Carolina to MATHEW ANSHEN of Edgecombe County, North Carolina, for 200 pounds, 287½ acres, originally granted to ABRAHAM LIPMAN, on Oconee River, Big Island Creek & another tract adj. JOHN COOK, HUGH HORTON, DAVID FELPS, WILLIAM LANIER (LS). Wit: JNO. HARBERT JP., THOMAS STEVENS.

Page 72: May 5, 1792, DAVID FELPS of Greene Co. to WILLIAM LANIER of same, for 60 pounds, 30 acres in Greene Co. DAVID FELPS (SEAL). Wit: GEORGE ROSS, THES. JACKSON. Proven: Feb. 11, 1795.

Pages 73-74: Oct. 30, 1794, BENJAMIN BRASWELL for 100 pounds, 100 acres on Rocky Creek, adj. STEPHEN JOHNSON, MARY PARKER, JAMES DANIELS, BENJAMIN BRASWELL (SEAL). Wit: J. LANFORD JP, JOSEPH PARMER?.

Page 74: Oct. 30, 1794, BENJAMIN BRASWELL of Hancock Co. to MARY PARKER, for 50 pounds, 100 acres, BENJ. BRASWELL (SEAL). Wit: JOSEPH PARMER, J. LANFORD JP.

Pages 75-76: Nov. 17, 1792, THOMAS ROBERTS & MARY his wife of Washington Co. to THOMAS HEATH of Wilkes Co. for 100 pounds, 287½ acres, adj. JAMES MCFARLAND, originally granted to JOHN JONES, Jan. 3, 1784, conveyed to JOSEPH REED then to THOMAS ROBERTS... THOMAS ROBERTS (SEAL), MARIA ROBERTS (SEAL). Wit: JOSEPH BONNER, HEN MITCHELL, SAMUEL NORTHINGTON.

Pages 76-77: Nov. 14, 1792, THOMAS ROBERTS to THOMAS HEATH for 50 pounds, 25 acres, adj. THOMAS ROBERTS & WILLIAM JACKSON. THOMAS ROBERTS (SEAL), MARIA ROBERTS (SEAL). Wit: HEN MITCHELL, SAMUEL NORTHINGTON, NANCY B. NORTHINGTON.

Pages 77-78: Jan. 19, 1795, THOMAS HEATH & SEALAH his wife of Warren Co. to WILLIAMSON BONNER & EDMUND HEATH Exors. of est. of NATHAN HEATH, dec'd. originally granted to JOHN JONES, land on Buffaloe Creek in Hancock Co. THOMAS HEATH (SEAL), SELAH HEATH (H) (SEAL). Wit: HEN. MITCHELL, JOHN FREEMAN, JOSEPH BONNER.

Pages 78-79: Jan. 19, 1795, THOMAS HEATH & SELAH his wife to WILLIAMSON BONNER & EDMD HEATH, Exrs. of NATHAN HEATH, for 50 pounds, 25 acres, on Buffaloe Creek. THOMAS HEATH (SEAL)., SELAH HEATH (X) (SEAL). Wit: HEN MITCHELL, JOHN FREEMAN, JOSEPH BONNER.

Pages 79-80: June 18, 1792, WILKINS SMITH of Columbia Co. to NATHAN HEATH of Sussex County, Virginia for 50 pounds, 200 acres, part of a 600 tract run in the name of CANDELOR, on a prong of Little Ogechee, adj. THOMAS WATLEY, ROBERT FLOURNOY, MICAH WATLEY, CHRISMAS & DANIEL WATLEY... WILKINS SMITH (SEAL). Wit: JOEL HEATH, PETER LEATH. JOHN HILL (X). Wit: The receipt of money.

Pages 81-82: June 4, 1794, WILLIAM ANDREWS to JOHN LEE for 35 pounds, adj. ORRICK, LEE, 150 acres, WM. ANDREWS (X) (SEAL). Wit: BENA. COWLING, CLARY LEE.

Pages 82-83: Feb. 16, 1795, LEONARD GORDY to ELIJAH MOORE, for 37 pounds, 150 acres on Rocky Creek, adj. JOSEPH HOWARD, ALLEN GAY, LEONARD GORDEY (SEAL). Wit: BENJAMIN SANFORD, J. SANFORD JP.

Pages 83-84: Oct. 25, 1794, JOHN WHITE to GEORGE WHITE for 30 pounds... JOHN WHITE & JANE his wife... 150 acres, in Hancock Co... originally granted to SANDERS WALKER, Dec. 13, 1785. JOHN WHITE (SEAL), JEAN WHITE (X) (SEAL). Wit: JAMES ORR, JAMES MCGAUGHY, DAVID DICKSON JP.

Page 84:   Oct. 2, 1794, JOHN LEDDALL DIXON & POLLY his wife of Washington Co. to ARTHUR DANNELLY of Hancock County for 100 pounds, 287½ acres on Rocky Creek, adj. WILLIAM WILDER, WILLIAM WALKER, granted Sept. 16, 1785... J. L. DIXON (SEAL), POLLY DIXON (SEAL). Wit: ANDERSON READING (X), HENRY HARRIS, ROBERT DAWSON.

Page 85:   Nov. 17, 1795, STEPHEN HORTON to THEODOSIUS TURK, for 150 pounds, 250 acres, originally granted to JOHN MCFARLAND, adj. JOHN COOK, SCARLETT, LACEY, on Island Creek, & Fort's land... STEPHEN HORTON (SEAL). Wit: JNO. HARBIRT JP., WILLIAM VINES (X).

Page 86:   Rec'd Dec. 10, 1791, from Mr. CHARLES STATHAM 100 pounds in full for a negro man slave named Jeff & his bro. Joe. EPHRAIM FERREL. Wit: J. L. DIXON, P. CLAYTON JP. Same, signed GEORGE RAGLAND.

Pages 86-87:   April 1, 1794, HENRY MCCOY & SALLY his wife of Hancock Co. to JOHN MCCOY for 40 pounds, 138 acres, granted to DANIEL MARSHALL WADE Washington Co. conveyed to HENRY MCCOY. HENRY MCCOY (SEAL), SALLY MCCOY (X) (SEAL). Wit: JOHN SMITH (X), ELIZABETH SMITH, HEN. GRAYBILL JP.

Page 87:   WILLIAM ANDREWS of Hancock Co. for 50 pounds to WARREN ANDREWS a gray horse and a gray mare. WILLIAM ANDREWS (SEAL). Wit: JAMES MORONEY, MARY GARISON? (X).

Pages 87-88:   WILLIAM ANDREWS for 250 pounds to WARREN ANDREWS... for negroes... WILLIAM ANDREWS (SEAL). Aug. 1, 1794. Wit: JAMES MERONEY, MARY GARNOR (X).

Page 88:   JUDKINS HUNT of Hancock Co. give to my dau. SARAH HUNT, 3 negroes. JUDKINS HUNT. March 16, 1795. Wit: FRANCIS ROSS, DAVID DICKSON JP.

Pages 88-89:   JUDKINS HUNT to son WILLIAM HUNT, 3 negroes, March 16, 1795. JUDKINS HUNT (SEAL). Wit: FRANCIS ROSS, DAVID DICKSON JP.
               JUDKINS HUNT to MILES GREENE 3 negroes (gift). March 16, 1795. (Same sig. and wit.)
               JUDKINS HUNT to dau. NANCY HUNT, 3 negroes, (same sing. & wit.)

Pages 89-90:   JUDKINS HUNT to son JUDKINS HUNT 3 negroes (same as above).

Page 90:   JUDKINS HUNT of Hancock Co. to dau. MARY HUNT, 3 negroes (same as above).
               JUDKINS HUNT to son JAMES HUNT, 3 negroes (same as above).

Pages 90-91:   Oct. 2, 1785, MICAJAH WILLIAMSON (Attorney for DANZA METCALF of Rutherford County, N.C.) of Wilkes Co. to WILLIAM WASHINGTON of Charleston, South Carolina, by letter dated July 11, 1785, to sell grant run on Bounty Warrant in the name of DANZA METCALF, adj. HENRY COUPS, ROBERT HARPER, 460 acres on Shoulderbone Ck. of Rocky Creek, M. WILLIAMSON (SEAL). Wit: P. CLYMA?, WILLIAM TRIPLETT.

Pages 91-92:   April 22, 1785, SAMUEL WILSON of Wilkes Co. to WILLIAM WASHINGTON of Charleston, S.C. for 200 pounds, 287½ acres in Washington Co. SAMUEL WILSON ( ) (LS). Wit: LEOD. PARK, HORATIO MARBURY.

Pages 93-94:   Oct. 3, 1785, MICAJAH WILLIAMSON (Attorney for WILLIAM METCALF of Rutherford County, N.C.) to WILLIAM WASHINGTON of Charleston, S.C. for 100 pds., 460 acres... MICAJAH WILLIAMSON (LS). Wit: WM. TRIPLETT, PETER CLYMA.

Pages 94-95:   Nov. 10, 1785, JAMES YORK to WILLIAM WASHINGTON of Charleston, S.C. 200 pounds, for 287½ acres, in Washington Co., Ga.... JAMES YORK (X) (LS). Wit: WM. TERRELL JP, HORATIO MARBURY.

Pages 95-96:   Nov. 27, 1787, HENRY COUP of North Carolina to WILLIAM WASHINGTON of Charleston, South Carolina, for 5 shillings, land on

Rocky fork of Shoulderbone Creek, adj. WIDDOW WOOTEN, DANZA METCALF, WILLIAM BRADY, 345 acres, HENRY COUP (H). Wit: BETTY BOIN, JOHN STEPTOE.

Page 96: Nov. 8, 1787, HENRY COUP to WILLIAM WASHINGTON for 100 pounds, 340 acres on Shoulderbone Creek. HENRY COUP (H). Wit: BETTY ROSIE (RORIE?), JNO. STEPTOE.

Pages 97-98: Nov. 11, 1793, WILLIAM MCINVAILL & ELIZABETH his wife, of Greene Co., to LAMUEL LAURENCE of Augusta, for 100 pounds, 178 acres, granted to WILLIAM LAMAR July 12, 1786... WILLIAM MCINVAILL (SEAL), ELIZABETH MCINVAILL (SEAL). Wit: THOMAS HARTON, EDMD. CROWDER.

Pages 98-99: Apr. 7, 1794, MICAJAH WILLIAMSON of Wilkes Co. to JOHN WEEKS of Hancock Co., 100 pounds, for 200 acres, on Powell's Creek, granted July 13, 1784. M. WILLIAMSON SEN. (SEAL). Wit: TURNSTALL ROAN (other illegible).

Page 99: Oct. 24, 1792, WILLIAM SHIELD & MARY his wife of Columbia Co. to JAMES WRIGHT, for 45 pounds, 191½ acres, part of grant to GEORGE ROSEBOROUGH, conveyed by his heirs to WILLIAM SHIELD, adj. WRIGHT, SANDERS, WILLIAM SHIELD (SEAL), MARY SHIELD (X) (SEAL). Wit: LEWIS BARNES JP.

Page 100: June 2, 1794, WILLIAM MINOR the younger of Hancock Co. to FRANCIS WILLIS Senr. for $800, equal to 186 pounds, 6 shillings & 8 pence... FRANCIS WILLIS of Gloucester Co., Virginia... 250 acres on Great Ogechee. WILL MINOR (SEAL). Wit: P. BOYL, JOHN MCKINZIE.

Page 101: May 5, 1794, MASEDITH PRICE of Hancock Co. to WILLIAM BEVIN of same, for 200 pounds, 287½ acres, on Buck Creek,... MEREDITH PRICE (SEAL). Wit: HUBBARD FERRELL (H), CHARLES WEBB, JOHN JONES (X)

Pages 101-102: Oct. 12, 1793, DEMPSEY STANDBY of Washington Co. to WILLIAM MURPHY, for 50 pounds, 50 acres on Dry Creek, adj. WM. SEL, WILLIAM FEW... DEMPSEY STANDBY (X) (LS). Wit: WILLIAM SEAL, ABNER PEARCE, HARMAN RUNNELS JP.

Pages 102-103: Nov. 10, 1794, WILLIAM GRIGGS to JOHN TRIPP of Hancock Co. for 50 pds. part of a tract formerly belonging to THOS. BELL where widow PRITCHETT now lives. WM. GRIGGS (SEAL). Wit: WM. BIGGINS, SHADRACH ROE, A. COMER JP.

Page 103: Dec. 15, 1792, JOHN ROBERTSON & SARAH his wife of Greene Co. to GEORGE STEPHENS of same, for 62 pounds, 10 shillings, 200 acres on Sandy Run Creek, adj. JESS CLEMENT, COOK, MADDOX... JOHN ROBERTSON (H) (SEAL), SARAH ROBERTSON (T) (SEAL). Wit: ROBERT BALDWIN, A. COMER JP.

Page 104: March 2, 1795, JAMES SCARLETT of Hancock Co. to J. K. POPE Extr. for MAJOR JOHN TRIPPE dec'd of same, for 100 pounds, 800 acres on Spring Creek, adj. SAMUEL ALLEXANDER, SANDERS, BECKOMS, JAMES SCARLETT (SEAL). Wit: JOHN WHATLEY (X), FANNY WATLEY (X).

Page 105: Feb. 10, 1795, WILLIAM POLLARD, Senr. of Washington Co. to JOHN MITCHELL of Hancock Co. for 5 shillings, 115 acres in Hancock Co. granted to WM. POLLARD, Senr. Sept. 22, 1785, Book OOO Fo. 460. WILLIAM POLLARD (SEAL). Wit: JNO. R. HOGIN, BENJN. TENNILLE JP.

Pages 105-106: Dec. 20, 1793, JOHN MCARTHY & MARY his wife of Columbia Co., to JOHN BARRON of Wilkes Co. for 100 pounds, land in Green Co. on Town & Island Creek... JOHN MCCARTHY (SEAL), MARY MCCARTHY (X) (SEAL). Wit: BENJ. REES, THOS. WHITE JP.

Pages 106-107: Jan. 6, 1792, NATHAN FOWLER of Wilkes Co. to JOEL REESE of Greene Co. for 100 pounds, 287½ acres on Fort Creek, adj. TOWNEHILL, MARSHALL granted Ma- 27, 1785... NATHAN FOWLER (LS). Wit: DANIEL HARMAN, BENJ. JENKINS JP.

Pages 107-108:   Feb. 10, 1795, WILLIAM POLLARD Senr. of Washington
Co. to HUGH FLANKIN of Hancock Co. for 5 shillings, 218½ acres part of a
grant to WILLIAM POLLARD, Senr... WILLIAM POLLARD (SEAL). Wit: JNO.
R. HOGINS, BENJN. TENPILLE JP.

Page 108:   Sept. 13, 1792, JOHN SHAKLEFORD of Columbia Co. to JOHN
PARKER of Elbert Co. for 10 pounds, 287½ acres in Greene Co. granted to
JOHN SHAKLEFORD Nov. 24, 1786... JNO. SHAKLEFORD (LS). Wit: JOHN WHITE
(X), BARTHM. THOMPSON.

Page 109:   Oct. 15, 1793, MICHAEL IKNON of Washington to NATHAN WILLIAMS
for 18 pounds, 200 acres on CAGG CREEK, adj. MARTIN, JERMANY BECKUM...
MICHAEL IKNOR (SEAL), NANCY IKNOR (SEAL). Wit: SAMUEL JOHNSON, CHARLES
JOHNSON.

Page 110:   1785, JACOB FORTUNE to WILLIAM WASHINGTON of Charleston,
South Carolina, 287½ acres in Washington Co., granted to sd. JACOB
FORTUNE Feb. 8, last... JACOB FORTUNE ( ) (LS). Wit: HORATION MARBURY,
DAVID ROLLING (X).
        Horatio Marbury, swore to deed in Richmond Co. before THOMAS
GLASCOCK.

Pages 111-112:   Oct. 9, 1785, WILLIAM MATHEWS of Richmond Co. to WILLIAM
WASHINGTON of Charleston, S.C. for 5 shillings, 287½ acres... WILLIAM
MATTHEWS (LS) ( ). Wit: NATHAN HARRIS JP., WM. YOUNG.

Page 112:   Oct. 10, 1785, WILLIAM MATTHEWS of Richmond Co. to WILLIAM
WASHINGTON of Charleston, S.C. for 100 pounds, 287½ acres in Washington
Co... WILLIAM MATTHEWS ( ) (SEAL). Wit: NATHAN HARRIS JP., JAMES
DANDLY (DANELLY?).

Pages 113-114:   Oct. 13, 1785, MESHACH MATTHEWS of Richmond Co. to
WILLIAM WASHINGTON of Charleston, S.C. for 5 shillings, 287½ acres...
MESHACK MATTHEWS (X) (SEAL). Wit: NATHAN HARRIS JP., WM. YOUNG.

Pages 114-115:   Oct. 10, 1785, MESHACK MATTHEWS to WILLIAM WASHINGTON,
287½ acres, for 100 pounds... MESHACK MATTHEWS (X). Wit: NATHAN
HARRIS JP., JAMES DANELLY.

Pages 115-116:   Sept. 5, 1785, MORDECAI BALDWIN of Wilkes Co. to
WILLIAM WASHINGTON of Charleston, S.C. for 5 shillings, 460 acres in
Washington Co... MORDECAI BALDWIN (LS) (M). Wit: JOHN KIMBROUGH,
CHARLES WILLIAMSON.

Pages 116-117:   Sept. 5, 1785, MORDECAI BALDWIN of Wilkes Co. to
WILLIAM WASHINGTON, for 500 pounds, lease for 1 year 460 acres on Shoulder-
bone Creek... MORDECAI BALDWIN (M) (LS). Wit: JOHN KIMBROUGH, M.
WILLIAMSON JP, CHARLES WILLIAMSON.

Page 118:   1785, WILLIAM MORRIS to WILLIAM WASHINGTON of Charleston,
S.C. for 200 pounds, 287½ acres, granted March 8, last. WM. MORRIS
(LS). Wit: HORATIO MARBURY, LEOD. PEAK.

Pages 119-120:   March 5, 1795, BENJAMIN THOMPSON & ANNE his wife, to
JOSEPH THOMPSON for 500 pounds, 380 acres on Powell's Creek, Ogechee...
BENJAMIN THOMPSON (SEAL), ANNE THOMPSON (SEAL). Wit: JESSE THOMPSON,
MALCOM JOHNSTON.

Pages 120-121:   Nov. 12, 1785, JAMES ADCOCK of Richmond Co. to WILLIAM
WASHINGTON for 200 pounds, 287½ acres, in Washington Co., JAMES
ADCOCK ( ) (LS), ELIZABETH ADCOCK ( ) (LS). Wit: JAMES HABLETON JP.,
NEHEMIAH JONES?.

Page 121:   April 9, 1794, DAVID FELPS & FELBY his wife, to AZARIAH
BUTTS, all of Hancock Co. for 100 pounds, 100 acres, land surveyed for
WILLIAM HORTON. BULL'S line, GEORGE GRAY'S line... DAVID FELPS (SEAL),
FELBY FELPS (SEAL). Wit: JOHN MCCULLOH, JOHN BUTTS (X).

Page 122: May 8, 1785, RICHARD CALL of Augusta to BENJAMIN THOMPSON of Wilkes Co. for 100 pounds, 500 acres... RICHD. CALL. Wit: R. MIDDLETON, JOHN GERMANY.

Page 123: BENJAMIN SIMS of Fairfield County, South Carolina to JOHN WOOTEN of same, one negroe girl, for 65 pounds, BENJN. SIMS. Wit: HARD WOOTEN (H), JOHN MOORE. Nov. 15, 1789. Test: WILLIAM LIGG (PIGG?).

Pages 123-124: Jan. 4, 1793, SAMUEL WILSON of Washington Co. to JACOB DUCKWORTH of same, for 80 pounds, land adj. ROBERT CHRISTMAS... SAMUEL WILSON (SEAL). Wit: ISUM PEACOCK, DEMUS WHITE, ROBERT WILSON.

Page 125: April 5, 1794, JOHN NEWNIM of Washington Co. to WILLIAM WELSH of Hancock Co. for 40 pounds, land on Turkey Creek, adj. VAN LOFTON's line... granted to JOHN NEWNIM May 16, 1793... JOHN NEWNIM (X) (LS). Wit: DAVIS LONG JP., JOHN DUNMAN (X).

Pages 126-127: Dec. 15, 1792, HADDON PARHAM & ARGEAN his wife of Wilkes Co. to MATHEW PARHAM of Columbia Co. 6r 48 pounds, 257 acres adj. REES, AR. SMITH. HADDON PARHAM (SEAL). Wit: JOHN PARHAM, ELIZABETH KELLY.

Pages 127-128: March 25, 1795, THOMAS LAMAR, Sheriff of Hancock Co., RICHARD CALL, land on head waters of Little Ogechee, 500 acres... against the Tenements of RICHARD CALL, sold to HENRY CANDLER at house of JOHN WHATLEY... THOMS. LAMAR Shff. H. C.. Wit: P. BOYLE, J. K. CANDLER.

Pages 128-129: Feb. 25, 1795, PERMAN FLOYD of Warren Co. to JONATHAN MILLER of Hancock Co. for 50 pounds, 287½ acres... PERAMAN FLOYD (SEAL). Wit: CHARLES LIGTHAM? (STATHAM), JOSEPH CARTER (X).

Pages 129-130: Feb. 5, 1795, JOEL MCCLENDON & LUCY his wife of Hancock Co. to THOMAS WYNNE for 70 pounds, 287½ acres, part of a grant to BENJAMIN MCCORMICK 1784... JOEL MCCLENDON (SEAL), LUCY MCCLENDON. Wit: JAMES REES, JOHN WYNNE (X).

Pages 130-131: June 18, 1791, HENRY HOUSTON of Greene Co. to NATHANIEL TATUM, for 100 pounds, land adj. JACKSON & by land surveyed for COL. WILLIAMSON, granted May 17, 1784. HEN. HUSTON (SEAL). Wit: HEN. GRAYBILL JP. SETH TATUM. Renunciation of dower by KEZIAH HOUSTON (X).

Page 131: DANIEL WOOTEN of Fairfield Co., S.C. for 80 pounds, to JOHN WOOTEN, a negro woman Cate Aug. 3, 1788.

Pages 131-132: Dec. 6, 1790, JAMES MORGAN of Washington to STEPHEN BROWN for 20 pounds, 200 acres, adj. WOOD WILKISON CARR?... JAMES MORGAN (SEAL). Wit: WILLIAM MORGAN, WILLIAM TANT (FANT?).

Pages 132-133: Nov. 20, 1792, THOMAS PICKERT of Washington Co. to AMRK STROUD, for 5 shillings, 500 acres, adj. JOHN PARKER, BENJAMIN THOMPSON... THOMAS PICKART (X) (SEAL). Wit: JOHN TAPLEY, JAMES HUDDLESTON.

Pages 133-134: March 9, 1795, AJONADAB REED of Hancock Co. to REUBEN REED of same, for 100 pounds, 300 acres on Powell's Creek... WIDDOW SPIKES, ROBERT BROWN, OAKES... AJONADAB REED (SEAL). Wit: THOMAS CRIDILLE, BENJAMIN REED.

Pages 134-135: July 4, 1794, JOHN LIDDALL DIXON of Washington Co. to PHILIP COOK of Hancock Co. for 60 pounds, 287½ acres granted to JAMES YORK, Sept. 16, 1785... sold to DIXON by JOHN DENNIS Tax Collector... on Rocky Creek, J. L. DIXON (SEAL). Wit: JOHN COOK Senr., JOHN COOK, Junr., JNO. HARBERT JP.

Pages 135-136: Nov. 18, 1794, SALLEY RAINS of Hancock Co., Ga. to STITH PARHAM of York Co., South Carolina, for 235 pounds... THOMAS

RAINS & SALLY his wife... JOHN TRIPPS Widdows... WIATT COLLIER'S line...
287½ acres... THOMAS RAINS (LS), SALLEY RAINS (LS). Wit: JAS. REES,
WILLIAM BIGGINS, FRANCIS MORLAND.

Pages 136-137:   June 2, 1792, JAMES MORGAN of Washington Co., to ASA
MORGAN of same, for 30 pounds, part of a grant to SAMUEL CAMP on Little
Ogeechee... Mr. BROWN's corner... JAMES MORGAN (SEAL). Wit: ABNER
PEARCY, HARMAN RUNNELS JP.

Page 137:   Oct. 9, 1793, GEROGE COTTON of Greene Co., to JOSIAH BEALLE,
for 37 pounds, six shillings & 8 pence... land adj. MOSES POWELL, 50
acres on Shoulderbone Creek, GEORGE COTTON (SEAL). Wit: JEREMIAH
BEALLE, LARTHY BEALIE.

Pages 137-138:   May 28, 1794, REUBEN REED of Hancock Co. to JOHN REED
of Wilkes Co., adj. BLAKEY's land, OATES odl line... REUBEN REED (LS).
Wit: JAMES SLAUGHTER, THOS. CREDILLE.

Pages 138-139:   May 29, 1794, AJONADAB REED of Hancock Co. to JOHN REED
of Wilkes Co. for 50 pounds, 100 acres in Hancock Co... AJONADAB REED
(LS). Wit: SAMUEL SLAUGHTER, THOMAS CREDILLE, ABRAHAM WOMACK JP.

Page 139:   June 26, 1790, RICHARD SIMMONS of Wilkes Co. to NATHANIEL
TATUM of Greene Co. for 60 pounds, 287½ acres... RICHARD SYMMONDS (LS).
Wit: NOYAL NELMS, JOHN MCCLAIN.

Pages 140-141:   March 9, 1794, ELIZABETH THOMPSON, widow of Warren Co.,
to JAMES HUTCHINSON of Hancock Co. for 10 pounds, 9 acres, part of 200
granted to ELIZABETH THOMPSON, Oct. 12, 1785... (not finished, no
signatures...).

Page 141:   Nov. 11, 1793, Rec'd of THOMAS HARTON 100 pounds for 3
negroes... WILLIAM MCINVAIL. Wit: EDMD. CROWDER, SAML. LAWRENCE.
Sworn to Juen 26, 1795.

Pages 141-142:   March 3, 1795, THOMAS LAMAR Sheriff of Hancock Co. to
PETER BOYLE & JAMES WOOD, against the good & Co. of RICHARD CALL, 500
acres on Little Ogechee, sold at house of JOHN WHATLEY, THOS. LAMAR
Shff. H. C. (LS). Wit: HEN. GRAYBILL JP., J. K. CANDLER.

Pages 142-143:   Jan. 31, 1795, JOHN RAGAN & SUSANAH his wife to JOHN
PIEARCE for 100 pounds, 390 acres on Island Creek, adj. STRICKLIN's,
RAGAN's, WALLER's, SCARLETT's, JOHN RAGAN (SEAL), SUSANNA RAGAN (SEAL).
Wit: JNO. HARBERT, SAMUEL SCOTT ( ).

Pages 143-144:   May 14, 1795, ASA SIMMONS of Oglethorpe Co. to WILLIAM
FREEMAN of Hancock Co. for 60 pounds 400 acres in Hancock, originally
in Washington, granted to MORDICAI CHANDLER, Sept. 20, 1792... GREY'S
land, BEIN'S LAND, CHACKIN'S land, also a tract to ABEDNEGO CHANDLER,
adj. the first. ASA SIMMONS (SEAL). Wit: MALCOM JNOSON, JOHN BURCH.

Pages 145-146:   Aug. 28, 1792, ABSALOM HANDS to FRANCIS TRAWICK &
JAMES YOUNGBLOOD, Deacons of the Baptist Church of the Watery Fork
of Buffelow, all of Washington Co., Ga., for 10 shillings, 3 acres, adj.
CHIRSMUS, signed ABSALOM ELAND (LS). Wit: JOHN BEAUCHAMP, BARY. POPE.

Pages 146-147:   Jan. 5, 1795, JAMES MORGAN of Hancock Co. to JOSEPH
THOMPSON of same for 100 pounds, 200 acres, granted to JAMES MORGAN,
one tract in Wilkes the other in Washington... JAMES MORGIN (SEAL),
CATEY MORGAN (X) (SEAL). Wit: JOHN TAPLEY, CHARLES PRICE, JACOB COLE,
H. RUNNELS JP.

Pages 147-148:   Nov. 28, 1793, DRURY THOMPSON & MARTHA his wife to
JONES PERSONS of Wilkes Co. for 100 pounds, land in Greene Co. on
Beaverdam Creek, adj. LAWRENCE's line, BERCHES line, ANDREW land 9 acres
cut off for Public Worship, 231 acres, 200 of which was granted to
ELIZABETH THOMPSON & 41 granted to MIDDLETON bought of Mr. HAMILL.. DREWRY
THOMPSON (SEAL), MARTHA THOMPSON (X) (SEAL). Wit: TURNER PERSONS,
JEREMIAH THOMPSON.

Page 150:   GEORGE BASSITT & ELIZABETH his wife of Wilkes Co. to JOHN
WRIGHT of Columbia Co. for 20 pounds, 287½ acres in Washington Co., adj.
KIMBROUGH, RAE, EVANS, Dated ___ 1792 (deed dim), GEORGE BASSITT (LS).
Wit: WILLIAM HARDWICH, THOMAS HARRY, JAMES WRIGHT.

Pages 150-151:   Oct. 20, 1792, SUSANNAH COLEMAND, late SUSANNAH ROSEBORO
widow of GEORGE ROSEBORO, dec'd... and DREADSIL PACE and Wife BETSEY,
late BETSEY ROSEBORO, dau. of sd. GEORGE... (deed partially obliterated).
Wit: BEN. OLIVER, Junr., JNO. HAMILL JP.

(These last few page No's uncertain due to poor condition of deeds,
the next positive pg. No. is 154.)

Page 151:   JOHN BOOTH of Greene Co., ZACHARIAH BOOTH, his son, 287 acres
where on he now lives... formerly intended property of son JOHN BOOTH...
JOHN SIMMONS line, July 27, 1793. JOHN BOOTH.

Page 154:   April 6, 1795, JAMES DOWDLE of Hancock Co. to JOHN WALLER
of same for 50 pounds, land on North fork of Island Creek, adj. lands
of JOHN RAGIN, 287½ acres... JAMES DOWDLE (SEAL), PRUDENCE DOWDLE (SEAL).
Wit: (not legible).

Page 155:   Oct. 1, 1795, JESSE CONNELL & PENELOPE his wife of Hancock
Co. to THOMAS COOPER of same for 100 pounds, 137 acres on Beaverdam
Creek of Ogechee... JESSE CONNELL (LS). Wit: HEN. GRAYBILL, JERARD
BURCH.

Page 156:   March 1, 1795, PETER JACKSON of Hancock Co. for 100 pounds,
to JAMES ORRICK, 200 acres at head of Powell's Creek in Hancock Co., part
of a grant Dec. 10, 1793... PETER JACKSON (SEAL). Wit: EDND CRIWDER,
AS. HARDY JP.

Pages 156-157:   July 8, 1794, ROBERT MIDDLETON of Augusta to JAMES
ORRICK, for 100 pounds, 37 acres, on Powell's Creek, part of a 1000 acre
tract, adj. JAMES HUTCHINSON's line... R. MIDDLETON (SEAL). Wit: JAS.
HARVEY JP., WM. LORD.

Pages 157-158:   Oct. 24, 1795, JOSEPH THOMPSON of Hancock Co. to
BENJAMIN THOMPSON Senr. of same, for 150 pounds, land adj. EDMD. CALLEY,
JOHN GREER, on Powell's Creek, 150 acres, granted to BENJAMIN THOMPSON
1784... JOSEPH THOMPSON (LS). Wit: HEN. GRAYBILL, JP., JESSE THOMPSON.

Pages 158-159:   Dec. 1, 1792, JOHN RAGAN of Greene Co. to JOHN PARKER
for 35 pounds, 143 3/4 acres on Island Creek, adj. Widow PARKER, JOHN
RAGAN, BATTLE's land... JOHN RAGAN (LS). Wit: JOHNE PARKER, A. COMER
JP.

Pages 159-160:   Nov. 6, 1790, JOHN PUGH & ELIZABETH his wife of Wilkes
Co. to BENJAMIN HUTCHINSON of Green Co. for 100 pounds... JOHN PUGH
(LS), ELIZABETH PUGH (X) (LS). Wit: WILLIAM HUTCHINSON, PETER HUTCHIN-
SON, A. COMER (acreage not given in above deed).

Pages 160-161:   June 20, 1785, WILLIAM WALKER of Wilkes Co. to PETER
COFFEE for 125 pds. 250 acres on Ogechee... WILLIAM WALKER (SEAL). Wit:
THOMAS CREDELLE, JAMES CAREY (X), JAMES KINDRICK.

Pages 161-162:   Oct. 12, 1795, PETER JACKSON of Greene Co. to JOHN
JOHNSTON, for 100 pounds, 200 acres on Powell's Creek, in Hancock Co.,
adj. SLAUGHTER, JAMES HARD, JOHN CAIN, PETER JACKSON (SEAL). Wit: JOHN
ROGERS, THOMAS CREDILLE, THOS. SPARKS, ABRAHAM WOMACK JP.

Pages 162-163:   Nov. 10, 1795, JAMES HARVEY & SARAH his wife to JOSEPH
COOPER all of Hancock Co., for 100 pounds, 250 acres on Beaverdam of
Ogechee, adj. NEEDHAM JERNIGAN, JOSEPH COOPER and others, JAMES HARVEY
(SEAL), SAREY HARVEY (SEAL). Wit: BETSEY GRAYBILL, HEN. GRAYBILL JP.

Page 163:   Dec. 2, 1795, SAMUEL BRASWELL of Hancock Co. to ARTHUR
DANIELLY, for 50 pounds, 200 acres in Washington Co. on Sandhill Creek,
SAMUEL BRASILL (SEAL). Wit: EDMOND ABERCROMBIE, EDWARD MOORE, Junr.,
HEN. GRAYBILL.

Page 164:   Jan. 4, 1796, WILLIS WHATLEY of Hancock Co. to JAMES LANGFORD
for 50 pounds, 50 acres... WILLIS WHATLEY (SEAL). Wit: JOHN HAMILTON,
DUKE HAMILTON.

Pages 165-166:   Sept. 4, 1785, WILLIAM BRADY of Wilkes Co. to WILLIAM
TRIPLETT of Augusta for 100 pounds, adj. DAVID METCALF, JAMES ALEXANDER,
287½ acres on Rocky Creek, WILLIAM BRADY (SEAL). Wit: P. CLYMA, JOHN
KING JP.

Pages 167:   Sept. 5, 1785, WILLIAM BRADY of Wilkes Co. to WILLIAM
TRIPLETT of Augusta, 287½ acres on Rocky Creek, WILLIAM BRADY (SEAL).
Wit: P. CLYMA, JOHN MCCARTY, JOHN KING JP.

Page 168:   July 6, 1792, JAMES ALFORD Gent. and SUZANNA his wife to
WILLIAM DICKSON for 100 pounds, 287½ acres, on Shoulderbone, adj. CHARLES
BURK, BARNETT... JAMES ALFORD (SEAL), LURANER ALFORD (SEAL. Wit:
FREDERICK ASHFIELD, JAMES WOODS.

(Apparently some pages missing here.)

Page 171 (?): To WILLIAM MINOR JUNR... R. BROOKE. Wit: E. LEISHMAN,
HUBARD BONNER. Jan. 23, 1795, JOHN DANIELLY of Washington Co. to JOHN
CURRIE & WILLIAM MINOR of Hancock, for 60 pounds, 254 acres (signatures
obliterated). JOHN DANIELY ( ) (SEAL). Wit: ROBERT MCGINTY, AARON
MCKENZIE. (Found on following page.)

Page 172:   Rec'd of WILLIAM MINOR at Augusta, a draft on Mr. JOSEPH
MILLER for 29 pounds, and on Mr. FREDK SIMMS for 21 pounds, for a mulatto
girl property of MATTHEW JOHNSTON. Signed: DAVID REID. Wit: JOSEPH
WARE, PHILIP CLAYTON JP.

Page 172:   Wilkes Co., Washington, Dec. 7, 1794, CHARLES WILLIAMSON sold
to WILLIAM MINOR, Junr. 2 Negroes, CHAS. WILLIAMSON. Wit: PETER
WILLIAMSON, Junr. (other wit. illegible.).

Page 173:   Feb. 13, 1794, THOMPSON COLMAN of Wilkes Co. to JAMES BONNER
of Hancock Co.... THOMPSON COLMAN & ELIZABETH his wife... for 100 pounds
287½ acres on Town Creek, adj. BISHOP, BECKCOME, MOSLEY, ISLAND, platt
obtained by SOLOMON BECKCOM of Washington Co., THOMPSON COLEMAN (SEAL).
Wit: JEREMIAH BONNER, ROBERT BONNER.

Pages 173-174:   June 24, 1795, JAMES BONNER of Hancock Co. to WILLIAM
MINOR of same, 321 Spanish milled dollars, 287½ acres (same as above)...
JAMES BONNER (SEAL). Wit: __ RUNNELS, JOHN CURRIE, JOHN MCKENZIE JP.

Page 175:   Jan. 28, 1795, BENJAMIN ANDERSON of Hancock Co. to JOHN
CURRIE & WILLIAM MINOR of same known as JOHN CURRIE & COMPANY, for 46
dollars, 46 acres granted to sd. ANDERSON 1790, adj. ROBERT FLOURNOY,
JOHN PINKSTON... BENJAMIN ANDERSON (SEAL). Wit: (names obliterated).

Page 176:   March 14, 1792, CHARLES BURKE of Wilkes Co. to ROBERT
ABERCROMBIE,for 100 pounds, granted to MICHAEL SMALLEY Feb. 21, 1785,
land on Shoulderbone Creek, of Oconee River... CHARLES BURK (B) (SEAL).
Sit: (names not given).
       Rec'd of WILLIAM F. BOOKER, $350, for negroes property of
WILLIAM MOORE, Dec. 1, 1795, THOMAS LAMAR, Shff. Wit: EDMD. CROWDER JP.,
EDWARD MOORE.

Page 177:   Rec'd of WILLIAM F. BOOKER $530 for negroes of WILLIAM MOORE,
Dec. 1, 1795, THOS. LAMAR Shff. (same Wit.). Snother receipt same as
above.

Pages 177-182:   Aug. 7, 1795, THOMAS GLASCOCK, Marshall of Dist. of
Ga. to FANNY FORSYTH of Richmond Co. relict of ROBERT FORSYTH, whereas
WILLIAM MCWHANN obtained a judgment against ROBERT FORSYTH, for $1485,
several tracts totalling 4424 acres, adj. BOGGY SHELMAN, FONTAIN, HENRY
LAND, THOMPSON, ADERSON, BEZMAN SHELMAN, tract adj. POWELL & COBB, tract
adj. FRANCIS BOYKIN, ANDREW ROE, EZEKIEL COBB... tract on Ogechee, tract
adj. WILLIAMSON's swamp... tract adj. HENRY WOODS, tract adj. JOSEPH
MCMATHIS, tract adj. BENJAMIN JONES, SIMEON JONES, tract adj. ROBERT
POLLARD, tract adj. GEORGE SMITH, tract adj. Mr. BRITTON... all foregoing
in Washington Co. tract in Camden Co. on Pagins Creek, tract on Great
Sattilla R., tract on Broad River in Franklin Co. adj. WILLIAM ADKIN,
tract adj. STAFFORD's land on Oconee R., adj. WILLIAM DEAN, tract in
Burke Co., adj. SAMUEL BARBER. THOMAS GERVINS, (References for all tracts
given, 29 in all.) THOMAS GLASCOCK, Marshall (LS). Wit: JOHN WILLSON
JP., ___ MIMMONS

Pages 182-183:   June 2, 1795, JAMES RICHARDS Sheriff of Richmond Co. to
FANNY FORSYTH for 28 pounds, 5000 acres in Greene Co., adj. JOHN PETER
WAGNON, originally granted to sd. WAGNON. JAS. RICHARDS (LS). Wit:
J. MIMMONS, ROBERT F. MURDOCK.

Pages 183-184:   July 14, 1787, JOHN PETER WAGNON & REBECCA to ROBERT
FORSYTH of Augusta, for 5000 pounds, granted 1786, adj. BRITTON's land,
J. O. WAGNON (LS), REBECCA WAGNON (LS). Wit: R. MIDDLETON JP, ___ COBBS,
JP.

Page 185:   May 17, 1790, CHARLES BURKE & PHEBE BURKE of Wilkes Co. to
ROBERT CHAMBERS of same for 250 pounds, 287½ acres in Greene Co. on
Shoulderbone Creek, CHARLES BURK (SEAL), PHEBE BURK (SEAL). Wit: M.
WADDEL, ALEXR. REID JUNR.

Pages 186:   JOHN POUND of Hancock Co. to JONATHAN THOMAS 80 barrels of
good, sound Indian Corn, 2 bay mares & colt for any claims... JOHN
POUND. Wit: JOEL POUND, JOHN CASELBERRY (C), RICHD. BONNER JP.
           An Inventory of the property of ELISHA GORE, now in jail of
Hancock County charged with horse stealing, a 3 year old boy and cash
Five and ¼ dollars. Oct. 1795.
           AARON MCKENZIE SENR. of Hancock Co. had his mark recorded
Dec. 23, 1795 which was a crop in each ear, and two slits in the right.
           JOEL MCCLENDON Esqr. had his mark recorded the same day, and
underslope in each ear and a hole in the right.

Pages 186-187:   (Deed very dim.) EDWARD PRICE to JAMES SHEPPARD.

Pages 187-188:   Jan. 16, 1796, EMANUEL WAMBERSIE of Savannah to HARMAN
LEHOY & JACOB LEHOY for 5 shilling, land on Ogechee originally granted
to JOHN PETER WAGNON... (deed dim). E. WAMBERSIE (LS). Wit: MICHL
F. HOUGHTON, PETER J. CARNES.

Page 189:   Feb. 7, 1794, JAMES SHEPPARD of Edgefield Co., South Carolina
to BRUCE GAITHER of Ga. for 55 pounds, land in Hancock Co. on Twelve
Mile Beaverdam, granted Oct. 13, 1785, adj. at time of survye, AARON
GRIER, MAJOR SHEPPARD's... JAMES SHEPPARD (SEAL). Wit: ALEXR. REID JP.,
J. NELSON.

Pages 189-190:   Dec. 31, 1795, ROBERT ABERCROMBIE of Warren Co. to
HENRY TURNER of Hancock Co. for 50 pounds, land on road from Sparta to
Chamber's mill, 191 acres, adj. SAMUEL HARRIS, JAMES WILLIAM GREEN,
WILLIAM DICKSON... ROBERT ABERCROMBIE (SEAL). Wit: GEO. HARGRAVES,
ETHD. WOOD JP.

Page 190:   Jan. 2, 1794, NATHAN BARNETT of Wilkes Co. to JOEL MCCLENDON
of Hancock Co. for 100 pounds, 187½ acres on Fort Creek, granted to
BENJAMIN MCCORMICK, sold to JOHN BURFORD, granted 1784... NATHAN BARNETT
(SEAL). Wit: STEPHEN KIRK, JOHN MARTIN (X)

Pages 190-191:   Jan. 2, 1794, NATHAN BARNETT to STEPHEN KIRK for 50
pounds, 100 acres on Fork Creek, granted to BENJAMIN MCCORMICK... NATHAN
BARNETT (SEAL). Wit: JOEL MCCLENDON, JOHN MARTIN (X).

91

Page 191:   Aug. 10, 1793, JOHN TRIPPE of Green Co. to JOHN WHITEHURST, for 40 pds., 50 acres... JOHN TRIPPE (SEAL). Wit: WM. BIGGINS, BETSY BIGGINS (X).

Page 192:   Jan. 29, 1796, HENRY PARRISH & MARYANN his wife of Hancock Co. to ARTHUR DANIELLY for $500, 287½ acres on Derrisoe Creek... HENRY PARRISH (X), MARYANN PARRISH (X). Wit: J. LANFORD JP.
          DANIEL RICHARDSON to dau. POLLY THOMAS, wife of WILLIAM THOMAS, negro woman... DANIEL RICHARDSON (SEAL). Wit: JNO. THOMAS, JUNR.

Page 193:   JOHN THOMAS, Junr., sold to WILLIAM THOMAS of Hancock Co. 3 negroes, JNO. THOMAS JUNR. (SEAL). Wit: JOSIAH THOMAS, SARAH THOMAS, R. THOMAS.
          Aug. 19, 1794, MOSES MATHEWS of Wilkes Co. to ZACHARIAH BOOTH of Hancock Co. for 100 pounds, 287½ acres on Rocky Creek... MOSES MATHIS SENR. (SEAL) (X). Wit: JOHN BOOTH, SENR., MOSES MATHEWS, JESSE MATHEWS.

Pages 193-194:   Aug. 3, 1795, JOHN BOOTH SENR. to JOHN JONES, for 5 pounds, 90 acres, JOHN BOOTH (SEAL). Wit: J. LANFORD.

Pages 194-195:   Dec. 26, 1794, DANIEL CONNER & MARTHA his wife to WILLIAM ADAMS, for 10 pounds, (acreage obliterated) DANIEL CONNER (SEAL), MARTHA CONNER (O) (SEAL). Wit: HENRY CHAMBERS, CORNELIUS CLARK, JAS. ADMS JP.

Pages 195-196:   March 26, 1794, SAMUEL REED SENR. of Hancock Co. to ABRAHAM REID for 100 pounds, 287½ acres on Twelve mile Beaverdam Creek, granted 1784, to STEPHEN BISHOP conveyed from him to SAMUEL REID Senr. SAML. REID (SEAL). AGNESS REID (X) (SEAL). Wit: LOWDY CARUTH, Mr. REID.

Pages 196-197:   Jan. 7, 1792, SAMUEL ELLIOTT of Green Co. to GEORGE PARKER, for 80 pds. land on Branches of Shoulderbone Creek, adj. JOHN MCCOY, granted Jan. 25, 1785, SAML. ELIOT (SEAL). Wit: JOHN JACK, JOHN SHACKELFORD, MOSES SHELBY.

Pages 197-198:   Nov. 27, 1795, MAJOR THOMAS GORDON of Newberry Co., South Carolina, to BENJAMIN GORDON of Hancock Co. for $300, 143 3/4 acres surveyed for GEORGE GRIZZLE, adj. THOMAS BRANTLY... THOS. GORDON (SEAL). Wit: JAMES ORR, JOHN TRIPPE, DAVID DICKSON JP.

Page 198:   THEODOCIUS TURK living on Island Creek having his mark entered on record is all follows viz. A smooth croop in the right ear and an upper and under keel in the left. Feb. 29, 1796.
          JOHN RAGAN, Esq. living in Island Creek his mark -- a crop off the right ear and an underslope in the left. Feb. 29, 1796.
          March 5, 1793, JOSEPH CARSON of Washington Co. to AUSTIN MORRIS for 85 pounds, 220 acres on Little Ogechee... JOSEPH CARSON (SEAL). Wit: JOHN BROWN, THOMAS RICKARD.

Page 199:   May 10, 1793, ROBERT TATE of Washington to AUSTIN MORRIS for 70 pounds, land originally granted to HENRY TATE, Jan. 17, 1787, HENRY TATE being old and of South Carolina gave power to attorney to ROBERT TATE. ROBERT TATE (SEAL). Wit: ALLEN JENKINS, P. BOYLE JP.

Page 1

JAMES CHRISTOPHER and JAMES HARVEY Admnrs. of HENRY GREYER?, dec'd.
Security, bond for 1000L=lbs Sterling, dated 12 May 1794.

NANCY LAWSON and JOHN THOMAS Admnr. of the estate of JOHN LAWSON, dec'd
and WILLIAM THOMAS Security, bond for 1000L=lbs Sterl. Dated 12 March
1796.

WILLIAM WRIGHT, JNR., Admnr. of estate of WILLIAM WRIGHT, SENR. and
THOMAS LOW Security - bond for 1000 lbs. Sterl. Dated 29 Feb. 1796.

JOHN BANK, Admnr. of the estate of JOHN NICHOLAS dec'd and JAMES HARVEY
and WALTER HAMILTON, Security, Bond for 1000L=lbs Sterl. Dated ?9th
April 1795.

SARAH PARKER, Admnr. of estate of JACOB dec'd and ALLEN BURTON, Security,
bond 1000L=lbs Sterl. Dated 13 Oct. 1794.

JANE STROTHER and RICHARD STROTHER, Admnr. of estate of JOHN STROTHER,
dec'd., THOMAS KING and JOHN STROTHER, JUNR. Security. Bond for 1000L=
lbs Sterl. Dated 11 June 1796.

THOMAS CLARK, Admnr. of estate of JOHN CLARK, JUNR. dec'd. and WILLIAM
CLARK and JESSE CLARK Securities. Bond for 1000L=lbs Sterl. Dated
30 Oct. 17__.

MARY WOOTIN and JAMES CATHELL Admnr. of estate of JOHN WOOTEN, dec'd
and ELIJAH CLARK and JESSE THOMPSON Securities. Bond 2000L=lbs Sterl.
Dated 16 Sept. 1794.

ELIZABETH MORRIS Admnx. and JOEL BUCKNER Admnr. of HENRY MORRIS, dec'd.
and JOHN STROTHER Security. Bond for 1000L=lbs. Sterl. Dated 21. Feb.
1795.

JANE HUNTER Admnx. of the estate of JOHN PINKLETON dec'd and JAMES
BONNER and DAVID PINKLETON Securities, bond for 1000L=lbs. Sterl.
Dated 1 Sept. 1796.

SARAH PRITCHETT and PHILIP PRITCHETT Admns. of estate of BENJAMIN
PRITCHETT dec'd. WM. TRIPPE and JESSE GREGG Securities. Bond for 1000L=
lbs. Sterl. Dated 9 Oct. 1795.

JOHN FLOYD Admnr. estate of GEORGE BULOCK (?) bond for 100L=lbs. Sterl.
Dated 10 May 1796.

DAVIS MCGEE Admnr. of estate of ELIJAH MCGLAMR.? dec'd and JOHN LAMAR
Security bond for 1000L=lbs. Sterl. Dated ___ Oct. 1794.

MATTHEW HARRIS and WM. COC___ Admnrs. of estate of WILLIAM HARRIS, dec'd.
and WILLIAM WEBB Security, bond for 1000L=lbs. Sterl. Dated 23 March
1796.

Page 2

EDMOND CROWDER Admnr. of estate of WILLIAM MCINVAIL and PETER BIRD and
WILLIAM BROWN, Securities, bond for 1000L=lbs. Sterl. Dated 23 Sept.
1795.

HENRY CHAMBERS, Admnr. of estate of JAMES CHAMBERS, dec'd. and ROBERT
CHAMBERS Security, bond for 1000L=lbs. Sterl. Dated 8 August 1794.

SARAH HUCKEBY, Admnx. of estate of THURSBY BROWN, dec'd. and LOYD KELLEY and WM. CHANDLER Securities, bond for $500, dated 30 Jan. 1802.

WILLIAM REES, Admnr. of WILLIAM PRIDE dec'd and HAMLIN LEWIS and EDMOND ABERCROMBIE Securities, bond for $1500 dated 30 Jan. 1802.

ARCHIBALD DEVEREUX, Admnr. of estate of JOSEPH M. WOOD, dec'd and URIAH THWEATT Securities, bond for $500, dated 3 Aug. 1801.

JOHN ACKWORTH obtained letters temporary to collect the estate of WILLIAM ESPEY, dec'd. Security JOHN FREEMAN and JAS. HALL, bond for $500, dated 25 July 1801.

JOHN ACKWORTH obtained letters temporary to collect estate of SAM MOORE, dec'd, Securities JOHN FREEMAN and JAS. HALL. Bond $500, dated 25 July 1801.

JOHN ACKWORTH obt. letters temporary to collect estate of THOMAS FINNY dec'd, Security JOHN FREEMAN and JAS. HALL. Bond $500, dated 25 July 1801.

JOHN ACKWORTH obt. letters temporary to collect estate of JOSEPH SCOTT dec'd., Securities JOHN FREEMAN and JAMES HALL. Bond $500, dated 25 July 1801.

BENJAMIN TEMPLE, Admnr. of estate of PETER TEMPLE dec'd., JOHN TURNER and JAMES BONNER, Securities, bond for $2000, dated 24 April 1802.

JAMES EVANS, Admnr. of estate of JOSEPH DOWDLE dec'd. and JOHN LUCAS, Security, bond $500 dated 1 Sept. 1801.

ANTHONY BUTTS, Admnr. of estate of JONATHAN JOHNS, dec'd., JOHN WILSON, AZARIAH BUTTS and JOHN BUTTS Securities, bond for $2000, dated 5 May 1802.

JONATHAN DAVIS, Admnr. of estate of ROBERT PICKARD dec'd. and SAM_EWING and JOEL BUCKNER, Securites. Bond for $500 dated 24 May 1802.

Page 3

WILLIAM EVERATT and JOHN EVERATT, Admnr. of estate of ALBRIGHT EVERATT dec'd. ROBERT STRIPLAND and DAVID EVERATT, Securities. Bond for $3000 dated 29 Nov. 1800.

FRANCES SHAKLEFORD and JAMES SHAKELFORD, Admnr. of estate of JOHN SHAKELFORD dec'd. and JOHN BAILEY and ALEXANDER REID, Securities, bond for $15000 dated July 12, 1800.

ARTHUR DANNELLY and GEORGE STEPHENS, Admnr. of estate of FRANCIS DANELLY dec'd. and JOSEPH WALLER and WM. GRIGGS, Securities, bond for $1000 dated 8 March 1801.

WILLIAM SPIKES, Admnr. of estate of BYRE BYNOM dec'd. and SHADRACK ROE, Security, bond for $500 dated 5 Jan. 1801.

STEPHEN WALLER and WILLIAM NEWSON, Admnr. of estate of BENJAMIN WALLER, dec'd. and WILLIAM NEWSON, Security for $100 dated 25 Oct. 1800. (Note: in microfilm copy WILLIAM NEWSON as an Admnr. looks as if it has been erased and his name later written as a Sec.)

REUBIN SLAUGHTER, Admnr. of estate of EDWARD WORHSAM dec'd. and WILLIAM HORTON Security, bond for $700 dated 28 March 1801.

RACHEL WALLER and JOSEPH WALLER, Admnr. of estate of CHARLES WALLER dec'd. and ARTHUR DANNELLY Securities. Bond for $500, dated 28 March 1801.

JOSEPH WOODWARD and AARON WOODWARD, Admnrs. of estate of ABRAHAM WOOD-WARD, Bond for 1000L=1bs. Sterl. Dated 15 Sept. 1797.

AQUILLA DAVIDSON and LOYD KELLEY, Admnrs. of estate of JAS. DAVIDSON and WILLIAM CHANDLER and DRURY COOK, Securities, bond for $2000 dated 24 April 1802.

WILLIAM GRIGGS, Admnr. of estate of THOMAS LYONS, dec'd. and JOSHUA ASHEY and JOHN GRIGGS, Securities, Bond for $600, dated 28 March 1801.

JOHN HICKS, Admnr. of estate of HENRY DUNN dec'd. and JOSEPH HOWELL and SOLOMON PHILIPS, Securities, bond for $2000 dated 6 Jan. 1800.

ROBERT RIVERS, Admnr. of HOSEA BRADFORD dec'd. and CHARLES MILLER and JOHN HUDMON, Securities, bond for $600, dated 6 Jan. 1800.

Page 4

EDMUND CORLEY obtained letters temporary to collect estate of ISHAM THOMPSON dec'd. by giving bond for $1500 dated 16 Jan. 1800. JAMES LUCAS and NEEDHAM JERNIGAN Sec.

RISDON MOORE, JUNR., Admnr. of estate of RISDON MOORE, SENR., dec'd. and RISDON MOORE, SENR. and ISAAC BENSON Security. Bond of $1000 dated 5 April 1800.

JAMES FAIL and PHILIP SPILLERS, Admnr. of THOMAS FAIL, dec'd and JOHN COOK and JOHN GRAY Securities in a bond of $2000 dated 7 June 1800.

MARY BOWEN, Admnr. with the will annexed on the estate of EPHRIAM BOWEN dec'd. and THOMAS LAMAR, JOSEPH HOWARD Securities. Bond for $2500 dated April 5, 1800.

SAML. TINSLEY, Admnr. of estate of ROBERT ALLEN dec'd and JNO WM. DEVEREAUX and ARCHIBALD DEVEREAU Securities, bond for $100 dated April 5, 1800.

ROSEY SWINNEY and NATHL. ROBERTSON, Admnr. of estate of JOHN SWINNEY dec'd. and ROBERT HILL and ELIJAH PALMORE securities. Bond for $20000, dated 25 April 1800.

NANCY MOORE, WM. CHANDLER and EDWARD MOORE, Admnr. of estate of EDWARD MOORE, dec'd. and BENJAMIN COOK and WILLIAM JONES Securities, bond for $1000, dated 23 Jan. 1799.

ROBERT WILL, ROBERT CLARK and NATHANIEL SLEDGE, Admnrs. of estate of BARKSDALE FOSTER and JOHN KELLY, JOHN BRIDGES and LEWIS BARNES, Securities Bond for $1500, dated 5 Jan. 1801.

WM. CLARK obtained letters temporary to collect estate of JESSE CLARK, dec'd. and WM. OWSLEY Security, bond for $1000 dated 2 Sept. 1799.

JANE CATHELL and ARCHIBALD SMITH, Admnr. of estate of JAMES CATHELL, dec'd and JEHU SMITH and JOHN MONTGOMERY Securities, bond for $6000. (No date.)

THOMAS HAWKINS, Admnr. of estate of THOMAS FARLEY dec'd and ABRAHAM MILES Security, bond for $1000 dated 1 June 1801.

Page 5

NANCY FREENEY, Admnx. of estate of ELIJAH FREENY dec'd and ROBERT MCGINTY and SAMUEL HALL Securities, bond for $10,000 dated 1 June 1801.

MARY LOCKHEART, CULLEN POPE and WILLIAM RABON, Admnrs. of estate of RICHARD LOCKHEART, dec'd and JESSE POPE Security, bond for $4000, dated 25 Oct. 1800.

REBEKAH SOUTHALL and NATHANIEL SLEDGE, Admnr. of estate of JOHN SOUTHALL dec'd. and DAVID ADAMS Sec., bond for $3000, dated 3 Sept. 1800.

HENRY HARRIS, Admnr. of estate of BENJAMIN HARRIS dec'd. and JOSEPH CHAPPELL and JOHN SLEDGE, Securities, bond for $3000, dated 15 Jan. 1803.

ROBERT CLARK obtained letters temporary to collect estate of JOHN BRIDGES dec'd. CORNELIUS CLARK Security, bond given for $800 and dated 1 March 1803.

BENJAMIN THOMPSON, Admnr. of estate of NATHANIEL PARHAM dec'd. and THOMPSON BIRD and CHARLES ABERCROMBIE Securities, bond for $2000, dated 15 Jan. 1803.

PATSEY COOPER and OBADIAH RICHARDSON, Admnr. of estate of THOMAS COOPER, JUNR. dec'd. and JESSE CONNELL and ZACHARIAH MIDDLETON Securities, bond for $1000 dated 1 June 1799.

MARY REDDOCK, WILLIAM REDDOCK, JOHN REDDOCK and ALEXANDER REDDOCK, Admnr. of estate of WILLIAM REDDOCK, dec'd. and THOMAS LAMAR and GEORGE THOMPSON Securities, Bond for $5000 dated 27 Sept. 1798.

GEORGE ROSSER one of the Admnrs. of estate of JOHN BREWER, SENR. dec'd. and JOHN BAILEY and SAML. REECE Securities, bond for 3000L=1bs. Sterl. dated 15 Nov. 1798.

JOHN C. PEAK, Admnr. of estate of Hubbard Sykes dec'd and WILLIAM HAMILTON and DUKE HAMILTON Securities bond for $500, dated 22 Oct. 1798.

Page 6

JOHN BREWER JUNR., Admnr. of the estate of JOHN BREWER Senr. dec'd. and ABSALOM HARRIS and ANDREW JETER Securities, bond for 3000L=1bs. Sterl. dated 15 Nov. 1798.

JEREMIAH BONNER and HUBBARD BONNER, Admnr. of estate of ROBERT BONNER, dec'd. and JAMES BONNER and JOSEPH BONNER Securities bond for 1000L=1bs Sterl. dated 4 March 1799.

DAVID DICKSON Senr., Admnr. of estate of DAVID DICKSON and JOHN DICKSON both dec'd and DAVID DICKSON, JUNR. Security bond for $500 dated 20 Feb. 1799.

JOHN HARBERT, JOHN COOK, PHILIP COOK, Admnrs. of estate of JOHN COOK dec'd and JOHN REGAN Security, bond for 3000L=1bs. Sterl. dated 5 June 1798.

CHARLES ABERCROMBIE and MATTHEW RABUN, Admnr. of estate of MART CHAMPION dec'd. ANDERSON COMER, WILLIAM RABUN Securities, bond for 1000L=1bs. Sterl. dated 30 Dec. 1797.

THOMAS H. LANGHAM, Admnr. of estate of TOBIAS MCCLURE dec'd. JOHN FREEMAN and SAMUEL HALL Securities, bond for 1000L=1bs. Sterl. Dated 23 Jan. 1797.

SUSANNAH HAMMOND, Admnx. of estate of MARTIN HAMMON dec'd. and JAMES TURNER Security for 500L=1bs. Sterl. dated 13 Feb. 1797.

HENRY JACKSON and JOHN JACKSON, Admnrs. of estate of BENJAMIN JACKSON dec'd. JOHN STURDIVANT, ALEXANDER REID and JESSE WARREN Securities, bond for $3000, dated 3 March 1798.

EDMOND BUTLER, Admnr. of estate of JOHN BUTLER dec'd. WM. BROWN & HUBBARD BROWN Securities bond for $3000 dated 6 April 1798.

DAVID MCGEE obtained letters temporary to collect and take care of the estate of ELIJAH MCGLAMRY dec'd and ARCHIBALD SMITH SENR., Security bond given for 100L=1bs Sterl. dated 21 Aug. 1794.

SUSANAH LAWSON, Admnx. of estate of FRANCIS LAWSON dec'd and ELLINGTON MORGAN and WILLIAM SPENCER Securities, bond for $8000 dated 28 May 1803.

DAVID HENRY, Admnr. of estate of STEPHEN HENRY dec'd. and ROBERT CLARK and ELIJAH PALMORE Securities, Bond for $600, dated 28 May 1803.

BENJAMIN EVANS and POLLEY EVANS, Admnrs. of estate of JOHN T. EVANS and WILLIAM SCOTT and ISAAC EVANS Securities, bond for $1000 dated 1 June 1801.

RICHARD FRETWELL, Admnr. of estate of BURWELL YARBROUGH dec'd and JESSE GRIGG Security, bond for $200 dated 26 March 1803.

ROBERT CLARK, Admnr. of estate of JOHN BRIDGES dec'd. and JOHN SLEDGE and DAVID HENRY Securities, bond for $1000 dated 26 March 1803.

REBEKAH JOHNSTON, Admnx. of estate of WILLIAM JOHNSTON dec'd and RICHARD B. FLETCHER, WILLIAM GARRETT and THOMAS JOHNSON Securities, bond for $6000 dated 26 March 1803.

HENCHIA LARY and LARY LARY, Admnrs. of estate of DARBY LARY dec'd. and JOSEPH HOWELL and JOHN HIX Securities, bond for $1500, dated 26 March 1803.

FANNY BUTLER, Admnx. of estate of EDMOND BUTLER dec'd and JOSEPH BARKSDALE and ABNER BARKSDALE Securities, bond for $4000 dated 28 May 1803.

RISDON MOORE SENR. and DAVIS MACGEE, Admnr. of estate of JOSHUA HENNERY dec'd. and LEVIN ELLIS and OBADIAH RICHARDSON Securites, bond for $500, dated 31 Oct. 1801.

ANDERSON COMER and JOHN BARRON, Admnrs. of estate of SAMUEL BARRON dec'd. and JAMES COMER and JOH ROE Securities, bond for $3000 dated 3 March 1802.

RISDON MOORE and DAVIS MCGEE obtained letters temporary to collect the personal estate of JOSHUA KENNERLY dec'd., their Securities are: OBADIAH RICHARDSON, and LEVIN ELLIS, their bond to amt. of $500, dated July 25, 1801. But they have since obtained letters of Administration.

Page 8

NICEY COLLINS and SAMUEL HA.. Admnrs. of estate of Truett Collins dec'd. and HAMLIN LEWIS Security, bond for $500, dated 30 Jan. 1801.

ISAAC FANN, Admnr. of estate of SARAH BROWN, dec'd and LOYD KELLEY and WILLIAM CHANDLER Securities bond for $500 dated 30 Jan. 1801.

Page 9

FRANCES SHAKELFORD and JOHN SHAKELFORD, Gdns. for EDMOND SHAKELFORD and FANNY SHAKELFORD and JEREMIAH MOORE Security, bond for $4000, dated 25 Oct. 1800.

JOHN SHAKELFORD, Gdn. for NANCY SHAKELFORD and BRICE GAITHER Security bond for $3000 dated 25 Oct. 1800.

JOHN COOK, Gdn. for HENRY COOK and ISAAC COOK and JOHN HARBERT Security, bond for $4000, dated 15 Jan. 1803.

JOHN GAY, Gdn. for THOMAS GAY and PETER GRAMER and LEONARD ABERCROMBIE Security, bond for $3000, dated 25 Dec. 1802.

WILLIAM BROWN, Gdn. for OBADIAH VEST, MORTON GRAY and THOMAS CARRELL Securities, bond for $300, dated 26 June 1802.

MANCIL WOMACK, Gdn. for JOHN WOMACK and JOHN ROGERS Security, bond for $3000, dated 29 May 1802.

BETSEY LYONS Gdn. for SALLEY LYONS, NELLEY LYONS and WILLIAM LYONS and JOHN TINGLE Security, bond for $500, dated 2 April 1803.

ROBERT RIVERS, Gdn. for WILLIAM HIX and ANDERSON COMER and JOHN GREGORY, Securities bond $6000, dated 28 May 1803.

MICHAEL HARVEY, Gdn. for EVAN HARVEY and WILLIAM SPENCER and LEONARD ABERCROMBIE Securities, bond for $800, dated 28 May 1803.

HENRY BEARD, Gdn. for SOLOMON PREWETT and ARTHUR DANNELLY and MICHAEL ROGERS Securities, bond for $400, dated 28 May 1803.

WILLIAM SPENCER, Gdn. for REBEKAH HARVEY and VERLINDER HARVEY and LEONARD ABERCROMBIE and MICHAEL HARVEY Securities, bond for $1500, dated 28 May 1803.

JOHN HARVEY, Gdn. for WILLIAM HENRY WRAY and RISDON MOORE JUNR. Security bond for $1420, dated 15 Jan. 1803.

RISDON MOORE, Gdn. for EVERTON KENNERLY and JEREMIAH MOORE security, bond for $500, dated 31 Oct. 1801.

JANE CATHELL, Gdn. for ELIZABETH VAUGHAN and SAMUEL SLAUGHTER Security, bond for $1500, dated 15 Dec. 1804.

EDWD. BROADNAX, Gdn. for LUCY B. BROOKING and WM. BRIADNAX Security, bond for $2000, dated 2 Feb. 1807.

JAMES HUFF, Gdn. for BURCHELL HUFF, WILLIAM HUFF and JAMES HUFF and ANDREW JETER Security, bond for $500, dated 8 Feb. 1805.

ARCHIBALD MARTIN, Gdn. for WYATT TURNER and URIAH THWEATT Security bond for $1000, dated 30 July 1805.

STEPHEN CLEMENTS, Gdn. for DAVID CLEMENTS and THOMAS FOARD Security, bond for $5000, dated 1 Oct. 1805.

REBECAH JOHNSTON, Gdn. for JOHN JOHNSTON, MALCHAM JOHNSTON and REBEKAH JOHNSTON and RICHARD FLETCHER Security, bond for $2000, dated 28 Jan. 1804.

JETHRO JACKSON, Gdn. for BETSEY SLEDGE and ROBERT CLARK Security bond for $2000 dated 5 Jan. 1807.

RICHMOND NOLLEY, Gdn. for NATHAN NOLLEY and JOHN LUCAS Security, bond for $1600 Dated 5 Jan, 1807.

CHARLES STEWART, Gdn. for WM. TYSON, AARON TYSON and CLARY TYSON and JOHN MILLER and JOHN HALL, Securities, bond for $1000, dated 5 Jan. 1807.

ELIZABETH REID, Gdn. for POLLEY REID, WM. REID and SALLEY REID and JAMS LOW Security, bond for $4000, dated 5 Jan. 1807.

E. B. BROUDNAX, Gdn. for EDWARD V. BROOKING and WM. BROADNAX Security, bond for $2000, dated 2 Feb. 1807.

JOHN WEEKS, Gdn. for RUTH STOVALL and JOSEPH COOPER Security bond for $2000, dated 7 July 1806.

ALLEN GREEN, Gdn. for THOS. B. GREEN and WILLIAM DAVENPORT and A. MYLES Security bond for $4000, dated 5 Jan. 1807.

JOSEPH COOPER, Gdn. for POLLEY STOVALL and PLEASANT STOVALL and JOHN WEEKS Security, bond for $5000, dated 7 July 1806.

WM. BROADNAX, Gdn. for J. W. BROOKING Security E. B. BROADNAX, bond for $2000, dated 2 Feb. 1807.

SOLOMON LANGSTON, Gdn. for BETSEY KINNEY and Security Bond for $4000, dated 6 April 1807.

SHERLEY SLEDGE, Gdn. for COLLEN SLEDGE and CHAPPEL SLEDGE Security bond for $2000, dated 5 Jan. 1807.

CHAPPELL SLEDGE, Gdn. for POLLEY SLEDGE, AMEY SLEDGE and PATTEY SLEDGE and SHERWOOD SLEDGE and (MINS?) SLEDGE Security, bond for $6000, dated 5 Jan. 1807.

THOMAS CROWDER, Gdn. for ROBERT TUCKER and SAMPSON DUGGAR Security, bond for $1000, dated 5 Jan. 1807.

REUBIN BATTLE, Gdn. for JAMES B. CAIN and ISAAC BATTLE Security, bond for $600 dated 5 Jan. 1807.

HINES HOLT, Gdn. for DANIEL NOLLEY and POLLEY R. NOLLEY and SIMON HOLT Security bond for $5000, dated 5 Jan. 1807.

POLLEY TUCKER, Gdn. for ELIZA TUCKER, PATSEY TUCKER, POLLEY G. TUCKER, LUCRETIA TUCKER, SALLEY C. TUCKER, AMANDA TUCKER and WM. DAVENPORT Security, bond for $3000, dated 5 Jan. 1807.

JOHN HUMPHRIS, Gdn. for WILLIAM MOORE and CHARLES ABERCROMBIE Security bond for $2000, dated 5 Jan. 1807.

BURWELL GREEN, Gdn. for BETSEY GREEN and DOLLEY GREEN and ANDREW BAXTER Security, bond for $3000, dated 4 Jan. 1807.

ALEXANDER BELLAMY, Gdn. for JAMES BONNER and JOHN DANIEL Security, bond for $4000, dated 5 Jan. 1807.

JAMES RUNNELS, Gdn. for HARRIOTT JONES, SELATA JONES and ALLEN JONES and RICHARD B. FLETCHER, bond for $2000, dated 5 Jan. 1807.

POLLEY JONES, Gdn. for GREEN JONES and ISAAC NEWSON Security, bond for $500, dated 6 July 1807.

RANDOLPH RUTLAND, Gdn. for THOMAS JONES RUTLAND and BENJAMIN WHITFIELD Security, bond for $800, dated 7 July 1806.

WILLIAM HUDSON, Gdn. for CHARLES HUDSON, POLLEY HUDSON, JOHN HUDSON, FANNY HUDSON, LEWELLIN IRBY HUDSON, WOODLEFF SCOTT Security, bond for $8000, dated 1 Dec. 1806.

EDMUND LAND, Gdn. for ELIZABETH D. CLARK and URIAH THWEATT and WILLIAM BARNES Security, bond for $8000, dated 7 April 1806.

ROBERT WILSON, Gdn. for LEVI WILSON and JOHN MURPHY Security, bond for $1500 dated 27 Aug. 1803.

NATHANIEL WALLER, Gdn. for SHERLEY WHATLEY and JOHN HERBERT Security, bond for $1000, dated 6 July 1807.

WILLIE HILLARD, Gdn. for WILLIAM DUNN, SUSANNAH DUNN and HENRY DUNN and GEORGE LARY Security, bond for $2000, dated 1 Oct. 1807.

HENRY POPE, Gdn. for JESSE EVANS and BENJAMIN J. HARPER Security, bond for $1000, dated 6 July 1807.

WILLIAM SCURLOCK, Gdn. for POLLEY PARKER and SALLEY PARKER and ROBT. CLARK Security, bond for $1500, dated 8 Feb. 1805.

ROBERT SIMS, Gdn. for CHRISTOPHER HARRISON and JAMES HARRISON and JOHN HENDERSON Security, bond for $1300, dated Jan. 7, 1805.

GEORGE SIMMS, Gdn. for JOSEPH WILLIAMS and WILLIAM WILLIAMS and GREEN SIMMS and BURWELL GREEN Securities, bond for $4000, dated 1 Dec. 1806.

STEPHEN CLEMENTS, Gdn. for STEPHEN CLEMENTS and THOMAS FOARD Security bond for $5000, dated 1 Oct. 1850.

GEORGE RACHELS, Gdn. for ELIZABETH HOLLOMAN and MILES RACHELS, bond for $200, dated 12 May 1804.

WILLIAM DAVENPORT, Gdn. for JOHN WILSON and TEREELL BARKSDALE Security bond for $2000, dated 1 Dec. 1806.

DOLLEY PETERSON, Gdn. for REBECCA ANN PETERSON, BALLE PETERSON, MARY PETERSON and M. D. PETERSON and THOMAS PETERSON and JOHN TURNER Securities bond for $40000, dated 1 Dec. 1806.

HUBERT REYNOLDS, Gdn. for THOMAS BONNER and JOHN HERBERT Securities, bond for $5000, dated 1 Dec. 1806.

REUBIN JONES, Gdn. for POLLEY SHIPP and JAMES H. JONES Security, bond for $1000, dated 19 Aug. 1805.

RICHARD P. BROWN, Gdn. for POLLEY P. BONNER and JOHN MCKINZIE, bond for $2000, dated 7 April 1806.

WILLIAM SIMMONS, Gdn. for RACHEL ONEAL and JOHN SIMMONS and THOS. MORRIS Security, bond for $1400, dated 21 July 1807.

ROBERT LUCAS, Gdn. for CHRISTOPHER HARRISON and JAMES HARRISON and HENRY LUCAS Security, bond for $1500, dated 1 June 1807.

JOHN WALLER JUNR., Gdn. for JOHN BUSH and JOHN WALLER SENR. & WM. SPENCER Securities, bond for $500, dated 12 May 1804.

EPPS BROWN, Gdn. for PHILIP BARNES and JAMES BARNES Security, bond for $2000, dated 12 July 1805.

RICHARD SARSNETT, Gdn. for JOSEPH SARSNETT, POLLEY SARSNETT and SALLEY SARSNETT and HENRY MITCHELL, WM. BIGGINS and ROBERT RAINES, bond for $3400, dated 21 July 1804.

JAMES WALLER, Gdn. for JOHN, NANCY, ALFORD, BETSY and ASA TRAMMELL and WILLIAM THOMAS Security, bond for $3000, dated 4 May 1807.

JAMES HOGG, Gdn. for JAMES HOGG and WILLIAM HOGG and DANIEL LOW and JOHN MCCULLER Securities bond for $2000, dated 12 May 1804.

THOMAS BARNES, Gdn. for ISAAC ONEAL and THOMAS BARNES Security bond for $1500, dated 8 Sept. 1807.

JOHN LEWIS, Gdn. for JOHN LEWIS BROOKING and EDWD. BROADNAX Security, bond for $2000, dated 6 April 1807.

GRACY HOLLEY, Gdn. for JOHN HOLLEY and ELIZABETH HOLLEY and MATTHEW DERKAM and WILLIAM SPENCER Security, bond for $3000, dated 8 Sept. 1804.

DANIEL (M) or (N) elson, Gdn. for THOS. WYNN and JOSEPH COOPER Security, bond for $3000, dated ___.

WILLIAM ALEXANDER, Gdn. for MARTHA A. CLARK and CHARLES ABERCROMBIE Security, bond for $8000, dated 7 April 1806.

JOHN DOWDLE, Gdn. for SALLY DOUDLE and HENRY MITCHEL Security, bond for $600, dated 27 August 1803.

SUSANNAH LAWSON, Gdn. for SALLEY LAWSON, ANNE LAWSON and FRANCIS B. LAWSON and MARTIN MARTIN and JECAMIA MOORE Securities, bond for $2000, dated 28 Jan. 1804.

AQUILLA SCOTT, Gdn. for DANIEL SCOTT and WM. LUCKETT Security, Bond for $600, dated 2 March 1807.

HARTWELL GARY, Gdn. for POLLEY GARY, WILLIAM GARY Security JOHN TURNER and RICHARD GARY, bond for $1500, dated 1 Dec. 1806.

WILLIAM HARGROVE, Gdn. for MASON (,?) WILLIAMSON, TURNER and JECAMIAH MOORE and DUDLEY HARGROVE Security, bond for $2000, dated 5 May 1806.

Page 17

ABITHA KENDRICK, Gdn. for SALLEY KENDRICK and MARY KENDRICK and WILLIAM SPENCER and MICHAEL HARVEY Securities, bond for $3000, dated 16 March 1805.

DANIEL LOW, Gdn. for POLLEY GILBERT and JOHN BATTER Security bond for $500, dated 13 July 1805.

PRESTLEY INGRAM, Gdn. for CHARLOTTE PENN and EPHRAIM WEST and GALE LEWIS Securities, bond for $1500, dated 8 Feb. 1805.

GEO. WILLIAMS, Gdn. for NANCY WILLIAMS, BUCKNER WILLIAMS, PATRICIA WILLIAMS and JUDGE WILLIAMS and JOHN MATTHEWS Security, bond for $5000, dated 6 April 1807.

LEVIN MOORE, Gdn. for NEWBILE MOORE and JOHN MOORE and ELIJAH MOORE Securities, bond for $1000, dated 29 Oct. 1803.

THEORIUS TURK, Gdn. for MELINDA TURK and WILLIAM TURK Security, bond for $2000, dated 16 March 1805.

JOHN BURS (?) Gdn. for LEONARD JONES and EDMUND CORLEY Security, bond for $500, dated 1 Oct. 1805.

JOHN WALLER SEN. Gdn. for SARAH BUSH and JOHN WALLER JUN. and WM. SPENCER, Securities, bond for $500, dated 12 May 1804.

WILLIAM MCLELLAN, Gdn. for ROBERT BRYANT and ELIZABETH BRYANT and REUBIN SLAUGHTER Security, bond for $2000, dated 16 March 1805.

Page 18

EDMUND GILBERT, Gdn. for PATSEY GILBERT and EDMUND GARRETT Security, bond for $240, dated 6 July 1807.

JOHN BUTLER, Gdn. for JOHN GILBERT and PATSEY GILBERT and DANIEL LOW Security bond for $500, dated 13 July 1805.

JAMES BIRD, Gdn. for ERWIN BIRD, NANCY BIRD and POLLEY BIRD and ALLEN BIRD Security bond for $2000, dated 8 Feb. 1805.

SUSANNA GARY, Gdn. for PATRICK GARY, ALFRED GARY and HENRY GARY and RICHARD GARD and HARTWELL GARY Securities, bond for $2000, dated 1 Dec. 1806.

EDMOND GILBERT, Gdn. for MATILDA G. GARRETT, NARCESSA E. GARRETT and EDMOND GARRETT Security, bond for $2000, dated 6 July 1807.

JOHN CROWDER, Gdn. for REBECAH STANTON, BETSEY STANTON, POLLEY STANTON and BATT STANTON and ROBERT RUTHERFORD Security, bond for $1600, dated 16 March 1805.

WILLIAM SAUNDERS, Gdn. for POLLEY, SALLEY, JUNSEY, ELIZA. and SHEPHRED SAUNDERS and CHARLES ABERCROMBIE Security, bond for $2000, dated 8 Feb. 1805.

ROBERT H. BONNER, Gdn. for THOMAS BONNER and JARRUS BONNER and DUKE HAMILTON Security, bond for $4000, dated 7 April 1806.

WM. STANTON, Gdn. for MARY SHORT STANTON and BATT SHORT STANTON and FRANCIS JETER and WILLIAM FARRELL Securities, bond for $1200, dated 7 July 1806.

Page 19

WILLIAM CLARK, Admnr. of JESSE CLARK dec'd and EVIN HARVEY and JAMES PRICK Security, bond for $4000, dated 7 Oct. 1799.

JOHN BROWN, Admnr. of JESSE BUTLER, dec'd and ALLEN BIRD Security bond for $800, dated 8 Sept.

SELETE ASKEYS, JOSIAH ASKEY, HARDY JERNAGAN, Admnrs. of URIAH ASKEY dec'd. and HENRY GRAYBILL Security, bond $2500, dated 10 April 1806.

AMEY G. GARRETT, Admnx. of WILLIAM GARRETT dec'd. and JAMES BYRUM and COLLIER BARKSDALE Securities bond for $2000, dated 2 June 1806.

DAVID MORGAN and JOHN BUCKER SEN., Admnrs. of JOHN SHURLY dec'd. and JOHN BROWN AND JO(IE?) BUCKER Securities, bond for $500, dated 11 May 1805.

JAMES HUFF and EPPS BROWN, Admnrs. of LUNDY HUFF dec'd and HINES HOLT and ROBT. CLARK Securities, bond for ___ 15 Dec. 1804.

JNO. W. DEVEREUX and SAMIEL DEVEREUX, Admnrs. of JOHN W. DEVEREUX dec'd. and JOHN FREEMAN Security bond for $2000, dated 7 July 1806.

ELIZABETH FOSTER and WILLIAM W. BREEDLOVE, Admnrs. of SAML. FOSTER and SAMUEL BREEDLOVE and JOHN BREEDLOVE JUNR. Securities, bond for $5000, dated 17 May 1806.

JAMES THOMAS, Admnr. of WM. RYAN Dec'd. and HERBERT REYNOLDS Security bond for $3000, dated 4 May 1807.

MILLEY CARSWELL and THOMAS JONES, Admnrs. of JOHN CARSWELL dec'd and JERARD BURCH, Security, bond for $5000, dated 7 April 1806.

Page 20

JAMES HUMPHRIES and ELIZABETH HUMPHRIES, Admnrs. of ISHAM HUMPHRIES dec'd. and DENNIS GRIFFIN and REUBIN BYRUM Securities, bond for $4000, dated 8 Sept. 1804.

CARLINE M. WOOD, Admnx. and THOMAS FRIEND and BENJA. THOMPSON, Admnrs. of JAMES WOOD dec'd., and JOHN TURNER and WILL. LEE Securities bond for $10,000, dated 4 May 1807.

PRISCILLA ROGERS and DEBENA CHAPMAN Admnrs. of MICHAEL ROGERS dec'd. and THOMAS HILL Security, bond for $8000, dated 1 Oct. 1805.

HARTWELL GARY, Admnr. of JAMES GARY dec'd. and JOHN TURNER and JOHN FREEMAN Securities, bond for $8000, dated 3 Feb. 1806.

ZACHARIAS MIDDLETON Exor. of HOLLAND MIDDLETON and ROBT. OWSLEY and JESSE CONNELL Security, bond for $2000, dated 23 July 1795.

DELITHA TYSON, Admnx. of JOB TYSON dec'd and JOHN HERBIRT and MILLER ABERCROMBIE Security bond for $12,000 dated 10 Dec. 1803.

JAMES W. GREENE, Admn. of WILLIAM COWARD, dec'd. and BOLLING HALL Security, bond for $300, dated 3 Feb. 1806.

WILLIAM SCURLOCK and DANIEL SCURLOCK Exors of JOSHUA SCURLOCK dec'd. and JOHN HAMILTON Security, bond for $1000, dated 18 Aug. 1795.

SUSANNA POTTER and H. HASWELL, Admnrs. of DANIEL POTTER and PHILIP RAWLS Security, bond for $2000, dated 1 May 1806.

Page 21

MINNS SLEDGE and BENJAMIN CHAPPELL, Admnrs. of JOHN SLEDGE dec'd and CHAPPELL SLEDGE Security, bond for $8000, dated 5 Jan. 1807.

CAHPPELL SLEDGE, Admnr. of ELIZABETH SLEDGE dec'd. and SHURLEY SLEDGE Security, bond for $10,000, dated 5 Jan. 1807.

MARY FULLER, Admnx. of ISAAC FULLER and ARTHUR YOUNGBLOOD and NATHL. YOUNGBLOOD Securities, bond for $2000, dated 5 Jan. 1807.

JOHN BAILEY and EDMOND ABERCROMBIE, Admnrs. of WILLIAM BAILEY dec'd. and WILLIAM BARNES and WILLIAM ALEXANDER Securities, bond for $2000, dated 7 Feb. 1806.

SAML. REID and ALEXANDER REID, Admnr. of ANDREW REID dec'd. and WILLIAM BARNES and JECAMIAH MOORE Securities, bond for $8000, dated 6 July 1807.

DUKE HAMILTON, Admnrs. of THOMAS GORDON dec'd. and THOMAS P. HAMILTON and JAMES THWEATT Securities, bond for $10,000, dated 6 July 1807.

ARCHD. M. DEVEREUX, Admnr. of WM. CARSON, JOHN JOHNSON and OWEN FOUR-HAND dec'd. and BOLLING HALL Security, bond for $200, dated 12 May 1804.

JOHN SLEDGE, Admnr. of PHILIP BARNHART dec'd and HENRY HARRIS Security bond for $600, dated 16 March 1805.

WILLIAM HUDSON and THOMAS HUDSON, Admnrs. of IRBY HUDSON dec'd. and WILLIAM THOMAS and WOODLIFF SCOTT Security, bond for $16,000, dated 5 May 1806.

Page 22

A. M. DEVEREUX, Admnr. of REUBIN ARMSTRONG dec'd. and WILLIAM BARNES Security, bond for $100, dated 15 Dec. 1804.

THOMAS SNOW, Admnr. of WILLIAM GILBERT and SAMUEL SNOW Security, bond for $200, 15 Dec. 1804.

ELIZABETH REID, SAMUEL REID and ALEXANDER REID of JOHN REID dec'd. and JOHN FREEMAN and WILLIE ABERCROMBIE Securities, bond for $6000, dated 8 Jan. 1806.

HENRY ROGERS and SALLEY MOBLY, Admnrs. of REUBEN MOBLY dec'd. and A. M. DEVEREUX Security bond for $1500, dated 21 July 1804.

VINES HARWELL, Admnr. of OWEN DAVIS dec'd. and JOHN SMITH Security bond for $4000 dated 1 Oct. 1805.

JOSEPH COOPER JUN. and THOMAS COOPER, Admnrs. of THOMAS COOPER dec'd. and JOSEPH COOPER Senr. and JOSIAH CARTER Securities, bond for 1000L=lbs. Sterl. dated 12 Feb. 1796.

SAMUEL HALL, Admnr. of VAN SWEARINGAM dec'd. and URIAH THWEATT and EPPS BROWN Securities, bond for $1000, dated 16 March 1805.

MARY KING and JOHN TINGLE, Admnrs. of WILLIAM KING dec'd. and MALACHI BRATLEY and WILLIAM PURIFY Securities bond for $1000, dated 27 Aug. 1803.

WILLIAM SANDERS and RICHARD SARSNETT, Admnrs. of WILLIAM WILCHER dec'd. and CHARLES ABERCROMBIE and BOLLING HALL Securities, bond for $3000, dated 15 March 1805.

Page 23

JOHN I. PORTER, Admnr. of WILLIAM ROACH, WILLIAM COULTER and JOHN SERGEANTS dec'd and JOHN FREEMAN Security bond for $100, dated 25 June 1803.

ELIZABETH WESTMORELAND, Admnx. of ISHAM WESTMORELAND dec'd. and THOMAS STERNBRIDGE Security, bond for $150, dated 30 Nov. 1803.

PRISCILLA BONNER, Admnx. of CHAPPEL BONNER dec'd. and JOSHUA CLOUD and DUKE HAMILTON Securities bond for $4000, dated 15 Dec. 1804.

JESSE MCKINNIE POPE and JAMES BISHOP Exors. of JOHN TRIPP dec'd. and WILLIAM BIGGINS and JOHN ROE Securities, bond for 2000L=lbs. Sterl., dated 20 Dec. 1794.

HENRY JACKSON and ROBERT N. MASS, Admnrs. of ISAAC JACKSON dec'd. and REUBIN SLAUGHTER Securities, bond for $20000, dated 16 March 1805.

SALLEY GILBERT and BIRD GILBERT, Admnrs. of MICHAEL GILBERT dec'd. and JACOB MOORMAN Securities bond for $10,000, dated 10 Dec. 1803.

CALEB OLIVER, Admnr. of SOLOMON OLIVER dec'd. and SOLOMON THORNTON and SAMUEL HAWKINS Security bond for $2000, dated 27 Aug. 1803.

PENELOPE BIRD, Admnx. of PETER BIRD dec'd. and ALLEN BIRD and JOHN LEE, JUNR. Securities, bond for $2000, dated 29 Oct. 1803.

Page 24

SARAH PATTERSON and JEFFERY BARKSDALE, Admnrs. of JOEL PATTERSON dec'd. and CHARLES ABERCROMBIE Security bond for $4000, dated 1 Dec. 1806.

HENRY JACKSON and JOHN JACKSON, Admnrs. of BENJAMIN JACKSON dec'd. and JOHN STURDIVANT and JESSE WARREN and ALEXANDER REID Securities bond for $3000, dated 3 March 1798.

POLLEY GARRETT and MICHAEL GILBERT, Admnrs. of HENRY GILBERT dec'd. and WILLIAM BARKSDALE and JACOB MOORMAN Securities, bond for $4000, dated 27 Aug. 1803.

BOLLING HALL, Admnr. of ROBERT PARHAM dec'd. and WILLIE ABERCROMBIE Securities bond for $6000, dated 15 March 1803.

ALLEN GREEN and BURRELL GREEN, Admnrs. of JAS. W. GREEN dec'd. and JAMES THWEATT and THOS. FOARD Securities bond for $12,000, dated 1 Dec. 1806.

RANSOM SWINNEY, Admnr. of J. DUDLEY SWINNEY dec'd. and NATHANIEL ROBERTSON Security bond for $4000, dated 2 Feb. 1807.

JAMES HUFF, Admnr. of WILLIAM HUFF dec'd. and THOMAS HUFF and DAVID MONCRIEF Securities, bond for $4000, dated 1 Dec. 1806.

FRANCIS ROSS and DAVID ADAMS, Admnrs. of JAMES ROSS dec'd. and CHARLES ABERCROMBIE and MAT. HAMILTON Securities, bond for $8000, dated 1 Dec. 1806.

JAMES SIMMONS, Admnrx. of WILLIAM HUDSON dec'd. and JEHU SMITH and ROBT. WEDDINGTON Securities, bond for $4000, dated 10 Dec. 1803.

Page 25

ELIZABETH SANDERS and JOSEPH D. FANNING, Admnrs. of WILLIAM SANDERS dec'd. and WILLIAM LOW and DARIL LOW Securities bond for $2000, dated 28 Jan. (1800 or 1804)

BENJAMIN CHAPPELL and HENRY HARRIS, Admnrs. of JOSEPH CHAPPELL dec'd. and ABSALOM HARRIS CHAPPELL SLEDGE Securities, bond for $10,000, dated 1 Dec. 1806.

SAMPSON DUGGAR, Admnr. of MOODY RAWLINGS dec'd. and TOMERLANE JONES Security bond for $240, dated 28 Jan. 1804.

ABRAHAM LAURENCE, Admnr. of JESSE BORAN dec'd. and JESSE M. POPE Security bond for $1500, dated 27 Aug. 1803.

DAVID and JAMES LEWIS, Admnrs. of JOHN LEWIS, JR. dec'd. and HENRY MITCHELL and FRANCIS LEWIS JUNR. Securities, bond for $8000, dated 28 Jan. 1804.

LARKIN SINGLETON, Admnr. of JOHN PEMBERTON dec'd. and JAMES HALL Security, bond for $1500, dated 2 May 1801.

WILLIAM MILES, Admnrs. of HILL CHAPMAN dec'd. and ABRAHAM MILES Security, bond for $1500, dated 1 June 1807.

DANIEL HUNT, Admnr. of JESSE COULTER dec'd. and ZACHARIAH BOOTH and GEORGE THOMPSON Security, bond for 1000L=lbs., dated 25 Jan. 1796.

WILLIAM INGRAM, Admnr. of JOHN INGRAM and ROBERT MORELAND Security bond for $3000, dated 27 Oct. 1803.

ABRAHAM WOMACK, Admnr. of WM. WOMACK dec'd. and JESSE MCKINNIE POPE Security bond $2000, dated 27 Aug. 1803.

Page 26

WILLIAM LOW, Admnr. of WILLIAM dec'd. and DANIEL LOW and LEWIS SMITH Securities, bond for $2000, dated 21 Jnly 1804.

JOHN HERBERT and HUBARD REYNOLDS, Admnrs. of ROBERT H. BONNER dec'd. and ALEX BELLAMY and RICHARD GARY Securities bond for $10,000, dated 1 Dec. 1806.

JAS. THOMAS and ELIJAH MOORE obtained temporary letters on estate of WILLIAM RYAN dec'd., FREDERICK GREEN Security bond for $2000, dated 9 March 1807.

SANDERS (?EVAN OR VAN) Admnr. of TALBERT EVANS dec'd. and EDWARD FLOWERS Security bond for $400, dated 6 July 1807.

MARTHA GODWIN, Admnx. of JONATHAN GODWIN dec'd. and AMOS BRANTLEY and JOHN GODWIN Securities, bond for $4000, dated 27 Aug. 1803.

THOMAS HARDING, Admnr. of SAM HARDIN dec'd. and JOHN TURK Security bond for $100, dated 2 Feb. 1807.

WILLIAM HURT and WILLI--WORSHAM, Admnrs. of THOMAS WORSHAM dec'd and JOHN LEWIS Security bond for $300, dated 1 Oct. 1804.

CHLOE FAIL and MALONE MULLINS, Admnrs. of JAMES FAIL, dec'd and W--- WILLIAMS and JOHN COOK Securities bond for $2000, dated 10 Dec. 1803.

ELIZA ROGERS and THOMAS DAWSON, Admnrs. of JOHN ROGERS, Security, bond for $15,000, dated 1 Dec. 1806.

ANN MARTIN and ALEXANDER MARTIN, Admnrs. of MARTIN MARTIN dec'd. and CH__ MCDONALD and SAMUEL HALL and TIMO. W. ROSSITER and WILLIAM SANFORD Securities bond for $100, dated 8 Sept. 1804.

Page 27

HANNAH MARCUS, Admnx. of JOHN MARCUS dec'd. and JOHN MCKINZEE and RICHD. G. BROWN Security bond for $10,000, dated 7 April 1806.

TAMERLANE JONES, Admnr. of WILLIS JONES, dec'd. and SAMPSON PUGGAR? Security bond for $1200, dated 28 Jan. 1804.

HEZEKIAH HOWELL, Admnr. of ROBERT ALLEN dec'd. and AMOS BRANTLEY Security bond for $10,000, dated __ Sept. 1806.

NANCY HOLT, SIMON HOLT, SENR., SIMON HOLT, JUNR. Admnrs. of ROBERT HOLT, dec'd. and HINES HOLT Security, bond for $4000, dated 3 Feb. 1806.

CAHPPELL SLEDGE, Admnr. of NATHANIEL SLEDGE dec'd. and MINS SLEDGE and EDWARD LANTON Securities, bond for $3000, dated 1 June 1807.

POLLEY HALL, Admnx. of ISAAC HALL dec'd. and SAMUEL HALL SENR. and JAMES HALL Securities, bond for $3000, dated 1 June 1807.

POLLEY TUCKER and THOMAS CROWDER, Admnrs. of FREDERICK TUCKER dec'd. and WILLIAM DAVENPORT, JOHN CROWDER Securities, bond for $8000, dated 2 June 1806.

ARCHIBALD MARTIN, Admnr. of JOHN PEARSON dec'd. and OLIVER SKINNER Security bond for $1000, dated 5 May 1807.

ALLEN GREENE, Admnr. of WILLIAM ANDERS dec'd. and JAMES W. GREENE and DAVID ADAMS Security bond for $2000, dated 3 Feb. 1806.

Page 28

DUKE HAMILTON, Admnr. of TABITHA HAMILTON dec'd. and THOMAS P. HAMILTON and JAMES THWEATT Securities, bond for $3000, dated 6 July 1807.

ISAAC HALL SENR., Admnr. of PHILIP DUNN dec'd. and HAMLIN LEWIS Security bond for $100, dated 22 Feb. 1807.

JAMES MITCHELL and JOHN MITCHELL, Admnrs. of SARAH MITCHELL dec'd and HENRY MITCHELL and ROBERT RAINS Securities bond for $10,000, dated 7 July 1807.

BENJAMIN RASBERRY, Admnr. of SHELDRAKE BROWN dec'd. and JAS. CUMMINGS Security bond for $400, dated 15 Dec. 1804.

JOHN BOOTH SEN., Admnr. of JOHN JONES dec'd. and JOHN BYAS Security, bond for $2000, dated 23 May 1798.

SARAH FAIL and STEPHEN STEPHENS, Admnrs. of ARTHUR FAIL dec'd. and TULLY CHOICE and JAMES HARVEY Securities, bond for $1500, dated 3 June 180_.

JOHN HUMPRIES, Admnr. of ELISHA ELLIS dec'd. and SETH KENNEDY and JAMES HALL Securities bond for $500, dated 2 May 1801.

NANCY J. CLARK, BOLLING HALL and WILLIAM ALEXANDER, Admnrs. of THOS. D. CLARK dec'd. and HONES HOLT and EDMUND ABERCROMBIE Securities bond for $30,000, dated 15 Dec. 1804.

Page 29

CHARLES ABERCROMBIE, Admnr. of SOLOMON BAREFIELD dec'd. and JEFFERY BARKSDALE Security, bond for $400, dated 2 March 1807.

DUKE HAMILTON, Admnr. of CHAPPELL BONNER dec'd. and ROBERT H. BONNER Security bond for $4000, dated 11 May 1805.

SALLEY NORWORTHY, Admnrx. of GEO. NORWORTHY dec'd. and JAMES THWEATT and HENRY MITCHELL Securities bond for $8000, dated 25 June 1806.

DANIEL NELSON and JOSHUA WINN,Admnrs. of STITH WINN dec'd. and JOHN GREGGS and JOSEPH COOPER Securities, bond for $3000, dated 1 June 1807.

LUCRETIA MINTON and JOHN COLBERT, Admnrs. of JOS. MINTON dec'd. and HARDY JERNIGAN and MILLS MINTON Securites bond for $2000, dated 1 Sept. 1806.

(Scratched out) JOHN S. PORTER, Admnr. of WILLIAM ROACH dec'd. and JOHN FREEMAN Security, bond for $100, dated 25 June 1803.

THOMAS P. HAMILTON and others Admnrs. of JOHN HAMILTON dec'd. and ROBERT RAINES and DUKE HAMILTON Securities bond for $6000.

REBECAH THOMAS, ISAAC NEWSOM and Admnrs. of ?TYSEY? THOMAS dec'd. and WILLIAM NEWSOM, HARDY JERNIGAN and BENJAMIN THOMPSON Securities, bond for $8000, dated 2 Nov. 1807.

Page 30

JOHN PERRY, Admnr. of WILLIAM FERRELL dec'd. and BIRD FERRELL Security, bond for $2000, dated 3 Nov. 1807.

LEONARD ABERCROMBIE, Admnr. of JOHN COMER dec'd. and ANDERSON COMER Security bond for $6000, dated 20 Oct. 1807.

ELLINGTON MORGAN, Gdn. for the persons and property of LEVEY CARSWELL, JOHN CARSWELL, ISHAM CARSWELL, MATTHEW CARSWELL, BETSEY CARSWELL and NANCY CARSWELL and WILLIAM S. MORGAN Security bond for $4000, dated 2 Nov. 1807.

WILLIS ROBERTS, Gdn. for the person and property of CHURCHILL ALLEN and WILLIAM MCLELLAN Security bond for $500, dated 7 Sept. 1807.

ABRAHAM WOOD, Gdn. for the persons and property of JOSEPH WOOD and POLLEY WOOD and MISAEL WOOD Security bond for $2000, dated 7 Sept. 1807.

DANIEL LOEW, Gdn. for the persons and property of JOHN GILBERT and JAMES WALLER Security bond for $200, dated 7 Sept. 1807.

DAVID PARKER, Gdn. for the persons and property of JOSHUA CATHEL, SALLEY CATHEL, JANE CATHEL, JAMES CATHEL, and JONATHAN CATHEL and ABRAM MILES Security bond for $2000, dated 7 Sept. 1807.

MISAEL WOOD, Gdn. for the person and property of PATSEY WOOD and ABRAHAM WOOD Security, bond for $1000, dated 7 Sept. 1807.

Page 31

BRITTON WILLIAMS, Gdn. for the person and property of WILLIAM ALLEN and JAMES HALEY Security bond for $500, dated 7 Sept. 1807.

SIMON HOLT JUNR. Gdn., for the persons and property of WILLIAM HOLT, DAVID HOLT, JOSEPH HOLT and SALLEY HOLT and SIMON HOLT, SR. Security bond for $4000, dated 1 Nov. 1807.

JOHN HAMILTON, Gdn. for the persons and property of WILLIAM HAMILTON and EVERARD HAMILTON and THOS. P. HAMILTON Security bond for $1200, dated 2 Nov. 1807.

Pages 32 and 33 are blank

Names of Executors & Admnrs.   Of What Estate   Date of

Robt. McGinty & John Herbert, Ex.   Levey Daniel, dec'd.   5 Jan. 180_

Pages 34-47

Pages 34-47 are the above listings which by and large are duplications of the before cited records. Hence, the next order will be to go to the records titled "Records of Wills, Inventories and Appraisements" following this and which begin on a "Page 2" next in order of sequence in this reel of microfilm and which contains Books A-AAAA.

Page 2:   An inventory of the Goods and Chattles, rights and credits of HENRY GREER deceased as they are appraised by WM. CLARK, HENRY GRAYBILL, NEEDHAM JERNIGAN and WM. MOSLEY appraisers appt'd by MYLES GREENE Reg. of Probate of Hancock Co. 9 June 1794. Valued at 65 lbs, 10 shillings and 4 pence.

Page 4:   Estate of HENRY GREER deceased as it was sold at public auction 21 June 1794. Sold for 51 lbs. 8 shill.

Page 8:   February 18, 1793, Hancock Co. Will of JOHN PARKER of above... weak in body... I give to my beloved wife the sum of 143 acres of land, whereon I now live... also all my household furn. and all my stock of horses and cattle, hogs during her lifetime and after her decease the 143 acres to be div. bet. three of my sons: JOHN PARKER, PETER PARKER and ELISHA PARKER to them and their heirs... to my son WILLIAM PARKER a tract on waters of dry Creek in Washington County the place whereon JOHN DENNIS now lives 87 acres to him and heirs... ordain my beloved wife SARAH PARKER my sole Extrx... and after my wife's decease I give and beq. to 4 of my children BETTY PARKER and WILLIAM PARKER and PETER PARKER and ELISHA PARKER a part of my estate such as my household furn. and stock to be div. with these my children that is married and gone from me which is JACOB PARKER, PRISCILLA CALLWAY and POLLEY PARKER and JOHN PARKER and what is left after my wife's decease of my household furn. and stock to be div. among all my children. Signed JOHN PARKER. Wit: LEONARD GORDY, GEORGE ROSS. Page 9 will sworn to 16 May 1794 bef. MYLES GREENE. Extrx. refused to Qualify.

Page 10:   Capt. JONATHAN ADAMS deposeth and saith that JAMES CHAMBERS being mortally wounded and unable to make a Will or Testament in writing desired his whole estate both real and personal to be div. bet. his brother HENRY CHAMBERS and his sister JANE CHAMBERS, to them and their heirs forever. Test. JOHN STURDIVANT. 16 June 1794 Capt. JONATHAN ADAMS swore to the above bef. MYLES GREENE, Register of Probates, Hancock Co.

Page 12:   Inventory of estate and Chattles of JAMES CHAMBERS in 1794 (month and day not stated) appraised by JAMES ADAMS, JOHN BREWER and FRANCIS ROSS, appraisers app'd by MYLES GREENE, Reg. of Pro. Est. valued at 106 lbs, 15s. 7p. 1/2. Mentioned is money due on a bond in name of HOWELL TATUM and PETER TATUM and also one tract of land cont. 287 1/2 acres on Richland Creek in Green Co. among the items listed. Cert. JAMES ADAMS, JOHN BREWER, FRANCIS ROSS.

Page 14:   Inventory of Estate and Chattles of JOHN WOOTEN dec'd. as appraised by JESSE THOMPSON, DANIEL LEWIS, ROBERT BLEAKNEY appraiser. Dated 3 Oct. 1794. Valued at 216 lbs. 3s, 4p.

Page 16:   Inventory and Appraisal of Estate and Chattles of ELIJAH MAGLAMERY late of Co. dec'd. Order for appraisal dated 7 Oct. 1794 and was made 29 Oct. 1794. Among items ment. are note due of SAMUEL TURNER, one on OBADIAH RICHARDSON. Valued at 31 lbs, 19 shillings, 4 pence 1/2. Inventory certified by RISDON MOORE, JOSHUA HENLEY, JOHN LAMAR.

Page 17: Inventory of Estate of JACOB PARKER deceased and appraisement
dated Oct. 23, 1794. Among household and other items is mentioned one
note against MARY PARKER for 3 lbs, 11 shillings. Also an account agst.
ROBERT MCGUINTY for 2 lbs, 10 shillings. 287 1/2 acres on Rocky Creek
whereon sd. widow PARKER now lives. Note agst. NATHANIEL WALLER and
CHARLES WALLER, note agst. LEONARD GORDY and JOSEPH HOWARD, note agst.
PRESSLEY SCURLOCK and WILLIAM SCURLOCK, note agst. ROBERT MCGUINTY and
ELISHA MORAN, note agst. TURNER HARWOOD and JESSE HARWOOD, note agst.
LITTLETON BEACHEM and JOSEPH HARWOOD, note agst. SARAH PARKER and JOSHUA
SCURLOCK and one note agst. JOSHUA SCURLOCK... Total estate app. at
271 lbs., 2 shillings, 10 pence. Signed by JOHN SIMMONS, WILLIS SPEIR,
JOHN RAGAN. Rec. 20 Dec. 1794.

Pages 19 & 22: Will of JOHN TRIPP of Hancock Co. dated 10 Nov. 1794...
being weak in body... I lend to my bel. wife SALLEY TRIPPE the use of
plantation whereon I now live dur. her life or widowhood... also lend
to loving wife 5 negroes (names them) together with one feather bed and
furn., including her riding mare and all the work horses and likewise
use of all my cattle, all to be lent to her dur. her nat. life... and
also a neg. woman SARAH and if SARAH has children the two first to my
2 oldest daughters SALLEY and LYDDAE and the next two to my daughters
ANN and POLLEY and at her death or marriage the plantation to descend
to my son SAMUEL TRIPPE... the negroes mentioned above to be div. among
all my children then living except old TONEY, him to be a free man under
the care of my son HENRY TRIPPE... to son HENRY TRIPPE all my land being
on South side of Fort Creek, slaves, bed and furn.; dau. SALLEY POPE one
neg. woman and all cattle etc. I have given her... dau. LYDDAE POPE
neg. woman and man and cattle, etc. I have given her... dau. ANN TRIPPE
2 negroes, bed... with its furn. and mare colt... dau POLLEY TRIPPE 2
negroes, feather bed and furn. and yearling mare... son JOHN TRIPPE all
that tract in fork of Fort Creek including that tract I purchased of
BENJAMIN PRITCHETTS Estate and 2 negroes, horse and feather bed and
furn.... son SAMUEL TRIPPE 2 negroes and manner plantation including the
plantation whereon FREDRICK EQUALS now lives... to son JOHN TRIPPE one
gun that was my fathers... sons JOHN and SAMUEL TRIPPE, to continue with
their mother until they come to age of 21 years. Appt's JESSEY MCKINNEY
POPE and JAMES BISHOP Exors. Signed JOHN TRIPPE. Wit: ROBT.
MORELAND, WM. BIGGINS, JOHN ROE. Two codicils added the first being
slaves given to sons JOHN and HENRY... 2nd. Codicil mentions 800 acres
of Piney land purchased of JAMES SCARLET to be sold and money div.=bet.
4 daus. SALLEY POPE, LYDDAE POPE, ANN TRIPPE and POLLEY TRIPPE... Will
and Codicils sworn to 20 Dec. 1794.

Page 23: Appraisal of property of JOHN LAWSON dec'd. 23 Oct. 1794.
Valued at 60 lbs. 3 shillings, 6 pence by DANIEL RICHARDSON, THADEUS
BEALLE and ANDREW BAXTER Appraisers. Appraisal on 23 Jan. 1795. Slaves
and other items not sold valued at 136L.

Page 24: Return of the Sale of part of the Estate of JOHN LAWSON sold
on Jan. 23, 1795. Total amt. 41 lbs, 16 shillings, 3 pence. Certified
by WALTER HAMILTON Clk. and JOHN THOMAS, Admnr. and NANCY LAWSON, Admmx.

Page 26: Will of RICHARD MOON of Hancock Co., Planter... beq. to my
son SIMON one shilling. 2nd. to my son RICHARD one shilling... 3rd.
to my oldest dau. MARY one shilling... 4th. to my dau. LOWREY one
shilling... 5th. to my dau. SUSEY one shilling... 6th. to my dau. HANNOR
one shilling... 7th to dau. NARGET one shilling... 8th to dau. RACHEL
one bay horse, one speckled cow and yearling, a bed and furn., pot,
plates, dish and basin which I give to my well bel. dau. RACHEL. I
beq. to my bel. wife SUSAN MOON my plantation I now live on, 125 acres
of land in Guilford Co., N.C. to be at her own disposal... also to wife
all my household furn., working tools, stock and after her death to be
div. among all my children. Appt. wife SUSANNAH Extrx. of Will. Dated
15 Jan. 1795. Signed: RICHARD MOON. Wit: THOMAS HILL, SETH TATUM.
Sworn to 27 Feb. 1795 bef. MYLES GREENE, Clk.

Page 27:   Notes due from Estate of JOHN LAWSON dec'd. brought in by
JOHN THOMAS and NANCY LAWSON Admnrs. and paid to: HUNT STALLINGS & CO.
of Augusta, another to ABRAHAM SIMS and another to A. MCMILLAN printer
to the state for advert. Esta. Sgn. MYLES GREEN.

Pages 29 & 31:   Inventory and Appraisement of part of Estate of JOHN
TRIPPE, dec'd. Shown to the appraisers by JAMES BISHOP, MCKINNEY POPE
Exors. Mentions: note of hand due on THOMAS LAMAR due Jan. 11, 1794,
WILLIAM WASHINGTON note on demand 19 Nov. 1793, JOSHUA SCURLOCK note on
demand 25 Dec. 1794, JAMES PRITCHETT note on demand 25 Dec. 1793, WILLIAM
SALLARD note on demand Nov. 1793, JAMES THOMAS note on demand 19 Jan.
1795, JAMES GREENE, note on demand 25 Dec. 1794, ROBERT BLACKLEDGE note
on demand 1 April 1788, due bill agst. AUGUSTEN HARRIS. Open Accounts:
mentions, ROBERT MORELAND, BENJAMIN BRAZIL, JOHN STURDIVANT, JAMES REES
SENR., MYLES GREENE, JESSE GRIGG, FRANCIS MORELAND SENR., ROBERT CHAMBERS,
ABEL JAMES, JOSHUA ROE, AUGUSTEN HARRISS, PHILIP PRITCHITT, WYATT
COLLIER, ISAAC MORELAND, FRANCIS ROSS, JAMES SCARLET, THOMAS RAINES,
RICHARD FRETWELL, WM. DIXON. Total valued at 1173 lbs, 1 shilling, 4
pence, 3/4. Certified under our hands: DAVID DIXON, JAMES THWEATT,
STEPHEN BISHOP, Appraisers. Page 33. Another part of Apprsmt. at 156
lbs., 18 shillings, 6 pence, 19 May 1795.

Page 32:   Inventory and Appaisement of Estate of RICHARD MOON SENR. dec'd
as appraised by us the subscribers on the 21 Feb. 1795. Valued at 20
lbs, 6 shilling, 9 pence and 15 lbs, 14 shillings, 2 pence. Signed:
NATHL. TATUM, THOMAS HILL, SETH TATUM.

Page 34:   Inventory of all the good and Chattles, rights and credits
of HENRY MORRISS dec'd. as they were appraised by JESSE VEASEY, JOHN
STROTHER and JOHN KIRK appraisers appt. by MYLES GREENE this 14 March
1795... Mentions: one note of hand of WM. MORGAN. One note of hand of
THADDEUS HOLT, one note of hand of GILBERT GAY and JAMES DOSSEN. Valued
at 80 lbs, 11 shillings, 0 pence. Cert. 14 April 1795 by the above
named men.

Pages 35, 39 & 42:   Memorandom of Sundry articles sold at public sale
this 10 July 1795 of the property of HENRY MORRISS dec'd. Persons who
bought were: ELIZABETH MORRISS, ELIZABETH MORRISS, WILLIAM BUCKNER,
JOHN BROWN, ELISHA WATLEY, MARTIN JOHNSON, WARD DARNEL, JOAB DURHAM,
JOHN TAPLEY, WILLIAM SEAL, RICHARD BONNER, JOHN DENNIS, JAMES MORRIS,
JOSEPH THOMPSON, PETER BOYLE, ISHAM HOGAN... and mentions rent of plantation of for 1805. Estate of HENRY MORRISS shows rents for 1807 and
1808 and repairs etc in 1809.

Page 36:   Inventory and Appraisement of Goods and Chattles rights
and credits of JOHN NICHOLAS dec'd. as appraised by the subscribers this
13 April 1795... Valued at 40 lbs. Signed: N. JERNIGEN, R. RUTLAND,
WM. MCINVAILL, bef. HENRY GRAYBILL.

Page 37:   Amount of the Estate of JOHN NICHOLAS dec'd as it sold at
public sale. Those mentioned as purchasers were: JNO BURCH, DOCTOR
DYAMPERT, NEEDHAM JERNIGAN, JOSHUA ASSHER, PETER BIRD, for total of 46
lbs, 1 shilling, ___ pence.

Page 38:   SARAH TRIPPE ratifies will of her husband JOHN TRIPPE dated
10 Nov. 1794 and asks this ratification to be recorded 3 July 1795.
Signed: SARAH (S) TRIPPE. Wit: DAVID DICKSON and JOHN HENDERSON.
Recorded 10 July 1795.

Page 40 & 41:   Will of HOLLAND MIDDLETON of Hancock County, Georgia...
to my son ZACHARIAH MIDDLETON, land in the county afrd. between the
beaver dam and the Greensborough road... to my wife MARY MIDDLETON, 1/3
of all my Estate real and personal or her Dowery at her option and no
more... to my daughter SARAH DICINSON, five shillings sterling exclusive
of all that I have already given her heretofore... to the heirs of my
daughter SUSANNAH BERRY, 5 shillings sterling, exclusive of property
heretofore given her and them... all remaining part of my Estate

equally divided between my son JOHN MIDDLETON, ROBERT MIDDLETON,
ELIZABETH MIDDLETON and MARY MIDDLETON, PARKS MIDDLETON and BENJAMIN
MIDDLETON... MARY MIDDLETON and son ZACHARIAH Exrs... HOLLAND MIDDLETON
(SEAL). Wit: RIDSON MOORE, JUNR., JONATHAN BLACK, ROBERT OWSLEY...
(Will not dated.)
        Appeared on 23rd of July 1795, ROBERT OWSLWY and RIDSON MOORE,
2 of subscribing witnesses... MYLES GREENE R. P. H. C.

Page 42:   Rec'd. of ZACHARIAH MIDDLETON and MARY MIDDLETON fees on Est.
of HOLLAND MIDDLETON, dec'd. 5 Apr. 1800.

Page 43:   A list of notes of hand: brought by JOEL BUCKNER, Exr. of
Est. of HENRY MORRISS, a note given to WM. MORGAN, a note given to
AARON FAGIN...a note given to THOMAS DILLARD, a note given to THOMAS
PICKARD, a receipt from A. MCMILLAN, Printer... proven accompt. by ASA
SIMMONS.

Page 44:   An inventory of part of Est. of JOHN LAWSON, dec'd., returned
to this office 12 Aug. 1795. Notes on THEOPHILUS THOMAS, WILLIAM
LAWSON, Kentucky, due 25 Dec. 1787, HEZEKIAH JOHNSON, one certificate
purchased of EZEKIEL STANLEY on Captain JAMES ALEXANDER... one certificate purchased of JAMES SHACKLEFORD, July 25, 1795. THADDEUS BEALL and
BARTER, DANIEL RICHARDSON.

Page 45:   Credit to NANCY LAWSON & JOHN THOMAS Admnr. of JOHN LAWSON,
dec'd. Inspection and cooperage of 2 HHds. of Tobacco... JOHN JACKS,
ROBERT SIMS Proven accompt again estate paid off. Brought in 28 Feb.
1801 Doctor J. NELSON, P. L. VANALEN, attorney fees, THOMAS P. CARNES
Attorney fees, ISAAC BENSON, JAS. TURNER, JOHN BARK, JNO. GRIFFIN,
SAMUEL DENT, MACMASTERS Receipt for cost of suit... ABRAHAM SIMS note,
A. MCMILLIAN for printing, HUNT STALLINGS note.

Pages 46-47:   Will of JOSHUA SCURLOCK of Hancock County, Ga., Sept. 14,
1794, being sick and weak in body... to my daughter ARGATHA WATTS, 5
shillings sterling... to son THOMAS SCURLOCK, 2 pounds sterling... to my
daughter ELIZABETH SCURLOCK... to son DANIEL SCURLOCK... to my dearly
beloved children namely, WILLIAM SCURLOCK, JAMES SCURLOCK, PRESLEY
SCURLOCK, JOSHUA SCURLOCK, DANIEL SCURLOCK, SARAH PARKER, LUCY NORMAN,
and ELIZABETH SCURLOCK all remainder of my property... JOSHUA SCURLOCK
(   ) (SEAL). Wit: JOHN HAMILTON, JP., WILLIAM HAMILTON, JOHN HAMILTON
JUNR. Proven Aug. 18, 1795.

Page 48:   A memorandum of Sundry articles sold at public sale, est. of
JACOB PARKER, dec'd. 21 Feb. 1795. Buyers; ELISHA HEARN, WILLIAM
PARKER, JOEL MCCLENDON, LITTLETON CARTER, JOSIAH DENNIS, WILLIAM
BEACHAM, SARAH PARKER, WILLIAM RYAN, 1000 weight of tobacco collected
of GEORGE ROSS. Vouchers brought WILLIAM BEAUCHAMP, WILLIAM RYAN, JOHN
RAGGANS.

Pages 49-51:   An inventory and appraisement of goods and chattles of
HOLLAND MIDDLETON 11 Aug. 1795. NEWDAY OWSLEY (SEAL), WILLIAM DENT
(SEAL), RISDON MOORE (SEAL).

Page 52:   An amt. of sales est. of HOLLAND MIDDLETON, Buyers: ZACHARY
MIDDLETON, MARY MIDDLETON, WM. WRIGHT, 21 Mar. 1801.

Pages 53-54:   A list of sale of part of the Est. of JOHN TRIPPE dec'd.
at public auction 9 Oct. 1795. Buyers: JOHN COOK, MARCUS RABY (ROBY?),
CULLIN POPE, THOMAS BARKLEY, ISAAC MORELAND, JAMES HOG, JESSEY THOMPSON,
HUBBARD FERREL, JOSEPH SPRADLING, WILLIAM EVANS, THOMAS WILCOX, JOHN
MORELAND, EPHRAIM MOORE, JOHN GRAY, WILLIAM LAWSON, WILLIAM HAMILTON,
JESSE POPE MCKINNEY, JOEL DICKERSON, JEREMIAH MCCARTY, CADER POWELL,
WELDON OWSLEY, LEWIS TIAS, ARCHIBALD TRAYLER, JAMES HUCKEBY, JOHN HUDMON,
HENRY TRIPPE, ELISHA WATLEY, ABRAM FAIRCHILD, PEYTON TUCKER, JOHN BREWER,
JAMES REES, JOHN ROE, JOHN MCGAHEE, JOHN WHITEHURST, JOSEPH TURNER,
ROBERT MORELAND, EDMUND DAY.

Pages 55-56:   Will of JAMES VIZEY of Hancock County, Georgia... being
in a sick and in a low state of health... to my loving wife ANN VEZE,
place whereon I now live till my youngest child comes of age... to my
beloved daughter ELIZABETH... to my son THOMAS VEZEY... to my son
WILLIAM VEZEY... to my daughter MAREY VEZEY... to my daughter SARAH
VEZEY... to son JAMES VEZEY and STEPHEN VEZEY... to my daughter ANN...
to my daughter CHARITY... friends ANN VEZEY and JOHNADAB READ, JOHN
VEZEY and JOHN WILLSON Exrs... 2nd. April 1795. JAMES VEZEY (SEAL).
Wit: FREDERICK WARD, JOHN WILSON. Proven: Dec. 1, 1795.

Page 57:   Part of estate of Maj. JNO. TRIPPE dec'd... no names.

Page 58:   Vouchers returned 2 June 1798. Est. of JOHN STROTHER dec'd.
note to JONES SHIVERS... JAS. THOMAS proven account... note of hand paid
to ULYSSES ROGERS... ANDEW BORLAND proven account, BOLAND MITCHELL,
1801 Sept. 1, JONES SHIVERS, JAS. STROTHERS, GEORGE STROTHERS, JOHN
STROTHER, THOMAS KING, PATTY STROUD, AARON STROTHER, JOEL MOODY. 1808..
July 8th, paid DAVID STROTHER, Jan. 6, 1812, paid RICHARD STROTHER,
Apr. 9, 1813, paid PATTY STROUD.

Pages 59-62:   Inventory of Est. of JOSHUA SCURLOCK dec'd as sold at
public auction 30 Oct. 1795. Buyers: PRESLEY SCURLOCK, WILLIAM SCUR-
LOCK, JAMES COWSON, WILLIAM BUZER, ISAAC DANIEL, ROGER THORNTON,
BENJAMIN JACKSON, JOSHUA SCURLOCK, WILLIAM FERREL, DANIEL SCURLOCK
BURWELL YARBROUGH, WILLIAM ROBINSON, JOHN BUZER, DAVIS LONG, CALEB
BAZER (?), JOHN STEEL, WILLIAM H. HARGRAVES, JOHN MITCHELL, WILLIAM RYAN
HENRY THORNTON, STEPHEN DYKES, WILLIAM SPEIR, SAMUEL HOLLEY, Capt.
RICHARD BONNER, JOSEPH REED, ISHAM HOGAN, JOHN HAMILTON, WILLIAM ROBINSON,
EPHRAIM BOWEN, ROBERT STEEL, PHILIP SPILLER, JOAB CURHAM, WILLIAM HENSON,
EDWARD ABBY, WILLIAM SALLAD.

Page 63:   An inventory & appraisement of good & C. of WILLIAM MCINVAIL,
late of county of Hancock, dec'd. as appraised by JAMES ORRICK, JERARD
BURCH, EDMUND CALLEY, HENRY GRAYVILL, 21 Oct. 1795. DANIEL CONNER
proven account against est. estate WM. MCINVAILS dec'd. to est. EDMUND
CROWDER dec'd.

Page 64:   A list of the sale of the estate of JOHN WOOTEN dec'd., sold
at public auction 1795. Buyers: JOHN SIMS, JAMES CATHELL, SAMUEL GILES,
JAMES PAUL. Signed: MARY WOOTEN, JAMES CATHELL, Admrs.

Page 65:   Vouchers brought by admr. of JOHN WOOTENS Estate... paid to
FRANCIS STUBBS... account to JOHN C. SLOCUMB... to WILLIAM RIGG... to
ISAAC JACKSON... to JESSE THOMPSON... WM. PIGGS, JOHN CAIN, STEPHEN
BISHOP, HARVEY WOOTEN, JOHN WILSON, H. HOTH Shff... WM. MINOR.

Page 66:   Inventory of estate of BENJAMIN PRITCHETT, dec'd, Dec. 31,
1795. Sgnd. JAMES THWEAT, JAMES WHITEHURST, JESSE MCKENNE POPE,
Appraisers.

Page 67:   Account sales, estate of BENJAMIN PRITCHETT, by PHILIP PRIT-
CHETT & SARAH PRITCHETT, Admr. Jan. 30, 1796. Names mentioned: WILLIAM
GRIGGS, BENJAMIN JACKSON, THOMAS WINN, ROBERT CARHAM, JOHN KELLEY, JOHN
MARSHALL.

Pages 68-73:   A list of sale of part of the estate of JOHN TRIPPE,
dec'd. Jan. 1, 1796. Buyers: STEPHEN BISHOP, HENRY LANIER, HENRY
TRIPPE, ALLEN POPE, FREDERICK ____?, JESSE MCKENNY POPE, SAMUEL POPE,
RICHARD RISPESS, JOHN SMITH, WILLIAM HURT, WILLIAM HARPER, WILLIAM
CURETON, JOSEPH HUTCHINSON, ROBERT BANEY, STEPHEN KIRK, JEREMIAH CASTLE-
BERRY, JAMES GREEN, JAMES BISHOP, JOHN COOK, ISHAM WHEELIST, MYLES GREENE,
THOMAS BRANTLEY, NATHANIEL WALLER, ALEXANDER CADENHAD, ANDERSON HARWELL,
JOHN BREWER, WILLIAM GRIGGS, PHILIP PRITCHETT, THOMAS BRANTLEY, FREDERICK
EQUALS, LEWIS BARNS, RICHARD HAMBLIN, WILLIAM FERREL, GEORGE VEST,
WILLIAM IVINS, ELISHA HEARN, JOEL REES, JULIAN SANDERS, Mr. FLOYD,
WILLIAM BROWN, THOMAS LILES, GEORGE REED, JAMES THWEATT, Doctor JEREMIAH
NELSON, CHARLES BURK, WILLIAM BIVENS, WILLIAM COWELL, ELISHA MOORE, ANNE
TRIPPE.

112

Pages 74-77:   Money collected estate of JOHN TRIPPE, for 1795. Names
JOSHUA ROE, JAMES PRITCHETT, WILLIAM BIGGINS, JAMES REES, WILLIAM
LALLAD (?), ROBT. CHAMBERS, FRANCIS ROSS, BENJAMIN BRAZEL, WILLIAM BIVINS,
Mr. FLOYD, WILLIAM WASHINGTON, THOMAS RAINS, JESSE GRIGG, RICHARD
HAMBLIN, WYATT COLLIER, WILLIAM FERREL, JAMES SCARLET, JAMES W. GREENE,
RICHARD FRETWELL, WILLIAM IVINS, ELISHA MOORE, WILLIAM BROWN, JULIUS
SANDERS, JACOB REES (Rev.), THOMAS LIALS, ROBT. MORELAND, CHAS. BURK,
HENRY TRIPPE, ELISHA HEANS, WM. DICKSON, WM. SCURLOCK, ELISHA HEARN,
JAMES PRITCHETT, PHILLIP PRITCHETT, WELDON OSWLEY, JOHN ROE, ARCHBL.
TRALER, MORRIS ROBY.

Page 78:   An account of expenditures, est. of JOHN TRIPPE dec'd. Jan.
5, 1796. Names: STEPHEN KIRK, SAML. BRAZEL, FRANCIS MORELAND, DAVID
ADAMS, JEREMIAH NELSON, BARRETT BREWER, THOMAS CUMMING BARNABETH POPE,
ABRAHAM BOWLAND, JNO. MITCHELL, JOHN STRAWDER, Mr. SPENCER, WILLIS
SPEIR, Mrs. NIPPIE, ROBERT MORELAND, WILLIAM DICKSON, BENJ. PRITCHETT,
HENRY GRAYBILL, BORELAND MITCHELL.

Pages 79,80,81:   Are blank.

Pages 82-84:   Will of THOMAS COOPER, of Green County, Ga., ... wife
SARAH COOPER, until my youngest daughter comes of age... daughter
ELIZABETH... son JOSEPH... land on Logdam Creek... daughter AGNESS... son
THOMAS... daughter POLLEY... Son JOHN... son MICAJAH... daughter SARAH...
land on Sandy Run... Exrs. THOMAS STOVALL, JOHN DILLARD, JOSEPH COOPER
JR., THOMAS COOPER JR., GEORGE HAMILTON & HENRY GRAYBILL, dated Aug. 20,
1793, THOMAS COOPER (SEAL). Wit: B. ANTHONY, JOSIAH CARTER, JOSEPH
COOPER. Proved by JOSIAH CARTER & JOSEPH COOPER, Feb. 13, 1796.

Page 85:   Is blank.

Pages 86-87:   Will of BETTY VAUGHAN of Hancock... to granddaughter
ELIZABETH BAUGHAN... MARY MOORE to divide my wearing apparel between my
daughter JEANE CATHELL and ELIZABETH SMITH... my son ISAAC VAUGHAN until
the said granddaughter ELIZABETH VAUGHAN comes of age... dated Jan. 31,
1796... BETTY VAUGHAN (SEAL). Wit: CHARLES MOORE, TAYLOR NELSON,
RISDON MOORE JUNR. Proven by RISDON MOORE JUNR., Feb. 15, 1796.

Pages 88-89:   Will of JAMES DOWDLE of Hancock Co... wife CREEDENCE
DOWDLE... daughter JEAN... three sons BARTHOLEOMEW JOHNSON, JOHN and
ROBERT... and my three daughters MARY, REBEKAH, and SARAH... friend
WILLIAM GREER, Exr... dated Dec. 1, 1795... JAMES DOWDLE (SEAL). Wit:
WILLIAM BUTLER, VALENTINE WARREN (+), MOURNING GERRETT (+). Proven by
WILLIAM BUTLER and MOURNING GERRETT April 22, 1796.

Pages 90-92:   Inventory and appraisement of good of JAMES DOWDLE, dec'd.
June 2, 1796... MICHAEL GILBERT, EDMUND BUTLER, PHILIP ALLEN, Appaisers.

Page 93:   Receipts from legatees of JAMES DOWDLE dec'd... rec'd.
PRUDENCE DOWDLE (X), June 2, 1796. Wit: MICHAEL GILBERT... rec'd.
STEPHEN WALLER (X), June 23, 1796.

Pages 94-97:   Inventory of goods of THOMAS COOPER, late dec'd., appraised
by EDMUND BUTLER, NEEDHAM JERNIGAN SENR. & JERARD BURCH. Notes on
JOSEPH COOPER JUNT. URIAH ASKEY & HENRY JERNIGAN, MOSES GOING, BENJAMIN
GILBERT, ISHAM WESTMORELAND, ARCHIBALD SMITH, JOHN LAMAR, OBADIER
RICHARDSON, JOHN DEYAMPER, PHILIP ALLEN, WILLIAM OUSLEY, JAMES BYNUM,
JOSEPH COOPER, SENR., land on Sandy Run, land on Logdam Creek...

Pages 98-99:   An account of goods and chattles of THOMAS COOPER sold
May 2, 1796... Buyers: JAMES BYNUM, JOSEPH COOPER, HENRY JERNIGAN,
ELIZABETH STOVALL, SARAH COOPER SENR., JAMES NESBIT, JAMES SHORTER,
BOLING ANTHONY.

Pages 100-101:   Inventory and appraisement of est. of WILLIAM WRIGHT
SENR., March 10, 1796... THOS LOW, THOMAS AYRES, appraisers.

Pages 102-103:   Account of sale of est. of WILLIAM WRIGHT SENR., April 6, 1796. Buyers: PETER JACKSON, ASA ALEXANDER, ROBERT SIMMS, WILLIAM WRIGHT, JOHN WILKERSON, GEORGE HALL, WILLIAM JACKSON, EPHRAIM BARNS, BRANDLE JACKSON, THOMAS CAMMELL, THOMAS AYRES, THOMAS LOWE, STEPHEN DANIEL, EZEKIEL STANLEY, EPHRAIM BARNS, LEVY DANIEL, JOSHUA MITCHELL.

Page 104: Blank.

Page 105:   Account of Receipts of Legatees of THOS. COOPER, Jan. 10, 1798. JAMES NEWBIY, GEORGE HAMILTON, JOHN WICKS, THOMAS LANCASTER, JOHN COOPER, JOHN WEEKS, JAS. COOPER, JOS COOPER, JOHN JACKS, JOHN LAMAR, JNO. MATHEWS, JAS. BYNUM.

Pages 106-107:   Amount sales of good and chatles of WILLIAM MCINVAIL, dec'd. Jan. 8, 1796 JESSE COLEMAN (X).

Pages 108-109:   Inventory of Estate of JESSE COULTER, appraiser by WILLIAM BEAUCHAMP, LITTLETON BEAUCHAMP and GEORGE THOMPSON.

Pages 110-111:   Amt. of sale est. of JESSE COULTER, Feb. 11, 1796, buyers not listed.

Numbering is not clear here..

Pages 111-114:   Feb. 10, 1796, JAMES ADAMS of Hancock Co... son DAVID... son JONATHAN... conveyed from DANIEL CONNER... sons JAMES and ROBERT... daughter POLLEY, land of watery fork of buffelo granted to RBOERT DAY... daughter JEAN... my daughter REBECCA deceased... MOLEY MONTGOMERY HILL, ALIVIA MOORE HILL, THOMAS ALEXANDER HILL, her children (REBECCA's)... JAS ADAMS (SEAL). Wit: ROBERT HILL, NOE DODDRIDGE, JOSEPH CHAPPELL, JAMES ALLIN. Proven by ROBERT HILL and NOE DODDRIDGE, July 21, 1796.

Pages 115-117:   Inventory and appraisement of goods of JAMES ADAMS... notes on NATHAN CULDER, DANL. MADDOX, WM. JOHNSTON, DANIEL COMER, MARK MCCLENDON, ARTHUR BEARDEN, THOS. MCCLENDON, SPENCER THOMAS.

Pages 118-120:   Will of BENJAMIN SHIP of Hancock Co... May 6, 1796... to son DAVID SHIP, 200 acres on head of Island Creek... to son RICHARD SHIP, land I now live, on south side of Lick Creek, adj. HOLCOMBS land... to son WILLIAM SHIP (after the death of my wife MAREY SHIP)... to son JOHN SHIP... to daughter CHRISTIAN SHIP... to daughter BETSEY SHIP... to daughter POLLEY SHIP... BENJN. SHIP (B) (SEAL). Wit: WILLIAM WASHAM (X), FRANCES SHIP ( ) her mark. Proven: by WILLIAM WASHAM & FRANCES SHIP, Aug. 3, 1796.

Pages 121-123:   Appraisal of goods of BENJ. CHIP... 29 Oct. 1796... Account to money received by executors of BENJ. SHIP, Jan. 1. 1798... Rec'd. of JESSE ASHLOCK, JAMES ORRICK, JOHN ADAMS, RICHARD SHIP SENR. & WM. SCOTT.

Page 124:   This day came Capt. MARTIN, THOMAS FARLEY and JOHN WHITNEY before JOEL MCCLENDON... GEORGE BULOW, late a physician in Capt. THOS. MARTIN's Company of the Federal Army was regularly discharged... dated Aug. 8, (year not given)... Signed: THO MARTIN, THO FARLEY, JOHN WHITNEY.

Page 125:   Account of sale of est. of BENJ. SHIP, March 31, 1801... Buyers: WILLIAM BIGGINS, JOHN LEE, JOEL HOLCOMBE, MARTHEW JONES, EBENEZER DAUGHTY, DAVID SMITH, REUBIN JONES, JOSEPH MINTON... MATT. RABUN, WM. BIGGINS, Exres.

Pages 126-127:   Will of THOMAS MOORE of Swift Creek (?), Hancock Co... LYDIA MOORE, wife all my goods... dated June 26, 1796... THOMAS MOORE. Wit: FRANCIS TRAWICK, JESSE TRAWICK, ROBERT TRAWICK. Proven by: FRANCIS TRAWICK and JESE TRAWICK, date obliterated.

Pages 128-129: Inventory and appraisal of goods of THOMAS MOORE, Aug. 30, 1796... appraisers FRANCIS TRAWICK (SEAL), SWAN THOMPSON (SEAL), WILLIAM BARNETT (SEAL).

Page 130: Blank.

Pages 131-132: Inventory and appraisement of est. of JOHN STROTHER, SENR. dec'd. Appraised by JAMES THOMAS, JONAS SHIVERS, JR., JOHN BUCKNER, July 12, 1796.

Page 133: Amt. sales of est. of JOHN STROTHER, dec'd. JEAN STROTHER & RICHARD STROTHER, Admnrs.

Pages 134-135: Will of MEREDITH PRICE, made Oct. 3, 1796... very sick and weak in body Exrs. ROBERT CHAMBERS, JOHN JON__ (JONES?)... to be equally divided between my wife and children (not named)... MEREDITH PRICE (SEAL). Wit: J. W. MONTGOMERY, ELIJAH LINGO. Proven by J. W. MONTGOMERY & ELIJAH LINGO, Oct. 28, 1796.

Pages 135-137: Appraisement of est. of MEREDITH PRICE, by JOHN BROWN, and _____ and ____ MILES (names very dim), Nov. 2, 1796.

Pages 138-140: Inventory and appraisement of est. of JOHN PINKERTON dec'd... dated Sept. 10, 1796, JAS. THWEATT, CHAS ABERCROMBIE, THOS. MITCHELL... Buyers: DAVID PINKERTON, PEGGY PINKERTON, MARY PINKERTON, RUTHA PINKERTON, ARTHUR LONG, JANE HUNTER.

Page 150: Hancock Co., Ga., Know that I, JAMES PINKSTON, relinquish all my interest in the est. of JOHN PINKSTON, SENR. dec'd., Dec. 6, 1816. JAMES PINKSTON (SEAL). Wit: JAMES H. JONES, JAMES W. ARMSTRONG JP.

Pages 151-152: Will of EDMD CROWDER, Nov. 14, 1796... being in a low state of health... unto my friend THOMAS GOOD... unto my niece NANCY TUCKER, daughter of FREDERICK TUCKER... EDMD CROWDER (SEAL). Wit: JOHN MURRAY, ANNE COOPER, SAML. LAWRENCE... codicil concern of MICHAEL & SIMS... notes due me from MICHAEL & LAWRENCE. Wit: JOHN MURRAY, ANNE COOPER.

Pages 153-154: Inventory of goods of EDMUND CROWDER, dec'd... Jan. 2, 1797... Appraisers, HENRY GRAYBILL, RANSOM HARWELL (?).

Pages 155-156: Will of JOHN CROXSON of Hancock Co., planter... wife HANNAH CROXSON... children JAMES NANCY (?) and BETSEY, Dec. 21, 1795... JOHN CROXSON (+) (SEAL). Wit: H. NICHOLSON, EDWARD BROWN, ALLEN BURTON. Proven 17 (?) Dec. 1796...

Pages 155-156: Inventory of est. of JOHN CROXSON, dec'd. made Feb. 18, 1797.

Next page is numbered 159 and is blank.

Pages 160-163: Inventory, appraisement and sale of goods of WILLIAM HARRIS, dec'd. Feb. 15, 1796. Appraisers THADEUS BEALL, JNO. BARKSDALE, JAMES DAVIS. Buyers: DRURY MITCHELL, JEREMIAH MCCARTER, ROBERT KELLEY, adn BURNS, HENRY MITCHELL, JOHN BELL, WM. WILEY, NATHL. CLAY, THOMAS HICHENBOTHOM, WILLIAM DICKERSON, GIAT (?) BEALL, JAMES DAVIS... a list of articles purchased by the widow of WM. HARRIS... MATTHEW HARRIS, Admr. Proven acct. of PETER DENT, THOS BAILEY, NATHL. TATUM, HENRY MILLER, SETH TATUM, JEREMIAH NELSON, THADEUS BEALL, JNO BURCH.

Pages 165-166: Amt. of sales est. of MEREDITH PRICE, brot from page 137; Buyers: NANCY PRICE, LEVIN HUTSON, HUBBARD PERREL (FERREL?), ROBERT CHAMBERS, THOMAS ILLIOT, PRESSLEY SCURLOCK ZACHARIAH PRICE, AARON MCKENZIE, SAMUEL PARKER, WM. BIVINS, WM. HARGRAVE, JAMES WALKER, HARDY WOOTEN, JOHN BROWN, J. MC. MONTGOMERY, JOHN TALLIAFERRO, JOHN JONES, JOSHUA BUCKHALTER, SAMUEL ROBINSON, JOHN PRICE, JAMES GOYNE PURNELL TRUETT, JNO. BOOTH, RICHD BARFIELD, JONA BLACK, A. DANNELLY, ROBERT OWSLEY, JAMES M. MONTGOMERY, JOSHUA BUCKHALTER, ELIJAH LINGO.

Pages 167-171:   Amt. brot from page 117, est. of JAMES ADAMS... Name
mentioned: MARK MCCLENDON, MICAJAH HARRY (?), WM. FLOURNOY, JAMES
HUCKABY, WM. ALLE, JOHN DUKE, WM. CURETON, ROBERT HILL, WM. DUNN, WM.
JOHNSTON, JOHN MCKISSICK, JOHN PEAVY, PHILLIP TURNER, WM. MARTIN, ISAAC
MCCLENDON, WALTER HAMILTON, RICHARD BEARDEN, NOE DODDRIDGE, THOMAS
MCCLENDON, HAWTHORN, June 9, 1797, REUBEN BLANKENSHIP, 12 Jul. 1800 DAVID
ADAMS, returned following... JOHN RYMES. Sale: Buyers: JONATHAN
ADAMS, WILLIAM CLARK, CORNELIUS CLARK, FRANCIS ROSS, JOHN MIDDLEBROUGH,
ROBERT CLARK, MARY ADAMS, ROBERT HILL, ISAAC MORELAND, MOSES WILEY,
JOSHUA SPRADLING, JOHN MCCAUTREY (?), MARK SANDERS, WILLIAM SELMAN, JOHN
MCCOY, JOHN WINSLET, BENNET IVEY... DAVID ADAMS, JONA ADAMS, MARY ADAMS,
Exrs.

Page 172: Blank.

Pages 173-174:   Will of DANIEL RICHARDSON of Hancock Co.... son THOMAS..
son OBEDIAH, daughter POLLEY THOMAS, daughter ELIZABETH HARRIS...
daughter CATY LAMAR... daughter NANCY DENT... daughter MARGRET WILLIAMS..
sons GABRIEL and ARMSTREAD... daughter SALLEY... friend JAMES BISHOP
and son OBADIAH RICHARDSON, Exrs... March 9, 1796... DANIEL RICHARDSON
(SEAL). Wit: DIXON HALL, STEPHEN BISHOP, LEWIS TYRES. Proven by
STEPHEN BISHOP & LEWIS TYRES, March 1, 1797.

Page 175: Inventory of est. of DANIEL RICHARDSON, appraised by
STEPHEN BISHOP, LEWIS TYRES, JAMES BISHOP, May 20, 1797.

Page 176: Blank.

Pages 177-179:   Will of BENJAMIN THOMPSON, SENR. of Hancock Co.... very
sick and weak in body... my dearly beloved wife ANNE... to my son JESSE
son WILLIAM... to my daughter RACHEL CUTCHING (CATCHING?)... sons
BENJAMIN THOMPSON, JOHN THOMPSON, ISHAM THOMPSON, GIDEON THOMPSON, JOSEPH
THOMPSON and the heirs of ZACHARIAH THOMPSON one dollar to each of them..
daughters REBECCA JONES, SUSANNAH MCINTOSH & NANCY CAWLY one dollar to
each... to grandsons BENJAMIN WOOD, JOSEPH WOOD one hundred dollars when
they come of age... wife ANNE, JESSE son, and friend HENRY GRAYBILL,
Exrs... May 12, 1796... BENJA. THOMPSON (SEAL). Wit: HEN. GRAYBILL,
SOLOMON JORDAN, JOHN GOODE. Proven by SOLOMON JORDAN and JOHN GOODE,
March 10, 1797.

Page 180: Iventory of est. of BENJAMIN THOMPSON, April 29, 1797.
Appraisers: PETER BOYLE, JOHN PINKSTON, CHAS ABERCROMBIE.

Page 181: Blank.

Page 182:   Amount of receipts on est. of BENJAMIN THOMPSON, by legatees.
BENJAMIN THOMPSON, JR., JAMES WOOD, ANNE THOMPSON, REBECKAH JONES,
SEYMORE CATCHING, SEYMORE CATCHING for WILLIAM THOMPSON.

Page 183:   Part of est. of EDMD CROWDER, brot from page 154: Signed:
HEN GRAYBILL, JAMES LUCAS, R. TARWELL (?).

Pages 184-185:   Will of NEWDAY OWSLEY of Hancock County... to wife
MARY ANN... to daughter PATSY (?) CONNELL... to son WILLIAM OWSLEY...
to son ROBERT OWSLEY... to ANNA OWSLEY, SARAH OWSLEY and CHLOE OWSLEY...
sons WM. & ROBT. Exrs... Oct. 16, 1796... NEWDAY OWSLEY (SEAL). Wit:
WILL. DENT, ZACHARIAS MIDDLETON, SAML. DENT. Proven April 10, 1797.

Pages 186-188:   Inventory of est. of NEWDAY OWSLEY, dec'd. Jan. 21,
1797, appr. by JONATHAN BLACK, AARON MCKENZIE, WM. MCKENZIE.

Page 189: Blank.

Pages 190-199:   Inventory and appraisement of est. of TOBIAS MCCLURE,
dec'd. Also sale included. Buyers: ABSALOM HARRIS, GAILE LEWIS, CHAS.
ABERCROMBIE, BRICE GAITHER, JOHN CHAPPELL, H. HOLT, J. CLEMONS, THADEUS
HOLT, JAMES PINKSTON, THOMAS JOHNSON, JOHN FREEMAN, NANCY LANIER, THOMAS
H. LAWGHAM, B. BALL, JAMES WOOD, W. ABERCROMBIE, A. BROELAND, Doctor

ROSITER, JOAB DERHAM, THOMAS DILLARD, ALLEN WHATTY, HILLARY PHILIPS, JOHN BREWER, THOMAS MOODY, ABRAM BORELAND, REUBEN HERNDON, BERYL. ANDERSON, BENJ. ANDERSON, RICHD. WHATTEY, J. PHILIPS, DAVID LONG, JULIUS SANDERS, THOMAS JOHNSON, J. LONG, ANDREW BORELAND, JOHN LEWIS, MICHAEL PEAVY, A. COMER, A. RISPASS, FRANCIS TRAWICK, STEPHEN BISHOP, SAML. HALL, M. MANGHAM, STEPHEN NOBLES, WM. CLOWERS, PARSON SKELLEY, BANALLY SHIVERS. WM. THOMAS LANGHAM, Admr.
   Claims against estate of TOBIAS MCCLURE... THOMAS H. LANGHAM, PETER L. VANALEN, ALLEN CAMRON.

Pages 200-202: Blank.

Pages 203: Inventory and appraisement of est. of MARTIN HAMMONS, dec'd. May 6, 1797. Debtos WILLIAM TURNER, JAMES TURNER... GEORGE STROTHER, WILLIAM HEARN, THOMAS TRAMMEL, appraisers.

Page 204: Blank.

Pages 205-206: Will of WILLIAM MINOR, Hancock County... to loving wife NANCY... to son WILLIAM the plantation we now occupy... 2000 acres in Washington County... 4000 acres in Montgomery County... purchased of STEPHEN NOBLES... two lots at Lexington... lot at shoals of Ogeechee... sold to WILLIAM WEST... BARRETT BREWER & JOHN HAMMETT to settle my accounts with JOHN FREEMAN... to my brother SAMUEL WRIGHT MINOR and my sister POLLEY MINOR of Maryland... all my lands in the state of South Carolina... my father WILLIAM MINOR of S.C. and my cousin JOHN MINOR of Hancock Co., Exrs... WM. MINOR (SEAL). Wit: H. NICHOLSON,HUBD BONNER, STEPHEN HOOKER. Will Dated June 4, 1797.

Pages 207-209: Blank.

Pages 210-211: Will of AARON MCKENZIE of Hancock County... wife JEMIMA, all my goods... Dec. 28, 1796... AARON MCKENZIE (SEAL). Wit: H. NICHOL-SON, THOMAS CALLAWAY (+), LUCY NICHOLSON (X). Proven June 29, 1797 by H. NICHOLSON.

Page 212: Inventory and appraisements of est. of AARON MCKENZIE, dec'd. Appraisers, JONATHAN BLACK, ROBERT OWSLEY, WM. GANTT, Aug. 29, 1797.

Page 213: Blank.

Pages 214-215: Will of ANDREW POGUE of Hancock Co... to wife, planta-tion where I now live... to my imprudent daughter MARY MORGAN, 5 shillings sterling... to daughter ELIZABETH when she reaches 18... to my son JOHN... my sons SAMUEL, ANDREW, ROBERT, DAVID & JOHN... wife MARY and friend JOHN ROGERS, Exrs... June 25, 1795... ANDREW POGUE (A) (SEAL). Wit: THOMAS CREDILLE, PEGGY B. CREDILLE, FABIAN M. CREDILLE. Proven Aug. 5, 1797 by PEGGY B. CREDILLE & FABIAN M. CREDILLE.

Pages 216-217: Inventory of est. of ANDREW POGUE, appraised Nov. 1, 1797, by JOHN ROGERS, SHEARWOOD WOMACK, PEYTON COFFEE.

Page 218: Blank.

Pages 219-222: Will of ABRAHAM WOMACK, June 2, 1797... to wife MARTHA.. my five youngest children, ELIZABETH, SARAH, LUCY, WILLIAM and JESSIE... my three sons in law WILLIAM STONE, CLEMENT GLENN and FRANCIS COLEMAN... for my son JOHN, 100 acres... JOHN REITS line... COEMAN's line... FRAZIERS Line... to my son SHEAWOOD WOMACK... to my son DAVID WOMACK... to my daughter SUSANNAH GLENN... to my daughter MARY COLEMAN... my grandaughter PATSEY HOWARD... sons SHEARWORD WORMACK, MANCIL WOMACK and JAMES H (K?) MCFARLAND, Exrs... ABRAHAM WOMACK (SEAL), MARTHA WOMACK (+). Wit: JOHN WHITE, THOMAS LIGHTFOOT, WALTER BROWN.

Pages 223-224: Inventory of est. of ABRAHAM WOMACK, dec'd., appraised Sept. 1, 1797 by JOHN ROGERS, A. JONADAB REED, PETER COFFEE.

Pages 225-226: Will of ROGER THORANTON, Dec. 5, 1796... to grandson
ISOM THORANTON... to son WILLIAM THORANTON, Land on Rocky Branch where
he now lives... to my wife CATHARIN, my dwellin plantation... between
my sons and daughters or their heirs... to my son JOHN THORANTON...
son LINSEY THORANTON... son HENRY and ZORABABLE WILLISON, Exrs... ROGER
THORANTON (SEAL) (X). Wit: ZOROBABEL WILLIAMSON, NATHL. WALLER,
CATHRANE WHATLEY (X). Proven by NATHL WALLER and CATHRANE WHATLEY
Sept. 1797.

Pages 227-228: Inventory and appraisement of est. of ROGER THORNTON,
dec'd. Sept. 28, 1797, JOHN HAMILTON, WILLIAM TALLARD, MARK SANDERS,
appraisers.

Pages 229-231: Sale of est. of ROGER THORNTON, dec'd. sold Nov. 4, 1803.
Buyers: not listed. HENRY THORNTON, ZORABABLE WILLIAMS, Exrs.

Pages 232-241: Inventory of est. of WILLIAM MINOR JUNR., late dec'd.
Lands: (1) 2000 acres in Washington County, Deed from JOHN HAMPTON,
Tax Collector, (2) four tracts in Montgomery County... grant to JNO
HUTCHINSON, (3) land granted to ELIJAH CLARK... two lots in Lexington,
deed from ROBERT MIDDLETON... lot in Lexington, deed from CHAS. STROTHER
... house and lot in Sparta, Hancock Co. 4 acres to WM. MINOR... NB
JOHN FREEMAN has got titles to this property since the decease of WM.
MINOR... deed from JOEL MCLANDON, 25 Dec. 1793, one lot at Montpelier...
one lot in Georgetown deed from ARTHUR FORT & wife... bounty to THOS.
MOSLEY, JR., 10 May 1785, deed from STEPHEN BISHOP & wife part of a
tract bought of A. BREED, sold to WILLIAM HIST, conveyed by JOHN MARCUS,
May 26, 1796. Bonds and Notes on JOHN CURRIE, HENRY ROGERS, HENRY
CHATMAN, REUBIN MOBLY, RICHMOND FERREL, AARON MCKINZIE, JOHN WALLACE
(Georgetown), PETER WILLIAMSON, WILLIAM WEST, ALLEN JENKINS, JESSE
THOMPSON, WILLIAM DENTON, THOMPSON BIRD, PETER WMSON... MILL MONK,
PHILLIP NEWTON, JOSEPH JOHN MARTIN, WILLIAM WILLIAMSON, GEORGE PURVIS,
DAVID WEATHERSPOON, JOSEPH DICKINSON, DANIEL MCLANE, BENJAMIN READY,
JOSHUA SEAL, HUGH SAXON, JOHN BLAKEN, BENJAMIN GILBERT, EDMUND BEARD,
JOHN BIRD, JOHN FENNING, DANIEL WALLER, JOHN PERMENTER, BARRETT BREWER,
WILLIAM HUTCHINSON, THOMAS MARTIN, AMBROSE CRAWFORD, SOLOMON NEWSOM,
EDWIN HARRIS, WILLIAM BENTON, EDMD. WALSH, ARTHUR LONG, WILLIAM WALLACE,
JOHN BEAMAN, JERE BONNER, HINES HOTT, D. Sheriff Hancock County, JOHN
GRIFFIN, BENJAMIN BRANHAM, WILLIAM J. HOBBY (Augusta), THOMAS SCHLEY,
JOSEPH HUTCHINSON, GEORGE HENNING, DAVID HILLHOUSE, JEHU CALLAWAY COOPER,
HENRY ROGERS, HUGH SAXON, GEORGE SIMPSON LENBURGH, THEOPHILUS HICKMAN,
JAMES CATHELL, JOHN KANSOLLAN, BENJAMIN PARKER, JEREMIAH BONNER, ROBERT
BLACKENY, JOHN KIMBRO, Blacksmith, BENJN. SIJS, ELIZABETH RILY widow,
JOHN FREEMAN, Sparta, JOHN R. HOGA, JOB TOWNSLY, LEWIS BAILEY, JAMES
GOYNE, ABNER WOOD, THOMAS HOLLIMAN, WILLIAM ROBERTSON, WILLIAM WILLSON,
gone to S. Carolina, AARON GEEGAN, ELIJAH WELLS, JAMES GRAYHAM, DAVID
MCALISTIN, JOHN BROWN, REUBEN MOBLEY, ROBERT LISCOE, JOHN STEVENDER,
HUGH FRANAKIN, DANIEL WALLER, LITTLETON REESE, EEVIN CALLAWAY, FANNY
FORSYTH, Augusta, ISHAM KARR, CHARLES MILL painter, WILLIAM SMITH Rock
landing, HENRY CHATMAN, MARY BAILEY, EDWARD BROWN, ROBERT BONNER, JOSEPH
MONTGOMERY, STEPHEN HOOKER, JOHN MARCUS, Washington Co., SEWALL HOLLAND,
PATSEY SIMS, ENOCH SEAL, ADAM KIMBROE, BENJAMIN READY, SILAS and CEASAR
HAWKINS... ROBERT MIDDLETON, JAMES JONES (son of WHISHY), BARTLEY
MCCRARY, JACOB PARKER, Capt. JAMES MCM. MONTGOMERY, JAMES CORSAN, JOHN
BOOTH, JOSHUA SEAL, JONATHAN DAY, JAMES VINSON, MARTIN NALL (?),
WILLIAM OWSLEY, SAML. SINQUEFIELD SENR., NATHL PACE, CALEB HERSON, JESSE
RILY, JACOB DENNIS, JOHN DOWNS (Cooper), Col. THOMAS LAMAR, JAMES RILY,
RICHARD BONNER, GABRIEL HUBERT, ROBERT JACKSON, ABRAHAM TAYLOR, JOSEPH
BONNER, MARTIN JOHNSON, JAMES COWDEN, JOHN DE GAMPERT (Columbia Co.),
CHARMES MCDONOLD (Ogechee), BAYARD WEATHERSPOON, WILLIAM WILLIAMSON,
Atty at Law, TEPLE LEA, JOHN WM. DEVEREUX (contractor), ARCHIBALD
BRYANT, CHARLES STOTHAM, WILLIAM RILY, MAJR. CHARLES WILLIAMSON, THOMAS
SHIELDS, Esqr. HENRY DIXON, JOHN B. WHITNEY, JAMES SEAGROVES, FERDINAND
PHINIGY, A. ALLEN (Shoal Ogechee), JOB ALLEN, COL. BENJA. FEW, Mrs.
SUSANNAH IRBY, CHARLES IRBY, dec'd., BENAJAH SMITH (once contractor),
MAJR. BUCKNER HARRIS, JAMES COOPER, AARON MCKINZIE assigned to JOSEPH
HUTCHINSON.

Pages 241-246:   Inventory of Goods on the House, appraised by JOHN
MITCHELL, JEAMES THWEATT & JAMES BONNER.

Pages 247-249:   Blank.

Pages 250-251:   Inventory of property of JAMES MCGAUGHEY, dec'd.,
appraised July 1, 1797.

Pages 252-253:   Blank.

Pages 254-255:   Account of sale of est. of JAMES DOWDLE late dec'd.,
Oct. 27, 1796, Buyers: BART JOHNSON, BENJN. GILBERT, EDWD WOODHAM, JAS.
HARVEY, JONATHAN MOORE, JAMES WALLER, JOHN GREER, JOSEPH HENRY, HENRY
GARRETT, JOHN COLBERT, JEREMIAH BELL, EPHRAIM SAMMONS, WM. KILGORE, JAS.
WALLER, JAS. TURNER, THOMAS CAVENER, SOLOMON LANKSTON, THOMAS MELVIN,
ROBERT KELLY, JONATHAN MOORE, WM. GILES, JONATHAN BLACK, JAMES HENRY,
JOSHUA ELLIS, STEPHEN WILLIAMS, RISDON MOORE, JOHN CALDWELL, JOHN
WILLIAMS, THOMAS DICKINSON, JOSEPH BARKSDALE, JOEL DICKINSON, WEMBORN
DICKINSON, DRURY ROGERS, JOSHUA KENNY, WM. KILGORE, DAVID SPHERES, JAS.
HALLER, STEPHEN NOBLES, JONATHAN MOORE, GEORGE WEST, EDMUND BUTLER, THO-
MAS MELVIN, JOSHUA CALVER, MICHL GILBERT, THOMAS GREENE, BENJ.   PEARCE,
NATHAN SMITH, STEPHEN WALLER, JESSE JOHNSON, ROBERT SIMMS, ISAAC ELLIS,
SARAH RAYFIELDS, JOHN WEEKS, JAS MCGEE, WM. OWSLEY, B. J. DOWDLE,
JOHN DOWDLE... WM. GREER, B. J. DOWDLE, Exrs.

Page 256:   Accounts return to office by Exrs. of JAS DOWDLE, Sept. 2,
1797, ___ LACY, Doctor RICHARD H. TAYLOR, JOHN DOWDLE.

Page 257:   Blank.

Pages 258-259:   Will of WILLIAM COLBERT... wife MIRIAM COLBERT...
daughter LUCY HAWKINS... son WILLIAM COLBERT... son JONATHAN COLBERT,
100 acres, part of tract where I now live... daughter ELIZABETH FAUSTER
son JOHN COLBERT... to ALEXANDER MCDOWELL ... grandson FEDERICK GERR
COLBERT... sons WILLIAM & JONATHAN and son in law THOMAS HAWKINS, Exrs.
Oct. 24, 1797, WILLIAM COLBERT (X) (SEAL). Wit: JOEL MCCLENDON JP,
JOHN BROWN. Proven Nov. 13, 1797.

Pages 260-261:   Appraisement of goods of WM. COLBERT, Nov. 13, 1797,
GEORGE LEE, ABRAHAM MILLS, JAMES WALKER, Appraisers.

Pages 262-263:   Receipts and expenditures on est. of JAS ADAMS for year
1797, returned Jan. 6, 1798. Paid tax in Green County... names mentioned
GODFREY MARTIN, JOHN BEEKER, SETH KENEDY, STERLING CATOE, JAMES WOOTEN,
MATTHEW GASTON, ROBERT BOLTON, THOMAS CUMMING, BENJ. HARRIS, ARCHIBALD
HATCHER, WILLIAM MARTIN, JOHN SHACKLEFORD, GEORGE SMITH, JAMES ROSS,
SPENCER THOMAS, SAML. HARRIS, ROBT. CUNNINGHAM, JAMES THWEATT, THOMAS
WYNN, BENJAMIN BRASEL, THOMAS GRIMES.

Page 264:   Receipts returned to this office, taken from the legatees of
WM. COLBERT, dec'd., returned by WM. COLBERT, Exr. April 15, 1799.
CLAIBURN FOSTER (legatee), ALEXANDER MCDONALD (legatee), JONATHAN COL-
BERT (legatee), Mrs. MIRIAM COLBERT (legatee).

Pages 265-271:   Inventory of goods, etc. of est. of ABRAHAM WOODWARD,
Sept. 20, 1797... list of goods in copartnership with ABRAHAM, AARON &
WILLIAM WOODWARD... list of goods in copartnership between ABRAHAM,
AARON, WILLIAM & JOSEPH... WILLDENT, HEN GRAYBILL, RISDON MOORE, Apprsrs.

Pages 272-273:   Blank.

Pages 274-275:   Will of MARK JACKSON, weak in body... to son ROBERT
JACKSON... wife MARTHA JACKSON... land in Hancock County... to my son
MARK JACKSON... sons WARREN JACKSON and EDMOND JACKSON... son HENRY
JACKSON... sons JOHN & JETHRO JACKSON, Dec. 1, 1797. MARK JACKSON (LS).
Wit: R. HARWELL, H. HILL, EPHRAIM JACKSON. Proved at a court held for
County of Brunswick, State of Virginia, will proved by HERBERT HILL &
EPHRAIM JACKSON, Dec. 25, 1797. Note: ments. "to son WILLIAM JACKSON"
which was omitted.

119

Page 276:   Inventory of est. of MARK JACKSON, March 3, 1798... names mentioned: JESSE WARREN, JAS BRIDGES.

Pages 276-279:   Inventory and appraisement of est. of BENJAMIN JACKSON dec'd., March 3, 1798. Appraisers: HENRY JACKSON, JOHN JACKSON, ALEXR. REED, JESSE WARREN, JOHN STURDIVANT.

Page 280:   List of bonds and notes belonging to MARK JACKSON & ROBERT JACKSON and WARREN JACKSON, orphans of MARK JACKSON, dec'd. Names mentioned: JOHN STURDEVANT, JETHRO JACKSON, REUBEN HERNDON, ANDREW JETER, SOLOMN BUTTS, ROBT RIVERS, ABSALOM HARRIS, JAMES HUCKABY, ANDERSON HARWELL, JAS RUEES SENR.

Page 281:   Vouchers on est. of JACOB PARKER, dec'd. brot from pg. 48. Names: HUBBERT REYNOLDS, MAR MARTIN, BOLLING HALE, JOSEPH HAMBRICK (legatee), EDWD BAYER, guardian for JOHN HAMBRICK, JAMES HAMBRICK, ARTHUR FOSTER's receipt for guardian from WM. HAMBRICK... BURWELL HAMBRICK, orphan of THOMAS HAMBRICK, dec'd. to WILLIAM RYAN.

Pages 282-283:   Amt. of sales on est. of BENJAMIN JACKSON, dec'd. March 3, 1798. Buyers: HENRY JACKSON, Mrs. PATSEY JACKSON, JAMES BRIDGES, SOLOMON MANGRAM, REUBIN WESTMORELAND, FRANCES LEWIS, JETHRO JACKSON, JOSEPH WESTMORELAND, MULES GREEN, ROBERT JACKSON, ALEXANDER REED, WILLIAM HUNT, WARREN JACKSON, JAMES HUCKEBY, MATTHEW BREWER, ZACHARIAH WILLIAMSON, WILLIAM SPENCER, FRANCIS LAWSON, JOHN STURDEVANT, ROBERT HILL, GALE LEWIS, JONATHAN HORAY, JACKSON HARWELL, JOHN BREWER, ROLLEY GREENE, JOHN HUDMAN, ANDREW JETER.

Pages 284-286:   Will of JAMES DANIELL of Hancock Co... to my son in law JAMES TAYLOR...to the heirs of my daughter SARAH and JAMES TAYLOR... to my son JOSE DANIELL, 300 acres on Congaree River... to son LEVY DANIELL, land in Washington County... wife NANCY DANIELL... land on Ocongy River, in Washington Co... unto WILLIAM HARDAGE... to son in law ROBERT HANDRICK, Land on Alligater Creek... to my granddaughter PATSEY HANDRICK... to my grandson JESSE DANIELL AUSTON, son of BETTY AUSTON, when he comes of age... JAMES DANIELL (SEAL), dated May 11, 1797. Wit: WM. BIGGINS, WM. JONES, JAMES H. JONES. Proven March 5, 1798.

Pages 287-289:   Inventory & appraisement of est. of JAMES DANIELL, April 2, 3 & 4, 1798.

Pages 290-291: Blank.

Pages 292-293:   Will of BARNABY POPE, of Hancock Co... May 10, 1795... to my daughter MARY POPE... to my daughter MOURNING CURREY's children... to my daughter MARTHA GIBSON's children... to my daughter LUCY CURSEY (CURREY?) children... to MARY POPES children... to son BARNABY MCKINNEY POPE... to my daughter JANE RUCHERS children... son HENRY NORMON POPE... THOMAS MOORE & JESSE MCKINNEY POPE Exrs... BARY POPE. Wit: HENRY TRIPPE, SARAH POPE. Proven by HENRY TRIPPE and SARAH POPE, ___ 1797.

Pages 294-295: Blank.

Pages 296-298:   Account of sales of est. of WILLIAM COLBERT, Feb. 9, 1798. Names: JONATHAN BLACK, BULAN JORDAN, JAMES WALKER, THOMAS HAWKINS, MOSES MILES, JONATHAN COLBERT, WILLIAM REDOCK, RANSOM LEIGH, MATHEW HAWKINS, WIDER COLBERT, JAMES MONTGOMERY, JOEL MCCLENDON, BARTLEY WALKER, WILLIAM SMITH, WILLIAM DENTON, JOHN LILES, HUBBARD FARRELL, MICHAEL ROGERS, JACOB BOZWORTH, BRITAIN JORDAN, ROBERT OWSLEY, SAMUEL MCGEE, ABRAHAM WALKER, RICHARD JENKINS, GEORGE LEIGH.

Page 299:   Blank.

Pages 300-301:   Will of JOHN WALKER, of Hancock Co... to son THOMAS and daughter ANN... land in Co. of ___, State of Maryland... land in Co. of Sussen, State of Delaware... brother THOMAS of Sussex Co., Delaware and NATHAN MELHVIN of Hancock Co., Ga., Exrs... March 7, 1798... JOHN WALLER (SEAL). Wit: P. BOYLE, JOAB DURHAM, JOHN CASTLEBERRY. Proven June 1, 1798.

Pages 302-303:   Blank.

Pages 304-305:   Will of PEYTON TUCKER of Hancock Co... to brother
BERRIMON TUCKER... to RICHARD BIGGINS, son of JOHN BIGGINS dec'd....
to LUCRETIA MORELAND... to SALLEY H. MORELAND... to WILLIAM BIGGINS...
WILLIAM BIGGINS and ROBERT MORELAND, Exres... Jan. 8, 1797. PEYTON
TUCKER (SEAL). Wit: ANDERSON HARWELL, WYATT COLLIER. Proven June 18,
1798.

Pages 305-306:   Inventory and appraisement of est. of PEYTON TUCKER,
Aug. 15, 1798... sale buyers: JOHN SHAKELFORD, WILLIE ABERCROMBIE...
names on receipts JOHN WHITEHURST, ROBERT MORELAND.

Pages 307-308:   Appraisement and sale of est. of JOHN BUTLER, dec'd.,
April 25, 1798. Buyers: NATHL KELLY, SAML. BRASWELL, GEORGE BUTLER,
JOHN PELLION, THOS. BRANTLEY, JAMES SAUDNERS, RUTH ONEAL, RICHD.
RESPASS, JESSE SANDERS, EDMOND BUTLER, JOHN BROWN, CALEB KENEDY, LEAVEN
TURNER, HUBBARD BROWN, DAVID YORK, ROBERT HILL, RICHD. GRAY, Doctor
ROSITER, PLANA SHORES, NATHAN DANIEL, DAVID WINYARD, WM. GILES, JOEL
REES, JEREMIAH SMITH, ANDREW JETER, JOHN STURDIVANT, JOHN ONEAL, STEPHEN
KIRK (?).

Page 310:   Inventory and sale of est. of JOHN JONES, recorded Aug.
17, 1798. Buyers: PRATER FUCA, JOHN BOOTH SENR., JOHN BOOTH JUNR.

Page 312:   List of proven accounts returned by ROBERT CHAMBERS and JOHN
JONES, Exrs. of est. of MEREDITH PRICE, dec. Aug. 31, 1798. Names:
ELIJAH LINGO, JOSHUA BUCKHALTER, SAMUEL WILSON, JAMES THWEATT, THOS.
MILES, N. W. MONTGOMERY, ABNER BARKSDALE, WILL MINOR, GEORGE SIMPSON,
NANCY PRICE, JOHN JONES, THOS CATES, THOS. PARROTT, MAR MARTIN, HUGH
SAXON, MYLES GRIMES, JOEL MCCLENDON, HENRY MCCOY, ROBERT CHAMBERS, JOHN
PRICE, W.? STITH, JUNR., JOHN GRIGGS, WM. HAY, BOLING HALL.

Pages 313-314:   Will of RICHARD HOLLAMAN of Hancock Co., planter...
daughter SARAH CURTON... son HARMON HOLLAMAN... CHARITY RACHEL, daughter.
WILLIAM, son land on Little Ogechee, 100 acres, to wife HARPY... daughter
ELIZABETH HOLLAMAN... July 23, 1798... RICHARD HOLLOMON (X) (SEAL).
Wit: HENRY TOWNSEND, JEHU GAULLINY. Proven Sept. 4, 1798.

Pages 315-316:   Blank.

Page 317:   Account of sale of est. of JOHN LAWSON, Jan. 1, 1803. Names:
FAVIAN CREDDLE, CHARLES GOSS, DUNCAN MCLEAN, Doctor LOCAIE, WM. REESE,
ELIZABETH BARNES, JERE NELSON, PATIENCE LAWSON, Mrs. DUGAN, JOHN LAWSON,
L. H. TAYLOR, GEO. STEWART.

JEFFERSON COUNTY, GA. WILLS

Book A 1777-1893

This book is completely typewritten with no explanation give as to who did the typing. It would appear that someone went through all the books in the Court House and picked out the Wills from various volumes and typed them in this one book. How it got to be named Book A is something of a mystery to your editor, and who it starts at 1777 instead of 1796 is still another mystery. This book does have an Index. In transcribing these Wills from these typed copies your editor has found what seems to be a great deal of errors in spelling and wording, which would make him tend to think that these may have been done by the W.P.A. in depression times. For those familiar with W.P.A. copies of legal records, one must remember that they were filled with many errors in transcription ommissions, as well as confusion with regards to relationships of persons named in original Wills, such as slaves often being mentioned as children instead of slaves. However, with nothing more to work with than these microfilm copies of the typed book, the reader is urged to use great care and caution if he finds a Will he is interested in and seek by some means to establish the persons in question.

Page 1:   Will of THOMAS ALEXANDER. Pro. 4 Sept. 1797. Made 16 Nov. 1778... weak in body. Wife MARTHA, JOHN WOODS, SR. & HUGH ALEXANDER to act and do for my wife and child, wife MARTHA one hors and saddle, son DAVID all my land and if it should please God to ad one more to my family, as it is in vue, then my cattle be equally divided bet. the three or whatever of them comes to yrs. of maturity. THOS. ALEXANDER. Wit: JAMES BRACKENRIDG, (TIMSON?) CARTER, JESS (I) CARE. JESSE CAREY swore to signing of Will on 15 Sept. 1797. ISAAC COLEMAN, R.P.

Pages 1-2:   Will of REASON WHITEHEAD. Made Sept. 8, 1780. Pro. Feb. 26, 1791. I REASON WHITEHEAD of Parish of St. George in Georgia, Planter, debts paid, Imprimis leave to dear and loving wife JANE WHITE-HEAD all my pers. est. and benefits arriving from my real Est., except such effects (as is after ment. and excepted) during her life and widowhood, and in case she chooses to marry, then 1/3 of all my pers. Est. Item: oldest son JOHN WHITEHEAD all my real Est., viz. lands with all improvements at death of his mother or her marriage, cattle, tools etc. Item: 2nd son REASON WHITEHEAD, 2 cows and calves and remaining 1/2 crops and joiner tools, also the value of my watch in a horse and the value of a saddle. Item: oldest dau. ELIZABETH, cows, calves, horse, saddle, feather bed and furn. etc. Item: 3rd dau. CATHERINE, one cow and calf. Item: 4th dau. JANE one cow and calf. Item: 5th dau. MARY one cow and calf. If son JOHN dies without heirs, his share to son REASON and if he dies without heirs, then to his sisters and if any daus. die bef. of age or marriage, then that portion equally divided bet. surviving children and at death of wife JANE all lands be valued and value thereof be div. among children, that each may have alike. Lastly, app't. wife JANE WHITEHEAD, JACOB WHITEHEAD and HUGH IRWIN to be my Extx. & Exors. Signed: REASON WHITEHEAD. Wit: 26 Feb. 1781 bef. JAMES IRWIN. Qual. by HUGH IRWIN 26 Feb. 1781, JA. WRIGHT. (The following being omitted are to be inserted at the "I leave & beq. to 2nd dau. SARAH 3 cows and calves and my Dun horse, one hunting saddle, one feather bed and furn. and one ewe and lamb." ... this was typed at bottom of transcribed copy, Ed.) Prob. bef. DANIEL MCNEIL, Reg. of Pro., Burke Co., Ga., who sd. he wrote the Will for REASON WHITEHEAD. Sworn to bef. DANIEL I. MURPHY, R.P.

Page 3:   Will of MISS MARTHA GREEN of Philadelphia. Made Jan. 1, 1798. This Will has already appeared on Page 85 of Wills 1796-1827, Books 1 & 3 in this issue.

Page 5:   Will of SAMUEL MCNEELEY. Made Nov. 15, 1796. Pro. April 11, 1797. I SAMUEL MCNEELEY of Jefferson County, farmer, very sick and weak

in body, gives and devises worldly Est. to dearly beloved Mother,
MARGARET MCNEELEY who he app'ts. Extx.   Wit: WILLIAM DANIEL' Sworn
to April 11, 1797, ISAAC COLEMAN, R.P.

Page 6:   Will of DAVID MCGOWAN. Made Sept. 12, 1796. Pro. March 3,
1798. I DAVID MCGOWAN of Jeff. Co., weak in body. Estate divided as
follows: to beloved wife ELIZABETH 5 shillings sterling; dau. MARY and
son JOHN all cattle now in their name; son WILLIAM to have 6 mos.
schooling ; to 3 children all rest of my Est. share and share alike.
Appt's. JOHN FEYL, JOHN ROGERS & HENRY MCCONKY sole Exors. Signed:
DAVID MCGOWAN. Sub. Wit. sworn to 3 March 1798, JOHN TOYIL, JOHN ROGERS.

Page 7:   Will of JOSEPH BEATTY. Made Nov. 12, 1796. Pro. Dec. 13,
1798. I JOSEPH BEATTY of Jeff. Co., weak, do this 12 Nov. 1796, make this
L.W.&T. to: son in law JAMES WILSON 100 acres to be taken off So. end
of tract where I now live; dau. JANE BEATY 100 acres, adj. afsd. being
part of same tract; son SAMUEL BEATY 150 acres for term of his nat. life
and after his decease same is devised to son WILLIAM BEATY and his heirs;
son WILLIAM BEATY all remainder of sd. tract of 150 acres; son in law
JAMES NORTON 5 shillings and remainder of land all all my stock of cattle
to be equally div. bet. sons SAMUEL & WILLIAM BEATY and dau. JANE BEATY.
Ordain son WILLIAM & BENJAMIN WHITAKER, Exors. Signed: JOSEPH BEATY.
Signed, Sealed & Del. bef. MATTHEW CARSWELL, JOHN WILLSONS, JAMES WARNOCK.

Page 8:   Will of WILLIAM JUNKINS. Made Feb. 4, 1777. Pro. March 19,
1799, being low in health, personal prop. sold at public sale and turned
into realm of money for the uses after mentioned.   3rd. money from sale
to dearly beloved Father JAMES JUNKINS in Parish of Learn, County of
Antrim & Kgdom of Ireland, also a certain tract cont. 100 acres lying
in Queensborough, in case of death of sd. Father bef. these things come
to his hands, I will and beq. all above money and land to my nephew
WILLIAM JUNKINS in Parish of Broad Island, Co. and Kingdom bef. recited,
4th. beq. to bros. SAMUEL, JAMES, THOMAS & JOHN JUNKINS to each one
shilling or 12 pence. Appt. ROBERT GIVENS & ANDREW BOYD my lawful
attorneys... and in case my father or nephew should never come to this
place to enjot the sd. land, then Attorneys to dospose of same and trans-
mit money as above directed. Signed: WILLIAM (X) JUNKINS. Wit:
WILLM. LITTLE, JR., RICHARD FLEETING, JOHN ANDERSON.
          Ct. of Ord. Jefferson Co., 3 May 1832, App. JOHN MANSON one
of Sub. Wit. to L. W. & T. of WILLIAM JUNKINS and saw same sign will...
and that he and RICHARD FLEETING and MATTHEW LYLE subs. their names as
Wit.

Page 9:   Will of MARY SMITH. Made Jan. 10, 1799. Pro. April 15, 1799.
I MARY SMITH of Lincoln County, Georgia, sick and weak... beq. to nephew
WILLIAM LEWIS CLEMENTS and his heirs all tract sit. on Rappahannock
River, Virginia, Richmond County, known by name of Folly... also another
tract adj. the Folly SAMPFORD; to my neice MARY CLEMENTS all Int. in
negroes and pers. Est. which my Mother was in possession of at present
which she has a life Est. in, equally div. bet. nephew and neice, JOHN
& MARY CLEMENTS. App't. WILLIAM CLEMENTS, Exor. Signed: MARY SMITH.
Wit: JOHN PUGESLY, LUCY PUGESLY, ANN (X) BUTLER.   JOHN PUGESLEY swore
to signing 15 April 1799, WILLIAM MCDANIEL, C.C.O.J.C.

Page 9:   Will of MILDRED PALMER. Made (no date)... Pro. (do not find
date; JOS. E. POSUR & WM. MCDOWELL have Wills filed here made and Pro.
Feb. 25, 1801.) I MARY PALMER... of sound mind... beq. 1st. grandau.
NANCY PALMER, dau. of EDWARD & ELIZABETH PALMER one negroe woman named
Rose and one bed, to my other granddau. being also the dau. of EDWARD &
ELIZABETH PALMER, named BETTY PALMER one feather bed, mare and colt, to
my graddau. being dau. of EDWARD & ELIZABETH PALMER named MARY PALMER I
leave one bed, the money arising from sale of tract of land which I
wold to ELIZABETH PALMER the sd. MARY PALMER mother which money she was
by agreement was to have pd. to me which I never received... I also
leave to my sd. grandau. ELIZABETH PALMER all the ready money I may be
possessed of at my decease and do name THOMAS SCOTT, JOHN SCOTT & WILLIAM
MCDOWELL & WILLIAM DEPHES, Exors. Signed: MILDRED (X) PALMER. Wit:
J. E. POSUR, WILLIAM MCDOWILL, WILLIAM MCGEHEE.

123

Page 10:   Will of THOMAS MCBRIDE: Made Oct. 11, 1799. Pro. Jan. 4, 1800. I THOMAS MCBRIDE of Jeff. Co., Planter, weak of body... beq. to my loving son JAMES all tract of land adj. SAMUEL GORDON on Dry Creek cont. 100 acres... dau. MARY, tract lying on Horse Creek be sold and div. as my Exors see cause... beloved wife should she marry, I allow her if those places are sold and raises as much as will purchase 2 negroes that she have one of them... if that cannot be done I allow her 50 acres and 3 cows and calves. My debts when collected put to best use for my small children. App't. Exors: loving Friend, GEORGE CARTER, THOMAS MCBRIDE & my loving son JAS. MCBRIDE & The Rev. DAVID BOTHWELL to assist when convenient by his advisers. Signed: THOMAS (X) MCBRIDE. Wit: DAVID BOTHWELL, GEORGE CARTER, WM. DOWELL, Clerk.

Page 11:   Will of BLASSINGAME HARVEY, SR.   Made Dec. 27, 1799. Pro. Feb. 27, 1800. I BLASSINGAME HARVEY, SR. of Jeff. Co. in low state of health... give lot in town of Louisville the lowest of Two No. _____ to son THOMAS HARVEY; dau. BETSY TUBERFIELD HARVEY wife to BLASSINGAME HARVEY, JR., 300 acres whereso they now live off of survey of DAVID RUSSELL... I give to their 5 children: GOLPHIN, BETSY TUBERFIELD, FRANCES, POLLY and TUBERFIELD HOLKUM HARVEY, 60 acres off of afsd. survey adj. & bet. the bef. ment. 300 acres & bef. ment. 250 acres... together with 4 negroes... be equally div. bet. all their children now born or to be born at death of sd. BETSY T. HARVEY. Item: Son, JOHN HARVEY, residue of that survey of DAVID RUSSELL on the side of Rocky Comfort, together with the mill & tract of land I now live on, say 350 acres all together, his mother having use of sd. land dur. nat. life... also to Son, JOHN, 2 negroes, a little house called TRIEKUM, cows, lot in town of Louisville... to son BILLY BLASSINGAME HARVEY all tract over Rocky Comfort adj. lands of ISAAC LOCHART & JOHN SHELLMAN's... 216 acres and whatever remains on So. side of Rocky Comfort, say 40 acres, 2 negroes and unimproved lot in Louisville adj. lot to his bro. THOMAS HARVEY. Item: Property of every kind I give to daus. POLLY KEY, SALLY PAWLETT & FRANCES BLACKMAN. Wife, Extx. and TANDY G. KEY & JOHN PAWLETT, Exors. Wit: JNO. PUGSLEY, PHILLIP CLAYTON. Rec. Book A, 29 July, 1801 and on Fos. 41, 42, 43, 44, 45, 46 & 47. JAS. BOZEMAN.

Page 13:   Will of POOL HALL: Made May 20, 1800. Pro. July 22, 1800. I, POOL HALL of Jeff. Co.,... very sick... 1st my dearly beloved wife SUSANNA one negro man and others... as for 2 daus. NANCY STANLY and ZELPHY HALL I give unto them 5 shillings each - POLL - all and singular my lands, hsld. farm, houses... and at her decease my son JAMES to have negro Frank and likewise after her decease the negro named Poll to be given to my 2 sons JOSEPH & REDDEN HALL... feather bed after wife's decease to son JOSEPH HALL. Wit: MICHALL FIELDS, EANIS FOUNTAIN, JAMES (X) HALL. WM. MCDOWELL, Clerk.

Page 14:   Will of ELIZABEHT PAULETT: Made July 7, 1799. Pro. July 21, 1800. I, ELIZABETH PAULETT of Jeff. Co.... to son RICHARD PAULETT 1/2 all money due me from THOMAS PAULETT for the hire of one negro man named Burnly, also 1/2 all money that may be due from sd. THOMAS PAULETT while he had management of my negro. Son: JESSE PAULETT the other 1/2 of all money due from above THOMAS PAULETT of Charlotte Co., in Virginia, also one feather bed and furn. horse. Appt's. sons RICH'D. PAULETT & JESSE PAULETT Exors. Signed: ELIZABETH (X) PAULETT. Wit: EDMUND BAILEY, JOHN REES (E), DAVID PAULETT.

Page 15:   Will of BENJAMIN JAMES: Made Sept. 6, 1797. Pro. Sept. 6, 1800. of Co. of Jeff., farmer, very sick and weak... to beloved wife SARAH during her nat. life 2 negroes and after her death to be property of SARAH DUBOSE. Also I beq. to bel. wife after decease her riding mare and saddle and I give & beq. to BENJAMIN JAMES my bel. son 3 negroes... beq. to youngest son JOHN JAMES 3 negroes... sons: JOHN JAMES and BENJAMIN JAMES all my lands, houses, horses, cattle etc. Dau. SARAH shall have wife's clothing. Make ISAAC DUBOSE & my eldest son BENJAMIN JAMES my Exors. Signed: BENJAMIN JAMES. Wit: MOSES NEWTON.

Page 15:   Will of Mrs. MARY PAULETT: Made May 9, 1800. Pro. Jan. 30, 1801. Give to dau. JEAN HARDWICK the wife of GARLAND HARDWICK all my

property of every kind with Sarah (a negro) and her children (names 8).
Appt. beloved brother JESSE PAULETT & my trust friend JOHN REEC & my
well beloved dau. JEAN HARDWICK my Exors. and Extx. Signed: MARY
PAULETT. Wit: JOHN VINNING, JR., WM. CLARK, JUDITH HARDWICK.

Page 16: Will of PATRICK MCNEELY: Made Dec. 25, 1800. Pro. Jan. 21,
1801. I, PATRICK MCNEELY of Jeff. Co. being very sick and weak... give
to loving wife PROCEDANCE MCNEELY 1/3 of pers. Est... to son PAUL
GRIMBLE MCNEELY another 1/3... dau. SARAH MCNEELY another 1/3. Signed:
PATRICK MCNEELY. Wit: GEO. INGRAM, RACHEL (X) CROSSLE (CROSSEL). Wit:
ELENOR (X) MCNEELY. An amendmentor Schoadle to the above Will if that
I allow my mother MARGARET MCNEELY 50 acres of my plantation with the
surplus land unmolliated her lifetime and then divided as Wit. my hand.
Same date and Wit's.

Page 17: Will of WILLIAM DAWKINS: Made Dec. 7, 1800. Pro. Jan. 30,
1801. "I WILLIAM DAWKINS, SR. of Jefferson Co... to beloved wife JANE
DAWKINS use of my plantation in Jeff. Co. adj. lands of SAMUEL ANDREWS...
to dau. DOLLY TARVER, wife of JACOB TARVER, 2 negros named Charlotte
and Sylvia... to JANE (Dau?) 2 negro girs Poll and Nelly... to dau. ELLEN
DAWKINS wife of GEORGE DAWKINS 2 negros namely Lucy and Venus... to dau.
CALEO GRAY wife of FREDERICK GRAY. Son WILLIAM DAWKINS 3 negros,
Solomon, Nan and Prince... son MICAJAH DAWKINS 3 negros Winny, Lewis
and Henry, 2 plantations and tract he now lives known by name of
David Woods tract adj. COBBS land as far as the road leading from SAMUEL
ANDREWS to Keys Mill, cont. 131 acres. Son WILLIAM DAWKINS all the
lower part of tract I now live on adj. lands of GEORGE DAWKINS... on a
straight line to Ogechee River... son FRANCIS DAWKINS 4 negros and all
the remaining part of my lands whereon I now live herein bef. left to
wife... and all my stock of creatures, hsld. furn. etc. to be kept together for support of my wife and maintainence and education of son
FRANCIS till he arrives at age of 21 or marry. After wife's decease I
beq. to son FRANCIS DAWKINS all my stock, plantation tools, hsld. furn.
etc. Appoint beloved wife JANE DAWKINS and my sons WILLIAM, MICAJAH
DAWKINS, Exors. Signed: WILLIAM (X) DAWKINS. Wit: JOSEPH TOMME
(TOMMY), HEZEKIAH GATES.

Page 18: Will of THOMAS ASKEW: Made Aug. 11, 1798. Pro. Jan. 30,
1801. "I, THOMAS ASKEW, being weakly and sick though of sound mind..."
to dearly beloved wife plantation with the woodlands from the little
branch to the upper side supposed to 1/2 of tract... during widowhood...
after that I order it to my son HENRY and his heirs... Wife to have
hsld. furn. but if she marry then same property to be divided bet. my
daus. SARA & WINIFORD (the way the following is written would give the
impression that these were children, but it seems to the editor that
they are slaves) ... (Cleo, Margert, Mary, Truzanna, Hallon, Katron),
2 negros to wife and then to son HENRY if he live to age of 21... after
wife's decease, remainder of negros to be divided amongst daus. 4th.
to beloved son WILLIAM other part of my land on south side of the little
branch that divides the tract... and one young negro girl Diana. To
dau. NANY 5 shillings and to dau. MILLEY 5 shillings and dau. ELIZABETH
5 shillings. Appoints SETH FOUNTAIN & my son WILLIAM Exors. Signed:
THOMAS ASKEW. Wit: JOHN WOODS, SETH FOUNTAIN, JAS. BOZEMAN, C.C.O.

Page 19: WILLIAM WOOD came into Court and produced a paper purporting
to be the L. W. & T. of ROBERT WOOD, dec'd. the same being duly proced.
& App. Ordered to be Recorded.

Page 20: Will of WILLIAM MCDOWELL: Made Feb. 13, 1801. Pro. Feb.
25, 1801. "I, WILLIAM MCDOWELL, of sd. Co., Clerk of Sup. Ct... thereof
being from an accidental cause in which Thank God, I have no imputation
to lay on myself in a most dangerous state of body but of sound mind...
during my disorder beyond the power of physical aid...1st. I forgive &
wish to be forgotten every unfortunate event which took place on Sat. the
7th. of Feb. instant and hope no prosecution will take place in the
occasion... convinced that the shot which injured me was not intended.
And more so, as it came from the hand of a friend, who I am convinced
would as soon have injured himself. 2nd. devise to my father JOHN

MCDOWELL and my uncle WILLIAM MCDOWELL, of the Town or neighborhood ⸺ in
Igdom. of Ireland. To father JOHN MCDOWELL the sum of $400 and to uncle
WILLIAM MCDOWELL $300. 3rd. Beq. to JAMES STUBBS & DOCTOR JOSIAH M.
STERRET of this town, my sincere friends & Exors of this Will all the
rest of my Est. divided share and share alike and not as joint tenants.
Dated 13 Feb. 1801. Wit: JAS. JACKSON, GARLAND HARDWICK, STEPHEN
JOHNSON.

Page 21: Will of JOHN WARREN: Made Sept. 24, 1797. Pro. April 29,
1801. First, beq. to beloved son THOMAS WARREN 5 shillings; 2nd. beq.
to son in law STEPHEN VAUGH 5 shillings; 3rd. to beloved grandson WILSON
WARREN one feather bed and furn., one colt and yearling etc. and $40
when he comes of age. To beloved wife MARY WARREN all remain.. of Est.
for lifetime and then to my beloved son in law BRITTAIN SMITH. Appt's.
son in law BRITTAIN SMITH sole Exor. Signed: JOHN (X) WARREN. Wit:
SAMUEL SMITH, SIMON SMITH, JAMES BOZEMAN, C.C.O.

Pages 21-22: Will of WILLIAM WILSON: Made Feb. 3, 1801. Pro. April
29, 1801... to beloved wife SUSANNA WILSON my woman slave Rhode and her
2 children and at wifes death they to devolve to my children... wife
SUSANNA to possess all real Est. during widowhood... also to wife
farming tools. Property devolving to children to be divided equally
bet. them... furn., tools, leather to be sold and money arising to be
appropriated to use of my children. Appt's. WM. CAWTHORN, Exor. & wife
SUSANNA WILSON, Extrx. Wife to give each child good bed & furn. at their
coming to years of maturity. Signed: WILLIAM (X) WILSON. Wit: MOSES
SPEIGHT, STEPHEN CAWTHORN, JAS. ROBINSON.

Page 23: Will of JOHN WILSON: Made July 31, 1797. Pro. June 1, 1801.
to wife ELIZABETH WILLSON all Est. at time of my decease, real & per.
and if sd. ELIZABETH WILSON should depart this life bef. my Honored
father HUGH WILLSON, then sd. property to belong to sd. HUGH WILSON, but
if ELIZABETH should survive sd. HUGH WILLSON, sd. prop. to be to her.
App't. wife ELIZABETH WILLSON & HUGH WILLSON, Exors. Wit: WILLIAM
PARSONS, JOHN PARKER, BENJAMIN WHITAKER. Signed: JOHN WILLSON.

Pages 23-24: Will of JOHN PARSONS: Made Aug. 18, 1801. Codicil
Nov. 23, 1800. Pro. June 30, 1801. "I, JOHN PARSONS, of Jeff. Co...
being somewhat sick and weake in body" ... to: Four youngest daus.
SARAH, PATSEY, WINIFRED & NANCY should reside with their mother until
they marry and one day of marriage be pd. by their mother out of the
afsd. sum of $1600 the sum of $350 each... but in case wife MARTHA
PARSONS my bel. wife should die bef. marriage of sd. daus... then the
$1600 or whatever part may not have been pd. or may be left after paying
portions of any of them that may be married but one and that one then
and that one might remain unmarried... to have balance that may remain
undivided. To son WILLIAM PARSON $400; 2nd. son JOHN PARSONS $500 &
$100 toward payment of his land which I expected to have pd. bef. this
time; to 3rd. son THOMAS PARSONS $450; to 4th son JAMES PARSONS $500 in
addition to small debt he owes me and which I hereby discount from his
proportion; to dau. CATHERINE FULTON's 3 children, PATSEY, BARBARA &
JAMES, $100 each; dau. MARY TOMKINS $300. Any remaining to be equally
div. bet. 4 sons: JOHN. WM., THOMAS & JAMES PARSONS. Appt's sons
WILLIAM & JAMES PARSONS, Exors. Signed: JOHN PARSONS. Wit: JOHN
WILLSON, THOMSON LAWSON. WILLIAM MCDOWELL, J.P. ex officio. Codicil:
to son in law THOMAS FULTON sum of 5 Spanish Mills __ Dollars for his
portion of my Est. real & personal.

Page 25: Will of JOHN VINING: Made April 26, 1801. Pro. April 26,
1801... "being weake and sick in body... to dau. SARAH JUMP the tract of
land where I live cont. 300 acres... and also all my stock of cattle...
to son CADAR VINING a negro woman Cloe... son WILLIAM VINING a negro boy
Dread... son SHADDRACK VINING a negro boy Ruffin... son JOHN VINING one
negro boy named Lake and negro gird named Juda... to ZACHARIAH VINING
the son of AMEY PEACOCK one neg. boy Jim when he arrives at 21... to
dau. ANN WILLIAMS wife of JOSEPH WILLIAMS a negro woman named Rosa,
feather bed I now lie on and bedstead and furn... to granddau. RODA
VINING, dau. of CADAR VINING one neg. girl child named Charity... to

grandson JOHN VINING, son of SHADRACK VINING one neg. girl Tressa... to
dau. ABEGILL FASLESS one feather bed & furn... sons JOHN and JESSE VINING
my wagon and 2 horses and stock of hogs... with a debt on JESSE PAWLETT.
Signed: JOHN (X) VINING. Wit: WM. HARDWICK, WILLIAM HANNAH, NANCY (X)
JUMP. Codicil... "if I die bef. present crop is finished, then Estate
to remain undivided til crop is finished. JAS BOZEMAN, C.C.O.

Page 26:   Will of JOSEPH JACKSON: Made June 28, 1800. Pro. Sept. 7,
1801. "I, JOSEPH JACKSON of Jefferson Co., being weake in body... debts
to be paid out of crop now a growing and then I lend 100 acres to my
son LEVY JACKSON bought of Mr. SHELMAN and 100 acres adj. the bluff on
the river and I also give him one negro boy Reese. Son JESSE JACKSON,
260 acres, 80 I had of MR. SHELMAN and 187 1/2 on the river joining
LEVEYE land and one negro girl Sarah, which he is to rec. at 21 years of
age... son JOSEPH JACKSON, 270 acres, 180 in bounty, where I now live and
70 I bought of MCNEAL and 20 bought of SHELMAN out of which legacy I
lend to my wife 50 acres for her life... son JOSEPH one negro boy named
Jacob... son JAMES JACKSON, 200 acres adj. WILLIAM FOKES, 109 on river
and 91 joining back side and one negro man named Gabe... I give my
dau. SARAH JACKSON (she married NATHAN BATTS) one negro girl Cherry and
one negro girl Lilly and one feather bed and furn... I lend to my wife
SARAH JACKSON one negro woman named Charlot and all my household furn...
give to dau. LUCY ASKEWY 5 cows and calves and also I give to my three
daughters JEMIMA WARNER, ARGENT COLEMAN and LUCY ASKEWY one negro woman
named Charlot after my wife's death... rest be sold and equally divided
bet. all my children after wife's death. App'ts. friend, JAMES WARNER
and son JESSE JACKSON, Exors. Signed: JOSEPH JACKSON. Wit: GEORGE
GRANBERRY, WM. HUBBARD, SHADRACK JACKSON. Notes show children as
VINNEY JACKSON, LENY ASKNEY or SUEY ASKNEY or LUCY ASKNEY: daus. JEMIMA
WARNER.

Page 28:   Will of DAVID BOTHWELL: Made June 13, 1801. Pro. Nov. 2,
1801. "I, DAVID BOTHWELL, being sick and in low condition... to bel.
wife JANE BOTHWELL the sole mangement of place where she now lives with
personal Est. and property during widowhood and to educate the children
as much as lies in her power... should she marry I give her a negro
wench named Cate, a young bay mare, 2 cows and calves... to bel. son
EBENEZER BOTHWELL 150 acres on Ogeechee adj. LAWSON and a negro girl
Nane with 1/2 a tract of land lying near the 8 mile branch adj. CLARKE
and BRYAN... 3rd. to bel. son JOHN BOTHWELL the other 1/2 tract on
Ogeechee and other half of tract on 8 mile branch together with girl
named Dinah... 4th. to bel. son JAMES BOTHWELL 1/2 of tract whereon she
now lives at his mothers death, together with negro boy George... 5th.
to bel. son DAVID BOTHWELL other 1/2 tract (note, said tract just
mentioned) and negro Jack. My wife now being pregnant shall she be
delivered and child survive my ___ it should have negro wench named
Penny and boy named Isaac. App't. well bel. wife JANE, JOHN PATTERSON,
Jr., and SAMUEL BOTHWELL my Extrx. and Exors... "We being present at the
Reverant DAVID BOTHWELLS last moments in this life... but his last
moments approaching fast, we did not present for his signature: SAML.
ROBINSON, J.P., WM. C. KENNEDY, JARED IRWIN, J.I.C., WM. IRWIN.

Page 29:   Will of ZACHARIAS FENN: Made Jan. 26, 1799. Pro. Jan. 10,
1802. "I, ZACHARIAS FENN, of Jeff. Co., Planter... to dau. MARTHA
BOUTON a neg. woman Nacy and 5 children (named), feather bed, furn. 4
cows and calves, 5 sheep, sow and pigs and 200 acres, being part of a
400 acres tract gtd. to SOLOMON ALLEN and also one mare bridle and
saddle in possession of her husband JOHN BOUTON... to dau. MARY DANIEL,
2 negroes (named), 200 acres part of 400 acre tract gtd. to SOLOMON
ALLEN, $500 in cash, one horse, saddle and bridle, feather bed and furn.
cattle, now in possession of her husband AMOS DANIEL... to son ELI FENN
$430 at his marriage or coming of age... to my six children, viz.
ELIZABETH, SARAH, HENRY, WINNEY, NANCY, DANIEL FENN $430 to each at
coming of age... also a stock of cattle at the Dead River on Oconee in
possession of Mr. ___ SWILLEY to be equally div. bet. 7 children, viz.
ELI, ELIZABETH, SARAH, HENRY, WINNEY, NANCY and DANIEL FENN as they come
of age. Wife NANCY FENN all remainder of real Est., slaves and 1000

acres lying in Washington Co., Sandy Run... also 937 1/2 acres in Jeff. Co. on Ogeechee River, FENN's Bridge. Exors: ____ MURPHY. Signed: ZACHARIAS FENN. Wit: JAMES MITCHELL, SAMUEL RICHMOND, WM. MCKAIN.

Page 30: Will of JOHN WOOD: Made ____. Pro. Dec. 6, 1802. (Note: Will can't be found, only the Probate.) Probate, Jefferson Co., Ga. At the Court for County afsd. on 6 Dec. 1802, personally appeared JOSEPH BARBER one of the subscribing witnesses to the annexed will and testament of JOHN WOODS deceased... swore that he was present and did see JOHN WOODS sign, seal and Pro. the same to be cont... (illegible).

Page 31: Will of BRITTAIN SMITH: Made Dec. 14, 1801. Pro. Feb. 1, 1802. "I, BRITTAIN SMITH, of Jeff. Co.... this 14th day Dec. 1801... beq. to son JOHN SMITH one negro boy named Will, one feather bed and furn. beq. to dau. MARY SMITH one negro woman Nell and negro girl Susan, one feather bed and furn... son JORDAN SMITH one negro boy named DANIEL, one feather bed and furn... beq. to son THOMAS SMITH one negro boy Jacob, negro girl Chaney, one feather bed and furn... to bel. dau. FANNY SMITH one negro girl Rachel and one negro girl Zilpha and also $50 in cash... land to be equally divided by line from river out to the rock line to my 3 sons... to nephew WILSON WARREN one feather bed and furn... remainder of Estate tail and personal shall be sold and put to use of raising my family white and black and schooling my children until youngest comes of age and the (rest?) be equally div. among my 5 worthy brothers: SIMON SMITH, JORDAN SMITH, Exors to my Will. Signed: BRITTAIN SMITH. Wit: THOMAS GARVIN, JNO. MARSHALL, JOSHUA (X) SMITH.

Page 32: Will of DANIEL DEES: Made Jan. 8, 1802. Pro. March 1, 1802, being sick and weak of body... to wife ELIZABETH to have the free informent of all my land... consisting of 2 tracts, meaning all that part of sd. land lying and being below or on the South eastern side of the Mill branch... also one negro man Bremus, one negro woman Easter and negro girl Jeffy, household and kitchen furn., plantation tools and bay mare, sorrel mare, stock and hogs... I lend to wife ELIZABETH until my son JOHN shall become the age of 21 one negro man... and I lend one negro woman, one negro boy, one negro boy and girl... beq. to son EDMON one silver dollar... beq. to son DREWRY all that part of above tract sit. on upper or N.E. side of Mill branch... also to son DREWRY one neg. man and one neg. boy... beq. to son HILLARD one negro boy to be delivered to him when my son JOHN shall leave cum to age of 21... beq. to son DANIEL one silver dollar... my wife a negro man "now in N.C." ... beq. to son JOHN all land sit. and lying on Lower S.W. side of Branch to be possessed by him sd. son JOHN when my sd. wife ELIZABETH shall or my decease... also I give to son JOHN one negro man, woman and 2 boys... rest is illegible... Wife, ELIZABETH, Extrx., Son DREWRY, Exor. Signed: DANIEL (X) DEES. Wit: THACHER VIVCON, JR., DUCET DEES,NANCY DEES, REBECCA CRAWFORD.

Page 33: Will of JESSE LOCK: Made March 16, 1802. Pro. May 3, 1802.. to wife NANCY LOCK all estate real and personal during widowhood and after that estate be equally div. bet. wife and my six children, namely: RICHARD, ELIZABETH, THOMAS, MARY and JOHN SURGENER and WINNIE. Appoints worthy wife and friends ARON LOWE, JAMES LAMAR, Extrx. and Exors. Signed: JESSE (X) LOCK. Wit: JORDAN SMITH, ISAAC (I) SEMMS. JAS. BOZEMAN, C.C.O.

Page 34: Will of SAMUEL ANDREW: Made March 16, 1802. Pro. July 5, 1802... being weak and sickly of body... to wife JENNY ANDREW my bay mare, saddle, bridle, a bed and furn. dur. nat. life and my 2 negro slaves... dau. PEGGY ANDREW my woman Alm and my mare, filly and a bed and furn... to son SAMUEL LAMONT ANDREW my boy Bob and woman slave Nanoe and tract of land I now live on and my mare and her colt and bed and burn. and one full one half of my smith tools and my farming utencils... to dau. NANCY my negro boy Davy and a bed and furn. and young mare... to dau. JENNY one negro boy Sammon, a bed and furn... and it is understood my son SAMUEL is to give his sister JENNY a mare out of his brood... son JOHN ANDREW negro boy and woman, young filly and bed and

128

and furn... and other 1/2 of smith tools and farming utencils... also my
tract of land cont. 125 acres adj. ISAAC RAWLS in this county and 100
acres adj. MATTHEW MCMILLAN in 96 Dist. S.C. Exors to see that my Mother
JANE ANDREW be provided with decent and comfortable support dur. her life
at proper charge of my estate... Nephew SAMUEL ANDREW $30... to pay for
his education... to Nephews SAMUEL GRANT and SAMUEL GILLAM $30 each for
their education. Exors: WILLIAM ANDREW and HUGH IRWIN. Signed:
SAMUEL ANDREW. Wit: ELIJAH (X) GIBSON, JAS. ROBINSON, ELIZABETH HODGES.
JAS. BOZEMAN, C.C.O. 5 July 1802, ELIZABETH HODGES swore to signature
of Will in Open Court.

Page 35: Will of STEPHEN POWELL: Made Nov. 11, 1802. Pro. Dec. 6,
1802... to bel. son JOHN POWELL one negro... 2nd. to bel. son FRANCIS
POWELL one negro... 3rd. to beloved dau. PATIENCE POWELL one negro...
to bel. dau. ELIZABETH PAGE a negro girl and 10 cows and calves, one
bounty of land on big Ohooppy called Mill Seat... Plantation and stock
in care of bel. son JOHN POWELL until bel. son FRANCIS POWELL comes of
age, then to be equally div. bet sons JOHN and FRANCIS POWELL. App'ts.
son JOHN POWELL and WILLIAM CAUTHORN Exors. Signed: STEPHEN POWELL.
Wit: GEORGE HENDRIX, THOMAS SPEIGHT and NANCY (X) SPIVEY. Rec. 16 Dec.
1802. Sworn to 6 Dec. 1802 in Open Ct. by GEORGE HENDRIX bef. JAS.
BOZEMAN, C.C.O.

Page 36: Will of RACHEL BLAIR: Made Oct. 1801. Pro. Dec. 20, 1802.
to loving mother ELIZABETH WHITE one bond agst. Estate of JOHN MCNEELY
dated 1773 and signed JOHN MCNEELY and Wit. by SAMUEL BLAIR and HUGH
MCNEELY cont. 20 lbs. Sterl. and all my clothing... and if my mother
never come from Europe I give and beq. all to my brother JOHN BLAIR and
DAVID WHITE. Appt's. WILLIAM MCNEELY Exor. Signed: RECHEL (X) BLAIR.
Wit: HUGH MCNEELY, RACHEL (X) CROSLEY. Pro. Sept. 6, 1802, sworn to in
Open Ct. 6 Sept. 1802 by RACHEL CROSLEY. JAS. BOZEMAN, C.C.O.

Page 37: Will of L. G. or HENRY GEORGE CALDWELL: Made Dec. 3, 1802.
Pro. Feb. 7, 1803... to bel. wife DRUSILLA CALDWELL, one negro boy and
one negro woman... to son WILLIAM RUFUS CALDWELL one negro man and one
negro woman... to dau. HENRIETTA CALDWELL one negro man and negro girl...
dau. MARIA CALDWELL one negro man and negro woman... Plantation whereon
I now live (lying on West side of Lambert Creek adj. ROBERT WARNOCK) to
remain for benefit of heirs for 7 years after my decease... and then to
be sold ... crops and property to be joint property of heirs. App'ts.
bel. wife Extrx. and trusty friends THOMAS FULTON and BANJAMIN WHITAKER
Exors. Signed: L. G. CALDWELL. Wit: JOHN CLEMENTS, THO. FULTON, B.
WHITAKER. 7 Feb. 1802 sworn to in Open Ct. by THOS. FULTON.

Page 38: Will of JAMES POWELL: Made Sept. 14, 1802. Pro. March 7,
1803... to dearly bel. brother WILLIAM POWELL $130; all rest of my Estate
personal and real to be equally divided bet. my two brothers DANIEL and
WILLIAM POWELL. Appt. worthy friend JOHN JOINER, Exor. Signed: JAMES
POWELLw Wit: JACOB HORN, BURREL ROSE. Sworn to in Open Ct. March 1803
by JACOB HORN bef. GEO. R. CLANTON, JAS. BOZEMAN, C.C.O.

Page 39: Will of THOMAS MERRIWETHER. Made Sept. 8, 1802. Pro. April
4, 1803. 1st. to brother JAMES MERRIWETHER a copy of my mother's
picture... 2nd. to neice SUSANNA PATTERSON the three following negroes
(named), all dau. of a negro woman slave Rhody... but if SUSANNA
PATTERSON dies before 21 years of age without issue, the 3 slaves to
neice JANE PATTERSON... to neice ELIZABETH CARSON a negro boy and a
negro girl... but if ELIZABETH CARSON dies before 21 years of age without
issue, then to neice JANE PATTERSON... to JULIA MARIA, dau. of my friend
JOHN BERRIEN a negro boy... residue of Estate real and personal, whether
in Virginia or Georgia to neice JANE PATTERSON. App'ts. neice JANE
PATTERSON Extrx. and friend JOHN BERRIEN Exor. Signed: T. MERIWETHER.
Wit: THO. CAMBER WALTON, DAVID FARIES, WM. CLARKE. Sworn to in Open
Ct. 4 April 1803 by WILLIAM CLARKE.

Page 40: Will of AARON POOL: (no dates given except date Will sworn
to below)... to wife and children a equal portion of money due me in

North Carolina as loan as can be collected and other debts due me...
wife to have her lifetime with the property and then at her death to be
div. equally among my children then living... my negro girl Jemiah
should be WILLIAM SMITHS... rest of property to be wifes as long as she
lives and then equally div. among children... and a cert. __ of land 87
acres of Pine land to wife... and WILLIAM SMITH to pay to the Colate
$50. App'ts. JESSE ELLENDER POOL and my son JOHN POOL my Exors.
Signed: AARON (X) POOL. Wit: WILLIAM KINCHEN, JR., ABRAM MOSS, WILLIAM
(X) PENNINGTON. 2 May 1803, WILLIAM PENNINGTON swore to in Open Ct.

Page 41:   Will of JONATHAN FOUNTAIN: Made July 16, 1803. Pro. Sept.
5, 1803... leaves sill to be sold and one horse and shop tools and one
gun... give rest of property to wife SARAH during widowhood, except one
feather bed to dau. PATTY... after death or marriage of wife, property
to be sold and equally div. bet. her and rest of children, excepting
dau. PATTY. Signed: JONATHAN (X) FOUNTAIN, SARAH (X) FOUNTAIN, WILLIAM
FOUNTAIN, JONAS MAYO, Exors. to Estate. Wit: BENJ. MAYO, ASA PARKER.
Sworn to in Open Ct. 5 Sept. 1803 by BENJAMIN MAYO.

Page 41:   Will of ROGER LAWSON: Made August 3, 1803. Pro. Nov. 9,
1803... Planter of Jeff. Co... to dearly bel. wife MARGARET LAWSON for
natural life or widowhood the plantation where now live called Mount
Pleasant, also my negro man Squire and negro woman, mare, colts, saddle
and 1/3 of household furn... if she marries again, to revert to my son
ANDREW BERRY LAWSON... to loving sons JOHN LAWSON, HUGH LAWSON or his
heirs, THOMPSON LAWSON and son-in-law JOHN GAMBLE $1.00 each... to dau.
HANNAH SPIERS $200 cash together with what I gave her at her marriage...
dau. MARY LAWSON one negro girl and negro boy, mare, saddle, furn. 1/3
stock and $100 cash... son ANDREW BERRY LAWSON and heirs all real Estate
together with that devised to bel. wife. App't. bel. wife MARGARET
LAWSON Extrx. and son-in-law JOHN GAMBLE, Exor. Signed: ROGER LAWSON.
Wit: CHAS. GACHET, ANDREW MOORE, JOSIAH M. STEWART, J.I.C. Sworn to
in Open Ct. 8 Nov. 1803 by Doct. JOSIAH M. STERRITT, JAS. BOZEMAN, C.C.O.

Page 43:   Will of ADAM CALHOUN: Made Nov. 15, 1803. Pro. Jan. 3,
1804. Tract I now live on with rest of real estate, wagons, horses and
my negro woman to be sold at public sale giving 12 mos. credit... to
dearly bel. wife ROSANNA the 11th. part of all my real and personal
Est. and also to have possession of my stock, cattle, hogs, sheep towards
raising the two youngest children til they should marry or come of age...
to son WILLIAM CALHOUN $20... to UNITY GOODWIN $10 and she to have 18
mos. schooling at expense of Est. App'ts. M. NEWTON and SAMUEL ALLEN,
Sole Exors. Signed: ADAM (X) CALHOUN. Wit: SAMUEL CALHOUN, DANIEL
KINGRY, JEREMIAH WILCHER. Sworn to in Open Ct.3 Jan. 1804 by SAMUEL
CALHOUN, bef. JAS. BOZEMAN, C.C.O.

Page 44:   Will of SAMUEL GORDON: Made Dec. 13, 1798. Pro. Jan. 19,
1805. "Planter" ... to bel. wife SARAH GORDON whilst being in chast
prudent manner a living support... with care and oversight of son JOHN
GORDON... at wife's decease my Exors shall sell sd. Plantation to the
best advantage and use of my sd. son JOHN... to wife and children JOHN &
SARAH, mare, colt, and hogs... to dau. MARY one hefer... dau. BETTY ANN
a hefer... dau. JANE, horse, bridle, saddle, feather bed and furn...
daus. JANE & SARAH all plantation lying bet. Buckhead and Dry Creek to
be equally div. bet. them...remainder of personal estate be for benefit
of family til such time as dau. SARAH shall marry and then she is to have
her equal share. App'ts. ROBERT BOYD and HENRY MCCONKEY, Exors. Wit:
JOHN FOIL, WM. KENNEDY, ANDREW MCCONKEY. Signed: SAMUEL GORDON. Sworn
to in Open Ct. 7 Jan. 1805 by JOHN BOYIL bef. JAS. BOZEMAN, C.C.O.

Page 45:   Will of JOHN ALLEN: Made Oct. 24, 1801. Pro. Jan. 25, 1805
To bel. wife JANE ALLEN everything she brought with her to me and also
increase of same... likewise use of my house and plantation dur. life...
likewise all clothing in house that is her own providing and the 1/2
of corn at time of my decease whether in field or cut... Grandau.
MARGARET FLEMING (Dau. of ROBERT FLEMING) plantation I now live on (after
death of wife)... to three grandchildren by JAMES MCCONKEY $120 each...
son-in-law JAMES MCCONKEY one hundred and fifty cents... son-in-law

ROBERT FLEMING one hundred and fifty cents... to WILLIAM FLEMING and
JOHN MARTIN all remaining part of my Est. to be equally div. bet. them
(except that WILLIAM FLEMING shall pay JOHN MARTIN out of his part $40
as he has 100 acres of land)... my best suit of wearing apparell to
grandson JOHN FLEMING. App'ts. BENJAMIN WHITAKER and MATHEW CARSWELL,
Exors. Signed: JOHN ALLEN. Wit: JAMES WILLSON, WILLIAM BEATTY,
WILLIAM HAIR. Sworn to in Open Ct. 23 Jan. 1805 by WILLIAM BEATTY.

Page 46:   Will of CHARLES MCCULLER: Made Feb. 9, 1805.   (No date of
Probate shown.) ... I, CHARLES LANSFORD MCCULLERS... to bel. wife
SUSANNA MCCULLERS the whole of my estate, real and personal for use of
schooling and raising my son HENRY BRYANT MCCULLERS and same to be in
her possession dur. lifetime or widowhood or until HENRY BRYANT MCCULLERS
arrives at age of 18 yrs., at which time he is to have 1/2 of above lent
to sd. SUSANNAH MCCULLERS during lifetime... if son HENRY BRYANT
MCCULLERS die without issue, then sd. wife SUSANNAH keep whole of above
and after her death if sister MARY MCCULLERS should be living, she to get
1/2 of property and other 1/2 bet. heirs of sd. SUSANNAH MCCULLERS.
App'ts. Brother BRYANT MCCULLER, Exor. Signed: CHARLES L. MCCULLER.
Wit: A. WOOD, JOSEPH (X) CHAIRS, E. WOOD.

Page 48:   Will of SAM MAYO: Made Dec. 24, 1804.   Pro. April 1, 1805..
to bel. wife MARTHA MAYO, feather bed and furn., and house and plantation
dur. her lifetime... to dec'd. dau. SARY ROSSE ehirs 5 shillings...
son HARMON MAYO my horse and bridle... sons BRITTIN MAYO and LEWIS MAYO
the whole of my land and plantation to be div. to their satisfaction and
also whole of plantation tools and each a feather bed and furn.... dau.
POLLY MAYO, feather bed and furn. and one dish... dau. ELIZABETH,
feather bed and furn. and one dish... son BRITTIN one yoke of oxen...
same to son LEWISS MAYO... then the stock of cattle to be equally div.
bet. my 3 daus. EASTER BROWN, POLLY MAYO and ELIZABETH MAYO.   Signed:
SAMUEL (X) MAYO. Wit: BENJAMIN MAYO, JONAS MAYO. Exors. were: HARMON
MAYO, BRITTIN MAYO, LEWIS MAYO. Sworn to in Open Ct. 1 April 1805 by
JONAS MAYO.

Page 49:   Will of GEORGE GRANBERRY: Made Aug. 11, 1804.   Pro. April
1805... to bel. wife SARAH GRANBERRY my riding cheare and harnesses
and one silver wath Nov,1-13-& at my wife's death the watch to son GEORGE
GRANBERRY... lend to son LOAMMI GRANBERRY my plantation on Ogeechee River
til son GEORGE comes of age and then sd. plantation be equally div. bet.
2 sons LOAMMI and GEORGE, but should GEORGE die bef. coming of age the
whole of land I give to LOAMMI... to dau. MARY MCCLENDAL 2 cows and
calves... dau. SARAH GRANBERRY, feather bed and furn. and one large
trunk and 1/2 of stock of cattle ... other 1/2 cattle to son GEORGE...
son LOAMMI GRANBERRY all household furn., plantation tools etc. for use
of schooling son GEORGE... my library of books be equally div. bet. all
my children vizt: ELIZABETH HERRINGTON, LOAMMI GRANBERRY, MARY MCCLENDAL,
SARAH GRANBERRY, GEORGE GRANBERRY. App'ts. son LOAMMI GRANBERRY, Exor.
Signed: GEORGE GRANBERRY. Wit: JOHN THOMPSON, JOHN COWART. Sworn to
in Open Ct. 1 April 1805 by JOHN COWART.

Page 50:   Will of JAMES PATILLO: Made May 11, 1804.   Pro. July 18,
1804... to bel. dau. MARTHA THOMAS one negro woman and another negro
woman, saddle, horse bridle, feather bed, furn. and one large covered
trunk... bel. dau. BETSEY a negro girl and negro boy, horse, saddle to
be worth $100... to bel. dau. MILLEY PATTILLO a negro girl and boy,
horse, saddle, bridle worth $100, feather bed, furn. trunk... to bel.
dau. NANCY PATTILLO two negroes (and same as given to other daus. just
described)... to bel. son GEORGE HENRY PATTILLO all tract of land I live
on cont. 200 acres... on his arriving at age of 21 and until then it is
considered an assylum for my family in common... also to bel. son, horse,
saddle, bridle equal $100 and the whole of my small library... son to
be kept in school til he is 18... Balance of estate to be sold for
maintainence of family til GEORGE HENRY comes of age of 21. App'ts.
friends DOUGLASS HANCOCK, DAVID THOMAS and JOHN THOMAS as Exors. Signed:
JAMES PATTILLO. Wit: CATHERINE (X) MURPHY, RICHARD BROWN, JOHN DARBY.
Sworn to in Open Ct. 18 July 1804 by RICHARD BROWN.

Page 51:   Will of Mrs. JANE MCBRIDE: Made Sept. 30, 1802, Pro. Nov.
1805... "I am fully satisfied with the division made bet. my sons SAMUEL
and JOHN, that is for JOHN to have negrow fellow Joe and negrow wench
Pat and SAMUEL to have $425 as his part of the negrows... to son JOHN a
negrow Polly and my part of the horses, cattle, hogs, household furn...
to dau. MARY my saddle and wheel and hat and body clothes and my large
Bible and Psalmbook and the Josplesonnets and (Roston?) on the Covenent
of Grace & $50 in money to be pd. by son JOHN... son THOMAS $50 to be
pad. by son JOHN... son WILLIAM $50 pd. by son JOHN. App'ts. sons
JOHN & THOMAS as Exors. Signed: JANE (X) MCBRIDE. Wit: ISAAC WOOD,
JAMES MCBRIDE, HUGH ALEXANDER, J.P. Sworn to in Open Ct. 4 Nov. 1805.

Page 52:   Will of EDWARD MOORE: Made Oct. 21, 1805. Pro. Nov. 4, 1805
my stock of cattle together with my mare, bridle, saddle and all property
shall be sold and equally div. bet.: MORNING PRICE, SUNTHA MORE, THOMAS
MORE, UNITY MORE, WILLIAM MORE, FERIBY MORE, MARY MORE. App'ts. friend
LOAMMI GRANBERRY as Exor. Signed: EDWARD (X) MORE. Wit: RICE (X)
PRICE, SYTHA (X) MORE, ANNA (X) MORE. Sworn to in Open Ct. 4 Nov. 1805
by RICE PRICE.

Page 53:   Will of JESSE LOFTLY: Made Oct. 7, 1804. Pro. Nov. 5, 1804
I JESSE LOFTLY... lend to bel. mother SARAH LOFTLY during natural life
all part of land above my plantation up Rocky Comfort beginning at mouth
of JESSE BRANCHE (a creek ? or person? Ed.) to WILLIAM ALLENS line, then
to WILLIAM BROWNS corner, supposed to be 200 acres... to bel. wife dur.
lifetime or widowhood, balance of land and support of my little children
and at her death or marriage, the land I live on be div. equally and
separate from mother's land, bet. my 2 sons DANIEL and WILLIAM LOFTLY...
to balance of personal estate lent to bel. wife SUSANNAH... at wife's
death or remarriage rest of Est. be equally div. bet. my 3 children:
NANCY, CEILA and PAGE LOFTLY. App'ts bel. brother RIGHT LOFTLY and
WILLIAM HARDWICK, Esq. as Exors. Signed: J. (X) LOFTLY. Wit: JOHN
VINING, DAVID INGRAM, JOHN LOFTLY. Memo: debts due JESSE LOFTLY at
his request I have set down: JOHN MARTIN $.75; NATHAN WEAVER... $1.00,
the school master MCDONALD $2.50, WILLIAM HICKMAN... $.75. Sworn to
in Open Ct. 5 Nov. 1804 by JOHN VINING.

Page 54:   Will of JAMES WARNOCK: Made June 11, 1804. Pro. Nov. 5,
1804... to well bel. wife JANE WARNOCK (all tract of land in Jefferson
Co. adj. MATTHEW CARSWELL and WILLIAM BEATTY, gtd. to JOSEPH BEATTY cont.
100 acres) and at her death or remarriage go to my dau. SARAH WARNOCK,
to son BERRY WARNOCK all tract of land which I live on cont. 150 acres
(lying on LAMBERTS creek, gtd. to ROBERT WARNOCK). App'ts. friends
MATTHEW CARSWELL and THOMAS FULTON, Exors. Signed: JAMES (X) WARNOCK.
Wit: JAMES WILLIAMS, JOHN ROGERS, B. WHITAKER.

Page 55:   Will of SOLOMON WOOD: Made Nov. 27, 1805. (No date of pro.
given.) ... to bel. wife ELIZABETH, six negroes, 4 horses, 15 cows and
calves, etc., 6 feather beds and furn. and all household furn. dur.
natural life and my stage wagon... to dau. ELIZABETH 4 negroes, horse,
bridle, saddle, $150, 10 cows and calves, 1 feather bed and furn. equal
that given to her sisters... to my 3 sons: GREEN WOOD, MARK RED WOOD
and JOHN WHITE WOOD, all my lands and negroes, 3 feather beds and furn.,
30 cows and calves, 3 horses etc. to be worth $150 each and sd. property
to be div. bet. them at GREEN's arriving at 21 years... also $500 each
for their education... remaining property to be equally div. bet. my
children: NANCY, POLLY, ELIZABETH, GREEN, MARK RED & JOHN WHITE. App'ts.
WILLIS BRAZIAL, THOMAS MITCHEL and GREEN WOOD, Exors. Signed: SOLOMON
WOOD. Wit: STEPHEN DUROWŸAS, JOHN COWARD.

Page 55:   Will of JOHN AKRIDGE: Made July 18, 1805. Pro. Jan. 6,
1806... to ELIZABETH AKRIDGE my wife all real and personal estate consisting of 200 acres, gtd. to ANDREW MACK, including grist mill and
cotton machine, dwelling houses and furn. therein... plantation and 3
negroes, cattle, horses... after her death the remainder of property to
be equally div. bet. lawful heirs of her body. App'ts. wife Sole Extrx.
Signed: JOHN AKRIDGE. Signed, sealed and proclaimed at L. W & T. of
JOHN AKRIDGE, SENR. Wit: JOHN MOCK, HAMPTON PARRISH. Sworn to in Open
Ct. 6 Jan. 1806 by JOHN MACK.

Page 56:   Will of RICHARD PEEL: Made Feb. 9, 1792.   Pro. Jan. 6, 1806.
"... of Burke Co..." ... to MARY my dearly bel. (wife?), the land I live
on and plantation, furn. and an equal divide of cattle together with JOHN
and JONATHAN to be forever enjoyed dur. life... to well bel. son WILLIAM
PEEL, 150 acres on waters of Rocky Creek and cattle now in his possession,
together with bed and bed clothes... son-in-law JOHN DONALSON 5 shillings
specie to be pd. at experation of one year after my decease... to bel.
son JOHN PEEL, 150 acres on waters of Rocky Comfort, mare and cattle now
in his possession... well bel. son JONATHAN PEEL the land wherein I now
live after his mothers decease with his divide of cattle. App'ts. "my
well bel. brother JOHN PEEL and my son WILLIAM, Exors." Signed: RICHARD
PEEL. Wit: JACOB JONES, JOHN PEEL, SAMUEL LITTLE. "This 18 Oct. 1793
read the before Legitty this L. W. & T., JOHN GAMBLE. Sworn to 6 Jan.
1806 in Open Ct. by JOHN PEEL." (Note by Ed.: says MARY his wife was
MARY GAMBLE, sister of JOHN GAMBLE and sister of ALICE GAMBLE who married
JOHN PEEL.)

Page 58:   Will of SHADRACK VINING: Made Dec. 11, 1805.   Pro. Jan. 6,
1806... to wife PHEREBE during life or widowhood full enjoyment of my
Estate both real and personal... after her death or widowhood the whole
of estate be equally div. among "my" children: Son, JOHN VINING (none
other named.) App't. JOHN BOUTIN & son JOHN VINING as Exors. Signed:
SHAD. VINING. Wit: JAMES MC CHASTAIN, JOHN BOUTIN, JOHN (X) MORGAN.
Sworn to in Open Ct. 6 Jan. 1806, JAMES M. CHASTAIN.

Page 58:   Will of JOHN WELLS: Made Dec. 23, 1805.   Pro. April 18,
1806... to dear and bel. wife SARAH WELLS, slaves and residue of my
estate that is perishable and the land and plantation whereon I now live.
... to dear and well bel. dau. MARTHA WELLS all tract of land I bought of
JACOB GODOWNS on north side of Big Creek on lower side of road and 3
slaves... to well bel. dau. SARAH WELLS, 200 acres land in Washington
County on waters of Big Creek, also 2 slaves... to my dearly and well
bel. son THOMAS WELLS all tract I bought of JOHN CLEMMANS, including my
Will Seal and down with the will run to where it empties into Big Creeke,
to RANKINS line and one slave... to well bel. dau. CATHERINE WELLS,
tract I bought of THOMAS FUZELL, except part given to son THOMAS, also
2 slaves... none of lands to be taken out of wife's possession til her
death or marriage... land I have bought of DAVID BROWN be sold to pay
debts... and as touching the part of NOAH HINTONS Estate that I has put
apart as being the lawful heir in behalf of my wife, I have impowered
my son-in-law DAVID BROWN to recover the same and equal distribution be
made among all my children. App'ts. wife SARAH and son THOMAS, Extrx.
and Exor. Signed: JOHN WELLS. Wit: JOHN BRYAN, WILLIAM WILLSON.
Sworn to in Open Ct. 3 Feb. 1806, JOHN BRYON.

Page 60:   Will of ANTHONY HANCOCK: Made March 8, 1806.   Pro. July 7,
1806... "of Jefferson Co., Ga." ... lend to wife SARAH HANCOCK dur. her
life plantation with personal property, except negroes hereafter devised
to sons: DUGLAS, MARTIN, THOMAS and JOHN HANCOCK, 4 negro boys equally
div. plus other negroes in the first three's possession... lend to dau.
SARAH SMITH dur. her lifetime and after her decease to the heirs of her
body one negro boy and girl ... lend to dau. NANCY CHEATHAM... and then
to her heirs, one negro girl ... lend to dau. JANE BROWN... and then to
her heirs 2 negro girls... son JOHN HANCOCK $100 cash... to sons and
daus. above and their heirs after their decease, the residue of estate
real and personal. Makes wife SARAH HANCOCK Extrx. and sons DUGLAS and
THOMAS HANCOCK, Exors. Signed: ANTHONY (X) HANCOCK. Wit: J. MERI-
WETHER, BENJAMIN BRYAN, CAREN BRANNON.

Page 61:   Will of JOHN DUPREE: Made Jan. 28, 1804.   Pro. Jan. 5, 1807.
"of Jeffer. Co." ... weak of body... to bel. wife REBECEK all estate
real and personal dur. her life, out of which just debts be pd. and
remainder for her support till death and then what remains be equally
div. amongst children... my plantation to be div. bet. my 5 sons equally
only my oldest son HAROD I allow him $200 more... I also allow my 3 daus.
LUCEY, CHARLOTTE and SARAH the sum of $20 each. App'ts. sons HAROD and
JAMES, Exors. Signed: JOHN (X) DUPREE. Wit: WILLIAM FLEMING, JEREMIAH
(X) WALKER, JEAN WASHINGTON (X) WARD (or WORD).

Page 62:   Will of WILLIAM BROWN: Made Aug. 18, 1806. Pro. Jan. 26,
1807 of Jeff. Co.... lend bel. wife ANN BROWN dur. nat. life or widowhood all my property real and personal for to support and maintain her
and to raise my children and on her death or remarriage, an equal div.
take place amongst my children: ELIZABETH, GEORGE R., NANCY, POLLY,
JANE, WILLIAM, JAMES, JOHN, SAMUEL and MATTHEW BROWN. App'ts. eldest
son GEORGE R. BROWN Sole Exor... and should in his judgment, with advice
and consent of his mother think it would be for advantage of his mother
and children, he is vested with full power to sell and convey my land,
cont. 174 acres. Signed: WM. BROWN. Wit: WM. HARDWICK, JUDITH (X)
HARDWICK, JUDITH HARDWICK.

Page 63:   Will of ISABELLA REID: Made Dec. 24, 1803 in Louisville
(Ga.). Pro. Feb. 24, 1807... of Jefferson Co.... real estate be sold
and monies be pd. to my dau. NANCY wife of JOHN BARON, $50... and to
ISABELLA BARON my granddau. of sd. NANCY BARON the sum of $250... to
son ROBERT REID 3 negroes and at his death sd. Mary, wench, be div.
among any female children of sd. ROBERT REID... to dau. MARY WOOLF, wife
of FRANCIS WOOLF dur. nat. life only and not to be controlled by her
husband or liable for his debts, negro wench Venus and her 5 children,
and at her death to female children of MARY WOOLF... to granddau. alias
MARY GORDON, MARY REID, dau. of MURRAY REED, dec'd. my negro girl Judy...
item, on condition that SUSANNAH REED, alias SUSANNAH STRINGER, alias
SUSANNAH ODUM, relict of MURRAY REED, dec'd. shall make and execute her
renunciation of dower of a plantation lying near Camden in So. Car. which
I have lately sold to WILLIAM ADAMSON; then and in that case, I give and
devise as follows to SUSANNAH REED, STRINGER, ODUM, the sum of $150; to
her dau. ISABELLA by MURRAY REED dec'd., $150... to each of her two
sons by MURRAY REED, viz. JACOB and MURRAY $150 and to her dau. SALLY by
sd. MURRAY REED dec'd., I give and beq. my negro girl Venus provided that
sd. SALLY pay to my Exors. the sum of $40 to assent in payment of the
other legacies... but if sd. SUSANNAH REED, STRINGER or ODUM should
refuse Ren. of Dower the above beq. to her and her children are made
void... and in case Ren. of Dower not complied with by SUSANNAH, I give
all the property etc. intended for her and her 4 children, to my 2 sons
ROBERT REED and JOHN REED and the children of my son ALEXANDER REED,
dec'd. and to be div. into 3 equal parts. App'ts. sons JOHN & ROBERT
REED, Exors. Signed: ISABELLA (X) REED. Wit: WALTER ROBINSON, A.
HAMMOND.

Page 64:   Will of WILLIAM INGRAM: Made Oct. 3, 1806. Pro. June 1,
1807... debts to be pd... to loving wife MARY INGRAM one mare, saddle,
bridle, 4 cows and calves... to bel. dau. AGNES $25 when she comes of
age with reasonable schooling... to bel. dau. JEAN, $25 when of age and
schooling... to son EDMOND one filly, saddle, bridle and reasonable
schooling when of age... son JOHN SPIRS, $25 and reasonable schooling
when of age... son WILLIAM, $25 and schooling when of age... dau.
ELIZABETH a negro woman to be sold or as Exors think best... to wife her
bed and furn... and my plantation I allow to be kept and cultivated to
raise my children til the youngest boy comes of age and then be equally
div. or sold and money equally div. among my 4 sons, viz: EDMOND,
JOHN SPEIRES, JOSIAH and WILLIAM. App'ts. wife MARY INGRAM and JOHN
INGRAM the Exors. Signed: WILLIAM INGRAM. Wit: SAMUEL BIGHAM, GEO.
INGRAM, JAMES WILLIAMS.

Page 66:   Will of ELIJAH PAGETT: Made July 5, 1805. Pro. July 6,
1807... to son WARREN PADGETT my lot and building in town of Louisville
and 2 cows and calves and $300... to dau. SUSANAH ROBINSON a sorrell mare
... son MOSES PADGETT 2 cows and calves and his choice of one of all my
horses... rest of estate real and personal to be equally div. among my
children without sale... and my old negro woman Patt which I wish to be
free from claim of any person... that she may act and do for herself.
App't. worthy friend SOLLOMON WOOD and son ELIJAH PADGETT, Exors.
Signed: ELIJAH PADGETT. Wit: SIMON SMITH, WILLIAM PADGETT, JOHN BRYAN.

Page 67:   Will of FREDERICK CLEM: Made May 19, 1806. Pro. Nov. 2,
1807 ... "in a low state of health... part of crops or effects be sold

to pay debts... to bel. wife MARY CLEM a childs part of all my estate, both goods and cattle, lands, etc. to hold dur. nat. life and at her decease the whole of Estate both personal and real to revert to my children, namely: FREDERICK my eldest son first I give and beq. to him the upper 100 acres on Reedy Creek and known by Orchard Tract, half of a 200 acres gtd. to JOSEPH MOCK and for him to receive it at 21 and a negro boy... if it is the will of the Lord to take him out of time without any heirs the sd. land, a negro be reverted back to his surviving brother and sisters namely: BETTY ANN CLEM, CATHERINE CLEM and EPHRIAM VALLENTINE CLEM... for each child to have sufficient schooling esp. the two boys and the whole of my estate to be div. equally amongst my surviving children at death of their mother. App'ts. THOMAS PEEBLES and WILLIAM MCGEEHEE, Exors. Signed: FREDERICK (X) CLEM. Wit: JOHN BLOODWORTH, HENRY CLEM, WILLIS HOWARD, SR.

Page 68:   Will of JAMES L. WILSON: Made Sept. 15, 1807.   Pro. Dec. 11, 1807 ... to bel. dau. SUSANNAH WILSON all my property of every description amongst which are my negroes, 5 of which I bought of MAJOR JAMES MONFORD of Wilkes County... negro bought of JOHN HULLING of sd. county and 3 from No. Car. ... none to be sold or exchanged for 4 years after my decease, unless dau. marry or move out of state... dau. SUSANNAH WILSON Sole Extrx. and she apply to my bel. friend Capt. JAMES MERIWETHER of Louisville for counsel and advice. Signed: JAMES L. WILSON. Wit: VAL. WALKER, A (RCHIBALD) HATCHER, M. (ARY) HATCHER.

Page 69:   Will of THOMAS DRAKE: Made March 1, 1794. Pro. April 30, 1808... "of Warren County and State of Ga., Blacksmith..." tract of land on Rocky Comfort cont. 300 acres and one tract on Ohopee to be disposed of by Exors to pay for education of my 4 children... bel. son FRANCES be put to apprentice to blacksmith trade... son LEMUEL DRAKE apprentice to Bricklayer... son EARLY DRAKE be put to his brother FRANCES and learn blacksmith trade... all property not yet ment. to be div. into 5 equal parts... my dearly bel. wife to have one part, bel. FRANCES DRAKE one part, bel. son LEMUEL DRAKE one part and bel. dau THENEY DRAKE one part and bel. son EARLY DRAKE one part... they to receive their part as they arrive at maturity or marriage... land and buildings and plantation where I now live to be disposed of and equally div.. and to be possessed by bel. wife during life. App'ts. bel. friends TANDY CLERK KEY and DANIEL EVANS and bel. wife SARAH DRAKE, Exors. Signed: THOS. DRAKE. Wit: JAMES BIBISON, JOHN FORE and PRISELLA FORE.

Page 70:   Will of SAMUEL MARSHBURN: Made Jan. 26, 1807.   Pro. Aug. 8, 1808... to bel. friends and relatives REBECCA formerly of Moore Co., N.C. the estate which now possessed of and all that I may possess at time of my decease for and dur. her nat. life... and at her death in case of her being married I beq. to heirs of her body share and share alike of all Estate she may rec. from me... and I have not heard of my friend and relative for some time... to the person to whom I intend to give my property is dau. of JOHN MILLER who was a resident of Cumberland Co., in N.C. Should REBECCA MILLER die without issue previous to my Exors settling affairs of my Est., I then give my sd. Est. both real and personal to my friend JAMES MILLER, brother of afsd. REBECCA MILLER and son of sd. JOHN MILLER and his heirs. Appt. friend JOHN BERRIEN of Louisville, JOHN MACPHERSON BERRIEN of Savannah in Ga., Exors. Will not signed. Wit: AM. H. ROBINSON, NATHAN BOZEMAN, WALTER ROBINSON.

Page 71:   Will of CHARLES MCALISTER: Made Aug. 2, 1808.   Pro. Sept. 5, 1808... I give and beq. agreeably to L. W. & T. of ELEANOR MCALISTER dec'd... to my dearly bel. grandchildren, viz: CHARLES, WILLIAM, GEORGE and MARGARET MCALISTER... all the articles herein named which were beq. by sd. ELEANOR MCALISTER to me for my use... dur. my nat. life... (and here he mentions household items and furn.) ... with all my wearing apparel. Appt's. ROBERT CRUTHER of Burke Co. and SAMUEL CLARK of Jefferson Co. as his Exors. Signed: CHARLES MCALISTER. Wit: ARTHUR CLARKE, WM. RONOLDSON, MICH. BURKE.

Page 72:   Will of HENRY COX (COCKS):   Made Aug. 10, 1807.   Pro. Nov. Term 1808, of Baldwin County... "I, HENRY COCKS, of Co. and State afsd...

being in low state of health... to bel. children: ELIZABETH CLEM, MARY NIX, SAREY COCKS, JOHN COCKS and ANN COCKS all my real and personal estate to be advertised and finally sold... and the money equally div. amongst the above named, except one feather bed and side saddle which I beq. to dau. ANN COCKS. Appt's DAVID CLEM, DAVID NIX, Exors. Signed: HENRY (X) COCKS. Wit: WILLIAM JOHNSON, JOHN (X) COCKS, JAS. CANTEY.

Page 73: Will of WILLIAM MATHEWS: Made June 11, 1798. Pro. Nov. 7, 1808. "This Indenture made 1798, June 11, I, WILLIAM MATHEWS of Jefferson Co. ... to bel. wife BATHSEBA all lands and plantation, furn. and a negro wench Patt, cattle, horses, hogs... as long as she lives single but if she marries then the 1/2 of Estate is hers only and other 1/2 to nephews WILLIAM MATTHEWS but if he lives with his aunt as long as she lives and doth a good part by her in taking care of all property till her death, then all falls to him... but if on contrary he is disobedient to his aunt, leaves her in distress my will is that he hath nothing but 3 years of schooling. Signed: WILLIAM MATTHEW. Wit: RUBEN BECKUM.

Page 74: Will of SAMUEL WALDEN: Made March 14, 1808. Pro. Jan. 2, 1809... to son HARRY, $1.00 to him and his heirs forever... dau. ELIZABETH ALLEN one negro woman... son REUBEN $1.00... son-in-law JOHN DAVIS $1.00... dau. MARY RAWLING $1.00... dau. TABETHA $1.00... son SAMUEL WALDEN, all my land and plantation I am possessed with cont. by estimation 530 acres and also negro man Zach, bed, bedstead, plow, horse... desire that crop is now on plantation or may grow thereon this season do belong to son SAMUEL WALDEN... to granddau. ELIZABETH one heifer... grandson LEML. heifer with calf... all moveable property not bef. beq. be sold to highest bidder and money arising be div. bet. children: HARRY, ELIZABETH, REUBEN, Grandau. PATTY DAVIS, my dau. POLLY, TABETHA, and son SAM'L... my negro man Warren to be free at my death and to live with son SAM'L to take care of him in his old age. Appt's. son-in-law SAM'L ALLEN, Sole Exor. Signed: SAM (X) WALDEN. Wit: JAMES MCDONALD, JOHN MORRIS, REBECAH (X) FOLK.

Page 75: Will of JOHN MCMAHAN: Made Jan. 9, 1803. Pro. May 1, 1809. "planter" ... to JAMES TRIMBLE and to each of his 5 children 5 shillings ... to JOHN HARTFIELD and his children 5 shillings... to MARRY MCGOWN my neice one horse to value of $100 and saddle... to bel. wife FANNEY the remaining part of my Estate during widowhood and if she marry again that MARRAY MCGOWN and JAMES TRIMBLE dau. MARGARET should have the 1/3 part of all my Est. Appt's. JOHN BIGGHAM, ROBERT FOYEL, ALEXANDER GORDON, Exors. Signed: JOHN MCMAHAN. Wit: JOHN BIGHAM, ALEXD. GORDON, ROBERT FAYIL.

Page 76: Will of JAMES SMITH: Made May 14, 1808. Pro. Sept. 4, 1809... to son JOHN one cow and calf when come of my loving wife during widowhood & after that to be equally div. amongst the rest of my children. Appt's. DAVID HOLLAWAY and loving wife Exors. Signed: JAMES (X) SMITH. Wit: JOHN ANDERSON, JESSE HOLLINGSWORTH.

Page 77: Will of MARBLE STONE: Made April 10, 1800. Pro. Feb. 9, 1810... to son SOLOMON STONE one negro woman... son LITTLEBERRY STONE 2 negroes, bed and furn... daus. BETTY WHEALLER, ANNEY MCANNALLY and NANCY STONE a negro woman... to 3 daus. and son LITTLEBERRY STONE all rest of household furn. to be div. by my bel. wife LUCY STONE at her discretion ... son LITTLEBERRY STONE rest of estate real and personal. Appt's. wife LUCY STONE, son LITTLEBERRY STONE and well bel. friend LITTLEBERRY BOSTICK and MIJAHAST TURNER, Exors. Signed: MARBIL STONE. Wit: JAS. HALL, ROSEY HALL, HANNAH HALL.

Pages 78-79: Will of JAMES BIGHAM. Made Jan. 27, 1810. Pro. April 4, 1810... I, JAMES BIGHAM SENR... to bel. wife JANE BIGHAM plantation dur. nat. life, tools, 20 cows etc... to proper use of sd. JANE BIGHAM and the 4 unmarried children while they remain unmar... also 2 negroes ... to son SAMUEL BIGHAM tract of land where he now lives cont. 80 acres, also one other tract known by name of Hally Land cont. 300 acres and 2 negroes... to dau. MARY ANN BROCKENRIDGE, wife of JOSEPH BROCKENBRIDGE

200 acres in the ahs woods to be taken out of South Side of a percent of land cont. 562 acres and 2 negroes to grandson JAMES BROCKENRIDGE, a son of MARYANN 4 cows and calves... to son JAMES BIGHAM, JR. my old plantation lying in oak woods cont. 243 acres... the the balance of the percent of land cont. 562 and 2 negroes... to dau. JANE BIGHAM, tract cont. 575 acres known by name of Shorses Place, 2 negroes and furn... to dau. SALLY POWEL, wife of WILLIAM POWEL, one tract cont. 164 acres, known by Wals Place, also one other tract cont. 200 acres, known as Mountain Place, lying on waters of Dewharts Creek on the Long Branch, cows... to dau. MARGARET BIGHAM, tract on waters of Rocky Comfort on Clear Creek cont. 800 acres, 3 negroes... to dau. ELIZABETH BIGHAM the plantation and land where I now live cont. 720 acres at the death of her mother but if ELIZABETH BIGHAM should marry bef. that time it will entitle her to 1/2 of plantation and lands and remainder at death of her mother... remainder of cattle equally div. bet. 4 unmar. children: JAMES, JANE and ELIZABETH BIGHAM... I also leave one part of land in Baldwin Co. to be sold and $200 used for schooling and clothing 2 youngest daus. or son. Appt's wife JANE BIGHAM, SAMUEL BIGHAM and WILLIAM POWELL, Exors. Signed: JAMES BIGHAM. Wit: JOHN VINING, EDMOND HERING, ROBERT MARTIN, JAMES MARTIN. Will read in presence of JOHN REAL, SR., JOHN GAMBLE SR. and JOSEPH KING on 7 May 1810.

Page 80-81: Will of ANDREW MCNEELY. Made Aug. 1, 1809. Pro. July 2, 1810... to wife ESTER $480... son-in-law JOHN WHIGHAM to build for her a good comfortable house on my plantation and son-in-law to furnish her with 40 bushels corn, 100 wgt. of clean cotton... to grandson JAMES ARCHER tract cont. 202 1/2 acres drawn by me in Wilkinson Co. in 1st. Land Lottery... to grandson ALEXANDER ARCHER 100 acres in Burke Co. on Burk Head orig. gtd. to JOHN WHIGHAM... to 2 granddaus. ELIZABETH and POLLY ARCHER $100 each... son-in-law JONATHAN ARCHER $1.00... dau. and son-in-law JOHN and AGNES WHIGHAM tract whereon I now reside... to the Rev. Mr. PORTER a minister, $10 a year for 5 years... son-in-law JOHN WHIGHAM and friend WILLIAM CLEMENTS, THOMAS PARSONS and ROBERT PATTERSON Exors. Signed: ANDREW MCNEELY. Wit: A. HAMMOND, SAMUEL BOTHWELL, DAVID BOTHWELL.

Page 81-82: Will of JAMES MCDONALD. Made March 7, 1810. Pro. Nov. 5, 1810... to dau. MARY KIRK one negro woman... son JAMES MCDONALD $1.00 ... son MATTHEWS MCDONALD $1.00... son JACOB MCDONALD have use of my negro man Will... Mr. JOHN MORRES of this neighborhood is bound as Security on Cert. of Obligation of my MATHEW MCDONALD and if he have to pay, my Exors. pay his back in full... remainder of estate be sold and equally div. bet. living heirs of MARY KIRKS, JARAD (or JACOB?) MCDONALD and MATTHEWS MCDONALD. Appt's. MOSSES NEWTON, Sole Exor. Signed: JAMES MCDONALD. Wit: JOHN MORRIS, SAMUEL BATEY, MARY (X) ROBINSON.

Pages 82-83: Will of BARNABAS GAY. Made Nov. 9, 1810. Pro. Jan. 7, 1811... to bel. wife MARY GAY all of personal and real estate now possessed of for term of widowhood and then to be equally div. bet. her and the heirs. Appt's. NEEDHAM LEE, THOMAS GAY, JR. Exors. Signed: BARNABAS (X) GAY. Wit: ELISHA (X) WHITE, THOMAS (X) MOSELEY, JUNR.

Pages 83-84: Will of MARY MCCULLER. Made June 22, 1805, probated Jan. 7, 1811... unto JULIUS CRITTIAN, son of SAMUEL CRITTIAN... to his sister ELIZABETH... MARY MCCULLER. Wit: DAVID DOUGLASS, JNO. R. BURTON.

Page 84: Will of ANN GANEWAY. Made Feb. 25, 1810, probated July 15, 1811... daughter SARAH REES wife of JOHN REES... friends GARDLAND HARDWICK, sole executor... ANN GANEWAY (X). Wit: GEO. W. HARDWICK, WM. HARDWICK, H. B. GREEN.

Pages 84-85: Will of WALTER ROBINSON. Made March 17, 1808, probated Oct. 8, 1811... wife JANE to have house and lot in town of Louisville where I now live... unto my eldest son ISAAC ROBINSON... son JACOB ROBINSON... son WILLIAM ROBINSON... to my dau. MARY ANN LAMAR... dau. ELISA MILTON... youngest son JESSE ROBINSON... WALTER ROBINSON. Wit: BENJ. BRYAN, BEN. GREEN, T. HANCOCK, J.P.

Page 85: Will of CHARLES KING. Made Aug. 2, 1811, probated Nov. 4, 1811... land in Jefferson County to be divided between my wife and two sons, RUFUS and MICHAEL KING, when the oldest son, RUFUS is of age... to my daughter ISBEL... to my son GERALDUS... $129 owing to me in the hands of THOMAS D. KING of Sampson County, North Carolina... I owe Mr. JOHN BOSTICK of Jefferson County, Ga.... my brother JOSEPH KING and my beloved wife UNITY KING, Executors... CHARLES KING. Wit: E. L. YOUNG, JNO. PUESLEY.

Page 86: Will of THATCHER VIVIAN, SR.   .... resides in County of Baldwin... no witnesses... note says see Records of Inferior Court... Vivions Bridge on Williamson Creek.

Pages 87-88: Will of CHARLES HARVEY. Made March 16, 1800, probated Feb. 13, 1812... wife FRANCIS HARVEY... to my son BLASSINGHAME HARVEY 200 acres on Georgetown Road and thence to Rocky Comfort Creek... to son JAMES H. HARVEY... to son THOMAS HARVEY, 100 acres in the Opoopee where ROBT. SPURLOCK now lives... to my son JOHN HOLCOMB HARVEY, 400 acres including the plantation whereon I now live... to my daughter ELIZABETH FRANCH... to grandson CHARLES FRENCH... to my daughter SALLY HARVEY... to daughter SUSANNAH HARVEY... wife FRANCIS, son BLASSINGAME, and son JOHN HOLCOMB HARVEY Exrs... CHARLES HARVEY, Wit: JNO PAULETT, JESSE PAULETT, DAVID PAULETT.

Pages 88-89: Will of JOHN RAIFORD. Made March 11, 1812, probated April 22, 1812... wife REBECCA RAIFORD... youngest son WILLIAM H. RAI- FORD land on Ogechee River... JACOB PAGE's land... to my daughter TEMPERANCE SCARBOROUGH... to my son ALEXANDER RAIFORD... EVER's old fied... land granted to ___ POLLARD... to my son BALDWIN RAIFORD... to my son JOHN S. RAIFORD, land called Elisha lands... to my son PHILIP RAIFORD, land adj. INGRAM... to my son ROBERT RAIFORD, land adj. WATSON land Stree, Calhoo and Scrutchin... to my three daughters SALLEY C., LUCY R. and ELIZA H. RAIFORD, land on Ogechee known as Bellyach tract, also lot number two, and 94 (294) twenty-fourth district, Wilkinson County. J. RAIFORD. Wit: JACOB PAGE, JOHN WOODS, DANIEL KING (X).

Page 90: Will of JAMES MCDANIEL. Made April 16, 1811, probated July 6, 1812... to brother JOHN MCDANIEL, to brother WILLIAM MCDANIEL... to MARY CALHOUN heirs... to MARTHA CALHOON... to SYNTHIA DEPRAY... to brother DENNIS & ENIS MCDANIEL... JAMES MCDANIEL. Wit: A. LEAPTROT, JOHN CORLY.

Page 91: Will of BENJAMIN COBERT SR. Made Jan. 22, 1811, probated July 6, 1812. ... in an advanced old age and low state of health... to my grandson JAMES PHILIP COBERT and my grandaughter SOPHIA COBERT... should there be any further issue by son BENJAMIN COBERT and his wife LOUISA... to my grandson JAMES PHILIP my libary ... my young friends JAMES JACKSON, ALEXANDER MERIWETHER and THOMAS MOORE BERRIEN, executors. BENJ. COBERT. Wit: J. MERIWETHER, JOHN BERRIEN, B. D. THOMPSON.

Page 92: Will of HENRY MEARS. Made July 19, 1812, probated Sept. 7, 1812, HENRY MEARS of Town of Louisville... to my son WILLIAM HENRY MEARS... to wife CHARITY MEARS... until my sd. son WILLIAM HENRY shall arrive at the age of 21... friends WILLIAM WRIGHT and BENJAMIN COBERT Exrs... HENRY MEARS. Wit: WM. HILTON, STARLING JORDAN, DENNIS GOODMEN.

Page 93: Will of JESSE JACKSON. Made July 12, 1812, probated Sept. 7, 1812... JASEY JACKSON being weak in body... mother (not named) is to pay debts... sister SARY BATTS... brother JAMES JACKSON... brother JOSEPH JACKSON... JAMES JACKSON, Exr. JESSE JACKSON. Wit: UNY COWERT (X), HENRY WALKER, WILLIAM COWART.

Pages 94-95: Will of VALLENTINE HATCHER. Made April 24, 1812, pro- bated Sept. 7, 1812, being weak in body... to my son JOHN HATCHER... to my daughter BETSY TANKISLY, to MARY HATCHER, widow of my son ARCHIBALT HATCHER... to my daughter SUSANNA MERIWEATHER... to my daughter RHODAKERR, formerly RHODA HAUS... to my daughter PATSY... to my grandson

ALEXANDER MERIWETHER... to my two grandsons ALEXANDER MERIWETHER and THOMAS HATCHER, 300 acres... to the children of JOSIAH HATCHER, and the children of my daughter SUSANNAH MERIWETHER... VALLENTINE HATCHER (X). Wit: WM. SCHLEY, JNO. P. HARVEY, BUCKETT D. THOMPSON. Exrs. JAS. MERIWETHER, LITTLEBERRY BOSTICK, ALEXANDER MERIWETHER.

Pages 95-96: Will of JOSEPH POSNER. Made Nov. 18, 1812, no probate date. I, JOSEPH GABRILL POSNER of Town of Louisville... wife SILVIA SIGMOND POSNER... my brother's son GEORGE P. SIGMOND, the son of Dr. JOSEPH P. SIGMOND, now living in Bath, Somersethsir, Kingdom of England.. to GABRIEL POSNER, the son of Dr. DAVID POSNER, my brother, now living in the Kingdom of Poland, and commonly called in that country, the Rev. Doctor DAVID, son of Doctor GABRIEL in Sheverzinze near Posend... to the heirs of my sister DIANA... J. G. POSNER. Wit: JOHN SCHLY, ALEXANDER GODDGAM, MICHAEL SCHLEY.

Pages 96-97: Will of Mrs. JANE ROBINSON. Made Feb. 18, 1812, probated March 1, 1813... being indisposed in body... to my sons ISAAC, JACOB, WM. H., JESSE... to my daughter ELIZA MILTON consort of COLONEL HOMER V. MILTON... bought of RLI. B. BROWNING... my daughter MARY ANN LAMAR... husband WALTER... Exrs. JACOB and WILLIAM HENRY ROBINSON... JANE ROBINSON (LS). Wit: T. HANCOCK, EBENESER A. DABERDEN.

Pages 98-99: Will of ROBERT BOYD. Made Aug. 5, 1811, probated Sept. 6, 1813... to my son WILLIAM BOYD, my plantation... as soon as my son ANDREW arrives at the age of twenty one... daughters NANCY and JANE BOYD... three sons ANDREW, ROBERT and SAMUEL C. BOYD... land in Baldwin County, Lot. 29 in the thirteenth district... WILLIAM CLEMENTS, SAMUEL CLEMENTS & WM. BOYD Exrs... ROBERT BOYD. Wit: JAS. BOYD, JAS. STONE.

Pages 99-100: Will of WM. PARSONS. Made June 17, 1813, probated Sept. 6, 1813... to LUCY ANDERSON now living with me... to my nephew WILLIAM PARSONS... to BENJAMIN ELIPHELET WHITAKER, son of BENJAMIN WHITAKER... to Mr. JOSEPH BRASSFIELD of Wake County, North Carolina land on Nuse River in North Carolina which I purchased from LUCEY REYNOLDS... to NANCY BRASSFIELD daughter of JOSEPH BRASFIELD of Nuse County, North Carolina... to BEDY BRASSFIELD, daughter of sd. JOSEPH, a mare I purchased from JOHN CLEMENTS... to POLLY BRASSFIELD, daughter of sd. JOSEPH BRASSFIELD... to BENY BRASSFIELD... WILLIAM PARSONS. Wit: WILLIAM MANSON, JOHN CROSSLE, HUGH MANSON.

Pages 100-101: Will of GEORGE COX. Made March 20, 1814, probated Sept. 5, 1814... being in a low state of health... to my wife RACHEL... to my daughter LAVICEY... my three sons DAVID COX, GRIFFEN L. COX and LORENZO C. COX... land I own in Wilkinson County, 5th Dist., No. 3, the other 15th. Dist., No. 90... when my youngest son comes of age ... my friend ELAM YOUNG and HENRY TURNER, SENR. Exrs. GEORGE COX. Wit: REUBEN TURNER, JOHN COOK, NOAH MINTON.

Pages 101-102: Will of WILLIAM FOUNTAIN. Made April 7, 1814, probated Oct. 2, 1814... being very old... to my son WILLIAM FOUNTAIN... unto JOHN LAND who married my daughter RUTHA... to my son EZALIAS FOUNTAIN... to my daughter EASTER LAND... to my grandson ISAAX, the son of SETH FOUNTAIN, dec'd... unto my wife MARY FOUNTAIN... to my granddau. ROZANNA... to ENOS FOUNTAIN, my still... the heirs of SETH FOUNTAIN dec'd... to my grandson WILLIAM FOUNTAIN, son of NOAH FOUNTAIN... AARON LOW and JOHNS MAYO SENIOR, my friends, Exrs... WILLIAM FOUNTAIN (X). Wit: JOHN FIELDS, ROBERT DODD, ROBERT LAND.

Pages 103-104: Will of RUSSEL BROWN. Made March 20, 1813, probated Nov. 7, 1814... advanced in years... my wife BETTY BROWN... my son RICHARD BROWN... to my daughter LUCKY ANDERSON... to my daughter MILLY MEA ALLY... among her four children ELIZABETH ANN MACWALLY, JANE ANDERSON MACWALLY, AMELIA ROBINSON MACWALLY, SUSANNAH WADKINS MACWALLY... to my daughter REBECCA WARNER... RUSSEL BROWN (X). Wit: N. L. BOSTICK, C. CHEATHAM, B. BROWN.

Page 105:   Will of MARTIN FOREMAN.   Not dated, probated Jan. 9, 1815..
weak in body... wife LEVISON FOREMAN... to JOHN HERRING, 25¢... SOLOMEN
WILLEY Exr... MARK FOREMAN. Wit: M. NEWTON, GEORGE R. BROWN, ELIZABETH
FRAMENR.

Pages 105-106:   Will of Mrs. MARGARIT CUDDY.   Made Jan. 5, 1815, pro-
bated Jan. 26, 1815... MARGARET CUDDY (widow)... to my grandson DAVID
M. MCCONKY, the son of HENRY & JANE MCCONKY... to my daughter JANE
FRASER... to my grandaughter MARGARET BOWER, the wife of EBENEZER BOWER.
DAVID M. MCCONKY, sole exr... lot adj. the estate of the late JAMES L.
LAISEUE... my son ROBERT FRASIR... affixed my seal in Louisville...
MARGARET CUDDY (X). Wit: JANE MCMURRY (X), WILLIAM FLEMING, WM. N.
HARMAN J.J.C.

Pages 106-107:   Will of CHARLES HUDSPETH.   Made Sept. 25, 1811, probated March 6, 1815... to CALEB WELCH 2/3 of tract, 200 acres after my
wife's death... MOSES NEWTON & RUBEN WALDEN, $250 after decease of my
wife... to SARAH KILB, one dollar... to BETSEY GRACE and NANCY HUDSPETH,
her daughter, each one dollar... not signed. Wit; WM. HURD, JAS.
JOHNS, WM. JOINER (X).

Pages 107-108:   Will of ABRAHAM LAFAVER.   Made Oct. 9, 1814, probated
March 6, 1815... being aged... wife DIANAH... to my son JOHN, the plan-
tation whereon I now live, son JAMP (?) lot on Turker Creek, in
Laurence County... to my daughter MARTHA, land in BEIER CREEK in Jeffer-
son County... wife and son JAMES Exrs... ABRAHAM LAFAVER. Wit: SAML.
M. BARR, NATHAN BARR.

Pages 108-109:   Will of JAMES BEATEY.   Made Oct. 25, 1813, probated
June 17, 1815... negroes TOBY and SUE to be free at my death... grand-
daughter ELEANOR LITTLE... to my granddaughter MARY LITTLE... to my
grandson JAMES LITTLE, son of ROBT. LITTLE... to my grandson ROBT.
LITTLE son of SAML. LITTLE... daughter ELIZABETH LITTLE... beloved wife..
daughter SARAH LITTLE... grandson ROBT. LITTLE of Chester District,
South Carolina and FORESTER LITTLE of Jefferson County, Ga., Exrs... JAMES
BEATEY. Wit: GEORGE STAPLETON SENR., THOMAS STAPLETON, GEORGE STAPLETON,
JUNR.

Page 110:   Will of WILLIAM FOLKES, SR.   Made Nov. 27, 1807, probated
July 3, 1815... to my wife MARGARET FOLKES, $60... to my daughter
PRISCILLA SANDERFORD...to my daughter MARTHA SPIVEY... to my son WILLIAM
FOLKES, JUNR... unto SOLOMON AUCOCK, one dollar... to heirs of my son
SOLOMON TOLKES... WILLIAM FOLKES. Wit: HENRY ASKEW, JAMES STONE,
FURSANNA ASKEW (X).

Pages 111-112:   Will of WILLIAM LOWERY.   Made July 9, 1815, probated
Sept. 4, 1815... very sick and weak in body... tract across the branch
from where I now live to be divided in to three equal parts to son
ANDREW LOWERY, son WILLIAM LOWERY, son GEORGE LOWERY... my daughter
MARTHA CLAM... son in law ELI LOFTIN... daughter MARTHA and THODA...
son CHRISTOPHER LAWERY... son in law MATHEW HUGHS... three notes upon
JOHN PEEBLES, SNR... judgments on THOMAS PENNINGTON and JOSEPH DARSEY...
son ROBERT LOWERY and GEORGE LOWERY Exrs... WM. LOWERY. Wit: ANDREW
FAMBLE, JONATHAN WINGATE, ANDY LOWERY.
          Sept. 4, 1815... ANDREW LOWERY quits claim unto the heirs of
WILLIAM LOWERY dec'd to tract of land.

Page 112:   Will of JESSE HATCHER.   Made Sept. 12, 1815, probated
Nov. 6, 1815... loving wife MILANCY HATCHER, 313 1/2 acres on which I now
live... my three sons namely ISHAM HATCHER, SOLOMON WILLIE HATCHER &
JAMES MARIAN HATCHER... JESSIE HATCHER (LS). Wit: WM. COOPER, LOUISA
FOREMAN. Another Will made same date mentions children: CINTHIA
SALETAY, IDON, JESSEY, DATEY LAMP HATCHER, SOLOMON WILLIE HATCHER, JAMES
MARION HATCHER. Wit: WM. COOPER, LOUISA FOREMAN.

Pages 113-114:   Will of JOHN BERRIEN.   Made Oct. 26, 1811, probated
Jan. 16, 1816... JOHN BERRIEN to town of Louisville... beloved wife

WILLIMINA SARAH ELIZA BERRIEN... until my youngest child arrives at
the age of twenty one... my sons JOHN MACPHERSON A. BERRIEN, THOMAS
MOORE BERRIEN, RICHARD MCALLESTER BERRIEN & JAMES WEENS MOORE BERRIEN
and my daughters SARAH LOWNDES CASEY, RUTH LOWNDES BERRIEN, JULIA MARIA
BERRIEN & ELIZA ANCIAUX BERRIEN and such future children as I may have...
I do not object the second marriage of my wife... Wit: J. MERIWEATHER,
T. HANCOCK, JOHN SHLY.

Page 115:   Will of JAMES H. CARR.   Made Feb. 20, 1816, probated Feb.
24, 1816... so WILLIAM HENRY CONLEY and JAMES HOWARD BOSTICK ten negroes.
... to BIRD TARVER... NICHOLAS C. CONLEY, NATHAN BOSTICK and BIRD
TARVER Exrs... JAMES CARR (X). Wit: LEWIS VENNON, THOMS. STREET, JM.
BERRYHILL.

Pages 115-116:   Will of HUGH MCNEELY.   Made March 3, 1816, probated,
no date... to son JOHN, land where my mother lives... to son SAMUEL
land where he now lives... to sons DANIEL and ANDREW the land I drew in
the 23rd District of Wilkinson, No. 7... to sons HUGH and WILLIAM the
plantation where I now live... to daughter RACHEL... to daughter MATHEW
... to daughters MARGARET and MARY... HUGH MCNEELY (X). Wit: RICHARD
LOCK, HENCHER WAREN, WILLIAM MURDOCK.

Page 117:   Will of NATHAN BARR.   Made June 1, 1815, probated March
4, 1816... wife ELIZABETH... sons JAMES and ALFRED... to son JOHN, one
lot of land in Putnam County on the Waters of Little Run... to my son
NATHAN two lots lying in Wilkinson originally... to my daughter SALLY...
sons SAMUEL and JOHN Exrs... NATHAN BARR. Wit: REUBEN TURNER, JNO
LAND, MRY TURNER.

Page 118:   Will of MARGARET MCNEELY.   Made March 8, 1816, probated
May 6, 1816... to my daughter MARGARET... to my grandson JOHN MCNEELY...
to my grandaughter AMY... to my son ANDREW... Exrs. JOHN MCNEELY,
WILLIAM MCNEELY... MARGARET MCNEELY (X). Wit: MATTHEW BISHOP.

Page 119:   Will of ISAAC HARRIS.   Made Oct. 8, 1812, probated July
term, 1816... being weak in body... my wife MARY ANN MARIA HARRIS... to
my said wife eight volumes of the Spectator... to son ADDISON HARRIS,
five volumes of the Life of Washington... to my daughter ELIZABETH
HARRIS, and a child with which my wife is now pregnant... before my son
ADDISON reaches the age of 21... friends DANIEL GREEN and JOHN SHLY
Exrs. IC HARRIS. Wit: JOHN SCHLY, BIRD TARVER, DANIEL GREEN.

Pages 120-121:   Will of JOHN MOORE.   Made May 9, 1815, probated Sept.
2, 1816... I, JOHN MOORE, planter... my first daughter MORNING PRICE...
my second daughter OLLIVE PARKER... my third daughter CINTHA PARKER...
beloved wife (not named)... to my daughter UNITY... daughter FERIBY...
daughter POLLEY... son WILLIAM MOORE, 150 acres... beloved wife ANNE...
WILLIAM WALKER and SETH PIERCE, Exrs. JOHN MOORE (X). Wit: MARTHA
BOON (X), MARYANN BOONE (X), STEPHEN PARKER (X), WM. WALKER JP.

Pages 121-122:   Will of JOHN PEEL, SR.   Made Sept. 16, 1816, probated
Nov. 4, 1816... weak in body... beloved wife SARAH... to my son-in-law
JOHN LEE and daughter MARY LEE his wife... son JOHN and daughter SARAH...
daughter SARAH PEEL... JOHN GAMBLE and RICHARD PEEL, Exrs. JOHN PEEL
(LX). Wit: R. L. GAMBLE, F. POUNCHER, WM. POWELL.

Pages 122-123:   Will of JOSEPH ALLEN.   Made Feb. 8, 1817, probated
March 3, 1817... being in a low state of health... wife CATHERINE... son
JOSEPH ALLEN, JR.... AVEX, CATHERINE & MARGARET my unmarried daughters..
daughter MARTHEW LAMP... son in law ROBERT MOUNTAIN... to my daughter
AVES ALLEN... Exrs. JOSEPH ALLEN JUNR. and WILLIAM POWELL... JOSEPH
ALLEN. Wit: WILLIAM POWELL, MICHAEL LAMP, JOSEPH ALLEN.

Pages 123-124:   Will of RACHEL GREEN... being in ill health... sons
JOHN & HINCHEY GREEN to inherit all portion of my property, the undivided
portion of my deceased husband's estate, JOHN GREEN... WARREN GREEN
and BENJAMIN SHERROD, Exrs... RACHEAL GREEN (X). Wit: HENCHE WARREN,
JOHN L. RAIFORD, WILLIAM MARSHALL.

141

Pages 124-125:   Will of MAJOR HOWELL COBB.   Made April 15, 1817, probated June 2, 1818... should my wife again marry, all property shall go
to my brother JOHN A. COBB... sister MARY FLOURNOY, her husband ROBERT
FLOURNOY... my sister MILDRED, wife of Col. WILLIAM JACKSON... to my
servant WILLIAM HILL... nephew HOWELL COBB, son of JOHN H. COBB.   Wit:
GARLAND HARDWICK, ROBERT STEVENS, JOHN BOUTIN.

Page 126:   Will of THOMAS BERRYHILL.   Made March 27, 1816, probated
March 3, 1817... THOMAS BERRIHILL being in a low state of health... to
my beloved brother SAMUEL... to my beloved brother ANDREW... to my
brother in law HENRY C. FUGUA... to my brother JOSEPH... to SARAH BERRI-
HILL, daughter of my brother SAMUEL... to POLLET BERRIHILL, son of my
brother ANDREW... to ANDREW AGUSTOS FUGUA... sister SUSANNAH and JOSIAH
SCRUTCHENS Exrs... THOMAS BERRYHILL.   Wit: ELONATHAN DAVIS, STEPHEN
GREEN.

Pages 126-127:   Will of NATHAN BOSTICK.   Made May 9, 1817, no probate
... NATHAN BOSTICK SENR... beloved wife MARTHA... to my son HILLERY...
to my daughter ELIZABETH... to my son FILMON... to my daughter POLLY...
my son HOMES children... MARTHA, MANDA, CARLINE, and LUWCY GWIN...
servants ADAM & MILLEY to live with WILLIAM HAYLES... sons JOHN, NATHAN
& FILMON and wife MARTHA Exrs... NATHAN BOSTICK.. Wit: WYLIE HAYLES,
HENRY GAY, DANIEL VENNEL JP.

Page 128:   Will of MARY DEBORAH MARBURY... Dated July 26, 1817, no
probate... from my first husband JOHN MARTIN... my property to be equally
divided between MARY D. SPENCER and HOMER V. MILTON... their uncle
HORATIO MARBURY, my present husband...MARY D. MARBURY.   Wit: JOHN
PUGHLEY, ELIZABETH HOLMS, WM. N. HARMAN.

Pages 129-131:   Will of JAMES MERRIWETHER.   Made Oct. 22, 1817, pro-
bated Nov. 3, 1817... of Town of Louisville, merchant... wife SUSANNAH
MERRIWETHER... my son ALEXANDER MERRIWETHER and JAMES ARCHIBALD MERI-
WETHER, and my daughter ELIZABETH MARIA MERIWETHER and LOUISA JENNETT
HARCHER BERRIEN, the wife of THOMAS MOORE BERRIEN Esq. attorney at law...
until each of the children shall attain the age of 21... T. MERRIWETHER.
Wit: JOHN BOSTICK, CHAS. CHEATHAM, WM. SCHLEY.

Pages 131-132:   Will of SARAH GRANBERRY.   Made Nov. 12, 1817, probated Nov. 26, 1817, to my daughter WINFRED... to my daughter SARAH...
to my son JOSEPH... to my son JAMES... my son JOSEPH JACKSON and NATHAN
BATTS HOLLWY Exrs... SARAH GRAMBARY (X).   Wit: WILLIAM FOKES, WINEFORD
FOKES (X).

Page 132-133:   Will of PHILEP SCOTT, shopkeeper, made Oct. 3, 1804,
probated Dec. 1, 1817... to my wife MARY SCOTT... my six children Viz.
JAMES and JOHN, FANNY, SUSAN, POLLY and SALLY... Exrs. wife MARY,
friends THOMAS HANCOCK, JOHN BERRIEN ... PHILIP SCOTT.   Wit: JOHN BOS-
TICK, WM. WRIGHT JP, JAS. BOGEMAN (?).

Pages 133-134:   Will of DANIEL THOMAS.   Made Jan. 16, 1812, probated
Dec. 1, 1817... in a low state of health... to my son BENJAMIN THOMAS...
daughter SALLY THOMAS... to BETSY ANN & SALLEY WRENN, daughters of my
daughter SUSANNAH WRENN... wife SUSANNAH THOMAS... son BLASSINGHAME and
BENJAMIN THOMAS Exrs... DANIEL THOMAS.   Wit: J. W. PAULETT, SALLY
PAULETT, BENJM. GOBERT JP.

Page 135:   Will of JOHN INGRAM.   Made Oct. 19, 1817, probated Dec. 1,
1817... to my wife ELLENDER... until my youngest child comes of age...
children JOHN and DAVID and my daughters MARY, JANE, NANCY, REBECKAH,
ELIZABETH A. SYNTHE, PHEABY, ABCENETH, SARAH, MORIAH, SAPHIAN... friends
JOHN INGRAM, DAVID INGRAM, WILLIAM FOUNTAIN and LEWIS DEAL Exrs... JOHN
INGRAM.   Wit: JOSEPH MARSHALL, JOHN MARSHALL, JOSEPH MARSHALL JUNR.

Pages 135-136:   Will of NATHAN BRASSEL.   Made Jan. 19, 1816, probated
Nov. 3, 1817... wife ELIZABETH BRASSEL... my son NATHAN... plantation in

Jefferson County... three sons BENJAMIN BRASSELE, WILLIAM BRASSEL, and NATHAN BRASSELL... on each of my youngest sons comes to age of 18 years. Viz., KINDRED, ELIAS & JAMES LITTLETON... NATHAN BRASSEL (X). Wit: M. NEWTON, CALEB WELCH, WILLIAM WELCH.

Pages 136-137: Will of JAMES ANDERSON. Made Oct. 3, 1815, probated Dec. 1, 1817... wife SUSANNAH ANDERSON... friend WILLIAM N. HARMAN, in trust for my grandson JAMES JACKSON THOMPKINS, son of THOMAS THOMPKINS, by my deceased daughter REBECCA W. THOMPKINS, formerly REBECCA W. ANDERSON... between my children, MARY J., SARAH C., CHARLES, RICHARD JORDAN and JAMES D. ANDERSON... JAMES D. ANDERSON when he arrives at the age of 21... negroes which RUSSEL BROWN JUNIOR brought from Virginia, formerly belonging to me... JAMES ANDERSON. Wit: ROBERT NORTHCUTT, JAMES CLARKE, THOMAS M. BERRIEN. Sept. 22, 1817 JAMES ANDERSON, being in a low state of health... in consequence of the death of my son JAMES D. ANDERSON... in consequence of the death of my children SARAH C. and JAMES D. ANDERSON... three surviving children MARY I., CHARLES and RICHARD JORDAN ANDERSON... JAMES ANDERSON (X). Wit: SAMUEL CLEMENTS, THOMS. S. MCKEE, BENJAMIN HUDSON.

Pages 139-140: Will of JAMES ARRINGTON. Made Nov. 13, 1813, probated Jan. 5, 1818... wife REBECCA ARRINGTON, land on which I now live... equally divided amongst all my children... JAMES ARRINGTON (X). Wit: D. BROWN, RUBEN BACKUM, WM. PATTERSON.

Pages 140-142: Will of THOMAS HANNAH. Made Feb. 13, 1817, probated April 8, 1818... to my wife ANN HANNAH, $1000... to my son WILLIAM HANNAH, 500 acres in Jefferson County... to the heirs of my son WILLIAM HANNAH begotten by his present wife (NANCY HANNAH)... to NANCY ALLEN, the wife of SHARRACK ALLEN... to my grandson THOMAS MCKIGNEY, the son of JAMES MCKEGNEY... to my grandson THOMAS HADDEN, the son of WILLIAM HADDEN... to my daughter ELLENDOR MCKEGNEY, the wife of JAMES MCKEGNEY... to the children of JAMES & ELLENDOR MCKEGNEY... to MARY CLARK, the wife of THOMAS CLARK (who is my granddaughter)... to my daughter ELIZABETH HADDEN, the wife of WILLIAM HADDEN... to the children of WILLIAM and ELIZABETH HADDEN, except the wife of THOMAS CLARK... THOMAS HANNAH (X). Wit: WM. HARDWICK, JOHN REES, SARAH REES (X).

Pages 142-143: Will of HOWELL COBB. Made April 15, 1817, probated June 2, 1818... wife (not named)... brother JOHN A. COBB... brother's son HOWELL COBB... when he arrives at the age of 21 years... sister MARY FLOURNOY... sister MILDRED, wife of Col. WILLIAM JACKSON... H. COBB. Wit: GARLAND HARDWICK, ROBERT STEVENS, JOHN BOUTIN... (identical with Will of pages 124-125).

Pages 144-146: Will of OWEN FORT. Made March 20, 1818, probated July 6, 1818, to my son OWEN J. FORT... to son ARTHUR P. FORT... to my granddaughter ELIZABETH FORT CAWTHOUR, the only child of my dear departed daughter late ELIZABETH FORT... my daughter LUCY SMITH... daughter RHODA... wife ELIZABETH FORT... son CHARLES M. FORT... CHARLES shall be executor when he shall arrive at the age of 17... OWEN FORT. Wit: DRURY WILSON, ISABEL REID, SARAH BLOUNT.

Page 146 + 1: Will of JOHN REESE. Made Jan. 29, 1816, probated April 5, 1819... wife SARAH REESE... friend HARLAND HARDWICK and wife SARAH Exrs... Wit: W. P. HARDWICK, DAVID PAULETT, FANNY HERRING (X). (This page was very dim.)

Pages 147-148: Will of MESHACK MATTHEWS, SR.... Made May 12, 1818, probated May 3, 1819... my beloved wife JANE MATTHEWS... her son JONATHAN MATTHEWS and her daughter RICEY JOINER... my two youngest daughters JANE & CHARLOTTE MATTHEWS... son MESHACK MATTHEWS JR. Exr... MESHACK MATTHEWS SENOR (X). Wit: JOHN CHAMPTION (X)., GEORGE STAPLETON SENR.

Pages 148-149: Will of JOHN P. HARVEY. Made Feb. 14, 1812, probated May 3, 1819... My sister SARAH PAULETT, wife of JOHN PAULETT... to my son EDWARD HAMILTON... my beloved wife JANE... my child or children... Wit: B. D. THOMPSON, JN. PAULETT, HENRY KEY.

Pages 149-150: Will of JANE ANDREW. Made March 16, 1816, probated May 3, 1819... to my son SAMUEL... a fourth part of 100 acres of land in Ninety Six District of South Carolina and 125 acres in Jefferson County, joining ISAAC RAWLS and others... to my daughter JANE... to my son in law GEORGE ROWLAND... my sisters three children JOHN WOOTEN, JANE WOOTEN & SPENCE WOOTEN... JANE ANDREW (X). Wit: MORRIS MURPHY, FREDRICK MORRSI, GEORGE C. HODGES.

Pages 150-151: Will of DAVID PUALETT. Made Jan. 4, 1810, probated June 9, 1819... friend WILLIAM HARDWICH, SENR., LITTLE BERRY BOSTICK SENR., JOHN REES, GARLAND HARDWICK, GEORGE HARDWICK and JESSE ROBINSON... DAVID PAULETT. Wit: THOMAS W. MCWATTY. L. BERRY BOSTICK JR., HARDY HARREL (X).

Pages 151-152: Will of RICHARD FLEETING. Made July 16, 1817, probated Nov. 3, 1819... to my wife MARGARET FLEETING... to my son RICHARD FLEETING the plantation where I now live... one tract 250 acres, dated March 15, 1790 and 100 acres purchased from JOHN WHIGHAM, April 4, 1793.. for my daughter ELIZABETH FLEETING, alias ELIZABETH ROAN 200 acres originally granted to JOSIAS GRAY for 250 acres, March 25, 1782, at that time adj. WILLIAM BLACK's land... to my daughter SARAH FLEETING 250 acres granted Feb. 29, 1804... to my son in law JOHN SPANN and my daughter CATHERINE SPANN... RICHARD FLEETING (X). Wit: ROGER L. GAMBLE, JOHN GIBHAM, JOHN IRWIN.

Pages 153-154: Will of WILLIAM HADDEN. Made Dec. 20, 1813, probated Dec. 27, 1819... my daughter SARAH CLEMENTS land on Chevises Creek, granted to SAMUEL GORDON, 150 acres... to my son THOMAS HADDEN, land I now live on Reedy Branch from HUTCHINS land toward Ogechee River until it strikes BOTHWILLS (?) line... to my wife MARY HADDEN... my daughter MARY HADDEN, son GORDON HADDEN, daughter MARGARET HADDEN, son WILLIAM HADDEN... WM. HADDEN. Wit: JOHN PARSON, ISOM MCCLENDON, ANDREW B. LAWSON.

Pages 154-155: Will of JOHN D. R. FIGG. Made Nov. 16, 1818, probated Jan. 19, 1820... unto my loving wife POLLY FIGG... 708 acres of land by original survey, adj. where I now live... store and books of accounts that is now in the hands of JOHN W. PATTON... to my sister MARTHA COX, all my fathers estate that is coming to me... wife and MUND GROSS and BRITTON JORDEN, exrs. JOHN D. R. FIGG. Wit: ABSOLEN PRYOR, JOHN WHIGHAM, JOHN BIGHAM.

Pages 155-156: Will of ELIZABETH JARVIS. Made Sept. 26, 1818, probated Sept. 4, 1820... to my daughter ELIZABETH ANN BOSTICK and her husband HILLARY BOSTICK, 25 acres, where I now live... to my grandson ALFRED R. JARVIS and PATRICK F. JARVIS, 202 1/2 acres in 16th District, Wilkinson County... HILLARY BOSTICK & NATHL. BEAL Exrs... ELIZABETH JARVIS. Wit: ELOISA BEAL, RHESA BOSTICK, NATHANIEL BEAL JUNR.

Pages 156-157: Will of DAVID MCCONKY. Made Nov. 10, 1820, probated Nov. 20, 1820... wife NANCY MCCONKY... by the L. W. & T. of my grandmother MAS. MARGARET CUDDY, all her estate... my mother JANE FRASIER, the use of the house and furniture... to my friend ALEXANDER MERITHER, BIRKET D. THOMPSON and ROGER L. GAMBLE, to provide for my mother... for the children of my sister MARGARET BOWERS, until they reach the age of 21 or marry... D. N. MCCONKY. Wit: WM. SCHLEY, WM. L. FOKES, J. MCCONKY.

Pages 158-159: Will of GEORGE INGRAM. Made Aug. 13, 1820, probated Nov. 20, 1820... to my wife MARGARET... land whereon I now live, 220 acres and 436 acres, adj. Warren County line and JOHN POWEL, JAMES WILLIAMS and lands belonging to the estate of WILLIAM INGRAM dec'd., to my grandson JOHN and GEORGE MARTAIN, sons of ROBERT MARTAIN, to be equally divided between them when they come of age... WILLIAM MARSHALL Esqr. and ETHELDRED FOUNTAIN and WILLIAM ANDERSON, my lawfull exrs... GEO INGRAM. Wit: DAVID ALEXANDER, ISRAEL CAUSEY, JOHN MCBRIDE (X).

Page 160: Will of ROBERT LOWRY. Made July 8, 1820, probated Dec. 4, 1820... to my loving companion PATIENCE LOWERY all my estate... to

to equally divided among all my loving and lawful sons and daughters...
JOHN WAY and WILLIAM WAY Exrs. ROBERT LOWR. Wit: ABS. PRYOR, GEORGE
WRIGHT, CHRISTOPHER LOWERY, WILLIAM LOWERY.

Pages 161-162: Will of ROBERT PIOR. Made Oct. 10, 1820, probated
Jan. 1, 1821... to my son JOHN PIOR a tract of land of 200 acres in
Burke County, represented by a plat to the grant of sd. land... to my
daughter SALLEY LIVINGSTON... to my daughter ELIZABETH MORE... to RACHAL
TRAVIS and unto RHODY TRAVIS... among the following heirs NANCY PIOR
and her four children ARRENOY, WILANTY, HEZEKIAH and NARISSAS PIOR... to
my four youngest children by deeds of gift vs. ARRENCY, WILANTY, HEZE-
KIAH and NARCISIOUR PIOR... ROBERT PIOR (X). Wit: JOHN BLACKSTONE, MOSES
BRINSON JUNR.

Page 162: Will of JOHN SANDERFER. Made March 5, 1820, no probate
date... to beloved wife PRISSELA SANDEFIR... JOHN SANDEFIR (X). Wit:
SUSAN POWELL, WILLIAM FOKES (SUSANNAH JACKSON testified that she saw
sd. JOHN SANDY sign seal, etc.).

Page 163: Will of JOHN COWART. Made Feb. 25, 1821, probated May 7,
1821... I cannot long survive in my present condition... my beloved
wife MICHAL COWART... land I purchased of SETH FOUNTAIN... land I purchased of JOHN SHELMAN JUNOR... to my oldest son WILLIAM COWART... land
lying north of ANDERSON's Branch... to my daughter SELAH N. COWART...
to my son JOHN W. COWART, 500 acres on water of Ogechee... to my son
THOMAS W. COWART... to JARED TOMLINSON 100 pounds sterling... to my
grand daughter TILEY ANN COSSEY, land lying between AMOS FOLKS and JOHN
W. COWART's land, on Ogechee... till it intersects Mr. J. FORSYTHE's
land... to my grand daughter SARAH AN TOMLINSON... to Bethel Church 100
dollars... 200 dollars for making a brick wall around my grave... JOHN
COWART. Wit: JAMES TOMPSON, GEORGE FOWLER (X), CELIA N. COWART.

Pages 163-164: Will of PLEASANT WALL HARGROVE. Made Sept. 6, 1820
probated July 2, 1821... being weak in body ... unto my nephew JOHN
HARGROVE CLAYTON, son of GEORGE R. CLAYTON, $500 cash for the purpose of
educating him... wife BETSY HARGROVE... wife and brother in law JAMES
JACKSON and WILLIAM SCHLEY Exrs... P. W. HARGROVE. Wit: RICHARD BROWN,
DANIEL HOOK, JOHN SHELLMAN, JR.

Page 164-166: Will of BENJAMINE WHITAKER. Made July, 1820, probated
Sept. 3, 1821... to my wife ANNE WHITAKER, plantation of which I now
live, 295 acres... for education of the children... to son ELI DANIEL
WHITAKER... daughters MARY CLEMENTS, ELIZABETH WHITAKER, ASSENTH ANNE
WHITAKER and REBECCA JANE FRANCES WHITAKER... my three sons, DAVID
EMANUEL WHITAKER, BENJAMIN ELIPHELET WHITAKER & ELI DANIEL WHITAKER...
land on Brushy Creek in Jefferson and Burke Counties... land on Lambert's
Creek, adj. CHEATHAM and others granted ELIPHELET WHITAKER... to my
daughter NANCY WHITAKER, when she arrives at twenty one or marries...
BENJAMIN WHITAKER. Wit: JAMES STONE, ROBERT LOWRY, MAMASSEY M. COPELAND.

Page 167: Will of ELIAS HODGES. Not dated, probated Nov. 5, 1821...
my beloved wife SARAH... to purchase a piece of land in Alabama sufficient to raise support for her and the children... son ELIAS... I am
indebted to Mr. COWART... my brothers RICHARD HODGES and GEORGE C.
HODGES Exrs... ILIAS HODGES. Wit: MOSES SINQUEFIELD, REBECCA I. WHEELER,
JOHN FLEMING JP.

Page 168: Will of JOHN MOUNTAIN. Made Nov. 4, 1821, probated Jan.
2, 1822... my daughter MARTHA MOUNTAIN... land whereon I now live at
the death of my mother... land I drew in Early County... land in
possession of WILLIAM FLANDERS... friends JAMES INGRAM SENR. and
BLASSINGAME THOMAS Exrs... JOHN MOUNTAIN. Wit: JOHN COLE, JOHN INGRAM.

Pages 169-170: Will of JOHN KENEDY. Made Sept. 1, 1821, probated
Jan. 9, 1822... to my son THOMAS, land on which I now reside, 250 acres...
to my granddaughter MARGARET BELL KENEDY... for support of my daughter
JANE (who is now a lunatic)... land in Twiggs County... to my son JOHN...
my daughter MARTHA, wife of BENJAMIN HALSEY... and to the orphan

145

children of my deceased son FRANCIS... to my son WILLIAM and my daughter
MARY, the wife of DANIEL MCNELLY, one dollar each... son THOMAS sole
executor... JOHN KENEDY (X). Wit: R. L. GAMBLE, H. ALEXANDER, DAVID
ALEXANDER.

Pages 170-171:   Will of JOB WOODMAN.   Made July 4, 1822, probated
July 17, 1822... to my niece TEMPERENCE D. WOODMAN... in possession of
my brother ENCHAL WOODMAN. (probably ENOCH)... to my niece MARY W.
WOODMAN... to my beloved sister in law LOIS WOODMAN... the clothing that
belonged to my deceased child... to my beloved wife WAITSILL G. WOODMAN,
JOB WOODMAN. Wit: ROGER L. GAMBLE, SAMUEL W. ROBBINS, LOYD BELT.

Pages 171-172:   Will of SION PENNINGTON.   Made Aug. 10, 1822, probated Nov. 4, 1822... to my wife ELIZABETH PENNINGTON... my following
named children ANNA M. PENNINGTON, MARY PENNINGTON and ELIZA PENNINGTON..
wife ELIZABETH and friends DOCTOR LLOYD BETT and JOSEPH LOWRY Exrs...
SION PENNINGTON. Wit: WINIFRED PARSONS, DAVID COTTER, JOHN G. BOSTICK.

Pages 172-173:   Will of SAMUEL IRWIN.   Made Oct. 19, 1822, probated
Nov. 4, 1822... to my mother JANE IRWIN... to my brother ROBERT IRWIN...
friend FORESTER LITTLE Exr.... SAMUEL IRWIN. Wit: JOHN DENDRY, JOHN
BRADY.

Pages 173-174:   Will of ELIJAH WARNER.   Made Nov. 2, 1822, probated
Nov. 12, 1822... to wife ELIZABETH, son WILLIAM and daughter JANE...
WILLIAM W. HARMAN and W. SOLOMON WILLY Exrs... ELIJAH WARNER. Wit:
LEWIS KENNON, MARGARET ALLEN, WILLIAM LIVINGSTON.

Pages 174-175:   Will of NOAH TURNER.   Made Sept. 19, 1822, probated
Nov. 18, 1822... wife NANCY L. TURNER, GREEN TURNER and all of her child-
ren... wife NANCY L. BYNE... her father LEWIS BYNE... my father HENRY
TURNER... until my children shall arrive to the age of 14... NOAH
TURNER. Wit: ANDREW HUDSON, SIMON JONES (X), CATY ROSS.

Page 175:   Will of STEPHEN POWEL.   Made Nov. 11, 1802, probated, no
date... named STEPHEN POWEL in body of will... to my son JOHN POWEL...
to my son FRANCIS POWEL... when my son FRANCIS comes of age... to my
daughter PATIENCE POWEL... to my daughter ELIZABETH PAGE... Exrs. son
JOHN POWEL and WILLIAM CAUTHORN. Wit: GEORGE HENDRIX, MANCY SPIVEY (X),
THOMAS SPEIGHT.

Pages 176-177:   Blank

Page 178:   Will of REUBEN POWELL.   Made Aug. 31, 1821, probated
March 3, 1823... to my wife REBECCA POWELL... land whereon I now live,
512 1/2 acres... to my son JASON POWELL and my youngest daughter
REBECCA HEATH, land in Hall County, lot #17, 10 Dist... to son-in-law
ARTHUR ROUNDTREE... to my daughter ELVE FLEMING... to my son THEOPHILUS
POWELL, $5 and to my daughter in law SARAH POWELL $5... land in Iarwin
County, drawn by REUBEN K. POWELL No. 259, 11th Dist... divided among
my children that survive me... REUBEN POWELL. Wit: ISAAC W. RAIFORD,
JOHN L. LOCKE, JOHN MURPHY.

Pages 178-179:   Will of ROBERT PATTERSON.   Made May 25, 1822, probated March 19, 1824... ROBERT PATTERSON SENR... to my son WILLIAM...
to my son JOHN... unto ANDREW BURY LAWSON, one dollar and to his two
children ROGER MCGIL and ELLENANOR WRIGHT $100... unto WILLIAM LITTLE
my son in law... unto my son in law SAMUEL FLEMING... unto my son in law
THOMAS WHIGHAM... to my son JAMES... to my daughter ELEANOR... unto my
daughter MARGARET SARAH... to my daughter ELIZA... land whereon I now
live to sons JAMES & ROBERT... to my five youngest children JAMES,
ELEANOR, ROBERT, MARGARET, and ELIZA... WILLIAM PATTERSON, JOHN PATTERSON
& WILLIAM LITTLE Exrs... ROBERT PATTERSON. Wit: PHILIP THOMAS, ELIJAH
ANDERSON, ELISHA CAMPBELL.

Pages 180-181:   Will of MAURICE RAIFORD.   Made April 28, 1824, probated Nov. 1, 1824... My lands in the state of Tennessee be sold by my

executor, and the effects be divided among nine of my children: ISAAC
W. RAIFORD, MATTHEW RAIFORD, MAURICE RAIFORD, LEXE RAIFORD, PENCY
WATSON, CAPE L. RAIFORD, ASENEATH RAIFORD, CAMPBELL RAIFORD, BAIDEN
C.M. (?) RAIFORD and for MAURICE and CAPEL to have one tenth part of sd.
effects extra between them... tract on south side of Williamson Swamp,
281 acres, granted to WELDON HOWSLEY, with 30 acres adj. sd. tract
granted to my self, and 100 acres adj. WILLIAM KENNEDY granted to myself,
and 500 acres lying in Tatnal County, on Beards Creek, granted to
SOLOMON WOOD and myself... to my youngest son BARDEN C.M. RAIFORD before
sd. son becomes of the age of 21 years... my daughter LEXE... MAURICE
RAIFORD. Wit: JOHN COX, JOHN POWELL J.J.C.

Page 182: Will of RUTH MULKY. Made May 16, 1816, probated July 6,
1823... to my daughter SARAH MULKEY, 15 acres whereon I now live in
Burke County, which fell to me by the death of my husband PHILLIP
MULKY, also 3 acres conveyed to me by JOHN CASON... good friend JOSEPH
HINES Exr... RUTH MULKY (X). Wit: L. BERRY BOSTICK, JACOB BOSTICK,
JESSE ROBINSON.

Page 183: Will of DAVID HOLLIWAY. Made May 24, 1818, probated Sept.
1, 1823. Georgia, Burke County... to my daughter LUCY TIMS children, all
the money that their father owes me... wife ELIZABETH HOLLIWAY... my
three daughters CHARITY HAIR, FERTY ANDERSON, SARAH SMITH... daughter
MARY HOLLINGSWORTH... DAVID HOLLIWAY. Wit: ELIZABETH COOK, ELIYAH
SMITH (X), WILLIAM COOK.

Page 184-185: Will of NICHOLAS COVENAH. Made Aug. 17, 1794, probated
Oct. 30, 1823... of State of Georgia and County of Burke... to wife
DORCAS CAVANAH 850 acres of land on Buckhead Creek in Burke Co., being
in 5 surveys, 300 acres where I now live including the plantation and
mill, 150 acres adj. it, transferred by JOHN BRADLEY to HENRY CAVANAH,
100 acres that was granted to JOHN SHATON, 200 acres granted to me and
200 acres in Screven County, on Deep Creek near the Sugar Leaf... to my
son CHARLES CAVANAH... to my daughter MARGARET CONNELLY, wife of PATRICK
CONNELLY, 350 where on the sd. PATRICK CONNELLY now lives, 100 acres in
the name of HENRY CAVANAH, 100 acres in the name of JOHN CABOURN, and
150 acres in the name of DANIEL MCMURPHY... NICHOLAS CAVANAH. Wit:
B. MCCULLER, JAMES HUGHES, MARY WINBERLY, ELIZABETH MCCULLERS.

Page 186: Will of JOHN WHIGHAM. Made May 29, 1823, probated Nov. 1,
1823 wife NANCY... to give unto ESTER MCNELLY an annuaty, given to her
by the Will of ANDREW MCNEELY, dec'd... to son in law ROBERT DONALSON
and his wife MARY... friends ROBERT DONALDSON and EBENEZER BOTHWELL.
Exrs... JOHN WHIGHAM (X) (LS). Wit: RICHARD K. BEAL, JOSIAH S. PATTER-
SON, ROGER L. GAMBLE.

Page 187: Will of SOLOMON WILLEY. Made July 13, 1821, probated Nov.
3, 1823, wife NANCY WILLEY... wife's sister RHODA HOLLOWAY... my
nephews MOORE FOREMAN, WILLEY HATCHER, WILLIAMS BIRD FOREMAN & JAMES
FOREMAN... niece THENEY HATCHER... LOMIS LAMP, SAMUEL L. ANDREWS, MOORE
FOREMAN and WILLIAM B. FOREMAN. Exrs... SOLOMON WILLEY. Wit: STEPHEN
MORGAN, HARRIET MORGAN, H. MORGAN.

Pages 188-189: Will of BENJAMIN WARNER. Made Jan. 15, 1820, probated Nov. 3, 1823... to my beloved wife CATHERINE WARNER... nine equal
parts that the following persons shall share... JAMES WARNER, my
daughter SUSANNAH, my daughter MARY, my daughter LYDA, my son SOLOMON
WARNER, my daughter CATHERINE, my daughter REBECKAH, my daughter SARY...
and my will is that my three grandsons PLEASANT WARNER, BENJAMIN WARNER
and JONATHAN D. G. W. WARNER should have one share... JOSEPH WILLIS and
JAMES WARNER. Exrs... BENJ. WARNER. Wit: JAMES GARNER, MORRIS MURPHY,
WM. PARADY.

Pages 189-191: Will of LITTLEBERRY BOSTICK SENR. Made Aug. 11, 1823,
probated November 3, 1823... unto my son RHESA BOSTICK... unto BETSY
BOSTICK the wife of JOHN BOSTICK, one dollar... reason is that her
husband JOHN BOSTICK deprived my daughter MATILDA G. BOSTICK of all her

property... to sons RHESA and LITTLEBERRY JUNR. in trust for the use
of my unfortunate son JEREMIAH... in trust for my son NATHANIEL BOSTICK..
to my daughter MARY ROBERSON, wife of JESSE ROBERSON... unto my daughter
SUSANNAH A. FLOURNOY, the wife of MARCUS FLOURNOY... to my daughter
MATILDA G. BOSTICK, wife of DON F. BOSTICK... to my granddaughter
ELIZABETH WATSON BEAL, dau. of MATILDA G. BOSTICK... LBERRY BOSTICK SENR.
Wit: JOHN M. SHELMAN, BENJM. GOBERT, M. SHELMAN.

Page 191:   Will of THEOPHILUS POWELL.   Made Sept. 16, 1823, probated
Dec. 11, 1823... to wife SARAH POWELL... that she have an equal share
with my children... SAMUEL FLEMING & JOSEPH PRICE Exrs... THEOPHILUS
POWELL. Wit: MILLES WATKINS, HARTWILL WATKINS, JASON POWELL.

Page 192:   Will of ANDREW DILLON.   Made Nov. 5, 1823, probated Jan.
9, 1824.... J. W. STILLWELL Exr... ANDREW DILLON JR. Wit: J. D. NEWTON,
PHP. S. LEMLE, RICHARD K. BEAL, ROBERT W. PATE.

Pages 192-193:   Will of RICHARD HODGES.   Made Jan. 21, 1823, probated
Feb. 11, 1824... to wife ELIZABETH HODGES... law suit to est. of JESSE
GORDON... to my daughter MARTHA HODGES... brother GEORGE C. HODGES
Exr... Wit: ANN GOODGAME (X), ANN BALLARD, JOHN HERRING.

Pages 193-194:   Will of JEFFERSON B. WELL.   SAMUEL W. RIBBINS,
JOSIAH SCRUTCHIN and DANIEL GREEN, being sworn that JEFFERSON B. WELLS,
a transient individual who departed this life in the County of Burke
on the 7th day of Nov. in the present year made the following Will...
my mother ___ DEAN of Gulhalo, Vermont have all my property... JAMES
MORRISON & ISAAC HINIS of the City of Savannah. Exrs... Sworn to March
11, 1824, SAML. W. ROBBINS, JOSEPH SCRUTCHIN, DANIEL GREEN, M. SHELMANE
J.J. CT., WM. N. HARMAN, J.J. CT.

Page 194:   Will of HENRY FOUNTAIN.   Made April 11, 1823, probated
Jan. 3, 1825... sickly a bit of body... to son HENRY FOUNTAIN. 100
acres on which I now live... I also desire that my wife LYDIA FOUNTAIN
live on the sd. land during her life... to my daughter MARY FOUNTAIN...
to son WILLIAM RILA FOUNTAIN... friend LUIS LAMPP Exr... HENRY FOUNTAIN.
Wit: JAMES RYLAND (X), ROBERT PITTMAN (X), A. B. VINING.

Page 195:   Will of MARY CLEMENTS, not dated.   Probated Sept. 5, 1825..
to my son JOHN CLEMENTS... to JOSIAH S. PATTERSON... to my daughters
RUTH, MARY and ELIZABETH... to JOHN CLEMENTS CHAMBERS... to son JOHN
land whereon I now live and a tract in Henry County... Mrs. WHITAKER,
Mrs. CLEMENTS and SARAH CLEMENTS... WILLIAM CLEMENTS and JOHN CLEMENTS
JUNR. Exrs. Wit: JOHN CLEMENTS.

Page 196:   Will of WILLIAM PERDUE.   Made May 21, 1823, probated
September 5, 1825, to my son JAMES PERDUE, 100 acres... to my son
BENGEMAN PERDUE, plantation where on he now lives... sons JOHN and NEWTON
PERDUE... WILLIAM PERDUE (X). Wit: ABRAHAM BEESLEY, GEORGE MOCK.

Page 197:   Will of STEPHEN MORGAN, SR.   Made Aug. 5, 1825, probated
Sept. 5, 1825... to brother JOHN MORGAN... my wife BETSY MORGAN,
supposed to be pregnant... MITCHEL HARDY & PLEASANT MORGAN, sons of JOHN
... ELIZA and WILLIAM children of my brother HARDY MORGAN... STEPHEN
MORGAN. Wit: JOHN BOUTIN, WM. N. HARMAN, D. GREEN.

Page 197-198:   Will of AQUILLA MATTHEWS, SR.   Made Oct. 1825, probated Nov. 7, 1825... being in a low state of health... to my wife
ELIZABETH MATTHEWS... 200 acres on which I now live... equally divided
between my children and grandchildren, my three grandchildren, the
children of my daughter NANCY FARMER, to draw one share equal to the
other children, and the children on my son WILLIAM... sons THOMAS
MATTHEWS and JAMES MATTHEWS Exrs... AQUILLA MATTHEWS SENR (X). Wit:
JONATHAN ROSS, JESSE P. JORDAN, D. T. SMITHE.

Pages 198-199:   Will of CATHERINE MCBRIDE.   Made Oct. 4, 1824, probated Nov. 9, 1825... to my eldest son JOHN MCBRIDE... to son JAMES J.

148

MCBRIDE... a small stock of cattle that is over the river... divided between my four sons equally when they come of age: JOHN, JAMES, THOMAS & WILLIAM G. MCBRIDE... CATHERINE MCBRIDE (X). Wit: ROBERT BOYD, JOSEPH BOYD, JOSEPH LOWRY.

Pages 199-200: Will of THOS PARSONS. Made Nov. 15, 1825, probated Jan. 16, 1826... wife DICE PARSONS, plantation on which I now live... for education of my children... to beloved son JOHN AVON PARSONS... to beloved son JAMES M. PARSONS... to beloved son THOMAS A. PARSONS... beloved son MATHEW JOSIAH PARSONS...rest of my children (not named)... THOMAS PARSONS. Wit: JNO PATTERSON, E. BOTHWELL, SAMUEL BOTHWELL.

Pages 201-202: Will of ROBERT FLEMING. Made Aug. 28, 1825, probated Sept. 26, 1826... wife SARAH FLEMING, house and lot I now occupy... between it and MATTHEW ROBERTSON lot... land in Monroe County, and land in the 18th district of Henry County, I bought of MICHAEL DEAREAUSA... land in Habersham County, bought of Widow MINTON... lot I purchased of JOHN MCBRIDE to be sold and proceeds divided among my wife and daughter JANE GLEMING and MARY FLEMING... plantation by the name of Woods Mill... lot I bought of heirs of ARTHUR CLARKE... land on the south side of Savannah Road, I bought of BENJAMIN JORDAN and JOHN BATTS... tract I bought of THOMAS HADDIN on Reedy Branch... swamp land I bought of BERRY LAWSON on the fork of Big Creek and Ogechee River... house and lot I bought of ADIN POWELL on the north side of the road known as the French Doctors house... to son in law MATHEW ROBERTSON... ASA HOLT and JOHN MURPHY Exrs. ROBERT FLEMING. Wit: JACOB FOREMAN, JAMES H. MAXWELL, JOHN G. BOSTICK.

Pages 202-203: Will of JOHN POWELL. Made May 20, 1825, probated Oct. 4, 1826... of Louisville in the State of Georgia... practioner of physick... to my beloved wife ANN D. POWELL... "in lieu of Dover and other claims..." of affectionate regard for one born under my roof... I give unto SARAH SEABORN REBECCA REED JONES, daughter of my friend the late SEABORN JONES, Esq. of Augusta, and granddaughter of my beloved wife, $100... to FREEMAN WALKER and ROBERT RAYMON REID of City of Augusta, in benefit for my dau. MARY MCKINE, wife of Col. JOHN MCKINNE of Augusta... JOHN POWELL. Wit: M. SHELMAN, WM. N. HARMAN, DAN HOOK.

Page 204: Will of ANNE PARSONS. Made March 13, 1826, probated Oct. 27, 1826... being sick and in a low condition... to son WILLIAM PARSONS $1... to daughter WINNEFRED COTTER and her husband GEORGE COTTER, $1... to daughter NANCY MCNEELY and husband HUGH MCNEELY, $1... lot of land drawn by myself, known as 15, in the 14th district of then Fayette County... to daughter MARTHA ANNE PARSONS... to my son SAMUEL LOUDEN PARSONS... to daughter MARY JANE PARSONS... four youngest children before arriving at maturity... friends ROGER L. GAMBLE and WM. BOTHWELL Exrs. ANNE PARSONS (X). Wit: SARAH BOYD, E. BOTHWELL.

Page 205: Will of HARRIS AUSTIN. Made Oct. 5, 1825, probated Nov. 7, 1825... wife ANNA... between her children now living... heirs of her body by me... Exrs. ANNA AUSTIN, SAMUEL BASS... HARRIS AUSTIN. Wit: WILLIAM WYLLY, CHARLES MATTHEWS (X).

Page 206: Will of ISAAC LAMB. Not dated, probated Jan. 1, 1827... my beloved wife CHARITY, 130 acres of land... money due me in state of South Carolina by THOMAS FULLALOVE to be collected by JOHN CORBET... to my beloved son JOHN LAMB, $10... ISAAC LAMB. Wit: MARY PENNINGTON (X). She testified as MARY ANN PENNINGTON. (There was a large LAMB family in Spartanburg and Union Districts, South Carolina during this period. BHH)

Pages 206-207: Will of JNO. ARRINGTON. Made Dec. 15, 1826, probated Jan. 18, 1827... land I live on to be divided into 3 equal parts... one share to son SHEROD... for daughter SARAH LAWRENCE, wife of ISHAM LAWRENCE... to my daughter MARY HAND 1/3 of land mentioned... two sons SHEROD and HENRY Exrs... JOHN ARRINGTON. Wit: ASHLEY PHILLIPS, PHILLIP BELCHER.

Pages 207-208: Will of JAMES INGRAM, SR. Made Sept. 19, 1823, probated Jan. 15, 1827... wife ELIZABETH INGRAM... my six sons JAMES L. INGRAM, JOHN INGRAM, ETHELDRED INGRAM, JESSE INGRAM, HENRY INGRAM, and CALVIN INGRAM... to daughter CHRISSY INGRAM... JAMES L. INGRAM, JOHN INGRAM and JAS. E. WHITFIELD Exrs... JAMES INGRAM SENR. Wit: SAMUEL HYSON, ARTHUR CHEATHAM.
    Widow makes petition that above will be declared void, since on 19th of Sept., 1823 when Will was made, his former wife and children were alive... testator recovered from his the sickness, wife and one son have departed this life... 15th Jan. 1827... MARY INGRAM, widow.

Pages 209-210: Will of WILLIAM CLARK. Made Feb. 1, 1827, probated March 5, 1827... Codicil made Feb. 1, 1827... wife MOTTY... to my son JOHN... to my son DAVID... 200 acres in Early County, 28th Dist... WILLIAM CLARK (X). Wit: JAMES WILLIAMS, JAMES M. KIGNEY... Codicil... to my grandson WILLIAM HADDAN, son of JOHN HADDAN and WINY my daughter... WILLIAM CLARK (X). (Same wit.).

Pages 210-211: Will of JOSHUA WATSON. Made Jan. 13, 1825, probated Dec. 27, 1827... to son MICHAEL WATSON, 450 acres, granted to JAMES AIRS and others, and adj. to lands of MAY... to my daughter REBECCA FITZ JARREL... to my daughter PENELOPE WIGGINS... to my daughter SARAH MAY... to my daughter TEMPERANCE ROWAN... to the children of my daughter CELIA ROSIER... MICHAEL WATSON and JOHN FITZ JARREL Exrs... JOSHUA WATSON (X). Wit: MAURICE RAIFORD, REUBEN Y. BURTS, CAPEL RAIFORD.

Pages 211-212: Will of SARAH BOTHWELL. Made Jan. 7, 1828, probated Jan. 16, 1828... to my daughter JANE L. BEAL, 539 acres in Jefferson County lately belonging to ADIN POWELL deceased, adj. to lands of RICHARD BROWN, HILLERY BOSTICK, JOHN MCDONALD and Mrs. MCNEELY... to my daughter MARY MATILDA FLEMING now a minor... to my brother JOHN and sister JANE's children... to MARY MATILDA FLEMING, land on north side of Savannah Road leading from Louisville, adj. WM. SCHLEY, SION PENNINGTON and others... to J. L. BEAL to be held in trust by ASA HOLT... friends ASA HOLT and DANL. HOOK, Exrs. SARAH BOTHWELL. Wit: HENRY B. TODD, M. BRINSON, JR., WM. N. HARMAN J.J. CT.

Pages 212-213: Will of WILLIAM ANDERTON. Made Feb. 1, 1818, probated Feb. 25, 1828... to my wife NANCY G.... unto my two sisters REBECCA and MARIA... Doctor DANIEL HOOK of Louisville, Exr.... W. ANDERTON. Wit: EDWARD FOLY, JOHN CLEMENTS, JR., DANIEL HOOKS.

Pages 213-216: Will of MORRIS MURPHY. Made Jan. 12, 1828, probated March 25, 1828... unto HOWELL HAY, nephew of my present wife... to SARAH THOMPSON, daughter of WILLIAM THOMPSON... to WILLIAM HARMAN, 300 acres of property formerly that of JOHN REESE, dec'd., on the north east side of Rock Comfort Creek in Jefferson County, adj. ELYAH HUDSON and others... in case of death of sd. HARMAN, CHARLES J. JENKINS SENR. to act as guardian... to DAVID HAY, nephew of my present wife... plantation on Rocky Comfort Creek together with land drawn by my wife in Lee County, first section to be divided among heirs of my wife's sister AGNES TALBOTT, that is HOWELL HAY, WILLIAM HAY, DAVID HAY, and MARTHA YOUNG... to my wife now SARAH MURPHY... to JAMES KOLT, land on which I now live, 290 acres adj. to TELFAIR and others... to JAMES MURPHY SINQUEFIELD... to MARY SINQUEFIELD wife of MOSES SINQUEFIELD, SENR. until ABEL KOLB comes of age... to ELIZABETH ELLIOTT's children... to MARY & SARAH, daughters of MOSES SINQUEFIELD, SR. to MOSES SINQUEFIELD, JR.... to HUGH LOYD, in trust for ABEL KOLB sons... Exrs. MOSES SINQUEFIELD, SR., CHARLES J. JENKINS, SR., and WILLIAM N. HARMAN... MORRIS MURPHY. Wit: SARAH HUDSON, ELYAH HUDSON, JACOB SHEPARD.

Pages 216-217: Will of WILLIAM MANSON. Made July 12, 1828, probated Nov. 3, 1828... wife POLLEY and children (not named)... daughter NANCY VINSON (or WINSON)... WILLIAM MANSON. Wit: BLASS THOMAS, W.B.G. THOMAS, CHARLOTTEY THOMAS (X).

Pages 217-218: Will of DENNIS WILLIAMS. Made June 18, 1823, probated Nov. 13, 1828... wife SARAH WILLIAMS, Plantation whereon ELIGA YOUNG

formerly lived, 200 acres adj. MUND GROSS and others... children NANCY,
BEATUS, GEORGE, BETSEY and MARYAN... son MUFREY D. WILLIAMS... son
ROBERT WILLIAMS... son JAMES WILLIAMS... friend ELAM YOUNG and PERRY
SINKFIELD Exrs... DENNIS WILLIAMS (X). Wit: MATT JORDAN, MUND GROSS,
JNO. HOLLAMAN.

Pages 219-220:   Will of WILLIAM CLEMENTS.   Made Dec. 24, 1818, probated Jan. 19, 1829... to son JAMES S. CLEMENTS, all that tract purchased
from the estate of MOSES ARCHER, except where the house stands... land
purchased from JANE BOYD... and 87 acres granted to myself... to daughter
ELIZABETH... to daughter MARY ANN... to daughter ISABEL NANCY LAWSON...
to wife SARAH... to ABRAM, the blacksmith tools... my sister MARY
PATTERSON... JOHN CLEMENTS and WM. BOYD Exrs... WILLIAM CLEMENTS. Wit:
WILLIAM CLEMENTS, MARY FLEMING, JOHN KENNADY, JOHN CLEMENTS.

Page 221:   Will of Mrs. PRISSY HATCHER.   Made Sept. 17, 1823, probated
May 4, 1829... to daughter PEGGY ANN JACKSON, wife of RICHARD JACKSON...
to grandson JOHN WILLIAMS WALKER JACKSON (son of PEGGY ANN and RICHARD
JACKSON)... Exr. General VALENTINE WALKER ... PRISSY HATCHER. Wit:
NEEDHAM LEE, LEWIS L. MCNAIR, SUSANNAH MCNAIR.

Pages 222-223:   Will of NOAH ADAMS.   Made Oct. 22, 1829, probated May
10, 1830... son NORVAL son JOHN... son NOAH... wife OPHA... sons in law
JOHN LIPTROT, HARDY WILLIAMS, GREEN H. HASLIP... daughter SARAH ADAMS...
son JAMES... daughter REBECCA... heirs of APSEY, MARY and JANE... NOAH
ADAMS (X). Wit: JAMES FIELDS, MILES FIELDS, MARY SPIRVY (X).

Pages 223-224:   Will of CALEB WELSH.   Made Aug. 28, 1826, probated
Jan. 11, 1830... to son ASA WELSH... to son WILLIAM WELSH... to daughter
ELIZABETH... to daughter FALBY... to daughter CYNTHIA... to daughter
JANE... to daughter MELINDA... to the four children of my deceased son
JAMES... son ASA and JOHN STARLING JUNR. Exrs... CALEB WELSH. Wit:
ISAAC D. NEWTON, JESS SCARBOUGH, JOHN H. NEWTON.

Pages 224-225:   Will of ELIZABETH HADDEN... to son BENJAMIN HADDEN...
now in the hands of JOHN STAPLETON... to son SAMUEL... son WILLIAM...
SAML & JOHN HADDEN... FOSTER LITTLE, Exr... ELIZABETH HADDEN (X). Wit:
JAMES STONE, WILLIAM D. STONE.

Pages 225-226:   Will of PRISCILLA SANDERFER.   Made Sept. 27, 1830,
probated Nov. 1, 1830... to SARAH FOKES, daughter of JOHN FOKES... my
sister MARTHA SPIVEY... to CLOE FOKES... friend ELIZABETH WALKER...
friend LITTLEBERRY BOSTICK Exr... PRISCILIA SANDERFER (X). Wit: HENRY
B. TODD, ANTHONY W. WALKER, MARTHA BOSTICK.

Pages 226-227:   Will of JOHN MCGOWEN.   Made Dec. __, 1828, probated
Nov. 22, 1830... to wife NANCY, 55 acres in Burke County... land in
Jefferson County on LAMBERT's Creek, adj. WHITAKER and others... 2
sons DAVID and WILLIAM G. MCGOWN... for purpose of raising my children..
friends BENJ. COBERT and ISRAEL CAUSEY... Wit: DAVID E. WHITAKER, PENTEN
TOMKINS.

Pages 227-228:   Will of SAMUEL CLEMENTS.   Made March 14, 1831, probated May 2, 1831... to daughter MARY A. J. CLEMENTS... to SAML. CLEMENTS
my grandson... to ELIZABETH ANN, my granddaughter... in possession of
my son JOHN until SAMUEL becomes 21... SAMUEL CLEMENTS. Wit: WM.
BOYD, WM. CLEMENTS, ISAAC MORRISON.

Pages 228-229:   Will of JOHN BIGHAM.   Made April 30, 1831, probated
Dec. 12, 1831... wife NANCY BIGHAM... JOHN BIGHAM and ELIZABETH ANN
BIGHAM... JOHN PARSONS and my daughter NANCY PARSONS... son JOHN BIGHAM,
the place where I now live, granted to WILLIAM H. GRAY and ELIZABETH
MCKIGNEY, adj. FLEMING and others... stock of cattle in Emanuel County...
JOHN CUNNING and THOMAS WHIGHAM... JOHN BIGHAM. Wit: JAMES FLEMING,
JOHN PENDRY, RICHARD F. PENDRY.

Pages 229-230:   Will of Dr. JOHN H. MASON.   Made Dec. 24, 1831, probated Jan. 16, 1832... I, JOHN BOUGH MASON... to brother THOMPSON MASON..

to brother in law THOMAS R. JOHNSON... to nephew JOHN HOUGH MASON... to brother THOMPSON MASON... to brother in law THOMAS R. JOHNSON... to nephew JOHN HOUGH JOHNSON... unto my nieces and nephews, and the children of THOMPSON MASON and of THOMAS R. JOHNSON and his wife SARAH ANN... my brother RICHARD BELLASON and my sister MARY B. MASON... to friend WM. P. HARDWICK... JNO. H. MASON. Wit: D. E. BOTHWELL, CHISLEY ATTAWAY, JOHN CLEMENTS JUR.

Pages 230-231: Will of WILLIAM SPIRES. Made Feb. 26, 1831, probated May 7, 1832... to little JOHN C. CHAMBERS, son of my brother in law JOHN CHAMBERS... cattle in the hands of JOHN DIXON... to nephew RICHARD TAYLOR SPEIRS... friends JAS. E. WHITEFIELD and JOHN CLEMENTS SENR. Exrs. WILLIAM SPIERS (X) (LS). Wit: JAS. E. WHITEFIELD, JOHN CLEMENTS, WM. W. MONTGOMERY.

Pages 231-232: Will of GEORGE FOWLER. Made March 10, 1832, probated May 7, 1832... to son GEORGE FOWLER... to my son JESSE FOWLER... to my daughter SARAH SPIVEY... wife NANCY FOWLER... my children SUSANNAH WAYNEWRIGHT, JOHN FOWLER, GEORGE FOWLER, JESSE FLOWLER, SARAH SPIVEY and heirs of TELITHE SUTTON... GEORGE FOWLER (X). Wit: ARCHIBALD BROWN (X), JOSHUA L. F. BLACK (X), ROBERT BLACK.

Pages 232-234: Will of WM. BATTS. Made May 16, 1832, probated July 16, 1832... to MORGAN ROGERS, NATHAN BATTS, SENR. and NATHAN BATTS JUNR., my Exrs., in trust for my wife SARAH... to my son JOHN... NATHAN BATTS, JR., ANN BATTS, JACKSON BATTS, my brothers and sister... JANE MARSH, the daughter of my wife SARAH... two tracts of land in Henry County... WILLIAM BATTS. Wit: EDWARD FOLEY, JOHN L. MARTIN, THOMAS FOLEY.

Page 234: Will of JOHN S. HOLDER. Made June 27, 1832, probated Aug. 7, 1832... son ASA HOLDER... land granted to MICHAEL S. HELMAN... corner on ANDREW GARTMAN's land... sons WILEY and WHITE HOLDER and daughter SARAH HAYS, lot 154 in the twelfth district of Carol County... wife MARTHA HOLDER, land adj. R. TILLMAN... JOHN HOLDER (X). Wit: JERTO ROGERS, BALDWIN RAIFORD, WM. GAUTMAN.

Page 235: Will of ELIZABETH CAUSEY, made July 19, 1832, probated Nov. 5, 1832... to son SHERROD CAUSEY... to son EZEKIEL CAUSEY... to sons ALLEN CAUSEY, EZEKIEL CAUSEY and SHERROD CAUSEY... land if I am a fortunate drawer... my daughter MATILDA ANN CAUSEY and her daughter SEYNTHA ANN CAUSEY... ELIZABETH CAUSEY (X). Wit: SHERROD ARRINGTON, JAS. E. WHITFIELD, SOLOMAN PHILLIP.

Page 236: Will of MARY SCOTT. Made May 31, 1832, probated Nov. 5, 1832... unto SALLY WATKINS, late SALLY SCOTT, as she hath been a dutiful child... to her husband ROBERT WATKINS... my late husband PHILLIP SCOTT.. friend ROBERT L. GAMBLE Exr... MARY SCOTT. Wit: ARCHL. CAMPBELL, JOHN M. GLAZE.

Page 237: Will of DAVID E. WHITAKER. Made Feb. 2, 1833, probated March 4, 1833... wife MARGARET L. (S?) WHITAKER... right and title to land in Early and Cherokee Counties... JOHN PATTERSON of Burk County and ROBERT PATTERSON of Jefferson County Exrs. DAVID E. WHITAKER. Wit: NEEDHAM LEE, JOHN B. LEE, JOHN W. W. JACKSON.

Page 238: Will of SAMUEL C. BOYD. Made Feb. 27, 1833, probated May 6, 1833... to my sister AGNES GORDON, 250 acres where I now live granted to JANE MATHERS, adj. HENDREY & GORDON... to SAMUEL GORDON, son of my sister AGNES, and his brothers ROBERT GORDON and WILLIAM GORDON... to SARAH GORDON... to WILLIAM BOYD, ROBERT BOYD and JANE MCBRIDE's children... my sister JANE MCBRIDE, amongst her children when they come of age... SAMUEL C. BOYD. Wit: JAMES FLEMING, SAML. DENNY, RICHARD G. PENDREY. N.B. lot 142, Sixth District, formerly Lee County... and lot in Cherokee County...

Page 239: Will of ELI HUDSON. Made Oct. 22, 1833, probated Nov. 4, 1833... daughter JANE has a slave given to her by her grandfather BRUCE, wife PENNY and my other children .... ELI HUDSON. Wit: SAML. M. BARR, E. G. HUDSON, JAMES ADAMS.

Page 240: Will of RICHARD HUDSON, SR. Made Aug. 1834, no probate date... unto my son ALFRED HUDSON... unto my two youngest daughters MARY HUDSON and NARCESSY HUDSON... unto my six youngest sons LITTLETON HUDSON, MATTHEW HUDSON, TOLIBER HUDSON, WILLIAM E. HUDSON, JAMES HUDSON and LAWSON HUDSON... to my wife MARTHA HUDSON... money coming to me from estate of RICHARD SPEIRS... sons HAMPTON HUDSON, ISAAC HUDSON, RICHARD HUDSON, JR., my daughters NANCY LOWERY, DECE PIPKIN, ELIZABETH HUDSON, SARAH DAVIS, MARY HUDSON and NACISSY HUDSON... CHRISTOPHER LOWERY and HARVEY PIPKIN Exrs... RICHARD HUDSON (X). Wit: D. T. SMITH, THAS. G. JORDAN, STERLING G. JORDAN.

Page 241: Will of JANE MOUNTAIN. Made March 2, 1839, probated Dec. 8, 1834... to JOHN BIGHAM, SR., and NANCY his wife... JOHN BIGHAM, SR. and JAMES BIGHAM, Exrs... JANE MOUNTAIN (X). Wit: JAMES FLEMING, JAMES BIGHAM, JOHN PARSONS.

Page 242: Will of SAMUEL FLEMING. Made Nov. 26, 1832, probated Dec. 8, 1834... plantation where I now live 108 acres... wife MARY FLEMING... children ELINOR W. FLEMING, SAMUEL J. FLEMING, WILLIAM O. FLEMING, MARY E. FLEMING, SARAH M. FLEMING... to JOHN F. BOYD and my daughter JANE... JAMES FLEMING, R. F. PENDRY, JOHN PENDRY.

Pages 243-244: Will of FREDERICK MORRIS. Made Oct. 18, 1832, probated Jan. 19, 1835... wife JANE, MORRIS... youngest daughter MARY JANE MORRIS... my daughter FRANCES MCGLOWHORN 180 acres... JAMES WHITFIELD, SAMUEL W. ROBBINS, and THOMAS PATERSON Exrs... FREDERICK MORRIS. Wit: ROBERT A. L. ATKINSON, CAMPBELL RAIFORD, JAMES E. WHITFIELD.

Pages 244-245: Will of ANN MONTGOMERY. Made July 12, 1834, probated Jan. 19, 1835... to ANN MONTGOMERY WHITFIELD... friend MARGARET B. KENEDY, daughter of FRANCIS KENEDY, dec'd., land in Early County... JAS. E. WHITFIELD and JONATHAN ROBINSON Exrs... ANN MONTGOMERY (X). Wit: ISOME EVANS, THOMAS KENADY, JONATHAN ROBINSON.

Page 245: Will of JOHN BOUTON. Made May 1, 1835, no probate date... wife FRANCIS BOUTON... Exrs.. HARDY MORGAN, JAMES CAIN... JOHN BOUTON. Wit: JAMES ADAMS, IRA G. JACKSON, JOHN H. DAVIDSON (X).

Pages 246-247: Will of NATHAN CHRISTIE. Made Apr. 16, 1835, probated July 6, 1835... beloved wife... son NATHAN G., son JOSEPH B., son GEORGE W., son BENJAMIN G., daughter MARGARET J. STEPHENS, granddaughter ELIZABETH MARY STEPHENS, daughter MARY F....N. CHRISTIE. Wit: I. C. FRANCIS, JORDAN R. SMITHE, JOHN N. KELLY.

Pages 247-248: Will of SAMUEL C. BOTHWELL, SENR. Made Feb. 5, 1828, probated July 25, 1835... becoming old and frail... son JAMES BOTHWELL and daughter JANE BOTHWELL... 700 acres granted to STOKES PEEL and others adj. lands of BIGHAM, BEEL, CUNNING and others... son SAMUEL C. BOTHWELL. grandson SAMUEL WILLIAM BOTHWELL, land formerly of Early County... SAMUEL BOTHWELL. Wit: JAS. R. HUDSON, JOHN W. BOTHWELL.

Pages 248-249: Will of ELIZABETH WALKER. Made Feb. 10, 1834, probated 1836... son ARTHUR daughter MARTHA ANN MARY BOSTICK... son ANTHONY WINSTON WALKER... to son CHARLES HENRY WALKER... plantation on Ogeechy River where son ARTHUR now resides and a note of hand given by L. B. BOSTICK... son ARTHUR and son in law LITTLE B. BOSTICK, Exrs... ELIZABETH WALKER. Wit: JNO. BOSTICK, HENRY WALKER, HENRY B. TODD, JP.

Pages 249-250: Will of MARGARET FLEETING. Made Feb. 22, 1836, probated May term, 1836 to MARY PENDRY wife of JOHN PENDRY... to my daughter MARGARET MANSON... to the children of my daughter CATHERINE SPAN... to my daughter SARAH LOWERY... to my grandaughter MARGARET LOWERY the daughter of JOHN LOWERY... ROGER L. GAMBLE, Exr... MARY FLEETING (X). Wit: EBENEZER BOTHWELL.

Pages 250-251: Will of THOMAS B. WELLS. Made July 1, 1836, probated July 18, 1836... until my second son DARIUS B. WELLS arrives at the age of 21... my eldest son JOHN R. WELLS... to educate my two youngest sons DARIUS B. WELLS and GEORGE TWIGGS WELLS... Exrs. MOSES BRINSON, JR., PHILLIP ROBINSON, JR., THOS. B. WELLS. Wit: PHILLIP ROBINSON, JOHN BELCHER, D. E. BOTHWELL.

Pages 251-252: Will of STEVEN DEUREAZEAUX... my negroes have chosen WILLIAM SHERROD as their master and JOHN W. BOTHWELL, JR.... (signature obliterated). Wit: ROBERT L. GAMBLE, JOHN WOODS, JAMES SHERROD.

Pages 252-253: Will of Mrs. ELIZABETH HUTCHENS. Made June 13, 1836, probated Nov. 8, 1836... brother WILY HUTCHENS... to my sister TIRECY HUGHES... to my nephews LEROYD. MOORE, WELSYE A. MOORE, LORENZO DOW MOORE, and my neice ELIZABETH MOORE... ELIZABETH HUTCHENS. Wit: JAS. CAIN, JAMES M. SINQUEFIELD.

Pages 253-254: Will of JOHN COLEMAN. Made July 22, 1836, probated Dec. 5, 1836, children RACHAEL JOHNSON, WILLIAMA COLEMAN, ELLENDER THOMAS, wife of WILLIAM B. G. THOMAS... land in Jefferson County on Rocky Comfort Creek, 100 acres known as ISAAC LEFEVER tract to grandson JOHN H. S. COLEMAN... JOHN COLEMAN. Wit: JAMES NEELY, CHARLES STEVENS, JOHN DARBY.

Pages 254-255: Will of ROBERT CROOKS. Made Oct. 16, 1836, probated Dec. 5, 1836... daughter MARGARET, wife of ROBERT R. BAILEY... daughter NANCY, wife of NATHAN STEVENS... son JOHN CROOKS... wife NANCY CROOKS... ROBERT CROOKS. Wit: PATRICK CAMPBELL, N. B. CLOUD, JONATHAN ROBERSON, J.J. CT.

Pages 255-256: Will of Mrs. SARAH MURPHY. Made Jan. 19, 1837, probated April 17, 1837. that I be interred by my first husband and mother... to JOHN HAY, son of HOWELL HAY to WILLIAM N. HARMAN, lot #43 in Lee County, 22nd District, now Stewart County... to HOWEL HAY, my nephew... to my brother DAVID HAY... to his sister MARTHA YOUNG... guardianship of CATO from GARLAND HARDWICK, who was appointed his guardian under Mr. REESE's Will... SARAH MURPHY (X). Wit: MARGARET FLEETIN (X), H. MORGAN, JOHN C. HARMAN.

Pages 256-257: Will of JOHN S. PERKINS. Made Aug. 2, 1837, probated Sept. 1837... wife DEVINA PERKINS... 160 acres in Cherokee purchase... 630 acres I sold in Washington County... interest I have in a survey in Early County, brother BRINSON L. PERKINS, Exr. JOHN S. PERKINS. Wit: HARDY C. MAUND, WM. W. MAUND, BENJM. AYER.

Pages 257-258: Will of ELIAS WIGGINS. Made May 24, 1837, probated Sept. 18, 1837... wife PENELOPE and children NANCY SALLEY, WALTON, EMALINE, and RUTHANY... until WALTON reaches the age of 23... son MICHAEL and daughter ELIZABETH ADKINS... son MICHAEL and JOHN LOVE, Exrs. ELIAS WIGGINS (X). Wit: MIACHEL WIGGINS, LABAN MOORE, DAVID ADKINS.

Page 259: Will of ALEXANDER GORDON. Made Nov. 17, 1838, probated Jan. 7, 1839... in low state of health... daughter JANE wife of JAMES J. BODY... all my lawful heirs... JOHN W. ALEXANDER, JOHN ROLLINGS, JR., and ELYAH ATTAWAY Exrs... ALEX GORDON. Wit: WILLIAM GORDON, DAVID WOODS, ELYAH ATTAWAY.

Page 260: Will of JOHN FLEMING. Made Jan. 12, 1837, probated Jan. 15, 1839... son JAMES FLEMING, plantation whereon I now live, 420 acres in two tracts, also 50 acres adj. land in Early County, 3rd District, #350, also a tract in Irwin County, 15th District, #107... wife JANE... grandsons JOHN FLEMING... JOHN FLEMING (X). Wit: NATHL. POLHILL, SAML. DENNY, NATHAN K. WHIGHAM.

Pages 260-261: Will of REBECCA POLHILL. Made Jan. 17, 1838, probated Dec. 3, 1838... to nephew WILLIAM H. BALDY, 700 acres where I now

live... to sister JANE M. POLHILL... sister ELIZABETH M. HAMILTON...
neice REBECCA ANN BALDY... neice REBECCA HAMILTON... nephews WM. H.
BALDY and THOS H. POLHILL, Exrs... REBECCA POLHILL. Wit: THOS. P.
BROWN, WILLIAM SWAN, ALICE BALDY.

Pages 261-262:   Will of EPHRAIM PONDER.   Made July 15, 1836, probated
Sept. 3, 1838... wife ELENDER PONDER... land on each side of Chaves
Creek, to be given to her sons WILLIAM and JOHN... my sons HEZEKIAH
PONDER and JAMES MOBLEY trustees... son EPHRAIM PONDER. son in law
ALEXANDER MCCOY, daughter CHARLOTTE MCCOY... son in law JOEL FUTRAL...
daughter MARY FUTREL... son RICHARD PONDER... to son HEZEKIAH, 500 acres
adj. WM. PATTERSON and JOEL FUTREL on waters of Buckhead... to son in
law WILLIAM MEALING... daughter MARTHA MEALING... daughter SUSAN MOBLEY..
to my grandchildren MARY ANN and JOHN HUDSON, children of my daughter
REBECCA HUDSON, 200 acres adj. ISAAC FARMER, TOLLIVER DILLARD and others.
daughter CHARLOTTE MCCOY, NANCY DAY, and MARY FUTREL... not to pay
debts of ALEXR. MCCOY, JOSEPH DAY or JOEL FUTREL.. EPHRAIM PONDER. Wit:
ROBERT L. GAMBLE, JOHN BEESLEY, S. B. TARVER.

Pages 263-264:   Will of CHARLES J. JENKINS.   Made June 14, 1828,
probated Aug. 13, 1828... beloved mother Mrs. SUSAN JENKINS... to
Baptist General Convetion, $100... to Baptist Convention of the State of
Georgia... Decons of Baptist Church Providence in Jefferson County...
to my young sister in the Lord, MARY ANN HARMAN... to my son CHARLES J.
JENKINS... CHAS. J. JENKINS. Wit: THOMAS M. PATTERSON, JOB HUNTER, ELI
HUDSON.

Pages 264-265:   Will of R. E. CUNNINGHAM.   Made Dec. 8, 1838, no
probated date... Executors JOHN P. EVE, GEORGE SCHLEY, CHARLES CUNNING-
HAM, J. F. BOTHWELL... frees slaves, mentions mulatte children and gives
them money... codicil made 10 Mar. 1841... R. E. CUNNINGHAM.

Pages 266-267:   Will of ELIZA MILTON.   Made Dec. 29, 1838, probated
Jan. 16, 1839... children JOHN MILTON and JANE ELIZABETH MILTON...
friend ROGER L. GAMBLE, Exr... (no signature). Wit: ALEDR. LOWERY,
I. R. SMITH, SAML. W. ROBBINS.

Pages 267-268:   Will of JOHN KING.   Made Dec. 2, 1838, probated Feb.
5, 1839... three youngest children, FANNY ANN, MARY ANN and JOHN CALVIN
KING... daughter SARAH INGRAM... daughter SOPHIA SHEROD... daughter
PRISCILLA KING... JESSE GLOVER, Exr... JOHN KING (X). Wit: ASA HOLT,
THOS M. PATTERSON, JESSE R. (?) MULLING.

Pages 268-269:   Will of AGATHA BEAL.   Made Feb. 18, 1838, probated
July 15, 1839... daughters ELIZABETH and SELIVER... children ELOISA
BOSTICK, NATHANIEL BEAL, LITTLEBERRY BEAL, CAROLINA REBECKAH BOSTICK...
LITTLEBERRY BEAL and JOHN BOSTICK, Exrs... AGGATHY BEAL (X). Wit:
ELSEY (?), JAS. LITTLE, MOSES BRINSON JUNR.

Pages 269-270:   Will of WILLIAM MARSHALL.   Made June 24, 1839, probated Sept. 21, 1839... to wife ANN MARSHALL, land where I now live,
1512 acres by resurvey of DANIEL STURGES and by JOHN LOVE, Meriwether
Tract... to nephew FRANCIS L. MARSHALL 200 acres... Exr. R. L. GAMBLE...
nephew and neice JOHN M. WOODS and VIANNA AUGUSTA MARSHALL... lands
called Canada Settlement... several tracts granted to REUBEN LAMB and
STEPHEN HOLLENSWORTH and others... Mother ANN MARSHALL... WM. MARSHALL.
Wit: JOHN LOVE, JNO BOSTICK, JOHN R. BOSTICK.

Pages 270-271:   Will of HENRY A. DODGE.   Made Sept. 15, 1839, pro-
bated Nov. 4, 1839... made by word of mouth... elder brother JOHN...
uounger brother RICHARD VARICK... servants of Mrs. STEED... to Mr.
NICOLL, my enjineering pencil... my mother (not named)... Mr. NICOLL and
Mr. HOUSTON, Exrs... Wit: JOHN W. HOUSTON, Exrs... Wit: JOHN W.
HOUSTON, JAS. EDW. NICOLL, PHILIP L. LEMILE.

Pages 271-272:   Will of JOHN TOMKINS.   Made May 9, 1836, probated
Jan. 20, 1840... son THOMAS TOMKINS... son SAMUEL TOMKINS and his
daughter FRANCIS... daughter ELIZABETH DONILSON, 40 acres I drew in

Cherokee in the gold lottery... son PARTIN TOMKINS, 250 acres in Early
County, #96 in 13th District... to daughter PATSEY MOY, 250 acres in
Early County, #220 in the 7th District... daughter EMILINE... son WILLIAM
land where I now live on Chiver Creek... to son MADISON, STEPHENS tract...
friend ASA HOLT... JOHN TOMKINS (X). Wit: WILLIAM CLEMENTS, JOHN FOLKS,
WILLIAM L. MURPHY.

Pages 272-273: Will of JETHRO ROGERS. Made Dec. 14, 1839, probated
July 6, 1840... to son ABEL GREEN ROGERS... my daughter LOUISZA... son
WILLIAM and daughter ANN... my younger children by my last wife (viz)
SARAHAN, REBECAH, JETHRO, WASHINGTON, MARY, EMILY, JULIA, ELIZABETH
and REBECAH WINFORD... wife MARY ROGERS... friend HENRY P? TURNER Exr...
JETHRO ROGERS (X). Wit: JOHN W. HOLDER, THOMAS LAMB (X), ISAAC NORRIS.

Pages 273-274: Will of THOMAS M. PATTERSON. Made July 16, 1840,
probated Nov. 16, 1840 to nephew THOMAS M. P. BELCHER, when he arrives
at 21... to my nieces and nephews except for my nephew JOHN D. WELLS...
wife MARY and HENRY B. TODD, Exrs... THOMAS M. PATTERSON. Wit:
ELIZABETH WOOTEN, Codicil made July 16, 1840 mentions niece MARY HOGG,
Wit: PHILIP L. LEMILE, JOHN PEEL.

Pages 275-276: Will of HARDY MORGAN. Made Sept. 7, 1840, probated
Oct. 5, 1840... daughter NANCY HATCHER... to great grandaughter MARY
ANN HARMAN... to my three grandchildren, the children of ELIJAH HUDSON,
ADRAIN, WILLIAM, JOHN and JANE... to JOHN C. HARMAN... to nephew
STEPHEN MORGAN... to daughter HARRIET, Jackson Tract, 650 acres... 400
acres near Providence meeting house... HARDY MORGAN. Wit: SAML. W.
ROBBINS, JAS. W. SINQUEFIELD, WILLIAM HUTCHINS (X).

Pages 276-277: Will of JOHN BOSTICK. Made Aug. 28, 1839, probated
Nov. 16, 1840... to my son in law MARTIN H. BROWN... to my son JOHN
RUFUS BOSTICK... land in old Early County, now Baker County, lot #9,
2nd District... to my son HUBERT H. BOSTICK, land in Lee County, lot
#62, 23rd District... to my wife ELDISA BOSTICK and my younger set of
children namely NATHANIEL BEAL BOSTICK, NATHAN LEROY BOSTICK, AGGATHA
ELIZABETH BOSTICK, RODOLPHUS LITTLEBERRY BOSTICK, ERASTUS OSEMUS BOSTICK.
Friends ASA HOLT, HENRY B. TODD, MOSES BRINSON, ROGER L. GAMBLE, Exrs..
JNO BOSTICK. Wit: NATHL. BEAL, ELIZABETH BEAL, JOHN R. BOSTICK.

Pages 278-279: Will of JAMES STONE. Made March 5, 1840, probated
Jan. 4, 1841... to wife NANCY STONE and son WILLIAM D. STONE... to
Ebenezer Church to be paid to JAMES FLEMING ... money due me from firm
of J. & W. D. STONE... to remember RUTH W. PEEL and brother JOHN...
JAMES STONE. Wit: JAMES WILLIAMS, LUCIUS Q.C.P. BROWN, RICHARD J.
BROWN.

Pages 279-280: Will of JAMES A. CARSWELL. Made May 18, 1841, pro-
bated Sept. 6, 1841... son EDWARD R. CARSWELL... daughter JANE E. KING..
minor children JAMES W. CARSWELL, LOUISA CARSWELL, CAROLINE M. CARSWELL,
MARTHA A. CARSWELL... wife LEVINS and son EDWARD, Exrs... JAMES A.
CARSWELL. Wit: CHARLES MATTHEWS, JUNR., CELIA BRINSON, WILLIAM J.
RHODES.

Pages 281-282: Will of LYDIA CROFTON. Made March 9, 1839, probated
Dec. 6, 1841... I, LYDIA CROFTON, wife of BENNET CROFTON, my three
children RICHARD WILLIAM LOWRY, MARY AGNES LOWRY, and ELIZABETH ROVERTA
LOWRY... ROGER L. GAMBLE, Exr... LYDIA CROFTON. Wit: ELIZABETH LOWRY,
MARGARET L. GAMBLE, JANE M. GAMBLE.

Pages 283-284: Will of WILLIS HOWARD, SR. Made Jan. 10, 1826, probated May 17, 1842... being aged... 300 acres on Reedy Creek, originally
granted to JOHN WALKER... to my son WILLIS, 146 acres originally granted
to myself... my daughter MARY, wife of JOSEPH MERCHANT... to my granddaughter SARAH CAROLINE HOBBS... 5 acres to Baptist Society for meeting
house... WILLIS HOWARD (X). Wit: JOHN SCHLY, JOHN WILLIAMS, MARY ANN
SHLY.

Pages 284-285:   Will of NANCY WRIGHT.   Made May 12, 1842, probated
July 4, 1842... to granddaughter WYLANTY DAVIS... to granddaughter
NACISSA DAVIS... to grandson WILLIAM P. DAVIS... 65 acres adj. JOHN WAY
and others... to daughter WYLANTY SMITH... to daughter NARCISSA SMITH...
NOAH SMITH, guardian for old Ben... ELBERT HUDSON and NOAH SMITH, Exrs..
NANCY WRIGHT. Wit: MOSES BRINSON, JR., WADDLE ALLEN, JOHN WAY.

Page 286:   Nuncupative Will of Dr. DAVID ROBERTSON.   Made June 17,
1842, probated Sept. 5, 1842... at the house of Dr. JOHN J. JENKINS...
"take care of the children... if there is anything left, let ELIZABETH
have it"... he died June 17, 1842... H. V. JOHNSON, E. H. HUNTER, JOHN
J. JENKINS.

Pages 286-287:   Will of SARAH ALEXANDER.   Made May 27, 1840, probated
Oct. 17, 1842... youngest son GREEN DAVID ALEXANDER... to granddaughter
MARY JANE LAWSON... sons JOHN W. ALEXANDER and WILLIAM S. ALEXANDER
lawful agent for her... SARAH ALEXANDER (X). Wit: ROBERT BOYD, THOMAS
A. MCBRIDE, SAMEL STEPHENSON.

Page 288:   Will of ELIZABETH BEAL.   Made Aug. 31, 1843, probated
Nov. 1843... three sisters ELOISA BOSTICK, CAROLINA T. BOSTICK, SILINER
BEAL... to ADAM BRINSON... to BENJAMIN BRISON... brother NATHANIEL...
brother LITTLE BERRY BOSTICK, Exr... ELIZABETH BEAL. Wit: PHILIP S.
LEMELE, ROGER K. DIXON.

Pages 288-289:   Will of ETHELDRED SMITH.   Made Nov. 18, 1843, pro-
bated May 6, 1844... wife NANCY SMITH... son NOAH SMITH... son RICHARD
SMITH... children of my son JORDAN SMITH, deceased... to daughter AMY
YOUNGBLOOD... to the children of my daughter PATSEY HUDSON, deceased...
to daughter POLLY OLIPHANT... to the children of my daughter NANCY
HARRIS... her husband SAMUEL H. HARRIS... DRED SMITH. Wit; R. W. JOHN-
SON, WADDLE ALLEN, J. W. ALLEN.

Page 290:   Will of Dr. BENNET HARRIS.   Made May 7, 1843, probated
Jan. 1, 1844... funds in the hands of WILLIAM A. CALDWELL of Charleston,
S.C. ... my wife REBEKAH ANN... "I owe to WILLIAM H. TURPIN, SENR. of
Augusta" ... to my son ROBERT... BENNET HARRIS. Wit: WILLIAM H. BALDY,
NATHL. POLHILL, ALICE BALDY.

Page 291:   Will of MARTHA HUDSON.   Made April 28, 1844, probated
Sept. 2, 1844... children now living LITTLETON HUDSON, MATHEW HUDSON,
MARY HUDSON, NARSISSA HUDSON, TOLAVEN HUDSON, LAWSON HUDSON, JAMES HUDSON
& WALTER HUDSON ... DAVID F. SMITH, Exr... MARTHA HUDSON (X). Wit:
PATIENCE TAYLOR (X), REUBEN ATWELL, D. F. SMITH.

Pages 291-292:   Will of THOS MCBRIDE.   Made Jan. 25, 1837, probated
Sept. 2, 1844... to son in law JOHN ROBBINS, tract on old Wilkinson,
lot #139, 2nd District also lot in Irwin County, #178 in 4th District...
to daughter in law JANE MCBRIDE, and my grandchildren now living with
her... grandson THOMAS A. MCBRIDE... land in Dry Creek and in Burke
and Jefferson... adj. MARY L. MCBRIDE's line... grandchildren ROBERT
B. MCBRIDE, SARAH ANN MCBRIDE, WILLIAM C. MCBRIDE, ELIZA CAROLINE MC-
BRIDE, and MARY ANN MCBRIDE... ALEXANDER GORDON and ROBERT BOYD, Exrs...
THOMAS MCBRIDE (X). Wit: WILLIAM M. LAWSON, ROGER M. LAWSON, ROBERT
BOYD J.P.

Pages 293-294:   Will of THOMAS P. PIERCE.   Made Dec. 24, 1844, probated Jan. 13, 1845... wife ASEY PIERCE... friend JAMES GRUBBS and son
THOMAS PIERCE, when he shall be old enough, Exrs... son JOHN... female
children (not named) ...THOS. PIERCE. Wit: WILLIAM T. ALLEN, LITTLETON
CROSS, P. B. CONNELLY.

Pages 294-295:   Will of JASON POWELL.   Made after June 4, 1834 and
before 1837, probate refused Jan. 13, 1845... wife ELIZABETH POWELL...
my son ISAAC POWELL... wife's brother ABRAM JOINER... JASON POWELL (L.S)
Wit: WILLIAM BECTON, HENRY P. WATKINS, J.P., JOHN R. WELLS, WM.
KILPATRICK. N. B. ABRAM JOINER, OBEDIAH PIERCE. (Refused probate
because none of witnessess could take necessary oath.)

Pages 295-296: Will of JOHN MORGAN. Made Feb. 15, 1845, probated March 3, 1845... son PLEASANT MORGAN... sons MITCHEL J. MORGAN, HARDY W. MORGAN... land in Early and Irwin Counties... one lot drawn by SUSAN CONELLY, a widow, #5 in the 11th district of Irwin County, 490 acres... one lot drawn by myself, #233, 5th district of Irwin County, 490 acres... one lot drawn by MARCUS FLOURNOY, #90, 17th District, Early County... to daughter BETSY MORGAN... to her son ELDRIDGE MORGAN... to my grandchildren SUSAN MORGAN and MARY ANN MORGAN, children of my son STEPHEN MORGAN, deceased... to my children JOHN H. MORGAN, CYNTHIA P. MORGAN, JESSE F. MORGAN, LOUISA W. MORGAN, ELIZA H. MORGAN and MARTIN W. MORGAN... until the youngest child becomes of age... land in Jefferson County... JOHN C. HARMAN and SAMUEL HANNAH, Exrs... JOHN MORGAN (X) (L.S). Wit: OWEN O. MOORE, B. J. BRANTLEY, PLEASANT WALDER, J.P.

Pages 297-298: Will of SION C. KIRKLAND. Made Nov. 18, 1842, probated March 25, 1845... son BENJAMIN L. KIRKLAND and his brothers... deceased son EDWARD C. KIRKLAND... friend EDWARD SWINEY, trustee for son BENJAMIN... son AUGUSTUS C. KIRKLAND... son RED W. L. KIRKLAND... SION C. KIRKLAND. Wit: ROGER L. GAMBLE, SHEROD ARRINGTON, EDWARD R. CARSWELL.

Pages 299-301: Will of Dr. DAVID A. LOWERY, made July 17, 1845, probated ... no date... ALEXDR LOWERY in body of Will... wife ELIZABETH LOWERY... to my sisters MARY GALLOWAY and SUSANNAH BOYD in South Carolina to brother JAMES LOWRY... to brother ROBERT LOWRY's child... to brother JOHN LOWRY's children in South Carolina... to JAMES ROBERT ALEXANDER LOWERY, youngest son of my brother Rev. JOSEPH LOWRY, deceased... to JOSEPHINE AMANDA LOWRY, daughter of my brother JOSEPH... to brother JOSEPH LOWRY's children now unmarried, viz. DAVID, LYDIA, GEORGIANA, ELIZER... to WM. S. LOWRY, JANE DARLEY, AGNES LEWIS, SARAH PATTERSON and SUSANNAH TRUMBLE, my brother JOSEPH's children... my stepson WILLIAMSON A. STOKES... Concord Church... to DAVID P? LOWRY, son of JOSEPH... Woodlawn Plantation which I got from WM. R. LOWRY... MARY A. LOWRY... oaken grove place I got from the estate of LYDIA CRAFTON, through Col. GAMBLE, trustee for said estate... niece ELIZABETH R. LOWRY... to ALEXANDER MURPHY son of JOHN MURPHY, now living in Hamilton Heirs County. to JOSEPH LOWRY PATTERSON, infant son of ROBERT and SARAH PATTERSON... Capt. EBENEZER BOTHWELL, ROBERT BOYD, Esq., WILLIAM S. LOWRY, Exrs. (signature and witnesses missing).

Pages 302-303: Will of ROGER L. GAMBLE. Made June 11, 1838, probated Jan. 10, 1848... to my niece JANE W. GAMBLE, JOHN & JAMES GAMBLE all that they owe me..." ... JAMES GAMBLE being crippled and diseased... to my sister HANNAH PATTERSON... to my son ROGER L. GAMBLE... to my daughter MARGARET L. GAMBLE... friends ASA HOLT, EBENEZER BOTHWELL and PATRICK B. CONNELLY, Exrs... ROGER L. GAMBLE (L.S.). Wit: OWEN MCDERMOTT, THOS H. POLHILL, JAMES T. BOTHWELL. Codicil made Nov. 24, 1840... nephews JAMES & JOHN are now dead.. niece JANE is now MILLER... I revoke their legacies... property in Louisville... ROGER L. GAMBLE (L.S.)

Pages 303-305: Will of SAMUEL B. TARVER. Made Dec. 7, 1846, probated Jan. 11, 1847... wife CHARLOTTE TARVER... land between Sandersville Road and the mill creek... to daughter ELIZABETH I. SMITH, my Oconee land in Washington County, between Deep Creek and Buckeye, joining BENNET B. SMITH... to daughter ISABELLA E. TARVER and her children, six lots in Stewart County, #33, #34, #35, #61 in 25th district, and #223 of 20th (?) district, Lee County when drawn now Stewart County... my grandson MARCELLUS, JOHN & ANDREW... to my daughter VIENNA A. SMITH... to my daughter CHARLOTTE M. A. SALTER and her children... land below Bagget's Creek, adj. BANKS, SPIER, WILLIAMSON Swamp, and A. E. TARVER... to my son ANDREW E. TARVER, land between Limestone Creek and the mill creek, adj. SMITH, FRANCES & W. C. SALTER in the counties of Washington and Jefferson, about 2000 acres... land joining CROOKS... son ANDREW and grandson BENJAMIN R. SMITH, Exrs... SAMUEL B. TARVER (L.S.). Wit: WILLIAM P. TAYLOR, ISAIAH JACKSON, J. W. BARBER.

Pages 305-307: Will of ANN MARSHALL. Made Aug. 7, 1846, probated May 15, 1847 being old and infirm... land where I now reside, 400 acres on Williamson Swamp... adj. MICHAEL WIGGINS, and estate of JAMES SPEAR to the children of my granddaughter MAHALA QUINNEY... to my son JOSEPH MARSHALL... to my grandchildren (heirs of my late son LEWIS MARSHALL), FRANCIS L. MARSHALL, WIRNNA AUGUSTA MARSHALL... to WILLIAM LOCKHART... to my grandson JOHN WOODS... to my friend Mrs. ANN DANIELS... JAMES L. DANIELS, Exr... ANN MARSHALL (X). Wit: HAMILTON RAIFORD, WILLIAM SHERRORD (X), MCCLENNA MOORE.

Page 307:   Will of BENJAMIN GOBERT, JR.   Made Oct. 7, 1839, probated Oct. 4, 1847... wife LOUISA... son JAMES P. GOBERT... son JAMES and ROGER L. GAMBLE Exrs... BENJM GOBERT. Wit: JAMES T. BOTHWELL, WM. L. LOWRY, WM. J. WHIGHAM.

Pages 308-309:   Will of SILAS ARRINGTON.   Made Oct. 2, 1847, probated Nov. 29, 1847... being of a tolerably advanced age... son WILLIS ARRINGTON... 450 acres partly described in a platt of my lands made by E. J. TARVER in August 1839... to my daughter ELIZABETH ARRINGTON... daughter THURSEA DAVIS... to son LEVIN ARRINGTON... my daughter MAHALA STEWART, wife of JAMES STEWART... land granted to JOHN PATTERSON... wife ELIZABETH ARRINGTON... SILAS ARRINGTON (X). Wit: JAMES T. BOTHWELL, JOSEPH T. PARKER, JAMES J. ARRINGTON.

Page 310:   Will of ELIZABETH POOL.   Made Sept. 3, 1847, probated Jan. 10, 1848... widow... my two youngest daughters MARY ANN MARTHA POOL and ELIZABETH JANE POOL... youngest son WILLIAM BRANTLEY POOL... friends JAMES POOL, JOHN BEASLEY and JOHN WREN, Exrs... ELIZABETH POOL (X). Wit: MAJOR H. WELLERS, JAMES ANDERSON, ISAAC POOL.

Page 311:   Will of LITTLE B. CORENAH.   Made Jan. 22, 1848, probated Jan. 31, 1848... wife and children (not named)... friend JAMES T. BOTHWELL, Exr... (no signature) Wit: WILLIAM HOUSER, H. B. GREGORY, LOVETT L. BROWN (X).

Pages 312-314:   Will of THOMAS STREET.   Made Oct. 1, 1846, probated Sept. 1, 1848... to be buried in the burying ground on my plantation where my children are buried... wife MARY STREET, the Pine Hill House... MARY HOGINS, my half sister... to the children of RICHARD STREET, deceased... MARTHA ASHLEY, one of the children of RICHARD STREET, her brother THOMAS STREET... to the children of WALDING BARBER, deceased... MARY BARBER, now MARY S. KINNER... SARAH BARBER, now SARAH WIGGINS... THOMAS BARBER, their brother... to the children of WILLIAM BARBER, deceased... to the children of GEORGE WADE BARBER... to LITTLE BERRY GRANT... to TEMPERANCE BROWN... stepson PATRICK B. CONNELLY... lands in the counties of Jefferson and Burke... THOS STREET. Wit: HARRIETT H. GLASCOCK, ELI MCCROAN, HENRY B. TODD.

Page 315:   Will of J. W. BATTS.   Made Aug. 28, 1847, probated March 18, 1849... mother SARAH BATTS... JOHN W. BATTS. Wit: ROBERT H. CATES, HENRY B. TODD, ELI MCCROAN.

Page 316:   Will of MATTHEW MARSHALL.   Made May 8, 1848, probated July 2, 1849... wife (not named)... brother in law MUND G. SCRUGGS and CHARLES H. BURKE, Exrs... M. MARSHALL. Wit: ELIZABETH SCRUGGS, ANN B. BURKE, EDWARD R. CARSWELL.

Pages 316-317:   Will of GODFREY KELLER.   Made 1838, probated July 30, 1849... unto BENJAMIN COOK, the husband of my daughter BETSEY... to wife SUSANNAH KELLY... my children EDNEY, ISAAC, JOHN & SARAH... JOHN HARRILL of Upson County, Exr... (no signature). Wit: L. B. HARMAN, NATHAN STEVENS, WILLIAM HARMAN.

Pages 317-318:   Will of ISHAM EVANS.   Made Feb. 9, 1842, probated Jan. 14, 1850... wife ELIZABETH... sons JOHN & LADSON when they become 21... my youngest children (not named)... ISAHM EVANS (L.S.). Wit: DAVID ROBERSON, FRANCIS B. MOUNTAIN, J. W. M. BERRIEN.

Pages 319-322:   Will of MOSES BRINSON, SR.   Made Feb. 18, 1848, probated Feb. 4, 1850... being of advanced age... my grandson HENRY T.

BRINSON... my son MOSES BRINSON... to HENRY STEPHENS, husband of SARAH
A. STEPHENS, formerly SARAH BRINSON, my daughter... friend JAMES T.
BOTHWELL... my granddaughter MARGARET E. PRITCHETT... my daughter ANNA
FREEMAN... grandson ISAAC BRINSON... land adj. RICHARD SMITH and est. of
WM. STREETMAN... daughter REBECCA J. JORDAN... land where JOHN FREEMAN
now lives... land adj. ISAAC FREEMAN CONNEL and others... land adj.
JOHN WAY & THOS MATTHEWS... to BENJAMIN PHILPS and to each of his three
children by my grandaughter NANCY... MOSES, MARGARET & SOPHIA JANE ...
to son MOSES BRINSON, JR. land adj. ELAM YOUNG, J. CONNEL and another
tract, part of the POPE tract on south side of the Quaker Road. adj.
JOHN WREN... at the death of AMELIA FARMER, my step-daughter... wife
APSABETH... MOSES BRINSON JR., WILLIAM W. YOUNG, and JOHN WREN, Exrs...
MOSES BRINSON SR. (X). Wit: WILLIAM H. STREETMAN, JOHN STREETMAN,
WALTER PARKER, AMAZON A. BRINSON. Codicil: In consequence of the death
of BENJAMIN PHILIP... to ISAAC FREEMAN, son of ANNA FREEMAN... my wife
and her daughter now Mrs. JOURDOW. Wit: CABEL A. WRIGHT, WALTER PARKER,
AMAZON A. BRINSON.

Page 332: Will of SARAH R. WRIGHT. Made May 13, 1851, probated
July 7, 1851... being of advanced age, very feeble in health... sisters
MARTHA WRIGHT and MARY HUNTER... niece SARAH WRIGHT, daughter of my
deceased brother AMBROSE WRIGHT... friend THOMAS H. POLHILL, Exr...
SARAH P. WRIGHT. Wit: STEPHEN S. PERKINS, IREDELL S. ERWIN. (In
heading of WPA copy mentions EDWARD W. HUNTER, nephew.)

Pages 333-334: Will of SARAH STREETMAN. Made Nov. 3, 1849, probated
Sept. 1, 1851... two brothers JOHN STREETMAN & JEREMIAH STREETMAN... my
sister MARTHA ROGERS and her children... brother WILLIAM H. STREETMAN
and my four sisters, HARRIET ROGERS, ELIZABETH STREETMAN, RUTH FARMER &
SAREPTA STREETMAN... my friend and relative WILLIAM U. YOUNG, Exr...
SARAH STREETMAN. Wit: E. B. HOOKS, MOSES BRINSON, JR., CATHERINE
CORBETT (X).

Pages 334-335: Will of JANE POLHILL. Made April 2, 1851, probated
Feb. 6, 1852... widow of NATHANIEL POLHILL, late of Jefferson Co... our
only son THOMAS H. POLHILL... my daughter REBECKAH M. POLHILL... to my
daughters, ELIZA G. BALDY, MARANN S. CAIN... to my grandchildren who
are children of my deceased daughter HENRITTA R. HARMAN... grandson JOHN
C. HARMEN... my grandsons NATHANIEL POLHILL BLADY, NATHANIEL THOMAS
HARMAN, JOSEPH H. POLHILL & JOHN C. HARMAN each to have one fourth arriv-
ing at the age of 21 or marrying... JOHN C. HARMAN's brother WILLIAM N.
HARMAN & sister CHARILLA J. HARMAN... JANE M. POLHILL. Wit: STEPHEN
S. PERKINS, IREDELL S. ERWIN, E. H. W. HUNTER.

Pages 336-344: Will of WILLIAM HUNT. Made Jan. 16, 1852, probated
March 1, 1852... to my wife ELIZABETH... plantation whereon I now live
containing 800 acres... to educate our two youngest children and WILLIAM
H. BRITT until they shall arrive at the age of 21 years of marry... to
friend ELBERT D. FAYLOR in trust for my daughter NANCY M. wife of OWEN
C. POPE... my daughter MARY ANN, wife of JAMES R. SMITH... daughter
REBECCA ANN, wife of CAPEL RAIFORD... my daughter MATHA ELIZABETH JANE...
my daughter SARAH ANN... my daughter GEORGIA ANN ELVIN... son WILLIAM
B. ... son JAMES RUSSELL... son JESSE B.... WILLIAM HUNT BRITT, son of
WILLIAM BRITT... WIHLIAM HUNT (L.S.). Wit: SAMUEL B. PALMER, JOSHUA R.
PRICE, DANIEL HARRIS. (This will headed Washington County, and proven
in Sandersville, Washington County, HAYWOOD BROOKINS, Ordinary.)

Page 345: Will of MUND G. SCRUGGS. Made Nov. 2, 1851, probated
March 9, 1852... wife ELIZABETH... dearly beloved WILLIAM G. SCRUGGS,
Exr. youngest children... MUND G. SCRUGGS. Wit: JOHN W. MURPHY, HUGH
L. BURKE, MARY L. MARSHALL.

Page 346: Will of MARTHA WRIGHT. Made May 3, 1852, probated Oct. 2,
1854... sister MARY HUNTER... nephew EDWARD H. W. HUNTER... nephew
HENRY G. WRIGHT... MARTHA WRIGHT (X). Wit: THOMAS H. POLHILL, STEPHEN
S. PERKINS, A. D. EVANS.

Page 347: Will of MARIAH JENKINS. Made July 9, 1851, probated July 5, 1852... of advanced years and somewhat infirm... son WILLIAM A. JENKINS... MARIA JENKINS. Wit: GURDON I. MILLER, ANNA M. MILLER, JOHN R. BOSTICK.

Pages 322-323: Will of WILLIAM SWAN. Made Jan. 7, 1850, probated Feb. 4, 1850... in a feeble state of health... to wife ELIZABETH SWAN... my three sons JABEZ M. SWAN, JOSHUA KEY SWAN & THOMAS SWAN, $125 for completing their education... my two sons JOHN SWAN and DANIEL SWAN... sons JACKSON SWAN... my son JOSIAH SWAN... sons SIDNEY & WILLIAM SWAN... W. SWAN. Wit: J. T. BOTHWELL, T. L. KEYS, J. JORDAN.

Page 324: Will of Mrs. NANCY SMITH. Probated May 6, 1850, made between Feb. 1 and Feb. 16, 1850... verbal Will taken by NOAH SMITH and SUSAN METZ... her grandson WILLIAM GROSS... NOAH SMITH, SUSAN METZ (X).

Pages 325-326: Will of WM. PARADISE. Made 1850, probated July 15, 1850... wife (not named)... sons JOHN D. PARADIS, daughter NANCY THIGPEN, granddaughter SUSAN WELLS & MARY THIGPEN... DARIUS B. WELLS, Exr... WILLIAM PARADISE (L.S.). Wit: JOSEPH PRICE, JESSE F. MORGAN, JOHN R. WELLS.

Pages 326-327: Will of SYLVIA CHISOLM. Made Dec. 18, 1838, probated Sept. 2, 1850... daughter MARY COLLEY, land whereon I now live... daughter ELIZABETH SHERROD... son WILLIAM TOMLINSON... grandsons JOSEPH & JOHN SHERROD, land in Henry and Cherokee Counties... friend HENRY I. TURNER, Exr... SILVERY CHISOLM (X). Wit: J. P. TURNER, JOHN R. CLARK, J. H. TURNER.

Pages 327-328: First Will of SILVIA CHISOLM. Made March 23, 1829... son WILLIAM CHISOLM... unto HENRY B. TODD and LITTLEBERRY BOSTICK in trust for my daughter ELIZABETH SHERROD and her children... my daughter MARY COLEY... granddaughter SARAH SHERROD daughter of ELIZABETH SHERROD.. SILVIA CHISOLM (X). Wit: JOHN BLECHER, WASHINGTON BELCHER, M. A. M. BOSTICK.

Pages 328-329: Will of NATHANIEL POLHILL. Made June 3, 1844, pro-bated Jan. 13, 1851, daughter ELIZA JANE BALDY... daughter HENRITTA A. HARMAN... to the children of my sons THOMAS H. POLHILL... to my daughter MARGARET S. POLHILL... daughter REBECKAH M. POLHILL... wife JANE M. POLHILL... grandson THOMAS NATANIEL POLHILL... NATHL. POLHILL (SEAL). Wit. B. B. CONNELLY, JAMES R. GOBERT, A. MCDONALD.

Pages 329-331: Will of WILLIAM WHIGHAM. Made May 3, 1848, probated May 5, 1851... wife MARY WHIGHAM, 200 acres laid off of my plantation... my daughter APENITH... for my grandchildren the children of SARAH ANDER-SON, afterward SARAH POLAND... to JOHN W. WHITHAM, the KING place... to THOMAS WHIGHAM, the DONALDSON tract... to NATHAN K. WHIGHAM, Land I bought of JOSEPH WHITHAM, the FLEETING tract, 250 acres... WARNER & HANNAH tracts... to WILLIAM P. WHIGHAM, land purchased by me of Col. THOMAS WHIGHAM, 500 acres adj. JOHN W. WHIGHAM & Mrs. BIGHAM land... to JANE DENNY... to MARGARET C. FLEMING... my grandaughter MARY JANE ANDER-SON... son NATHAN... WILLIAM WHIGHAM. Wit: JAMES T. BOTHWELL, ROBERT J. PENRY, ENOCH FARMER.

Pages 348: Will of MERENDA THOMPSON. Made May 10, 1852, probated July 5, 1852, wife TOLETHA THOMPSON... until my youngest child reaches 21... MERRENDER THOMPSON. Wit: JONATHAN HUFF, JOHN GAY, ELIZABETH LUCKY (X).

Pages 348-349: Will of SARAH MOYE. Made Dec. 17, 1845, probated July 5, 1852... son BENAJAH A. MOYE... afflicted son JAMES MOYE... plantation where I now reside, 550 acres... SARY MOYE. Wit: HAMILTON RAIFORD, ROBERT W. DANIEL, HENRY G. GARRETT.

Page 350: Will of ELIZABETH JORDAN. Made June 21, 1852, probated Sept. 6, 1852... having reached a respectable old age... sons THOMAS G.

JORDAN and STERLING G. JORDAN... my daughters MARY BYNE and NANCY LOWE...
my grandchildren DENNIS LOWE, FREDERICH LOWE, STERLING LOWE and
LERTRETRICE LOWE... to my daughter SARAH ROGERS... (no signature)...
Wit: REUBEN ATWELL, JOHN S. WILLSON, JAMES M. JORDAN.

Pages 351-352: Will of JAMES C. TRIMBLE. Made Aug. 6, 1850, probated Oct. 4, 1852... wife (not named)... children as they may become
of age or marry... brother JOSEPH L. TRIMBLE... cousin EDWARD R. CARSWELL,
Exr... JAMES C. TREMBLE, Wit: JOHN W. CLARK, W. M. WOODS, JAS N.
CARSWELL.

Pages 352-353: Will of SELINA BEAL. Made Oct. 19, 1852, probated
Nov. 1, 1852... Nuncupative Will... WILLIAM HOUSER, NATHANIEL B. BOSTICK
and ERATUS O. BOSTICK were present Oct. 15, last Friday night, 1852, 8
hours before the said SELINA BEAL died... Mrs. ELOISA BOSTICK, sister...
sister Mrs. CAROLINE BOSTICK... child SAVANNAH.

Pages 353-354: Will of WILLIAM CALHOUN. Made Feb. 2, 1849, probated
Dec. 6, 1852... to my son JAMES CALHOUN... for my granddaughter MARY
TALLULA CALHOUN, daughter of my son WILLIAM, deceased... daughter MARTHA
A. L. TARRENSE, 318 acres including the MARSHALL tract... son THOMAS S.
CALHOUN... daughter SUSANNER W. M. MOORE, where HENRY J. MOORE her
husband now lives... son ROBERT M. CALHOUN... wife MARTHA CALHOUN...
490 acres in Lownedes County, and 240 in Cherokee... cattle in Emanuel
(?) County... son JORDAN W. ... BENJAH S. CARESWELL, Exr... WILLIAM
CALHOUN (X). Wit: HENRY G. GARRET, GREEN L. FOKES, P. A. MOYE.

Page 355: Will of GREEN ROGERS. Made Aug. 17, 1852, probated Jan. 4,
1853... of county of Burke... brother WILLIAM ROGERS... GREEN ROGERS.
Wit: SARAH BATTS (S), MARY POPE (X), ELI M. BROWN.

Pages 356-357: Will of DANIEL T. SMITH. Made Oct. 22, 1852, probated
Jan. 10, 1853... daughter SARAH M. PIPKEN... daughters ELIZA A. ATWELL
and GOWZADY I. SWAN... daughter ADELINE A. SMITH... my five unmarried
sons DAVID T., JAMES M., PATRICH M., JOHNATHAN & WILLIAM E... my
oldest son JEFFERSON C. SMITH... to son JEFFERSON, land whereon JEFFERSON
now lives, has been bought and partly paid for from JAMES PARKER, but no
title has yet been made... wife FRANCIS SMITH... son in law REUBEN
ATWELL, Exr... D. T. SMITH. Wit: GEO. H. SCHLEY, W. W. HUGHES, NOAH
SMITH, J. J. Ct.

Pages 358-359: Will of HENRY B. PIPKIN. Made June 12, 1844, probated
Feb. 7, 1853... wife and children (not named)... until my youngest son
comes of age... son JOHN G. PIPKIN and friend EBENEZER BROWN, Exrs...
H. P. PIPKIN. Wit: E. R. CARSWELL, WM. H. BALDY, E. W. JOHNSON.

Pages 359-360: Will of JOHN C. HARMAN. Made Jan. 1, 1848, probated
May 2, 1853... to be buried between the graves of my wives SARAH ANN
and HENRIETTA ADELINA HARMAN near the Church and Academy in Louisville...
daughter MARY ANN HARMAN to make her equal to the children of my second
wife HENRIETTA... all of my children, MARY ANN, WILLIAM NEARE, CHARILLA
JANE, NATHANIEL THOMAS and JOHN CUMMING HARMAN... wife HENRIETTA gave to
her son WILLIAM NEARE her watch with her maiden name on the back... unto
REBECKAH M. POLHILL, her sister's children HENRIETTA (wording not clear)
JOHN C. HARMAN. Wit: SARAH LIVINGSTON, MARTHA G. YOUNG, HOPKIN WAR.

Pages 360-361: Will of JAMES GUNN. Made June 1, 1844, probated May
2, 1853... three children KEZIAH, WILLIAM and BENHEBA GUNN... 100 acres
in Jefferson County granted to JARED IRVIN and one acre granted to
JOHNATHAN KEMP, 202½ acres in Telfair County, granted to BENJAMIN
JORDAN... son JOHN GUNN and WILLIAM U. YOUNG, Exrs... JAMES GUNN. Wit:
JOHN W. LAFAVOR, ROBERT LOWERY, NATHL. POLHILL.

Pages 361-362: Will of JOSEPH MARSHALL. Made Nov. 12, 1839, probated
May 28, 1853... wife SARAH MARSHALL... friend EDWARD R. CARSWELL, trustee
for children SARH JENKINS, wife of NICHOLAS JENKINS and MAHALY QUINEY,
wife of HINSON QUINNEY... JOSEPH MARSHALL. Wit: WILLIAM HADDEN, MOSES
BRINSON, JR., JOHN W. ALEXANDER.

Page 363: Will of Mrs. MARY WHIGHAM. Made Sept. 17, 1852, probated Jan. 9, 1854... widow of WILLIAM WHIGHAM... to be buried in the family burying ground... daughter MARGARET G. FLEMING... to son WILLIAM P. WHIGHAM... daughter SENETH E. ARRINGTON, wife of ABNER ARRINGTON... MARY WHIGHAM. Wit: WILLIAM J. WHIGHAM, ENOCH FARMER, ROBERT J. LEE (X).

Pages 364-365: Will of MARY PATTERSON. Made April 22, 1851, probated Jan. 9, 1854... niece MARY A. J. ALEXANDER and her heirs... to niece ISABEL MCKIGANEY and heirs... relative ELIZA MCBRIDE... to nephew JAMES S. CLEMENTS, paid out by WILLIAM CLEMENTS... relative WILLIAM JOHN CLEMENTS... nephew WILLIAM CLEMENTS... MARY PATTERSON (X). Wit: WILLIAM T. MARSHALL, JOHN W. ALEXANDER.

Pages 365-366: Will of PENELOPE HUDSON. Made April 26, 1854, no probate date... being of advanced age and feeble health... friend MOSES BRINSON in trust for my son JAMES C. HUDSON, all my land on which I now live 996 acres... to JANE FARMER and CAROLINE CLARK, wives of ENOCH FARMER and PHILIP CLARK... daughter Mrs. ELIZABETH MATTHEWS... children of my deceased daughter SARAH WHIGHAM... PENNY HUDSON (X). Wit: E. B. HOOK, I. T. JORDAN, H. I. FARMER.

Page 367: Will of FRANCIS B. MOUNTAIN. Made Dec. 21, 1853, probated July 3, 1854... wife SARAH ANN... my brothers and sisters children viz. JOHNATHAN MOUNTAIN children, THOMAS H. MOUNTAIN children, POLLY NAS-WORTHY children... THOMAS A. MCBRIDE and GEORGE NASWORTHY, Exrs... FRANCIS B. MOUNTAIN. Wit: JAMES GORDON, ROBERT OATS, WILLIAM CLEMENTS.

Pages 368-372: Will of JAMES WILLIAMS. Made Jan. 9, 1851, probated July Term, 1854... of old age... wife MARY WILLIAMS... son LAWSON WILLIAMS... land where I now live... upper corner of my son JOHN's fence.. land granted to JAMES TRIMBLE, 200 acres on east side of Durharts Creek.. 196 acres granted to myself... land granted to GEORGE INGRAM, purchased by me from NATNAIEL SAMPLE JUNR. estate, 430 acres joining the tract granted to myself... land granted to myself and brother MILES, 700 acres... grandson JAMES WILLIAMS, son of my deceased son JOHN W. WILLIAMS 150 acres granted to my on Durharts Creek... grandsons WILLIAM WILLIAMS & NEWTON WILLIAMS (sons of my deceased son JOHN)... land on north side of Indian Creek in Waren County, Ga.... daughter in law CASSEY WILLIAM (widow of my deceased son JOHN B. WILLIAMS)... grandchildren TEMPERANCE MCDANIEL, CLAYTON STEPHENS, SAMINO MANSON and NATHAN STEPHENS, children of my deceased daughter ELIZABETH STEPHENS, the former wife of ROBERT STEPHENS... daughter SARAH ANN LITTLE, notes I hold against the estate of her deceased husband FOSTER LITTLE... son in law JOHN HADDEN... for children of my deceased daughter NANCY HADDEN, viz. NEWTON, POLLY ANN, JANE, THOMAS & JOHN... son JEFFERSON WILLIAMS, 50 acres granted to my-self adj. Warren Line... brother JOHN B. WILLIAMS... my son SIMEON WILLIAMS, two tracts of land... land I bought from the estate of WILLIAM HANNAH... to son JAMES M. WILLIAMS, land containing three hundred acres, known as the PITMAN land on Rocky Comfort, Jefferson County... to son in law JOHSUA WILLIAMS, my daughter POLLY ANN WILLIAMS, wife of JOSHUA WILLIAMS... grandson FRANKLIN WILLIAMS, son of LAWSON WILLIAMS, part of the GRAVES land below Persion Branch and Persimon Pond ... to grandson THOMAS WILLIAMS, son of LAWSON... to grandson JOHN WILLIAMS son of LAWSON... to my granddaughter NANCY WILLIAMS, daughter of LAWSON... to granddaughter PAULINE JANE WILLIAMS daughter of LAWSON... to grand-daughter SARAH EMALINE WILLIAMS, daughter of LAWSON... grandson MADISON AUGUSTUS WILLIAMS, son of LAWSON... to grandson SIMEON, son of SIMEON, land I bought of ROBERT I. PUGESLY and SIDNEY PUGESLY... to grandson WILLIAM WILLIAMS, son of JEFFERSON WILLIAMS... to grandson ANDY WILLIAMS son of MADISON WILLIAMS... JAMES WILLIAMS. Wit: JOHN C. HARMAN, JAMES W. MCKIGNEY, JAMES MCKINGNEY.

Page 373: Will of RICHARD J. BROWN. Made April 29, 1855, probated Aug. 6, 1855... verbal Will taken by JAMES J. BROWN, SAMUEL A. DENNY, LUCIUS C. D. BROWN, AUGUSTUS J. PUGESLEY & A. WHIGHAM were present of Apr. 29, 1855 at the residence of RICHARD J. BROWN, some hours before his death... his wife ELIZA BROWN, and children ELIZABETH J. BROWN, BURREL J. BROWN, LOUISA BROWN, SARAH F. BROWN, MARTHA BROWN and RICHARD J. BROWN... son SAMUEL D. BROWN.

Page 373-374:   Will of THOMAS MATTHEWS not copied, but probated Nov.
Term, 1855... produced by CHARLES MATTHEWS, executor... three wit-
nesses and said Will and Codicils WILLIAM A. BRINSON, WILLIAM A. HAYLES
& MICHAEL KING... 5 Nov. 1855.

Pages 374-376:   Will of JAMES MATTHEWS.   Made Aug. 9, 1849, probated
Nov. 5, 1855... wife ELIZABETH MATTHEWS... to CHARLES MATHEWS JR. in
trust for MARGARET A. J. THOMPSON, child of LEMUEL THOMPSON, land on
Reedy Creek... adj. land of RHESA J. FARMER and others 270 acres... in
trust for ELIZABETH MCGAINS, land originally in Early County 250 acres,
#129, 12th dis. drawn by myself... in trust for my daughter JULIA
ELIZABETH, Kelly place... to my daughters MARTHA M. CHEATHAM, MARGARET
A. J. WEEKS, & JULIA E. MATHEWS... DAVID T. SMITH, trustee of MARTHA M.
CHEATHAM... friends HENRY P. TODD, CHARLES MATHEWS JUNIOR, DAVID T.
SMITH & THOMAS MATHEWS, Exrs... JAMES MATHEWS (X). Wit: R. J. FARMER,
JAS. W. CLARK, L. D. MATHEWS.

Pages 377-378:   Will of ROBERT BOYD, JR.   Made Dec. 1, 1855, no
probate date... of advanced age... wife RUTH W. BOYD and three youngest
children JACENTHA CAROLINE, AGNES LUTETEA and ELLEN SOPHRONIA WRIGHT...
my children WILLIAM, SARAH E., ANN A. & ROBERT J. BOYD... son SAMUEL
BOYD... ROBERT BOYD. Wit: WILLIAM L. LOW, ROBERT B. MCBRIDE, THOMAS A.
MCBRIDE.

Pages 378-380:   Will of LITTLEBERRY BOSTICK, JR.   Made Aug. 1, 1855,
probated Nov. 5, 1855... wife MARY ANN MARTHA BOSTICK... daughter MARY
ANN RHODES, JULIA ANN BOSTICK, EMMA LOUISA BOSTICK and son RHESA BOS-
TICK, CHARLES A. W. BOSTICK and ALBERT ADDISON BOSTICK... son in law
WILLIAM W. RHODES, husband of my daughter MARY ANN... daughter MARGARET
FRIERSON... my deceased daughter ELIZABETH W. RAIFORD, her daughter
MARY ANN ELIZABETH FREDONIA RAIFORD... friends ARTHUR B. WALKER and
A. R. WRIGHT, Exrs... L. BERRY BOSTICK (L.S.). Wit: E. H. HUNTER,
W. F. DENNY, W. A. HAYLES.

Page 381:   Will of JESSE GLOVERS.   Made Oct. 19, 1855, probated Feb.
4, 1856... wife MARTHA GLOVER and her children, should she have any...
my sister MARY FERGERSON and her children and the children of my deceased
brother RICHARD GLOVER... friends GEORGE MILLER & THOS. H. POLHILL,
Exrs. of my last will and testament... the grave of my late deceased
wife enclosed... JESSE GLOVER (X). Wit: WILLIAM ROLLINS, WM. SINQUE-
FIELD, EDMUND CLARK.

Pages 382-383:   Will of THOMAS KENEDY.   Made Aug. 6, 1848, probated
May 5, 1856... being of advanced age... wife HESTER KENNEDAY... son JOHN
HARMAN KENDAY... son JOHN THARMERS KENEDEAY... to my sister MARY BOYED
three children... daughter SARAH CLEMENS... granddaughter SAREAH LOWERY
granddaughter MARY KENEDAY... neighbours BENIJAH A. MOYE and OBEDIE
PEACE, Exrs... THOMAS KENEADY. Wit: HAMILTON RAIFORD, HENRY G. GARRETT,
ROBERT W. DANIEL.

Pages 384-385:   Will of MARY LEMLE.   Made June 4, 1856, no probate
date... advanced in life... son in law ROGER R. DIXON, land on Rocky
Comfort Creek, adj. lands of JOHN JORDAIN, AMBROSE R. WRIGHT and others..
my late son Dr. PHILIP S. LEMLE... daughter ELISA F. DIXON... I have
omitted my other two daughters ... MARY LEMLE. Wit: A. B. COFFIN,
J. T. BOTHWELL, CHARLES J. JENKINS.

Pages 386-387:   Will of JAMES A. PARKER.   Made June 6, 1856, probated July 7, 1856... wife DIANAH... to my grandson JAMES R. STEVENS,
son of NATHAN STEVENS, JOSEPH R. PARKER his trustee... two sons in law
HENRY P. WATKINS and JEFFERSON SMITH, Exrs... JAS. A. PARKER. Wit:
J. I. MILLER, WM. HOUSER, W. P. JORDAN.

Pages 387-388:   Will of WILLIAM LITTLE.   Made Oct. 3, 1853, probated
Jan. 11, 1857... wife NANCY... son ROBT. P. LITTLE, my fathers family
Bible... to son in law DAVID G. PHILLIPS... what I have given to my
other children ROBT. P. LITTLE and WM. D. STONE... WM. LITTLE (SEAL).
Iit: ROBT. PATTERSON, JOSEPH B. AVRET, JAMES PATTERSON.

Pages 388-389: Will of Mrs. MILLY PIERCE. Made Oct. 30, 1856, probated
Jan. 12, 1857... being of very adbound age... son OBED PIERCE... grandson JOHN COWARD, son of my departed daughter UNITY COWARD... each of my
daughters CLAUISA BARGINIER, HESTER KENNEDY, NANCY MOORE and MARY MILLER.
friend THOS H. POLHILL, Exr. MILLY PIERCE (X). Wit: C. TORRANCE,
ROBERT STEVENS, AZANIAH COWART.

Pages 390-391: Will of WILLIAM PARKER. Made July 7, 1856, probated
Feb. 7, 1857... to each of my children JOSEPH G. PARKER, AQUILLA WESLY
PARKER, THOMAS D. PARKER, MARTHA EVANS wife of PHILIP J. EVANS,
DIALSHA ELIZABETH MOSELY, wife of THOMAS MOSELY, ANN MARY STEVENS, wife
of EDMUND N. STEVENS, FRANCIS L. PARKER and the children of my deceased
son JAMES A. PARKER, the children of my deceased daughter SARAH JORDAN,
wife of STERLING G. JORDAN... WILLIAM PARKER (X). Wit: TOM P. DAVID,
E. R. CARSWELL, THOS H. POLHILL.

Pages 392-393: Will of BRYANT LAWM. Made Jan. 6, 1854, probated
Sept. 7, 1857... being of advanced age... wife MARIA with whom I have
lived, 350acres on west side of Pond drain... my son WILLIAM SILAS...
son ELI HOLLAND... daughter CENEY FRANCES... my brother and sisters by
deed, 200 acres... sisters ELIZABETH,THAROLOTTE or CELIA, if they marry..
hogs known as the SILAS WATKINS hogs... friend ANDREW TARVER, Exr...
BRYANT LAMB. Wit: C. TORRANCE, THOMAS W. LAMB (X), JAMES S. SPEIR J.P.

Pages 393-395: Will of WILLIAM BARGINNIER. Made Sept. 1, 1857, pro-
bated Dec., 1857... being of advanced age... wife CLARISA... son JOHN
BARGINNIER and daughter's children, ELIZABETH PARKER now wife of
FRANCIS PARKER... son SETH BARGINNIER. to my granddaughter GEORGIAN
BARGAINNIER, dau. of my son JOHN... granddaughter EMILY BARGINNIER,
daughter of my son JOHN... granddaughter BESHADA PARKER, daughter of my
son in law FRANCIS PARKER... to granddaughter SARAH PARKER, daughter of
FRANCIS... to granddaughter CLAUISA BARGINNIER, daughter of JOHN... to
WILLIAM PARKER, son of FRANCIS... to grandson MARCUS PARKER, son of
FRANCIS... to grandson OBEDIAH BARGINIER, son of JOHN... to WILLIAM
BARGINNIER, son of JOHN... WILLIAM BARGINNIER (X) (LS). Wit: JOHN W.
BOTHWELL (L.S.), WILLIAM TARVER (L.S.), WAILLIAM A. HARPER, J.P. (L.S.).

Pages 396-397: Will of JAMES FLEMING. Made Dec. 23, 1857, probated
March 1, 1858... wife LOUISA H. FLEMING... son JAMES G. FLEMING...
children of my brother WILLIAM FLEMING and children of my brother
BENJAMIN F. FLEMING... friend EDWARD H. W. HUNTER, Exr... guardian of
person and property of my son JAMES G. FLEMING until he is fourteen
years old... JAMES FLEMING (SEAL). Wit: WILLIAM A. WILKINS, JOSEPH
H. WILLIMS, ROBERT JORDAN.

Pages 397-398: Will of LEVINIA CARSWELL. Made Feb. 22, 1858, pro-
bated Nov. 7, 1864... daughter CAROLINE M. WHIGHAM... son JAMES W.
CARSWELL... granddaughters AMANDA WHIGHAM, ADDELLA DENNY, LUCIE L.
CARSWELL... children EDWARD R. CARSWELL, JAMES W. CARSWELL, CAROLINE M.
WHIGHAM, LOUISA L. DENNEY and the children of my deceased daughter JANE
E. KING... LEVINIA CARSWELL (L.S.). Wit: REBECCA P. JORDAN, JOSHIA
T. JORDAN, MOSES BRINSON.

Pages 398-399: Will of DAVID HOWARD. Made April 8, 1858, no probate
date... knowing that I must shortly depart from this world... brother
WILLIS HOWARD JR. trustee for ANDREW JACKSON MARTIN THOMPSON... to ALLEZ
BEATMAN CORDELIA THOMPSON... 128½ acres in Glasscock County, adj. estate
of JERTHRAM HOBBS, deceased, JOHN F. RIVERS and others, and GREEN B.
THOMAS' place, partly in Glasscock and partly in Jefferson Counties...
adj. BENJAMIN HADDEN, WILLIS HOWARD and others... to DAVID L. HOWARD...
to DAVID PHILIPS... to all my lawful heirs, JOHN HOWARD, WILLIAM HOWARD,
MENJAH PHILIPS, JOHN F. RIVERS, JOHN RUSSEL, WILLIS HOWARD, WILLIAM
CLARK, and JAMES STAPLETON... brother in law JOHN F. RIVERS, Exr...
DAVID HOWARD. Wit: HENRY BALEY, JAMES H. RAYBUN, WILLIS PHILLIPS,
THOMAS RAYBUN.

Pages 400-401: Will of THOMAS HADDEN, SR. Made Aug. 31, 1857, probated Oct. 18, 1858... beloved wife (not named)... daughter MILLY... sons

165

BENJAMIN, SAMUEL & THOMAS... to ELIZABETH VININGS children, to wit WILLIAM & MARY, SARAHANN WILLIAMS, ELDA MATILDA WILLIAMS, MARY RABURN, MILLY HADDAN & MARGARETT ALLEN... THOMAS HADDEN. Wit: THOMS R. HAMMETT of Warrent Cty, LOUIS RABRON (T) of Warren Cty, and GEORGE STAPLETON, SNR. of Jefferson Cty.

Pages 401-402: Will of SARAH BATTS. Not copied, probated Feb. 7, 1858... ROGER L. GAMBLE, Exr. Wit: ELI M. BROANE.

Pages 402-405: Will of MOSES BRINSON, Jr. Made June 30, 1859, probated Sept. 5, 1859... having arrived at an advanced age... wife ZELPHIA A. BRINSON ... children by my first wife... my daughter AMAZON A. PILCHER, and her husband THOMAS J. PILCHER... daughter SYLYIA H. SEAY and her husband REUBEN F. SEAY... friends ROBERT PATTERSON, JAMES T. BOTHWELL, and son in law THOMAS J. PHILCHER, and son JOHN W. BRINSON, Exr... MOSES BRINSON. Wit: JOHN GAY, CALEB W. YOUNG, GEORGE W. FARMER. Codicil: JOHN W. BRINSON guardian for EBENEZER B. BRINSON... either ROBERT PATTERSON or MITCHEL BROWN guardian for my youngest daughter SARAH BRINSON... as I do not know whether my wife will remain or return to Houston County... plantation where I now live, 1400 acres adj. J. T. JORDAN, J. T. WAY and others... FLOURNOY tract, adj. ABLE RUSSEL, LAVINA ANDERSON and to her... tract where JESSE JOHNSON now lives, adj. JOHN FREEMAN... one lot in Wilkerson County.

Page 406: Will of ANDREW MCDERMOTT. Made Oct. 24, 1859... to OWEN MCDERMOTT, husband of BRIDGETT MCDERMOTT... should she die before her youngest child arrives at the age of 21... friends JAMES P. GOBER, Dr. EDWARD W. HUNTER and LINDSEY C. WARREN Exrs... A. MCDERMOTT. Wit: JAMES P. GOBERT, E. H. W. HUNTER, L. C. WARREN. (No probate date.)

Page 407: Will of GERALDINE E. JOHNSON. Made Sept. 14, 1859, probated Nov. 23, 1859... Bibb County, State of Georgia... Whereas by the L. W. & T. of my father LARKIN GRIFFIN, I am impowered to make a Will, in the event of my death without children... now on a visit to my friend in Macon... to my husband BURRET R. JOHNSON... GERLADINE E. JOHNSON. Wit: GEO M. LOGAN, L. N. WHITTLE, PETER SOLOMON.

Pages 408-410: Will of JOHN FREEMAN. Made Feb. 7, 1857, probated Jan. 9, 1860... having arrived at an advanced age... wife ANNA FREEMAN son ISAAC FREEMAN... son MOSES FREEMAN... grandchildren, children of my daughter NANCY JOHNSON... son in law JESSE JOHNSON... friend MOSES BRINSON and son ISAAC FREEMAN, Exrs... JOHN FREEMAN (L.S.). Wit: JOSHUA T. JORDAN, ETHELDRED A. WASDEN, JOHN W. BRINSON. Codicil: granddaughter GEORGANNA FREEMAN, dau. of MOSES FREEMAN... son MOSES BRINSON having died... friend HENRY FARMER, Exr. of this codicil, dated Nov. 8, 1859... Wit: JAMES W. CLARK, CHARLES MATTHEW, ISAAC F. ADKINS.

Pages 410-411: Will of A. B. L. Fleming. Made April 27, 1860, probated June 3, 1860... sister SARAH E. FLEMING... brother W. W. FLEMING... brother JOHN FLEMING... brother SAMUEL FLEMING... A. B. L. FLEMING. Wit: W. P. WHIGHAM, W. C. POLAND, R. L. GAMBLE.

Pages 411-413: Will of JOSEPH PRICE. Made Dec. 15, 1856, probated May 7, 1860 wife ELITIA PRICE... children of JOHN VINING, dec'd. who was the husband of my daughter HEPHEZIBAH VINING, also deceased... granddaughter HEPHIZIAH T. VINING (now LOGUE)... my daughter REBECCA HADDEN, deceased, her two children JOSEPH T. and ELITEA R. HADDEN... son in law SAMUEL HADDON, husband of sd. daughter REBECCA... daughter HANNA HADDEN.. son JOSEPH PRICE... son JOSHUA R. PRICE... daughter JUDY WISE... land adj. WILLIAM WILCHER, BENJAMIN COXWELL and others... JOSEPH PRICE. Wit: JAS CAIN, NOAH B. COVINGTON, G. F. HUDSON.

Pages 413-415: Will of INDIA G. PARKER. Made Sept. 25, 1860, probated Nov. 5, 1860... in body of Will INDIANA G. PARKER, being of advanced age... daughter SARAH ELIZABETH GROSS... son JOHN T. GROSS... son AUGUSTUS B. GROSS... son in law BENJAMIN F. FLEMING... friend DAVID E. HODO... INDIANA G. PARKER. Wit: RHESA BOSTICK, JOHN B. WATKINS, ELISHA S. MALLONY.

Pages 415-417: Will of SAMUEL FLEMING. Made Sept. 6, 1858, probated Oct. 1, 1860... advanced in years... son WILLIAM FLEMING... my daughter MARY ANN GREEN... wife ELVIRA FLEMING... son OLIVER... son ALIRD... son BENJAMIN F.... children ALLEN, MARTHA FLEMING and my grandson JAMES G. FLEMING (son of JAMES FLEMING, deceased)... SAMUEL FLEMING. Wit: E. H. W. HUNTER, I. R. POWELL, JAMES J. BROWN, J. J. Ct.

Pages 417-419: Will of SILAS HERINGDINE. Made Jan. 15, 1849, probated July Term... exclude my son JAMES WILLIAM HERRINGDINE... each of my female children... wife... to SILAS SMITHART HERRINGDINE, Exr... SILAS HERRINDGDINE. Wit: THOMAS M. TURNER, HENRY ROGERS, L. S. STEWART. CAVEAT! .. JAMES W. HERRINGDINE, an heir of sd. SILAS... at time of said Will the said SILAS HERINGDINE was not of sound mind and disposing memory and was unduly influenced... (This will was headed Hancock County.)

Pages 419-420: Will of ROGER L. WHIGHAM. Made Oct. 27, 1860, probated Dec. 3, 1860... brothers FRANKLIN WHIGHAM and WILLIAM WHIGHAM... ROGER L. WHIGHAM (L.S.). Wit: JAMES J. BROWN, WILLIAM T. WHIGHAM, JAMES G. CAIN.

Pages 420-421: Will of RHODA JORDAN. Made May 16, 1861, no probate date... children JOHN G. JORDAN, ROBERT JORDAN, SUSANNAH JORDAN, LEVICY JORDAN, and MARY B. JORDAN... daughter EMILY MILLER... daughter ELIZA-BETH T. MURPHY... RHODA JORDAN (LS). Wit: JAMES G. CAIN, GURDON I. MILLER, WM. I. ARRINGTON.

Pages 421-423: Will of JOHN W. LEFAVER. ... being advanced in life.. made Apr. 27, 1859, probated Oct. 9, 1861... daughter MARTHA (GERVIS, GROSS?)... sons WILLIAM... daughter MARGARET VOSS... daughter RUTHA WILLIAMS... friend JAMES HAMAR, Exr... wife SARAH... daughter SARAH, deceased... JOHN W. LAFAVOR. Wit: THOMAS J. HARVEY, SIMEON WILLIAMS, MITCHEL WALDEN.

Pages 423-424: Will of ANN DANIEL. Made Oct. 16, 1861, no probate date... to ROBERT NICHOLAS DONAVAN, son of my step daughter NANCY C. DONAVAN... a watch formerly the property of his grandfather JAMES D. DANIEL... to my sister MARIA HARDON... to my brother JOHN PERRY... to my niece CHARY BRANTLY TARVER... sister in law MARY DANIEL, wife of my brother in law ROBERT W. DANIEL... to MARIA CELESTIN DONAVAN, daughter of NANCY C. DONAVAN... ANN DANIEL. Wit: L. A. TARVER, C. S. WISE, ELI MCCROVAN.

Pages 424-426: Will of WILLIAM J. R. CARSWELL. Made March 3, 1862, no probated date... wife SARAH ANN and daughter EMILY ADELINE, lot in town of Louisville... nephew WILLIAM JOHN DOUGLAS, son of WILLIAM H. DOUGLAS and my deceased sister ELIZABETH A. DOUGLAS... a claim against the estate of Mrs. SARAH J. MOORE... WILLIAM J. R. CARSWELL. Wit: JAMES A. DENNY, SM. B. SIKES, JAS. J. BROWN, J. J. Ct.

Pages 426-427: Will of MOSES FREEMAN. Made June 15, 1861, probated Jan. 13, 1862... daughter GEORGE A. FREEMAN... wife LUNA A. FREEMAN... brother ISAAC F. FREEMAN, Exr... MOSES FREEMAN (L.S.). Wit: SYDNEY B. SWAN, W. S. WREN, B. F. TAYLOR.

Pages 427-428: Will of OSBORN WALDEN. Made Sept. 7, 1861, probated Jan. 14, 1862... being of advanced age... nephew THOMAS M. WALDEN, my watch when he reaches age of 21... law suit I have in Marietta, Cobb County, Ga... sisters LARENA & EMILY WALDEN and my brother IRA WALDEN... OSBORN WALDEN. Wit: WILLIAM G. LYON, PLEASANT WALDEN, JOB R. HUNTER.

Pages 429-430: Will of A. B. GROSS. Made Dec. 23, 1861, probated Feb. 3, 1862... AUSTIN B. GROSS... sister SARAH F. GROSS... brother JOHN T. GROSS... sister MARY A. FLEMING, wife of BENJAMIN FLEMING... A. B. GROSS (L.S.). Wit: RHESA BOSTICK, HARVY P. WATKINS, T. W. MOSELEY.

Pages 430-431: Will of WILLIAM BOYD. Made March 14, 1862, no probate date... about to enter the service of my beloved county in the Army of

the Confederate States... my share in the firm of BOTHWELL & BOYD...
sister SARAH E. BOYD... brother SAMUEL BOYD... brother ROBERT J. BOYD...
half sister JACUTHA? CAROLINE... half sister SOPHRONIA WRIGHT BOYD...
friend and kinsman WILLIAM D. STONE Exr... Mrs. RUTH W. BOYD's house...
WM. BOYD (L.S.). Wit: SAMUEL A. DENNY, W. B. SIKES, JAS. J. BROWN,
J. J. Ct.

Page 432:   Will of R. C. ROBBINS.   Made May 14, 1862, no probate
date... ROBERT C. ROBBINS... mother Mrs. SUSAN A. ROBBINS... friend
LINDSAY C. WARREN, Exr... R. C. ROBBINS. Wit: WM. W. HOLT, NICHOLAS
DIEHL, W. B. SIKES.

Pages 433-434:   Nuncupative Will of JOHN SHEPPARD.   Made May 19, 1862,
probated July 30, 1862... taken by ROBERT W. HOLES & HENRY WALDEN... wife
MARTHA... son HENRY SHEPPARD, KINABREW place... four daughters AMANDA
G., NANCY E., SUSAN R., & SARAH J. SHEPPARD... made about 14 days before
his death.

Pages 434-435:   Will of LOUCIOUS Q. C. D. HANNAH.   Made August 6,
1862, no probate date... wife and children (not named)... to PLEASANT
WALDEN in trust for wife... L. Q. C. D. HANNAH. Wit: ALONZA J. HOLMES
JP, WILLIAM HANNAH, WM. R. THOMPSON.

Pages 435-436:   Will of JOHN F. SPEIR.   Made June 14, 1861, probated
Oct. 6, 1862... my sister ELMINA E. SPEIR... sister SARAH M. DONAVAN,
wife of WILLIAM DONAVAN... friend ALLEN W. TARVER... brother WILLIAM A.
SPEIR... friend SPENCER G. SPIVEY, Exr. JOHN F. SPEIR. Wit: Z. Z.
BOSTICK, JAMES STRATFORD, WILLIAM A. WILKINS.

Pages 437-438:   Will of ROBERT JORDAN.   Made June 19, 1861, probated
Oct. Term, 1862... sister EMILY MILLER... to ELIZABETH MURPHREE...
nephew ROBERT MURPHREE... my other sister SUSAN JORDAN, LEVICY JORDAN &
MARY R. JORDAN and my brother JOHN G. JORDAN... ROBERT JORDAN L.S.,
Wit: F. A. SINQUEFIELD, SAMUEL A. DENNY, WILLIAM A. WILKINS.

Page 438:   Will of COUNSEL D. WISE.   Made Oct. 15, 1862, no probate
date... mother SARAH WISE... uncle ROBERT W. DANIEL, Exr... COUNSEL D.
WISE (L.S.). Wit: A. J. LOCKHART, BRYANT BEESLEY, E. MCROAN.

Pages 439-440:   Will of EDWARD R. CARSWELL.   Made Nov. 25, 1862, no
probate date... daughter CORNELIA E. CARSWELL, my piano... son REUBEN W.
CARSWELL... daughter MARY E. LESTER... mother of my beloved wife Mrs.
MARTHA WALKER... and aunt of my beloved wife Miss REBECCA WALKER... my
deceased daughter ELLA M. PITTS, on her marriage with JAMES H. PITTS...
daughter MARTHA R. HUDSON, wife of JAMES C. HUDSON... MARY E. LESTER,
widow and ROBERT C. LESTER... uncle WILLIAM J. RHODES... E. R. CARSWELL
(L.S.). Wit: JAMES A. FLEMING (L.S.), A. I. DAVID (L.S.), JAS. W.
CARSWELL (L.S.)

Pages 441-442:   Will of LIDIA BECTON.   Made April 21, 1855, probated
Jan. 12, 1863... sons ROBERT STEPHENS and JONAS STEPHENS, land adj.
H. P. WATKINS, Dr. HUNTER and others... to WILLIAM STEPHENS, one dollar..
sons JONAS, ROBERT STEPHNS & CURREM BECTON... friends HENRY P. WATKINS
and JAMES T. BOTHWELL, Exrs... LYDIA BECTON (X). Wit: JAMES M. CROSS,
NATHAN STEVENS, THOMAS H. POLHILL.

Pages 442-443:   Will of JAMES DENTON.   Made March 11, 1862, probated
March Term, 1863... wife ADALINE DENTON... my children (not named)...
THOS I. HAMMETT, THOS STAPLETON, Exrs... JAMES DENTON. Wit: KENDOL
MCTYEIR, MOSES DENTON, LOUIS RABUN (X).

Pages 444-445:   Will of WM. A. SPEIR.   Made Jan. 13, 1863, probated
June 1, 1863... I desire that the body of my brother JOHN F. SPEIR be
brought home... each of the children of my sister SARAH M. DONOVAN...
nephew WILLIAM R. ROBERSON... to Laurence Lodge of Free Mason at Betheny..
to Miss AUGUSTA BELEE COFFIN... ANDREW E. TARVEF, Exr. WM. A. SPEIR.
Wit: WILLIAM A. PRITCHARD, M. A. WELKILIH, J. S. SPEIR.

Pages 445-446: Will of SHERWOOD ALLEN. Made August 1863, no probate date... wife (not named)... son W. H. ALLEN... son RICHMOND, son WARREN.. to NANCY E. BIGHAM, wife of JAMES A. BIGHAM... land in Montgomery County, 550 acres... to lots in Louisville, #18 & #19... no signature... Wit: ROBERT P. LITTLE, MITCHELL WALDEN, ROBERT SAMPLES.

Pages 446-447: Will of ROBERT ROBERSON. Made Sept. 5, 1863, probated Oct. 5, 1863... to son CARLOS D. ROBERSON, note on JAS. J. BROWN & ELIZABETH BROWN... wife ELIZA ANN ... friend EDWARD H. W. HUNTER, Exr. ROBERT ROBERSON. Wit: R. R. DIXON, J. J. BROWN J. J. Ct., NICHOLAS DIEHL.

Page 448: Will of R. G. WEEKS. Probated Dec. 7, 1863, not copied... Wit: STERLING G. JORDAN, GEORGE R. PALMER & THOMAS G. JORDAN.

Pages 449-450: Will of SHERROD ALLEN. Made Aug. 31, 1863, probated Dec. 7, 1863... to my wife... same as on Pages 445-446.

Pages 450-451: Will of THOMAS WALSH. Made June 18, 1861, probated Dec. 15, 1863... to father JAS. WALSH of County of Silgo, Ireland... mother ANN WALSH of Co. of Silgo, Ireland... brother JOHN of same... brother MARTIN of same... brother MATHEW of same... brother LUKE of same... brother MICHAEL of same... sister BRIDGET WALSH, now LONDY of same... and other children born if any... friends THOS. D. KEY, JESSE BEALL, Exrs... THOS. WALSH. Wit: JOHN M. ROBERTS, PETER MCGOWAN, JAS. J. BROWN J.P.

Pages 452-453: Will of WILLIAM WEEKS. Made August 13, 1860, probated Feb. 1, 1864... of County of Richmond... wife NANCY WEEKS... land on Big Brier Creek, 115 acres, adj. MARCUS J. EVANS, ELI STEART & JAMES PATTERSON... four children MARY ARRINGTON, MISSOURI LANDON, WILLIAM WEEKS, BENJAMIN WEEKS... daughter MARTHA PARKER... grandson RUFUS WEEKS.. Exrs, friend JAMES CAWLEY... WILLIAM WEEKS (X). Wit: JAS MCNAIR, ZECHARIAH ATKINSON, AVERY ATKINSON.

Pages 453-454: Will of HENRY WALDER. Made March 8, 1854, no probate date... wife MINERVA WALDEN... youngest son WILLIAM WALDEN... land known as JOHN WALDEN... to LINNEY ANN ELIZABETH MCCOY... divided between son PLEASANT WALDEN, QUILLA SAMMONS, wife of BENJAMIN SAMMONS, and son WILLIAM... HENRY WALDEN (X). Wit: B. S. CARSWELL, W. B. SIKES, G. T. MILLER.

Pages 454-455: Will of BENJAMIN F. TAYLOR. Made April 9, 1864, no probate date... wife NANCY TAYLOR... with whom I have lived for 10 years, 500 acres adj. CARSON, W. WREN and others... 5 children ABSALOM, ALICE, BENJAMIN, FRANKLIN, SARAH LEWELLEN, FRANCIS... eldest son ABSALOM, when he reaches 21... friends L. N. OLIPLANT, and JOHN S. WILSON, Exrs... B. F. TAYLOR (L.S.). Wit: NOAH S. TARVER, S. B. TEMPLETON, E. C. TARVER, J. A. FLEMING.

Pages 456-457: Will of GEORGE W. BELCHER. Made Aug. 17, 1864, no probate date... Fulton County, State of Georgia... sons GEORGE & WILLIAM... wife and children, when my son WILLIAM shall arrive at 21... friends JOHN G. JORDAN and WILLIAM A. STOKES, Exr... J. W. BELCHER. Wit: W. R. MILLER, R. M. LAWSON, SHERWOOD ARRINGTON, J. P. Ct.

Pages 457-458: Will of JOHN KELLY. Made Aug. 28, 1864, probated Oct. 3, 1864... wife MARY A. KELLY and minor children... son CHARLES KELLY, Exr... JOHN N. KELLY. Wit: R. A. GARVIN, OLIN MCDERMOTT, NICHOLAS DIEHL.

Pages 458-460: Will of JAS. S. SPEIR. Made July 16, 1864, probated Nov. 7, 1864... wife NANCY ANN... all my children, namely, JAMES, AUGUSTUS, SPENCER, LEISTTENTON, JOHN, CALDWELL, LENLER, ANN, WILLIAM, MONTGOMERY & ELIZABETH ELMINA (not punctuated in Will... later mentions his 6 children... son JAMES AUGUSTUS and wife NANCY ANN Exrs... J. S. SPEIR. Wit: R. W. DANIEL, M. MURPHY, WINFIELD M. RIVER, W. J. GREEN.

Pages 459-460:   Will of ARTHUR R. CHEATHAM.   Made Aug. 29, 1864,
probated Jan. 9, 1865... wife (not named)... son LEWIS... daughter in
law ELIZABETH wife of son ELI F. CHEATHAM... grandson EDWIN JUDSON BURCH,
son of WM. BURCH... daughter CAROLINE MALLORY, share to son in law
EZEKIEL T. MALLORY... sons ARTHUR R. & JOHN W. CHEATHAM, Exrs... A. R.
CHEATHAM (L.S.). Wit: JOHN R. COOK, ANDREW J. COOK, B. A. MOYE.

Pages 461-462:   Will of ABEL RUSSELL.   Made Dec. 24, 1858, probated
Oct. 29, 1874... being of advanced age... son JOHN, 200 acres... to
CHARLES 500 acres where he now lives... POWELL Line... to daughter MARY
MCGAHEE, wife of ANDREW JACKSON MCGAHEE... daughter CATHERINE NORTON,
wife of ANDREW J. NORTON... wife ELIZABETH... son MOSES, 500 acres where
I now reside... son CHARLES RUSSELL... ABEL RUSSEL (L.S.). Wit: V. A.
HATCHER, WILLIS HOWARD, JR., BASTEN R. BASTON, WILLIAM GAY.

Pages 462-464:   Will of MARY PERDUE.,   Made Nov. 17, 1858, codicil made
Feb. 21, 1871, probated Aug. 6, 1873 and Sept. 1, 1873... daughters
ARTIMUS M. HUDSON and NARCISSA N. CASON... children MARY V. PERDUE, wife
of JAMES PERDUE, ROBERT W. PERDUE, ARTIRNIS M. HUDSON, wife of ALFRED S.
HUDSON & NARCISSA N. CASON, wife of JAMES M. CASON... sons JAMES M. and
ROBERT PERDUE, Exrs... MARY PERDUE (X) (L.S.). Wit: FREEMAN A. ARRING-
TON, WILLIAM G. GRIFFIN, THOMAS N. POLHILL, JAMES G. CAIN. Wit: to
codicil: J. W. BRINSON, MICHAEL KING, JOSHUA R. JORDAN.

JEFFERSON COUNTY, GA. WILLS

1796 - 1827 Books 1 & 3

Page 1: Appraisement of Estate of EDWARD PALMER, dec'd. Appraisers: JOHN BOSTICK, ISAAC RAWLS, PETER CHASTAIN. Returned October 24, 1796, by ELIZABETH PALMER, Administratrix. Total Value 15/82/1/2.

Pages 2-3: Appraisement of Estate of JOHN COHOON, dec'd. Total Value 298/62/1/2. Appraisers: JOHN BRYAND, M. RAIFORD & ELIJAH PAGETT. Returned January 26, 1797 by MARY COHOON, Administratrix.

Pages 4-5: Last Will & Testament of SAMUEL MCNEELEY, dec'd. SAMUEL MCNEELEY of County of Jefferson, gives to dearly beloeved mother MARGARET MCNEELEY whom he ordains his Extx., and leaves his cards, messages and testaments, together with all his other property, disallows and revokes any other Wills, Testaments, etc. by him before made. Written: 15 Nov. 1796. Signed: SAMUEL MCNEELEY. Wit: WM. DANIEL, MARGARET MCNEELEY.

Page 6: Probate of Will of SAMUEL MCNEELEY bef. ISAAC COLEMAN, Reg. of Probate for Jefferson County on April 11, 1797. WILLIAM DANIEL, qualified as Witness.

Page 7: Inventory of Estate of SAMUEL MCNEELEY, dated July 13, 1797. Value: 485/621/2 Appraisers: WILLIAM BARRON, HUGH ALEXANDER, WILLIAM HADDEN, GEORGE INGRAM. Returned by MARGARET MCNEELEY.

Pages 8-10: Register of Probate Office, 8 June 1796. Appointed this day JESSE WOMACK and made application for Letters of Admn. on Estate of ROBERT COOPER, dec'd. Citation gtd. in due form. JOHN GIBSON on 21st. same month appears bef. me and objected to giving of Letters to sd. WOMACK, alledging that he the said GIBSON with SARAH COOPPER the dau. of afsd. ROBERT COOPER had been previously appt'd and still were the Admnrs. of all goods, etc., of ROBERT COOPPER dec'd. and show the same for cause why Letters of Admn. should not be gtd. to JESSE WOMACK. And at same time lodged in my office an Inv. and Appraisement of sd. Est. taken and made in presence of the Adma. Page 9, Granted to show as afsd. (and this controversy was sent to the Superior Court for final determination. Dated 10 March 1797, ISC. COLEMAN, R.P.

Page 9: Evidence in Sup. Ct. awarded Admn. to JOHN GIBSON if he appears in the Court within 60 days and if not, then Admn. may be gtd. to any competent person who may apply for same. Signed: W. FEW. JOHN GIBSON came and received Letters of Admn.

Page 10: Inventory & Appraisement of Est. of ROBERT COOPER, dec'd., Dec. 5, 1783, 55/16/4. Appraised by: MATTHEW MARSHAL, JOHN PIERCE, JOHN BREANK. Returned by JOHN GIBSON, Adm'tor. 5 June 1797.

Page 11: Last Will & Testament of THOMAS ALEXANDER, dec'd. Signed 16 Nov. 1770. "I THOMAS ALEXANDER, weak of body but of perfect mind & memory, make, ordain & app't. in my stead my wife MARTHA, JOHN WOOD, Senr. & HUGH ALEXANDER to act and do for my wife and child as if I were bodily present, i.e., debts to be paid; 2nd I leave to my wife MARTHA ALEXANDER one house, sadle; 3rd I leave to my son DAVID all my land and if it should please God to ad one more to my family as it is in vue, then my cattle to be equally divided bet. these three or whatever of them comes to the years of munwrity and further saith not..." Signed: THOMAS ALEXANDER. Wit: JAMES BROOKERIDGE, VINSON CARTER, JESSE (-) CERO.

Page 12: Personally appeared bef. me JESSE CARO and saith he saw THOMAS ALEXANDER assign the within Instrument of writing as his Last Will & Testament. Sworn 4 Sept. 1797, bef. ISC. COLEMAN, R.P. Signed: JESSE (-) CARO.

Page 12: WILLIAM MCDOWELL, Reg. of Probate. The whole of the Estate of THOMAS ALEXANDER appraised to the above amount: $146.00. Appraisers: JOSEPH CHAIRS, ROBT. DONALDSON, JOHN MARSHALL. Returned 4 Dec. 1797.

Pages 13-14: By WILLIAM MCDOWELL, Reg. of Pro. of Jefferson County, "Whereas JACOB TOWNSHEND late of this State, dec'd. lately died Intestate having while he lived and at time of his death divers goods, chattels, rights and credits within this State of Ga., I desiring that the goods, chattels, rights, etc. of sd. dec'd. may be well and truly administered, converted and disposed of do hereby grant unto ABNER HAMMOND in whose Fidelity in his Behalf, I do very much confide full power and authority, by these presents to Admnr. the goods, of sd. dec'd. stood obliged, to make a true Inventory, thereof and exhibit the same unto Reg. of Pro. to be recorded." ABNER HAMMOND constituted Admnr. of sd. dec'd. 20 Feb. 1798.

Page 15: WILLIAM MCDOWELL, Reg. of Pro. for Jefferson Co., directs Appraisement and Inv. be made and reported to sd. Admnr. on or bef. 20 May next ensuing this date.

Page 16: Warrant of Appraisement of Est. of JACOB TOWNSHEND del. to ABNER HAMMOND, Admnr. of Est. was ret. by him no property to be found and another warrant issued 7 June 1798. WILLIAM MCDOWELL, R.P., J.C.

Page 18: New Appraisement directed on 2 Jan. 1798 and above ret. and no property found this 7 June 1798.

Page 19: WILLIAM MCDOWELL, Reg. of Pro. "Whereas RICHARD ROWELL of this State dec'd. lately died Intestate with goods, chattels, etc., sd. MCDOWELL requested full accounting of Est. and for such to be converted and disposed grants to GEORGE TARVER full power to administer all goods of the estate and to pay debts and to make a true Inv. of same and exhibit in Reg. of Pro. Office to be recorded bef. 22 May next ensuing. Dated 22 Feb. 1798.

Pages 22-23: By ISAAC COLEMAN, Reg. of Pro. of Jefferson County. To ABNER HAMMONDS, administrator, whereas STEPHEN SULLIVAN of Jefferson County late of this State, dec'd. lately died Intestate having goods, etc. within the State, Power of Admn. is gtd. for audit and for admn. do grant unto ABNER HAMMOND the Power of Administrator. HAMMOND to make Inv. to be filed in Reg. of Pro. Office to be Rec. bef. 2 Jan.next ensuing. Dated 2 Oct. 1797. ISAAC COLEMAN.

Pages 26-27: By WILLIAM MCDOWELL, Reg. of Pro. of Jefferson Co., "Whereas JAMES NESSELS late of this state dec'd. died Intestate, was possessed of goods, etc. Power to be Administrator of Est. gtd. to MATTHIAS DALTON to pay all debts... make Inv. and be Rec. bef. 24 June next ensuing. Dated 24 March 1798.

Page 28: By WILLIAM MCDOWELL, Reg. of Pro., directs Appraisement be made and Del. to MATTHIAS DALTON bef. 24 Juen next. Dated 24 March 1798.

Pages 30-31: Will of DAVID MCGOWAN of Jefferson County "... weak in body... devise and dispose of such worldly estate God has blessed me with in the following manner: First - to beloved wife ELIZABETH 5 shillings sterling, Daughter, MARY, and my son, JOHN, all the cattle now in their names. Likewise to my son, WILLIAM, the 2 cows and their increase that are at DANIEL WARDS and out of the rest of my moveable Est. that my son WILLIAM first of all shall have 6 months schooling, likewise I give and beq. to my 3 children , all the rest of my Est. both lands and chattels to be divided share and share alike." App'ts. as Exors: JOHN FOGIL, JOHN ROGERS & HENRY MCCONKY. Signed: DAVID MCGOWAN. Wit: JOHN ALLEN, JOHN ROGERS, JOHN FOGIL. Subscribed 3 March 1798 by JOHN FOGIL and JOHN ROGERS.

Page 35: 3 March 1798, Last Will & Testament of DAVID MCGOWAN was proved.

Page 36:   By ISAAC COLEMAN, Reg. of Pro. Jefferson Co., 4 Sept. 1797,
Last Will and Testament of THOMAS ALEXANDER late of Jefferson Co. was
proved.

Page 37:   ISAAC COLEMAN, Reg. of Pro.   "These are to authorise and
empower you three whose names are underwith to repair to all such parts
and places within this state as you shall be directed thence unto by
MARTHA YEATON, Executrix of the Est. of THOMAS ALEXANDER late of this
County dec'd. ... and to make Appraisal of any goods MARTHA YEATON shall
show you, on or bef. Dec. 4 next." Dated Sept. 14, 1798.

Pages 38-39:   ISAAC COLEMAN, Reg. of Pro. of Jefferson County.   "To
HORATION MARBURY Admnr. Whereas ROBERT SAMPSON of sd. county, late of
this state dec'd. lately died Intestate," he is directed to be Admnr.
of all Est. pay all debts, make Inv. and exhibit same in Reg. of Pro.
Office to be Rec. bef. 15 March next ensuing. Dated 15 December 1796.

Page 40:   Appraisal of Estate of ROBERT SAMPSON directed to be made
bef. 15 March next, Dated 15 Dec. 1796.

Page 42:   WILLIAM MCDOWALL, Reg. of Pro., directs any 3 or the 4
appraisers to go whereever in State the Exors. of Est. of DAVID MCGOWAN
may direct. Dated Aug. 4, 1796.

Page 45:   WILLIAM MCDOWALL, Reg. of Pro., directs Appraisers to go
whereever ABNER HAMMOND, Exor. of Est. of STEPHEN SULLIVAN may direct
and ret. same bef. 7 Sept. 1798. Dated June 7, 1798.

Page 48:   WILLIAM MCDOWALL, Reg. of Pro. directs App's of Est. of JACOB
TOWNSHEND may be directed to go by ABNER HAMMOND and ret. same bef. 7
Sept. 1798.

Page 50:   Memorandum - "of the Est. and Effects of RICHARD ROWALL,
late of State dec'd. to 8 months and 18 days service done under Command
of Lt. GEORGE TARVER.
                            $57 - 27¢
"We are of opinion that the above claim is with the sum of $40. Wit:
30 April 1798, Signed: ISOM (Y) ROSS, JAMES HARVEY, JONATHAN MATTHEWS.

Page 51:   The Estate of THOMAS ALEXANDER to MARTHA YEATON. Maintainence
and schooling of one child 17 years at $30 per year - $510; Maint. and
schooling of other child 5 years at $30 per year - $150; expences
attending the admn. and taxes paid - $30. Dated 26 May 1798, HORATIO
MARBURY, J.P.

Page 52:   WILLIAM MCDOWALL, Reg. of Pro., directs Appraisers of Est.
of DAVID MCGOWAN to continue appraisal under direction of JOHN FOGIL,
JOHN ROGERS & HENRY MCCONKEY to be Rec. bef. 3 Nov. 1798. Dated 3 Aug.
1798.

Pages 53-55:   Inventory on Est. of DAVID MCGOWAN ret. appraisal req.
bef. 3 Nov. 1798, they were THOMAS FELTON, ROBERT FLEMMING and WILLIAM
KENNEDY. Pages 54-55: Estate was appraised at $405.00.

Pages 56-57:   WILLIAM MCDOWALL, Keeper of the Rec. at Court of Ordinary,
Jefferson Co. "Whereas ABNER BLACKMAN of state dec'd, lately died
Intestate", appt's. with consent of the Inferior Court grants STEPHEN
BLACKMAN as sole Admr. of Estate. Wit: The Hon. MICHAEL SHELMAN one of
the Judges of our Inf. Ct. for Jefferson County. Dated 27 Aug. 1798.

Page 58:   Will of JOSEPH BEATTY of Jefferson County, "weak of body...
do this 12 Nov. 1796... make and put my Last Will and Testament... I
give to my son in law JAMES WILSON, 100 acres to be taken off So. side
of tract where I now live, give to daughter, JAN BEATTY, 100 acres next
adj. afsd. being part of same tract, also I give unto my son, SAMUEL
BEATTY, 150 acres for and during his natural life and after his decease
I devise same to my son WILLIAM BEATTY and his heirs forever. Also, I

give to my son WILLIAM BEATTY all the remainder of same tract being 150 acres, also I give my son in law JAMES NORTON 5 shillings and the remainder of the land and all my stock of cattle to be equally divided (by the Exors of my L.A.&T.) bet. my sons SAMUEL & WILLIAM BEATTY and my daughter JAN BEATTY and I make my son WILLIAM BEATTY & BENJAMIN WHITAKER, Exors. Signed JOSEPH BEATTY. Wit: MATTHEW CASWELL, JOHN WILSON, JAMES WARNOCK. Sub. & sworn to in Open Ct., MATHEW CASWELL, Rec. 12 Dec. 1798.

Page 61:   Estate of ROBERT COOPER, dec'd. by JOHN GIBSON, cash paid following persons: MRS. RANDALSON, JAMES BLACK, MARGARET MCNEELEY, SAM CLEMENTS, ROGER LAWSON. Total paid on all items: 77 - 10 - 2.
        JOHN GIBSON states Est. of ROBERT COOPER indebted to him for sum fo 77 lbs., 10 shillings and two pence. Sworn 14 Dec. 1798. Signed: JOHN GIBSON. Wit: HORATIO MARBURY.

Page 62:   JOHN GIBSON dismissed as Admnr. of Est. 14 Jan. 1799 by WILLIAM MCDOWALL, KRCO.

Page 63:   December 12, 1798. Will of JOSEPH BEATTY, dec'd. was proved.

Page 65:   Will of MARY SMITH of Lincoln County, Georgia. Dated 10 Jan. 1799. "being sick and weak but of sound mind, make this my L. W. & T., Imprimis, I give and beq. to beloved nephew WILLIAM LEWIS CLEMENTS and his heirs all my right and title in a tract of land situate and being on Rappahannock River, Virginia, Richmond County, known by the name of The Folly, also all my right and title to another tract adj. The Folly, SAMFFORDS, further it is my will and desire that my Exor. if he thinks proper may sell the above land and apply the money arising from sale to the benefit of my nephew WILLIAM LEWIS CLEMENTS. Item, I give and beq. to nephew JOHN SMITH CLEMENTS and my niece MARY CLEMENTS all the right, title and interest which I have in Negroes and personal Est. which my mother has in her possession at present which she has a life Estate in, equally divided bet. my nephew and neice JOHN & MARY CLEMENTS. Exor: my friend WILLIAM CLEMENTS. Signed: MARY SMITH. Wit: JOHN PUGESLY, LUCY PUGESLY, ANN (X) BUTLER. Sub. 15 April 1799, WILLIAM MCDOWALL, C.C.O

Page 67:   WILLIAM MCDOWALL, C.C.O. "Whereas JONATHAN PAULK late of County, dec'd. died Intestate, Inf. Court appt's. ELIZABETH PAULK to admn. Est. and make Inv. and Appraisement to be Rec. bef. 2 July 1799. Dated 2 April 1799.

Page 69:   WILLIAM MCDOWALL, directs Appraisement to be made under direction of ELIZABETH PAULK bef. 2 July 1799. Dated 2 April 1799.

Page 70:   ABSALOM COURSEY, EZEKIEL ALKRIDGE sworn to do true Appraisers, they swear bef. DANIL CANNEL, J.P. 18 May 1799.

Page 71:   Items of the Real and Personal Estate of JONATHAN PAULK, dec'd. valued at $257.30 were valued at the house on 18 May 1799 by ABSALOM COURSEY, EZEKIEL ALKRIDGE & DAN'L CANNEL. Dated 19 June 1799.

Page 73:   Inferior Court, July Term 1799 - July 19, 1799
        Present The Honorable MICHAEL SHELMAN, THACKER VIVIAN, DOUGLAS HANCOCK, Esq's.

        MARY PRINCE, Applicant)
            the Estate of   )   Administration
        SYLVANUS PRINCE, dec'd)
                Vs.
        GEORGE PRINCE   )   Caveator

        Court appointed MARY PRINCE as Admnx. of Est. of SYLVANUS
            PRINCE
            Granted
        MOSES NEWTON   )
            &   )   Securities
        HEZEKIAH GATES   )

Page 74: WILLIAM MCDOWALL, Applicant for Letters of Admn. on Est. of JOHN MURRAY, dec'd.

****

SAMUEL ANDREWS, Applicant for Letters of Admn. Est. of ROBERT SPENCE, dec'd.
Granted
THOMAS WHITEHEAD) Securities
JOSEPH CHEARS)

****

MARY SUMMERLIN, Applicant for Letters of Admn. on Est. of OWEN SUMMERLIN, dec'd.
Granted
THOMAS TINSLEY)
EPHRIAM CHANCE) Securities

Page 75: RICHARD ROWELL and MARTHA ROWELL, Applicants for Letters of Admn. on Estate of ELIJAH GROUT, dec'd.
Granted
WILLIAM INGRAM)
JOHN EVERS) Securities

****

LEVI SMITH, Applicant for Letters of Admn. on Est. of JAMES U. SIMMONS, dec'd and a Caveat entered by THOMAS SIMMONS
Ordered
That the Caveat be sustained and the Admn. be gtd.
THOMAS SIMMONS

Page 76: HUGH ALEXANDER)
Vs.) For Letter Dismissing
MARTHA YEATON)
Admnx. of
THOMAS ALEXANDER, dec'd.

The defendant came into Open Court and Ack. that HUGH ALEXANDER, Exor. of Est. of THOMAS ALEXANDER, dec'd. should be finally discharged.
12 July 1799   MARTHA YEATON

****

WILLIAM SETTLE this day applied for Letters of Admn. on Est. of WILLIAM JUNKIN, dec'd. August 7, 1799.

Page 77: Court of the Ordinary, February 4, 1800
Present: The Honorable RICHARD G. GRAY, DOUGLAS HANCOCK, MICHAEL SHELMAN

WILLIAM STEPHENS, Exor. of L. W. & T. of CHARLES WATSON & JOHN TEBEAU, principal devisee of same
Vs.
CHURLEY BOSTICK
Continued

****

MARY STEVENS & NATHAN POWELL
Vs.
WILLIAM STEVENS, dec'd.
Granted

JOSEPH MARSHALL on the Est. of JOSEPH MARSHALL, dec'd.
application withdrawn

JOSEPH MARSHALL on Est. of MATTHEW MARSHALL, dec'd.
Granted

Page 78:   Inferior Court, 1800 February 4:

ANN HARGROVE applicant on the Est. of JOHN HARGROVE, dec'd. -
Granted.

MARY MCNAIR & SAMUEL MCNAIR, Applicants for Letters of Admn.
on Est. of GILBERT MCNAIR, dec'd. - Granted

KEZIAH TINSLEY, applicant for L. of Admn. Est. THOMAS TINSLEY,
dec'd. ordered that the clerk issue L. of A. and the Appl.
on his applying to him and giving such Sec. as may be
approved by any member of Court.

ELISHA CAMPBELL an orphan of the age of 13 made Application
to this Court to be bound apprentice to ABRAM LAFAVOR to
learn the planting business. Ordered that sd. ELISHA
CAMPBELL be bound to sd. ABRAM LAFAVOR for the term of 5
years.

Page 79:   ELIZABETH ASKEW, Applicant for L. of A. on Est. of WM. ASKEW,
dec'd. - Granted

JOSEPH MARSHALL, applicant for L. of A. on Est of MATTHEW
MARSHALL, dec'd. Ordered: that such be gtd. by the giving
of Sec. approved by any of Ct.

WILLIAM LITTLE, Applicant for L. of A. on Est. of WILLIAM
JUNKIN, dec'd. the death of WILLIAM LITTLE, Applicant in
this case being suggested to the Court, the application was
dismissed.

Page 80:   JAMES MCBRIDE, Exor. of L. W. & T. of THOMAS MCBRIDE, dec'd.
Ordered: that the Exors. named in L. W. & T. of sd. MCBRIDE
is as many of them may apply is the Clerk of Ct. shall be
qual. to Execute the sd. Will and give such Sec. as may be
approved.

JOSEPH CHAIRS, Applicant for Letter of Guardianship for
JAMES GREEN an orphan in a state of minority. - Granted.

Page 80:   JAMES TROWELL on the behalf of ARON BARROW made application
to this Ct. to bind the sd. ARON BARROW being an orphan of
age of 14 years to learn the Taylor trade.
Ordered:
that sd. ARON BARROW be bound an apprenticeship to the sd.
JOSEPH WHITE during the term of 7 years and that sd. JOSEPH
WHITE oblige himself to teach him the art and mysteries of
the Taylor trade and give him one year of schooling.

Page 81:   POLLY BURNEAY a person of Colour made application in this Ct.
to be admitted to the choice of a Gdn.
Ordered:
that sd. POLLY BURNEY be placed in hands and care of JOHN
DOWNES he giving bond with suff. sec. is to be approved of
by any one member of this Ct. to provide her with good &
suff. clothes and provisions and produce her bef. the next
Ct. of Ord. to be held in and for Co. of Jeff. to be subject
to the order of sd. Ct. and that he the sd. JOHN DOWNES be
Entitled to the services of above sd. POLLY BURNAY during the
vacation of sd. Ct. as payment.
DOUGLASS HANCOCK, Z. LAMAR, W. SHELMAN

Page 82:   Court of the Ordinary, Jefferson County, February 27, 1800:
                    Present: RICHARD D. GRAY
                              DOUGLASS HANCOCK
                              ZACHARIAH LAMAR

           WILLIAM WOOD came into Ct. & produced a paper purportedly to
           be the L. W. & T. of ROBERT WOOD, dec'd., the same being duly
           proved and approved.
                        ORDERED TO BE RECORDED

           DRUSILLAR HARVEY and TANEY C. KEY & JOHN PAULELL & Exor. &
           Exec. of L. W. & T. of BLASSINGAME HARVEY came into Ct. &
           produced a paper in writing purportedly to be the L. W. & T.
           of sd. B. HARVEY, dec'd. the names being duly approved and
           allowed ordered to be recorded.

Page 83:   Jefferson Court of Ordinary, July 21, 1800 met according to
           Law.   Present: RICHARD D. GRAY
                              DOUGLASS HANCOCK
                              ZACH. LAMAR

Page 85:   Will of MARTHA GREEN: "Be it remembered that I MARTHA GREEN
           of City of Philadelphia, Gentlewoman being of sound mind and
           memory ... do make this my L. W. & T. Item: I give unto
           MARIA ANN POLLARD the dau. of my nephew THOMAS GREEN POLLARD
           the sum of $350 specie... to be kept at Int. until sd.
           MARIA attain to full age of 18 yrs. & Int. be applied toward
           her education & support... otherwise the Int. to be at her
           disposal as soon as she attains age of 18 yrs... but if she
           departs then principal & Int. go to SOPHIA MCCORMICK, the
           dau. of my beloved neice SARAH MCCORMICK... Item: To
           SOPHIA MCCORMICK the dau. of my sd. neice SARAH the like sum
           of 250 lbs. specie (with same limitations as in gift to MARIA)
           also to SOPHIA MCCORMICK an undivided tract in State of Pa.,
           beginning at Mouth of Pennipock Creek and running South along
           River Delaware cont. 11 acres & 1/4... but if SOPHIA departs
           then Principal and Int. & lands go to next eldest dau. of
           sd. SARAH MCCORMICK and for want of such dau. then to next
           eldest child of sd. SARAH... I give for use of the poor
           widows, Hospital of Christ Church congregation, Philadelphia
           the sum of 50 lbs... Item: I give & devise unto my brother-
           in-law WILLIAM POLLARD, Esq. an annuity of 50 lbs. per annum
           during term of his nat. life and I do charge my plantation in
           lower Dublin Township with payment of sd. annuity. Item:
           Wearing appearel, trinkets to sd. neice SARAH MCCORMICK. Item:
           Rest of Est. not otherwise disposed unto my friends WM. TODD,
           Sr. and WILLIAM TODD, Esq. their heirs and assigns in trust
           only... neice SARAH MCCORMICK... as that her present husband
           DAVID MCCORMICK or any other husband who... shall not have
           any right or Int. whatsoever therein, neither shall the admnrs
           be subject to or liable for his debts... I nominate sd.
           WILLIAM F. TODD, WM. TODD, Sr. & DAVID MCCORMICK, Exors.
           Dated 1 January 1798. Signed: MARTHA GREEN. Wit: JAMES
           CUMMING, ROBERT MCCORMICK, JOHN HOOD.

Page 90:   Jefferson Co., Ga., Will of ISAAC LAMB: I ISAAC LAMB (of the
           state and Co. afsd.) do make & ordain this my L.W.&.T. as
           following: Viz. First, I will to my beloved wife CHARITY LAMB
           all my stock of horses, cattle & hogs & my household & kitchen
           furn. and one hundred and 30 acres of land on which I now live
           adj. HOWARD SLY, also the money which is due me in South
           Carolina by THOMAS FULLALOVE and is to be collected by JOHN
           CORBET, also I will to my beloved son JOHN LAMB $10.00. Signed
           ISAAC LAMB. Wit: MARY (X) PENNINGTON. Rec. June 16, 1827.

Page 91:   MARY PENNINGTON swore she saw ISAAC LAMB sign his will.
           Sworn to 1 Jan. 1827, MARY ANN PENNINGTON.

JEFFERSON COUNTY, GA.
GRAND JURORS - JULY 3RD., 1797

1. Thomas Fulton
2. Tandy G. Key
3. Moses Newton
4. John Dupree
5. Elisha Ward
6. Luke Besman
7. George Tarver
8. Vinson Rowell
9. Blass Harvey, Sen.
10. Joseph Jackson
11. Samuel Andrews
12. William Calhoun
13. Thomas Neely
14. Thacker Vivian
15. James Spurlock
16. Thompson Lawson
17. Roger Lawson
18. Joseph Spencer
19. Robert Reed
20. David Wood
21. George Granberry
22. Samuel Clements
23. Richard Rowell
24. Thomas Cox
25. John Bemen
26. John Vining
27. Thomas Johnston
28. Stephen Powell
29. Solomon Wood
30. Hezekiah Gates
31. Robert Fleming
32. Jesse Lock
33. James Stubbs
34. Simmons Fowler
35. Ashley Wood
36. Benjamin Browning
37. Robert Fulward
38. John Paulett
39. John Rogers
40. William Guilliam
41. William Fleming
42. John Cowart
43. Horatio Marbury
44. Locharich Fenn
45. John Sapp
46. James Neely
47. Stephen Morgan
48. Benjamin Whitaker
49. Charles Rhodes
50. John Vining
51. John J. Schley
52. Morrice Raiford
53. John Barron
54. Charles Gaehett
55. Robert Patterson
56. Joseph Hampton
57. William Clements
58. James Chartain
59. Michael Ashley
60. Samuel Bothwell
61. Valentine Hatcher
62. Virgin Vivion
63. Thomas Whitehead
64. Joseph Allen
65. Phillip Clayton
66. Peter Charlain
67. Charles Harvey
68. John Shellman
69. George Stapleton
70. Phillip Calhoon
71. Nathan Powell
72. John Wood
73. Richard Gray
74. James Spivey
75. William Coleman
76. Matthew Cassaele
77. Thomas Shields
78. John Gamble
79. Jesse Paulett
80. Daniel Sturgess
81. Thomas Collier
82. William Blackman
83. William Pollard
84. William Paulett
85. John Boyd
86. Joseph Chairs
87. Joseph Darsey
88. Bird Tarver
89. John Neely
90. Robert Flemming
91. Charles C. Jenkins
92. John Hargrove
93. William Peel
94. Charles Reynolds
95. William Vining
96. Phillip Richardson
97. Benjamin Green
98. John Moreland
99. Benjamin Ogbert
100. John Clements
101. Alexander Carswell
102. William McGehee
103. Thomas Rogers
104. Jesse Vining
105. Manus Lemle
106. John Cobbs
107. Samuel Benedix
108. Hardy Morgan
109. George Prince
110. Daniel Connel
111. Abner Hammond
112. Cherry Bostick, Jr.
113. William Brackett
114. Andrew Hampton
115. Joseph White
116. Pattrick Connally
117. John Pugerly
118. Samuel Little
119. Cherly Bostick
120. Walter Robinson
121. Alexander Love
122. John Bryant
123. Jesse Wammock
124. William Pitman
125. Zachariah Lamar
126. James Merrywether

127. William Hadden
128. Owen Fort
129. David Jameson
130. James Parsons
131. David Terry
132. Josiah M. Stenett
133. Samuel Little
134. Samuel Barber
135. John Raiford
136. Michael Shelman
137. Gilbert McNair
138. John Few
139. Eliaha Nail
140. Joseph G. Posney
141. John Peel
142. Francis McMurray
143. John Marshall
144. Douglass Hancock
145. Zachariah Gray
146. John Whitehead
147. John Fleming
148. Robert Pryor
149. Lendsey Coleman
150. John Scott
151. Hugh Alexander
152. John Herrington
153. William McBride
154. Richard Paulett
155. Levi D. Smith
156. Peter J. Carnes

JEFFERSON COUNTY, GA.

JULY 3, 1799

A LIST OF PERSONS LIABLE TO SERVE AS PETIT JURORS

FOR THE ENSUING YEAR.

1.	Joseph Scott	61.	James Williams
2.	Jesse Lofly	62.	Joseph Branham
3.	Wm. Hadden	63.	John Martin
4.	James McKigney	64.	John McMahan
5.	James Farless	65.	Jesse Glover
6.	William Martin	66.	William Ingram
7.	Edmund Baily	67.	Nathaniel Sample
8.	Dan McNeel	68.	Samuel Sample
9.	Robert Broddy	69.	John Green
10.	Saml. Gates	70.	John Kennedy
11.	Adam Taply	71.	Jesse Price
12.	John Little	72.	Sphraim Kennedy
13.	Saml. McCandless	73.	Benjamin Davis
14.	John Irwin	74.	Saml. Montgomery
15.	Deucksen Wooten	75.	Charles Cavannah
16.	William Hannah	76.	William Kennedy
17.	James Branham	77.	Lewis Kennedy
18.	James Martin	78.	John Kennedy
19.	Francis Coleman	79.	James Kennedy
20.	John Wammock	80.	Jesse Cary
21.	John Coleman	81.	Saml. Carter
22.	John Rheese	82.	Andrew Berryhill
23.	Patrick McCullough	83.	Alexander Cary
24.	Nathaniel Sample	84.	Page Tally
25.	William Duncan	85.	Robert Little
26.	William Clerk	86.	Robert Boyd
27.	William Allen	87.	Saml. Boyd
28.	Thomas Hannah	88.	Andrew Boyd
29.	Simon Barden	89.	Nathaniel Whitaker
30.	David Ingram	90.	John Rise
31.	James Rogers	91.	Abraham Baily
32.	William Harsing	92.	Sphraim Chance
33.	Stephen Stevens	93.	William Fountain
34.	John Martin	94.	Phileman Chance
36.	Bennett Abbett	95.	Stephen Durezeaux
37.	Daniel More	96.	Benjamin Mayo
38.	Jesse Dykes	97.	Harmon Ross
39.	Benjamin Samons	98.	Reuben Ross
40.	John Morris	99.	Jonas Mayo
41.	Thomas Wasden	100.	Jacob Horn
42.	John Anderson	101.	Shoemake Holden
43.	Isaac Lockhart	102.	John Land
44.	William Ford	103.	Jonathan Fountain
45.	Jesse Hatcher	104.	William C. Bonds
46.	John Rogers	105.	Hugh McNeely
47.	Adam Calhoon	107.	Alexander Berryhill
48.	John Rowland	108.	Jesse Jump
49.	William Lyons	109.	Thomas Kennedy
50.	Nathaniel McMickin	110.	Robert Montgomery
51.	William Harris	111.	John Gibson
52.	Andrew Bush	112.	George Ingram
53.	Robert Wood	113.	Joseph Marshall
54.	William Brown	114.	Nicholas Baker
55.	John Candle	115.	William Baker
56.	George Varner	116.	Bullain Smith
57.	Thomas Douglass	117.	Samuel McBride
58.	Davis Shares	118.	John McBride
59.	Sanders Bush	119.	Robert Greaves
60.	Kidar Vining	120.	Thomas Girvin

121. Joshua Smith	190. Thomas Tinsley
122. William Crane	191. Daniel Girtman
123. John Kennedy	192. Spires Canman
124. Isaac Sumner	192. Redding Hall
126. Richard Parker	193. Dempsey Hall
127. Francis Brown	194. James Hall
128. Archibald Little	195. Joseph Hall
129. Samuel Gibson	196. Samuel Page
130. Richard Sumner	196. Jacob Colson
131. Eyesem Franklin	197. William Leggett
132. Moses Horn	198. John Powell
133. Robert Merrell	199. Samuel Sandford
134. John Padgett	200. Benjamin Sanford
135. Joseph Barber	201. Malachi Goff
136. Andrew Ronaldson	202. John Berryhill
137. Francis Flanders	203. Richard Kersey
138. William Manson	204. Nathan Ross
139. Thomas Peebles	205. James Simons
140. John Foyle	206. Willeam Wilson
141. Robert Foil	207. James Weeks
142. Robert Warnock	208. Garriel Picknen
143. Robert Stone	209. Menan Coleman
144. James Warnock	210. Aquilla Low
145. John Parker	211. Hugh Lambert
146. Thomas Tanner	212. Abraham Pierce
147. John Stephenson	213. Luke Sloughter
148. William Parsons	214. Thomas Hardy
149. John Wilson	215. Robert Maxwell
150. John Tomkins	216. Felix Maxwell
151. Stephen Webb	217. James Jones
152. Daniel Thomas	218. Harwood Dupree
153. Matterson Thomas	219. John Dupree
154. William Kennedy	220. Jesse Aycock
155. John Bigham	221. John Truelock
156. Thomas Mountain	222. Henry Jourdan
157. James Manson	223. William Boon
158. John Whigham	224. Jesse Hammock
159. John Manson	225. William Folks
160. John Lowry	226. John Hammock
161. Richard Fleeting	227. William Folks
162. Frederick Clemson	228. Reuben Powell
163. Hugh Gilmore	229. Jennings Cattle
164. Alexander Whigham	230. George Ubanks
165. William Whigham	231. Abel Sutton
166. Isaac Fountain	232. Peter Smith
167. Henry Land	233. John Fleming
168. Samuel Mayo	234. James Henesey
169. Bartholomew Girtman	235. Hugh Donaldson
170. John Densen	236. James Hunt
171. Herman Mayo	237. John Cook
172. James Robinson	238. Charles Henry
173. Michael Cahoon	239. Milbourn Cowart
174. Samuel Hammock	240. Jacob Godown
175. Thomas Askew	241. Robert Tilman
176. John Ingram	242. William Pennington
177. John Brock	243. Jesse Brown
178. William Brock	244. Peter Hauthorn
179. Abram Herring	245. Stephen Thompson
180. Arthur Herring	246. Aquilla Matthews
181. John Burton	248. John Turner
182. Richard Rise	249. Henry Turner
183. John Merchant	250. Samuel Briggs
184. John Tinsely	251. William Matthews
185. Peter Durrezeaux	252. William McGlawlin
186. John Thompson	253. Strander Crawford
187. James Hall	254. Caleb Wright
188. Henry Stapleton	255. Hugh Wilson
189. Alimeleck Sutton	256. Samuel Stater

257.	Gideon Thompson	335.	John Manning
258.	Charles Collins	336.	David Young
259.	William Young	337.	Abraham Roberts
260.	Abraham Lafever	338.	Samuel Little
270.	David Brown	339.	William Speirs
271.	Revel Evans	340.	John Turner
272.	William Darsey	341.	James Harris
273.	Jesse Slater	342.	Daniel McNeel
274.	Henry Cowart	343.	Jacob Jones
275.	John Webb	344.	John Lee
276.	George Henderson	345.	Isaac Jones
277.	Walter Graham	346.	Richard Sharer
278.	Davis Hallaway	347.	Thomas Herring
279.	Jesse Hollingsworth	348.	Jacon Robinson
280.	Archibald Culbreath	349.	John Rogers
281.	Elijah Wasden	350.	Shadrack Lee
282.	Levi Bush	351.	William Thomas
283.	Hall Hudson	352.	Micaijah Paulk
284.	Archibald Boyd	353.	Thomas Leak
285.	George Spivey	354.	Thomas Gay
286.	Absalom Pryor	355.	Barnabas Gay
287.	Alexander Douglass	356.	Rezin Colly
288.	Reuben Beckham	357.	Price Bradshaw
289.	John Downes	358.	John Akridge
290.	Ebenezer Jenks	359.	William Young
291.	Jacob Peterson	360.	Saml. Slocendl
292.	George Johnston	361.	John Brokenridge
293.	Isaac Rawls	362.	James Young
294.	Louis Voicle	363.	Jacob Young
295.	Job Townsly	364.	James Johnston
296.	David Thomas	365.	Absalom Coursey
297.	Eli Browning	366.	John Baggs
298.	William Gould	367.	William Pardue
299.	Peter Matthews	368.	Richard Corbitt
300.	John McDonald	369.	Jesse Purvis
301.	George Mclejahn	370.	John Mock
302.	Wm. Wright	371.	Thomas Russell
303.	Nethaniel Simons	372.	Orendalus Watson
304.	Maurice Gilbert	373.	William Jones
305.	Simon Day	374.	Daniel Marks
306.	Daniel McDowell	375.	Isaac Dubose
307.	Richard Wingate	376.	Reuben Walden
308.	Henry Beatty	377.	John Campbell
309.	James Bigham	378.	William Jereman
310.	William Clark	379.	Nathan Braswell
311.	John Little	380.	Richard Davis
312.	John Donaldson	381.	Joseph Smith
313.	William Donaldson	382.	John Davis
314.	Ephraim Peebles	383.	James Dubose
315.	Matthews Bailey	384.	Joseph Price
316.	Moses Brysnon	385.	Jesse Thomas
317.	Ezekiel Akridge	386.	William Andrews
318.	Thomas Mosely	387.	William Wood
319.	William Morgan	388.	Soloman Willie
320.	James Temples	389.	James McMullin
321.	Andrew Collins	390.	John Armstrong
322.	Samuel Bloodworth	391.	James Harvey
323.	David Kelly	392.	Joseph Temmy
324.	John Cunning	393.	Charles Coats
325.	William Thompson	394.	William Coats
326.	Robert Little	395.	George Smith
327.	Shadrack Evans	396.	Samuel Walden
328.	John Lewis	397.	Moses Dean
329.	Jesse Newton	398.	Henry Cox
330.	Ebenzer Fulgam	399.	Gardner Ubanks
331.	William Baker	400.	John Ubanks
332.	Elkhanah Loften	401.	Drury Harris
333.	William Lowry	402.	Morris Murphy
334.	Jacob Farmer	403.	Shadrach Vining

404. John Smith
405. Benjamin Warner
406. Willie Williams
407. Duett Dees
408. Stephen Kent
409. James Warner
410. Joseph Bozman
411. George Jones
412. Simon Smith
413. Nocholas Padgett
414. Elijah Padgett
415. David Douglass
416. William Walker
417. Elisha Ward
418. Samuel Ward
419. David King
420. Edmund Price
421. William Dawkins
422. Charles Hudspeth
423. William Oliver
424. John Kelly
425. John Daukins
426. William Baker
427. Jeremiah Welcher
428. Nathaniel Williams
429. Henry Walden
430. John Widener
431. John Coleman
432. William Dawkins
433. John Darby
434. Stephen Chance
435. Meedjah Dankins

WARREN COUNTY MARRIAGE RECORDS
Book A

EDITOR'S NOTES: (1) As stated before in publishing marriage records of other old counties, there was no law in Georgia requiring the return and recordation of marriage licenses until 1806, and before then there was no law specifically requiring the issuing officer to keep any list or record of the marriage licenses he issued. It can therefore be seen that the existing lists of marriage licenses issued found in old Georgia court-houses do not show if and when the parties named in a license were ever actually married or not, that is, prior to 1806. But it is generally assumed by genealogists that they were duly married especially if subsequent public records or private records like family Bibles indicated or showed that they were married. And after the new law came into effect in 1806, the records of licenses show that many of them were never returned to the issuing officer with entry of marriage entered thereon, so that it would appear clergymen and J.P.'s were very slow or ignorant or indifferent in complying.

(2) As a result of the foregoing circumstances none of the licenses for the first ten or fifteen years given any indication where the parties were married or by whom. Simply the names and the date of license were shown. Neither was the county or counties of residence of the contracting parties shown.

(3) In the first marrage book beginning with 1794, the manner of listing the licenses issued, was to draw a line down the middle of the page and then draw lateral lines about 1½ or 2 inches high, thus forming little boxes in which the names and the date of a license were entered. The lower parts of several of the pages were cut off and gone as far back as sixty years ago. The cutting off was evidently done with scissors and followed the box lines, thus giving rise to the idea that it was done maliciously or destroy a record of a license or possibly by some person or persons who wanted the little boxed-in records for family records or souvenirs. It has been so long that probably it will never be known how and why parts of the pages were removed.

(4) Warren County marriage records have heretofore been published in other publications, and normally GGM does not publish that which has been already been published in some other magazine or book, but finding errors in the published lists, GGM feels justified in printing them in this magazine. The Editor has attempted to make a few corrections in the spelling of names in the original record. For example, William Hart's name was written in the original record as "Hert" but by reference to deed records and other public records it can be seen that the correct name as "Hart", and that name appears in Parenthesis with a question-mark after it. Limited time in the Warren Court House recently made it impossible for the Editor to closely check the spellings in each license for errors.

Name of Groom	Name of Bride	Date of License
Nathan McG. Tilby	Sarah Jacobs	March 1, 1794
Phillip Logan	Leah Littleton	March 29, 1794
Presley Sanford	Polly Wynne	April 4, 1794
Nathan Bruton (Brewton?)	Nancy Fontaine	May 18, 1794
Benjamin Howard	Nancy Moore	June 7, 1794
Thomas Luckett	Betsy Sims	June 22, 1794
Nicholas Williams	Betsy Baker	June 22, 1794
William Hert (Hart?)	Mary Bass	June 27, 1794
James George	Mary Hardin	June 29, 1794
Dempsey Hood	Charity Hill	Aug. 5, 1794
Barton Atchison	Prudence Hill	(Date lost off)
Mark Hardin	Frances Newsom	(Date lost off)

Name of Groom	Name of Bride	Date of License
Ezekiel Alexander	M___ Neal	(Date lost off)
Robert McTier	Polly Chandler	Aug. 30, 1794
John Hays	Betsy Meadows	Sept. 9, 1794
Philip Barnheart	Rachel Williams	Sept. 10, 1794
Malcolm Johnston	Ann Burnley	Oct. 8, 1794
William Elliott	Elizabeth Burns	Nov. 10, 1794
Hugh Rees	Elizabeth Newsom	Nov. 19, 1794
Isaac Bankston	Polly Goings	Dec. 2, 1794
Silson Thrower	Betsy Mash (Marsh?)	Dec. 6, 1794
Ambrose Peavy	Viney (Lavina?) Rowland	Dec. 10, 1794
Walter Newman	Argent Culpepper	Dec. 16, 1794
Joseph Carter	Frances Wynne	Dec. 21, 1794
Joseph Williamson	Agnes Williams	Dec. 24, 1794
William Breed	Frances Brantley	Dec. 25, 1794
William Matthews	Sibia (Sibbiah?) Green	Dec. 26, 1794
James Mitchell	Lucena Heath	Dec. 31, 1794
Littleberry Strange	Nancy Lawton	Dec. 31, 1794
Henry Bonner	Mary Vaughn	Jan. 30, 1795
John Addison Johnston	Nancy Clerk (Clark?)	Feb. 13, 1795
Gideon George	Tabitha Burnley	March 4, 1795
Thomas Cary	Elizabeth Ellis	March 26, 1795
Peter Ryan	Fanny Walker	March 21, 1795
Richard Moore	Jean Jones	March 31, 1795
Nathaniel Perritt	Nancy Hill	March 31, 1795
John Thompson	Nancy Grimsley	March 31, 1795
Dixon Perryman	Ann Vining	March 31, 1795
William Sanders	Betsy Dennis	May 26, 1795
Ephriam Peebles	Sarah Drake	June 2, 1795
Joshua Moses	Sarah Mims	(Date lost off)
John Brantley	Rebecca Hill	June 22, 1795
William Newman	Hannah Simmons	July 29, 1795
James Bray	Betsy Neal	Oct. 18, 1795
Daniel Hutchinson	Nancy Burkhalter	Oct. 25, 1795
Samuel Newman	Anna Lovett	Oct. 20, 1795
Robert Black	Viney (Lavina?) Bruton	March 18, 1795
Elias Blunt	Phoebe Shaw	March 20, 1795
James Branham	Sally Tommy	June 18, 1795
James Farlis	Abegail H___is	Sept. 24, 1795
James Chastain	Sarah Morgan	Sept. 28, 1795
Drury Thompson	Susannah Anglin	Oct. 27, 1795
Hillery Fowler	Mary O'Neal	Nov. 1, 1795
Thomas Cocks	Susannah Peavy	Nov. 3, 1795
John Cobb	Mary Hargrove	(Date lost off)
James Elliott	Susannah Harris	(Date lost off)
George Dawkins	Elinor Dawkins	- - 1796
Jesse James	Phoebe Brewer	- - 1796
Alexander McCarty	Patsy Franklin	Feb. 15, 1796
John Rhodes	Phoebe Thompson	March 20, 1796
Isaac Heart (Hart?)	Sarah Buffington	May 10, 1796
Jonathan Nobles	Jean Dicken	May 24, 1796
Benjamin Harding	Mourning Smith	June 6, 1796
Michael Harvey	Polly Clower	July 30, 1796
John Saxon	Nancy Rogers	Aug. 13, 1796
John Greeson	Mary Ann Coughhsan (sic)	Aug. 20, 1796
John Moore	Ann Moore	Oct. 1, 1796
Richard Hutchinson	Charity Golden	March 4, 1796
William Perry	Nancy Abbott	- - 1796
Turner Parsons (Persons?)	Sally Williams	- - 1796
Christopher Preston	Millie Wadley	- - 1796
Stephen Sayager (sic)	Pollie Middlebrooks	June 10, 1796
David Golden	Elizabeth Harbuck	June 10, 1796
John McCray	Charity Fugett	Feb. 20, 1797
James Bonner	Sally Hill	March 8, 1797
Wood Moreland	Sally Heath	April 11, 1797
George M. McClung	Anny Whatley	April 13, 1797
William Ward	Milliford Whiting	(Date lost off)

Name of Groom	Name of Bride	Date of License
William Wilder	Elizabeth Hotnel	July 4, 1797
William Watson	Abegail Torrence	July 6, 1797
Michael Horn	Elizabeth Carter	Aug. 28, 1797
Benjamin Crenshaw	Pollie Hight	Aug. 14, 1797
Walter Fitzsimmons	Kesia (Keziah?) Butt	Aug. 10, 1797
Jesse Matthews	Pollie Peebles	Oct. 20, 1797
Benjamin Shepard	Cassandra Montray	Oct. 4, 1797
James Weeks	Pollie Carter	Nov. 21, 1797
David Mims	Betsy Broom	Dec. 27, 1797
Thomas Wilkins	Rebecca Ford	Dec. 27, 1797
Samuel Loughlin	Cele (Celia?) Zachary	Dec. 29, 1797
Jesse Duberry	Pollie Duberry	Oct. 10, 1797
John Forrest	Amelia Beall	Jan. 5, 1797
George Cotton	Sallie Cary	Dec. 26, 1797
Edward Short	Catherine Sims	Jan. 20, 1797
William Mims	Elizabeth Hilton	Jan. 20, 1797
William Hunt	Elizabeth Bass	Jan. 26, 1797
Rowland Green	Betsey Bass	Jan. 30, 1797
James Simmons	Polly Alexander	Jan. 31, 1797
Elijah Horn	Polly Boothe	Jan. 2, 1797
Thomas Fontaine	Sally Threewitts	Feb. 14, 1797
William Lloyd	Pollie Coling	Feb. 20, 1797
Alexander Flewellin	Thessey (Thereasa?)Peebles	Feb. 22, 1797
John McCoy	Mary Fontaine	April 15, 1797
Willie Grissle	Sarah Hadley	April 27, 1797
Samuel Fickling	Susannah Jones	May 12, 1797
Littleberry Petillo (Patillo?)	Mary Ann Simpson	May 26, 1797
Thomas Mitchell	Mary Wall	(Date lost off)
Edward Castleberry	Patsy Heath	(Date lost off)
Rowland Dixon	Nancy Ross	(Date lost off)
William Heath	Sallie Bonner	Feb. 21, 1798
James Taylor	Nancy Moore	Aug. 11, 1798
John Kilgore	Nancy Bishop	Sept. 22, 1798
Joshua Renolds (Runnolds?)	Sarah James	Oct. 17, 1798
Isaac Ball	Sally Wheeler	Oct. 18, 1798
Henry Williams	Elizabeth Goodwin	Nov. ___, 1798
John Parker	Rachel Kelly	Nov. 10, 1798
James Cotton	Martha Perryman	Nov. 9, 1798
Samuel Ledbetter	Martha Crittenden	Nov. 30, 1798
Solomon Brown	Betsy Mims	Dec. 23, 1798
John Sims	Rebecca Harris	Dec. 26, 1798
Jacob Dansby	Catherine Baker	May 27, 1798
William Davis	Peggy Manning	Feb. 27, 1799
Luke Patrick	Sally Brewer	(Date lost off)
William Williams	Elizabeth Crook	Feb. 5, 1799
Johnston Runnolds	Anna Nobles	March 13, 1799
Matthew Davis	Sarah Logan	May 5, 1799
Moses Gatling	Avy Rose	May 14, 1799
Thomas Doles	Susannah Yarbrough	May 20, 1799
Dr. Ignatius Sims	Henrietta Thompson	June 7, 1799
Hilton Peavy	Nellie Peavy	June 13, 1799
Ephriam Bishop	Betsy Moore	June 17, 1799
Alexander Hunter	Lydia Wynne	June 26, 1799
Robert Bonner	Elizabeth Heath	July 2, 1799
John Oliver	Sarah Low (Lowe?)	July 4, 1799
John Keener	Mary McKindley	July 6, 1799
Henry Avent (Avant?)	Sarah Vining	July 9, 1799
Elisha Poor (Poore?)	Polly Lunsford	July 8, 1799
Nathan Jackson	Priscilla Sanders	July 18, 1799
Robert Bennett	Polly Glasgo (Glasgow?)	July 17, 1799
Charles Rayburn	Dory (Dora?) Williford	July 18, 1799
Merrit Mitchell	Sally Hutchison	July 19, 1799
Leonard Desieur	Polly Malone	(Date lost off)
Elijah Conner	Polly Upton	Aug. 14, 1799
Frederick Glover	Nancy Jones	Sept. 3, 1799
James Hilburn	Nancy Jackson	Sept. 17, 1799

Name of Groom	Name of Bride	Date of License
Stephen Todd	Sibella Williams	Sept. 20, 1799
Jones Kendrick	___ Lawrence	Oct. 7, 1799
John Griffin	Elizabeth Costly	Oct. 15, 1799
Jonathan Hagathy	Ferreby (Fairiby) Cook	Oct. 16, 1799
Samuel Newman	Anna Lovett	Oct. 27, 1799
Peter Peavy	Vevinah Aarons	Nov. 2, 1799
James Davison	Mary Butler	Nov. 15, 1799
John Henry	Amy Bishop	Nov. 15, 1799
Lewis Wright	Patsy Heath	Nov. 18, 1799
Elisha Neal	Nancy Yarbrough	Nov. 30, 1799
Jonas Ray	Biddy (Obedience?)Ellington	Dec. 11, 1799
Stafford Williams	Sarah Dismukes	Dec. 16, 1799
Robert Wynne, Jr.	Jennie Perkins	Dec. 17, 1799
John Reed	Betsy Low (Lowe?)	Dec. 25, 1799
Matthew Mims	Ursie Harville	Dec. 27, 1799
Daniel Crenshaw	Selethe Cook	Dec. 27, 1799
Lanier Humphreys	Susannah Spinks	Jan. ___, 1800
Fisher Gaskins	Rhody Row (Rhoda Rowe)	Jan. 17, 1800
Robert Bowman	Peggy Dove	Jan. 21, 1800
James Williams	Peggy Slatter	Jan. 23, 1800
Aaron Smith	Elizabeth Abercrombie	Jan. 21, 1800
John Thrasher	Sarah Bearden	Jan. 25, 1800
James Darnall	Polly Davis	Feb. 5, 1800
Thomas Madox (Maddox?)	Polly Neal	Feb. 10, 1800
Aaron Jones	Dicy Willaby (Willoughby?)	Feb. 12, 1800
John Gibson	Fanny Fluellen (Flewellin?)	Feb. 22, 1800
William Jones	Bershaba (Bathsebeba) Abercrombie	Feb. 22, 1800
Austin Pruitt	Nancy Yarbrough	Feb. 27, 1800
Azariah Butts	Elizabeth Doles	March 4, 1800
Nathaniel Pruitt	Polly Perkins	March 16, 1800
James Dunnoway (Dunaway?)	Sarah Lee	March 30, 1800
Asa Newsom	Nancy Newsom	April 6, 1800
Joseph Miller	Alice Woolsey	April 7, 1800
Charles Oliver	S. Templene	April 27, 1800
Seth Woolsey	Honor Miller	May 5, 1800
William Kellum	Deborah Stubbs	May 10, 1800
William Thompson	Sarah Scott	May 12, 1800
Sherod Barden	Elizabeth Fickling	June 25, 1800
Reubin Lockett	Sarah Hill	June 27, 1800
Andrew Walker	Naomi Moore	July 10, 1800
Moses Boynton	Tabitha Chapman	July 14, 1800
Goodwin Mitchell	Elizabeth Cox	July 15, 1800
William Taylor	Elizabeth Hutchison	Aug. 5, 1800
James Williams	Nancy Wilkinson	Aug. 12, 1800
Solomon Thompson	Frances Parker	Aug. 18, 1800
John Harrison	Elizabeth Newman	Aug. 24, 1800
Laban Chapman	Hannah Richardson	Aug. 30, 1800
William Willis	Mary Eades	Oct. 18, 1800
William Richardson	Peggy Aaron	Oct. 28, 1800
John Williams	Nancy Camp	Nov. 24, 1800
Pierce Crossly	Susannah McCowan	Nov. 2, 1800
Micajah Darden	Dicy Darden	Nov. 10, 1800
Elijah Anglin	Susannah Wheeler	Nov. 19, 1800
William Jones	Ketrina Abercrombie	Nov. 26, 1800
Joseph Hancock	Mary Brady	Nov. 25, 1800
William Simmons	Sarah Wright	Dec. 3, 1800
Furney Griffin	Elizabeth Norton	Dec. 3, 1800
Jacob Clowers	Sally Darden	Dec. 7, 1800
William Flournoy	Nancy Wallace	Dec. 24, 1800
Austin Baker	Maret? Hern?	Dec. 24, 1800
Charles Webb	Polly Hackett?	Dec. 25, 1800
Isaac Daniel	Polly Johnston	Dec. 25, 1800
Peter Mullins	Tabitha Wynne	Jan. 8, 1801
James Gibson	Rachel Waggoner	Jan. 9, 1801
John Hollis	Frances Pembleton	Jan. 12, 1801

Name of Groom	Name of Bride	Date of License
Isaac Revison?	Sarah Cody	Jan. 7, 1801
Samuel Howell	Patsy McCrary	Jan. 17, 1801
Jeremiah Uaniel	Patsy Edmondson	Jan. 17, 1801
William Landrum	Agnes Smith	Jan. 23, 1801
William Jones	Susannah Parham	Jan. 17, 1801
Pleasant Moorman	Nancy Beall	Jan. 15, 1801
Elijah Grenade	Zilpha Dove	Jan. 21, 1801
Alexander Avera	Jane Curry	Jan. 24, 1801
John Gilpin	Cleary (Clara?) Bond	Feb. 9, 1801
Ephriam Ivy	Celia Finch	Feb. 9, 1801
Nathaniel Hutchinson	Rebecca Harbuck	Feb. 1, 1801
Willis Roberts	Apsilla Alexander	Feb. 2, 1801
William Wade	Sally Simons	March , 1801
Thomas Lovett	Elizabeth Johnston	March 8, 1801
Thomas Simmons	Rebecca Simmons	March 17, 1801
Francis F. Risher (Raskin?)	Elizabeth Threewits	March 24, 1801
Cullen Alford	Pheriby Wooten	April 10, 1801
Timothy Matthews	Patsy Fluellin	April 13, 1801
John P. Jones	Mary Puckett	May 4, 1801
Thomas Bowman	Deborah Wall	May 18, 1801
William Hutchinson	Patsy Burkhalter	June 2, 1801
Josephus Tucker	Susannah Tucker	June 11, 1801
Charles Stewart	Elizabeth Moore	June 11, 1801
John Peavy	Patsy Bearden	June 20, 1801
Henry Hadley	Elizabeth Matthews	June 10, 1801
Leroy Mims	Elizabeth Benton	June 16, 1801
John Thomas	Phoebe Guyland?	June 26, 1801
Gardiner Smith	Rebecca Nobles	July 1, 1801
Hugh Logan	Nancy Tuning	July 5, 1801
James Hardin	Nancy Morgan	July 9, 1801
John Moore	Margaret Digby	July 11, 1801
Henry Harris	Patsy Marshall	July 12, 1801
Anderson Ball	Phoebe Jenkins	Aug. 2, 1801
Jeremiah Crane	Mary Weldon	Aug. 12, 1801
Jesse Dennis	Nancy McGraw	Sept. 24, 1801
Phillip Johnston	Mourning Howell	Oct. 22, 1801
Joshua Stephens	Polly Britt	Oct. 24, 1801
William Brooks	Mary Simms	Oct. 28, 1801
John Keener	Mary McKindley	Oct. 24, 1801
Samuel Rutherford	Elizabeth Carroll	Nov. 5, 1801
William Gardiner	Sallie Neal	Nov. 29, 1801
John Breed	Lucy Dennis	Dec. 8, 1801
James Wood	Caroline Matilda Buffin	Dec. 28, 1801
John Poor	Sallie Hobson	Dec. 29, 1801
Dinkins Ivey	Lydia Hogans	Jan. 1, 1802
Arthur Taylor	Sarah Williams	Jan. 2, 1802
Henry Walker	Fanny Parham	Jan. 5, 1802
David Whatley	Frances Poor	Jan. 2, 1802
Marritt Wheeler	Rebecca Kemp	Jan. 7, 1802
Charles Dean	Ann O'Briant	Jan. 9, 1802
Henry Prince	Polly Pace	Jan. 8, 1802
Andrew Hodges	Elizabeth Potter	Jan. 22, 1802
John Hill	Elizabeth Moore	Feb. 13, 1802
Benjamin Oliver	Nancy Rose (Ross?)	Mar. 8, 1802
John Wilson	Celia Howell	Mar. 13, 1802
Thomas Davis	Nancy Short	Mar. 13, 1802
James Howell	Rebecca Dunaway	Mar. 17, 1802
James Armstrong	Phoebe Simmons	Apr. 17, 1802
Isom (Isham) Boman	Peggy Greesom	Apr. 25, 1802
Job Todd	Gracy Williford	Apr. 29, 1802
Henry Brewer	Nancy Doles	May 16, 1802
John Cox	Rachel Stephens	May 19, 1802
George Cooper	Linnie Parrish	June 2, 1802
Henry Moss	Sally Gardner	June 8, 1802
Nicholas Highland	Lydia Hartsfield	June 10, 1802
Hardy Newsom	Charity Wright	June 5, 1802

Name of Groom	Name of Bride	Date of License
Francis Walker	Sallie Thorn	July 1, 1802
William Keener	Vashti Gibbs	July 10, 1802
Daniel Connell	Pollie Smith	July 2, 1802
William Butler	Elizabeth Woodward	July 14, 1802
John Sullivant	Sallie Pierce	July 27, 1802
Silas Todd	Pollie Lindsey	July 28, 1802
Baalam Brooks	Mary McGlamery	Aug. 11, 1802
William Tait	Sallie Howard	Aug. 17, 1802
John Fowler	Zilpha Howell	Aug. 22, 1802
John Wynne	Elizabeth Harris	Sept. 7, 1802
*Jacob Fair	Sally Hays	Sept. 8, 1802
*John Robertson	Jennie Berry	Oct. 4, 1802
*William Proctor	Peggy Brady	Oct. 11, 1802
*David Morgan	Peggy W. Brady	Oct. 17, 1802
*Shemei Drake	Nancy White	Oct. 18, 1802
*Michael Row (Rowe)	Susannah Hathorne	Oct. 19, 1802
*Joshua Mitchell	Patsy Williams	Nov. 1, 1802
Henry Hill	Beady Walker	Dec. 11, 1802
David Castleberry	Sarah Howard	Dec. 14, 1802
Claiborne Ogletree	Betsy Gibson	Dec. 15, 1802
Bailey Hays	Mary Stubbs	Dec. 15, 1802

EDITOR'S NOTE: Miss Helen Prescott about 1909-1910 compiled and published Warren County marriages down through 1805, in Vol. III of "Historical Collections of Joseph Habersham Chapter, D.A.R." (which book has already been referred in this issue in connection with Greene County Marriages). About 1930-34, the late Mrs. John L. Davidson of Quitman, at that time State Historian of the Georgia Society, D.A.R., compiled Warren County Court-House records for publication as had been done by her with the Wilkes County records (and which Wilkes records were published) however, her Warren records were never published. She had a copy of the book just mentioned above, by Miss Prescott, and she added the dates of licenses in her copy as Miss Prescott did not show the dates. A few years ago many old Warren County record books including marriage records, were laminated and rebound by the State Dept. of Archives & History, and the records were then returned to the Warren County Court-House where they are now. The Editor recently checked the list in Miss Prescott's book and the dates added in the margin by Mrs. Davidson, with the re-bound book of Warren County Marriages in order to see if Miss Prescott had overlooked any, and was surprised to find about thirty-five of the marriages listed by Miss Prescott missing from the first book of Marriages in the Ordinary's Office of Warren County. They were there when Mrs. Davidson added the dates in her copy of the Prescott book, about 1930-34, but are not to be found in records now, so that sometime in the last 30-odd years about thirty-five of the marriages have been lost of the old book. Those missing ones are indicated in the list herewith published, by an asterisk (*) appearing just before the groom's name. Remember, the dates are those of when the licenses were issued.

Name of Groom	Name of Bride	Date of License
Tolliver Cox	Frances Davison	Dec. 20, 1802
Allen Davis	Rebecca Cahoon	Dec. 21, 1802
John Smith	Patsy Staton	Dec. 25, 1802
John Rogers	Nancy Swain	Dec. 28, 1802
Thomas Flake	(Missing)	Jan. 10, 1803
Samuel Davis	Polly Verdin	Jan. 14, 1803
James Wade	Charity Cooper	Feb. 6, 1803
Benjamin Humphreys	Sally Dickens	Feb. 15, 1803
Doctor Lockett	Mary Hill	Feb. 20, 1803
John Patterson	Sally Lockett	Feb. 20, 1803
Charles H. Deveraux	Polly Bruton	Feb. 22, 1803
Robert McCrary	Treacy Rogers	Feb. 21, 1803
Thomas T. Walker	Phoebe Medlock	Mar. 19, 1803

Name of Groom	Name of Bride	Date of License
James Smith	Nancy Villiams	March 24, 1803
George Parham	Betsy Hill	March 29, 1803
Abel James	Sarah Miller	March 28, 1803
Hartwell Heath	Nancy Parham	March 29, 1803
James Hogwood	Polly Harvill	March 30, 1803
Leaven McGee	Mary Dunn	April 9, 1803
William Slatter	Mary Crawford	April 3, 1803
*David Williams	Peggy Nixon	April 1, 1803
Hyram Perry	Nancy Flake	April 11, 1803
Isaac Williams	Rhoda Jones	April 24, 1803
Moses Catlin	Chloe Row (Rowe?)	April 16, 1803
Samuel Harris	Betsy Wells	April 16, 1803
Edward Harper	Hannah Yarbrough	May 21, 1803
Moses Fillingim	Nancy Fillingim	May 25, 1803
Robert Night	Elizabeth Bird	June 9, 1803
Moses Williams	Mary Hardy	June 10, 1803
Jeremiah Perry	Elizabeth Walker	June 27, 1803
Robert Parker	Hannah Hutchins	July 7, 1803
James Neves	Concord Hambleton	July 19, 1803
*Mordecai Malone	Penny Edmondson	July 27, 1803
Bray Warren	Hetty Mitchell	Aug. 2, 1803
James Burt	Rebecca Burt	Aug. 6, 1803
Robert Daniel	Holland Row	Aug. 20, 1803
David Dove	Elizabeth Finch	Aug. 21, 1803
Henry Atchison	Winnie Hill	Aug. 30, 1803
William Chambliss	Martha Robertson	Sept. 19, 1803
Isaac Barbaree	Nancy Smith	Sept. 21, 1803
George Fickling	Ephathan? Barden	Sept. 27, 1803
Daniel James	Elizabeth Gibson	Oct. 8, 1803
James Minton	Sarah Pool	Oct. 15, 1803
James Crissap	Sarah McCoy	Oct. 18, 1803
Howell Hight	Penny Wall	Nov. 3, 1803
James Threewitts	Sally Fontaine	Nov. 8, 1803
Levin Stanford	Nelly McGee	Nov. 20, 1803
James Bailey	Sarah Johnson	Dec. 6, 1803
Jesse Miller	Patsy Dennis	Dec. 15, 1803
Richard Fletcher	Athy Hardin	Dec. 31, 1803
Henry Cocroff (Lecross?)	Peggy Sandford	March 26, 1804
John Hardy	Sucky Mullins	Jan. 24, 1804
Samuel Harrold	Susannah Harrall	Jan. 13, 1804
Jonathan Fuller	Jincy Hodges	Jan. 23, 1804
David Sallis	Letty Nichols	Jan. 6, 1804
William Ansley	Ann Ray	Feb. 6, 1804
Arnold Atcheson	Patsy Gibson	Feb. 11, 1804
Edward Jenkins	Eliza Sheffield	Feb. 14, 1804
William Murray	Mary Rayburn	Feb. 14, 1804
James Heath	Elizabeth Heath	Feb. 26, 1804
William D. Wright	Nancy Heath	March 6, 1804
William Bird	Mary Matthews	March 8, 1804
*William Ewell	Judith Higginbotham	March 14, 1804
*Joseph Hill	Nancy Finsh	April 24, 1804
Benjamin Walker	Patsy Butler	May 8, 1804
Amos Wheeler	Charlotte Findle (Tindall)	May 14, 1804
Elias Beall	Polly Neal	May 19, 1804
David Jones	Lydia Row (Rowe)	May 24, 1804
Thomas Low (Lowe?)	Elizabeth Rose (or Rowe?)	June 13, 1804
Nathan Davis	Catherine Rogers	July 26, 1804
Josiah Draper	Sophia Stanford	Aug. 2, 1804
John Russell	Elizabeth Murphy	Aug. 15, 1804
William White	Sarah Hogans	Aug. 16, 1804
James Cody	Elizabeth Adams	Aug. 17, 1804
John Purge	Winnie Thurman?	Aug. 18, 1804
John Rowland	Nancy Wilson	Aug. 27, 1804
John Anglin	Nancy Edmondson	Sept. 15, 1804
John Atchison	Rebecca Jenkins	Sept. 27, 1804
Benjamin Carpenter	Polly Jackson	Sept. 15, 1804

Name of Groom	Name of Bride	Date of License
Thomas Redless	Nancy Smith	Sept. 29, 1804
Washington Hardaway	Sally Cody	Oct. 1, 1804
John Hardaway	Patsy Rose (Rowe)	Oct. 1, 1804
Ishmael Broom	Nancy Myhand	Oct. 16, 1804
John Wade	Jerusha Taylor	Oct. 31, 1804
Dudley Peebles	Susannah Peebles	Jan. 7, 1804
Thomas Hinton	Patsy Duckworth	Dec. 11, 1804
Dennis Brooks	Elvy Stanford	Dec. 12, 1804
James Ansley	Elizabeth Jones	Dec. 18, 1804
Thomas Harriss	Jincy Wynne	Dec. 19, 1804
Henry Harris	Concord Carter	Dec. 22, 1804
*Aaron Grier, Jr.	Polly Grier	Dec. 22, 1804
*Ephriam McGee	Elizabeth McGlamery	Dec. 24, 1804
*Samuel Moses	M. Dennis	Dec. 24, 1804
Robert Taylor	Mary Chambers	Dec. 27, 1804
Joab Brooks	Delilah Langford	Dec. 27, 1804
William Hoof	Tabitha Burson	Dec. 28, 1804
John Sheffield	Susannah Hight	Sept. 27, 1804
Whitfield Tucker	Eliza Darden	Dec. 3, 1804
Thomas Terry	Polly Faulks	Jan. 7, 1805
William Ward	Susannah Wynne	Jan. 7, 1805
Hugh Blair	Polly Lee	Jan. 14, 1805
Samuel Barksdale	Lucy Bunkley	Jan. 16, 1805
Orren Parker	Nancy Hutchins	Jan. 21, 1805
*James Handley	Sally Henry	Jan. 23, 1805
William Bunkley	Betty Slatter	Jan. 26, 1805
Richard Lovett	Sally Johnston	Feb. 4, 1805
*Ambrose Murphy	Sarah Horn	Feb. 12, 1805
Matthew Harris, D.D.	Mrs. Susannah Jones	Feb. 12, 1805
John Benton	Viny (Lavina?) Morris	Feb. 13, 1805
Barnard Fickling	Rebecca Moore	March 6, 1805
Joseph Leonard	Millie Howell	March 6, 1805
James Wheeler	Lasey? (Cassy?) Kinsey	March 16, 1805
Joel Lasseter	Mary Beasley	March 21, 1805
William Hoof	Sallie Breed	March 25, 1805
Thomas Williams	Polly Ivy	March 26, 1805
Adam Broom	Mary S. Wheeler	March 30, 1805
John Wilson	Martha Dismukes	April 2, 1805
David Chapman	Milly Chapman	April 10, 1805
Nicholas Booty	Sallie Locke	April 15, 1805
Neill Ferguson	Tabitha Chapman	April 29, 1805
Richard Hopkins	Hannah Smith	May 5, 1805
John Crokett	Pheriba Payne	May 8, 1805
Joseph Hill	Elizabeth Heath	May 23, 1805
John Moore	Elizabeth Davis	May 24, 1805
William B. Allison	Alla Hutchins	May 28, 1805
Micajah Perry	Polly Banks	May 31, 1805
Nathan Harris	Rhoda Champion	June 1, 1805
*James Turner	Elizabeth Morris	June 1, 1805
*Vincent Wheeler	Nelly Nixon	June 3, 1805
*Daniel Eades	Charity Watson	June 3, 1805
*Jeremiah Holden	Jenny Gunn	June 17, 1805
*Isham Reese	Polly Rogers	June 8, 1805
*Thomas Jones	Sarah Mitchell	June 22, 1805
*John K. Revers?	Sally Burkhalter	June 22, 1805
*Benjamin Matthews	Polly Jones	July 4, 1805
Moses Williams	Edy Barrow	July 4, 1805
Thomas Jones	Kizzy Bazemore	July 4, 1805
John Blount	Sally Pruitt	July 8, 1805
Ambrose Hably? (Abley?)	Elizabeth Parham	July 8, 1805
John Quinn	Mary Tapper	July 11, 1805
Littleberry Bagwell	Winnie Castleberry	July 11, 1805
Jones Burkhalter	Kizzy Basemore	July 12, 1805
Reubin Nantz	Rosanna Sanders	July 13, 1805
*John Johnston	Elizabeth McNabb	July 16, 1805
*Robert Oliver	Patience Pitts	July 16, 1805

Name of Groom	Name of Bride	Date of License
*Phillip Brooks	Nancy Sherley	July 25, 1805
*David Benagin?	Nancy Zachary	Aug. 13, 1805
*Phillip Brantley	Rebecca Harbuck	Sept. 5, 1805
*Ebenezer Bird	Betsy Bryson	Sept. 10, 1805
Willie Dorman	Frances Crawford	Sept. 11, 1805
Churchwell Gibson	Mary Brantley	Sept. 11, 1805
Daniel Culpepper	Jemima Wright	Sept. 24, 1805
Byrd Pruitt	Rebecca Turner	Oct. 7, 1805
Ambrose Shillings	Polly Fields	Oct. 26, 1805
John Lynn	Viney (Lavina?) Ivy	Oct. 28, 1805
Richard Murphy	Effie McDuffie	Oct. 30, 1805
*Winfrey Lary	Phoebe Richards	Nov. 2, 1805
*John Matthews	Mary Smith	Nov. 12, 1805
*Zachary Hobson	Leamander Grenade	Nov. 18, 1805
*Joshua Williams	Peggy Filligin	Nov. 6, 1805
*James Buckelaw	Elizabeth James	Nov. 7, 1805
*James Rowland	Polly Pearson	Nov. 6, 1805
Spencer Seals	Elizabeth Burnley	Nov. 25, 1805
John McDaniel	Charlotte Nichols	Nov. 27, 1805
Henry T. Anthony	Pollie Lovell	Nov. 30, 1805
Jonathan Dunaway	Elizabeth Dennis	Dec. 7, 1805
James Cooke	Rebecca Potts	Dec. 13, 1805
Benjamin Napier	Pollie Williford	Dec. 13, 1805
Samuel M. Smith	Elizabeth M. Hill	Dec. 15, 1805
William McNash	Pollie Hatcher	Dec. 17, 1805
George Dashiel?	Nellie Stanford	(Date lost off)
Harden Chambers	Vicy Kinney	(Date lost off)
William Davidson	Sarah Geaslin	Dec. 26, 1805
Adam Livingston	Patsy Womack	Dec. 28, 1805
John Womack	Sarah Lewis	Aug. 12, 1805

EDITOR'S NOTE: The above concludes the list as printed in the Miss Prescott book in 1910, with addition of dates of licenses added by Mrs. Davidson, and some corrections made by the Editor. This list is down through 1805. In 1806 the new law went into effect requiring the return of licenses to the issuing officer with the entry of the officiating minister or officer showing when the marriage took place. It was, however, as late as 1810 (in Warren County) before the new law began to be generally complied with. As a result, it will be noticed in the remainder of the list in this issue the dates given are those of the issuance of the license, and such dates are preceded with two asterisks, thus (**). Those not so marked, are dates of marriage.

Ambrose Chapman	Elizabeth Stone	**Jan. 13, 1806
Murphy Champion	Kinsy? Newsom	**Jan. 18, 1806
Burrell Maybrunk?	Marion? Newsom	**Jan. 18, 1806
William Darden	Pollie Dewberry	**Jan. 20, 1806
Joseph Grenade	Catherine Johnson	**Jan. 27, 1806
Bishai Breed	Nancy Barber	**Feb. 2, 1806
John Ward	Nancy Jones	**Feb. 2, 1806
William Jackson	Dandace B__ (torn)	**Mar. 22, 1806
Benjamin M__ (torn)	Polly Hill	**Feb. 3, 1806
John Boy__ (torn)	Lydia Welle__ (torn)	**Apr. 2. 1806
Amos Waggoner	Betsy Millirons	**June 15, 1806
Thomas Hall	Patsy Finch	**June 25, 1806
David Holeman	Patsy Gibson	**Jan. 17, 1806
William Brown	Polly Owen	**Feb. 21, 1806
Aaron Livingston	Jean Allen	**Feb. 5, 1806
William Green	Elizabeth Darden	**Mar. 25, 1806
William Snelling	Elizabeth Pickard	**Apr. 15, 1806
Amos Parsons	Patsy Gardiner	**Apr. 8, 1806
Note: At this point in the record it seems that six marriages are lost.		
Nathan Sherley	Mary Brooks	**May 13, 1806
Nathan Culpepper	Fannie Gardiner	May 27, 1806
David Jones	Mary Mendenhall	May 14, 1806
Cleveras? Andrews	Elizabeth Jones	May 26, 1806

Name of Groom	Name of Bride	Date of License
Thomas Jones	Pollie Matthews	**May 2, 1806
Alexander Perryman	Jane W. Vining	**June 4, 1806
Solomon Castleberry	Rebeckah Lovett	**June 14, 1806
Samuel Hyde	Caty Gibson	**June 18, 1806
Andrew R. Stephens	Margaret Grier	**July 7, 1806
Simon Herrold	Jenny Rushin	July 10, 1806
Thomas Jones	Polly Matthews	**May 21, 1806
Joshua Windham	Elizabeth Jones	**July 11, 1806
Joshua Draper	Elizabeth Morgan	Aug. 10, 1806
William Shaw	Hannah Hodgerson	**Sept. 8, 1806
Silas Buckholts	Sarah Roberts	**Sept. 19, 1806
William Cooper	Elizabeth Slater	**Sept. 29, 1806
John Littleton	Elizabeth Kinsey	Oct. 2, 1806
Charles Stewart	Henrietta Hargraves	Oct. 1, 1806
Walter Beall	Rebecca Neal	Oct. 22, 1806
Jonathan Newman	Cary (Carrie?) Lovett	**Oct. 26, 1806
Henry Conaway	Nancy Turner	Nov. 9, 1806
James Hutchens	Susannah Castleberry (alias Susannah Morris)	**Nov. 13, 1806
William Jones	Patience Davis	Nov. 16, 1806
Elijah Horn	Margaret Nugent	**Nov. 21, 1806
Benjamin Matthews	Rebekah Pierson (Pierson?)	**Dec. 6, 1806
Archibald Little	Mary Butrel	**Dec. 15, 1806
Moses Butt	Eliza Brown	Dec. 30, 1806
John Digby	Blenda Slade	**Dec. 1, 1806
John Chaffing	Clotilda Darden	**Dec. 15, 1806
Anson Highfield	Fanny Burge Heath	Mar. 28, 1806
John Beville	Franky Boynton	Sept. 4, 1806
Samuel Johnston	Rosamond Spinks	Dec. 3, 1806
David Rhodes	Mary Justice	July 11, 1806
Ebenezer Bird	Petsey Byrom	Feb. 25, 1806
John Ross	Polly Matthews	**Dec. __, 1806
William Paulk	Henrietta Buckholts	**Dec. 24, 1806
John Roberson	Sally Harris	**Jan. 20, 1807
Moses Ivey	Elizabeth George	**Jan. 26, 1807
Theophilus Hill	Rebeccah Gibson	Jan. 28, 1807
Thomas Huston	Lucy Boynton	Jan. 31, 1807
Robert Culpepper	Pheriba Wright	Feb. 8, 1807
Joshua Howell	Jennie Darden	Feb. 9, 1807
Nathaniel Brooks	Drusilla Morris	Feb. 7, 1807
Benjamnin Chapman	Patsy Slaid (Shaw?) not plain	**Feb. 25, 1807
David Bailey	Milly Johnston	**Mar. 5, 1807
Joel Kinsey	Tabitha Johnston	**Mar. 5, 1807
Robert M. Cunningham	Emily M. Bird	Mar. 24, 1807
Robert Sheffield	Anne Hight	**Mar. 24, 1807
William Torrence	Mary Scott	Apr. 5, 1807
John Moneyham	Elizabeth Millirons	Apr. 12, 1807
Benjamin Weatherby	Mildred Bonner	Apr. 7, 1807
Asa Chapman	Synthia Lockett	Apr. 7, 1807
William Gibson	Polly Duckworth	June 17, 1807
Abram Hill	Catherine Gibson	**June 9, 1807
William Few	Hannah Anders (Andrews?)	June 13, 1807
Ebenezer Smith	Clary (Clara?) Rogers	June 17, 1807
John Davidson	Linsey Smith	July 16, 1807
John Howard	Sarah Jones	**June 30, 1807
Rie? (or Pue?) Newsom	Dicy Newsom	July 13, 1807
Terrence Ivey	Polly George	July 21, 1807
Isaac Pate	Rachel Gibson	**Aug. 6, 1807
James Lynn	Nancy Harbuck	Aug. 13, 1807
James Ricketson	Jane Simpson	Aug. 24, 1807
Robert Tait	Sally Oliver	**Aug. 25, 1807
Allen Carter	Sally Edmonds	Sept. 3, 1807
William Mullens	Fanny Williams	Sept. 30, 1807
David Jones	Elizabeth Shamling	Aug. 4, 1807

Name of Groom	Name of Bride	Date of License
Thomas Draper	Rebekah Granade	Sept. 5, 1807
Joseph Baker	Rachel Wade	**Sept. 11, 1807
Myrick Hunneycutt	Polly Linch	Sept. 11, 1807
Elisha Smallwood	Nancy Davis	**Sept. 15, 1807
Thomas Grimes	Polly Bunkley	Sept. 24, 1807
James McCormick	Catherine Oliver	**Oct. 5, 1807
Joel Smith	Sarah Banks	**Oct. 10, 1807
Jacob Harbuck	Sally Rickerson	Oct. 15, 1807
John Morris	Sally Carter	Nov. 4, 1807
Henry Loyless	Lavinah Carter	Nov. 5, 1807
Samuel Jones	Elizabeth Neal	**Oct. 5, 1807
James Johnston	Polly Jarrett	**Nov. 6, 1807
James Jenkins	Sally Flake	**Oct. 8, 1807
James Crowder	Hannah Burnley	Nov. 19, 1807
Hardy Pitts	Drusilla Neal	Nov. 18, 1807
Thomas Gibson	Patsy Neal	Nov. 18, 1807
James Vaughan	Elizabeth Darden	**Nov. 23, 1807
William Myhand	Nancy Lock	Nov. 23, 1807
David Adams	Polly Johnston	**Nov. 27, 1807
John Myrick	Verilinda Harris	Nov. 29, 1807
Nelson Gunn?	Jane Reynolds	Dec. 24, 1807
John C. Turner	Sally Fluellen	Dec. 23, 1807
Henry Wilson	Mary Stanford	Jan. 15, 1807
William Barrow	Rebeckah Heath	Aug. 13, 1807
Price Willis	Nancy Coleman	Dec. 18, 1807
Daniel Dennis	Nancy Breed	**Dec. 29, 1807
John Killabrew	Patsy Lindsey	**Dec. 29, 1807
Joseph White	Winnie Wheeler	Jan. 4, 1808
Dingley (Wrigley?) Lokey	(blank) McGee	**Jan. 7, 1808
James Lesly	Eliza Bird	Jan. 13, 1808
John Hutcheson	Fanny Smith	Jan. 16, 1808
Abner Bailey	Elizabeth Parker	Jan. 19, 1808
Lewis Wright	Nancy Hill	Jan. 21, 1808
John Kellam	Nancy Rigby	**Jan. 23, 1808
John Lewis	Patsy Waggoner	**Jan. 27, 1808
Peter Clower	Loveny Mitchell	**Jan. 28, 1808
John Walker	Polly Moore	Feb. 3, 1808
David Lynn	Lucy Kinsey	Feb. 18, 1808
Elijah Gosea (sic)	Hixy Avent (sic)	Feb. 19, 1808
John Brooks	Nancy Nunn	**Feb. 16, 1808
Young Seymore	Teletha Cohoon	Feb. 25, 1808
James Cobb	Ann Jones	**Feb. 25, 1808
John Bonner	Catherine Haynes	Feb. 25, 1808
John McCrary	Amelia Beall	**Feb. 27, 1808
William Wynne	Lucy Harris	Mar. 13, 1808
Lemuel McCrery	Jinney Beall	**Mar. 8, 1808
George Cotton	Rebeccah Pennington	Mar. 17, 1808
William Wynne	Lucy Harris	**Mar. 12, 1808
Samuel Geesling	Mary Smith	Apr. 2, 1808
Dickinson Culpepper	Franky Wynne	Apr. 10, 1808
Elijah Jones	Margaret Beall	**Apr. 9, 1808
John Bunkley	Mariah Barksdale	Apr. 9, 1808
John Sanders	Lucinda Malone	Apr. 12, 1808
Solomon Draper	Lucy Dennis	**Apr. 27, 1808
Henry Carlton	Nancy Moore	Apr. 27, 1808
Henry Harbuck	Hester Greeson	Apr. 21, 1808
Thomas Battle	Polly Baker	Apr. 17, 1808
William Harbuck	Hannah Merritt	Apr. 14, 1808
John Butts	Tempy Green	May 18, 1808
William Ball	Elizabeth Gray	June 6, 1808
William Shoder? (not plain)	Polly King	May 28, 1808
Moses Jackson	Rebackah Strother	May 17, 1808
Lemuel Wynne	Lucy Fretwell	June 23, 1808
William Taylor	Sally Rose	June 2, 1808
Isom Wheeler	Eddea Smith	June 12, 1808
Daniel Thomas	Lavinah Smith	June 19, 1808
Wright Mims	Eliza Kendall	June 29, 1808

Name of Groom	Name of Bride	Date of License
Henry Brown	Aley Burnley	June 23, 1808
Sims Kelly	Polly Kemp	**June 28, 1808
Josiah Sallis	Patience Jones	**June 6, 1808
William Dunaway	Lavinah Brewer	**July 28, 1808
Thomas Deason	Cythia Averit (Averil?)	**July 2, 1808
Benjamin Bryant	Polly Brazil	Aug. 7, 1808
John Matthews	Polly Rogers	Aug. 7, 1808
Bala (sic) Hardin	Betsy Cox	**Aug. 9, 1808
Hardy Green	Elizabeth Jones	**Aug. 9, 1808
John Woods	Patsy Culpepper	Aug. 2, 1808
Dennis L. Ryan	Mary Haynes	Aug. 30, 1808
Samuel Pearson	Patience Jones	**Sept. 2, 1808
Windor Hillman	Gracy McMath	**Sept. 10, 1808
David Herrington	Elizabeth Holaday	Sept. 12, 1808
Littleberry Little	Rebecca Newsom	Sept. 15, 1808
Jeremiah Pool?	Milly Hancock	**Sept. 24, 1808
John Rigby (Wrigley?)	Elizabeth Kelly	**Sept. 27, 1808
Gideon Beddingfield	Henrietta Ball	Oct. 9, 1808
Benjamin Hardin	Patsy Cox	**Oct. 9, 1808
John Green	Nancy Daniel	June 29, 1808
William Henry	Nancy Drake	**Oct. 2, 1808
Insil? Farr	Catherine Smith	**Oct. 4, 1808
Michael Rogers	Elender McFarlin	Oct. 22, 1808
James Ledbetter	Sally Camp	**Nov. 12, 1808
John Wright	Temperance Ogletree	Nov. 13, 1808
James Butt	Patsy Jones	**Nov. 19, 1808
Robert Ellis	Martha Granade	Dec. 3, 1808
Benjamin C. Gancy?	Caroline Bird	Dec. 8, 1808
Jesse Davidson	Peggy King	Dec. 4, 1808
William Luckett	Jane Sims	**Dec. 1, 1808
Wadkins Davis	Sarah Matthews	**Dec. 6, 1808
Richard Barrow	Betsey Jones	Dec. 29, 1808
Clody Camp	Mary Harwell	**Dec. 19, 1808
Silas Pace	Margaret Sell(Sill?)	Jan. 5, 1809
Daniel Burgin	Polly McGee	**Dec. 13, 1808
John King	Mary Jackson	**Dec. 27, 1808
John Runolds	Patsy Herold	**Dec. 21, 1808
Robert Fleming	Polly Watson	**Dec. 29, 1808
Lovett Smith	Eliza Fort	**Dec. 29, 1808
Dunwoodie Dozier	Eliza Chapman	**Dec. 31, 1808
John Tharp	Elizabeth Hatcher	**Jan. 2, 1809
John Gibson	Elizabeth Dozier	**Jan. 7, 1809
Lewis Harrell (Howell?)	Crisa Farr	Jan. 26, 1809
John Vining	Polly Hubert	Jan. 5, 1809
Aaron Johnston	Jessie Freeman	**Jan. 13, 1809
Willis Randle	Millie Moore	Jan. 17, 1809
James Powell	Nancy Williams	Jan. 22, 1809
Highland Livingston	Sarah Cardal	**Jan. 22, 1809
Allen Anders (Andrews?)	Dicy Allen	Jan. 23, 1809
John Rushing	Suckey Gardner	**Jan. 30, 1809
James J. Dale	Hester Duckworth	Feb. 9, 1809
Solomon Warner	(Bride's name blank)	**Feb. 9, 1809
Stephen Granberry	Eliza Spurling	**Feb. 18, 1809
William Mitchell	Rebecca Newsom	**Feb. 23, 1809
Amos Johnston	Sally Bishop	**Feb. 11, 1809
Henry Adams	Rebecca Sanders	**Feb. 13, 1809
Willis Hobbs	Polly Pool	**Feb. 20, 1809
Leonard Pratt	Elizabeth Brooks	**Feb. 14, 1809
Renay Eades	Elizabeth Harden	**Mar. 2, 1809
Amos Newsom	Nancy Adams	**Mar. 3, 1809
John Smith	Elizabeth Camp	**Mar. 13, 1809
Parot Rouse	Mary Mash	**Mar. 15, 1809
Granville Moody	Anna Harris	**Mar. 23, 1809
James Armstrong	Rachel Coleman	**Apr. 12, 1809
William Holland	Elizabeth Fluellin	**Apr. 15, 1809
William Reese	Lettice McCrery	May 20, 1809

Name of Groom	Name of Bride	Date of License
Richmond Dennis	Frances Jones	**May 31, 1809
Daniel Rowland	Eliza Harville	**June 1, 1809
Joseph Johnston	Polly Darden	June 6, 1809
John Green	Nancy Daniel	**June 28, 1809
Jeptha Brantley	Lucy Persons	**July 12, 1809
Robert Chapman	Polly Stone	**July 17, 1809
Samuel Ansley	Mary Tillman	**July 21, 1809
Willoughby S. Hill	Nancy A. Tharp	**Aug. 2, 1809
John Matthews	Polly Rogers	**Aug. 4, 1809
John Chambers	Obedience Ledbetter	**Aug. 7, 1809
Hardy Pace	Succy (sic) Turner	**May 20, 1809
Elbert Bishop	Eleanor Stanford	Sept. 5, 1809
(Married by A. Crawford, M.G., in Columbia County.)		
Lemuel Koats (or Roats?)	Lavina Flinn	**Sept. 11, 1809
Crawford Newsome	Elizabeth Newsome	**Sept. 14, 1809
John Harrison	Elizabeth Smith	Sept. 22, 1809
Middleton Usry	Polly Newsome	Sept. 2, 1809
David Herrington	Elizabeth Holaday	**Sept. 13, 1809
Jacob Willis	Sally Rogers	**Sept. 17, 1809
Anthony Jones	Sarah Barrow	Sept. 24, 1809
Joshua Rowe	Elizabeth Rigby	**Feb. 23, 1809
William Pile	Hannah Cloud	Oct. 12, 1809
Daniel Kinsey	Levicy Davidson	**Oct. 9, 1809
William Teddley	Polly Perry	Oct. 29, 1809
Bird Gilbert	Sally Spinks	**Oct. 19, 1809
Henry Chambless	Rachel Dannelly	**Oct. 6, 1809
Gideon Beddingfield	Henrietta Bull	**Oct. 9, 1809
Benjamin Matthews	Sally Wilmouth	**Oct. 12, 1809
James Jackson	Sally Beall	**Nov. 2, 1809
Drury Pate	Sarah Johnston	**Nov. 17, 1809
William Byrom the 2nd.	Isabella Akins	Nov. 15, 1809
Michael Deason	Polly Deason	Nov. 26, 1809
John James	Polly Parish	Nov. 23, 1809
James Sallis	Rebeckah Ivy	Dec. 12, 1809
James Gafford	Elizabeth Dickens	Jan. 2, 1810
William McNeill	Peggy Bailey	Jan. 25, 1810
James Rogers	Sophia Cooksey	Jan. 25, 1810
Francis Benton	Susannah Holland	Jan. 6, 1810
William Warner	Patsy Neal	**Feb. 6, 1810
Jacob Johnston	Patsy Smith	Feb. 18, 1810
Jesse Williams	Milberry Wheless	Feb. 12, 1810
Willis Hobbs	Polly Pool	Feb. 22, 1810
Elisha Gardner	Elizabeth Rushin	**Mar. 4, 1810
Perry Powell	Nancy Lyon	Mar. 22, 1810
James Standford	Polly McGee	Mar. 18, 1810
Edmond Johnston	Sally Crenshaw	Mar. 17, 1810
Edwin Baker	Nancy Baker	May 13, 1810
James Littleton	Lydia Tydwell	**May 17, 1810
Stephen Grizzle	Elizabeth Harrison	May 27, 1810
John Parham	Catherine Dansby	Oct. 7, 1810
Abner Abbett	Susannah Averett	Nov. 15, 1810
Willis Terry	Jinsy Edwards	Aug. 26, 1810
Stephen W. Bembry	Petheny Garrett	**Aug. 7, 1810
(Bromley?)		
Abner Norris	Peggy Davis	Aug. 4, 1810
Thomas Lockhart	Tempy Rogers	**Sept. 4, 1810
William Greeson	Sucky Hill	**Sept. 5, 1810
Warren Barrow	Polly Heath	Oct. 17, 1810
William Newsom	Frances Hardaway	Oct. 1, 1810
Timothy Reading	Fannie Hardaway	**Nov. 12, 1810
James Lockett	Sally Darden	Dec. 13, 1810
Michael Moore, Esq.	Polly Smith	**Jan. , 1811
Lewis Krinze?	Gatsy M. Wingate	Sept. 15, 1810
John Daniel	Elizabeth Hutchins	Oct. 2, 1810
John Hutchins	Sally Irby	Sept. 28, 1810
James Hicks	Polly Hutchins	Oct. 2, 1810

Name of Groom	Name of Bride	Date of License
William Northen	Rebecca Watherby	Oct. 3, 1810
John Matthews	Sally Moore	Dec. 18, 1810
Hardy Hopson	Patsey Turner	Jan. 24, 1811
James Gray, Jr.	Betsey Hadley	Jan. 10, 1811
Caswell Ball	Betsy Parham	Jan. 10, 1811
Aaron Jackson	Elizabeth Fleming	Jan. 15, 1811
Fisher Ghaskins (Gaskins)	Polly Lacy	Jan. 17, 1811
William McMath	Polly Amos	Jan. 23, 1811
Hampton Pariah	Sally Smith	Jan. 31, 1811
Presley Spinks	Martha Jones	Jan. 31, 1811
Michael Moore, Esq.	Nancy Smith	Jan. 3, 1811
William Gunn	Pleasant Stephens	Feb. 3, 1811
James Bonner	Nancy Bonner	Feb. 19, 1811
Archelaus Wilson	Sarah Wilson	Mar. 7, 1811
Thomas Ivy	Peggy Gibson	Oct. 18, 1810
Joseph Wright	Polly Walker	Apr. 11, 1811
Joseph Rhodes	Sally Rhodes	Apr. 8, 1811
Henry McNease	Polly McNease	May 5, 1811
Jared Wright	Dicy Cobb	Aug. 1, 1810
John Turner	Nancy Parham	May 16, 1811
John Hygh?	Elizabeth Harris	May 27, 1811
Harris McKinney	Jincy Ivey	May 17, 1810
William Blount	Mrs. Elizabeth Wright	May 17, 1810
George W. Hardwick	Mary Fontaine	June 27, 1810
Irby Dewberry	Temperance Heath	Aug. 1, 1810
Robert Hill	Sarah Hill	July 11, 1811
Jonah Brook	Sally Wall	Feb. 5, 1805
Allen Duckworth	Theresa Rees	Dec. 4, 1810
William Doster	Margaret Edge	Aug. 6, 1810
William Grace	Elizabeth Coxwell	Aug. 24, 1811
Thomas Avera	Tabitha Davis	Sept. 11, 1811
Moses McKinney	Harriet Burgholder	Sept. 21, 1811
Elijah Dickens	Susannah Jackson	Oct. 15, 1811
John Coffield	Harriet Jackson	Oct. 15, 1811
John Lock	Rosy Morris	Nov. 5, 1811
Allen Dykes	Polly Bledsoe	Nov. 7, 1811
Wiley Hight	Nancy Brantley	Dec. 19, 1811
Joseph Mil'n Semmes	Mary Torrence, widow	Jan. 16, 1812
James Gray of Jones Co.	Susannah Cody	Jan. 20, 1812
James Peek	Peggy Swain	Jan. 25, 1812
Samuel Yarbrough	Mrs. Nancy Manning	Jan. 4, 1812
Fielding Hill	Isabella Gibson	Jan. 30, 1812
Richard Stonestreet?	Mary Dicken	May 10, 1812
John Smythe	Elizabeth Peevy	May 4, 1812
Britton Carroll	Winifred Benton	Feb. 6, 1812
Bolland Lacy	Phalby? Peevy	Feb. 25, 1812
Moses Ivy	Sarah Banks	Mar. 10, 1812
Thomas Myhand	Susannah Benton, widow	June 25, 1812
William Abbett	Penelope Newsom	Aug. 9, 1812
John Henderson	Polly King	Aug. 24, 1812
John White	Rachel Carter	Nov. 24, 1812
Theophilus Miller	Charity Davis	Dec. 9, 1812
James Harbuck	Martha Harris	Dec. 24, 1812
Robert Armstrong	Priscilla Dennis	Dec. 31, 1812
John McEwen	Lucy Morris	Jan. 28, 1813
John Davidson	Elizabeth May	Jan. 18, 1813
Elijah Boynton	Elizabeth Jackson	Feb. 18, 1813
James Armstrong	Lavina Harbuck	Feb. 21, 1813
Churchwell Roey?	Sally Parrish	Mar. 4, 1813
Thomas Fisher	Epsy Burkhalter	May 23, 1813
William Denmark	Mary Cockrum	May 30, 1813
John Gibson	Clarissa Britt, widow	June 8, 1813
Thomas Shambless	Nelly McNiece	June 23, 1813
William Harrell	Milly Barrow	June 24, 1813
Dolphin Davis	Jemima Kendall	July 15, 1813

Name of Groom	Name of Bride	Date of License
Abraham Grierson	Susannah Sheffield	Aug. 3, 1813
Nicholas Andrews	Marcella Ransom	Aug. 18, 1813
Nathan Maffett	Elizabeth Blount	Sept. 2, 1813
Orian Davis	Polly Parker	Sept. 23, 1813
Henry B. Thompson	Louisa Sophia Cratin	Oct. 26, 1813
James McCarty	Drusilla Ghesling	Dec. 2, 1813
Charles Moore	Elizabeth Ellington	Dec. 22, 1813
Thomas Tieson	Drusilla Mays	Dec. 21, 1813
James M. Bates	Elizabeth Ghesling	Dec. 21, 1813
John Smith	Nancy Anderson	Dec. 30, 1813
Ishmael McDaniel	Sallie Harvill	June 2, 1813
Ira Weaver	Martha Rowland	Jan. 12, 1814
Thomas Davis	Temperance Matthews	Feb. 11, 1814
John Battle	Jane Allen	Feb. 24, 1814
Gilham Smith	Patsy Sturdivant	Mar. 20, 1814

WARREN COUNTY DEED BOOK A

NOTE: This BOOK A is actually several older books transcribed in 1853.
This transcription may account for some errors. In this Book
the older ones were transcribed as follows:

Pages 1-85 Old Book A   Pages 286-540 Old Book D
Pages 85-131 Old Book B   Pages 540-636 Old Book E
Pages 131-286 Old Book C

Page 1: ALLEN DORMAN of Warren Co., Ga. to WILEY DORMAN one negro man
Simon and one negro woman Sook for 100 pounds Dec. 10, 1794.
Wit: JOHN CASTLEBERRY, ASA CASTLEBERRY. Rec. Apr. 12, 1796.

Pages 1-2: THOMPSON BIRD of Wilkes Co., Ga. to JOHN PEAK of Burke
County (now Warren) one negro girl Sal. Oct. 1, 1795.
Wit: PETER B. TERRELL, JOHN HUNTER. Ack. Apr. 30, 1796.

Page 2: MARK HARDIN of Warren Co., Ga. to MARTIN HARDIN of same place,
for 50 pounds, a negro man Slave Brister? Feb. 28, 1795.
Wit: J. HARDIN.

Pages 2-3: Warren Co., Ga., WILLIAM DRYDEN admr. & JAMES BLUNT are
held and firmly bound unto SEPTIMUS WEATHERBY, Judge of
Probate of said county. Aug. 24, 1796. WILLIAM DRYDEN, admr. of est.
of JNO. DRYDEN, dec'd. (bond to insure true administration of est.)
WILLIAM DRYDEN (X), JAMES BLUNT, Test: THOMAS DESTOR? Rec. April 12,
1796.

Pages 3-4: Warren Co., Ga., ANNA J. JOHNSTON, WM. BRYON adms. GEORGE
SMITH & BURLEY bound unto SEPTIMUS WEATHERBY 1000 pounds,
Sept. 12, 1795. admr. of est. of MALCOM late of this Co., dec'd.
ANNA J. JOHNSTON (SEAL), WM. BYROM (SEAL), GEO. SMITH (SEAL), STEPHEN
BURLEY (SEAL). Wit: LEONARD FRETWELL.

Page 4: JOSEPH CARSON of Wilks Co., Ga., for 182 dollars paid by
JOHN GIBSON of Warren Co., a negro girl Celie, Jan. 2, 1796,
JOSEPH CARSON (SEAL). Wit: ISA TUCKER. Ack. Jan. 3, 1796. Rec.
Apr. 12, 1796.

Page 5: WILLIAM SLATTER of Warren Co., Ga. to MARY FEW of same Co.,
a negro woman Charity, a young negro woman Pegga. 430 silver
dollars. Feb. 22, 1796. WILLIAM SLATTER (SEAL), Wit: EDMOND WALSH,
Ack. Feb. 22, 1796, Wit: ELIZABETH DYSART(m)JOHN DYSART Ack. March 16,
1796, Rec. May 10, 1796.

Pages 5-6: Received at Augusta Nov. 17, 1795 of JOHN FOX 200 dollars
for a negro boy slave Kinchen. BENJA. HILL (SEAL). Wit:
JAS. F. WALKER. Rec'd at Augusta Jan. 15, 1796 of Mr. HENRY PEEBLES
250 dollars for negro boy Kinchen. JOHN FOX (SEAL). Test: JAMES
STALLINGS, JAMES HAY. Ack. Jan. 18, 1796, Rec. May 12, 1796.

Page 6: State of Georgia, Wilkes County, now Warren, Sept. 29, 1791,
SARAH MIMS bound to JOHN BALL for 100 pounds. a certain
tract of land joining to said BALLS land & ZADOCK RODANS land, where
MARY MIMS now lives, lying on Rocky Comfort. SARAH MIMS (X), MARY
MIMS (X). Wit: JOHN MIMS. Rec. May 18, 1796.

Page 7: Warren Co., Ga., PIERSON YOUNG, admn. and JACOB YOUNG bound
unto SEPTIMUS WEATHERBY, 300 pounds Jan. 18, 1796. est. of
_____ BURTON, late of this Co., dec'd. PIERSON YOUNG (SEAL), JACOB
YOUNG (SEAL), Rec. May 18, 1796.

Pages 7-8: Warren Co., Ga., by virtue of a Writ of Fierefacias directed
to me, taken unto Execution, four negroes (Viz) Mill & her
child PHILLIS, SARAH & DANIEL, of the property of BENJAMIN DICKSON,

dec'd, and thereon a Sale in Market when VINSON JOHNSON became the purchaser, and paid 150 pounds. B. HODO Shff., June 12, 1795. Test: HENRY MITCHELL, Rec. July 8, 1796.

Page 8:   PETER GOODWIN, Warren Co., Ga., 250 pounds paid by WYCHE
          GOODWIN of same Co., one negro man Mark, negro woman Phillis, negro girl Chancy, negro child boy Anthony, sone Sorrel Mare, one horse, June 12, 1795. PETER GOODWIN (SEAL), Wit: CORNELIUS CARDION (M), JAMES CRISUP (X). Ack. March 8, 1796, Rec. Aug. 18, 1796.

Page 9:   RANDOLPH REVILL of Warren Co., Ga., to MARTIN HARDIN, sold a
          Molatto boy slave Austin, Aug. 23, 1796. RANDOLPH REVILL
(SEAL). Wit: MARK HARDIN, LEML. PRUITT J.P. Rec. Sept. 6, 1796.
          Richmond County, Ga., JOSEPH MAY of St. and Co., aforesd. sold to RICHARD WHATLEY, one negro boy Jim for 40 pounds. Nov. 8, 1782. JOSEPH MAY (4‚), Wit: JAMES BOWIE, SALLIE BOWIE. Rec. Oct. 7, 1796.

Page 10: State of Ga., Warren Co., FRANCIS HILL, admr., SOLOMON
          SLATTER and RICHARD FELTCHER Esq. bound to SEPTIMUS WEATHERBY,
Oct. 3, 1796, est. of RICHARD HILL, dec'd. FRANCES HILL (Ɵ) (SEAL), R. B. FLETCHER (SEAL), SOLM. SLATTER (SEAL), Test: WILLIAM MIMS (Z), Rec. Oct. 20, 1796.

Page 11: Warren Co., Ga., BARBARA LUCAS & JAMES CALDWELL, Admr. and
          SAMUEL YARBROUGH & JOSEPH PEARY bound to SEPTIMUS WEATHERBY.
May 13, 1796, est. of WILLIAM LUCAS, dec'd. BARBA (sic) LUCAS (X), JAMES CALDWELL, SAMUEL YARBROUGH, JOSEPH PEARY (£). Rec. Oct. 20, 1796.

Pages 11-12:   Warren Co., Ga., ELIZABETH GOODWIN, Amnx., WYCHE GOODWIN,
               WILLIAM DEANE bound unto SEPTIMUS WEATHERBY. July 19,
1796, est. of PETER GOODWIN dec'd ELIZA. GOODWIN (SEAL), WYCHE GOODWIN (SEAL), WILLIAM DEANE (SEAL). Rec. Dec. 16, 1796.

Pages 12-13:   Warren Co., Ga., REUBEN, Admr. and GEORGE WEATHERBY bound
               to SEPTIMUS WEATHERBY. Oct. 18, 1796, est. of LAZARUS
GURLEY, dec'd. REUBEN JONES (SEAL), GEORGE WEATHERBY (SEAL), Rec. Dec. 16, 1796.

Pages 13-14:   Warren Co., Ga., RICHARD CURRIE & BENJAMIN WARNER,
               Admnrs., CARY CURRIE & NORVELL ROBERTSON bound to SEPTIMUS
WEATHERBY. Oct. 3, 1796. est. of JOHN CURRIE, dec'd BENJAMIN WARNER (SEAL), RICHARD CURRIE (SEAL), NORWELL ROBERTSON (SEAL), CARY CURRIE (SEAL). Test: ETHELRED THOMAS.

Page 14: Received of Mr. JOEL THRUWITTS one thousand weight of
          Tobacco being his part in paying a note off, which he and
his mother in law (the widow COX) gave for rent. I say rec'd. by me in 1790. Dec. 31, 1791 WM. SILLAVAN. Test. JAMES BOON. Sworn to by JAMES BOON Dec. 16, 1796. Rec. Dec. 26, 1796.

Pages 14-15:   Warren Co., Ga., RICHARD COCKS, Admr. and THOMAS COCKS
               bound unto SEPTIMUS WEATHERBY, Jan. 8, 1796. est. of
THOMAS HARDIN, dec'd RICHARD COCKS (SEAL), THOS. COCKS (SEAL), Rec. Feb. 16, 1797.

Pages 15-16:   JOSEPH MAY, Washington Co., Ga., to SOLOMON NEWSOM of
               Warren Co., Ga., six negroes, 33 head of cattle, 4 horses,
two bay mares, two colts, four feather beds Sept. 1, 1796. $1288.57 paid on or before the Jan. 1, 1799. JOSEPH MAY (SEAL), THOS. SHIELDS, J.P., Rec. Feb. 18, 1797.

Page 16: Franklin Co., North Carolina, Rec'd of ETHELRED THOMAS of
          Warren Co., Ga., $250 for negroes May 13, 1790. Jan. 25,
1797. JAS BARROW (SEAL). Test: BYRD JARRELL, JOHN ROBINSON. Act. Feb. 9, 1797. Rec. Feb. 10, 1797.

Page 17: JOHN WHITWORTH of King William Co., Virginia, and SAMUEL
          WHITWORTH of Warren Co., Ga., for 20 pounds from JAMES JONES

200

Pages 17-18:   Wilkes County, Georgia, know all men by these presents
                that whereas ELIANDER, ELIZABETH & CATHERINE KILGORE,
and JAMES & MARY ALISON, ROBERT KILGORE, Junr., and RONERT KILGORE,
Senr. as guardian for JOHN KILGORE, we being, the wife and heirs of
RALPH KILGORE, dec'd of the county and state aforesaid.. tract of land
in County of Columbia, Ga.. in the possession of one JOEL HANDBY, JOSEPH
EVANS, and RICHARD BUFFINGTON.. we appoint WILLIAM STARK (or his attorney)
of Columbia Co., to recover said land.. Feb. 3, 1791 ELIANDER KILGORE
(SEAL), ELIZABETH KILGORE (SEAL), CATHARINE KILGORE (SEAL), JAMES ALISON
(SEAL), MARY ALISON (SEAL), JOHN KILGORE (SEAL). Wit: JOHN OWENS,
DAVID HEDGEPETH, ELIZABETH WELLS (X) (WILLS?). Rec. April 14, 1798.

Page 19:   RICHARD SMITH have sold to JOSEPH WHITE a certain Negro girl
            for $200, March 17, 1798. RICHD SMITH S Wit: T. HARMON, A
GRIER J.P.

Pages 19-20:   Warren Co., Ga., JANE VAUGHN, Admx. and SAMUEL ALEXANDER
               bound to SEPTIMUS WEATHERBY.. "this 27th day 1797" est.
of ALEXANDER VAUGHN, dec'd. JANE VAUGHN (SEAL), SAML. ALEXANDER (SEAL)
Test. A. GRIEL?, Rec. July 16, 1798.

Page 20:   Warren County, Ga., LOVINAH WHEELER Admx., ICHABOD COX &
           EDMD DISMAKES bound to SEPTIMUS WEATHERBY Jan. 24, 1798.
est. of SION WHEELER, dec'd. LOVINAH WHEELER (SEAL), ICHABOD COX (SEAL),
EDMUND DISMAKES (SEAL) July 16, 1798.

Page 21:   Warren County, Ga., MARY COOPER, Admx., HARMOND WILKERSON
           & PETER CASTLEBERRY bound to SEPTIMUS WEATHERBY May 16, 1798.
est. of JAMES COOPER, dec'd. MARY COOPER (LS), HARMON WILKERSON (LS),
PETER CASTLEBERRY (LS). Jly. 17, 1798. (Rec. date)

Pages 21-22:   Warren Co., Ga., DAVID NEAL, Admr., JOHN HOBSON bound to
               SEPTIMUS WEATHERBY March 7, 1797.. est of ZECHARIAH HEROLD,
dec'd.. D. NEAL (LS), JNO HOBSON (LS). Rec. July 17, 1797.

Pages 22-23:   Warren Co., Ga., JAMES SCOTT, Admn. and WILLIAM BYROM,
               Esq. bound to SEPTIMUS WEATHERBY. Nov. 9, 1796. est.
of GEORGE HAWTHORNE, dec'd. JAMES SCOTT (SEAL), WM. BRYOM (SEAL).
Rec. July 17, 1798.

Pages 23-24:   Warren Co., Ga., SARAH WYNNE, Admx., BENJAMIN WYNNE,
               Admr. and WILLIAM ROBERTSON bound to SEPTIMUS WEATHERBY.
Oct. 3, 1797.. est. of JOHN WYNNE Esq. dec'd. SARAH WYNNE (SEAL),
BENJAMIN WYNNE (SEAL), WM. ROBERTSON (SEAL) Test: JOHN MAUTREY. Rec.
July 17, 1798.

Pages 24-25:   Warren Co., Ga., WILLIAM COX, Admr. SARAH THRUWITS,
               Admx., THOMAS COX bound to SEPTIMUS WEATHERBY, Oct. 5,
1797. est. of JOEL THRUWITS dec'd. WM. COCKS (SEAL), SALLAY THRUWITTS
(SEAL), THOS COCKS (SEAL), TO (F.?) PERSONS, Rec. July 17, 1798.

Pages 25-26:   Warren Co., Ga. JAMES DOUGLASS, Admr. HARMAN PERRYMAN
               & JOSHUA VINING bound to SEPTIMUS WEATHERBY, April 12,
1798. est. of REVD. JEPHTHAN VINING. dec'd. JAMES DOUGLASS (SEAL),
HARMAN PERRYMAN (SEAL), JOSHUA VINING (SEAL). Rec. July 17, 1798.

Page 26:   Warren Co., Ga., GEORGE FRANKLIN, Admr. & ALEXANDER SMITH
           bound to SEPTIMUS WEATHERBY Feb. 9, 1797... est. of WILLIAM
FRANKLIN, dec'd. GEORGE FRANKLIN, ALEXANDER SMITH. Rec. July 17,
1798.

Page 27:   DAVID WALKER of Jefferson Co., Ga., to JOHN BRUTON for $800?,
           one negro man, one negro woman, one mare, a stock of hogs,
my corn, cotton and remaining part of any crop Nov. 1, 1798 DAVID
WALKER (SEAL) Wit: AALLEY BRUTON, BENJAMIN BRUTON J. P. Rec. Dec. 28,
1798.

Pages 27-28:   Warren Co., Ga., SARAH HILL, Exrx., WYATT BONNER and
               ADAM JONES bound to SEPTIMUS WEATHERBY Feb. 16, 1796.
est.. of JOSEHUA HILL, dec'd SARAH HILL (X) (SEAL), ADAM JONES (SEAL),
WYATT BONNER (SEAL). No recording date.

Page 28:   JAMES COLTON of Warren Co., Ga., for $350 to STERLING JONES
           a negro wench March 8, 1798. JAMES COLTON (SEAL). Wit:
TURNER PERSONS & ISAIAH TUCKER. Proven: Mar. 4, 1799, Rec. March 5,
1799.

Page 29:   Warren Co., Ga., THEOPHILUS HICKMAN of Edgefield Co., South
           Carolina for $1000 to JOHN RURKIN of Warren Co., Ga., one
negro man Nash, Dec. 27, 1798. THEOPHILUS HICKMAN (SEAL). Wit:
LARKIN CHIVERS (X), WILLIAM SIMMONS, D. MACLEAN.
           Warren Co., Ga., personally appeared before me WM. BRYOM,
Justice of the Peace for Co. afrsd. WILLIAMS SIMMONS to Swear that he
saw DUNCAN MCLEAN, LARKIN CHIVERS and ENOCH RENTFROE sign their names
before me April 23, 1799, WM. BRYOM J.P. Rec. Apr. 25, 1799.

Pages 29-30:   Georgia. LEWIS WRIGHT, HENRY HILL, LEVI PRUITT, JOHN
               GIBSON, REDDICK BASS, AMOS WRIGHT, ISAIAH TUCKER & REUBEN
JONES bound the his Excellecy JARED IRWIN, Governor and Commander in
and over said state, $20,000 Dec. 1, 1797. The above bounden LEWIS
WRIGHT was, on that last General Election Duly Elected Sheriff for the
County of Warren in said State and HENRY HILL appointed his lawful
deputy. Rec. April 25, 1799.

Pages 30-31:   JOHN CURRIE, Admr. and BARRETT BROWN bound to SEPTIMUS
               SEATHERBY April 17, 1799...est. of JANE BURNS dec'd.
JNO. CURRIE (SEAL). Rec. Oct. 29, 1800.

Pages 31-32:   Warren Co., Ga., LYDIA HARTFIELD, BENJAMIN HOWARD bound
               unto the Judges of the Court of Ordinary Aug. 11, 1800...
est. of GEORGE HARTFIELD, dec'd LYDIA HARTFIELD (SEAL) BENJA. HOWARD
(SEAL). Rec. Oct. 29, 1800.

Page 32:   Warren Co., Ga., DANIEL MCCOWAN and THOMAS JONES bound to
           Court of Ordinary July 18, 1799. JOHN SINN, Admr. of est.
of FUGUS SINN, dec'd. Signed FERGUS SINN (SEAL), THOS. JONES (SEAL).
Rec. Dec. 2, 1800.

Page 33:   Warren Co., Ga., FREDERICK DANIEL, WILLIAM MIMS bound to
           Court of Ordinary, July 18, 1799...est. of JOHN THOMAS,
dec'd. FREDERICK DANIEL (SEAL), WM. MIMS (SEAL). Rec. March 3, 1800.

Pages 33-34:   Warren Co., Ga., SUSANNA BUTLER, Admx. BEAL BUTLER, ENOS
               BUTLER bound to Court of Ordinary, July 18, 1799. Est.
of NOBLE BUTLER, dec'd. SUSANNA BUTLER (SEAL), BEAL BUTLER (SEAL),
ENOX BUTLER (SEAL). Rec. Dec. 3, 1800.

Pages 34-35:   Warren Co., Ga., JONATHAN HARGATHY, Admr. and EDWARD
               HILL, bound to Court of Ordinary Apr. 7, 1800. est. of
ISAAC COOK, dec'd. JONATHAN HARGATHY (SEAL), EDWARD E. HILL (SEAL).
Rec. Dec. 3, 1800.

Page 35:   Warren Co., Ga., JONATHAN HAGARTHY and EDWARD HILL bound to
           Court of Ordinary July 18, 1799. JONATHAN HARGATHY guardian
for PERRYBY COOK, SELETHY COOK, daus. of ISAAC COOK, dec'd JONATHAN
HAGARTHY (SEAL), EDWARD E. HILL (SEAL), Rec. Dec. 4, 1800.

Page 36:   Warren Co., Ga., AMOS PERSON, HOLLY WALKER, Admrs., NICHOLAS
           WILLIAMS and RICHARD HEATH bound to Court of Ordinary Apr.
20, 1800. Est. of JOEL WALKER, dec'd. AMOS PERSONS (SEAL), HOLLY
WALKER (SEAL, RICHD HEATH (SEAL), N. WILLIAMS (SEAL), Rec. Dec. 4, 1800.

Pages 36-37:   Warren Co., Ga., DAVID NEAL & SAMUEL NEAL, Admrs. JAMES
               MCCORMAC & JOSEPH DUCKWORTH bound to Court of Ordinary
Feb. 18, 1800. Est. of THOMAS NEAL, dec'd. DAVID NEAL (SEAL), SAMUEL
NEAL (SEAL), JAMES MCCORMACK, JAS. DUCKWORTH (SEAL), THOS. NEAL (SEAL).
Rec. Dec. 4, 1800.

Pages 37-38:   Warren Co., Ga., JOHN VANCE & MILLEY MCGEE bound to
               SEPTIMUS WEATHERBY Jan. 14, 1799...est. of JAMES VANCE
dec'd. JOHN VANCE (SEAL), MILLEY (MILEY) MCGEE (SEAL). Rec. Dec. 4,
1800.

Page 38:   Rec'd of DANIEL CULPEPPER $500 for Negro boy slave JOHN,
           Dec. 3, 1804. JOHN GIBSON (SEAL). Test. ISAIAH TUCKER clk.,
CHURCHILL GIBSON. Rec. Jan. 1, 1805.

Page 39:   DRURY MCCULLARS this 10th day of June 1805 certifies his
           mark and brand to be as follows, Viz., a swallow fork in each
ear & a hole in the left, and brand thus entered on record the date
above written J. TUCKER, Clk.
           Warren, Ga., SARAH GOLDWIN of the Co., and State aforesd.
for $2 paid by RICHARD HUTCHINSON a negro girl Priss June 23, 1800.
SARAH GOLDWIN (S), JO. R E I D, J. HODE J.P. Rec. Jan. 7, 1806.

Pages 39-40:   Warren Co., Ga., MICHAEL BURKHATTER, Admr., STERLING
               GARDNER, BASIL WRIGHT bound to SEPTIMUS WEATHERBY, July
3, 1797, est. of DAVID NUSAM, dec'd. MICHAEL BURKHATTER, BASIL WRIGHT,
STERLING GARDNER. Rec. Feb. 17, 1808. Test. JAMES JONES.

Pages 40-41:   Warren Co., Ga., THOMAS JONES, Admr., with will annext,
               BENJAMIN MITCHAEL & SOLOMON NEWSOM bound to SEPTIMUS
WEATHERBY Feb. 3, 1799. est. of WENNY PINSON, dec'd. THOMAS JONES,
BENJAMIN MITCHAEL, SOLOMON NUSAM. Rec. Feb. 17, 1808.

Pages 41-42:   Warren Co., Ga., SARAH ROSE & EDMOND ROSE, Admr. & WORMLEY
               ROSE & SAHD. FLEWILLEN bound to Judges of Court of
Ordinary, Feb. 9, 1801. Est. of WILLIAM ROSE, dec'd. SARAH ROSE,
EDMOND ROSE, W. E. ROSE, SHAD. FLEWILLIN. Rec. Feb. 18, 1808.

Page 42: Warren Co., Ga., NANCY BURSON, ISAAC BURSON, Admr. JOHN
          ENGLISH, MICHAEL CODY bound to Court of Ord. Aug. 11, 1801.
Est. of JONATHAN BURSON, dec'd. NANCY & ISAAC BURSON (SEAL), JOHN
ENGLISH (SEAL), MICHAEL CODY (SEAL). Rec. Feb. 18, 1808.

Page 43:   Warren Co., Ga., ROBERT RUTHERFORD, Admr., ROBERT ABERCROMBIE
           & HENRY SHELTON bound to Court of Ord. Feb. 10, 1801, est.
of ABNER MITCHELL, dec'd. ROBERT RUTHERFORD (SEAL), R. ABERCROMBIE
(SEAL), HENRY SHELTON (SEAL). Rec. Feb. 18, 1808.

Pages 43-44:   Warren Co., Ga., REUBEN BARROW & HUGH REESE & DAVID
               NUSAM bound to Court of Ord. June 8, 1801. Est. of
JAMES BARROW, dec'd. REUBEN BARROW (SEAL), HUGH REESE (SEAL), DAVID
NUSAM (SEAL), Rec. Feb. 19, 1808.

Pages 44-45:   Warren Co., Ga., ASA WRIGHT, JONSTON WRIGHT & BLAKE
               PEARCY bound to Court of Ord. June 8, 1801. Est. of
SAMUEL WRIGHT, dec'd. ASA WRIGHT, JOHNSTON WRIGHT, BLAKE PEARCY.
Rec. Feb. 19, 1808.

Pages 45-46:   Warren County, Ga., ROBERT ABERCROMBIE, JOSEPH HARREL
               (HOWEL?), MATHEW HUBERT Esqr., & JAMES JONES, Aug. 10,
1801. Est. of ARCHIBALD KEMPSEY, dec'd. ROBT. ABERCROMBIE, JOSEPH
HOWEL, M. HUBERT, J. JONES. Rec. Feb. 19, 1808.

Pages 46-47:   Warren Co., Ga., LYDIA NAPPER, SAMUEL RIDGEDELL, Admr.
               with will annexd. SOLOMON NUSAM, Senr. & ELISHA BROWN,
bound to Court of Ord. Feb. 8, 1802. Est. of JAMES NAPPER, dec'd
LYDIA NAPPER, SAMUEL RIDGEDELL, ELISHA BROWN, SOLLOMON NUSAM. Rec.
Feb. 21, 1808.

Page 47:   Warren Co., Ga., ROBERT ABERCROMBIE, Admr. MATHEW HUBERT,
           Esqr., WILLIAM FLOURNOY bound to Court of Ord. Feb. 8, 1802.
Est. of WILLIAM C. ABERCROMBIE, dec'd. R. ABERCROMBIE, WM. FLOURNOY,
M. HURBERT. Rec. Feb. 21, 1808.

Page 48:   Warren Co., Ga., JACOB BULL, MARK HARDIN & JESSE BULL bound
            to Court of Ord. Feb. 9, 1802. Est. of ELI BULL, dec'd.
JACOB BULL (SEAL), MARK HARDIN (SEAL), JESSE BULL (SEAL), Rec. Feb. 21,
1808.

Pages 48-49:   ELIJAH WORTHEN, MARGARET HOLLIDAY, JAMES HARVIL, WILLIAM
                WORTHEN, JOSEPH HARVIL bound to Court of Ord. May 14, 1802.
Est. of AMBROSE HOLLIDAY, dec'd. ELIJAH WORTHEN, MARGARET HOLLADAY,
JAMES HARREL, JOSEPH HARREL, WILLIAM WORTHEN. Rec. Feb. 22, 1808.

Pages 49-50:   Warren Co., Ga., WILLIAM FLOURNEY, Admr. ROBERT ABERCROM-
                BIE, JOHN B. FLOURNOY bound to Court of Ord., May 3, 1802.
Est. of JACOB FLOURNEY, dec'd. WILLIAM FLORNOY, ROBERT ABERCROMBIE,
JOHN B. FLORNOY. Rec. Feb. 22, 1808.

Pages 50-51:   Warren Co., Ga., SAMUEL WINSLET, JOHN WILLIAMS, Admrs.
                SOLOMON LOCKET, JOSEPH BELL, MART. HARDIN, HOWEL HIGHT,
bound to Court of Ord. May 3, 1802. Est. of JOHN CARSON, dec'd. SAMUEL
WINSLET, JOHN WILLIAMS, JOSIAH BELL, SOLOMON LOCKET, HOWEL HIGHT, MARK
HARDIN.

Pages 51-52:   Warren Co., Ga., ELIZABETH MURPHY, JOHN MURPHY, JOHN
                WILSON & JOHN RUSHEN bound to Court of Ord. June 1, 1802.
Est. of EDWARD MURPHY, dec'd. ELIZABETH MURPHEY, JOHN MURPHEY, JOHN
RUSHEN, JOHN WILSON. Rec. Feb. 24, 1808.

Pages 52-53:   Warren Co., Ga., MARY PARKER, SOLOMON THOMPSON, JOHN
                MARTHEWS & AMOS PERSONS bound to Court of Ord. Feb. 15,
1803. Est. of JAMES PARKER, dec'd. MARY PARKER, SOLOMON THOMPSON, JOHN
MATHEWS, ANOS PERSONS. Rec. Feb. 24, 1808.

Page 53:   Warren Co., Ga., SAMUEL COOPER, JOEL HEATH & THOMAS HUTCHISON,
            bound to Court of Ord. Feb. 15, 1803. Est. of JAMES BISHOP,
dec'd. SAMUEL COOPER, JOEL HEATH, THOMAS HUTCHISON. Feb. 25, 1808.
(Rec.)

Page 54:   Warren Co., Ga., DAVID NEAL, REUBEN JONES, JOHN MCORMICK,
            bound to Court of Ord. April 11, 1803. Est. of SAMUEL NEAL,
dec'd. DAVID NEAL (SEAL), REUBEN JONES (SEAL), JOHN M. CORMICK (SEAL).
Rec. Feb. 25, 1808.

Pages 54-55:   Warren Co., Ga., STEPHEN LAWLENCE, JOSEPH CARTER, bound
                to Court of Ord. April 11, 1803. Est. of NATHAN WESTON,
dec'd. STEPHEN LAURENCE, JOSEPH CARTER. Rec. Feb. 26, 1808.

Pages 55-56:   Warren Co., Ga., ALSEY LEE, Admx., THOMAS ROGERS, WILLIAM
                PILCHER bound to Court of Ord., Aug. 9, 1803. Est. of
RICHARD LEE, dec'd. ALSEY LEE (X) (LS), THOMAS ROGERS (LS). Rec.
Feb. 26, 1808. Also WM. PILCHER (X) (L.S.).

Pages 56-57:   Warren Co., Ga., DAVID NUSAM, THOMAS DENT, ROBERT MOSES,
                JODAY NEUSOM, WILLIAM USRY bound to Court of Ord. Oct. 17,
1803. Est. of SOLOMON NEWSOM, Junr. dec'd. DAVID NEWSOM, THOMAS DENT,
WILLIAM URSERY, JOEDAY NEWSOM. Rec. Mar. 1, 1808.

Pages 57-58:   Warren Co., Ga., TULLEY BIGGS, JOHN RUSHING & WILLIAM
                SIMMONS, bound to Court of Ord. Oct. 17, 1803. Est. of
WIGGINS KILLEBREW, dec'd. TULLEY BIGGS, JOHN RUSHING (X), WM. SIMMONS.
Rec. May 31, 1808.

Pages 58-59:   Warren Co., Ga., SAMUEL BARKSDALE, PINKITHMAN HARVEY,
                STEPHEN BURNLEY, MICHAEL HARVEY & JOSIAH BEALL, bound
to Court of Ord. Est. of JOHN BARKSDALE, dec'd. SAMUEL BARKSDALE,
PINKITHMAN HARVEY (SEAL), STEPHEN BURNELY (SEAL), MICHAEL HARBEY (SEAL),
JOSIAH BEALL (SEAL). Rec. May 31, 1808.

Pages 59-60:   Warren Co., MARY WAGGONER, JAMES WAGGONER, GEORGE
                WAGGONER, AAROM LIPHAM, WILLIAM WAGGONER & SOLOMON
SLATTER bound to Court of Ord. Dec. 4, 1803. Est. of HENRY WAGGONER,

dec'd. MARY WAGGONER (X) (SEAL), JAMES WAGGONER (SEAL), GEORGE WAGGONER (SEAL), WILLIAM LIPHAM (SEAL), SOL SLATTER (SEAL), AAROM LIPHAM (SEAL) Rec. Dec. 17, 1808.

Page 60:   Warren Co., Ga., MARY SELL, JAMES DAVIS & JEREMIAH BURKHATTER,
           bound to Court of Ord... Jan. 2, 1804. Est. of THOMAS SELL,
dec'd. MARY SELL (X) (SEAL), ISAAC DAVIS (X) (SEAL), JEREMIAH
BURKHATTER (SEAL). Rec. Dec. 17, 1808.

Pages 60-61:   Warren Co., Ga., RHODA BATTLE & COL. SAMUEL ALEXANDER,
               COL. ROBERT ABERCROMBIE, MICAJAH LITTLE, bound to Court
of Ord. Feb. 12?, 1804. Est. of JOHN BATTLE Esq. dec'd. SAMUEL
ALEXANDER (SEAL), RHODA BATTLE (SEAL), R. ABERCROMBIE (SEAL), MICAJAH
LITTLE (SITTLE?) (SEAL). Dec. 17, 1808.

Pages 61-62:   Warren Co., Ga., ELIZABETH ROQUEMORE, DAVID ROBERTSON &
               WILLIAM USSORY bound to Court of Ord. Feb. 14, 1804. Est.
of JAMES ROQUEMORE, dec'd ELIZABETH ROQUEMORE (X) (SEAL), DAVID
ROBERTSON (SEAL), WILLIAM USSERY (X) (SEAL). Rec. Dec. 20, 1808.

Pages 62-63:   Warren County, Ga., HANAH CHAPMAN, WILLIAM CHAPMAN &
               ROBERT PARKER bound to Court of Ord. Feb. 15, 1804. Est.
of LABOURN CHAPMAN, dec'd. HANAH CHAPMAN (X) (SEAL), WILLIAM CHAPMAN
(SEAL), ROBERT PARKER (SEAL). Wit: T. PERSONS. Rec. Dec. 20, 1808.

Page 63:   Warren Co., Ga., ELIZABETH MYRICK, THOMAS EDMONSON & SEPTIMUS
           WEATHERBY bound to Court of Ord. Feb. 15, 1804. Est. of
OWEN MYRICK, dec'd. ELIZABETH MYRACK (SEAL), THOMAS EDMONSON (SEAL),
SEPTIMUS WEATHERBY (SEAL). (Apparently a diff. S. Weatherby from Judge
of Ord. Court.)

Pages 63-64:   Warren Co., Ga., JOHN NEVES & SHADRACK FLEWELLIN bound
               to Court of Ord. Feb. 15, 1804. Est. of DANIEL NEVES,
dec'd. JOHN NEVES (SEAL), SHADRACK FLEWELLIN (SEAL). Wit: T. PERSONS.
Rec. Dec. 21, 1808.

Pages 64-65:   Warren Co., Ga., JOHN MARTIN & JOSEPH MCKINLEY bound to
               Court of Ord. Dec. 15, 1804. Est. of WILLIAM MCKINLEY,
dec'd. JOHN MARTIN (SEAL), JOSEPH MCKINLEY (SEAL), Rec. Dec. 21, 1808.

Page 65:   Warren Co., Ga., ROBERT PARKER, JAS. MATHEWS & SOLOMON
           THOMPSON bound to Court of Ord. Feb. 15, 1804. Est. of
WILLIAM PARKER, dec'd. ROBERT PARKER (SEAL), JAMES MATHEWS (SEAL),
SOLOMON THOMPSON (SEAL), Rec. Dec. 21, 1808.

Page 66:   Warren Co., Ga., ELIZABETH JONES, JOHN NUNN, WILLIAM JONES
           bound to Court of Ord. Dec. 15, 1804. Est. of HENRY JONES,
dec'd. ELIZABETH JONES (X) (SEAL), JOHN NUNN (SEAL), WILLIAM JONES
(X) (SEAL). Rec. Dec. 15, 1808.

Pages 66-67:   Warren Co., Ga., SALLY GUSLING, BENJAMIN GUSLING, JOHN
               MOSES & JAMES GRAY bound to Court of Ord. Aug. 15, 1804.
Est. of WILLIAM GUSLAND, dec'd. BENJAMIN GUSLAND (X) (SEAL), SALLY
GUSLAND (X) (SEAL), JOHN MOSES ( ) (SEAL), JAMES GRAY (SEAL). Rec.
Dec. 21, 1808.

Pages 67-68:   Warren Co., Ga., NATHANIEL WARD & MICHAEL BURKHATTER,
               bound to Court of Ord. Aug. 15, 1804. Est. of WM.
MORRISON, dec'd. NATHANIEL WARD (X) (SEAL), MICHAEL BURKHATTER (X)
(SEAL), Rec. Dec. 21, 1808.

Pages 68-69:   Warren Co., Ga., MARY DUBERRY, HENRY DUBERRY & JACOB
               DARDEN bound to Court of Ord. Dec. 10, 1804. Est. of
JESSE DUBERRY, dec'd. MARY DUBERRY (X) (SEAL), HENRY DUBERRY (SEAL),
JACOB DARDEN (SEAL), Rec. Dec. 22, 1808.

Page 69:   Warren Co., Ga., WILLIAM JONES & JAMES JONES, Admrs. &
           MICHAEL BURKHATTER & WILLIAM DENT bound to Court of Ord. Dec.
10, 1804. Est. of JAMES JONES, dec'd. WM. JONES (SEAL), JAMES JONES
(SEAL), MICHAEL BURKHATTER (X) (SEAL), Rec. Dec. 22, 1808.

Page 70:   Warren Co., Ga., MARGARET BEASLEY, ROBERT BEASLEY, JAMES GRAY,
            bound to Court of Ord. Jan. 6, 1805. Est. of RICHARD BEASLEY,
dec'd. MARGARET BEASLEY (X) (SEAL), ROBERT BEASLEY (SEAL), JAMES GRAY
(SEAL), Rec. Dec. 22, 1808.

Pages 70-71:   Warren Co., Ga., SARAH NEWSOM & MICHAEL BURKHATTER bound
                to Court of Ord. Feb. 14, 1805. Est. of JOHN NEWSOM,
dec'd. SARAH NEWSOM (X) (SEAL), MICHAEL BURKHATTER (M) (SEAL). Rec.
Dec. 22, 1808.

Pages 71-72:   Warren Co., Ga., MARY STOW, ROBERT JENKINS, Senr. &
                JEREMIAH BELL bound to Court of Ord. Feb. 14, 1805. Est.
of MICAJAH STOWE, dec'd. MARY STOWE (X) (SEAL), ROBERT JENKINS (SEAL),
JEREMIAH BELL (SEAL). Rec. Dec. 23, 1808.

Page 72:   Warren Co., Ga., ELIZABETH PRUIT, BURD PRUIT, JOEL NEAL,
            ISAIAH TUCKER & HARDIN PRUIT bound to Court of Ord. Est. of
LEVI PRUITT, dec'd. (Dated Mar. 4, 1805), ELIZABETH PRUITT (SEAL),
BURD PRUITT (SEAL), ISAIAH TUCKER (SEAL), HARDIN PRUITT (SEAL). Rec.
Dec. 23, 1808.

Page 73:   Warren Co., Ga., MARY WAGGONER, DAVID WAGGONER, GEORGE
            WAGGONER, GEORGE WAGGONER, Junr., & WILLIAM WAGGONER, bound
to Court of Ord. Aug. 14, 1805. MARY WAGGONER (X) (SEAL), DAVID W.
WAGGONER (SEAL), GEORGE B. WAGGONER (SEAL), GEORGE WAGGONER (SEAL),
WILLIAM WAGGONER (SEAL). Rec. Dec. 23, 1808.

Pages 73-74:   Warren Co., Ga., WINNEFRED BENTON, LEROY MIMS & JOHNSTON
                WRIGHT bound to Court of Ord. Aug. 14, 1805. Est. of
AARON BENTON dec'd. WINNYFRED BENTON (X) (SEAL), LEROY MIMS (X) (SEAL),
JOHNSTON WRIGHT (SEAL). Rec. Dec. 23, 1808.

Pages 74-75:   Warren Co., Ga., ZACHERIAH BOOTHE, JOHN HICKS &
                RICHARD CURRY bound to Court of Ord. Dec. 14, 1805. Est.
of JOHN K. CANDLER, dec'd. ZACHARIAH BOOTHE (SEAL), JOHN HICKS (SEAL),
RICHARD CURRY (X) (SEAL). Rec. Dec. 23, 1808.

Page 75:   Warren Co., Ga., LOUISA ROPER, JOHN ROPER & FADDY WHITTINGTON
            bound to Court of Ord. March 3, 1806. Est. of JAMES ROPER,
dec'd. LOUISA ROPER (SEAL), JOHN ROPER (SEAL), FADDY WHITTINGTON (X)
(SEAL). Rec. Dec. 23, 1808.

Page 76:   Warren Co., Ga., SAMUEL JACKSON & JOHN MCGLANEY bound to
            Court of Ord. May 5, 1806. Est. of SAMUEL RUTHERFORD dec'd.
SAMUEL JACKSON (SEAL), JOHN MCGLAMERY (X) (SEAL), Rec. Jan. 4, 1809.

Pages 76-77:   Warren Co., Ga., JESSE WHITE & SAMUEL ALEXANDER bound to
                Court of Ord. May 5, 1806. Est. of SHERRID DRAKE, dec'd.
JESSE WHITE (SEAL), SAMUEL ALEXANDER (SEAL). Rec. Jan. 4, 1809.

Pages 77-78:   Warren Co., Ga., HANNAH JONES, HENRY WILLIAMS & ISAAC
                DAVIS bound to Court of Ord. July 7, 1806. Est. of
AQUILLA JONES, dec'd. HANAH JONES (X) (SEAL), HENRY WILLIAM (SEAL),
ISAAC DAVIS (ψ) (SEAL). Rec. Jan. 4, 1809.

Page 78:   Warren Co., Ga., MARY JARNETT, JAMES EDGE & NEHEMIAH EDGE
            bound to Court of Ord. Sept. 1, 1806. Est. of ALEXANDER
JARNETT, dec'd. HANAH JARNETT (X) (SEAL), JAMES EDGE (-) (SEAL),
NEHEMIAH EDGE (X) (SEAL). Rec. Jan. 5, 1809.

Page 79:   Warren Co., Ga., BENJAMIN S. WOODWARD & HARMAN PERRYMAN
            bound to Court of Ord. Nov. 3, 1806. Est. of FRANCIS WOOD-
WARD, dec'd, BENJAMIN S. WOODWARD (SEAL), HARMAN PERRYMAN (SEAL),
Rec. Jan. 5, 1809.

Pages 79-80:   THADIUS BEALE, Junr., ELIAS BEALE & THADIUS BEALE,
                bound to Court of Ord. Dec. 2, 1806. Est. of JOSEPH
BEALE, dec'd. THS. BEALE (SEAL), ELIAS BEALE (SEAL), THADIUS BEALE
(SEAL), Jan. 5, 1809 (Rec. date).

Pages 80-81:   Warren Co., Ga., ABSALOM NAPPER, JOHN BURKHATTER, HENRY
                 HARBUCK, JEREMIAH BURKHATTER, bound to Court of Ord.
Jan. 5, 1807.   Est. of DRURY NAPPER, dec'd. ABSALOM NAPPER (SEAL),
JOHN BURKHATTER (X) (SEAL), HENRY HARBUCK (+) (SEAL), JERM. BURKHALTER
(SEAL). Rec. Jan. 25, 1809.

Page 81:   Warren Co., Ga., SAMUEL ALEXANDER & JOHN SIMMONS bound to
             Court of Ord. March 2, 1807. Est. of JAMES HIFFLIN, dec'd.
SAMUEL ALEXANDER (SEAL), JOHN SIMMONS (SEAL), Rec. Jan. 25, 1809.

Page 82:   Warren Co., Ga., WINNYFRED ATCHINSON & CHARLES ATCHINSON &
             GEORGE HARGRAVES bound to Court of Ord. March 2, 1807.
Est. of JAMES ATCHINSON, dec'd WINNYFRED ATCHINSON (SEAL), CHARLES
ATCHINSON (SEAL), GEORGE HARGRAVES. Rec. Jan. 25, 1809.

Pages 82-83:   Warren Co., Ga., NANCY DARDEN, JETHRO DARDEN, JACOB
                 DARDEN, JETHRO DARDEN, Senr. & WILLIAM DARDEN bound to
Court of Ord. May 4, 1807. Est. of STEPHEN DARDEN, dec'd. NANCY
DARDEN (SEAL), JETHRO DARDEN (SEAL), JACOB DARDEN (SEAL), JE. DARDEN
(SEAL). Rec. Jan. 25, 1807.

Pages 83-84:   Warren Co., Ga., THOMAS PERSON, RACHEL PERSONS, TURNER
                 PERSONS & WORMBY ROSE bound to Court of Ord. May 4, 1807.
Est. of JOSIAH PERSONS, dec'd. THOS PERSONS (SEAL), RACHEL PERSONS (X)
(SEAL), T. PERSONS (SEAL), W. B. ROSE (SEAL), Rec. Jan. 25, 1809.

Pages 84-85:   WILLIAM SLATTER of Warren Co., Ga., for $550 paid by
                 JACOB DARDEN of same Co. & State a negro woman 7 three
children, WM. SLATTER (SEAL). Wit: RICHMD. TERRELL, L. BATTLE.
Proven: Feb. 13, 1809

Pages 85-86:   State of Ga., May 7, 1795 PETER GOODWIN of Warren Co.,
                 & THOMAS DAWSON of Co. & State aforesd for 100 pounds
paid by THOMAS DAWSON a parcel of land lying in Warren Co., on Joe's
Creek, bounded by MOON's land, the Trading Road and F. DANIELLY's
land surveyed for PETER GOODWIN in 1794, also that other tract or
parcel of land containing 2000 acres bounded by BAILEY PARKERS, E.
THOMAS, Joe's Creek and on all other sides by GOODWIN's land... was
granted in fee simple to the said PETER GOODIN, JOSHUA JONES, EZEKIEL
ABBOTT, by his Excellency GEORGE MATHEWS, Gov. of sd. State bearing date
May 2, 1795, and duly registered in the Office of the Sec'y of State
in Book OOOO... PETER GOODWIN. Rec. May 10, 1795.

Pages 86-87:   Ga., Nov. 16, 1796, JOSHUA MOSES of State of Tennessee
                 and Sumner County and WILLIAM JOHNSON of Warren Co., Ga.,
JOSHUA MOSES to WILLIAM JOHNSON for $60 a parcel of land in Warren
Co., on west side of Rocky Comfort, near JAMES DAVIES, bound by BOWLING,
JOSHUA MOSES (LS). Wit: TURNER PERSONS & JONES PERSONS. Ack. Nov.
18, 1796. Rec. May 26, 1796.

Page 87:   Ga., Dec. 28, 1795 ALLEN WHATLEY & BENJAMIN FULLER, of the
             State of Ga., & County of Hancock of one part and WILLIAM
COCKS of the Co. of Warren the other part for 67 pounds paid by
WILLIAM COX a parcel of land lying in Warren Co., having such form and
marks natural & artificial as are expressed, in the platt surveyed the
10th of Sept. 1788 by JOHN TORRENCE for WILLIAM COX (originally the claim
of THOMAS FULLER, dec'd & granted to WILLIAM COX & bounded by unknown
lands & SAMUEL NEWMAN's land, by JOHN MCCRARY's land, by BIAN. BLAKELY's
land, and by ISAAC BALL's land)... ALLEN WHATLEY (SEAL), BENJAMIN FULLER
(SEAL). Wit: ETHELDRED THOMAS, ISAAC BALL. Proven: May 20, 1797.
Rec. May 26, 1797.

Pages 88-89:   State of Ga., Oct. 20, 1794, JOSIAH TATTNELL, NICHOLAS
                 LONG & PHILIP CLAYTON, Commissioners appointed to carry
into effecy "an Act to amend an act pointing the mode under "which
property reverting to the State shall be disposed of "passed on the 20th
day of December 1793, of the first, and ABRAM JONES & WILLIAM POE of the
County of Richmond and Town of Augusta of the second part. "Confiscating

the Estate of such persons as are therein declared guilty of treason...
"did sell unto WILLIAM KELLY in fee for a valuable consideration all
that Tract of Land containing 300 acres, in the County of Wilkes (now
Warren) on the N. side of Ogeechee River, at the mouth of Long Creek
adj. lands of REUBEN BARROW, which said tract of Land of three hundred
acres had been found to be the property of EDWARD CRAWFORD, a person
named in the sd. act., confiscated to & in the State of Ga., N. LONG
(SEAL), R. CLAYTON (SEAL). Wit: R. WILKINSON J.P., GEOR. R. CLAYTON.
Rec. June 29, 1795.

Page 90:   State of Ga., July 29, 1789 JOSEPH SMITH of Burk County, Ga.,
            and FITZMANUEL HUNT of Richmond Co., Ga., for 50 pounds paid
by FITZMANUEL HUNT that tract of land lying on the waters of Reedy
Creek, adj. land of JAMES TEMPLE, containing 200 acres was granted to
the said JOSEPH SMITH Jan. 27, 1789... JOSEPH SMITH (T.T.) (SEAL). Wit:
JAMES EDWARD, MORDECAI EDWARDS, SARAH HUNT. Proven March 2, 1795.
Rec. June 29, 1795:

Pages 91-92:   Ga., Jan. 21, 1795, BENJAMIN ROSE & SARAH ROSE (his wife)
                of Columbia County, Ga., of the one part and ZACHARIAH
LANDRUM of Warren Co., the other part for 30 pounds sterling paid by
ZACHARIAH LANDRUM for a tract of land 100 acres, situated in Warren Co.,
joining what is call the old line parth, dividing formerly Wilkes &
Richmond Countys, BEN REESE land & JACOB BURKHATTERS land, the same
being a part of twelve hundred & fifty acres tract, formerly run for and
claimed by Governor JAMS. WRIGHT, and sold by confiscation & deed of
conveyance to JOHN GARRETT the 13th day of Sept. 1785 and from the said
JOHN GARRETT unto the said BEN REESE by indenture dated 27 June 1796...
BENJA. REESE, SARAH REESE. Wit: CHARLES GUSLING (-), THOMAS WHITE,
J.P. Rec. July 14, 1795.

Page 92:   Ga., WILEY DORMAN of Warren Co., for 100 pounds paid by
            ALLEN DORMAN of same place the following slaves: Simon, Luke,
a negro wench, a bright bay mare, June 9, 1795. WILIE DORMAN (SEAL),
Test. RICHMOND CASTLEBERRY, Proven June 10, 1795. Rec. July 14, 1795.

            Warren Co., Ga., MOSES THOMPSON & SECRETARY POWELL sworn
            that the left ear of said MOSES THOMPSON was bitt off in a
fight between said THOMPSON and GIDEON THOMPSON in the month of October
(sic) 1795, MOSES THOMPSON (X), Rec. July 14, 1795.

Pages 92-93:   Ga., July 13, 1795 between WILLIS PERRY and KIDDY his
                wife of the first part and JAMES ELLIOTT all of Warren
Co., for sum of $300 paid by JAMES ELLIOTT a tract of land lying in the
sd. co., on WM's Creek adj. ROBERT HILL, JACOB DARDEN, bounded by
ROGERS, bound by WILLIS PERRY, bound by MICAJAH STONE, 113½ acres.
WILLIS PERRY (SEAL), KIDDY PERRY (X) (SEAL). Wit: TURNER PERSONS,
JACOB DARDEN. Proven July 14, 1795. Rec. July 15, 1795.

Pages 93-94:   Sept. 1, 1791, BENJAMIN RUS of Columbia Co., Ga., and
                HUGH RUSE of Wilkes Co., Ga., BENJAMIN RUS and SARAH his
wife, paid by HUGH RUS (REESE?) tract of land 210 acres, land belonging
to WILLIAM DAVISON, being part of a 1250 acre tract formerly for and
claimed by Gov. JAMES WRIGHT... BENJAMIN RUS (SEAL), SARAH RUS (SEAL),
Wit: FERGUS S. LIN, JAMS. MCCORMICK, J.P.

Page 95:   July 10, 1795, JAMES DAVIS & LYDIA his wife of Warren Co.,
            Ga., and PHILIP LOGAN of same co. and state, for 77 pounds,
3 shillings, and 4 pence paid by PHILIP LOGAN 200 acres on waters of
Rocky Comfort, bound by vacant land, plat to the Grant annexed bearing
date the 11th Aug. 1784. JAMES DAVIS (X) (L), LYDDIA DAVIS (X) (LS).
Wit: JOSEPH PEARCY ( ), JONATHAN THOMPSON, MATHEW HUBERT JP. Rec.
July 28, 1795.

Pages 95-96:   JOHN HARDAWAY of Warren Co., Ga., (but formerly of the
                County of Dinwoddie in the common Wealth of Virginia)
appoint Senior JNO. GLASS of the County of Mecklinburg and common
wealth of Virginia my true & lawful attorney... my father THOMAS
HARDAWAY's Estate of Dinwiddie County... Aug. 9, 1795. JOHN HARDAWAY
(L). Rec. Aug. 13, 1795.

Pages 96-97:   Ga., March 10, 1795 CLABOURN NEWSOM of Warren Co., and
               RANDOL NEWSOM of same, for 10 pounds... tract of land
100 acres joining sd. CLAYBORN NEWSOM, JAS. MCCORMICK, EDMOND CODY, &
MOSES MCKINNE...being a part of a 600 tract granted to SOLOMON NEWSOM
July 29, 1785, and lyes on the north E. corner of sd. tract. CLAYBORN
NEWSOM (L), Rec. Aug. 14, 1795.

Pages 97-98:   Feb. 19, 1795, THOMAS JOHNSON, of Columbia Co., Ga., and
               JOHN BREWTON of Warren Co., 10 pounds paid by sd. JOHN
BRUTON, a tract of land of W. side of Beach Tree Creek, ROBERT BOLLING's
land, UPTON's land, 200 acres. THOMAS JOHNSON (SEAL). Wit: EDMUND
BUGG, BENJAMIN BRUTON (X). Rec. Aug. 31, 1795.

Pages 98-99:   Ga., March 27, 1795, WILLIAM BUSH Senr. and MOURNING his
               wife and JOHN BRUTON of Warren Co., for 10 pounds tract
of land in Warren Co., (tho formerly called Richmond) on W. side of
Beech Tree Creek, bounded by THOMAS JOHNSON at the original survey.
WILLIAM BUSH (SEAL), MOURNING BUSH (X) (SEAL). Wit: ISAAC TISON,
THOS. LANCASTER (L). Rec. Aug. 31, 1795.

Page 100:   State of Ga., Wilkes Co., CARTER NEWSOM of State and Co.,
               aforesd, sold unto SOLOMON NEWSOM Senr., four Negroes.
Feb. 4, 1792. CARTER NEWSOM (X), JOEDAY NEWSOM, JOHN NEWSOM. (Wit)
Rec. Oct. 18, 1795.

Pages 100-101:   Nov. 6, 1794, THOMAS ELLIT and ELIZABETH his wife, of
                 Warren Co., Ga., and ZACHARIAH GRAY of same, for 5
pounds, a tract of land containing 5 acres on Duharts Creek, being part
of 100 acres granted to ANN PTIOT and part of 125 acres granted to
ZACHARIAH GRAY, THOMAS ELLIOTT (SEAL), ELIZABETH ELLIOTT (SEAL). Wit:
R. D. GRAY, JOSIAH CARPENTER ( ). Rec. Oct. 28, 1795.

Pages 101-102:   July 16, 1793 ABRAM HELTON of Washington Co., Ga., and
                 PRECIOUS CAIN CRENSHAW of Wilkes Co., for 50 pounds,
land on Ogechee in Wilkes Co., bounded by STEPHEN BISHOP's land, MATHEW
HUBBERT's land, JOHN COXES land, being part of a tract granted to
ABRAM HELTON by the Gov. EDWARD TELFAIR, June 2, 1791, ABRAM HELTON
(SEAL). Wit: SAMUEL HARPER JP., RICHD. GRIMSLEY. Rec. Oct. 29, 1795.

Page 102:   JOSEPH LANDRUM of Wilkes Co., Ga., sold to SUSANNAH LANDRUM
            of same all my personal estate that I this day possess.
July 27, 1795, JOSEPH LANDRUM (X) (SEAL). Wit: MARY WALL (M), SAMUEL
LANDRUM. Rec. Nov. 9, 1795.

Page 103:   Ga., Sept. 1, 1795, JOHN MOSES Junr., of Warren Co., Planter,
            and GEORGE CLIFTON of same, 100 pounds for 220 acres between
the road leading from Mitchell's Mill to Watson's Mill on Little Sweet
Water and Bever Dam Creek of Briar bounded by PETER GOODWIN's land
EVEN THOMAS, BEN GHEASLIN, PETER HODE, JOHN MOSES land. JOHN MOSES
(SEAL). Wit: JAS. MCCORMICK JP. Rec. Sept. 25, 1795.

Page 104:   Warren Co., Ga., Nov. 27, 1795, LEVI PRUITT & ELIZABETH his
            wife, and AMOS WRIGHT all of Warren Co., 24 pounds for land
being part of a 300 acre tract bounding PRISCILLAE JONES land containing
40 acres more or less granted by Gov. ELBERT WHITE, Wilkes Co., Oct.
12, 1785. L. PRUITT (SEAL), ELIZABETH PRUITT (SEAL) Wit: ELISHA WRIGHT,
GEO. WEATHERBY JP. Rec. Nov. 30, 1795.

Pages 105-106:   Ga., Dec. 10, 1793, BARNEY MOLOY, of Burke Co., Ga.,
                 and THOMAS HANNON Burk Co., for 40 shillings, a tract
of land in County of Burk (now Warren) bounded by vacant land, BIGHAM's
land Sample's land... granted to said MOLOY Dec. 11, 1793 by EDWARD
TELFAIR, Pres. of Executive Council of sd. state. BARNEY MOLOY (SEAL)
his mark thus T. Wit: WILLIAM HANNOR, TARRY MOLOY. Rec. Jan. 9, 1796.

Pages 106-107:   Ga., July 13, 1793, RICHARD KERSEY of Burk Co., and
                 THOMAS HANNOR of same, for 31 pounds nine shillings, and
4 pence a tract of land 250 acres in Co. of Burk (now Warren) bounded W.

by Hervey's Mill Creek, which was granted to the sd. ROBERT KERSEY
June 18, 1793. RICHARD KERSEY (X) (SEAL). Wit: WILLIAM PORTER,
WILLIAM HANNAH. Rec. Jan. 9, 1796.

Pages 107-108: Ga., Aug. 14, 1794, JOHN DRYDEN of Warren Co., and
HENRY BALEY of same, for 8 pounds, a tract of land 57
acres on Lambeth's Creek, JOHN DRYDEN (X) (SEAL). Wit: DAVID TERRY,
JOHN PEEL, JOHN MCCOY. Rec. Jan. 10, 1796.

Pages 108-109: Ga., Jan. 17, 1796 JOHN WATSON of Warren Co., and
WILLIAM WOOD of same. 100 acres on Bryar Creek (formerly Wilkes Co.) now Warren, originally granted to RACHEL WELLS, June
17, 1789, and conveyed to JOHN WATSON June 19, 1789. JOHN WATSON (SEAL).
Wit: CLABURN NEWSOM, JOHN BAYN. Rec. Feb. 1, 1796.

Page 110: Oct. 10, 1795, BENJAMIN PORTER of Wilkes Co., and JOHN
MYRICK of Warren Co., BENJAMIN PORTER and PATSEY CLAIBORNE
his wife, for $120 paid by JOHN MYRICK, a tract of land on Rocky Comfort,
being part of a tract granted to JOHN HILL, which said 150 acres of land
was sold by JOHN CLARK, Esqr. (then sheriff of Wilkes County), B. PORTER
(SEAL), PATSEY C. PORTER (SEAL). Wit: R. WORSHAM JP, WM. STONE.
Rec. Feb. 3, 1796.

Page 111: Ga., April 4, 1794, WILLIAM GREENWOOD Junior of City of
Charleston, Esqr. and JOHN COURSE of Augusta, for 75 pounds
sold to JOHN COURSE, a tract of land being in Warren Co., lately taken
out of Wilkes Co., bounded at the time of survey by land of WILLIAM
OATES and vacant, originally surveyed for and granted to THOMAS SCOTT
and also all that other tract containing 200 acres bounded at the time
of survey by THOMAS SCOTT's land and vacant land, lately purchased at
Sheriffs Sale by the said WILLIAM GREENWOOD as the property of ANDREW
MCLEAN, Esqr., dec'd. WM. GREENWOOD, Jr., (SEAL). Wit: JOHN WILLSON
JP., JOHN WILLSON, Junr. Rec. Feb. 3, 1796.

Page 112: Ga., May 10, 1794, JOHN COURSE of Augusta and SOLOMON NEWSOM
of Warren Co., for 150 pounds, 250 acres in Warren Co.,
lately taken out of Wilkes Co. JOHN COURSE (SEAL). Wit: PHILIP CLAYTON
JP, JOHN GARRETT. Rec. Feb. 3, 1796.

Page 113: June 27, 1795, JOHN MASH of Warren Co., JOHN MANNON of same,
for 10 pds. 350 acres of land, in Warren Co., (in Richmond
Co., at time of survey) bounded by RANDOL RAMSEY's land and vacant land
at the time of survey, originally to JOSEPH MAY by his Excellency
GEORGE HANDLEY, May 28, 1788, surveyed by ANDERSON CRAWFORD, March 16,
1787. JOHN MASH (SEAL). Wit: ROBERT BARTON, JAMES BARTON. Rec.
Feb. 4, 1796.

Pages 114-115: May 20, 1795, JEREMIAH WILCHER of Warren Co., Ga., and
PHILIP GIBBS of same, 100 pounds sterling, 225 acres
on a Branch of Big Creek of Ogechee, bounding by WILSON's land granted
July 23, 1788 and registered in Book QQQ, fol. 134. JEREMIAH WILCHER
with his wife JANE, JEREMIAH WILCHER, (H) (SEAL). Wit: NORVELL
ROBERTSON, JOHN LAWSON JP. Rec. Feb. 4, 1796.

Pages 115-116: Jan. 9, 1792, SAMUEL JOHNSON of Warren Co., and JOHN
WILSON of Columbia Co., Ga., for 50 pounds paid by
JOHN WILSON a tract of land 300 acres in Columbia Co., (now Warren)
on Joes Creek of Ogechee bounding S.E. WILCHER, VAN's and vacant
lands, WALKER's, b. JOSEPH MCKINLEY's. SAMUEL JOHNSON (SEAL), MARY
JOHNSON (X) (SEAL). Wit: PHILIP GIBBS, WILLIAM RUNNER (∧). Rec.
Feb. 4, 1796.

Pages 116-117: April 23, 1795, JAMES THOMAS of Hancock Co., Ga. to
WILLIAM CAMPBELL of Warren Co., 150 pounds for a tract
of land on both sides of Long Creek of Ogechee 322½ acres granted to
JAMES THOMAS Oct. 5, 1785. JAMES THOMAS (T) (SEAL). Wit: P. BURNS,
WILLIAM GRANTHAM. Rec. Feb. 8, 1796.

Pages 117-118:   Ga., May 5, 1795, WILLIAM CAMPBELL of Green Co., to
                 SAMUEL CAMPBELL of same, for 200 pounds a tract of
land in Warren Co., both sides of Long Creek of Ogechee, 322½ acres
granted to JAMES THOMAS Oct. 5, 1785. WILLIAM CAMPBELL (SEAL). Wit:
JAMES CAMPBELL, PETER BURNS. Rec. Feb. 8, 1796.

Pages 118-119:   Ga., Sept. 21, 1795, SAMUEL CAMPBELL of Green Co., and
                 JAMES BOON of Warren Co., for 150 pounds (the same
tract as above). SAML. CAMPBELL (SEAL). Wit: P. BURNS, T. H. BUYNES.
Rec. Feb. 8, 1796.

Pages 119-120:   Warren Co., Ga., ELIZABETH KELLY, JOHN CARSON & JOHN
                 GIBSON of State and Co. aforesd. bound to SEPTIMUS
WEATHERBY, April 19, 1794. Est. of JOHN KELLY, dec'd. ELIZABETH
KELLY (SEAL), JOHN CARSON (SEAL), JOHN GIBSON (SEAL). Rec. April 20,
1795.

Pages 120-121:   Warren Co., Ga., PHEBE HILL, Admx. RICHARD HILL &
                 BENJAMIN HILL bound to SEPTIMUS WEATHERBY, May 1, 1795.
East. of THOMAS HILL, dec'd. PHEBE HILL (X) (SEAL), RICHARD HILL (SEAL),
B. HILL (SEAL)ʳ] Rec. Sept. 20, 1795.

Pages 121-122:   Warren Co., Ga., JOSEPH BOON, JAMES BOON, Exrs., ELISHA
                 PRUITT and JOHN HILL bound to SEPTIMUS WEATHERBY May 19,
1794. Est. of THOMAS BOON, dec'd. JOSEPH BOON (SEAL), JAMES BOON (SEAL),
ELISHA PRUITT (SEAL), JOHN HILL (X) (SEAL). Test. JOHN MYRICK. Rec.
April 20, 1795.

Pages 122-123:   Warren Co., Ga., PRISCILLA BAKER, Admx, WILLIS PERRY
                 of Warren Co., and JAMES THOMAS of Hancock Co., bound
to SEPTIMUS WEATHERBY Oct. 15, 1794. Est. of CHARLES BAKER, dec'd
PRISCILLA BAKER (X) (SEAL), WILLIS PERRY (SEAL), JAMES THOMAS (T) (SEAL).
Rec. Apr. 20, 1795.

Pages 123-124:   Warren Co., Ga. HENRY GRAYBILL Esq. Admr. & AARON BENTON
                 bound to SEPTIMUS WEATHERBY Nov. 19, 1794. Est. of
SAMUEL HELTON, dec'd. HEN. GRAYBILL (SEAL), AARON BENTON (SEAL). Rec.
Apr. 20, 1795.

Pages 124-125:   Warren Co., Ga., ADAM JONES & NATHANIEL MYRICK bound
                 to SEPTIMUS WEATHERBY Dec. 18, 1794. Est. of JESSE
CAMBLE, dec'd, ADAM JONES (SEAL), NATHANIEL MYRICK (SEAL). Rec. Apr. 20,
1795.

Page 125:   Warren Co., Ga., ALEXANDER MOORE, JAMES REYLEY & HENRY
            REYLEY bound to SEPTIMUS WEATHERBY Jan. 5, 1795. Est. of
MORDECAI MOORE, dec'd. ALEXR. MOORE (SEAL), JAMES RALEY (SEAL), HENRY
RALEY (SEAL). Test. JOHN SALLIS. Rec. Apr. 20, 1795.

Page 126:   Warren Co., Ga., SAMUEL SLOCUM, Admr. and ORANDATUS WATSON
            bound to SEPTIMUS WEATHERBY Feb. 2, 1795. Est. of SETH
SLOCUM, dec'd. SAMUEL SLOCUM (SEAL), ORONDATUS WATSON (LS). Rec. Apr.
23, 1795.

Pages 126-127:   Warren Co., Ga., HENRY MITCHELL, Admr. of Est. of
                 HAWTHORNE, decd of this Co. bound to SEPTIMUS WEATHERBY,
March 5, 1795. HENY. MITCHELL (SEAL). Rec. Apr. 22, 1795.

Pages 127-128:   Warren Co., Ga., RICHARD CASTLEBERRY, WILLIAM NEWSOM
                 and MARK LITTLETON bound to SEPTIMUS WEATHERBY Apr. 11,
1795. Est. of SAMUEL NEWMAN, dec'd. RICHARD CASTLEBERRY (SEAL),
WILLIAM NEWMAN (O𝟴) (SEAL), MARK LITTLETON (SEAL). Test. MARCOM INSON.
Rec. Apr. 23, 1795.

Pages 128-129:   Warren Co., Ga., SUSANNAH STROTHER & DAVID KELLY, bound
                 to SEPTIMUS WEATHERBY, Apr. 20, 1795. Est. of
WILLIAM STROTHER, dec'd. SUSANNAH STROTHER (X) (SEAL), DAVID KELLY (SEAL)
Rec. Apr. 23, 1795.

Page 129:   Ga., May 16, 1795, BENJAMIN RUS of Columbia Co., Ga., and
             JACOB SMITH of Warren Co., for 32 pounds 10 shillings, paid
by JACOB SMITH for tract of land 100 acres in Warren Co., bounded on
one side by BENJAMIN RES's Mill Creek, part of a tract originally
grant to Sir JAMES WRIGHT. BENJAMIN RUS (SEAL). Wit: DORSEY HOWARD,
THOS. WHITE JP. Rec. July 17, 1795.

Page 130:   June 9, 1795, LAZARUS GURLEY of Warren Co., Ga., to JOSEPH
             BOON of Washington Co., for 100 pounds, a tract of land
200 acres more or less in Warren Co., originally granted to JAMES
BREWER on April 5, 1787. LAZARUS GURLEY (SEAL). Wit: L. PRUITT JP.
Rec. July 13, 1795.

Pages 130-131:   April 25, 1791, JOSEPH BONNER of Wilkes County (now
                  Warren), Ga., from THOMAS KEMP and LUCY his wife of
Washington Co., for 100 pounds land in Wilkes Co. on Ogechee River
bounded by lands of BOYLES and vacant land. THOMAS KEMP (X). Wit:
WILL MINOR, ROBERT BONNER. Rec. (no date of rec.).

Pages 131-132:   Ga., Sept. 1, 1794, CORNELIUS MCCARDEN of Wilkes Co.,
                  to LIGHFOOT WILLIAMS of Columbia Co., for 32 pounds,
a tract of land 100 acres in Warren Co. on waters of Bryar Creek
originally surveyed for CORNELIUS MCCARDION Oct. 23, 1787. CORNELIUS
MCCARDEON (SEAL). Wit: JESSE BURGEN, HENRY WILLIAMS. Rec. Feb. 1,
1796.

Page 133:   Ga., April 13, 1794, FREDERICK MCMURRIN to JAMES SANDERS
             for 160 pounds a tract of land being 200 acres more or less.
FREDERICK MCMURRIN (SEAL), ELIZABETH MCMURRIN (SEAL). Wit: ROBERT
BARNETT, JOHAM STRANGE. Rec. Feb. 1, 1796.

Page 134:   June 12, 1792, DANIEL MCMURPHY and SUSANNAH his wife of
             Richmond Co., Ga., to NICHOLAS JONES of Columbia Co., Ga.,
for 80 pounds, 400 acres more or less in Co. of Columbia (now Warren)
in Wrightsborough Township adj. lands of JOHN CARSON, sold as the
property of Sir JAMES WRIGHT by Comm. of confiscated Estates to DANIEL
MCMURPHY on Jan. 2, 1784. DANIEL MCMURPHY (SEAL), SUSANNAH MCMURPHY
(SEAL). Wit: JAMES TAYLOR, ROBERT JAMISON. Rec. Feb. 9, 1796.

Page 135:   Nov. 14, 1795, JOSEPH PERRY (son of DYAL PERRY) and
             PATIENCE PERRY (his wife) of Warren Co., Ga., to THOMAS
BUCHANAN of Hancock Co., Ga., for 45 pounds land in Warren Co., on
Waters of Long Creek, bounded by WALLER's land and vacant land, origin-
ally granted to PHILIP LOGAN June 10, 1786. JOSEPH PERRY (ℐ) (SEAL),
PATIENCE PERRY (SEAL). Wit: HENRY GREEN, THOMAS COCKS, GEORGE
WEATHERBY JP. Rec. Feb. 12, 1796.

Page 136:   Sept. 9, 1794, WILLIAM ORR of Washington Co., Ga., to
             THOMAS HANNAH of Burk Co., Ga., for 40 shillings, 200 acres
in Co. of Burk (now Warren) bounded by ALLEN's land and ROWE's land,
MOTT's land, originally granted to WILLIAM ORR Sept 4, 1786. WILLIAM
ORR (SEAL), JENNY ORR (LS). Wit: WILLIAM HADDEN, ISABELLA ALEXANDER
(A). Rec. 10, 1796.

Page 137:   Deed of Gift, THOMAS HANNAH of Warren Co., Ga., for consid-
             eration of love, good will and affection I bear toward by
beloved dau. ELIZABETH HADDEN of same state and Co., a tract of land
350 acres on Duhart's Creek, bounded by WILLIAM KENNEDY's land, ALLEN's
& vacant land, by SAMUEL SAMPLES & MOTTS, WILLIAM ROWE's land. Dec. 8,
1795. THOMAS HANNAH (X) (SEAL). Wit: WILLIAM PORTER, WILLIAM HANNAH.
Rec. Feb. 12, 1796.

Pages 137-138:   Ga., Dec. 28, 1795, JAMES BOON and LAZARUS GURLEY of
                  Warren Co., Ga., and THOMAS NEAL of same for 65 silver
dollars, paid by THOMAS NEAL land in Warren Co., & on GOLDING's fork,
beginning where Augusta Road crosses sd. fork, bound by WORNLEY ROSE's
land, containing about 75 acres, being part of tract originally granted
to JOHN GRANTHAM. JAS. BOON (SEAL), LAZARUS GURLEY (SEAL). Wit:
BURNER PERSONS & STERLING GARDNER. Rec. March 5, 1796.

Pages 138-139:   Warren Co., Ga., Feb. 22, 1796, MICHAEL BURKHATTER and
                  MARGARET his wife to STARLING GARDNER for 100 pounds
land on east side of Little Rocky Comfort, by NICHOLAS HAREBUCK's land,
MICHAEL BURKHATER (M) (SEAL), MARGARET BURKHATER (X) (SEAL). Wit:
TURNER PERSONS, THOMAS NEAL. Rec. March 31, 1796.

Page 140:   Warren Co., Ga., Feb. 29, 1796, JOHN BURKHATTER, JACOB
             BURKHATTER, JOSHUA BURKHATTER, JEREMIAH BURKHATTER, ISAAC
BURKHATTER, JESSE BURKHATTER, MICHAEL BARBUCK, NICHOLAS HARBUCK, &
DANIEL HUTCHERSON, of Warren Co. to MICHAEL BURKHATTER of same for 300
dollars a tract of land on GOLDING's Creek. JOHN BUCKHATTER (SEAL),
JACOB BUCKHATTER (X) (SEAL), JOSHUA BUCKHATTER (X) (SEAL), JEREMIAH
BUCKHATTER (X) (SEAL), MICHAEL HAREBUCK (X) (SEAL), JESSE BUCKHATTER,
NICHOLAS HAREBUCK (∼) (SEAL), DANIEL HUTCHERSON (SEAL). Wit: TURNER
PERSON, ETHELDED THOMAS, CLARK BLANDFORD. Rec. April 5, 1796.

Pages 141-142:   Ga., Feb. 29, 1796, MICHAEL BUCKHATTER, ISAAC BUCK
                  HATTER, JOHN BUCKHATTER, JACOB BUCK HATTER, JOSHUA
BUCKHATTER & JESSE BUCKHATTER, JEREMIAH BUCKHATTER of County of Warren
& Hancock Co., to NICHOLAS HAEBUCK of Warren Co., 300 dollars, tract
of land on Golding's Creek. MICHAEL BUCKHATTER (M), JOHN BUCKHATTER
(SEAL), JACOB BUCKHATTER (SEAL), JOSHU BUCKHATTER (X) (SEAL), ISAAC
BUCKHATTER (∅) (SEAL), JESSE BUCKHATTER (∅) (SEAL), JEREMIAH BUCKHATTER
(X) (SEAL). Wit: TURNER PERSON, ETHELDRED THOMAS, CLARK BLANFORD.
Rec. Apr. 1, 1796.

Pages 142-143:   Ga., Nov. 25, 1793, HENRY GREEN, Junr. of Wilkes (now
                  Warren) Co., to RICHARD HEATH of same for 40 pounds
lands on Hart's Creek, along JESSE STANFORD's line, by Estimation 200
acres. HENRY GREEN (X) (SEAL). Wit: ELISHA HUNT, JAMES GREEN. Rec.
April 1, 1796.

Pages 143-144:   Oct. 11, 1790, MICHAEL WHATLEY of Wilkes (now Warren
                  Co.) to JOEL WALKER of same for 200 pounds 2 tracts of
land on Middle Creek containing by Estimation 400 acres.. being part
of land granted to JOHN CASTLEBERRY Feb. 29, 1784 and land granted to
HENRY CASTLEBERRY Aug. 31, 1785. MICHAEL WHATLEY (X) (SEAL), CHRISTIANA
WHATLEY (SEAL). Wit: HENRY PEEBLES, JONES PERSONS. Rec. April 2, 1796.

Pages 144-145:   Ga., Feb. 14, 1795, JOHN DRYDEN of Warren Co., to
                  SHADRACH LEE of same, for 52 pounds, 10 shillings,
350 acres more or less on Lambeth's Creek, bound by JOHN CUNNING's land.
JOHN DRYDEN (≴) (SEAL). Wit: DAVID TERRY, JOHN BOZAR. Rec. April 5,
1796.

Pages 145-146:   Ga., Oct. 12, 1795, GEORGE SMITH and wife FRANCES, of
                  Warren Co., and HENRY BURNLEY of Hancock Co., 125
pounds, 180 acres, originally granted to MOSES POWEL, Senr. Sept. 5,
1783, on Ogechee River. LEWIS POWEL's line, JESSE BUNKLEY's line.
GEO. SMITH (SEAL), FRANCES SMITH (SEAL). Wit: JESSE BUNKLEY, HENRY
BYROM, WM. BYROM JP. Rec. (no date).

Pages 146-147:   Ga., Aug. 12, 1791, JAMES HARVEY & ELIZABETH his wife
                  of Co. of Burke (now Warren), to JOHN REACE of same,
for 10 pounds, 50 acres on Rocky Comfort, bounded by Dubox's land,
originally granted to JAMES W. HAREY Aug. 10, 1788. JAMES HARVEY (SEAL),
BETTEY HARVEY (SEAL). Wit: CHARLES HARVEY JP. Rec. April 5, 1796.

Pages 147-148:   Ga., Dec. 12, 1789 ISAAC DUBOSE of Burke Co., (now
                  Warren) to ROBERT WOOD of same, for 20 pounds, land in
Burke Co., on Rocky Comfort, originally granted July 29, 1785. ISAAC
DUBOSE (SEAL), SARY DUBOSE (SEAL). Wit: CHARLES HARVEY JP., JOHN
_____. Rec. April 6, 1796.

Page 148:   Ga., April 25, 1795, JAMES SIMMS, Esq., of Columbia Co., to
             ANDERSON CRAWFORD of same a tract of land for 5 shillings,
(formerly the Co. of Richmond but now Warren) adj. lands of JOSEPH
MCKINLEY, original grant July 17, 1794. JAMES SIMMS (SEAL). Wit:
THOMAS MOORE JP. Rec. Apr. 6, 1796.

Page 149:   Oct. 23, 1795, HENRY CHAMPION of Warren Co., Ga., to ELISHA
             BROWN of same, for 20 pounds land on Brier Creek, 100 acres
more or less. HENRY CHAMPION (SEAL). Wit: ROBERT ISAACS, JOHN KENT.
Rec. April 6, 1796.

Page 150:   Ga., Feb. 7, 1795, WILLIAM STARK of Columbia Co., Ga., to
             JAMES NAPIER of Warren Co., Ga., WILLIAM STARK purchased
253 acres at Sheriff's sale in Co. of Wilkes but now Warren, adj. JAMES
WAGONERS, ROBERT JACKSON & sd. JAMES NAPPIERS lands. WM. STARK (SEAL).
Wit: DRURY MURPHEY, WM. CLAIBORNE, ELISHA BROWN (𝓑). Rec. April 6,
1796.

Pages 150-151:   Feb. 17, 1795 DAVID BLACKSHEAR of Washington Co., Ga.,
                  to BENJAMIN CHAPMAN of Warren Co., for 50 pounds, 200
acres in Warren Co., originally granted Jan. 25, 1785. DD. BLACKSHEAR
(SEAL). Wit: JOSEPH KING, SUSA BUSH, JOHN BUSH JP. April 6, 1796.

Pages 151-152:   Ga. Feb. 27, 1796, MICHAEL BUCKHATTER, JOHN BUCKHATTER,
                  JACOB BUCKHATTER, JOSHUA BUCKHATTER, ISAAC BUCKHATTER
& JESSE BUCKHATTER of Warren Co. & Hancock Co., to JEREMIAH BUCKHATTER
of Warren Co., for 200 silver dollars, land on Goldin's Creek. MICHAEL
BUCKHATTER (𝑛) (SEAL), JOHN BUCKHATTER, JACOB BUCKHATTER, JESSE
BUCKHATTER, JOSHUA BUCKHATTER, ISAAC BUCKHATTER. (All with (SEAL), ed.)
Wit: CLARK BLANDFORD, DANIEL HUTCHERSON, HENRY HAREBUCK. Rec. April
6, 1796.

Page 153:   Ga., June 2, 1795 BENJAMIN RUS of Columbia (now Warren)
             Co., to EDMOND HAYES of same for 100 pounds, a tract of land
sd. co. part of a tract originally granted to Sir JAMES WRIGHT, 1288
acres, by an act of confiscation, conveyed to JOHN GARRETT and then to
BENJAMIN RUS June 29, 1786. BENJA. RUS (SEAL). Wit: JONATHAN SMITH,
THOS. WHITE JP. Rec. April 6, 1796.

Page 154:   Nov. 25, 1795, MARTIN COX of Warren Co. to SAMUEL POWEL of
             same for 22 pounds, 200 acres on jumping Gulley, granted to
MARTIN COX July 1787. MARTIN COX (X) (SEAL). Wit: NEWEL ROBERTSON,
SALLY ROBERTSON, JOHN SAUSON JP. Rec. April 7, 1796.

Page 155:   Ga., Dec. 30, 1794, MOSES POWELL Junr., and his wife SARAH
             of Hancock Co., and MOSES POWELL, Senr. and his wife
ELIZABETH & BENJAMIN POWELL and his wife MARY to GEORGE SMITH of Wilkes
Co., (MOSES POWELL Senr. of Warren Co.), for 150 pounds tract of land
in Warren Co. on Ogechee, 180 acres more or less. MOSES POWELL (SEAL),
SARAH POWELL (X) (SEAL), BENJAMIN POWELL (SEAL), MARY POWELL (X) (SEAL),
MOSES POWELL (SEAL), ELIZABETH POWELL (𝓭) (SEAL). Wit: JAS. ROGERS,
JESSE BUNKLEY, STEPHEN BURNLEY, WM. BYROM JP, HENRY BURNLEY. Rec.
April 17, 1796.

Page 156:   Ga., Nov. 6, 1795 JOHNSON WRIGHT, Planter of Warren Co., to
             JACOB SHOUSE of same for 15 pounds 150 acres in Warren Co.
Poioson Branch or Brier Creek. JOHNSON WRIGHT. Wit: ROBERT ISAACS,
JOHN SHOUSE (𝓜). Rec. April 11, 1796.

Pages 157-158:   Aug. 19, 1789, WM. NICHOLS of Co. of Wilkes (now
                  Warren), Ga., to PETER CASTLEBERRY of same, for 120
pounds a tract of land 100 acres on Rocky Comfort Creek. Granted to
WILLIAM NICHOLS Nov. 25, 1789. WILLIAM NICHOLS (SEAL). Wit: HUGH
RUS JP., BENJAMIN RUS. Rec. April 11, 1796.

Pages 158-159:   Nov. 20, 1791, JEREMIAH OATES of Washington Co., Ga.
                  and JAIN his wife to WILLIAM BYROM of Wilkes Co. (now
Warren) for 100 pounds, 100 acres on Red. Lick Creek. Granted to sd.
OATS on Nov. 24, 1786. JEREMIAH OATS (SEAL), JANE OATS (SEAL). Wit:
JOSEPH THOMPSON, SAMUEL SINQUIFIELD. Rec. April 11, 1796.

Page 159:   Whereas ROBERT MIDDLETON did sell unto WILLIAM BYROM a
             tract of land in Wilks County (now Warren) containing 100
acres on Lick Creek including the plantation where said BRYOM now lives

which land was originally granted to JEREMIAH OATS & the said OATS has
conveyed the same to sd. BYROM where will appear by a Deed, bearing the
date the twenty eighth of November in the Year of our Lord One Thousand
Seven Hundred & Ninety One, but doubts having arisen in the mind of
Sd. BYROM respecting the Legality of Said Titles & whereas the said
Middleton wishing to give Sd. BRYOM full satisfaction respecting the
same, likewise to give the Sd Bryom good Security for guaranteeing the
same now Know Ye that we ROBERT MIDDLETON, ROBERT FOURNOY & WILLIAM
ONSLEY, doth bind ourselves & heirs to the Sd. Byrom his heirs and
Assigns that in case the Sd. Titles prove deficient and that the Sd.
Byrom his Heirs or assigns should loose the Sd. land, that then & in
that case, we the said ROBERT MIDDLETON, ROBERT FLOURNOY & WILLIAM
ONSLEY doth oblige ourselves our Heirs to make the damages good the
said Byrom his heirs or assigns in the penal sum of 200 pounds sterling
money in case of failure as above mentioned given under our hands this
Eighth of October 1792. ROBERT MIDDLETON (SEAL), R. FLOURNOY (SEAL),
WILLIAM ONSLEY (SEAL), Test: JESSE BUNKLEY, RICHD. FRITWELL, HENRY
BYROM. Rec. April 11, 1796.

Pages 159-160:   Sept. 27, 1788 DAVID HOLLIMON of Wilks Co. (now Warren)
to WILLIS PERRY of the same, planter, for 80 pounds land on William's
Creek 300 acres granted May 4, 1786. DAVID HOLLIMON (X) (SEAL). Rec.
April 11, 1796.

Pages 160-161:   Sept. 27, 1788, SAMUEL HOLLIMAN of Wilks Co. (now
                 Warren) to WILLIS PERRY of same for 10 pounds land on
William's Creek 20 acres at the corner of AARON PARKER's fence.
SAMUEL HOLLIMON (X) (SEAL). Rec. April 11, 1796.

Pages 161-162:   JOSHUA PERRY of Franklin Co., North Carolina for
                 natural love and good will I have for my friend WILLIS
PERRY hath given a tract of land lying in Wilkes (now Warren) Co. on
waters of Hardin's Creek of Little River bounding on lands of ABRAHAM
HAMMACK, granted to JOSHUA PERRY 400 acres Sept. 22, 1784. Jan. 24,
1786. JOSHUA PERRY. Wit: JOEL PHILLIPS, BURRELL PERRY. No Rec. date.

Pages 162-163:   Ga., Wilkes Co. (now Warren). Jan. 25, 1792. JAMES
                 JONES to JOHN GIBSON for 30 pounds, 200 acres more or
less on Middle Creek, bounded by WHATLEY's land, Miller's land, Widow
JONES... JAMES JONES (SEAL). Rec. April 25, 1796.

                 JAMES JONES to JOHN GIBSON for 60 pounds, 258 acres
originally granted Sept. 29, 1784. JAMES JONES (SEAL) Rec. April
25, 1796.

Page 164:   March 21, 1795, AMOS GREEN of Wilkes Co., to ISAIAH TUCKER
            of Warren Co., for 20 pounds a tract of land in Warren Co.,
on Middle Creek, bounded by PRUITT's land, HARDIN's land 27 acres more
or less, whereon DAVID JONES formerly lived. AMOS GREEN (SEAL). Wit:
JESSE ARMSTRONG, WHITEFIELD TUCKER. Rec. Dec. 3, 1796.

Page 165:   Warren Co., Ga., Nov. 12, 1794, JOHN BARTON, late of sd.
            co. to JOHN TORRENCE of Columbia Co., for 40 pounds a tract
of land in Warren Co.. on Beach Tree Creek bounded by ROBERT BARTON's
land, SOLOMON NEWSOM's land, and vacant land 150 acres originally
granted to JOHN BARTON Sept. 10, 1786. JOHN BARTON (SEAL). Wit:
ANTHY. NEAL, DAVID NEAL. Rec. April 7, 1796.

Pages 166-167:   Ga., April 27, 1796 NICHOLAS LONG of Wilkes Co. to
                 MARTIN HARDIN of Warren Co., for 100 pounds, a tract
of land 400 acres on Rocky Comfort and other branches of Ogechee,
granted to NICHOLAS LONG... N. LONG (SEAL). Wit: R. WORSHAM, STOKELY
MORGAN. Rec. April 7, 1796.

Pages 167-168:   March 31, 1796 HENRY GREEN Senr. of Warren Co., to
                 ELISHA HUNT of same for 20 silver dollars, land on
Rocky Comfort, bounded by BENTON SPESE? ELISHA HUNT, originally granted
to H. GREEN Sept. 20, 1790. HENRY GREEN (SEAL). Wit: JEREMIAH
MATHEWS, ANDREW KING. Rec. May 18, 1796.

Pages 168-169:   Jan. 1, 1796, WILLIAM BASS of Warren Co., to ASA
                  TINDELL of same, for 12 pounds, land joining EZEKIEL
WILLIAM, 25 acres, WILLIAM BASS (SEAL). Sit: ALEXANDER BASS, Senr.,
ALEXANDER BASS Junr., WM. BYROM JP. Rec. May 18, 1796.

Pages 169-170:   April 22, 1793, JOHN BARTON of Wilkes Co., to ROBERT
                  BARTON, of same, for 30 pounds, a tract of land 150
acres, being part of a 300 acre grant to JOHN BARTON Sept. 31, 1787.
JOHN BARTON (SEAL). Rec. May 21, 1796.

Pages 170-171:   Jan. 2, 1796, BENJAMIN BRASWELL of Hancock Co., to
                  HENRY HARDIN of Warren Co. for 100 pounds, 150 acres
more or less in Warren Co., formerly granted to JOHN DOWER?, July 3,
1773, conveyed to JOSEPH MADDOCK... BENJAMIN BRASWELL (SEAL). Wit:
ISA. TUCKER, MARK HARDIN JP. Rec. May 23, 1796.

Pages 171-172:   May 9, 1796, RACHEL MCCULLERS of Warren Co., to JAS.
                  COBB of same, for 100 pounds 133 1/3 acres, being part
of a tract surveyed for RACHEL COBB (now RACHEL MCCULLERS) and granted
August 13, 1788... RACHEL MCCULLERS (B) (SEAL). Wit: ABSALOM COBB,
JACOB COBB. Rec. June 7, 1796.

Pages 173-174:   Wilkes Co., Ga., To all to whom these presents may
                  come GREETING: Know Ye, that whereas WILLIAM MCCULLERS
of the state and county aforesd. Planter, by an intermarriage with
RACHEL COBB, late widow and Relict of JOSEPH COBB, Farmer late of Sd.
County and State dec'd, became seized and possessed of a right of
Inheritance in one third part of a Tract of land... on the water of
Brier Creek containing two hundred acres as the Dower of the said
Rachel, which said Land was originally claimed, possessed, improved
and occupied by the said JOSEPH COBB in his lifetime and at his decease,
and hath been since surveyed for and confirmed to the Sa. Rachel Cobb,
by a Grant from the hand his Honor GEO. HANDLEY, Esqr. Gov & dated
Aug. 13, 1788, recorded Book QQQ fo. 352 the 10 of the same... WILLIAM
MCCULLERS and Rachel his wife for and inconsideration of 15 pounds
paid by EZEKIEL COBB, son of the said Rachel and Joseph Cobb, hath
sold him 200 acres... WM. MCCULLERS (SEAL), RACHEL MCCULLERS. Wit:
JNO.TORRENCE JP, JAMES MCCORMICK JP. Rec. June 7, 1796.

Pages 174-175:   April 15, 1796, EZEKIEL COBB of Columbia Co., Ga., to
                  JAMES COBB of same for 20 pounds, 66 acres & 2/3,
surveyed for RACHEL COBB... EZEKIEL COBB (SEAL). Wit: FRANCIS GRUBBS,
ELIZABETH JONES. Rec. June 13, 1796.

Pages 175-176:   Ga., Jan. 18, 1794 WILLIAM COCKS of Warren Co., to
                  JOEL THRUITTS of same for 50 pounds, tract of land,
part of which was granted to WILLIAM COCKS... Drury's Mim's Branch...
100 acres more or less. WILLIAM COCKS (SEAL), HANNAH COCKES (-) (SEAL).
Wit: THOMAS COCKS, JAMES COCKS. Rec. June 14, 1796.

Pages 176-177:   August 1, 1795, JAMES MCCORMICK and MARY his wife of
                  Warren Co., Ga., to JOSEPH MCMATH of same, for 30
pounds, land in Warren Co. (formerly Wilkes) on Bryar Creek bounded by
THOMAS JONES, WILLIAM WHARE, RUS... 300 acres granted to JAMES
MCCORMICK July 22, 1795, BOOK PPPP fol. 746. JAS. MCCORMICK (SEAL),
MARYANN MCCORMICK (SEAL). Wit: JOHN GRANT, D. NEAL. Rec. June 14,
1796.

Page 178:   Ga., Jan. 25, 1793, SILAS MONK of Washington Co., to THOMAS
             FREND of County of Wilkes (now Warren), for 50 pounds,
land in Wilkes Co. (now Warren). SILAS MONK (SEAL). Wit: JOSEPH
MARTIN, WM. C. ABERCROMBIE. Rec. June 15, 1796.

Page 179:   Ga., Jan. 1, 1795, JOHN MANNON & ELIZABETH his wife, of
             Warren Co., to PARSONS POW, Merchant, for land on Bryar
Creek, bound by THOMAS MERCER, WILLIAM SMITH... 200 acres. JOHN
MANNON (⌘), ELIZABETH MANNON (()). Wit: ROBERT ISAACS, SAMUEL
AVERA. Rec. July 1, 1796.

Page 180:   Same parties as above, land in Warren Co., on Little Bryar's
             Creek, 100 acres, more or less bounded by WALTER JACKSON,
PELEG ROGERS. (Same Signa. and Wit. as above.)

Pages 180-181:   Warren Co., Ga., Feb. 15, 1794, MARY RIGDON to JOHN
                 NIXON... sd. MARY RIGDON delivers her son ENOCH RIGDON
to care of sd. JOHN NIXON until he arrives at age 21, guardian, one
year's schooling... MARY RIGDON (X) (SEAL), JOHN NIXON (SEAL). Wit:
ELISHA PRUITT JP, MOUNTAIN HILL. Rec. July 22, 1796.

Pages 181-182:   Warren Co., Ga., Feb. 15, 1796, ELISHA PRUITT,
                 collector of Co. of Warren, to CHARLES GATES, Land at
public sale for 10 shillings, land (Burk Co. when surveyed) containing
200 acres bounded by CHARLES HARVEY's land, CHARLES GATES... plat
signed by GEO. MATHEWS, March 31, 1795. ELISHA PRUITT (LS). Wit:
JAMES MCCORMICK JP. Rec. Aug. 24, 1796.

Pages 182-183:   Dec. 1, 1795, ELIZABETH BROMTEY Senior, JOHN CROMLEY,
                 ELIZABETH CROMLEY, Junior, WILLIAM ESSORY & KATHERINE
his wife & MARY CROMLEY, heirs of WALENTINE CROMLEY, dec'd of County
of Washington and some in Co. of Screven, to JOHN MYRICK, Jr. of Warren
Co., for 50 pounds, a tract of land bounded by JOEL KING, WILLIAM DAVIS,
NATHANIEL MYRICK, JOHN MYRICK 200 acres more or less. Rec. in Sec'y
BOOK UUUU, Folio 737. ELIZABETH CROMLEY Senr. (LS), ELIZABETH CROMLEY
Junr. (LS), JOHN CROMLEY (LS), WM. ESSORY (LS), KATAY ESSORY (LS),
MARY CROMLEY (LS). Wit: GEO. WEATHERBY JP. ANRHN. CROMLEY, SOL GROSS.
Rec. Aug. 26, 1796.

Page 184-185:   April 2, 1796, JOHN MYRICK of Warren Co., Ga., to
                 GEORGE WEATHERBY of same, for 50 pounds, land on Rocky
Comfort, bound by JOHN DAVIES land, 112 acres, more or less, JOHN
MYRICK (LS). Wit: CHRISTOPHER BUSTIN, NATHANIEL MYRICK, ANDREW KING
JP. Rec. Aug. 27, 1796.

Pages 185-186:   Oct. 3, 1796, JOHN MAY, JAMES COBB, BALAAM MAY, BECKOM
                 MAY, ELIZABETH MAY, MARY MAY & SARAH MAY of Wilkes Co.,
Ga., to ISAAC BALL, of same, for 200 pounds, land on Bever Dam Creek,
bound by SAMUEL NEWMAN, JOSEPH MAY, ISAAC BALL, WILLIAM HEATHRON, 600
acres by Est. JOHN MAY, BALAAM MAY, JAMES COBB, SUSANNAH COBB. Wit:
WM. AVERIT, JONATHAN YOUNGBLOOD, ELISHA PRUITT, REBECKAH BALL. Aug.
27, 1796.

Pages 186-187:   Ga., May 12, 1794, JOSEPH BOON of Warren Co., to
                 ISAAC BALL of same, for 50 pounds, 200 acres bounded
by WM. TERCH... JOSEPH BOON (SEAL). Wit: JOHN TALIAFERRO, JOHN
MYRICK. Rec. Aug. 27, 1796.

Pages 187-188:   Ga., March 1, 1794, DAVID HILLHOUSE of Wilkes Co. to
                 JOHN BAKER of Warren Co., for 100 pounds, land on
William's Creek in Warren Co., 750 acres more or less, DAVID HILLHOUSE.
Wit: HENRY MOUNGER JP, JOHN HENLEY, JOHN HENLEY, Junr. Rec. Aug. 27,
1796.

Page 189:   Ga., March 6, 1792, JOHN TOWNSEND & JANE TOWNSEND his wife,
             of Wilkes Co., to BARNABAS JONES of same for 100 pounds,
174 acres (100 acres under the head right of CHARLES BREWER) (74 acres
run for JOHN TOWNSEND) JOHN TOWNSEND (SEAL), JANE TOWNSEND (SEAL).
Wit: JAMES CALDWELL, THOMAS HEATH, JOSEPH BONNER, SAMUEL YARBROUGH.
Rec. Aug. 27, 1796.

Page 190:   Ga., Sept. 22, 1795, MARY FULLAR to ALLEN WHATLEY for 20
             dollars, 350 acres in Warren Co. on Rocky Comfort bounded
by SAMUEL NEWMAN, JOHN MCCRARY, BLAN BLACKLEY, and heirs of JOHN MAY...
MARY FULLAR (SEAL). Wit: None but Mary Fullar sworn. Rec. Aug. 27,
1796.

Page 191:   Feb. 9, 1796, JOHN ELIJAH OPHELL of Notches District to
             JOSIAH CARTER of Warren Co., Ga. (later JOHN ELIJAH OFIELD)
for 50 pounds land on Walker's Branch, water of Ogeeche R. 200 acres

more or less, bounded by SAUNDERS WALKER's, granted to JOSIAH CARTER, Oct. 25, 1784 in Co. of Wilkes, JOHN ELIJH. OPHELL (SEAL), Wit: B. ANTHONY, WM. BYROM JP. Rec. Aug. 27, 1796.

Page 192:   Oct. 4, 1794, JOHN MCDANIEL of Warren Co. to HENRY SHELTON
            of same, for 50 pounds, land where ELIZABETH JOHNSON now
liveth, on East side of Rocky Comfort, 166½ acres by Estimation, granted
to JOHN MCDANIEL July 22, 1785. JOHN MCDANIEL (SEAL), MARY MCDANIEL
(SEAL). Wit: ZACHARIAH HARRILL, WILLIAM SMITH. Rec. August 29, 1794.

Page 193:   July 16, 1789, PETER PARKINS of Wilkes Co., Ga., to JAMES
            REED of same, for 30 pounds, in Wilkes Co. (now Warren)
granted to PETER PARKINS ISA. TUCKER, JOHN REED. Rec. Aug. 29, 1796.

Page 194:   Nov. 21, 1789 ISHAM WESTMORELAND from JAMES REED, 30 pounds
            pd. by ISHAM WESTMORELAND, 100 acres more or less bounded
by PETER PARKINS, JOHN PARKINS & WHEELIS, granted to PETER PARKINS
Dec. 13, 1788. JAMES REED. Wit: JOSEPH WHITE. SARAH WHITE. Rec.
Aug. 27, 1796.

Page 195:   Dec. 31, 1795 JAMES GREEN of Warren Co., Ga., to JAMES
            PARKER of same, for 25 pounds, 200 acres more or less,
granted to JAMES GREEN Dec. 4, 1790. JAMES GREEN (SEAL). Wit: H.
PEEBLES, LADOCK RODEN. Rec. Aug. 29, 1796.

Page 196:   Dec. 21, 1795 WILLIAM SULLIVAN of Pendleton Co., South
            Carolina to LAZARUS GURLEY of Warren Co., Ga., for 100
pounds, 300 acres more or less, bounded by STERLING JONES, Golden Fork
Creek, THOMAS NEAL, MCCRARY... WILLIAM SULLIVAN (SEAL). Wit: GEORGE
YOUNG, WILLIAM BROOKS. Rec. Sept. 1, 1796.

Page 197:   Jan. 6, 1796, LAZARUS GURLEY to JAMES BOON of Warren Co.,
            100 pounds for land (same land as above) LAZARUS GURLEY
(SEAL). Wit: ISHAM STRANGE, FRANCIS BECK. Rec. Sept. 2, 1796.

Pages 197-198:   Feb. 15, 1796 HOWELL JARROT of Wilkes Co., Ga., to
                 JOSIAH PERSON of Warren Co. for 70 pounds, 375 acres
in Warren Co., on Harts Creek, bounded by SHAW & WEBB, DYSART... half
of a tract granted to SAMUEL CRESWELL & SOLOMON BAREFIELD. Oct. 15,
1785. HOWELL JARRETT. Wit: B. SMITH, AMBROSE EDWARDS. RDc. Sept. 2,
1796.

Pages 198-199:   May 14, 1794, REUBEN ALLEN to GEORGE GRANDBERRY for
                 40 pounds, 100 acres on south side of Joe's Creek,
granted to REUBEN ALLEN Oct. 1, 1785. REUBEN ALLEN (SEAL). Wit:
MOSES GRANDBERRY, RICHD. CURRY. Rec. Sept. 2, 1796.

Pages 199-200:   May 5, 1795 ELISHA BIGGOT of Prov. of South Carolina to
                 WILLIAM DOWNS of Prov. of Ga. and Wrightsborough
Township for 100 pounds land 100 acres more or less in Wrightsborough
Township in Parish of St. Paul's bounded by JOHN SLATER, and vacant land
originally granted to ELISHA BIGGOT June 7, 1794... ELISHA BIGGOT (SEAL).
Wit: ALEXANDER MILLER, JAM: BOWERS. Rec. Sept. 5, 1796.

Pages 200-201:   Feb. 1794 WILLIAM DOWNS to WILLIAM BERRY for 100 pounds
                 in Warren Co. (formerly Wrightsborough Township in
Parish of St. Paul's) (same as above). WM. DOWNS (SEAL). Wit:
STEPHEN HOGE, WM. HOGE, HIRAM JOHNSON JP. Rec. Sept. 5, 1794.

Pages 201-202:   Feb. 19, 1791, RICHARD BONNER of Green, Ga., to
                 WILLIAM BERRY of Richmond (sic) Co., Ga., for 200
pounds, 100 acres more or less in Richmond Co. bound by HUGHIN's
originally granted to sd. RICHARD BONNER Jan. 24, 1791. RICHARD BONNER
(SEAL). Wit: ABNER MITCHELL, JOHN PARHAM. Rec. Sept. 5, 1796.

Pages 202-203:   Feb. 26, 1794, WILLIAM HOGE of Columbia Co. to WILLIAM
                 BERRY of Warren Co., Ga., for 100 pounds 100 acres in

Co. of (sic) Warren (formerly Richmond) bounded by Williams' Creek, SLATTER's and BIGGOT's land, DOBBIN's land, and vacant land, granted to WILLIAM HOGE Feb. 8, 1786. WILLIAM HOGE (SEAL). Wit: WALTER DRANE.

Pages 203-204: Ga., Nov. 22, 1792, JAMES YARBROUGH of Wilkes Co., to JAMES GOLIGHTLY of same for 60 pounds, 185 acres in Co. of Wilkes (now Warren), bounded by JOHN ZACHARY, JAMES THWEATT, THOMAS JONES, or granted to JAMES YARBOROUGH Aug. 10, 1785. JAMES YARBOROUGH (SEAL). Wit: FANNEYE MITCHELL, H. J. MITCHELL. Rec. Sept. 6, 1796.

Pages 204-205: Ga., Nov. 13, 1794 BENJAMIN FEW of Columbia Co. to BENJAMIN HAMP of Warren Co. and WILLIAM BIRD of same for 850 pounds, land in Warren Co. on Ogechee bounded at time of survey by DENNIS... 200 acres... grant to ISAAC DENNIS April 26, 1787 conveyed to BEN. FEW Oct. 22, 1794.. BENJN. FEW. Wit: JNO. WALLACE, H. FEW, ZACHH. COX. Rec. Sept. 6, 1796. Wife RACHEL FEW.

Pages 206-207: Ga., Dec. 4, 1794, JOWEL FEATHERSTONE & PAMELIA FEATHERSTONE of Warren Co. to WILLIAM BIRD & BENJAMIN AUGUSTUS HAMP of same for 5 pounds, one acre in Warren Co. bounded by BENJAMIN UPTON and the SHOALS tract, formerly property of BENJAMIN FEW, now sd. BIRD & HAMP, HOWELL FETHERSTONE (SEAL), PAMELA FETHERSTONE (SEAL) Wit: BENJA. JPTON, JNO HAMILL JP. Rec. Sept. 6, 1796.

Pages 207-208: Ga., Jan. 22, 1795, BENJAMIN UPTON and JUDITH his wife of Warren Co., to WILLIAM BIRD & BENJAMIN AUGUSTUS HAMP of same for 5 shillings, on Ogechee a tract of land, BENJAMIN UPTON (SEAL), JUDITH UPTON (SEAL). Wit: DUNCAN MCLEAN, JNO. HAMILL JP. Rec. Sept. 6, 1796.

Pages 208-209: Feb. 17, 1794, NEAL DOUGHTERTY & THOMAS COWAN of Columbia Co., Ga., to MOUNTAIN HILL and JESSE ARMSTRONG of Warren Co., Ga., for 50 pounds, 450 acres joining REDDICK BASS, JOHN WHATLEY, JOHN GILROW, CULPEPPER & PEEBLES... NEAL DAUGHTERTY (SEAL), THOS. COWAN (SEAL). Wit: L. PRUITT JP, JOHN TALIAGERRO. Rec. Sept. 22, 1796.

Pages 209-210: Wilkes Co., Ga., Oct. 22, 1787, EZEKIEL MILLAR and SARAH his wife to JOHN NIXON for 30 pounds, 100 acres bounding JOHN WELLS & EZEKIEL MILLAR... EZEKIEL MILLAR (SEAL), SARAH MILLAR (SEAL). Wit: L. PRUITT JP., JOSEPH MILLAR, JOSEPH BATTSON. Rec. Sept. 22, 1796.

Pages 210-211: Ga., Feb. 16, 1796, JONATHAN MCCRARY of Hancock Co., to WORMLEY ROSE of Warren Co. for 280 silver dollars a tract of land in Warren Co. on Whetstone Creek, 280 acres more or less JONATHAN MCCRARY (SEAL). Wit: CHAPPEL HEATH, TURNER PERSONS. Rec. Nov. 9, 1796.

Pages 211-213: Oct. 5, 1795, Heirs, Representatives and Distributors of RALPH KILGORE, dec'd (to wit) ELIZABETH KILGORE, KATHERINE KILGORE, JAMES & MARY ALLISON & ROBERT KILGORE, Junr. to WILLIAM STARK of Columbia Co. for 200 pounds (Dollars at 4 shillings and 8 pence) 350 acres in Columbia Co. bounded by Little River, EVAN's land, HOWARD's, WHITTOCK's & DOUGLASS's... ELIZABETH KILGORE, CATHARINE KILGORD, JAMES ALLISON, MARY ALLISON. Wit: WM. SALLY, THOS. J. MOORE. Rec. Nov. 10, 1796.

Pages 213-214: Nov. 18, 1795, JOHN BARTON of Lawrence Co., Ga., to WILLIAM JOHNSON of Warren Co. for 40 pounds, 230 acres on Stamp Branch of Ricky Comfort... JOHN BARTON (SEAL). Wit: JOSEPH WALKER, REUBEN WALKER, VINCENT A. THARP JP. Rec. Dec. 2, 1796.

Pages 214-215: Dec. 5, 1796, JOSEPH RICHARDSON of Warren Co. to ARCHIBALD LACY for 100 dollars, 100 acres, being part of a tract granted JOHN COX. Rec. in Secretaries Office BOOK OOO, pg. 380. bounded JACK COMER, STEPHEN BISHOP... JOSEPH RICHARDSON (£) (SEAL). Wit: L. RPUITT JP, HARMON PERRYMAN. Rec. Dec. 6, 1796.

Pages 215-216:   Warren Co., Ga., JORDAN LACEY swears that he bought
                  a tract of 200 acres on Rocky Creek from JOSEPH
RICHARDSON. Dec. 3, 1796. JORDAN LACEY swears that he did sell on
March 15, 1792 to JOHN HAMPTON, then of Washington, who since that
date by report removed to the Southward and a certain bay Mare four feet
eight inches high for which the said JOHN HAMPTON did give and deliver
to JORDAN LACEY a note of hand payable Oct. 1, wherein JOHN FINNEY was
signed as Security for 3500 of Augusta Inspected tobacco payable to
the said JORDAN LACEY on order. Sept. 14, 1796. Rec. Dec. 6, 1796.

Pages 216-217:   Oct. 3, 1790 JOHN COX of Richmond Co., to JOSEPH
                  RICHARDSON of Wilkes Co. for 35 pounds, land on Rocky
Creek bounded by J. CARTER, STEPHEN BISHOP, ABRAHAM HILLON, 200 acres
more or less originally order to sd. JNO. COX. July 3, 1786, granted
March 22, 1787 Recorded Book OOO folio 304... JOHN COX (SEAL). Wit:
JAS. BISHOP, ZECHERIAH LANDRUM. Rec. Dec. 6, 1796.

Pages 217-218:   Ga., Dec. 5, 1790, JOSEPH RICHARDSON of Warren Co. to
                  EDMOND WALSH of Hancock Co., for 25 pounds, land on
Rocky Creek, bounded by STEPHEN BISHOP & ABRAHAM HELTON HEATH, 100
acres more or less part of 200 acres bought from ARCHIBALD LACEY...
JOSEPH RICHARDSON (ⴤ) (LS). Rec. Dec. 6, 1796.

Pages 218-219:   Feb. 15, 1793, JOSEPH DAVIES of Wilkes Co., Ga., to
                  JEREMIAH MATHEWS of same for 20 pounds land on Rocky
Comfort Creek. RUTHERFORD's land, 100 acres granted to JAMES COCKRHAM
1786. JOSEPH DAVIDSON (SEAL). Wit: JOHN MYRICK, ELISHA WRIGHT.
Rec. Dec. 7, 1796.

Pages 219-220:   Jan. 26, 1796, JOEL KING & MARY KING to AMBROSE HADLEY
                  all of Warren Co., for 400 silver dollars land on
Whetstone Creek, originally granted to sd. KING... JOEL KING (K) (SEAL),
MARY KING (K) (SEAL). Wit: JOHN HAWTHORNE, SOLOMON SLATTER. Rec.
Dec. 7, 1796.

Pages 220-221:   Dec. 4, 1794, PETER MAHONE of Warren Co. to JOHN
                  SNELLING for 50 pounds, land on Ogechee 175 acres,
part of 500 acres granted to JOHN KELLY, July 3, 1787, PETER MAHONE (🕂).
Wit: JACOB FLOURNEY, JAMES ELLETT. Rec. Dec. 7, 1796.

Pages 221-222:   Sept. 22, 1795, ELEAZER MOBLEY of Warren Co., to
                  FRANCIS BECK of same for 50 pounds, land near GOING's
Mill, originally granted to GEO. BREWER Oct. 29, 1789. ELEAZER MOBLEY
(EM SEAL). Wit: LEWIS HARVIE, SAMUEL FIELDS. Rec. Dec. 8, 1796.

Pages 222-223:   Jan. 3, 1788 THOMAS GAMBILL and wife SUSANNAH of Green
                  Co. to JOHN PARRISH of Wilkes Co. for 35 pounds paid
by PARRIAH, 200 acres adj. B. FEW, GEORGE COOPER, Widow COULLARS, JOHN
EDMONDSON & HENRY PARRISH. THOMAS GAMBILL (LS), SUSANNAH GAMBILL (LS).
Wit: GEO. BREWER, HENRY PARRISH. Rec. Dec. 8, 1796.

Pages 223-224:   May 4, 1789, JOHN LEDBETTER of Wilkes Co. to FREDERICK
                  LEDBETTER of same for 25 pounds, land on Ogechee,
granted to JOHN LEDBETTER May 15, 1785.. JOHN LEDBETTER (SEAL). Wit:
SOLOMON NEWSOM, ARTHUR FORT JP. Rec. Dec. 8, 1796.

Pages 224-225:   Feb. 25, 1796, ISAAC LEDBETTER of Washington Co. to
                  WILLIAM JORDAN of Warren Co. for 25 pounds, 130 acres,
part of 200 acres granted to ISAAC LEDBETTER May 13, 1790... ISAAC
LEDBETTER (SEAL). Wit: JNO. CURRIE, JNO. HAMILL JP. Rec. Dec. 8, 1796.

Pages 225-226:   March 2, 1795, WILLIAM FRANKLIN and wife MARY to
                  ALECK SMITH all of Warren Co. for 20 pounds, land on
Brier Creek bounding WILLIAM WHITE, DAVID ROBISON, 100 acres, part of
a tract of 200 granted... WILLIAM FRANKLIN (SEAL), MARY FRANKLIN (SEAL).
Wit: ROBERT ISAACS, BENJAMIN SMITH. Rec. Dec. 9, 1796.

Pages 226-227:   March 7, 1794 THOMAS STARK Senr. of Wilkes Co., to
                  JOHN WHITLOCK of Columbia Co. THOMAS STARK & ELIZABETH
his wife, for 120 pounds, 150 acres originally granted to ABRAHAM DENNIS
July 3, 1770. THOMAS STARK (SEAL), ELIZABETH STARK (SEAL) (X). Wit:
JOSEPH WHITLOCK & STEPHEN STAPLE. Rec. Jan. 2, 1797.

Pages 228-230:   Oct. 5, 1775, JOSEPH BROWN & ANNE his wife of Wrights-
                  borough Township, Parish of St. Paul, to ABRAHAM JOHNSON
Junr. of same for 90 pounds, lease for 1 year, 300 acres of Carsons
Creek, bounded by JOHN CARSON, granted to JOSEPH BROWN March 2, 1773.
JOSEPH BROWN (SEAL), ANNE BROWN (SEAL). Wit: JNO SUGGS, WM. WHATLEY,
JOSEPH MADDOCK JP. Rec. Feb. 18, 1797.

Pages 230-232:   Almost identical to above Rec. Feb. 13, 1797.

Pages 232-233:   Feb. 29, 1796 MICHAEL BURKHATTER, JOHN BURKHATTER,
                  JACOB BURKHATTER, JOSHUA BURKHATTER, JEREMIAH BURK-
HATTER, ISAAC BURKHATTER, JESSE BURKHATTER of Warren Co. to DANIEL
HUTCHISON of same for 100 dollars, land bounded by STARLING GARDNER,
JOSEPH RICHARDSON & GOLDEN's fork, 200 acres. (all above BURKHATTERS
signed with (SEAL). Wit: P. HODO, WM. CORAN, CLARK BLANDFORD. Rec.
13, 1796.

Pages 233-234:   Nov. 15, 1796, WILLIAM MIMS & NAOMI, his wife, of
                  Warren Co., to HENRY KENDALL of Columbia Co. for $300
land on Rocky Comfort, 100 acres, half of a 200 acre grant to WILLIAM
MIMS... WILLIAM MIMS (SEAL), NAOMI MIMS (SEAL). Wit: T. PERSONS, GEO
WEATHERBY. Rec. Feb. 13, 1797.

Pages 234-235:   Dec. 18, 1796 WILLIAM BARNETT, Admr. of est. of
                  WILLIAM BARNETT of Columbia Co., dec'd to JOHN MADDOX,
sold at Columbia Court House $185.72 land in Warren Co. 184 acres.
WM. BARNETT (SEAL). Wit: MARY A. CRAWFORD, PETER CRAWFORD JP,
Columbia Co., Rec. Feb. 15, 1797.

Pages 235-236:   Dec. 17, 1795, ROBERT JENKINS of Warren Co. to MICAJAH
                  STONE of same for $1500, land on Williams' Creek in
Warren Co., 320 acres, granted to ROBERT JENKINS Oct. 7, 1785, Rec. in
BOOK JJJ, folio 49. ROBERT JENKINS (SEAL). Wit: JOHN JENKINS, WILLIAM
JENKINS, ROBERT JENKINS. Rec. Feb. 15, 1797.

Pages 236-237:   March 28, 1786, THOMAS BETHANY of Wilkes Co. to JOHN
                  JONES of same for 10 pounds, land in Wilkes Co. (now
Warren) 200 acres, granted Sept. 29, 1784... THOMAS BETHANY. Wit:
SUSANNAH DAVIES, ROBT. RUTHERFORD, JOHN RUTHERFORD JP. Rec. Feb. 15,
1797.

Pages 237-238:   Aug. 21, 1792, JOHN JONES of Wilkes Co. to WILLIAM COX
                  of same, for 200 pounds 2 tracts of land in Wilkes Co.
(now Warren) 200 acres, conveyed to JOHN JONES from THOMAS BETHANY
March 28, 1786, located to BETHANY Aug. 12, 1784, registered in Book
EEE, folio 64... the second 200 acres conveyed to JOHN JONES by JOHN
RUTHERFORD Jan. 10, 1792, who located it April 4, 1785, Reg. in Book
JJJ, folio 869. JOHN JONES (SEAL). Wit: JOHN MYRICK, GEO. WEATHERBY
(SEATHERLY?) Rec. Feb. 16, 1797.

Page 239:   April 1, 1793, SAMUEL NEWMAN of Wilkes Co. to WILLIAM COCKS
             of same, for 7 pounds for 10 acres in Wilkes Co. (now
Warren) bound by JOEL KING, DRURY MIMS... SAMUEL NEWMAN (SEAL). Wit:
THOMAS COCKS & WALTER NEWMAN. Rec. Feb. 16, 1797.

Pages 239-240:   May 24, 1796, JOHN J. WELLS to ELISHA WRIGHT of Warren
                  Co., for 10 pounds land on Rocky Comfort in Warren
Co., 20 acres, bound by JOSEPH MILLAR... JOHN J. WELLS (SEAL), MARY
WELLS (SEAL). Wit: JOSEPH WRIGHT, JOSEPH MILLAR. Rec. March 11, 1797.

Pages 240-241:   Sept. 14, 1795, NICHOLAS JONES & JEAN his wife to
                  MATHEW PARHAM of Co. of Warren for 50 pounds, 230 acres

ELISH ROBERT's land, GRAY's land, NICHLAS JONES (SEAL), JEAN JONES (SEAL).
Wit: G. ? FRANKLIN, JOHN WILLIAMS. Rec. March 11, 1797.

Pages 241-242:   Jan. 2, 1797, WILKINS SMITH of Warren Co. to MATHEW
                 PARHAM of same, for $201.37, 200 acres granted to
THOMAS SMITH, Senr. WILKINS SMITH. Wit: ZEPH. FRANKLIN, WYATT
BONNER. Rec. March 29, 1797.

Pages 242-243:   Jan. 25, 1791, JOHN FULLER of Washington Co., Ga., to
                 DREWRY MIMS of Wilkes (now Warren) Co. for 100 pounds,
200 acres in Wilkes Co., granted Aug. 2, 1786... JOHN FULLER. Wit:
WILLIAM MIMS. Rec. March 29, 1797.

Pages 243-244:   1793, JOHN FULLER of Washington Co. to DREWRY MIMS
                 of Wilkes Co. for 25 pounds, 50 acres in Wilkes Co.
(now Warren) granted March 2, 1791. JOHN FULLER. Wit: RACHEL TENNILLE,
BENJ. TENNILLE JP. Rec. March 30, 1797.

Pages 244-245:   Sept. 3, 1796, DREWRY MIMS & ELIZABETH his wife to
                 TURNER PERSONS for $118, land on Whetstone Creek
bound by THOMAS FULLER, JNO. FULLER, 50 acres granted to JOHN FULLER.
March 2, 1791... DREWRY MIMS (M) (SEAL), ELIZABETH MIMS, Wit: JAMES
DARNEL, JOHN LOWE. Rec. March 30, 1797.

Pages 245-246:   Sept. 3, 1796, DREWRY MIMS & ELIZABETH to TURNER PERSONS
                 for $460, 200 acres more or less granted to JOHN FULLER
Aug. 2, 1796... DREWRY MIMS (M) (SEAL), ELIZABETH MIMS. Wit: JAMES
DARNEL, JOHN LOWE. Rec. March 30, 1797.

Pages 246-247:   Dec. 31, 1795, WILLIAM JOHNSON & ROSANNAH his wife of
                 Warren Co. to ASA TINDALL of same for 75 pounds land
bounded by EZEKIEL WILLIAMS, WM.BASS, DAVID CROCKETT, 200 acres more
or less, the north part of a grant of 500 acres to DAVID FELPS Dec. 4,
1790. WM. JOHNSON (SEAL). Wit: WILLIAM BYROM JP. Rec. April 1, 1797.

Pages 247-248:   June 13, 1792, JOHN DUNAWAY of Wilkes Co. (now Warren)
                 to WILLIAM DUNAWAY for 50 pounds, about 41 acres part
of a 400 acre tract granted to JOHN DUNAWAY Oct. 13, 1785... corner of
JACOB DUCKWORTH's... JOHN DUNAWAY (X) (SEAL). Wit: JAS. MCCORMICK JP.
Rec. April 1, 1797.

Pages 248-249:   March 15, 1797, WM. DUNAWAY to JOSEPH DUCKWORTH for
                 $90, 41 acres 9above) WM. DUNAWAY. Wit: SALLY HODO,
P. HODO JP. Rec. April 1, 1797.

Pages 249-250:   March 1, 1792, RICHARD SMITH of Washington Co. to
                 NEEDHAM SMITH of Wilkes Co. (now Warren), 100 acres
more or less, for 25 pounds. RICHARD SMITH (R) (SEAL). Wit: JOEDAY
NEWSOM, CARTER NEWSOM. Rec. April 5, 1797.

Pages 250-251:   May 20, 1795, SEPTIMUS WEATHERBY of Warren Co. to
                 AMBROSE EDMONDSON of Halifax Co., North Carolina for
90 silver dollars, land in Warren Co. bound by J. MYRICK, JAS. MILLER,
granted April 19, 1790. SEPTIMUS WEATHERBY (SEAL). Wit: TURNER PERSON,
THOMAS NEAL. Rec. April 5, 1797.

Pages 251-252:   July 7, 1795, BENJAMIN JACKSON of Hancock Co., Ga. to
                 JAMES ROQUEMORE of Warren Co., Ga., for 40 pounds,
200 acres on Little Brier Creek, adj. MERCER, BENJAMIN JACKSON (SEAL).
Wit: DREWRY MURPHEY, WILLIS WHATLEY. Rec. April 6, 1797.

Pages 253-254:   JAMES ROQUEMORE, Senr. for love, good will & affection
                 to son PETER ROEQUEMORE (sic), my eldest son, land
on Little Bryar Creek, my next eldest son JAMES ROQUEMORE, Junr. one
half of profit and increase of my wench Dinah,, 250 acres in Co. of
Lincoln adj. JAMES GREEN & BENJAMIN BENTLEY and one horse, saddle and
6 head of cattle.. my next eldest son THOMAS ROQUEMORE... same as to
JAMES... my eldest Dau. POLLY ROQUEMORE, half of profit of Negro wench,

Luce, 6 head of cattle, half of my household furniture... to my son, JOHN ROQUEMORE half of profit of above Luce, 287½ acres in Montgomery County, adj. JAMES YORK & JOHN GARRETT.. my wagon and gear... to my Dau. ELIZABETH ROQUEMORE negro wench Rose, saddle & 6 head of cattle, half of my household furniture. March 31, 1797, JAMES ROQUEMORE (SEAL). Wit: WM. B. MURPHY, DRURY MURPHEY. Rec. April 7, 1797.

Pages 254-255: Town of Warrenton, Ga., April 8, 1797, STERLING GARDNER of Warren Co. & POLLEY his wife to Judges of Inferior Court & their successors in office, land on Goldwin's Creek on Road to Augusta, for laying off into lots, for erecting Public Building. STARLING GARDNER (SEAL), POLLEY GRADNER (SEAL). Rec. April 10, 1797.

Pages 255-256: Sept. 17, 1796, JACOB DARDEN of Warren Co. to JOHN BUSTIN for $230... land in Warren Co. on William's Creek, part of 900 acre tract granted to MR. MURRAY on which JOHN BAKER, Esq. now lives... JACOB DARDEN (SEAL). Wit: ROBT. HILL, N. WILLIAMS, T. PERSONS. Rec. Apr. 11, 1797.

Pages 256-257: Dec. 29, 1791, ROBERT BARNETT of Wilkes Co. to JOHN MCMURRIN of same for 100 pounds, 200 acres in Wilkes Co. (now Warren) on Long Creek adj. land of BERRY, granted Jan. 24, 1791... ROBERT BARNETT (SEAL). Wit: ANDWE. BERRY JP., GOBSON BERRY. Rec. April 11, 1797.

Page 257: Sept. 27, 1796, JAMES SANDERS to JAMES LOWE all of Warren Co. for $550, 200 acres JAMES SANDERS (SEAL), HEREN SANDERS (SEAL). Wit: D. PERRYMAN, THOMAS BANKSTON, M. HUBBERT JP. Rec. April 11, 1797.

Page 258: Dec. 23, 1796, MARK HARDIN of Warren Co. to JOHN GIBSON of same for $1250, 140 acres on Middle Creek adj. LEVI PRUITTS, LEMUEL PRUITT, TUCK & MCLINVALE... MARK HARDIN (SEAL). Wit: LEWIS WRIGHT, ISAIAH TUCKER. Rec. Dec. 2, 1797.

Page 258-259: WILLIAM SANDERS to son HENRY SANDERS for natural love and good will ... all my household furniture & c. April 10, 1797. Rec. 17 ___ 1797. WILLIAM SANDERS (X) (SEAL).

Pages 259-260: April 15, 1795 WILLIAM STARK of Columbia Co. to SAMUEL COOPER of Warren Co., for 20 pounds, 100 acres bounded by CARSON & BISHOP, JAMISON's old survey... WM. STARK (SEAL), Wit: NOBLE BUTLER, WM. JOHNSON. Rec. May 8, 1797.

Pages 260-261: April 15, 1795, WILLIAM STARK to JOHN BISHOP of Warren Co., for 20 pds, 100 acres adj. J. HILL, STARK, CARSON, GRAY's old line... part of old survey granted to JAMES GRAY conveyed Feb. 26 last, to STARK... WM. STARK (SEAL). Wit: NOBLE BUTLER, WM. JOHNSON. Rec. May 8, 1797.

Pages 261-262: Feb. 2, 1797, LITTLEBERRY CREWS of Hanover Co., Virginia to JAMES JONES of Warren Co., for $500 land on Bryar Creek... originally granted to ISAAC BALL Aug. 26, 1788... LITTLE BERRY CREW. Wit: MATTW. HUBERT JP., TURNER PERSONS & STARLING JONES. Rec. May 22, 1797.

Pages 262-263: Nov. 9, 1796, MARY MIMS of Warren Co. to JOHN BALL of same for $30, land on Rocky Comfort Creek, MARY MIMS (S) (SEAL). Wit: LEWS. BRANTLEY, WM. JOHNSON. Rec. May 22, 1797.

Pages 263-264: March 26, 1796, NATHANIEL COATS, Esq. collector of Tax for Co. of Wilkes to DAVID HILLHOUSE of Town of Washington, and County & State aforesd. 900 acres of land in Wilkes County in the name of GEORGE MURRAY in arrears for taxes up to the year 1788, exposed to public sale where DAVID HILLHOUSE bought it for 10 pounds. NATHANIEL COATS (SEAL). Wit: FRANIS GORDON, DAVID TERRELL. Rec. May 22, 1797.

Pages 264-265: Jan. 14, 1793, WILLIAM BREWER of Wilkes Co. to JESSE
COLES of same for 55 pounds, 120 acres in Wilkes Co.,
adj. JAMES BISHOP, DAN. REYNOLDS... WILLIAM BREWER, ELIZABETH BREWER
(SEAL). Wit: FRANCIS CALLAWAY & MATTW. BREWER. Rec. May 22, 1797.

Pages 265-266: Sept. 2, 1791, SAMUEL CAMP of Wilkes to ENOCH RENTFROE
of same for 12 pounds, land in Wilkes Co. (now Warren),
on Joe's Creek adj. JOHN TABOR, RENFROE's, 200 acres more or less,
originally grant Jan. 22, 1789 to sd. CAMP. S. CAMP (SEAL). Wit
ANDW. BURNES, JONATHAN MILLER. Rec. May 22, 1797.

Pages 266-267: May 8, 1794, PHILIP GIBS of Warren Co., to LARKIN
CHIVERS of same, for 45 pounds, PHILIP GIBS & PHEBE
his wife... land on waters of Fort's Creek, 250 acres. PHILIP GIBBS
(SEAL), PHEBE GIBBS (SEAL). Wit: JOHN WILSON, NATHAN RENTFROE.
Rec. May 22, 1797.

Pages 267-268: March 25, 1797, RACHEL POWELL of Richmond Co. to COL.
CHAS. POLK of Co. of McLinburg in North Carolina for
85 pounds, 250 acres in Warren Co. on Bryar Creek, granted to RACHEL
POWELL... RACHEL POWELL (*Q*) (SEAL). Wit: A. HOBSON, SAMUEL KENNEDY.
Rec. May 22, 1797.

Pages 268-269: Feb. 4, 1797, ROBERT STANFORD to JESSE STANFORD for
$25.00, on both sides of Little Sweet water, 100
acres. ROBERT STANFORD (SEAL). Wit: PETER HODO, JOHN WILSON JP.
Rec. May 22, 1797.

Pages 269-270: March 23, 1790, STEPHEN MITCHELL of Richmond Co. to
ENOCH RENTFROE of Wilkes Co. CELIA, wife of STEPHEN
MITCHELL, for 100 pounds, land on Joe's Creek in Wilkes Co. 150 acres,
vacant on all sides when surveyed July 3, 1787. STEPHEN MITCHELL (X)
(SEAL), SELAH MITCHELL (X) (SEAL). Wit: ADAM JONES, THOMAS ROGERS &
THOMAS FARMER. Rec. May 23, 1797.

Pages 270-271: Nov. 19, 1796, JAMES ROGERS of Warren Co. to JOSIAH
CARTER of same, for 17 pounds, 2 shillings & six
pence, land on Ogechee, 10 acres... JAMES ROGERS (SEAL). Wit: JAMES
HENDERSON, THOS. POORE, WM. BYROM JP. Rec. May 23, 1797.

Pages 271-272: April 16, 1794, ROBERT SYNNE of Warren Co. to THOMAS
POORE, of same, for 100 pounds, 222 acres on a branch
of Ogechee. ROBERT WYNNE, ELIZABETH WYNNE. Wit: JAMES LUCAS, AUGUSTUS
COTTEN & WM. BYROM JP. Rec. May 23, 1797.

Pages 272-273: March 27, 1797, GEORGE DYKES of Warren Co. to ISAAC
BLUNT of Washington Co., Ga., for $50, 300 acres, part
of a grant to GEORGE DYKES, Jan. 14, 1797. GEORGE DYKES (SEAL). Wit:
JOHN LAWSON JP, MOSES GRANDBERRY. Rec. May 23, 1797.

Pages 273-274: 1790, STEPHEN MITCHELL of Richmond Co., Ga., to THOMAS
JONES of Wilkes Co., Ga., for 50 pounds, land on west
side of Long Creek, originally granted to STEPHEN MITCHELL adj. NATHAN
FOWLER March 17, 1785. STEPHEN MITCHELL (SEAL), SELAH MITCHELL (SEAL),
Wit: ADAM JONES, THOMAS ROGERS. Rec. May 23, 1797.

Pages 274-275: March 23, 1790, STEPHEN MITCHELL & SELAH his wife to
ADAM JONES, for 50 pounds, land on Long Creek in Co.
of Wilkes (now Warren), 150 acres granted to STEPHEN MITCHELL. Aug. 13,
1786, adj. ARTHUR FORT... STEPHEN MITCHELL (SEAL), SELAH MITCHELL (SEAL).
Wit: THOMAS ROGERS, TOMAS FARMER, ENOCH RENFROE. Rec. May 23, 1797.

Pages 275-276: March 29, 1796, NATHAN FOWLER of Warren Co. to ADAM
JONES for 25 pounds, land on Long Creek... Brady Branch
originally granted to sd. NATHAN FOWLER, 1788... NATHAN FOWLER (SEAL)
Wit: ANDERSON BERRY, ZEPHANIAH FOWLER. Rec. May 24, 1797.

Pages 276-277:   May 17, 1797, JAMES THOMAS of Hancock Co. to ADAM
                   JONES of Warren Co. for $65, on Long Creek of Ogechee.
P. ADAM JONES, Junr... JAMES THOMAS (T) (SEAL). Wit: SAML. CAMP.
Rec. May 24, 1797.

Pages 277-278:   July 8, 1796, EDWARD BLACK of Warren Co. to JOHN
                   RUSHING of same for 30 pounds, land in Warren Co.,
100 acres originally granted to EDWARD BLACK Oct. 12, 1785. EDWARD
BLACK (SEAL). Wit: NATHAN RENFROE, LEVI MATTHEWS. Rec. May 24, 1797.

Page 278:   May 18, 1797, JOHN HILL of Warren Co., to HOWELL HIGHT $500,
              200 acres surveyed for JOHN HILL and Recorded in Book T
July 4, 1775, adj. P. BRANTLEY, ADAM JONSON... JOHN HILL (SEAL). Wit:
LEVI PRUITT JP. Rec. May 24, 1797.

Pages 278-279:   Jan. 1, 1795, JOSEPH PEVAY of Warren Co. to ABRAHAM
                   HEATH of same, for 30 pounds, 50 acres on Long Creek,
adj. JOSEPH PEVAY, JOHN ACRES, JOSEPH PEAVEY (SEAL). Wit: JOHN CHAPPELL
& WILLIAM HEATH. Rec. June 12, 1797.

Pages 279-280:   Nov. 7, 1795, WILLIAM THOMSON to JOHN RUSHING all of
                   Warren Co., for 50 pounds... land on Fort's Creek in
Warren Co., granted to SAMUEL CAMP Jan. 22, 1789. WILLIAM THOMPSON
(SEAL). Wit: NATHAN RENFROE, LARKIN CHIVERS. Rec. May 25, 1797.

Pages 2802-81:   April 17, 1797, RICHARD CASTLEBERRY of Warren Co. to
                   JOHN HIX for $500, 150 acres by est., part of a tract
granted to JOHN FULSOM... RICHARD CASTLEBERRY (SEAL), ANN CASTLEBERRY
(SEAL). Wit: JACOB FLOURNOY, JEREMIAH SALEY, JOHN CASTLEBERRY, HENRY
HARDIN JP. Rec. May 25, 1797.

Pages 281-282:   Jan. 14, 1797, JOHN WHITLOCK & TABITHA his wife of
                   Oglethorpe Co., Ga., to THOMAS BUTTRILL of Columbia
Co., Ga., for 82 pounds, 100 acres part of a tract granted to JOHN &
ABRAHAM DENNIS July 3, 1770 in Warren Co., on Little River, adj. RALPH
KILGORE... sold by JOHN & ABRAHAM DENNIS to THOMAS STARK then to JOHN
WHITLOCK. JOHN WHITLOCK (SEAL), TABITHA WHITLOCK (SEAL). Wit: JAMES
MCFARLAND, WILLIAM DOZER, JOHN DOZER & WM. CLAIBORNE. Rec. May 25, 1797.

Pages 282-283:   Oct. 27, 1795, DAVID MERIWETHER, Esqr. Receiver of Tax
                   Returns for the Co. of Wilkes to CHARLES CARTER...
1792 sold for payment of taxes of BENJAMIN PORTER... 200 acres in Warren
Co., originally granted to ABRAHAM DENNIS... DAVID MERIWETHER (SEAL).
Wit: R. Worsham JP. Rec. May 25, 1797.

Pages 283-284:   Dec. 1, 1795, CHARLES CARTER of Wilkes Co. and JANE
                   his wife from BENJAMIN PORTER for 5 shillings, 200
acres on Little adj. JOSEPH EVANS, BENJAMIN HARDIN, BENJAMIN PORTER,
KILGORE's Creek... granted to ABRAHAM DENNIS, then sold by DAVID
MERIWETHER... CHAS. RO. CARTER (SEAL). Rec. May 25, 1797.

Pages 284-285:   Feb. 21, 1791, JOHN D. YOUNG of State of South
                   Carolina to JOHN HULL of Richmond Co., Ga., for 50
pounds, 200 acres on Rocky Comfort, granted to ABSOLEM JACKSON Feb.
25, 1786. Adj. WILLIAM LANDRUM, SHADRACK SMITH... JOHN D. YOUNG (SEAL).
Test: PHILIP GIBBS, JOHN LAWSON. Rec. May 26, 1797.

Page 285:   Dec. 28, 1796, JOHN HULL of Camden Co., Ga., to BYRD PRUITT
              of same state & co. of Warren, for 50 pounds, 200 acres on
Rocky Comfort, part of 400 acres granted to ABSOLEM JACKSON, Feb. 25,
1786, adj. SHARDACH SMITH, WILLIAM LANDRUM... JOHN HULL (X) (SEAL).
Wit: JOHN LAWSON JP., CHAS. M. LAWSON. Rec. May 26, 1797.

Page 286:   Feb. 4, 1797, ROBERT STANFORD to SPENCER OWEN of Warren
              Co., for 50 dollars, 200 acres on both sides of Little
Sweet Water, part of 300 acres granted to ROBERT STANFORD Oct. 29, 1795.
ROBERT STANFORD (LS). Wit: P. HODO, JOHN WILSON. Rec. May 26, 1797.

Page 287:   June 6, 1797, JOHN HENRY PICKARD of Warren Co. to JEREMIAH
            SPURLIN of same, for $70, 80 acres in Warren Co. part of
200 acres granted to PATRICK BRADDY, Nov. 28, 1796, Rec. in BOOK YYYY,
folio 488... JOHN H. PICKARD (X). Wit: JNO. CURRIE, CLABORN CRAWFORD.
Rec. July 17, 1797.

Page 288:   March 26, 1796, PATRICK BRADY, Senr. of Warren Co. to
            JOHN HENRY PICKARD of same, for $100, land on North side of
Joe's Creek, adj. JOHN HATCHER's, 100 acres, granted to PATRICK BRADY
Rec. BOOK JJJ, folio 426... PATRICK BRADY (P) (SEAL). Wit: JOHN
HATCHER, JOHN SPURLIN. Rec. July 24, 1797.

Page 289:   Dec. 21, 1796, PATRICK BRADY to HENRY PICKARD, for $200,
            200 acres in Warren Co. (in Richmond when surveyed)...
PATRICK BRADY (𝟮) (SEAL). Wit: FRANCIS DANIELLY, JEREMIAH SPURLIN.
Rec. July 24, 1797.

Page 290:   July 4, 1796, GEORGE GRANDBERRY of Jefferson Co. to GEORGE
            DYKES of Warren Co. for 30 pounds, 300 acres on Joe's
Creek, being part of two tracts one granted to GEORGE GRANDBERRY
May 24, 1796, the other granted to REUBEN ALLEN Oct. 1, 1785, adj.
ELIAKIM TISON, BUCKELOW, RICHARD CURRY... GEORGE GRANDBERRY (SEAL).
Wit: JOHN LAWSON JP, MOSES GRANDBERRY. Rec. July 24, 1797.

Pages 290-291:   April 21, 1797, JOHN RUTHERFORD of Washington Co., to
                 NICHOLAS WILLIAM of Warren Co. for $700, land on both
sides of Rocky Comfort Creek, all of 400 acres except for one acre sold
to a certain Mr. Davies with a further reserve of ten square feet
including a grave... adj. at time of survey CLARK, JOSEPH MIMS... JOHN
RUTHERFORD (SEAL). Wit: FREDERICK MORRRIS & MORTAN MINTER. Rec.
July 25, 1797.

Pages 291-292:   June 3, 1797, HENRY KINDALL & ELIZABETH his wife of
                 Warren Co. to NICHOLAS WILLIAM of same, for $345, for
land on Rocky Comfort adj. JOHN BALL, KID's land, WILLIAM MIMS, 100
acres half of a 200 acre tract granted to WILLIAM MIMS, conveyed by
MIMS to KINDALL... HENRY KENDALL (SEAL), ELIZABETH PENNY KINDALL (SEAL),
Wit: TURNER PERSON, RICHD. B. FLETCHER JP. Rec. July 25, 1797.

Pages 292-293:   Feb. 20, 1797, JOHN TORRENCE (farmer) to JAMES BRAY
                 (planter) for $85, land on Rocky Comfort, adj.
NATHANIEL FULSOM, STARLING JONES, AMOS WRIGHT, and part of a survey
this day conveyed to DAVID COX, part of a tract granted to JOHN
TORRENCE April 7, 1789. Recorded BOOK GGG (SSS?) Fol. 72, this convey-
ance for 60 acres... JOHN TORRENCE (SEAL). Wit: SOL. SLATTER, ELISHA
HURT JP. Rec. July 26, 1797.

Pages 293-294:   May 1, 1791, BRITAIN MCCULLERS of Washington Co. to
                 JOHN NUNN of Wilkes Co. for 100 pounds, 143 acres on
both sides of Little Brier Creek... adj. WILLIAM SMITH... B. MCCULLERS.
Rec. July 26, 1797.

Pages 294-295:   Feb. 6, 1796, JAMES BALEY of Warren Co. to WILLIAM
                 SHIRLEY of same for 50 pounds, 150 acres part of a
tract granted to JAMES BALEY March 5, 1787, on Little Creek... JAMES
BALEY (SEAL). Wit: J. GRIZARD, WILLIAM KITCHEN, L. PRUITT JP. Rec.
July 27, 1797.

Pages 295-296:   July 12, 1795, JONATHAN ANDERSON of Hancock Co., to
                 JAMES W. GREEN of Warren... JONATHAN ANDERSON did
obtain a grant in his own name, or in the name of WILLIAM & JONATHAN
ANDERSON Sept. 29, 1784 for 200 acres, the upper half being JONATHAN's
for 75 pounds pd by sd. GREEN adj. JOSHUA ROE, THOMAS VININGS, JOHN
ANGLIN, CHILDREY's (now JAMES BISHOP's)... JONATHAN ANDERSON (SEAL).
Wit: DIXON PERRYMAN, WILLIAM ANDERSON. Rec. July 27, 1797.

Pages 296-297:   Sept. 21, 1792, WILLIAM SMITH and PATTY his wife of
                 Washington Co., to DANIEL ATKINS of Wilkes Co. for 60

pounds, 70 acres on Little Bryar Creek, adj. JOHN MAYNOR, JACKSON, WILLIAM SMITH... WILLIAM SMITH (SEAL), PATTY SMITH (P) (SEAL). Wit: ROBERT ISAACS, JOSEPH ADKINS. Rec. July 27, 1797.

Pages 297-298: May 22, 1797, CLAIBORN NEWSOM to JAMES MECKUM for $2, 120 acres on Big Bryar Creek... CLABORN NEWSOM (SEAL), HESTER NEWSOM (X) (SEAL). Wit: MOSES MCKINNEY. Rec. July 31, 1797.

Pages 298-299: July 24, 1794, JEREMIAH DUCKWORTH of Warren Co., to JACOB DUCKWORTH of Hancock Co. for 150 pounds, part of two tracts of 200 acres each, granted to sd. DUCKWORTH & MARGARET DAVISON or their head rights, being part of the survey that sd. DUCKWORTH sold to JAMES CARTER, where sd. CARTER now lives, lying on a little branch of Bryar Creek adj. WILLIAM NICHOLS, JAMES MAY, JACOB DUCKWORTH & JOHN DUNAWAY... JEREMIAH DUCKWORTH (SEAL). Wit: JOSEPH DUCKWORTH, JAMES DRAPER, JESSE BURGEN. Rec. Aug. 8, 1806.

Pages 300-301: June 15, 1797, JACOB DUCKWORTH of Hancock Co. to JOSEPH DUCKWORTH of Warren Co. for 400 pounds, 374 acres, lying on Bryar Creek. JACOB DUCKWORTH (⊕) (SEAL). Wit: ARTHUR FORT, RANDAL DUCKWORTH. Rec. Aug. 8, 1806.

Page 301: Nov. 26, 1796, JAMES THWEATT of Hancock Co. to DIXON PERRYMAN of Warren Co. for $130, 147 acres on Ogechee. JAMES THWEATT (SEAL). Wit: ABNER BANCKSTON, FRANK LAWSON JP. Rec. Aug. 2, 1797.

Page 302: June 19, 1797, ELEAZER MOBLEY to JOHN MCMURRIN, both of Warren Co., for $550, 180 acres on Ogechee... on Georgetown Road (Beck's corner), formerly a line of KELLY's, THOMAS FRIEND's line, formerly FEW's, part of a grant to GEORGE BREWER, Junr. Nov. 25, 1788. ELEAZER MOBLEY (E) (SEAL). Wit: ROBERT BARNET, JELSON BERRY. Rec. Aug. 2, 1797.

Pages 302-303: Jan. 26, 1797, ARTHUR FAIL of Hancock Co. to JOHN SMITH of Warren Co. for 128½ (not specified dollars or pounds), land adj. MOSES GRANDBERRY, Rocky Comfort Creek, ALLEN, SIMS, 200 acres... ARTHUR FAIL (SEAL). Wit: SALLEY ROBERTSON, NOWELL (NORVELL?) ROBERTSON JP. Rec. Aug. 15, 1797.

Pages 303-304: March 3, 1797, CHRISTOPHER PRITCHELL of Halifax Co., North Carolina to WILLIAM HEATH of same, land in Warren Co., Ga., on Ogechee, 200 acres CHRISTOPHER PRITCHETT (SEAL). Wit: JAMES DAVISON (X), NANCY HEATH. Rec. Aug. 15, 1797.

Pages 304-305: April 23, 1796, SAVAGE LITTLETON of Warren Co. to TIMOTHY LANDRUM of same, for 30 Guineas, 116 acres in Warren Co. adj. SHELTON, HOWARD, SOLOMON NEWSOM, granted April 20, 1796. Rec. in BOOK XXXX, folio 140. SAVAGE LITTLETON (SEAL), NANCY LITTLETON (SEAL). Wit: JOHN BURKHATTER, JAS. MCCORMICK. Rec. Aug. 15, 1797.

Pages 305-306: Sept. 3, 1791, JESSE CONNELL & PENELOPE his wife of Green Co., to JAMES ROGERS of same for 200 pounds, land in Wilkes Co. (now Warren), on Redlick Creek of Ogechee, bounded by MOSE POWELL Senr., JEREMIAH OATES & vacant land, granted Aug. 2, 1786... JESSE CONNELL (SEAL), PEN. CONNELL (X) (SEAL). Wit: WILLIAM WYNNE, R. MIDDLETON, JAS. HARVEY JP. Rec. Aug. 19, 1797.

Pages 306-307: Dec. 24, 1796, FRANCIS DANIELLY of Hancock Co. to JEREMIAH SPURLING of Warren Co. for 100 pounds 200 acres on Joe's Creek, being part of a 400 acre grant to JNO. TABOR... FRANCIS DANELLY (SEAL), ELIZABETH DANILLY (SEAL), Wit: SAMUEL BRADY, HENRY PICKARD (X). Rec. Aug. 19, 1797.

Pages 307-308: JOSIAH CARTER of Wilkes Co. for love, good will and affection to my dau. ELIZABETH HENDERSON, wife of JAMES HENDERSON of same Co., 200 acres part of survey for sd. CARTER of 600 acres, July 17, 1784, and part of a survey of April 9, 1793, beginning at FRAZER's Hickory corner, on east side of north fork of Walker's Branch... DAVID LOCKETT's line... WILLIAM DISMUKES line... JOSIAH CARTER (SEAL). Wit: JOHN VEAZEY, JOHN WYNNE JP. Rec. Aug. 19, 1797.

Pages 308-309:   May 27, 1797, WILLIAM WEST of Warren Co., to RICHMOND TERRELL of same, for $10, land adj. THOMAS's, THOMAS SMITH, CASTLEBERRY, 300 acres more or less, WILLIAM WEST (SEAL). Wit: MATHEW MCCRARY, WILLIS ROWLAND. Rec. Aug. 19, 1797.

Pages 309-310:   May 27, 1797, WILLIAM WEST of Warren Co. to RICHMOND TERRELL, for $1200, 500 acres adj. GRADNER's & FOWLER's, BAKER's, LINSICUM's, BERRY's, NUGENT's, WILLIAM WEST (LS), MARSES WEST (X) (LS). Wit: MATHEW MCCRARY, WILLIS ROWLAND. Rec. Aug. 19, 1797.

Pages 310-311:   May 10, 1789, SAMUEL CAMP of Wilkes Co. to WILLIAM RUSHING for 10 pds. land on Fort's Creek, 250 acres part of a tract of 750 acres granted to sd. CAMP Jan. 22, 1789. S. CAMP (SEAL). Wit: JNO. RUSHING, WM. THOMSON. Aug. 19, 1797.

Pages 311-312:   Aug. 13, 1796, JOHN MOUTREY of Warren to JOHN DUBERRY of same, for 40 pounds, part of a survey for WILLIAM SPIKES Oct. 16, 1784, granted to SPIKES Sept. 27, 1787. JOHN MOUTREY (LS). Wit: ROBERT SYNNE, WILLIAM ROBERTSON, WILLIAM BYROM JP. Rec. Aug. 19, 1797.

Pages 312-313:   Jan. 14, 1797, JOSEPH MATHEWS from WILLIAM ANGLING all of Warren Co., for 15 pounds, 100 acres where JOSEPH MATHEWS now lives, part of a 300 acre grant to JACOB MERCER July 29, 1785, adj. Widow POWELL's land, Bryar Creek, sd. grant conveyed from JACOB MERCER & JEABY his wife to HENRY CHAMPION Sept. 1, 1791... WILLIAM ANGLIN (SEAL). Wit: CHAS. MAYBERRY, JAS. MCCORMICK JP. Rec. Aug. 19, 1797.

Pages 313-314:   Oct. 6, 1795, STEPHEN NOBLES of Warren Co. to EPHRAIM DICKEN of same for 100 pounds, 200 acres in Warren Co. adj. JAMES BISHOP, RUNNELS, WILLIAM NOBLES, WILLIAM LUCAS... grant to STEPHEN NOBLES... STEPHEN NOBLES (SEAL). Wit: JESSE DOLES, WILLIAM NORTHERN. Rec. Aug. 19, 1797.

Pages 314-315:   July 18, 1797, WILLIAM BYROM collector of taxes to CHARLES MAYBERRY of Columbia Co., land of ABRAHAM PENNINGTON, 240 acres sold May 17, 1797 at public sale, because of taxes for the years 1795... 150 acres sold for 213½ cents. WM. BYROM (LS). Wit: JOHN WILSON JP, HENRY KENDALL. Rec. Aug. 21, 1797.

Pages 315-316:   Oct. 7, 1796, MOSES HILL to JESSE RICKETSON, both of Warren Co., Ga., for $100, 200 acres adj. ISAAC SIMONS, and vacant land at time of survey, granted to MOSES HILL Aug. 19, 1790. MOSES HILL (M) (SEAL). Wit: JOHN GRENADE, PETER HODO JP. Wit: Aug. 21, 1797. (Rec.).

Pages 316-317:   April 13, 1793, DIXON HALL & NANCY his wife of Greene Co., to JAMES ROGERS of Wilkes Co., for 50 pounds, 200 acres in Wilkes Co. (now Warren),on Long Creek, originally granted to JAMES WADSWORTH Oct. 1, 1784... laters says DIXON HALL & ANNA his wife... DIXON HALL (SEAL). Wit: MALCOM JNO. SEN., DANIEL MITCHELL, HENY. MITCHELL. Rec. _____ 1797.

Pages 317-318:   1797, RHESA HOWARD of Columbia Co. to HENRY HIGHT of Warren Co., for $192, land on Hart's Creek, adj. old Richmond County line, 192 acres, part of a 777 acre grant to RHESA HOWARD June 4, 1796... R. HOWARD. Wit: ISAIAH TUCKER, LEML. PRUITT JP. Rec. Oct. 13, 1797.

Pages 318-319:   Sept. 25, 1797, LEWIS BRANTLEY of Warren Co. to AMBROSE HADLEY of same, for $500, land on Rocky Comfort Creek, 200 acres, granted to JOHN DAVIES... LEWIS BRANTLEY (SEAL). Wit: T. PERSONS & DAVID BROOM, L. PRUITT JP. Rec. Oct. 14, 1797.

Pages 319-320:   Jan. 30, 1798, GEORGE BREWER of Hancock Co., to JOSEPH
                  HILL of Warren Co. for $400, land on Rocky Branch of
Williams Creek, land surveyed for ROBERT JENKINS... Now the property of
JOHN RUDISELL... WILLIAM WHITE's line... 160 acres originally granted to
BENJAMIN SCOTT, Dec. 17, 1784. Rec. in BOOK FFF, Folio 16. GEORGE
BREWER (SEAL). Wit: LUCS. WRIGHT, JNO. TORRENCE. Rec. May 30, 1798.

Pages 320-321:   Oct. 27, 1796, SOLOMON BAREFIELD of Hancock Co. to
                  WILLIAM BAREFIELD of Warren Co., for 150 pounds, land
on Hart's Creek, 300 acres. SOLOMON BARFIELD (SEAL). Wit: LOYD
KELLY JP, MARK GONDER. Rec. June 13, 1798.

Pages 321-322:   Dec. 20, 1786, BENJAMIN THOMPSON & ANN his wife of
                  Green Co., to JOHN JONES of Wilkes Co. for 50 pounds
287½ acres, land in Washington Co., on Cowpen Creek of Little Ogechee.
granted to BENJAMIN THOMPSON June 27, 1786. BENJA. THOMPSON (SEAL),
ANNE THOMPSON (A) (SEAL). Wit: JAMES THOMPSON, JACOB JACKSON (J),
Proven: April 4, 1798. Rec. June 15, 1798.

Pages 322-323:   LAZARUS GURLEY of Warren Co. 300 acres on fork of Rock
                  Comfort, to WILLIAM SULLIVAN adj. lands of THOMAS NEAL,
ISAAC MCCRARY & JAMES JONES (the same land that WILLIAM SULLIVAN sold
to LAZARUS GURLEY) until such time as a note of 6000 weight of Inspected
Tobacco, due Nov. 1, 1796. Dec. 21, 1795. LAZARUS GURLEY (SEAL).
Wit: WILLIAM BROOKS, THOMAS NEAL GIBSON. Rec. Oct. 17, 1797.

Pages 323-324:   Jan. 19, 1797, REUBIN JONES of Warren Co. to STARLING
                  JONES of same, (mentions REBECCA JONES, wife of REUBEN)
148 acres on Rocky Comfort, adj. SARAH GOLDING's, HAWTHORNE, WRIGHT,
granted to REUBEN JONES, Jan. 9, 1797. Rec. BOOK ZZZZ, Fo. 115.
REUBIN JONES (SEAL), REBEKAH JONES (X) (SEAL). Wit: WM. JONES, JAMES
JONES. Rec. Nov. 1, 1797.

Pages 324-325:   Nov. 25, 1795, HENRY CHAMPIONS Senr., farmer to JOHN
                  KENT, farmer of Warren Co. for 60 pounds, land on west
Bryar Creek... bounded by the new road leading from Providence Iron-
works on Sweet Water to Waynesborough, land formerly that of Widow
POWELL, now JESSE MATHEWS, granted to JACOB MERCER July 29, 1785,
conveyed to CHAMPION Sept. 1, 1791... 100 acres more or less, HENRY
CHAMPION (H). Wit: JOHN TORRENCE, JESSE MATTHES. Relinquish of Dower
by MARY CHAMPION. Rec. Nov. 1, 1797.

Page 326:   JOHN CHAMPION to JOHN KENT in Warren Co., for 10 pounds,
             land on Main Bryar Creek... granted to CHAMPION the 25th
inst., Nov. 30, 1795, JNO. CHAMPION (X). Wit: JNO. TORRENCE, WM. WHITE,
JOSEPH WHITE. Nov. 2, 1797.

Page 327:   May 18, 1797, JOSEPH ARMSTRONG from WILLIAM CORUM for $30,
             50 acres, part of 420 granted to WM. CORUM, May 16, 1797,
on Brushy Fork of Cold Brier Creek... WM. CORUM (SEAL). Wit: EVAN
THOMAS, BENJA. GUSLING (X), ROBERT WILLIS. Rec. Nov. 2, 1797.

Pages 328:   March 19, 1796, EZEKIEL ALEXANDER of Warren Co. to WM.
              CRENSHAW of same, for $80, land on William's Creek and
Carson's Creek, 80 acres more or less. EZEKIEL ALEXANDER, NANCY
ALEXANDER. Wit: WM. SMITH, PETER HELTON (V). Rec. Nov. 2, 1797.

Pages 328-329:   May 2, 1797, SOLOMON NEWSOM of Warren to EDWARD KINSEY
                  of same for $707, 230 acres granted April 26, 1797,
registered in BOOK ZZZZ, Fo. 575... SOLOMON NEWSOM (SEAL), Wit: JAS.
MCCORMICK JP, A. THARP? JP. Rec. Nov. 2, 1797.

Pages 329-330:   Nov. 14, 1792, JESSE SANFORD, of Green Co., to THOM.
                  HEATH, for 50 pds. 255 acres on Rocky Branch in Wilkes
Co., originally granted to JESSE SANFORD... JESSE SANFORD (SEAL). Wit:
CADWALL RAINES, WYATT COLLIER. Ack. Nov. 14, 1792. Rec. Nov. 4, 1797.

Page 331:   Sept. 18, 1797, JOHN DISMUKES, Senr. to EPHRAIM DISMUKES
            for $200, 200 acres granted to sd. JOHN DISMUKES July 9,
1787... JOHN DISMUKES (SEAL). Wit: SEPTIMUS WEATHERBY, WILLIAM DISMUKES.
Rec. Nov. 5, 1797.

Page 332:   Feb. 17, 1796, MOUNTAIN HILL & ELIZABETH his wife, JESSE
            ARMSTRONG & AMIVIL his wife, all of Warren Co. to RICHARD
SUMMONS of same for $162, 152 acres in Warren Co. MOUNTAIN HILL (SEAL),
ELIZABETH HILL (SEAL), JESSE ARMSTRONG (SEAL), AMIVIL ARMSTRONG (SEAL).
Rec. Nov. 5, 1797.

Pages 332-333:   Oct. 17, 1797, SAMUEL OZBORN of Warren Co. to WILLIAM
                 OZBORN his son, for $100, land in Wilkes Co., (now
Warren), on Long CREEK, part of a 300 acre grant to sd. OZBORN Feb. 19,
1790... SAMUEL OZBORN (X) (SEAL). Wit: FANNEY FRIEND, WM. FLAKE (X).
Rec. Nov. 5, 1797.

Pages 333-334:   March 22, 1796, IGNATIUS FEW of Columbia Co., Ga., to
                 JAMES SOCTT of Warren Co. for 206 pounds, 10 shillings,
300 acres in Warren Co... I, FEW (SEAL). Wit: W. WILEE?, DAVIS MAHU,
WM. H. LEE. Rec. Nov. 8, 1797.

Pages 334-335:   Sept. 18, 1797, JOHN DISMUKES Senr. of Warren Co., to
                 JOHN DISMUKES, Junr. for $200, land on Hardin's Creek
& Ogechee, 100 acres, adj. SION WHEELER & EPHRAIM DISMUKES line...
JOHN DISMUKES (SEAL). Wit: SEPTIMUS WEATHERBY, WM. DISMUKES. Rec.
Nov. 8, 1797.

Pages 335-336:   Sept. 18, 1797, JOHN DISMUKES to PETER DISMUKES, for
                 $200, land adj. ANDREW KING, EDMOND DISMUKES, SAMUEL
JOHNSON, SION WHELIS & JOHN DISMUKES, Junr. 100 acres... JOHN DISMUKES
(SEAL). Wit: SEPTIMUS WEATHERBY, WM. DISMUKES. Rec. Nov. 9, 1797.

Pages 336-337:   Aug. 16, 1797, DIAL PEARY & HANNAH his wife of Warren
                 Co. to THOMAS HEATH of same, for $750, 300 acres on
Long Creek, adj. JOHN F. FLOURNOY, DIAL PEARY (q) (SEAL). Wit: HEN.
MITCHELL JP, FANNY MITCHELL, Relinquish of dower by HANNAH PEARY (X).
Rec. Nov. 9, 1797.

Pages 337-338:   Aug. 25, 1797, JOHN DEYAMPERT & MARY his wife to
                 HENRY HARDIN, for $400, 100 acres in Warren Co. on
Middle Creek... JOHN DEYAMPERT (SEAL), MARY DEYAMPERT (SEAL). Wit:
GAD HARRISON, THOS. WHITE JP. Rec. Nov. 9, 1797.

Pages 338-339:   Aug. 5, 1797, BENJAMIN FEW & RACHEL his wife of
                 Columbia Co., Ga., to HENRY HARDIN of Warren Co., for
$200, 100 acres in Warren Co... land formerly of JNO. DEYAMPERT, adj.
FEW's land... BENJ. FEW (SEAL), RACHEL FEW (SEAL). Wit: WM. FEW,
THOS. WHITE JP. Rec. Nov. 9, 1797.

Pages 339-340:   Sept. 9, 1795, ANTHONY CRUMLEY of Warren Co. to LEWIS
                 BRANTLEY of same, for 30 pounds, land on Whetstone
Creek... adj. FULSOM, KING, FULSOM... 200 acres... ANTHONY CRUMLEY (X)
(SEAL). Wit: THOS. LAW, THOS. COCKS, YOUNG MIMS (X). Rec. Nov. 9,
1797.

Page 340:   Feb. 2, 1795, GEORGE BREWER, of Warren Co. to ABRAHAM
            PERKINS of same, for 100 pounds, land on Williams's Creek.
Parham's Spring... originally granted to BENJAMIN SCOTT, Dec. 17, 1784,
willed to SHADRACH KINNEBREW and conveyed to BREWER July 10, 1792.
GEORGE BREWER (B) (SEAL). Wit: JOSEPH WHITE, THOS. HILL. Dec. 2,
1797 (Rec.).

Pages 341-342:   Dec. 26, 1790, SAMUEL OSBURN of Wilkes Co. (now Warren)
                 to JAMES WHITE of same, for 20 pounds, land on Long
Creek of Ogechee, adj. JOHN HUTCHINS's, TORRENCE's line, MATHEW GRANT,
100 acres, part of 300 granted to SAMUEL OSBORN April 9, 1790. SAMUEL
OSBORN (-) (SEAL). Wit: S. CAMP, MARY CAMP. Rec. Dec. 6, 1796.

Page 342:   STEPHEN MITCHELL for love, etc. toward my loving son
             STEPHEN MITCHELL do give, 5 negroes. Nov. 4, 1797.
STEPHEN MITCHELL (X). Wit: MOSES FORT, ARTHUR FORT JP, Rec. Dec. 6,
1797.
             STEPHEN MITCHELL to dau. LIEUCRESIA NEEL, lawfully begotten
in wedlock... one Negroe Cleo in the County of Washington, Nov. 4, 1797.
STEPHEN MITCHELL (X). Rec. Dec. 6, 1797. Wit: MOSES FORT, ARTHUR FORT
JP.

Page 343:   STEPHEN MITCHELL of Warren Co. to dau. SUSANNAH HARVELL,
             lawfully begotten in wedlock of County of Washington, one
Negro woman. STEPHEN MITCHELL (X). Dated and Wit. as above.
             STEPHEN MITCHELL of Warren Co. to SALLY COATMAN, alias
MITCHELL, of Washington Co., one negro girl. STEPHEN MITCHELL (X).
Dated and wit. as above.

Page 344:   Oct. 13, 1797, STEPHEN MITCHELL of Warren Co. and his wife,
             to THOM. FARMER of same, for 40 pounds, land in Warren Co.
on Fort's Creek adj.JNO. DILL, 250 acres... SEIAH, wife of STEPHEN
MITCHELL, STEPHEN MITCHELL (X) (SEAL). Wit: SUSANNAH FORT, ARTHUR
FORT JP. Rec. Dec. 6, 1797.

Pages 344-345:   Warren Co., Ga., Oct. 23, 1797, CLEMENT FORBES of Pitt
                  Co., North Carolina (planter) to PHILIP GIBBS of
Warren Co., (planter), for 500 silver dollars, 350 acres on Rocky
Comfort Creek, patent by RICHARD BARROW Senr., the grants bearing date
Aug. 2, 1774... CLEMENT FORBES (SEAL). Wit: ARTHUR DRUE, ABSALOM
BARROW, MEBRY BARROW (X). Wit: MILBREY BARROW. Rec. Dec. 7, 1797.

Pages 345-346:   Jan. 15, 1796, WILLIAM DAVIS of Warren Co. to LEWIS
                  BRANTLEY of same, for 80 pounds, 200 acres on Rocky
Comfort Creek, adj. JOEL KING, DREWRY THOMSON... WILLIAM DAVIES (SEAL).
Wit: JOHN SLATTER, ROBERT MOSES. Rec. March 17, 1800.

Pages 346-347:   March 13, 1797, NATHANIEL WILLIAM of Warren Co. to
                  JOHN WILLIAMS of same, for $150, land on cat tail
fork of Rocky Comfort, 100 acres, part of a 200 acre tract granted to
JOHN AUSTON, Aug. 10, 1785, adj. JAMES PARKER, A. F. ELLEN...
NATHANIEL WILLIAMS (X) (SEAL). Wit: PETER RAIN, ABRAHAM PERKINS.
Rec. Dec. 17, 1797.

Pages 347-348:   March 26, 1796, BRIAN MCCLENDON of Warren Co. to
                  JOSEPH GRIZARD, for 30 pounds, 390 acres on Rocky
Comfort... BRIAN MCCLENDON (SEAL). Wit: WM. EARNEST, SARAH RALEY.
Rec. Dec. 15, 1797.

Pages 348-349:   State of South Carolina: JOHN HUNTER of Greenville Co.
                  for 100 pounds, to MATHEW MCCRARY of the County
Laurence (Laurens?), land in Town of Wrightsborough in State of Georgia,
No. 15, also a tract of land in parish of St. Paul's, being part of the
reserved for the people called Quakers containing 200 acres, at time
of original survey bounded by vacant lands on all sides, Nov. 6, 1770,
registered in Secretary's office, Book I, p. 198. Nov. 24, (no year).
JOHN HUNTER (SEAL). Wit: SAMUEL EWING, ROBT. MCCRARY, BARTLEY
MCCRARY. Rec. Dec. 15, 1797.
                  (There was a MCCRARY family in Laurens Co., S.C. from
before the Revolution, among whom were at least one Mathew. BHH)

Pages 349-350:   Dec. 13, 1796, JOHN WHITLOCK of Oglethorp Co., Ga. to
                  JOHN CLABORNE Senr. of Warren Co. for $225, 50 acres,
originally granted to JOHN DENNIS, 1770 adj. DOYLE, KILGORE's Creek,
THOMAS PORTER... JOHN WHITLOCK (SEAL). Wit: PERRY G. YOUNG, JOHN
W. CLAIBORNE. Rec. Jan. 15, 1798.

Pages 350-351:   Dec. 27, 1796, JOHN HARMON of Warren Co. to PLEASANT
                  WALKER of same, 100 acres on William's Creek...
PLEASANT WALKER (SEAL). Wit: ROBT. HILL, BENJ. CHAPMAN. Rec. Jan. 15,
1798.

Pages 351-352:   Feb. 22, 1796, PLEASANT WALKER of Warren Co. from
                 MATHEW JONES of Hancock Co. for 40 pounds, 100 acres in
Warren Co., MATHEW JONES (SEAL). Wit: JOHN PEYAMPERT, EDMD. CROWDEN
JP. Rec. June 15, 1798.

Pages 352-353:   Nov. 21, 1797, JOHN HARMON of Warren Co. to JOHN BUSTIN,
                 of same, for $40, land on William's Creek, 20 acres
J. HARMON (SEAL). Wit: ROBT. HILL, A. GRIER JP. Rec. Jan. 15, 1798.

Pages 353-354:   Nov. 20, 1797, J. HARMON of Warren Co. to JOHN BUSTIN
                 of same, $200 for 100 acres on William's Creek... J.
HARMON (SEAL). Wit: ROBT. HILL, HANS PETAGREW. Rec. Jan. 18, 1798.

Pages 354-355:   Jan. 9, 1797, PLEASANT WALKER to JOHN HARMAN for 10
                 pounds, 20 acres on William's Creek... PIERCE BAILEY
now lives... PLEASANT WALKER (SEAL). Wit: RICHD. SMITH, PEACE BAILEY.
Rec. Jan. 18, 1798.

Pages 355-356:   Jan. 9, 1797, PEARCE BAILEY of Warren Co. to PLEASANT
                 WALKER,for 10 pounds, land on William's Creek...
PEARCE BAILEY (𝐁) (SEAL). Wit: J. HARMAN, RICHD. SMITH. Rec. Jan. 18,
1798.

Pages 356-357:   Dec. 26, 1797, THOMAS CHILDREY of Warren Co. to AQUILAR
                 JONES, for 30 pounds, 120 acres, originally granted
to CHILDREY Nov. 25, 1788. Rec. BOOK QQQ, fo. 597... THOMAS CHILDREY
(SEAL). Wit: HENRY WILLIAMS, JOHN BAYN JP. Rec. Jan. 18, 1798.

Page 357:   Sept. 7, 1797, JAMES MCCORMICK to MICHAEL CODA, for $200,
                 300 acres, granted July 22, 1795, adj. ISAAC BALL, SMITH,
HUGH REISE, Rec. BOOK PPPP, Fol. 747... JAS. MCCORMICK (SEAL). Wit:
JOHN SALLIS, P. HODO JP. Rec. Jan. 21, 1798. Also signed Mary Ann
MCCORMICK (M).

Page 358:   Dec. 26, 1797, JOHN WATSON of Warren Co. to ROBT. STANFORD
                 of same, for 520 silver dollars, 100 acres on White's
Creek, originally granted to Sd. JOHN WATSON, 1772, BOOK I, fol. 572.
JNO. WATSON (SEAL). Wit: JONATHAN BURSON, AQUILA JONES. Rec. Jan.
21, 1798.

Pages 359-360:   Dec. 13, 1791, MOSES HILL to JONATHAN BURSON, MOSES
                 HILL & HANNAH his wife... for 50 POUNDS, land in
Wilkes Co. (now Warren)... adj. JOHN DUNAWAY & DUCK's, J. FEW, MCCARDE's,
granted Oct. 14, 1788. MOSES HILL (𝓊) (SEAL), HANNAH HILL (Z) (SEAL).
Wit: ALEXR. MCDOUGAL, JOHN SMITH. Rec. Jan. 21, 1798.

Pages 360-361:   Jan. 24, 1795, EZENIAH VERDIN & JANE his wife of
                 Warren Co., Ga., to JAMES OSBORNE of same, for 40
pounds, 100 acres... adj. WM DUPRESE, WILLIAM NICHOLS, PETER CASTLEBERRY,
EZENIAH VERDIN (SEAL), JANE VERDIN (SEAL). Wit: SAMUEL TEDDERS, WM.
LEM Senr. Rec. Jan. 21, 1798.

Pages 361-362:   Nov. 25, 1797, WILLIAM COCKS of Washington Co., Ga.,
                 to CHRISTOPHER BUSTIN of Warren Co., for $236, land
on Rocky Comfort Creek... adj. HARMAN PERRYMAN, 100 acres, part of
200 granted to THOMAS BETHANY & the land whereon RICHARD COCKS now
lives... WM. COCK (SEAL). Wit: TURNER PERSONS, GEORGE TURNER. Rec.
Jan. 21, 1798.

Page 362:   Dec. 29, 1797, JONATHAN BURSON of Warren Co. to ROBERT
                 STANFORD, of same, for $50, 12 acres of land, out of tract
of 200 originally granted to sd. BURSON July 29, 1785, Rec. BOOK HHH,
fol. 94, White's Creek... JONATHAN BURSON (SEAL). Wit: PHILLIP GIBBS,
JOHN BAYN JP. Rec. Jan. 20, 1798.

Pages 363:   Warren Co., Ga., WILLIAM SANDERS to ZELSON? BERRY, land
                 where I now live, for $60... WM. SANDERS (SEAL). Wit:
GARRET BERRY, JOHN A JOHNSON, BURL. JONES. Rec. Jan. 20, 1798.

Pages 363-364: Feb. 27, 1796, AMOS STEWART & PATSEY his wife of
              Wilkes Co. to DEBERA CHAPMAN of Warren Co. for 370
silver dollars... adj. William's Creek, Capt. MURRAY's 200 acres more
or less originally granted to RICHD. CURETON... AMOS STEWART (SEAL),
PATSEY STEWART (SEAL). Wit: JONES BONNER, WM. TAYLOR. Rec. Feb. 21,
1798.

Pages 364-365: Jan. 20, 1797, SOLOMON BAREFIELD of Hancock Co. to
              JESSE BAREFIELD of Warren Co., for 100 pounds land on
Hart's Creek, 200 acres... SOLOMON BAREFIELD (SEAL). Wit: MATTH. WOOD,
JOHN RUNNELS JP. Rec. Feb. 21, 1798.

Pages 365-366: Oct. 7, 1795, MOSES GOING & AGGY his wife to WM.
              STITH Junr. for $2000, land on North side of Ogechee,
465 acres, part of 780 acres granted to IGNATIUS FEW, March 2, 1791..
MOSES GOINGS (SEAL), AGNESS GOINGS (X) (SEAL). Wit: ROBT. ABERCROMBIE,
WM. FRIEND, WM. STITH. Rec. Feb. 21, 1798.

Pages 366-367: Dec. 26, 1792, JOHN MIMS of Washington Co., Ga., to
              RICHARD HILL of Wilkes Co. (now Warren) for 200 pounds,
land adj. JESSE HARPER, CHAS. WILLIAMS, 200 acres located by sd. JOHN
MIMS, March 15, 1788. Rec. BOOK UUU, fo. 436. JOHN MIMS (X) (SEAL),
ANNE MIMS (SEAL). Wit: JOHN BALL, THOS. CAVINAH.. Rec. Feb. 25, 1798.

Page 368: Oct. 5, 1796, LEWIS POWEL & CATHERINE his wife of Warren
          Co. to HENRY BURNLEY of Hancock Co., for 150 pounds, 231½
acres, originally granted to MOSES POWEL Senr., Sept. 5, 1783, adj...
JAMES ROGERS, BUNKLEY... LEWIS POWEL (SEAL). CATHARINE POWEL (✗) (SEAL).
Wit: JAMES LUCAS, JESSE BURNKLEY, WM. BYROM JP. Rec. Feb. 25, 1798.

Pages 368-369: Sept. 1, 1797, LIGHTFOOT WILLIAMS of Lincoln Co.,
              N.C. to HENRY WILLIAMS Junr. of Warren Co., Ga., for
32 pounds, 100 acres, part of 200, on Briar Creek, granted to CORNELIUS
MCCARDEN Oct. 3, 1787... LIGHTF. WILLIAMS (SEAL). Wit: BENJAMIN
VINHOWN? (X), HENRY WILLIAMS, JOHN BAYN JP. Rec. Feb. 25, 1798.

Pages 369-370: Jan. 17, 1797, JOHN BURKHATTER of Warren Co. to STARLIN
              WILLIAMSON of same... JOHN BURKHATTER & SARAH his wife.
for 35 guineas, 150 acres, part of a 300 acre grant to JARED IRWIN,
Esq. June 4, 1790... adj. JOSEPH BURSON, LANDRUMS, CASTLEBERRIES, GIBBS,
Rec. BOOK XXXX, fol. 234. JOHN BURKHATTER (SEAL), SARAH BURKHATTER (X)
(SEAL). Wit: JOHN WILLIAMS, JAS. MCCORMICK JP. Rec. Feb. 25, 1798.

Pages 370-371: Nov. 25, 1797, WILLIAM HICKSON of Columbia Co. to
              WILLIAM BERRY of Warren Co. for $300, 100 acres
originally granted to JAMES HABERSHAM Feb. 2, 1773... WILLIAM HICKSON
(W) (SEAL). Wit: JAMES WILLIS JP. Rec. March 3, 1798.

Pages 371-372: Oct. 4, 1797, FRANCES HILL, Admx. of est. of RICHARD
              HILL, Decd., to STARLING GARDNER of Warren Co., for
$100, land on Whetstone Creek, adj. JESSE WHITE, HENRY PEEBLES, 100
acres... FRANCES HILL (X) (her mark) (SEAL). Wit: T. PERSONS, H.
PEEBLES, R. B. FLETCHER JP. Rec. April 6, 1798.

Page 372: Oct. 4, 1797, FRANCES HILL, admx. of est. of RICHARD HILL,
          dec'd to STARLING GARDNER for 700 Spanish Mill Dollars,
200 acres on Whetstone Creek, originally granted to JOHN MIMS, Oct. 17,
1785. FRANCES HILL (X) (SEAL). Wit: (same as above). Rec. Apr. 6,
1798.

Page 373: Oct. 4, 1797, FRANCES HILL to STARLING GARDNER, for $300,
          200 acres, granted to JOHN MIMS Sept. 12, 1791... FRANCES
HILL (X) (SEAL). Wit: T. PERSONS, H. PEEBLES, R. B. FLETCHER JP.
Rec. April 6, 1798.

Pages 373-374: Nov. 10, 1796, JOHN LANDRUM, to IGNATIUS FEW for 100
              pounds, land in Warren Co. on Rocky Comfort, adj.
JOHN HILL... originally granted to JOHN LANDRUM, Aug. 17, 1786 JOHN
LANDRUM (SEAL). Wit: THOS. HUNT, JOHN HUDNELL. Rec. Apr. 15, 1798.

Pages 374-375: Feb. 11, 1797, IGNATIUS FEW to THOMAS BURK (BUSH?)
land on Rocky Comfort (same as above), for 100 pounds..
I. FEW (SEAL). Wit: JOHN LEE, JAMES BOND. Rec. April 15, 1798.

Pages 375-376: May 17, 1794, JAMES GILMORE of Warren Co. to PETER
COX, of same, for 80 pounds, 194 acres on Middle Creek.
adj. Richmond County line, ANSLEY's, granted to JAMES GILMORE. Dec. 30,
1788, Rec. BOOK RRR, fol. 90. JAMES GILMORE (X) (SEAL), ANN GILMORE (X)
(SEAL). Wit: JOHN GILMORE, JOSEPH STUBBS, MARK HARDIN JP. Rec.
April 19, 1798.

Page 377: May 17, 1794, JAMES GILMORE to PETER COX, for 20 pounds,
land on Upton's Creek, surveyed March 6, 1787, Rec. BOOK
VVV, fol. 199... (signatures & wit. same as above).

Pages 378-379: Aug. 6, 1794, JOHN MAYNOR of Warren Co. to ISAAC
MARCHANT of same, for 15 pounds, land on Little Briar
Creek, 173 acres... JOHN MAYNOR (SEAL). Wit: ISAAC H. & SAML.
REDGWELL?, (later RIDGEWELL). Rec. Apr. 25, 1798.

Page 379: Sept. 27, 1797, JOSEPH ARMSTRONG to JESSE RICKETSON for $45,
for 50 acres, adj. DAVIES, HILL, CORUM, WILLIS, part of a
400 acre tract granted to WILLIAM CORUM May 16, 1797... JOSEPH ARMSTRONG
(SEAL). Wit: REUBEN JONES, PETER HODO JP. Rec. Apr. 30, 1798.

Page 380: March 4, 1795, JOHN PEARY of Warren Co. to JOSEPH DAVIDSON,
blacksmith, for 50 pounds, 100 acres on south fork of
Briar Creek, half of a 200 acres tract granted to JOHN PEARY... JOHN
PEARY (O) (SEAL). Wit: WILLIAM PLEASANT, M. HUBERT JP. Rec. Apr. 30,
1798.

Pages 380-381: Nov. 18, 1797, JOSEPH DAVIDSON of Warren Co. to JESSE
RICKETSON for $30, 100 acres on south fork of Briar
Creek, half of a tract granted to ISAAC SIMONSON Sept. 6, 1785. Rec.
BOOK HHH, fo. 490... JOSEPH DAVIDSON (SEAL). Wit: JAMES CARTER, JOHN
BAYN JP. Rec. May 1, 1798.

Pages 381-382: Oct. 17, 1797, JOSEPH SMITH of Columbia Co. to JOHN
GRENAID of Warren Co. for $100, 200 acres granted to
JOSEPH SMITH April 29, 1797, adj. RUSE, MCCORMICK, BALL, HILL... JOSEPH
SMITH (SEAL). Wit: WILLIAM FU?, P? HODO JP. Rec. May 1, 1798.

Pages 382-383: May 17, 1794, JAMES GILMORE to MARY MORRIS for 4
shillings per acre, 4 acres and a half on Middle
Creek adj. GILMORE, granted to JAMES GILMORE Dec. 3, 1788, BOOK RRR fo.
80... JAMES GILMORE (SEAL), ANN GILMORE (X) (SEAL). Wit: JACK STUBBS,
MARK HARDIN JP. Rec. May 2, 1798.

Pages 383-384: March 16, 1798, THOMAS COCKS of Warren Co. to JOHN
PARHAM of same, for $200, land on Rocky Comfort Creek,
130 acres... THOMAS COCKS (SEAL). Wit: JNO. MATHEWS. Rec. May 2,
1798.

Pages 384-385: Oct. 24, 1797, STARLING GARDNER of Warren Co. to
ROBERT JENKINS for $1500, land on Little Rocky Comfort,
adj. DANIEL HUTCHERSON, 300 acres, reserving 7 acres for public utility.
STERLING GARDNER (SEAL). Wit: TURNER PERSONS, SHADRACH F. ELLEN.
Rec. May 2, 1798.

Pages 385-386: Feb. 16, 1798, ROBERT JENKINS to RICHARD HEATH, $1714
and 25 cents, land on Williams's Creek, adj. MICAJAH
STONE, BURREL PERRY... 400 acres... ROBERT JENKINS (SEAL). Wit:
TURNER PERSONS JP, STERLING GARDNER. Rec. May 2, 1798.

Page 386: Feb. 11, 1798, ROBERT JENKINS of Warren Co. to BURREL PERRY
for $400, 100 acres on William's Creek... ROBT. JENKINS.
Wit: T. PERSONS, J. BETTLE. Rec. May 2, 1798.

Page 387:   Oct. 1, 1790, JAMES ROWLAND of Richmon Co. to PETER COCKS
             of same but now Warren Co. for 60 pounds, 200 acres origi-
nally granted to JAMES ROWLAND, Sept. 1787. Reg. BOOK II Page 104,
No. 221, on Sweet Water Creek, JAMES ROWLAND (SEAL). Wit: JOSEPH
STUBBS, RICHARD SMITH (R). Rec. May 4, 1798.

Page 388:   Nov. 2, 1793, JOHN SMITH Senr. of Wilkes Co. to REUBEN
             MAGEE of Columbia Co. (now Warren) for 100 pounds, 180
acres, part of a 200 acres granted to NICHOLAS WHITE Sept. 24, 1784,
on both sides of Beaver Dam Creek, fork of Bear Creek, part in Wilkes
and part in Columbia... JOHN SMITH Senr. (W) (SEAL), SARAH SMITH (W)
(SEAL). Wit: JOHN BAYN JP, JOHN SMITH Junr. Rec. May 4, 1798.

Pages 388-389:   Oct. 7, 1797, WILLIAM COX of Washington Co. to THOMAS
             COCKS of Warren Co. for $3.00, land on Rocky Comfort
Creek, adj. KING... being part of 2 surveys, 130 acres, one granted to
THOMAS BETHANY the other to JOHN RUTHERFORD... WILLIAM COCKS Senr.
(SEAL). Wit: RICHARD COCKS, R. PERSONS. Rec. May 4, 1798.

Page 390:   March 3, 1798, GEORGE DYKES of Warren Co. to REDDIN RAT-
             CLIFF of same for $60, 300 acres... GEORGE DYKES (SEAL).
Wit: REBEKAH BISHOP (G). Rec. May 4, 1798.

Pages 390-391:   Aug. 30, 1797, GIBSON FLOURNOY of Warren Co. to
             BENJAMIN WHEELER of same for $400, 200 acres, half of
grant to JOHN GRANTHAM Aug. 4, 1789. GIBSON FLOURNOY (SEAL), PATTEY
FLOURNOY (X) (SEAL). Wit: WM. SIMS, M. HUBERT JP. Rec. May 9, 1798.

Pages 391-392:   Nov. 10, 1794, JOSEPH MILLER of Warren Co. to LEMUEL
             PRUITT of same, for 30 pounds, land on Middle Creek,
adj. LEVI PRUITT, SAMUEL PRUITT, MARK HARDIN, THOMAS WEEKLEY... 90
acres, JOSEPH MILLER (SEAL). Wit: L. PRUITT JP, REUBEN MEADOWS.
Rec. May 9, 1798.

Pages 392-394:   Jan. 24, 1798, THOS. ANSLEY & REBECCA his wife to
             ABEL ANSLEY of Warren Co. for $200, land on Still
Creek, formerly known as Upton's Creek, part of 2 surveys granted to
THOMAS ANSLEY, one 150 acre Jan. 19, 1785, the other May 24, 1787...
JOHN LANDRUM's original survey... THOM. ANSLEY Junr., JOSEPH HODGINS'
line, 330 acres... THOMAS ANSLEY (SEAL), REBECCA ANSLEY (SEAL). Wit:
JOSEPH LANDRUM, JOSEPH ANSLEY, JOHN WILSON JP. Rec. May 9, 1798.

Pages 394-395:   June, 1796, ANN STEWART of Warren Co. to CABAL STEPHENS
             of same, for 10 pounds, land on Rocky Comfort, surveyed
for ANN STEART, adj. JOHN LAWSON's line... 100 acres whereon she now
lives... ANN STEWART (X) (SEAL). Wit: SAMUEL POWELL, ROBT. THOMPSON,
no rec. date.

Pages 395-396:   April 15, 1797, PROPER HORTON & SARAH his wife to
             JACOB FLOURNOY, for $500, 225 acres more or less,
PRSOR HORTON (SEAL), SARAH HORTON (SEAL). Wit: ALLEN DORMAN, JAMES
COZART, EDWARD KELLY. Rec. May 10, 1798.

Pages 396-397:   March 17, 1798, ELISHA PRUITT to AMOS PERSONS for
             $25, land on Middle Creek, adj. MCINVALE, TUCKER,
EZEKIEL MILLER, 38 acres... ELISHA PRUITT (SEAL). Wit: LEML. PRUITT
JP. Rec. May 10, 1798.

Pages 397-398:   March 15, 1798, HUGH REESE of Warren Co. to JOSEPH
             MCMATH of same, for $100, all that land granted Aug.
17, 1785, 100 acres on Briar Creek, in Wilkes Co. (now Warren) adj.
WILLIAM WHAIR, NEWSOM. Rec. BOOK JJJJ (III?), HUGH REES (SEAL),
Relinquish of dower ELIZABETH REES (X). Wit: BENJAMIN REES, JAS.
MCCORMICK JP. Rec. June 20, 1798.

Pages 398-399:   Oct. 18, 1790, STEPHEN MITCHELL & CELIA his wife of
             Richmond Co. to REUBEN WINFREY of Wilkes Co., for 50
pounds, land on Long Creek, 150 acres adj. NATHAN FOWLER, THOMAS JONES.
STEPHEN MITCHELL (X) (SEAL). Wit: ADAM JONES & KINCHEN NEWSOM. Rec.
June 21, 1798.

Pages 399-400:   REBECKAH PARHAM of Warren Co. to son GEORGE PARHAM,
                 one negro man Tom, April 2, 1798, REBECAH PARHAM (X).
Wit: JOHN MATTHEWS, POLLY MATTHEWS. Rec. June 20, 1798.

Pages 400-401:   May 15, 1798, CALEB STEPHENS of Warren Co. to BETHIAR
                 STEWART for 10 pounds, land on Rocky Comfort, surveyed
for ANN STEWART... 100 acres... CALEB STEPHENS (SEAL). Wit: MOSES
GRANDBERRY, NOWELL ROBERTSON JP. Rec. June 20, 1798.

Pages 401-402:   Jan. 24, 1797, WALTER NEWMAN of Wilkes Co. to JOHN
                 SLATTER of Warren Co. for 200 pounds, land on Rocky
Comfort, adj. JONES PERSONS, HARMAN PERRYMAN, WILLIAM COCKS, MCDONALD,
DARNAL, 90 acres and 43 acres (2 tracts), WALTER NEWMAN (SEAL), ARGEN
NEWMAN (SEAL). Wit: GEO. WEATHERBY, SOLOMON SLATTER, R. D. FLETCHER
JP. Rec. June 20, 1798.

Pages 402-403:   April 5, 1796, DAVID NEAL, Esqr. Sheriff of Warren Co.
                 to JAMES WHITE & DAVID ROBERSON Senr. of Columbia Co.,
for $12,000 against WILLIAM FRANKLIN as Ex. of Last W. & T. of
EBENEZER STERNS, sale of 100 acres including the conference of Main
Briar Creek & Sweet Water, 100 acres originally granted to sd. STERNS
Oct. 26, 1784, Rec. BOOK EEE, Fol. 279, Rec. in BOOK B Surveyor's Office
Richmond Co.. D. NEAL's W. C. (LS). Wit: ROBERT WHITE, JNO. TORRENCE.
Rec. July 10, 1798.

Pages 403-404:   March 26, 1798, JOHN CAMPBELL of Green Co. to PETER
                 BUCKHATT of Warren Co. for $500, land on William's
Creek, adj. REUBEN ROGERS, 134 acres... JOHN CAMPBELL (LS). Wit:
MICAJAH PERRY, RICHARD BUTLER. Rec. July 10, 1798.

Pages 404-405:   April 6, 1798, THOMAS BOHANNON & SELAH his wife, to
                 EDMUND JOHNSON, land on Long Creek adj. WALLER, 100
acres... THOMAS BOHANNON (SEAL), SELAH BOHANNON (SEAL) Wit: JOHNSON
WRIGHT, ROBERT JOHNSON. Rec. July 10, 1798.

Pages 405-406:   Sept. 3, 1795, JOHN CAMPBELL of Warren Co. to RICHARD
                 BUTLER of same, for 50 pounds, land on Williams's
Creek, 100 acres... JOHN CAMPBELL (SEAL). Wit: JOHN RUDACIL, IGNATIUS
SIMMES. Rec. July 11, 1798.

Pages 406-407:   May 9, 1798, JOHN LANDRUM, Senr. to JOSEPH LANDRUM,
                 Junr. for 100 dollars, land on Upton's Creek, part of
550 acre grant to JOHN LANDRUM Aug. 17, 1785. BOOK HHH, fo. 262, adj.
THOMAS ANSLEY's, JOHN LANDRUM (LS). Wit: JOHN COX, JOHN WILSON JP.
Rec. July 11, 1798.

Pages 407-408:   March 5, 1798, WILLIAM CORAM to ROBERT WILLIS $100,
                 for 142 acres, on head of Briar Creek, adj. RICHERSON's,
PETER HODO's... WILLIAM CORAM (LS). Wit: JOHN LOWE, P. HODO, JP.
Rec. July 11, 1798.

Pages 408-409:   Oct. 11, 1797, JOHN KENT to JOSEPH BURSON FOR $200,
                 150 acres, adj. JAMES NAPIER, SAMUEL RIDGDEL, WILLIAM
JONES, granted Nov. 11, 1788. Reg. BOOK QQQ, fo. 546, JOHN KENT (X)
(SEAL). Wit: WM. B. MURPHEY, VINCENT A. THORP JP. Rec. July 12, 1798.

Page 409:   Feb. 20, 1797, JOHN TORRENCE to DAVID COCKS, for 25 pounds,
            land on Rocky Comfort, bounded by FULSOM, MIMS, AMOS WRIGHT,
JAMES BRAY, part of a grant to JOHN TORRENCE April 7, 1789, BOOK SSS
fol. 72, JNO. TORRENCE (SEAL). Wit: HUGH REESE, JOHN BAKER JP. Rec.
July 12, 1798.

Page 410:   May 17, 1798, JOHN RUSHING to WILLIAM SIMMONS for $130 land
            on Fort's Creek, adj. JONATHAN MILLER, LONG, 150 acres, part
of a grant to SAMUEL CAMP Jan. 22, 1789, BOOK JJ, Fo. 319, JOHN RUSHING
(X) (SEAL). Wit: JNO. CURRIE, THOMAS FRIEND JP. Rec. July 13, 1798.

Page 411:   May 14, 1796, PETER CASTLEBERRY & CATHERINE his wife to
             MATHEW MCCREERE, for 30 pounds, land on Long Creek, 130
acres, PETER CASTLEBERRY (SEAL), CATHARINE CASTLEBERRY (X) (SEAL).
Wit: DAVID CASTLEBERRY, CLABUN CASTLEBERRY. Rec. July 13, 1798.

Page 412:   Jan. 6, 1798, WILLIAM NEAL of Wilkes Co. to JOHN BRANTLEY
             of Warren Co. for $210, 100 acres, adj. Old Indian Path and
Hart's Creek, originally granted to JOHN WELCH July 3, 1770 by deed,
confirmed to ROBERT WALDER by JOHN WELCH Dec. 3, 1773... WILLIAM NEAL
(SEAL), ANNA NEAL (SEAL). Wit: HENRY HIGHT, LARKIN BRANTLEY. Rec.
July 13, 1798.

Page 413:   Nov. 16, 1797, OWEN MYRICK of Warren Co., to EZEKIEL MILLER
             of same for $170, adj. VINING, MICHAEL THOMAS, 170 acres,
OWEN MYRICK (LS). Wit: TURNER PERSONS, WM. ROSE. Rec. July 14, 1798.

Pages 413-414:   May 1, 1790, NEWDAY ONSLEY of Green Co. to ROBERT
                  FLOURNOY, of Wilkes Co. for 500 pounds, 200 acres on
Ogechee, adj. JOHN WYNNE, JESSE CONNEL, ABRAHAM REDDIX... NEWDAY ONSLEY
(SEAL), MARYAN ONSLEY (SEAL). Wit: ADM. BOWDREE, STEPHEN BURLEY.
Rec. July 14, 1798.

Pages 414-415:   June 9, 1798, ROBERT FLOURNOY of Jefferson Co., Ga.,
                  to ROBERT WYNNE, of Warren Co. for one dollar, but more
for a deed of conveyance made some time in year 1797, 200 acres more or
less, on Ogechee bound by... (same as above) ROBERT FLOURNOY (SEAL).
Wit: JOHN MITCHELL JP, CHARLES ABERCROMBIE. July 14, 1798.

Pages 415-416:   Aug. 18, 1797, SOLOMON NEWSOM Senr. of Warren Co., Ga.,
                  to ARTHUR MATHEWS, of same for one dollar, for use and
benefit of the Methodist Society one acre to be laid out where the said
MATTHEWS shall think best... SOLOMON NEWSOM (SEAL). Wit: JOSEPH
WALKER, BENJMAIN BURTON JP. Rec. July 14, 1798.

Pages 416-417:   Jan. 6, 1798, VINCENT ALLEN THARP of Warren Co. to
                  ARTHUR MATTHEWS of same for $60, 200 acres, adj. COBB,
THORP, TRANT, SOLOMON NEWSOM, ABBOT, granted Sept. 15, 1797, V. A. THARP
(SEAL), SARAH THARP (T) (SEAL). Wit: EDWARD MATTHEWS, BENJN. BURTON
JP. Rec. July 16, 1798.

Pages 417-418:   March 13, 1797, ROBERT JENKINS of Warren Co. to
                  JONATHAN LOCKE of same, for $500, 200 acres in Wilkes
Co. (now Warren), adj. COOK's line, ROBT. JENKINS (SEAL), SARAH
JENKINS (+) (SEAL). Wit: ELISHA HURT JP, WILLIAM LAYNE (X). Rec.
Aug. 3, 1798.

Pages 418-419:   Oct. 22, 1795, LEWIS BRANTLEY & SUSANNAH his wife of
                  Hancock Co., to SHADRACH FLEWILLIN of Warren Co. for
75 pounds, land on Whetstone Creek, grant of 200 acres (except for 50)
Aug. 10, 1785... LEWIS BRANTLEY (SEAL). Wit: TURNER PERSONS, JOHN
LOWE. Rec. Aug. 8, 1798.

Page 419:   March 7, 1797, JOHN SEYBOLD, of Wilkes Co. to SEPTIMUS
             WEATHERBY of Warren Co. for $200, land on head branches of
Hart's Creek, 280 acres, JOHN SEYBOLD (SEAL). Wit: SILAS GRIGG, GEO.
WEATHERBY. Rec. Aug. 10, 1798.

Page 420:   March 9, 1797, MARY MANN of Warren Co. to ARTHUR FORT of
             same for $150, land on Ogechee River, 100 acres, MARY MANN
(X) (SEAL). Wit: BARRET BREWER, RICHARD WHITEHEAD. Rec. Aug. 13, 1798.

Pages 421-422:   Nov. 2, 1791, JOHN JONES of Wilkes Co. to ARTHUR FORT
                  of same, for 50 pounds, land in Washington Co.,
originally granted to BENJAMIN THOMPSON June 27, 1786. Rec. BOOK KKK,
fo. 174, from BENJAMIN THOMPSON & wife ANN to JOHN JONES... JOHN JONES
(SEAL). Wit: W. STITH, PEYTON T. STITH. Rec. Aug. 13, 1798.

Pages 422-423: May 26, 1798, SOLOMON NEWSOM, Senr. of Warren Co. to WILLIAM GAZA of same, for $300, 108 acres, the southwest corner of a 687½ acre tract granted April 15, 1797. SOLOMON NEWSOM (SEAL). Wit: BENJ. BURTON JP, JAMES MCCORMICK JP. Rec. Aug. 14, 1798.

Pages 423-424: Aug. 15, 1797, MILLEY GRIMSLEY of Hancock Co. to PARKS KING of Warren Co. for 60 pounds, 200 acres, MILLIE GRIMSLEY. Wit: Z. BOOTH JP, JAMS. WORKS. Rec. Sept. 13, 1798.

Pages 424-425: Sept. 3, 1796, JOHN MCDANIEL of Warren Co. to JOHN MYRICK, for $600, land on Rocky Comfort adj. JOSEPH MAY, heirs of JOSEPH (deceased), 600 acres surveyed for JOHN MAY (dec'd) and conveyed to ISAAC BALL... JOHN MCDONALD ( )(LS). Wit: NATHANIEL MYRICK, GEO. WEATHERBY. Rec. Sept. 15, 1798.

Page 426: Nov. 3, 1797, JOSHUA JONES of Warren Co. to JOHN MYRICK, for $400, 179 acres, adj. CHARLES DARNELL, THOMAS NEAL, HENRY SHELTON, JOSEPH BOON, THOMAS WEST, THOMAS & JOHN MYRICK, granted to JOSEPH MAY Sept. 14, 1789, BOOK SSS Fo. 505, JOSHUA JONES (SEAL), SARAH JONES (X) (SEAL). Wit: E. THOMAS, RICHD. COX. Rec. Sept. 18, 1798.

Page 427: Jan. 3, 1798, JOHN MYRICK Senr. to JOHN MYRICK Junr. for $300, 180 acres on Rocky Comfort. JNO. MYRICK (SEAL). Wit: THOMAS FLIN, GEO. TWEATHERBY. Rec. Sept. 15, 1798.

Page 428: March 5, 1798, JOSEPH BOON of Washington Co. to JOHN MYRICK Junr. of Warren Co. for $500, 200 acres on Rocky Comfort, land granted to JAMES BREWER, July 2, 1788. Rec. BOOK QQQ... JOSEPH BOON (SEAL), Wit: SEPTIMUS WEATHERBY, THOMAS DAVIS (X). Rec. Sept. 18, 1798.

Page 429: Oct. 18, 1788, JAMES ALFORD of Wilkes Co. to HENRY COOPER of same, for 25 pounds, land on Long Creek of Ogechee, granted March 25, 1787, adj. Widow LANSACUM's... JAMES ALFORD (SEAL), Wit: S. CAMP, MARY CAMP. Rec. "26th of 1798".

Pages 430-431: July 2, 1798, LEMUEL PRUITT & CATY PRUITT his wife of Warren Co., to CHURCHILL GIBSON of same, for $1000, land on middle fork of Upton's Creek, adj. BISHOP's survey, THOMAS WEAKLEY, LEVI PRUITT, JAMES MCINVALE, JOSEPH BREED... LEMUEL PRUITT (SEAL), CATY PRUITT (SEAL). Wit: ISAIAH TUCKER, LEVI PRUITT JP. Rec. Sept. 26, 1798.

Pages 431-432: Nov. 16, 1789, WILLIAM WILCHER of Richmond Co. to JEREMIAH WILCHER for 100 pounds, land (now in Warren Co.), granted to sd, WILSHER July 20, 1787... WILLIAM WILSHER (SEAL), MARY WILSHER (SEAL). Wit: PHILLIPS GIBBS, ALLEN BROWN (X). Rec. Sept. 27, 1798.

Pages 432-433: April 22, 1791, JOHN LEDBETTER of Wilkes Co., to JOHN CURRY of Burke Co. for 40 pounds, 100 acres on Big Creek of Ogechee (Burke Co., now Warren)... JOHN LEDBETTER. Wit: P. BOYLE, BENJA. JENKINS JP. Rec. Sept. 28, 1798.

Pages 433-434: Jan. 28, 1792, WILLIAM KEENER of Columbia Co. to JEREMIAH WILCHER of same, for 30 pounds, 100 acres in Columbia Co. on a branch of Big Creek, whereon WILLIAM LYONS formerly lived, adj. JOSEPH PAINTER, WARLOCK, WILLIAM WILCHER, WILLIAM KEENER, 2 granted 1788 & 1789... WILLIAM KEENER (K) (SEAL), RACHEL KEENER (X) (SEAL). Wit: JOSEPH BURSON, JACOB KEENER, WILLIAM LYONS. Rec. Sept. 29, 1798.

Page 434: Oct. 28, 1797, DANIEL KINGREY of Warren Co. to the heirs of JOHN CURRY, dec'd of Jefferson Co., for 50 pounds, land in Warren Co. on Ogechee River... DANIEL KINGREY (SEAL). Wit: CAREY CURRY, NORWELL ROBERTSON JP. Rec. Oct. 3, 1798.

Page 435:   Dec. 30, 1797, JEREMIAH WILSHER of Jefferson Co. to
              NATHANIEL WILLIAMS Senr... for $100, land whereon sd.
WILLIAMS now lives, on Little Creek of Big Creek in Warren Co., granted
to WILLIAM WILSHER July 20, 1787... JEREMIAH WILSHER (-) (SEAL),
JENNE WILSHER (+) (SEAL). Wit: ABRAHAM YERTA, JOHN WILLIAMS, NORVELL
ROBERTSON JP. Rec. Oct. 4, 1798.

Pages 435-436:   Dec. 30, 1797, JEREMIAH WILSHER of Warren Co. to
                   WILLIAM WILLIAMS, for $100 (tract bought from WM.
KEENER). JEREMIAH WILSHER (-) (SEAL), JENNE WILSHER (X) (SEAL). Wit:
(same as above). Rec. Oct. 5, 1798.

Pages 436-437:   Dec. 30, 1797, JEREMIAH WILSHER of Jefferson Co. to
                   NATHANIEL WILLIAMS, for $100, 74 acres, adj. WARLOCK
WILSHER, surveyed July 11, 1777. JEREMIAH WILSHER (-) (SEAL), JENNE
WILSHER (X) (SEAL). Wit: (same as above). Rec. Oct. 5, 1798.

Pages 437-438:   Dec. 13, 1792, HONOUR ANDERSON (widow) of Wilkes Co.
                   to JAMES WILLIAMS, GREEN... whereas the said HONOUR
ANDERSON (widow) did obtain a grant in her own name (or by mistake in
the name of HANNAH ANDERSON) Sept. 29, 1784, for 200 acres, in Wilkes
Co. (now Warren) on both sides of Long Creek, near Ogechee, adj.
WILLIAM & JOHN ANDERSON... for 75 pounds pd by JAMES W. GREEN, all that
tract except that that has been indentured to JOSHUA ROE... HONOUR
ANDERSON (X) (SEAL). Wit: EZEKIEL MILLAR, ANNE VINING. Rec. Oct. 8,
1798.

Pages 438-439:   Sept. 22, 1796, JOHN MOSES of Warren Co. to WILLIAM
                   HOWARD, for 40 pounds 200 acres in Warren Co. adj.
SAMUEL NEAL, JOHN MOSES, Junr., MICHAEL BURKHATTER... JOHN MOSES (SEAL),
Wit: JOHN MOSES Junr., DAVID THOMAS (X). Rec. Oct. 9, 1798.

Pages 439-440:   July 24, 1797, JOHN MOSES of Warren Co. to WILLIAM
                   HOWARD, $10, a tract of land taken up by KIAH BUSSEY,
sold to ROBERT MOSES, which JOHN MOSES bot of his father, 15 acres...
JOHN MOSES (SEAL). Wit: EVAN THOMAS, NATHAN CASTLEBERRY (X), P.
HODO JP. Rec. Oct. 25, 1798.

Pages 440-441:   Oct. 24, 1796, EDMOND NUGENT of Washington Co. to
                   HENRY COOPER of Warren Co... EDMOND NUGENT & MARY his
wife... for $50, 21½ acres... COOPER's Spring Branch... EDMUND NUGENT
(SEAL), MARY NUGENT (N) (SEAL). Wit: BENJAMIN PERRY, ARTHUR JENKINS.
Rec. Oct. 26, 1798.

Pages 441-442:   Jan. 29, 1796, HENRY GREEN, Senr. & ELIZABETH his wife,
                   of Warren Co. to BENTON SPIER of Hancock Co. for $184,
land on Rocky Comfort, adj. PARKINS, JOHN COOK, THOMAS SEAL... 123¼
acres... HENRY GREEN (SEAL), ELIZABETH GREEN (X) (SEAL). Wit: ELISHA
HUNT, JAMES GREEN. Rec. Nov. 15, 1798.

Pages 442-443:   Oct. 22, 1798, ELISHA WRIGHT to HENRY & WILLIAM
                   SANDERS Jurn. all of Warren Co. for $50, 60 acres on
Rocky Comfort... GOLDING's line... ELISHA WRIGHT (SEAL). Wit: JOHN J.
WELLS, RICHD. B. FLETCHER JP. Rec. Nov. 15, 1798.

Pages 443-444:   Sept. 7, 1798, EDMUND HAYES of Warren Co. for $75, to
                   PETER COX, 50 acres adj. SANDERS, PETER DAVIS,
EDMUND HAYES (LS). Wit: MICHL. CODY (X), P? HODO JP. Rec. Nov. 16,
1798.

Pages 444-445:   Sept. 1, 1797, SOLOMON BARFIELD of Hancock Co. to JOHN
                   HARMAN of Warren Co. for 50 pounds, 157 acres on
Williams's Creek... SOLOMON BARFIELD (SEAL). Wit: SOLOMON BARFIELD,
Junr., LOYD KELLY JP. Rec. Nov. 16, 1798.

Pages 445-446:   Oct. 24, 1795, STEPHEN MITCHELL of Warren Co. to
                   WILLIAM DEANE of same, for 80 pounds, 100 acres on

239

Rocky Comfort, granted Nov. 5, 1788... STEPHEN MITCHELL (X) (SEAL).
Wit: SA. HARVILLE, JAMES MCDADE. Rec. Nov. 17, 1798.

Pages 446-447:   Oct. 7, 1790, JOHN PITMAN of Richmond to JOHN MOUTREY
                  of same, for 100 pounds, land 200 acres in Wilkes Co.
(now Warren)... JOHN PITMAN (SEAL), EUNICE PITMAN (SEAL). Wit: JAMES
SIMMS JP, JOEL MOUTREY. Rec. Nov. 19, 1798.

Page 447:   Oct. 26, 1796, NATHANIEL WARD of Warren Co. to SAMUEL
             BARFIELD of Hancock Co. for 50 pounds, 150 acres on Williams
Creek... NATHANIEL WARD (X) (SEAL), Wit: LLOYD KELLY JP, JOHN
WAGGONNER. Rec. Nov. 19, 1798.

Pages 447-448:   Oct. 17, 1797, SAMUEL OSBORNE of Warren Co. to WILLIAM
                  FLAKE of same, for $150, 100 acres on Long Creek...
SAMUEL OSBORNE (X) (SEAL). Wit: WILLIAM OSBORN (X), FANNEY FRIEND.
Rec. Nov. 21, 1798.

Pages 448-449:   Sept. 18, 1798, ISAAC BALL of Warren Co. to JOHN
                  MYRICK for $400, part of a 600 acres grant on North
side of Rocky Comfort, granted to Heirs of JOHN MAYS April 1, 1786,
BOOK JJJ, fo. 673. ISAAC BALL (SEAL). Wit: NANCY THOMAS, E. THOMAS.
Rec. Nov. 21, 1798.

Pages 449-451:   Aug. 7, 1797, DAVID NEAL Esqr. Sheriff of Warren Co.
                  JAMES W. GREEN of Hancock Co. did in the Inferior
Court of Warren County, obtain a Judgment against GEORGE WEATHERBY for
the sum of... said Sheriff was commanded to levy on the Godds and
chattels, etc... 122 acres on Rocky Comfort for $53, D. NEALS, W. C.
(SEAL). Wit: JOHN LOWE, FRANCIS STAINBACK. Rec. Nov. 21, 1798.

Pages 451-452:   Sept. 7, 1797, BURREL ROGERS, SAMUEL STOKES & JAMES
                  HENDRICK of Washington Co. to JOHN THYMES of Warren,
for 40 shillings, 100 acres granted in the name of DRURY ROGERS, surveyed
July 19, 1784... BURREL ROGERS (LS), JAMES KENDRICK (LS), SAMUEL STOKES
(LS). Wit: MANSIL WOMAK, JORDAN BKER. Rec. Nov. 26, 1798.

Pages 452-453:   April 15, 1790, WILLIAM BREWER of Wilkes Co. to
                  DANIEL RUNNALS of same, for a certain sum, 60 acres in
Wilkes Co. (now Warren), adj. NATHAN BREWER, NOBLES BISHOP, PARK KING...
WILLIAM BREWER (SEAL). Wit: PARKS KING, GEO. BREWER. Rec. Nov. 26,
1798.

Pages 453-354:   April 9, 1798, JAMES MCDADE of Warren Co. (planter)
                  for 50 pounds to ROBERT BARTON, 100 acres on Rocky
Comfort... JAMES MCDADE (S), ELIZABETH MCDADE. Wit: JAMES BARTON,
SAMUEL BEATTY. Rec. Nov. 27, 1798.

Pages 454-455:   Jan. 26, 1796, CHRISTOPHER WILLIAM of Hancock Co. to
                  DANIEL SANDERS & ARDIN SANDERS of Warren Co. for 30
pounds, 160 acres, part of a tract of 200 acres, granted to sd. WILLIAMS
1796... CHRISTOPHER WILLIAMS (SEAL), MARGARET WILLIAMS (SEAL). Wit:
THOS. HEATH (X), JOHN JENKINS, MATTH. BREWER. Rec. Nov. 27, 1798.

Pages 455-456:   Nov. 30, 1797, WILLIAM DAVIDSON of Warren Co. to ARDEN
                  SANDERS of same, for $150, 100 acres   originally
granted to JOHN PARKINS April 12, 1791... Widow COWEN,   HENRY GREEN...
WILLIAM DAVIDSON (M) (SEAL). Wit: JOHN WILLIAMS, DANIEL SANDERS,
E. HURT JP. Rec. Nov. 27, 1798.

Page 456:   March 17, 1798, ARDIN SANDERS of Warren Co. to DANIEL
             SANDERS for $100, half of a tract of 160 acres bought
jointly of CHRISTOPHER WILLIAMS, Jan. 26, 1796... ARDEN SANDERS (X) (SEAL)
Wit: JONES PERSON, RD. B. FLETCHER JP. Rec. Nov. 27, 1798.

Page 457:   Oct. 4, 1791, JOHN WEAVER & ELIZABETH his wife of Wilkes
             Co. to ELISHA PRUITT, for 40 pounds, 100 acres, originally
granted to sd. WEAVER Jan. 22, 1789. JOHN WEAVER (SEAL), ELIZABETH

WEAVER (SEAL). Wit: JOSIAH COKS JP, L. PRUITT, JP. Rec. Nov. 28, 1798.

Pages 457-458: July 7, 1790, JAMES JONES & ELIZABETH his wife to
        ELISHA PRUITT, for 30 pounds, land on Middle Creek,
52 acres... JAMES JONES (SEAL), ELIZABETH JONES (X) (SEAL). Wit: M.
HARDIN, JESSE ARMSTRONG. Rec. Nov. 28, 1798.

Page 459: March 15, 1798, ELISHA PRUITT, Esqr. Receiver of Tax for
        Warren Co., to MOSES DARDIN, selling for non-payment of
taces by HUGH FRANKLIN, 400 acres on Hart's Creek, land surveyed for
HENRY CANDLER or PETER LOWRENCE, adj. VARFIELD WILDER, RHESA HOWARD,
JAMES COBB... ELIS. PRUITT (SEAL). Wit: MOUNTAIN HILL, JOEL CLOUD.
Rec. Nov. 29, 1798.

Pages 460-461: March 15, 1798, ELISHA PRUITT Esqr. Collector of Tax.
        to MOSES DARDEN... non-payment of BENJAMIN FEW...
200 acres adj. HIGHT, DARLING MCDONALD, JAMES COBB, BRANTLEY... ELISHA
PRUITT (SEAL). Wit: (same as above). Rec. Nov. 29, 1798.

Page 461: March 15, 1798, MOSES DARDEN to ELISHA PRUITT for $21,
        land bought of sd. PRUITT, 400 acres on Hart's Creek...
MOSES DARDEN (SEAL), Wit: MOUNTAIN HILL, JOEL CLOUD. Rec. Nov. 29,
1798.

Page 462: March 15, 1798, MOSES DARDEN to ELISHA PRUITT, land, 200
        acres... (same as bought from PRUITT)... MOSES DARDEN (SEAL).
Wit: JOEL CLOUD, MOUNTAIN HILL. Rec. Nov. 30, 1798.

Pages 462-463: Articles of agreement between ELISHA PRUITT & MOSES
        DARDEN in a certain tract of land on Hart's Creek, adj.
lands of PHILIP BRANTLEY, HOWELL HIGHT, COX and others, 600 acres
which was sold for Tax due. Witnessed our hands March 15, 1798...
if land is lost, deed is not considered to be Warranted. MOSES DARDEN,
ELIS PRUITT. Wit: (same as above). Rec. Nov. 30, 1798.

Pages 463-464: March 15, 1798, ELISHA PRUITT to PHILIP BRANTLEY, for
        $325, land on Hart's Creek 368 acres... ELIS. PRUITT
(SEAL), Wit: LEML. PRUITT JP. Rec. Nov. 30, 1798.

Page 464: March 20, 1798, ELISHA PRUITT to LEMUEL PRUITT, for $10,
        20 acres on Middle Creek adj. LEMUEL PRUITT, MARK HARDIN,
ELISHA PRUITT... ELIS PRUITT (SEAL). Wit: HENRY HARDIN JP. Rec.
Nov. 30, 1798.

Pages 464-465: March 17, 1798, ELISHA PRUITT to JOSIAH DARDEN $350,
        200 acres on Hart's Creek... ELISHA PRUITT (SEAL).
Wit: HENRY HARDIN JP, LEML. PRUITT JP. Rec. Nov. 30, 1798.

Pages 465-466: 1798 ELISHA PRUITT to LEMUEL PRUITT for $500, 195 acres
        on Hart's Creek... ELIS PRUITT (SEAL), Wit: HENRY
HARDIN JP. Rec. Nov. 30, 1798.

Pages 466-467: March 24, 1798, WILLIS PERRY to Deacons of Williams's
        Creek Church both of Warren County, for $10, 2 acres..
WILLIS PERRY (SEAL). Wit: JOHN BAKER JP, LEML. PRUITT JP. Rec. Dec.
1, 1798.

Pages 467-468: Nov. 9, 1798, JOHN HARMAN of Warren Co. to JOSIAH
        N. KENNEDY, 157 acres, granted to SILAS MERCER Aug.
8, 1792, adj. PIERCE BAILEY, WILLIAMS, ZECHARIAH SHUFFIELD... J.
HARMAN. Wit: EPHRAIM SMITH & TILMAN NIBLET. Renunciation of Dower by
MARY HARMAN (X). Rec. Dec. 1, 1798.

Pages 468-469: Nov. 5, 1798, HUGH REESE of Warren Co. to HARDY NEWSOM
        of same, for $200, 100 acres on Big Bryar Creek,
granted to BAZIL LAMAR, Feb. 11, 1785, from BAZIL LEMAR to CHARLOTTE
NICHOLS, who became the wife of HENRY GLOVER... BRAY WARREN, JAMES

CARTER, JAMES MAY dec'd... HUGH REES (LS). Wit: JAS. MCMATH, JAS. MCCORMICK JP. Rec. Dec. 11, 1798.

Pages 469-470: SAMUEL ALEXANDER of Wilkes County... to my loving friend and relation PHEREBY WOOTON, her heirs, etc... (as my wife's hsare of sd. estate), Oct. 28, 1791, SAML. ALEXANDER. Wit: DUNCAN CAMPBELL, ARTHUR BELL. Rec. Dec. 19, 1798.

Page 470: ASA ALEXANDER of Green Co., Ga., for love, good will etc... to my loving friend and relation ASENATH WOOTEN of Wilkes Co., (as my wife's share of sd. estate)... A. ALEXANDER (SEAL). Wit: JOHN WILKINSON, ABNER WILKINSON. Rec. Dec. 19, 1798.

Pages 470-471: Dec. 8, 1797, JOHN NIXON & FRANCES his wife to JOSEPH CARSON of Wilkes Co. for $500, 100 acres on Middle Creek in Warren Co., adj. JOHN WELLS, EZEKIEL MILLER,... JOHN NIXON (SEAL), FRANCES NIXON (X) (SEAL). Wit: RICHD. CARTER, WILLIS PERRY, HENRY HARDIN JP. Rec. Jan. 12, 1799.

Pages 471-472: April 6, 1796, JOSEPH MILLER & ANN his wife to WILLIAM DENNIS, 100 acres on Middle Creek for 23 pounds... JOSEPH MILLAR, ANN MILLAR (H) (SEAL). Wit: THOMAS WEAKLEY, ELIZABETH PRUITT, L. PRUITT JP. Rec. Jan. 12, 1799.

Pages 472-473: Dec. 19, 1798, WILLIAM CORAM to JESSE RICKETSON, for $34, 34½ acres on Branch of Big Bryar Creek, adj. ROBERT WILLIS... WM. CORAM (LS). Wit: L. PRUITT JP, NATHANIEL THOMPSON. Rec. Jan. 12, 1799.

Page 473: Dec. 1, 1797, JOHN GIBSON to REDDICK BASS, both of Warren Co. for $400, 200 acres on Middle Creek, granted Feb. 28, 1788... JOHN GIBSON (SEAL). Wit: A. PERSONS, L. PRUITT JP. Rec. Jan. 16, 1799.

Pages 474-475: May 18, 1798, REUBEN WINFREY of Columbia Co., to WALTER SLAUGHTER of Warren Co. for $700, adj. NATHAN FOWLER, MITCHELL, S. CAMP, ADAM JONES, 200 acres granted March 17, 1786 to STEPHEN MITCHELL and also part of 275 acres granted Aug. 13, 1788 to sd. MITCHELL, conveyed Oct. 18, 1790 to REUBEN WINFREY... REUBEN WINFREY (SEAL). Wit: ADAM JONES Senr., THOMAS JONES. Rec. Jan. 16, 1799.

Pages 475-476: July 27, 1798, JAMES STAPLER of Columbia to HENRY PEEBLES of Warren for $2000, 300 acres on Middle Creek, granted to sd. JAMES STAPLER, heir of AMOS STAPLER, March 4, 1785, Adj. JESSE HARPER, J. CASTLEBERRY... JAMES STAPLER (SEAL), JNO. MATHEWS, P. MATHEWS, Rec. Jan. 17, 1799.

Page 476: ROBERT FORD of Warren Co. to relation JOHN FORD, Junr., a mare, Dec. 20, 1798. ROBERT FORD (R) (SEAL). Wit: ISAIAH TUCKER, HENRY HILL. Rec. Jan. 17, 1798.

Pages 476-477: Dec. 20, 1794, JOHN WALTON of Columbia Co. to THOMAS YOUNG of Bryan, for 5 shillings, 1000 acres on Middle Fork of Upton's Creek, formerly in Richmond Co. originally granted to sd. THOMAS YOUNG... JOHN WALTON (SEAL). Wit: JOHN CARTER WALTON, BENJ. SKEINE. Rec. Jan. 18, 1799.

Pages 477-478: I JOHN WALTON of Columbia Co. held unto THOMAS YOUNG of Bryan for 1000 sterling... concerning relinquish of dower on above deed. Rec. Jan. 18, 1799.

Pages 478-479: Sept. 22, 1796, RICHARD WHATLEY & FRANCES his wife of Warren Co. to JOHN THOMAS of same, for 50 pounds, 125 acres on Middle Creek... RICHD. WHATLEY (X) (SEAL), FRANCES WHATLEY (SEAL). Wit: GIDION GEORGE, RICHD. CARTER. Rec. Jan. 23, 1799.

Pages 479-480:   Jan. 2, 1798, WYATT BONNER of Warren Co. to THOMAS
                 FONTAIN, for $400, 200 acres granted to MARY MCDONALD,
ALEY MCDONALD & DARLING MCDONALD. Sept. 9, 1784, WYATT BONNER (SEAL).
Wit: JONES BONNER, Z. FRANKLIN. Rec. Jan. 29, 1799. (ANNE mentioned
as wife of WYATT BONNER, above).

Pages 480-481:   Feb. 5, 1799, JEFFREY BARKSDALE & PHEBE his wife,
                 of Hancock Co. to JAMES GEORGE of Warren Co. for 50
pounds, 100 acres on Middle Creek, surveyed Dec. 8, 1772, Rec. BOOK I,
JEFFERY BARKSDALE (B) (SEAL), PHEBE BARKSDALE (X) (SEAL). Wit:
GIDION GEORGE, JOSEPH BRANKLEY (X). Rec. Feb. 6, 1799.

Pages 481-482:   March 30, 1798, THOMAS YOUNG of City of Savannah,
                 Gentlemen, to HENRY HARDIN of Warren Co., planter, for
$1500, land granted to sd. THOMAS YOUNG, Oct. 4, 1774, 1000 acres,
Wrightsborough Township, Pariah of St. Paul, by old Indian line &
path, FRANCIS GREEN, JOHN DOVER... THOS. YOUNG (S), ELIZA. YOUNG (S).
Wit: MATT. MCALLISTER, Mayor of Savannah, THOMAS YOUNG, Junr. Rec.
Feb. 15, 1799.

Pages 482-483:   Jan. 27, 1797, SARAH TAYLOR of Wilkes Co. to JAMES
                 BISHOP of same, for 5 shillings, land on Middle Ck.,
adj. WILLIAM ANDERSON (now Miller's land, 100 acres, granted March 3,
1784... SARAH TAYLOR (ᴖ) (S). Rec. Feb. 18, 1799.

Pages 484-485:   July 10, 1793, JAMES BISHOP to JOSEPH BREED, for 30
                 pounds, 100 acres on Middle Creek (same as above) JAMES
BISHOP (B) (SEAL). Wit: E. PRUITT, E. PRUITT. Rec. Feb. 19, 1799.

Pages 485-486:   Oct. 25, 1795, JOSEPH BEASLEY & MARY his wife to JOSEPH
                 BREED, for 2 pounds, land on a branch of Childrea's
Creek, being waters of Middle Creek. Surveyed by ROBERT CRISWELL,
Dec. 6, 1792. Rec. BOOK MMMM, 100 acres... JOSEPH BEASLEY (L) (X),
MARY BEASLEY (X) (X). Wit: WM. BREED, JOSHUA MILLER, THOS. WEEKLEY.
Rec. Feb. 19, 1799.

Pages 486-487:   Oct. 24, 1793, WILLIAM COCKS & HANNAH his wife of
                 Wilkes Co. to DIAL PEAVEY of same, for 50 pounds, land
on west side of Rocky Comfort, adj. JAMES PARSONS... 154 acres (2
reserved for use of mill), WILLIAM COCKS (LS), HANNAH COCKS (ℋ) (LS).
Wit: DANIEL COCKS, JOSEPH DAVIDSON. Rec. Feb. 20, 1799.

Pages 487-488:   June 14, 1798, DIAL PEAVEY of Warren Co. to JOHN
                 PARHAM of same, for $450, land on west side of Rocky
Comfort, adj. BOHANNAON, CHRISTOPHER BUSTIN, 130 acres... DIAL PEAVEY
(LS). Wit: T. PERSONS, SHADRACH FELLIN. Rec. Feb. 20, 1799.

Page 488:   Nov. 7, 1798, CHRISTOPHER BUSTIN of Warren Co. to JOHN
            PARHAM for $500, land on Rocky Comfort, adj. HARMAN PERRYMAN,
118 acres, C. BUSTIN (SEAL). Wit: JNO. MATHEWS, AMBROSE HADLEY (X),
R. B. FLETCHER JP. Rec. Feb. 20, 1799.

Pages 488-489:   Dec. 25, 1798, JOSEPH MILLAR of State of South Carolina,
                 Vinton County, to HENRY PEEBLES of Warren Co. for $20,
land on Middle Creek, adj. Augusta Road, FREDERICK DENNIS, 5 acres,
JOSEPH MILLAR (SEAL). Wit: FREDK. DANIEL (X), THOMAS FORD (X). Rec.
Feb. 20, 1799.

Pages 489-490:   Oct. 10, 1791, BENJMAIN JENKINS of Washington Co. to
                 ARTHUR JENKINS of same, for 100 pounds, land on Ogechee
River, 200 acres, part of 340 granted to JOHN LEDBETTER, April 19, and
conveyed to ISAAC LEDBETTER, May 13, 1790... BENJA. JENKINS (SEAL).
Wit: ISAAC HILL, HEN GARDNER, JAMES STUBBS JP. Rec. Feb. 25, 1799.

Pages 490-491:   July 1, 1797, ARTHUR JENKINS of Warren Co. to BENJAMIN
                 UPTON of same for $430, land on Ogechee River...
LITTLETON CHAMBLESS... GLASCOK's line... part of 340 acres granted to
JOHN LEDBETTER... ARTHUR JENKINS (SEAL). Wit: RICHARD WHITEHEAD,
WILLIAM JENKINS. Rec. Feb. 21, 1799.

243

Page 492:   Nov. 20, 1794, GEORGE DYKES of Warren Co. to BENJAMIN UPTON,
             for 40 pounds, 200 acres on Rocky Comfort, adj. THOMAS
JOHNSON, WILLIAM BUSH, GEORGE UPTON, granted to ROBERT WILKINS May 31,
1788, then conveyed to JAMES HICKY, then to ISAAC BLOUNT, then to
DYKES... GEORGE DYKES (SEAL). Wit: SUSANNA HAMILL, JNO. HANILL JP.
Rec. Feb. 22, 1799.

Pages 492-493:   Jan. 5, 1793, GEORGE UPTON of Columbia Co. to BENJAMIN
                  UPTON of Wilkes Co. for 100 pounds, land on Rocky
Comfort in Burk & Columbia (now Warren Co.), originally granted to
RICHARD BARROW, conveyed to JOHN GRIESON, sold by JOHN DENNIS, Sheriff,
to GEORGE UPTON, 1785, 320 acres... GEORGE UPTON (SEAL). Wit: GEO.
WALKER, SEABORN JONES. Rec. Feb. 22, 1799.

Page 494:   March 3, 1794, Rec'd. of CHAS. ABERCROMBIE, a bond in my
             favour to WILLIAM DUPIUES, JOSEPH DUPIES, & GEORGE NICHOLS,
an agreement made Dec. 11, 1789, signed by JOHN MITCHELL, HENRY GRAYBILL,
MATTHEW RABUN, ADNW. BAXTER, SAMUEL ALEXANDER, ANDREW BURNES, THOMAS
HARRIS, WILLIAM THEDFORD, JEREMIAH BONNER, ROBERT ABERCROMBIE.
Wit: SAMUEL SAXON, JOHN SAXON. Rec. Oct. 18, 1698.

Pages 494-495:   Jan. 25, 1798, EDMOND WALSH of Hancock Co. to JOEL
                  MCLENDON for $150, on Rocky Branch of Ogechee adj.
STEPHEN BISHOP, ABRAHAM HELTON, HEATH, 100 acres, part of a tract of 200
laid off that JOSEPH RICHARDSON formerly lived on,... ED. WALSH (SEAL).
Wit: THO. MARTIN, SAML. MCGEHEE. Rec. Feb. 24, 1799.

Pages 495-496:   Aug. 6, 1798, DAVID FELPS of Hancock Co. & FALBY FELPS
                  his wife to WILLIAM DISMUKES of same for $430, 160
acres on Ogechee, adj. WILLIAM & STEPHEN LAWRENCE, ESTHER JEFFREYS,
KINGS, AND PERRYS, originally granted to DAVID FELPS, REC BOOK ZZZZ,
fo. 288... DAVID FELPS (SEAL), FALBY FELPS (SEAL). Wit: SARAH HILL,
JOHN WILSON JP. Rec. March 22, 1799.

Page 497:   March 10, 1795, BRITTON MCCULLERS of Burke Co. to JOHN
             NUNN of Warren Co.... BRITTON & PATTY his wife... for 50
pounds, land surveyed for BRITTON MCCULLERS, Dec. 9, 1789. BOOK ZZZ,
fo. 262, B. MCCULLERS (SEAL), PATTY MCCULLERS (SEAL). Wit: CHARNICK
THARP, AARON BENTON. (mentions Jackson's line) Rec. March 22, 1799.

Pages 498-499:   April 2, 1797, BENJAMIN A. HAMP of Warren Co. to
                  WILLIAM BIRD of same for $3000, 100 acres on Ogechee
River, granted to BENJAMIN FEW Jan. 20, 1786, conveyed to BIRD & HAMP,
Nov. 13, 1794, one other tract 200 acres, granted to ISAA (C?) DENNIS,
April 26, 1787, one other acre conveyed by HOWELL FETHERSTONE &
PERMELA his wife, to BIRD & HAMP Dec. 4, 1794... BENJAMIN UPTON &
JUDITH Lis wife... BENJA. A. HAMP (SEAL). Wit: WILLIAM STITH, WILLIAM
BIRD Junr. Rec. March 22, 1799.

Pages 499-500:   April 29, 1797, PETER MAHONE of Hancock Co. to
                  STEPHEN MARSHALL of Warren Co. for $260, land on
Rocky Comfort, 200 acres adj. HILL's... PETER MAHONE (X) (SEAL). Wit:
D. PERRYMAN, ANDW. KING JP. Rec. April 25, 1799.

Page 500:   March 21, 1799, DAVID COCKS of Warren Co. to HENRY HADLEY,
             for $195, land on Whetstone Creek... NATHANIEL FULSOM,
MIMS, AMOS WRIGHT, JAMES BRAY, 100 acres... DAVID COCKS (SEAL). Wit:
T. PERSONS, SHADK. FLEWELLIN, ELISHA HURT JP. Rec. April 26, 1799.

Page 501:   Jan. 20, 1799, SOLOMON NEWSOM Senr. to SAMPSON IVY for
             $387, 129 acres, ADH. MCKINNIE... SOLOMON NEWSOM &
ELIZABETH his wife... SOLOMON NEWSOM (SEAL), ELIZABETH NEWSOM (SEAL).
Wit: H. THARP JP, BENJ. BRUTON JP. Rec. April 26, 1799.

Pages 501-502:   May 20, 1797, JACOB FARR to JOHN FARR both of Warren
                  Co., for $10, 100 acres, part of a 200 grant to
JACOB FARR March 24, 1797, adj. WILLIAM DUCKWORTH, E. LEONARD, N.
THOMPSON, JAMES SMITH... JACOB FARR (X) (SEAL). Wit: SALLEY HODO,
PETER HODO JP. Rec. April 27, 1799.

Pages 502-503: Feb. 7, 1799, JOHN FARR to NATHANIEL THOMSON, for $200, (land conveyed above)... JOHN FARR (X) (SEAL). Wit: DORCAS CHANDLER (X), JOHN BAYN JP. Rec. April 30, 1799.

Pages 503-504: May 23, 1797, GEORGE COOPER of Warren Co. to BENJAMIN COOPER of same, for $200... GEORGE COOPER & ELIZABETH his wife... 75 acres on Long Creek. GEORGE COOPER, (G) (SEAL), ELIZABETH COOPER (X) (SEAL). Wit: THOS VINING, M. HUBERT JP. Rec. April 30, 1799.

Pages 504-505: Nov. 19, 1796 M. JEREMIAH MATHEWS, of Warren Co. to JESSE MATTHEWS for 200 Spanish milled dollars, land adj. RUTHERFORD, 130 acres, part of a grant to JAMES COCKRUM 1786... JEREMIAH MATHEWS (SEAL). Wit: ELISHA WRIGHT, H. HILL. Rec. May 4, 1799.

Page 505: Aug. 6, 1788, SAMUEL CRESWELL to WM. POE, both of Wilkes Co. for 100 pounds, 375 acres on Hart's Creek, formerly granted to AARON CINQUEFIELD, SOLOMON BARFIELD... SAMUEL CRESWELL (SEAL). Wit: JOSEPH COOK, M. WILLIAMSON JP. Rec. April 30, 1799.

Page 506: Jan. 12, 1799, CHARLES MCDONALD of Hancock Co., to MATHEW MCCRARY of Warren Co., for $220, 195 acres on Rocky Comfort, granted to sd. MCDONALD 1786,... CHARLES MCDONALD (SEAL). Wit: JOSEPH HOWARD, ISAAC HEARN. Rec. May 10, 1799.

Page 507: I, SEABORN JONES of City of Augusta, attorney at Law, relinquish all claim to land sold by CHARLES MCDONALD, Jan. 14, 1799. SEABORN JONES (SEAL). Wit: JNO POWELL, W. STITH JP. Rec. May 10, 1799.

Pages 507-508: April 23, 1798, NATHAN FOWLER & NANCY his wife, to MATHEW MCCRARY on Ogechee, 19½ acres, granted to NATHAN FOWLER March 7, 1797... NATHAN FOWLER (SEAL). NANCY FOWLER (X) (SEAL). Wit: WILLIS ROWLAND, ZEPHANIAH FOWLER. Rec. May 10, 1799.

Pages 508-509: Feb. 20, 1799, MARTHA CASTLEBERRY, PETER CASTLEBERRY, CLAIBORN CASTLEBERRY of Warren Co. to MATHEW MCCRARY of same, for $50, land 100 acres on Long Creek of Ogechee granted to MARTHA CASTLEBERRY, Dec. 22, 1791... MARTHA CASTLEBERRY (X) (SEAL), PETER CASTLEBERRY (SEAL), CLABURN CASTLEBERRY (SEAL). Wit: ARTHUR JENKINS, COLLINS ON WATERS (X). Rec. May 13, 1799.

Pages 509-510: Aug. 11, 1798, ANDREW KING of Warren Co. to STEPHEN MARSHALL Rf same for $450, land on Rocky Comfort, 39 acres... THOMAS SEALS... THOMAS & CHARLES SEALS... ANDREW KING (SEAL). Wit: JNO. MATHEWS, ELISHA HURT JP. Rec. May 13, 1799.

Pages 510-511: May 28, 1798, WILKINS SMITH of Edgefield County, South Carolina, to ROBERT MOORE of Warren Co., for $70, 50 acres on Little River... MULKEY's land... WILKINS SMITH (SEAL). Wit: WM. STARK, JOHN DOZER, LEONARD DOZER (X). Rec. May 14, 1799.

Page 512: June 26, 1797, EDMOND WALSH to CORNELIUS O'KEEFE of Carruk on suir and Kingdom Tulon, for love and affection of sd. EDMOND doth bear to his Sister MARY WALSH alias, O'KEEFE, wife of sd. CORNELIUS, 100 acres on Rocky Branch of Ogechee... EDM. WALSH (SEAL). Wit: WILLIAM KINCHEN, WILLIAM FELPS, JNO. HARBISH JP. Rec. May 15, 1799.

Pages 512-513: Feb. 23, 1799, JOSEPH CARSON of Wilkes Co. to WILLIAM HILL of Warren Co. for $240, 100 acres on Middle Creek... JOHN WELLS & MILLER... JOSEPH CARSON (SEAL). Wit: JOHN TINDALL, SALLEY MORROW, EVVING MORROW JP. Rec. May 15, 1799.

Pages 513-514: Jan. 21, 1794, GARLAND MORGAN & DELILA AGEN & JEAN MORGAN, MARY MORGAN & SARAH MORGAN to JOHN KELLY for

100 pounds, 300 acres on Ogechee River, granted 1787, GARLAND MORGAN (X) (SEAL), DELILA OGAIN (SEAL), JEAN MORGAN (X) (SEAL), MARY (M) (SEAL), SARAH MORGAN (SEAL). Wit: LEWIS BRADY, JAMES YOUNGBLOOD (X), KEADER KEATEN. Rec. May 15, 1799.

Pages 514-515:   May 10, 1790, WILLIAM BUSH & MOURNING his wife, of Wilkes Co. to JOEL TAPLEY of Richmond Co., for 12 pounds, 200 acres in Richmond Co., on east side of Beachtree Creek, adj. ANDREW CRANFORD, BOWLINGS, THOMAS JOHNSTON, granted May 28, 1788... WILLIAM BUSH (SEAL), MOURNING BUSH (M) (SEAL). Wit: JAMES HOMPHILL, EVIN TAPLEY. Rec. May 15, 1799.

Pages 516-517:   Oct. 21, 1798, JOB SPRINGER & LYDIA his wife, admr. & admx. of est. of JAMES MAY, dec'd... to EDMOND FEARS 487½ acres in Franklin County, granted to JOHN JARRETT, conveyed to WILLIAM CLARK, then to NICHOLAS BOWER... JOB SPRINGER (X) (SEAL), LYDIA SPRINGER (X) (SEAL). Wit: H. G. CALDWELL, JOSEPH WRIGHT (X). Rec. June 6, 1799.

Pages 517-518:   April 25, 1790, PELEG ROGERS of Wilkes Co. to JOHN MANNON of same, for 50 pounds, 100 acres, on Little Bryar Creek, bounded by WALTER JACKSON... PELEG ROGERS. Wit: BENJAMIN JACKSON, ISAAC NEWTON. Rec. June 29, 1799.

Pages 518-519:   April 25, 1790, PELEG ROGERS to JOHN MANNON for 50 pounds, 100 acres on Little Bryar Creek, half of a 200 acre grant to JOHN MAYNOR Feb. 22, 1786, adj. WALTER JACKSON... PELEG ROGERS (same wit. as above). Rec. June 29, 1799.

Pages 519-520:   April 4, 1794, WILLIAM GREENWOOD Junr. of City of Charleston to JOHN COURSE of Augusta, land 800 acres for 60 pounds, granted to JAMES JACKSON, ROBT. CROOKE & ALEXAND MCINTOSH, purchased as property of ANDREW MCLEAN at Sheriff's sale... WILLIAM GREENWOOD Junr. (SEAL). Wit: JNO. WILSON JP, JNO WILSON Junr. Rec. May 16, 1799.

Pages 520-521:   Aug. 6, 1794, JOHN MAYNOR of Warren Co. to JOHN MANNON, for 15 pounds, 100 acres, part of a 200 acre grant on Little Bryar Creek... JOHN MAYNOR. Wit: ISAAC HILL, SAMUEL RIDGDELL. Rec. June 29, 1799.

Pages 521-522:   March 4, 1794, SOLOMON LOCKETT of Warren Co. to STEPHEN DARDEN for 100 pounds, land on Williams's Creek, adj. JACOB DARDEN, JOHN CAMPBELL, ROBERT CAREY, ROBERT HILL... SOLOMON LOCKETT (SEAL). Wit: T. LOCKETT, JACOB DARDEN. Rec. July 1, 1799.

Pages 522-523:   July 15, 1793, ROBERT MOSES Senr. of Wilkes Co. to PETER FOODWIN of Columbia Co. for 130 pounds, 160 acres adj. EVAN THOMAS, EPHRAIM POOL, JOHN MOSES, part of 400 acres granted to sd. MOSES May 29, 1785... ROBERT MOSES (SEAL). Wit: PETER HODO, ROBT, MOSES Junr. Rec. July 1, 1799.

Pages 523-524:   May 17, 1799, LEWIS WRIGHT Sheriff of Warren, to SAMUEL YARBOROUGH, since SAMUEL YARBOROUGH did obtain a Judgment for $222, against the admr. of WILLIAM LUCAS, 400 acres on Ogechee, adj. JOHN COX, BISHOP, NOBLE, RYLEY, CAMP, & SANFORD, granted to WILLIAM LUCAS Nov. 25, 1797, by publick sale, for $135... LEWIS WRIGHT (SEAL). Wit: T. PERSONS, SAML. ALDEXANDER JP. Rec. July 2, 1799.

Pages 524-525:   March 10, 1797, PROSSER HORTON to ALLEN DORMAN, later PROPER HORTON... for $800, land on Ogechee 200 acres... PROPER HORTON (SEAL). Wit: W. STITH Junr., JOHN HOBSON, JOHN HENNESSEY. Rec. July 2, 1799.

Pages 525-526:   May 3, 1797, JAMES HENDERSON & ELIZABETH his wife to ICHABOD COX, for 25 pounds, 100 acres on Ogechee,

LIPHAM's line, FRAZER's line... JAMES HENDERSON (SEAL), ELIZABETH
HENDERSON (SEAL). Wit: WM. BYROM Junr., JOHN HARRIS, WM. BYROM JP.
Rec. July 3, 1799.

Pages 526-527:   May 20, 1797, WILLIAM COX of Washington Co. to JOHN
                  TURNER of Warren Co. for $600, 250 acres on Whet Stone
Creek, adj. SAMUEL NEWMAN, heirs of MAY, THREEWIT's... WILLIAM COCKS.
Wit: TURNER PERSONS, WORMLEY ROSE, Relinquish of dower by HANNAH
COCKX (-) (SEAL). Rec. July 3, 1799.

Pages 527-528:   May 16, 1799, LEVI PRUITT to THOMAS PARHAM, for $130,
                  52 acres on Cannon's Creek, originally granted to
LEVI PRUITT, Dec. 21, 1791, L. PRUITT (SEAL). Wit: LEML. PRUITT JP,
PETER PARHAM. Rec. July 3, 1799.

Pages 528-529:   Jan. 21, 1799, DAVID RUNNERLS of Jackson Co. to
                  OBADIAH FLOURNOY of Warren Co. for $200, 60 acres on
Ogechee, adj. NATHAN BREWER, BISHOP, granted to WILLIAM BREWER June,
1789... DAVID RUNNELS (SEAL). Wit: SAMUEL JOHNSON. Rec. July 23,
1799.

Pages 529-530:   Feb. 9, 1799, WILLIAM TYLER of Columbia to SAMUEL
                  JOHNSTON of _____, for 100 pounds, land on Redlick
Creek, granted to ANDREW FRAZE, Feb. 2, 1785, from sd. FRAZE to THOMAS
CARR, thence to TYLER... WM. TYLER (SEAL). Wit: MARY LOVELL, WILLIAM
LOVELL. Rec. July 23, 1799.

Pages 530-531:   Feb. 28, 1799, SAMUEL JOHNSON & ELIZABETH his wife,
                  for $400, to FLEMEN HODGES, land originally granted to
ANDREW FRAZER, 300 acres. SAMUEL JOHNSON (SEAL), BETSY JOHNSON (SEAL).
Wit: J. KENNEDY. Rec. July 25, 1799.

Pages 531-532:   Oct. 16, 1798, SAMUEL ALLEN Senr. of Greenville Co.,
                  South Carolina to JESSE DYKES of Jefferson Co., Ga.,
for $128.57½, land on Joe's Creek, 15 acres, granted to SAMUEL ALLEN
July 18, 1787... SAMUEL ALLEN (SEAL). Wit: JOSEPH HOWELL (X),
NORVELL ROBERTSON JP. Rec. July 25, 1799.

Page 532:   May 18, 1799, JACOB BURKHATTER of Warren Co. to HUGH
             ARMSTRONG of same, for $200, 100 acres, adj. LANDRUM, HUGH
REESE, SANDERS, THOMAS CHILDREA's... JACOB BURKHATTER (SEAL). Wit:
P. HODO JP, JOHN WILSON JP. Rec. Sept. 20, 1799.

Pages 532-533:   Warren Co., Ga., JOHN GAZA, NATHAN BOUTEN & JOSHUA
                  GAZA have received of BENJAMIN & JEMIMA BRUTON, Adm. of
est. of FRANCIS FONTAINE, then Junr. (dec'd). $75.10½... JOHN GAZA,
NATHAN BRUTON, JOSHUA GAZA. Wit: SARAH FONTAINE, EDMD. MATHEWS. Rec.
Nov. 1, 1799.

Pages 533-534:   July 7, 1797, NATHAN HARRIS of Columbia Co. to
                  FREDERICK LITTLE of Burke Co. for $220, 200 acres
originally granted to ELIZABETH COOMS, for Co. of Richmond (now Warren),
adj. River Ogechee, SIMS... NATHAN HARRISS (SEAL). Wit: PETER ZUALLS,
JOHN ZUALLS. Rec. Nov. 26, 1799.

Page 535:   May 14, 1796, JOSEPH MILLER to JOHN J. WELLS, for 50 pounds,
             150 acres on Rocky Comfort, WEATHERBY, ELISHA WRIGHT...
JOSEPH MILLER (SEAL). Wit: L. PRUITT, THOMAS WEEKLEY. Rec. Nov. 26,
1799.

Pages 535-536:   June 28, 1785, Wilkes Co., Ga., I, WILLIAM KELLY of
                  aforsd. give unto JOHN KELLY, 100 acres whereon JOHN
KELLY now lives, WILLIAM KELLY (SEAL), (𝖠). Wit: ISHAM GARDNER,
JOHN JONES.
             This is to certify that I have relinquished & forever
quit claim under my Father WILLIAM KELLY, Senr. all my Right, Title &
Interest in the within mentioned Tract of 100 acres... Aug. 9, 1786.
JOHN KELLY ( ) (SEAL). Wit: JOHN LEDBETTER, JOHN LEDBETTER. Rec.
Nov. 26, 1798.

Page 537:   Jan. 28, 1797, RICHARD WHATLEY of Warren Co. & BENJAMIN FEW
             of Columbia Co. to RICHARD CARTER of Warren Co., for 50
pounds, 100 acres, RICHD. WHATLEY (X) (SEAL), BENJAMIN FEW (SEAL). Wit:
FRANCIS WOODWARD, R. HOWARD JP. Rec. Nov. 27, 1799.

Page 538:   March 28, 1797, MOSES GOING & AGNESS his wife to SAMUEL
             HOWELL, for 100 pounds, land on Long Creek, adj.BANKSON,
REILY, PARISH, granted to EDMOND NEWGENT Sept. 5, 1784,.. MOSES GOING
(SEAL), AGNESS GOING (X) (SEAL). Wit: ISAAC BANCKSTON, ROBT. JOHNSON.
Rec. Nov. 27, 1799.

Pages 539-540:   Jan. 19, 1799, JONES PERSONS to AMBROSE HADLEY, for
                 $30, land on Rocky Comfort, adj. WM. DAVIES, JOHN
MYRICK, 12½ acres, JONES PERSONS (LS). Wit: ELISHA HURT JP, R. B.
FLETCHER JP. Rec. Nov. 27, 1799.

Pages 540-541:   Nov. 4, 1798, JAMES SIMMONS & MARY his wife, to
                 JACK S. DAVENPORT, all of Warren Co. for $60, 200
acres, adj. JAMES HOGG... JAMES SIMMONS (SEAL), MARY SIMMONS (SEAL).
Wit: RICHARD DEVENPORT, WM. BYROP, WM. BUNKLEY, Rec. Nov. 27, 1799.

Page 541:   REUBEN BANKS of Garrard County, Kentucky, constitute my
             well beloved SAMUEL CAMP of Warren Co., Ga., my attorney,
interest and claim in 130 acres in Jackson County, Ga. Sept. 12, 1799.
REUBEN BANKS (SEAL).
             BENJAMIN LETCHER, Clerk of Court for Garrard Co. certify that
WM. G. BRYANT & WM. JENNINGS Esqrs. before me when power of attorney
was acknowledged. BENJA. LETCHER.
             Rec. Oct. 31, 1799.

Page 542:   Hancock Co., Ga., Dec. 18, 1797, JAMES GOLIGHTLY to JOHN
             CASWELL of Warren Co. for $100, adj. THOMAS JONES... JAMES
GOLIGHTLY (SEAL). Wit: HEN. MITCHELL, JJ., WM. CHANDLER, JOHN ZACKRY.
Rec. Nov. 27, 1799.

Pages 542-543:   Nov. 19, 1791, ALEXANDER STEEL of Washington Co. to
                 LITTLETON CLAMBLESS of Wilkes Co. for 10 pounds, 50
acres on Ogechee River, purchased by STEEL from JOHN LEDBETTER, May
28, last... ALEXANDER STEEL (X) (SEAL). Wit: DUNCAN MCLEAN, BENJA.
JENKINS JP. Rec. Nov. 28, 1799.

Pages 543-544:   Sept. 14, 1795, RICHARD STORY of Warren Co. to JOHN
                 HAMBLETON, for 15 pounds, 50 acres on north side of
Bryar Creek, part of 200 acres granted to NEEDHAM SMITH, Jan. 7, 1787
BOOK LLL, fo. 349, RICHARD STORY (R) (SEAL), ELIZABETH STORY (≡) (SEAL).
Wit: VINCENT A. THARP. Rec. Nov. 28, 1799.

Pages 544-545:   Sept. 10, 1798, RANDEL NEWSOM to BENJAMIN ADAMS for
                 $300, 300 acres, adj. CLABORN NEWSOM, JAMES MCCORMICK,
EDMOND CODY, MOSES MCKINNE, Fart of 600 acres granted to SOLOMON
NEWSOM July 29, 1785... RANCEL NEWSOM (X) (SEAL). Wit: TILMAN MCKINNEY,
P. HODO JP. Rec. Nov. 28, 1799.

Pages 545-546:   Aug. 19, 1799, JOHN ____ Senr. to BARTON ATACHSON, 140
                 acres, adj. EDWARD HILL, THOMAS BUSH, JOHN HILL, for
$240... JOHN HILL (SEAL). Wit: THOS. HILL, EDWARD HILL (E), Rec. Nov.
28, 1799.

Pages 546-547:   JOHN MCGAW of Battemore County, Maryland make JOHN
                 TRAVIS of Warren Co., Ga., my attorney. JNO. MCGAW
(SEAL). Wit: HAS. BOND, JOHN ROCKHOLD.
             Haiford Co., Maryland, Nov. 13, 1798. JAMES BOND.
Rec. Nov. 28, 1799.

Pages 547-548:   Oct. 23, 1797, JOHN KELLY to JOHN HILLSON for 100 pounds
                 300 acres, granted May 21, 1787. JOHN KELLY (SEAL),
ELIZABETH KELLY (X) (SEAL). Wit: THOMAS PHILIPS, BENJAMIN ARRANDELL.
Rec. Oct. 28, 1799.

Pages 548-549: July 13, 1799, SOLOMON NEWSOM & ELIZABETH his wife to MOSES MCKINNEY for $600, 500 acres on both sides of Big Bryar Creek, granted to sd. NEWSOM July 29, 1795, BOOK JJJ fo. 92... SOLOMON NEWSOM, ELIZABETH NEWSOM (LS). Wit: BENJA. BRUTON JP, WILLIAM CASON JP. Rec. Nov. 28, 1799.

Pages 549-550: SARAH CHILDREE, widow of WILLIAM CHILDREE, WILLIAM HODGEM, WILLIAM DAVISON & HANNAH CHILDREE & FRANCIS CHILDREE, children and heirs of aforesd. WILLIAM CHILDREE, dec'd, quit claims unto THOMAS CHILDREE & WILLIAM CHILDREE of County of Warren... land on Long Creek adj. JOHN ANGLIN, ANDERSON, MATHEW HUBERT, JAMES BISHOP, 200 acres... SARE CHILDREE (X) (SEAL), WM. DAVIDSON (X) (SEAL), WM. HODGEN (--) (SEAL), FRANCES CHILDREE (-) (SEAL), HANAH CHILDREE (X) (SEAL). Wit: JOSEPH HODGEN, EVANS PHELAN. Rec. Nov. 29, 1799.

Page 551: Jan. 20, 1798, JACOB BURKATTER, of Warren Co. to THOMAS CHILDREY, for $200, 110 acres, adj. JOSEPH DAVISON... JACOB BURKHATTER (LS). Wit: ROBERT HODGIN, P. HODO JP. Rec. Nov. 29, 1799.

Pages 551-552: Dec. 27, 1789, WILLIAM GLOVER & LUCY his wife to ROBERT THOMPSON for 100 pounds, land on Indian Creek, granted to WILLIAM GLOVER, Aug. 26, 1788, adj. FRANCIS GRUBBS, JOEL TAPLEY... WILLIAM GLOVER, LUCY GLOVER (X). Wit: JOHN VENSON, ALLEN GLOVER & JOHN LAWSON. Rec. Nov. 29, 1799.

Page 553: May 14, 1790, JOEL TAPLEY & MARY his wife of Richmond Co. to ROBERT THOMPSON for 60 pounds, land on Deep Creek granted to sd. TAPLEY Jan. 3, 1786, JOEL TAPLY (LS). Wit: EZEKIEL SMITH, JOHN RAGLAND. Rec. Nov. 29, 1799.

Pages 554-555: Feb. 25, 1799, BENJAMIN REESE & SARAH his wife of Columbia Co., for $200, 236 acres, granted to SIR JAMES WRIGHT and confiscated etc... BENJ. REES (LS), SARAH REES (LS). Wit: REUBEN REES, P. HODO JP. Rec. Nov. 29, 1799.

Pages 555-556: Sept. 9, 1799, HARDY NEWSOM to JACOB BURKHATTER, for $300, 100 acres on Big Bryar Creek, granted to BASEL LAMAR Oct. 11, 1785, adj. JAMES CARTER, BRAY WARREN... HARDY NEWSOM (H) (LS). Wit: P. HODO, HUGH REES. Rec. Nov. 29, 1799.

Pages 556-557: May 29, 1792, JESSE MILLAR of Wilkes Co. to JAMES GEORGE of Columbia Co., land on Middle Creek, adj. JAMES BISHOP, 100 acres, JESSE MILLAR (SEAL), ELIZABETH MILLAR (X) (SEAL). Wit: ISAIAH TUCKER, JOSHUA MILLAR, HENRY HARDIN. Rec. Nov. 29, 1799.

Pages 557-558: June 7, 1787, RICHARD WHATLEY of Warren Co. & BENJAMIN FEW of Columbia Co., for $200, 92 2/10 acres to JAMES GEORGE... BENJ. FEW (SEAL), RICHD. WHATLEY (X) (SEAL). Wit: RICHD. CARTER, JAMES GEORGE Junr. Rec. Nov. 30, 1799.

Pages 558-559: Feb. 2, 1799, JOHN THOMAS & PHEBE his wife, to JAMES GEORGE for 150 silver dollars, land on Middle Creek, 120 acres... JOHN THOMAS (X) (SEAL), PHOEBE THOMAS (X) (SEAL). Wit: GIDION GEORGE, JOSEPH GEORGE. Rec. Nov. 30, 1799.

Pages 559-560: April 21, 1795, RICHARD WHATLEY & FRANCES his wife to JAMES GEORGE for 50 pounds, 125 acres on Middle Creek.. RICHARD WHATLEY (W) (SEAL), FRANCES WHATLEY (X) (SEAL), Wit: RICHD. CARTER, M. HARDIN. Rec. Nov. 30, 1799.

Pages 560-561: Nov. 29, 1799 JUDITH GEORGE, DRURY BENKS, LEWIS GARNER, JESSE GEORGE, JAMES GEORGE, RICHARD GEORGE, JOSEPH GEORGE & ISAIAH TUCKER of Warren Co. to GIDION GEORGE, 125 acres on Middle Creek for 150 silver dollars, JUDITH GEORGE (X) (SEAL), DRURY BANKS, LEWIS GARNER, JESSE GEORGE (X), JAMES GEORGE, RICHARD GEORGE, JOSEPH GEORGE (X), ISAIAH TUCKER, guardian for MORRISS. Wit: RICHD. CARTER, LEML. PRUITT JP. Rec. Nov. 30, 1799.

Pages 561-562:   Nov. 29, 1799, JESSE GEORGE, GIDEON GEORGE, RICHARD
                  GEORGE, JOSEPH GEORGE, DRURY BANKS, LEWIS GARNER,
JUDITH GEORGE & ISAIAH TUCKER, guardian for JOHN NORRIS, to JAMES
GEORGE all of Warren Co. (except for LEWIS GARNER, who is a resident of
Moore Co., North Carolina), for $200, 73 acres on Middle Creek, surveyed
Dec. 8, 1772, to JAMES BISHOP... (same signatures & wit as above)
Rec. Nov. 30, 1799.

Pages 562-563:   Nov. 29, 1799, same as above except to RICHARD GEORGE,
                  for $400, 100 acres on Middle Creek. Rec. Nov. 30,
1799.

Pages 563-564:   Nov. 26, 1799, RICHARD CARTER of Warren Co. to GIDEON
                  GEORGE... TEMPE wife of RICHARD CARTER... for $560,
112 acres on Middle Creek... RICHD. CARTER (SEAL). TEMPEY CARTER (X)
(SEAL). Wit: JOSEPH RUCKER, WHITEFIELD TUCKER. Rec. Nov. 30, 1799.

Pages 564-565:   Nov. 29, 1799, JUDITH GEORGE, DRURY BANKS, LEWIS
                  GARNER, JAMES GEORGE, GIDEON GEORGE, RICHARD GEORGE,
JOSEPH GEORGE & ISAIAH TUCKER for $450, to JESSE GEORGE, 90 acres on
Middle Creek... Rec. Nov. 30, 1799.

Pages 565-566:   Nov. 29, 1799, (same as above except to JOSEPH GEORGE,
                  for 125 silver dollars, 125 acres on Middle Creek...
Rec. Nov. 30, 1799.

Pages 566-567:   Nov. 20, 1799, JESSE GEORGE, JAMES GEORGE, GIDEON
                  GEORGE, RICHARD GEORGE, JOSEPH GEORGE, DRURY BANKS,
LEWIS GARNER & ISAIAH TUCKER to HENRY HARDIN for $30, land originally
granted to JAMES BISHOP, 27 acres... Rec. Nov. 30, 1799.

Pages 567-568:   Nov. 20, 1799, (same as above to PHILIP BRANTLEY, for
                  $2000, land granted to JAMES BISHOP... Wit: WM.
BREED, LEML. PRUITT JP. Rec. Dec. 2, 1799.

Pages 568-569:   Nov. 22, 1799, WILLIAM JOHNSTON to THOMAS BUCKHANNON,
                  land on Rocky Comfort, adj. TORRENCE, JAS. DAVIES,
DIAL PERSONS, 171 acres, for $500... WILLIAM JOHNSTON (SEAL). Wit:
ISAIAH TUCKER, T. PERSONS. Rec. Dec. 2, 1799.

Pages 569-570:   Jan. 6, 1797, HUGH REES to JACOB BURKHATTER for 50
                  pounds, 210 acres, adj. WM. DAVIES, BENJAMIN REES,
granted to Gov. JAMES WRIGHT, deed to JOHN GARROTT... HUGH REES (LS),
ELIZABETH REES (X) (LS). Wit: BENJAMIN REES, P. HODO JP. Rec. Dec.
2, 1799.

Pages 570-571:   March 24, 1799, WILLIAM RICHARDSON to MICHAL PEAVY, for
                  $500, 121 acres on Long Creek of Ogechee, survey
belonging to WILLIAM RICHARDSON & HANNAH RICHARDSON (orphans of JAMES
RICHARDSON, dec'd). WILLIAM RICHARDSON (R) (SEAL). Wit: J. PEAVY,
WILLIAM MIMS. Rec. Dec. 2, 1799.

Pages 571-572:   Feb. 15, 1798, WILKINS SMITH of Columbia Co. to JOHN
                  TRAVIX, for $500, land granted to WILLIAM DOWNS, Esqr.
July 23, 1784, 134 acres, W. SMITH (SEAL). Wit: NANCY DOZER, WILLIAM
DOZAR. Rec. Dec. 2, 1799.

Pages 572-573:   Sept. 27, 1799, JEREMIAH DUCKWORTH to son & dau. JAMES
                  & NELLY CARTER, land on White's Creek, adj. THOMAS
ANSLEY's, JESSE CARTER, JOHN WILSON, 133 acres, JEREMIAH DUCKWORTH (SEAL).
Wit: JNO. WILSON JP, MARY WILSON (M). Rec. Dec. 2, 1799.

Pages 574-575:   Oct. 12, 1798, SAMUEL ALLEN of Greenville Co., South
                  Carolina, to JAMES ALLEN of Warren Co., Ga., land on
Poe's Creek, 200 acres. SAMUEL ALLEN, Dec. 3, 1799. Wit: SAML.
POWELL, NORVELL ROBERTSON JP.

Pages 575-576:   Oct. 3, 1799, JAMES ALLEN to JAMES JOHNSON, for $50,
                   60 acres granted to JAMES ALLEN, Feb. 27, 1799. JAMES
ALLEN (SEAL). Wit: SALLY ROBERTSON, NORVELL ROBERTSON JP. Rec. Dec.
3, 1799.

Page 576:   Oct. 3, 1799 JAMES ALLEN to JAMES JOHNSON, for $100, 50
              acres on Joe's Creek, conveyed from IRWIN & ROBERT IRWIN
to SAMUEL ALLEN, Sr. and divided into equal parts, one to sd. JAMES
ALLEN... JAMES ALLEN (SEAL), Wit: SALLEY ROBERTSON, NORVELL ROBERTSON
JP. Rec. Dec. 3, 1799.

Page 577:   Jan. 21, 1797, JOSEPH HODGIN of Warren Co. to THOMAS
              CHILDERS, of same, for 30 pounds, land on north west side
of my Spring Branch to the line of (formerly) JAMES BILMORE's 100 acres,
JOSEPH HODGIN (X) (SEAL). Wit: JOHN WILSON JP. Rec. Dec. 4, 1799.

Pages 577-578:   June 1, 1797, ABRAHAM HEATH & WINNEY his wife of
                   Warren Co. to WILLIAM GRIZZLE of same, for $500, 387
acres on Rocky Comfort, ABRAHAM HEATH (X) (SEAL), WINNEY HEATH (X)
(SEAL). Wit: ELISHA HURT JP, THOMAS FONTAINE. Rec. Dec. 4, 1799.

Pages 578-579:   Dec. 8, 1798, JOHN BUSTIN to JAMES SMITH (blacksmith)
                   for $400, land on Williams's Creek... JOHN BAKER's
land... SAXON's land... MOSES DARDEN... 100 acres, granted to GEORGE
MURRY, sold for taces to DAVID HILLHOUSE... JOHN BUSTIN (SEAL). Wit:
JOHN TORRENCE, A. GRIER JP, JOHN BAKER JP. Rec. Dec. 5, 1799.

Pages 579-580:   Nov. 24, 1798, WILLIAM JOHNSON to JOHN BALL for $500,
                   land on Rocky Comfort, AMBROSE HADLEY, Perit's Creek..
WILLIAM JOHNSON (X) (SEAL). Wit: JNO. MATHEWS, LEWIS BRANTLEY. Rec.
Dec. 5, 1799.

Pages 580-581:   July 20, 1799, WILLIAM MIMS to JOHN BALL for $200, 23
                   acres on Rocky Comfort, WILLIAM MIMS (N) (SEAL). Wit:
JOHN MATHEWS, R. B. FLETCHER JP. Rec. Dec. 5, 1799.

Pages 581-582:   June 21, 1798, GEORGE BREWER of Hancock Co. to JOSEPH
                   WHITE of Warren Co., for $200, land on Williams's
Creek, adj. IGN. FEW, BURREL, PERRY, JOSEPH HILL, originally granted to
BENJAMIN SCOTT, 400 acres, Dec. 17, 1784,.. GEORGE BREWER. Wit:
ROLEN BREWER, MATTHEW BREWER. Rec. Dec. 6, 1799.

Pages 582-583:   THOMAS LT. HALL of Warren Co. to dau. REBECKAH DOWDY
                   of Lancaster County, South Carolina, a Negro wench
Phillis, a boy named Cezr, boy, girl, and others. THOMAS LT. HALL
(SEAL). Wit: T. PERSONS, ABR. FLEWELLIN. Rec. Dec. 10, 1799.

Page 583:   Sept. 20, 1799, HUGH ARMSTRONG to HARDY NEWSOM for $250,
              100 acres adj. LANDRUM, HUGH REES, SAUNDERS, THOMAS CHILDREA,
HUGH ARMSTRONG. Wit: Z. LANDRUM, HUGH REES. Rec. Dec. 11, 1799.

Page 584:   Nov. 20, 1799, HENRY HARDIN to JOHN GIBSON for $30, land
              originally granted to JAMES BISHOP on Middle Creek, HENRY
HARDIN (SEAL). Wit: WILLIAM BREED, LEML. PRUITT JP. Rec. Dec. 11,
1799.

Pages 584-585:   Nov. 20, 1799, JOHN GIBSON to PHILIP BRANTLEY, for
                   $1000, 10 acres on Middle Creek... JOHN GIBSON (SEAL).
Wit: WM. BREED, LEML. PRUITT JP. Rec. Dec. 12, 1799.

Pages 585-586:   Feb. 21, 1793, ROBERT FLOURNOY of Green Co. to JOHN
                   COBBS, of Columbia Co., for 1000 pounds, land on
Clower's Branch in Wilkes Co. adj. BENJAMIN SIMMONS, JOHN WYNNE,
LEONARD FRETWELL, ROBERT WYNNE, THOS. PATE, SMITH, PERKINS, JESSE
WARREN... 250 acres, lying around the tract of JOHN AUSTIN, and 400
acres of cleared ground... R. FLOURNOY (SEAL). Wit: W. WILLIAMSON,
ROWD. STONE. Rec. Dec. 12, 1799.

Pages 586-587:   July 6, 1793, JOHN COBBS, Senr. of Columbia Co. to
                  NATHANIEL COKE of Richmond Co., for 500 pounds land
on Ogechee, 1000 acres (same as above)... JOHN COBBS (SEAL), Wit:
CHARLES F. RANDOLPH, WM. LONGSTREET JP. Rec. Dec. 12, 1799.

Pages 587-588:   Nov. 20, 1799, HENRY HARDIN & SARAH his wife to JOHN
                  GIBSON for $700, 640 acres on Upton Creek, originally
granted to THOMAS YOUNG Oct. 4, 1774... HENRY HARDIN (SEAL). Wit:
(none). Rec. Dec. 12, 1799.

Pages 588-589:   Oct. 3, 1799, JOHN GIBSON to JACOB TURKNETT, for $300,
                  140 acres, adj. ISAIAH TUCKER, CHURCHILL GIBSON,
JAMES MCINVALE... JOHN GIBSON. Wit: J. TUCKER, HENRY HARDIN, Rec.
Dec. 12, 1799.

Pages 589-590:   Dec. 29, 1797, JOHN RUDISELL for $2000, to ABNER CHAP-
                  MAN, bought of THOMAS DAVIS and others by deed,
March 10, 1795, JOHN RUDISELL (SEAL). Wit: DAVIS CHAPMAN, A. GRIER JP,
RICHD SMITH. Rec. Jan. 14, 1800.

Pages 590-591:   Feb. 4, 1797, BENJAMIN FEW of Columbia Co., & RICHARD
                  WHATLEY of Warren Co. for $700, to WILLIS PERRY of
Warren, land on Middle Creek, granted to RICHARD WHATLY, Aug. 7, 1795,
BENJM. FEW (SEAL), RICHARD WHATLEY (SEAL). Wit: I. FEW, JAMES GEORGE.
Rec. Jan. 28, 1800.

Pages 591-592:   Jan. 26, 1799, ISAAC BLOUNT of Washington Co. to
                  MOSES GRANDBERRY, land granted to GEORGE DYKES, 900
acres, for $50, 300 acres of sd. grant... ISAAC BLOUNT (SEAL). Wit:
GEORGE GRANDBERRY, PHILIP DILLARD JP. Rec. Jan. 28, 1800.

Pages 592-593:   Jan. 9, 1798, JOHN MYRACK Senr. of Warren Co. to
                  NATHANIEL MYRICK Senr. for $300, 72½ acres, JNO.
MYRICK (LS). Wit: SEPTIMUS WEATHERBY, OWE MYRICK. Rec. Jan. 28, 1800.

Page 593:   Nov. 17, 1798, LEWIS BRANTLEY to NATHANIEL MYRICK for $200,
             land on east side of Whetstone Creek, 50 acres... LEWIS
BRANTLEY (SEAL). Wit: ELISHA HURT JP, T. PERSONS. Rec. Jan. 29, 1800.

Page 594:   Dec. 29, 1797, MOSES GRIER to ABNER CHAPMAN for $50, land
             on Williams's Creek, originally granted to JOHN O'NEAL,
Oct. 13, 1785, to MOSES GRIER by deed May 13, 1787, 11 acres... MOSES
GRIER (LS). Wit: AGA. SCOTT, AARON GRIER. Rec. Jan. 29, 1800.

Pages 595-596:   Dec. 28, 1797, JOB SPRINGER & LYDIA his wife (now the
                  wife of sd. SPRINGER but late the wife of JAMES MAY,
dec'd) JOSEPH DAVIDSON & WINNEY (one of the heirs of MAY dec'd) and
DARCUS MASSE and LYDIA MAY, heirs of sd. JAMES MAY to JACOB BURKHATTER
for $300, land on Bryar Creek... JOB SPRINGER (X), LYDIA SPRINGER (X),
JOSEPH DAVIDSON (X), WINNY DAVIDSON (X), DARCUS MAY (X), MASSY MAY (X),
JAMES MAY, LYDIA MAY (X). Wit: RICHARD HUTCHINSON, RP. HODO JP.
Rec. Jan. 31, 1800.

Page 596:   WILLIAM DEPUIS, JOSEPH DEPUIS & GEORGE NICHOLDS of Warren
             Co. appoint our friend ROBERT ABERCROMBIE attorney to ask,
demand, etc. from CHARLES ABERCROMBIE of Hancock Co. the penalty of
the Bond given to us on March 3, last, July 17, 1794. WILLIAM DUPUIS
(SEAL), JOSEPH DEPUIS (X) (SEAL), GEORGE NICHOLS (SEAL). Wit: ROBERT
JENKINS, SIMEON VANWINKLE. Rec. Jan. 31, 1800.

Pages 596-697:   Sept. 17, 1798, BYRD PRUITT to LEVI PRUITT for 5
                  shillings, land on Rocky Comfort, part of a tract
where BYRD PRUITT now lives... BYRD PRUITT (SEAL). Wit: GEO. HARGRAVES,
J. B. HARDIN. Rec. Feb. 1. 1800.

Pages 597-598:   April 1, 1798, JOHN MYRICK Senr. to OWEN MYRICK (son
                  of sd. JOHN) for $300, 377 acres on Rocky Comfort,
JOHN MYRICK Senr. (SEAL). Wit: NATHL. MYRICK, WILLIAM FINCH, Rec.
Feb. 5, 1800.

Pages 598-599:   Jan. 21, 1800 WILLIS PEVEY to RICHARD CARTER for 100
                 silver dollars, land on Middle Creek, adj. JOSEPH
BREED, 200 acres, WILLIS PEVEY (SEAL). Wit: GIDEON GEORGE, HUGH
ARMSTRONG. Rec. Feb. 5, 1800.

Pages 599-600:   Dec. 3, 1798, LEVI PRUITT & ELIZABETH his wife to
                 ISAIAH TUCKER, for $1350, 2 tracts on Middle Creek, adj.
WIGHT, ANDERSON, originally granted to ABSOLAM ISLANDS, 260 acres...
LEVI PRUITT, ELIZA PRUITT (SEAL). Wit: JOHN GIBSON, HENRY HILL,
RICHD. B. FLETCHER JP. Rec. Feb. 6, 1800.

Pages 601-602:   July 25, 1797, JOHN GIBSON to ISAIAH TUCKER...
                 marriage contract between said TUCKER and my beloved
daughter SALLEY GIBSON (now SALLEY TUCKER), land on Middle Creek, adj.
JAMES MCINVALE, AMOS PERSON, THEES HOWARD, CHURCHIL GIBSON, 161 acres,
JOHN GIBSON Senr. (LS). Wit: BARIEY BARRET, WHITEFIELD TUCKER. Rec.
Feb. 17, 1800.

Pages 602-603:   Dec. 28, 1799, WILLIAM DAVIDSON to PETER PARHAM for
                 $260, adj. NATHANIEL SMITH, 115 acres... WILLIAM
DAVIDSON (X) (LS). Wit: PHELAN, MARTIN HAYES. Rec. Feb. 18, 1800.

Pages 603-604:   Aug. 31, 1797, ROBERT ABERCROMBIE to WARREN ANDREWS
                 for $480, 227 acres, Ryal's Branch... ROBERT ABER-
CROMBIE (SEAL). Wit: JOSEPH MCGINTY, M. HUBERT JP. Rec. Feb. 18,
1800.

Page 604-605:   Jan. 2, 1800, WILLIAM NOBLE to WARREN ANDREWS, for
                $1000, land on Ryal's Branch of Ogechee River, 200
acres, part of a tract granted to WILLIAM NOBLES, Jan. 3, 1785...
WILLIAM NOBLE (SEAL). Wit: ROBT. ABERCROMBIE, W. C. ABERCROMBIE.
Rec. Feb. 19, 1800.

Pages 605-606:   Oct. 21, 1793, MOSES GOING of Wilkes Co. to WARREN
                 ANDREWS, for 100 pounds, 100 acres, part of 780 granted
to IGNATUS FEW, 1791... MOSES GOING. Wit: ROBERT ABERCROMBIE, JOHN
OLIVER. Rec. Feb. 20, 1800.

Page 606:   Nov. 14, 1796, NATHAN STUBBS of Columbia Co., to WYATT
            BONNER, for $107, for 100 acres granted to NATHAN STUBBS...
NATHAN STUBBS (SEAL). Wit: Z. FRANKLIN, JNO. WILLIAMS. Rec. Feb.
27, 1800.

Page 608:   Feb. 11, 1800, MICHAEL CODY & MARY his wife, to JOHN FREEMAN
            for $500, 300 acres, granted to JAMES MCCORMICK, 1795, BOOK
PPPP, fo. 747, ad. ISAA BALL, SMITH, HUGH REES... MICHAEL CODY (X) (SEAL),
MARY CODY (X) (SEAL). Wit: MOSES NEAL, PETER HODO. Rec. Feb. 27, 1800.

Pages 609-610:   Aug. 10, 1791, HENRY COX & MARY his wife of Columbia
                 Co. to WYATT BONNER for 50 pounds, 200 acres, adj.
WILDER, originally granted to ALEX MCDANIEL, MARY MCDANIEL & DARLING
MCDANIEL Sept. 9, 1784... HENRY COX (X) (SEAL), MARY COX (C)(SEAL),
ALEY MCDANIEL (S) (SEAL), DARLING MCDANIEL (X) (SEAL). Wit: JOHN
OLIVER, JAMES WHEELER (X). Rec. Feb. 27, 1800.

Pages 610-611:   May 8, 1799, JOHN MOSES to GEORGE CLIFTON for $200,
                 228 acres on north side of the road leading from
Mitchell's Mill to Watson's Mill on Sweet Water, adj. MOSES,... JOHN
MOSES (SEAL). Wit: JOEL NEAL, PETER HODO JP. Rec. Feb. 27, 1800.

Pages 611-612:   Oct. 16, 1798, SAMUEL ALLEN of Greenville Co., South
                 Carolina to MASTEN COX of Warren Co., Ga., for $100,
200 acres, adj. JESSE DYKES, ISHAM PEACOCK... granted to sd. ALLEN
March 31, 1786... SAMUEL ALLEN (SEAL). Wit: NANCY POWELL, NORVELL
ROBERTSON JP. Rec. Feb. 27, 1800.

Pages 612-613:   Jan. 22, 1798, WILLIAM ALLEN of Dunkham Co., North
                 Carolina to MARTIN COX of Warren Co., Ga., for 20

pounds, 5 shillings, 115 acres on Joe's Creek, granted to SAMUEL ALLEN, July 12, 1787... WILLIAM ALLEN. Wit: SALLEY ROBERTSON, NORVELL ROBERTSON JP. Rec. Feb. 27, 1800.

Pages 613-614: Jan. 18, 1800, MOSES GRIER to ABNER CHAPMAN, for $100, 90 acres on Williams's Creek, adj. AARON GRIER, MCLAUGHLIN, HAMMAC, FLEMING... MOSES GRIER (SEAL), MARY GRIER (X) (SEAL). Wit: A. GRIER JP, DEBERA CHAPMAN. Rec. Feb. 27, 1800.

Pages 614-615: Jan. 18, 1800, MOSES GRIER to ABNER CHAPMAN for $1200 land on Williams's Creek, adj. MCLEAN, ROGERS, MOSES GRIER (SEAL), MARY GRIER (X) (SEAL). Wit: AARON GRIER JP, DEBERA CHAPMAN, ROBERT GRIER. Rec. Feb. 27, 1800.

Pages 615-616: Dec. 2, 1796, JOHN PERKINS of Hancock Co., to ISHAM BOMAN of Warren Co. for 50 pounds, 100 acres on Rocky Comfort, adj. NATHANIEL WILLIAMS, PERKINS, AARON BENTON, BENJA. DEES, JONATHAN LOCK, granted to JOHN PURKINS, Aug. 1, 1791, BOOK UUU, fo. 624. JOHN PARKINS (LS). Wit: WM. GILLELAND, ROBERT BOMAN. Rec. March 17, 1800.

Pages 616-617: Dec. 18, 1799, BENJAMIN SMITH of Warren Co. to JOHN SMITH for $43, 100 acres, part of a 200 acre tract in Wilkes Co., when surveyed, now Warren Co., on Briar Creek... BENJAMIN SMITH (M) (SEAL). Wit: DAVID WHEELER (X), ISHAM WHEELER (A), Rec. March 17, 1800.

Pages 617-618: EBENEZER STARNES for 20 pounds to BENJAMIN SMITH, land on north side of Brier Creek, adj. WM. WAMMACKS, 200 acres, Nov. 20, 1787... EBENEZER STARNES (SEAL), Wit: WM. WAMMACK (W), B. MCCULLARS. Rec. March 17, 1800.

Page 619: Aug. 19, 1799, JAMES W. GREEN of Hancock Co. to AMBROSE HADLEY of Warren Co. for $280, land on south side of Rocky Comfort, 112 acres, adj. JOHN BALL, VALENTINE CROMLEY's, JOHN DAVIS... JAMES W. GREEN (LS). Wit: JOHN NEVES, FRANCIS STANBACK. Rec. March 17, 1800.

Page 620: March 15, 1800, JOHN BALL of Warren Co. to JOHN MATHEWS for $500, 228 acres on Rocky Comfort Creek, adj. WM. MIMS... JOHN BALL (LS). Wit: T. MATHEWS, H. CANDLER. Rec. Mar. 17, 1800.

Pages 620-621: Nov. 3, 1798, WILLIAM NEWMON of Warren Co. to JONES PERSONS, for $100, land on Rocky Comfort, adj. RUTHERFORD, 100 acres, WILLIAM NEWMON (X) (SEAL). Wit: T. PERSONS, WILLIAM GUSLING. Rec. March 18, 1800.

Pages 621-622: Aug. 12, 1789, Judges of Inferior Court, ARTHUR FORT, JOHN LAWSON, LEVI PRUITT, SAMUEL ALEXANDER & WILLIAM STITH to SOLOMON SLATTER, TURNER PERSONS, SHAD. F. ELLIN & AMOS PERSONS for $82.50, a lot in the Town of Warrenton, 26,964 sq. ft... L. PRUITT (LS), SAML. ALEXANDER (LS), JOHN LAWSON (LS). Wit: D. NEAL, HENRY HARDIN JP. Rec. Mar. 18, 1800.

Pages 622-623: Aug. 12, 1799, Judges of Inferior Court of Warren Co., (same as above on both parts), for $52, a lot 26,964 sq. ft. (same signatures). Wit: SEPTIMUS WEATHERBY. Rec. March 18, 1800.

Pages 623-624: Aug. 24, 1798, SOLOMON BAREFIELD of Hancock Co. to JOHN RUDDSILLE of Warren Co. for $100, 375 acres, originally granted to SAMUEL CRESWELL, Oct. 1785... SOLOMON BAREFIELD (SEAL). Wit: A. SCOTT, DUNCAN MCCOWEN. Rec. April 15, 1800.

Pages 624-625: Oct. 12, 1797, JOHN DAVIS of Warren Co. to NICHOLAS WILLIAMS of same, for $114, 76 acres on Rocky Comfort adj. LOCKE, RUTHERFORD, BALL, MIMS, 75 of which was granted 1795, the other acre bought of JOHN RUTHERFORD... JOHN DAVIS (ID). Wit: JOHN MATHEWS, ABRAHAM ROE. Rec. April 24, 1800.

Page 625:   June 20, 1799, WILLIAM MIMS & NEOMA his wife to NICHOLAS
             WILLIAMS, for $500, 100 acres on Rocky Comfort... WILLIAMS
MIMS (2) (SEAL), NAOMI MIMS (SEAL). Wit: JOHN MATHEWS, SOL. SLATER.
Rec. April 24, 1800.

Pages 626-627:   Dec. 23, 1799, BENJAMIN SMITH to WILLIAM MCCOWLES, of
                  Richmond Co., for $257, 200 acres originally in
Wilkes Co. granted Jan. 25, 1787... BENJAMIN SMITH (X) (SEAL), LUCY
SMITH (X) (SEAL). Wit: JAMES ROQUEMORE, JOSEPH WHITE. Rec. April 24,
1800.

Pages 627-628:   Sept. 25, 1786, ROBERT CHRISTMAS of Green County,
                  Gent. to SIMON SALTER of Richmond Co., for 100 pounds,
one year's lease on a tract of land... R. CHRISTMAS (SEAL). Wit:
LEW JONES, CHARLES LENN. Rec. April 25, 1800.

Pages 629-630:   Sept. 25, 1786, ROBERT CHRISTMAS to SIMON SALTER for
                  5 shillings, land on Hart's Creek, granted 1786, adj.
ASKINUS' land... ROBERT CHRISTMAS (SEAL). Wit: LEW JONES, CHARLES LINN.
Rec. April 29, 1800.

Pages 630-631:   Oct. 3, 1786, SIMON SALTER to JOHN PINKSTON for 100
                  pounds a year's lease, (same land as above). SIMON
SALTER (S) (SEAL). Wit: LEW JONES, CHARLES LIN. Rec. April 29, 1800.

Pages 631-632:   Dec. 12, 1798, JOHN PINKSTON of Washington Co. to
                  JOSIAS RANDAL for $400, 200 acres in Warren Co., JOHN
PINKSTON (X) (SEAL). Wit: JOSIAS WRIGHT, ARCHD. SMITH. Rec. April
29, 1800.

Pages 632-633:   March 7, 1799, LEWIS WRIGHT, Sheriff of Warren Co. to
                  MOSES GOING, whereas HENRY CANDLER & MOSES GOING each
obtained a judgment in Inferior Court against WILLIAM SANDERS, 352
acres, the greater part of a grant to IGNATIUS FEW, June 18, 1793,
adj. WOOTEN, WILLIAMS, ALEXANDER... LEWIS WRIGHT (SEAL). Wit:
ANDERSON BERRY, JNO. MCMURRAIN (X). Rec. May 5, 1800.

Pages 634-635:   May 11, 1799, HADDON PARHAM & JOEL HEATH to JOSIAS
                  WRIGHT, for $300, land, adj. BOWMAN, CHRISTMAS, ANDREW
KING (now in hands of JOSIAS WRIGHT)... HADDON PARHAM (SEAL), JOEL
HEATH (SEAL). Wit: RAYSTON HEATH, RICHD. B. FLETCHER JP. Rec.
June 6, 1800.

Page 635:   May 27, 1797, JOHN MOUTREY to BURREL BROOM for 300 silver
             dollars, 200 acres, adj. KINGS, BOHANNONS, MARSHALLS...
JOHN MOUTRAR, JOEL MOUTRAY (SEAL). Wit: AMBROSE EDMONDSON, JOHN
MYRICK. Rec. June 6, 1800.

Page 636:   April 7, 1800, JAMES DAVIES of Warren Co. to JOHN BALL of
             same for $50, 100 acres, part of a tract granted to Widow
PETTER, on Rocky Comfort adj. Widow MIMS, STEPHEN WRIGHT, JOHN TORRENCE.
JAMES DAVIES (ϙ) (SEAL). Wit: WOOD MORELAND, DAVID BROOM, JOHN
MATHEWS J. J. C. Rec. June 6, 1800.

Pages 1-2:   Jan. 10, 1801, JAMES BUSH of Warren Co. to WILLIAM GAZA
             of same, for $600, 380 acres, part of two surveys granted
to BAXTER JORDAN conveyed to sd. BURK by three different deeds, adj.
ABBOTT's land, lands granted to AVERETT & BUSH, JACOB BROOKS land,
to the branch below BARTON's... JAMES BURK (##) (LS), Wit: JOEDAY
NEWSOM, JAS MCCORMICK JP. Rec. July 14, 1801.

Pages 2-3:   March 8, 1797, FRANCIS & DENNIS DOYLE of Savannah,
             Merchants, to WILLIAM ANGLIN of Warren Co. for $150, 100
acres in the Parish of St. Paul, adj. ABSOLUM JACKSON, Williams' Creek..
FRANCIS DOYLE (LS), DENNIS DOYLE (LS). Wit: FRANCIS MALLARY, JOHN
CUNNINGHAM, WILLIAM JONES. Rec. July 14, 1801.

Pages 3-4:   April 25, 1798, WILLIAM ANGLING of Wilkes Co. to ROBERT
             MATHEWS of same, for $200, 100 acres (same as above)...
WILLIAM ANGLIN (LS). Wit: JOHN DIXSON, SOLOMON DIXSON. Rec. July
14, 1801.

Pages 4-5:   May 13, 1801, DAVID NEAL & JOYCE his wife to ARTHUR
             MATHEWS for $50, land on SW side of Little Brier Creek,
surveyed July 13, 1797... DAVID NEAL (LS), JOYCE NEAL (LS). Wit:
REUBEN REESE, JAS. MCCARMICK. Rec. July 15, 1801.

Page 5:   April 20, 1801, ROBERT MATHEWS of Wilkes Co. to SOLOMON
          MATHEWS of Warren Co. for $500, 100 acres on Williams Creek...
ROBERT MATHEWS (X) (LS). Wit: RONERT PARKER, JAMES BURT (BURK?).
Rec. July 15, 1801.

Page 6:   Feb. 14, 1801, BENJAMIN REESE & SARAH his wife of Columbia
          Co., to HUGH REESE of Warren Co. for $100, 47 acres, granted
to JAMES WRIGHT and sold under the act of confiscation to JOHN GARRETT
Sept. 20, 1785, adj. land owned by HUGH REESE... BENJAMIN REESE (LS),
SARAH REESE (LS). Wit: MATHEW MCCRARY, P. HODO JP. Rec. July 15, 1801.

Page 7:   April 25, 1801, WILLIAM FRANKLIN & MARY his wife of Warren
          County, to WILLIAM COWLER of Columbia Co. for 25 pounds, 135
acres, adj. HICK SMITH, land surveyed for ABSALOM JACKSON... (Signed)
GEORGE FRANKLIN Administrator (LS). Wit: GEORGE HERNDON JP, WILLIAM
WHITE Senr., Rec. July 15, 1801.

Pages 7-8:   May 16, 1801, JOHN WATSON of Columbia Co. to THOMAS
             CHILDREA of Warren Co. for $100, 25 acres, JOHN WATSON
(LS). Wit: EDWARD SILLS (R), JOHN WILSON JP. Rec. July 15, 1801.

Pages 8-9:   Sept. 25, 1798, GEORGE GRANBERRY of Jefferson Co. to
             REUBEN BARROW of Warren Co. for $40.80, land on Joe's
Creek, Rocky Comfort, 100 acres, part of a tract granted to GEORGE
GRANBERRY May 24, 1796, adj. GEORGE DYLES... GEORGE GRANBERRY (SEAL).
Wit: BENJAMIN WARNER, MOSES GRANBERRY. Rec. Aug. 1, 1801.

Page 9:   April 25, 1801, WILLIAM FRANKLIN (deed not completed)...

Pages 9-10:   March 3, 1801, JOHN BAITS to JOSEPH EVANS for $540, 88
              acres on south side of Little River, adj. WILLIAM BERRY,
HARDIN, ... JOHN BIATS (LS), JEMIMA BAITS (X) (LS). Wit: THOMAS
PORTER JP, JAMES WILLIS JP. Rec. Aug. 1, 1801.

Pages 10-11:   Feb. 9, 1801, JEREMIAH BUKHALTER & DORCAS his wife to
               HUGH REESE, for $650, 147 acres on Golding Creek. adj.
MICHAEL BUKHALTER, HAIRBUCK, STERLING GARDNER... JEREMIAH BUKHALTER (LS),
DARCAS BUKHALTER (LS). Wit: JAMES MECAM, SAMPSON IVY, P. HODO. Rec.
Aug. 1, 1801.

Page 11-12:   May 29, 1801, HUGH REESE & ELIZABETH his wife to JACOB
              BUKHALTER, for $600, 147 acres on Golding Creek... HUGH

REESE (LS), ELIZABETH REESE (X) (LS). Wit: LAW D. RYAN, JOEDAY NEWSOM JP. Rec. Aug. 1, 1801.

Pages 12-13:   Oct. 24, 1796, JAMES BOON of Warren Co. to PRIOR GARDNER of Halifax Co., North Carolina for $675, 322½ acres on both sides of Long Creek... JAMES BOON (SEAL). Wit: T. PERSONS, WORMLEY ROSE. Rec. Aug. 3, 1801.

Page 13:   June 23, 1797, MASS GOING & AGNES his wife of Warren Co. to PRIOR GARDNER of same for $500, 92 acres on Long Creek of Ogechee, granted to JOHN EDMUNDSON March 6, 1790, MOSES GOING (LS), AGNES GOING (X) (LS). Wit: REUBEN WINFREY, SAMUEL HOWELL. Rec. Aug. 5, 1801.

Page 14:   Oct. 16, 1800, MOSES GOING of Wilkes Co. to SAMUEL ALEXANDER of Warren Co. for $100, 352 acres on Ogechee, at time of survey in Wilkes Co., but now part in Wilkes and part in Warren, granted to IGNATIUS FEW June 18, 1793, formerly belonging to WILLIAM SANDERS... MOSES GOING (LS). Wit: M. ALEXANDER, J. BANKSTON. Rec. Aug. 25, 1801.

Page 15:   JOEL MCCLENDON bound to EDMUND WALSH for 200 pounds, Jan. 25, 1790... in case of trouble in title of 100 acres of land.. (headed Hancock Co., Ga.,)... JOHN MCCLENDON (SEAL). Wit: SAML. MCGEE, EPHRAIM MOORE JP. Rec. Sept. 3, 1801.

Pages 15-16:   Aug. 15, 1801, WILLIAM STITH of Warren attorney, to ROBERT BALTON & JOHN BALTON of Savannah... STITH indebted to sd. BALTON's for $1122.26... 460 acres on Ogechee in Warren Co. adj. lands of ROBERT ABERCROMBIE, WARREN ANDREWS, & RICHARD SHIP called Mayfield... WILLIAM STITH (LS). Wit: JAS. H. SCOTT, CURTIS BALTON. Rec. Sept. 7, 1801.

Page 17:   Oct. 25, 1798, WILLIAM HOWARD of Warren Co. to JACOB TOMLIN for $200, 100 acres in Warren Co. adj. SAMUEL NEAL, THOMAS SPRINGER, JOHN MOSES Junr... WILLIAM HOWARD (LS). Wit: JAMES TOMLIN, BENJAMIN HOWARD. Rec. Oct. 3, 1801.

Page 18:   Jan. 29, 1799, JACOB TOMLIN to MICHAEL FLINN for $210, 100 acres, adj. SAMUEL NEAL, HOWARD & SPRINGER, JOHN MOSES Junr. JACOB TOMLIN (LS). Wit: JAMES TOMLIN BS, JAS MCCORMICK JP. Rec. Oct. 3, 1801.

Pages 18-19:   Dec. 28, 1799, DAVID CASTLEBERRY of Hancock Co. to EDWARD CASTLEBERRY, for $250, 112 acres on Ogechee, granted to HILL BARNES 184 acres, April 3, 1787, DAVID CASTLEBERRY. Wit: JOSEPH HOWEL, CALLINSTON WATERS. Rec. Oct. 3, 1801.

Pages 19-20:   Feb. 9, 1801, ETHELRED THOMAS of Warren Co. to PETER NEWSOM, for $100, 110 acres on south side of Watery Branch... E. THOMAS (LS). Wit: J. PRUITT, WM. BYROM. Rec. Nov. 5, 1801.

Pages 20-21:   Nov. 1, 1799, PETER NEWSOM to SOLOMON NEWSOM for $165, 148 acres, granted to SOLOMON NEWSOM Jan. 16, 1786... SOLOMON NEWSOM (LS). Wit: JOHN NEWSOM, WILLIAM CASON JP. Rec. Nov. 5, 1801.

Pages 21-22:   Oct. 9, 1801, WOOTEN O'NEAL of Wilkes Co. to JONATHAN HAGUTY ofr $500, land on Ogechee adj. EMERY ROGERS, DAVID FELPS, THOMAS LOCKET, 170 acres... WOOTEN O'NEAL (LS). Wit: D. HUBERT, DELPHY HUBERT (X). Rec. Nov. 5, 1801.

Pages 22-23:   Aug. 30, 1800, JOHN O'NEAL of Washington to WOOTEN O'NEAL of Wilks Co. for $500, (same as above)... JOHN O'NEAL (X) (LS). Wit: JESSE ONEAL, SAMUEL THOMPKINS. Rec. Nov. 5, 1801.

Page 23:   State of Ga., Warren Co. by NORWELL ROBERTSON one of the Justices appointed to keep the peace in and for the county aforesaid, NATHAN BRIDGES personally appeared before me and being duly sworn deposeth and saith, that on a certain time, when an appeal case was depending & determined between JAMES DURHAM appellant & EDWARD MURPHEY respondent which of record appears to have been on the 21st day of Feb. last in an affray with BENJAMIN GATES he the said NATHAN BRIDGES did seize and with his teeth bite off a part of the left ear of the said BENJAMIN GATES which confession on Oath the said NATHAN BRIDGES doth Voluntarily make and of his own free will acknowledge. Dec. 1, 1801. NATHAN BRIDGES. Rec. Dec. 3, 1801.

Pages 23-24:   Nov. 25, 1800, HENRY COOPER of Warren Co. to ARTHUR JENKINS for $76, 132 acres on Long Creek, part of 200 granted to EDWARD NUGENT April 28, 1794,... HENRY COOPER (X) (LS). Wit: S. CAMP, RICHD. TERRELL. Rec. Dec. 4, 1801.

Pages 24-25:   Dec. 22, 1796, JOHN RICE of Warren Co. to RICHARD SMITH, for 100 pounds, 150 acres on Hardin's Creek, adj. RICE's line... JOHN RICE (LS). Wit: THOS. CREDILLE, WILLIAM JERWIN. Rec. Dec. 4, 1801.

Pages 25-26:   Oct. 12, 1799, BENTON SPIER of Warren Co. to ARDIN SANDERS for $200, land on Rocky Comfort, adj. JOHN COOK, JOHN PERKINS, THOMAS SEALOE's (?) line... BENTON SPIER (LS). Wit: JOHN WILLIAMS, WILLIAM LOGUE (X). Rec. Dec. 4, 1801.

Pages 26-27:   Dec. 23, 1797, DAVID CASTLEBERRY of Jackson Co. to MARK LITTLETON of Warren Co. for $5, land in Warren Co. adj. RICHARD CASTLEBERRY, granted to WILLIAM BARNETT May 24, 1787, DAVID CASTLEBERRY (LS). Wit: ALEXR MASON JP, JACOB LITTLETON. Rec. Dec. 4, 1801.

Page 27:   JOHN MANNING of Warren Co. for $175, to JOHN CHAMPION, JOHN MANNING & ELIZABETH his wife... part of tract on Deep Creek, originally granted to JOSEPH MAY, May 28, 1788. JOHN MANNING (X) (LS) ELIZABETH MANNING (X) (SS). Wit: JOHN GAZA, WILLIAM JONES (X). Rec. Dec. 16, 1799.

Pages 27-28:   July 18, 1801, JOHN SAXON to MICAJOH DARDEN, for $350, 129 acres, part of 200 granted to ANDREW BURNS?... May 15, 1797, adj. land granted to MOSES GRIER... JOHN SAXON (SS). Wit: JOHN ROGERS, WILLIAM DARDEN. Rec. Dec. 5, 1801.

Page 29:   Apr. 2, 1801, JOHN TORRENCE to ANSIL PARISH for $200, land on Long Creek of Ogechee, where the Public Road from Stith's Mill on Ogeechee to Augusta crosses to said Creek, bounded JESSE JAMES, JOHN EDMONDSON, ROBERT JOHNSTON, originally run for CHARLES MCCULLAR, dec'd... part of a grant of 350 to sd. THOMAS April 17, 1789... 104 acres... JOHN TORRENCE (SS). Wit: JOEL NEAL, JAS. MCCORMICK. Rec. Dec. 5, 1801.

Page 30:   PHILIP POOL of Warren Co. for good will to my son HENRY POOL give a sorrel horse... PHILIP POOL (SS). Wit: JOHN BRUTON. Rec. Dec. 5, 1801. Made Sept. 26, 1801.

Pages 30-31:   Nov. 23, 1799, HANNAH RICHARDSON of Warren Co. to PETER PERRY of same, for $150, 116 acres on Long Creek, HANNAH RICHARDSON (H), (SS). Wit: JOEL NOUTREY, ABSALOM (ABRAHAM?) PERRY (P). Rec. Dec. 5, 1801.

Page 31:   Jan. 6, 1801, PETER HODO to DREWRY MCCULLERS of Warren Co. for $100, 100 acres on west side of still house Branch, part of 200 purchased of BENJAMIN RICHISON, adj. JONES, HEARSLING? where RICHARD CODY now lives... PETER HODO Jr. (SS). Wit: RICHD HODO, JAS. MCCORMICK, JAMES CARTER JP. Rec. Dec. 5, 1801.

Page 32:   Aug. 21, 1801, ALEXANDER SMITH of Washington Co. to ELIJAH SMITH of Warren Co., ALEXANDER SMITH & wife MOTHEW, 100 acres

258

in Warren Co. on Brier Creek... ALEXANDER SMITH (X), MOTHEW SMITH (X).
Wit: JONAH N. KENNEDY, CHARLES RAY. Rec. Dec. 23, 1801.

Pages 32-34:   Dec. 4, 1784, EDWARD PILCHER to ROBERT MCCLARY for 80
                pounds, 150 acres in Burk Co. on Ogechee River, adj.
YARBROUGH, originally granted Feb. 7, 1775 to EDWARD PILCHER... EDWARD
PILCHER. Wit: WM. WALKER, JOSEPH HAMPTON. Renunciation of dower.
LYDIA PILCHER... Rec. Jan. 9, 1802.

Pages 34-35:   Nov. 11, 1795, LAZEROUS PHILLIPS & WINNEYFORD his wife
                to BLAKE PERRY for 100 pounds... (later) BLAKE PERRY...
part of 200 acres tract, granted to BUCK POWEL July 3, 1787...
LAZERUS PHILLIPS (X) (SS), WINNEYFRED PHILLIPS (X) (SS). Wit: JNO
CODY, WM. MUSGROVE, SENTARY? POWEL (P). Rec. Jan. 28, 1802.

Pages 35-36:   Nov. 26, 1792, OWEN MCGARR & ANN his wife of Richmond
                Co. to REUBEN JACKSON of Columbia Co. for 150 pounds,
80 acres on Ogechee, granted Feb. 3, 1785... OWEN MCGARR (X) (SS), ANNE
MCGARR (X) (SS). Wit: JNS LAMAR, JOSEPH HUBS. Rec. Jan. 20, 1802.

Pages 36-37:   Dec. 1, 1801, REUBEN JACKSON of Warren Co. to JOHN
                RUSHING of same, for $1000, 150 acres on Ogechee, granted
to sd. JACKSON May 24, 1787, REUBEN JACKSON (SEAL). Wit: JNO C. CURRIE
ARTHUR FORT JC. Rec. Jan. 21, 1802.

Pages 37-38:   May 8, 1801, DAVID GOLDING of Warren Co. to STARLING
                JONES, for $80, 20 acres on Golding's Creek, DAVID
GOLDING (X). Wit: SAM. BEALL, JOHN MATHEWS. Rec. Jan. 21, 1802.

Pages 38:   Jan. 25, 1800, JAMES JONES of Washington to AMOS PERSONS of
            Warren for $240, land on Middle Creek along a line agreed
upon by EZEKIEL MILLER & J. JORDAN WATTS, 100 acres... JAMES JONES (SEAL)
Wit: JESSE ARMSTRONG, SAML. PRUITT JP. Rec. Jan. 31, 1802.

Page 39:   June 25, 1801, PETER HODO & SALLY his wife of Warren Co. to
            DRURY MCCALLARS of same, for $20, 200 acres adj. WM. MAYS,
Widow MAYS, ROBT. WILLIS... PETER HODO (SEAL), SALLY HODO (SEAL).
Wit: JAMES CODA, WM. CORAM, L. PRUITT. Rec. Dec. 2, 1802.

Pages 39-40:   Dec. 23, 1800, POLLY HOBART (HOBALT?), for $300 to
                SAMPSON WILDER land on Hart's Creek, adj. WM. WAGGONER,
MARTHA BULASTER, 50 acres... POLLEY HOBELT (X) (SEAL). Wit: DARLING?
MCDANIEL, A. PERSONS JP. Rec. Feb. 2, 1802.

Page 40:   June 7, 1801, BUCKNER DARDEN of Pickering County, Mississippi
            Territory, to HENRY PEEBLES of Warren Co., Ga., for $360
tract of land on Middle Creek... BUCKNER DARDEN (SEAL). Wit: ?
ROSE, STARLING JONES

Page 41:   Jan. 7, 1800, JOEL MCCLENDON of Hancock Co. to THOMAS HEATH
            of Warren Co. for $275, land on Rocky Branch of Ogechee, adj.
STEPHEN BISHOP, ABRAHAM HILTON, 100 acres, part of 200 including the
plantation whereon WM. CHEATAM now lives, agreeable to a plat given
from JOSEPH RICHARDSON to EDMUND WALCH,... JOEL MCCLENDON (SEAL).
Wit: M. HUBERT, WM. HEATH, JAMES HEATH. Rec. Feb. 3, 1802.

Pages 41-42:   Wilks Co., Ga., SOLOMON BARFIELD of Washington Co. for
                love to son in law SAMPSON WILDER & SARAH his wife,
dividing line between sd. WILDER & CHARLES WEBB, 110 acres... SOLOMON
BARFIELD Feb. 14, 1792. Wit: L. PRUITT JP. Rec. Feb. 3, 1802.

Pages 42-43:   Dec. 22, 1801, THOMAS PATE only heir of JOHN PATE, dec'd
                of Jackson Co. to WILLIAM ROBERTSON of Warren Co. for
$200, 200 acres on Ogechee, granted to JOHN PATE on July 20, 1786...
THOMAS PATE (SEAL). Wit: WILLIAM HEADEN, JAMES HENDRIE JP. Rec.
Feb. 5, 1802.

Page 43:   Oct. 20, 1799, ROBERT PUGH & ALCEY PUGH his wife to ICHABOD
            COX for $625, 153½ acres on west side of Little River, adj.
JOHN IRWIN, WILLIBY HAMMOCK, CASEY COX... ROBERT PUGH (SEAL), ALCEY
PUGH (SEAL). Wit: JOHN MCGINTY, ASA COX, JOHN BAKER. Rec. Feb. 6,
1802.

Page 44:   Jan. 29, 1800, MARK LITTLETON of Warren Co. to JACOB LITTLETON
            for $500, land adj. FLOURNOY, JOHN SNELLING, WM. BREWER,
229 acres, part of 100 acres granted to sd. MARK Nov. 9, 1799, part of
500 granted to JNO KELLY July 3, 1787, and conveyed to sd. MARK Sept.
21, 1793, and part of 104 acres granted to WM. BARNETT, May 24, 1787,
and bequeathed to JOHN MADDOX, sold to DAVID CASTLEBERRY then to
MARK LITTLETON Dec. 3, 1799... MARK LITTLETON (SEAL). Wit: BENJ.
OLIVER Jr., RICHMOND CASTLEBERRY Senr. Rec. Feb. 10, 1802.

Page 45:   Oct. 27, 1792, SARAH MCKINLEY of Columbia Co. to JOHN CLOWER
            for 40 pounds, 200 acres on Ogechee, granted to SAMUEL
BRASWELL Feb. 2, 1786, sold to SYLVANUS ROBESON then to SARAH MCKINLEY
SARAH MCKINLEY (SS). Wit: JAMES RYAN, THOS. WHITE JP. Rec. Feb.
11, 1802.

Page 46:   July 5, 1797, MATTHEW PARHAM of Warren Co. to NATHANIEL
            PARHAM, son of MATTHEW of Hancock Co. for love & affection
gives 130 acres, including part of a 200 acre grant to THOMAS SMITH...
line made for ELISHA ROBERTS now HENRY WALKER... MATHEW PARHAM (SEAL).
Wit: PATSEY FRANKLIN (X). Rec. Feb. 11, 1802.

Pages 46-47:   Dec. 17, 1801, JOHN SALLIS of Warren Co. to MOORE CARTER,
               for $50, 14 acres, part of grant to JOHN SALLIS May 8,
1801... adj. DUNAWAY, JAMES CARTER... JOHN SALLIS (SEAL). Wit: JNO.
HASAWAY?, JOEDAY NEWSOM JP. Rec. Feb. 12, 1802.

Pages 47-48:   Dec. 31, 1801, SEPTIMUS WEATHERBY of Warren Co. to
               THOMAS FONTAINE, for $400, land on Hart's Creek, 280
acres... adj. WORMLEY ROSE, JAMES PARHAM, PETER PERKINS, THOMAS BRANNON.
SEPTIMUS WEATHERBY (SEAL). Wit: J. MATHEWS JP. DAVID COX. Rec.
Feb. 12, 1802.

Pages 48-49:   Aug. 20, 1801, RICHARD SMITH of Warren Co. to JESSE
               DEWBERRY for $400, land on Warden's Creek, 150 acres,
RICHARD SMITH (SEAL). Wit: JAMES HENSERSON, ALSEY SANDERS, JNO.
BATTLE JP. Rec. Feb. 15, 1802.

Page 49:   Feb. 19, 1801, JACOB LITTLETON of Warren Co. to WILLIAM
            FLOURNOY of same for $400, 240 acres, deed from MARK
LITTLETON to son JACOB, part of 100 granted to JOHN KELLY, July 3,
1787, and part of 184 acres granted to WM. BARNETT May 24, 1787...
JACOB LITTLETON (SEAL). Wit: MARK LITTLETON, THOS. FRIEND JP. Rec.
Feb. 15, 1802.

Pages 49-50:   Nov. 12, 1799, JOHN CLOWER to PETER CLOWER for $200,
               200 acres in Wilks Co. (now Warren) on Ogechee, adj.
SAMUEL BRASWELL... JOHN CLOWER (SEAL). Wit: JACOB CLOWER, RANSOM
HOWEL JP. Rec. Feb. 15, 1802.

Pages 50-51:   Dec. 21, 1801, JONES PERSONS of Warren Co. from HAMMOND
               WILKINSON of Montgomery Co. for $500, land on Rocky
Comfort, adj. BEASLEY, VERDIN, PELEG ROGERS, 150 acres, granted to
JOSEPH HIGGINBOTHAM May 24, 1787... HAMMOND WILKERSON (SEAL). Wit:
J. PERSONS, A. PERSONS JP. Rec. Feb. 15, 1802.

Page 51:   Aug. 12, 1801, JOSHUA ROE of Warren Co. to RICHARD ROE of
            same for $200, 80 acres, adj. HEATH, WILTON, JAMES PEARCY
on west side of Long Creek, originally granted to ABRAHAM WILTON...
JOSHUA ROE ( ) (SEAL). Wit: H. HUBERT, M. HUBERT JP. Rec. July 16,
1802.

Pages 51-52:   April 10, 1801, DAVIS NEAL of Warren Co. admr. of the
                est. of his Father THOMAS NEAL... to JAMES MECOM for $500,
543 acres, granted Sept. 16, 1785 on Brier Creek, adj. NEWSOM POOL,
another grant for 143 acres May 24, 1796... DAVID NEAL (SEAL). Wit:
JOEL NEAL, JAMES MCCORMICK JP, JAMES NEAL. Rec. Feb. 16, 1802.

Pages 52-53:   Oct. 13, 1795, THOMAS CURTON of Warren Co. to ROBERT
                PUGH of Wilkes Co. for 70 pounds, 153½ acres on Beaver-
dam of William Creek, adj. JOHN TRAVIS, WILLIBE HAMMOCK, part of a
grant to THOMAS CURENTON April 9, 1792... THOMAS CURETON (X) (SEAL).
Wit: JEH PUGH, R. CHRISTMAS. Rec. Feb. 16, 1802.

Pages 53-54:   Feb. 19, 1801, ELIZABETH OREELY of Augusta in Richmond
                Co. to REUBEN MAGEE of Warren Co. for $450, 904½ acres
on Brier Creek, granted March 10, 1797 BOOK ZZZZ fol. 449... property
of JOHN JAMIESON sold for Taces sold unto ELIZABETH GROVE, now
ELIZABETH OREALY, adj. STANFORDS, PHILIPS, CARTER, GRAY, STAY...
ELIZABETH O RIELEY (X) (SEAL). Wit: DAVID B. BUTLER JP, JAS. PERRY.
Rec. Feb. 16, 1802.

Pages 54-55:   Feb. 9, 1801, SIMS WRIGHT Sheriff of Warren Co. to
                MINSAH? HUBERT for $325, 191½ acres on Long Creek...
LEWIS WRIGHT (SEAL). Wit: BENJAMIN WELLS, M. HUBERT JP.

Page 55:   JOSHUA ROE for $60 to JOHN FLOURNOY, 19 acres in Warren Co.
            on Augusta Road, adj. THOMAS DOLE... JNO. FRANCIS FLOURNOY..
JOSHUAH ROE (‡) (SEAL). Wit: JOSIAH BEALEE, M. HUBERT JP. Rec.
Feb. 17, 1802.

Pages 55-56:   Oct. 13, 1799, JOHN TORRENCE to HUGH ARMSTRONG for $300,
                9 acres on Middle or Town Creek, granted to WM. SCOTT
Dec. 21, 1791, and part of a survey originally granted to THOMAS WHITE
March 29, 1795, 300 acres, on old Richmond Co. line, adj. GIDEON
GEORGE... JOHN TORRENCE (SEAL). Wit: THOS. SELL, R. HUTCHINSON,
HENRY HARDIN JP. Rec. Feb. 23, 1802.

Pages 56-57:   Dec. 11, 1799, PARKS KING & MARY his wife of JOHN F.
                FLOURNOY for $80, land adj. SAMUL. YARBROUGH, MATTHEW
HUBERT, 40 acres... PARKS KING (P) (SEAL). MARY KIN (R) (SEAL). Wit:
FRANCIS FLOURNOY, ARCHIBOLD LARY (LACY?). Rec. Feb. 23, 1802.

Pages 57-58:   Jan. 12, 1802, THOMAS CHILDREA of Warren Co. to JAMES
                WILSON for $75, 25 acres on White's Creek, originally
granted to JACOB WATSON... THOMAS CHILDRE (LS). Wit: JESSE CARTER,
JOHN WILSON JP. Rec. Feb. 23, 1802.

Page 58:   Jan. 28, 1802, THOMAS CHILDRE of Warren Co. to JAMES WILSON
            for $125, part of 200 granted to THOMAS CHILDREN Dec. 17,
1784... JOHN WILLIAMS line, White's Creek, THOMAS CHILDRE (SEAL). Wit:
JESSE CARTER, JOHN WILSON JP. Rec. Feb. 23, 1802.

Page 59:   Oct. 23, 1799, THOS. WHITE of Columbia to JOHN A. TORRENCE
            of Warren Co. for $340, land in Childrea's fork of Middle
Creek, granted to THOS. WHITE March 29, 1795, 300 acres... THOS WHITE
(SEAL). Wit: WM. SHOST?, JESSE BUTT JP. Rec. Feb. 24, 1802.

Pages 59-60:   Jan. 29, 1802, THOS. CHILDRE of Warren Co. to EDWARD
                SILLS of same, for $200, granted to sd. CHILDRE 1784,
200 acres... THOS. CHILDRE (SEAL). Wit: JESSE CARTER, JNO. WILSON.
JP. Rec. Feb. 25, 1802.

Pages 60-61:   Nov. 13, 1800, GEORGE CLIFTON to JAMES GRAY for $2000,
                2 surveys on each side of road from Warrenton to Watson's
Mill on Sweet Water, 448 acres, adj. EVIN THOMAS on Beaverdam Creek,
FLINN, MOSES... ROBERT MOSES... GEORGE CLIFTON (X) (SEAL). Wit: THOMAS
DENT, G. W. COTTON. Rec. Feb. 24, 1802.

Page 61:   July 5, 1800, DAVID HUBERT & DELPHY his wife to NATHAN JONES
            of Columbia Co. for $156, 100 acres, on Rocky Comfort of

Ogechee, in Warren Co., adj. JOHN BUTT, STEPHEN WRIGHT, JAMES COTTON, STEPHEN MARSHALL, JOHN W. JACKSON. DAVID HUBERT (SEAL). DELPJY HUBERT (X) (SEAL). Wit: JOHN ANGLIN, M. HUBERT JP. Rec. Feb. 24, 1802.

Page 62:   Jan. 29, 1802, WILLIAM ROBERSON of Warren Co. to PETER
             PEARRY of same, for $300, (later spelled PETER PEAVEY)....
150 acres on Long Creek, granted to JOHN PATE July 20, 1786. deeded to
WILLIAM ROBERSON by THOS. PATE only heir of sd. JOHN... WILLIAM ROBERSON
(SEAL). Wit: JOHN HAYES (X), ANDREW KING JP. Rec. Feb. 25, 1802.

Pages 62-63:   Feb. 23, 1801, JAMES MCCORMICK of Warren Co. to DAVID
               NEAL of same, for $300, 1250 acres in Warren Co. adj.
E. POOL, THOS. NEAL, THOS. JONES, JAS. GRAY, PHILLIP POOL, CASTLEBERRY,
NEWMAN, CRESWELL... except for abt. 40 acres grantes to JAMES CRESWELL..
JAMES MCCORMICK (SS). Wit: JOEL NEAL, J. NEAL. Rec. Feb. 25, 1802.

Pages 63-64:   Jan. 5, 1801, SOLOMON NEWSOM Senr. JOHN NEWSOM & SOLOMON
               NEWSOM Junr. of Warren Co. to DAVID NEAL for $1200, 400
acres granted to sd. SOLOMON NEWSOM April 8, 1785. adj. BURKHALTER,
HOWARD... SOLOMON NEWSOM (SEAL), JOHN NEWSOM (SEAL), SOLOMON NEWSOM
(SEAL). Wit: JOEDAY NEWSOM, JOEL NEAL, JAMES MCCORMICK JP. Rec. Feb.
25, 1802.

Pages 64-65:   Jan. 14, 1799, JESSE ARMSTRONG & CHURCHILL GIBSON to
               DANIEL CULPEPPER all of Warren Co.for $300, 250 acres on
Middle Creek, adj. RICHARD SAMONS, JNO. GILBSON, originally granted to
JOHN TORRENCE, Dec. 13, 1788... JESSE ARMSTRONG, CHURCHILL GIBSON (SEAL).
Wit: ISA. TUCKER, HENRY HILL. Rec. Feb. 25, 1802.

Pages 65-66:   Nov. 2, 1795, HENRY CANDLER to HENRY WAGGONNER for 10
               pounds, 126 acres, adj. CANDLER, HENRY WAGGONNER, part
of a 250 grant... HENRY CANDLER (SEAL). Wit: J. H. CANDLER, W.
STITH. Rec. Feb. 25, 1802.

Page 66:   JOHN HUDSON to JACOB BEALL, $300 for one negro, May 17, 1799,
           JOHN HUTSON (SEAL). Wit: MARY BOND, JESSE BUTT JP. Rec.
Feb. 26, 1802.
           Another deed identical to above except reads JACOB BULL.

           Ga., this certifies that I permitted JNO. DUNAWAY to sell
unto JOHN ENGLISH all that land formerly sold to THOS. ADCOCK, 62
acres, surveyed 1792, originally granted to JOHN DUNAWAY, in Wilks Co.
(now Warren). Dec. 10, 1798. (Signature illegible). Wit: JOHN
RAYN. Rec. Feb. 26, 1802.

Page 67:   Sept. 9, 1800, ISAAC BALL of Warren Co. to HARMAN PERRYMAN
           for $600, 200 acres, adj. land of JAMES COOPER dec'd ISAAC
BALL (SEAL). Wit: JACOB CASTLEBERRY (J). E. THOMAS. Rec. Feb. 26,
1802.

Page 68:   Richmond Co., Ga., Rec'd from Mr. SAMUEL ALEXANDER, Senr.
           a letter to THOMAS B. NORNES of Charleston attorney,
requesting of him to give Mr. WILLIAM ROBERTSON of Wynton Co. a full
discharge against the judgment obtained against him at Orangeburgh
Court he the said ROBERSON paying and satisfying all necessary charges,
I the under named STEPHEN SMITH do therefore acknowledge myself when a
full discharge is given to the said ROBERSON to be justly indebted to
him the said ALEXANDER for whatever the amount may be due on the
hudgement... July 3, 1788. STEPHEN SMITH. Wit: E. ALEXANDER, W. H.
CASTELLAW.
           State of S.C., Co. of Wynton, W. H. CASTELLAW swore to above
June 10, 1789. W. DUNBER JP. Rec. March 3, 1802.

Pages 68-69:   March 5, 1802, ADAM HARDIN of Washington to WILLIAM
               PORTER of Warren Co. for $100, land adj. E.____ WHEELER,
all that tract except for 12 acres in the name of A. JACKSON...
ADAM AHRDIN (X) (SEAL). Wit: ZARED IRWIN JP, JOHN BRUTON. Rec. March.
11, 1802.

Pages 69-70:   Dec. 25, 1801, THEOPHILUS HOWEL of Warren Co. to SAMUEL
               ALLEN for $100, 250 acres adj. JOSEPH HOWEL, W. GRAY,
JNO HOWEL, granted to THEOPHILUS HOWEL Dec. 17, 1801. THEOPLILUS
HOWEL (I) (SEAL). Wit: SALLEY ROBERTSON, NORVELL ROBERTSON JP. Rec.
March 11, 1802.

Page 70:   I hereby relinquish and make over to HENRY GOLDEN all my
           right title interest and claim to any undivided part of a
tract of 515 acres on Golden's Creek, being the tract formerly owned
by my deceased husband at presently DAVID GOLDIN, REUBEN JONES & the
sd. HENRY GOLDEN. Witn: SARAH GOLDIN (S). Rest: GEO. HARGRAVES,
JOHN TORRENCE. Rec. March 11, 1802.

Pages 70-71:   I Sarah GOLDING of Warren Co. for natural love to my
               dau. REBEKAH JONES give a negro boy... SARAH GOLDING (S)
July 26, 1799. Wit: ELISHA WRIGHT, CLARK BLANDFORD. Rec. March 11,
1802.

Page 71:   July 26, 1799, HUTCHINSON, DAVID GOLDING & RICHARD GREEN to
           REUBEN JONES for $300, land on Golding Creek, adj. WILLIAM
BURKHALTER, granted to heirs of HENRY GOLDING 500 acres, Apr. 15, 1791..
RICHD. HUTCHINSON (SS), DAVID GOLDING (X) (SS), RICHARD GREEN (SEAL).
Wit: ELISHA WRIGHT, CLARK BLANDFORD. Rec. June 1, 1803.

Page 72:   May 20, 1788, THOMAS WOOTEN of Wilks Co. to JAMES MCCORMICK,
           for 50 pounds, 280 acres granted to THOMAS WOOTEN July 3,
1787, adj. JACKSON, HOWELL, HOWARD, JONES... THOMAS WOOTEN (SEAL). Wit:
NATHL. COATS, DAVID NEAL... Rec. Mar. 25, 1802.

Page 73:   Aug. 11, 1794, GEORGE UPTON of Warren Co. to JAMES MCCORMICK,
           for 50 pounds, 150 acres on Ricky Comfort Creek, in Richmond
Co. (now Warren), granted July 3, 1787... GEORGE UPTON (SEAL). Wit:
HUGH REES, DAVID NEAL. Rec. Mar. 25, 1802.

Page 74:   Jan. 5, 1795, WILLIAM SMITH of Washington Co. to JAMES
           MCCORMICK... WILLIAM SMITH obtained a grant for 200 acres
Jan. 7, 1786, where McClains Branch runs into Brier Creek... sold for
30 pounds. WILLIAM SMITH (X) (SEAL). Wit: HARDY SMITH, SAMUEL SMITH.
Rec. March 25, 1802.

Pages 74-75:   Feb. 7, 1799, SARAH HILL of Warren Co. to ASA TINDAL
               for $100, tract granted in the name of DAVID PHELPS,
where the road crosses the line between said tract & STEPHEN
ALURENCE, where SARY HILL now is living, 30½ acres.. SARAH HILL (SEAL).
Wit: JOHN HILL, STEPHEN LAURENCE. Rec. March 25, 1802.

Pages 75-76:   Oct. 17, 1801, JOHN HOBSON Sheriff of Warren Co. to
               LEWIS WRIGHT, 19½ acres on Long Creek... property of
WILLIAM RUBY (REELEY?)... JOHN BACON & HENRY HILL, adj. ROBERT BARNET..
JOHN HOBSON (SEAL). Wit: HENRY HARDIN JP, E. THOMAS. Rec. March 21,
1802.

Pages 76-77:   Feb. 1, 1800, JOHN RUDICILLE from SAMPSON WILSER for
               $600, 300 acres on Hart's Creek... SAMPSON WILDER (SS),
Wit: ROBT. PERRYMAN, HENRY HARDIN JP. Rec. March 26, 1802.

Pages 77-78:   April 22, 1795, SAMUEL NORTHINGTON of Oglethorpe Co. to
               JOHN MICHAEL & SAMUEL AURENCE for 10 pounds, 600 acres on
Ogechee, formerly property of JOHN FREEMAN, deed of JOHN CLARK High
Sheriff of Wilks Co... SAMUEL NORTHINGTON (SEAL). Wit: EDMD. CROWDER,
other name illegible. Rec. March 26, 1802.

Page 78:   Sept. 2, 1793, JOHN CLARK Esqr. Sheriff of Wilkes Co. to
           SAMUEL NORTHINGTON for 53 pounds (same land as above) adj.
MOSES GOING, STEPHEN NOBBS, WILLIAM NOBBS, WILLIAM LUCAS, JOSEPH BONNER,
RICHARD SHIP... JOHN CLARK (SEAL). Wit: H. MOUNGER JP. Rec. March
26, 1802.

Page 79:   SARAH GOLDING for natural love to son HENRY GOLDING give a
            negro wench, July 26, 1799. SARAH GOLDING (ᘯ) (SEAL). Wit:
ELISHA WRIGHT, CLARK BLANDFORD. Rec. March 29, 1802.

Pages 79-80:   Feb. 6, 1798, ETHELDRED THOMAS to NEWELL WARD for $200,
                500 acres, part of a 600 acres survey on Rocky Comfort
granted to ETHELRED THOMAS, adj. SOLOMON NEWSOM, ROBERT BARTON... E.
THOMAS (SEAL), NANCY THOMAS (SEAL). Wit: JOHN LOWE, JAMES MCCORMICK
JP. Rec. March 29, 1802.

Page 80:   Feb. 17, 1799, RICHARD BEASLEY to ROBERT PERRYMAN for $60,
            land adj. SHERDAN, 50 acres. RICHARD BEASLEY (8) (SEAL).
Wit: LEML. PRUITT, RICHARD GINN.

Pages 80-81:   Oct. 1, 1798, NATHAN FOWLER of Wilkes Co. to ADAM JONES
                & EDMUND NUGENT elder for a Baptist congregation now
Imbodied and united in church government on Long Creek, for 5 shillings,
2 acres. NATHAN FOWLER (SEAL). Wit: DAVID NEAL, JAMES MCCORMICK JP.
Rec. March 29, 1802.

Pages 81-82:   Dec. 15, 1797, JONES KENDRICK of Warren Co. to ICHABOD
                COX for $270, land on north fork of Williams Creek,
called the Beaverdam, adj. THOMSON's line, 100 acres... JONES KENDRICK
(SEAL). Wit: JOSEPH COHAN?, CASEY COX. Rec. March 29, 1802.

Pages 82-83:   Jan. 3, 1798, ALEXANDER MCCARTER of Warren Co. to CARY
                COX for 100 pounds, land on north fork of Williams Creek.
corner on ROBERT PER's land... JOHN HOG COTTON's line, 150½ acres...
ALEXANDER MCCARTER (SEAL). Wit: JAMES KENDRICK, ICHABOD COX. Rec.
March 30, 1802.

Page 83:   March 17, 1801, ICHABOD COX of Warren Co. to CARY COX for
            $100, land on north fork of Williams Creek, called Beaverdam,
25 acres... ICHABOD COX (SEAL). Wit: JOHN TRAVIX, JOHN SMITH (X).
Rec. March 30, 1802.

Pages 83-84:   Jan. 2, 1793, HARRIS BRANHAM to SAMPSON WILDER for 25
                pounds, 50 acres on Hart's Creek, in Wilks Co., part of
a grant to POLLY BURLASTON Dec. 10, 1788... HARRIS BRANHAM (SEAL), (∇).
Wit: MOUNTAIN HILL, ELISH PRUITT. Rec. March 30, 1802.

Pages 84-85:   Feb. 2, 1801, JOHN EADY of Warren Co. to THOMAS BAZMORE
                for $500, 483 acres on Brier Creek, adj. MERCER's land,
JOHN EADY (SEAL), MARGETT EADY (X) (SEAL). Wit: ROBT NIXON, DRURY
MURPHEY. Rec. March 31, 1802.

Pages 85-86:   Feb. 12, 1801, JOHN HOBSON of Warren Co. to HENRY
                HARRISS (?), for $800, on Ogechee River, granted to
JOSEPH RAELEY June 13, 1791, 200 acres.. JOHN HOBSON (SEAL). Wit:
ANDREW KING JP. Rec. March 30, 1802.

Page 86:   Dec. 14, 1801, AMOS WRIGHT Sr. of Warren Co. to STARLING
            JONES,for 616 Spanish milled dollars, 308 acres AMOS WRIGHT
(SEAL) (𝕏). Wit: ELISHA WRIGHT, JOHN MATTHEWS JP. Rec. March 30,
1802.

Page 87:   Nov. 15, 1798, WILLIAM WILDER to SAMPSON WILDER both of
            Warren Co. for $100, 58 acres on Hart's Creek, adj. GILES
DEWBERRY... WILLIAM WILDER (X) (SEAL). Wit: I. TUCKER, WHITEFIELD
TUCKER. Rec. March 31, 1802.

Pages 87-88:   Aug. 13, 1800, JOHN CASWELL of Warren Co. to SIMON
                HOWELL for $225 (later appears to be HARRELL), land adj.
THOS. JONES, 100 acres... JOHN CASWELL (SEAL). Wit: SAMUEL HARRELL,
GRAY HARRELL. Rec. March 31, 1802.

Pages 88-89:   April 4, 1801, WILLIAM SCOTT of Columbia Co. to JOHN
                 TORRENCE of Warren Co. for $20, nine acres, on Middle
Creek, bounded on north by Richmond Co., land surveyed for RICHARD
WHATLEY, THOMAS WHITE, now property of sd. TORRENCE... WM. SCOTT,
Wit: JAMES HARDIN, JOHN HARDIN. Rec. Apr. 20, 1802.

Page 89:   JAMES SMITH bound to EBENEZER SMITH for $500, condition if
             JAMES SMITH should pay $250 before March 1, 1802, the bound
shall be void... JAMES SMITH (SEAL). Wit: WM. TORRENCE, JOHN TORRENCE.

Pages 90-91:   JAMES SMITH boundin penal sum of $500... to EBENEZER
                 SMITH 100 acres, adj. JOHN BAKER, MOSES DARDAN, GEROGE
HARRIS, JOHN SIMONS, PEARCE BAILEY on Williams Creek,.. JAMES SMITH
(SEAL). Wit: WILLIAM TORRENCE, JNO TORRENCE. Rec. April 23, 1802.
Deed dated Jan. 2, 1801.

Pages 91-92:   Dec. 11, 1786, JOHN MADDOX of Richmond Co. to JOHN
                 OLIVER for 50 pounds, 200 acres in Wilkes Co. on Little
River, granted to ARNOLD ATKINS Aug. 10, 1785, made over to SEPTIMUS
WEATHERBY, adj. CRESWELL's land... JOHN MADDOX. Wit: DAVID MILLER,
ABRAHAM PERKINS, R. HOWARD JP. Rec. Apr. 29, 1802.

Pages 92-93:   Dec. 9, 1801, JOHN OLIVER to BENJAMIN OLIVER for 200
                 pounds, 200 acres on Ogechee... to BENJAMIN OLIVER Senr.
originally granted to MARY WALL Nov. 25, 1786, by sd. WALL to GEORGE
WAGGONNER then to BENJAMIN OLIVER Senr., then to JOHN OLIVER Aug. 14,
1783... JOHN OLIVER (SEAL). Wit: ROBERT OLIVER, H. CANDLER JJC.
Rec. Apr. 29, 1802.

Page 93:   WILLIAM HAMILTON & THEOPHILUS HARGRAVE of Charles Co.,
             Maryland & GEORGE HARGRAVE of Warren Co., Ga., for $780.
paid by HUGH REESE of Warren Co. negroes... WM. HAMILTON, THOS. HAR-
GRAVE, GEO. HARGRAVE (SEALS). Wit: J. STEADMAN, RICHD. HILL. Rec.
April 30, 1802.

Pages 93-94:   July 15, 1800, LEVI PRUITT of Warren Co. to JOHN MC-
                 CORMICK for (amt. not legible) 200 acres, the west part
of a 350 acre tract granted to JOHN TORRENCE March 21, 1789, across
Rocky Comfort, adj. JOSEPH HIGGANBOTHAM, sold to BYRD PRUITT, conveyed
to LEVI PRUITT Sept. 17, 1798... L. PRUITT (SEAL). Wit: D. NEAL,
SAML. PRUITT, JAMES MCCORMICK JP. Rec. May 8, 1802.

Pages 94-95:   Jan. 17, 1802, JAMES SMITH to EDMOND JOHNSTON for $550,
                 300 acres on Brier Creek, adj. GUSLIN, HODO, south part
of a 1000 acre grant to PETER HODO Dec. 15, 1798... JAMES SMITH (SEAL).
Sit: D. STURDIVANT, ELISHA WRIGHT. Rec. May 8, 1802.

Pages 95-96:   Sept. 29, 1790, ABSOLEM BEARDEN & HANNAH his wife of
                 Wilkes Co. to JOHN MCCORMICK of same for 67 pounds, 200
acres adj. FULLER (now HARRELL's land) and Rocky Comfort Creek, surveyed for sd. BEARDEN Nov. 5, 1784... ABSOLUM BEARDEN (X) (SEAL),
HANNAH BEARDEN (H) (SEAL). Wit: BIRD PRUITT, DAVID NEAL, JAMES
MCCORMICK JP. Rec. May 8, 1802.

Page 96-97:   July 11, 1801, JAMES GEORGE & POLLY his wife of Warren Co.
                JAMES GONAD for 400 silver dollars, 120½ acres adj.
JAMES GEORGE, DRURY BANKS, WILLIAM DAVIDSON... JAMES GEORGE (SEAL),
POLLY GEORGE (X) (SEAL). Wit: RICHARD HUTCHINSON, NATHANIEL HUTCHINSON.
Rec. May 17, 1802.

Pages 97-98.   Sept. 10, 1797, NICHOLAS LONG & REBECCA his wife of Wilks
                 Co. to WILLIAM BIRD of Warren Co. for $876, 122 acres in
Warren Co. adj. CURRIE, LEDBETTER, CAMP, CHAMBLESS, FEW, JORDAN...
N. LONG (SEAL), R. LONG (SEAL). Wit: THOS COLLINS, THOS. ORAM JP.
Rec. May 10, 1802.

Page 98:   JOSEPH RILAH of Washington Co. for 100 pounds paid by JOHN
             FREEMAN on Wilks Co. sell 200 acres on north side of Ogechee

Dec. 16, 1791... JOSEPH RILEY (X) (SEAL). Wit: RICHARD SHIP, THOS. BANKS Junr. Rec. May 16, 1802.

Page 99:   Feb. 27, 1792, HENRY MCCOY of Green Co. to JOHN FREEMAN of Wilks Co. for 100 pounds, 400 acres in Wilks Co., HENRY MCCOY (SEAL). Wit: DAVID BANKSTON, R. ABERCROMBIE. Rec. May 2, 1802.

Page 100:   Nov. 2, 1801, JOSEPH WILLIAMSON of Warren Co. to THOMAS MADDOX of same, for $180, 172 acres granted to JOSEPH WILLIAMSON May 8, 1801, adj. E. THOMAS, NEWMAN, LANDRUM, MOOR, PRUITT, HARDIN... JOSEPH WILLIAMSON (SEAL). Wit: JAMES NEAL, JAMES MCCORMICK JP. Rec. June 24, 1802.

Pages 100-101:   Oct. 14, 1799, RICHARD BEASLEY of Warren Co. to THOMAS MADDOX of same, for $300, 100 acres granted to GEORGE NEWMAN May 21, 1786... BOOK JJ Fol. 132-133... RICHARD BEASLEY (B) (SEAL). Wit: D. NEAL, JAS. MCCORMICK JP. Rec. June 14, 1802.

Pages 101-102:   Oct. 14, 1799, RICHARD BEASLEY to THOMAS MADDOX for $300, 200 acres granted to JAMES WAGGONNER Sept. 17, 1787, adj. NEWMAN, JACKSON sold to sd. BEASLEY May 22, 1790... RICHARD BEASLEY (B) (SEAL). Wit: D. NEAL, JAS. MCCORMICK JP. Rec. June 14, 1802.

Page 102:   June 1, 1802, LEWIS WRIGHT of Warren Co. to RICHARD HEATH of same, for $500, 200 acres on Rocky Comfort, adj. TORRENCE, PERKINS, Augusta Road... originally granted to WILLIAM BOMAR Apr. 20, 1786... LEWIS WRIGHT (SEAL). Wit: ZACHARIAH BEAL (BUAL?), TIMOTHY METTHEWS JP. Rec. June 15, 1802.

Page 103:   Oct. 18, 1796, MARTIN HARDIN to MARK HARDIN for 100 pounds, 400 acres on Rocky Comfort, granted to NICHOLAS LONG... MARTIN HARDIN (SEAL). Wit: RANDOLPH BEVILL, JAMES HARDIN JP. Rec. June 16, 1802.

Page 103-105:   Aug. 1, 1707 (sic), JAMES MCFARLAND of Richmond Co. to PATRICK DOYLE for 34 pounds, lot #43 in Wrightsboro, in the province of Ga., adj. ABSOLUM JACKSON, Williams Creek... JAMES MCFARLAND. Wit: JAMES WHITFIELD JP, EZEKIEL ALEXANDER... Rec. June 16, 1802.

Pages 105-106:   THOMAS HATHHORN bound to JOHN ZACHARY for 50 pounds, 1794... condition of land title, adj. BED CARR PERRYMON, THOMAS JAMES (JONES?), 250 acres... THOMAS HATHHORN (SEAL). Wit: HENRY MITCHELL, THOMAS JONES. Rec. June 19, 1802.

Pages 106-107:   Warren Co., Ga., EZEKIEL ALEXANDER of sd. Co. saith that the annexed papers contains a true copy of mortgage given by STEPHEN SMITH to SAMUEL ALEXANDER, Sen. for 3 negroes... June 8, 1801. EZEKIEL ALEXANDER

Page 107:   MOSES ALEXANDER swears that annexed paper is a true copy of a mortgage given to SAMUEL ALEXANDER Sen. by STEPHEN SMITH for 3 negroes. June 9, 1801.

Page 107:   Jan. 11, 1802, ISAAC BURSON to JONATHAN BURSON of Warren Co. for $200, 100 acres on Brushy fork of Brier Creek, adj. Widow DAVIS & E. TARLOR? ... ISAAC BURSON (SEAL). Wit: ISAAC BURSON, P. HODO JP. Rec. July 19, 1802.

Page 108:   April 19, 1802, STARLING GARDNER of Warren Co. to MARTIN HARDIN for $500, a parcel of land in Warrenton, No. 1, on Union Street... STARLING GARDNER (LS). Wit: GEORGE HARGRAVES, LEWIS WRIGHT. Rec. July 19, 1802.

Pages 108-109:   Jan. 19, 1801, MOSES MCKINNY to WILLIAM SMITH of Warren Co. for $300, 100 acres, adj. NEWSOMS Old Fort where TILMAN MCCINNY Now lives, adj. BENJAMIN ADAMS, EDMUND CODY, on

Brier Creek... MOSES MCKINNY (SEAL). Wit: MOSES NEAL, P. HODO, JP. Rec. July 19, 1802.

Pages 109-110: May 14, 1801, MOSES MCKINNEY & MARY his wife to JACOB WATSON of Columbia Co. for $425, 100 acres on Big Brier Creek, adj. JOSEPH WATSON, JACOB WATSON... MOSES MCKINNEY (SEAL), MARY MCKINNEY (SEAL). Wit: JOSEPH WATSON, P. HODO JP. Rec. July 19, 1802.

Pages 110-111: Feb. 6, 1802, DAVID MCCOY of Wilks Co. to ROBERT MOORE Senr. of Warren Co. for $275, 100 acres on Williams Creek adj. WILLIAM N. ALISON, WILLIAM BERRY, granted to ZACHARIAH PHILLIPS Nov. 1, 1774... DAVID MCCOY (SEAL). Wit: WILLIAM KIRKLAND (X), ROBERT MATHEWS. Rec. July 26, 1802.

Page 111: DUDLY RUNNELS of Caswell County, North Carolina for 50 pounds sell to BENJAMIN HUBERT one yellow Negro boy, Dec. 13, 1785. BY. RUNNELS (LS). Wit: M. HUBERT, JOHN TALBERT. Rec. Aug. 31, 1802.

JOHN PARHAM to beloved son PETER PARHAM give my stud horse, Aug. 9, 1802, JOHN PARHAM (X) (SS). Wit: Z. FRANKLIN, HARTWELL JONES. Rec. Aug. 31, 1802.

Pages 111-112: JESSE MILLER of Warren Co. for good will and affection to my son THEOPHILAS MILLER of same Co. give a negro girl, July 28, 1802. JESSE MILLER. Wit: EZEKIEL MILLER, M. HUBERT JP. Rec. Sept. 3, 1802.

Page 112: JESSE MILLER to son JOSHUA MILLER Junr., a negro girl July 28, 1802, JESSE MILLER (same wit. as above). Rec. Sept. 6, 1802.

Pages 112-113: JESSE MILLER to son EZEKIEL MILLER a negro girl, Nov. 7, 1801, JESSE MILLER (SEAL). Wit: JOSEPH BREED, ISIAH TUCKER. Rec. Sept. 7, 1802.

Page 113: Nov. 21, 1800, JOSEPH GEORGE to EZEKIEL MILLER... SUSANNAH GEORGE wife of JOSEPH ... for $100, 100 acres... JOSEPH GEORGE (X) (SEAL), SUSANNAH GEORGE (X) (SEAL). Wit: HENRY HARDIN, GIDEON GEORGE, JESSE MILLER. Rec. Sept. 7, 1802.

Pages 113-114: May 9, 1801, ASA COX to JOHN GILPIN for (amt. not given), land on north fork of Williams Creek, called Beaverdam, adj. MCLAUGHLIN, THOMAS LOCKETT?, CARY COX, land where CARY COX now lives, 50 acres... ASA COX (SEAL), MIRIAH COX (X) (SEAL). Wit: CARY COX, MARTHA COX (X), JOHN BATTLE JP. Rec. Sept. 8, 1802.

Pages 114-115: Oct. 7, 1800, JOHN FLETCHER to WILLY HARRIS both of Warren Co., for $300, land on Rocky Comfort, 100 acres, adj. EDMUNDSON, WELLS, BENJ. WELLS spring, WRIGHT, JOHN FLETCHER (SEAL), MARTHA GLETCHER (X) (SEAL). Wit: WORMLEY ROSE, AMBROSE EDMUNDSON, STARLING GARDNER. Rec. Sept. 8, 1802.

Pages 115-116: April 6, 1802, JNO SALLIS & JAMES GRAY to DRURY MIMS for $1400, 400 acres granted to DRURY & DAVID MCCULLERS Sept. 23, 1784, adj. Widow THOMAS, COOPER, ? CHADY MCCULSAR?, Widow ANDERSON... JOHN SALLIS (SEAL), JAMES GRAY (SEAL). Wit: HUGH REESE, JAS. MCCORMICK JP. Rec. Sept. 8, 1802.

Page 116: I received of E. THOMAS six negroes... to get his right from JAMES HARRISON in South Carolina, May 30, 1791... SOLOMON NEWSOM. Wit: JESSE PITTMAN, JOEDAY NEWSOME. Rec. Oct. 19, 1802.

Pages 116-117: SOLOMON NEWSOM Senr. received a bill of Sale of ETHELRED THOMAS in 1790 for negroes, recorded in Wilks Co., I resign all claim to sd. negroes. Oct. 18, 1802. SOLOMON NEWSOM. Wit: JOEDAY NEWSOM JP, JAS MCCORMICK. Rec. Oct. 19, 1802.

Page 117:   EDWARD GREEN of Warren Co. for affection to my son WM.
             B. GREEN give all my cattle, household furniture... Sept.
28, 1802, EDWARD (EDMOND?) GREEN (LS). Wit: BRYANT MARCHANT, WM.
B. MURPHY. Rec. Nov. 4, 1802.

Pages 117-118:   Sept. 14, 1802, JONATHAN BURSON & ELIZABETH his wife
             for $350, to BEVERLY ESTHERS, 100 acres, originally
granted to ISAAC BURSON, adj. HINSUG, ELIZABETH DAVID & EDWARD TAYLOR,
JONATHAN BURSON (SEAL), ELIZABETH BURSON (X) (SEAL). Wit: W. D.
BUNKLEY, D. STURDIVANT, O BEALLE. Rec. Nov. 5, 1802.

Pages 118-119:   May 16, 1800, JESSE BARFIELD of Warren Co. to ELISHA
             HURT of same, for $675, two tracts on Hart's Creek,
adj. JOHN HOWARD, AARON CINGEFIELD, originally granted to SOLOMON
BARFIELD 1774, 100 acres part of a tract of 500 granted to SOLOMON
BARFIELD Sept. 24, 1784, adj. PETER HODO, .. JESSE BARFIELD (SEAL).
Wit: H. GRIEF, RD. B. FLETCHER JP. Relinquish of dower by HANNAH
BARFIELD (X). Rec. Nov. 5, 1802.

Page 120:   Feb. 3, 1802, DAVID ROBERTSON of Richmond Co. to JOHN
             MATHEWS of Warren Co. for $50, 50 acres on Big Brier Creek,
originally granted to ABSOLEM JACKSON surveyed in April 1787... DAVID
ROBERSON (SEAL). Wit: JOHN SMITH (X), THOS. WESTBAY. Rec. Nov. 5,
1802.

Pages 120-121:   PETER PERKINS of Warren Co. for $100 pd. by WILLIAM
             WHITE of same, for one negro girl... PETER PERKINS (P)
(SS). Wit: T. MATTHEWS JP. Rec. Nov. 8, 1802.

Page 121:   Aug. 6, 1802, WILLIAM RIGBEE to THOMAS RIGBEE of Warren Co.
             for $200, 122 acres on Ogechee River originally granted to
JOSEPH CARTER, adj. RICHARD ROE, conveyed by JAMES THWEATT to sd.
RIGBEE... WILLIAM RIGBEE (X) (SEAL). Wit: JOHN BLAKELY, FISHER GASKIN
(I). Rec. Nov. 8, 1802.

Page 122:   JOSHUA ROE & SARAH his wife of Warren Co. to WILLIAM HEATH
             & THOMAS DOLES of same for $4, 1 acre on Long Creek wife
Carter's line on Augusta Road... JOSHUA ROE (Ŧ) (SEAL), SARAH ROE (X)
(SEAL). Wit: JOSEPH DELOOCH, SAML. YARBROUGH. Dec. 31, 1801. Proven
Aug. 28, 1802

Pages 122-123:   Dec. 31, 1801, JOSHUA ROE & SARAH his wife to THOMAS
             DOLES, for $87, land on Long Creek, originally granted
to ABRAM HELTON... 35 acres, adj. RICHARD ROE, CARTER, JOSHUA ROE (Ŧ),
SARAH ROE (X). Wit: JOSEPH DELOOCH, SAMUEL YARBROUGH.

Pages 123-124:   June 18, 1801, THOMAS BAHANNON to THOMAS DOLES for
             $350, part of a grant to JOSIAH CARTER, adj. to
EDMONDSON's line... widow SEERR's (?) line, JAMES PEAY's line... PARKS
KING... THOMAS BOHANNON (SEAL), WILE BOHANNAN (S) (SEAL). Wit: SAML.
JOHNSTON, ACHD. LAY.

Page 124:   Nov. 6, 1802, WILLIAM HUTCHINSON & MARTHA his wife, formerly
             BURKHALTER, both of Warren Co. to JOSEPH FICKLING of State
of South Carolina for $800, land on Golding Creek, adj. NICHOLAS
HARBUCK, MICHAEL HARBUCK, PERIMON, 187 acres. WILLIAM HUTCHISON (SEAL),
MARTHA HUTCHINSON (X) (SEAL). Wit: STARLING JONES, JOHN MATTHEWS JP.

Pages 124-125:   Feb. 14, 1801, FRANCIS BECK to JOHN RUSHING, for $250,
             125 acres on Rocky Comfort, adj. VERDEN, FRANCIS BECK
(SEAL). Wit: H. CANDLER, THOS. FRIEND JP.

Page 125:   July 28, 1794, RICHARD BROOKS FLETCHER of Warren Co.
             relinquish claim to a negro girl unto WILLIAM CULPEPPER
Senr., bill of sale given by WILLIAM JOHNSTON, Montgomery Co., North
Carolina. RICHD. B. GLETCHER (SEAL). Wit: DANIEL CULPEPPER, HADDUN
PARHAM.

Page 126: Oct. 25, 1799, NATHANIEL FOULSOM to SOLOMON SLATTERS for $200, land on Whetstone Creek, 100 acres adj. FLEWELLEN's line... NATHL. FOULSOM (X) (SEAL), OETHER FOULSOM (X) (SEAL) (her mark). Wit: JOHN MATTHEWS, SHARAK F. ELLEN.

Pages 126-127: Nov. 24, 1801, JAMES PARKER to ROBERT PARKER, for $1000, paid by JOSEPH WHITE, JAMES MATTHEWS & ROBERT PARHAM, 120 acres granted to JAMES GREEN & ABNER T. ELLEN by them deeded to JAMES PARKER. JAMES PARKER (SEAL). Wit: T. MATTHEWS JP, OWEN PARKER

Page 127: April 26, 1802, JNO & WM. LEE acting as guardians to HANNAH, ANDREW & MOSES her brother both children of our Mother, rec'd from THOMAS BUSH and our Mother his wife ELIZABETH full portion of the legacy of WM. FEW Senr. to his dau. ELIZABETH and the heirs of her body... JOHN LEE (SEAL), WM. LEE (SEAL). Wit: STARLING GARDNER, THOS. H. SANDWICH.

Page 127-128: Oct. 15, 1801, STEPHEN MITCHEL of Liberty Co., Ga., to AMBROSE HOLLIDAY of Warren Co. for $2000, 750 acres, several grants, one to RICHARD CRUTCHFIELD 100 acres, one to JOHN COLEMAN, Oct. 11, 1785, one granted to ROGERS QUALLS 200 acres, one granted to THOMAS YARBROUGH, 100 acres Oct. 27, 1783 & one granted to YARBROUGH for 1000 acres, and one to STEPHEN MITCHEL (X) (SEAL). Wit: BARRETT BREWER, HUGH TAYLOR, SOLOMON BEEKCOM... SELAH MITCHEL (X) renunciation of dower.

Page 129: Oct. 28, 1802, JOSEPH MAY of Washington Co., deed of gift to dau. ELIZABETH NEWSOM... negroes... JOSEPH MAY (HHf) (SEAL). Wit: ISAAC HURT, JOEDAY NEWSOM JP. Jan. 6, 1800, JOSEPH GISSARD of Warren Co. to WILLIAM EARNEST for $100, land on Rocky Comfort, adj. CHARLES MCCALLISTER, WM. KIYCHING, RICHD BEASLEY... sd. JOSEPH GRIZARD. JOS. GRIZARD. Wit: L. PRUITT J I C, JOHN NEWSOM.

Pages 129-130: A judgement has been obtained in the name of the Exr. of the estate of WILLIAM GLASCOCK agnst. the Admr. or ADAM HILES, dec'd, debt is in part the est. of JOHN BIDDINGFIELD in favor of MARY & JOHN BEDDINGFIELD, heirs of sd. JNO dec'd... July 26, 1796. ROBERT WALTON, ABRAHAM JONES. Wit: JAMES MASE, C. SEABEMAN. Richmond Co., Ga. Consod Seaberman swore to above Dec. 31, 1796.

Pages 130-131: Feb. 11, 1802, JACOB CAIN of Wilks Co. to JOHN RHYMER, for $600, land on Ogechee, adj. FATHA WOOLEN, 100 acres later JOHN RYMES, JACOB CAIN (SEAL). Wit: JOHN BUSH, WILLIE JONES.

Pages 131-132: Feb. 16, 1802, COLLIN WOOTEN & Wife FATHA to JOHN RHYMES, 100 acres on Ogechee, for $500. COLLIN WOOTEN (SEAL), FATHA WOOTEN (Ч) (SEAL). Wit: WILLIE JONES, DANIEL MORRIS.

Page 132: March 8, 1801, JOHN HILL of Jackson Co., Ga., to JNO RYMES of Warren Co., for $800, 250 acres, granted to JOHN HILL, Feb. 1788. JOHN HILL (SEAL). Wit: WOOTEN ONEAL, JOHN PATTLE JP.

Page 133: Jan. 8, 1802, JONATHAN HAGOTHY to JOHN RHYMES for $500, land on Ogechee, adj. THOS LOCKET, 170 acres, JONATHAN HAGOTHY (SEAL). Wit: JOHN BURK Sr., JNO BURK (may be BUSH).

Pages 133-134: Aug. 8, 1802, THOMAS DOLES & wife of Warren Co. to JOHN LAMAR of Hancock Co. for $600, land on Ogechee near BURCHES MILLS, 128 acres. THOMAS DOLES (SEAL), SUSANNAH DOLES (X) (SEAL). Wit: JOHN MARSHALL, M. HUBERT JP.

Pages 134-135: Jan. 23, 1802, BENJAMIN COOPER to WILLIAM COOPER for $60, land on South side of Long Creek, 15 acres. BENJAMIN COOPER (X) (SEAL). Wit: JAMES FILLING IM, ROBERT FILLING IM (X).

Page 135:   Nov. 6, 1801, JOHN GIBSON to NOAH BUTTS, for $500, 129½
             acres on Middle Creek, adj. WILLIS PERRY, JAMES GEORGE &
others, part of a 1000 acre tract granted to THOMAS YOUNG, and by him
conveyed to HENRY HARDIN and from him to sd. GIBSON, JOHN GIBSON (SEAL).
Wit: ISAIAH TUCKER JP, HIRAM PERRY.

Page 136:   Jan. 16, 1801, JOHN CALDWELL of Columbia Co. to ROBERT
             JOHNSTON of Warren Co. for $428, 200 acres adj. DIAL PEARY,
granted to JAMES COLDWELL Oct. 10, 1785, and willed by sd. JAMES
CALDWELL to JOHN CALDWELL... JOHN COLDWELL (Ɖ) (SEAL). Wit: D.
HUBERT, THOS VINING.

Pages 136-137:   May 9, 1801, ASIA COX to JOHN GILPIN, (amt. blank)
                  land adj. JOHN MCLAUGHLEN, THOMAS SUCKET, 14 acres.
ASIA COX (SEAL), MIRAH COX (X) (SEAL). Wit: JOHN BATTIE JP, CASY
COX, MARTHA COX.

Pages 137-138:   Jan. 31, 1802, JOHN RUSHING to SAMUEL S. KELLY, for
                  $250 (later appears SAMUEL SKELLY)... 125 acres on
Rocky Comfrt, adj. VERDIN. JOHN RUSHING (X) (SEAL). Wit: EPHA.
RENFROE, NORVELL ROBERTSON JP, JOHN HATCHER JP.

Page 138:   Jan. 20, 1800, ANDREW MCCLARY & JAMES MCCLARY, SAMUEL
             MCCLARY of State of North Carolina & County of McBourge
(Mecklinburgh???) to ELIJAH WARTHEN of Washington Co., Ga., for $500,
150 acres in Warren Co. on Ogechee, adj. MURPHEY, granted to EDWD.
PILCHER by KING GEORGE 3rd, then to ROBERT MCCLARY & his heirs.. from
them to ELIJAH WARTEAN... ANDREW MCCLEARY (SEAL). Wit: PHILIP RAWLS,
RICHARD WARTHEN, M. WARTHEN JP.

Page 139:   Jan. 15, 1801, JOHN DYSART of Hancock Co. to PATRICK
             SHANNON of Wilks Co. for $500, granted to IGNATIUS FEW, Jan.
21, 1785 in Wilks Co., but now in Warren, 200 acres JOHN DYSART (SEAL).
Wit: AQUILLA SCOTT, JAMES BOND, SOLOMON ELLIS.

Pages 139-140:   Jan. 1, 1799, HENRY GRAYBILL of Hancock Co. to WILLIAM
                  HEATH of Warren Co., for $100, 100 acres on Long Creek,
originally granted to JAMES HITTON (?) Jan. 24, 1791, HENR GRAYBILL
(SEAL). Wit: S. DUGGEN, EVAN HANSY.

Page 140:   Nov. 13, 1802, AMOS WRIGHT to REUBEN JONES, $400, 169 acres
             on Golding Creek, AMOS WRIGHT (A) (SEAL). Wit: JESSE
MATTHEWS, JOHN MATTHEWS JP.

Pages 140-141:   Jan. 23, 1802, SOL MATTHEWS to ROBERT PARKER, for $800,
                  100 acres on Williams Creek, SOLOMON MATTHEWS. Wit:
ARCHABALD FLEWELLEN, JOHN MATTHEWS J Q P.

Pages 141-142:   Dec. 18, 1802, THOMAS ANSLEY of Warren Co. to son
                  SAMUEL ANSLEY for love and affection, part of an 800
tract on Brier Creek, originally granted to THOMAS ANSLEY while sd.
County was included in Wilkes, May 24, 1787, adj. JEREMIAH DUCKS,
153 acres THOMAS ANSLEY (SEAL). Wit: MOORE CARTER, ALLEN CARTER, JAS.
CARTER JP.

Pages 142-143:   Jan. 14, 1795, JOHN SLATTER of Pendleton Co., S.C. to
                  JOHN BATES of Warren Co., Ga., for 225 pounds specie,
land in St. Paul's Parish in Warren Co., originally granted to JOHN
SLATTER, Sr., adj. J. EVANS, JOHN SLATTER (SEAL). Wit: WITHERS SMITH,
ABRM JOHNSTON JP. (Plat indicated bordering on WM. BERRY, MENDENALLS)

Pages 143-144:   Jan. 1, 1801, VEINSON JOHNSTON & SUSANNAH his wife to
                  GEORGE TURNER for $600, 230 acres on Long Creek of
Ogechee, adj. CHILDERS line, VINSON JOHNSON (SEAL), SUSANNAH JOHNSON
(X) (SEAL). Wit: JOHN C. TURNER, SAMUEL JOHNSON.

Page 144:   Nov. 16, 1802, JOHN MIMS, Junr., WM. MIMS, Junr. & MATHEW
MIMS to WOOD MORELAND of Hancock Co., for $279, land on
Rocky Comfort, adj. JOHN BULL, STEPHEN WRIGHT, ARCHD. FLEWELLEN, 125
acres JOHN MIMS (X) (SEAL), WM. MIMS (X) (SEAL), MATTHEW MIMS (X) (SEAL).
Wit: ISHMEAL BROOKS, DAVID MIMS. (Deed was headed Washington Co., Ga.)

Page 145:   June 16, 1801, JOHN TORRENCE to JAMES WILLIAMS for $500, on
waters of Long Creek, originally granted to JOHN TORRENCE,
corner of land originally run for CHARLES MCCULLARS, now held by
ROBERT JOHNSON, land run for DAVID & DRURY MCCULLARS, now occupied by
THADUIS BEALL, JOHN TORRENCE (SEAL). Wit: JESSE JAMES, IRESUM (?)
BAITS, JOHN MATTHEWS JP.

Page 146:   Nov. 24, 1802, MARGARET GREEN to JESSE CARTER, for $262, 150
acres on White's Creek, part of a 450 acre tract originally
granted to JEREMIAH DUCKWORTH, June 27, 1786. MARGARET GREEN (SEAL).
Wit: JOHN BAYNE, JEREMIAH BURKHALTER.

Page 147:   Sept. 19, 1801, PATRICK SHANNON of Wilks Co. to DANIEL
VAUGHN of Warren Co., for $525, 200 acres originally to
IGNATIUS FEW in Jan. 1785. PATRICK SHANNON (SEAL). Wit: THOS PORTER,
JAMES BAUGHAN.

Page 148:   March 2, 1802, ROBERT SYNNE, Senr. of Warren Co. to DANIEL
MITCHEL of Hancock Co. for $300, land on Lick Creek of
Ogechee, adj. WM. ROBERTSON, CLEMENT WYNN... Lack granted to ABRAM
RIDDICK, ROBERT WYNNE (LS). Wit: D. W. ZACHARY, STEPHEN W. BARNLEY.

Page 149:   April 16, 1801, NORVELL ROBERTSON to RICHARD CURREY, for
$4, 135 acres on Rocky Comfort Creek, granted to NORVELL
ROBERTSON, Feb. 15, 1799, adj. ELIZABETH CASTLEBERRY, JOSEPH HOWEL...
MOSES GRANDBERRY, NORVELL ROBERTSON (LS). Wit: RICHARD TERRELL,
JOHN HATCHER JP.

Page 150:   Feb. 21, 1801, JOSEPH HARVEL to RICHARD CURRY, for $15, 100
acres, adj. RICHARD CURRY & vacant land... JOSEPH HARVELL
(LS). Wit: NORVELL ROBERTSON JP, JOHN HATCHER JP.

Pages 150-151:   Nov. 9, 1800, IGNATIUS FEW of Columbia Co. to CLAI-
BORNE CASTLEBERRY of Warren Co., for $200, 166 acres
on Long Creek, part of a 400 acre tract granted to IGNATIUS FEW Sept.
23, 1784. I. FEW (LS). Wit: COLLENSON WATERS, WILLIAM ROUGHSAW.

Pages 151-152:   May 4, 1799, ARTHUR FORT of Ogechee, to JOHN HAMILL
of Georgetown in the Co. of Warren, for 5 shillings
7 acres on Fort's Creek, UPTON's line, part of a grant to ARTHUR FORT,
Feb. 3, 1785, then in Wilkes Co. ARTHUR FORT (SEAL), SUSANNAH FORT (SEAL).
Wit: RICHD. WHITEHEAD, I. (J?) S. DIXON.

Pages 152-153:   July 1, 1799, ARTHUR FORT & SUSANNAH his wife to JOHN
HAMILL, for $85.72, lot in Town of Georgetown #23 &
#24, bound by GREEN STREET & MCCORMICK STREET, ARTHUR FORT (SEAL),
SUSANNAH FORT (SEAL). Wit: RICHARD WHITEHEAD, J. S. DIXON.

Page 154:   Feb. 19, 1791, ARTHUR FORT & SUSANNAH his wife of Ogechee
to JOHN HAMILL, Merchant for 20 pounds sterling, lots #20
and #25, lot in possession of JOHN HENLY, ARTHUR FORT (SEAL), SUSANNAH
FORT (SEAL), JOHN HAILL (SEAL). Wit: JNO. BARNHILL, JOHN HENLEY.

Pages 155-156:   March 29, 1800, BENJAMIN UPTON & JUDITH his wife, both
of Rocky Comfort, to JOHN HAMILL of George Town for $1,
12 acres on Augusta, adj. ARTHUR FORT & sd. JOHN HAMILL, BENJAMIN
UPTON (SEAL). Wit: BENJAMIN BEUTON JP, NORVELL ROBERTSON JP.

Pages 156-157:   May 15, 1802, WILLIAM ANSLEY of Green Co. to ROBERT
FLOURNOY, for 50 pounds, land in Warren County (for-
merly Wilks), 100 acres, adj. J. AUSTON & WYNNE, formerly MIDDLETON's...
WILLIAM ANSLEY (SEAL). Wit: ELIZA ANSLEY, JOHN CONNEL.

Pages 157-158:   Feb. 27, 1801, JESSE CONNEL of Hancock Co. to WILLIAM
                  ANSLEY, land on Rocky Creek, 163 acres, adj. at time of
survey, PATES, SPIKES, AUSTIN & MIDDLETONS, reference to a grant June
17, 1788. JESSE CONNILL (SEAL). Wit: R. MIDDLETON, JOEL DICKINSON,
R. FLOURNOY.

Page 158:   Sept. 1, 1802, MICHAEL WATLEY of Green Co. to FEDRICK
             DANIEL of Warren Co. for $100, on Middle Creek, granted
Oct. 14, 1788. MICHAEL WHATLEY (X) (SEAL). Wit: WM. DANIEL, JOHN
J. WELLS, NATHAN CULPEPPER.

Page 159:   Nov. 17, 1802, JACOB TURKNETT to CHURCHILL GIBSON of Warren
             Co., for $400, land on Middle Creek, adj. ISAIAH TUCKER,
GIBSON & MOUTAIN HILL. JACOB TURKARET (SEAL). Wit: ISAIAH RUCKER,
Clk. Supr. Ct., WHITEFIELD TUCKER.

Pages 159-160:   State of Georgia, Wilkes County, JOSEPH COOK bound to
                  BENJAMIN HOWARD, for $5000, do sell Negroes, June 8,
1788 JOSEPH COOK (SEAL). Wit: THOMAS RICHARDSON, before L. PRUITT,
J. I. C.

Pages 161-162:   June 1, 1790, SOLOMON NEWSOM of Wilks Co. to FREDRICK
                  NEWSOM & ASA NEWSOM & JOEDAY NEWSOM & WILLIAM NEWSOM
Jr. & DAVID NEWSOME of same, whereas SOLOMON NEWSOM Senr. did obtain
a tract of land 750 acres, made over from SAMUEL HART Feb. 2, 1786,
adj. RUTHERFORD, BENJAMIN FEW, Oke____ (?) River, for 50 pounds, sd.
tract with house, SOLOMON NEWSOM (LS). Wit: JAS. MCCORMICK JP. WYCHE
GOODWIN JP.

Page 162:   Feb. 5, 1801, JAMES BISHOP of Hancock Co. to VINSON JOHNSTON
             of Warren Co. for $800, land on Long Creek, originally
granted to CHILDREN and deed from CHILDRES heirs to sd. BISHOP, containing 226½ acres, adj. JOHN ANGLERS, HUBERT's line, YARBROUGH's line,
JAMES BISHOP (SEAL). Wit: FRANCES STANTACK, M. HUBERT JP.

Page 163:   Dec. 9, 1802, CHRISTOPHER HINTON & AMBROSE EDMUNDSON to
             HUGH REESE, relinquish claim on Grave Yeard in the n. side
of Big Brier Creek, 60 feet square. CHRISTOPHER HINTON (SEAL), AMBROSE
EDMUNDSON (SEAL). Wit: BENJAMIN REESE, JOHN BURKHALTER.

Pages 163-164:   Feb. 24, 1800, ROBERT MOORE to JACOB BUTT, for $170,
                  50 acres, originally granted to THOMAS SMITH, dec'd,
adj. at time of survey, SMITH & DOYLE, MULKEY. (Plat in book). ROBERT
MOORE (LS). Wit: JONES KENDRICK, ROBERT BURTIN, ELI BULL.

Page 164:   July 16, 1790, DAVID MCCOY of Wilks Co. to ASA COX of
             Warren Co. for $14, land adj. THOMAS LOCKET, JOHN MCLAUGHLIN,
14 acres. DAVID MCCOY (SEAL). Wit: THOMAS LUCKETT, JOHN HAMMAC, JAS.
PATTERSON JP.

Page 165:   Dec. 27, 1799, CARY COX to ASA COX, for $150, land on north
             fork of Williams' Creek, called Beaverdam Creek, CARY COX
& MARTHA his wife, CARY COX (LS), MARTHA COX (X) (LS). Wit: ICHABUD
COX, MOSES CRAFFORD, JOHN BATTLE JP.

Pages 165-166:   JOHN PARHAM to son THOMAS PARHAM... wife ELIZABETH
                  deed of gift. Aug. 9, 1802, JOHN PARHAM (X) (LS). Wit:
Z. FRANKLIN, HARTWELL JONES. Proved by ZEPHANIAH FRANKLIN.

Page 166:   Aug. 9, 1802, JOHN PARHAM to THOMAS PARHAM, for $100, 334
             acres whereon sd. JOHN PARHAM now lives, part of a 600
acre grant to JOHN JAMISON, sold by commissioners of confiscated property
to JOHN GARNETT & bounded at time of survey by HOLLAND MIDDLETON &
Augusta Road, line run by TIMOTHY MATTHEWS, Esqr., JOHN PARHAM & wife
ELIZABETH. JOHN PARHAM (X) (LS). Wit: Z. FRANKLIN, HARTWELL JONES.

Pages 167-168:   March 3, 1803, BENJAMIN BRUTON of Montgomery County,
                  to WILLIAM SIMPLES of Warren Co., for $850, 200 acres

on Rocky Comfort, containing 214 acres granted to BENJAMIN BURTON Feb. 2, 1791 & a tract granted to sd. BRUTON Dec. 13, 1802 & 200 acres granted in name of ROBERT GRAY. BENJAMIN BRUTON (LS), JEMIMA BRUTON (X) (LS). Wit: BENJ. UPTON, JOHN SMITH (X).

Pages 168-169:   March 20, 1802, BENJAMIN UPTON & JUDITH his wife of Rocky Comfort, to WILLIAM BIRD of Shoals of Ogechee, for $600, 1 acre & one road on Shoals of Ogechee, adj. sd. BENJ. UPTON, HOWELL FEATHERSTONE, in decision of court UPTON against BIRD & HAMP, granted to PERRIMAN FLOYD... BENJAMIN UPTON (LS), JUDITH UPTON (LS), Wit: WM. SIMPLER, MATTHEW GRANTHAM (M), N. ROBERSON JP.

Pages 169-170:   Feb. 7, 1803, THOMAS BOMAN to JOHN GREISON (?), for $500... later appears to be JOHN GUSON, 127½ acres on Harts Creek, adj. BRANKLEY, COBBS, HENRY COX, VARFIELD, originally granted to JAMES COBBS, and another granted to ELISHA PRUITT, THOMAS BOMAN (X) (SEAL). Wit: LEML. PRUITT, THOMAS JONES.

Pages 170-171:   March 3, 1803, WILLIAM SEMPLER to SAMUEL ALLEN for $230, 250 acres on Harts Creek, 100 originally granted to JAMES BLOUNT/ conveyed to LENKIN CHEVUS (?), to JOHN HARTWELL and then to JOHN BROOKS, then to WILLIAM SIMPLER., 125 acres granted to JOHN HOLLANDSHEAD, then conveyed to JOHN EMBREE, then to JOHN HAMILL (HARRILL?), then to JOHN BROOKS, then to WILLIAM SIMPLER. WILLIAM SEMPLER (SEAL). Wit: BENJA. UPTON, N. ROBERSON.

Pages 171-172:   Feb. 4, 1801, ISAAC BURSON to JOSHUA DAVIS for $300, 100 acres on s. side of Brushy Fork of Brier Creek, part of a 200 acre grant to ISAAC BURSON, July 29, 1788, ISAAC BURSON (LS). Wit: RICHARD HODO, PETER HODO JP.

Pages 172-173:   March 15, 1798, ELISHA PRUITT to THOMAS BOMAN, for $250, land on Harts Creek, adj. BRANTLEY, COBBS, HENRY COX, BARFIELD, 127½ acres, originally granted to JAMES COBBS, ELISHA PRUITT (LS). Wit: JOEL CLOUD, MOUNTAIN HILL.

Page 173:   March 5, 1803, ABRAHAM SALLS from JOHN MCCORMICK for $400, 400 acres on Deep Creek, granted to JOHN MCCORMICK Sept. 1, 1797, JOHN MCCORMICK (SEAL). Wit: THOMAS EDMUNDSON, CHARLES STEWART.

Pages 173-174:   Jan. 24, 1803, JOHN MULKEY of State of Ga. to JACOB BALL of Warren Co. for $250, on Waters of Little River, 100 acres, granted to WALTER JACKSON, July 3, 1770 & sold to JOHN MULKEY May 3, 1780, (later appears to be JACOB BULL), JOHN MULKY (LS), JOB COHUN, BIDDY MULKEY (X) (LS). Wit: DAVID MERCER, WILLIAM BERRY, JT.

Pages 174-174:   May 13, 1801, JOSHUA JONES of Washington Co. to LARKIN SHIVUS, for $53, 220 acres on Joe's Creek, adj. GOODWIN, JOSHUA JONES (SEAL). Wit: JOHN C. CURRIS, MOSES FORT (Plat in book.)

(There are two pages numbered 174.)

Pages 174-175:   March 11, 1797, ANDREW JETER & MARY his wife, of Hancock Co., to ABNER FLEWELLEN of Warren Co. for $200, 100 acres on Rocky Comfort, adj. JOHN PERKINS. ANDREW JETER (SEAL), MARY JETER (SEAL). Wit: JNO. MATTHEWS, HENRY REED (X).

Pages 175-176:   Dec. 31, 1802, JOHN WILLIAMS to JOHN MIDAY, for $400, 124½ acres on Carsons Creek, part of a tract formerly belonging to JOHN CARSON Senr., dec'd... JOHN WILLIAMS (SEAL). Wit: Z? FRANKLIN, AMOSE JOHNSTON (X). (Plat in book.)

Page 176:   Nov. 10, 1802, ABNER F. ELLEN (FLEWELLEN?), to TIMOTHY MATTHEWS, 60 acres on Rocky Comfort, ABNER F. ELLEN (SEAL). Wit: JOHN MATTHEWS, JP., E. HURT J. I. C.

Pages 176-177:   March 19, 1793, CHRISTOPHER WILLIAMS of Wilks Co. to
                 ABNER F. ELLEN, for 50 pounds, land on west side of
Whetstone Creek, adj. JOHN RUTHERFORD at time of survey, granted to
JOHN MIMS, Feb. 6, 1787, part of a 200 acre tract, 130 acres. CHRISTO-
PHER WILLIAM (SS). Wit: ELISHA HURT, JEREMIAH MATTHEWS.

Pages 178-179:   Jan. 19, 1803, DAVID HUBERT of Hancock Co., to JOHN F.
                 FLOURNOY of Warren Co. for $130, 32 7/10 acres. DAVID
HUBERT (LS). Wit: JOHN MATTHEWS JP, M. HUBERT JP. (Plat in book.)

Pages 179-180:   Oct. 9, 1802, NATHAN MARSH & ELIZABETH his wife, to
                 JOHN CHAMPION, for $600, 350 acres, adj. RANDAL RAMSAY
(?), & vacant land, granted to JOSEPH MAYj May 28, 1788, conveyed to
JOHN MARSH, then to WILLIAM DEAN, then to NATHAN MARSH, formerly in
Richmond Co., NATHAN MARSH (∧) (LS), ELIZABETH MARSH (LS). Wit:
DANIEL BUTLER, JOHN GAGE.

Page 180:   Warren County, Ga., I hereby certify that in an affray
            between myself and WILLIAM GARDNER on the nineteenth day
of December, 1800, I unlickily bit off a piece of his left Ear. April
13, 1801, JOHN LAW (LS). Wit: T. PERSONS, J. PERSONS.

Pages 180-181:   Feb. 7, 1801, JOHN SAXON to SAMUEL FLEMING for $400,
                 land on Williams Creek, adj. JOHN PRATEN, RICHARD
BUTLER, ICHBOD COX, REUBEN ROGERS, DARDEN FLEMING old tract, 168½
acres, JOHN SAXON (LS). Wit: HENRY BONNER, ELISHA DARDENS (X).

Pages 182-183:   April 8, 1801, SAMUEL HOWEL to THOMAS FRIEND, $400,
                 100 acres on Long Creek, of Ogechee, adj. GARDNER,
PARISH, originally granted to EDMUND NUGENT, Sept. 25, 1784, SAMUEL
HOWEL (LS). Wit: WM. GARDNER, PRYOR FARDNER JP.

Pages 183-184:   Feb. 26, 1803, HENRY GOLDING of Warren Co. to WILLIAM
                 BARDIN of the same, 176 acres on Rocky Comfort, granted
originally to heirs of HENRY GOLDING dec'd, April 15, 1797, HENRY
GOLDING (X) (LS). Wit: STARLING JONES, REUBEN JONES.

Pages 184-185:   Oct. 20, 1794, JOHN LEDBETTER of Washington Co. to
                 WILLIAM BIRD of Warren Co. for 150 pounds, 25 acres in
Warren Co. formerly Wilkes, granted to NICHOLAS LONG Sept. 1786, adj.
FEWS line, DENNIS line, FREDERICK LEDBETTER's line, JOHN LEDBETTER (LS),
Wit: RICHD. WHITEHEAD, LEWIS GRAVES (X).

Pages 185-186:   Columbia Co., Ga., Feb. 28, 1801, FRANCIS JONES to
                 RICHARD GREEN, 250 acres on Upton's Creek, for $100,
granted to FRANCIS JONES by King George III, FRANCIS JONES (LS). Wit:
MATHEW MCCRARY, WILLIAM DAVIDSON.

Page 186:   Warren Co., Ga. Know all men by these presents that I
            SARAH GOLDING have delivered to RICHARD GREEN & his wife
SARAH & her heirs, one negro child for $4. SARAH GOLDING (LS) (X). Wit:
AMOS GREEN, THOS SELLS.

Pages 187-188:   July 12, 1802, JOHN WILSON to MARGARET GREEN for $100,
                 150 acres, adj. DUCKWORTH, JOHN WILSON (LS). Wit:
RICH M. HUNT (?), SARAH HUNT.

Page 188:   Oct. 6, 1801, THOMAS FOUNTAIN, FRANCIS RISHER & JAMES THRE-
            WITS to TURNER PERSONS, for $350, adj. CHARLES DARNELL,
PERSON's spring, THOMAS FONTAIN (LS), FRANCIS F. RISHER (LS), JAMES
THREEWITS (LS). Wit: SOL. SLATER, ELISHA HURT JP.

Page 189:   Dec. 6, 1801, WORMLEY ROSE & SUSANNAH his wife, to TURNER
            PERSONS, for $700, 300 acres on Whetstone, adj. WOODS line,
land originally granted to JONATHAN LAPER, July 22, 1785. WORMLEY ROSE
(LS), SUSANNAH ROSE (LS). Wit: JOHN C. TURNER, LUCY TURNER.

Page 190:   Nov. 24, 1801, ABNER F. ELLEN to JAMES PARKER for $200, 123
            acres ABNER F. ELLEN (LS). Wit: ROBERT PARKER, JOHN
MATTHEWS JP.

Pages 190-191:   March 20, 1803, RICHARD SLAUGHTER to SAMUEL NEWMAN for
                $200, part of 400 acres granted to IGNATIUS FEW, Sept.
23, 1784, on Long Creek, RICHARD SLAUGHTER (LS). Wits: JONES PERSON,
HENRY CANDLER J. I. C.

Pages 191-192:   Sept. 14, 1801, CLABORN CASTLEBERRY of Jackson County
                to RICHARD SLAUGHTER, for $200, adj. MEDLOCK, part of a
grant to IGNATIUS FEW, Sept. 23, 1784. CLABORN CASTLEBERRY (LS).
Wit: ZEPHANIAH FOWLER.

Pages 192-193:   Jan. 20, 1802, ABRAHAM PERKINS to TIMOTHY MATTHEWS for
                $400, 94 acres, adj. PARKENSES Spring, ATCHESON spring,
part of a grant to BENJAMIN SCOT Dec. 17, 1784, conveyed to SHADRACH
KENNETRUE, then to GEORGE BREWER, then to ABRAHAM PERKINS by deed Feb.
2, 1794. ABRAHAM PERKINS (LS). Wit: WM. BOELT (?), WM. WHITE (X).

Pages 193-194:   Feb. 10, 1803, JOSEPH WATSON to Cumbia Co. (Columbia?),
                to JOSEPH WATSON of Warren Co. for $920, on n. side of
main prong of Big Brier Creek, adj. NEWSOM, JOSEPH WATSON, Wit:
WILLIAM SMITH, JOS. CARTER JP.

Pages 194-195:   Hancock Co., Ga., Feb. 7, 1800, JAMES THWEAT to
                BARBARA LUCUS, for $50, 50 acres in Warren Co. on
Ogechee, adj. PEAVEY, THOS. BOHANNON, JAMES THWEATT (LS). Wit: THOS.
BOHANNON, JOSEPH PEAVY (T).

Pages 195-196:   Dec. 8, 1801, ANDREW KING, Esqr. of Warren Co. to
                CHARLES REYNOLDS of Jefferson Co., for $400, ANDREW
KING & ELIZABETH his wife, 100 acres on Harden's Creek, part of a
grant to IGNATIUS FEW Sept. 15, 1784, adj. JNO. DISMUKES, EDMD DISMUKS,
JNO. BATTLE, PETER DISMUKES, ANDREW KING (LS), ELIZABETH KING (X) (LS).
Wit: SEPTIMUS WEATHERBY, EDMOND DISMUKES. (Plat in book.)

Pages 196-197:   May 14, 1801, MOSES MCKINNY to JOSEPH WATSON of Columbia
                Co., for $920, 170 acres on n. side of main prong of
Big Brier Creek, adj. NEWSOM, MOSES MCKINNEY (LS), MARY MCKINNEY (LS).
Wit: JACOB WATSON, P HODO JP.

Page 197-198:   Feb. 12, 1800, JOHN WATSON of Columbia Co. to ROBERT
                STANFORD of Warren Co. for $350, 75 acres granted to
JACOB WATSON 1772, Book 1, fo. 572 across White's Creek, JOHN WATSON (LS)
Wit: JESSE BURGEN, JOHN BAYNE JP.

Page 198:   June 6, 1800, JONATHAN BURSON to ROBERT STANFORD, for $40,
            6 acres, part of a 200 acre tract granted to sd. BURSON
July 29, 1785, on White's Creek, JONATHAN BURSON (LS). Wit: SHAILY
BAINE, JOHN WILSON JP, JOHN BAYNE.

Page 199:   June 6, 1800, ROBERT STANFORD to STEPHEN STANFORD of
            Columbia Co., for $50, land adj. MAYS, R. STANFORD, STEPHEN
STANFORD, originally granted to JONATHAN STANFORD, Nov. 28, 1795.
ROBERT STANFORD (LS). Wit: CHARLES BAYNE, JOHN BAIN, JOHN WILSON JP.

Page 199-200:   CONCORD HAMILTON, appoints HENRY KINDAL attorney, to
                sue for a negro which has been out of his possession
for some time. June 25, 1803. CONCORD HAMILTON (LS). Wit: WILLIAM
DARNELL, JOHN MATTHEWS JP.

Page 200:   January 8, 1803, JACOB WATSON to MICHAEL CODY, for $360,
            72 acres on Big Brier Creek, on w. side of dry fork,
JACOB WATSON (LS). Wit: P. HODO, RICHARD HODO.

Page 201:   Feb. 15, 1800, JOHN GIBSON to PHILIP BRANTLEY, for $375, 100
            acres on Middle Creek, adj. WILLIS PERRY, DRURY BANKS.
JOHN GIBSON (LS). Wit: ISAIAH RUCKER, WILLIS PERRY.

Pages 201-202:   JAMES JONES for natural love to grandson JOSEPH F.
                 JONES, son of WILLIAM JONES, a negro girl. JAMES JONES
(LS), Wit: T. PERSONS, A. PERSONS. April 6, 1803.

Pages 202-203:   April 10, 1803, ANN STEART to JERUSHA STUART & POLLY
                 STUART, for $100, 100 acres on Deep Creek, part of a
300 acres tract when surveyed in Columbia County & Richmond County,
but now in Warren County granted to sd. ANN STUART, by Gov. EDWARD
TELFAIR, line run for BETHSIA STUART, ANN STUART (X) (LS). Wit: JESSE
PITTMAN, WM. ALLEN, JOEDAY NEWSOM JP.

Pages 203-204:   March 14, 1803, WILLIAM HODGIN & AGNESS his wife to
                 JOHN BEDDINGFIELD, 125 acres part of a grant to JOHN
HODGIN, father of aforesaid WILLIAM HODGINS, now occupied by JOSEPH
HODGIN & JOHN LANDRUM adj., in Counties of Warren & Columbia (plat
annexed) also a tract adj. HENRY WILLIAMS & JOHN COX, originally granted
to ROBERT HODGIN 7 conveyed to sd. WILLIAM HODGIN by WILLIAM DAVERSON,
June 20, 1800... PETER COX, WILLIAM HODGEN (LS), AGNESS HODGEN (X) (LS).
Wit: CAMMT. THOMAS, JOHN P. BACON.

Pages 205-206:   April 27, 1803, JOSEPH WILLICE to JERUSHA STUART, for
                 $40, land on Rocky Comfort, 20 acres, part of a grant
to ALEXANDER CASWELL, now is poss. of JOEL WILLICE, known as BENSON
tract. JOEL WILLIS (LS). Wit: MOSES GRANDBERRY, N. ROBERSON JP.

Page 206:   Dec. 1, 1801, JOHN MATHEWS Exr. of L. W. & T. of BURRELL
            BROON dec'd, to ANDREW KING, 200 acres, JOHN MATTHEWS (LS).
Wit: N. WILLIAMS, ___ STITH JP.

Pages 206-207:   May 21, 1803, RICHARD CURRY of Hancock Co. to CARY
                 CASEY of Warren Co. for $700, land on Joe's Creek, adj.
NORVELL ROBERSON, REUBEN BARROW, GEORGE DYKES & MOSES GRANBERRY, 480
acres. RICHARD CURRY (X) (LS). Wit: AMOSE TRAVIS, N. ROBERSON JP.

Pages 207-208:   Feb. 10, 1803, JOHN DYSART of Hancock Co. to JAMES
                 THREWITS of Warren Co. for $500, land adj. FEW, JOHN
CULLAR (?), BRANNON, CHRISTMAS, 195 acres. JOHN DYSART (LS). Wit:
DAVID THOM, JOEL MCLENDON, JOHN MILES JP.

Pages 208-209:   Oct. 21, 1802, EDWARD PLEASANT MORGAN to LEWIS HILSON
                 & AARON HILSON for $20, 300 acres on Ogechee River,
granted May 1, 1784, land took up by the head right of JESSE MORGAN, and
willed to GAILAND MORGAN & the other part to HENRY MORGAN, EDWARD P.
MORGAN (SEAL). Wit: J. GILES, WILLEY G. BRADDY (X), JAMES JOHNSON (S).

Pages 209-210:   Deed of gift, Sept. 12, 1803, BENJAMIN MOORE of Warren
                 Co., Planter, to JAMES TAYLOR Wheelright & planter to
son in law JAMES TAYLOR and wife NANCY, all his negroes, kitchen
furniture, cattle, etc. BENJAMIN MOORE (SS). Wit: THOMAS EDMUNDSON,
BENJ. HOWARD Junr.

Page 210:   RATFORD BUTT, HENRY WALKER, WILLIAM JONES, GEORGE PARHAM,
            ELIZABETH PARHAM & HARTWELL HEATH, legal heirs of THOMAS
PARHAM dec'd late of Halifax Co., North Carolina, all of Warren Co. for
$400, sold a negro woman & children to JOHN PARHAM. Sept. 3, 1803.
RATFORD BUTT (LS), HENRY WALKER (LS), WILLIAM JONES (LS), GEORGE PARHAM
(LS), ELIZABETH PARHAM (X) (LS), HARTWELL HEATH (LS). Wit: L. PRUITT
J. I. C.

Pages 210-211:   Sept. 24, 1801, MARY MCCOLLISTER to WILLIAM BALE, for
                 $100, 50 acres on Rocky Comfort, granted to JOHN DARDEN
Aug. 17, 1786. MARGARET MCCALLISTER (X) (LS). Wit: L. PRUITT, EDWARD
SHIRLEY.

Pages 211-212:   Oct. 28, 1803, DAVID GOLDING of Warren Co. to SAMUEL
                 FICKLING of St. Paul's Parish, Charleston District,
South Carolina for $800, land in Warren Co., on Golding's Creek, 108½
acres. DAVID GOLDING (X) (LS), ELIZABETH GOLDIN (X) (LS). Wit:
FRANCIS FICKLING, REUBEN JONES.

Page 212:   WILLIAM HAMILTON & THEOPHILAS HARGRAVES of Charles County,
             Maryland & GEORGE HARGRAVES of Warren Co., Ga., for $500
paid by REUBEN JONES sold a negro man. WILLIAM HAMILTON, THEOPHILAS
HARGRAVES, GEORGE HARGRAVES. March 27, 1802.

Pages 212-213:   Nov. 1, 1803, ALEXANDER PERRYMAN, HARMAN PERRYMAN,
                  BENJAMIN HOWARD, Junr. & ETHELRED THOMAS acknowledged
themselves indebted to the governor... if ALEXANDER PERRYMAN does not
perform duties of sheriff.   ALEXD. PERRYMAN (LS), HARMON PERRYMAN (LS),
B. HOWARD Junr. (LS), E. THOMAS (LS). Wit: L. PRUITT JIC, JNO.
TORRENCE J. I. C., ELISHA HURT, J. I. C.

Page 213:   Oct. 25, 1802, JOHN MCCORMICK to JOHN JOHN DARK, for $100,
             120 acres, part of a 150 acre tract conveyed from JOHN
BIRKHALTER to sd. JOHN MCCORMICK, Jan. 16, 1797, JOHN MCCORMICK (LS).
Wit: RANDAL DUCKWORTH, JAS. MCCORMICK JP.

Pages 214-215:   PETER PERKINS, late of Warren Co., made L. W. & T.
                  March 6, 1800, making JOHN TORRENCE & JOHN BAKER Exrs.
sold to JOHN DARDEN highest bidder, land on WILLIAMS Creek, part of 2
original surveys, 196 acres, by virtue of a grant to DREAD WILDER, for
350 acres, made Dec. 9, 1784, conveyed to sd. dec'd May 17, 1787, and
fifty more acres, remainder of a tract of 200 granted to sd. dec'd Oct.
30, 1788, adj. IGNATIUS FEW, WILLIAM WHITE, heirs of ROBERT PARKER dec'd
TIMOTHY MATTHEWS & by FONTAINS land... to JETHRO DARDEN. JNO. TORRENCE
(LS), JOHN BAKER (LS). Wit: ROBERT HILL, DEBERA CHAPMAN, SOLOMON
LOCKET JP.

Pages 215-216:   May 14, 1787, DREAD WILDER of Wilks Co. to PETER
                  PERKINS, for 36 pounds, six shillings sterling, 196
acres in Wilks Co., adj. BENJAMIN SCOTT, PETER PERKINS, MARY MCDANIEL
or CHILDRENS land, being part of a tract granted to DREAD WILDER, 350
acres, Dec. 9, 1784. DREAD WILDER (X) (LS). Wit: CHARLES LUM, JAMES
CHRISTMAS, SAMPSON WILDER.

Pages 217-218:   July 20, 1802, BENJAMIN MOORE of Warren Co. to JAMES
                  TAYLOR of Hancock Co., for $700, 150 acres on Rocky
Comfort, granted to sd. BENJAMIN MOORE May 24, 1786, BENJAMIN MOORE
(LS). Wit: THOMAS EDMUNDSON, EDMOND E. TAYLOR.

Page 218:   Nov. 20, 1803, CHRISTOPHER BUSTIN of Warren Co. to BENJAMIN
             WRIGHT of Washington Co., for $600, 175 acres on s. side
of Rocky Comofrt, formerly property of JOHN DAVIS, conveyed by him to
NICHOLAS WILLIAMS and from him to CHRISTOPHER BUSTIN. C. BUSTIN (LS).
Wit: DAVID BROOM, JOHN MATTHEWS JP.

Page 219:   July 20, 1802, BENJAMIN MOORE of Warren Co. to JAMES TAYLOR
             of Hancock Co., for $300, half of a 200 acre grant to sd.
MOORE, on Rocky Comfort. BENJAMIN MOORE (LS), Wit: THOMAS EDMUNDSON,
EDMUND E. TAYLOR.

Pages 219-220:   June 4, 1803, JOHN DUNAWAY & JONATHAN DUNAWAY to JOHN
                  ENGLISH, 50 acres on Brier Creek, adj. J. CARTER,
EDMUNDS, DUNAWAYS line. Wit: MOORE CARTER, JAMES CARTER. JOHN
DUNAWAY (X), JONATHAN DUNAWAY (X).

Page 221:   Oct. 18, 1803, JOHN MATTHEWS to CHRISTOPHER BUSTIN, for
             $350, 71 acres on Rocky Comfort Creek, adj. JACKSON's line.
JOHN MATTHEWS (SEAL). Wit: DAVID BROOM, ISHMEAL BROOM.

Pages 221-222:   July 14, 1803, NICHOLAS WILLIAMS to CHRISTOPHER BUSTIN
                  for $150, 75 acres on Rocky Comfort Creek, originally
granted to JOHN RUTHFORD, conveyed by him to JNO. DAVIS, then to
NICHOLAS WILLIAMS, N. WILLIAMS (SEAL). Wit: BUTTON PEARMORE (PEARMON?),
JOHN MATTHEWS JP.

Page 222:   Rec'd of CHRISTOPHER BUSTIN of Warren Co. $400, for a negro
             girl. Dec. 3, 1803, STEPHEN WRIGHT (SEAL). Wit: DAVID
BROOM, ARCHD. FLEWELLEN JP.

Pages 222-223:   June 15, 1800, SAMUEL CAMP to RICHARD SLAUGHTER for
                 $300, 138 acres on Long Creek, granted to sd. CAMP.
Nov. 23, 1792. S. CAMP (SEAL). Wit: SAMUEL NEWSOM, ARTHUR FORT JC.

Pages 223-224:   Dec. 17, 1801, HENRY HADLEY of Warren Co. to DAVID
                 MIMS for $170, 100 acres on Whetstone Creek, adj.
FULSOM, HENRY HADLEY (LS). Wit: ARCHILUS F. ELLEN, JOHN MATTHEWS JP.

Page 224:   Dec. 9, 1803, DAVID MIMS to SHADRACK F. ELLEN for $150,
            100 acres on Rocky Comfort. DAVID MIMS (X) (LS). Wit:
DAVID BROWN, ASCHELUS F. ELLEN JP.

Pages 224-225:   Dec. 24, 1803, MARK HARDIN to JOHN TORRENCE for $600,
                 400 acres on Rocky Comfort, adj. JOEL MATTHEWS, JACOB
DANSBY, land granted to ABRAHAM REDDICK, by lands of JOHN TORRENCE
originally granted to NICHOLAS LONG on March 2, 1791, conveyed April
27, 1791, to MARTIN HARDIN, then to MARK HARDIN Oct. 18, 1796. MARK
HARDIN (SS). Wit: WM. HARISS, G. GEORGE.

Pages 225-226:   MOSES BUTT late of Halifax Co., North Carolina but now
                 of Warren Co., Ga., for love to my son WILLIAM BUTT,
of Warren Co., to give property in State of N.C. Dec. 6, 1802. MOSES
BUTT (LS). Wit: POLLEY MATTHEWS, JOHN MATTHEWS JP, E. HURT.

Page 226:   Dec. 26, 1803, HARDIN SANDERS of Tattnall Co., Ga., to
            JAMES MYHAND of Warren Co., for $500, 223 acres on Rocky
Comfort, adj. JOHNATHAN LOCK, ANDREW BUSH & WM. BUTTS. HARDEN SANDERS
(X) (SEAL). Wit: STEPHEN MARSHALL, JOHN MATTHEWS JP.

Page 227:   Nov. 12, 1803, JOSEPH FICKLIN & ELIZABETH his wife of St.
            Paul's Parish, Colliton District, South Carolina to BERNARD
WOODS of same, for $800, 187 acres on Golding's Creek, adj. NICHOLAS
HAIRBRECK, MICHAEL HAIR BACK (HARBUCK?), JOSEPH FICKLING (LS), ELIZABETH
FICKLING (LS). Wit: WM. S. BARDIN, MARY BARDIN.

Pages 227-228:   Jan. 21, 1802, WILLIAM PILCHER of Warren Co. to JOHN
                 HEATON sf same, for $129, land in Warren Co. on Big
Ogechee, originally granted to WILLIAM PILCHER, dec'd 200 acres, the
sd. WILLIAM PILCHER claim supposed to be 25 acres more or less to hold
part of JOHN HEATON... WILLIAM PILCHER (⊙) (LS). Wit: THOMAS JACKSON,
BENJAMIN GATES.

Pages 228-229:   Oct. 26, 1801, LEWIS PILCHER & REASE PILCHER to
                 RICHARD LEE, for $200, land on Ogechee, granted to
WILLIAM PILCHER, dec'd... LEWIS PILCHER (𝒫) (LS), REASE PILCHER (↪)
(LS). Wit: THOMAS JACKSON, BENJAMIN GATES, B. ROBINSON.

Pages 229-230:   Jan. 21, 1802, RICHARD LEE to JOHN HEATON for $325,
                 land granted to WILLIAM PILCHER on Ogechee, 75 acres.
RICHARD LEE (X), AYLSEY LEE (𝓁). Wit: THOS. JACKSON READER (?)
KEATON.

Pages 230-231:   March 10, 1803, WALTER SLAUGHTER to JOHN RUSHIN for
                 $1000, land on Long Creek, adj. ADAM JONES, MITCHELL,
A. JONES, FOWLER (from plat), SAMUEL TURNER's line, 300 acres granted to
sd. WALTER SLAUGHTER May 8, 1798. WALTER SLAUGHTER (SEAL). Wit: S.
CAMP, JOHN LEDBETTER Senr.

Pages 231-232:   Jan. 13, 1803, JOHN MICHAEL & SAMUEL LAURENCE & ANN
                 MICHAEL of state aforesaid & VINSON JOHNSON of Warren
Co. for $100, land on Ogechee 600 acres, formerly adj. MAPE, GOINGS,
STEPHEN NOBLES, WILLIAM NOBLES, WILLIAM LUXUS & JOSEPH BONNER, JOHN
MICHAEL (L), SAMUEL LAURENCE, ANN MICHAEL (LS). Wit: R. ABERCROMBIE,
JAMES HARVEY.

Pages 232-233:   Sept. 18, 1801, JOSEPH WHITE to LEWIS WRIGHT for $600,
                 land on Williams Creek, adj. heirs of JOHN CHAPMAN,
BURREL PERRY, JOSEPH HILL, JOSEPH HILL, FEWS land, 100 acres. JOSEPH
WHITE (LS). Wit: SOLOMON THOMPSON, ROBERT PARKER, TOM MATTHEWS JP.

278

Pages 233-234:   March 10, 1803, RICHARD SLAUGHTER to JOHN RUSHIN, for
                   $150, part of 138 acres on Long Creek, granted to
SAMUEL CAMP, Nov. 23, 1792, conveyed to sd. RICHARD June 15, 1800.
RICHARD SLAUGHTER (X) (LS). Wit: S. CAMP, JNO. LEDBETTER Senr.

Pages 234-235:   July 12, 1800, THOMAS JONES to RICHARD SLAUGHTER, for
                   $30, land on fork of Long Creek, part of 200 acres
grant to JOHN MICHAEL March 17, 1786. THOMAS JONES (X) (LS). Wit:
SAMUEL ALLEN (X), THOMAS FRIEND JP.

Pages 235-236:   March 10, 1803, RICHARD SLAUGHTER to JOHN RUSHING for
                   $50, land on Fork of Long Creek, 80 acres, part of 200
granted to JOHN MICHAEL March 17, 1786, RICHARD SLAUGHTER (X). Wit:
S. CAMP, JOHN LEDBETTER Senr.

Pages 236-237:   Columbia Co., Ga., July 5, 1800, ANDREW CRAWFORD to
                   JOHN RUSHING for $97, land on n. side of Ogechee, part
of a tract of 337 granted to sd. CRAWFORD, 65 acres. A. CRAWFORD (LS).
Wit: THS. W. MURRELL, J. APLING J. I. C.

Pages 237-238:   Dec. 24, 1800, SAMUEL CAMP to WALTER SLAUGHTER, for
                   $130, land on Long Creek, part of 500 acres granted
to WILLIAM KELLY March 15, 1785, conveyed to sd. CAMP Aug. 9, 1786,
also a part of 40 acres granted to sd. CAMP, 65 acres total. S. CAMP
(LS). Wit: THOS FRIEND, PRYOR GARDNER JP.

Page 238:   June 15, 1800, SAML. CAMP to CADER HARRILL, for $95, land on
              Fort's Creek, part of 750 acres granted to sd. CAMP Jan. 22,
1789, 220 acres. S. CAMP (LS). Wit: SAMUEL NEWMAN, ARTHUR FORT JC.

Pages 238-239:   Nov. 22, 1787, ANDREW KIDD of Wilks Co. to LUDWELL
                   ARMSTRONG of Washington Co., for 50 pounds, 100 acres
part of 200 granted, adj. DRURY MIMS, WILLIAM MORRIS. ANDREW KIDD (LS).
Wit: JNO. RUTHERFORD, HUGH ARMSTRONG.

Pages 239-241:   Jan. 17, 1804, WILLIAM NANCE of Warren Co. to JOHN
                   MORELAND of Jefferson Co. for $2000, all goods, furni-
ture & household stuffs. WILLIAM NANCE (LS). Wit: WILLIAM CLARK,
WILLIAM HARDWICK JP.

Page 241:   RICHARD BEASLEY deed of gift to son DAVID BEASLEY, 2 tracts
              of land 233½ acres, on Rocky Comfort, RICHARD BEASLEY (R)
(LS). Wit: THOS EDMUNDSON, L. PRUITT JIC. Jan. 16, 1804.

Pages 241-242:   RICHARD BEASLEY to son ROBERT BEASLEY 207½ acres on
                   Rocky Comfort, Jan. 16, 1804,RICHARD BEASLY (R) (LS).
Wit: THOS. EDMONDSON, L. PRUITT J.I.C..

Pages 242-243:   April 25, 1803, JAMES ROQUEMORE Senr. to SHEDRICK
                   POTTS, for $20.5020 (?) acres on Little Brier Creek,
originally granted to BENJMAIN JACKSON, 1785. JAMES ROQUEMORE (LS).
Wit: BAINES CARTER, THOMER (?) WARD.

Pages 243-244:   Oct. 28, 1802, JOSEPH MATTHEWS to SHADRICK POTTS for
                   $270, 82 acres on Big Brier Creek, adj. DAVID ROBERSONS,
ROCQUEMORE. JOSEPH MATTHEWS (W). Wit: THOS WESTBUY, JAMES
ROCQUEMORE.

Pages 244-245:   THOMAS OSTEEN of Buck Co., Ga., for 27 pounds, pd. by
                   WILLIAM MARLOW, sell 100 acres, July 23, 1793, THOMAS
OSTEEN (T) (LS). Wit: JOHN DAVID, ROBERT MARLOW.

Page 246:   March 20, 1801, PHILIP GIBBS to REUBEN BARROW, 100 acres
              known as SAMUEL POWEL improvement on the Big Road about 6
miles below Georgetown, part of a grant to REASE PRICE, paid $60.
PHILLIP GIBBS (LS). Wit: JOHN BARROW, JAMES BARROW.

Page 246:   HUGH REESE to REUBEN JONES for $800, a negro & 4 children,
             Aug. 14, 1803, HUGH REES. Wit: GEO. HARGRAVES, HILL
CHAPMAN.

Page 247:   Jan. 15, 1803, JOHN MATTHEWS to SHARDRACK POTTS, for $55,
             50 acres on Big Brier Creek, adj. JOSEPH MATTHEWS,
FRANKLIN's line, part of a grant to ABSOLEM JACKSON, April 1787. JOHN
MATTHEWS (X) (LS). Wit: PETER ROCKMORE, THOMAS WESTBAY.

Pages 248-249:   Oct. 29, 1798, JOHN WILSON to PETER QUALLS for $300,
             300 acres adj. GIBBS, JAS MCKINLEY, or granted to
SAMUEL JOHNSTON April 19, 1790. JOHN WILSON (LS), MARGARET WILSON (6)
(LS). Wit: LEWIS GRADY, JOHN QUALLS.

Page 249:   WILLIE DORMAN & ALLEN DORMAN to AMOS TRAVIS, three negroes
             for 700 silver dollars. Nov. 16, 1801. WILLIE DORMON,
ALLEN DORMON. Wit: WILLIAM MCDOWEL, JOHN SMITH (L).

Pages 250-251:   Aug. 20, 1803, ISAAC BALL to ETHELRED THOMAS for $2000,
             land on both sides of Rocky Comfort, adj. JOHN MYRICK,
JOSEPH BOON, JOHN TURNER BALL, part of two tracts granted to heirs
of JOHN MAYS. Warrant dated Nov. 12, 1785... ISAAC BALL & SARAH his
wife... ISAAC BALL (LS), SARAH BALL (X) (LS). Wit: NOYAL NELMS,
CASWELL BALL.

Pages 251-252:   Dec. 28, 1797, KEADER KEATON to JOHN KEATON, for $1,
             50 acres, part of the tract bought of GIDION ALLEN.
KEADER KEATON (LS). Wit: JACOB GILES, KEADER KEATON.

Page 252:   Warren Co., Ga., GEORGE JOHNSTON of Columbia Co. to JOSEPH
             EVANS & WILLIAM BERRY, Admr. of est. of MARMADUKE MENDINGHALL,
dec'd, $157, to mortgage following property -- negroes. GEORGE JOHNSON.
Wit: JOHN EVANS, Aug. 6, 1803. Also Wit: JACOB BULL, Jr.

Page 253:   MALLICHI CULPEPPER of Elbert Co. sold to RUBEN BARROW one
             negro woman, for $600, MALLISHI CULPEPPER (X). Wit:
ALEXANDER AVERA, JAMES BARROW.

Pages 253-254:   July 1, 1803, WILLIAM STARK of Columbia Co. to JOHN
             DOZER, Sr. of Warren Co. for $1050, 350 acres on Little
River, originally surveyed for RALPH KILGORE & vacant on all sides at
time fo survey, at present adj. EVANS, HARDE & BALL, BULL:... later says
JAMES DOZER Senr. WM. STARK (LS), ELIZABETH STARK (X) (LS). Wit:
JENEY G. WILLIS, JAMES WILLIS JP.

Page 254:   RICHARD DUNS to RICHARD BARROW, for $400, negro woman and
             child. Feb. 20, 1797, RICHARD DUNS. Wit: DAVID BLACKSEAR
JP.

Page 255:   Oct. 17, 1803, JOSEPH HARVILL to ROBERT STANFORD Junr. for
             $100, 100 acres part in Warren & part in Columbia Co., part
of a 300 acre tract adj. JOSEPH CARTER, MULLIN ANSLEY & JAMES CARTER.
JOSEPH HARVELL (LS). Wit: JESSE STANFORD, JOHN BAYN JP.

Pages 255-256:   Oct. 21, 1803, ROBERT STANFORD to JESSE STANFORD both
             of Warren Co., for $100, 98 acres adj. HONDS OWENS
& sd. JESSE STANFORD (Plat in deed.) ROBERT STANFORD (LS). Wit:
LEWIS STANFORD, P. HODO.

Pages 256-257:   Jan. 10, 1799, LEWIS BRADY to JOHN KEATON for 10
             pounds, 200 acres on Pilcher's Creek, adj. MITCHEL
HOLODAY, PILCHER, MARLOW, part of a tract granted to LEWIS BRADY March
5, 1792, LEWIS BRADY (LS). Wit: PETER QUALLS, NORVELL ROBERTSON JP.

Pages 257-258:   July 20, 1795, THOMAS JACKSON Planter to JOHN KEATON
             Planter, for 40 pounds, 100 acres on Ogechee River
granted March 7, 1786. THOMAS JACKSON (LS), LUDICE JACKSON (LS). Wit:
JESSE KEATON, ROBERT DICKENS.

Pages 258-259:   Feb. 19, 1804, JOHN PARHAM Senr. to THOMAS PARRHAM
                  for $100, land on Carsons Creek, adj. THOMAS PARHAM,
LEWIS PARHAM, NICHOLAS JONES, and a tract in dispute between HENRY
CANDLER & ROYSTES HEATH, HENRY WAGGINES & JOHN BISHOP. JOHN PARHAM.
Wit: SHADRICK FLEWELLEN, JOHN MATTHEWS.

Page 259:   Feb. 11, 1804, JACOB BUCKHALTER to BENJAMIN REESE for $300,
             100 acres on s. side of Big Brier Creek, adj. WARREN MC-
GOMMERY BROOKS, JACOB BUCKHALTER (LS), MARY BUCKHALTER (LS). Wit:
P. HODO, JOEDAY NEWSOM JP.

Page 260:   Jan. 23, 1804, MARROCK HUBERT to JESSE JAMES for $500, 191½
             acres on Long Creek, MANOAK HUBBARD (LS). Wit: BAILLOTT
SIMMS, THOMAS FRIEND JP.

Pages 261-262:   Jan. 8, 1798, THOMAS CHILDRE Senr. to JOHN WILLIAMS
                  for 25 pounds, 50 acres on White's Creek, adj. JOHN
WATSON, JACOB WATSON, JONATHAN BASONS Mill, JONES, STANFORD, THOMAS
CHILDRE (LS). Wit: JOHN WATSON, ROBERT STANFORD, HENRY WILLIAMS.

Page 262-263:   Jan. 13, 1803, JOHN WATSON Senr. of Columbia Co. to
                 ROBERT STANFORD, land in Columbia & Warren Counties
originally surveyed for JOSEPH MADDOCK and part of JOHN WATSON, adj.
MATHESES line, COWPEN line, JOHN WATSON (LS). Wit; JOHN STANFORD,
FLITHA HUKE (?).

Pages 263-264:   Dec. 29, 1803, JOHN BAYN to WILLIAM BROWN, for $240,
                  86 acres, part of a 200 acre tract originally granted
to PRISCILLA MAYS and part granted to AQUILLA JONES, JOHN BAYN (LS).
Wit: ROBERT STANFORD, GEORGE DUNAWAY.

Pages 264-265:   May 16, 1800, ROBERT STANFORD from MOSES HILL, for $160,
                  100 acres on White Creek, on n. side of Beaverdam
Branch, land originally granted to IGNATIUS FEW. MOSES HILL (X) (LS).
Wit: JAMES CARTER, JOHN WILSON JP.

Pages 265-266:   July 18, 1798, WILLIAM BYROM Collector of Taxes, to
                  ELIZABETH DOW, (DOVE?) of Richmond Co., sold for back
taxes the amount of $6, 904½ acres to ELIZABETH DOVE adj. JAMESON,
PHILIPS, CASTER, GRAY, STORY... originally granted to JOHN JAMERSON...
WILLIAM BYROM (LS). Wit: J. WILSON JP., JAS. MCCORMICK JP.

Pages 265-266:   Oct. 21, 1803, ROBERT STANFORD to REUBEN MCGEE for
                  $88, 88 acres on White Creek, ROBERT STANFORD (LS).
(Plat included) Wit: JESSE STANFORD, P. HODO.

Pages 266-267:   Jan. 8, 1802, JOHN DIXON of Wilks Co. to NATHANIEL
                  MYRICK of Warren Co. for $1000, land on Williams
Creek, 300 acres. JOHN DIXON (LS). Wit: SEPTIMUS WEATHERBY, JOHN
PEAVEY (X).

Pages 267-268:   Dec. 2, 1795, JACOB MARTIN Senr. to JAMES FARLESS for
                  60 pounds, sterling, 300 acres on Deep Creek, in two
surveys, one granted to JOEL TAPLY, adj. LAWSON... conveyed by WM.
SIMS Deputy Sur. Aug. 7, 1795. JACOB MARTIN. Wit: JOHN LAWSON JP,
C. DAWSON (LAWSON?).

Pages 268-269:   Nov. 3, 1797, JAMES FARLESS to JOSEPH WILLIAMS of
                  Jefferson Co., for 65 pounds, 300 acres on Deep Creek,
land granted to JOEL TAPLEY April 19, 1790. JAMES FARLESS (LS). Wit:
JOHN LAWSON JP, JAMES WILLIAMS.

Page 269:   DAVID COOK of Richmond Co. bound to DUKEY BUCKSHIRE for
             500 pounds, to insure good title to land on Carsons Creek,
adj. JAMES GRAYSTONE, JOHN CARSON 100 acres. DAVID COOK (LS). Wit:
EZEKIEL STANLEY, ALBENIA STANLEY. Aug. 31, 1787. DUKEY BURKSHIRE (LS).
Wit: JONATHAN JONES. Dec. 6, 1787 I do hereby assign all my right of
within obligation unto SAMUEL COOPER, THOS. HOLDEN. Wit: JOSEPH
FRANKLIN.

Page 270-271:   Feb. 24, 1804, PHILIP LOGAN of Washington Co. to
                TURNER PERSONS for 500 dollars, land on Rocky Comfort
adj. DAVID HUBERT, 102 acres, part of a 200 acre grant to JAMES DAVIS
(plat included). PHILIP LOGAN (LS). Wit: WM. SAFOLD, WM. HARRELL.

Pages 271-272:   Jan. 5, 1802, AUSTIN PRUITT to LEVI PRUITT for $1400,
                 350 acres, originally granted to JOHN TORRENCE, March
21, 1789 (1769?), another 100 acres originally granted to ABSOLEM JACK-
SON, Oct. 12, 1785, then to JOHN D. YOUNG, then to JOHN HALL, then to
BIRD PRUITT, then to AUSTIN PRUITT. AUSTIN PRUITT (LS). Wit: JAMES
MCCORMICK Junr. JAS MCCORMICK JP.

Pages 272-273:   Feb. 7, 1804, WM. WARD to NEWIT WARD for $350, half of
                 a tract of 750 acres granted to JAMES ROLEY March 5,
1787, WILLIAM WARD (𝄢) (LS). Wit: JOHN ONAL, HANNAH ONAL (X). N.
ROBERTSON JP, JOHN HUTCHINSSON JP.

Pages 273:   March 5, 1804, WILLIAM CORAM to JESSE RICKETSON for $400,
             237 acres where sd. CORAM now lives, adj. CLARK BLANFORD,
ROBERT PULLEN, ELISHA WRIGHT, WILLIAM CORAM (LS). Wit: GEO. HARGRAVES,
D. BUSH (BURK?).

Pages 274-275:   Oct. 16, 1788, JOHN MANION of Richmond Co. to JOHN
                 WILSON for 90 pounds, 200 acres on Briar Creek, adj.
JEREMIAH DUCKWORTH, JOHN MANION (𝄢) (LS), ELIZABETH MANION (T) (LS).
Wit: MAURICE HUNT, SARAH HUNT.

Pages 275-276:   Feb. 6, 1804, GIDEON GEORGE & TABITHA his wife to
                 HUGH ARMSTRONG for $250, 113 acres, adj. MILLER, JOHN
THOMAS, HUGH ARMSTRONG, DENNIS & LEWIS, GIDEON GEORGE (LS), TABITHA
GEORGE (LS). Wit: DRURY BANKS, JOHN BAYN JP.

Pages 276-277:   Dec. 28, 1797, KEADER KATON Senr. to KEADER KEATON Jr.
                 for $1, granted to KEADER KEATON adj. Ogeechee R.,
surveyed 1796. KEADER KEATON (LS), HESTER KEATON (LS). Wit: JACOB
GILES, JOHN KEATON.

Pages 277-278:   Dec. 28, 1797, KEADER KEATON Sr. to KEADER KEATON Jr.
                 for $175, 170 acres. KEADER KEATON (LS). Wit: (same
as above).

Page 278:   LEVI PRUITT to keep free land to JOHN TORRENCE, adj.
            land of RICHARD BEASLEY. March 8, 1803. L. PRUITT (LS).
Wit: W. ROSE, H. PEEBLES, H. CANDLER J. I. C.

Pages 278-279:   MATTHEW ENGLISH Senr. being in a cedlining and low
                 state of health, having one dau. in like condition
JENNY, possessed of land, cattle, etc. I give to son MATTHEW ENGLISH
Jnr. for taking me & my dau. JENNY under his care. MATTHEW ENGLISH
Senr. (E), MATTHEW ENGLISH JR. (X). Wit: ELIA (?) MEDLOCK, JAS.
MCCORMICK J. I. C.

Pages 279-280:   April 17, 1804, MATTHEW ENGLISH Senr. to MATTHEW
                 ENGLISH Jr. for $500, 200 acres originally to BROCK
DAVIS Dec. 31, 1787, on a branch called Stump Brank, Rocky Comfort, now
adj. AVERL, WILDER, RABUN, conveyed by sd. DAVID & his wife to
MATTHEW ENGLISH Senr. May 17, 1793. MATTHEW ENGLISH (O). Wit: CHA.
MEDLOCK, JAS MCCORMICK.

Pages 280-282:   JOHN REEDIFIELD & AQUILLA SCOTT adj. all their account
                 up to the present from March 16, 1792, the commencement
of a Verbal Copartmnership... SAMUEL RINGSELIE (LS), A. SCOTT (LS).
Wit: JAMES MCMULLIN, PETER HILL. Oct. 27, 1803. Names included in
accounts: THOS. DAVID, J. STUBBS, JNO COBBS, R. HEATH, E. SHORT, M.
AMOS, AMOS GREEN, JOSIAH DARDE, N. PERRY, WILLIAM PERRY, JOHN RODGERS,
P. BAILEY, HILLERY THOMPSON, BERRY CHAPMAN, BENJ. WILEY, NOLAND,
COCKETT, CLEMMONS, ONEAL, RICHERSON, BEVIN (?).

Pages 282-283:   Jan. 10, 1799, RICHARD STORY to PETER WILLIAMS for
                  30 pounds, 200 acres on both sides of Whites Creek,
adj. STORY, LYDIE GYES, JAMERSON, JAMES SMITH, surveyed Dec. 5, 1787.
RICHARD STORY (R) (LS). Wit: THOMAS SMITH, JOHN BAYN JP.

Pages 283-285:   Dec. 31, 1802, JOSEPH GUY to PETER WILLIAMS for $30,
                  10 acres, part of a tract of 200 acres granted to
ELISHA GUY Dec. 16, 1784, on White's Creek, JOSEPH GUY (LS). Wit: JOHN
BAYN, JAMES CARTER JP.

(There was no page numbered 284)

Pages 285-286:   Sept. 21, 1803, EDWARD STORY to PETER WILLIAMS, for
                  $400, 100 acres on Brier, formerly in Wilkes Co., now
Warren Co. originally granted to RACHEL WELLS, from her to JOHN WATSON
Sept. 20, 1792, adj. SMITH, Widow GUY's, MAYS, EDWARD STORY (£) (LS).
Wit: SALLY ROBERT, JOHN BAYN JP.

Pages 286-287:   Dec. 22, 1800, JOHN WOOD to PETER WILLIAMS for $125,
                  75 acres, part of a 200 acre grant to JOHN JAMERSON,
Sept. 20, 1787, on Big Brier Creek, JOHN WOOD (LS). Wit: JOHAM
WHEELER (X), JOHN BAYN.

Page 287:   Jan. 22, 1803, FEDRICK DANIEL of Warren Co. to ANSIL MCKINNY
             for $500, land on Middle Creek, adj. ELISHA WRIGHT, 120
acres. FEDERICK DANIEL (X) (LS). Wit: L. WRIGHT, JOHN MATHEWS JP.

Page 288:   Nov. 18, 1798, WILLIAM WOOD to EDWARD STORY for 34 pounds,
             100 acres, originally granted to RACHEL WELLS, June 17,
1789, sold to JOHN WATSON Sept. 24, 1792, adj. Widow GUY's, SMITH, MAYS,
WILLIAM WOOD (LS), MARY WOOD (X) (LS). Wit: JOHN WOOD, JOHN BAYN JP.

Page 289:   Jan. 28, 1804, RUBEN MAGEE to PETER WILLIAMS for $50, 10
             acres on White Creek, part of 904 acres granted to J.
JAMMERSON March 10, 1798, adj. Widow GUY's, corner of land grante to
B. STORY. RUBEN MAGEE. Wit: JOHN WATSON Junr. JOHN BAYN JP.

Pages 289-290:   JACOB DANSBE, in Wilks Co. now Warren 200 acres, to
                  son DANIEL DANSBE, adj. ZACHARIAH SHEFFIELD, ABRAM
REDICKS, NICHOLA ONG, JOHN GRECIS. JACOB DANSBE (£) (LS). Wit:
LEVINIA MORRISS (⌐), JOHN BAKER.

Page 290:   JOHN ZACHARY to JAMES ZACHY one negro boy, JOHN ZACHRY (LS).
             Wit: SIMON HARRELL, M. HUBERT JP. Dec. 10, 1803.

Page 291:   JOHN ZACHARY to ABNER ZACHRY, negro boy. JOHN ZACHRY (LS).
             Dec. 10, 1803. Wit: SIMON HARRELL, M. HUBERT JP.

Pages 291-292:   Feb. 23, 1803, ABSALOM HORN to JAMES LEDBETTER, for
                  $250, lot in Georgetown, conveyed by SAMUEL KELLY
to ABSALEM HORN, Feb. 6, 1802. ABSALAM HORN (LS). Wit: ISAAC LED-
BETTER, LEWIS GRIFFIN.

Pages 292-293:   Feb. 13, 1804, WILLIAM THOMAS to ABEL JAMES, land
                  obtained by deed from JEPTHAH VINING April 20, 1794,
husband of MARY THOMAS who did obtain in her own name a grant May 12,
1786 for 100 acres on Long Creek of Ogechee, adj. BULLAR, ANDERSON,
JOSHUA ROSS, VINING formerly JONES' for $400... WILLIAM THOMAS &
WILLIAM BULL's land... WILLIAM THOMAS (LS). Wit: JESSE JAMES, MANOAK
HUBERT.

Pages 293-294:   July 30, 1801, DIXON PERRYMAN of Columbia Co. to JOHN
                  SEXTON of Warren Co. for $350, 147 acres on Ogechee,
part of a survey granted to JOSIAH CARTER... DIXON PERRYMAN (LS). Wit:
HIRAM HUBERT, D. H. ZACHARY.

Page 294:   July 26, 1802, JOHN SAXTON of Wilks Co. to JOSEPH DUNN, for
             $500, 147 acres... PEVEY's line... originally granted to
JOSIAH CARTER, JOHN SAXON (LS). Wit: HENRY THOMPSON, JESSE LACY JP.

Page 295:   April 15, 1804, JOSEPH DUNN to LITTLE BRYAN of Wilks Co. for
            $300, land on Ogechee, originally granted to JOSIAH CARTER.
JOSEPH DUNN (LS). Wit: EDWARD CROWILL, DRURY GOYAN (X).

Page 296:   HUGH REESE Senr. to dau. POLLY BUCKHALTER give her a negro
            girl. HUGH REESE (LS). Wit: SOLOMON NEWSOM, JOEDAY
NEWSOM JP.

Pages 296-297: Nov. 15, 1802, JOSEPH WHITE & ROBERT PARKER, to JAMES
            MATTHEWS, for $500, land originally granted to JAMES
GREEN & ABNER F. ELLEN, 120 acres. JOSEPH WHITE (LS), ROBERT PARKER
(X) (LS). Wit: SOLOMON THOMPSON, JAMES PARKER.

Pages 297-298: Feb. 1, 1803, DIXON PERRYMAN of Columbia Co. to JAMES
            ZACHERY of Warren Co., for $400, 200 acres on both
sides of Long Creek, granted to JOHN SMITH Sept. 20, 1787, adj. HAYS'
line. DIXON PERRYMAN (LS). Wit: JOHN ZACHERY, M. HUBERT JP.

Page 298:   Feb. 18, 1802, JOHN CRATON & MARY his wife to JAMES ELLIOTT,
            for 170 acres, remainder of that bought of WILLIS PERRY,
on Williams Creek, JNO CRATIN (LS), MARY AN CRATIN (LS). Wit: THOS
LUCKETT, SOLOMON LOCKETT.

Pages 299-300: Sept. 30, 1800, MICIJAH STONE to JAMES ELLIOTT, for $40,
            6 acres on Williams Creek, part of a 320 acre grant to
ROBERT JENKINS, Oct. 5, 1785. MICAJAH STON (X) (LS), Wit: JOHN
ROGERS, ROBERT GRIER, SOL. LUCKETT JP.

Page 300:   HERMAN PERRYMAN to MARY PERRYMAN a negro woman (no money
            mentioned). HARMAN PERRYMAN (LS), Feb. 1, 1797. Wit: D.
PERRYMAN, ALSEY HARRIS.

            LEVTI PRUITT relinquished claim to a negro girl to his sister
NANCY WILLIAMS. March 5, 1804. L. PRUITT (LS). Wit: JNO. TORRENCE.

Page 301:   May 3, 1796, JESSE EMBREE of Montgomery Co. to HENRY HARP
            for 50 pounds, 100 acres on Rocky Comfort. JESSE EMBREE
(LS), ANNA EMBREE (LS). Wit: JOHN HOWARD JP, JAMES HARDIN JP.

Page 302:   Sept. 10, 1800, ABRAHAM PURKINS to JOHN BENTON & ELI
            BENTON for $200, 100 acres on Rocky Comfort. ABRAHAM
PERKINS (LS). Wit: TIMOTHY MATTHEWS, AARON BENTON.

Pages 302-303: "21st day of ____ 1799" JOHN DUNAWAY to EDWARD
            DUNAWAY, for $50, 50 acres, adj. TAYLOR, JONATHAN
DUNAWAY, ENGLISH. JOHN DUNAWAY (X) (LS). Wit: GEORGE DUNAWAY, PETER
HODO JP.

Page 304:   Jan. 19, 1803, EDMUND DUNAWAY to JOSHUA STANFORD, Jnr. for
            $200, 50 acres, adj. TOLLER, CARTER, JONATHAN DUNAWAY,
EDMUND DUNAWAY (X) (LS). Wit: JAMES CARTER.

Page 305:   Sept. 13, 1803, WILLIAM RUSHING of Washington Co., to JOHN
            RUSHING, 250 acres for $500, adj. MITCHEL's line, Fort
Creek, EDWARD BLACK, WILLIAM RUSHING (W) (LS). Wit: SAML. CAMP,
WMSON J. CRAWFORD.

Page 306:   Nov. 26, 1803, JOHN LANDRUM Sr. of Warren Co., to JOSHUA
            STANFORD, for $980, 280 acres originally granted to sd.
JOHN LANDRUM Aug. 17, 1785. JOHN LANDRUM (LS). Wit: ROBERT STANFORD,
JOHN BAYNE JP.

Page 307:   ANCIL PARISH gift to dau. DICY ALRAGE, cattle branded WP.
            ANSIL PARISH (L), Aug. 13, 1804. Wit: L. PRUITT, WM.
LEVETT JP.

Pages 307-308:   Sept. 21, 1803, GEORGE CLIFTON to JESSE CARTER for
                  $500, 225 acres part of 3 surveys held by sd. CLIFTON.
GEORGE CLIFTON (X) (LS). Wit: JAMES MECUM, RANDAL DUCKWORTH.

Pages 308-309:   Oct. 19, 1803, CLABORN NEWSOM of Columbia Co. to JESSEE
                  CARTER of Warren Co., for $1200, 300 acres on Big Brier
Creek, adj. BASS, ADAMS, and SALLIS (?). CLABORN NEWSOM (LS), NESTER
NEWSOM (X). Wit: JAMES CODY, PETER HODO, DANL. STARNES.

Pages 309-310:   Sept. 21, 1803, JOSEPH M. MATH (MCMATH?), to JESSE
                  CARTER, for $40, 20 acres, adj. EPHRAIM IVEY. JOSEPH
MCMATH (LS), ELIZABETH MCMATH (X). Wit: JAMES MECUM, RANDAL DUCKWORTH.

Pages 310-311:   Aug. 6, 1793, PHILIP POOL & MARY POOL Exrs., and NEW
                  TAPLEY, ELIZABETH TAPLEY, JUDITH WILDER & WM. TAPLEY,
heirs of JOEL TAPLEY, dec'd. to HENRY HARP, for 12 pounds sterling, 50
acres in Columbia County on Rocky Comfort Creek, part of a grant of
287½ acres granted to HERIS of MARK TAPLEY, Aug. 15, 1788. PHILIP POOL,
MARY POOL (X), NEW TAPLEY (N), ELIZABETH TAPLEY (X), JUDITH WILDER (つ).
Wit: JOHN WILDER, WILLIAM GRAY.

Pages 312-313:   Sept. 20, 1802, RICHARD SLAUGHTER to ENOCH ELLINGTON,
                  for $100, 76 acres adj. BARNET's Hickory, WM. BREWER's
line, part of a 138 acre grant to SAMUEL CAMP, June 15, 1800. RICHD.
SLAUGHTER (X) (LS). Wit: WALTER SLAUGHTER, BARTON ATCHINSON, JOSIAH
ELLINGTON (X). (Plat included)

Pages 313-314:   RICHARD SHIP of Hancock Co., to VINCENT JOHNSTON for
                  $200, 200 acres on Ogechee, adj. JOHN HODSON, origin-
ally granted to MATTHEW HUBERT, April 10, 1804. RICHARD SHIP (LS).
Wit: JNO J. DAVIDSON, DREWRY JACKSON.

Page 314:   Sept. 21, 1804, PETER P HODO to JOSHUA DRAPER, for $20, 20
             acres on Upton's Creek, adj. GRENAD R. HODO & JAMES SMITH.
P. HODO (LS). Wit: WILLIAM MOZLEY, JACOB JOHNSON.

Page 315:   Sept. 17, 1804, JOHN WILLIAMS to LEVEN STANFORD, for $250,
             50 acres on White's Creek, originally granted to THOMAS
CHILDRES Senr. from him conveyed to JOHN WILLIAMS from him to LEVIN
STANFORD. JOHN WILLIAMS (LS). Wit: ROBERT STANFORD, JOHN BAYN JP.

Pages 315-316:   THOMAS JONES & SARAH JONES appoint JOHN ALEXANDER of
                  Darlington District, South Carolina attorney, to
receive from Mrs. PARKER (tho now married to a man unknown, living in
the State of North Carolina, Salisbury District) from est. of STEPHEN
POOL Senr., dec'd of State of South Carolina, Nov. 1, 1804. THOMAS
JONES (T) (LS), SARAH JONES (J) (LS). Wit: WILLIAM CASON, CARTER
SAWYER (G).

Pages 316-318:   BENJAMIN HOWARD, Jr. bound to BENJAMIN HOWARD Senr.,
                  for $2500 on or before April 1, 1804... involving
certain negroes. BENJAMIN HOWARD Jnr. (LS). Wit: ASA HARFIELD, JAMES
TAYLOR.

Page 319:   Nov. 10, 1804, JAMES BRAY to GEORGE PARHAM for $600, land on
             Long Creek, 200 acres originally granted to THOMAS HAWTHORN.
JAMES BRAY (LS). Wit: WILLIAM PITTS, HARDY PITTS, JOHN PARHAM.

Pages 319-320:   NATHANIEL ALEXANDER SMITH formerly of that part of
                  Wilks Co. that is now Warren, did in 1789 decease
interstate, legal heirs and Legatees are his wife MARY SMITH, dau. NANCY
SMITH, son JAMES SMITH... did own land on Greens Creek (or Childres
Creek, adj. old line of Richmond Co., lands of WILLIM SCOTT, THOMAS
ANSLEY... 550 acres... since then NANCY SMITH has intermarried with
ISAAC BARBERIC of Warren Co., ... division of property... ISAAC BARBERIC
(X) (LS), NANCY BARBERIC (X) (LS). Wit: JNO. TORRENCE, D. NEAL JP.

Pages 321-322:   Jan. 12, 1800, ABRAHAM PERKINS to WILLIAM BUTT, for

$200, land on Rocky Comfort, 100 acres, part of a 200 acre tract to JOHN PERKINS. ABRAHAM PERKINS (LS). Wit: T. MATTHEWS JP, WILLIAM WHITE (X).

Pages 322-323: March 15, 1791, PETER COX & DEBORAH his wife to JOHN COX all of Columbia County, for 5 shillings sterling, land in Columbia & Wilkes Counties chiefly in Columbia, in St. Paul's Parish, 300 acres originally to the sd. DEBORAH STUBBS, now DEBORAH COX, adj. HENRY WILLIAMS, heirs of JOHN HODGENS, dec'd, JAMES GILMORE & BENJAMIN REESE... PETER COX (LS), DEBORAH COX (LS). Wit: BENJAMIN WATSON, BENJAMIN HARRISON, WM. THOMAS JP. (Plat included..) JOSEPH STUBBS, JOHN COX, chain bearers.

Pages 324-325: Jan. 3, 1803, VINSON & SUSANNAH JOHNSON to GEORGE TURNER, for $500, 113 acres on north side of Long Creek, part of a grant to CHILDRES, deed from him to BISHOP then to VINSON JOHNSON... line between SAMUEL JOHNSON & VINSON JOHNSON (LS), SUSANNAH JOHNSON (X) (LS). Wit: E. HARPER, SAML. JOHNSON.

Page 325: Jan. 10, 1803, ABRAHAM HEETH to STEPHEN MARSHALL for $500, 102 acres on Rocky Comfort, adj. WILLIE GRIZZEL, JOHN LOCK, ABRAHAM HEETH (LS). Wit: ABRAHAM CARD, ANDREW KING JP, WM. B. SHIVER (?).

Page 326: April 18, 1803, MARGARET MCALLISTER widow to CHARLES MCALLISTER her son, for $50, 50 acres on Rocky Comfort, part of a survey granted to JOHN DORDEN, Aug. 17, 1786, then sold to NOEL THORNTON, and by sd. THORNTON & his wife to MARGARET MCALLISTER. MARGARET MCALLISTER (X) (LS). Wit: WILLIAM BOKE, BOOZ. (?) KITCHING.

Page 327: Washington Co., Ga., Jan. 2, 1802, GEORGE FRANKLIN to DAVID ATKINS, for $250, 100 acres on Big Brier Creek, originally granted to the Rev. WILLIAM FRANKLIN, GEORGE FRANKLIN (LS). Wit: DAVID HARRIS, GEORGE HERNDON JP.

Pages 327-328: MARTIN HARDIN of Tattnall Co., for the friendship I have for LEWIS WRIGHT give all that tract of Brier and Middle Creeks, 350 acres, surveyed Feb. 17, 1795 and granted to me Nov. 18, 1800... M. HARDIN (LS). Wit: SAMUEL KITCHIN, JESSE EMBREE J. I. C.

Pages 328-329: Oct. 22, 1803, LEWIS WRIGHT Sheriff of Warren Co., to WILLIAM BIRD... whereas AMOS WRIGHT did before the Justices of Capt. Dushing obtain a judgment against JOHN WALLACE... whereas WALLACE lived on the river Ogechee, on a tract originally granted to PAMELLA HORN, Sept. 14, 1789, 100 acres... sold to the best bidder WILLIAM BIRD, LEWIS WRIGHT (LS). Wit: JOSIAH BEALL, JOHN MATHEWS JP.

Pages 329-330: Feb. 20, 1801, SAMUEL COBBS to DANIEL ATKINS for $50, 78 acres, surveyed by JAS MCCORMICK & bargained to JOHN MIM (?) (NUNN), from him to SAMUEL COBBS, adj. CHRISWELL, ROBINSON & ATKINS. SAMUEL COBBS (S) (SEAL). Wit: WM. B. MURPHY, WILLIAM CASON JP.

Pages 330-331: July 19, 1804, NEWIT WARD to JOHN BROOKS, for 200 pounds, 50 acres, part of a grant to JAMES RAILY, March 5, 1787. NEWIT WARD (X) (LS). Wit: WILLIAM EARNEST, WILLIAM SHURLEY.

Pages 331-332: Nov. 20, 1800, WILLIAM WOOD to DANIEL ATKINS, for $13, 13 acres, part of a 143 acre grant made Dec. 4, 1790, to BRITTAIN MCCULLERS, on Little Brier Creek, WILLIAM WOOD (SEAL). Wit: WILLIAM CASON JP, N TATHARP (N. T. ATHARP?).

Pages 332-333: Jan. 4, 1796, WILLIAM MADDOX of Richmond Co., to THOMAS FERRY for 10 pounds sterling, 362 acres originally granted to JOHN BARNETT, July 17, 1794 on Brier Creek, formerly Wilkes Co., now Warren Co., WILLIAM MADDOX (LS), ANN MADDOX (LS) Wit: JNO. BURNETT, A. CRAWFORD JP.

Pages 333-334:   Jan. 8, 1805, ELIZABETH LANDRUM Widow to JACOB TAYLOR
                  LANDRUM, for love and affection to her son... 100
acres adj. JOHN MCCORMICK, HOWARD, TAYLOR, WILLIAM LANDRUM, ELIZABETH
LANDRUM (X) (LS). Wit: BENJ. HOWARD Jnr., THO. DARK, MARY HOWARD.

Pages 334-335:   Dec. 8, 1804, THOMAS ANSLEY to JAMES ANSLEY, for $1,
                  land in Warren Co., part of a 1050 acre grant to THOS.
ANSLEY, May 24, 1787, adj. SMITH... THOS ANSLEY (LS). Wit: MORGAN
MALLOWN, JAMES CARTER JP.

Pages 335-336:   Oct. 12, 1801, PETER QUALLS to HENRIETTA NANCE for
                  $450, 300 acres on Joe's Creek, of Ogechee, adj. GILLS,
(GIBBS?), WALKERS, JAS & MCKINLEY... originally granted to SAMUEL
JOHNSTON April 19, 1790. PETER QUALLS (LS), NANCE QUALLS (X)(LS).
Wit: JOHN BRIDGES, BRITAIN BRIDGES.

Pages 336-337:   JAMES R. SOMMERS sold to HENRY DINSALL a negro man,
                  for $500, Jan. 19, 1805. JAMES R. SOMMERS (LS). Wit:
ARCHD. FLEWELLEN JP, STARLING GARDNER JP.

Pages 337-338:   Dec. 20, 1802, JOHN MOSES Jnr. to JOHN BURKHALTER, for
                  $1500, 500 acres adj. MOSES, NEWSOM, DARR, JOHN MOSES
MINER, GRAY, part of a grant to HESEKIAH BUSSEY and part of a tract to
HODO Sept. 1784, conveyed from BUSSEY to ROBERT MOSES, Senr., from
HODO to JOHN MOSES Junr... JOHN MOSES (LS). Wit: JAMES MECAN, SAMUEL
MOSES.

Pages 338-339:   Dec. 8, 1804, JAMES ANSLEY from THOS. ANSLEY for $250,
                  287½ acres on Middle Creek & Upton's Creek, part of a
grant to THOS ANSLEY, Jan. 19, 1785... WILLIAM ANSLEY's line... THOS
ANSLEY (LS). Wit: MORGAN MELLOWN, JAMES CARTER JP.

Pages 339-340:   Jan. 11, 1805, JETHRO DARDEN to JAMES MATTHEWS for $51,
                  land on William's Creek, adj. PARKER's line, WILKINSES
line, 27 acres... JE. DARDEN (LS). Wit: THOS FOUNTAINE, TIMOTHY
MATHEWS JP.

Pages 340-341:   Oct. 20, 1801, BENJAMIN UPTON to MOSES GRANBERRY for
                  $5, 171 acres on Rocky Comfort Creek, granted to sd.
BENJAMIN UPTON July 22, 1801, BENJM. UPTON (LS). Wit: MICK COSTLY,
NORVELL ROBERTSON JP.

Pages 341-342:   Dec. 12, 1803, WOOD MORELAND to SOLOMON MATHEWS,
                  $403, land on Rocky Comfort Creek, adj. JOHN BALL.
STEPHEN WRIGHT, ARCHD. F. ELLEN, 124 acres... WOOD MOURLAND (LS). Wit:
ISHMEAL BROWN, HOUSEMAN PASMORE (X).

Pages 342-343:   Dec. 4, 1801, JOHN LEDBETTER to LITTLETON CHAMBLESS
                  for $200, 50 acres, granted to sd. LEDBETTER April 19,
1790. JOHN LEDBETTER Senr. (LS). Wit: J. WOODSON, WILLIAMSON
CRAWFORD.

Pages 343-344:   May 19, 1804, MOSES GRANBERRY to GEORGE GRANBERRY, 200
                  acres at mouth of the mill branch of Rocky Comfort,
part of 2 other tracts, one granted to ARTHUR FAIL, the other to
JOHN SMITH... MOSES GRANBERRY (LS). Wit: FRANCIS WISE, DANIEL
SIMPSON (S).

Pages 344-345:   Jan. 20, 1801, JOHN SMITH to MOSES GRANBERRY for $500,
                  290 acres on Rocky Comfort Creek, JOHN SMITH (LS).
Wit: WILLIAM MCDOWEL, NORVELL ROBERTSON JP.

Pages 345-346:   Dec. 22, 1804, CHARLES MCCALLISTER to JAMES EASTWOOD
                  for $90, land adj. ADGENIAH VERDIN, WILLIAM BOWLES,
RICHD WHEELER, originally granted to JOHN DARDEN, conveyed to me by
MARGARET MCCOLLISTER. CHARLES MCCALLISTER (LS). Wit: T. PERSONS,
JNO. STALLING.

Page 346:   Jan. 3, 1806, ROBERT BEASLEY from DAVID BEASLEY, for $200,
            the two Flewelling tracts on Rocky Comfort, 233 acres.
DAVID BEASLEY (LS). Wit: GEO. HARGRAVES J. I. C., C. D. STUART.

Page 347:   State of North Carolina, I, JAMES MOORE of Halifax Co. for
            $285, to JEREMIAH BUTT of Warren Co., Ga., a negro. JAMES
MOORE (LS). Wit: NOEL (JOEL?) PITTS.

Pages 347-348:   WILLIAM LOWE to son THOMAS LOWE, give negroes and 130
                 acres on Long Creek. WILLIAM LOWE (LS). Wit: J.
OLIVER, H.CANDLER J. I. C.

Pages 348-349:   Aug. 17, 1796, JOHN SIMMONS to JESSE BUNKLEY for 50
                 pounds, 186 acres, adj. sd. BUNKLEY, LEWIS POWELL,
part of a 200 acre grant to MOSES POWELL, Dec. 20, 1785, sold by POWELL
to BORUM then to BENJAMIN SIMMONS, willed by him to JOHN SIMMONS. JNO
SIMMONS (LS). Wit: WM. BYROM JP, WM. LOVELL, HENR. MICHALL.

Pages 349-350:   June 3, 1805, JESSE BUNKLEY & KEZIA LUCAS widow
                 whereas, JOSHUA BUNKLEY dec'd, late of Charlotte Co.,
Virginia, bequeath unto MILDRED BUNKLEY, his then wife, but now lately
MILDRED RUTLAND, certain negroes... she has lately departed this life...
sd. JESSE & KEZIA being of full age decided to divide the negroes...
JESSE BUNKLEY (LS), KEZIA BUNKLEY (LS). Wit: JOHN LUCAS, Junr.,
SAML BARKESDALE, TERRELL BARKESDALE.

Pages 350-351:   Oct. 25, 1788, JOHN HARVEY & MARGARET HARVEY his wife
                 to JESSE BUNKLEY, for 267 pounds, on North Ogechee
in Wilkes County, part of a grant to sd. JOHN HARVEY, adj. MOSES POWELL,
SIMMONS... JOHN HARVEY (LS), MARGARET HARVEY (X) (LS). Wit: BENJAMIN
SIMMONS (X), ISREAL BURNLEY, RANDOLPH RUTLAND.

Page 352:   Oct. 15, 1803, JOHN PARKER to JOHN & THOMAS KELLYS, for
            $200, 51 acres... part of a tract of 373 acres belonging to
JOHN KELLEYS, dec'd, father of RACHEL PARKER, wife of JOHN. JOHN P.
PARKER (LS), RACHEL PARKER (X) (LS). Wit: JAMES WAGGONER, DAVID W.
WAGGONER.

Pages 352-353:   JOHN ASHWERT authorizes JOHN FRANCIS FLOUNOY his
                 lawful attorney, for his father's estate in the state
of Virginia, Feb. 11, 1805. JOHN ASHWEST (?). Wit: ARCHELUS FLEWELLEN,
SOLOMON LOCKET JP.

Pages 353-354:   April 5, 1794, JOHN HOBSON son & heir to MATHEW HOBSON
                 dec'd, to JOHN LYDDALE DIXON of Washington Co., Ga.,
for 100 pounds, property in Pittsylvania County, Virginia, land patented
to MATHEW HOBSON, Aug. 6, 1792. JOHN HOBSON (LS). Wit: JOHN HENNESS'Y,
JOHN HAMMILL Not Pub & JP.

Pages 354-355:   Oct. 21, 1799, JESSE BROOK to HEZEKIAH WILLIAMS for
                 $200, land on Rocky Comfort, 100 acres... JESSE BROOKS
(LS). Wit: JAS. GRIZZARD, JOHN MCCLUNG.

Pages 355-356:   May 24, 1803, PHILIPS GIBBS to WILLIAM KENOR Jnr. for
                 $800... WILLIAM KENOR & VASHTI his wife, land adj.
WALKER on Little Creek, WILLIAMS' line... PHILIP GIBBS (LS). Wit:
ELHANON GIBBS, ZACHEUS GIBBS (W).

Pages 356-357:   July 10, 1795, WM. BERRY Senr to JILSON BERRY planter,
                 for 100 pounds, 100 acres on Long Creek, originally
granted to WILLIAM BERRY Senr. in part of his head right 1785...
WILLIAM BERRY (LS). Wit: PRESLEY BERRY, MARY BERRY, ANDERSON BERRY,
JARROT BERRY.

Pages 357-358:   Oct. 13, 1790 BAXTER POOL of Richmond County, mechanic,
                 and ANN his wife to NOAH KELSEY, for 225 pounds, 450
acres in Wilks County, adj. THOMAS ANSLEY, COLLINS, granted to EDMUND
BUGG HICKS, Oct. 24, 1787, B POOL (LS), ANN POOL (LS). Wit: EDWD.
RANDOLPH, THO. WATKINS JP.

Pages 358-359:   Dec. 7, 1789, EDMUND BUGG HICKS of Richmond Co. to
                  BAXTER POOL CARPENTER, for 30 pounds sterling, 150 acres
(same tract as above)... EDM HICKS (LS). Wit: JAMES BROWN, ROBERT
DUCK.

Pages 359-360:   March 15, 1802, JOHN WILLIAMS of Winston County, South
                  Carolina & WILLIAM WILLIAMS of Burke County, Ga., to
NOAH KELSEY of Burk Co., Ga., for $3000, 350 acres on Evans Creek of
Ogechee, originally to EZEKIEL WILLIAM dec'd, Oct. 5, 1785 (date of
grant), willed to his son JOHN WILLIAMS and in case of his death without
heirs to his son WILLIAM WILLIAMS, two tracts totalling 500 acres,...
JOHN WILLIAMS (LS), WILLIAM WILLIAMS (LS). Wit: ROBERT IVERSON JP.

Page 361:   Jan. 9, 1792, JOSEPH BRYAN to NOAH KELSEY of Richmond Co.,
             for 225 pounds, 450 acres in Wilkes County, granted to
EDMUND B. HICKS, conveyed to BAXTER POOL, then to NOAH KELSEY, then to
JOSEPH BRYAN Dec. 29, 1790... JOSEPH BRYAN. Wit: THOS WATKINS JP.

Pages 362-363:   Nov. 20, 1804, WILLIAM GAZA Blacksmith to SOLOMON
                  NEWSOM, Junr., for $400, about 302 acres, granted to
SOLOMON NEWSOM Senr. dec'd, April 15, 1797, WILLIAM GAZA (LS). Wit:
AARON GAZA, JOEDAY NEWSOM JP.

Pages 363-364:   Jefferson County, Mississippi. HENRY MANDEN, appoints
                  WILLIAM COLLINS of same place attorney on the est. of
HENRY MANDUE (?), Sept. 29, 1804. H. MANDUE (LS), Wit: JESSE WITHERS.
JOHN HENDERSON for Miss. Territory, City of Natchez.

Pages 364-365:   Dec. 3, 1802, ANDERSON BERRY to BILSON BERRY, for $200
                  part of a 215 acre grant to SAML. CAMP, Feb. 9, 1790.
ANDERSON BERRY (LS). Wit: WILLIAM KELLIBREW, ARTHUR JENKINS, WILLIAM
ELLIS.

Pages 365-366:   Dec. 29, 1804, SAMUEL S. KELLY to JOHN RUSHING for
                  $250, 125 acres on Rocky Comfort, adj. VERDIN...
Wit: JOHN HATCHER, N. ROBERTSON JP, SAMUEL SKELLY (SAMUEL S. KELLY?).

Pages 366-367:   Dec. 7, 1804, ENOCH RENTFROE, to JOHN RUSHING for $500,
                  land on Joe's Creek, adj. TALOR PORT oak, ... later
says BENTFROE... plat included, part of land granted to STEPHEN PRITCHARD
Aug. 13, 1788, and part of a grant to SAML. CAMP. ENOCH RENTFROE (LS).
Wit: WILLIAM SHURLEY, LARKIN CHIVERS (X).

Pages 367-368:   Aug. 13, 1804, ENOCK ELLINGTON to WILLIAM CRAWFORD for
                  $200, land adj. Long Creek, WILLIAM BREWER, RICHARD
LOVETT, part of 138 acres granted to SAML. CAMP (Plat included).
ENOCK W. ELLINGTON (LS). Wit: JAMES LEDBETTER, CLABORN CRAWFORD.

Pages 368-369:   April 18, 1801, AMBROSE HADLEY to HENRY KINDALL for
                  $5, land in Rocky Comfort, AMBROSE HADLEY (X) (LS). Wit
T. PERSONS, JNO MATHEWS J. I. C.

Page 369:   JOHN LOWE of Hancock Co., Ga., sell to WILLIAM LOWE a slave
             for $450, JOHN LOWE (LS). Wit: THOMAS LOWE.

Pages 369-370:   Oct. 11, 1803, JOHN MYRICK to HENRY KINDALL for $400,
                  292 acres on Whetstone Creek, JOHN MYRICK (LS). Wit:
ALEXANDER F. ELLEN, JOHN MATHEWS JP.

Page 370:   WILLIAM LOWE to THOMAS LOWE, a negro for $450. WILLIAM LOWE
             (LS). Wit: E. THOMAS, H. CANDLER J. I. C.

Page 370-371:   1793, JOHN TALIAFERO of Wilks Co. to CHARLES DANSLE of
                  same... JOHN TALIAFERO & MARY his wife... later CHARLES
DARNELD, 125 acres for 45 pounds, adj. MAYS, MCDANIEL, BALL, THOMAS
FULLER, granted 1787, JOHN TALIAFERRO (LS), MARY TALIAFERRO (LS), Wit:
JONES PERSONS, JONATHAN MCRARY.

Pages 371-372:   March 27, 1804, JOSEPH GRIZARD to SILAS TODD for $400
                 part of a tract granted to BREAN MCCLENDON, "Feb. 15,
last," adj. HUBBERT, MORE, SHURLEY on Rocky Comfort... JOSEPH GRIZARD
(LS). Wit: JOHN BROOKS, WILLIAM EARNEST.

Pages 372-373:   EDWARD HOGANS of Washington Co., to RICHARD BEASLEY
                 of Warren Co., negroes, no amt. stated. Jan. 1, 1794.
EDWARD HOGAN (E) (LS). Wit: FRANS. BECK, JAMES BEASLEY.

Pages 373-374:   March 19, 1799, ALEXANDER FLEWELLEN of Warren Co. to
                 HENRY KINDALL for $20, 300 acres on s. side of
Whetstone Creek, ALEXANDER F. ELLEN (LS). Wit: JOHN MATHEWS, AMBROSE
HADLEY (X).

Page 374:   Nov. 24, 1803, JEREMIAH BEALL to GEORGE COTTON, for $600,
            adj. STITH, NEAVES & KELLY, 100 acres on Golding Creek.
JEREMIAH BEALL (LS). Wit: JAMES MECUM, JEREMIAH BEALL.

Page 375:   Feb. 13, 1805, JEREMIAH BEALL to GEORGE COTTON for $100,
            20 feet square where Cotton's Store house stands. JEREMIAH
BEALL (LS). Wit: JAS. MCCORMICK. Other Wit. illegible.

Pages 375-376:   Jan. 11, 1805, JETHRO DARDEN to TIMOTHY MATHEWS for
                 $60, land on Williams' Creek, 18 acres JE. DARDEN (LS).
Wit: THOS FOUNTAIN, JOHN BROOKS.

Pages 376-377:   Jan. 21, 1805, RICHARD SAMMON to REDDICK BASS for $457,
                 land on Middle Creek, adj. JOHN GIBSON's line,
CULPEPPER's line, 450 acres originally granted to JOHN TORRENCE Dec. 30,
1787. RICHARD SAMMON (LS). Wit: LAUR. D. BRYAN, HENRY HILL.

Pages 377-378:   June 22, 1804, LEVI PRUITT to THOMAS MADDUX for $45,
                 30 acres, (plat included)... granted in 1785 to JOHN
YOUNG, adj. MADDOX, LANDRUM & MOORE... L. PRUITT (LS), E. S. PRUITT (LS).
Wit: THOMAS EDMUNDSON, MAS MCCORMICK JP.

Pages 378-379:   May 26, 1803, PHILIP GIBBS to RICHARD WHITE NANCE for
                 $100, land part of a tract granted to JEREMIAH WILCHER
on Big Creek of Ogechee, adj. Walker's Branch.. VANCE's line... PHILIP
GIBBS (LS), PHEBE GIBBS (,) (LS). Wit: THOMAS MILES, ISAIAH EELAND.

Pages 379-380:   HUGH MCGEE, dec'd.. schedule of property... against est.
                 of WILLIAM FEW dec'd... Jan. 14, 1805. WILLIAM NANCE,
CATHERINE NANCE... JULIA MCGEE heir of HUGH MCGEE dec'd.

Pages 380-381:   Aug. 10, 1801, NICHOLAS POOL to WILLIAM LOCKET for
                 $130, 50 acres on Williams' Creek. WILLIAM LUCKET (LS).
Wit: WILLIAM CHAPMAN, WM. SMITH.

Page 381:   April 13, 1805, STEPHEN MARSHALL to ELISHA HURT for $100,
            land on s. side of Rocky Comfort Creek, 50 acres STEPHEN
MARSHALL (LS). Wit: JESSE MATHEWS, STARLING GARDNER JP.

Page 382:   Legal heirs of JOHN HUTCHINSON dec'd of Warren Co. to
            SOLOMON THOMPSON, for $800, 200 acres on Mill Creek of Little
River, originally granted to JOHN WHITSILL, Junr. July 3, 1770,
transferred by deed to sd. JOHN HUTCHINS Sept. 26, 1774, bound at
present by JACOB BULL, JOSIAH HARDING, WILLIAM BERRY. July 21, 1804.
THOMAS HUTCHINS (LS), ELIZABETH EWIN, ROBERT PARKER (LS), HANNAH
PARKER (LS), ALEJAMA HUTCHINS (X-her mark), NANCY HUTCHINS. Wit:
WILLIAM BERRY JP, JAMES MATHEWS.

Pages 383-384:   Whereas in 1789 NATHANIEL ALEXANDER SMITH a citizen of
                 the part of Wilkes Co., known as Warren, deceased
interstate without a will, leaving legal and legitimate heirs, MARY
SMITH his wife, a daughter NANCY SMITH & one son JAMES SMITH... land on
a branch of Greens Creek, otherwise called Childres Creek adj. WILLIAM

SCOTTS, THOMAS ANSLEY and by the line of Richmond County, surveyed for
the sd. SMITH 1785... MARY the widow now has intermarried with WILLIAM
TARVER... WILLIAM RAVER & MARY sell for $160 land to JACOB DARDEN,
their third of the 550 acres. WILLIAM TARVER (T) (LS). Wit: WILLIAM
TORRENCE, JOHN BAKER, JOHN TORRENCE. (Plat included.)

Page 385:   SAMUEL FICKLING to son BAR W. FICKLING negroes... (later)
             BARNARD W. FICKLING... my two daughters ANN JONES &
ELIZABETH FICKLING. SAM FICKLING (LS). Wit: ARCHD. FLEWELLEN, SHAD.
FLEWELLEN. Jan. 26, 1805.

Pages 386-387:   April 23, 1801, JAMES MOSSMAN, Exr. of JAMES MCKAY,
                  dec'd to THOMAS YOUNG Esqr. of Chatham Co., 500 acres,
in Parish of St. Paul, now Columbia Co., adj. JOSIAH SAUDNERS, originally
granted to JAMES MCKAY, Dec. 6, 1774... Mr. LAWSON was granted on Dec.
15, 1797, Exrs. of estate... JAMES MOSSMAN Esqr. (LS). Wit: GEO. W.
NICHOLS, THOS YOUNG, Junr.

Pages 388-389:   June 4, 1805, JEREMIAH BEALL & ELIZABETH his wife for
                  25 cents and diver causes to SOLOMON SLATTER, JOHN C.
TURNER, WORMLY ROSE, WILIE HARRIS & NICHOLAS WILLIAMS as trustees one
acre of land near Warrenton... for building of a Meeting House, for the
Methodist Society... the house be for the Baptist, Presbyterian or any
other Sect. or Denomination whatsoever, who believes in the Gospel...
JEREMIAH BEALL, ELIZABETH BEALL (LS). Wit: STEPHEN MARSHALL, ANDREW
KING JP.

Page 389:   April 15, 1801 JOSHUA REYNOLDS to JOHN VERDIN for $300, 50
             acres on Rocky Comfort Creek, adj. WILCHER, RICHARD BEASLEY..
JOSHUA REYNOLDS (LS). Wit: L. PRUITT, J. I. C., SAMUEL BEALL.

Pages 389-390:   May 14, 1803, HENRY HARRIS & MARTHA his wife to
                  JOHN HOBSON, for $900, 200 acres on Ogechee River, adj.
MATHEW HUBBERT, then in Wilkes County & granted to JOSEPH RIELY, June
13, 1791, HENRY HARRIS (LS). Wit: PETER CLOUR, ANDREW KING.

Pages 390-391:   March 12, 1805, JEREMIAH & JOSIAH BEALL to JOHN
                  MATHEWS for $150, one acre, JEREMIAH BEALL (LS), JOSIAH
BEALL (LS). Wit: GEO. HARGRAVES J. I. C., JAMES BYNUM.

Pages 391-392:   Oct. 30, 1804, SAMUEL STORY to MOSES HILL for $150, land
                  formerly granted to NEEDHAM SMITH, Jan. 7, 1787 corner
made by sd. HILL & JOHN HAMILTON... SAMUEL STORY (S) (LS). Wit:
SAML. STORY (S), WM. CASON JP.

Page 392:   PETER HODO for natural affection to my five children, NEAL,
             AUGUSTUS, PETER, BALDWIN, HUTHCERSON, MARGUESS LAFAYETTE &
INDIANIA... a negro girl. P. HODO. Wit: BENJAMIN REESE, JACOB
BURKHALTER May 12, 1805.

Pages 393:   SAMUEL FICKLING to grand daughter ELIZABETH F. JONES, dau.
              of STARLING JONES, a negro woman. Dec. 17, 1804. SAMUEL
FICKLING. Wit: ARCHS. FLEWELLEN, SHAD. FLEWELLEN.

Pages 393-394:   April 17, 1804, LEWIS WRIGHT Planter to MILLY CHAPMAN
                  (Widow) for $12, land on Williams' Creek, originally
granted to BENJAMIN SCOTT, Dec. 17, 1784. LEWIS WRIGHT (X) (LS).
Wit: WILLIAM CHAPMAN, STEPHEN BUTT.

Pages 394-395:   Aug. 12, 1803, HARBERT SIMS to WILLIAM WADE, for $200,
                  granted to BARTLETT SIMS Senr. dec'd, willed to sd.
HARBERT SIMS, adj. BARLOTT SIMS Junr., LEW SMELLING, and the River Road
of Ogechee, 90 acres. HARBERT SIMS (LS). Wit: WILLIAM BROOKS,
BARTLOOTT SIMS.

Pages 395-396:   Clarke County, Ga., March 20, 1805, WILLIAM WILKINS to
                  JAMES MATHEWS of Warren Co. for $100, 50 acres on
Hart's Creek, originally granted to PETER PERKINS. WILLIAM WILKINS (X)
(LS). SARAH WILKINS (◔) (LS). Wit: ELIZABETH KELLIM (?), JOSHA BROWNING
JP.

Pages 396-397:   PETER PERKINS to grandson JOHN WILKINS son of WILLIAM
                  & SARAH WILKINS now an infant or minor, land on Hart's
Creek, adj. JOSEPH WHITE, SOLOMON THOMPSON & THOMAS FONTAINE, 50 acres,
originally granted to myself Dec. 30, 1788. PETER PERKINS (X) (LS).
Wit: SOLOMON THOMPSON, TIMOTHY MATHEWS JP, JNO. TORRENCE J. I. C.

Pages 397-398:   Dec. 15, 1804, ELIZABETH WESTMORELAND Amdx. of est. of
                  ISHAM WESTMORELAND of Hancock Co., to MARY PARKER
Admx. & SOLOMON THOMPSON Admr. of est. of JAMES PARKER dec'd both of
Warren Co., for $500, land on Williams Creek, part of a grant to PETER
PERKINS Dec. 13, 1788. ELIZABETH WESTMORELAND (X) (LS). Wit: JACOB
LOCKETT, GEORGE CLOWER (X).

Pages 398-399:   Feb. 18, 1804, JAMES WHEELER to JOHN FONTAINE Planter
                  for $225, 50 acres on Williams' Creek, part of a 200
acres grant to SUSANNAH WALL (Widow) and vested in the sd. WHEELER by
his intermarriage with the sd. SUSANNAH. Granted April 9, 1784. JAMES
WHEELER (X) (LS), SUSANNAH WHEELER (X). Wit: JNO TORRENCE J. I. C.,
DAVID COX, SOLOMON LOCKETT JP. (Plat included.)

Pages 400-401:   Feb. 6, 1804, JOHN GREESON Snr. to LUCY THOMPSON Snr.
                  & LUCY THOMPSON and ALEXANDER DO, for $900, land on
Williams Creek, granted by Pattent to GEORGE PALMORE, April 8, 1785,
adj. BERRY CHAPMAN, JAMES WHEELERS. JOHN GREESON (LS). Wit: THOS
FONTAIN, JOSIAS WRIGHT.

Pages 401-402:   Feb. 21, 1805, JOHN FONTAINE to JAMES ALLEN for $250,
                  50 acres on Williams's Creek, granted to SUSANNAH WALL
(Widow)... JOHN FONTAINE (LS). Wit: THOS FONTAINE, DAVID COX.

Pages 402-403:   April 13, 1805, SAMPSON WILDER to FRANCIS RISHER for
                  $250, 50 acres adj. GILES BERRY, Wilders Branch,
JAMES WAGONER, SAMPSON WILDER (LS). Wit: A. PERSONS, JNO TORRENCE
J. I. C.

Pages 403-404:   May 4, 1787, GEORGE PALMER & his wife of Burk Co., Ga.,
                  to JOHN GRESON of Wilks Co., for 86 pounds, 200 acres
on Williams Creek, GEORGE PALMER (LS), MARY PALMER (P)(LS). Wit: HALL
HUDSON, WILLIAM JONES, MARY JONES.

Pages 404-405:   Jan. 11, 1805, JETHRO DARDEN to JOHN FONTAIN for $230,
                  117 acres on Williams Creek, adj. PARKER, FEW,
WILKINS, part of a tract formerly belonging to PETER PERKINS, JE
DARDEN (LS), ELLENDER DARDEN (X) (LS). Wit: JOHN BROOKS, TIMOTHY
MATHEWS JP.

Pages 405-406:   Jan. 11, 1805, JETHRO DARDEN to THOMAS FONTAIN, for
                  $350, 87 cares on Hart's Creek... WILLIAM WILKINS
line... JE DARDEN (LS), ELLENDER DARDEN (X) (LS). Wit: JOHN BROOKS,
TIMOTHY MATHEWS JP.

Pages 406-407:   PETER HODO to his five children NEAL, AUGUSTUS, PETER,
                  BALDWIN HUTCHERSON, INDIANNA GUEN & MARQUES la FAYETTE.
cattle, etc.. P. HODO (LS). Wit: GEO. HARGRAVES. May 22, 1805.

Pages 407-408:   Dec. 14, 1802, CHARLES LINN to WILLIAM SMYTH, for $500,
                  280 acres formerly in Richmond Co., now Warren,
originally granted to CHARLESS LINN, Sr., dec'd, left by him to his
son JOHN Dec. 30, 1788, sd. son JOHN since deceased... purchased by
his brother FERGUS Dec. 18, 1801, and 70 acres by purchase from BAILEY
WILKERSON in right of his wife JANE LYNN and other acres purchased from
his sister ANN LINN... CHARLES LYNN (LS). Wit: JOHN HARDIN, DANL.
MCCOWAN.

Pages 408-409:   Dec. 28, 1801, BAILEY WILKERSON of Columbia Co. to
                  CHARLES LINN, for $100, land adj. JAMES WRIGHT, 70
acres, 1/5 of tract granted to CHARLES LINN Senr., containing 350 acres.
BAILEY WILKERSON (LS), JINCY WILKERSON (LS). Wit: AQUILLA HOWARD,
THOS WHITE JP.

Pages 409-410:   Dec. 28, 1801. FURGUS LINN of Columbia Co., to CHARLES
                 LINN, for $100, 1/5 of grant to CHARLES LINN, Senr.
FURGUS LINN (LS). Wit: AQUILLA HOWARD, THOMAS WHITE JP.

Pages 410-411:   Columbia Co., Ga., CHARLES LINN to WILLIAM SMITH, for
                 $70, 1/5 of a grant to CHARLES LINN, bought of
JOHN NEYLAND & ELIZABETH his wife (formerly ELIZABETH LINN)... CHARLES
LINN (LS). Wit: BAILEY WILKERSON, THAD. BEALL.

Pages 411-412:   Dec. 22, 1802, ANN LYNN of Columbia Co., to CHARLES
                 LINN, for $60, 1/5 of grant to CHARLES LINN Snr...
ANN LINN (LS). Wit: THAD BEALL, GEORGE JONES.

Pages 412-413:   Feb. 21, 1803, JOHN NEYLAND & ELIZABETH his wife of
                 Columbia Co., for $70, 1/5 of grant to CHARLES LINN...
J. NEYLAND (LS), ELIZABETH NEYLAND. Wit: BAILEY WILKERSON, THD. BEALL.

Pages 413-414:   Jan. 28, 1805, WILLIAM SMITH of Columbia to HENRY COX
                 of Warren Co., for $400, 350 on Carsons Creek, origin-
ally granted to CHARLES LINN Snr... WILLIAM SMITH (LS). Wit: WALTER
DENT, THOS. WHITE JP.

Pages 414-415:   May 18, 1797, HARRISON JONES to GEORGE WALKER of
                 Augusta, for $100, 200 acres in then Columbia Co., now
Warren, adj. MCDANIEL, on Deep Creek, granted to HARRISON JONES Feb. 10,
1797. HARRISSON JONES (LS). Wit: NICHOLAS WARE, EZEKIEL MILLER, T.
PERSONS.

Pages 415-416:   March 5, 1803, STEPHEN STANFORD of Columbia Co., to
                 JOSEPH HARVILL & wife PATSY for $30, 100 acres on
White's Creek, in Warren & Columbia Counties, part of a 300 acre tract
that JOSEPH MATTOX conveyed to sd. STEPHEN STANFORD, adj. JESSE CARTER,
JAMES MULLEN ANSLEY & JAS. CARTER... STEPHEN STANFORD (C) (LS). Wit:
JOHN BAYN, JESSE CARTER.

Pages 416-417:   Aug. 13, 1805, HARDY NEWSON of Warren Co. to ISAAC
                 BROOKS, for $250, 100 acres adj. LANDRUM's line, HUGH
REES's line, SAUNDERS line, THOMAS CHILDRES... HARDY NEWSOM (H) (LS).
Wit: NATHANIEL THOMPSON, JOHN BAYN JP.

Pages 417-418:   June, 1805, ALEXR PERRYMAN Sheriff of Warren Co. to
                 WILLIAM EARNEST... suit of WILLIAM PITTS against JAMES
EASTWOOD, for $50 highest bid, land on Rocky Comfort 60 acres, part of
a 100 acre survey to JOHN DARDEN... A PERRYMAN (LS). Wit: THOMAS
KENT, D. NEAL JP.

Pages 418-419:   May 13, 1805, ALEXANDER PERRYMAN Sheriff to DAVID NEAL.
                 suit of DAVID NEAL against WILLIAM TODD for $36,
Rocky Comfort Creek, 50 acres bound by land where the relick of WILLIAM
KITCHENS Senr. dec'd, now resides... WILLIAM BROOKS, ALEXR. PERRYMAN
(LS). Wit: WM. GAZA, H. CANDLER J. W. C.

Page 420:   May 19, 1804, HENRY KINDAL to LAURENCE KITCHINGS for $90,
            plat made Nov. 25, 1788 (acreage not given)... HENRY
KINDALL (LS). Wit: SAMUEL PITTS, WILLIAM SLATER.

Pages 421-422:   Jan. 14, 1802, BENJAMIN KATON to RICHARD LEE for $510,
                 182 acres on Big Ogechee... BENJAMIN KEATON (X) (LS).
Wit: THOMAS ROGERS, JOHN KEATON.

Pages 422:   April 26, 1803, WILLIAM KITCHINGS to JAMES EASTWOOD, for
             $175, 150 acres, adj. SANFORD, MCCLENDON, BRYANT... a
grant to WILLIAM KITCHINGS, April 22, 1803... WILLIAM KITCHINGS (LS).
Wit: T. PERSON, JONES PERSONS.

Pages 423-424:   June 5, 1805, ALEXANDER PERRYMAN Sheriff to WILLIAM
                 PITTS suit of JOHN PARHAM Guardian for sd. PITTS,
against JAMES EASTWOOD... for $120, 50 acres on Rocky Comfort. ALEXR.
PERRYMAN (LS). Wit: T. PERSONS, JNO STALLINGS.

Pages 424-425:   May 16, 1799 IGNATIUS FEW of Columbia Co., to TIMOTHY
                   LEE for 47 pounds, 100 acres on Long Creek, land
granted to IGNATIUS FEW Sept. 23, 1784... (Plat included.) I FEW (SEAL),
Wit: JOHN ROBERTSON, SAML. BUFFINGTON.

Pages 425-426:   Jan. 24, 1800, TIMOTHY LEE to SAMUEL CAMP for $300,
                   100 acres on Long Creek, part of a 350 acre grant to
IGNATIUS FEW Sept. 23, 1784. TIMOTHY LEE (T) (LS). Wit: J. WOODSON,
JACOB LITTLETON, THOS FRIEND JP.

Pages 426-427:   CLOUDSLEY CAMPT for $230, 50 pd by SAMUEL CAMPT cattle,
                   Dec. 31, 1804. CLOUDSLEY CAMP (LS). Wit: MANOAH
HUBBARD, THADDEUS CAMP, H. CANDLER J. W. C.

Pages 427-428:   Feb. 22, 1793, PHILLIP LOGAN of Wilks Co. to DIXON
                   HALL of Green County, for 45 pounds, 100 acres on Long
Creek, of Ogechee, PHILIP LOGAN (LS). Wit: JOSEPH PAVEY (X), WYATT
COLLIER.

Pages 428-429:   May 23, 1797, NICHOLAS LONG of Wilks Co. to SAMUEL
                   CAMP of Warren Co., for $100, adj. CHAMBLESS, LONGE,
(plat included), granted to NICHOLAS LONG April 26, 1787... N. LONG
(LS). Wit: WILLIAM MALLOREY, CARAH CAMP.

Pages 429-430:   Oct. 19, 1802, CORNELIUS WHILLINGTON of Hancock Co.
                   to SAMUEL CAMP of Warren Co., for $340, CORN
WHITTINGTON (LS). Wit: SUZANAH TALBERT, ALEXR. MONTGOMERY, JESSE
TALBERT JP.

Pages 430-431:   JOHN HOBSON for $900, to VINSON JOHNSTON, 200 acres on
                   Ogechee, adj. MATHEW HUBERTS, land granted to JOSEPH
ROILEY (then in Wilks Co.)... JOHN HOBSON (LS). Wit: W. MARSHALL,
JOEL STURDIVANT, JOHN HATCHER JP.

Pages 431-432:   Oct. 17, 1803, BENJMAIN PORTER of Wilkes Co. to WILSON
                   WOODRUFF of South Carolina, for $1500, 203 acres
granted to ABRAHAM DENNIS (originally in Richmond Co.) on Little River,
adj. SMITH, SHITESDIES, JOSEPH EVANS... BENJA PORTER (LS). Wit: JOHN
COURSE J. I. C., WILLIAM POE.

Pages 432-433:   Jan. 11, 1805, BENJAMIN HARRISON to WILLIAM MILLIRONS
                   part of a 230 acre granted July 11, 1795. BENJAMIN
HARRISON (X) (LS). Wit: REUBEN REESE, JOHN BROOK ( ).

Page 433:   March 31, 1804, JOHN NIDAY to JESSE STUBBS for $400, land on
              Carson's Creek, 124½ acres, part of a large survey, late the
property of JOHN CARSON, Snr. dec'd and sold by JOHN WILLIAMS to JOHN
NIDAY, adj. heirs of JOSHUA HILL, BUTLER & COOPER (plat included) &
DAVIDSON. JOHN NIDAY (LS). Wit: CHAS. PORTER JP.

Page 434:   May 17, 1805, JAMES WEEKES to SAMUEL JOHNSTON for $100,
              24½ acres, on Red Lick Creek, one of the Waters of Ogechee,
adj. ROBERT SANFORDS land originally granted to ISAAC BUSH, SAMUEL
JOHNSON's line originally granted to ANDREW FRAZIER. JAMES WEEKS (LS).
Wit: WM. BYROM, WM. BRYROM Junr.

Pages 435:   Jan. 17, 1805, ASA COX to MOSES DARDEN for $520, 100 acres
               on Williams Creek, part of a grant of 950 acres to GEORGE
MURRAY, 1784. ASA COX his seal (LS), Wit: ROBERT HILL, SOLOMON
LOCKETT JP.

Page 436:   Sept. 27, 1805, WILLIAM MAY's of Warren Co. to BEVERLY
              HESTER, for $270, land granted to ISAAC BURSON 1784,
surveyed Aug. 12, 1784, adj. JNO BURKHALTER, WALKER, Brier Creek, E.
KIMSEY, WILLIAMS MAYS (LS). Wit: CHARLES D. STUART, M. HUBERT JP.

Pages 436-437:   April 24, 1805, RICHARD HODO of Columbia Co., to
                   JOSHUA DRAPER of Warren Co., for 25 dollars, 20 acres

land originally granted to RICHARD HODO, 150 acres May 13, 1805. RICHARD HODO (LS). Wit: HENRY WILLIAMS, JOHN BAYN JP.

Pages 437-438: Nov. 24, 1803, JOHN TORRENCE to MARK HARDIN, for $600, tract on Childres Creek, adj. HANNAH SMITH, land granted to THOMAS YOUNG, land sold to HUGH ARMSTRONG, land granted to THOMAS MASER, and land of WILLIAM SCOTT... part of 2 surveys, the easternmost part of 300 acres granted to THOMAS WHITE, March 29, 1785 and conveyed to sd. TORRENCE Oct. 23, 1799, and a survey of 300 acres granted to JOHN TORRENCE, April 23, 1803... JOHN TORRENCE (LS). Wit: WM. HARRESS, G. GEORGE JP.

Pages 439-440: May 5, 1804, JAMES SMITH, Blacksmith to ASA COX planter, for $500, 100 acres on Williams Creek, adj. GEORGE HARRIS, JOHN SIMS, PIERCE BALEY, JOHN BAKER, MOSES DARDEN, part of 950 acres granted to JOE MURRY, 1784, conveyed to JOHN BAKER, then to JACOB DARDEN, then to JOHN BUSTIN then to above JAMES SMITH... JAMES SMITH (LS). Wit: EBENEZER SMITH, EBENEZER TORRENCE, JNO TORRENCE J. I. C. W. C.

Page 440: March 10, 1805, MATHEW PARHAM to EDWARD PARHAM for $300... (later written EDMUND PARHAM)... 200 acres, adj. to heirs of NATHL PARHAM dec'd, on Kilgore's Creek, GEORGE HENRY's land... MATHEW PARHAM (LS). Wit: Z FRANKLIN JP, HENRY WLAKER, JAMES PARHAM (X).

Page 441: Dec. 27, 1804, WILLIAM BURKHALTER & REBEKAH BURKHALTER, both of County of Edgefield, South Carolina to CLARK BLANDFORD, of Warren Co., for $600, 200 acres on Rocky fort, adj. SARAH GOLDING. WILLIAM BURKHALTER (LS), REBEKAH BURKHALTER (X) (LS). Wit: PETER RYAN, JOHN LYON (justice of Quorem for Edgefield Dist. S.C.)

Pages 442-443: Aug. 13, 1794, ROBERT MARLOW Planter, JOSEPH MARLOW, Planter, PRESILLAH MARLOW & CHARITY MARLOW of Hancock Co., to THOMAS JACKSON Planter, of Warren Co., for 70 pounds sterling 100 acres on Ogechee, adj. PILCHER and vacant land at time of survey, granted 1786. ROBERT MARLOW (LS), JOSEPH MARLOW (LS), PRESILLAH MARLOW (X) (LS), CHARITY MARLOW (X) (LS). Wit: ROBERT DICKINS, SISANOH JACKSON (X).

Pages 443-444: May 24, 1798, KEDER KEATON & SARAH his wife to THOMAS JACKSON, for $210, 150 acres on Keaton's Mill Creek, adj. JOHN KEATON MARLOW's land and connects land known as ALLEN TRACT... SARAH KEATON (X) (LS), KEADER KEATON (LS). Wit: JESSE KATON, JOHN L. HILLSON.

Pages 444-445: Jan. 10, 1801, SAMUEL STUBBS to WYATT BONNER for $50, 20 acres, adj. ADAM JONES, GEORGE PARHAM, SAML. STUBBS (LS). Wit: Z. FRANKLIN, ANN A O BREIN.

Pages 445-446: Nov. 12, 1803, ROBERT DICKINS to THOMAS JACKSON for $350, 150 acres except for one that is reserved for the use of WILLIAM BIRD Senr & BENJAMIN A. HARRESS on the shoals of Ogechee, granted to JOHN WATKINS 1786, recorded BOOK HHH, Folio 850, adj. WILLIAM CHAMBERS & SIMS. ROBERT DICKINS (LS). Wit: N. ROBERTSON, JOHN HATCHER JP.

Pages 446-447: Sept. 14, 1804, WILLIAM CHAMBERS for $50, 8 acres on Georgetown Road, MCKENNELLY's stake corner, granted to sd. CHAMBERS Nov. 23, 1801, WILLIAM CHAMBERS (X). Wit: JOHN HATCHER, N. ROBERTSON JP.

Page 447: Sept. 14, 1804, WILLIAM CHAMBERS to THOMAS JACKSON, for $150, 150 acres, granted to sd. CHAMBERS 1797. WILLIAM CHAMBERS (X) (LS). Wit: JOHN HATCHER, N. ROBERTSON JP.

Page 448: Nov. 10, 1800, JOHN WILLIAMS to GEORGE PARHAM for $54, 53 acres, adj. to a grant to JOHN CARSON, adj. ROBERT BONNER's land. JOHN WILLIAMS (LS). Wit: JONES BONNER, WYATT BONNER.

Pages 449-450:   Feb. 20, 1800, JOHN CARSON to GEORGE PARHAM for $685,
                 228 acres, surveyed pursuant to a warrant from JAMES
HABERSHAM Esqr. surveyed Feb. 19, 1772, land on both sides of Carson's
Creek, (plat included)... JOHN CARSON (LS). Wit: Z. FRANKLIN, W. HILL.

Pages 450-451:   Dec. 21, 1805, JONES PERSONS to JOSEPH HOWARD, for $600,
                 150 acres on Rocky Comfort, adj. WILCHER at time of
survey... adj. RICHARD BEASLEY, conveyed to JONES PERSON by JOHN BERDIN
Dec. 3, 1804. JONES PERSONS (LS). Wit: JOS DUCKWORTH JP, T. PERSONS.

Pages 451-452:   JOHN HOWELL to son JOHN, cow and calf, to dau. MORNING
                 furniture, to ELIZABETH HOWEL.. to DEMPSEY HOWELL...
to JOEL HOWEL... I have given to my sd. children... Sept. 25, 1803. JOHN
HOWEL (LS). Wit: BENJA. PURKINS, DANIEL BUTLER.

Pages 452-453:   O HENRY CRITTENDON of Washington Co., to JOHN SPEED of
                 Richmond Co., impounding JOHN SPURLING... Richmond
County, North Carolina, Dec. 10, 1803 HENRY CRITTENDON (LS). Wit:
BARNED (?) BROWN. (Later appears to be BARRUT BROWN.)

Page 453:   Dec. 3, 1804, JOHN VERDIN to JONES PERSONS, for $65, tract
             on south side of Rocky Comfort, originally granted to
DPUIS conveyed to JOSEPH HOWARD then to JOSHUA REYNOLD then to sd.
VERDIN, adj. RICHARD BEASLEY, 50 acres. JOHN VERDIN (LS) ( ). Wit:
T. PERSONS, T. FLEWELLEN, D. NEAL JP.

Pages 454-455:   Sept. 7, 1805, JESSE SANFORD of Hancock Co. to THOMAS
                 MOODY of Warren Co., for natural good will and affec-
tion, part of a 790 acre grant to sd. SANFORD, 200 acres, JESSE SANFORD
(LS). Wit: JOHN PINKSTEN, WILLIAM SANFORD.

Pages 455-456:   Dec. 6, 1803, JEREMIAH BEALL of Warrenton & ELIZABETH
                 his wife to DAVID BUSH, for $50, land in Warrenton,
adj. Court House, JEREMIAH BEALL (LS), ELIZABETH BEALL (LS). Wit: D.
NEAL, L. PRUITT J. I. C.

Pages 456-457:   Jan. 20, 1806, WILLIAM AVERITT to REUBEN REESE, for
                 $200, 145 acres on southeast side of Stamp branch, adj.
AARON ATARIS, WILLIAM AVERITT... WILLIAM AVERETT (LS) (X). Wit:
E. THOMAS, DAVID NEAL JP.

Pages 457-458:   Sept. 7, 1798, EDMUND HAYS to PETER DAVIS for $75, 50
                 acres, adj. PETER COX... EDMUND HAYS (LS). Wit:
PETER COX, PETER HODO JP.

Page 458:   JOHN LEE, WILLIAM LEE & MARY LEE children of ELIZABETH BUSH
             and heirs of GREENBERRY LEE, dec'd, all being of lawful age.
portion of our Grandfather's estate to his daughter ELIZABETH our
Mother. JNO LEE (LS), WILL LEE (LS), MARY LEE (LS). Wit: STERLING
GARDINER, THOS K. SANDWICH. April 26, 1802.

Page 459:   JOHN & WILLIAM LEE acting as guardians to HANNAH, ANDREW &
             MOSES (both children of our Mother) have this day received
of THOMAS BUSH & our mother his wife ELIZABETH the full and ample
portion of the legacy of WILLIAM FEW Senr. to his dau. ELIZABETH &
heirs of her body. JOHN LEE (LS), WM. LEE (LS). Wit: STERLING
GARDNER, THOS K. SANDWICH.

Pages 459-460:   March 20, 1804, JOHN VANCE to PETER DAVIS for $52,
                 land adj. P. COX, 15 acres. WILLIAM SMITH. Wit: THOS
WHITE JP.

Pages 460-461:   Sept. 10, 1799, BENJAMIN REESE of Columbia Co., to
                 THOMAS SELL, for $114, land in Warren Co. adj. HARDIN's
line, LANDRUMS line, SCOTT's line. BENJ. REESE (LS). Wit: CATHERINE
WHITE, THOS J. WHITE JP.

Pages 461-462:   This day rec'd satisfaction for sum of $2500, Dec. 10,
                 1805, BENJAMIN HOWARD Sr. Wit: JOHN MOORE, JAMES
TAYLOR.

Pages 462-463:   Jan. 10, 1801, WYATT BONNER to SAMUEL STUBBS, for $50,
                 28 acres, adj. DANIEL MCCOWEN, ENOS BUTLER. WYATT
BONNER (LS). Wit: Z. FRANKLIN JP, ANNA OBRIEN.

Pages 463-464:   March 14, 1805, SAMUEL STUBBS & MARY his wife, to
                 THOMAS HAYNES for $1350, land on Upton's Creek (now by
the name of Hart's Creek)... several plats and deeds, the first and
second granted to PETER HART by Sir JAMES WRIGHT, the first July 5, 1770,
the second Nov. 6, 1770, and third a part of a tract granted to sd.
SAMUEL STUBBS, Aug. 24, 1796, adj. DANIEL MCCOWEN, JOEL CLOUD & others,
200 acres. SAMUEL STUBBS (LS), MARY STUBBS (LS). Wit: JOEL REVIS,
Z. FRANKLIN JP.

Pages 464-465:   June 24, 1797, NATHAN STUBBS of Columbia Co., to
                 SAMUEL STUBBS, for $400, two surveys that first 100
acres in Warren County (formerly Richmond, St. Paul's Parish) on
Upton's Creek, surveyor plat made Aug. 31, 1769, and annexed to the
grant to PETER HART, Nov. 6, 1770, the second grant made July 5, 1770...
NATHAN STUBBS (LS). Wit: Z FRANKLIN, THOS WHITE JP.

Page 466:   March 16, 1805, PETER COX Senior to PETER DAVIDSON for $750,
            adj. IVY & BENNEFIELD, land purchased by sd.COX of JAMES
GILMORE, PETER COX (LS). Wit: ROBERT LAZENBY, THOS. HOWARD, SAMPSON
S. STEELE JP.

Pages 466-467:   HENRY BONNER Jr. to ASA CHAPMAN for $400, land on
                 Williams Creek, originally granted to sd. HENRY BONNER
Jr., HENRY BONNER (LS). Wit: ZACHD. FLEWELLEN JP, TIMOTHY MATHEWS JP.
July 12, 1805.

Pages 467-468:   THOMAS BAZMORE of Warren County sold a negro girl to
                 JOHN SMITH, Feb. 7, 1806. THOMAS BAZMORE. Wit:
JOSEPH WHITE, ISHAM WHEELER (X), JAME MCCORMICK JP.

Pages 468-469:   Oct. 31, 1805, JOSEPH HOWARD to SAMUEL HALL for $600,
                 193 acres on Rocky Comfort, adj. LYNN, OZBURN, CASTLE-
BERRY, MCCRARY, granted to sd. JOSEPH HOWARD July 30, 1802. JOSEPH
HOWARD (LS), AMELIA HOWARD (LS). Wit: MATTHEWS MCCRARY, GEORGE WAYNE.

Pages 469-470:   Nov. 25, 1803, JOHN TORRENCE to WILLIAM SCOTT of
                 Columbia Co., for $100, 100 acres, adj. MARK HARDIN,
land granted to THOMAS WHITE, now the property of sd. HARDIN, the
northeast part of a 300 acre grant to sd. TORRENCE April 23, 1803.   JNO
TORRENCE (LS). Wit: WM. HARRISS, G. GEORGE JP.

Pages 470-471:   This indenture made by an order of the court of
                 Richmond County, Jan. 11, 1806, between DAVID ROBINSON,
JOHN WILSON, FITZ M. HUNT, Admr. of DAVID ROBERTSON, dec'd, to WILLIAM
M. COWLES, for $370, 245 acres adj. DANL. ATKINS, SHADRACH POTTS,
ROQUEMORE, originally granted to ABSOLAM JACKSON April 1787. DAVID
ROBERTSON (LS), J. WILSON (LS), FITZ M. HUNT (LS). Wit: J. KENNON,
THOS WESTBAY.

Pages 471-472:   Oct. 27, 1805, WILLIAM SCOTT of Columbia Co. to
                 MARY SELL, Admrx. of est. of THOMAS SELL, dec'd of
Warren Co., for $214, 170 acres on Childres Creek, WILLIAM SCOTT (LS).
Wit: JOHN QUIN, WILLIAM HARRIS, JOHN SCOTT (+). (Plat included.)

Page 472:   HENRY PEEBLES to dau. BETSEY PEEBLES, 8 negroes, for natural
            love. H. PEEBLES (LS). Feb. 5, 1806. Wit: A. PERSONS,
STERLING GARDNER JP.

Page 472:   HENRY PEEBLES for love to son WILLIAM H. PEEBLES, 8 negroes.
            H. PEEBLES. Wit: A. PERSONS, STERLING GARDNER JP.

Page 473:   ALEXANDER JARRETT for love to wife MARY JARROTT... lands,
            goods & chattels. Feb. 10, 1805. ALEXANDER JARROTT. Wit:
SOLOMON MATHEWS, NOEL MATHEWS, ROBT. GRIER.

            SAMUEL SKELLY, for $750, to JOHN RUSHING, five negroes.
Feb. 1, 1806, SAMUEL SKELLY (LS). Wit: R. WHITEHEAD, H. CANDLER.

Page 474:   JOHN GUTHRIE of Buncomb County, North Carolina to NATHAN
            DAVIS of Warren Co., Ga., for $250, 89 acres, adj. BRIER
& WHITE's Creek, originally granted to RICHARD SMITH, adj. HAMBLETON.
JOHN BUTHRIA (LS). Wit: WILLIAM CASON JP, WILLIAMSON ROWLAND. March
20, 1805.

Pages 474-475:   March 3, 1806, IGNATIUS FEW of Columbia Co., to
                 JOSEPH HILL of Warren Co., for $500, 171 acres, part of
a 200 acre grant to ISHAM WHEELAS, Dec. 16, 1793. I. FEW (LS). Wit:
JOHN TORRENCE J. I. C., M E HURT J. I. C.

Pages 475-476:   Jan. 20, 1806, GEORGE BREWER of Baldwin Co. to JOSEPH
                 HILL of Warren Co., for $50, 9 acres on Williams
Creek, GEORGE BREWER (X) (LS). Wit: WOOD MORELAND, MARK HEATH.

Pages 476-477:   April 27, 1803, JERUSHA STEWART to JOEL WILLIS for
                 $40, 20 acres on Rocky Comfort, part of a grant to
ANN STEWART, Jan. 8, 1793... BENSON tract... JERUSHA STEWART (X) (LS).
Wit: MOSES GRANBERRY, NORVEL ROBERTSON JP.

Page 477:   Feb. 24, 1806, BENJAMIN OLIVER of State of Virginia to
            JOB WILDER, for $300, 200 acres on Hart's Creek, BENJAMIN
OLIVER Senr. (LS). Wit: BENJ. OLIVER Junr. SAMPSON WILDER.

Page 478:   July 4, 1805, HENRY CASTLEBERRY of Clark Co. to JOHN
            HARDAWAY of Warren Co.,for $100, 84 acres, adj. MOSES &
DU KS, CASTLEBERRY, NEAL... HENRY CASTLEBERRY (LS). Wit: CHARLES
HARVELL, DAVID NEAL JP.

Pages 478-479:   June 25, 1805, WASHINGTON HARDAWAY to JOHN HARDAWAY,
                 for $50, 31 acres, part of a tract granted to JOHN
BURKHALTER and sold to STARLING WILLIAMSON on Jan. 17, 1797, then sold
to WASHINGTON HARDWAY, Nov. 1, 1804. WASHINGTON HARDAWAY (LS). Wit:
JOHN BIRKHALTER, DAVID NEAL JP.

Pages 479-480:   Nov. 1, 1802, HENRY CASTLEBERRY & SARAH his wife to
                 JOHN DARDAWAY, Blacksmith, for $400, 200 acres granted
to HENRY CASTLEBERRY, Sept. 14, 1789, adj. land granted to SAMUEL NEAL,
and land now owned by WILLIAMSONS & DARK. HENRY CASTLEBERRY (LS),
SARAH CASTLEBERRY (X) (LS). Wit: ROBERT MOSES, JAS. MCCORMICK JP.

Pages 480-481:   Feb. 25, 1806, JEREMIAH BEALL Merchant of Warrenton
                 to HENRY DENDALL for $1000, 50 acres on Broad St., adj.
NICHOLAS HAIRBUCKS, JACOB BIRKHALTER, GEORGE HARGRAVES GARDNER, JEREMIAH
BEALL (LS), ELIZABETH BEALL (X) (LS). Wit: T. PERSONS, JOHN C. TURNER,
WM. C. DUNKLEY.

Pages 482-483:   Feb. 17, 1806, WYATT BONNER & ANN his wife to THOMAS
                 HAYNES for $870, 100 acres granted to NATHAN STUBBS,
and sold to WYATT Nov. 14, 1796 and 56 acres adj. other tract lately
occupied by JOEL REEVES, part of a grant to sd. WYATT BONNER, one of
original corners BUTLER's and 20 acres granted to SAML. STUBBS, adj.
ADAM JONES' old tract. WYATT BONNER (LS), ANN BONNER (LS). Wit:
J. STITH, Z. FRANKLIN JP.

Pages 484-485:   May 9, 1803, FRANCIS DOYLE of Savannah, Merchant, and
                 DENNIS DOYLE to JACOB BULL, for $375, land in Parish
of St. Paul, now Warren Co., 250 acres, adj. ISAAC & JOHN DENNIS, Little
River, RALPH KILGORE, DENNIS MILES and vacant land. FRANCIS DOYLE (LS),
DENNIS DOYLE (LS). Wit: ROBERT FISHER, JOHN S. ZACHARY, WILLIE JONES.

Pages 485-486:   Oct. 8, 1792, ALEXANDER CASWELL & MARY his wife to
            JOHN LAWSON... CASWELL of Burk Co., LAWSON of Columbia
Co., for 50 pounds, 150 acres, adj. land grant to ROGER LAWSON, land
granted to ALEXANDER CASWELL, June 17, 1789 in Columbia Co., ALEXD.
CASWELL (LS), MARY CASWELL (X) (LS). Wit: JOHN BENSON, THOMPSON
LAWSON.

Pages 486-487:   Dec. 21, 1804, WILLIAM JONES heir of JAMES JONES, dec'd,
            to JAMES JONES & SUSANNAH JONES, widow & relict of
JAMES JONES, dec'd, for $2800, two tracts one in Warren Co., on Goldings
Creek, bound at time of survey by JACKSON, 200 granted to JONATHAN JONES,
the other tract adj. it, 198 acres. WM. JONES (LS). Wit: T. PERSONS,
SHAD FLEWELLEN.

Page 488:   Jan. 4, 1805, JEREMIAH BEALL to GEORGE COLE for $50, lot
            in Warrenton. JEREMIAH BEALL (LS). Wit: GEO HARGRAVES,
DAVID BUSH.

Pages 488-489:   SUSANNAH JONES, widow of JAMES JONES for $1400, to
            JAMES JONES land on Goldings Creek, adj. GRANTHAMS,
SUSANNAH JONES (LS). Wit: NANCY SLATER, W. STITH, E. HURT J. I. C.

Pages 489-490:   Jan. 11, 1802, BENJAMIN UPTON to TOBIAS UPTON 220
            acres, adj. ISAAC LEDBETTER, L. CHAMBLESS, on Ogechee
and Rocky Branch (Plat included)... granted to JOHN LEDBETTER, and
conveyed to ISAAC LEDBETTER... BENJAMIN UPTON (LS). Wit: WILLIAM
HANCOCK, N. ROBERTSON JP.

Page 491:   Feb. 7, 1800, JAMES THWEATT to THOMAS BOHANNON for $200,
            part of a survey to JOSIAH CARTER, adj. EDMONDSON, Widow
LUCAS, PEAVEY, JAMES THWEATT (LS). Wit: PETER PEAVY ( ), JOSEPH
PEAVY (P).

Pages 492-493:   Feb. 19, 1801, JOHN LAWSON & ALICE his wife, to JOEL
            WILLIS, for $1000, 200 acres on Rocky Comfort, and
Deep Creek, granted to ROGER LAWSON and granted to ALEXANDER CASWELL.
JOHN LAWSON (LS), ALICE LAWSON (LS). Wit: J. LAWSON, NORVEL LAWSON JP.

Page 493:   Aug. 4, 1800, JEREMIAH BEALL to THOMAS DENT for $200, 3/4
            of an acre, adj. to Publick Lot. JEREMIAH BEALL (LS).
Wit: RICHARD DENT, JAS MCCORMICK JP, L. PRUITT J. I. C.

Pages 494-495:   May 6, 1806, DAVID NEWSOM adj. of SOLOMON NEWSOM dec'd
            to THOMAS DENT, for an order of inferior court at
Warrenton... land adj. BUTT, DAVID NEAL, 149½ acres... DAVID NEWSOM (LS).
Wit: GRESHAM SMITH, THOS FRIEND JP.

Page 495:   WILLIAM LOWE, to son JAMES LOWE three negroes for natural
            love, etc. WILLIAM LOWE, 1803. Wit: JOHN OLIVER, J.
CANDLER J. I. C.

Pages 495-496:   Jan. 4, 1805, JOHN CLABORN to JACOB BULL for $130,
            50 acres granted to JOHN DENNIS, 1770 adj. CLABORN's
Spring Branch, on Kilgore's Creek, DOYLE, KILGORE, a dividing line made
by THOMAS PORTER 1791... land whereon THOMAS BUTTRILL now lives.
JOHN CLABORN Senr. (LS). Wit: JOS. EVANS, STANTON PORTER, CHAS PORTER
JP.

Pages 496-497:   Dec. 5, 1805, JOEL WILLIS of Warren Co. to BENJAMIN
            BLEDSOE of Columbia Co., for $1000, 200 acres on
Rocky Comfort and Deep Creek. JOEL WILLIS (LS). Wit NORVEL ROBERTSON,
GEO DYKES JP.

Page 498:   Jan. 13, 1786, THOMAS STAPLER of Jackson Co., to WILLIAM
            KENOR of Warren Co. for $30, 200 acres on Joe's Creek,
granted to CANDLER, Feb. 9, 1790. THOMAS STAPLER (LS). Wit: AMOS
STAPLER, WM. NORMAN JP.

Pages 498-499:   May 20, 1806, WILLIAM KENOR Senr. of Warren Co. to
                  BARNET SMIDER of Washington Co. for $100, 500 acres in
Richmond Co., when surveyed but now in Warren, granted to HENRY CANDLER,
Feb. 9, 1790, adj. land where PELEG GREEN formerly lived... WILLIAM
KENOR Senr. (LS). Wit: GEORGE GRANDBERRY, GEORGE DYKES JP.

Pages 499-500:   July 10, 1795, JOHN DYSART of Warren Co. from IGNATIUS
                  FEW of Columbia Co., for 65 pounds, 200 acres on
Williams Creek, granted to sd. FEW Jan. 21, 1785. I. FEW (LS). Wit:
JNO. W. DEVEREUX, MARK CANDLER.

Page 501:   April 9, 1806, JESSE MATHEWS of Baldwin Co., to ELISHA HURT
             of Warren Co., for $105, 42 acres on north side of Rocky
Comfort Creek, JESSE MATHEWS (LS). Wit: A. PERSONS, STERLING GARDNER
JP.

Pages 501-502:   Feb. 9, 1801, HILTON PEEVY to WILLIAM BLUNT, for $275,
                  110 acres on Long Creek of Ogechee, HELTON PEEVY (*)
(LS). Wit: STEPHEN MARSHALL, JAMES ZACHARY.

Page 503:   Feb. 22, 1802, WILLIE GRIZZLE to WILLIAM BLUNT for $100, 49
             acres on Long Creek, adj. DAVID HUBERT's line... WILLIE
GRIZZLE (LS). Wit: ABRAHAM CARD, JNO MATHEWS J. I. C.

Pages 503-504:   ZACHARIAH TUCKER of Lincoln Co., Kentucky, nominate my
                  friend ISAIAH TUCKER of Warren Co., Ga., as lawful
attorney... money from est. of JOHN PIERCE Junr, dec'd... of the City
of Augusta, Ga., April 8, 1806. ZACHARIAH TUCKER (LS). Wit: T.
PERSONS, A. PERSONS.

Pages 504-505:   Jan. 30, 1805, WILLIAM KENOR, Junr. to HARDY HARREL,
                  for $300, 200 acres on Walker's Branch, then down to
Little Creek, to Williams line. WILLIAM KENOR (LS). Wit: JOHN
WILLIAMS, WM. KENOR (K).

Page 505:   JOSIAH BEALL sold to HENRY SHELTON, 2 negroes for $630,
             June 11, 1805, JOSIAH BEALL. Wit: JOHN MATTHEWS.

Page 506:   WILLIAM WRIGHT sold to HENRY SHELTON for $325, negro March
             22, 1803. WILLIAM WRIGHT. Wit: MARK HARDIN Junr. THOS.
DENT.

Pages 506-507:   April 8, 1806, HENRY MOSES of Baldwin Co. to STERLING
                  GARDNER, land on Whetstone Creek, adj. RICHD. HILL,
120 acres. HENRY MOSES (LS). Wit: BENJ. HURT, ARCHL FLEWELLEN J. I. C.

Page 507:   Nov. 1, 1804, THOMAS SMITH to HENRY WILLIAMS Junr... for
             $550, 172½ acres, the 220 acres that sd. SMITH conveyed to
ELIJAH LEONARD 27½ acres, adj. THOMPSON & LEONARD... originally
granted to ELIJAH LEONARD, June 25, 1800. THOMAS SMITH (LS). Wit:
RHESE JONES & JNO BAYNE JP.

Page 508:   Aug. 6, 1800, ELIJAH LEONARD to THOMAS SMITH for $200, 200
             acres on Brier Creek, adj. to grant of 600 acres made to
sd. LEONARD... ELIJAH LEONARD (LS). Wit: MICHAEL CODY (X), JOSEPH
LEONARD, PETER HODO JP.

Pages 509-510:   Feb. 28, 1804, JAMES WHEELER to JAMES ALLEN of
                  Columbia Co., Planter, for $1000, tract on Williams
Creek, adj. at time of survey by CURETON's land, a part of the same
survey conveyed to JOHN FONTAIN, and land surveyed for JOHN GREYSON
(GREGSON?), Richmond Co. line, 150 acres, originally granted for
SUSANNAH WALL (widow) on April 29, 1784 by right vested in WHEELER by
his marriage to sd. SUSANNAH WALL... JAMES WHEELER (X) (LS), SUSANNAH
WHEELER (X) (LS). Wit: JOHN FONTAIN, SOLOMON LOCKETT JP.

Page 510-511:   July 28, 1806, AMOS PERSONS to ROBERT BEASLEY for $525
                 (spanish milled dollars) 100 acres, part of a 200 acre

grant to ELIJAH PETERS Jan. 7, 1786, conveyed to BENJAMIN MOORE then to THOMAS EDMONDSON then to PERSONS. AMOS PERSONS (LS). Wit: JAMES GRAY, ISAAC BALL JP.

Pages 511-512:   May 12, 1797, GEORGE BREWER to WILLIAM WHITE, $100 for 40 acres, adj. IGNATIUS FEW, PERKINS, HEATH, part of a 400 acre grant to BENJAMIN S____, Dec. 17, 1784. GEORGE BREWER (LS). Wit: ROLEN BREWER, JOSEPH WHITE.

Page 512:   JAMES NORTHINGTON to JOHN ZACHARY a negro. JAMES NORTHINGTON Test: JNO STEWART, RANSOM DUKE, GEORGE OWEN JP.

Pages 513-514:   Whereas THOMAS HARTON did make obligation to JOHN ZACHARY... tract of land 250 acres and sd. HARTON died intestate, HENRY MITCHELL of Hancock Co. is admr... land adj. when surveyed JAMES YARBROUGH... HENRY MITCHELL (LS). Wit: JOHN CROWDE J. I. C.,   J. B. CROWDER.

Page 514:   July 10, 1792, SHADRACH KENNEY BREW of Wilks Co. to GEORGE BREWER for 150 pounds, land on Williams Creek, 400 acres, adj. JENKINS, WILDER. SHADRACH KENNEY BREW (LS). Wit: JOSEPH WHITE, JOHN SHROPSHIRE JP.

Page 515:   Jan. 14, 1801, PHILIP LOGAN of Mongomery Co., to RANDAL WOOLSEY of Warren Co., for $200, 90 acres adj.WILLIE GRIZZLE, DAVID HUBERT, JAMES COTTON & NATHAN JONES, on Rocky Comfort part of 200 acres granted to JAMES DAVID by a patent. PHILIP LOGAN (LS). Wit: EDMUND JOHNSON, ROBERT JONESON.

Page 516:   MARY SMITH, widow, to son ABISHA BREWER for love, etc. 500 acres taken up by husband ALEXANDER SMITH, dec'd. MARY SMITH (X) (LS). Wit: ALARY SIMONS (M her mark). Jan. 5, 1798.

Pages 516-517:   Nov. 8, 1802, MATHEW PARHAM to JAMES PARHAM for $1, 100 acres, adj. GEORGE HEWEY, Permetau Branch, land granted to MULKY... part of a tract granted to NICHOLAS JONES. MATHEW PARHAM (LS). Wit: Z FRANKLIN, REBEKAH WALKER (X).

Pages 517-518:   June 3, 1805, ISHAM WHEELAS of Green Co., to TIMOTHY MATHEWS of Warren Co., for $50, adj. PERKINS, SCOTTS, part of a tract granted to ISHAM WHELAS Dec. 16, 1793. ISHAM WHELES (LS). Wit: IGNATIUS SIMMES, JOSEPH HILL.

Page 518:   WILLIAM CULPEPPER of Warren Co. to son DANIEL CULPEPPER for love, etc. negroes. WILLIAM CULPEPPER (✔) (LS). Wit: WILLIAM CULPEPPER, ISIAH TUCKER.

Pages 519-520:   Jan. 11, 1806, CHARLES RAYBORN Planter to ABRAM SAULS for $225, 200 acres on the dividing ridge between Brier Creek, (formerly Wilks Co.) and Rocky Comfort, CHARLES RAYBORN (X) (LS). Wit: JOHN MATHEWS, FRANCES CHANDLER (X).

Page 520:   Dec. 16, 1800, PHILIP GIBBS sold to JOHN BRIDGES, 100 acres on Big Creek, known as ELIACON TYSOM improvements, originally granted to REACE PRICE, PHILIP GIBBS (LS). Wit: BENJAMIN BRIDGES, JAMES WHEELER (ᑐ).

Pages 520-521:   March 8, 1805, JOHN BRIDGES to EVAN THOMAS 100 acres, part of 200 acres granted to REACE PRICE and conveyed to PHILIP GIBBS, adj. Mr. GREEN, JOHN BRIDGES (L SEAL). Wit: N. ROBERTSON JP, JOHN HATCHER JP.

Page 521:   Jan. 31, 1806, EVAN THOMAS to MARTIN KEINER, part of a grant to REECE PRICE, conveyed to GIBBS then to BRIDGES... EVAN THOMAS (SEAL). Wit: JOSHUA GRANTHAM, LARKIN CHEVIRS, GEORGE DYKES JP.

Page 522:   Nov. 17, 1806, HENRY KENDALL to SAMUEL & THOMAS KILE, 1000
            acres in Jackson and Franklin Counties, for $300, (Signed):
HENRY KINDALL, THOMAS KILE, SAMUEL KILE. Wit: JAS. KIEL, T PERSONS JP.

            ELIZABETH PREWITT, widow of LEVI PRUITT Esqr. for $5,
received of JOHN MCCORMICK, right to lands of husband. July 21,, 1806.
ELIZABETH PRUITT. Wit: JAMES MCCORMICK JP.

Pages 522-523:   Aug. 22, 1792, ELIZABETH LANDRUM of Wilks Co. (widow)
                 to JOHN MCCORMICK, for 50 pounds, 100 acres granted to
ELIZABETH LANDRUM, Aug. 10, 1785, adj. BUSSON, HOWARD's line...
ELIZABETH LANDRUM (D) (LS). Wit: JAMES RAY, JAMES MCCORMICK JP.

Page 524:   Nov. 13, 1805, RICHARD HODO of Columbia Co., to MICHAEL CODA
            for $236, 102 acres, WILLIAM HUGG, part of a 150 acre grant
to PETER HODO Senr. RICHARD HODO (SEAL). Wit: JAMES WILSON (J),
JOHN BAYN JP.

Pages 524-525:   Sept. 4, 1806, SAML. FICKLING & BARNARD WOOD FICKLING
                 to REUBEN JONES, for $1500, land on Goldings Creek,
adj. REUBEN JONES, CLARK BLANDFORD & ELISHA WRIGHT, granted to heirs of
HENRY GOLDIN deceased, 285 acres, except about 20 acres sold to STARLING
JONES, SAMUEL FICKLING (SEAL), BARNARD W. FICKLING (SEAL). Wit: GEO.
HARGRAVES, ELISHA HURT J. I. C.

Pages 525-526:   Feb. 13, 1806, JOHN FRANCIS FLOURNOY to BENJAMIN CARR,
                 for $1500, land adj. MATHEW HUBERT, LAMAR, 291½
acres. JOHN F. FLOURNOY (SEAL). Wit: ALEXR. PERRYMAN, M. HUBERT.

Pages 526-527:   May 3, 1806, JOHN ONEAL to WM. SIMPTER for $600, 194½
                 acres adj. JAMES BUSH, ROBERT BARTON, JOHN ONEAL & WM.
WILLIAMS... JOHN ONEAL (SEAL). Wit: REUBEN REESE, NATHAN DUCK.

Pages 527-528:   Jan. 7, 1800, ELIJAH WILLIAMS to WILLIAM MAYS, for
                 $220, 200 acres on Brier Creek, granted to BYRD
BRASWELL, April 3, 1794, adj. Widow MAYS, WILLIAM MAYS & E. TAYLOR.
ELIJAH WILLIAMS (X). Wit: P. HODO.

Pages 528-529:   Jan. 14, 1805, JOHN MAGLAMMERY to JOHN PEIRSON for $250,
                 100 acres originally to BUHLAM MAY, Dec. 14, 1790.
JOHN MAGLAMMERY (W) (LS). Wit: JAMES PEIRSON, JOHN BAYN JP.

Pages 529-530:   July 18, 1806, JESSE JAMES of Baldwin Co. to THOMAS
                 FRIEND for $600, land on waters of Long Creek, 191½
acres. JESSE JAMES (LS). Wit: SAMUEL BUFFINTON, PHILIP COOK JP.

Pages 530-531:   March 12, 1805, JOHN GUTHRIA of BUNCKUM (Buncombe) Co.,
                 North Carolina, to JAMES PEERSON of Warren Co., Ga.,
for $600, 300 acres on Big Brier Creek, adj. JESSE STORY originally
granted to RICHARD SMITH, July 12, 1787... JOHN GUTHRIA (LS). Wit:
WILLIAMSON ROWLAND, WM. CASON JP.

Pages 531-532:   Nov. 6, 1803, CATHERINE SMITH, SARAH FARR, JOHN
                 MCCARTHY, MARY MCCARTHY, JACOB JOHNSON, DORCAS JOHNSON,
CASSANDRE SMITH, JOSEPH SMITH & ELIZABETH SMITH of Counties of Columbia
and Warren to JACOB SMITH of Warren Co., for 60 silver dollars, land on
Middle Creek... CATHARINE SMITH (X), SARAH FARR (X), JOHN MCCARTHY,
MARY MCCARTHY, CASANDER SMITH,(X), JACOB JOHNSON, DORCAS JOHNSON (X),
JOSEPH SMITH, ELIZABETH SMITH, JAMES GRANADE, CATHERINE GRENADE, JONA-
THAN SMITH, PEREBY SMITH. Wit: WILLIAM DUCKWORTH, GIDEON GEORGE JP.
(All above signatures were parties of the first part selling to JACOB
SMITH.)

Page 533:   Dec. 10, 1801, JOHN MCGLAMARY from JOHN HOOD Senr. for
            $300, 100 acres granted to BALKAM MAY Dec. 4, 1790. JOHN
HOOD (LS). Wit: JEAN CASON (X her mark), WILLIAM CASON JP.

Pages 533-534:   Dec. 10, 1801, JOHN MCGALMARY from JOHN HOOD of
                  Richmond Co., for $200, 10 acres, part of a grant to
JAMES BROOKS. JOHN HOOD (X) (LS). Wit: JEAN CASON, WILLIAM CASON.

Pages 535-536:   Dec. 7, 1793, ABEL JAMES of Wilks Co. to MORDICAI
                  MOORE MASON, for 15 pounds sterling, 200 acres on Rocky
Comfort, surveyed for JESSE SANFORD, and conveyed to ABEL JAMES. ABEL
JAMES (LS). Wit: WM. GRIFFIN BERRY, JESSE JAMES, SARAH JAMES (X)

Page 536:   I relinquish all my title to negroes... to GRESHAM SMYTH.
             Signed JOSEPH HUTCHINSON (LS). Wit: JOHN DANTIGNAL JP.

Page 537:   June 25, 1805, WASHINGTON HARDAWAY to THOMAS MADDOX, for
             $50, 25 acres, part of a 150 acre grant to JOHN BURKHALTER
and sold to STERLING WILLIAMSON, Jan. 17, 1797. WASHINGTON HARDAWAY
(LS). Wit: L. WRIGHT, D. NEAL JP.

Pages 537-538:   Dec. 25, 1803, NICHOLAS HARIBUCK to JAMES JONES Senr.
                  for $65, 14½ acres on Golding's Creek, NICHOLAS HAIRBUCK
(O) (LS). Wit: GEO. HARGRAVES, JOHN MATHEWS JP.

Pages 538-539:   Oct. 18, 1806, RICHARD SHIRLEY to RANDAL JOHNSON for
                  $100, 50 acres on Rocky Comfort, granted to THOMAS
MCCLENDON, RICHARD SHIRLEY (LS). Wit: WILLIAM SIMMONS, JOHN HATCHER JP.

Pages 539-540:   Jan. 14, 1805, JOHN MCGLAMARY to JOHN PIERSON for $50,
                  10 acres on Brier Creek, part of 215 acres granted to
JANE BROOKS, July 22, 1795, conveyed to J. HOOD, JOHN MCGLAMARY (W)
(LS). Wit: JAMES PIERSON, JOHN BAYNE JP.

Page 540:   Oct. 19, 1803, CLABORN NEWSOM of Columbia Co., to JOHN ADAMS
             for $432, (later named as BENJAMIN ADAMS)... 102 acres adj.
SMITH, WATSON, MCKEWN, BASS & ADAMS, CLABORN NEWSOM (LS). Wit: JAMES
CODY, P. HODO.

Page 541:   May 3, 1806, JOHN BROOKS to WILLIAM SIMPLER for $300, 100
             acres, adj. ROBERT BURTON, JOHN BROOKS (D) (LS). Wit:
REUBEN REESE, NATHAN DUCK.

Page 542:   Sept. 6, 1802, CLABORN NEWSOM of Columbia Co. to DREWRY BASS
             of Warren Co., for $200, adj. ADAMS, FREEMAN, SALLIS,
CLABORN NEWSOM (LS). Wit: P. HODO, EPHRAIM IVEY.

Page 543:   June 10, 1806, JAMES WILLIAMS to RICHARD SAMMONS for $450,
             part of a 350 acre grant to Long Creek, to JOHN TORRENCE,
conveyed to sd. JAMES WILLIAMS June 16, 1801. JAMES WILLIAMS (LS).
Wit: T. PIERSON , RICHARD BRAY, ISAIH TUCKER JP.

Pages 544-546:   Dec. 10, 1796, JOHN CHAPPEL of Green Co. to SEPTIMUS
                  WEATHERBY, for $500, land on Rocky Comfort, adj. land
granted to NATHAN SPIKES, adj. land granted to WILLIAM SPIKES, 130
acres. JOHN CHAPPEL (LS). Wit: HARMON PERRYMAN, PETE MAHONE.

Pages 545-546:   Oct. 1805, THOMAS ANSLEY Senr. to WILLIAM ANSLEY for
                  $100, 327 acres where the sd. WILLIAM ANSLEY now lives
adj. COX, MORRIS, DAVIS, THOS ANSLEY (LS). Wit: JOSEPH ANSLEY, ABEL
ANSLEY.

Pages 546-647:   Dec. 15, 1806, JOHN MOSES of Washington Co., to SAMUEL
                  MOSES of Warren Co., for $500, land granted to PHILIP
POOL & HEZEKIAH BURSEY, on Brier Creek, adj. JAMES GRAY, JOHN MOSES (LS).
Wit: JOHN MOSES, ROBERT MOSES.

Pages 547-548:   Nov. 13, 1806, JOSEPH MCMATH of Warren Co. to MICHAEL
                  BURKHALTER, for $500, land on Turkey Creek in Baldwin
County, 202½ acres. JOSEPH MCMATH (LS). Wit: GEO HARGRAVES, THOMAS
GIBSON.

Pages 548-549:   Dec. 30, 1806, EDMUND CODY to THOMAS PATE for $465, land granted to ISAAC BALL, Feb. 9, 1790, EDMUND CODY (X) (LS). Wit: JOHN BAYNE, WASHINGTON HARDAWAY.

Pages 549-550:   Dec. 14, 1805, ALEXANDER MOORE Amr. of est. of MORDECAI MOORE, dec'd to RANDOLPH JOHNSON for $100, 200 acres on Rocky Comfort Creek, surveyed for JESSE SANFORD, conveyed to ABEL JAME... ALEXANDER MOORE (LS). Wit: JAMES JOHNSON, LEWIS JOHNSON.

Pages 550-551:   Jan. 4, 1804, ROBERT PULLIN of Green Co., to EDWARD TAYLOR, $81 acres. ROBERT PULLIN (SEAL). Wit: BENJAMIN BRIANT (X), JOHN M. NEAL (X).

Pages 551-552:   Aug. 8, 1803, WILLIAM JOHNSON to RANDOLPH JOHNSON, for $350, 150 acres on Rocky Comfort Creek, WILLIAM JOHNSON (8). Wit: REUBEN REESE, AARON ALDRED (X).

Pages 552-553:   Nov. 13, 1805, CHURCHWELL GIBSON to MARGARET BARRETT and her two youngest sons HENRY & CHARLES BARRETT, more commonly known by the names of HENRY & CHARLES GIBSON, for natural love, etc... lands conveyed to me by LEMUEL PRUITT & JACOB TURCONETT, adj. lands of JOSEPH BREED, RICHARD GEORGE, JOHN BREED, ISAIAH TUCKER & MOUNTAIN HILL. CHURCHWELL GIBSON (LS). Wit: ISAIAH TUCKER JP, HENRY GIBSON.

Pages 553-554:   HENRY BONNER Junr. to ABNER CHAPMAN for $300, 100 acres. HENRY BONNER (SEAL). Wit: WM. BERRY, T. MATHEWS JP.

Page 554:   HENRY JONES bound to LEVEN MCGEE for $100, Jan. 17, 1803, make lawful rights to 270 acres on road from Augusta to George Town, adj. JOHN NUNN, ISAAC HART. HENRY JONES (X) (SEAL). Wit: WM. CASON JP.

Pages 554-555:   Nov. 23, 1804, MARY PACE to JOHN PACE for $292, 143 3.4 acres, adj. REESE GREEN, SEEL & BURKHALTER... MARY PACE (X). Wit: JAMES TAPPER, SILAS PACE (X).

Pages 555-556:   March 19, 1806, SUSANA BUTLER, relict of NOBLE CUTLER dec'd, DANIEL MCCOWAN, BEALL BUTLER, JESSE BUTLER, ENOS BUTLER, NOBLE BUTLER, WILLIAM BUTLER, ELI BUTLER, LEVI BUTLER, EDITH BUTLER & HIRAM, heirs of sd. NOBLE BUTLER, dec'd all of Warren Co., except BEALL & WM. who are residents of Columbia Co. to THOMAS HAYNE Senr. of Warren Co., for $1000, 100 acres granted to JAMES HOWELL, Dec. 6, 1774, conveyed to sd. NOBLE BUTLER, by JAMES HOWELL & ELIZABETH his wife... (plat included)... adj. DANIEL MCCOWAN & JOEL CLOUD, heirs of SAMUEL HART, EZEKIEL ALEXANDER, AMOS JOHNSON, JOHN WILLIAMS, ZEPHANIAH FRANKLIN & JESSE STUBBS. (Signed) SUSAN BUTLER, DANIEL MCDOWAN, BEALL BUTLER, JESSE BUTLER, ENOS BUTLER, NOBLE BUTLER, WILLIAM BUTLER, ELI BUTLER, LEVI BUTLER, EDITH BUTLER, HIRAM BUTLER (all seals). Wit: THOMAS HAYNES JUTN. Z FRANKLIN JP.

Pages 557-558:   Dec. 3, 1800, ZACHARIAH SUFFIELD to JOEL MATHEWS for $500... SOLOMON SAXON... ZACHARIAH SHUFFIELD (SEAL). Wit: STEPHEN W. BURNLEY, BENJAMIN MATHEWS.

Pages 558-559:   Nov. 25, 1803, BENJAMIN REESE of Columbia Co., to MARY PACE, for $273, 136 acres. BENJR. R. (LS). Wit: JOHN PACE, HUGH REESE.

Pages 559-560:   Jan. 5, 1807, SAMUEL WILLIAMS of Richmond Co., to MOSES HILL, for $300, 100 acres on Brier Creek, originally granted to RACHEL WILLIS, June 17, 1789. SAMUEL WILLIAMS (X) (SEAL). Wit: J. BAYNE, JOHN WILLIAMS.

Pages 560-561:   May 8, 1805, ZACHARIAH SHEFFIELD to ROBERT SHEFFIELD for $300, 100 acres, part of 2 surveyed of 100 each to Z. SHEFFIELD. ZACHARIAH SHEFFIELD (SEAL). Wit: BENJAMIN CRENSHAW, CLEMENT WYNNE, JNO TORRENCE J. I. C.

Pages 561-562:   I, JOHN PACE, for $400, sell to RANDOLPH IVY land on
                Childres Creek, 133½ acres, adj. MARY SILLS, GREEN,
BURKAHLTER, REES (Plat included)... JOHN PACE (LS). Wit: JERM.
BURKHALTER, CHARLES JONES. Jan. 31, 1807.

Page 562:   Jan. 31, 1807, JOEL LASITER & POLLY his wife to ROBERT
            BEASLEY, for $175... interest of MARGARET BEASLEY widow of
RICHARD BEASLEY... JOEL LASITER, POLLY LASITER (X). Wit: JAMES MC-
CORMICK Junr., D. NEAL JP.

            JOHN HOBSON for $600, sold to ALLEN DORMAN, negro Nov. 12,
1805, JOHN HOBSON. Wit: JONAS SHIVERS, STERLING GARDNER JP.

Page 563:   Jan. 3, 1807, JOHN BUCKHALTER, to EDWARD KINNY for $100,
            91 acres (plat included)... JOHN BUCKHALTER. Wit: E. THOMAS,
STERLING GARDNER JP.

Pages 563-564:   July 16, 1787, JAMES HOWELL & ELIZABETH his wife of
                Richmond Co., formerly Parish of St. Paul, for 40
pounds sterling, to NOBLE BUTLER, 100 acres granted to sd. JAMES HOWELL,
1774, JAMES HOWELL (LS), ELIZABETH HOWELL (X) (LS). Wit: THOS WHITE
JP, R. HOWARD JP.

Pages 565-566:   July 16, 1787, JAMES HOWELL to NOBLE BUTLER for 50
                pounds, 200 acres, adj. JOEL CLOUD, SAMUEL HART,
ABRAHAM JOHNSON. JAMES HOWELL (LS), ELIZABETH HOWELL (X) (LS). Wit:
THOS WHITE JP, R. HOWARD JP.

Pages 567:   Sept. 2, 1805, JOHNSON WRIGHT to WILLIAM JONES, for $600,
            200 acres on Rocky Comfort Creek, granted to JOHN GRANTHAM
(400 acres), March 4, 1789, JOHST WRIGHT (SEAL). Wit: ABNER LOCKE,
ROYSTER HEATH.

Pages 568:   June 7, 1806, MOSES GRANBERRY to BENJAMIN UPTON & JOHN
            P. MARTIN, trustees of the Baptist Church known as Church
of Christ at Fellowship, for Good will to Baptist Society in General,
land on Granberry's mill branch... MOSES GRANBERRY (SEAL). Wit:
WILLIAM O HILL, N. ROBERTSON, GEORGE DYKES JP.

Pages 569-570:   Feb. 19, 1802, DAVID ROBERTSON Senr. to ISHAM WHEELER
                for $400, 200 acres granted to WILLIAM WAMMACK. July
12, 1787, conveyed from him to FITZHU HUNT and then to DAVID ROBERTSON,
on Briar Creek... DAVID ROBERTSON. Wit: DAVID WHEELER (✿), THOS.
WESTBAY.

Page 570:   Feb. 9, 1807, JOHN ZACHARY to RICHARD SMITH for $400, 162
            acres adj. SOLOMON WARD & HARDY CHAMBERS. JOHN ZACHARY (LS),
SARAH ZACHARY (X) (LS). Wit: JESSE ZACHARY, D. H. ZACHARY JP.

Pages 571-572:   Jan. 16, 1807, JOSEPH HUTCHINSON of Augusta, to HENRY
                HARDIN, for $350, 520 acres, granted to MARTIN HARDIN,
sold by the Sheriff of Warren Co., to sd. JOSEPH HUTCHINSON, JOSEPH
HUTCHINSON (LS). Wit: GEO. W. EVANS, JOHN HARDIN, JOHN D'ANTIGNAC JP.

Page 572:   Nov. 1, 1803, WILLIAM FEW to NOVELL ROBERTSON, for $325,
            212 acres, granted to GEORGE UPTON 1787, and conveyed by him
to sd. FEW, W. FEW (LS). Wit: J. WHEELER, I FEW JP.

Page 573:   Jan. 11, 1806, PHILIP BRANTLEY & ANN his wife to HENRY
            HARDIN, for $200, 114 acres on Middle Creek, PHILIP BRANTLEY
(LS), NANCY BRANTLEY (X) (LS). Wit: HIRAM PERRY, JEPHTHA BRANTLEY,
BENJA. BRANTLEY.

Pages 573-574:   Sept. 3, 1805, ALEXANDER PERRYMAN Sheriff to JOSEPH
                HUTCHINSON, of Augusta, for $101, ALEXR. PERRYMAN
(SEAL). Wit: J. HAMILL, JOEDAY NEWSOM.

Pages 574-575:   JACOB WATSON to WILLIAM SMITH, for $112, 28 acres adj.
                 MICHAEL CODA, part of a 1000 acre tract known as Fort
tract... JACOB WATSON (SEAL). Wit: JOHN SAUNDERS, WILLIAM CASON JP.

Pages 575-576:   April 2, 1807, WILLIAM SMITH to EDMUND CODY, for $1400,
                 128 acres, adj. MICHAEL CODY... WILLIAM SMITH (SEAL).
Wit: WILLIAM D. BUNKLEY, E. HURT J. I. C.

Page 576:   Whereas HARMAN PERRYMAN made a bill of sale Feb. 1, 1797 to
            MARY PERRYMAN for a negro... April 8, 1807, MARY PERRYMAN
(X) (LS). Wit: A. PERRYMAN, CASWELL BALL.

Page 577:   Jan. 9, 1805, NATHAN BREWER to THOMAS BOHANNON, for $250,
            50 acres on Ogechee River... NATHAN BREWER (X) (LS). Wit:
JESSE DOLES, WM. HARDWICK.

Pages 578-579:   GEORGE THE THIRD... grant unto ROGER LAWSON, 200
                 acres in Province of Georgia, March 3, 1767. JAS.
WRIGHT (LS). (Entire grant copied in will book.)

Pages 579-580:   May 22, 1789, ROGER LAWSON & MARGARET his wife to
                 JOHN LAWSON for 100 pounds, grant to sd. ROGER LAWSON,
1767. ROGER LAWSON (LS), MARGARET LAWSON (X) (Plat included). Wit:
ANN BEATTY, WM. LAWSON JP.

Page 581:   EZEKIEL ALEXANDER to JAMES ALLEN for $500, 80 acres on
            Williams Creek, on a line agreed upon by PETER HELTON &
WILLIAM CRESHAW. EZEKIEL ALEXANDER (LS). Wit: WYATT BONNER, HESTER
WOODYARD (X).

Pages 581-582:   Dec. 16, 1803, CHARLES DARNELL to HENRY KENDALL, for
                 $700, 160 acres on Rocky Comfort, adj. ISAAC BALL,
ETHELDRED THOMAS. CHARLES DARNEL (LS). Wit: HANNAH HARRISON, J.
PERRYMAN.

Pages 582-583:   Nov. 29, 1806, HENRY KINDALL to JACOB CASTLEBERRY, for
                 $600, adj. TURNER PERSONS on Whetstone Creek, JOHN
MYRICK, JOHN SLATTERS, granted to BLAND BLACKLEY, July 3, 1787, 120
acres. HENRY KENDALL (LS). Wit: T. PERSONS, EDMOND PARHAM.

Pages 583-584:   Oct. 26, 1802, MARTIN HARDIN of Tatnall Co., to JAMES
                 HUTCHINSON of Campden County, for $520, adj. HOWARD &
WHATLEYS land, granted Nov. 13, 1801, 520 acres. MARTIN HARDIN (LS).
Wit: JOSEPH JACKSON, SOLOMON MOBLEY.

Pages 584-585:   Dec. 5, 1806, WILLIAMSON CRAWFORD to JOHN RUSHING for
                 $200, 76 acres on Long Creek, (plat included) granted
to SAML. CAMP. Nov. 23, 1792. WILLIAMSON CRAWFORD (X) (LS). Wit:
J. RUSHIN, JAS. LEDBETTER.

Pages 585-586:   Jan. 5, 1807, JACOB CASTLEBERRY to TURNER PERSONS, for
                 $300, land on east side of Whtestone Creek, adj.
THOMAS NEAL, JOHN MYRICK... JACOB CASTLEBERRY (SEAL). Wit: ISAAC
BALL JP., SEPTIMUS WEATHERBY.

Pages 586-587:   Dec. 8, 1806, DOCTOR LOCKETT to JOSIAH CARTER, for $100,
                 part of a tract granted to HENRY GRAYBILL, on Ogechee,
8 4/10 acres. DOCTOR LOCKETT (LS). Wit: WM. BYROM Junr., JOHN BYROM.

Pages 587:   Rec'd May 13, 1807, STEPHEN JONES' $600, for negroes. Wit:
             ROBT. B. DANIEL AGT., for L. DANIEL, WILLIE DANIEL. Test:
GEO. HARGRAVES, DAVID NEAL JP.

Pages 587-588:   JAMES MATHEWS appoint ISHAM MATHEWS of Hallifax County,
                 North Carolina lawful attorney, to receive from LEWIS
DANIEL of Hallifax Co., N.C., debts due me... June 3, 1807. JAMES
MATHEWS (LS). Wit: ELISHA HURT J. I. C., JAMES MYHAND.

Pages 588-589:   Dec. 21, 1804, JAMES JONES, admr. & SUSANNAH JONES widow of JAMES JONES, dec'd to WILLIAM JONES one of the heirs of est. of JAMES JONES, for $2000, land adj. AMY MCCOLOURS... a tract granted to ISAAC BALL, ... JAMES JONES (LS), SUSANNAH JONES (LS). Wit: T. PERSONS, S. FLEWELLIN.

Pages 589-590:   Feb. 27, 1807, ROBERT CARRY & his wife RUTHANNA to HEZEKIAH COOKSEY, for $500, land on Williams Creek, 250 acres, adj. to grant to HENRY CANDLER... land granted to BOLING CURETON conveyed to ANN CARRY then to ROBERT CARRY. ROBERT CARRY (SEAL), RUTHANNA CARRY (X) (SEAL). Wit: WALTER NALLY, GEORGE STEWART, SOLOMON LOCKETT JP.

Page 590:   Feb. 7, 1807, ABNER FLEWELLIN of Baldwin Co. to SAMUEL POSEY for $900, 200 acres granted to JOHN PERKINS, Feb. 9, 1790, also part of a tract granted to ABNER FLEWELLEN, Nov. 21, 1806, also part of a tract to JOHN MIMS, which was bought of CHRISTOPHER WILLIAMS, supposed of be 142 acres... land adj. ORRAN PARKER, TIMOTHY MATHEWS, AB. FLEWELLEN (SEAL). Wit: GEORGE HARGRAVES, ARCHD. FLEWELLEN J. I. C.

Page 591:   Nov. 23, 1804, ANN CARRY to ROBERT CARRY, for $500, 250 acres on William Creek, adj. CANDLER, granted to BOLING CURETON... ANN CARRY (X) (SEAL). Wit: ROBERT GRIER, A. GRIER.

Pages 591-592:   JAMES JONES Admr. & SUSANNAH JONES widow for $1800, granted.. slaves... to WILLIAM JONES. JAMES JONES (SEAL) SUSANNAH JONES (SEAL). Wit: FLEWELLEN, T. PERSONS.

Pages 592-593:   HENRY HIGHT for $387, to ROBERT CULPEPPER, land on Hart's Creek, 182½ acres (plat included). Jan. 6, 1807. HENRY HIGHT (SEAL). Wit: DANIEL CULPEPPER, WILLIAM HARRISS, WILLIAM CULPEPPER.

Pages 593-594:   Jan. 29, 1802, WILLIAM ROBERSON to SEPTIMUS WEATHERBY for $100, 50 acres on Long Creek of Ogechee, granted to JOHN PATE, 200 acres, July 20, 1786, deeded to WILLIAM ROBERSON by THOMAS PATE only heirs of sd. JOHN PATE, dec'd. Dec. 22, 1801. (Plat included). WILLIAM ROBERSON (LS). Wit: JOHN HAYSE (?) (X), ANDREW KING JP.

Page 594:   Dec. 26, 1806, STEPHEN MARSHALL to ELISHA HURT for $100, land on Rocky Comfort, adj. JOHN LOCK, JOHN W. JACKSON. STEPHEN MARSHALL (SEAL). Wit: DAVID MIMS (X), JEREMIAH DAVIDSON (X).

Page 595:   May 12, 1807, WILLIAM JONES & BARSHABA his wife to BARNARD W. FICKLING for $3200, 400 acres on Brier Creek, granted to ISAAC BALL, Aug. 26, 1788. WILLIAM JONES (LS) BARSHABA JONES (LS). Wit: SUSANNAH HARRIS, REUBEN JONES.

Page 596:   July 15, 1807, JAMES SUTTY a free person of colour, had himself enrolled. T. PERSONS.

Pages 596-597:   April 17, 1802, ENOCH W. ELLINGTON to JOHN MCKINZIE, for $70, 200 acres, on the waters of Hart & Joe's Creeks, adj. BLUNT's line (now CONNER's), SPURLINGS part of a 570 acre grant to JOHN HOLLINGSHEAD July 30, 1791. ENOCH WARD ELLINGTON (LS), Wit: NORVELL ROBERTSON JP, JOHN HATCHER JP.

Pages 597-598:   Oct. 12, 1805, THOMAS HAWTHORN to THOMAS RIGBA, for $200, land on Kegg Creek, in Washington Co., part of a 500 acre grant to ALEXANDER ARMSTRONG. THOMAS HAWTHORN (SEAL). Wit: JAMES ROE, DAVID RIGBY.

Pages 598-599:   Jan. 6, 1802, JOHN ANGLING & MARY his wife to FRANCIS STAINBACK for $400, 89 acres originally granted to sd. JOHN ANGLIN. JOHN ANGLIN (LS), MARY ANGLIN (X) (LS). Wit: WILLIAM FLOURNOY, MATHEW HUBERT JP.

Pages 599-600: July 21, 1807, JOHN OLIVER & SALLY his wife & BENJAMIN OLIVER Junr. & NANCY his wife to FRANCIS STAINBACK, for $600, 170 acres on Long Creek, of Ogechee, part of two tracts to JOHN ANGLIN. JOHN OLIVER (LS), SARAH OLIVER (LS) BENJ. OLIVER Jur. (LS), NANCY OLIVER (LS). Wit: EDMUND ROSE, MATHEW HUBER JP.

Page 600: Feb. 5, 1801, JAMES BISHOP of Hancock Co. to FRANCIS STAINBACK, for $30, 10 acres, granted to CHILDERS on n. side of Long Creek. JAMES BISHOP (X) (LS). Wit: JAMES W. GREEN, MATHEW HUBERT JP.

Pages 600-601: Jan. 12, 1804, JOHN ANGLIN & MARY his wife to ROBERT & JOHN OLIVER 170 acres on Long Creek... JOHN ANGLIN (LS), MARY ANGLIN (X) (LS). Wit: BEN. OLIVER JNT., HENRY ANGLIN.

Pages 601-602: Dec. 22, 1806, BENJAMIN WRIGHT to ARCHILAUS FLEWELLEN for $900, land on s. side of Rocky Comfort Creek, adj. JOHN LOCK, NICHOLAS WILLIAMS (part of an old survey that DAVID MIMS now lives on), JOHN DAVIDSON formerly lived, conveyed to NICHOLAS WILLIAMS, then to CHRISTOPHER BUSTIN, BENJ. WRIGHT (LS). Wit: ZACHEUS BURT, JAMES BURT.

Pages 602-603: Dec. 29, 1801, GEORGE MORRIS to HOWEL WILLIAMS, land adj. ELISHA HURT, JOHN LOCK, NICHOLAS WILLIAMS, JESSE MATHEWS. GEORGE MATHEWS (LS). Wit: N. WILLIAMS, ELEY WILLIAMS.

Pages 603-604: Jan. 5, 1805, JOHN BALL of Washington Co., to ARCHILEUS FLEWELLEN for $350, 91 acres on Rocky Comfort ... JOHN BALL (LS). Wit: ABRAM BRINKLEY, BENJ. WRIGHT.

Pages 604-605: June 12, 1802, JAMES BROOKS to JOSEPH DAVIDSON, for $200, 100 acres on Rocky Comfort, granted to BAXTER JORDAN, Nov. 5, 1788. JAMES BROOKS (LS). Wit: JOHN MAY, JOHN MCKINZIE.

Page 605: MARTHA SMITH to son WILLIAM SMITH land and stock, etc. MARTHA SMITH (X) (LS). Wit: PARSONS POE, JOSEPH WHITE.

Page 606: Nov. 17, 1792, CHARLES COLLINS of Burk Co., Ga., for 216 pounds to JOHN DICKENS of Columbia Co., 50 acres in Columbia Co., adj. LEWIS BRADY... CHARLES COLLINS (CC) (LS). Wit: THOS JACKSON, ROBERT DICKSON (X).

Pages 607-608: June 28, 1807, LEWIS BRADY to JOHN DICKEN for $450, part of 990 acres granted to sd. LEWIS BRADY, July 28, 1798. LEWIS BRADY (SEAL). Wit: JAMES SAUNDERS, THOMAS STOKES.

Pages 608-609: June 8, 1805, ARTHUR DAVIS to FEREGRINE YOUNG, for $250, originally granted to Jan. 9, 1797, 100 acres on Williams Creek, conveyed by grantee SAMUEL ALEXANDER to WILLIAM LOCKETT. ARTHUR DAVIS (LS). Wit: TIMOTHY MATHEWS JP, SOLOMON LOCKETT JP.

Pages 609-610: JAMES FRENCH to WILLIAM FEW for $150, adj. when surveyed to IGNATIUS FEW & THREWITS... JAMES FRENCH (IF) (LS). Wit: MARK HEETH, SOL. LOCKETT JP.

Pages 610-611: Dec. 29, 1806, WILLIAM HUGG to MICHAEL CODY for $564, 188 acres, granted to RICHARD HODO and part to PETER HODO. WILLIAM HUFF (SEAL). Wit: JAMES SMITH, WILLIAM BREED.

Pages 611-612: DAVID HARRINGTON of Washington Co., Gerrots Dist., appointed THOMAS RIGBY to draw in the land lottery, Jan. 9, 1807. DAVID HERRINGTON (X). Test: HENRY JONES.

Pages 612-613: Jan. 20, 1804, JOHN MACMURRINS to THOMAS HARRISON, 200 acres adj. KILLEBREW, BERRY, GARDNER & LOVETT, JOHN MCMURRIN (X) (SEAL). Wit: GOBSON BERRY, PRYOR FRANDNER JP.

Page 613: Oct. 11, 1804, WILLIAM GARDNER to THOMAS HARRIS for $100, 16½ acres. WM. GARDNER (SEAL). Wit: PRYOR GARDNER JP, FANNIA GARDNER.

Pages 613-614: Sept. 17, 1806, PETER QUARLS to JOHN MOOR of Washington Co., for $450, 115 acres on Joe's Creek, granted to SAMUEL ALLEN, Sr., PETER QUARLS (SEAL). Wit: ALEXANDER CLUERA (?), GEORGE DYKES JP.

Pages 614-615: Dec. 4, 1804, LUKE WILLIAMS to TILMAN NESBITT for $160, land on head waters of Williams Creek, adj. JOHN BAKER, PIERCE BAILEY, ASA COX, STAFFORD WILLIAMS... (later TILMAN NEBLETT)... originally granted to MICAJAH STONE, and transferred to sd. LUKE WILLIAMS, LUKE WILLIAMS (L) (SEAL). Wit: AUG BAKER, JOHN TORRENCE J. I. C.

Pages 616-617: Dec. 4, 1804, LUKE WILLIAMS to STAFFORD WILLIAMS, for $250, land conveyed by LUKE WILLIAMS to TILMAN NEBLETT. LUKE WILLIAMS (L). Wit: JNO TORRENCE.

Pages 617-618: April 13, 1798, MICAJAH STONE to LUKE WILLIAMS, for $250, land on Williams Creek, MICAJAH STONE (SEAL). Wit: JAMES SMYTH, EBENEZER SMYTH, JOHN BAKER JP.

Page 618: This is to certify that ELENDER RIDGEDIL sold to JOHN MCCORMICK to lands purchased on the Oconee River. Nov. 25, 1806. ELENDER RIDGEDIL (£) (LS). Wit: PAUL MCCORMICK.

Page 619: Feb. 19, 1805, JOHN MATHEWS of Hancock Co. to JAMES BIRT of Warren Co., for $500... ZACHEUS BURT's corner... JOHN MATHEWS (LS), land on Rocky Comfort. Wit: ZACHEUS BURT, WM. BANKS (X).

Page 620: Nov. 20, 1802, JOHN MATHEWS to ZACHEUS BURT for $800, 130 acres on Rocky Comfort. JOHN MATHEWS (LS). Wit: THAD. FLEWELLIN, E. HURT J. I. C.

Page 620: ABRAM HEATH to son WILLIAM gift of a negro. ABRAM HEATH (X) (LS). Wit: WM. BLUN, ANDREW KING JR.

Page 621: State of South Carolina, MICHAEL SWICORD for $500, sell to ALEXANDER PERRYMAN a negro. June 27, 1805. MICHL. SWICORD (LS). Wit: GRESHAM SMITH.

Pages 621-622: Nov. 3, 1807, JOSHUA JONES & ELIZABETH his wife to WILLIAM BIRD of Shoals of Ogechee, for $400, 201½ acres. JOSHUA JONES (X) (LS), ELIZABETH JONES (X) (LS). Wit: WM. B. CROWDER, JAMES MCCORMICK JP.

Pages 622-623: Jan. 1, 1804, WILLIAM CHAMBERS & wife to WILLIAM BIRD, land adj. JOSEPH MCKINLEY, RICHARD BULLOCK 150 acres, for $27, WILLIAM CHAMBERS (LS). Wit: WILSON BIRD, THOMAS CARRELL.

Pages 623-624: April 4, 1807, BENJAMIN A HAMP to WILLIAM BIRD, for $1400, 100 acres granted to BENJAMIN FEW, and sold to sd. BIRD; another tract 200 acres granted to ISAAC DENNIS, another tract granted to BENJAMIN UPTON and sold by sd. UPTON & wife JUDITH, also land in town of Lexington... JACOB DENNIS... also 1000 acres granted to BENJAMIN HAMP May 10, 1797. BENJAMIN A. HAMP (LS). Wit: WILSON BIRD, AZANA BIRD.

Page 625: May 8, 1806, LEWIS WRIGHT to RICHARD HEATH for $600, adj. I. FEW, BURREL PERRY, HILL, CHAPMAN. LEWIS WRIGHT (LS). Wit: STERLING GARDNER, CHAS MATHEWS.

Pages 626-627: Dec. 23, 1802, JAMES JOHNSON to ALEXANDER AVERA, for $500, 110 acres, part granted to JOSEPH QUIN, part of JAMES ALLEN, adj. WALLDEN, JOSEPH HOWELL, JAMES WILLIS Senr., WM. MCKINLEY, JAMES JOHNSON (S) (SEAL). Wit: ARTHUR AVERA, ARTHUR C. GREEN, THOMAS JACKSON, JOHN HATCHER JP.

Page 627:   LEWIS WRIGHT for $500, to RICHARD HEATH... negroes... May 3,
              1806. LEWIS WRIGHT (LS). Wit: T. MATHEWS, JOS HILL.

Page 628:   Sept. 7, 1805, JESSE SANFORD of Hancock Co. to WILLIAM
              SANFORD Senr. & RACHEL his wife, for love and affection.
186 acres on Hart's Creek, to revert to him at their decease. JESSE
SANFORD (LS). Wit: B. HUBERT, HUBERT REYNOLDS JP.

Pages 628-629: Jan. 16, 1797, JOHN BURKHALTER to JOHN MCCORMICK, for
                30 guineas, 150 acres granted June 4, 1796. JOHN
BURKHALTER (LS), SARAH BIRKHALTER (X) (LS). Wit: JOHN WILLIAMS, JAS.
MCCORMICK JP.

Pages 630-631: JOSEPH EVANS of Columbia Co. to WILLIAM BERRY of Warren
                Co., for $3000, 2 tracts, one granted to JOHN HOWARD,
1770; and another 88 acres. JOSEPH EVANS (LS). Wit: WM. B. ALLISON,
ANDW. B. STEPHENS.

Pages 631-632: Feb. 24, 1791, EMPEROR WHEELER of Wilks Co. to JAMES
                BEASLEY, for 100 pounds, land surveyed for sd. WHEELER
Dec. 7, 1786. EMPEROR WHEELER (X) (LS), CATHERINE WHEELER (X) (LS).
Wit: JAMES GRAY, RICHARD BEASLEY.

Pages 632-633: Jan. 20, 1806, JOHN BATES to WILLIAM BERRY, for $1500,
                312 acres on Little River. JOHN BATES (SEAL). Wit:
J. RIVIERE, WILLIAM BIMES, THOMAS BERRY.

Pages 633-634: Dec. 14, 1803, JOSEPH EVANS to WILLIAM BERRY, for $100,
                land on Williams Creek. JOSEPH EVANS (SEAL). Wit:
DRATIUS SIMMS, WM. B. ALLISON.

Pages 634-635: Jan. 3, 1808, JOHN MCCORMICK to JACOB LANDRUM for $200,
                100 acres granted to ELIZABETH LANDRUM Aug. 10, 1785,
adj. HOWARD, BUSSON, conveyed to JOHN MCCORMICK by sd. ELIZABETH LANDRUM,
Aug. 22, 1792. JNO MCCORMICK (LS), SALLY MCCORMICK (LS). Wit: THOS
DARK, JAS MCCORMICK JP.

Pages 635-636: Dec. 28, 1807, NEWITT WARD to ARTHUR MATHEWS, for $20,
                15 acres adj. CORVAN, ENGLISH... NEWIT WARD (X) (SEAL).
Wit: STERLING GARDNER JP, SOL SLATTER.

Pages 636:   Dec. 28, 1807, ETHELDRED THOMAS to ARTHUR MATHEWS, for $300,
              200 acres on Stamp Branch of Rocky Comfort. E. THOMAS
(SEAL). Wit: SOL SLATTER, STERLING GARDNER JP.

Pages 636-637: Feb. 25, 1807, LEWIS BRADY to son CULLEN LEWIS BRADY
                for natural love, 250 acres adj. WILLIS GILES BRADY's,
LEWIS BRADY (SEAL). Wit: JOS GRIZARD, WILLEY GILES BRADY (X).

Pages 637-638: NOAH BUTT for $150 to ROBERT CULPEPPER, 37 acres on
                Hart's Creek... Jan. 28, 1808, NOAH BUTT (LS). Wit:
DANIEL CULPEPPER, WILLIAM CULPEPPER.

Pages 638-639: Aug. 2, 1804, ABSALAM COBB of Hancock Co. to CHARLES
                MCCALLISTER of Warren Co. for $200, 93 acres, part of
a tract of 200, granted to BAXTER JORDAN, Nov. 25, 1788. A COBB (LS),
Wit: H. NICHOLSON, JOAB BROOKS.

ADMINISTRATOR'S BONDS IN DEED BOOK A

The following Administrator's Bonds were recorded in this Deed Book "A", by mistake, the law then as now requiring same to be recorded in the office of the Court of Ordinary (formerly, prior to 1799, called the Register of Probate office). It will be observed that a few administrator's bonds appear in the abstracts already printed and in the foregoing pages of this installment. The following are the other bonds recorded in Deed Book "A":

Page	Estate of	Admrs.	Date	Sureties
30	Burns, Jane	John Currie	Apr. 17, 1797	Barrett Brewer
31	George Hartfield	Lydia Hartfield	Aug. 11, 1800	Benj. Howard
32	John Linn	Fergus Linn	Jul. 18, 1799	Thomas Jones
				Daniel McCowan
33	John Thomas	Frederick Daniel	Jul. 18, 1799	William Mims
33	Noble Butler	Susannah Butler	Jul. 18, 1799	Enos Butler
34	Isaac Cook	Jonathan Hagarty	Jul. 18, 1799	Edward Hill
36	Joel Walker	Holly Walker and	Apr. 20, 1800	Richard Heath
		Amos Persons		Nicholas Williams
36	Thomas Neal	David Neal and	Feb. 18, 1800	Jas. McCormick
		Samuel Neal		Jos. Duckworth
37	James Vance	John Vance	Jan. 14, 1799	Milby McGee
39	David Newsom	Michael Burkhalter	July 3, 1797	Sterling Gardner
				Basil Wright
40	Winnie Pinson	Thomas Jones	Feb. 3, 1799	Benj. Mitchell
				Solomon Newsom
41	William Rose	Sarah & Edmond Rose	Feb. 9, 1801	Shadrach Fluellin
42	Jonathan Burson	Nancy Burson and	Aug. 11, 1801	John English
		Isaac Burson		Michael Cody
43	Abner Mitchell	Robert Rutherford	Feb. 10, 1801	R. Abercrombie
				Henry Shelton
43	James Barrow	Reubin Barrow	June 8, 1801	Hugh Reese
				David Nusom
44	Samuel Wright	Asa Wright	June 8, 1801	Johnson Wright
				Blake Pearcy
45	Archibald Kenpsey	Robt. Abercrombie &	Aug. 10, 1801	Matthew Hubert
		Joseph Howell		James Jones
46	James Nepper	Lydia Nepper and	Feb. 8, 1802	Elisha Brown
		Samuel Ridgedill		Solomon Newsom
47	Wm. C. Abercrombie	Robert Abercrombie	Feb. 8, 1802	Wm. Flournoy
				M. Hubert
48	Eli Bull	Jacob Bull	Feb. 9, 1802	Mark Hardin
				Jesse Bull
48	Ambrose Holliday	Elijah Worthen and	May 4, 1802	William Worthen
		Margaret Holliday		
49	Jacob Flournoy	William Flournoy	May 3, 1802	Robt. Abercrombie
				John B. Flournoy
50	John Carson (Cason?)	Samuel Winslet and	May 3, 1802	Josiah Bell
		John Williams		Solomon Lockett
51	Edward Murphy	Elizabeth Murphy and	June 1, 1802	John Rushin
		John Murphy		John Wilson
52	James Parker	Mary Parker and	Feb. 15, 1803	John Matthews
		Solomon Thompson		Amos Persons
53	James Bishop	Samuel Cooper	Feb. 15, 1803	Joel Heath
				Thos. Hutchinson
53	Samuel Neal	David Neal	Apr. 11, 1803	Reubin Jones
				John McCormick
54	Nathan Wootten	Stephen Lawrence	Apr. 11, 1803	Joseph Carter
55	Richard Lee	Alsy Lee	Aug. 9, 1803	Thomas Rogers
				Wm. Pilcher
56	Solomon Newsom, Jr.	David Newsom	Oct. 17, 1803	Thomas Dent
				Wm. Ursery et. al
57	Wiggins Killebrew	Tully Biggs	Oct. 17, 1803	John Rushing
				Wm. Simmons
58	John Barksdale	Samuel Barksdale, Pink Harvey Stephen Burnley	Oct. 22, 1803	Michael Harvey
				Josiah Beall

Page	Estate of	Admrs.	Date	Sureties
59	Henry Waggoner	Mary James, Geo. Waggoner & Aaron Lippham	Dec. 4, 1803	William Lipham Solomon Slatter
60	Thomas Sell	Mary Sell	Jan. 2, 1804	Isaac Davis Jere. Burkhalter
60	John Battle	Rhoda Battle & Col. Samuel Alexander	Feb. 13, 1804	Robt. Abercrombie Micajah Little
61	James Roquemore	Elizabeth Roquemore	Feb. 14, 1804	David Robertson
62	Labourn Chapman	Hannah Chapman	Feb. 15, 1804	Wm. Chapman Robert Parker
63	Owen Myrick	Elizabeth Myrick	Feb. 15, 1804	Thos. Edmondson Septimus Weatherby
63	Daniel Neves	John Neves	Feb. 15, 1804	Shadrach Flewellin
64	William McKinley	J hn Martin	Dec. 15, 1804	Joseph McKinley
65	William Parker	Robert Parker	Feb. 15, 1804	Jas. Matthews Solo. Thompson
66	Henry Jones	Elizabeth Jones	Dec. 15, 1804	John Nunn William Jones
67	William Geesland	Sally & Benj. Geesland	Aug. 15, 1804	John Moses James Gray
67	William Morrison	Nathaniel Ward	Aug. 15, 1804	Michael Burkhalter
68	Jesse Duberry	Mary & Henry Duberry	Dec. 10, 1804	Jacob Darden
69	James Jones	Wm. & James Jones	Dec. 10, 1804	Michael Burkhalter Thos. Dent
70	Richard Beasley	Robt. & Margaret Beasley	Jan. 26, 1805	James Gray
70	John Newsom	Sarah Newsom	Feb. 14, 1805	Michael Burkhalter
71	Micajah Stone	Mary Stone	Feb. 14, 1805	Robert Jenkins Jeremiah Bell
72	Levi Pruitt	Elizabeth & Bird Pruitt	Mar. 4, 1805	Isaiah Tucker Hardin Pruitt
73	James Waggoner	Mary, David W. & George B. Waggoner	Aug. 14, 1805	Geo. Waggoner Wm. Waggoner
73	John Benton	Winnifred Benton	Aug. 14, 1805	Leroy Mims Johnson Wright
74	John K. Candler	Zachariah Booth	Dec. 14, 1805	Richard Curry
75	James Rosser	Louisa Rosser	March 3, 1806	John Whittington Faddy Whittington
76	Daniel Rutherford	Samuel Jackson	May 4, 1806	John McGlamery
76	Sherrod Drake	Jesse White	May 5, 1806	Samuel Alexander
77	Aquilla Jones	Hannah Jones	July 7, 1806	Henry Williams Isaac Davis
78	Alexander Jarnett	Hannah Jarnett	Sept. 1, 1806	James Edge Nehemiah Edge
79	Francis Woodward	Benj. S. Woodward	Nov. 3, 1806	Harmon Perryman
80	Napper, Drury	Absalom Napper John Burkhalter	Jan. 5, 1807	Henry Harbuck Jeremiah Burkhalter
81	James Hefflin	Samuel Alexander	Mar. 2, 1807	John Simmons
82	James Atchinson	Wingfield Atchinson Charles Atchinson	Mar. 2, 1807	Geo. Hargraves
82	Stephen Darden	Nancy & Jethro Darden	May 4, 1807	Jacob Darden William Darden
83	Josiah Persons	Thomas Persons & Rachel Persons	May 4, 1807	Turner Persons Wormsley Rose
119	John Kelly	Elizabeth Kelly	Apr. 19, 1794	John Carson John Gibson
100	Thomas Hill	Phoebe Hill	May 1, 1794	Richard Hill
121	Thomas Boon	Joseph Boon and James Boon	May 19, 1794	Elisha Pruitt John Hill
122	Charles Baker	Priscilla Baker	Oct. 15, 1794	Willis Perry James Thomas
123	Samuel Helton	Henry Graybill	Nov. 19, 1794	Aaron Benton
124	Jesse Camble	Adam Jones	Dec. 18, 1794	Nathaniel Myrick
125	Mordecai Moore	Alexander Moore	Jan. 5, 1795	James Raley
126	Seth Slocum	Samuel Slocum	Feb. 2, 1795	Orandatus Watson

Page	Estate of	Admrs.	Date	Sureties
127	Thomas Horton	Henry Mitchell	Mar. 5, 1795	None
127	Samuel Newman	Richard Castleberry William Newman	Apr. 11, 1795	Mark Littleton
128	William Strother	Susannah Strother	Apr. 20, 1795	David Kelly

Page 8: ABERCROMBIE, ROBERT, dec'd. Admr's. Bond dated May 4, 1812, of NANCY ABERCROMBIE, WILLIAM JONES and AARON SMITH, Admrs.

Page 51: ANDREWS, WARREN, dec'd. Bond dated March 23, 1818, of PAYTON BAKER, Admr. JEREMIAH BEALL and JAMES PACE, securities.

Page 92: ALEXANDER, SAMUEL, dec'd. Bond dated Sept. 10, 1822, of MOSES ALEXANDER, Admr. Securities: JOSEPH HILL.

Page 97: ALLEN, SAMUEL, dec'd. Bond of SHERWOOD ALLEN, Admr., dated March 3, 1823; securities, GIDEON ALLEN, BENJAMIN ALLEN.

Page 114: AKINS, WILLIAM, dec'd. Bond of JOSEPH D. MCFARLAND and JAMES BAILEY, Admrs., dated Jan. 5, 1824. Sureties: NELSON GUNN, BENJ. CRENSHAW.

Page 114: AKINS, JOHN, dec'd. Bond dated Jan. 5, 1824, of JOHN AKINS as Admr. de bonis non with will annexed. Surety: BENJAMIN HURT.

Page 121: ARMSTRONG, HUGH, dec'd. Admrs. Bond dated March 1, 1824, of SHERMAN ARMSTRONG, Admr. SURETIES; JESSE ARMSTRONG, EDWARD KINSEY, SAM'L S. HILLMAN.

Page 128: ALLEN, ELISHA, dec'd. Admrs. Bond dated Nov. 8, 1824, of GEO. T. ALLEN. Sureties: ABEL FUNDERBURK, GEO. KELLUM, BENJAMIN ALLEN.

Page 234: ANDREWS, ELBERT P., dec'd. Bond dated May 5, 1834, of JOHN MOORE, Admr. Sureties: PETER CODY, SION HILL, JOSEPH FORD.

Page 5: BURKHALTER, JOHN, JR., dec'd. Bond dated Dec. 2, 1811, of JOHN BURKHALTER, Admr. Surety: HARDY PITTS.

Page 13: BENTON, FRANCIS, dec'd. Bond of THOMAS MYHAND, Admr., dated May 3, 1813; WILLIAM MYHAND, surety.

Page 15: BAILEY, PIERCE, dec'd. Bond of JENNIE BAILEY, Admx., dated Nov. 1, 1813; ELISHA ALLEN, JOSEPH JOHNSTON and BENJ. CRENSHAW, sureties.

Page 19: BROOKS, HENRY, dec'd. Bond of CHARLES BROOKS, Admr., dated June 6, 1814; THOMAS MADDUX, surety.

Page 23: BEALL, BENJAMIN B., dec'd. Bond of ROBERT A. BEALL, Admr. dated Dec. 5, 1814; A. MONCRIEF and CHAPPELL HEATH, securities.

Page 30: BONNER, WYATT, dec'd. Bond of JAMES BONNER, Admr., dated Sept. 4, 1815; WILLIAM BROWN and DAVID SALLIS, securities.

Page 34: BROTHERS, ELISHA, dec'd. Bond of ANDREW C. HORN, temporary Admr., dated Nov. 21, 1815; JOSIAS VINCENT, surety.

Page 52: BARTON, ROBERT, JR., dec'd. Bond of WILLIAM BARTON, Admr. dated Sept. 7, 1818; ROBERT BARTON, NATHAN MARSH, sureties.

Page 55: BROOKS, JOAB, dec'd. Bond of MARTIN KINSEY, Admr., dated Nov. 2, 1818; JOHN KITCHENS, surety.

Page 58: BASS, BATSON, dec'd. Bond of ZADOCK BASS, Admr., dated March 9, 1819; JOHN FONTAINE, JEREMIAH BUTT, NATHAN BODDIE, sureties.

Page 59: BECKWITH, JOHN, dec'd. Bond dated July 2, 1819, of WILLIS BECKWITH, Admr. Surety: BENJAMIN CRENSHAW.

Page 63:   BALL, ISAAC, dec'd. Bond dated Sept. 17, 1819, of HARDY PITTS and ARCHALAUS BUTT, Admrs. Surety: JAMES LOYLESS.

Page 71:   BRADY, JAMES, dec'd. Bond dated Nov. 6, 1820, of WILLIAM SHIVERS, Admr. Sureties: JONAS SHIVERS and VINSON JOHNSON.

Page 77:   BATTLE, RHODA, dec'd. Bond dated May 7, 1821, of HART-WELL BATTLE and JAMES LANGDON, Admrs. Sureties: ELISHA ALLEN, WILLIAM DARDEN.

Page 88:   BARKSDALE, WILLIAM, dec'd. Bond dated July 2, 1821, of MARY BARKSDALE, Admx. Sureties: EBENEZER BIRD. ZACHARIAH DARDEN.

Page 99:   BROOKS, CHARLES, dec'd. Bond dated May 5, 1823, of HENRY LOCKHART and JOHN FONTAINE, Admrs. Sureties: SAMUEL HALL and JOEL NEAL.

Page 100:   BEALL, MANNAN, dec'd. Bond of ELIJAH JONES and JOHN MCCRARY, Admrs. Sureties: SAMUEL HALL and HENLEY JONES. Dated May 5, 1823

Page 101:   BAKER, BLAKE, dec'd. Bond dated May 5, 1823, of DANIEL HUTCHINSON and IDEY BAKER. Sureties: WILLIAM HARBUCK and BENJ. SANDI-FORD.

Page 102:   BAILEY, JOHN, dec'd. Bond dated May 5, 1823, of JAMES BAKER as Admr. Sureties: BENJAMIN CRENSHAW and HARTWELL BATTLE.

Page 115:   BRAY, RICHARD, dec'd. Bond dated Jan. 5, 1824, of LUCY BRAY and AMOS WRIGHT, Admrs. Sureties: HARTWELL HEATH and JOSEPH WRIGHT.

Page 126:   BRAY, DR. RICHARD, dec'd. Bond dated Sept. 6, 1824, of HENRY B. THOMPSON, Admr. Sureties: SOLOMON LOCKETT and JOHN FONTAINE.

Page 123:   BATTLE, JOHN, dec'd. Bond dated March 1, 1824, of JOHN L. MARTIN as Admr. Surety: HARTWELL BATTLE.

Page 165:   BUTT, ARCHELAUS, dec'd. Bond dated Dec. 28, 1827, of JOHN BUTT, Admr. Surety: JOHN MOORE.

Page 185:   BAILEY, JAMES, dec'd. Bond dated Feb. 17, 1830, of PIERCE BAILEY, Admr. Sureties: EBENEZER BIRD, DAVID S. ANDERSON.

Page 238:   BRYANT, BENJAMIN, dec'd. Bond dated March 3, 1834, of ADAM JONES, Admr. Sureties: ELIJAH JONES, STEPHEN JONES.

Page 240:   BLOUNT, JAMES M. dec'd. Bond dated March 3, 1834, of WILLIAM H. and EMILY BLOUNT, Admrs. Sureties: HENRY H. CHAPMAN and JAMES A. CHAPMAN, also PETER CODY and EDMUND CODY.

Page 220:   BAKER, EDWIN, dec'd. Bond dated Nov. 5, 1832, of NANCY BAKER and JOHN HARRIS, Admrs. Sureties: ARCHIBALD SEALS and JETHRO DARDEN.

Page 173:   BYROM, WILLIAM, dec'd. Bond dated Sept. 1, 1828, of BENJAMIN HURT, Admr. Sureties: WILLIAM HURT and STARLING GARDNER.

Page 131:   BEALL, ELIZABETH, dec'd. Bond dated Feb. 1, 1825, of ELIJAH JONES, Admr. Sureties: JOHN VEAZEY and JOHN MCCRARY.

Page 46:   CRAWMAN, WILLIAM, dec'd. Bond dated Sept. 1, 1817, of MARY CROWMAN, Admx. Sureties: HEZEKIAH JONES, THOMAS WAGGONER.

Page 76:   CHAPMAN, BENJAMIN, dec'd. Bond dated March 5, 1821, of ROBERT and ABNER CHAPMAN, Admrs. Sureties: ASA CHAPMAN, BENJAMIN HILL.

Page 109:   CODY, DAVID, dec'd. LUCRETIA CODY, Admx. Admr's Bond dated Nov. 17, 1823; sureties, CHURCHILL GIBSON, WM. B. HUNDLEY, PETER CODY.

Page 124: CHAMBLESS, JOSEPH, dec'd. ADAM JONES, JR., Admr. Admr's bond dated April 7, 1824; sureties, ELIJAH JONES, CHRISTOPHER CHAMBLESS.

Page 139: CODY, DAVID, dec'd. CHURCHILL GIBSON and PETER CODY, sureties on the bond of LUCRETIA CODY, Admx. (now LUCRETIA SHERMAN), released from the bond at their request and new bond given Oct. 4, 1825, with ELI G. SHERMAN, JOHN G. WINTER and JOSEPH DENSON as sureties.

Page 161: CAMP, SAMUEL, dec'd. Bond dated Oct. 2, 1827, of GARRARD CAMP, Admr. Sureties: THADDEUS CAMP, SAMUEL HALL.

Page 223: CODY, MICHAEL, dec'd. Bond dated Jan. 8, 1833, of REBECCA CODY as Admx. Sureties: THOMAS LOCKETT, ELIAS WILSON.

Page 228: CULPEPPER, NATHAN, dec'd. Bond dated March 4, 1833, of SAMPSON R. CULPEPPER, Admr. Sureties: JESSE BEALL, ELIJAH JONES.

Page 230: CODY, GREEN, minor son of MICHAEL CODY, dec'd. Bond of PETER CODY, Guardian, dated May 6, 1833.

Page 171: CULPEPPER, WILLIAM, dec'd. Bond dated March 21, 1828 of RICHARD HEATH, Admr. Sureties: LEWIS JACKSON, THOMAS SEALS.

Page 164: COSBY, NANCY, dec'd. Bond of MORDECAI JOHNSON, Admr., dated Jan. 7, 1828. Sureties: HOWELL HIGHT, SEABORN DOZIER.

Page 47: DARDEN, JACOB, dec'd. Bond dated Nov. 3, 1817, of ABNER DARDEN and DAVID DARDEN, Admrs. Sureties: ROBERT HILL, WILLIAM DARDEN. On Sept. 4, 1826 the administrators of this estate were required to give a new bond which they did with JOHN HARRIS and JAMES CLAXTON as sureties. (page. 142)

Page 53: DAVIDSON, GEORGE H., dec'd. Bond dated Oct. 5, 1818 of ARTHUR MONCRIEF as Admr., with JOHN BUTT, security.

Page 86: DUCKWORTH, SAMUEL, dec'd. Bond dated Feb. 4, 1822, of JOSEPH CULPEPPER, Admr. Sureties: EDWARD KINSEY and WILLIAM TERRY.

Page 107: DARDEN, WILLIAM, dec'd. Bond dated Nov. 17, 1823, of JETHRO DARDEN, Admr. Sureties: SOLOMON LOCKETT.

Page 180: DARDEN, Ann, dec'd. Bond of JETHRO DARDEN, Admr., dated March 2, 1829. Sureties: SEPTIMUS TORRENCE and JAMES BAILEY.

Page 225: DENNIS, CATHERINE, dec'd. Bond dated Dec. 4, 1832, of DANIEL DENNIS, Admr. Sureties: FIELDING HILL, GAZAWAY DUCKWORTH.

Page 193: DENSON, BENJAMIN, dec'd. Bond dated Jan. 3, 1801, of JOHN B. BOYD, Admr. Security: STARLING J. PATE.

Page 146: DUCKWORTH, WILLIAM, dec'd. Bond of JOSEPH LEONARD, Admr., dated Jan. 2, 1827. Sureties: DAVID CODY, SAMUEL STORY.

Page 245: DARDEN, JONATHAN, dec'd. Bond of WILLIAM STONE, Admr., dated Nov. 3, 1834. Sureties: SOLOMON LOCKETT, SEPTIMUS TORRANCE.

Page 69: EDWARDS, ROBERT, dec'd. Bond of WILLIAM EDWARDS and THOMAS AVERA, Admrs., dated Nov. 6, 1820. Sureties: HENRY HIGHT, RICHARD BRAY.

Page 125: EDMONDSON, AMBROSE, dec'd. Bond of WILLIAM G. EDMONDSON, Admr. dated Sept. 6, 1824. Sureties: HACKAKIAH MCMATH, HENRY HINTON.

Page 197: EDMONDSON, WILLIAM, dec'd. Bond dated Feb. 14, 1831, of WILLIAM HURT, Admr. Sureties: HENRY HARRIS, NATHAN TURNER.

Page 61: FORD, JOSEPH, dec'd. Bond dated July 5, 1819, of WILLIAM W. FORD, Admr. Sureties: JEREMIAH BUTT, KENDALL MCTYEIRE, JAMES NEAL SR.

Page 104: FOWLER, NATHAN, dec'd., "formerly a citizen of this part of Wilkes now Warren County." Admr's bond dated June 30, 1823 of ZEPHANIAH FOWLER, temporary Admr., de bonis non of a certain undivided part of said estate. Surety: ELIJAH JONES.

Page 106: FINCH, ICHABOD, dec'd. Bond of LEVI MAY, Admr., dated Sept. 1, 1820. Sureties: JAMES ROWLAND, THOMAS ROWLAND.

Page 116: FLEWELLIN, ARCHELAUS, dec'd. Bond dated Jan. 5, 1824, of THOMAS FLEWELLIN, temporary Admr. Sureties: WM. H. BLOUNT, JAMES SHIVERS, THOMAS BERRY.

Page 152: FLEWELLIN, NANCY, dec'd. Bond dated March 5, 1827, of JAMES FLEWELLIN, Admr. Sureties: JAMES SHIVERS, HENRY HIGHT, WILLIAM HURT

Page 221: GRENADE, ADAM, dec'd. Bond dated Nov. 5, 1832, of JOSEPH ANSLEY, Admr. Sureties: GEORGE W. RAY and AARON ADKINS.

Page 10: GREGORY, HOWELL, dec'd. Bond dated March 2, 1812, of FRANCIS BEALL, Admr. Surety: SAMUEL BEALL.

Page 14: GRENADE, BENJAMIN, dec'd. Bond dated Sept. 6, 1813, of JAMES GRENADE, Admr. Surety: JEREMIAH BURKHALTER.

Page 88: GRAY, JAMES, SR., dec'd. Bond dated May 6, 1822, of JAMES GRAY, Admr. Sureties: THOS LOCKETT, MICAJAH ROGERS, DAVID SALLIS.

Page 91: GIBSON, JOHN, dec'd. Bond dated Sept. 16, 1822, of PERSONS BASS, Admr. Sureties: SAMUEL FULLER, THOMAS GIBON.

Page 98: GRIZZLE, WILIE, dec'd. Bond dated May 5, 1823, of THOMAS GIBSON, Admr. Sureties: ARTHUR MONCRIEF, GERRARD CAMP.

Page 129: GRIZZLE, THOMAS W., dec'd. Bond dated Jan. 24, 1825, of LETTICE GRIZZLE, Admx. Sureties: WILLIAM H. BLOUNT, LEWIS JACKSON.

Page 145: GRAY, AMY, dec'd. Bond dated Oct. 7, 1826, of JAMES GRAY as Admr. Surety: JOHN DAVIDSON.

Page 168: GLOVER, ELIZABETH, dec'd. Bond dated March 3, 1828, of FREDERICK GLOVER, Admr. Sureties: ISHAM GLOVER, LARKIN GLOVER.

Page 181: GRIERSON, ABRAM, dec'd. Bond dated April 25, 1829, of SUSANNAH GRIERSON, Admx. Sureties: HOWELL HIGHT, AMBROSE HEATH.

Page 218: HILL, JOSEPH, dec'd. Bond dated Oct. 3, 1832, of ZEPHANIAH FRANKLIN, Admr. Sureties: Q. L. C. FRANKLIN, DAVID MIMS, D. DENNIS.

Page 187: HARRISON, BERRYMAN H., dec'd. Bond dated April 17, 1830, ZEPHANIAH FRANKLIN, Admr. Sureties: HENRY HIGHT.

Page 74: HARRISON, DINWIDDIE R., dec'd. Bond dated Jan. 29, 1821, of ADAM JONES, Admr. Sureties: DANIEL OWENS, JOHN MOORE, ASA CHAPMAN.

Page 11: HARRIS, MISS OLIVE, dec'd. Bond dated Sept. 12, 1812, of JOHN BAKER, Admr. Sureties: NICHOLAS WILLIAMS, THOMAS BATTLE.

Page 21: HARDAWAY, JOHN, Esq., dec'd. Bond dated July 4, 1814, of WASHINGTON HARDAWAY, Admr. Surety: JOHN BURKHALTER.

Page 22: HARBUCK, JOHN, dec'd. Bond dated Nov. 7, 1814, of WILLIAM HARBUCK, Admr. Surety: JAMES NEAL.

Page 29: HOPKINS, JOSHUA, dec'd. Bond of SUSANNAH HOPKINS, Admx., dated July 3, 1815. Sureties: CHAPPELL HEETH, JOSEPH ROBERTS.

Page 38:   HEATH, ADAM, dec'd.   Bond of RICHARD HEATH and PETER CLOWER as Admrs., dated May 6, 1816. Sureties: HARDY PITTS, BENJAMIN SANDIFORD.

Page 67:   HEATH, MARK, dec'd.   Bond of HENRY HEATH, Admr., dated Aug. 7, 1820. Sureties: JOSEPH HILL, CHAPPELL HEATH.

Page 145:   HUFF, ABNER, dec'd.   Bond of JONATHAN HUFF, Admr., dated Dec. 4, 1822. Sureties: MIDDLETON HUFF and WILLIAM STANDFORD.

Page 149:   HILL, MOUNTAIN, dec'd.   Bond of AMBROSE HEETH, Admr., dated Jan. 14, 1827. Sureties: ABNER ROGERS, JOHN WRIGHT.

Page 156:   HOLDER, WILLIAM, dec'd.   Bond of LYDIA HOLDER, Admx., dated Sept. 3, 1827. Sureties: JOHN MAYS, JOSHUA LAZENBY.

Page 158:   HINTON, CHRISTOPHER, dec'd.   Bond of HENRY HINTON, Admr., dated Sept. 3, 1827. JOHN MAYS, surety.

Page 207:   HEETH, EDMOND P., dec'd.   Bond dated Nov. 7, 1831, of PETERSON HEETH, Admr. Sureties: CURTIS LOWE, D. DENNIS, NICHOLAS H. JONES.

Page 192:   HARBUCK, WILLIAM, dec'd.   Bond dated Nov. 13, 1830, of WILLIAM HARBUCK, Admr. Sureties: MICHAEL HARBUCK, JAMES HARBUCK.

Page 213:   HEATH, RICHARD, dec'd.   Bond dated May 21, 1832, of GEO. W. C. SHIVERS, Admr. Sureties: STARLING J. PATE, JOHN L. BURK-HALTER.

Page 20:   JONES, SAMUEL, dec'd.   Bond dated June 6, 1814, of HARDIN PRUITT, Admr. Surety: THOMAS MADDUX.

Page 81:   JOHNSON, ROBERT, dec'd.   Bond dated Sept. 10, 1821, of LITTLETON JOHNSON, Admr. Sureties: EDMOND JOHNSON, JOHN P. CARR.

Page 122:   JONES, JULIUS C., dec'd.   Bond dated March 1, 1824, of JOHN JONES, Admr. Surety: HENRY GIBSON.

Page 167:   JONES, WILLIAM, dec'd.   Bond dated Jan. 7, 1828, of RICHARD H. JONES, Admr. Bondsmen: HARTWELL HEATH, LEWIS PARHAM.

Page 199:   JOHNSON, HENRY, dec'd.   Bond of VINSON JOHNSON, Admr., dated April 5, 1831. Sureties: JAMES T. DICKEN, WILLIAM HURT.

Page 200:   JOHNSON, WILLIAM, dec'd.   Bond dated July 4, 1831, of WILLIAM JOHNSON, Admr. Bondsmen: JAMES JOHNSON, RANDOLPH JOHNSON.

Page 150:   JOHNSON, JACOB, dec'd.   Bond of JACOB SMITH, Admr., dated Feb. 14, 1827. Sureties: JOHN SMITH, JAMES GRENADE.

Page 136:   KINSEY, EDWARD, dec'd.   Bond of JAMES GRAY, temporary Admr., dated May 2, 1825. Sureties: JOHN FONTAINE, JOHN LITTLETON. (page 138) Bond of JAMES GRAY, permanent Admr., dated Jan. 24, 1825. Sureties: JOHN W. KINSEY, ROBERT BLACK.

Page 37:   KINSEY, DANIEL, dec'd.   Bond of May 6, 1816, of EDWARD KINSEY, Admr. Sureties: JEREMIAH BURKHALTER, WILLIAM USSERY.

Page 118:   KINSEY, WILLIAM, dec'd.   Bond dated Feb. 2, 1824, of JOHN W. KINSEY, Admr. Sureties: ABNER MCCORMICK and WILLIAM CASTLEBERRY.

Page 130:   KINSEY, MARTIN, dec'd.   Bond dated Jan. 24, 1825, of DELILAH KINSEY, Admx. Sureties: JOHN W. KINSEY and ROBERT BLACK.

Page 62:   LITTLETON, ALEXANDER, dec'd.   Bond of JAMES LOYLESS, Admr., dated Sept. 13, 1819. Surety: JAMES CODY, JR.

Page 112: LOCKETT, WARREN, dec'd. Bond of SOLOMON LOCKETT, Admr., dated Dec. 2, 1823. Sureties: JAMES ELLET, ASA CHAPMAN.

Page 205: LUCKETT, WILLIAM R., dec'd. Bond dated Nov. 7, 1831, of GUSTUS LUCKETT, Admr. Sureties: MARTIN GRIFFIN, JAMES DEWBERRY.

Page 236: MONROE, THOMAS, dec'd. Bond dated March 3, 1834, of ANDREW BUSH, Admr. Sureties: WILLIAM HARBUCK and SPENCER SEALS.

Page 17: MARKS, JOSEPH, dec'd. Bond dated Feb. 7, 1814, of MARY MARKS as Admx. Sureties: EDWIN BAKER, SOLOMON OGDEN, WILLIAM TEDDLIE, ANSEL MCKINNEY.

Page 33: MORRIS, JOHN, dec'd. Bond of BENJAMIN REES, Admr., dated Nov. 6, 1825. Sureties: JEREMIAH BURKHALTER and DAVID SALLIS.

Page 68: MAYES, WILLIAM, dec'd. Bond dated Sept. 4, 1820 of MERCY MAYES as Admx. Sureties: JOSHUA DRAPER, JEREMIAH BUTT, HENRY WILLIAMS.

Page 119: MYRDON, JOHN, dec'd. Bond dated March 1, 1824 of WILLIS RHYMES, Admr. Surety: MICAJAH ROGERS.

Page 153: MAY, NATHAN, dec'd. Bond of REUBIN MAY, Admr. dated May 7th, 1827. Sureties: WILLIAM CASTLEBERRY and ELIJAH JONES.

Page 177: MATTHEWS, ARTHUR, dec'd. Bond dated Dec. 2, 1828, of EDWARD MATTHEWS, Admr. Sureties: WILLIAM CASTLEBERRY, FRANCIS HARDAWAY.

Page 83: MESSER, NATHANIEL S., dec'd. Bond of PHILANDER O. PARIS, Admr., dated Dec. 3, 1821. Surety: JOHN W. A. PETTIT.

Page 41: MCCRERY, MATTHEW, dec'd. Bond of JOHN MCCRERY and SAMUEL HALL, Admrs. dated July 1, 1816. Sureties: HENRY KENDALL SR., THOMAS WILLIAMS.

Page 120: MCKINNEY, KINCHEN, dec'd. Bond of JOHN BURKHALTER, Admr., dated March 1, 1824. Surety: MOSES MCKINNEY.

Page 135: MCCOY, CHARLES, dec'd. Bond of REUBIN JONES, Admr., dated Apr. 4, 1825. Sureties: SPIVEY FULLER, ROYSTER HEETH.

Page 141: MCDOWELL, SAMUEL, dec'd. Bond of JOHN G. WINTER, Admr., dated Dec. 5, 1825. Surety: JEREMIAH BUTT.

Page 144: MCCULLERS, DAVID, dec'd. Bond of WILLIAM BALL, Admr., dated Dec. 4, 1826. Bondsman: JOHN W. KINSEY.

Page 6: NEAL, DAVID, Esq., dec'd. Bond of JAMES MADDOX and THOMAS MADDOX, Admrs. Sureties: THOMAS NEAL, JOHN HARDAWAY, REUBIN JONES.

Page 18: NEAL, JEHU, dec'd. Bond of THOMAS MADDOX, Temporary Admr. dated March 15, 1814. Surety: JAMES NEAL. Bond of THOMAS MADDOX and REBECCA NEAL. Permanent Admrs., dated June 6, 1814 (same page).

Page 42: NEAL, SAMUEL, dec'd. Bond dated Aug. 19, 1816, of JAMES NEAL, JR., Temporary Admr. Surety: JAMES NEAL. (p. 242) Bond of JAMES JOHNSON, Admr., dated Aug. 5, 1834; sureties: WILLIAM JOHNSON, WILLIAM ENGLISH.

Page 66: NEWSOM, JOHN, dec'd. Bond of GIDEON NEWSOM, Admr., dated Feb. 7, 1820. Sureties: JOSHUA NEWSOM, HENRY NEWSOM.

Page 189: NELSON, ANDREW, dec'd. Bond dated July 5, 1830, of ANDREW BUSH, Admr. Surety: SEABORN DOZIER.

Page 7: ORR, NOBLE, dec'd. Bond dated May 4, 1812 of HAMILTON GOSS as Admr. Surety: GEORGE HARGRAVES.

Page 3:   PHILLIPS, THOMAS, dec'd. Bond dated Nov. 4, 1811, of WILLY GILES BRADY, JOSEPH PHILLIPS, JOHN PHILLIPS, Admrs. Surety: CULLEN LEWIS BRADY.

Page 4:   PARHAM, JOHN, dec'd. Bond of ELIZABETH PARHAM and SAMUEL PITTS, Admrs., dated Nov. 4, 1811. Sureties: JOHN TURNER, HARDY PITTS.

Page 45:   PARHAM, JAMES, dec'd. Bond of EDMOND PARHAM, Admr., dated April 5, 1817. Surety: ROBERT BONNER.

Page 49:   PARHAM, ELIZABETH, dec'd. Bond of JOHN C. TURNER and SAMUEL PITTS, Admrs., dated Dec. 22, 1817. Sureties: WILLIAM H. BLOUNT, HENRY DEWBERRY.

Page 69:   PERKINS, SARAH, dec'd. Bond of JETHRO DARDEN, SR., Admr., dated Nov. 1, 1819. Surety: SAMPSON WILDER.

Page 96:   PERSONS, HENRY, dec'd. Bond of GRIGSBY E. THOMAS, Admr., dated Jan. 6, 1823. Sureties: JEREMIAH BUTT, ARTHUR MONCRIEF.

Page 104:   PARRISH, JOHN, dec'd. Bond dated Sept. 1, 1823, of GERARD CAMP as Admr. with the will annexed. Sureties: BENJ. SANDEFORD, BENJAMIN HURT.

Page 160:   PERSONS, TURNER, dec'd. Bond of AMOS J. PERSONS, Admr., dated Dec. 1, 1827. Sureties: HENRY LOCKHART, G. W. PERSONS, SAMUEL PITTS, NICHOLAS W. PERSONS and JAMES FLEWELLEN.

Page 186:   PARHAM, LEWIS, dec'd. Bond of FANNY PARHAM and NATHANIEL PARHAM, Admrs., dated Nov. 2, 1829. Sureties: DAVID MIMS, HARTWELL HEATH.

Page 155:   PATE, DRURY, dec'd. Bond of JOSEPH LEONARD, Admr., dated Sept. 3, 1827. Sureties: STITH HARDAWAY and BENJAMIN THOMPSON.

Page 190:   PORTER, RICHARD, dec'd. Bond of HENRY LOCKHART, Admr., dated Aug. 10, 1830. Surety: ARTHUR MONCRIEF.

Page 214:   PEEBLES, MARY, dec'd. Bond of JOHN MOORE, Admr., dated July 3, 1832. Sureties: THOMAS P. F. THREEWITS, JAMES HARRIS.

Page 34:   ROSE, STEPHEN, dec'd. Bond of HARDY PITTS, Admr., dated Dec. 4, 1815. Surety: JAMES NEAL.

Page 182:   ROGERS, REUBIN, SR., dec'd. Bond of JOHN ROGERS, Admr., dated May 4, 1829. Sureties: HENRY HIGHT, WILLIS DARDEN.

Page 202:   REESE, EDMOND, dec'd. Bond of DAVID MIMS, Admr., dated July 4, 1831. Sureties: SPIVEY FULLER and FELIX D. FRANKLIN.

Page 195:   REES, TALBOT S., dec'd. Bond of ZEPHANIAH FRANKLIN, Admr., dated Jan. 2, 1830. Surety: WILLIAM HURT.

Page 251:   ROBERTS, ELISHA, dec'd. Bond of WILLIS ROBERTS, Admr., with the will annexed, dated March 2, 1835. Sureties: ELISHA P. BOLTON, MOSES JOHNSON, LARKIN B. ROBERTS.

Page 257:   RICKETSON, JESSE, dec'd. Bond of THOS. P. F. THREEWITTS as Admr., dated May 4, 1835. Sureties: HENRY LOCKHART, THOMAS GIBSON.

Page 262:   STINSON, MICHAEL, dec'd. Bond of WILLIAM CASTLEBERRY, as Admr., dated Aug. 24, 1835. Sureties: PETER USREY, WILLIAM H. BRINCKLEY.

Page 132:   SMITH, THOMAS, dec'd., late of Richmond now Warren County. Bond of SPIVEY FULLER, Temporary Admr., dated Feb. 25, 1825. Sureties: CURTIS LOWE and NATHAN BEALL.

Page 1:   STITH, MILLIE, dec'd. Bond of JOHN HOBSON, Admr., with the will annexed, dated Feb. 4, 1811, that is, "with the will of WILLIAM STITH, dec'd., annexed." Sureties: SOLOMON LOCKETT, TIMOTHY MATTHEWS.

Page 259:   STANDFORD, WILLIAM, dec'd. Bond of ELISHA BURSON, Admr., dated July 6, 1835. Sureties: HUGH MONTGOMERY, MANN DUNEVENT?.

Page 32:   SALLIS, JOHN, dec'd. Will of DAVID SALLIS and JOHN SALLIS, Admrs., dated Nov. 6, 1815. Sureties: JAMES NEAL, ISAAC BURSON, WASHINGTON HARDAWAY.

Page 35:   STURDIVANT, DANIEL, dec'd. Bond of GEORGE HARGRAVES, Admr., dated Feb. 5, 1816. Surety: CHAPPELL HEATH.

Page 35:   SALLIS, JOSEPH, dec'd. Bond of GALBY MATTHEWS, Admr., dated May 5, 1817. Surety: DAVID SALLIS.

Page 46:   STRODDAR, SHADRACK, dec'd. Bond of LETITIA (or LETTICE?) STRODDAR, Admr., dated Sept. 14, 1816. Surety: WILLIAM GOYNE.

Page 60:   SALLIS, JOSEPH, a minor, dec'd. Bond dated July 5, 1819, of GALBY MATTHEWS, Admr. Surety: JOHN SALLAS.

Page 79:   STEVENS, OWEN B., dec'd. Bond of ROSS STEVENS, Admr., dated Sept. 10, 1821. Sureties: BENJAMIN WYNNE, BENJAMIN HURT.

Page 80:   STEVENS, AQUILLA, dec'd. Bond of ROSS STEVENS, Admr., dated Sept. 10, 1821. Sureties: BENJAMIN WYNNE, BENJAMIN HURT.

Page 94:   STONE, MICAJAH, dec'd. Bond of WILLIAM STONE, Admr. de bonis non, dated Nov. 18, 1822. Sureties: JOSEPH HILL, HENRY HEATH.

Page 95:   STONE, MARY, widow, dec'd. Bond of WILLIAM STONE, Admr., dated Nov. 18, 1822. Same sureties as last above.

Page 148:   SHIVERS, JONAS, dec'd. Bond of JAMES SHIVERS, Admr., dated Jan. 2, 1827. Sureties: EDWIN BAKER, JAMES FLEWELLIN, SAMUEL PITTS, JOS. ROBERTS.

Page 174:   STANFORD, JESSE, dec'd. Bond of REUBIN STANFORD, Admr., with the will annexed, dated July 11, 1828. Sureties: WILLIAM B. HARRIS, RICHARD S. LAZENBY.

Page 24:   THOMPSON, JAMES B., dec'd. Bond of HENRY B. THOMPSON, Admr., with the will annexed, dated Oct. 3, 181y. Sureties: CHAPPELL HEATH, JOS. M. SEMMES.

Page 43:   THOMPSON, JOHN, dec'd. Bond of NATHANIEL THOMPSON as Admr., dated Jan. 6, 1817. Sureties: JAMES NEAL SR., PEYTON BAKER.

Page 48:   TRAVIS, JOHN, dec'd. Bond of AMOS TRAVIS, Admr., dated Dec. 1, 1817. Sureties: SIMEON TRAVIS, LAWRENCE KITCHENS.

Page 73:   THOMPSON, NATHANIEL, dec'd. Bond of NANCY THOMPSON, Admx., dated Jan. 29, 1821. Sureties: MICHAEL CODY, SR., STEPHEN THOMPSON.

Page 84:   TUCKER, ISAIAH, dec'd. Bond of CHURCHILL GIBSON, Admr., with the will annexed, dated Dec. 13, 1821. Sureties: ASA CHAPMAN, JOHN FONTAINE.

Page 85:   TUCKER, GERMAIN, dec'd. Bond of FRANCES H. TUCKER and WILLIAM B. HUNDLEY, Admrs., dated Dec. 22, 1821. Sureties: PHILANDER PARRIS, HENRY GIBSON of Columbia County.

Page 127:   THOMAS, WILLIAM, dec'd. Bond of HARDY PITTS, Admr., dated Sept. 6, 1824. Sureties: ELIJAH JONES, ROBERT PALMER.

Page 137: TERRY, THOMAS, dec'd. Bond of JAMES MCC. CASON, Admr., dated July 4, 1825. Sureties: WILLIAM CASON, HUGH MONTGOMERY.

Page 140: TODD, LEWIS, dec'd. Bond of AARON ENGLISH as Admr., dated Dec. 5, 1825. Sureties: MATTHEW ENGLISH, JOHN ENGLISH.

Page 154: TURNER, JOHN, dec'd. Bond of JAMES TURNER, Admr., dated October 6, 1827. Sureties: KENDALL MCTYAIRE, ABRAM GRIERSON.

Page 159: THOMPSON, MOSES, dec'd. Bond of HANNAH THOMPSON and MOSES THOMPSON (JR.), Admrs., dated December 1st, 1827. Sureties: GILES SMITH and JONATHAN HUFF.

Page 217: THOMAS, STEWART, dec'd. Bond of BELL (or BILL?) THOMPSON Admr., dated Aug. 14, 1832. Sureties: SAMUEL NEWMAN, DANIEL DENNIS.

Page 2: THOMPSON, DAVID, dec'd. Bond of JOHN AIKENS, Admr., dated July 1, 1811. Sureties: JOHN BYROM and WILLIAM BYROM.

Page 211: TURLEY, PATRICK, dec'd. Bond of HUGH WARD, Admr., dated March 5, 1832. Sureties: IGNATIUS SEMMES, THOMAS TURLEY, HENRY HARE.

Page 16: WAGGONER, GEORGE, dec'd. Bond of GEORGE B. WAGGONER, Admr. with the will annexed, dated Nov. 1, 1813. Sureties: GEORGE MITCHELL, HENRY DEWBERRY, DAVID W. WAGGONER.

Page 25: WRIGHT, AMOS, dec'd. Bond of RACHEL WRIGHT, JOSEPH WRIGHT and AMOS WRIGHT (JR.), Admrs. with the will annexed, dated April 3, 1815. Sureties: REDDICK BASS, CHAPPELL HEATH.

Page 26: WRIGHT, LEWIS, Esq., dec'd. Bond of SOLOMON LOCKETT and NANCY WRIGHT, Admrs., dated April 3, 1815. Sureties: CHAPPELL HEATH, JACOB DARDEN.

Page 27: WRIGHT, ASAPH, Esq., dec'd. Bond of JOHN BUTT, Admr., dated March 6, 1815. Surety: CHAPPELL HEATH.

Page 39: WHITE, JOSEPH, dec'd. Bond of ROBERT WHITE, Admr., dated May 6, 1815. Sureties: AARON DENTON, JOHN HAMILTON.

Page 50: WOODWARD, FRANCIS, dec'd. Bond of BENJAMIN T. WOODWARD, Admr. dated March 23, 1818. Sureties: ISHAM WOODWARD, WILLIAM JACKSON.

Page 50: WHITE, WILLIAM, dec'd. Bond of JETHRO DARDEN, SR., Admr., dated March 23, 1818. Surety: JAMES VAUGHAN.

Page 53: WRIGHT, JOHN, dec'd. Bond of JOSEPH WRIGHT and AMOS WRIGHT as Admrs., dated Sept. 21, 1818. Surety: JOHN FONTAINE.

Page 54: WILLIAM, HENRY, SR., dec'd. Bond of HENRY WILLIAMS, Admr., dated Oct. 24, 1818. Surety: GEORGE W. HARDAWAY.

Page 57: WAGGONER, MARY, dec'd. Bond of ZACHEUS WAGGONER, Admr., dated Jan. 4, 1819. Sureties: DAVID W. WAGGONER and GEORGE B. WAGGONER.

Page 75: WILLIAMS, JOHN, dec'd. Bond of WINGFIELD COSBY, Admr., dated Jan. 29, 1821. Surety: FREDERICK B. HEETH and RICHARD DOZIER.

Page 89: WIGGINS, PETER, dec'd. Bond of REBECCA WIGGINS and REUBIN MAY, Admrs., dated May 6, 1822. Sureties: JOEL NEAL, PETER MAY.

Page 90: WADE, MARY, dec'd. Bond of JAMES ENGLISH as Admr., dated May 6, 1822. Surety: JOHN USRY.

Page 93: WILDER, WILLIAM, dec'd., "formerly of Wilkes County." Bond of SAMPSON WILDER, Admr. de bonis non, dated Sept. 24, 1822. Surety MOSES ALEXANDER.

Page 105: WILSON, JOHN, dec'd. Bond of JOSEPH LEONARD, Admr., dated Sept. 1, 1823. Surety: HENRY WILSON, DAVID CODY.

Page 120: WOOD, WILLIAM, dec'd. Bond of JOSEPH WOOD, Admr., dated March 1, 1824. Sureties: HARRIS WOOD, MARY WOOD, THOMAS JONES.

Page 151: WILSON, JOHN M., dec'd. Bond of HENRY WILSON, Admr., dated Feb. 14, 1827. Sureties: HENRY WILLIAMS, JOSEPH LEONARD.

Page 178: WILSON, JEREMIAH, dec'd. Bond of HENRY WILSON, Admr., dated Jan. 5, 1829. Sureties: ELIAS WILSON, JOSEPH LEONARD.

Page 226: WRIGHT, DRUSILLA, dec'd. Bond of JOSEPH WRIGHT, Admr., dated Feb. 12, 1833. Sureties: HENRY HIGHT, SOLOMON WILDER.

Page 232: WRIGHT, AMOS (JR.?), dec'd. Bond of WILLIAM CASTLE-BERRY and JOSEPH WRIGHT, Admrs., dated Sept. 24, 1833. Sureties: JOSEPH LEONARD, EDMOND CODY, ISHAM R. BURKHALTER, J. L. BURKHALTER, VINCENT E. RIVERS, EZRA CASTLEBERRY.

Page 252: WALTON, ROBERT, dec'd. Bond of Q. L. C. FRANKLIN, Admr. dated March 2, 1835. Sureties: WILLIS ROBERTS, LARKIN B. ROBERTS.

Page 255: WILLIAMS, JOHN, dec'd. Bond of MARY WILLIAMS, Admx., dated March 2, 1835. Sureties: SHADRACK BRADSHAW, WOODSON BRADSHAW.

Editor's Note: The reader will remember that administrations are granted on estates where the decedent died without a will. In cases where there is a will probated and the executor named in the will dies, resigns or fails to qualify, the Court will appoint an Admr. "with the will annexed." Where there is a previous administration and a new admin-istrator is appointed, he is referred to as the Admr. "de bonis non."

ADMINISTRATOR'S BONDS IN DEED BOOK "A"

(ERRONEOUSLY RECORDED IN DEED RECORDS)

Page 30: JOHN CURRIE, Admr. of JANE BURNS estate. Dated April 17, 1797. Surety: BARRETT BREWER.

Page 31: LYDIA HARTFIELD, Admx. of GEORGE HARTFIELD estate. Dated Aug. 11, 1800. BENJAMIN HOWARD, security.

Page 32: FERGUS LINN, Admr. of JOHN LINN estate. Dated July 18, 1799. THOMAS JONES and DANIEL MCCOWAN, sureties.

Page 33: DANIEL FREDERICK, Admr. of JOHN THOMAS estate. Dated July 18th, 1799. WILLIAM MIMS surety.

Page 33: SUSANNAH BUTLER, Admr. of NOBLE BUTLER estate. Dated July 18, 1799. BEALL BUTLER and ENOS BUTLER, sureties.

Page 34: JONATHAN HAGERTY, Admr. of ISAAC COOK estate. Dated ___, 1799. EDWARD HILL, security.

Page 35: JONATHAN HAGERTY, Guardian of PERREBY COOK and SELETHA COOK, minor daughters of ISAAC COOK dec'd. Dated July 18, 1799. EDWARD HILL, surety.

Page 36: HOLLY WALKER and AMOS PERSONS, Admx. and Admr. of JOEL WALKER estate. Dated April 20, 1800. RICHARD HEATH and NICHOLAS WILLIAMS sureties.

Page 36: DAVID NEAL and SAMUEL NEAL, Admrs. of THOMAS NEAL estate. Dated Feb. 18, 1800. JAMES MCCORMICK & JOSEPH DUCKWORTH, sureties.

Page 37:   JOHN VANCE, Admr. of JAMES VANCE estate. Dated Jan. 14, 1799. MILBY MCGEE, security.

Page 39:   MICHAEL BURKHALTER, Admr. of DAVID NUSOM (NEWSOM?) estate. Dated July 3, 1797. STERLING GARDNER and BASIL WRIGHT, sureties.

Page 40:   THOMAS JONES, Admr. of WINNIE PINSON estate. Dated Feb. 3, 1799. BENJAMIN MITCHELL, SOLOMON NEWSOM, sureties.

Page 41:   SARAH ROSE and EDMOND ROSE, Admrs. of WILLIAM ROSE estate. Dated Feb. 9, 1801. Sureties: WORMSLEY ROSE, SHADRACH FLUELLIN.

Page 42:   NANCY BURSON and ISAAC BURSON, Admrs. of JONATHAN BURSON estate. Dated Aug. 11, 1801. JOHN ENGLISH and MICHAEL CODY, securities.

Page 43:   ROBERT RUTHERFORD, Admr. of ABNER MITCHELL estate. Dated Feb. 10, 1801. R. ABERCROMBIE and HENRY SHELTON, securities.

Page 43:   REUBIN BARROW, Admr. of JAMES BARROW estate. Dated June 8, 1801. HUGH REESE and DAVID NUSOM (NEWSOM?), sureties.

Page 44:   ASA WRIGHT, Admr. of SAMUEL WRIGHT estate. Dated June 8, 1801. JOHNSTON WRIGHT and BLAKE PEARCY, securities.

Page 45:   ROBERT ABERCROMBIE & JOSEPH HOWELL, Admrs. of ARCHIBALD KENTSEY (KINSEY?) estate. Dated Aug. 10, 1801. MATTHEW HUBERT, JAMES JONES, sureties.

Page 46:   LYDIA NEPPER and SAMUEL RIDGEDELL, Admrs. of JAMES NEPPER estate, with the will annexed. Dated Feb. 8, 1802. ELISHA BROWN, SOLOMON NEWSOM, sureties.

Page 47:   ROBERT ABERCROMBIE, Admr. of WILLIAM C. ABERCROMBIE estate. Dated Feb. 8, 1802. WILLIAM FLOURNOY and M. HUBERT, sureties.

Page 48:   JACOB BULL, Admr. of ELI BULL estate. Dated Feb. 9, 1802, MARK HARDIN and JESSE BULL, sureties.

Page 48:   ELIJAH WARTHEN and MARGARET HOLLIDAY, Admr. and Admx. of AMBROSE HOLLIDAY estate. Dated May 4, 1802. JOSEPH HOWELL and WM. WARTHEN sureties.

Page 49:   WILLIAM FLOURNOY, Admr. of JACOB FLOURNOY estate. Dated May 3, 1802. ROBERT ABERCROMBIE and JOHN B. FLOURNOY, sureties.

Page 50:   SAMUEL WINSLET and JOHN WILLIAMS, Admrs. of JOHN CARSON estate. Dated May 3, 1802. JOSIAH BELL, SOLOMON LOCKETT, HOWELL HIGH, MARK HARDIN, sureties.

Page 51:   ELIZABETH MURPHY and JOHN MURPHY, Admrs. of EDWARD MURPHY estate. Dated June 1, 1802. JOHN RUSHIN and JOHN WILSON, sureties.

Page 52:   MARY PARKER and SOLOMON THOMPSON, Admrs. of JAMES PARKER estate. Dated Feb. 15, 1803. JOHN MATTHEWS, AMOS PERSONS, sureties.

Page 53:   SARAH COOPER, Admx. of JAMES BISHOP's estate. Dated Feb. 15, 1803. JOEL HEATH, THOMAS HUTCHINSON, sureties.

Page 53:   DAVID NEAL, Admr. of SAMUEL NEAL's estate. Dated April 11, 1803. REUBIN JONES, JOHN MCCORMICK, sureties.

Page 54:   STEPHEN LAURENCE, Admr. of NATHAN WOOTTEN estate. Dated April 11, 1803. JOSEPH CARTER, surety.

Page 55:   ALSEY LEE, Admx. of RICHARD LEE estate. Dated Aug. 9, 1803. THOMAS ROGERS and WILLIAM PILCHER, sureties.

Page 56:   DAVID NEWSOM, Admr. of estate of SOLOMON NEWSOM JR., dec'd. Dated Oct. 17, 1803. Sureties: THOMAS DENT, WILLIAM URSERY, JOEDAY NEWSOM.

Page 57:   TULLY BIGGS, Admr. of WIGGINS KILLEBREW estate. Dated Oct. 17, 1803. Sureties: JOHN RUSHING, WILLIAM SIMMONS.

Page 58:   SAMUEL BARKSDALE, PINKITTIAM HARVEY, STEPHEN BURNLEY, Admrs. of JOHN BARKSDALE estate. Dated Oct. 22, 1803. Sureties: MICHAEL HARVEY, JOSIAH BEALL.

Page 59:   MARY SELL, Admx. of THOMAS SELL estate. Dated Jan. 2, 1803. ISAAC DAVIS, JEREMIAH BURKHALTER, sureties.

Page 59:   MARY JAMES and GEROGE WAGGONER and AARON LIPHAM, Admrs. of HENRY WAGGONER estate. Dated Dec. 4, 1805. WM. LIPHAM, SOLOMON SLATTER, SURETIES.

Page 60:   RHODA BATTLE and COL. SAMUEL ALEXANDER, Admrs. of JOHN BATTLE estate. Dated Feb. 13, 1804. ROBERT ABERCROMBIE and MICAJAH LITTLE, sureties.

Page 61:   ELIZABETH ROQUEMORE, Admx. of JAMES ROQUEMORE estate. Dated Feb. 14, 1804. Sureties: DAVID ROBERTSON and WILLIAM USSERY.

Page 62:   HANNAH CHAPMAN, Admr. of LABOURN CHAPMAN estate. Dated Feb. 15, 1804. WILLIAM CHAPMAN, ROBERT PARKER, sureties.

Page 63:   ELIZABETH MYRICK, Admr. of OWEN MYRICK estate. Dated Feb. 15th 1804. THOMAS EDMONDSON and SEPTIMUS WEATHERBY, sureties.

Page 63:   JOHN NEVES, Admr. of DANIEL NEVES estate. Dated Feb. 15, 1804. SHADRACH FLEWELLIN, surety.

Page 64:   JOHN MARTIN, Admr. of WILLIAM MCKINLEY estate. Dated Dec. 15th, 1804. JOSEPH MCKINLEY, security.

Page 65:   ROBERT PARKER, Admr. of WILLIAM PARKER estate. Dated Feb. 15th, 1804. JAMES MATTHEWS, SOLOMON THOMPSON, sureties.

Page 66: ELIZABETH JONES, Admx. of HENRY JONES estate. Dated Dec. 15, 1804. JOHN NUNN and WILLIAM JONES, sureties.

Page 67:   SALLIE and BENJAMIN GEESLAND, Admrs. of WILLIAM GEESLAND estate. Dated Aug. 15, 1804. JOHN MOSES, JAMES GRAY, sureties.

Page 67:   NATHANIEL WARD, Admr. of WILLIAM MORRISON estate. Dated Aug. 15, 1804. MICHAEL BURKHALTER, security.

Page 68:   MARY and HENRY DUBERRY, Admrs. of JESSE DUBERRY estate. Dated Dec. 10, 1804. JACOB DARDEN, surety.

Page 69:   WILLIAM JONES and JAMES JONES, Admrs. of JAMES JONES estate. Dated Dec. 10, 1804. MICHAEL BURKHALTER, THOMAS DENT, securities.

Page 70:   MARGARET BEASLEY and ROBERT BEASLEY, Admrs. of RICHARD BEASLEY estate. Dated Jan. 26, 1805. JAMES GRAY, surety.

Page 70:   SARAH NEWSOM, Admx. of JOHN NEWSOM estate. Dated Feb. 14, 1805. MICHAEL BURKHALTER, surety.

Page 71:   MARY STONE, Admx. of MICAJAH STONE estate. Dated Feb. 14, 1805. ROBERT JENKINS, JEREMIAH BELL, sureties.

Page 72:   ELIZABETH PRUITT and BIRD PRUITT, Admrs. of LEVI PRUITT estate. Dated March 4, 1805. ISAIAH TUCKER, HARDIN PRUITT, sureties.

Page 73:   MARY WAGGONER, DAVID W. WAGGONER and GEO. B. WAGGONER, Admrs. of JAMES WAGGONER estate. Dated Aug. 14, 1805. GEO and WM. WAGGONER, sureties.

Page 73:   WINNIFRED BENTON, Admx. of JOHN BENTON estate. Dated Aug. 14, 1805. LEROY MIMS, JOHNSTON WRIGHT, sureties.

Page 74: ZACHARIAH BOOTH, Admr. of JOHN K. CANDLER estate. Dated Dec. 14, 1805. Security: RICHARD CURRY.

Page 75: LOUISA ROSSER, Admx. of JAMES ROSSER estate. Dated Mar. 3, 1806. JOHN ROSSER and FADDY WHITTINGTON, sureties.

Page 76: SAMUEL JACKSON, Admr. of SAMUEL RUTHERFORD estate. Dated May 5, 1806. JOHN MCGLAMERY, surety.

Page 76: JESSE WHITE, Admr. of SHERROD DRAKE estate. Dated May 5, 1806. SAMUEL ALEXANDER, surety.

Page 77: HANNAH JONES, Admx. of AQUILLA JONES estate. Dated July 7, 1806. HENRY WILLIAMS, ISAAC DAVIS, sureties.

Page 78: HANNAH JARNETT, Admx. of ALEXANDER JARNETT estate. Dated Sept. 1, 1806, JAMES EDGE and NEHEMIAH EDGE, sureties.

Page 79: BENJ. S. WOODWARD, Admr. of FRANCIS WOODWARD estate. Dated Nov. 3, 1806. HARMON PERRYMAN, surety.

Page 79: THADDEUS BEALL and THADDEUS BEALL, Jr., Admrs. of JOSEPH BEALL estate. Dated Dec. 2, 1806. ELIAS BEALL also an Admr.

Page 80: ABSALEM NAPPER and JOHN BURKHALTER, Admrs. of DRURY NAPPER estate. Dated Jan. 5, 1807. HENRY HARBUCK and JEREMIAH BURKHAL-TER, sureties.

Page 81: SAMUEL ALEXANDER, Admr. of JAMES HEFFLIN estate. Dated March 2, 1807. JOHN SIMMONS, surety.

Page 82: WINGFIELD ATCHINSON and CHARLES ATCHINSON, Admrs. of JAMES ATCHINSON estate. Dated March 2, 1807. GEORGE HARGRAVES, surety.

Page 82: NANCY DARDEN and JETHRO DARDEN, Admrs. of STEPHEN DARDEN estate. Dated May 4, 1807. Sureties: JACOB DARDEN, JETHRO DARDEN, WM. DARDEN.

Page 83: THOMAS PERSONS and RACHEL PERSONS, Admrs. of JOSIAH PERSONS estate. Dated May 4, 1807. TURNER PERSONS, WORMSLEY ROSE, sureties.

Page 119: ELIZABETH KELLY, Admx. of JOHN KELLY estate. Dated Apr. 19, 1804. JOHN CARSON, JOHN GIBSON, sureties.

Page 120: PHOEBE HILL, Admx. of THOMAS HILL estate. Dated May 1, 1794. RICHARD HILL, surety.

Page 121: JOSEPH BOON and JAMES BOON, Admrs. of THOMAS BOON estate. Dated May 19, 1794. ELISHA PRUITT and JOHN HILL, sureties.

Page 122: PRISCILLA BAKER, Admx. of CHARLES BAKER estate. Dated Oct. 15, 1794. WILLIS PERRY, JAMES THOMAS, sureties.

Page 123: HENRY GRAYBILL, Admr. of SAMUEL HELTON estate. Dated Nov. 19, 1794. AARON BENTON surety.

Page 124: ADAM JONES, Admr. of JESSE CAMBLE estate. Dated Dec. 18, 1794. NATHANIEL MYRICK, surety.

Page 125: ALEXANDER MOORE, Admr. of MORDEEON? (Possibly MORDECAI?) MOORE, estate. Dated Jan. 5th, 1795. JAMES and HENRY RALEY, sureties.

Page 126: SAMUEL SLOCUM, Admr. of SETH SLOCUM estate. Dated Feb. 2, 1795. ORONDATUS WATSON, surety.

Page 127: HENRY MITCHELL, Admr. of THOMAS HARTON (HARDIN?) estate. Dated March 5, 1795. No name of surety signed to bond.

Page 127: RICHARD CASTLEBERRY, WILLIAM NEWSOM (signed WM. NEWMAN) Admrs. of SAMUEL NEWMAN estate. Dated April 11, 1795. MARK LITTLETON, surety.

Page 128: SUSANNAH STROTHER, Admx. of WILLIAM STROTHER estate. Dated April 20, 1795. DAVID KELLY, surety.

Note: This first book of wills extends from 1794 to 1810. No date of probate is shown for many of the wills, but the date may be obtained from the minutes. The Minute Book will give the dates for the period covered by the book (ending 1807), though it should be borne in mind that some wills may not be mentioned on the minutes and on the other hand some (or rather just a few) mentioned in the minutes, do not appear in the will book. They may show up in the deed records yet to be published, as sometimes wills were mistakenly recorded in the deed records. Date of probate of a will is important to the genealogist to show that the decedent died between the date of making the will and the date the will was probated.

Page 1: BENJAMIN HUBERT, Last Will and Testament, dated May 1, 1793; probated July 6, 1794. Gives to his wife MARY all estate, real and personal, for her support; at her death their youngest son, DAVID HUBERT, to have 100 acres to include the plantation where testator then lived, also a slave Bob, son DAVID to pay testator's three daughters, FANNIE RUNNELS, POLLY RUTHERFORD and HESTER RUNNELS a specified sum of money. Grandson, HUBERT RUNNELS, at the death of wife MARY to have a cow and calf, a small shotgun and 100 acres known as the Brewer tract. At death of said wife MARY, all property other than the above, to be divided into eight lots and drawn for; son, WILLIAM HUBERT to have first draw; son MATTHEW HUBERT to have two draws; then POLLY RUTHERFORD, HESTER RUNNELLS, sons GABRIEL HUBERT, DAVID HUBERT, and JACOB WILLIAMS to draw in the order named. If daughter FANNIE dies before her mother, her part to fall to my said grandson HUBERT RUNNELLS. Executors: JOHN RUTHERFORD, MATTHEW HUBERT and DAVID HUBERT. Witnesses: MATTHEW HUBERT, ELIJAH RUNNELLS, GIBSON FLOURNOY.

Page 3: JAMES YOUNG. Last Will and Testament, dated June 4, 1794; no date of probate. Gives to wife (unnamed), 5 shillings; to his beloved son, JOHN FEWOCKS, 300 acres on Ready Creek, waters of Brier Creek, two slaves, horses, household furniture & c., for his lifetime. Final division of estate to go to JACOB, JAMES, WILLIAM and JOHN PEARSON YOUNG, and WILLIAM BOWLING (BOWLAND). WILLIAM YOUNG JR., to receive certain cattle. Witnesses: SAMUEL SLOCUMB, WILLIAM YOUNG SR., LOUISA CORBITT. Note: Relationship, if any, of the YOUNGS and BOWLING to the testator shown.

Page 5: JACOB HORN, planter, of Richmond County, Ga. Last Will and Testament dated May 1, 1793; probated July 6, 1794. Gives to wife MARGARET for her lifetime, a slave Jennie, cattle and other personal property. Gives to son JOHN HORN a ewe and lamb; to son, JESSE HORN, 200 acres, being the western part of the tract on which testator lives, together with slave Ann; to son, ISAAC HORN, 200 being the eastern part of the said homeplace tract, together with horse, &c. To daughter, ELIZABETH HENDERSON, a ewe and lamb; and the same to daughter, MARY POWELL; to daughter, MARTHA HORN, a mare called Gin, and to daughter, ELLINOR HORN, the increase of said mare; to daughter, SARAH HORN, a cow named Cherry. Executors: Sons, JOHN and JESSE HORN. Witnesses: ROBERT PATTERSON, JOHN BARBERER (or BARBERIE?), ABEL LENNARD.

Page 8: BETTY FLUWELLIN. Last Will and Testament dated March 28, 1794; no date of probate. Bequeaths to sons, HOWELL, WILLIAM ABNER and SHADERICK FLUWELLIN five shillings each; to son, ALEXANDER FLUWELLIN, two slaves for his lifetime; to ELIZABETH, daughter of SOLOMON SLATTER, at his death, but if she dies without heirs, then to be divided among all testatrix's own children; gives to son, the said ALEXANDER, "all my right to the land I now live on, or any other land I have a right to, together with all my pewter, household goods, &c." Gives to daughter, NANCY SLATTER, a saddle, flax-wheel and wearing apparrell. Witnesses: SEPTIMUS WEATHERBY, DANIEL GRANTHAM, NANCY SLATTER.

Page 11:   HARDY WESTER, of Warren County. Last Will and Testament,
dated May 18, 1795; probated July 8, 1795. Gives to his wife FANNY, his
horses, household goods including his pewter, three shotguns, punch-bowl,
cotton and linen wheels, and $29.00 in money. No land mentioned. To
daughters, NANCY and ELIZABETH WESTER, five shillings each. Executors:
Wife, FANNY WESTER & SAMPSON IVY.

Page 9:   BENJAMIN SIMMONS, planter. Last Will and Testament, dated
Mar. 16, 1795; probated April 11, 1795. Gives to son, JAMES SIMMONS,
200 acres originally granted MOSES POWELL, SR., and deeded by him to testator, adjoining the land where testator lives; to daughter, REBECKAH
SIMMONS, a slave named Beck, a bed &c., to be hers upon her reaching her
majority or marriage. Residue of estate is devised to son, JOHN SIMMONS,
he to pay son, HENRY SIMMONS, Ł 150 upon him reaching his majority, and
also pay to daughters POLLIE and JINCEY SIMMONS $300.00 each upon each
of them becoming of age or marriage; also to provide testator's wife LUCY
SIMMONS with a "genteel maintenance for her widowhood on the place where
I now live." Executors: JAMES SIMMONS and JOHN SIMMONS. Witnesses:
MALCOLM JOHNSON, JOHN SIMMONS, JOHN WYNNE, J.P.

Page 14:   GAHAZI DAVIS, "known by this name, alias GAHAZI SHOCKLEY."
Last Will and Testament dated Nov. 9, 1795; probated Dec. 18, 1795.
Devises to BARSHEBA GRANARD, a sorrel mare Nell; to brother, NATHAN
SHOCKLEY, "known by the name of NATHAN DAVIS", all of testator's land &c.
Executor: REUBIN MCGEE of said county. Witnesses: P. HODO, THOMAS
ANSLEY, JAMES SMITH.

Page 16:   NATHANIEL HOOD. Last Will and Testament, dated Nov. 17,
1795; probated Feb. 1, 1796. Gives his entire estate of his brother,
JOHN HOOD, who is also named Executor. Witness: WILLIAM HARDIN.

Page 17:   THOMAS DRAKE, blacksmith. Last Will and Testament dated
March 1, 1794; no date of probate shown. He gives or directs that a
tract of 300 acres on Rocky Comfort Creek and a tract of land on the
Ohoopee be sold and the proceeds used to educate testator's four children.
He directs that his son, FRANCIS DRAKE, be apprenticed to a blacksmith to
learn that trade. His son, LEMUEL BRAXTON DRAKE, to be apprenticed to a
bricklayer to learn that trade; and son, EARLY DRAKE, be apprenticed to
his brother FRANCIS. He directs that his property be divided into five
parts, one each to his wife SARAH and the sons above named and daughter,
THENEY DRAKE. Executors: Friends, TANDY CLARK KEY, DANIEL EVANS, and
wife, SARAH DRAKE. Witnesses: JAMES ROBINSON, JOHN FOVE?, PRISCILLA
FOVE?.

Page 19:   DAVID LOCKETT. Last Will and Testament dated Jan. 7, 1796;
probated March 12, 1796. He directs that his estate be kept together for
use of his wife (not named) and the children under age; that a still
be bought, and that the money received from sale of his tobacco be put out
at interest. Provides for youngest children WINFREY, REUBIN, DOCTOR and
SALLY LOCKETT, giving them Ł30 each. The land bought of DANIEL PHELPS to
be sold except 50 acres whereon "my sister, GIPSON, lives." "My bounty
land warranty" to go to two youngest sons REUBIN and DOCTOR LOCKETT. He
directs that all his estate be kept together until son DOCTOR comes of
age. Son, DAVID, to have a bed and other items. Certain lands with three
slaves are given to his wife. Residue to be divided between my children
SOLOMON, THOMAS, ABNER, DAVID, WINFREY, REUBIN, DOCTOR and SALLIE LOCKETT;
and son, THOMAS, to have the land where he now lives. Executors: Sons,
SOLOMON and THOMAS LOCKETT. Witnesses: ALEXANDER BASS and HENRY PEEK.

Page 21:   SAMUEL MOORE of Warren County. Non-cupative will, sworn
to Setp. 7, 1795, by CAPT. SOLOMON NEWSOM, who says that on the evening
of the 1st inst., SAMUEL MOORE, now dec'd., sent for him, deponent, and
deponent arrived at MOORE's home the next day and found him in his perfect senses but very ill; that MOORE told him he was desirous of making
his will as soon as he could get JODY NEWSOM. He said that MOORE wished
nothing sold of his estate but that his wife and children have all the
income until they the children were of age; that all the estate should be

in the hands of his wife and JODY NEWSOM and "to bedealt out to the children as they become of age, and they in their discretion should sell his land and the proceeds with what is due him from COL. LEWIS, be invested in two young negroes." Sworn to before WYCHE GOODWIN, J.P., and L. PRUITT, J.P.

Page 22: SAMUEL NEWMAN of Washington Co., Ga. "being very sick. Last Will and Testament dated (undated); no date of probate shown. Says his oldest daughter, ANN LOOKER (or LOOPER) received her portion of his estate at her marriage. Devises to his son, WALTER, certain land, he to pay to "my daughter" MARY NEWMAN and to my son, JOHN NEWMAN, 20 shillings. To son, WILLIAM, he gives 100 acres of "the old tract." To daughter ZILPHA, L10 at her majority (legal age). To sons, LENNARD & JONATHAN, 200 acres each in Burke County. Son, WILLIAM, to have testator's stock, farming tools &c., till testator's daughters ELIZABETH & MARGERY NEWMAN come of age. He directs son, WALTER, to make TITLES to THOMAS MCDOWD to certain land on Stephenson's Creek. To his grandson, ALASON NEWMAN, 40 shillings. He designates son, WILLIAM, to be his "attorney-at-law" (evidently meaning executor - Editor).

Page 24: EPHRIAM KING of Warren County. Last Will and Testament dated May 4, 1795; probated April 1, 1796. Gives to his wife, ELIZABETH, the plantation of 50 acres whereon he lives, with all personal estate, for her lifetime, and at her death to be divided between my children, ISAAC, MARY, JOEL and JAMES. SHADRACK FLUWELLIN to be executor. Witnesses: JOHN HAWTHORN, JOEL KING.

Page 25: CHARLES MEDLOCK. Last Will and Testament, dated Dec. 9, 1796; probated Jan. 2, 1797. Gives to his wife, AGATHA, a horse, saddle and his household goods outright, and also his slaves Jane and Dinah for her lifetime and at wife's death said Dinah to become the property of his son, GEORGE, and his daughter, ANN JORDAN, to have the said Jane. To his granddaughter, POLLY JORDAN, he gives his slave Violet. To his grandson CHARLES MEDLOCK, he gives his slaves Will and Richmond together with horse, bedding, &c., to remain in possession of testator's son, GEROGE, until CHARLES becomes of age. To granddaughter, SUSAN MEDLOCK, he gives his slaves Adam and Eve on the same condition. To his granddaughter AGATHA HALEY, he gives a slave named Millie on same terms. To his granddaughter, POLLY MEDLOCK, he gives his slave Tamar. Executors: wife, AGATHA, son, GEORGE MEDLOCK, and son-in-law, WILLIAM JORDAN. Witnesses: JOSEPH HOWELL, JAMES TAYLOR, GEORGE TAYLOR.

Page 27: WINNEY PINSON. Last Will and Testament dated March 14, 1798; probated May 26, 1798. To her son, EDWARD PINSON, she gives all her estate consisting of cattle and household goods. Witnesses: EASTON MCDONALD, THOMAS JONES.

Page 29: ROBERT HINTON. Last Will and Testament dated April 15, 1798; probated (no date shown). Gives his estate to his half-brother, CHRISTOPHER HINTON, and to his own sister, POLLY KITCHEN. Witnesses: ELISHA HURT, AMBROSE EDMONDSON.

Page 31: JOHN MONTRAY. Last Will and Testament dated Nov. 26, 1795. No date of probate shown. Gives to his daughter, CASSANDRA MONTREY, his horse, hunting-saddle, cow, pewter, dishes, dutch oven &c. Residue of estate to remainder of his children, JOHN MONTRAY, SALLY WELLS, LEWIS MONTRAY, JOEL MONTRAY, MARY PEAVY and LEAH CARTER. Executrix: Daughter, CASSANDRA MONTREY. Witness: SEPTIMUS WEATHERLY, Register of Pro.

Page 33: THOMAS SMITH. Last Will and Testament dated Nov. 20, 1796; probated Dec. 29, 1797. Says he is in a low state of health. Devised to his mother, PHOEBE SMITH, a slave named Robin for her lifetime, same to be sold after her death and proceeds equally divided between JAMES, the son of WILKINS SMITH, and JAMES, son of JOHN TRAVIS when they become of age. To JOHN TRAVIS, my horse and saddle. To sister, MOURNING HARDEN, all my part of estate of my father, THOMAS SMITH, deceased. Friend, JOHN TRAVIS, appointed executor. Witnesses: JONES KENDRICK, JOHN JARRETT.

Page 34:   JOHN CHAPMAN. Last Will and Testament dated May 15, 1798,
probated Dec. 14, 1798. Gives to his wife MILLIE all his slaves, household goods, cattle, etc., for her lifetime or widowhood, she to support
their children out of the estate and furnish those not married a horse
&c., whenever they become 21 or marry. Executors: DEBERA CHAPMAN and
ABNER CHAPMAN. Witnesses: BENJAMIN CHAPMAN and SOLOMON LOCKETT.

Page 37:   BURRELL BROOM. Last Will and Testament dated Nov. 15,
1798; probated March 4, 1799. Directs his executors to sell 200 acres on
Long Creek purchased of MONTRAY, saddles, dutch oven and other items.
Gives to son, ISHMAEL $25.00, his gun and "great coat"; to sons, ADAM
and RUFUS BROOM, $35.00 each; to daughter, ELIZABETH MIMS, a feather bed
and furniture. Directs that his corn be equally divided between his wife,
MARTHA, and sons, ADAM, ISHMAEL and RUFUS. Gives to his wife, MARTHA,
the land he owns on Rocky Comfort he purchased of DRURY MIMS; also cow
and calf, feather bed, pot, frying pan &c., "provided she takes care of
it; if not same to be sold by his executors and proceeds equally divided
among his five children; DAVID BROOM, ELIZABETH MIMS, ISHMAEL BROOM,
ADAM BROOM & RUFUS BROOM. He directs that his land and other property in
North Carolina be sold and proceeds and $12.00 due testator by DEMPSEY
FLUWELLEN be equally divided between above five children. Executors:
JOHN MATTHEWS, DAVID BROOM. Witnesses: HENRY KENDALL and LEROY MIMS and
SEPTIMUS WEATHERLY, Register of Probates.

Page 38:   JAMES BEASLEY, SR., Last Will and Testament dated May
14, 1799; probated June 3, 1799. Gives to his wife, ANN, all his estate,
real and personal, for her lifetime, and at her death to be divided among
their children RICHARD, WILLIAM ELIZABETH, HENRY, JAMES, BURRELL & POLLY.
Executors: RICHARD BEASLEY (son), and son-in-law, WILLIAM EARNEST.
Witnesses: L. PRUITT, JAMES BEASLEY, WM. HOWARD.

Page 41:   THOMAS LENT HALL. Last Will and Testament dated Nov. 13,
1799; probated Nov. 23, 1799. Gives to his wife, LYDIA, all his household furniture &c. "that I may not have already given to my daughter,
REBECCA DOWDY. Executors: Wife, LYDIA and RICHARD BROOKS FLETCHER.
Witnesses: DANIEL SAUNDERS, MARY WILKINS.

Page 42:   JOHN HILSON, SR. Last Will and Testament dated Oct. 3,
1800; no date of probate shown. He directs that his land be equally
divided between his four sons, LEWIS, AARON, JOHN and WILLIAM HILSON, and
that all his cattle be equally divided among his eight children and wife
DIANNA (other children unnamed in will). Executors: "my loving wife,
DICY HILSON" and AARON and LEWIS HILSON. Witnesses: THOMAS PHILLIPS,
LEWIS HILSON.

Page 43:   GEORGE MEDLOCK. Last Will and Testament dated Oct. 2,
1800; no date of probate shown. Gives to daughter POLLY when 18 years of
age, a slave named David; to his daughter, AGATHA, when she becomes 18,
two slaves; to son, GEORGE deLAFAYETTE all his real estate when he is 21;
all of said property to remain in possession of my wife, FERIBEE, during
her widowhood; she to receive one-fourth of estate if she marries.
Executors: EZEKIEL SMITH and JOHN SMITH, and son, GEORGE MEDLOCK, when
he becomes of age. Witnesses: WILLIAM BARDEN, JR., GEORGE TAYLOR &
ASA CASTLEBERRY.

Page 45:   THOMAS DOVE. Last Will and Testament dated Feb. 5,
1801; no date of probate shown. Gives all his estate to wife, ANIDORITHY.
Witnesses: SEPTIMUS WEATHERLY, DAVID DOVE, THOMAS DOVE, JR.

Page 46:   PETER HODO (signed PETER HODOSON). Last Will and Testament dated May 6, 1799; no date of probate shown. Gives to son, RICHARD
HOD, 150 acres of the land where testator now lives, the remaining two-
thirds for the use of his wife, SUSANNAH HODO, for her lifetime or widowhood, then to said RICHARD. Gives to son, PETER HODO, a horse. Residue
of estate to wife, SUSANNAH, for her lifetime with same passing at her
death to testator's children, ANN CORAM, ELIZABETH CULLERS, PETER HODO,

MARY CODAY, RICHARD HODO (with exception of a bed to NATHANIEL HODO, son of RICHARD) to be equally divided between said children. Executors: Sons, PETER and RICHARD HODOSON. Witnesses: JAMES SIMPSON, JOHN BAYNE.

Page 47: GEORGE COOPER. Last Will and Testament dated Jan. 25, 1802; no date of probate shown. Gives to wife, ELIZABETH, the land whereon he now lives, together with all his personal estate, for her lifetime for widowhood, then to be divided between sons, WILLIAM and JOSEPH COOPER. To sons, GEORGE and BENJAMIN and daughters, ELIZABETH, REBECCA, MARY and SARAH, five shillings each. Executors: Sons, BENJAMIN and GEORGE COOPER. Witnesses: JARVIS and ROBERT FILLINGIM.

Page 48: WILLIAM KENDALL of Washington Co., Ga. "Sick and weak in body." Last Will and Testament dated Dec. 22, 1801. No date of probate. Gives to daughters BETSY and SALLY KENDALL, a slave named Jim, two feather beds and other household items and $200.00 in cash, to be equally divided between them, when either marries or becomes of age. If they are not ill-treated they may remain with rest of the family. Residue of estate to remain in possession of his wife, HOLLENBURY, for her lifetime or widow-hood, then to go to and be divided between his other three daughters, PRISCILLA, JEMIMA and SUSANNAH KENDALL if they are of age at that time. Executors: JEREMIAH KENDALL, PHILLIP BRANTLEY & ADAM JONES. Witnesses: JOSEPH NUNN, SUCKEY KENDALL, JOHN LEWIS.

Page 50: JAMES NAPIER. Last Will and Testament dated Jan. 30, 1798; no date of probate. His children DRURY (the eldest son), CALEB NAPIER, PHOEBE BROWN and CREESA (LUCRETIA?) RIDGEDALL, to have all his estate at the death of testator's wife (unnamed in will). He directs that MARTHA PRESLEY and BENJAMIN NAPIER (evidently children) shall have nothing as they have already received their portions years ago. Gives feather bed to granddaughter, SARAH SMITH. No executor named. Witnesses: V. T. A. THARP, J.P., & WILLIAM CASON.

Page 51: JOSEPH BURSON "expecting shortly to depart this life." Last Will and Testament dated Oct. 28, 1801; no date of probate shown. Gives to "my well beloved companion, MARY BURSON, all his land, horses &c., for her lifetime, and at her death to pass to his eldest son, JONATHAN; to son, ISAAC, and daughters, LYDIA, PHOEBE, RACHEL, PEGGY and POLLY, he gives 50¢ each. Residue of estate to be divided between sons, JOSEPH & JESSE and daughter, ALSE, and granddaughters, POLLY, SALLY, and NANCY "now living with me." "Written in my own house and in the pre-sence of God." Executors: MARY & JOSEPH BURSON. Witnesses: CHARLES THARP, WILLIAM BLOODWORTH and MATTHEW BAILEY.

Page 52: DAVID DAVIS of Wilkes Co., Ga. Deed of Gift dated May 3, 1787 (evidently treated as a will and probated, no date shown.) Gives to his daughters, MARY, SARAH and ANN DAVIS and SUSANNAH ARMSTRONG one shilling each; to daughter, STERLING PATTY DAVIS, and to WILLIAM SIMMONS, a cow and calf each; to JOHN DAVIS, 200 acres where donor lived. Residue of his estate he gives to his wife, ELIZABETH, she to have possession of the land until the children all come of age or marry. Witnesses: ROBERT MOSES, ISAAC BURSON.

Page 53: MOSES MCKINNIE, SR. Last Will and Testament dated Dec. 3, 1801; no date of probate shown. He gives all his estate to wife, POLLY, for her lifetime or widowhood, then to pass to and be equally divided between his children, ANSELEM, MASON, MOSES JR., HARRIS, WILLIAM, HINCHEN, POLLY, NANCY & MATTHEW MCKINNIE; the youngest son, TILLMAN, to have his part of any overplus of the legacies to the other children. Executors: Wife, POLLY, son, TILLMAN MCKINNIE & JODEY NEWSOM. Witnesses: ROBERT MOSES, JR., HENRY HARRIS.

Page 55: PHILLIP POOL. Last Will and Testament, dated Sept. 19, 1801; no date of probate shown. Gives to wife, MARY, all his estate for her lifetime, and after her death to be divided between their five young children to-wit: MARY GRAYBILL, EPHRIAM, HENRY & JAMES POOL, and SUSANNAH CAPPS. Executors: Wife, MARY, and son-in-law, HENRY GRAYBILL. Witnesses: JOHN BRUTON, WILLIAM PORTER.

Page 56:   HARDY TODD.   Last Will and Testament dated Dec. 23, 1801; no date of probate shown. To son, SILAS TODD, one gun, a cow and other items. To son, JOBE, a feather bed and other items. Residue to estate to wife (unnamed) and after her death to above-named sons, except to daughter MOURNING, daughter ANNA, son HARDY, to WILLIAM HARNO TODD and WINNIE, five shillings each. No executor named. Witnesses: EDWARD SHIRLEY, RICHARD SHIRLEY, JOHN BROOKS.

Page 57:   HENRY HILL.   Last Will and Testament dated Aug. 8, 1801. Gives to his brother BENJAMIN WILLIAMS a slave named George and a note against him for Ł8. Gives to ASA CHAPMAN (relationship not stated) a slave named Will and blacksmith tools; and to TABITHA CHAPMAN, a horse, bed and all money on hand. Executor: Friend ABNER CHAPMAN. Witnesses: JOHN ROGERS, A. GRIER, ROBERT GRIER.

Page 58:   PETER PERKINS "being very sick." Last Will and Testament dated March 26, 1801, no date of probate shown. Bequeaths to wife, SARAH, a slave named Caeser, said slave to be sold at her death and proceeds divided between testator's two sons, JOHN & ABRAHAM PERKINS. He gives $10 each to his grandsons JOHN DAVIS & PETER PERKINS. Residue of estate to be sold at the death of his wife and proceeds to be equally divided among his children viz., JENNY CLOWERS, ABEGAIL KIDD, JOHN PERKINS, ABRAM PERKINS, ELEANOR DARDEN, JEMIMA WHITE, SARAH WILKINS, ELIZABETH NEAL and the children of NANCY GREATHOUSE, deceased. He gives $8.00 to the trustees of the society called Quakers in the District of Wrightsborough to be used for repairing the enclosure around the burial ground at the meeting house. Executors: JOHN TORRENCE and JOHN BAKER. Witnesses: SOLOMON THOMPSON, JOHN WILLIAMS, __ (torn) TORRENCE.

Page 61:   JAMES ROQUEMORE, JR., "being weak in body." Last Will and Testament dated April 30, 1803; no date of probate shown. Devises to son PETER the land whereon he, PETER, lives; to son, JAMES ROQUEMORE, JR., the land whereon he lives; to wife, ELIZABETH, the use of the plantation whereon she now lives and at her death the same to pass to and be equally divided between his two sons, THOMAS & JOHN ROQUEMORE. He devises all his slaves to his wife, ELIZABETH, for her lifetime, and at her death to be divided, the slave Dinah to go to daughter, POLLY PEARSON, and the slave Rachel to go to ELIZABETH ROQUEMORE (daughter), together with a feather bed each, woman's saddle and bridle and horse each, in discretion of wife. No executor named. Witnesses: THOMAS BAZEMORE, THOMAS WESTLAY, SHADRICK POTTS.

Page 62:   WILLIAM BARDEN.   Last Will and Testament dated April 6, 1803; no date of probate. Gives to wife, MARY, all his estate for her lifetime. At wife's death, a slave named Viney to go to sons, WILLIAM & JOHN SHEROD BARDEN. Gives to daughters MARY B. & SARAH W. BARDEN $1.00 each. Gives to daughter EPTHATHAN, a slave named Hannah at wife's death, together with all other undevised property. If she dies without heirs then to go to sons, WILLIAM & SHEROD. Executors: Wife, MARY BARDEN & JAMES JONES, SR. Witnesses: T. PERSONS, A. PERSONS.

Page 64:   BARTLETT SIMMS, SR. Last Will and Testament dated March 20, 1802; no date of probate shown. He gives to his wife Catherine all his estate for her lifetime and at her death his homeplace lands to pass to his two sons, BARTLETT & HARBERT. To daughter, CHARLOTTE, he gives a bed and other items. No executor. Witnesses: FRANCIS BECK & ALEXANDER SNELLINGS.

Page 65:   MOSES BUTTS of Halifax Co., N.C., "being sick in body." Last Will and Testament dated March 19, 1800; probated in Halifax Co., N. C., Nov. Term, 1803 on the oaths of JOSEPH WRIGHT and DUDLEY COUNSEL. Certified copy dated Nov. 24, 1803, recorded in Warren County, Ga. He devises all his land on the north and south sides of Rocky Swamp to his three sons, WILLIAM, MOSES & ELDRIDGE BUTTS to be theirs when ELDRIDGE becomes of age. He directs all his estate to be kept together until said ELDRIDGE becomes of age, "in order to raise my younger children viz., MOSES, ELDRIDGE & SUCKY, then to be divided between his five children

NANCY, WILLIAM, MOSES, ELDRIDGE & SUCKY BUTTS. Certain slaves are devised to each of above named children and to son NOAH BUTTS. Executors: Friend, WILLIAM MCDANIEL, and sons, WILLIAM & MOSES BUTT. Witnesses: JOSEPH WRIGHT, DUDLEY COUNSEL & JAMES MOORE.

Page 68: ENOCH RENFROE, planter, "being weak of body." Last Will and Testament dated Aug. 7, 1802; no date of probate. Devises to son, ENOCH, 150 acres on Joe's Creek, whereon testator now lives. Originally granted STEPHEN MITCHELL in 1783 and 200 acres adjoining being part of a grant to SAMUEL CAMP in 1789. Gives to SARAH RENFROE, widow of son JOEL, five shillings, and $10 to her daughter NANCY. Gives to his beloved children, MARY HANCOCK, STEPHEN RENFROE, NATHANIEL RENFROE's widow JANE BAKER, MARGARET RENFROE, SARAH RUSHIN, and JOHN RENFROE's widow MARTHA, $5.00 each; to NANCY, daughter of MARTHA RENFROE $10.00; to RACHEL RUSHING, LYDIA CHIVERS, WILLIAM RENFORE, NATHAN RENFROE, ENOCH RENFROE and MARTHA MATTHEWS, each a one-eleventh of all of testator's estate except those receiving certain named sums. Executors: ENOCH RENFROE & JOHN RUSHING. Witnesses: VINCENT DAVIS, WILLIAM SIMMONS & ELIJAH CONNER.

Page 70: JOHN MYRICK, SR., planter, "being very sick." Last Will and Testament dated May 12, 1803; no date of probate. Gives to his daughter SALLY WEATHERBY, a slave named Bob, a slave Lucy and a slave Littleton, "in fee simple." He directs that his slave Robin be set free after 18 months following his death. To son, JOHN, a slave named Charity; to his grandchildren, the heirs of deceased son OWEN MYRICK, two slaves named Molly and Betty and "little Sarah", when said grandchildren become of age. He gives to ELIZABETH, widow of son OWEN MYRICK, a cow and calf; to daughter, NANCY FINCH, a slave named Tamar, also slaves Jack and Bet; and at said NANCY FINCH's death said slaves to go to BETSY & PATSY FINCH. Gives to daughter REBECCA FLINN, slaves named Peggy and Briton; and to son NATHANIEL MYRICK a slave named Big Sarah and her child Celia. Executors: Son, NATHANIEL MYRICK and friend, JOHN MYRICK. Witnesses: ANDREW KING, ELIZABETH KING.

Page 71: ZACHARIAH SUMMERALL of Warren County. Last Will and Testament dated Dec. 4, 1803; no date of probate. He directs that the debts due him be collected and the money collected be lent to his cousin, WILLIAM ANDERSON. Directs that all his money be delivered to his uncle JESSE DOLES after payment of debts. Directs that his Aunt ELIZABETH and his cousin SALLY ANDERSON to have a "habit pattern out of the store." Remainder of his money with saddle and bridle to be divided between testator's three cousins POLLY & BENJAMIN DOLES & JOHN ANDERSON, "BENNY to have saddle." No exeuctor named. Witness: JOHN MARSHALL.

Page 72: MARGARET HOLLADAY. Last Will and Testament dated Mar. 11, 1803; no date of probate. Bequeaths to her daughter, SARAH, $300.00 and all the money due testatrix from the estate of her late husband (unnamed). Gives to her daughter, ELIZABETH MURPHY, $300.00 "in considertation of her friendship and tenderness to me in my declining years." Devises to son, DENNIS LINDSEY and his wife LUCY; to son ELIJAH WARTHEN and wife NANCY; to son WILLIAM BATIE and wife REBECCA, $1.00 each. Residue from estate of my late husband to be equally divided between my sons, JAMES, JOHN, EDWARD & SAMUEL HARVILL; to the heirs of my son JOSEPH, deceased, one dollar. Executors: Son, JAMES HARVILL & SOLOMON BECKDORS?. Witnesses: THOMAS ABBOTT, POLLY ABBOTT & SOLOMON BECKCOM.

Page 73: JOAB BROOKS. Last Will and Testament dated March 17, 1804; no date of probate. Devises all his property to his wife, CATRICK, for her lifetime or widowhood, then to be divided between his children POLLY, JOHN, MICAJAH, BETSY, ALLEN, JENNY TERRELL, MARTIN & WILLIAM BROOKS. Executors: Wife and MICAJAH BROOKS. Witness: SEPTIMUS WEATHERLY, Clerk Court of Ordinary.

Page 74: WILLIAM TRAVIS "being low in health." Last Will and Testament dated Feb. 25, 1805, probated Aug. 13, 1805. Gives to his wife ABIGAIL the use of 650 acres of land on Rocky Comfort Creek, five

slaves, all his household goods, for her lifetime or widowhood; then at
her death or remarriage all the land to go to his son, SIMEON "being all
the land I own in Georgia" and where I now live," also said SIMEON's
choice of his chemistry books. Gives to his son, ASA TRAVIS, a slave
named Tango; to son AMOS TRAVIS, a slave named Ester; to daughter,
SIDDIE TRAVIS, a slave named Nancy; to daughter, LIDDY ALBRITTON $3.00;
to the heirs of his deceased daughter, POLLY MCK___ (torn) $3.00; to the
heirs of his deceased son GIDEON TRAVIS $3.00. Mention made of debt due
testator by ELIJAH ROSAR. Testator's three sons to be executors.
Witnesses: JOHN HERRING, JOHN SMITH, MARTHA POWELL.

Page 75: ROBERT STANDFORD "in a low state of health." Last Will
and Testament dated May 7, 1805; probated Oct. 15, 1805. Gives to his
sisters, HETTY STANDFORD and IBBY BURKE, all his estate. Executor:
JOHN BAYNE. Witnesses: JESSE STANDFORD, MARY MILLER, JOHN BAYNE.

Page 76: JOHN BROWN of Greene Co. Last Will and Testament dated
Jan. 31, 1805; probated March 4, 1805. Devises to his brother EDMUND
BROWN of S. C., certain slaves; to his brother, WILLIAM BROWN, of Ga.,
certain slaves; to JOHN DUKE, son of my brother-in-law BURNLEY DUKE, two
slaves. He devises to a girl of color named Millie "whom I have legally
emancipated agreeably to an Act passed in Virginia," four slaves together
with his money and bonds. Executors: SAMUEL M. SMITH, WALTER LEE,
HENRY & WILLIAM JONES; "I earnestly entreat them to take good care of
the above named girl Milly." Witnesses: DAVID BUSH, GEORGE HARGRAVES,
JAMES LOYLESS.

Page 78: HENRY HARP. Last Will and Testament dated March 26,
1805; probated April 22, 1805. Gives to his wife SUSANNAH, 200 acres
being his homeplace, for her lifetime or widowhood, then to go to his
daughter NANCY together with all his cattle, furniture, etc. To his
daughter, SALLY NEWSOM, he gives cattle and other stock and 100 acres
"which she must clear out of the office" (that is, take out the State's
grant and pay the grant fees - Editor.) Executors: Wife, SUSANNAH, and
SOLOMON BEDDINGFIELD. Witnesses: MARTIN STREETMAN, JESSE WARD, CHARLES
BEDDINGFIELD.

Page 79: DRURY MCCULLERS, planter, "being very sick." Last Will
and Testament dated Aug. 5, 1806; probated Feb. 2, 1807. Gives to his
wife, ELIZABETH, for her widowhood his homeplace property. He directs
that "all the land below the Stillhouse branch be equally divided between
my two sons, DRURY ALLEN MCCULLERS and HYRUM MCCULLERS." The land above
said branch he gives to his daughter, FAITHA. To his daughter, ELIZABETH,
he gives 200 acres adjoining WILLIAM MAYS and ELIJAH WILLIAMS. Executors:
JAMES GARY & MICHAEL CODY. Witnesses: JAMES SMITH, JOHN SALLIS &
EDMUND CODY.

Page 81: PETER NEWSOM. Last Will and Testament dated Mar. 19,
1805, probated March 3, 1806. Gives to his wife RHODA, sons FIGROUS?
and RIX? "and the nine youngest children (unnamed). Executors: Wife,
RHODA, and brother, JOHN NEWSOM. Witnesses: ASA NEWSOM, DAVID NEWSOM,
J.P., ROBERT BARTON.

Page 83: SAMUEL PARKER. Last Will and Testament dated Oct. 26,
1806; probated Jan. 5th, 1807. He devises all his estate, real and
personal, to his wife, MOLLIE, for her lifetime or widowhood, and then
the residue after her death or remarriage to be divided into seven parts
and one part given to each of his daughters, BETSY PARKER, SUCKY PARKER,
& MATHOLOMEW PARKER, and sons, JOHN S. PARKER, SAMUEL THOMAS PARKER &
NATHAN PARKER, the daughters to receive theirs as they marry and the sons
to receive theirs when and as they become of age. Executors: Wife,
MOLLIE, and JOHN REEVES. Witnesses: BARRETT BREWER, FRANCIS BEALL,
HENRY RALEY.

Pages 85: JOSEPH BREED. Last Will and Testament dated April 27,
1807; probated May 4, 1807. Gives to his son, WILLIAM, the tract of land
whereon WILLIAM now lives. He says that he has already given his son,
JOHN, his portion of his estate. To daughters SARAH HOFF & PRISCILLA

GEORGE and to son, AVERA BREED, $100.00 each; to daughters NANCY &
CATHERINE BREED, $125.00 each. Executors: Son, WILLIAM BREED and son-
in-law RICHARD GEORGE. Witnesses: ISAIAH TUCKER, THEOPHILUS HILL,
ABRAHAM HILL.

Page 87: NATHAN DAVIS. Last Will and Testament dated Jan. 31,
1807; probated Sept. 7, 1807. He gives $250.00 to "the supposed daughter
of GEHERIN DAVIS, deceased, which (whom) I had by BARSHEBA GRANADE now
BARSHEBA SMITH which she had before she married THOMAS SMITH." Remainder
of his estate he directs to be equally divided between EPHRIAM MCGEE,
NELLY STANFORD, wife of LEVAN STANFORD, and MARY, LEAH, ELIZABETH and
SARAH MCGEE, children of REUBIN MCGEE. No executor named. Witnesses:
WINDER HILLMAN, EDWARD MCGLAMORY AND THOMAS STORY.

Page 88: BARNABAS JONES "finding myself in a very low state of
health and wishing to distribute my property to my liking" etc. Last
Will and Testament dated June 11, 1806; probated November 3, 1806. To
his wife, PATSY, for her widowhood he gives 182½ acres of land, five
slaves, tools, cattle &c., then the residue after her death and after
their youngest child PHILLIP becomes of age to be divided between children
HENRY, ANTHONY, NANCY, ELIZABETH, JOHN, PATSY, BARNABAS, POLLY AND
PHILLIP. Executors: Wife, PATSY, and sons, HENRY & ANTHONY JONES.
Witnesses: JOSEPH ROBERTS, JOSEPH BONNER.

Page 89: JAMES DOZER. Last Will and Testament dated Sept. 27,
1804; probated January 4, 1808. He devises to the heirs of his deceased
son WILLIAM, a slave Joe which they already have in their possession. He
gives to his son, JOHN, the land whereon he lives and a slave named Jenny.
To son, JAMES, he gives the 100 acres of land on which he lives, and a
slave named Ben; to son, LEONARD, he gives a slave named Lizzie; to son,
THOMAS, 100 acres of land where he now lives and a slave Primus; to son,
RICHARD, 100 acres of land adjoining JOSEPH EVANS, and a slave Dicy.
He directs that his wife, MARY, to have possession of their homeplace
plantation for her lifetime then the same to go to the son, WOODY DOZIER,
together with a slave named "Hamlin." To daughter, ELIZABETH MOSS (or
MORRIS? torn) he gives a slave named Dave and the residue of his estate.
Executors: Sons, JOHN & JAMES DOZER (or DOZIER). Witnesses: WILLIAM
BERRY, SALLY BERRY, THOMAS BERRY.

Page 93: ABRAHAM JOHNSTON (also spelled JOHNSON). Last Will and
Testament dated Sept. 27, 1803; probated March 4, 1806. To son ROBERT,
he gives 100 acres on Long Creek adjoining ROBERT's land. To sons, AMOS
& WILLIAM, he divises the tract of land whereon he (testator) lives, same
lying on the road from Wrightsborough to Washington (Ga.); it is stated
that WILLIAM lives on his part of the land. To son, AMOS, a walnut table
and corner cupboard, and to son, WILLIAM, a silver tablespoon. To sons,
CALEB & ABNER, $100.00 each. To daughters, TACY? SAMPLES, MARGARET
HUNT, ELIZABETH THOMAS & CATHERINE ARNETT, $50.00 each. To granddaughter,
SARAH DAY, he gives his large family Bible; to grandson, ABRAHAM (minor
son of dec'd. son ABRAHAM) $50.00, same to be put out at interest for him
and if he dies without issue then same to be paid to CYRUS, son of my
son WILLIAM JOHNSON. Executors: Sons, WILLIAM & AMOS JOHNSON. Witnesses: EZEKIEL ALEXANDER, THOMAS WHITE, THOMAS SOMERS.

Page 95: THOMAS NEAL. Last Will and Testament dated Sept. 2, 1807;
probated Jan. 1, 1808. Gives to wife, SARAH, for her lifetime or widowhood the homeplace property. At her death his two stills to go to their
son, ELISHA NEAL, together with nine slaves in fee-simple. To daughter,
POLLIE GRADNER, he gives four slaves; to daughter, DINAH PARSONS, he
gives three slaves; to daughter, BETSY (ELIZABETH) BRAY, he gives three
slaves; to son, ELISHA, four other slaves; to daughter SALLIE GARDNER
$25.00; to daughter, REBECCA BEALL, he gives three slaves; to daughter,
PATSY NEAL, three slaves; to daughter, DRUSILLA NEAL, three slaves.
Executors: His trusty friends; WORMSLEY ROSE & ELISHA NEAL. Witnesses:
SHADRICK FLEWELLIN, SOLOMON SLATTER.

Page 96: WILLIAM STITH, Attorney-at-law, being "weak of body."
Last Will and Testament dated March 9, 1807; probated Jan. 4, 1808. To

MARY TILLMAN (relationship not shown) he gives $150.00. Remainder of
estate to his wife MILLIE and her heirs, she to be the sole executrix.
Witnesses: JOHN STITH, JOHN HENNESSY, HARTWELL JONES.

Page 97: ABRAHAM HEATH. Last Will and Testament dated Nov. 23,
1807; probated Jan. 4, 1808. He devises to his son, JOHN, three slaves;
to daughter, SALLIE CHAPPLE, four slaves; to son, BENJAMIN, three slaves;
to son, WILLIAM, two slaves; to granddaughter, POLLIE CLOWER, a slave
named Sarah; to grandson, STEPHEN B. CLOWER, a slave named Isaac; to
granddaughter, LINNIE CLOWER, a slave named Sam; to grandson, GREEN
CLOWER, a slave named Charles; to grandson, ABRAHAM H. CLOWER, a slave
named Millie; to son, ADAM HEATH, 200 acres of land for which he has
titles; to daughter, ELIZABETH, two slaves; to daughter, POLLIE HEATH, a
slave and a bed; to daughter FRANCES B. HIGHFIELD, a slave named Sylvia;
to son, RICHARD HEATH, a slave named Jacob, a horse, bed, and other small
items; to grandson, ABRAHAM HEATH CHAPPLE, a slave named Ephriam; to wife,
WINNIFRED, certain slaves; also to wife certain land for her widowhood
or lifetime; and after her death, same to go to sons, RICHARD & ABRAHAM
HEATH. Executors: Son, ADAM HEATH, SOLOMON SLATTER & ELISHA HERT.
Witnesses: STEPHEN W. BURNLEY, BRITAIN BLOUNT, MARY GARRETT.

Page 99: RICHARD HEATH. Last Will and Testament dated May 26,
1807; probated Jan. 4, 1808. Gives to wife, REBECCA, the land he purchased from ROBERT JENKINS, for her lifetime or widowhood and four slaves
outright; to son, CHAPPELL HEATH, 200 acres of land on the south side of
the Augusta Road, purchased of LEWIS WRIGHT, together with slaves; to son,
MARK, the testator's chances of drawing land in the late purchase from
the Indians, together with a slave named Dred; to daughter, ELIZABETH
HILL, three slaves; to daughter, SARAH MORELAND, two slaves; to daughter
NANCY WRIGHT, two slaves; to daughter TEMPY HEATH, two slaves, bed,
horse and other small items; to son, HENRY HEATH, 150 acres of land
purchased of BURREL PERRY, together with slave Ben; to daughter REBECCA
HEATH, two slaves, bed, &c.; to son, RICHARD, at the death of my wife
REBECCA, 250 acres where testator lives and two slaves; to grandchildren,
NANCY, FAITHY?, JAMES HENRY & BETSY WRIGHT, 100 acres of land purchased
of LEWIS WRIGHT and six slaves, bed, furniture, etc. To daughter, PATSY
WRIGHT, $20.00. Executors: Son, CHAPPELL HEATH, JOSEPH HILL. Witnesses:
WILLIAM BAKER, JOHN BAKER, ABRAHAM HEATH.

Page 101: CHARITY POWELL. Last Will and Testament dated Dec. 30,
1807 probated Jan. 4, 1808. Gives to daughter, BETSY, her best feather
bed; she gives her other feather bed to POLLY SUTTON, daughter of ABSALOM
& PHOEBE SUTTON; and another feather bed to BECKY MILES, dau. of THOMAS
MILES and wife MOURNING. Residue to be divided between her six children,
daughter BECK; son POGUE? (torn); son WILLIAM; son NATHAN. Executors:
GEORGE DYKES, MOSES GRANBERRY.

Page 102: MOSES GRANBERRY. Last Will and Testament dated Jan. 24,
1808; probated March 7, 1808. He bequeaths to his wife, BETSY, 150
acres of land to include the plantation where he lives, and the household goods, &c., as a support to her and the children during her widowhood.
To daughters, POLLY, PATSY, BETSY & NANCY GRANBERRY, all of his property
both real and personal; to step-son, JAMES POWELL $30.00 on the day of
his marriage, and to the heirs of his daughter, DULANY RATCLIFFE,
deceased, $10.00. Executors: Sons, GEORGE & SETH GRANBERRY, and NOWELL
ROBERTSON. Witnesses: GEORGE DYKES, JOHN SMITH, BENJAMIN UPTON.

Page 103: WILLIAM CULPEPPER. Last Will and Testament dated Aug.
22, 1806, probated March 7, 1808. He confirms the gifts he had made to
his children (unnamed). To his son, DANIEL CULPEPPER, he gives $2.00; to
son, WILLIAM CULPEPPER, 200 acres lying on Carson's Creek where he now
lives; to son-in-law, RICHARD B. FLETCHER, he give $2.00. Residue of
estate devised to daughter, ARGEN PARHAM, together with chance in the 1806
Land Lottery. Executor: Son, DANIEL CULPEPPER. Witnesses: WILLIAM
CULPEPPER, DICKERSON CULPEPPER, ISAIAH TUCKER.

Page 105: EZENIAS VERDON "being very old." Last Will and Testament dated Aug. 14, 1808, probated Sept. 5, 1808. To his wife, WINNIE,

her choice of his cattle, pewter, deds &c., and also $70.00. Residue of estate to be divided between his two sons, THOMAS & JOHN VERDON. To son, WILLIAM VERDON, he gives $300.00 and notes due by THOMAS DAVIS. Executors: Wife, WINNIE, and son, JOHN VERDON. Witnesses: REUBIN REESE, EDWARD MATTHEWS, AARON ALDRED.

Page 106: THOMAS FONTAINE. Last Will and Testament dated Jan. 7, 1808; probated Nov. 7, 1808. To his wife, SALLIE, he gives a slave named Sealey, $500.00 in cash (proceeds of sale of a slave named Ned), and a child's share of the household goods, to be hers in fee simple; she to live with testator's family for her life or widowhood and be supported. He directs that his sister, SALLIE FONTAINE, be allowed to live with the family and be supported out of his estate. He directs that his property be held together intact until his youngest child is of age, then to be equally divided between his children (not named). Executors: ELISHA HERT, JAMES ALLEN, and brother JOHN FONTAINE. Witnesses: CADER WORLEY, WILLIAM TAYLOR, SALLIE FONTAINE. Subjoined to the record of the will is a renunciation by SALLIE FONTAINE "one of the legatees", whereby she relinquishes all her claim in and to the estate of THOMAS FONTAINE (it is not clear whether she was testator's wife or sister, both having the same name in the will).

Page 109: THOMAS ANSLEY. Last Will and Testament dated Dec. 13, 1808; probated March 6, 1809. To his wife, ZEBECCA, he gives his home-place property, also live stock and slaves, household goods &c., as needed by her for her support during her lifetime or widowhood. To son, ABEL ANSLEY, he gives 400 acres adjoining JOSHUA STANDFORD, SAMUEL ANSLEY and DUCKWORTH, located near the road to Watson's old mill, ABEL to give the refusal of said land to his brothers if sold by him. To son, WILLIAM ANSLEY, he gives $100.00 above an equal share in his estate. To his grandson, SAMUEL DUCKWORTH, son of testator's daughter, REBECCA DUCKWORTH, he gives a slave. Upon the death or remarriage of his wife, he directs that all his estate be equally divided between the following persons: ABEL, SAMUEL, THOMAS, WILLIAM, JOSEPH & JAMES ANSLEY, REBECCA & SAMUEL DUCKWORTH, and BENJAMIN HARRISON "my wife'd eldest son." Executors: Sons, ABEL, SAMUEL, THOMAS & JOSEPH ANSLEY. Witnesses: DAVID STANDFORD, JOSEPH STANDFORD, MACKLIN SILLS.

Page 112: NICHOLAS BOOTY. Last Will and Testament dated Nov. 7, 1809; probated Jan. 1, 1810. Says he "is laboring under a heavy afflic-tion." To wife, SARAH, he gives his land whereon he lives, all plantation tools &c., household goods and two slaves, for her lifetime or widowhood, and thereafter to go "to the three children I had by her, JOHN LOCK BOOTY, ELIZABETH DENT BOOTY & MARTHA BOOTY." He gives "to my two dear children by my first wife, POLLIE and BENJAMIN BOOTY" he gives two slaves, feather beds and other items, and directs them to remain with his wife, SARAH, until they become 21 years of age or marry. Executrix: Wife, SARAH, "assisted by ELISHA HERT." Witnesses: JOHN ROBERTS, WARREN BARROW, RICHARD BARROW.

Page 113: BENJAMIN OLIVER. Last Will and Testament dated May 7, 1809; probated July 3, 1809. He gives to his wife, SARAH, all of his estate for her lifetime, and at her death he gives a slave named REUBIN to his son, JOHN OLIVER; to son, BENJAMIN, 25¢; to son, ROBERT, 100 acres where testator lived, adjoining ADAM JONES and ROBERT ABERCROMBIE; to son, TERRY OLIVER, a slave, bed &c.; to son, JAMES, he gives a slave, bed, &c.; to daughter, PATSY ROGERS, a slave named Rachel "now in possession of my son-in-law, JAMES ROGERS," to the children of deceased daughter, NANCY CANDLER, a slave named Sylvia; to daughter SARAH TATE, a slave named Nell; to daughter, MARY OLIVER, a slave named Till, also bed and other small items; to daughter, ERMINE OLIVER, a slave named Epps and feather bed. Executors: Wife, SARAH, WILLIAM FOURNOY & THOMAS FRIEND. Witnesses: GREEN ANDERS, JAMES LOWE, THOMAS LOWE, WILLIAM H. BLOUNT.

Page 115: JOEL HEATH. Last Will and Testament dated March 3, 1810; probated May 7, 1810. He gives to son, AMBROSE HEATH, half of the homeplace lands where testator lives, two slaves, and half of all his

tools, furniture &c., and to son, HARTWELL HEATH, he gives the other half
of same, together with four slaves. To son-in-law, ROBERT BONNER, he
gives two slaves. He directs his son, HARTWELL, to pay to his (testator's)
son, ROSTER, and son-in-law, PETER CLOWER, $50 within 12 months after
testator's death. Executors: Son, HARTWELL, and ROBERT BONNER. Witnesses: JOHN HANSON, ORIN PARKER, HENRY WALKER.

 Page 117: JOHN BARROW. Last Will and Testament dated Dec. 26,
1809; probated March 5, 1810. He bequeaths to his sons, JOHN & GEORGE
BARROW, and daughters, MARY BOYD and CELIA DAVIS, five shillings "and
what they have already received." To his wife, JEMIMA, he gives all his
estate, real and personal, for her lifetime or widowhood, except a slave
and a bed with curtains to be hers in fee-simple. To son, RICHARD, a
slave "Sam"; to son, THOMAS, a slave Moses; to son, WARREN, a slave
named Luke; to son, WILLIAM, a slave Daniel; to daughter, MILLIE BARROW,
a slave named Lila; to daughter, SARAH JONES, a slave Rhese, all to be
had and received after the death or remarriage of his wife. To his son,
MICAJAH BARROW, he gives (after his wife's death or remarriage) 195
acres being testator's homeplace. Executor: STEPHEN W. BURNLEY.
Witnesses: SIMON HARRELL, MICAH HARRELL and WILLIAM HOLLAND.

 Page 119: JAMES CARTER. Last Will and Testament dated May 9,
1807; probated May 6, 1811. He gives to son, JESSE, two slaves; to daughter, SARAH HODO, a slave Orphe; to son, MOORE CARTER, he gives two slaves
and 100 acres of land where testator resides; to son, ISAAC, he gives
three slaves, and 137 acres of a 275 acre tract bought of BENJAMIN WARREN,
the other half of said 275 acres to go to testator's son, ALLEN CARTER.
To daughter, ELIZABETH BURSON, he gives a slave; to daughter, RENNY, he
gives a slave; to daughter, PENELOPY DAVIS, he gives a slave. To
BARTHENY CARTER (relationship not state) he gives a slave Phyllis, bedstead, saddle, &c. To son JAMES CARTER, he gives slaves and 395 acres
of the land where he (testator) lives; to wife, ELIZABETH, he gives seven
slaves for her lifetime or widowhood, and after her death or remarriage,
to be equally divided between his children. Executors: Son, JESSE
CARTER; son, MOORE CARTER; JACOB SMITH (these referred to as "my children") and JOHN BAYNE. Witnesses: V. T. A. THARPE, WILLIAM CASON, J.P.

WARREN COUNTY, GEORGIA
WILL BOOK "B" 1811-1829

Note: Arranged alphabetically by Testator's name.

Page 25: AKINS, JOHN. Last Will and Testament dated March 11, 1814, probated May 2, 1814. Directs that his estate be kept together and may be disposed of as becomes necessary in order to support and educate his children viz: WILLIAM, JAMES, BENJAMIN, ISABELLE, THOMAS, POLLY, MARIAH and MATILDA AKINS (evidently minors - Editor) and his wife, WINNIFRED. Executors: WILLIAM BYROM, WILLIAM AKINS. Witnesses: JOHN WILSON, SR., JOHN WILSON JR., JESSE BATTLE.

Page 50: ANDERSON, WILLIAM. Last Will and Testament dated June 3, 1819; probated July 5, 1819. Bequeaths to wife, SARAH, for her life-time his homeplace with the improvements together with certain slaves, and after her death to be divided between his five youngest children JOHN, WILLIAM, SALLY BETSY, ISAAC. To his daughter, NANCY SMITH, five slaves. To his daughter, POLLY ROPER, four slaves. To his son, JOHN, a slave named Harry. To son, WILLIAM, a slave named Aaron. Executors: Wife, SARAH, JOHN ANDERSON and HENRY CARLETON. Witnesses: ANN CARLTON, ELIZABETH LOWE, HAMPTON W. PARISH.

Page 74: ANSLEY, ABEL. Last Will and Testament dated March 7, 1822; probated May 6, 1822. Gives to his wife, LYDIA, for her lifetime the home plantation and the appurtenances. To son, JESSE ANSLEY, 119 acres where he now lives adjoining JOSHUA STANFORD. To son, MORRIS ANSLEY, 130 acres originally granted to THOMAS ANSLEY and adjoining JAMES CARTER. Testator says both tracts of said land have already been conveyed by him to said sons by deeds of gift. To daughter, MARY REDDISH for her lifetime, 45 acres originally granted THOMAS ANSLEY (testator's father) between the lands given sons JESSE and MORRIS (above). To daughter, ANN CARTER, 53 acres adjoining above land. To daughter, PEGGY ANSLEY, the remainder of testator's 400 acre tract of land, together with bed and otherhousehold items. To son, ASA ANSLEY, 86 acres formerly belonging to MARY MORRIS, adjoining CARY JOHNSON and WM. ANSLEY. To son, ISAIAH ANSLEY, a tract of land adj. BENJ. HARRISON and JOSEPH STANFORD on Upton's Creek. To sons, THOMAS and ABEL ANSLEY, 200 acres "of the survey I now live on." To daughters, LYDIA and REBECCA ANSLEY, balance of said land. Executors: LYDIA ANSLEY and ELIAS WILSON. Witnesses: JAMES ANSLEY, JOHN ANSLEY and WILLIAM HARRISON.

Page 184: ADAMS, JAMES. Last Will and Testament dated Sept. 5, 1828; probated Jan. 5. 1829. Bequeaths to his brother, DAVID ADAMS, all of his estate consisting of cattle &c. in hands of JOHN ADAMS. Mention made of note due him by EALY BROOKS. Executor: His brother, DAVID ADAMS. Witnesses: RIVERS REESE, RICHARD REESE, THOMAS NEAL.

Page 12: BUSH, THOMAS. Last Will and Testament dated Sept. 25, 1804; probated Nov. 2, 1812. Gives to his son JOHN BUSH and daughter, JANE RICHARDS, a dozen silver tablespoons and teaspoons each, to bought out of his estate. Residue of his estate to his wife, ELIZABETH, for her lifetime, and at her death to be divided between his three children, ELIZABETH, MARTHA and ANN, minors. Executors: Wife, ELIZABETH, son, JOHN BUSH, and DR. WILLIAM LEE. Witnesses: SEPTIMUS WEATHERBY, STEPHEN W. BURNLEY, JACK S. DAVENPORT.

Page 14: BARROW, REUBIN. Last Will and Testament dated Aug. 17th 1812; probated Nov. 3, 1812. Gives to his wife, MILBRE, 100 acres in Pulaski County being part of Lot 323, together with half of his planta-tion &c., for her lifetime or widowhood "or good behavior." To son, JAMES BARROW, the other half of his said plantation and the 100 acres in Pulaski County at his wife's death. To granddaughter, NANCY BARROW (dau. of JAMES BARROW), a slave. To his son, JOHN BARROW, the "remainder of the tract he lives on." To son, ABSALOM BARROW, a slave named Bob. To daughters, FERRIBY and EADY, each a cow and other items. Executors: Sons, JAMES and ABSALOM BARROW. Witnesses: BENJ. BLEDSOE, RICHARD BLEDSOE, GILES BLEDSOE, WILLIAM BRANNEN.

Page 15:   BIRD, WILLIAM "of the Shoals of Ogeechee and State of Georgia." Last Will and Testament dated Oct. 22, 1812; probated March 1, 1813. To his son, WILLIAM BIRD, he gives "my holsters and pistols only." To his wife, CATHERINE BIRD, his double riding-chair: and he directs that a horse and harness be kept for her use together with the use of a servant "to visit occasionally as she does now" and "hopes she will be satisfied as she will be at no expense as long as she lives at the Shoals; he directs that if she should claim a dower of his estate, she must then support herself. To the children of his daughter, EMILY M. CUNNINGHAM, the sum of $2,000.00 (there seems to have been two children - Editor). To the two children of his daughter, CAROLINE YANCEY, the sum of $2,000.00. To his daughter, ELIZA LESLEY, $1,000.00 in cash. To granddaughter, CAROLINE FRANCES LESLEY, and to the daughters of testator, ARIANA, CATHERINE and LOUISA BIRD, $2,000.00 each as each marries. Two sons, JOHN and FITZGERALD and the above named daughters to be educated at the expense of the estate, both said sons to be sent to DR. WADDELL'S School, JOHN to be taught geometry especially, and FITZGERALD to study medicine later. After above legacies are paid, his three sons, WILSON, JOHN and FITZGERALD BIRD, to have all his real estate &c. Executors: MAJ. NICHOLAS LONG, HUGH TAYLOR, DR. WILLIAM TERRELL and son, WILSON BIRD. Witnesses: S. CAMP, JOHN HUGHES, NATHAN MOTT, J. THOMPSON, ELISHA BROTHERS.

Page 34:   BAKER, JOHN "in a low state of health." Last Will and Testament dated Feb. 1, 1816; probated Feb. 12, 1816. Gives to his wife PATTY, his slaves, household goods, the house where he lives and the land he owns on Still Branch adjoining WM. BAKER and JOHN TORRENCE, for her lifetime or widowhood, and then to his sons, WILLIAM, AUSTIN, EDWIN, PEYTON, JONATHAN and HENRY BAKER and his (testator's) daughter, POLLY BATTLE. To daughter, ELIZABETH WILLIAMS, a slave named Judy already in her possession. Executors: Wife, POLLY, and sons, EDWIN and JONATHAN BAKER. Witnesses: JOHN TORRENCE, JOHN W. TORRENCE, SEPTIMUS TORRENCE.

Page 39:   BRANTLEY, PHILLIP, JR. Last Will and Testament dated July 24, 1811; probated Sept. Term 1817. He directs that all his estate be kept together for duration of his wife's widowhood or as long as she has any of their children to support; then to be equally divided among and between his said wife REBECCA BRANTLEY, and children, LARKIN, CYNTHIA, LAVINA JONES, HARRIS and KATY BRANTLEY. Executors: Brothers, JEPTHA and BENJAMIN BRANTLEY. Witnesses: WILLIAM PORTER, FIELDING HILL, HENRY HIGHT.

Page 73:   BEALL, FRANCIS, "very sick in body" etc. Last Will and Testament dated Feb. 14, 1822, probated Feb. 23, 1822. Gives all his estate to his wife, SARAH, for her lifetime or widowhood with authority to her to dispose of and equally divide among "all the children as they become of age, taking care to educate them. Wife to be sole executrix. Witnesses: ARTHUR JENKINS, EVANS MCCRARY and SAMUEL BEALL.

Page 79:   BEALL, ROBERT. Last Will and Testament dated March 20, 1822; probated Sept. 16, 1822. Gives to wife, ELIZABETH, the land on Long Creek adjoining ELIJAH JONES and ZEPHANIAH FOWLER, being the place where he resides, together with all his slaves, farming implements &c. Same to be hers for her lifetime or widowhood, provided all the children (unnamed) remain with her. Gives to grandchildren, ELIZA, AMANDA and EMILY NEAL "with any other children my daughter, ELIZA NEAL, may have" several slaves and 1/6th of the remainder of the estate. To daughters, EVELINA, MARY, PRISCILLA and CAROLINE BEALL, slaves and other items as they become of age or marry. Executors: Wife, ELIZABETH, and ELIJAH JONES. Witnesses: HENDLEY JONES, NATHAN JONES, WILLIAM JONES, WM. FOWLER, THOS. GORDON.

Page 86:   BEALL, MANNAM. Last Will and Testament dated Aug. 9, 1814; probated May 5, 1823. Gives to wife FRANCES for her lifetime the plantation where he lives, together with four slaves; and after her death same to go to his surviving children at that time. Residue of his estate to his seven children viz: FRANCIS, ROBERT, SAMUEL and ELIZABETH BEALL, JEAN MCCRARY, MARGERY JONES and MILLIE MCCRARY. No executor named. Wit: NATHAN CASTLEBERRY, ASA LYNN, HENLEY JONES.

Page 93: BUNKLEY, JESSE. Last Will and Testament dated Aug. 16, 1823; no date of probate shown. Gives to wife, ALLEY, sixteen head of slaves for her lifetime or widowhood and then to be divided between his children, LUCY BARKSDALE, JOHN BUNKLEY, JOSHUA BUNKLEY, JAMES BUNKLEY, ALBERT G. BUNKLEY, MATILDA BUNKLEY now MATILDA TOWNS. Executors: Wife, ALLEY, and son, ALBERT G. BUNKLEY. Witnesses: HENRY BROWN, ARCHIBALD SEALS, RICHARD BURNLEY.

Page 95: BAKER, PATTY. Last Will and Testament dated Dec. 19, 1823; probated Jan. 5, 1824. Gives to son, HENRY BAKER, the loan for two years of the plantation where he (testator) lives, then same to be sold and divided among all my children except ELIZABETH WILLIAMS, viz: WILLIAM, AUSTIN, EDWIN, PEYTON, JONATHAN and HENRY BAKER and POLLY BATTLE. Directs that the lot of land drawn by her in the late land lottery, being Lot 144, 2nd Dist. of what was then Monroe Co., be sold and proceeds divided among his legatees. No executor named. Witnesses: SAMUEL TORRENCE, JOHN W. TORRENCE, STPTIMUS TORRENCE.

Page 101: BRANTLEY, PHILIP. Last Will and Testament dated Mar. 18, 1819; probated June 7, 1824. Devises to daughter, CATHERINE PRUITT, $200.00; to daughter PHOEBE HIGHT, $5.00" as an evidence of my affection and because of provision hereafter made for her son, FIELDING HILL." Gives to son, JOHN BRANTLEY, $400.00; to sons, BENJAMIN and JEPTHAH BRANTLEY and daughters, FRANKY BREED and HANNAH WALKER and grandson, FIELDING HILL, 9 slaves. Residue of his estate to wife, POLLY, daughter POLLY GIBORN and grandchildren, LARKIN, CYNTHIA, LAVINA, JONES, HARRIS and CATHERINE BRANTLEY. Executor: Friend, DENNIS L. RYAN. Witnesses: HENRY CONAWAY, THOMAS HAYNES, MARTHA M. HAYNES.

Page 134: BARKSDALE, HENRY, "being very sick." Last Will and Testament dated Aug. 24, 1826; probated Sept. 4, 1826. Gives to son, JEFFERSON BARKSDALE, a slave named Simon; to brother, HORATIO BARKSDALE, a slave named William; to JOHN M. BARKSDALE, testator's watch. To JOHN M. BARKSDALE, son of SAMUEL, and JOHN BARKSDALE, son of TERRELL, testator's draw in the present land lottery. Gifts of various items of personal property to LOUISA, SUSAN and ALLCY BARKSDALE (relationship not shown). Executors: SAMUEL and HORATIO BARKSDALE. Witnesses: ALBERT G. BUNKLEY, LUCY BARKSDALE, NATHAN TUCKER.

Page 162: BUTTRILL, THOMAS. Last Will and Testament dated July 20, 1825; probated Sept. 12, 1827. Gives to wife, PEGGY, 100 acres of land (homeplace) together with all his slaves and farming implements, household goods &c. and his draw in the present state land lottery, all to be hers for her lifetime, and at her death to be divided between their two sons, WILLIAM and THOMAS T. BUTTRILL and the heirs of their daughters, POLLY LITTLE and NANCY J. MCCRARY. Portion given son, WILLIAM, to be his on condition he returns before the death of testator's wife. Executors: Wife, PEGGY, son, THOMAS T. BUTTRILL and RICHARD DOZIER. Witnesses: WILLIAM G. STARKE, HENRY DOZIER, QUINTIUS L. C. FRANKLIN.

Page 186: BASS, REDDICK. Last Will and Testament dated Dec. 12, 1828; no date of probate shown. Gives to his wife, OBEDIENCE, 287½ acres of land (home-place) in Warren County on Middle Creek, and four slaves, for her lifetime, then to be divided between daughters NANCY BASS and ELIZABETH MCTYEIRE and grandchildren NARCISSA and REDDICK MCTYEIRE, NANCY FULLER BASS, and JANE the daughter of BUCKNER BASS, and sons PERSONS, LARKIN and BUCKNER BASS. Executors: JOHN FONTAINE, LARKIN BASS, KENDALL MCTYEIRE. Witnesses: D. DENNIS, ELIJAH MALLARD, JOHN D. GIBSON.

Page 29: CASTLEBERRY, NATHAN, "being sick and very weak." Last Will and Testament dated Sept. 20, 1814; probated Nov. 7, 1814. Gives to wife, MARY, all his property for her lifetime, then to be divided between all his children (who are unnamed and who it appears are minors). Executors: Wife, MARY, and SAMUEL NEWMAN. Witnesses: BENJ. OLIVER, J. OLIVER, RICHARD LOVITT, AMBROSE KILLINGSWORTH.

Page 54: CULPEPPER, DANIEL. Last Will and Testament dated Apr. 3, 1819; probated Sept. 13, 1819. Gives to wife, SARAH, for her widowhood

the homeplace, his slaves and household goods; to son, WILLIAM, 125
acres whereon he now lives; confirms to his sons, DANIEL and ROBERT,
Lot No. 72 in 11th Dist. formerly Baldwin now Jones County containing
202½ acres; to son, JOSEPH, he gives 250 acres where said JOSEPH now
lives; to sons, DICKERSON, BENJAMIN and MARINER CULPEPPER, and daughters,
MARTHA CULPEPPER and ARGIN (ARGENT?) NEWMAN $780.00 each; to sons, JOSEPH
and WILLIAM CULPEPPER $280.00 each. Executors: Sons, BENJAMIN and
MARINER CULPEPPER. Witnesses: WILLIAM PORTER, JOHN BENTON, DANIEL
DENNIS.

Page 105: COOKSEY, HEZEKIAH, planter. Last Will and Testament
dated June 3, 1817; probated Jan. 3, 1825. Gives to daughters, MARY
SEMMES and SOPHIA ROGERS, certain slaves already in their possession; to
son, THOMAS, the land whereon he (THOS.) lives together with an adjoining
tract bought of DR. IGNATIUS SEMMES: to son, HEZEKIAH, under age,
testator's homeplace plantation and 200 acres adjoining bought of ROBERT
CAREY. Executors: Son, THOMAS COOKSEY, and nephew, WALTER NALLY.
Witnesses: HENRY B. THOMPSON, WM. R. LUCKETT, JOHN DEWBERRY.

Page 118: CHAPMAN, ASA. Last Will and Testament dated Oct. 19,
1825; probated Nov. 7, 1825. Gives to son HENRY H. CHAPMAN, under age,
a certain part of his tavern-lot in town of Warrenton located on the Public
Square, and a horse and saddle and bridle, to replace one given him by
his (HENRY'S) grandfather, ALFORD. Balance of estate to be and remain
in possession of his wife, CYNTHIA, and their children, HENRY H., JAMES,
SOLOMON, EMILY, BRADFORD, MARTHA and ASA CHAPMAN, minors. Should wife
marry again he directs that WM. R. LUCKETT, CAPT. ROBERT HILL, MOSES
ALEXANDER, HENRY B. THOMPSON and LEROY HOLT appraise and set aside 1/8th
of the estate to her "which must include the manor house on my plantation.
Executors: Wife, CYNTHIA, SOLOMON LOCKETT, HENRY H. CHAPMAN, JOHN
FONTAINE. Witnesses: HENRY LOCKHART, JEREMIAH SWAIN, THOMAS GIBSON.

Page 124: CODY, JAMES. Last Will and Testament dated Nov. 2, 1825.
Probated Dec. 5, 1825. Directs that all his property be kept together
in possession of his wife, ELIZABETH, for her lifetime, for her support,
then to be divided between their children EDMOND, BENJAMIN, ROBERT, CELIA,
ELIAS, CHRISTOPHER C., CATHERINE, ANNALIZAR, LUCRETIA and JAMES CODY,
minors at the time. Executors: BARNETT CODY and GEO. W. HARDAWAY.
Witnesses: MICHAEL CODY, PETER CODY, DANIEL DENNIS.

Page 111: CARY, ELPTHINSTON?. Last Will and Testament dated Jan.
8, 1821; probated March 7, 1825. Gives to his wife ELIZABETH his homeplace plantation purchased of SAMUEL HEMING, for her lifetime, together
with certain slaves in fee simple. At her death the property to be
divided between JAMES CAREY's wife NANCY and her heirs, ELISHA CARY's
children, and the children of HENRY B. THOMPSON viz: JOSEPH, BENJAMIN
LANCASTER THOMPSON, GEORGE H. THOMPSON, NANCY ANN THOMPSON. Executors:
Wife, ELIZABETH, and HENRY B. THOMPSON. Witnesses: M. ALEXANDER, ADAM
MILLER and ROBERT GRIER.

Page 31: DEWBERRY, IRBY, SR. Last Will and Testament dated Jan. 8,
1816; probated Feb. 5, 1816. Gives all his estate to his wife, MARY,
for her lifetime or widowhood, then to be divided between children,
ELIZABETH, wife of BENJAMIN WYNNE, FRANCES wife of CLEMENT WYNNE, the
three daughters of SARAH WYNNE, dec'd., former wife of PETER WYNNE, viz:
NANCY, ELIZABETH and FRANCES WYNNE; POLLIE DARDEN, THOMAS DEWBERRY, JOHN
DEWBERRY and JAMES DEWBERRY. Says he gives no legacy to his three grandsons, the sons of SARAH WYNNE, dec'd., "as they are able to make their
own way." Executors: Son-in-law, BENJAMIN WYNNE, and son-in-law,
WILLIAM DARDEN. Witnesses: BENJAMIN CHAPMAN, ZACHARIAH DARDEN, HENRY
B. THOMPSON.

Page 84: DANIELLY, ANDREW. Last Will and Testament dated Dec. 27,
1822; probated Jan. 22, 1823. Gives to his wife, RHODA, for her lifetime
or widowhood, the 200 acre tract where he lives adjoining PETER CASTLE-
BERRY and POLLIE PARKER, together with certain slaves, household goods,
etc. To daughters, RACHEL and JANE CHAMBLESS, certain sums of money.

Remainder of slaves to go his children, MACD., JOHN, ARTHUR, FRANCIS and ANN DANIELLY. Unto each of his 2nd wife's children (unnamed) certain items of personal property. Executors: Wife, RHODA, and son, MAC D. DANIELLY. Witnesses: SAMUEL HALL, JOHN PARKER, ENOCH FARMER.

Page 140: DURDEN, JESSE. Last Will and Testament dated Nov. 21, 1826, probated Jan. 2, 1827. He gives life-estate in his land, cattle, etc., to his wife, CHRISTIAN, and after her death to PRISCILLA, POLLIE and CALVIN, children of ARCADA HEARN (relationship, if any, not shown). Executor: HENRY GIBSON of Columbia County. Witnesses: WM. B. HUNDLEY, JOAB SPIVEY, THOMAS W. BATTLE.

Page 89: FAGALIE, WILLIAM. Last Will and Testament dated June 24, 1822; probated July 7, 1823. Gives to his wife, LUCY, for her lifetime or widowhood the land whereon he lives, being 772 acres, &c., then to go to his five sons, JOHN, WILLIAM, JAMES, ROBERT and FRANKLIN FAGALIE. To daughter, MARY FAGALIE, feather bed, etc. To daughter, CASSA WILLIAMS, cows &c. To daughters, BARBARA and FANNIE FAGALIE, when of age, a feather bed and other items, each. He directs that the six youngest children, viz., BARBARA, WILLIAM, JAMES, ROBERTSON, FRANKLIN and FANNIE be educated. Executors: JAMES WILLIAMS and GRAY CUMMINGS. Witnesses: JOSEPH WILLIAMS, JR., JOHN FAGALIE and JOHN W. VANZE.

Page 97: FLEWELLEN, ARCHULAUS. Last Will and Testament dated June 13th, 1821. Caveat filed when it was offered for probate Jan. Term. 1824, of court, caveat filed by THOMAS PERSONS on account of erasures and interlineations. Will ordered probated April Term. 1824, and admitted to record. To son, JAMES FLEWELLEN, testator gives the slaves and money he has already given him. To son, THOMAS FLEWELLEN, certain slaves &c., "above the other gifts already made him." To grandson, THOMAS FLEWELLEN PERSONS, six slaves and other items., now in possession of his father THOMAS PERSONS, same having been given by testator to CIBELL PERSONS, the mother of THOMAS (JR.) after her marriage. To his daughter, MARTHA FLUELLEN (sic) seven slaves, etc. To wife and "My three youngest children E NOS RUSSELL FLEWELLIN, LAWRENCE AUGUSTUS FLEWELLEN and MARYANN FLUELLEN, minors, 25 head of slaves, livestock &c., and the use of the home place of testator of 600 acres. Executors: Sons, JAMES and THOMAS FLUELLEN and DENNIS L. RYAN. Witnesses: JOHN S. HEATTS, GEORGE B. WAGGONER and JOHN TORRENCE.

Page 40: GOYNNE, WILLIAM. Last Will and Testament dated Jan. 4, 1816, probated Sept. 1, 1817. He gives certain sums of money to his grandchildren, JOHN and MOUNT HERMAN GOYNNE, sons of his son HIRAM. He directs that his home, lands, &c., be kept as a home for his wife (unnamed) and after her death to go to his son HIRAM. Son, TYRA GOYNNE, he gives a bed and other items to. To his daughters, REBECCA DICK and ALICE KING, and sons JOHN, DRURY, WILLIAM and HARDY GOYNNE, he gives $1.50 each. No executor named. Witnesses: JOSEPH JOHNSTON, OBEDIENCE RAY, HARTWELL BATTLE.

Page 107: GRIER, AARON. Last Will and Testament dated Sept. 16, 1824; probated Oct. 20, 1824. To his daughter, ELIZABETH, he gives a slave, household goods, &c. To his son ROBERT GRIER, he gives lot of land #140, 13th Dist. of old Wilkinson County, and $50 in cash. To his grandchildren, AARON G. and ALEXANDER STEPHENS, each $400.00 when the younger is 18 years of age. To his daughter, KATHERINE FINDLEY, he gives slaves named CLARY and AILEY. To his son, AARON W. GRIER, he gives one-half of his homeplace lands with certain slaves; and to his son THOMAS GRIER, he gives the other half. To his sons and daughters he gives his library of books. Executors: Sons, ROBERT and AARON W. GRIER. Witnesses: MOSES ALEXANDER, WILLIAM WRIGHT and WASHINGTON DARDEN.

Page 43: HARDEN, MARK. Last Will and Testament dated Apr. 13, 1813, probated Nov. Term. 1817. He gives to his sons, HENRY, MARK, MARTIN, JAMES and JOHN HARDEN, and daughters, POLLY GEORGE, JUDITH WILLIS, and SALLIE HARDIN $2.00 each. All the residue of his estate he gives to his wife FRANCES and their two daughters, PATSY and NANCY HARDEN, and son, WILLIAM HARDEN, "to be used by them in common" and after wife's death to be divided between said PATSY, NANCY and WILLIAM. Executors: ISAIAH TUCKER, RICHARD FLESHER and wife FRANCES HARDEN.

Page 57: HIGHT, HOWELL, SR. Last Will and Testament dated Feb. 2, 1821; probated Feb. 13, 1821. To his wife, ANNE HIGHT, his homeplace of 580 acres, with the livestock and slaves, for her lifetime. To sons, HOWELL, WILEY, GILBERT HIGHT and daughters, SALLY JOHNSON, POLLY CREN-SHAW, SUKEY GRIERSON and ANNE SHEFFIELD, one eighth of his estate each. To son, JULIUS HIGHT, $30.00 in cash. To his grandchildren (children of his son JULIUS), viz., LUCINDA, ALFRED, SUKEY, HENRY, HOWELL, NANCY, ELIZABETH, EDNA, CORNELIUA and WILLIAM, the land on Hart's Creek where the said JULIUS now lives, together with land lot 74, 7th District of Wilkinson County drawn by testator in the land lottery, together with one-eighth of testator's estate, when the youngest of said children is of age; said son, JULIUS, to be trustee for his said children. To testator's grandchildren, PASCAL CRENSHAW, ELIZABETH GRIERSON (late ELIZABETH CRENSHAW), and SALLIE JOHNSON (children of testator's daughter SALLIE JOHNSON), one eighth part of testator's estate. To his (testator's) grandchildren LUCY, SALLY and ZILLA ANN SHEFFIELD, DELILAH, PEYTON, FRANCES CAROLINE and WYATT OLIVER GRIERSON (children of testator's daughter, SUKY GRIERSON) one-eight part of his estate. Executor: CHURCHILL GIBSON. Witnesses: HENRY HILL, ROBERT BONNER, DENNIS L. RYAN.

Page 30: HEATH, WILLIAM. Last Will and Testament dated Dec. 12, 1813; probated July 4, 1814. Gives to his son, JOHN, a "bay filly" and other items. Residue of estate to his wife, SARY, for her lifetime or widowhood, then to wife (if in life) and "my children" (unnamed). Executor: Brother, JOHN HEATH. Witnesses: WILLIAM BARROW and JOHN KELLUM.

Page 62: HARRIS, GEORGE. Last Will and Testament dated Oct. 20, 1817; probated Sept. 3, 1821. Gives to his sons EZEKIEL, THOMAS, BENJA-MIN and JOHN HARRIS, certain items of furniture and feather bed each. He directs his lands all be sold (including homeplace tract) and proceeds divided between the following legatees, SALLY ELLIOTT one share; the children of SAMUEL HARRIS, dec'd. son, one share; REBECCA SIMS one share; children of daughter ANN MOODIE that may be living at his decease, one share; MALINDA MYRICK, one share; and sons, EZEKIEL, THOMAS, BENJAMIN and JOHN HARRIS, one share each. "All ready money at my decease to be divided between my wife, CATHERINE, and the above named legatees." He gives the homeplace to his wife, CATHERINE for her use for her lifetime. Executors: Sons, THOMAS and JOHN HARRIS. Witnesses: ROBERT HILL, SR., MOSES DARDEN, JESSE DARDEN.

Page 85: HILLMAN, REV. WINDER. Last Will and Testament dated Oct. 25, 1823; probated March 3, 1823. Gives to ELIZABETH HILLMAN (not yet 16) daughter of JOSHUA HILLMAN, a slave. Gives to son, JOSHUA HILLMAN, all money owing to testator. To son, SAMUEL HILLMAN, testator's watch and half of his library (wife having first choice of same) and the land testator drew in the lottery lying in Early County, SAMUEL to pay the grant fees for said land. Residue of his estate to his wife, GRACY, in fee simple. Executors: Wife, GRACY, and SAMUEL HILLMAN. Witnesses: DRURY BANKS, SARAH WALKER, ROBERT WALKER.

Page 90: HAYNES, THOMAS. Last Will and Testament, dated June 25, 1823 probated Nov. 3, 1823. Gives to sons, CHARLES EATON HAYNES and THOMAS HAYNES, certain slaves; and to said sons in trust for his daughter CATHERINE BONNER and her children, $300.00 and slaves to daughter FRANCES BONNER, and slaves to daughter ELIZABETH ROBINSON. He gives SLAVES to his daughters, MARY RYAN and SUSANNAH LIVINGSTON. To son, WILLIAM PEYTON HAYNES, testator's homeplace. To daughter, MARTHA M. DOZIER, certain slaves. Executors to sell and dispose of testator's land in Wayne County at their discretion. Executors: CHARLES EATON HAYNES and THOMAS HAYNES (sons), and son-in-law, DENNIS L. RYAN. Witnesses: ZEPHANIAH FRANKLIN, G. D. FRANKLIN and H. A. FRANKLIN.

Page 121: HILL, ROBERT, SR. Last Will and Testament dated May 16, 1825; probated Oct. 7, 1825. Gives to daughters SARAH HILL and

TEMPERANCE DARDEN and son BENJAMIN HILL, two slaves each; to sons, SION and ABNER HILL, two slaves and bed each; to son, SEABORN HILL, two slaves, bed, and testator's homeplace; to sons BENJAMIN, ROBERT JR., and ABNER, lot of land #63 in Gwinnett County containing 250 acres. (Wife not mentioned). Executors: SION HILL, ROBERT HILL JR. Witnesses: ELBERT DARDEN, HENRY W. DARDEN, JOHN HARRIS.

Page 129: HARBUCK, NICHOLAS. Last Will and Testament dated Oct. 5, 1822; probated July 3, 1826. Gives to wife, BARBARA, the land whereon he lives, for her lifetime, then to be divided between daughters, C. E. GOLDING, REBECCA BRANTLEY, MARY HUTCHINSON and her children, BARBARA and NICHOLAS HUTCHINSON; SUSAN GEESLING and her children REDIAN GREEN and ANNA BARBARA TEESLING and their brothers and sisters; ANNA HARBUCK and her son GREENBERRY LEE HARBUCK; and to daughter LAVINIA ARMSTRONG and daughter ANNA HARBUCK, daughter LAVINIA to have a certain sum above equal share "because she is infirm." Executors: Wife, BARBARA, HENRY SHELTON, JEREMIAH BUTT, WILLIAM HARBUCK, JR., and THOMAS GIBSON. Witnesses: MICHAEL HARBUCK, WILLIAM HARBUCK and THOMAS GIBSON.

Page 136: HAMILTON, JOHN, SR. Last Will and Testament dated June 14th 1826; probated Sept. 4, 1826. Gives to wife, MARY, the land on Big Brier Creek where he lives, together with all perishable property, for her lifetime or widowhood, except $200 to daughter MARY. After wife's death or remarriage estate remaining to "my children" (unnamed), except that son, DANIEL HAMILTON, is to received the 40 acres he owns on Big Brier Creek, Executors: E. PERRYMAN SR., and AARON ADKINS. Witnesses: E. PERRYMAN, JESSE STORY, AARON ADKINS.

Page 191: HURT, ELISHA, planter. Last Will and Testament dated March 24, 1829; probated April 6, 1829. He gives to son BENJAMIN HURT all the land purchased from JOSEPH J. BATTLE; and to son, WILLIAM HURT, the land testator purchased from RICHMOND TERRELL, one-third each of his slaves and other personalty, in possession of his son, WILLIAM and ELISHAMA WORTHEN. The remaining third to go to the heirs of deceased daughter, POLLY BAKER, viz., LEONORA AKINS (formerly BAKER), ELIZA WORTHEN (nee BAKER), PRISCILLA, CIDNEY M., ELISHA H. and BENJ. H. BAKER. He gives to his son-in-law, AUSTIN BAKER, $5. Executors: BENJAMIN and WILLIAM HURT. Witnesses: BENNET YEATS, JAMES PILCHER, LARKIN GLOVER.

Page 33: IVEY, SAMPSON. Last Will and Testament dated Feb. 28, 1814; probated Feb. 5, 1816. Gives to his wife, MILLIE, his home plantation for her lifetime, then to go to his five children; THOMAS IVY, POLLY WILLIAMS (nee IVY), JINCY MCKENNEY (nee IVY), ELIZABETH and CHARLOTTE IVY. Executor: Son, THOS. IVY. Witnesses: BARNARD W. FICKLING, MOSES MCKENNEY, JOHN LEWIS.

Page 21: JACKSON, LOWE "very sick in body." Last Will and Testament dated May 6, 1813, probated July 5, 1813. Gives his entire estate to wife, AILEY JACKSON, in fee-simple. Executor: JOHN RUSHIN, SR., itnesses: VINCENT DAVIS, JOSEPH MURRAY.

Page 165: KING, ELIZABETH. Last Will and Testament (undated); probated Nov. 5, 1827. Gives all her slaves to the heirs of her daughters, MARY POYTHRESS and SARAH ZACHRY. Residue of estate to son, WILLIAM JACKSON. Executor: JAMES T. DICKEN. Witnesses: JOHN B. HARRELL, JAMES T. DICKIN.

Page 2: LOCK, JONATHAN, "very sick in body." Last Will and Testament dated Dec. 24, 1810, probated March 4, 1811. Gives to his wife, MARY, the home plantation for her lifetime or widowhood. If she marries, she is to take her third of the estate, instead of under the will. At her death or remarriage the land where he lives and a lot of land he drew in the 7th District of Wilkinson County to be sold and divided among his four children, ABNER, MANCEY, JOHN and JESSE LOCK. Executors: Wife, MARY, and son, JOHN LOCK. Witnesses: ELISHA HURT, ANDREW BUSH and JAMES BUSH.

Page 9:   LASSITER, BLAKE, of Halifax Co., N.C.   Last Will and
Testament dated Aug. 21, 1809, probated in Warren Co., Oct. 8, 1811.
Gives to WILLIS LASSITER of Warren Co., Ga., certain slaves and a right
to others in possession of WILLIAM G. GRIMES in Greene Co., Ga. Witnesses: SEPTIMUS WEATHERBY, HENRY COCROFT.

Page 37:   LOWE, WILLIAM, of Halifax Co., N.C.   Last Will and Testament dated Sept. 12, 1814; probated in Warren Co. May 6, 1816.   Gives to
NANCY YARBOROUGH (relationship, if any, not shown) the plantation whereon he then lived, with all his livestock, etc., also $400.00 of his money
in the hands of KINCHEN WHEELESS.   Witnesses: WILLIAM ANDERSON, SARAH
ANDERSON, MARY ANDERSON.

Page 83:   LACY, ARCHIBALD.   Last Will and Testament dated Sept. 21,
1822, probated Nov. 4, 1822.   Gives all his estate ot his wife, SARAH,
for her lifetime, and after her death to their daughter, POLLIE, to have
certain property and residue to his six children, ELIZABETH, JOHN, MARTHA,
NANCY, PLEASANT, SARAH, and grandson RANDOLPH LACY.   Executors: PLEASANT
M. LACY and GERARD CAMP.   Witnesses: HIRAM HUBERT, VINSON JOHNSON and
JAMES T. DICKENS.

Page 126:   LOCK, JOHN.   Last Will and Testament dated May 19,
1823; probated March 6, 1826.   Gives to his son, JAMES LOCK and daughter
SARAH BOOTY $1.00 each; to daughter, REBECCA LOCK, a cow and calf; to
daughters REBECCA, ELIZABETH and LIDDY LOCK all the remainder of his real
and personal property.   Executors: Daughters, ELIZABETH and LYDIA LOCK.
Witnesses: WILLIAM LANGHAM, BENJ. B. LANGHAM and LEWIS JACKSON.

Page 138:   LATIMER, REBECCA (wife of WILLIAM LATIMER of Warren Co.)
Last Will and Testament dated Aug. 27, 1823, probated Nov. 16, 1826.
Says that by virtue of her marriage contract made with husband when they
married, she makes this her last will and testament.   Gives to her son,
CHARLES LATIMER, 400 acres of the land on which she lives, for which land
he is her Trustee; such portion to include any houses he may choose, also
his choice of her slaves, given in consideration of his "particular atten-
tion to me and the care of the family."   To daughter, MARIA FURLOW, a
slave named Cato.   Residue of her estate to be divided between her five
sons, WILLIAM MARSHALL LATIMER, CHARLES LATIMER, SAMUEL MARCUS LATIMER,
JAMES LATIMER and HORACE AUGUSTUS LATIMER.   Executor: Son, CHARLES
LATIMER.   Witnesses: ROBERT A. BEALL, JEREMIAH PERRY, WALKER PERRY.

Page 114:   MCMATH, JOSEPH.   Last Will and Testament dated Aug. 24,
1824, probated Sept. 5, 1825.   To his wife, ELIZABETH, he gives 100 acres
where he lives, with all his personal property, for her lifetime, then to
be divided "amongst my heirs."   He gives a "special bequest" of $500.00
to his granddaughter, SALLY BARBAREE.   Executors: Wife, ELIZABETH, and
son, WILLIAM MCMATH.   Witnesses: HACHALIAH? MCMATH, ELIJAH MCMATH, CLA-
BURN WALL.

Page 169:   MCCORMICK, JOHN.   Last Will and Testament dated Jan. 22,
1828; probated March 3, 1828.   Gives to his wife, SARAH, the land where
he lives "provided she will not convey any part or the whole of it to
any person except my own children or grandchildren."   He gives to his son,
JAMES MCCORMICK land lot #82 in the 13th District of Irwin County, and
$300.00 in cash.   To his daughter, SUSANNAH DUCKWORTH, $50.00 in cash.
To son, PAUL MCCORMICK, a certain part of testator's home place in fee
simple.   To daughter, SCENA CODY, another part of his homeplace.   To his
grandchildren (children of POLLY CODY) viz., SARAHANN, ABNER, GREEN,
MARY, SCENA and MICHAEL, a slave.   To sons PAUL and ABNER H., and daughter
SCENA CODY, land lots 106 and 237 in 13th Dist. and lot #92 in 10th Dist.
of Early Co.   To GEORGE MCCORMICK "alias GEORGE KITCHEN, son of SARAH,"
lot #87, 30th Dist. Lee County.   Executors: Wife, SARAH, son PAUL and
BARNETT CODY.   Witnesses: THOS. GIBSON, WM. P. BUTT, JOHN REYNOLDS.

Page 188:   MAGEE, REUBIN.   Last Will and Testament dated Apr. 11,
1818; probated May 4, 1829.   Gives to his son EPHRIAM MAGEE, 423 acres
where he now resides.   Residue of his estate to his wife, ELIZABETH, for
her lifetime or widowhood then to be divided as follows: To daughter,
MARY E. STANFORD, certain slaves, she to pay daughter, SARAH M. MAGEE,

347

a certain amount to equalize legacy; to daughter, ELIZABETH L. EDMONDSON, the land he bought of MOSES HILL; to grandson, JAMES MAGEE, the son of LEAH, $250.00 if and when of age; $50.00 to Sweetwater Church. Residue to be divided between his five daughters, ELENDER and MARY E. STANFORD, LEAH N. PEARSON, ELIZABETH L. EDMONDSON and SARAH M. MAGEE. Executors: Wife, ELIZABETH and son-in-law THOMAS EDMONDSON. Witnesses: ROBERT LAZENBY, JOHN MITCHELL and WILLIAM STANFORD.

Page 28: NEAL, SARAH, "low in health." Last Will and Testament dated Oct. 27, 1814, probated Oct. 3, 1814 (sic). She gives certain slaves to her daughters, ELIZABETH BRAY, DIANNA PERSONS, REBECCA BEALL, PATSY GIBSON, SARAH GARDNER and DRUSILLA PITTS, and son ELISHA NEAL. To granddaughter, FRANCES GARDNER, a slave named Caty. Executor: HARDY PITTS. Wit: FREDERICK W. MASTERS, JOHN C. TURNER.

Page 5: PITTS, WILLIAM. Last Will and Testament dated Aug. 2, 1811; probated Sept. 2, 1811. To "my dearly beloved mother" (unnamed) he gives one-third of his estate, and one-third each to his brothers, SAMUEL and HARDY PITTS, except minor bequests to his sister, PATIENCE OLIVER, sister NANCY PARHAM "now NANCY TURNER," brother, MATTHEW PARHAM, sister REBECCA PARHAM, each to have $1.00. Executors: SAMUEL and HARDY PITTS. Wit: RADFORD BUTT, JOHN LEWIS, SELAH HADLEY.

Page 43: PEAVY, JOSEPH, SR. Last Will and Testament dated Aug. 25, 1810; probated Nov. 3, 1817. Gives to his wife, ANN, all his estate for her lifetime, then to be divided between "all my children" (unnamed); except a horse and saddle to grandson, WADE HAMPTON PEAVY, and bed and mattress &c., to daughter, MARY PEAVY. Executors: Wife, ANN, son ABRAHAM PEAVY. Wit: STEPHEN W. BURNLEY, PARTHENA BURNLEY.

Page 77: PATE, HARBERT. Last Will and Testament dated March 12, 1822; probated May 6, 1822. Gives to his wife, CHARLOTTE, the land where he lives with its appurtenances for her lifetime, then with all other land he owns to go to his three sons, DAVID, EDMUND and CORDY N. PATE. To daughters, POLLY RAY and ELIZABETH BROOM, beds already in their possession; to said sons and daughter NANCY PATE, beds, etc. To son-in-law, JOHN RAY, $1.00. Executors: DAVID PATE, EZEKIEL F. BROOM and THOMAS GIBSON. Witnesses: THOMAS LEWIS and JOHN W. JACKSON.

Page 80: PARRISH, JOHN. Last Will and Testament dated Aug. 23, 1819; probated May 5, 1823. Gives a slave to his wife, ELIZABETH, to sons, HAMPTON, WILLIAM and ALLEN PARRISH, daughters LINNEY COOPER, SALLY ROWE, POLLY JAMES and DICY SMITH, $5.00 each; to his son, ANSELM, a horse; to grandchildren, JOHN and THOMAS PARRISH (sons of said HAMPTON PARRISH), WILSON and EPSEY PARRISH (son and dau. of said WILLIAM), to JOHN and ELIZABETH COOPER (children of said LINNEY), to LUCINDA and JOHN FLOYD ROWE (children of said SALLY), to JAMES and WILEY JAMES (sons of said POLLY) $50.00 each. Residue of estate to be divided between his sons, ALLEN and ANSELM and daughters, ELIZABETH and PATSY. Executor: THOMAS FRIEND. Witnesses: BENJAMIN SANDIFORD, BENJ. F. FRIEND, JOHN O. FRIEND, MOSES GATLIN.

Page 104: POSEY, THOMAS. Last Will and Testament dated Apr. 24, 1824. No date of probate shown. Gives all estate to his mother, REBECCA LEWIS, and brothers, SAMUEL MARCUS POSEY (a minor) and LEMUEL POSEY. Executors: SION HILL and SAMUEL MARCUS POSEY. Witnesses: JAMES SMITH, NANCY SMITH, REBECCA SMITH.

Page 176: PALMER, ROBERT. Last Will and Testament dated Nov. 5, 1826; probated July 7, 1828. Gives to his wife, WINNIFRED all the land where he lives, being 1028 acres, with his slaves and other personal property, also lot 376, 12th District of Irwin County (when drawn) to be hers for her lifetime or widowhood, "provided she supports and educates all my children and sets off to each of my sons at his majority a suitable portion of the land," and the daughters to have certain other types of property. Children not named in will. Executors: HARDY PITTS and ABSALOM T. DAWKINS. Witnesses: MARY ENNIS, IRA NEAL, THOMAS GIBSON.

Page 49: ROBERTS, ELISHA. Last Will and Testament dated May 10, 1818; probated March 6, 1819. He directs that his wife, MARY, possess and enjoy his whole estate for her lifetime as a support for herself and his three younger children (unnamed). At her death his son, JOSIAS RANDOL ROBERTS to have the slave Lewis, and residue of the estate to be divided equally among all his children (unnamed). Executor: Friend, ZEPHANIAH FRANKLIN. Witnesses: SARAH CLOUD, MARY RYAN, DENNIS L. RYAN.

Page 38: SANDERS, ABRAM. Last Will and Testament dated July 17, 1817; probated Sept. 1, 1817. Gives all his estate to his wife, MARY, for her lifetime or widowhood, then to be divided between his "beloved" children, JAMES SANDERS, ABRAM SANDERS, REBECCA SANDERS, MARY THOMPSON, SARAH GRANADE, CHARLEY SANDERS and ANNA SANDERS. Executors: Wife, MARY, and son, JAMES SANDERS. Witnesses: JOHN HOWARD, ABEL ANSLEY, THOMAS CORAM.

Page 46: STAINBACK, FRANCIS, planter. Last Will and Testament dated Sept. 5, 1817; probated March 23, 1818.. Gives to his "beloved spouse" NANCY STAINBACK the use of the land where he lives for her life-time, and half of all his personal property in fee simple. To his nephew, DAVID STAINBACK, he gives one-third of the other half of the personal property; and the remaining two-thirds of one-half to his nephew GEORGE STAINBACK and nieces, NANCY ROBINSON and ELIZABETH CHISHOLM (children of his brother, THOMAS STAINBACK). To MARY RADCLIFFE (rela-tionship not shown) and her heirs, certain slaves and the land whereon he lives at wife's death; and to ELIZABETH PACE and DOLLY OXFORD and the heirs of their bodies, he gives certain slaves. Executors: WARREN ANDREWS and GEORGE TURNER. Witnesses: WILLIAM ANDERSON, EPHRIAM IVY, HARBERT PATE.

Page 47: SWAIN, JOB. Last Will and Testament (undated); probated Mar. 1st, 1819. Gives to his wife, SUSANNAH his home plantation with its appurtenances for her widowhood or until his son JOHN is of legal age. Also wife SUSANNAH he gives 14 slaves for her widowhood, then to pass to his sons, RICHARD, JAMES and WILLIAM SWAIN when of age. To daughter, NANCY ROGERS, he gives a slave "Sherman." To son, THOMAS SWAIN one "square" of land in Telfair County which he, testator, bought of UNDERWOOD. To son, JOSIAH SWAIN, certain slaves. To son, RICHARD SWAIN, one "square" of land in Pulaski County, being lot 344, drawn by BARTON ATCHESON, together with slaves, to his daughter, MARGARET PEEK, he gives two slaves. To his son, JOHN SWAIN, he gives certain land and slaves. Mentions his four youngest children as being RICHARD, JAMES, WILLIAM and JOHN. Executors: Wife and son, RICHARD SWAIN. Witnesses: NOAH KELCEY, CHARLES ATCHISON, THOMAS DOSTER.

Page 116: SNIDER, BARNETT. Last Will and Testament dated Sept. 26th, 1820; probated Nov. 2, 1825. Gives to his wife, ELIZABETH, the plantation where he lives, for her lifetime, then to be equally divided between sons, JACOB and BARNETT and daughter, ELIZABETH JOANNE. He gives a cow to FANNY THIGPEN (no relationship stated). He gives his perishable property to his daughter, ELIZABETH. Executor: JOHN MCCOY. Witnesses: JAMES BARFIELD, JOSEPH PHILLIPS, JOHN MCCOY.

Page 128: STANFORD, JOSHUA, SR. Last Will and Testament dated May 4, 1825; probated May 1st, 1826. He gives to son, JOSEPH STANFORD, the home place; to granddaughter, HARRIET DESHIELD, a cow and calf. Residue of his estate to his eight children viz: LEVI, JOHN and JOSHUA STANFORD, SOPHIA DRAPER, LEVIN STANFORD, MARY WILSON, ELLENDER LAZENBY and SARAH ANSLEY. Executor: Son, JOSEPH STANFORD. Witnesses: JOHN WILLSON, BENJAMIN HARRISON, WILLIAM HARRISON.

Page 143: SHIVERS, JONAS. Last Will and Testament Sept. 6, 1825, probated Dec. 4, 1826. He gives to his son, BARNABY, son WILLIS, son WILLIAM, son THOMAS, and grandson JONAS SHIVERS (son of BARNABY) certain sums of money; to his granddaughter MARTHA HIBLER (daughter of WILLIAM SHIVERS), a certain slave; to granddaughter LILLY ANN SHIVERS, a certain slave; to granddaughter NANCY SHIVERS (daughter of WILLIS SHIVERS) a

349

slave; to grandson GEORGE W. C. SHIVERS (son of WILLIS) the sum of $500 in cash, and a like amount to grandson OBEDIAH SHIVERS (son of WILLIS); to his son JAMES SHIVERS, forty head of slaves, and the tract of land where he (testator) lives, and his land in Hancock County. Residue of estate to his son JAMES SHIVERS. Executor: Son, JAMES SHIVERS. Witnesses: C. E. HAYNES, GIDEON HAGOOD, JOSEPH ROBERTS, LITTLEBERRY LUCKIE.

Page 147: STANFORD, JOSEPH. Last Will and Testament dated March 26, 1827; no date of probate shown. Gives to his wife, MARGARET, for her lifetime or widowhood the land where she resides, and his other lands on Little Sweetwater Creek and on the Greensborough Road, and all his perishable property. To his son, CHRISTOPHER STANFORD, the tract of land known as the MITCHELL tract, with cattle &c. To his son-in-law, HENRY HAND, $5.00. To his son, ISAIAH STANFORD, he gives his personal property and homeplace at the death of his said wife, MARGARET. Executor: Wife, MARGARET. Witnesses: THOS. W. BATTLE, JAMES WATSON, HILLERY LANGFORD.

Page 172: SMITH, JOHN C. Last Will and Testament dated Nov. 13, 1827; probated March 3, 1828. Gives a slave each to his daughters, FRANCES, SARAH and MARTHA and sons, WILLIAM, BENJAMIN and JOHN SMITH. Residue of estate to his wife, NANCY, to be hers until the children arrive at their majority or marries. Executor: JOHN B. ANDERSON. Witnesses: WILLIAM SHIVERS JR., WM. W. ANDERSON, JESSE E. SMITH.

Page 174: STANFORD, JESSE. Last Will and Testament dated Sept. 20th, 1819; probated Feb. 4, 1828. Gives to his wife, PARTHENA, his homeplace property; to son, REUBIN, the remainder of his real estate, and the home-place after his wife's death. To his grandson, JESSE RUARK, lot of land #174 in 11th District of Wilkinson County containing 202½ acres; to his daughter, EBBE RUARK, an equal share in all his undevised property at his death. Gives to EMILY MASH, a featherbed formerly belonging to her grandmother, BETHANY MASH, now my beloved wife, BETHANY STANFORD, No executor. Witnesses: ESTHER MCDONALD, WILLIAM MCDONALD, ANDREW MC-DONALD. (Editor's note: An error was evidently made in abstracting this will, as his wife in one place is referred to as PARTHENA, and in another place as BETHANY. Knowing the short of these two names as I do, the probability is it is one and the same person the "short" of PARTHENA being "THENEY" and of BETHANY "THANEY.")

Page 23: THOMPSON, LUCY. Last Will and Testament dated July 6, 1813; probated Feb. 7, 1814. Gives to her daughter LUCY KERR, a slave for her lifetime, then to be the property of AUGUSTUS THOMPSON KERR, son of said LUCY KERR. Gives the residue of her estate to her son, ALEXANDER THOMPSON, he to be the executor. Witnesses: JAMES ALLEN, ZITHA ALLEN, MARIAH ALLEN.

Page 26: THOMPSON, JAMES B. Last Will and Testament dated Dec. 3, 1813; probated July Term, 1814. Gives to his wife, PRISCILLA, all his estate for her lifetime or widowhood. Upon her death or remarriage, one-half of the estate shall go to nephew, JAMES THOMPSON, JR., except land lots 231 and 238 in Wilkinson County, to nephew WILLIAM THOMPSON, JR., with my gun and powder horn "which was his father's in his lifetime." To godson, JOSEPH W. LUCKETT, a horse, saddle and bridle. To his cousin, JOSEPH BROOKS, of Jasper Co., testator's clothes. Executors: WM. R. LUCKETT and brother, HENRY B. THOMPSON. Witnesses: HENRY B. THOMPSON, WM. R. PUCKETT and GEORGE LEWIS.

Page 66: TUCKER, ISAIAH. Last Will and Testament dated Aug. 9, 1821; probated Nov. 5, 1821. Says he is in business with his son, GERMAIN TUCKER, to whom he gives $5.00 "in addition to former gifts made him." To his granddaughter, ELIZABETH TUCKER (daughter of son, JOHN, dec'd.), to WALTER LUCAS, who married testator's daughter, BETSY TUCKER, and to daughter, LUCRETIA CODY, and to daughter, NANCY HOLCOMBE, he gives $5.00 "in addition to former gifts made to them." To his son, EDMOND TUCKER, daughters, LOUISA and JULIA TUCKER, sons MATTHEW and MARK TUCKER and daughter, MIRIAM TUCKER, he gives each $1400.00 in cash and a feather bed. Said sons, EDMOND MATTHEW and MARK being under age. Testator directs that his son, EDMOND, be sent to Augusta Academy to be educated. He requests that MIRIAM be placed with her uncle and aunt HENRY and MARY GIBSON and that they educate her. Executor: Son, GERMAIN TUCKER. Witnesses: JOHN BREED, CHURCHILL GIBSON, D. DENNIS.

Page 109: TARRY, THOMAS. Last Will and Testament dated Nov. 10, 1824; probated Jan. 24, 1825. To "his relatives" SAMUEL TARRY and GIDEON FLEWORNAN he gives $1 each. Remainder of his estate including 100 acres of land, he gives to his wife, HANNAH, in fee simple. Executors: Wife, HANNAH, and JAMES MCCASON. Witnesses: WILLIAM CASON, JAMES MCCASON.

Page 150: TORRENCE, JOHN. Last Will and Testament dated May 14, 1825. Codicil dated June 8, 1827. Recorded Sept. 6, 1827. To his wife, JEMIMA, he gives his large family Bible and all other divinity books, also life estate in his home and farm property; and he directs that if his son, SEPTIMUS TORRENCE and family continue to live there, he shall share it. To his son, SAMUEL TORRENCE, 350 acres and the improvements where he (SAMUEL) lives. To son, JOHN WISTON TORRENCE, 110 acres where he now lives (that is, where the son now lives). To granddaughter CAROLINE W. TORRENCE (daughter of son WILLIAM TORRENCE, dec'd.) 284 acres where said WILLIAM lived at his death, her mother, MARY SEMMES, widow of JAMES M. SEMMES, "to equally enjoy it." To his son, EBENEZER TORRENCE, he gives 537 acres, he to pay CAROLINE W. and said JOHN W., a certain sum each to equalize legacies. To daughters MARY WHITE and ABIGAIL WATSON, 600 acres he owns in Washington County, they to release all claim to lot #30, 22nd Dist. of Early County drawn in the name of their deceased brother, BENAJAH TORRENCE. Mention made of claim to 1000 acres in Jackson County drawn in name of GEORGE WEATHERBY, and land lot #177, 2nd Dist. Early Co., drawn in testator's own name. Executors: Sons, EBENEZER, SAMUEL and SEPTIMUS TORRENCE. Codicil provisions: Because of deficiency in eyesight of son, JOHN WISTON TORRENCE, he gives him land lot #88 in Carroll Co., drawn by testator in 1827 land lottery, also lot 146 in 18th District of Lee County. He appoints son, EBENEZER TORRENCE, of Greene Co., as executor. Witnesses: BENJ. BLEDSOE, JOHN FONTAINE, THOMAS GIBSON.

Page 69: UPTON, BENJAMIN. Last Will and Testament dated Jan. 28, 1813; probated Nov. Term, 1821. He directs that his wife, JUDITH, may use all his estate as she pleases for her lifetime, and at her death the homeplace to be divided between his two daughters, REBECCA CHALKER and OBEDIENCE BRANNON. Residue to his other children, SARAH HIGHNOTT (or HIGHNOTE?), NANCY MURRAY, TOBIAS UPTON, POLLY CONNER. Executors: NEVILLE ROBERTSON, SIMEON TRAVIS and SAMUEL ALLEN. Witnesses: SELINA MURRAY, CHARLOTTE MURRAY, ALEXANDER AVERA.

Page 1: WRIGHT, AMOS. Last Will and Testament dated Apr. 18, 1810; probated Jan. 7, 1811. To his wife, RACHEL, he gives all his estate in Warren County for her lifetime or widowhood. If she remarries then all the estate except the land to be divided among his children viz: ELISHA, BASIL, LEWIS, JOSEPH, AMOS, JAMES, LUCY, CHLOE and DRUSILLA WRIGHT. To his grandson JOSEPH RYAN he gives money for "a good education," He directs his land in Wayne County be sold. To his son, JOHN, he gives one French crown (sic). No executor named. Witnesses: DANIEL STURDIVANT, JEREMIAH BUTT, JOHN BUTT.

Page 6: WAGGONER, GEORGE. Last Will and Testament dated Feb. 6, 1797; probated Sept. 2, 1811. Gives to his wife, ELIZABETH, his entire estate except five shillings each to his children, WILLIAM, SARAH WEBB, JAMES, HENRY, MARY SHAW, JOHN, GEORGE, and BECKY WARD. Executors: Wife, ELIZABETH, and WILLIAM SMITH. Witnesses WILLIAM LUCKETT, CHARLES WEBB, JOHN MCCRAY.

Page 10: WYNNE, ROBERT. Last Will and Testament dated April 22, 1811; probated Dec. 2, 1811. Gives to his daughter, LUCY MULLINS; son, CLEMENT WYNNE; daughter, ELIZABETH WALKER; son, PETER WYNNE; daughter, MARY WALKER; son, ROBERT WYNNE; son, DUDLEY WYNNE; daughter, NANCY WYNNE; daughter, SUSANNAH EDWARDS; daughter, LYDIA HUNTER, five shillings each.

To daughters, PATSY and CYNTHIA WYNNE, a feather bed and other small items each. The residue of his estate to be equally divided among "my six last children," viz., WILLIAM WYNNE, FRANCES CULPEPPER, THOMAS WYNNE, PATSY WYNNE and CYNTHIA WYNNE. Executors: CLEMENT WYNNE and JACK S. DAVENPORT. Witnesses: HARDY HOBSON, JAMES PEAVY, FRANCIS BENTON.

Page 44: WHITE, WILLIAM. Non-cupative Will made the day of his death, Feb. 2, 1818; probated Feb. 7, 1818. Gives to his sons, GREEN and AUSTIN WHITE, a horse each; to sons, TIMOTHY, MATTHEW and WILLIAM WHITE, $100.00 each; to daughters, NANCY, PEGGY, UNITY and BETSY WHITE, a feather bed each. Remainder of estate to be equally divided between all of said children. JETHRO DARDEN, witness, swore to the above as being said WHITE'S spoken will, sworn to before D. DENNIS, J.P.

Page 81: WHEELER, BENJAMIN. Last Will and Testament dated Mar. 21, 1817; probated Nov. 14, 1822. Gives to his wife, MARY, one-fourth of the lands where he lives, to include the residence, for her life time or widowhood. The other three-fourths he gives to his three sons MERRITT, VINSON and JAMES jointly. He gives two feather beds now in possession of MARY SIGNOR BROOM to her two daughters, SARAH and TEMPY BROOM. Residue of his estate to be equally divided between his three daughters, SARAH BALL, SUSANNAH ANGLIN and MARY SIGNOR BROOM. Executors: ISAAC BALL, JAMES WHEELER. Witnesses: JOHN HUBERT, HANNON HUBERT.

Page 167: WILLSON, DAVID. Last Will and Testament dated Oct. 15, 1827; probated Jan. 7, 1828. He directs that all his estate be kept together until his youngest child becomes of age, and to be in charge of his wife, ANN, for her lifetime or widowhood; if she should remarry, then she to receive only a child's part. He directs that his daughter, HARRIET LAZENBY, having already received property from him that his other children (not named) be made equal to that which she has received. Executors: Wife, ANNE; brother, JOEL WILSON and JOHN M. LAZENBY. Witnesses: WILLIAM DRANE JR., RICHARD E. LAZENBY, JOHN R. STANFORD.

Page 181: SYNNE, CLEMENT. Last Will and Testament dated Nov. 5, 1825; probated Jan. 16, 1829. Gives to his wife, FRANCES, all his estate for her lifetime or widowhood except $500.00 in cash to daughter, SALLY WYNNE. He says he confirms gifts of land theretofore made to his sons, JAMES and IRBY WYNNE, and daughter, MARY JOHNSON (nee MARY WYNNE). Executors: Sons, JAMES and IRBY WYNNE. Witnesses: BENJAMIN ALLEN, WILLIAM WYNNE, BENJAMIN HART.

Record for Wills, Court of Ordinary of Warren County, by Zephaniah
Franklin, Clerk. 1829

Pp. 1-3: L. W. & T. of THOMAS REYNOLDS of the State of Georgia, and recently of Burke County..that my body be buried in the County of
Columbia near to the grave of my father...to brother REUBEN Y. REYNOLDS,
my mills in Burk County on Brushy Creek & 220 A of Oak and Hickory land
in Burk County, adj. to sd. Mill tract, known as the RUTLEDGE tract, also
300 A in Jefferson County on Brushy Creek, purchased from the heirs of
SAMUEL SLATER decd., & 100 A of Pine land adj. heirs of DAVID BROWN decd,
ROBERT ALLEN SENR., T. DILLARD & others in Burk and Jefferson Counties &
negroes (named)...to my brother WALKER REYNOLDS, tract in Burke County,
known as my residence, 1237 A adj. SMITH, ROBINSON, DILLARD & others, &
tract in Lee County, 10th dist., #226 & negroes (named)...unto ESTHER ANN
MAHARRY, negro Henry & others...to EMMA STONE, negroes (named)...to
MARGARET STONE, negro girl Barbary..to my dear cousin MARY STONE 2 negroes
(named) & $500 in cash...to ALEXANDER STONE, negro Jerry...to my friend
WILLIAM STONE, $1000 in cash...to an old negro woman AMY(belong to my
borther WALKER), $40...bro WALKER & REUBEN Y., Exrs...26 June 1829. THOMAS
REYNOLDS (LS), Wit: PIERSON PETTIT, EDMUND TUCKER, JOSEPH E. GIBBS, JAMES
HIGGINBOTHAM. Proven 7 Sept 1829. Rec. 15 Nov 1829.

Page 4: L. W. & T. of JOEL CLOUD, 16 Aug 1817. To son JOEL JR., two tracts
on Harts Creek & land purchased of THOMAS BOWDRE, 193 A...home to
single daughters (not named)...son JOEL, Exr...JOEL CLOUD (LS), Wit:
RICHARD DOZIER, NATHAN BEALL, WELLS WALKER, WM. BERRY. No prov. date.
Rec. 8 Mar 1830.

Pp. 5-6: Georgia, Warren Co.: L. W. & T. of HENRY PEEBLES..to wife POLLY
PEEBLES, 300 A purchased of JAMES STAPLER, adj. MRS. WALKER, 34
A adj. the other tract granted to JESSE WRIGHT, with tract I now live on
300 A & 18 Negroes (named) & at her death it to be divided between her
three children, FRANCES, ROBERT C. & NANCY C. MORELAND...to my granddaughter CLARA B. GILBERT, $50...remainder to be divided among my other grand-
children...wife POLLY & friend SOLOMON LOCKETT, Exrs...24 Aug 1829...H.
PEEBLES (LS), Wit: GEORGE COTTAN, DENNIS L. RYAN, THOMAS GIBSON. Proven
1 Mar 1830. Rec. 9 Mar 1830.

Page 7: L. W. & T. of ANN CORUM, dated 11 Apr 1829...to THOMAS CORUM, (no
relationship stated), lot #206, 10th Dist., 1st Section, Lee Co.,
which she drew in 1827 Land Lottery...ANN CORAM (X) (LS), Wit: JASON
HAYS (X), WILLIAM M. CORUM, THOMAS YOUNG. Provated 1 Mar 1830. Rec. 9
Mar 1830.

Page 8: L. W. & T. of MASSA MAYS of Warren Co., to my daughter ELIZABETH
DAVIDSON & sons GEORGE NICHOLS, 7 negroes (named)...to son ALFRED
MAYS, 100 A, the HARDAWAY tract, adj. CASTLEBERRY...my children ELIZABETH
DAVIDSON, GEORGE NICHOLS, LYDIA HOLDER, WILLIAM MAYS, ANNA SELL, & ALFRED
MAYS...WILLIAM CASTLEBERRY, Exr...8 Apr 1830...MASSA MAYS (X-hermark)
(SEAL), Wit: HENRY THOMSON (X), NATHAN PATE, WILLIAM CASTLEBERRY. Proven
3 May 1830. Rec. 21 June 1830.

Pp. 9-11: L. W. & T. of PRYOR GARDNER of Warren Co...whereas JOSEPH DENSON
and REDDING LEWIS became security for BENJAMIN SANDEFORD and my-
self to ANDREW STEWART at the instance of ANDREW STEWART against sd. BEN-
JAMIN SANDEFORD, each of them to be paid out of my estate...to WILLIAM
GARDNER, negroes (named)...to my daughter SARAH POWELL, formerly SARAH
HARRIS, negro Kesiah and $10...to my daughter FANNEA CULPEPPER, negroes
(Named) & $100...to son ELISHA GARDNER, now decd, negro Isaac...to daughter
SUCKEY RUSHING, negroes (named)...to grandson PRYOR GARDNER, son of STER-
LING GARDNER, decd, negroes (named)...to daughter POLLY Jerry...to daughter ELIZABETH BEAZEY, negro (named)...remainder divided
among MARTHA SANDEFORD, WILLIAM GARDNER, FANNEA CULPEPPER, SUCKY RUSHING,
POLLY P. HEETH, ELIZABETH VEAZEY, SARAH HARRIS(daughter of SARAH POWELL)...
HARRY HEATH & JOHN VEAZEY, Exrs...1 Feb 1827...PRYOR GARDNER (SEAL), Wit:
MARY R. GIBSON, THOMAS GIBSON, OBADIAH C. GIBSON.
Codicil: to daughter ELIZABETH VEAZEY, tract of 200 A I now live on
adj. JILSON BERRY, ASA McCRARY, 26 Dec 1848. Wit; MARY R. GIBSON, THOMAS
GIBSON, STERLING GARDNER. Prov. 5 July 1830. Rec. 13 Sept 1830.

Pp. 12-13: L. W. & T. of ADAM JONES...to son SEABORN JONES, tract where I
now live, 262 A & tract where I formerly lived, the BRADY field
...wife NANCY JONES to remain on it as long as she lives...to son NATHAN
JONES, tract on Long Creek, Coursey branch, adj. SAMUEL BEALL & negroes
(named)...the balance of my children THOMAS JONES, PATSY FOWLER, AARON
JONES, ELIZABETH GLOVER, SIMON JONES, ELIJAH JONES, STEPHEN JONES, ADAM
JONES, SUSANNAH CHAMBLESS...son ELIJAH, ADAM, STEPHEN, Exrs...14 Oct 1826.
ADAM JONES (A) (SEAL), Wit: JOHN McCRARY, AUGUSTUS BEALL, WILLIAM JONES.
Prov. 1 Nov 1830. Rec. 30 Nov 1830.

Page 14: L. W. & T. of STEPHEN MARKS of Warren Co....wife SUSANNAH. .son
ROBERT MARKS...my other children JANE, SAMUEL & SUSANNAH...138½
A I now live on purchased from JOHN VANCE & tract # 362, 15th Dist. of Ear-
ly County drawn by me divided among my four children...wife SUSANNAH &
son SAMUEL, Exrs...29 July 1830. STEPHEN MARKS (LS), Wit: TIMOTHY GRANALE,
CARY JOHNSTON, ELIAS WILSON. Prov. 12 Oct 1830. Rec. 30 Nov 1830.

Pp. 15-16: L. W. & T. of EDWARD BOOTH...to granddaughters ELLEN & MARY
ALDRED, minor daughters of son in law WILLIAM ALDRED; to WILLIAM
ALDRED and CATHERINE CHALKER (relation not stated), 137½ A granted to
JAMES ABBOTT & 47½ A granted to JOSEPH ABBOTT...9 May 1831...EDWARD BOOTH
(SEAL), Wit: JAMES PACE, BENJAMIN IVY, HARDY PITTS. Proven 8 Aug 1831. Rec.
3 Nov 1831.

Pp. 17-18: L. W. & T. of SUSAN JONES of Warren Co....to son NICHOLAS JONES
...two children FELIX GILBERT JONES & NANCY HEATH JONES, to
send them to school...to daughter ELIZABETH JONES...to sons THOMAS P.
JONES, JESSE SMITH JONES, WILLIAM P. JONES & daughter MATILDA HENRY, formerly MATILDA JONES...son NICHOLAS, Exr....10 May 1831...SUSAN JONES (X)
(SEAL), Wit: THOMAS PERSONS, HARTWELL HEATH, AMBROSE HEATH. Proven by all
3 wit. 5 Sept 1831.

Page 18: Probate of SAMUEL T. HILLMANs will. see Page 20 for will. Rec.
8 Nov 1831. Proven by ELIZABETH HILLMAN & KATHERINE SELL.

Page 19: L. W. & T. of WILLIAM SIMPLER of Warren Co....to wife CLARA, all
estate real & personal... 1 Oct 1831...WM SIMPLER (LS), Wit:
RACHEL SWINT (X), JOHN SWINT (X), THOMAS GIBSON. Proven by GIBSON 17 Oct
1831. Rec. 8 Nov 1831. THOMAS NEEL, J. I. C., JOHN WINTER, J. I. C.

Page 20: L. W. & T. of SAMUEL HILLMAN of Warren Co....to wife GRACY HILL-
MAN, all estate real & personal not devised in this will...to my
mother FRANCIS HILLMAN, land bought of CLAYTON HUFF, near CALEB HILLMANs
House...at her death divided between SAMUEL, son of CALEB HILLMAN & WINTON,
son of JOSHUA HILLMAN...negro Chester to my mother...my brothers daughters
FRANCES, GRACY, MARTHA, MARY, ANNY & ELLEN HILLMAN, daughters of JOSHUA &
SUSAN, ELIZA, LUCY, ORMOND(?), daughters of CALEB...to my Brother EZEKIEL,
tract in 4th Dist. Early Co., drawn by WINDER HILLMAN...to nephew JOHN
HILLMAN...friends BILLINGTON SANDERS & ROBERT DAZENBY, Exrs...18 Oct 1831
...SAMUEL T. HILLMAN (LS), Wit: DAVID COOPER, ELIZABETH HILLMAN, KATHERINE
SELL. See page 18 for probate.

Pp. 21-22: L. W. & T. of JOHN HYMAN of Warren Co., planter...to daughter
MARY HYMAN...daughter HARRIET HYMAN...to the four children of
my son AARON HYMAN...my son HENRY HYMAN...son WILLIAM HYMAN...until the
death of my wife RODA HYMAN...to the heirs of ELIZABETH NORRIS...to the
heirs of MASON SMITH...to the heirs of AARON HYMAN...to the heirs of MAR-
THA HARRELL...to HENRY HYMAN...to WILLIAM HYMAN...to MARY HYMAN...to
HARRIET HYMAN...each 1/8 part...son in law SAMUEL SMITH & son WILLIAM,
Exrs...18 Nov 1831...JOHN HYMAN (SEAL), Wit: HARRIET HYMAN (X), LITTLETON
JOHNSON, J. P. Proven by both wit. Rec. 10 Jan 1832.

Page 23: L. W. & T. of THOMAS W KENT of Warren Co....to wife SALLY, all
estate real & personal and at her death to ASA WILLIAM KENT...2
July 1831...THOMAS W KENT (X). Exrs. WM COOPER, JOHN WOOD, Wit: ANDERSON
WALKER (X), LAWRENCE KITCHENS. Proven 5 Mar 1832. Rec. 8 Mar 1832.

Pp. 24-25: L. W. & T. of EDMUND CODY of Warren Co....to daughter SARAH
HARDAWAY, $700...to grandson ROBERT CODY...to the children of
my son JAMES CODY: EDMUND, BENJAMIN, ROBERT, CELIA, ELIAS, CHRISTOPHER C.,
ELIZA, LUCRETIA & JAMES, as they arrive at 21 years...to grandson ALBERT

L. CODY, $500...son BARNETT CODY...son BARNETT & G. W. HARDEWAY, Exrs....
15 Aug 1831. EDMUND CODY (X), Wit: PETER CODY, JAMES HIGGINBOTHAM, DRURY
A. McCULLERS. Prov. by DRURY A. McCULLERS. Rec. 9 Mar 1832.

Pp. 26-28: L. W. & T. of MICHAEL CODY, dated 3 Aug 1831; probated 7 May
        1832...to wife REBECCA, 1335½ A including the PRIOR tract,
whereon I now live adj. WASHINGTON HARDAWAY, EDMUND CODY & others & 42
negroes (named)...to the children of my son JAMES CODY...to the children
of my daughter ELIZABETH NEEL...to my daughter ELIZABETH 489 A on Big Brier
Creek, adj. McMATH, HODO, & others...to PETER CODY in trust for my son
GREEN CODY...to my oldest set of children & grandchildren...to sons
JAMES, PETER, GREEN, MICHAEL M., and JEPTHA M., (last two being minors)
...daughters ELIZABETH NEAL and LOUISA AMANDA CODY...to grandson JAMES
MADISON GRAY, when he becomes 21...Exrs. wife and son PETER CODY....
MICHAEL CODY (X) (SEAL), Wit: EZEKIAL HILLMAN, WILLIAM CASTLEBERRY,
DRURY A. McCULLERS. Rec. 25 May 1832.

Pp. 29-30: L. W. & T. of REUBEN ROGERS...to wife ELIZABETH ROGERS, 494 A
        ...two daughters MARY H. ASBURY & ELIZABETH C. ROGERS...to wife
negroes (named)...to MARY A. ASBURY, lot # 135, 1st Dist., Early Co. &
10th Dist., # not recollected...wife ELIZABETH & RICHARD V. ASBURY, Exrs...
13 June 1832...REUBEN ROGERS (SEAL), Wit: EDWARD HARPER, MILES CARY (+),
JETHRO DARDEN. Rec. 14 Nov 1832.

Pp. 30-31: L. W. & T. of EPHRAIM SPRINKS of Warren Co., all estate of wife
        LOUISA SPRINKS...30 Oct 1832. EPHRIAM SPRINKS (LS), Wit: .
ISAIAH COX, MARTHA WILSON (O), THOMAS GIBSON. Rec. 14 Nov 1832.

Pp. 31-32: L. W. & T. of JAMES NORRIS of Warren Co.....to son WILLIAM
        NORRIS, $5...to grandson THOMAS NORRIS, son of WILLIAM NORRIS
... to son in law MOSES ADAMS, $1 and no more..remainder of estate to be
sold and divided among children: ABNER NORRIS, ELIZABETH MILBURN(?), JAMES
NORRIS, HENRY MATHEWS & wf MARGARET...to son THOMAS NORRIS & children of
my son WILLIAM NORRIS...21 Aug 1832. JAMES NORRIS (SEAL), Wit: SOLOMON
NEWSOM, THOS MONROE, J. L. W. WILSON. Prov. 6 May 1833. Rec. 16 Aug 1833.

Pp. 32-33: L. W. & T. of RICHARD WIGGINS of Warren Co., to son WILLIAM
        WIGGINS, $1...to son AMOS WIGGINS $1...to son in law REUBEN
MAY, $1...to REBECCA HALIWAY(?), formerly REBECCA WIGGINS, & heirs of my
son PETER WIGGINS, $1...to SALLY WIGGINS, $25 when she arrives at the age
of 21...to wife LAVINA WIGGINS, all estate real & personal until my son
RICHARD ROE FRANKLIN HINES WIGGINS, arrives at the age of 21....& then
1/3 of estate...until my daughter MARTHA MARY SARAH ANN MAHALA WIGGINS,
arrives at the age of 21...JEREMIAH WILEHAN(?) AMOS WIGGINS, & REUBEN MAY,
Exrs...6 Sept 1832. RICHARD WIGGINS (SEAL), Wit: REUBEN MAY, G. H. WOR-
THEN, JEREMIAH WELCHER, J. P. Prove by all three wit. 16 Apr 1833.

Page 34: Warren Co.: L. W. & T. of JOEL NORRIS....all estate to wife
        FANNY NORRIS...21 Aug 1833...JOEL NORRIS (X), Wit: JAMES JOHN-
STON, WM. P. BUTT. Proven by both witnesses and also REBECCA JOHNSON, who
was present but not a subscribing witness, Nov. term. Rec. 12 Nov 1833.

Pp. 35-36: Warren Co.: Nuncupative Will of MARTHA MILLER...made in the
        latter part of 1832 and the early part of 1833 and at differ-
ent times since...all estate to grand neice MARY ANN DAVIS, when she arrives at the age of 21... Sworn 8 July 1833, G. DENNIS. Sworn to by
REBECCA BRANTLY, JESSE PERRY, & DRUCILLA HOBSON. Rec. 3 Nov 1833.

Pp. 37-38: L. W. & T. of ARTHUR JENKINS of Warren Co....to wife NANCY,
        land where I now live & negroes (named)...to daughter SARAH
BURKHALTER, Negroes (named)...to daughter LUCY REESE, lot in Houston Co.,
#93, 6th Dist....my five children BENJAMIN JENKINS, MORDECAI JENKINS,
MARY HOLLIMAN, ELIZABETH LOWE & SARAH BURKHALTER...9 Feb 1834...ARTHUR
JENKINS (SEAL), Wit: ADAM JONES, JOHN McCRARY, JESSE M. ROBERTS. Proven
by all three wit. Rec. 2 June 1834.

Pp. 39-40: Wilkes Co.: L. W. & T. of JAMES ELITT of Warren Co....one negro
        to the children of JULIA COOPER...one negro to the children of
SARAH WARE...to my daughter CATHERINE ELLITT, a negro...to my daughter
BARTHENA ELLITT, $200 or a negro...to wife SARAH ELLITT...to the children
of MATILDA FLINT...to the children of JULIA COOPER...to the children of

LUCINDA COOPER...to JAMES R. ELLITT...to JESSE M. ELLITT...sons CORNELIUS
ELLITT & GEORGE H. ELLITT...Brother in law JOHN HARRIS & son JESSE, Exrs.
...2 Oct 1830...JAMES ELLETT (LS), Wit: OBADIAH FLOURNOY, JOSEPH W.
COOPER, SAMUEL FLOURNOY, J. P. Proven by COOPER & SAMUEL FLOURNOY 3 Mar
1834.

Pp. 40-43: L. W. & T. of NICHOLAS WILLIAMS...to wife ELIZABETH WILLIAMS,
tract I now live on in Warren County on waters of Rocky Comfort,
adj. STARLING GARDNER, VINCENT JOHNSON, BIRCH ROBERTS & THOMAS GIBSON, 829
A & 33 slaves (named)...to ELVILAH SLATTER, widow of JOHN SLATTER & her
daughter FRANCES, a negro Levi...to NICHOLAS W. PITTS, Negroes (named)...
to PRUDENCE PERSONS & her sister CYNTHIA, 475 A in Warren County on waters
of Brier Creek, adj. MOSES McKENNIE, JOHN BURKHALTER & others, & negroes
(named)...to my sister SARAH PERSONS, $500...to LOUISA DRAKE, $500...to
the children of MARIA FLUELLEN, wife of THOMAS FLUELLEN, $500...to JOHN
PITTS, my nephew, $1000...to my nephew NESTOR PITTS, $1000...to NICHOLAS
SOOSBY, son of REBECCA WHITEHEAD, $500...to NICHOLAS BODY, son of GEORGE
BODY, $500...to ELIZABETH FLUELLEN, daughter of SARAH PERSONS, $500...to
OBADIAH C. GIBSON in trust for his brother JOHN GIBSON, $100...to STARLING
GARDNER JR in trust for THOMAS GIBSON, Jr., son of THOMAS GIBSON, $100...
to JOHN W PERSONS, AMOS J. PERSONS, GEORGE W. PERSONS, NICHOLAS W PERSONS,
JAMES T. PERSONS, LUCIUS S. PERSONS, REMIS A. PERSONS, ROMULUS C. PERSONS,
children of SARAH PERSONS, 1065 A on Middle Creek adj. ROBERT WALTON &
others, known as my Wrightsborough place, & 590 A in the 2nd Dist, Appling
Co., #434 & 202½ A in 11th Dist., Henry Co., #155 & negroes (named)...26
Jan 1834...NICHOLAS WILLIAMS (LS), Wit: THOMAS GIBSON, LEWIS JACKSON,
STERLING GARDNER JR. Codicil: to NANCY BROOM, wife of RUFUS BROOM, $500.
Proven by THOMAS GIBSON & STERLING GARDNER 3 Mar 1834. Rec. 12 June 1834.

Page 44: L. W. & T. of MARCUS POSEY of Warren Co., 20 Mar 1831...to brother SAMUEL POSEY, $50 provided he claims the same in 12 months, if
not to be divided between my four half-brothers and sisters (hereafter
named)...to my mother REBECCA LEWIS, the residue of my estate...WILLIAM
M. LEWIS, WALTER F. LEWIS, ALFRED A. LEWIS & MARY M. LEWIS(evidently the
half-brothers and sister earlier mentioned)...MARCUS POSEY (SEAL), Wit:
JOHN MOORE, JOSEPH FORD, ARTHRU MONCRIEF. Proven by all three wit.

Pp. 45-46: L. W. & T. of BENJAMIN ALLEN (apparently a nuncupative will)...
to THOMAS J. ALLEN, 109½ A adj. JAMES GREEN(?), L. L. ALLEN &
others...all balance of estate to be managed by Exr. until my youngest
child comes of age...tract of land I drew in Cherokee Gold & Land Lottery
...son THOMAS ALLEN...THOMAS J. ALLEN, Exr...Proven by REBECCA ALLEN,
JAMES B. MARTIN, ELISHA ALLEN & JOSEPH ALLEN, made by BENJ. ALLEN 4 Oct
1834 at his place of residence in Warren County. Sworn to 3 Nov. 1834.
Rec. 17 Nov 1834.

Pp. 46-47: L. W. & T. of WILEY HARRIS of Warren Co...to wife JANE HARRIS,
all estate real & personal & to pay my daughter ELIZABETH HIGH
$20...rest divided among "all my children"...wife JANE & son WILLIAM, Exrs.
...22 Sept 1834...WILEY HARRIS (LS), Wit: PERRONS WALKER, WINFIELD WRIGHT,
THOMAS GIBSON. Proven 3 Nov 1834 by WINFIELD WRIGHT. Rec. 17 Nov 1834.

Pp. 48-49: L. W. & T. of MARY ROBERTS of Warren County...son WILLIS ROBERTS,
son SHERROD ROBERTS, son THOMAS ROBERTS, son EDWARD ROBERTS, $1
each...to daughter NANCY FRANKLIN, $100...to son JESSE ROBERTS, $1...to
son JOSIAH RANDALL ROBERTS $1...to son ELISHA ROBERTS, all crop of corn,
cotton, wheat, rye & oats...to daughter MARY ROBERTS, negro Isaac...other
negroes (Named) to be sold & divided between ELISHA ROBERTS my youngest
son, & the children of my son JOSIAH RANDALL ROBERTS...Elisha Roberts,
Exr...23 Sept 1834...MARY ROBERTS (X) (LS), Wit: EATON P BROWN, WILLIAM
CLARK, J. L. C. FRANKLIN J. I. C. Proven 5 Jan 1835. Rec. 28 Jan 1835.

Page 50: L. W. & T. of EBENEZER BIRD of Warren County, 24 Jan 1835...in
presence of HIRAM HUBERT, JOSEPH ROBERTS & BENJAMIN F. HUBERT
(apparently a nuncupative will)...all estate of wife ELIZABETH BIRD...
daughter MARY ANN SWAIN, land on Williams Creek & negroes (named)...Rec.
19 Mar 1835.

Pp. 51-52: L. W. & T. of PEOPLES IVY of Warren Co....to daughter MARTHA
IVY, negroes (named) & 1/2 of Household plantation, adj. SMITH
...to daughter DICY THOMAS, Negro Sam...to daughter DICY THOMAS in trust

for my daughter SUSAN McCRARY...provided she pay a note & interest held
by DICY THOMAS against ASA McCRARY...to my grandchildren, children of
MOSES IVY, tract where my son MOSES now lives, adj. ROBERT WALTON...to
ELIZBAETH McCRARY, $100...to my wife, 15 A & negroes (named)...to grand-
children, children of JESSE W. IVY, $50 each...daughter DICY & THOMAS
GIBSON, Exrs...19 Oct 1834. PEOPLES IVY (SEAL), Wit: BURCH M. ROBERTS,
BENJAMIN R. PALMER, JOHN GIBSON. Proven 4 May 1835. Rec. 18 May 1835.

Page 53: L. W. & T. of FRANCES HILMON of Warren County...to son EZEKIEL
        HILMON, lot of 202½ A, Muscogee County, 23d Dist., #240...& if
he should leave no heirs, divided between my two grandsons SAMUEL H.
SIMPSON & EZEKIEL H. CARR...to my granddaughter FRANCES CARR, one feather
bed, etc...to ELENOR HILMON, one bed, two sheets, etc...to FRANCES SIMP-
SON, one trunk...to FRANCES HILMON, one heifer...to SAMUEL H. SIMPSON, one
white cow...to son EZEKIEL HILMON, rest of cattle...son EZEKIEL, Exr...
27 June 1832. FRANCES HILMON (X-her mark) (LS), Wit: D. DENNIS, V. A.
SMITH, DAVID CARR (X). Proven 4 May 1835. Rec. June 1835.

Page 54: L. W. & T. of FRANCES PARHAM of Warren County...to daughters
        EPSEY PARHAM, SARAH PARHAM, MARIAH ANTINET PARHAM, & FRANCES
ELIZA PARHAM, until the youngest becomes of age...to son ERASTUS PARHAM,
bed & furniture and negro Waymon...to son NATHANIEL PARHAM...17 Apr 1833...
FRANCES PARHAM (X-her mark) (LS), Wit: ROBT LAZENBY, ELIZABETH LAZENBY.
Proven 28 Dec 1835. Rec. 18 Mar 1836.

Page 55: L. W. & T. of JOHN McLAUGHLIN of Warren County...to wife ELENOR
        McLAUGHLIN, all estate real & personal...pension received of
the United Stated for Revolutionary Services...wife ELENOR & ARON W.
GRIER, Exrs...10 Dec 1835...JOHN McLAUGHLIN (X) (LS), Wit: ARON W. GRIER,
GUSTUS LUCKETT, THOS GRIER. Prov. 7 Mar 1835. Rec. 19 Mar 1836.

Pp. 56-57: L. W. & T. of RICHARD WALDEN of Warren County...to wife MARY
        WALDEN during her widowhood, land where I now live, also the
GIBS tract, 175 A & 150 A known as the Legare(?) tract, & part of the
BRADDY tract & 6 negroes...daughter PERMILY ALLENs part to be put for the
use of her children...my two daughters MELINDA & PHALBEE WALDEN, bed,
quilts, etc....my son ALFRED, negro Tom...to son in law EDWARD ALLEN, $5
...AMOS WALDEN, WILLIAM G. WALDEN & HENRY WALDEN, Exrs...RICHARD WALDEN
(R) (LS), Wit: NANCY WELCHER (X), JEREMIAH WELCHER, LARKIN WELCHER.
Proven 4 Jan 1836, Rec. 27 Mar 1836.

Pp. 57-58: L. W. & T. of JAMES DEWBERRY of Warren County...to wife LUCY
        all proceeds after my debts are paid...ABNER DARDEN & my wife
LUCY, Exrs...8 Apr 1836...JAMES DEWBERRY, Wit: T. FOSTER, G. T. TOWNS &
BENJAMIN WYNNE. Proven 2 May 1836. Rec. date not given.

Page 58: L. W. & T. of MATILDA IVY of Warren Co....brother SEABORN JONES
        FLAKE to have all...MATILDA IVY, Wit: WM. L. TUCKER, GILHAM M.
SMITH, JOHN BLACK (X). Proven 5 Sept 1836. Rec. 8 Oct 1836.

Pp. 59-60: L. W. & T. of BENJAMIN HARRISON of Warren County...to wife
        ABIGAIL HARRISON, plantation whereon I now live, 75 A...to son
BENJAMIN HARRISON, 50 A, to be laid off the WM ANSLEY tract adj. MORRIS
ANSLEY, STANFORD, WILSON...to my daughter ELIZABETH HARRISON, 50 A on S
side of tract willed to my son BENJAMIN...to son JOHN, balance of WM.
ANSLEY TRACT, & 37 A adj. LAZENBY, IVY & WILSON...tract in Upson Co.,
drawn by MARY MORAN widow, Williams Dist., #95, 16th Dist...for the use of
DAVID GEORGE COOPER...to son WM HARRISON, 1/4 part of sd. land, adj. #92...
to daughter MARY SMITH, 1/4 part of sd. land...to daughter NANCY ANSLEY,
1/4 part...to daughter REBECCA ANSLEY, remaining part adj. #128...to son
inlaw JAMES ANSLEY, husband of Rebecca, I rented a part of sd. tract for
1831 & he removed to the same, where he remained for 1832 and has not
paid any rent for that year or the present year...my executors to collect
$60 for 1832 and for the present year...son in law ABEL ANSLEY & WM
HARRISON, Exrs...19 Jan 1833...BENJAMIN HARRISON (LS), Wit: ELIAS WILSON,
MORRIS ANSLEY, JAMES MOORE.

Pp. 61-62: L. W. & T. of REESE JOHNSON of Warren Co...to wife FRANCES
        JOHNSON, all estate during her widow hood; if she marries, 140
A and a child's part of remainder of estate..."when my children come of
age"...31 July 1835...REESE JOHNSON (LS), Wit: JAMES(?) L. RYAN, A.

MUNCRIEF, THOMAS GIBSON. Proven 1 Nov 1836. Rec. 7 Nov 1836.

Pp. 63-64: L. W. & T. of SOLOMON LOCKETT of Warren County...to wife PAT-
SEY LOCKETT, 14 negroes (named) & HOLOMON Tract on which I
live, 400 A & tract I bought of MRS. RIGHT(?) & orphans, & cattle...to
granddaughter REBECCA A. LOCKETT, negroes (named) & $150...to son URIAH
T. LOCKETT, all land I got of my daughter CYNTHY CHAPMAN & of THOMAS GREER
...to my son JAMES LOCKETT, my daughter CYNTHY CHAPMAN, COLLER & URIAH
T. LOCKETT and granddaughter REBECCA LOCKETT...sons JAMES & URIAH, Exrs.
...9 July 1836. SOLOMON LOCKETT (LS), Wit: RICHARD V. ASBURY, SION HILL,
ANN B. WALKER. Proven 24 Oct 1836. Rec. 22 Nov 1836.

Pp. 65-67: L. W. & T. of NANCY ABERCROMBIE of Warren County...to daughter
NANCY CARLTON, 1/5 of my estate & to her children EMMILY &
EDWARD...to my daughter SARAH MATHEWS, 1/5 of my estate and at her death
to her children...to my daughter SARAH MATHEWS one other 1/5 of my estate
which I intended for my deceased daughter POLLY THOMAS...to my four grandchildren ELIZA, CAROLINE, EMELINA & ADELINA, children of my deceased
daughter REBECCA FICKLAND, 1/5 of my estate...Exrs. to manage for EMELINA
& ADELINA until they marry or come of age...to my grandchild CAROLINA,
and grandchildren EMELINA & EDMUND, children of my deceased daughter
MILLY RANDALL, 1/5 of my estate...DANIEL CHANDLER & THOMAS GIBSON, Exrs.
...12 Oct 1833...NANCY ABERCROMBIE (LS), Wit: DANL CHANDLER, GRAY A.
CHANDLER, ALFRED M. MATHEWS. Proven 2 Nov. 1836. Rec. 4 Jan 1837.

Page 68: L. W. & T. of WM B DENNIS of Warren County...nuncupative will
made by him at his usual place of abode at the house of D.
DENNIS, two or three days before his death, 15 Oct 1836...his brother
RICHMOND A. DENNIS to have his horse & refle...land to be sold and money
divided among his brothers and sisters...his father D. DENNIS, Exr...10
Nov 1836...CATHERINE BREED (X), LEONA B. HEETH, HARRIETT L. DENNIS,
RICHMOND A. DENNIS, NANCY DENNIS. Rec. 2 Feb 1837.

Pp. 69-70: Exemplification taken from Hancock County, taken 1837. Monday
7 Nov 1836. L. W. & T. of JOSEPH ROBERT, late of this county,
deceased, produced in court by BURCH M. ROBERTS...to son COLEMAN ROBERTS,
5 negroes (named)...to son DANIEL W. ROBERTS, negroes (named)...to daughter BETSEY RANSOM, negroes (named) & $400...to the children of my wife's
daughter FANNY WRIGHT , 5 negroes (named), now in possession of my step
daughter...to son JESSE M. ROBERTS, 4 negroes (named)...to REBECCA A.
JEFFRIES, 5 negroes (named)...to mywife CLARISSA ROBERTS, remainder of
estate, land, negroes, etc....28 Oct 1832. JOS ROBERTS (SEAL), Wit:
LITTLEBERRY RUCKER, GEORGE W. C. SHIVERS, REUBEN TAMPLIN, SOLOMON RAIN-
WATER. Rec. 19 Apr 1837. For balance of exemplification see Book E
Inventories p. 611, 12, & 13. Clk.

Pp. 71-72: L. W. & T. of WILSON DAWSON of Warren County...2 lots I drew
one district & the number not recollected (Gold) the other
10th dist., & 1st section, No. 134 (Land) be sold and put on interest for
my two sons ISAAC DAWSON & HARMON DAWSON...to son in law WILLIAM DEMANY,
$1...to son in law JOHN WOOD, $1...to son in law, STEPHEN ROGERS, $1...to
wife PRUDENCE, residue of my estate...my three daughters REBECCA DAWSON,
MARIAM DAWSON, & ADALINE DAWSON...8 Jan 1834...WILSON DAWSON (X) (SEAL),
Wit: WILLIAM F. BROOM (X), MARY BROOM, LITTLETON JOHNSON, J. P. Rec. Apr
1837.

Pp. 72-73:L. W. & T. of THOMAS ANSLEY of Warren County... to son JOHN
ANSLEY, 38 A where he has formerly lived...to son TILMAN ANSLEY
bay mare, $30 paid to JNO C. HOLCOMBE and $450 paid to THOMAS J. HARDAWAY
...to son ALFRED ANSLEY...to son JAMES ANSELY...to daughter MALINDA, who
intermarried with JAMES LAVENDER...to son WILLIAM ANSLEY...to son
RICHMOND A. ANSLEY...to daughter ELIZABETH ANSLEY...to son SAMUEL ANSLEY
to have more schooling...to son JOSEPHUS R. ANSLEY, to have more schooling
...sons JAMES & WILLIAM, Exrs...31 July 1837...THOS ANSLEY (LS), Wit:
THOMAS J. HARDAWAY, THOMAS WILSON, ABEL ANSLEY. Proven 17 Oct 1837.

Pp. 74-75: L. W. & T. of MATHEW ENGLISH of Warren County...to son ARON
ENGLISH in trust for my daughter OLIVE SCRUGGS, wife of WILL-
IAM G. SCRUGGS & negro Epsey...daughter GINSEY HOBBS...my daughter SARAH
ALDRED...son JOEL ENGLISH...son JOHN ENGLISH, negroes (named)...son
THOMAS ENGLISH, land on which I now live...granchildren ABNER NORRIS,

WILLIAM NORRIS, & CHAPMAN NORRIS, children of my daughter NANCY MORRIS...
son WILLIAM ENGLISH...daughters ELIZABETH KITCHENS, OLIVE SCRUGGS, SARAH
ALDRED, & JINSEY HOBBS & granchildren to receive $50...25 Nov 1837...MATHEW
ENGLISH (X) (LS), Wit: BENJAMIN MATTHEWS (X), HENRY POOL (X), JOHN MOORE.
Proven 18 Jan 1838.

Page 76: Nuncupative will of WILLIAM HEETH of Warren County who departed
this life 14 Apr 1838...his mother SARAH HEETH to take charge of
his two children SUSAN ANN HEETH & SARY JANE HEETH until said children
arrive at lawful age...HENRY HEETH, Exr...17 Apr 1838...Test; JOHN HEETH,
M. H. HEETH, HENRY HEETH. Rec. 9 May 1838.

Pp. 77-79: L. W. & T. of SAMUEL STORY of Warren County...to the children
of my first wife: JAMES STORY, JANE PERRYMAN who married JAMES
PERRYMAN, ELIZABETH USRY who married CARROLL USRY, MAHALY BOSWORTH who
married RICHARD BOSWORTH, MTILDA WHITE who married JAMES WHITE, FALEA
BURNLY who married HENRY BURNLY, MARY BRADSHAW who married WOODSON BRAD-
SHAW, BENJAMIN A. STORY; and LITTLETON B. STORY & WM. R. STORY of my
second wife to be equal...the other children of my second wife to have,
$125 paid by my wife STACY...500 A on White Creek, & 10 negroes (named)
divided amorg all my children, to wit the children aforesaid and FRANCINA,
REBECCA, ANDREW J. ELIZA ANN, MARTHANN, WITANTY, SAMUEL & SANDERS W.
STORY & any children that may hereafter be born of my wife STACY....28
July 1835...SAMUEL STORY (SEAL), Wit: ELISHA BURSON, ELISHA PERRYMAN JR.,
ISAAC BURSON. Proven May term 1838. Rec. 6 June 1838.

Pp. 79-81: L. W. & T. of STEPHEN W. BURNLEY of Warren County...to daughter
CAROLINE JOHNSON, Negro Milley...to daughter TERESA BARKESDALE
negros (named)...to daughter HARRIET HOWARD, Negro Eady and her children
...to son JAMES LAURENCE BURNLEY, negroes (named)...to son PERRY JACKSON
BURNLEY, negroes (named)...to my mother in law MARY GARRET, Negroes (named)
...to sons JAMES LAURENCE and PERRY JACKSON, tract I now live on 678 A &
adj. tracts of 600 A on mill creek, 250 A granted to KNIPPER, 300 A granted to BROOK, 300 A to WELCH, 200 A granted to PRATT, & 73 A granted to
myself & grist mill, saw mill, cotton gin, etc...20 May 1837...STEPHEN W.
BURNLEY (LS), Wit: JACOB A. H. RIVIENE, F. M. NUNN, ELISHA BURSON. Proven
May term 1838. Rec. 6 June 1838.

Pp. 82-83: L. W. & T. of MOSES McKINNEY of Warren County...to daughter
ELVIRA HALL, 8 negroes (named)...to son KINCHEN, tract where
he now lives in Warren County, on Rockey Comfort adj. THOMAS LOCKETT, JOHN
W. KINSY & others, 600 A & negroes (named)...to son HENRY McKINNEY, tract
where I now live in waters of Brier Creek, adj. DAVID E. HODO, BENJAMIN
ADAMS, PRUDENCE PERSONS & others, 750 A & negroes (named)...to granddaugh-
ter HARRIET MARTHA HALL, a girl Julian...to grandson SAMUEL MOSES HALL,
$300 when he attains the age of 21...son KINCHEN McKINNEY, JOEL HALL &
WILLIAM HARRIS, Exrs...13 Jan 1838...MOSES McKINNEY (LS), Wit: JAMES HALL,
THOMAS IVEY, ROBERT D. CODY. Proven 2 July 1838. Rec. 7 July 1838.

Pp. 84-85: L. W. & T. of JACOB SMITH of Warren County...to wife CHRISTIAN
SMITH, 5 negroes (named) on the plantation whereon I now live
on S side branch running between me and where JANE SMITH now lives, also
waggon, still, eight day clock, etc....to grandchildren MARTHA JETER, MARY
FARR, CYNTHIA FARR, REBECCA FARR & JACOB FARR, all the land I purchased
of ISAAC DAVIDSON on Childries Creek & tract adj. to it purchased of
REUBEN MCGEE, 350 A & to my daughter CATHERINE, mother of said children
...to my daughter MARTHA JOHNSTON, tract where she lives of 262 A...to
grandson VINSON SMITH, tract adj. where I live on Oliver's Creek...to
grandson HILLMON SMITH, land on E side Oliver's Creek...the daughter of
JOHN SMITH decd, my granddaughter NANCY COLLIER, EPSEY SMITH, ELIZA SMITH,
EMALY SMITH & MARTHA JANE SMITH, as they arrive at lawful age...to grand-
son JOHN R. SMITH...to MOSES JOHNSTON, a relation that I raised...WILLIAM
CASTLEBERRY & ELIAS WILSON, Esrs...19 May 1836...JACOB SMITH (LS), Wit:
TIMOTHY GRANAD, ISAIAH IVY, GIDEON GRANADE, Proven 7 Nov 1836.

Pp. 86-87: L. W. & T. of JOHN CLARK of Warren County...all estate to be
sold and used for the schooling of my children WILLIAM T. CLARK,
MARY ANN CLARK, JAMES R. CLARK & JOHN W. CLARK...also negroes (named)....
to WILLIAM F. HEATH, son of my sister ELIZABETH HEATH of CAss County....
THOMAS DYER, Exr....estate sold to B. T. HARRISON...5 Dec 1838...JOHN
CLARKE (LS), Wit: JOEL CLOUD, ERASTUS PARHAM, EVANS McCRARY, J. P. Proven
Jan. term 1839.

Pp. 88-89: L. W. & T. of DANIEL SHOWS of Warren County...to wife MARY
SHOWS, 4 negroes (named) & 200 A, East of the long branch, etc.
...to my grandson THOMAS GREEN HARDAWAY, a negro to reamin in possession
of his grandmother until he calls for him...all unnamed property to my
children: LINNY McMATH who married ELIJAH McMATH, EPSY HUNT who married
HOWELL H. HUNT, NANCY STORY who married WILLIAM R. STORY, MARY SWINT who
married JOHN SWINT, and MARY WILLIAMS my granddaughter who married
SHADRACK F. WILLIAMS & my three grandsons THOMAS GREEN HARDAWAY, JOHN
MADISON HARDAWAY & DANIEL HOLCOMBE HARDAWAY...ELISHA BURSON(?), Exr...
22 Sept 1838...DANIEL SHOWS (X) (SEAL), Wit: SAMUEL SMITH, JOHN BURSON,
MANN DUNEVENT. Proven 26 Nov 1838.

Pp. 90-92: L. W. & T. of MARY ANDREWS of Warren County...son MONCLABORN
(?) ANDREWS, $1...son EDWIN R. ANDREWS....(will very dim)...16 Oct 1838...
MARY ANDREWS (+) (LS), Wit: THOS L LATIMER, WILLIAM HARREL, STERLING
EVANS. Codicil 17 Jan 1839 (also quite dim)...names daughter SARAH A.
BAKER, granddaughter JOSEPHINE JOHNSON. Proven 6 May 1839. Rec. 30 May
1839.

Page 93: L. W. & T. of SARAH NESBIT, widow of the late JOHN NESBIT of
Warren County...friends AARON KENDRICK & JOHN C BYRD, Exrs. &
trustees for daughter AIRIAND THERMOSSESS MOORE & her infant daughter
ARIAND MOORE...2 Jan 1830...SARAH NESBIT (+) (LS), Wit: JESSE PERRY, JONA-
THAN GRESHAM, WILLIE J. FULLER. Proven 4 Mar 1839.

Pp. 94-95: L. W. & T. of ROBERT FLEMING...to wife CYNTHIA FLEMING, 500 A
on waters of Williams Creek, adj. LOCKETT, CULPEPPER & others
...until my son ARTHUR shall arrive at the age of 21...negroes (named) &
lot in Warrenton...ROBERT FLEMING (LS), Wit: CHRISTOPHER C. LEWIS, BRAD-
FORD T. PARKER, EDMUND W. BUTT. Proven 23 July 1839. Dated 7 June 1839.

Pp. 95-96: L. W. & T. of MICAJAH ROGERS of Warren County...to wife MARTHA
the three tracts on which I now live granted to GIBBS, HOWARD & FLEWELLEN
& negroes (named)...for my three youngest children when they come of age
....grandson MICAJAH WILSON...son JOHN ROGERS, Exr...5 Oct 1839...MICAJAH
ROGERS (LS), Wit: REUBEN W. LOCKETT, WM. R. BATT, WM. H. PITTS. Proven
4 Nov 1839.

Pp. 97-98: L. W. & T. of ISHAM WHEELER of Warren County...to be buried in
the burying ground on the premises where I now live...to my son
JOHN WHEELER, $100, & the worth of two cows DAVID EVANS has had...son in
law HUGH EVANS...DAVID & HUGH EVANS, sons in law...wife EDY WHEELER, son
DAVID WHEELER, & SON DILLY(?)...daughter MARY WHEELER...land adj. JOHN
ADKINS...to DAVID WHEELER, land adj. HUGH MONTGOMERY & SAMUEL STORY on
big brier creek...the balance to my sisters now living SARAH & ELIZABETH
WHEELER, including the house they live in...ISHAM WHEELER (X), Wit: HUGH
MONTGOMERY, BENJAMIN BROOKS, JAMES MONTGOMERY. Dated 3 Dec 1839. Proven
6 Jan 1840. Rec. 15 Jan 1840.

Page 98: L. W. & T. of EDWARD HARTY...to mother MARY, all estate real &
personal...(nuncupative will)...sworn to by JAMES HARTY, MARY ANN
HARTY & JOANA HARTY, 3 Jan 1842. ADAM JONES, J. I. C., JOHN HARRIS, J. I.
C., THOS L. LATIMER, J. I. C. PATRICK N. MADDUX, C. C. O. Rec. 10 Jan
1842.

Page 99: L. W. & T. of JOHN MAYE of Warren County....wife to have tract
on which I now live 50 A, also four negroes (named)...at wife's
death to be sold and divided among my children...JACOB to have a bay horse
...to my daughter MOSEY one feather bed and furniture...alson one to my
son JOHN and to JACOB...three tracts of land, I have one in the county of
Randolph and one in Muscogee County and in Cherokee County when drawn to
be sold and divided among my children...WILLIAM MAYS, & D. DENNIS, Exrs...

27 Aug 1838...JOHN MAYES (LS), Wit: D. DENNIS, WILLIAM MAYES, ELISHA HOLI-
DAY. Prov. 6 Jan 1840. Rec. 15 Jan 1840.

Page 100: L. W. & T. of ANN CATHARINE QUISENBY of Warren County...negro
Jane and her increase to my father JAMES QUISENBY during his
natural life, and at his death to go to my brother JAMES LEWIS QUISENBY...
SEABORN DOZIER, My Exr...4 Jan 1840...ANN CATHARINE QUISENBY (X). Wit:
SUSAN E. HUTCHINGSON, SEABORN DOZIER. Proven 4 May 1840. Rec. 6 May 1840.

Pp. 101-102: L. W. & T. of MONCLAIBORN ANDREWS of Warren County...my wife
SARAH ANDREWS shall have the raising and educating my children
...to her all estate goods, land, houses, negroes, etc...to my son WARREN
ANDREWS $1600...to my youngest daughter MARY $2000...As there is a probability that my wife SARAH will in the course of six months have a child or
children, I give to it or them each $2000......the children of JOHN BUTT
and the children of JOHN MOORE of Warrenton...SARAH ANDREWS, Extx, JOHN
MOORE, Ext....17 Mar 1840...M. ANDREWS (LS), Wit: HENRY HARE, WM. MOORE,
ALBERT PARIS. Proven 4 May 1840. Rec. 6 May 1840.

Pp. 103-104: L. W. & T. of EPHRAIM IVEY of Warren County...to wife CELIA
one negro Jack, negro woman Mason, negro woman Hanna, the
house I now live in and 100 A wherever she sees cause to take it, etc....
to JOHN LYNN SR., $200 for my daughter LAVINA...to be equally divided
among the living children of my daughter REBECCA SALLAS, one negro woman
NANCY, and her increase, 90 A more or less adj. REBECCA CODY...to JAMES
SALLAS, $5 and no more...to my daughter POLLY SALLAS, $100...to the three
oldest sons of MILLY MILLIER $100 each when they come of age...to CLEMMON
MOLLIER, $5 and no more...remainder to be equally divided among my five
living sons RANDOL IVY, THOMAS, ADAM, BENJAMIN and STERLING...sons THOMAS
& ADAM IVEY, Exrs...30 Oct 1838...EPHRAIM IVEY (LS), Wit: ALBERT PARIS,
ELIPHALET HALE, JOHN MOORE. Proven 6 July 1840. Rec. 9 July 1840.

Pp. 105-106: L. W. &. T. of BENJAMIN GEISLING of Warren County...to wife
RHODA GEESLING the house and 5 A immediately around it where
my son FLEMING now lives...to son FLEMING GEISLING, tract whereon I now
live cont.   250 A reserving out of it 5 A where my wife will live...to
son BENJAMIN GEISLER, a negro Sam...to my daughter MAHALY GFISLING, negro
Harriett & negro Harry...to my daughter MARY FEISLING, negroes Stephen and
Lizz...negro man Phil be sold to the highest bidder & proceeds paid over
to my daughter NANCY DUGGIN...I wish it expresely understood by my Executors that the purchaser of Phil shall not carry him out of the neighborhood of his wife...balance be divided equally between my wife, children
and grandchildren: the children of my daughter PRISILLA; the children of
my daughter BETSEY; the children of my son HIRAM; NANCY DUGGIN, BENJAMIN
GEISLEING, MAHALA BEISLING, FELMING GEISLING, MARY GEISLING and wife RHODA
...sons BENJAMIN &.FLEMING, Exrs...20 Dec 1838...BENJAMIN GEISLING (B)
(SEAL), Wit: STOKES P IVEY, THOMAS WILSON, CHAPMAN P. MADDOX, J. P. Proven
19 Aug 1840. Admitted to record Sept. Term 1840. Rec. 22 Sept 1840.

Pp. 106-107: L. W. & T. of JEREMIAH BUTT SENIOR...body be interred decent-
ly near wife and children at the church burial ground around
the graves I wish a stone wall to be erected by my Executors in a suitable
manner...sons EDMUND W. BUTTS estate....children MELMOND M. BUTT, WILLIAM
P BUTT, MARTHA B BANKS, JEREMIAH BUTT JUNIOR, SUSAN A. JONES and JOSEPH H.
BUTT...sons JEREMIAH to remain in the house where I now live...
MELMOND M. BUTT, WILLIAM P.BUTT & JAMES JONES, Exrs...8 May 1840...JEREMIAH
BUTT (SEAL), Wit: JOSEPH W. THOMAS, ALBERT PARIS, ROBERT W HUBERT. Sworn
to 7 Sept 1840. Rec. 22 Sept 1840.

Pp. 108-109: L. W. & T. of JAMES ROGERS SENR of Warren County...to wife
MARTHA ROGERS, tract of land as it now stands...to my three
grand sons DOCTOR FRANKLIN, HENRY RUFUS and JOBIAH BURNETT (sons of my
son JOHN ROGERS)...half of tract whereon my son JAMES ROGERS resides to
my two grand daughters AMANDA JANE and MARIAH ANTONETT, daughter of my
son JAMES...at my wifes death negroes Austin and Marenda to be divided
amongst my grandchildren for maintaining them and educating them...son
JOHN ROGERS & RICHMOND BURNLEY, Exrs...10 Aug 1840...JAMES ROGERS (SEAL),
Wit: SAM BARKSDALE, GREEN BAKER, THOS SEALS. Proven 7 Sept 1840. Rec.
23 Sept 1840.

Pp. 109-111: L. W. & T. of MRS. ANN F. MUNCRIEF of Warren County...to my
            niece MARY ANN LOCKHART, wife of HENRY LOCKHART, negroes
(named), my new carriage and all furniture which I may leave in the house
of DOCTR. HENRY LOCKHART, also one pair of Silver candlesticks, one silver
tray & snuffers and three china flower vases...to my niece ANN F.YOUNG
wife of EDWARD YOUNG, five negroes which are in the possession of the said
EDWARD YOUNG (named) and one half pint Silver cup, one pair silver candlesticks and one Silver punch ladle...to my niece SUSAN M. BILLUPS, wife of
JOHN BILLUPS, one sett Silver table Spoons and one Silver pepper castor....
to my niece ELIZABETH B. BILLUPS, wife of ROBERT BILLUPS, one sett silver
Table spoons and one silver pepper castor...to my niece ELLEN A. YOUNG,
wife of WILLIAM YOUNG, one dozen silver dessert Spoons,one punch ladle and
pair sugar tongs...to my niece JANE L. GUNBY wife of ROBERT GUNBY, one
large silver ladle, one dozen silver tea spoons and one salt spoon...to
the following persons, children of HENRY LOCKHART & my niece MARY LOCKHART
to ROWENA MALVINA LOCKHART; to ANN E. LOCKHART; to RICHARD H. LOCKHART; to
ROBERT A. LOCKHART; to MARY CORNELIA LOCKHART & ELLEN JANE LOCKHART, $600
to purchase a negro...my sister ELIZABETH ANN HIGDON, $400...to my niece
SUSAN M. BILLUPS, $1000...to my niece MARY ANN ELY, wife of CHARLES A.
ELY, $300...to my niece JANE L. GUNBY, $1800...to my niece ELIZABETH ELLE-
NOR OGILSBY, wife of URBAN B. OGILSBY, $300...to my niece AUGUSTA BEALL
SMITH, wife of STODDARD W. SMITH, $300...my niece MARY JANE SHIELDS, wife
of MATTHEW SHIELDS, $300...to FLORIDA BEALL, daughter of the late ROBERT
A. BEALL, $600...HENRY LOCKHART, Exr...3 July 1840...ANN F. MUNCRIEF (LS)
Wit: WM. P. BUTT, EASON D. HUDSON, JOSEPH W. THOMAS, CHAPMAN F. MADDUX.
Proven 7 Sept 1840. Rec. 26 Sept 1840.

Pp. 112-113: L. W. & T. of DAVID McCOY SENR of Warren County...each of my
            daughters that I have not already given, have a bed and fur-
niture & bridle & saddle...the negroes I lent to my daughter MARTHA BROOKS
be divided into eight equal shares, 1/8 part to MARTHA BROOKS, 1/8 to RE-
BECCA HARBUCK. 1/8 to my grandchildren MARTHA ANN & ALPHEUS BROOKS...the
other five parts to my children DAVID, SARAH, CAROLINE, ELIZA and FRANCES
...my children DAVID & SARAH McCOY and SAMUEL HALL, Exrs...8 June 1840....
DAVID McCOY (SEAL), Wit: RICHD V. ASBURY, ENOS N. HILL, HARDY HOPSON (X).
Proven 4 Jan 1841. Rec. __ Jan 1841.

Pp. 114-117: L. W. & T. of NATHAN BEALL of Warren County...to wife MARTHA
            T. BEALL, tract on which I now live on N side Greensboro
Road adj. SHOCKLY, HARRISON, to include all lands I hold on the South of
the Washington & Greensboro Roads, at her death to my daughter ELIZABETH
F. BEALL and the Heirs of her body...also Negroes (named)...my four children JOHN H. BEALL, ROMALDIES GREEN BEALL, WILLIAM M LEWIS who intermarried with my daughter ANN and ELIZABETH F. BEALL...to son JOHN H. BEALL,
tract on which he now resides, lying on the north sides of the Washington
and Greensboro Road, formerly owned by CHARLES EVANS, now by SHOCKLEY &
HARRISON adj. tract and negroes (named)...to son RAMALDUS GREEN BEALL,
tract where he now resides & negroes (named)...to son in law WILLIAM M.
LEWIS, negroes (named)...to my daughter ELIZABETH FRANCES BEALL, at the
death of her mother, the tract on which I now reside and negroes (named)
...son JOHN & son in law WM M. LEWIS, Exrs...6 Feb 1841...NATHAN BEALL
(SEAL), Wit: CURTIS LOWE, DAVID W. LOWE, HENRY W. MASSENGALE. Proven
3 May 1841. Rec. 4 May 1841.

Page 118: L. W. & T. of WILLIAM SHURLEY of Warren County...all estate to
            wife ELIZABETH SHURLEY and at her death to be equally divided
amongst all my children to wit, EDWARD SHURLEY, MAHALEY PARKER wife of
SAMUEL PARKER, CHARLES SHURLEY, NATHAN SHURLEY, THOMAS SHURLEY, NATHANIEL
SHURLEY, MARY SHURLEY, WILLIAM SHURLEY & ELIZABETH SHURLEY....sons EDWARD
& THOMAS Exrs...19 Oct 1841...WILLIAM SHURLEY (SEAL), Wit: CHARLES RALEY,
W. M. BALES & ADAM JONES J. I. C. Proven 3 May 1841. Rec. 5 May 1841.

Pp. 118a-120: L. W. & T. of BENJAMIN WYNNE SENR....to wife ELIZABETH WYNNE
            all property, both real and personal, during her life....
to daughter NANCY STEPHENS, 1/10 part of estate...to CECILLA WYNNE, wife
of JOHN WYNNE, 1/10 part of estate...to IRBY WYNNE, one bed and furniture
and 1/10 part of estate...to THOMAS WYNNE, 1/10 part of estate...to LEMUEL
WYNNE, 1/10 part of estate...to BENJAMIN WYNNE, 1/10 part of estate...to
SARAH RUNNELS my daughter. 1/ 10 part of estate...to daughter MARY WYNNE,
1/10 part of estate...to my daughter MARTHA DARDEN. 1/ 10 part of estate...

free from the use of her husband JESSE DARDEN...to my grandchild LORENZO
D. RUNNELS, 1/10 part of estate...to my grandchild LEMUEL WYNNE, the son
of WILLIAM WYNNE decd., 1/ 10 part of estate...except $100 to MARY GREGORY,
wife of BENJAMIN GREGORY...JOHN HARRIS, THOMAS WYNNE, Exrs...16 Aug 1839...
BENJAMIN WYNNE SR. (LS), Wit: JETHRO DARDEN, JOHN W. HARRIS, BENJN. CREN-
SHAW. Proven 6 Sept 1841. Rec. 7 Sept 1841.

Pp. 120-121: L. W. & T. of DANIEL ADKINS of Warren County...to my daughter
ALECY MATTHEWS, two negroes (named)...to my son ARON ADKINS
$300 for the use of my daughter ALECY MATTHEWS...her husband JOHN MATTHEWS
shall not have any power over said property...to my daughter NANCY ADKINS
$300...remainder of property to be divided among all my children JOHN
ADKINS, ARON ADKINS, the children of my daughter MACY ANSLEY decd., ELIZA-
BETH NEWSOM, NANCY ADKINS, SARAH NEWSOM, MARY HART, PENELOPE ADKINS &
JOSEPH ADKINS...24 Oct 1838...DANIEL ADKINS (LS), Wit: NIMROD NUNN, WM.
P. BUTT, DANIEL F. ADKINS. Proven 15 Nov 1841. Rec. __ Nov 1841.

Page 122: L. W. & T. of HARDY PITTS of Warren County...to wife DRUCILLA,
the house plantation where I now live with all stock, negroes,
etc...to my daughter SARAH what she has already received...to my daughter
ELIZABETH what she has already received and negroes (named)...to my son
THOMAS N. what he has already received...to my son WILLIAM H. C. what he
has already received...remainder divided among my four youngest children:
HARDY A., AMANDA M., WALTER VAN B., and MARY D....wife to be guardian of
youngest children...wife, sons THOMAS N., WILLIAM H. C., and HARDY A., with
friend THOMAS GIBSON, Exrs...2 March 1840...HARDY PITTS (LS), Wit: S. G.
HARRELL, ROBT A. HILL, R. K. MORELAND. Proven 1 Nov 1841. Rec. 2 March
1842.

Pp. 124-125: L. W. & T. of BELITHA RUARK of Warren County...to wife NANCY
RUARK, my land and plantation whereon I now reside...to my
son THOMAS RUARK, one horse...to son JACKSON RUARK, one horse...to my
four daughters that are now living with me ELIZABETH, PARSEY, LINNY and
AMANDA, one bed and furniture...at the death of my wife plantation to be
divided between my sons THOMAS RUARK & JACKSON RUARK...after the decease
of my wife, my three daughters SALLY MORGAN, POLLY INMAN and LETTY MAGRAW
to have $10 each...ELISHA BURSON, Exr...22 Jan 1842...BELITHA RUARK (LS),
Wit. F. M. NUNN, WM. O. SMITH (X), ELISHA BURSON. Proven 3 May 1842. Rec.
6 May 1842.

Pp. 125-126: L. W. & T. of NANCY ADKINS, Georgia, Warren County, August
2d 1842...to son ABSALOM, the oldest sorrel mare & all hogs,
cattle, etc...to daughter MARTHA, the spotted mare, etc...to son LAZARUS,
colt and heifer...to son DANIEL, $50...to son ANDREW, one bed & furniture,
etc...JOSEPH ADKINS & son ABSALOM JACKSON Exrs...son ABSALOM JACKSON keep
the children together & give the boy each one years schooling...NANCY
ADKINS (X) (LS), Wit: ISAAC HART, JR., JOSEPH ADKINS, DANIEL F. ADKINS.
Porv. 5 Sept 1842. Rec. 22 Sept 1842.

Page 127: L. W. & T. of SARAH ELLIOTT of Warren County...to my daughter
PARTHENA, a negro Joe...to my grandchildren, the children of
HARRIS ELLIOTT and LUCINDA COOPER and PARTHENA ELLIOT...to JOSEPH COOPERS
children...to JAMES WARES children...to CORNELAS ELLIOTTS children...to
RHODES ELLIOTTS children...JOHN HARRIS & B. F. HUBERT, Exrs...29 Apr 1841...
SARAH ELLIOTT (LS), Wit: RICHARD V. ASBURY, JAMES CARY, CATHARINE STONE
(X). Prov. 5 Sept 1842. Rec. 22 Sept 1842.

Pp. 128-129: L. W. & T. of GEORGE TURNER of Warren County...to son NATHAN
TURNER, and two sons in law JOHN P. CARR and ROBERT W. HUBERT,
Exrs...to wife HARRIET, plantation 600 A with household & kitchen furni-
ture, farming utensils, etc....to son WARREN, negro Martha...to my daughter
NANCY, negro Adaline...all children to have an equal portion of estate...
to the children of my daughter LUCY decd...children of my daughter MARTHA
decd...to daughter MARY...to the heirs of my son GEORGE...to daughter
NANCY...1 Oct 1842...GEORGE TURNER (X) (SEAL), Wit: STARLING EVANS, JESSE
IVEY, STARLING J. PATE, WM. W. ANDERSON. Prov. 7 Nov 1842. Rec. 18 Nov
1842.

Pp. 130-132: L. W. & T. of THOMAS GIBSON of Warren County...to my wife
MARY, late MARY LEMMES (SEMMES?), negroes (named)...DR. SEMMES
estate, by JAMES R. BROOK, Admr. of said estate....my five youngest have

363

had less education, and therefore must have more property...the two young-
est sons have done more work, and perhaps the three girls may. The six
oldest children are as near equal as I care for...JOHN to keep negro Emily
...MARY E. to keep Violet & Martha A. Ellin...OBADIAH C. GIBSON, Exr...
THOMAS GIBSON (LS), Dated 7 Sept 1842, Wit: R. K. MORELAND, DRUSILLA PITTS,
AMANDA M. PITTS. Proven 24 Nov 1842.
Codicil: My wife MARY is unwilling to continue with my children upon my
plantation...son OBADIAH C. may be under of selling a part because the
ROBERTS place was bought to employ under my own direction....7 Sept 1842...
dated 8 Oct 1842...THOMAS GIBSON (LS), Wit: P. N. MADDUX, EDMUND CODY, WM.
R. LOWE. Codicil prov. 24 Nov 1842. Rec. __ Jan 1843.

Page 133: L. W. & T. of WILLIAM PROCTOR of Warren County...to my brother
          BEDER PROCTOR all property both real and personal...6 March 1843
...WILLIAM PROCTOR (X) (LS), Wit: FRANCES PROCTOR, P. O. LEARY, JAMES R.
BROOKS, J. P. Proven 5 Apr 1843. Rec. 18 Apr 1843.

Pp. 134-135: L. W. & T. of STERLING JONES of Warren County...to wife PAT-
             SEY, the lot on which we live including the Stable lot,
bounded by the public Square, the Augusta Road, the lot conveyed by me
in trust for my daughter MRS ROGERS and by NEAL & CHAPMAN, the Rose tract
of land, 200 A...to my son ANDREW JACKSON JONES, negroes (named)...for
the benefit of my daughter ADELINE SMITH...to my sons ANDREW JACKSON &
STERLING W, slaves (named)...to son STERLING WASHINGTON, slaves (named)...
my children MRS. MANA ROBERTS, SARAH SATTERWHITE, SUSAN BOLER, SAMUEL,
JAMES & WILLIAM JONES ...wife PATSEY & son ANDREW JACKSON JONES, Exrs...5
Nov 1843...STARLING JONES (SEAL), Wit: J. A. CHAPMAN, W. H.BLOUNT, NATH.
C. SAYRE. Rec. Apr 1843.

Pp. 136-137: L. W. & T. of RICHARD LOVETT of Warren County...Exrs.: ADAM
             JONES, & son DAVID LOVETT...all the cotton I have six bags in
Augusta and four at the Gin be sold and money applied to payment of debts
...I have lately sold a piece of land unto HENRY POOL JUNR for $281.25 to
be paid by him on 25 Dec next...to my children that has left me JAMES
LOVETT, EDY DAVIS, ANNA HARRISON, SARAH BALES, REBECCA HOWELL, CRISSA WOOD
and MAHALA HOWELL...daughter JANE LOVETT now living with me...sons DAVID
& JOHN LOVETT...13 Feb 1843...RICHARD LOVETT (X) (SEAL), Wit: HENRY POOL
JUNR (X), EPHRAIM POOL (X), JESSE M. JONES. Prov. 1 May 1843. Rec. June
1843.

Pp. 138-140: L. W. & T. of ELIZABETH WILLIAMS of Warren County...to TEMPY,
             JOHN, PEYTON, WILLIAM BELICIA, AMANDA & NANCY BAKER, the
children of HENRY BAKER & ELIZABETH his wife and all the legitimate children hereafter born of sd. ELIZABETH & HENRY BAKER, 1000 A in Warren Co.,
whereon I now live, adj. WM. LOWE, THOMAS GIBSON & others & negroes (named)
...to WILLIAM BAKER, 50 A where he now lives of the 1000 A tract...to
JONATHAN BAKER, WILLIAM BAKER and the legitimate children as specified,
all persons estate...HENRY BAKER, my beloved brother...JOHN HARRIS, HENRY
BAKER, Exrs...15 July 1842...ELIZABETH WILLIAMS (X) (SEAL), Wit: JOHN
HARRIS, JESSE PATE, MICHAEL BARROW (X). Proven July term 1843. Codicil:
dated 17 Nov 1842.

Pp. 141-142: L. W. & T. of ZEPHANIAH FOWLER of Warren County...to son
             TERAH W. FOWLER, two negroes (named)...to son ADAM J. FOWLER,
two negroes (named)...to sons LEVI & JAMES FOWLER, 2 negroes each (named)
...to wife MARTHA FOWLER, three negroes (named), cattle, etc., tract of
land where I now live..children WILLIAM FOWLER, NATHAN FOWLER, TERAH W.
FOWLER, ADAM J. FOWLER, LEVI FOWLER & JAMES FOWLER...sons WILLIAM & NATHAN,
Exrs...27 Oct 1832...ZEPHANIAH FOWLER (SEAL), Wit: ELIJAH JONES, SEABORN
JONES, ADAM JONES, J. P. Prov. 4 Sept 1843. Rec. 7 Sept 1843.

Pp. 142-143: L. W. & T. of JAMES DRAPER of Warren County...to wife OBEDIENCE
             DRAPER, all lands, negroes, stock, etc...my daughter NANCY
H. TARVER...Wife OBEDIENCE, Extx...15 March 1841, JAMES DRAPER (SEAL), Wit:
JOHN MOORE, HENRY HINTON, JOHN D. BUTT. Prov. 4 Sept 1843. Rec. 7 Sept
1843.

Pp. 143-144: L. W. & T. of CLEMENT WYNNE of Warren County...to sister MARY
             JOHNSON, negro (named) & $200...to niece SUSAN MORRIS, negro
Malinda...to FRANCES ADKINS, negro Sally...to LOUISA WYNNE, daughter of

JAMES WYNNE, negro Rose...to ALBERT WYNNE, son of JAMES WYNNE, negro Bill
...to ABNER WYNNE, son of JAMES WYNNE, negro Caroline...to LOKEY ANN
WYNNE, daughter of JAMES WYNNE, negro Martha...to LUCINDA WYNNE, daughter
of JAMES WYNNE, negro Nancy...to ELIZABETH WYNNE, daughter JAMES WYNNE, ne
gro...to my brothers JAMES WYNNE, IRBY WYNNE, ELEMUEL WYNNE, ROBERT
WYNNE & sister ELIZABETH BUNN, all money, notes & account...brother JAMES
WYNNE, Exr...15 Oct 1843...CLEMENT WYNNE (SEAL), Wit: JOSEPH C. JOHNSON,
GEORGE W. DARDEN, DAVID GREEN (X). Prov. 13 Nov 1843.

Page 145: L. W. & T. of FRANCIS PROCTOR of Warren County...to son BEDA
         PROCTOR, six negroes (named) and for my grandchildren JAMES &
FRANCIS PROCTOR...to my daughter FETUAH COOKSEY my horse Ned...son BEDA,
Exr...13 Aug 1843...FRANCES PROCTER (SEAL), Wit: RICHARD V. ASBURY, WALTER
F. LEWIS, JESSE M. ELLIOTT. Porv. 1 Jan 1844.

Pp. 146-147: L. W. & T. of PATRICK NORTON...land, negroes, etc. to wife
         HONORA and to my children PHILIP OCONNEL NORTON, PATRICK
HENRY NORTON, SARAH CATHERINE NORTON, JOHN THOMAS NORTON, MARY ELLEN NOR-
TON, and if there should be further issue, all to share alike...until our
youngest child be of age...JOHN HARTY, HUGH WARD, Exrs...14 Oct 1843...
PATRICK NORTON (LS), Wit: MICHAEL RYAN, PATRICK RYAN, JAMES RYAN (X).
Prov. 5 Mar 1844. Rec. 7 Mar 1844.

Pp. 147-148: L. W. & T. of RANDOLPH IVY of Warren County...to son in law
         GEORGE W. HILLMAN, $5 and no more...to daughter EVALINA HILL-
MAN'S children: CEMANTHA ANN HILLMAN, ROANNA HILLMAN, WILLIAM HENRY HARRI-
SON HILLMAN and COALMAN W. HILLMAN, $25 each...remainder of estate divided
among my living sons ISAIAS IVY, OLIVER IVY, LAZARUS IVY, ZACHEUS IVY,
BRADFORD IVY, LEVI IVY, JEPTHA IVY and JOEL IVY...sons ZACHEUS and LAZARUS
Exrs...16 Apr 1844...RANDOLPH IVY (LS), Wit: ANDERSON IVY, FREEMAN W.
REED, ELIAS WILSON. Prov. 6 May 1844. Rec. June 1844.

Pp. 149-150: L. W. & T. of ISAAC HART, SENIOR, of Warren County...my daugh-
         ters SARAH ADKINS, PHEBE PEEBLES, MARY HOBBS, MILBRY HOBBS &
ELIZABETH TARRY (& their heirs) have negroe girls I have already given
them, $100 each...to son SAMUEL HART, one half of 250 A purchased at pub-
lic sale of the estate of SOLOMON NEWSOM decd...to son BARNABAS HART, $700
...$600 of which is paid...to son ISAAC HART, $700 all of which is already
paid...to son WILLIAM HART, other half of above tract...to son VINCENT
HART, $700...to son SOLOMON HART, $100...AARON ADKINS, son in law, & son
ISAAC, Exrs...27 Jan 1838...ISAAC HART (LS), Wit: JOHN ADKINS, ELISHA
BURSON, DANIEL F. ADKINS. Prov. 1 July 1844. Rec. 17 July 1844.

Pp. 151-152: L. W. & T. of THOMAS LOCKETT of Warren County...to son REUBEN
         WINFREY LOCKETT 2 negroes (named) & $500...to son SOLOMON
LOCKET, 2 negroes (named)...to granddaughter TEMPERANCE R. CAULDING, 2
negroes (named), good bed & furniture, $80 horse, if she dies before law-
ful age...to THOMAS LOCKETT, $500...to wife TEMPERANCE LOCKETT, all rest
of estate...to son SOLOMON LOCKETT, after death or marriage of my wife,
lot of land on which son REUBEN W. LOCKETT Now lives in Marion County,
202½ A...to my four youngest children CULLEN R. LOCKETT, THOMAS LOCKETT,
REUBEN W. LOCKETT & SOLOMON LOCKETT, $500 each...all my children: MARTHA
LEWIS, GREEN H. LOCKETT, OSBORN LOCKETT, CULLEN R. LOCKETT, THOMAS LOCKETT,
REUBEN W. LOCKETT & SOLOMON LOCKETT...wife TEMPERANCE & sons CULLEN &
THOMAS, Exrs...24 May 1841...THOMAS LOCKETT (SEAL), Wit-: ADAM JONES, JOEL
HALL, JEPTHA M. CODY. Prov. 1 July 1844. Rec. 18 July 1844.

Pp. 153-154: L. W. & T. of HENDLEY JONES JR. late of the county of Marion
         but now of Warren County...I am the lawful owner of an Execu-
tion issued from the Superior Court of Muscogee County in favor of E.
McKINSEY, Admr. of the estate of GEORGE SMITH, late of Columbus, decd., vs
WILLIAM JONES of Muscogee County amoungtin to $437.50 and left in the hands
of the sheriff of Muscogee County...to my brother BENJAMIN JONES, for use
of WILLIAM HENDLEY JONES & THOMAS, son of my brother WILLIAM JONES of
Muscogee County...contract between myself and GRAY HARRIS of Muscogee
County, I am the lawful owner of tract in 10th dist. of Muscogee Co., 71
A, said HARRIS agreeing before 2 wit.: WILLIAM HOLLIS and DRURY POOL...
for benefit of my brother WALKER JONES...at the final settlement of my
estate, $50 to MARY HALL and WILLIAM HALL, $25 each they being children
of MATTHEW HALL...to my sister DRUCILLA JONES, my gold watch & $50...to my

sister GILLY HUDSON $50...my brothers: BENJAMIN JONES, OSCAR P. JONES, FRANCIS(?) M. JONES, WILLIS B. JONES, THOMAS J. JONES...my sister MARY LIGHTFOOT...17 Sept 1844...HENDLEY JONES (SEAL), Wit: ADAM JONES, STEPHEN JONES, JOHN VEAZEY. Prov. 4 Nov 1844. Rec. 8 Nov 1844.

Pp. 155-156: L. W. & T. of SAMUEL SMITH of Warren County...to wife DELILAH SMITH,all lands, estates, etc...son JEREMIAH, to return home to manage plantation with his mother...son JOSEPH, to remain with his mother until 21...son JEREMIAH SMITH, Exr....27 Jan 1845...SAMUEL SMITH (SEAL), Wit: ELISHA PERRYMAN, ELISHA BURSON, THOMAS NORRIS (X). Prov. 5 May 1845. Rec. 9 May 1845.

Pp. 156-158: L. W. & T. of JAMES GRANADE of Warren County...to son TIMOTHY GRANADE, negro Alfred...to son STEPHEN GRANADE, negro, and tract where he now lives known as my old place...son MARTIN and his family, land on Sweet water, in Columbia Co., known as my Sweet water Mill tract, and tract adj. it known as MAGEE tract, 400 A total...son TIMOTHY GRANADE, agent to property...to son JAMES GRANADE, negro and tract he lives on in Wilkinson Co...to grandson COLUMBUS GRANADE, one negro Ben...to daughters ANN & SUSAN GRANADE, tracts I now live on, 235 A...to daughter RACHEL WALLS negro Anny...to daughter RHODA GEESLING, negro Sary...to son in law JOSEPH HOWELL, negro Judy...to 3 grandchildren CAROLINE ELLIS, AMANDA IVY & ADAM ELLIS, $20 each...MARY GRANADE has heretofore recd. $1300...son TIMOTHY GRANADE, Exr....25 Oct 1843...JAMES GRANADE (LS), Wit: ELIAS WILSON, JOHN F. JOHNSON, NICHOLAS C. BACON. Prov. 3 Nov 1845. Rec. 6 Nov 1845.

Pp. 158-159: L. W. & T. of ESTHER J. WRIGHT of Warren County, being of advanced age...to sister MARTHA SAMMONS, tract on waters of Middle Creek adj. THOMPSON & MAYS...29 Nov 1845. Wit: SAMUEL HALL SEN., STERLING G. CULPEPPER, S. R. CULPEPPER. Prov. 6 Jan 1846.

Pp. 160-162: L. W. & T. of ELIZABETH FLEWELLIN of Warren County...to sister SARAH PERSONS, $2000...to ELIABETH FLEWELLIN, daughter of my sister SARAH PERSONS, $1000...to WILLIAM SHIVERS SENR., $2000, for the use of ELIZABETH SHIVERS, wife of GEORGE W. C. SHIVERS and her children...to NICHOLAS W. PITTS, NESTOR PITTS & JOHN PITTS, FRANCES SHIVERS & NANCY BROWN, children of my sister MARTHA, $1200 each...to my sister REBECCA WHITEHEAD, $50 because she is wealthy not that I love her less...to ANN BOZEMON, daughter of my sister REBECCA WHITEHEAD, $2000... to the sons of my sister WHITEHEAD by her marriage with ALEXANDER SARSBY, $6000share and share alike...to MARIA FLEWELLIN, wife of THOMAS FLEWELLIN, $1000...to sister FRANCES DRAKE, $65000...to my sister LUCY BODY, $7500... to ALFORD BATTLE, son of my sister MARY, $50, not that I like him less but because he is already wealthy and only one child...to my sister MARYS grand child by her marriage with WILLIAM ARRINGTON a daughter now living with ALFORD BATTLE, $500...to the children of MARTHA SHARP by her first marriage with FORT, $200 to be equally divided among them...to MARYANN COLIER, $1000...to WILLIAM BATTLE, son of my sister MARY, $1000...to FREDERICK BATTLE, brother as above, $1000...to the children of LARKIN BATTLE, $1000...to NICHOLAS ARRINGTON, son of my sister MARY, $1000...to ELIZABETH BODDIE, daughter of my sister MARY...to THOMAS BATTLE son of my sister MARY, $1000...to ELIZABETH BODDIE, daughter of my sister MARY, negroes (named)...to THOMAS BATTLE, son of my sister MARY, negroes (named) ...to NESTOR & JOHN PITTS, negroes (named)...to JOHN H. DRAKE, FRANCES DRAKE and CALVIN DRAKE, negroes (named)...to MARYANN COLLIER, negroes (named)...to LAURENCE BATTLE, negroes (named)...to sister SARAH PERSONS, $1000 more...all my lands at the Court house in Warrenton to be sold and proceeds to the children of my sister REBECCA by her marriage with ALEXR SARSBY and the children of my sister LUCY......THOMAS BATTLE, Exr...19 Feb 1839...ELIZABETH FLEWELLIN (LS), Wit: JAMES A. CHAPMAN, CHAPMAN F. MADDUX, STODDARD W. SMITH.. "We the special Jury find that this paper contains the Will of ELIZABETH FLEWELLIN Decd & find the cost against the Caveators. JEREMIAH PERRYMAN, foreman. Rec. in 1846. The above will was executed at the March Term 1845. The caveat was overruled & it was carried to the Sup. Court.

Page 163: L. W. & T. of JAMES BULLOCK of Warren County...to SUSAN B. STEED, formerly SUSAN B. DANIEL niece of my wife, all personal and real estate...her husband and my friend WILLIAM P. STEED, Exr...21 Apr 1843... JAMES BULLOCH (LS), Wit: ELISHA BURSON, HILLERY LANGFORD, JOHN W. MADDOCK.

Prov. 6 July 1846.

Page 164: L. W. & T. of SARAH HEETH of Warren County...2nd item omitted
because it is illegal...3d item omitted by order of court...
balance of estate both real and persons be sold and divided among the 4
children: HENRY, JOHN, MARTHA(?) H. children and WILLIAM children...to
son HENRY HEATH, 1/4 part...to son JOHN HEETH 1/4 part...to son WILLIAM"s
children SARAH JANE & SUSAN ANN, 1/4...to son MATHA H. HEETH 5 children:
WILLIAM HENRY, CAROLINE ALISA, JOHN THOMAS, HARRIETT ELVIRA, SARAH ANN
1/4 part...to granddaughter SARAH JANE HEETH, one bed and furniture...
to son HENRY HEETH, Exr...3 Feb 1846...SARAH HEETH (X) (SEAL), Wit: FREDER-
ICK HAUTHORN, J. P. BENJAMIN A. HEETH. Prov. 7 Sept 1846.

Page 165: Blank.

Pp. 166-167: L. W. & T. of WILLIAM JONES of Warren County...to son HENRY
AUGUSTUS JONES, tract of land on which I now reside, 494 A
one lot in Appling County, 10 A in Hall County joining Gainesville &
slaves (named)...my daughter ELIZABETH THOMAS JONES, one bed, etc & slaves
(named)...daughter MARY SUSANNA HARPER, her husband JAMES N. HARPER...to
son HENRY AUGUSTUS, daughter MARY SUSANNA and daughter ELIZABETH THOMAS,
50 shares of Alabama City Stock...son HENRY AUGUSTUS JONES, DOCTOR
JAMES S. JONES and WILLIAM H. JONES, Esqr. of Richmond Co., Exrs...19 Jan
1843...WILLIAM JONES (SEAL), Wit: W. R. LOWE, RICHARD D. HAYS, JOHN MOORE.
Prov. 2 Nov 1846.

Page 168: L. W. & T. of WILLIAM BAKER of Warren County...my interest in
the estate of my sister ELIZABETH WILLIAMS and of my mother
MARTHA BAKER, shall be divided into five equal shares, four of which I
give to my wife CELIA BAKER and to my son GREEN BAKER, STEPHEN BAKER &
EDWIN BAKER in trust for my son JOHN BAKER...also Negro Seaborn...STODDARD
W. SMITH, Exr...WILLIAM BAKER, dated 1 Aug 1846, Wit: W. R. LOWE, ISAAC
L. ANDERSON, JOSEPH H. WRIGHT. Prov. 2 Nov 1846.

Pp. 169-171: L. W. & T. of JOHN HARRIS of Warren County...to my sister
ANNA MOODY, tract of land whereon she now resides, 50 A adj.
MEADOWS, BAILEY & WYNNE...to my niece CATHERINE MOODY, $150, when she
arrives at age 21 or marries...to brother EZEKIEL HARRIS, $275...to brother
THOMAS HARRIS, whatever amount of notes & account I hold against him...
to niece LUCINDA COOPER, the wife of THOMAS COOPER and her children, $300
...to friend and neighbour ABNER DARDEN, my library of books, maps and
Periodicals...to my niece MARY J. HARRIS (who lives with me), tract of
land I now live on, and tract lately purchased of THOMAS SIMMES, known
as the MICASA DARDEN tract 230 A, and both tracts adj. BAILEY, CHAPMAN,
& others...also to sd. MARY negroes (named)...negroes Bob, Nelson & Lewis
and 10 tracts of land (described) be sold...ABNER DARDEN, Exr...22 Dec 1846
...JOHN HARRIS (LS), Wit: JAMES WYNNE, HUGH WARD, WILLIAM F. DARDEN, JOHN
THOMPSON. Prov. 1 March 1847.

Page 172: L. W. & T. of AARON JACKSON of Warren County...to son SAMUEL,
JOHN, AARON & MANUEL JACKSON, one horse, etc. each...to my
daughters MARY, LYDIA, JANE, CATHERINE & CHARLOTTE JACKSON...to my 8 children MARY,JANE, SAMUEL, JOHN, CATHERINE, AARON, MANUEL & CHARLOTTE...
to the children of LYDIA TAYLOR, to wit: JAMES, ELIZABETH, AARON & WALKER
and all other children she may lawfully have...18 June 1840...AARON
JACKSON (LS), Wit: N. H. JONES, FELIX B. JONES (X), LEWIS JACKSON. Rec.
1847.

Page 173: L. W. & T. of LEVI McCRARY of Warren County...to brother JASPER
McCRARY, my shot gun and two chests...to LEVI McCRARY, son of
my brother ASA, $100...to brothers JASPER McCRARY, ISAAC McCRARY, EZRA
McCRARY, and ASA McCRARY, balance of estate...22 Apr 1845...LEVI McCRARY
(LS), Wit: NAPOLEON B. THOMAS, WILLIAM IVY (X), THOMAS JONES. Prov. 22
July 1847.

Page 174: L. W. & T. of JACOB ALLEN of Warren County...to wife and five
children: JAMES, JACOB, WILLIAM, MARY & JOSEPH the house I now
live in for a dwelling place until the youngest one is 21 years of age...
STODDARD W. SMITH, Exr...9 July 1847...JACOB ALLEN (LS), Wit: THOMAS P. F.
THREEWITS, AMON COBB, MATTHEW SHIELDS. Prov. 6 Sept 1847.

Pp. 175-176: L. W. & T. of DANIEL F. ADKINS of Warren County...29 Apr 1846
...to brother WILLIAM L. ADKINS of the State of Texas, negroes
(named), all notes, tract on Big Briar Creek in Columbia Co...to sister
MARY ANN ADKINS, negroes (named)...W. L. ADKINS of Texas, Exr....DANIEL F.
ADKINS (LS), Wit: AARON ADKINS, WILLIAM R. STORY, LAZARUS JACKSON. Prov.
3 May 1847.

Pp. 177-178: L. W. & T. of JILSON BERRY of Warren County being of advanced
age...to wife MARY with whom I have lived in the strictest
quiet for 35 years, negroes (named) 150 A, a part 6f which is cleared and
in cultivation...wife MARY, Extx...16 July 1847...JILSON BERRY (X) (LS),
Wit: JOHN J. PILCHER, JAMES PILCHER, NATHAN CULPEPPER. Prov. 1 Nov 1847.
Rec. 1847.

Pp. 178-179: L. W. & T. of AMOS JOHNSON of Warren County...real & personal
estate to be kept in the hands of wife MARTHA M. JOHNSON, for
rearing and support of children...lot belonging to me in Lumpkin Co...
wife and STODDARD W. SMITH, Exrs...25 Oct 1847...AMOS JOHNSON (LS), Wit:
WM. L. WESTON, W .W. SWAIN, JAMES STONESTREET (X). Prov. 6 Dec 1847.

Pp. 180-181: L. W. & T. of JOHN WILSON of Warren County, being of advanced
age...to son DAVID WILSON, what I have already given him and
negro Mariah...two slaves for benefit of my daughter SARAH SCOTT, I will
to JOHN SCOTT in trust for sold and separate use of my daughter SARAH,
not to be controlled by her husband WILLIAM SCOTT...to son ELIAS WILSON,
negro man Randle and tract in Lee County...to daughter REBECCA DRANE, and
her children Negroes (named)...to daughter ELIZABETH WILSON, negro Fanny,
& others (named) and land in Columbia County on Todd branch...heirs:
SARAH SCOTT, ELIAS WILSON, REBECCA DRANE and JOEL WILSON...son ELIAS
Exr...24 Apt 1846...JOHN WILSON (X) (LS), Wit: JOHN F. JOHNSON, MARION
IVEY, NICHOLAS C. BACON. Prov. 1 March 1847.

Pp. 182-184: L. W. & T. of HENDLEY JONES of Warren County, being far advanced in life...wife MARY JONES all property...to my youngest son THOMAS J. JONES, negro David...my children: BENJAMIN JONES, FRAN-
CIS JONES, & WILLIS P. JONES...daughter DRUCILLA HARDAWAY...GILLEY
HILSON(daughter?)...to WILLIAM JONES, $1200 in land...to son in law MAT-
THEW HALL, negro value at $400...to BAKER JONES...to WALKER JONES...to
WILLIAM S. LIGHTFOOT...to son in law MIDDLETON HILSON...to OCAR P. JONES...
to grandchildren WILLIAM HALL, MARY JANE HALL and JAMES MADISON HALL,
children of my daughter PRISCILLA HALL decd., $150 when they arrive of age
...unto my grand Daughter living with me SUSAN JONES, daughter of my son
WALKER JONES, $100...to granddaughter TEMPERANCE HILSON, $100...to OSCAR
JONES...wife MARY, Exrs with friend ADAM JONES...15 Sept 1847...HENLY
JONES (SEAL), Wit: ADAM JONES, JASPER McCRARY, TERAH W. FOWLER. Prov. 1
May 1848.

Pp. 185-187: L. W. & T. of THOMAS MADDUX of Warren County...to wife MARY
MADDUX, 4 negroes (named), also land on N side long branch,
adj. PATRICK N. MADDUX, on the Shoal Road, rocky Comfort Creek...daughter
JOICY WOODING...children: PATRICK N. MADDUX, CHAPMAN F. MADDUX, LAVINIA
BUTTS, DAVID N. MADDUX, LUCIOUS W. MADDUX...tract in Gwinnett Co., Early
Co., drawn by JOHN MASH also one in Early Co., drawn by JOICY NEFL...11
Dec 1847...THOMAS MADDUX (SEAL), Wit: AUGUSTUS BEALL, COLUMBUS C. CODY,
JESSE M. ROBERTS, J. I. C. Prov. 4 Sept 1848. Rec. 11 Sept 1848.

Page 188: L. W. & T. of JUDITH CLEARY of Warren Co....a head and foot
stone to my grave...to the Church of the Purification of the B.
V., Locust Grove, Warren County, $100, also to the contingent fund of
said church, $5...to Rev. PETER WAHLEN, pastor of said church, $20 and
the balance of said estate to my son ANDREW WHOLAHAN...HUGH WARD, Exr...
19 Feb 1849...JUDITH CLEARY (X) (LS), Wit: ELISHA E. CARY, BRIEN MAGUIRE,
MARGARET MANAHY. Prov. 5 March 1846. Rec. May 1849.

Page 189: L. W. & T. of ANNA MOODY of Warren County...daughter CATHERINE,
all household furniture, etc...remainder to be divided among
my children...14 Nov 1848...ANNA MOODY (X), Wit: ABNER DARDEN, F. W.
HLFRIEND(?), WILLIAM LOVE. Prov. May 1849.

Pp. 190-191: L. W. & T. of THOMAS RIVERS of Warren County, being of ad-

vanced age...to wife MARY with whom I have lived in quietness for a great
while, a certain portion of the plantation whereon I now live...the remain-
der divided into 6 shares and one share each to my son WILLIAM, daughter
HARRIETT MEGAHEE, daughter SUSAN RABORN, son THOMAS J. RIVERS, son
JOHN F. RIVERS, son FRANCIS M. RIVERS...sons JOHN & FRANCIS, Exrs...13
March 1847...THOS RIVERS (LS), Wit: H. N. WALKER, CARTER NEWSOME, MAYBERRY
HOWELL. Prov. 3 Sept 1849. Rec. Sept 8th 1849.

Pp. 191-192: L. W. & T. of SION HILL...to wife SUSAN HILL, all property
until the youngest child becomes of age, and then an equal
division between each of the children...wife, Extx...13 Feb 1839...SION
HILL (SEAL), Wit: RICHARD V. ASBURY, JESSE M. ELLIOTT, ELISHA P SMALLWOOD
(X).Prov. 14 Jan 1850. Rec. 28 Jan 1850.

Pp. 192-193: L. W. & T. of JOHN W. JACKSON of Warren County...sons AARON,
NATHAN & THOMAS...20 Feb 1846...son LEWIS JACKSON, $1...son
AARON, Exr...JOHN W. JACKSON (X) (LS), Wit: NATHANIEL PARHAM, SAMUEL F.
JACKSON, JOS. W. THOMAS. Rec. 1850.

Pp. 193-194: L. W. & T. of SARAH BAREFIELD alias SARAH WILDER of Warren
County...to sister MARY WYNNE, $5...to brother WILLIAM
WILDER, $25...to brother SOLOMON WILDER, $25...to brother CHARLES WILDER,
$25...to sister NANCY CLOUD, two negroes (named)...to niece MAY FALL, 2
negroes (named)...tract of land on watters of Harts Creek, adj. JERRY
PERRY, CHARLES WILDER & others 249 A also the one half of the mill and
mill lot 8A, divided between ELIZABETH HALL, CHARLES WILDER, NANCY
CLOUD & heirs of SOLOMON WILDER...brother CHARLES, Exr...9 Apr 1838....
SARAH BAREFIELD Alias SARAH WILDER (X), Wit: SARAH STONE, MATILDA TORRENCE,
SEPTIMUS TORRENCE. (No prov. or rec. date given.)

Pp. 195-196: L. W. & T. of JEREMIAH MAY of Warren County...to wife LYDIA
MAY, the tract of land on which I now live, 130 A, then to
my son JOHN N. MAY...to son ALLEN MAY, 60 A adj. STEPHEN JONES, THOMAS L.
VEAZY & others...daughter BASHA BURNETT & WILLIAM HILLSON, children begot-
ten by me my present wife before marriage with her and LOUISIANNA GREEN,
JOHN N. & ALLEN MAY...son STEWART J. MAY & daughter CINNA MAY...daughter
SPICY MAY...JEREMIAH MAY (X) (LS), 8th May 1850. Wit: JESSE M. JONES,
STEPHEN JONES, THOMAS J. VEAZY."(See Minutes of Court July Term 1850."

Pp. 196-198: L. W. & T. of BENJAMIN CRENSHAW of Warren County...to wife
POLLY CRENSHAW, negroes (named), all the lands whereon we
now live containing 1000 A...to my daughter ANN ALLEN, negroes (named)...
to my daughter ELIZABETH BAKER, negroes (named)...to my daughter MARY
ALLEN, negroes (named)...to my grandchildren, children of my son BENJAMIN
CRENSHAW decd., three negroes and lot in Early County, #441, 21st dist.,
250 A...to son HENRY CRENSHAW, negroes (named)...to son JOSEPH CRENSHAW,
negroes (named)...to grandson BENJAMIN BECKWITH, tract of land on which
he now lives in Taliagerro Co., 116 A and $400...to my granddaughter
MARY ANN DARDEN, three negroes, and then to be divided among ELISHA
ALLENS children and her children by ELBERT DARDEN...250 A and a fractional
survey in the cherokee purchase drawn by JOSEPH ALLEN, be sold...LINTON
STEVENS, Esq. of Crawfordville, Exr...13 June 1850...BENJAMIN CRENSHAW
(SEAL), Wit: JETHRO DARDEN, JAMES WYNNE, HOWEL HIGHT. Prov. 8 July 1850.
Rec. July 1850.

Pp. 198-199: L. W. & T. of WILLIAM HILL of Warren County, being advanced
age...to my daughter WINIFRED LESTER, negro & plantation
whereon I now reside 383 A known as the STANBACK place...to my daughter
VIRGINIA HUBERT, $350...remainder divided among my son WADE, the children
of my deceased ROBT HILL, daughter WINIFRED LESTER, VIRGINIA HUBERT & the
children of NANCY BUTT...friends JAMES THOMAS & THOMAS L. LATIMER, Exrs...
29 Oct 1847.WILLIAM HILL (SEAL), Wit: JOHN T. JONES, JOHN R. EVANS, THOS
L. LATIMER. Prov. 2 Sept 1850. Rec. Sept. 1850.

Pp. 199-201: L. W. & T. of MARCIA ANN CRETIN, of Warren County...to my
daughter SUSAN BEAMAN, the plantation whereon I now reside
on the waters of Beaverdam Creek, & negroes (named)...to my daughter
ELIZABETH MATILDA WILKINSON, negro Malinda & her 3 children...to my daughter LOUISA SOPHIA THOMPSON, negroes (named)...to my great granddaughter
MARTHA ELIZABETH GRIFFIN, negroes (named)...to the REV. PETER WHELAN, for

the use of the parsonage one bedstead & bedding...to each of my grandsons
RICHARD STOKES, JOHN STOKES & JOHN CRETIN, $1 each...grandsons JAMES WILK-
INSON & JOHN THOMPSON, Exrs...22 June 1850...MARCIA ANN CRETIN (LS), Wit:
JOHN HARTY, E. W. ALFRIEND, J. McMAHON. Prov. 2 Sept 1850. Rec. Sept 1850.

Pp. 201-202: L. W. & T. of GEORGE M. HUFF of Warren County...to wife UNITY
            HUFF, all estate...to son JONATHAN J. G. HUFF, $200...to
daughter NANCY HUFF negro Frances...3 Dec 1850...GEORGE M. HUFF (X) (SEAL),
Wit" D. H. HOBBS, HUMPHREY HOOD (X), JONATHAN HUFF (=). Prov. 6 Jan 1851.
Rec. 14 Jan 1851.

Pp. 203-204: Warren County...deed of gift & will...5 Sept 1844...between
            RHODA HARRIS of one part and ELIHARRIS the younger son of
said RHODA...for natural love & affection negroes (named); part of said
RHODA's interest in the estate of NATHAN HARRIS, decd., which lies between
HENRY P. HARRIS & WILLIAM HARRIS & ISAAC HARRIS...to son HENRY P. HARRIS,
tract where I now live...son ISAAC HARRIS, HENRY P. HARRIS & WILLIAM HARRIS
...RHODA HARRIS (X) (LS), Wit: HENRY P. HARRIS, WM. L. HARRIS, JOHN LAND.
Rec. 1850. N. B. The above & foregoing Deed of Gift & Will was decided
on in Superior Court October Term 1850. See records of said court for
explanation. See also minutes of court of ordinary for Sept term 1850.

Pp. 204-205: L. W. & T. of ELIJAH CONNER SR., of Warren County...to son
            ELIJAH CONNER, JR., living with me and taking care of me in
my old age...the whole of my estate..20 Sept 1849...ELIJAH CONNER (X)
(SEAL), Wit: THOMAS J. CHULY, ROBERT E. MILLER, ADAM JONES SR. Prov. 3
March 1851.

Pp. 205-206: L. W. & T. of ALFRED WALDEN 30 Dec 1850...wife MARY WALDIN
            to have all property...then to be equally divided among the
children...ALFRED WALDEN (LS), Wit: AMOS WALDEN, LARKIN WILCHER, J. P.
Prov. 5 May 1851. Rec. 8 May 1851.

Pp. 206-207: L. W. & T. of THOMAS NORRIS of Warren County...to my son
            JAMES NORRIS, one iron grey Horse...to son SOLOMON NORRIS,
one grey colt...to son JOHN NORRIS, one sorrel colt...to my beloved SUSAN
NORRIS, all lands, negroes, etc......my children: JAMES NORRIS, SEALY
NORRIS, CHARITY NORRIS now CHARITY JONES, SOLOMON NORRIS, MARY NORRIS,
JOHN NORRIS & NANCY NORRIS...wife SUSAN, Extx...5 Jan 185_...THOMAS
NORRIS (X) Wit: ELISHA PERRYMAN, DAVID E. HODO, HAZEAL G. BURSON. Prov.
5 May 1851. Rec. 5 May 1851.

Pp. 208-209: L. W. & T. of JOHN LINN of Warren County...to my daughter
            NANCY RAINWATER, wife of SOLOMON RAINWATER, equal portion
of my estate...785 A and about 13 negroes to wife MILLY, then divided
amongst my five children JAMES S., DRUCILLA ANN, LUCRETIA, JOSEPH C. ,
SARAH ANN & EMILY GABRIELLA...26 Mar 1851...JOHN LINN (LS), Wit: GEORGE
W. DICKSON, JAMES A. SHIVERS, EDWARD W. POTTS. Prov. July term 1851. Rec
7 July 1851.

Pp. 210-211: L. W. & T. of SEABORN JOHNSON of Warren County, being of
            Middle age...to wife NANCY with whom I have lived in the
strictest quiet for two years, my lot of land in Warren County where I
now live, 270 A & negroes (names and ages given)...to my child which my
wife is now pregnant with...my brother AMOS JOHNSON and friend WILLIAM G.
SCRUGGS, Exrs...15 May 1851...SEABORN JOHNSON (LS), Wit: WILLIAM JOHNSON.
JOHN C. REESE, ASA JOHNSON, TILLMAN POOL. Prov. 7 July 1851. Rec. 9 July
1851.

Pp. 212-214: L. W. & T. of BARNARD W. FICKLIN of Warren County...to my
            granddaughter ADELINE GIBSON, $400...to my grand daughter
ELLEN LYNCH...to the children of THOMAS J. & CARLINE WHEELER, each $200...
the balance to my daughter ADELINE LYNCH, wife of DR. EDWARD F. LYNCH
...to the children of WINGFIELD & EMELINE WRIGHT (the later deceased)...
to the children of HENRY & ELIZA GIBSON (the later now deceased)...unto
DR. AUGUSTUS C. ROGERS in trust for his wife REBECCA, $100...friends
THOMAS P. F. THREEWITS & ARCHIBALD M. JACKSON, Exrs...14 June 1851...B. W.
FICKLING. Provn 5 Aug 1851. Codicil: to grandson JAMES WRIGHT, son of
WINGFIELD WRIGHT, negro (named)...1 July 1851...B. W. FICKLING, Wit:
JAMES A SHIVERS, WILLIAM H. SMITH, EDWARD H. POTTS(?). Rec. 8 Aug 1851

Pp. 215-216: L. W. & T. of NANCY THOMPSON of Warren County, widow of
NATHANIEL THOMPSON....estate divided into equal shares and
distributed as follows: to sons BENJAMIN THOMPSON, STEPHEN THOMPSON,
NATHANIEL THOMPSON, BELL THOMPSON, & POLHILL THOMPSON each one share...
to my daughter MARY GIBSON, her children THOMAS C. GIBSON, EHNRY Z. GIBSON
& WILLIAM B. GIBSON...son BELL, Exr...26 Sept 1845...NANCY THOMPSON (X)
Wit: EDWARD CODY, GEORGE W. HARDAWAY, STODDARD W. SMITH. Prov. 1 Sept
1851 . Rec. 5 Sept 1851.

Pp. 217-218: L. W. & T. of JAMES TODD of Warren County...to son HENRY TODD
negroes (names and ages given)...to son JOHN M. C. TODD,
negroes...to son JAMES N. TODD, all the land in Warren County & negroes...
to son JESSE B. TODD, negroes...to grandchildren, the children of my
daughter NANCY decd be taken care of by my son JAMES H. TODD viz. my
grandson JOHN REESE, ELIZABETH my grand daughter, and grandson JFSSE PEESE
when the youngest comes of age...to my son WILLIAM TODDS children, $5...
15 Apr 1851...JAMES TODD (X), Wit: WILLIAM G. SCRUGGS, MARCUS A. L. WIL-
SON, SETH WILSON. Rec. 1 Sept 1851.

Pp. 219-222: L. W. & T. of JOHN SWINT SENR of Warren County...to wife
RACHAEL SWINT with whom I have lived in peace and harmony
for upwards of 30 years, tract I now live on & negroes (named)...to my
daughter LUCY...all my children: JOHN SWINT JR., WILLIAM SWINT, BASDALE
SWINT, MARY MONTGOMERY, MARTHA STORY, LUCY ANN SWINT...land in Irwin Co....
to son JOHN SWINT JR., 100 A adj. JOHN SWINT, RHODA HARRIS, and 2 negroes
...to son BASDALE, tract adj. tract I now live on...to daughter MARTHA
STOREY, negroes (named)...8 Nov 1847...JOHN SWINT SENR (X) (LS), Wit:
ADAM JONES, WILEY CENTER, CEARO GRIBSON. Prov. 13 Oct 1851. Rec. 24 Oct
185.

Pp. 222-225: The new act to carry into effect the Amended
Constitution of the state in reference to the ordinari's of
said state and for other purposes.

L. W. & T. of CHARLES WILDER of Warren County...all negroes of sufficient
discretion to choose their masters...my brothers WILLIAM & SOLOMON WILDER
...each negro five good suits of clothing...to my nephew RABRUN M. WILDER,
228 A that tract on which my Brother WILLIAM WILDER formerly lived, until
the youngest child of my Bro. SOLOMON & WILLIAM WILDER may come of age...
my nephew AUGUSTUS D. WILDER...to sell to SAMUEL HALL, MARION BROWN or
JOEL CLOUD...my brothers WILLIAM WILDER, SOLOMON WILDER, NANCY CLOUD,
& ELIZABETH HALL each one dollar and no other part...friend and neighbour
KINDLE McTYRE & WILLIAM GIBSON, Exrs...17 Jan 1852...CHARLES WILDER (LS),
Wit: SAMUEL A. GEESLING, JOSHUA H. GEESLING, W. G. DUCKWORTH.   Proven
Feb. term 1852. Rec. 13 Feb 1852.
This last will Recorded namely Charles Wilders will has bin Transcribed
and Recorded in a new book...May 20th 1842.

END

THE FIRST MINUTE BOOK - WARREN INFERIOR COURT

The Inferior Court handled or had jurisdiction of all estates in Georgia until 1852 when the office of Ordinary in each county was created and estates, guardianships, wills, marriage licenses, and such matters were transferred to that office where they have been since. The Inferior Court in its original jurisdiction, had in addition to the just mentioned matters, jurisdiction over all county affairs including the levying of taxes, opening and closing and maintenance of public roads, and other duties now performed by the Boards of County Commissioners. The Court also had the jurisdiction over suits on notes, accounts and c., and other civil cases similar to the jurisdiction now exercised by County Courts. The Inferior Court had its own clerk (usually the same person who was Clerk of the Superior Court.) The Clerk was required to keep two sets of minutes, one of which dealt with estates and orphans and guardianships, and the other with county affairs, including judgments rendered in civil suits. The following is an abstract of the first Minute Book dealing with estates, dating from 1794 and extending until 1807. The pages were unnumbered. The date given at the commencement of each item or paragraph is that of the date of the minutes:

Sept. 20, 1794 - The will of THOMAS DRAKE was proved by the oath of JAMES ROBISON and admitted to probate.

Oct. 3, 1794 - Letters of administration with the will annexed were granted HHABUKKUK WRIGHT on the estate of ADAM HILL, deceased.

May 10, 1795 - The will of HARDY WESTER was admitted to probate, and FANNIE WESTER and SAMPSON IVEY qualified as executors of same.

May 10, 1795 - PHOEBE HILL applied for letters of dismission as Admx. on the estate of THOMAS HILL, deceased.

June 9, 1795 - SAMUEL SLOCUMB, Admr. of estate of SETH SLOCLUMB, applied for letters dismissory.

Aug. 12, 1795 - ANNA TERRELL JOHNSTON applies for letters of administration on estate of MALCOLM JOHNSTON. Application was grated Sept. 12, 1795.

Oct. __, 1795 - PEARSON YOUNG applies for administration on the estate of ROBERT BUR___ (torn off and lost). Same was granted Dec. 15, 1795. JACOB YOUNG, surety on administrator's bond.

Nov. 9, 1795 - The will of GAHAZI DAVIS, alias SHOCKLEY, was proved by the testimony of PETER HODO, Esq., one of the subscribing witnesses and admitted to probate. REUBIN MCGEE qualified as executor.

Sept. 7, 1795 - SAMUEL MOORE's will was duly proven and admitted to probate. OLIVE MOORE and JODA NEWSOM qualified as executors, Dec. 18, 1795.

Feb. 16, 1795 - SARAH HILL applies for letters of administration on the estate of JOSHUA HILL, deceased. Adam Jones and WYATT BONNER to be securities of the administratrix' bond.

Feb. 1, 1796 - The will of NATHANIEL HOOD was proved on the oaths of the subscribing witnesses, WILLIAM HARDIN and SAMPSON IVY.

Jan. 2, 1797 - The will of GEORGE MEDLOCK was proved by the testimony of JAMES TAYLOR and GEORGE TAYLOR, subscribing witnesses, and letters testamentary ordered to issue to GEO. MEDLOCK (JR.).

Feb. 16, 1797 - JANE VAUGHN applied for letters of administration on the estate of ALEXANDER VAUGHN (or VAUGHAN). Same was later granted, and SAMUEL ALEXANDER accepted as surety on her bond.

May 27, 1797 - Michael Burkhalter applies for letters of administration on estate of DAVID NEWSOM. Same was duly granted and BASIL WRIGHT and STERLING GARDNER accepted as securities on the administrator's bond.

July 18, 1797 - WILLIAM COCKS and SALLY THREEWITS apply for administration on estate of JOEL THREEWITS. Duly granted and THOMAS COCKS and TURNER PERSONS, accepted as sureties on bond.

July 28, 1797 - SARAH NIBB WYNNE and BENJAMIN WYNNE apply for letters of administration of JOHN WYNN's estate. Duly granted, WILLIAM ROBERSON surety on their bond.

Nov. 17, 1797 - DIXON PERRYMAN and JAMES DOUGLAS apply for administration on estate of REV. JEPTHA VINING. JAMES DOUGLAS only was appointed, and HARMON PERRYMAN and JOSHUA VINING were accepted as securities on his bond.

Dec. 26, 1797 - CASSANDRA MONTRAY applied for letters testamentary on the will of her deceased father, JOHN MONTRAY.

Dec. 29, 1797 - JOHN TRAVIS applied for letters testementary on the will of THOMAS SMITH, deceased, and offered the same for probate. It was proved on the oath of JONES KENDRICK and admitted to probate.

Apr. 13, 1798 - MARY COOPER applies for administration on the estate of JAMES COOPER, deceased, and same was granted. HARMON WILKINSON and PETER CASTLEBERRY, sureties on her bond.

April 26, 1798 - ELIZABETH GOODWIN applies for letters of administration on estate of PETER GOODWIN, dec'd. Duly granted.

June 4, 1798 - JESSE KITCHEN applies for letters testamentary on will of ROBERT HINTON and offered the will for probate. It was proven on oaths of ELISHA HERT and AMBROSE EDMONDSON, subscribing witnesses. The latter was accepted as surety on the administrator's bond.

Oct. 20, 1798 - THOMAS JONES applies for letters of administration with the will annexed on estate of WINNEY PINSON. A caveat was filed Dec. 4, 1798 by JOHN KELLY, and he was appointed with BENJ. MITCHELL and SOLOMON NEWSOM, sureties.

Dec. 6, 1798 - JOHN VANCE applies for letters of administration on the estate of JAMES VANCE, dec'd. Same was granted, with Milby McGree, surety on bond. Inventory and Appraisement in this matter was filed April 10, 1799.

Dec. 14, 1798 - Letters testamentary were ordered granted to DEBERA CHAPMAN as executrix of the will of JOHN CHAPMAN, and the will admitted to probate it being proven by oath of BENJAMIN CHAPMAN, a subscribing witness.

March 4, 1798 - JOHN MATTHEWS was granted letters testamentary as executor on the will of BURRELL BROWN, the will being proven by the oath of LEROY MINIS, a subscribing witness, and admitted to probate.

Jan. 10, 1799 - SHADERICK FLUWELLIN, Executor of the will of EPHRIAM KING, dec'd., applied for letters dismissory. Same was granted March 2, 1799.

Apr. 24, 1799 - PHERIBY COOK and JONATHAN HAGERTY apply for administration on estate of ISAAC COOK, dec'd.

July 18, 1799 - JONATHAN HAGERTY applied for guardianship of PHERIBY and CELETHY COOK, orphans of ISAAC COOK, EDWARD HILL security on bond, and was duly appointed.

Apr. 29, 1799 - WILLIAM STITH JR., applies for administration on estate of WILLIAM STITH, SR., and was duly appointed.

May 16, 1799 - FERGUS (FERGUSON?) LINN applies for administration on estate of JOHN LINN. Same was granted July 8, 1799, and DANIEL MCCOWAN and THOMAS JONES accepted as sureties on bond.

April 20, 1799 - FREDERICK DANIEL applies for administration on estate of JOHN THOMAS, and was duly granted July 18, 1799, with WM. MIMS, surety.

May 16, 1799 - SOPHIA TRENT applies for administration on estate of JOHN TRENT, deceased, and was appointed July 18, 1799.

May 27, 1799 - SUSANNAH BUTLER applied for administration on estate of NOBLE BUTLER, dec'd., and she was appointed July 18, 1799, with ___ BEALL and ENOS BUTLER, sureties on her bond.

June 3, 1799 - RICHARD BEASLEY and WILLIAM EARNEST, the duly nominated executors of the will of JAMES BEASLEY, SR., offered the will for probate, and it was proven by oaths of WILLIAM HOWARD and JAMES BEASLEY, and ordered recorded; and they were appointed executors of the will.

July 1, 1799 - The will of HENRY MCNIECE, deceased, was proven by the oath of EDMOND HAYS, a subscribing witness, and admitted to record. No executor was mentioned in the minutes. Note: This will is not recorded in the will book.

Dec. 24, 1799 - DAVID NEAL and SAMUEL NEAL apply for administration on estate of THOMAS NEAL, dec'd. They were appointed Feb. 11, 1800, JAMES MCCARAN? and JOSEPH DUCKWORTH, sureties on their bond.

Nov. 29, 1799 - LYDIA HALL and RICHARD B. FLETCHER, Esq., apply for letters testamentary on the will of LIEUT. THOMAS HALL, dec'd. The will was proven by the testimony of DANIEL SAUNDERS and MARYANN WILKINS, subscribing witnesses, and ordered recorded.

July 10, 1800 - JOHN HORN, executor of will of JACOB HORN, was granted letters of dismission.

Feb. 10, 1800 - LYDIA NAPPER (NAPIER?) applied for letters of administration with the will annexed on will of JAMES NAPPER (NAPIER?).

Feb. 10, 1800 - ISAAC BURSON applies for letters of administration on estate of DAVID DAVIS, and was duly appointed.

Feb. 11, 1800 - A. PERSONS and LITTLEBERRY WALKER apply for administration on estate of JOEL WALKER, and were duly appointed, with NICHOLAS WILLIAMS, RICHARD HEATH and AMOS PERSONS, securities on bond.

Feb. 11, 1800 - JONATHAN HAGERTY was appointed Admr. of estate of ISAAC COOK, dec'd., with EDWARD HILL, surety on his bond.

April 7, 1800 - JOSHUA BUTT, SR. applies for administration on estate of JOSHUA BUTT, JR.

April 7, 1800 - FRANCES HILL, Admx. of RICHARD HILL, dec'd., applies for letters dismissory.

March 18, 1800 - LYDIA HEARTFIELD applies for administration on estate of GEORGE HEARTFIELD. She was appointed Aug. 11, 1800, BENJAMIN HOWARD, surety on bond.

Aug. 11, 1800 - JOHN TRAVIS, Executor of will of THOMAS SMITH, was granted letters of dismission.

Aug. 11, 1800 - REUBIN MCGEE, Executor of will of GAHAZI DAVIS, applied for letters dismissory.

Aug. 11, 1800 - ALEXANDER FLUWELLIN, Admr. of BETTY FLUWELLIN estate, applies for letters dismissory.

Aug. 25, 1800 - RADFORD and JOHN BUTTS apply for administration on the estate of JOSHUA BUTTS, dec'd. They were appointed Oct. 6, 1800, with SOLOMON SLATTER and GEORGE PARUM (PARHAM?) as sureties on their bond.

Sept. 24, 1800 - WILLIAM BERRY and JAMES MITCHELL were appointed temporary administrators on estate of ABNER MITCHELL, deceased. Permanent letters of administration were granted ROBERT RUTHERFORD, Apr. 28, 1801. Inventory of estate filed April 28, 1801. ROBERT ABERCROMBIE and HENRY SHELTON, sureties on bond.

Feb. 11, 1801 - LYDIA HARTFIELD, Admx. of estate of GEORGE HARTFIELD, was granted letters dismissory.

Oct. 17, 1800 - RICHARD CASTLEBERRY and WILLIAM NEWMAN were granted letters of dismission from their administration of SAMUEL NEWMAN estate.

Nov. 9, 1800 - ASA WRIGHT applied for administration on estate of SAMUEL WRIGHT, deceased. He was appointed June 8, 1801, with JOHNSTON WRIGHT and BLAKE PEARCY, sureties on his bond.

Nov. 19, 1800 - REBECCA KEMP applied for administration on estate of HIPPLE (or NIPPLE) KEMP, dec'd. She was appointed Feb. 9, 1801, with SETH WOLSEY surety on her bond as Admx.

Dec. 4, 1800 - SARAH ROSE and EDMOND ROSE apply for administration on estate of WILLIAM ROSE, dec'd. They were appointed Feb. 9, 1801, with SHADRICK FLUWELLIN, surety on their bond.

Aug. 10, 1801 - FRANCES HILL, Executrix of HENRY HILL estate, was granted letters dismissory.

Feb. 9, 1801 - The will of THOMAS HILSON, dec'd., was proven by the oath of THOMAS PHILLIPS, a subscribing witness, and admitted to record. Note: This will does not appear of record in the will book.

Feb. 9, 1801 - The will of GEORGE MEDLOCK, dec'd. was proved by the oath of GEORGE TAYLOR, a subscribing witness, and admitted to record.

Feb. 9, 1801 - REUBIN BARROW applies for administration on estate of JAMES BARROW, dec'd. He was appointed June 8, 1801, DAVID NEWSOM, surety on bond.

Feb. 10, 1801 - COL. ROBERT ABERCROMBIE and JOSEPH HOWELL apply for administration on estate of ARCHIBALD KINSEY and were duly appointed; MATTHEW HUBERT and JAMES JONES sureties on bond.

Aug. 2, 1801 - JACKY DAVENPORT was granted letters dismissory from his administration of the MALCOLM JOHNSTON estate.

March 1, 1801 - DAVID HUBERT applies for administration on estate of JOHN COOK, dec'd. He was appointed June 8, 1801, with JOSEPH BOWER and ABNER FLUWELLIN, sureties on his bond.

March 10, 1801 - PATTY NEAL applies for admn. on estate of SAMUEL NEAL dec'd., and was appointed Aug. 10, 1801, JAMES MCCORMACK, surety on her bond. Note: The minutes later show that PATTY NEAL'S bondsman, MC-CORMACK, was released at his request as her surety, and she being unable to furnish new bond, DAVID NEAL was appointed Amr., March 9, 1803.

Jan. 10, 1801 - The will of THOMAS DOVE as proven by the oaths of DAVID DOVE and THOMAS DOVE, and admitted to probate.

Dec. 1, 1801 - JACOB BALL applies for administration on estate of ELI BULL, and was appointed Feb. 9, 1802, M. HARDIN, JESSE BULL, sureties.

April 14, 1801 - NANCY BURSON and ISAAC BURSON apply for administration on estate of JONATHAN BURSON, dec'd. They were appointed Aug. 11, 1801, sureties on their bond, JOHN ENGLISH, MICHAEL CODY.

Jan. 1, 1802 - ZILPHIA HOGINS and JAMES HOGINS apply for administration on estate of ROBERT HOGINS, dec'd.

Nov. 2, 1801 - ROBERT ABERCROMBIE applies for administration on estate of WILLIAM C. ABERCROMBIE, and was appointed Feb. 10, 1802; WILLIAM FLOURNOY and M. HUBERT, sureties on bond.

Dec. 1, 1801 - HARDY SMITH applies for administration of estate of JAMES NAPPER (NAPIER). On Feb. 7, 1802, LYDIA NAPIER and SAMUEL RIDGEDALE were appointed administrators with the will annexed. SOLOMON NEWSOM SR., and ELISHA BROWN were accepted as sureties on their bond.

Jan. 20, 1802 - SAMUEL WINSLETT and JOHN WILLIAMS apply for administration on estate of JOHN CARSON, and were appointed May 3, 1802; sureties on bond, SOLOMON LOCKETT, JOSIAH BEALL, MARK HARDIN, HOWELL HIGHT.

Jan. 23, 1802 - WILLIAM FLOURNOY applies for letters of administration on estate of JACOB FLOURNOY, and was appointed Feb. 19, 1802; ROBERT ABERCROMBIE and JOHN B. FLOURNOY, sureties on his bond.

Feb. 19, 1802 - ELIZABETH TODD and JOB TODD apply for Admn. of estate of HARDY TODD with the will annexed, and offered the will for probate which was proved.

Feb. 10, 1802 - POLLY MCKINNEY offered the will of MOSES MCKINNEY for probate, and it was admitted to record; she qualified as Executrix of same.

March 1, 1802 - Letters Testamentary were granted on the will of WILLIAM KENDALL, dec'd., to JEREMIAH KENDALL and HENRY KENDALL and PHILLIP BRANTLEY, as executors, and they were qualified, and the will was admitted to probate.

Feb. 9, 1802 - MARY BURSON and JOSEPH BURSON offered the will of JOSEPH BURSON for probate and it was duly proven, and they qualified as executors.

March 9, 1802 - PRESLEY SPINKS applies for administration on estate of BENJAMIN DICKEN, dec'd., with the will annexed. A caveat (objections) was filed by RICHARD SNIPES in behalf of himself and LEWIS DICKEN.

March 2, 1802 - The will of PHILLIP POOL, deceased, was duly probated and letters testementary ordered to issue to MARY POOL and HENRY GRAYBILL, executors.

March 2, 1802 - HENRY GRAYBILL was granted letters dismissory from his administration of the JAMES HILTON estate.

March 2, 1802 - Letters dismissory were ordered to issue to MATTHEW HUBERT and DAVID HUBERT and JOHN RUTHERFORD on their administration of the estate of BENJAMIN HUBERT, deceased.

May 3, 1802 - The will of GEORGE COOPER was duly proven by the oath of JAMES FILLINGIM, one of the subscribing witnesses.

May 3, 1802 - The will of DAVID DAVIS, dec'd., was duly proven by the oath of ROBERT MOSES, a subscribing witness, and it was ordered recorded.

May 3, 1802 - ELIZABETH MYRICK applies for letters of admn. on estate of OWEN MYRICK, dec'd. She was appointed Feb. 15, 1804; THOMAS EDMONDS and SEPTIMUS WEATHERBY, sureties on her bond.

Feb. 24, 1802 - ELIZABETH MURPHY applied for administration on estate of EDWARD MURPHY, dec'd. She was appointed June 1, 1802; JOHN RUSHING and JOHN WILSON, securities on her bond.

March 29, 1802 - MARGARET HOLLADAY applied for letters of admn. on estate of AMBROSE HOLLADAY. On May 3, 1802, she with ELIJAH WORTHEN were appointed Admrs. with JAMES HARVILL, WILLIAM HARVILL and JOSEPH HARVILL, sureties on bond.

Aug. 5, 1802 - THOMAS HUTCHINS applies for administration on estate of JOHN HUTCHINS, and was appointed Feb. 15, 1803; SOLOMON THOMPSON and JOEL HEATH, sureties on his bond.

June 10, 1802 - JOHN MATTHEWS, Esq., applies for letters of administration on estate of STEPHEN FLUWELLIN, dec'd. HENRY KENDALL, JESSE MATTHEWS, sureties.

Jan. 13, 1803 - FREDERICK NEWSOM applies for administration on estate of DAVID NUSOM (NEWSOM) deceased.

Jan. 13, 1803 - MARY PARKER and SOLOMON THOMPSON apply for administration on estate of JAMES PARKER, dec'd. JOHN MATTHEWS and AMOS PARSONS, sureties on bond.

Feb. 16, 1803 - The will of PETER PERKINS dec'd., was proven by the oath of SOLOMON THOMPSON, and letters testamentary ordered to issue to JOHN BAKER and JOHN TORRENCE as executors.

Feb. 16, 1803 - ELIZABETH NEWSOM, FREDERICK NEWSOM, SOLOMON NEWSOM and DAVID NEWSOM apply for letters of administration on estate of SOLOMON NEWSOM, deceased; and were duly appointed, Aug. 1803. Pending granting of same, JODY NEWSOM was appointed temporary Admr. Oct. 17, 1803; DAVID NEWSOM was appointed Admr., THOMAS DENT, ROBERT MOSES SR., WILLIAM URSERY, JODY NEWSOM, sureties on bond.

Nov. 25, 1802 - JOHN BISHOP and SAMUEL COOPER apply for administration on estate of JAMES BISHOP, and were appointed Feb. 15, 1803; JOEL HEATH and THOS. HUTCHINS, sureties on bond.

Jan. 25, 1803 - ROBERT PARKER applies for admn. on estate of WILLIAM PARKER, deceased.

Feb. 15, 1803 - WILLIAM WHITE applies for administration on estate of WILLIAM WHITE, SR., and was duly appointed; JACOB BURKHALTER and WILLIAM MATTHEWS, sureties on bond. On July 6, 1807, letters dismissory were duly granted to WM. WHITE, Admr. on said WILLIAM WHITE, SR., estate.

Feb. 23, 1803 - STEPHEN LAWRENCE applies for administration estate of NATHAN WOOTTEN, and was appointed with JOSEPH CARTER, surety on bond.

May 2, 1803 - JAMES BOND applies for administration on estate of PETER BOND, deceased.

June 21, 1803 - ALCY LEE applies for letters of administration on the estate of RICHARD LEE, dec'd. She was appointed with THOMAS ROGERS and WILLIAM PILCHER, sureties on her bond.

Aug. 9, 1803 - TULLEY BRIGGS applies for administration on estate of WIGGINS KILLEBREW, dec'd. JOHN RUSHIN, surety on bond.

Aug. 10, 1804 - JOHN NEAVES applies for letters of administration on the estate of DANIEL NEVES (NEAVES). SHEDRICK FLUWELLIN, surety on bond.

Aug. 9, 1803 - MARTHA SELLS applies for administration on estate of THOMAS SELLS. ISAAC DAVIS and JEREMIAH BURKHALTER, sureties on bond.

Aug. 9, 1803 - ELIZABETH ROCKMORE applies for administration with the will of JAMES ROCKMORE, testate. The will was probated and she was appointed with DAVID ROBERTSON and WILLIAM USSERY, sureties on her bond.

Oct. 17, 1803 - JOHN RUSHIN and ENOCH RENFROE, JR., were granted letters testamentary on the will of ENOCH RENFROE, SR., and the will was probated.

Oct. 17, 1803 - The will of WILLIAM BARDIN, dec'd., was proved, and MARY BURDIN qualified as executrix of same.

Sept. 19, 1803 - SAMUEL BARKSDALE and PINKETHMAN HARVEY apply for administration on estate of JOHN BARKSDALE, dec'd. On Oct. 22, 1803, the above applicants with STEPHEN BURNLEY were appointed Admnrs., MICHAEL HARVEY, JOSIAH BEALL, sureties.

Oct. 22, 1803 - AARON LIPHAM, JAMES WAGGONER and GEORGE WAGGONER apply for temporary administration on estate of HENRY WAGGONER, dec'd. and were appointed; WILLIAM WAGGONER and SOLOMON SLATTER, securities on bond.

Dec. 5, 1803 - JOHN MARTIN applies for administration on estate of WILLIAM MCKINLEY, dec'd. He was appointed, with JOSEPH MCKINLEY, surety on bond.

Dec. 5, 1803 - FREDERICK and SARAH NEWSOM apply for administration on estate of JOHN NUSOM (NEWSOM), and were appointed; MICHAEL BURKHALTER, surety on bond.

Jan. 2, 1804 - HANNAH CHAPMAN applies for administration on estate of LABAN CHAPMAN, and was appointed with WILLIAM CHAPMAN. ROBERT PARKER, sureties.

Dec. 29, 1803 - NATHANIEL WARD applied for admn. on estate of WILLIAM MORRISON, deceased, and was appointed; MICHAEL BURKHALTER, surety on bond.

Jan. 11, 1804 - RHODA BATTLE and SAMUEL ALEXANDER apply for administration on estate of JOHN BATTLE, and were appointed; ROBERT ABERCROMBIE and MICAJAH LITTLE, sureties on bond.

Jan. 23, 1804 - RICHARD FLETCHER applies for administration on estate of THOMAS LENT HALL, and was appointed in 1806.

Jan. 23, 1804 - The will of JOHN MYRICK was admitted to probate, and JOHN MYRICK JR., and NATHANIEL MYRICK qualified as executors.

March 5, 1804 - THOMAS JONES was appointed temporary administrator of the estate of HENRY JONES, dec'd. Sureties on bond: JOHN NUNN, WILLIAM JONES.

Jan. 22, 1804 - SALLY GEESLAND and BENJAMIN GEESLAND were appointed temporary Admrs. on estate of WILLIAM GEESLAND, dec'd. JOHN MOSES, JAMES GRAY, sureties.

Sept. 6, 1804 - The will of JOAB BROOKS was duly probated, and his widow and WILLIAM BROOKS qualified as executors.

Sept. 6, 1804 - A warrant of appraisement was issued in re: MOSES BUTTS, SR., estate; MOSES and WILLIAM BUTTS, Admrs.

April 13, 1805 - TULLY BIGGS was granted letters dismissory from his administration of the WIGGINS KILLEBREW estate.

Sept. 6, 1804 - MICHAEL HARBUCK was appointed temporary administrator on estate of DAVID NUSOM (NEWSOM), deceased.

Oct. 1, 1804 - HENRY DUBERRY and HARRIS MCFARLING were appointed temporary administrators on estate of JESSE DUBERRY, deceased. On Dec. 11, 1804, POLLY and HENRY DUBERRY apply for permanent letters of administration on the estate.

Oct. 24, 1804 - JAMES DAVISON was appointed temporary admr. on estate of RICHARD BUTLER, deceased.

Oct. 1804 - WILLIAM JONES and JAMES JONES were appointed temporary Admrs. of estate of JAMES JONES, SR., MICHAEL BURKHALTER, THOMAS DENT, sureties on bond.

Dec. 11, 1804 - MARY STONE was appointed temporary administratrix on the estate of MICAJAH STONE; ROBERT JENKINS and JEREMIAH BEALL, sureties on her bond.

Dec. 11, 1804 - MARGARET and ROBERT BEASLEY were appointed temporary Admrs. on estate of RICHARD BEASLEY, deceased. JAMES GRAY, surety on their bond.

Jan. 7, 1805 - ELIZABETH PRUITT and BYRD PRUITT were appointed temporary Admrs. on estate of LEVI PRUITT, deceased; ISAIAH TUCKER, JOEL NEAL, HARDEN PRUITT, sureties on bond.

Jan. 8, 1805 - MARY WAGGONER, DAVID W. WAGGONER and GEO. B. WAGGONER were appointed temporary Admrs. on estate of JAMES WAGGONER, dec'd., GEORGE WAGGONER and WILLIAM WAGGONER, sureties on bond.

Jan. 28, 1805 - THOMAS HUTCHINS, Admr. of JOHN HUTCHINS estate, was granted letters of dismission.

March 4, 1805 - The will of JOHN BROWN was duly probated and SAMUEL M. SMITH qualified as executor.

March 6, 1805 - JOHN KELLY was appointed temporary Administrator of estate of THOMAS RHODEN PINSON, deceased.

March 9, 1805 - ZACHARIAH DEASON was appointed temporary Administrator on estate of BENJAMIN DEASON, deceased.

May 24, 1805 - WINNIFRED BENTON was appointed temporary administratrix on estate of AARON BENTON, deceased. LEROY MIMS and JOHNSTON WRIGHT, sureties.

Aug. 13, 1805 - BENJAMIN HOWARD was appointed temporary Administrator on estate of WILLIAM KITCHEN, SR., deceased.

Aug. 14, 1805 - ALEXANDER MOORE was granted letters dismissory from his administration of the MORDECAI MOORE estate.

Aug. 14, 1805 - The will of WILLIAM TRAVIS, deceased, was duly probated and AMOS TRAVIS qualified as executor of the same.

Sept. 3, 1805 - ZACHARIAH BOOTH as the greatest creditor, was appointed temporary Administrator on estate of JOHN K. CANDLER, deceased; JOHN HICKS and RICHARD CURRY, sureties on his bond.

Oct. 15, 1805 - The will of HENRY HARP, dec'd., was proven by the oaths of JESSE WARD and CHARLES BEDDINGFIELD, subscribing witnesses; and SUSANNAH HARP and SOLOMON BEDDINGFIELD qualified as executors.

Oct. 15, 1805 - The will of ROBERT STANDFORD was duly probated.

March 3, 1806 - RADFORD BUTT and JOHN BUTT, Admrs. on estates of JOSHUA BUTTS, SR., and JOSHUA BUTTS, JR., were granted letters of dismission.

March 3, 1806 - The will of PETER NEWSOM was duly probated.

March 3, 1806 - The will of SAMUEL HEART, dec'd., was duly proven by the oaths of SEPTIMUS WEATHERBY and JOHN MYRICK, and ISAAC HEART quali-fied as Executor. The will and the proceedings were then returned to Washington Co. (Note: This would indicate the testator died a resident of Washington Co., and on account of convenience of the subscribing witnesses who probably lived in Warren Co., the will was sent to Warren to be proven; such a course would not now be proper.)

March 24, 1806 - JESSE WHITE was appointed temporary Admr. on estate of SHIMEI DRAKE, deceased; SAMUEL ALEXANDER, surety on bond.

July Term. 1806 - The will of ABRAHAM JOHNSTON was proven on the oath of EZEKIEL ALEXANDER, and was duly probated.

July Term. 1806 - The will of JOHN MYRICK, SR., was offered for probate. The Court heard the testimony of the subscribing witnesses, and a caveat having been filed, appointed THOMAS FLINN was temporary administrator, whereupon the case was appealed to the Superior Court by consent, July 7, 1806.

Jan. 31, 1806 - SAMUEL JACKSON was appointed temporary administrator on estate of SAMUEL RUTHERFORD; JOHN MCGLAMERY, surety on bond.

Jan. 31, 1806 - Letters dismissory were granted to ROBERT ABERCROMBIE, Admr. on the estate of WILLIAM C. ABERCROMBIE, deceased.

Jan. 4, 1806 - DANIEL PERRYMAN was appointed temporary Admr. on the estate of MONTFORD PERRYMAN, deceased.

May 5, 1806 - ASA WRIGHT was granted letters of dismission from his administration of the SAMUEL WRIGHT estate.

May 5, 1806 - DAVID NEAL was granted letters of dismission from his administration of the THOMAS NEAL estate.

June 14, 1806 - MARY JARRETT was appointed temporary administratrix on estate of ALEXANDER JARRETT, dec'd.

Oct. 11, 1806 - THADDEUS BEALL JR., and ELIAS BEALL were appointed temporary administrators on estate of JOSIAH BEALL, dec'd. THADDEUS BEALL, SR. surety on their bond.

Sept. 1, 1806 - BENJAMIN S. WOODARD was appointed temporary administrator on estate of FRANCIS WOODARD: HARMON PERRYMAN, surety on bond.

Nov. 3, 1806 - ABSALOM NAPPER and JOHN BUCKHALTER were appointed temporary administrators on estate of DRURY NAPPER, deceased. HENRY HARBUCK and JEREMIAH BUCKHALTER, sureties on their bond.

Nov. 3, 1806 - The will of BARNABAS JONES was probated on the oath of JOSEPH BONNER, a subscribing witness; and PATTY JONES qualified as executrix.

Jan. 1, 1807 - WINNIFRED ATCHISON was appointed temporary administratrix on estate of JAMES ATCHISON, deceased; GEORGE HARGRAVES, surety on her bond.

Jan. 5, 1807 - JOHN BAYNE, executor of will of ROBERT STANDFORD, was granted letters dismissory.

May 4, 1807 - ISAIAH TUCKER, surety on the bond of BYRD PRUITT and ELIZABETH PRUITT, Admrs. of estate of LEVI PRUITT, deceased, having been relieved as bondsman at his request, the administrators were cited to attend the next term of the Court and give new bond, as in default thereof they would be removed.

Jan. 5, 1807 - The will of SAMUEL PARKER, dec'd., was duly probated; and MARY PARKER qualified as executrix.

Feb. 2, 1807 - The will of DRURY MCCULLERS was probated on the oaths of JOHN SALLIS and JAMES SMITH, subscribing witnesses.

Feb. 2, 1807 - SAMUEL ALEXANDER as the greatest creditor, applies for letters of administration on the estate of JAMES HEFLIN as the will of the deceased could not be proven. He was duly appointed March 2, 1807; JOHN SIMMONS, surety.

May 4, 1807 - Letters dismissory were ordered issued to JANE VAUGHN as Admx. on estate of ALEXANDER VAUGHN (VAUGHAN) deceased.

May 30, 1807 - MARTHA JONES was appointed temporary administratrix on estate of THOMAS JONES, dec'd. Permanent administration on said estate was granted to her and JOHN LAMAR, July 6, 1807; BENJAMIN SANDEFORD and MATTHEW HUBERT, sureties on their bond.

March 30, 1807 - NANCY DARDEN was appointed temporary administratrix on estate of STEPHEN DARDEN, dec'd. She and JETHRO DARDEN were appointed permanent administrators, May 4, 1807. Sureties on bond; JACOB DARDEN, JETHRO DARDEN and WILLIAM DARDEN.

Sept. 7, 1807 - Justices of the Court present and presiding: JOHN TORRENCE, ELISHA HURT, HENRY CANDLER, ARCHELAUS FLEWELLIN. ELEANOR SPANN applied for administration on FRANCIS SPANN's estate and was appointed Admx., notice having previously given as required by law. Sureties on bond accepted: JOHN BRUTON, WYATT BONNER.

Sept. 7, 1807 - REUBIN MCGEE and EPHRIAM MCGEE applied for administration with will annexed on estate of NATHAN DAVIS. Notice having been given they were appointed Admrs. with will annexed, and duly qualified. PETER BUCKLES and JOSEPH WHITE accepted as sureties on bond.

Nov. 2, 1807 - SEPTIMUS WEATHERBY applied for administration of estate of GEORGE WEATHERBY and was appointed and qualified. Sureties accepted on bond: JOHN MYRICK and G. SMITH.

Jan. 4, 1808 - RHODA BATTLE appeared before the court and made choice of her third of the estate of JOHN BATTLE, dec'd.

Jan. 4, 1808 - MILLY STITH petitioned for Letters Testamentary on the will of WILLIAM STITH, and offered the will for probate. On the testimony of the subscribing witnesses JOHN STITH, HARTWELL JONES, JOHN HENERY. She duly qualified as executrix.

Jan. 4, 1808 - JAMES DOZIER and JOHN DOZIER applied for Letters Testamentary on will of JAMES DOZIER dec'd., and offered the will for probate. On the testimony on the subscirbing witnesses WILLIAM BERRY and THOMAS BERRY the will was probated, and petitioners qualified as executors of the same.

Jan. 4, 1808 - STERLING GARDINER and WALTER BELL applied for administration with the will annexed, on estate of THOMAS NEAL dec'd., and offered the will for probate. On testimony of the subscribing witnesses SHADRACH FLEWELLIN and SOLOMON SLATTER it was probated and petitioners were appointed Admrs. with the will annexed, and duly qualified.

Jan. 4, 1808 - CHAPPLE HEATH and JOSEPH HILL applied for administration with the will annexed, on estate of RICHARD HEATH dec'd. Will was probated on testimony of the subscribing witnesses JOHN BAKER, WM. BAKER. Petitioners were appointed Admrs. with will annexed, and qualified.

Jan. 4, 1808 - WILLIAM B. ALLISON petitioned for administration with the non-cupative will attached, on estate of MARGARET ALLISON, and petitioned for the probate of the will. On the testimony of the witnesses REBECCA WALKER, MARY HUSKEY and ELIZABETH HUSKEY as to the spoken will of dec'd., the will as probated, and petitioner was appointed. Sureties on his bond: WILLIAM BERRY, JOHN ALLISON.

Jan. 4, 1808 - GEORGE DYKES petitioned for administration with the non-cupative will annexed on estate of CHARITY POWELL, and was appointed.

Jan. 4, 1808 - LEWIS WRIGHT and JOSEPH WRIGHT petitioned for administration on estate of JESSE WRIGHT dec'd. Notice having been given and there being no objections he was appointed. AMOS WRIGHT, surety on bond.

Jan. 4, 1808 - LORANY MITCHELL petitioned for administration on estate of JAMES MITCHELL, dec'd intestate. She was appointed and qualified. Sureties accepted on her bond: WILLIAM BERRY, JOSEPH BOWEN.

March 7, 1808 - JOSEPH WRIGHT and CHLOE WRIGHT on their petition, were appointed Admrs. on estate of DR. WARRISS? D. RYAN, dec'd. and qualified. Surety on their bond: BASIL WRIGHT.

March 7, 1808 - NOWELL ROBERTSON and GEORGE GRANBERRY presented the will of MOSES GRANBERRY dec'd., for probate. It was duly probated and they were appointed executors of the will, and qualified.

March 7, 1808 - CHARLES LOGUE was appointed Admr. on estate of NATHANIEL WILLIAMS dec'd. Surety on his bond: NOWELL ROBERTSON.

March 7, 1808 - JOHN SLATTER was appointed Admr. on estate of JAMES SLATTER dec'd. Surety accepted on his bond: JOEL SLATTER.

March 7, 1808 - NOWELL ROBERTSON was appointed Admr. on estate of JAMES WILLIS, SR., dec'd. Sureties on his bond: JAMES WILLIS, GEO. GRANBERRY.

March 7, 1808 - DANIEL CULPEPPER offered for probate the will of WILLIAM CULPEPPER dec'd. It was duly probated and he was appointed Executor of same.

March 7, 1808 - LEVAN MCGEE presented his petition praying for a deed to be made to him in terms of a Bond for Title made to him by HENRY JONES in his lifetime, whereby he agreed to make him title for 270 acres of land lying on both sides of the Georgetown-Augusta Road dated Jan. 17, 1803. Rule Nisi issued directing ELIZABETH JONES, Admx. of dec'd., to show cause at next term why same should not be made.

March 7, 1808 - ISAIAH TUCKER asked to be released as a bondsman on the bond of ELIZABETH PRUITT and BIRD PRUITT as Admrs. of LEVY PRUITT. They were directed to show cause at next term why he should not be released as prayed.

March 7, 1808 - ELIAS BEALL and THADDEUS BEALL, Admrs. of JOSIAH BEALL estate, were granted leave to sell three slaves of the estate in order to pay the debts of the estate.

March 7, 1808 - MICHAEL BURKHALTER petitioned to be released as surety on bond of SARAH NEWSOM, Admx. of JOHN NEWSOM. Rule Nisi issued directing said SARAH to show cause at next term, etc.

March 7, 1808 - JOHN RUSHIN and JAMES WILLSON petitioned to be released as sureties on bond of ELIZABETH ROSSER (formerly ELIZABETH MURPHY) Admx. on estate of EDWARD MURPHY. Rule Nisi issued, etc.

May 2, 1808 - BENJAMIN OLIVER JR., applied for administration on estate of PETER OLIVER. He was appointed and qualified. JOHN OLIVER, surety.

May 2, 1808 - THOMAS CARR caveats to appointment of TURNER PARSONS as Admr. on estate of REUBIN BRIT__ (illegible) on the ground that PARSONS is not next of kin or a creditor of dec'd., also on the further ground that he, CARR, is already Admr. by appointment in Columbia County where dec'd. died and where his property lies. Caveator says PARSONS is said to be authorized by persons calling themselves heirs and who reside in Connecticut and are not heirs.

July 4, 1808 - MARY PARKER, SOLOMON THOMPSON, Asmrs. of JAMES PARKER estate, were dismissed, the estate having been fully administered.

July 4, 1808 - RHODA CHAPMAN and TEMPERANCE CHAPMAN, minors over age of 14 years, chose MILLIE CHAPMAN to be their Guardian, and she was appointed.

July 4, 1808 - JEREMIAH BEALL and THOMAS BEALL were appointed Admrs. of estate of THADDEUS BEALL, dec'd. THOMAS PENNINGTON, surety on their bond.

Sept. 5, 1808 - JANE VAUGHAN, Admx. of ALEXANDER VAUGHAN's estate, was dismissed, having administered the estate.

Sept. 5, 1808 - Likewise, ADAM JONES and PRISCILLA his wife, Admx. of CHARLES BAKER's estate, were dismissed.

Sept. 5, 1808 - JOHN J. ZACHRY was appointed Admr. of EDMOND WIGGINS estate, and qualified. GEORGE HARGRAVES and TIMOTHY MATTHEWS, sureties.

Sept. 5, 1808 - WINNIFRED VERDUN and JOHN VERDUN presented for probate the will of JOHN VERDUN, dec'd. It was probated and they qualified as Executors.

Nov. 7, 1808 - The will of THOMAS FONTAINE was probated on the testimony of the subscirbing witnesses CADER WESLEY and SALLY FONTAINE. JAMES ALLEN qualified as Executor. ELISHA HART Esq., and JOHN FONTAINE named executors in the will, relinquished their right to serve, and SALLY FONTAINE relinquished her rights as a legatee.

Nov. 7, 1808 - REBECCA POSEY was appointed and qualified as Admx. on the estate of SAMUEL POSEY, deceased.

Jan. 2, 1809 - ARCHELAUS FLEWELLIN and ELIZABETH WRIGHT were appointed Admrs. on WILLIAM WRIGHT's estate, and duly qualified.

Jan. 2, 1808 - SALLY JONES was appointed Admx. on TAMERLANE JONES estate.

Jan. 2, 1808 - JAMES MARTIN was appointed Admr. on WILLIAM MCKINLEY's estate.

Jan. 2, 1808 - LITTLEBERRY LITTLE was app'td Admr. on NATHANIEL NEWSOM's estate.

Jan. 2, 1808 - EMELIA BEALL, relict of THADDEUS BEALL, came forward and made choice of her third part of estate as dower.

Jan. 2, 1808 - NICHOLAS WILLIAMS was appointed Admr. of NOEL PITTS' estate.

March 6, 1809 - POLLY TORRENCE was appointed Admx. on WILLIAM TORRENCE estate.

March 6, 1809 - REBECCA DUCKWORTH and JOSEPH DUCKWORTH were appointed Admrs. on estate of WILLIAM DUCKWORTH's estate.

March 6, 1809 - The will of THOMAS ANSLEY was duly probated, whereupon ABEL ANSLEY, SAMUEL ANSLEY, THOMAS ANSLEY and JOSEPH ANSLEY qualified as executors of the will, being named as such in the will.

March 6, 1809 - JOHN FONTAINE came forward and qualified as joint executor with JAMES ALLEN on the will of THOMAS FONTAINE, dec'd.

March 6, 1809 - SEVERN BUKIE (or RUKIE, almost illegible) was appointed Admr. of estate of WILLIAM MCKINLEY and qualified as such.

May 1, 1809 - MARY NEWSOM was appointed Admx. on DAVID NEWSOM's estate.

May 1, 1809 - ASA NEWSOM was appointed Admr. de bonis non on estate of SOLOMON NEWSOM, dec'd., succeeding DAVID NEWSOM, deceased Admr.

July 3, 1809 - SARAH OLIVER and THOMAS FRIEND Esq. offered for probate the will of BENJAMIN OLIVER SR. and it was probated and they wualified as Executors of the same.

July 3, 1809 - ROBERT JENKINS and ANSON BEALL were appointed Admrs. on estate of ROBERT JENKINS, and qualified as such.

July 3, 1809 - LETTICE MCCRARY was appointed Admx. on MATTHEW MCCRARY's estate.

July 3, 1809 - JAMES OLIVER was appointed Admr. with BENJAMIN OLIVER JR., on the estate of PETER OLIVER dec'd., and qualified as such.

Sept. 4, 1809 - THOMAS HUTCHINS, Admr. of JOHN HUTCHINS estate was dismissed.

Sept. 4, 1809 - PHILLIP BRANTLEY was appointed Admr. of DAVID GOLDEN's estate.

Sept. 4, 1809 - JOHN DRAKE was appointed Admr. of MATTHEW DRAKE's estate.

Nov. 6, 1809 - WILLIAM B. ALLISON and CLAYTON HURKEY? (not plain) were appointed Admrs. on Estate of FREDERICK HURKEY?, dec'd.

Nov. 6, 1809 - JOSEPH DUCKWORTH and RANELLA? DUCKWORTH were appointed Admrs. on estate of JEREMIAH DUCKWORTH, deceased.

Nov. 6, 1809 - HENRY KENDALL, Executor of will of WILLIAM KENDALL, dec'd. was granted leave to sell a negro belonging to the estate.

Jan. 1, 1810 - WARREN BARROW and RICHARD? BARROW, witnesses to the will of NICHOLAS BOOTY, dec'd., testified to the execution of the will.

Jan. 1, 1810 - ELIZABETH CODY and NATHANIEL HUTCHINSON were appointed Admrs. of estate of RICHARD CODY, and duly qualified as such.

Jan. 1, 1810 - NATHANIEL HUTCHINSON applies for an order authorizing the Admrs. of DAVID GOLDEN's estate to make him a deed conveying land on Hart's Creek in this county, in terms of Bond for Title made him by GOLDEN in the latter's lifetime. Citation was ordered to issue thereon, and be published.

March 5, 1810 - The will of JOHN BARROW SR., was probated, and STEPHEN W. BURNLY qualified as Executor of the same.

March 5, 1810 - MARY CASTLEBERRY was appointed Admx. on JACOB CASTLEBERRY estate.

March 5, 1810 - TIMOTHY MATTHEWS was appointed Admr. on estate of WILLIAM BRITT.

May 7, 1810 - The will of JOEL HEATH was probated in due form, and HARTWELL HEATH and ROBERT BONNER qualified as Executors of same.

May 7, 1810 - Mrs. ANNA DARDEN, widow of STEPHEN DARDEN, made choice of her third of the estate.

May 7, 1810 - CHURCHWELL GIBSON was appointed Guardian of ISABELLA, WILLIAM and MARGRATE BARNETT, in place of ISAIAH TUCKER.

July 3, 1810 - NANCY BONNER was appointed Admx. on WYATT BONNER estate.

July 3, 1810 - ROBERT THOMPSON JR., was appointed Admr. on ROBERT THOMPSON estate.

July 3, 1810 - GEORGE PARHAM was appointed Admr. on WILLIAM HILL's estate.

July 3, 1810 - Mrs. REBECCA DUCKWORTH, relict of WILLIAM DUCKWORTH, dec'd., made choice of her third of the estate.

July 3, 1810 - PHILLIP BRANTLEY, Admr. of DAVID GOLDEN estate was authorized to make deed to NATHANIEL HUTCHINSON in compliance with bond for title made by dec'd. to HUTCHINSON, as petitioned for by latter.

Nov. 5, 1810 - JOHN MURPHY, Admr. of EDWARD MURPHY estate, was dismissed.

Nov. 5, 1810 - The will of DAVID RAGLIN was probated and admitted to record.

Jan. 7, 1811 - JOSEPH WRIGHT and CHLOE RYAN, Admrs. of LAURENCE D. RYAN's estate were dismissed, having closed out the estate.

Jan. 7, 1811 - The will of AMOS WRIGHT was probated in due form.

Feb. 4, 1811 - JOHN HOBSON was appointed Admr. of Mrs. MILLIE HEATH, de benesse (sic) and qualified as such. He was authorized to sell the negroes of deceased. It is stated she was sole heir of WILLIAM STITH, dec'd.

Mar. 4, 1811 - The will of JONATHAN LOCK was probated in due form, and MARY LOCK and JOHN LOCK qualified as Executors of same.

Mar. 4, 1811 - JOHN LAMAR, Admr. of THOMAS JONES estate, was dismissed.

Mar. 4, 1811 - ELIZABETH MYRICK, widow of OWEN MYRICK, comes into Court with her minor son, NATHANIEL MYRICK and agrees that if he lives with her and be under her direction and in her service until he is 21 years old, she will not make any charge against him in the final settlement of the estate of his said father OWEN MYRICK, for any support furnished him until he is 21.

May 6, 1811 - JOHN TORRENCE qualified as Clerk of the Court of Ordinary.

May 6, 1811 - The will of JAMES CARTER was duly probated, and MOORE CARTER, JESSE CARTER, JACOB CARTER, qualified as Executors of same. JOHN BAYNE also named by the will as an Executor, declined to serve.

July 1, 1811 - JOHN AIKINS was appointed Admr. of DAVID THOMPSON's estate.

July 1, 1811 - NOAH KELSEY, Guardian of the orphans of JOHN BATTLE was ordered to come into court by next term and give bond.

July 1, 1811 - WILLIAM B. ALLISON, Admr. of FREDERICK HUSKY, was dismissed.

July 1, 1811 - MOORE CARTER was appointed guardian of JAMES CARTER, a minor son (over 14 years of age) of JAMES CARTER, dec'd.

Sept. 2, 1811 - DEBORA CHAPMAN, Admx. of JOHN CHAPMAN, applied for dismission.

Sept. 2, 1811 - THOMAS CHAPPELL, Admr. of SION WHELESS estate, was dismissed.

Sept. 2, 1811 - WILLIAM PITTS' will was probated and the Executor named in the will (not named in the Minutes) was duly qualified.

Sept. 2, 1811 - The will of GEORGE WAGGONER was duly probated.

Sept. 2, 1811 - WYLIE JILES BRADY was appointed Guardian of JOHN JILES, a minor over 14 years of age, and he qualified as such Guardian.

Sept. 2, 1811 - ELIZABETH PARHAM and SAMUEL PITTS apply for administration on estate of JOHN PARHAM, dec'd.

Oct. 8, 1811 - The will of BLAKE LASSETER, dec'd., of Halifax Co., N.C. was presented and was probated here on oath of Henry Cocroft.

Oct. 8, 1811 - NICHOLAS WILLIAMS was appointed Guardian of NICHOLAS WILLIAMS PITTS, an orphan over age of 14 years, by his choice; and was also appointed by the Court as Guardian of NANCY WILLIAMS PITTS, NESTOR PITTS, SOLOMON PITTS, JACK PITTS, ELIZABETH PITSS, minor children of NOEL PITTS, dec'd., late of State of N.C. Said Guardian qualified, giving bond in sum of $10,000 with STERLING GARDNER as surety on his bond.

Nov. 4, 1811 - ELIZABETH PARHAM and SAMUEL PITTS were appointed Admrs. of estate of JOHN PARHAM, on giving bond in sum of $20,000.

Nov. 4, 1811 - WILEY G. BRADY was appointed Admr. of THOMAS PHILLIPS estate, together with JOSEPH and JOHN PHILLIPS, sons of the dec'd.

Nov. 4, 1811 - GEORGE WASHINGTON RAY, a minor bound out to WILLIAM ANSLEY until he is 21 years old. ANSLEY required to give bond for $500, and to give said minor when he is 21 a good horse, bridle and saddle and a decent suit of clothes, also give him two years' schooling.

Nov. 4, 1811 - JOHN E. LITTLE, Admr. of MICAJAH LITTLE estate, and ROBERT ABERCROMBIE apply to be released as bondsmen on bond of SAMUEL ALEXANDER and RHODA BATTLE, Admrs. of JOHN BATTLE estate. Citation was ordered to issue for next term, etc. (Note: MICAJAH LITTLE had signed the bond during his lifetime, with ABERCROMBIE.)

Nov. 4, 1811 - LEWIS PARHAM petitions for an order directing JAMES BONNER, Admr. in right of his wife, and NANCY CONNER, Admx. of WYATT BONNER estate to make him title to 100 acres in compliance with Bond for Title made PARHAM in the lifetime of dec'd. Citation ordered to issue for next term, directing Admrs. to show cause if any they can why they should not be required to make the deed, as prayed.

Nov. 4, 1811 - JAMES BONNER and NANCY BONNER, Admrs. of WYATT BONNER estate were granted leave to sell a negro slave of the estate.

Nov. 4, 1811 - JOHN BLAKEY was appointed Guardian for JESSE, SARAH and LEVI BLAKEY, minor children of said JOHN BLAKEY, they being over 14, having chosen him to be their Guardian; and he was also appointed Guardian of MARY, JOHN, SUSANNAH, MARY, JOHN and NANCY BLAKLEY, his minor children under age of 14 years.

Dec. 2, 1811 - JAMES BONNER was appointed Guardian of SARAH PARHAM HILL, age over 14 years, at her request.

Dec. 2, 1811 - JAMES NEAL and THOMAS MADDUX were appointed Admrs. of estate of DAVID NEAL, dec'd. Their bond was fixed at $10,000.

Dec. 2, 1811 - The will of GEORGE WAGGONER, dec'd. was probated in due form.

Dec. 2, 1811 - JOHN BURKHALTER, SR., was appointed Admr. of estate of JOHN BURKHALTER JR., dec'd. Bond was fixed at $1,000.

Dec. 2, 1811 - Mrs. ELIZABETH PARHAM, widow of JOHN PARHAM, came into court and made choice of her part of the estate, by taking one-third of the real estate, and a child's part of the personal property.

Dec. 2, 1811 - MATTHEW and REBECCA PARHAM, orphans (over 14 years of age) of JOHN PARHAM, chose JOHN C. TURNER as their guardian. He was appointed.

Dec. 2, 1811 - TURNER PERSONS, SHADRACH FLEWELLIN, ARCHELAUS FLEWELLIN, WILLIAM BLOUNT, JOHN MYRICK were appointed partitioners to divide the estate of JOHN PARHAM, dec'd., between the heirs.

Dec. 2, 1811 - ARCHELAUS FLEWELLIN was appointed Guardian of HELLENA, SALLY, WINNIFRED and NANCY WRIGHT, orphans of WILLIAM WRIGHT, dec'd.

Dec.2, 1811 - RACHEL RUFF and JACK RUFF, minor persons of color, were bound out to DAVID MIMS. It is stated that RACHEL will be 12 years old in February next, and JACK will be 10 next April. FANNY, JUDITH and BETHENA RUFF, minor children of colour, were bound out to BENAJAH WYNNE until they are 18. FANNY will be 18 next March, JUDITH will be 15 in Dec., and BETHANA two years old in July.

Dec. 2, 1811 - ELISHA HURT, TURNER PERSONS, RADFORD BUTT, SHADRACH FLEWELLIN and JOHN C. TURNER were appointed partitioners to divide the estate of WILLIAM WRIGHT dec'd., among the heirs.

Dec. 2, 1811 - The will of ROBERT WYNNE was duly probated.

Feb. 3, 1812 - The Admrs. of WYATT BONNER estate were directed to make
title to LEWIS PARHAM as per his petition previously filed.

Feb. 3, 1812 - The Admrs. of GEORGE WEATHERBY, deceased, were granted
leave to sell the real estate of the dec'd.

Feb. 3, 1812 - ISAIAH TUCKER, DANIEL CULPEPPER, STERLING GARDNER, NICHOLAS
FLEWELLIN and HENRY HIGHT were appointed partitioners to divide and turn
over to JOSEPH WRIGHT, his part or moeity of two-thirds of the personal
property of dec'd.

Feb. 3, 1812 - Mrs. MARTHA PITTS came into court and made choice of a
child's part for her share of the estate of her dec'd. husband NOEL
PITTS.

Feb. 3, 1812 - CLEMENT WYNNE qualified as Executor of will of ROBERT
WYNNE, dec'd.

Feb. 3, 1812 - Received and approved the report of partitioners appointed
to divide the estate of JOHN PARHAM.

Feb. 3, 1812 - Received and approved the report of partitioners appointed
to divide the estate of WILLIAM WRIGHT.

Feb. 3, 1812 - PETER CLOWER, Admr. in right of his wife, on estate of
JAMES MITCHELL, dec'd., was dismissed, having wound up the estate.

Mar. 2, 1812 - Inventory of the HOWELL GREGORY estate was received; and
F. BEALL was appointed permanent Admr. of the estate.

Mar. 2, 1812 - WILLIAM TAYLOR, age 11 years next Sept., son of WILLIAM
and PATSY TAYLOR, was bound out to SOLOMON THOMPSON until age of 21
years. THOMPSON was directed to give bond and to give the child a years
schooling and when 21 to give him a good horse, saddle, bridle and a
decent suit of Sunday clothes.

Mar. 2, 1812 - Miss JINCY WAGGONER, age over 14, orphan of HENRY WAGGONER,
chose WILLIAM MCFARLIN as her Guardian and he was appointed.

Mar. 2, 1812 - ANTHONY JONES was appointed Guardian of BARNABAS JONES,
POLLY JONES, PHILLIP JONES, minor children under 14, of BARNABAS JONES,
dec'd.

May 4, 1812 - JAMES WAGGONER, orphan of HENRY WAGGONER, made choice of
WILLIAM MCFARLAND as his Guardian succeeding WYATT BONNER, his deceased
guardian; said orphan being over 14 years old.

May 4, 1812 - Leave to sell 230 acres of land was granted Admrs. of
DAVID THOMPSON.

May 4, 1812 - NANCY ABERCROMBIE, WILLIAM JONES, AARON SMITH, were
appointed temporary Admrs. of COL. ROBERT ABERCROMBIE, dec'd.

May 4, 1812 - JOHN JONES and MARTHA JONES, orphans (over 14) of BARNABAS
JONES, made choice of HENRY JONES as their Guardian and he was appointed.

May 4, 1812 - WILLIAM HODGINS, about 8 years of age, was bound out to
RICHARD BRAY until he is 21, to learn the carpenter's trade. BRAY was
directed to give the boy two years schooling, and when 21 to give him a
decent suit of Sunday clothes and a common set of carpenter's tools.

May 4, 1812 - WILLIAM MCFARLIN was appointed Guardian of JAMES WAGGONER
and JINCY WAGGONER, orphans of HENRY WAGGONER dec'd.

May 4, 1812 - Mrs. NANCY ABERCROMBIE, the widow of ROBT. ABERCROMBIE,
WILLIAM JONES and AARON SMITH were appointed temporary Admrs. of estate
of dec'd. Bond was fixed at $50,000.00. EZEKIEL SMITH of Hancock
County and SOLOMON LOCKETT were approved as sureties.

July 6, 1812 - JOHN HOBSON, Admr. of COL. WILLIAM STITH's estate was granted leave to sell tract of 300 acres in this county and a tract of 250 acres situated in Camden County.

July 6, 1812 - WILLIAM B. ALLISON, Admr. of estates of FREDERICK HUSKY and of MARGARET ALLISON, was dismissed, having closed out said estates.

July 6, 1812 - Mrs. NANCY ABERCROMBIE, WM. JONES and AARON SMITH were appointed permanent Admrs. of COL. ROBT. ABERCROMBIE estate, and bond was fixed at $50,000.

July 6, 1812 - HENRY WILSON, JOHN WILSON and JAMES WILSON were cited to show cause at next term in Sept., why JOHN ROLLING should not recover pay from them for keeping WILLIAM WILSON four months in 1811.

Aug. 12, 1812 - The Court convened in special session this date and appointed a committee from the five Justices of the Court to attend Mrs. ELIZABETH WAGGONER, the widow of GEORGE WAGGONER, and administer the oath and qualify her as Executrix on said will, she being infirm and unable to come to court, or leave her residence.

Sept. 7, 1812 - ANTHONY JONES and HENRY JONES were granted Letters of Guardianship for the orphans of BARNABAS JONES.

Sept. 7, 1812 - SILAS BURKHOLTS was appointed Guardian of LINNY RAYSE?, a minor.

Sept. 7, 1812 - The Court dismissed the case of JOHN ROLLIN seeking payment for four months keeping of WILLIAM WILSON, "one of the list of county pensioners."

Nov. 2, 1812 - The will of RUBIN BARROW, dec'd., was probated on the testimony of BENJAMIN BLEDSOE and WILLIAM BRANNEN, subscribing witnesses.

Nov. 2, 1812 - JOHN BAKER, temporary Admr. of estate of Miss OLIVE HARRIS, dec'd., was appointed permanent Admr.

Jan. 1, 1813 - ARCHELAUS FLEWELLIN, Admr. of WILLIAM WRIGHT, dec'd., was dismissed.

Mar. 1, 1813 - POLLY, REBECCA and SAMUEL DUCKWORTH, minor children of WILLIAM DUCKWORTH, dec'd., being age of over 14, chose JOSEPH DUCKWORTH as their Guardian, and he was appointed. At the same time the Court appointed him Guardian for NELLY, JOSEPH and GAZAWAY DUCKWORTH, minor children of dec'd., under the age of 14. "This to apply only to their part of the divident due from the estate of their grandfather, JEREMIAH DUCKWORTH, dec'd."

Mar. 1, 1813 - The executrix of will of SAMUEL PARKER, was granted leave to sell 257 acres of land in this county owned by dec'd.

Mar. 1, 1813 - Mrs. NANCY ABERCROMBIE caveats to application for leave to sell lands of ROBERT ABERCROMBIE, dec'd.

Mar. 1, 1813 - WILSON BIRD presented the will of WILLIAM BIRD, dec'd., for probate and it was duly probated and he qualified as Executor of same.

Mar. 1, 1813 - JOHN BAKER, SOLOMON LOCKETT, AARON GREER were appointed partitioners to divide the personal property of estate of STEPHEN DARDEN.

Mar. 1, 1813 - Mrs. JOICE NEAL, widow of DAVID NEALE, Esq., chose a child's part of the estate for her part of the estate.

Mar. 1, 1813 - The Admrs. of DAVID NEAL estate were granted leave to sell a certain lot in town of Warrenton, and 100 acres whereon the grist and saw mills are located, also 150 acres of pine land.

Mar. 1, 1813 - JOHN TORRENCE qualified as Clerk of Court of Ordinary.

May 3, 1813 - WILLIAM ANSLEY was appointed Guardian of his daughter, EPSY ANSLEY.

May 3, 1813 - THOMAS MYHAND was appointed Admr. of FRANCIS BENTON's estate.

May 3, 1813 - ANN DARDEN was appointed Guardian of NICHOLAS DARDEN and MOSES (or possibly MONS? not plain) DARDEN, orphans (over 14) of STEPHEN DARDEN; and of MATILDA CLOWERS, minor dau. of JACOB CLOWERS.

July 5, 1813 - The will of LOWE JACKSON was probated in due form.

July 5, 1813 - REUBIN ROGERS was appointed Guardian of JOHN EMERSON, a minor over 14, at the latter's request. Bond fixed at $4000.

Sept. 6, 1813 - JAMES GRENADE was appointed Admr. of BENJ. GRENADE, dec'd. & qualified.

Sept. 6, 1813 - TIMOTHY MATTHEWS was appointed Guardian of JESSE BUTT and SALLIE BUTT, orphans (over 14) of WILLIAM BUTT, having been chosen by them; and the Court appointed him Guardian of NANCY BUTT and WILLIAM BUTT, orphans (under 14) of said WILLIAM BUTT, dec'd.

Sept. 6, 1813 - Leave to sell 50 acres was granted the Executrix of SAMUEL RUTHERFORD.

Sept. 6, 1813 - A Rule was issued against ELIZABETH GREEN (formerly JONES) and HARDY GREEN, her present husband, Admrs. of HENRY JONES, dec'd., requiring them to appear at next term and show cause why they have not made their returns as required by law.

Sept. 6, 1813 - JAMES ROGERS, a minor, was bound out to JOSHUA STANDFORD until he is 21, to learn the shoemaker's trade. Said minor will be 11 years old next February.

Nov. 1, 1813 - SOLOMON LOCKETT, Esq., SOLOMON THOMPSON, ARCHIBALD FLE-WELLIN, WILLIAM LATIMER and ROBT. A BEALL were named as partitioners to divide the personal property of WILLIAM BUTT estate, so far as respects the widow's part.

Nov. 1, 1813 - The will of JOHN DRAKE was duly probated.

Nov. 1, 1813 - JAMES BAILEY was appointed Admr. of PIERCE BAILEY estate.

Nov. 1, 1813 - MAHALA STORY, orphan of ASA STORY, was bound to LEVI STANFORD until she is 16 years old, she now being 7 years old the 7th of this month.

Nov. 1, 1813 - G. B. WAGGONER was appointed Admr. with will annexed on estate of GEORGE WAGGONER, dec'd.

Nov. 1, 1813 - The Clerk of the Court of Ordinary of Hancock Co., re-ceived and recorded the estate proceedings in the matter of the GEORGE MEDLOCK estate which had been transferred there.

Jan. 7, 1814 - WILLIAM DRAKE of North Carolina qualified as Executor of will of JOHN DRAKE, late of this county deceased.

Feb. 7, 1814 - The surviving Admrs. of JAMES WAGGONER estate were cited to show cause why WILLIAM WAGGONER should not be released on surety on their bond at next term.

Feb. 7, 1814 - The report of partitioners to divide the personal estate of STEPHEN DARDEN, dec'd., was received and approved.

Feb. 7, 1814 - MARY MARKS was appointed Admx. on JOSEPH MARKS estate.

Feb. 7, 1814 - The will of Mrs. LUCY THOMPSON was probated, and ALEXANDER THOMPSON qualified as Executor of same.

Feb. 7, 1814 - Mrs. CATHERINE BIRD, widow of COL. WILLIAM BIRD, gave notice that she would file claim to her dowry in the lands of the estate and a take a child's part in the personal estate.

Mar. 7, 1814 - The report of partitioners to divide the WILLIAM BUTT estate among the heirs, was received and adopted.

May 2, 1814 - The will of JOHN AKIN was probated in due form.

May 2, 1814 - CASWELL WRIGHT, orphan of ISAIAH WRIGHT, was bound out to DANIEL HUTCHINSON for a term of four years, to learn the blacksmith trade.

May 2, 1814 - MELTON WRIGHT, orphans of said ISAIAH WRIGHT, was bound out to WILLIAM A. FULLER for a term of 3 years to learn blacksmithing.

May 2, 1814 - WILLIAM BYROM, Esq., and WILLIAM AIKENS qualified as executors of the will of JOHN AKINS, dec'd.

June 6, 1814 - CHARLES BROOKS applied for Admr. on HENRY BROOKS estate.

June 6, 1814 - HARDEN PRUITT applied for Admn. on SAMUEL JONES estate.

June 6, 1814 - THOMAS MADDUX applied for admn. on JOHN NEAL'S estate.

July 4, 1814 - The will of JAMES THOMPSON was duly probated.

July 4, 1814 - The will of WILLIAM HEATH was duly probated.

July 4, 1814 - Leave to sell the realty of WILLIAM BUTT dec'd., consisting of 450 acres was granted.

July 4, 1814 - HARRIS PARRISH, age 9 years of 22nd Dec., next, was bound out to PHILANDER O. PARISH to learn the carriage-maker's trade, and to remain so bound until he is 21 years old.

Sept. 6, 1814 - CHARLES BROOKS, Admr. of HENRY BROOKS estate, was dismissed.

Sept. 6, 1814 - HARDIN PRUITT was appointed Guardian of his own minor children who are entitled to legacy left them by their grandfather JAMES MCCORMICK, Esq., deceased.

Sept. 6, 1814 - JAMES NEAL, JR., was appointed Guardian of the three minor children of SAMUEL NEAL, dec'd., insofar as relates to legacy left them by their late grandfather JAMES MCCORMICK, dec'd.

Oct. 3, 1814 - The will of SARAH NEAL was duly probated.

Oct. 3, 1814 - H. B. THOMPSON was appointed Admr. of JAMES B. THOMPSON with will annexed.

Nov. 7, 1814 - ARCHELAUS FLEWELLIN, Admr. of WILLIAM WRIGHT estate was granted leave to sell 320 acres on Rocky Comfort in this county.

Nov. 7, 1814 - Mrs. MARTHA HARDAWAY, widow of JOHN HARDAWAY, came into court and made choice of a child's part for her share of the estate.

Nov. 7, 1814 - WILLIAM HARBUCK qualified as Admr. of JOHN HARBUCK estate.

Nov. 7, 1814 - REBECCA NEAL, widow of JOHN NEAL, chose a child's part for her share.

Nov. 7, 1814 - The will of NATHAN CASTLEBERRY was duly probated.

Nov. 7, 1814 - THOMAS MADDUX was appointed Guardian of STITH and THOMAS HARDAWAY orphans of JOHN HARDAWAY.

Nov. 15, 1814 - Amicable settlement was made between ELIZABETH MYRICK, widow and Admr. of OWEN MYRICK, dec'd., and NATHANIEL MYRICK, son and legatee of dec'd.

SOME GEORGIA COUNTY RECORDS

YOW 63
YOWN 72
ZACHARY 30,65,186,192,219,
    266,271,283,298,383,
    300,301,305
ZACHERY 34,284
ZACHRY 59,70,71,73,3,41,
    51,346
ZACKRY 248
ZILLUER 63
ZILLUN 63
ZIMMERMAN 27
ZUALL 247